Interpreting Canada's Past

J. M. Bumsted

Interpreting Canada's Past

Volume Two
Post~Confederation

Second Edition

Toronto

OXFORD UNIVERSITY PRESS

1993

Oxford University Press, 70 Wynford Drive, Don Mills, Ontario M3C 1J9

Toronto   Oxford   New York
Delhi   Bombay   Calcutta   Madras   Karachi   Kuala Lumpur
Singapore   Hong Kong   Tokyo   Nairobi   Dar es Salaam
Cape Town   Melbourne   Auckland   Madrid

and associated companies in
Berlin   Ibadan

This book is printed on permanent (acid-free) paper ⊖ .

Canadian Cataloguing in Publication Data

Main entry under title:

Interpreting Canada's past

2nd ed.
Includes bibliographical references.
Contents: v. 1. Before confederation. — v. 2. After
confederation.
ISBN 0-19-540946-9 (v. 1) ISBN 0-19-540947-7 (v. 2.)

1. Canada — History. 2. Canada — Social conditions.
I. Bumsted, J. M., 1938–

FC170.I58 1993   971   C93-093566-7
F1026.I57 1993

Contents

Acknowledgements viii

Preface xi

I. Government and Politics, 1867–1914 1

1. Federal Politics after Confederation 2
   Gordon T. Stewart

2. Politics in Quebec after Confederation 30
   Brian Young

3. Provincial Rights and Dominion-Provincial Relations 43
   Christopher Armstrong

4. The West and Louis Riel 64
   J.M. Bumsted

5. The Economy of Atlantic Canada 75
   Eric W. Sager

6. The Settlement of Western Canada 91
   Wendy Owen

7. Race in Victorian Canada 107
   Judith Fingard

II. Society and Culture, 1867–1914 135

8. Industrialization and the Family 136
   Bettina Bradley

9. Sport and Canadian Society after Confederation 166
   Colin D. Howell

10. Canada and its Native Peoples 189
    Sarah Carter

11. Canadian Nationalism 215
    Carl Berger

12. Women and Reform 237
    Carol Bacchi

13. Canadian Education before the Great War 254
    Marta Danylewycz and Alison Prentice

14. Urban Reform 275
    Margaret W. Andrews

15. The Rise of Organized Labour 296
    Gregory S. Kealey

16. Immigration and Ethnicity 331
    Ross McCormack

III. From World War I to World War II 353

17. Canada and the Great War 354
    Timothy H.E. Travers

18. Quebec and the Great War 378
    Suan Mann Trofimenkoff

19. Women and Work 395
    Graham S. Lowe

20. Regional Political Protest in the 20s 421
    Ernest R. Forbes

21. Nationalism in the 20s 445
    Mary Vipond

22. The Canadian Economy in the Great Depression 467
    R.B. Bryce

23. The Rise of Tourism 487
    Ian McKay

24. Political Protest in the Canadian Depression 513
    Peter R. Sinclair

25. Origins of the Welfare State in Canada 532
    Alvin Finkel

26. Women in the Labour Force in World War II 558
    Ruth Pierson

27. Dieppe, 1942 594
    Bruce Loring Villa

IV. After 1945 619

28. The Beginnings of Post-War Nationalism in Quebec 620
    Michael D. Behiels

29. The 'Modernization' of Newfoundland 636
    Ralph D. Matthews

30. The Conduct of External Relations under Diefenbaker 662
    John F. Hilliker

31. The Canadian Constitution 681
    David Milne

32. Aboriginal Land Claims 704
    William R. Morrison

Acknowledgements

MARGARET W. ANDREWS. 'The Emergence of Bureaucracy: The Vancouver Health Department, 1866–1914', *Journal of Urban History* 12, 2 (Feb. 1986), 131–55. © Sage Publications Inc. Reprinted by permission.

CHARLES ARMSTRONG. 'The Mowat Heritage in Federal-Provincial Relations'. Reprinted by permission of the author.

CAROL BACCHI. 'Race Regeneration and Social Purity: A Study of the Social Attitudes of Canada's English-Speaking Suffragists', *Histoire sociale/Social History* XI, 22 (Nov. 1978). Reprinted by permission.

MICHAEL D. BEHIELS. 'Cité Libre and Nationalism' from *Prelude to Quebec's Quiet Revolution: Liberalism versus Neo-Nationalism 1945–1960*. Reprinted by permission of McGill-Queen's University Press.

CARL BERGER. 'The True North Strong and Free'. Reprinted by permission of the author.

BETTINA BRADBURY. 'The Family Economy and Work in an Industrialized City: Montreal in the 1870s', *Canadian Historical Association Historical Papers* (1979). Reprinted by permission of the Canadian Historical Association and the author.

R.B. BRYCE. 'The Canadian Economy in the 1930s: Unemployment Relief under Bennett and Mackenzie King' in Duncan Cameron, ed., *Explorations in Canadian Economic History: Essays in Honour of Irene M. Spry* (1985). Reprinted by permission of University of Ottawa Press.

J.M. BUMSTED. 'The "Mahdi" of Western Canada? Louis Riel and His Papers', *The Beaver Magazine* 67, 4 (Aug.–Sept. 1987). Reprinted by permission of *The Beaver Magazine*.

SARAH CARTER. 'Demonstrating Success: The File Hills Farm Colony'. This article first appeared in *Prairie Forum* 16, 2 (Fall 1991). It is reprinted with the permission of the Canadian Plains Research Center, University of Regina.

MARTA DANYLEWYCZ and ALISON PRENTICE. 'Teachers' Work: Changing Patterns and Perceptions in the Emerging School Systems of Nineteenth- and Early Twentieth-Century Central Canada'. Reprinted from *Labour/Le*

WILLIAM R. MORRISON. 'The Comprehensive Claims Process in Canada's North: New Rhetoric, Old Policies' in Kenneth S. Coates and William R. Morrison, eds, *For Purposes of Dominion: Essays in Honour of Morris Zaslow* (Captus Press, 1989). Reprinted by permission.

WENDY OWEN. 'The Cost of Farm-Making in Early Manitoba: The Strategy of Almon James Cotton as a Case Study', *Manitoba History* 18 (Autumn 1989). Reprinted by permission of the Manitoba Historical Society.

RUTH ROACH PIERSON. 'Women's Emancipation and the Recruitment of Women into the Canadian Labour Force in World War II', *Canadian Historical Association Historical Papers* (1976). Reprinted by permission of the Canadian Historical Association and the author.

ERIC W. SAGER. 'Buying Cheap and Selling Dear: Merchant Shipowners and the Decline of the Shipping Industry in Atlantic Canada' in Peter Baskerville, ed., *Canadian Papers in Business History*. Reprinted by permission of the Public History Group, University of Victoria.

PETER R. SINCLAIR. 'Class Structure and Popular Protest: The Case of Western Canada', *The Canadian Journal of Sociology* 1 (1975). Reprinted by permission of The Canadian Journal of Sociology.

GORDON T. STEWART. 'Political Patronage Under Macdonald and Laurier 1878–1911', *American Review of Canadian Studies* X (1980). Reprinted by permission.

TIMOTHY H.E. TRAVES. 'Allies in Conflict: The British and Canadian Official Historians and the Real Story of Second Ypres (1915)', *Journal of Contemporary History* 24 (1989). © 1989 Sage Publications Ltd. Reprinted by permission.

SUSAN MANN TROFIMENKOFF. 'The Prussians are Next Door: Quebec and World War I' in *The Dream of Nation: A Social and Intellectual History of Quebec* (1983) by Susan Mann Trofimenkoff. Reprinted by permission of Gage Educational Publishing Company.

BRIAN LORING VILLA. 'How Canada Became Involved', from *Unauthorized Action* by Brian Loring Villa. Copyright © Brian Loring Villa 1989. Reprinted by permission of Oxford University Press Canada.

MARY VIPOND. 'The Nationalist Network: English Canada's Intellectuals and Artists in the 1920s', *Canadian Review of Studies in Nationalism* V (Spring 1989). Reprinted by permission.

BRIAN YOUNG. 'Federalism in Quebec: The First Years After Confederation' from *Federalism in Canada and Australia: The Early Years* edited by Bruce W. Hodgins, Don Wright, and W.H. Heick (Waterloo: Wilfrid Laurier University Press, 1978), pp. 97–108. Used by permission.

Preface

The past few years have seen some profound changes in the writing and interpretation of Canadian history, in both the subjects being explored and the methodologies and conceptualizations used to illuminate them. Canadian historians have been asking new questions and investigating new subjects and at the same time examining old themes, such as reform, political constitutional revision, and military history, from new perspectives. While the new history is most stimulating, it often does not t easily into the traditional patterns of Canadian historical scholarship. Worse still, it has in conceptual and methodological terms often gone well beyond the comprehension of all but the most committed specialists. The result is a serious dilemma for those teaching the new history to undergraduate students. Much of the best scholarship is inaccessible both physically and intellectually to neophyte historians. This collection of readings, concentrating on modern Canada since Confederation, represents one attempt to address the problem.

While Canadian historians have not on the whole been given to explicit theorizing, it is plain that new developments and a new methodology inform much of the scholarship of the past decade. Conceptually one direction has been towards the recognition of the complexities of economic and social structures within Canada. A generation ago the study of social class was regarded as one of the great neglected areas of Canadian historical scholarship. Today nearly all Canadian historical analysis owes some debt to Marxism, although not all historians would agree on the results. Along with studies of economic and social structure has come a corresponding emphasis on previously neglected elements of the population, such as women and native peoples. Also important over the past few years has been the in uence of the international trend toward cultural studies, in which cultural matters are explored in ways that go well beyond the traditional query, Is there a Canadian Culture?

The study of society and its cultural manifestations, for example, requires the generation of evidence drawn from not only literary sources (letters, diaries, etc.) but also such non-literary sources as legal records, vital statistics, and census data. Cultural studies have encouraged the use of various theories of language, aesthetics, and textural analysis in dealing with artifacts previously not regarded as important. As scholarship has turned increasingly to a study of those people once thought to be on the margin of Canadian society, and often relatively inarticulate, the importance of new sorts of evidence and of new ways of examining old evidence became apparent. The computer has made possible the collection of much new data, but quantification has not been the only new technique employed, and many of the essays in this collection testify to the possibility of non-quantitative production of new evidence, often by reading the old with fresh eyes.

Not surprisingly, many of the new practitioners in the Canadian historical enterprise are associated with disciplines outside traditional history. Indeed the expansion of historical scholarship, as well as the teaching of history, outside departments of history, have been major developments in recent years. At almost any Canadian university, courses in Canadian history—albeit with a specialized focus—are taught in departments of economics, geography, law, and women's studies, among other locations. This collection should prove of value in such courses as well as in the standard Canadian history surveys normally offered in history departments.

As well as expanding historical horizons with new questions and new empirical techniques, recent Canadian scholarship has greatly extended the geographical scope of investigation. Much of the best and most innovative work of the past few years has focused on regions and localities peripheral to the central Canadian heartland, and no compilation that ignores the resurgence of local and regional historiography, or the excellent work being done on these regions, can satisfactorily reflect the present state of scholarship. Studies of both the Atlantic region and the West are well represented within these pages, not as any concession to regional sensibilities but because, to a considerable extent, they have been on the frontiers of current scholarship.

One basic assumption underlying this book is that teachers of courses in Canadian history are already providing for their students a broad chronological and interpretative framework and adequately covering familiar ground. Introductory courses, almost by definition, must consider the traditional issues that have concerned scholars for generations, and each instructor has no doubt worked out an acceptable approach to these standard historiographical questions. The predecessor of this collection received some notoriety on the editorial page of one of Canada's leading newspapers not very long ago, when it was attacked for not providing adequate coverage of the battles of World War II. The critic, who was an academic, ought to have known better. But it is worth emphasizing here that this collection is not a survey text, but a supplementary collection of recent writings in Canadian history—most of them either implicitly or explicitly revisionist—that will introduce students to insightful discussions about traditional and current scholarly issues. The selections range widely, and however unexpected some of them may be, all have been selected for their potential utility in a typical introductory course in Canadian history, and in some cases also for the provocative arguments they raise.

In preparing this volume one other criterion for selection has been absolutely critical. One of the ironies of modern Canadian history is that research intended to get beyond traditional male élites engaged in traditional male élite activities—chiefly politics and war—to topics appropriate for all Canadians has lost contact with its audience. Historians have become increasingly specialized in vocabulary and narrow in focus, filling the pages of learned journals with articles for fellow specialists, not the average Canadian reader. I have thus attempted to select only work that addresses the larger audience of informed Canadians, of which students in our introductory courses are representative.

Obviously no two people would choose the same set of selections. I hope that the one I have made here will prove not only broadly representative of the best (and mainly recent) scholarship on early Canada, but illuminating and accessible as well.

J.M. BUMSTED
St John's College,
University of Manitoba.

I

Government and Politics

1867–1914

1

Federal Politics after Confederation

Gordon T. Stewart

The role of political parties in governing the new nation was not a central question in the debates over Canadian Confederation in the 1860s; but organized parties (as opposed to unorganized factions or special-interest groups in the legislatures of British North America) had emerged in the wake of responsible government and were not likely to disappear in the new federal system. The basis of party organization was patronage, which cemented relations between those who ran for public office and those who worked to get them elected to positions of power. The years between Confederation and the First World War were the heyday of political patronage in Canada. During this period, when reform of the government bureaucracy along the lines of a merit system (such as had occurred in Britain and the United States) was slow in developing, two highly articulated political parties emerged. The Conservatives and the Liberals approached patronage

similarly: both national parties seemed to be guided by the American motto 'to the victor belong the spoils.' Whichever party was in power had many appointments and honours (such as the title QC for lawyers) at its disposal.

Gordon Stewart examines patronage practices before the First World War, first describing the workings of the system and then discussing some of its implications. He points out that because of the relatively slow growth of industrial capitalism in Canada (especially in relation to that of the United States and Great Britain) government appointments continued to be much sought after, especially by the professional middle classes, and 'the public service was the biggest single area of attractive, secure, and prestigious employment' in the nation. Stewart argues that this situation confirmed the status of the professional middle classes. Moreover, the patronage system tended to obscure racial and regional differences and to increase political stability. On the other hand, the system encouraged localism to the detriment of national questions, and enabled the parties to mediate ethnic issues privately, rather than discuss them publicly and come to terms with them. While the system may have suited the period before 1911, Stewart concludes, it was not designed to deal with the changing circumstances of Canada as a modern state.

Does Stewart's analysis suggest that existing appointees were fired to make room for party faithful? If not, was it a 'spoils system'? To what extent does Stewart's treatment give consideration to the provincial parties? Why, and to whom, were public appointments so attractive? Are Stewart's arguments for the impact of patronage on localism and race relations persuasive? How was the patronage system unsuited to Canadian conditions in the twentieth century?

This article first appeared, titled 'Political Patronage under Macdonald and Laurier 1878–1911' in *American Review of Canadian Studies* X (1980), 3–26.

It is standard knowledge that patronage was endemic to Canadian politics in the 1867–1911 period. Source-books for undergraduate students contain sections on patronage, and the major historians who have written about these years refer to the ubiquitous nature of patronage, describing it as the natural currency of public life.[1] Professor W.L. Morton has pointed out that the cabinet minister of the time, 'a beneficiary of patronage himself . . . was well disposed towards being a dispenser of patronage. Indeed it was the power to distribute patronage that in the main gave his office meaning and substance.'[2] In his authoritative account of this period Professor Peter B. Waite remarks of Mackenzie Bowell, minister of customs throughout the entire span of Macdonald's administrations from 1878 to 1891, that his 'principal preoccupation was patronage'.[3] As well as these reminders from respected modern scholars, the official records of the period offer testimony to the pervasiveness of patronage. Commissions to investigate the civil service were established in 1880–1, 1891–2, 1907–8, and 1911–12, and all drew attention to the 'patronage evil'.[4] In 1909 the Department of Marine and Fisheries had the doubtful honour of being the object of a separate investigation and it failed to disappoint its critics, revealing widespread practices not only of patronage but also of corruption.[5] Newspapers, periodicals, and parliamentary debates are full of dramatic stories, charges, and countercharges concerning patronage. Major political scandals of the time, involving national figures such as Charles Rykert and Hector-Louis Langevin, revolved round issues of patronage.[6] Because of this kind of evidence it is now common knowledge that patronage was of central importance to Canadian political life. Yet there has been no study made of the workings and significance of patronage. Professor Hodgetts has noted this odd gap in Canadian historical studies. 'It is somewhat curious', he writes, 'that the practice of patronage has never been the subject of sustained analysis on the part of Canadian social scientists and historians'.[7] This article is an attempt at such an analysis.

I

A useful and informative starting point for examining the mechanics of the patronage system is to look at John A. Macdonald's own constituency of Kingston. The picture that emerges from the Kingston patronage evidence shows that patronage was distributed by the party on a bureaucratic-like basis. Appointments and contracts were not distributed hurriedly but invariably followed discussion between local party leaders in Kingston and the member of parliament (in this case Macdonald) in Ottawa. Those party activists seeking posts in the public service or public contracts made application, usually in writing, to the executive committee of the local Conservative Association. The committee considered all the applications, weighed the contributions of each applicant to the party's electoral campaigns, and then passed on a recommendation to Macdonald who in turn would pass on the name to the appropriate cabinet minister for formal action. In no case in the correspondence was consideration given to the applicant's qualifications—the sole criterion was service to the party.[8]

Within the executive committee there was formal discussion over each piece of patronage. The local party, through its executive committee, functioned almost as an employment agency for party workers. In 1889, for example, Edward Smythe, a barrister and president of the Liberal-Conservative Association, discussed with Macdonald various jobs in the Kingston post office. Smythe informed Macdonald that the committee had now filled all but one of the current vacancies. 'That will leave', he noted, 'a vacancy among the letter carriers that we will subsequently fill up.'[9] Two months earlier Macdonald had written to the executive committee to inform the local party leaders of changes in the Kingston post office that would open up new jobs. These developments, Smythe replied, 'received the hearty recommendation of our Executive Committee'.[10] When the committee discussed the distribution of such posts, the merits of the candidates were discussed exclusively in terms of their work in the local party organization. Writing in January 1891 in connection with the application of William A. Newlands for a clerkship in the post office, J.A. Metcalfe explained that 'his [Newland's] father and brother are active workers in the Conservative interest and William A. is a good Conservative.' Metcalfe added that Newlands had followed the proper procedure, having 'applied through the Executive Committee'.[11] Once Macdonald received the recommendation from the committee, he passed it on to the cabinet minister in charge of the appropriate department. In response to one such recommendation to the Customs Department, the minister, Mackenzie Bowell, sent a note to Macdonald explaining he had signed the necessary papers implementing the requested appointments. Mackenzie Bowell pointed out that neither of the two individuals recommended had 'passed the "qualifying" examinations' and therefore could not be employed as landing-waiters or clerks. But they still received posts in the customs service.[12] Local party considerations took precedence over questions of qualifications.

Because party considerations were paramount it was essential for any applicant to show a solid record of work in local electoral campaigns. An example of these values occurred over the position of second engineer at the federal dry-dock facility in Kingston. Thomas McGuire, a local party notable, had been told 'the Conservative Association have recommended' Joseph Levitt for the post. McGuire wrote in support of Levitt and warned Macdonald about two other aspirants for the job who should be rejected because they had made contact with the Liberal 'enemy'. Those other two, wrote McGuire, 'are Heretics while Levitt is one of the Faithful as that term is understood by the archbishop'.[13] In another case the importance of long, faithful, and uncontaminated party service was emphasized. In this instance the record of the family as a whole was considered. A 'claim of patronage has been brought before the Executive Committee', wrote J.A. Metcalfe to Macdonald. 'I do not admire the tone of the letter yet as the old man and his sons have never gone grit I feel kindly disposed toward them.'[14] During the winter of 1890–1 similar considerations dominated discussion of a vacancy for a staff officer in the militia. In December 1890 S.M. Conger, president of the Prince Edward County Liberal-Conservative Association, pressed the claims of his candidate, Colonel Graveley. Conger wrote of Graveley that he was not only 'a most efficient military officer . . . he is more . . . he is a staunch Conservative and has made many sacrifices for the party'.[15] Another endorsement of Graveley came from R.R. Pringle of Cobourg, who reminded Macdonald that 'as far as this riding is concerned he [Graveley] has always worked well and he certainly sacrificed himself when he ran for the local [elections] when nothing but defeat stared him in the face.'[16] Writing from Port Hope, another correspondent addressed himself to the essential point—Graveley deserved the appointment because of 'his service to the party'.[17]

The fact that service to the party was the most important element in appointments did not make Macdonald's or the committee's task any easier, for in many cases there were several suitable party workers seeking a post. In such cases it was difficult to make a recommendation without causing dissent and factionalism in the local organization. In other cases local party notables might either try to dominate the executive committee or try to by-pass the committee and deal directly with Macdonald on patronage issues. All these factors appeared over the appointment of a landing-waiter in the customs service at Kingston, a case that well illustrates some of the local complexities involved in distribution of patronage. In this instance John Gaskill of the Montreal Transport Company, a prominent local Conservative, had ignored the work of the executive committee and had pressed his own candidate on Macdonald. On January 8, 1891, Macdonald was warned by George Fitzpatrick of the consequent trouble—'Gaskill is raising a row and I hear that the Executive Committee had a real lively time yesterday. The Kilkenny Election was nothing to it.'[18] Fitzpatrick sent a telegram to Macdonald asking that the appointment be held up until a local solution to the conflict was found. The situation was more tangled because Gaskill's candidate had been 'insulting' to the executive committee. The committee's viewpoint was put by John McIntyre who explained to the Prime Minister that 'we are all anxious to do what we can for the party . . . but I know the majority of the Committee will feel greatly humiliated if Gaskill is allowed to reverse every recommendation that is made.'[19]

The Kingston patronage letters also reveal that Macdonald and local party leaders did not deal simply with appointments but also were actively involved in promotions within the public service and even in the creation of new posts to satisfy the patronage demands within the party. In September 1889, for example, John Haggart, Postmaster General in Ottawa, replied to the Prime Minister concerning the promotion of a clerk within the postal service. Macdonald himself had requested the promotion after hearing from the executive committee, and Haggart was willing to comply except that there was no vacancy to which the clerk could be promoted. Haggart, however, went on to suggest a solution. He could do what Macdonald requested by 'providing in the Estimates for the coming year a first-class clerkship in the Inspectors office at Kingston'.[20] There was no discussion about the necessity of a clerkship; it was simply to be created in the interests of the local party.

From this Kingston evidence we begin to get an idea of the workings of patronage, particularly the relationship between Ottawa and the localities. The Member of Parliament, in this case Macdonald, made the formal and final decision about appointments from the Kingston area as he passed on names to other cabinet ministers. Usually the MP received the nomination from the local executive committee. It was assumed that the local party organization, by its executive committee, was the normal channel through which patronage business flowed. When acting on patronage matters the committee did so in a formal way, receiving and reviewing applications, weighing credentials, passing resolutions, and forwarding the recommendations to the MP at Ottawa. One final point to emerge is that the structure of the patronage system, as revealed in the Kingston evidence, excluded outsiders from sharing in contracts and appointments. The patronage was given only to local figures who could prove their loyalty to the local party organization.

II

The Kingston evidence, while informative, may not be typical because of Macdonald's position as Prime Minister. This may have led him to leave much of the daily patronage business in the hands of the local leaders. It is therefore essential to examine other evidence to assess whether this pattern was representative.

One report during the period revealed a good deal about the day-to-day workings of the patronage system. This was the investigation in 1909 by Judge Cassels into the Department of Marine and Fisheries. A basic point made in the report was that since 1867 the department had been used by both the Conservatives and the Liberals, when they were in power, for partisan purposes. Positions and contracts were given to reward party activists. Regular 'patronage lists' drawn up by the MP and local party leaders were kept on file so that business could be directed to party faithful. 'The system', noted the report,

> seems to have been handed down from one administration to another since Confederation . . . It is apparently based on the old maxim of 'to the victor belong the spoils' utterly ignoring the fact that the money to be disbursed is mainly contributed by the people generally and not the money of the political followers of the party at the time being in power.[21]

During the course of the investigation the activities of the department's office in Halifax provided detailed evidence on how the system worked. In the case of Halifax the MPs were active in the regular distribution of jobs and contracts. The report explained that

> patronage in Halifax extended beyond the mere naming of the merchants and others who should comprise the patronage list. It extended to the nomination by the members of Parliament representing the constituency of individuals or an individual to whom orders were to be given.[22]

The questioning of witnesses showed the way things were managed. When work needed to be done or supplies furnished 'then the members would recommend . . . that the orders should be given to A, B, C, or D as the case may be'. Mr Jonathan Parsons, the Department's chief agent in Halifax, explained that this was done 'under the rules of patronage'. He further explained that these rules applied 'from year to year and from month to month every year'. On every occasion a contract was to be placed the MPs 'would designate . . . which merchant or manufacturer or dealer particular orders should be given to'. The questioning concluded:

Q: That has been the case?
A: Yes.
Q: Each time?
A: Yes.

Q: So it is not your independent judgement that was exercised from time to time as to where the work should be done or by whom material should be furnished; that was done upon the recommendations?
A: By the member of parliament having the patronage.[23]

The evidence also showed that aside from this regular management of patronage the MPs authorized 'taking on an employee' because they 'had the patronage'.[24]

The 1909 Report on the Department of Marine and Fisheries confirmed the assessment made the previous year by a civil service inquiry that the organization of the department, comprehensively influenced by patronage, had 'few redeeming features'. The Commission of 1908 had made a broad investigation of the public service outside the home departments in Ottawa and had concluded that these outside agencies were entirely at the disposal of the party in power. 'As a rule,' the commissioners explained,

> in the outside service . . . politics enter into every appointment and politicians on the spot interest themselves not only in the appointments but in the subsequent promotion of the officers . . . in the outside service the politics of the party is of greater importance in making appointments and promotions than the public interests of the Dominion.[25]

In each locality the MP and the party leaders regarded appointments and contracts as their exclusive right to be used to reward local party workers. 'In practically no case,' the commissioners discovered, 'is it possible to fill a vacancy in one locality by a transfer from another.'[26] In the Inland Revenue department, for example, 'political appointments as in other branches of the public service, prevail and as a rule the officers in one district are confined to that one district'. In Montreal all the appointments in the customs service were made 'at the insistence of the members of parliament for the district'. Indeed throughout the entire customs service the commissioners concluded that each riding was 'looked upon as local patronage' and that posts were awarded to local people only.[27] In his evidence Dr Barrett, inspector of Inland Revenue at Winnipeg, explained the active role MPs took in preserving local patronage exclusively for local party use. Barrett described how when a post became available 'the member for the constituency says, "No, I will not allow any one outside my constituency to go in there." ' In Winnipeg as in Kingston, the names for appointments were 'generally given by the Liberal Association of Winnipeg'. Barrett emphasized that 'when the Conservatives were in power they did the same thing.'[28] In their general observations on this kind of evidence, the commissioners concluded that 'each locality was separately guarded'.[29] Even the national party leader could not interfere with this local exclusivity. Writing to a party worker who had asked for a position outside his own constituency, Wilfrid Laurier pointed out how hard this would be to arrange. 'I need not tell you,' wrote the Prime Minister, 'that it is always difficult to bring an outsider into a locality.'[30]

It is important to note that this type of patronage distribution exclusively to party activists was not confined to minor posts in the customs or postal services and other such branches of the federal bureaucracy but operated at all levels. This can be demonstrated by looking at Macdonald's policies in making appointments to the bench and the bar. County judgeships and the earning of the title of Queen's Counsel (QC) were sought-after plums in the legal profession and were at the disposal of the party in power. As with the customs-service workers and post-office employees the positions in the judiciary were given by the party in power primarily on the basis of the candidate's service to the party. An example of the essential relationship between party service and advancement in the legal profession is contained in correspondence from 1887 between John Small and John A. Macdonald. Small wrote a confidential memorandum to the Prime Minister with a list of barristers eligible for QCs, and set out against each name the reasons for his recommendation:

> Michael Murphy: defeated candidate 1882 . . . attended meetings in recent elections . . . Roman Catholic;
> Daniel Defoe: strong supporter, always took a prominent part in political movements;
> James Reeve: did good work in the last election;
> James Fullerton: takes the platform in the interests of the party;
> George Blackstock: has contested elections;
> Emerson Coatsworth: rising young barrister, pillar of the Methodist Church, a strong Temperance advocate, President of the Liberal Conservative Association for his ward, was my agent in the last election.[31]

These candidates for QC had varied characteristics—some Roman Catholic, others Methodist, some with long legal experience, others just beginning to become noted in the profession—yet each shared one necessary qualification without which any other would be useless. In one way or another all had worked for their local Conservative parties either by running as candidates, being speakers or canvassers, or drawing up and scrutinizing the voters' lists. It was this kind of information on good hard party work that Macdonald looked for when creating a new batch of QCs. And these criteria were well understood throughout the party. In October 1889 Robert Birmingham, the Secretary-Treasurer of the Liberal-Conservative Union of Ontario, sent Macdonald 'the names of a few legal friends who rendered us special service in the recent campaign in the hope that you might be able to repay them with the much sought after QC'.[32]

The next step up beyond QC was county judgeships, and these too were distributed with the party's interest in mind. The context in which the awarding of judgeships was discussed can be seen from a case involving the Prime Minister, Frank Smith, the Senator who was the most important Ontario Catholic in the party, and B.L. Doyle, a party worker seeking a promotion to the bench. Doyle set forth his qualifications which rested on the premise that his 'services to the Party for the last 15 years entitled me to something'. He then proceeded to recount the details of this party work, emphasizing that he had 'stood by the party in the darkest hours of its severest trials [and] fought for it when it was down and persevered in the desperate struggle on behalf of our principles till the victory again crowned our efforts'. Doyle then went on to describe the election campaigns, particularly the one of 1878, in which he had done a great deal to get out the Catholic vote. He concluded his letter with the blunt request—'I want a County Judgeship.'[33] This request was endorsed by Senator Frank Smith, who confirmed that Doyle had indeed done all the party work he claimed to have done over the years. Smith wrote of Doyle that he was 'a plucky, active man whom I know to have worked hard for his party'. Therefore, concluded the Senator, 'he deserves to get what he asks.'[34] Macdonald was unable to satisfy Doyle immediately because of some rival candidates but he did promise to do what he could, and in January 1880 Doyle was appointed junior judge of Huron county.[35]

Other evidence from the Macdonald papers confirms this pattern of judicial appointments related to partisan activity. In November 1883 Robert Smith, QC, was recommended for a vacant judgeship in Huron. He was considered deserving of such honour because he was 'ever willing to go where duty to his party called him'. In April 1885 H.C. Gwyn applied to the Prime Minister for a vacant judgeship on the grounds that he had been

> actively identified with the party . . . and up to a year ago and for seven or eight year previously [was] the Secretary of the Liberal-Conservative Association of North Wentworth . . .[36]

In May 1884 a Conservative MP recommended J.M. Hamilton of Sault Sainte Marie for a judgeship, explaining that Hamilton was 'very much esteemed throughout Algoma and it is of some political importance that he should be appointed'.[37] About a year later another Conservative MP, N.C. Wallace, in recommending Edward Morgan, a barrister, for a junior county judgeship in York, explained that Morgan had 'fought, bled and almost died for the Party and has very much stronger claims than anyone else that has been proposed for the position'.[38] In the summer of 1887 A.M. Boswell, a party leader in Toronto, after reporting to Macdonald about party fund-raising, turned to judicial patronage and recommended N.C. Stewart for a junior judgeship in that city. Stewart, explained Boswell, was 'an out and out Conservative and as steady as a rock. At one time he was not a cold water man but now he is all right.'[39]

This evidence concerning the legal profession confirms that at all levels of public employment, from judgeships down to landing-waiters in the customs service, the party in power distributed patronage only to those who had worked for the party. It was not enough simply to be a contributor to party funds or an occasional canvasser but necessary to prove a long period of active, dedicated work in the ridings. The immutability of this standard was well illustrated by a case from London, Ontario, that developed in the spring of 1900. It concerned the family of John A. Donegan, who had volunteered to fight in the Canadian contingent in the Boer War. Donegan had been killed in South Africa, leaving a widow and two sons in London. There were some efforts to find jobs for the two boys to help support the family, and James Sutherland, a Liberal MP, had written to local party leaders in London asking their views of the proposal to find posts for the Donegan boys. It might be expected that in this part of Ontario the sons of war dead in South Africa would receive sympathetic treatment but the local party balked and refused to consider them for any posts. In response to Sutherland's inquiries, George Reid, a local party leader, explained that

> as for making a position for either of the Donegans in this locality, it would be very unpopular, they have never been Friends of ours in any particular and [it] would never do to appoint any one who has not been identified with the work of the party. . . . To appoint him for any position purely [and] simply because his father was killed in Africa would be to my mind very absurd.[40]

Reid also pointed out that the man who was doing most to find jobs for the Donegans was not a party supporter. If he had been, that might have been a reason to give the Donegans something to reward a party worker but, warned Reid, there was no point in helping the Donegans' backer for 'he is a strong supporter of the enemy and of no use to us whatsoever.'[41]

A comprehensive example of the normality of these expectations is contained in some private correspondence between Laurier and Roy Choquette concerning the Liberal party in the district of Quebec. Following the Liberal victory in 1896, Laurier had asked Choquette to report on the patronage requirements of the local party in the Quebec area. Choquette was to sound out party notables and send Laurier 'une liste des nominations . . . sur lesquels nos amis insistent le plus pour le moment'. On September 12 Choquette sent Laurier a detailed list of demands by Quebec Liberals:

> Voici ce qui en est: L'Hon. M. Joly [controller of Inland Revenue] devrait immédiatement remplacer le Dr Fiset de St Sauveur par le Dr Coté, et ce, pour faire plaisir à nos jeunes amis de Québec M. l'Orateur devrait remercier de ses services M. Fournier, pour satisfaire M. Talbot, et en même temps le Ministre des Chemins de fer devrait faire l'échange des stations de l'Intercolonial entre Castonguay de St Charles et M. Roy de St Moise. M. l'Orateur devrait encore destituer un nommé Gagnon, messager sessional pour donner satisfaction à M.

LaForest, notre candidat contre Costigan. M. Paterson [minister of customs] ou
Joly devrait remplacer Philéas Dubé, de Fraserville, officier du Douane, par M.
Amédé Gagan de St Arsène comté de Témiscouata . . .[42]

Choquette then continued, in the same matter-of-fact manner, to list further
patronage requirements of other important local Liberals, each of whom,
typically enough, had specific rewards in mind for himself and his fellow-
workers:

Pour faire plaisir à l'ami Lemieux, un nommé Baudin, gardien de phare de la
Grande Rivière, et qui a voulu le battre à son arrivée à cet endroit, devrait être
remercié de ses services et remplacé par M. William Bisson.
    L'ami Fisset attend avec impatience, ce qui lui est promis depuis longtemps,
la nomination du Dr Ross de Ste Flavie, à la place du Dr Gauvreau, partisan
bleu enragé, comme médecin du port à la Pointe au Père; et la nomination du
Dr Boullion, de Matane, à la place du Dr Pelletier comme médecin du port à
cet endroit.
    L'ami Angers aimerait avoir la réinstallation immédiate de M. Joseph Gau-
dreau, comme maître de poste à Grands Fonds, Malbaie.[43]

Choquette ended this list of patronage requirements by briskly noting his
own demands. 'Quant à moi,' he wrote, 'si l'ami Fisher [minister of agri-
culture] pouvait me nommer Desiré Vezina à la place de Zephiron Danceuse
comme homme de police à la Grosse Ile, et l'ami Mulock [postmaster gen-
eral] me nommer M. Georges Gagné, maître de poste à St Pierre, à la place
de madame C. Dienne, j'en serais bien content.'[44]

The working of the patronage system as revealed by these examples continued right down to the eve of World War I. The Royal Commission that
investigated the civil service in 1911–12 uncovered the same practices that
their predecessors had described in the 1880s and 1890s. One particular
interchange between the commissioners and a witness laid out clearly the
mechanics of the patronage system. The witness was Robert G. MacPherson,
postmaster at Vancouver. He was asked how appointments were made to the
staff and the following exchange took place:

A: Appointments are made through recommendations by the patronage committee or the members supporting the government.
Q: Do they communicate directly with you when vacancies occur?
A: No. I will apply for one or two men to the department at Ottawa who
authorize the appointment of men who shall be recommended by the member
of parliament or the patronage committee as the case may be.[45]

From the other side of Canada, on Prince Edward Island, came evidence of
how the system worked there. Thomas Mann, agent at Charlottetown for
the Department of Marine and Fisheries, explained that appointment and
purchasing worked 'by patronage'. If a position fell vacant, 'the members

supply a list of men they want put on and if they are suitable I put them on. . . . ' In the matter of buying supplies these were purchased 'from the patronage people'. The questioning continued:

Q: You have a list.
A: It is not a list from the government, just from the local members. They do the same as when the other government was in power. They have their friends to go and so have these.
Q: You have a patronage list.
A: A patronage list of friends to go to the same as before.[46]

The evidence in this section has provided an overview of the workings of the patronage system in the years between 1878 and 1911. There emerges a remarkable similarity in how the system worked under Macdonald and Laurier and a remarkable stability in a system that had the same structure in 1912 as it did in the 1880s. From Vancouver to Halifax, from London to Quebec, from Winnipeg to Prince Edward Island, Conservative and Liberal administrations of the period used their power in the same way. Federal posts and contracts were given to local party activists in a regular, time-honoured manner. Although the actual decisions on patronage were made by the cabinet ministers in Ottawa, the evidence shows that much of the work in terms of identifying applicants and proposing candidates was done by the local party organization, usually working through a committee. It is also clear that the patronage system applied to all levels of the public service from judgeships down to temporary positions in the post office. The system had become so rooted a part of Canadian political culture that it was considered legitimate and normal. It was only late in the period with the Royal Commission of 1911–12 that serious questions were raised about the impact of so extensive a system of patronage on Canadian governments and their effectiveness in dealing with the needs of society.[47]

III

To understand all the ramifications of the patronage system it is essential to relate it to the structure of Canadian society during this period. The first and most fundamental point to make here is that Canada was a small-town, rural society which was only beginning to be changed by the consequences of industrialization and urbanization. Professor Waite has reminded us of this basic fact in his authoritative study of the period between 1873 and 1896. The rural nature of Canada, he writes, 'must be kept continually in mind when considering the character and setting of Canadian life. The conservativeness of the French-Canadian countryside is well known, its resistance to social change is as strong as its political allegiances, but so much of Canada was similar. . . . Canada was rural.'[48] In 1881 the census classified 81 per cent of the population as rural. By 1911 it was down to 56 per cent, still over half the population. But even that figure does not tell the whole story. The census for 1911 shows that out of a total population of 7,206,643 there were 5,507,214 Canadians living in rural areas or in towns with less than 30,000. As late as 1911 about 76 per cent of the Canadian population was living in small-town or rural conditions.[49]

One characteristic related to these conditions is that Canadian society was localistic. Professor Gibson has remarked on this quality of Canadian society, pointing out that 'at Confederation and for many years afterwards, the Canadian people, a small and widely dispersed population, formed a simple and individualistic society, exhibiting strong local loyalties.'[50] The evidence on patronage cited above shows again and again how social and political leaders in each locality were anxious to keep 'outsiders' from moving in to their traditional sphere of influence. An insight into the isolation and localism of Canadian society in this period is provided by the memoirs of the historian A.R.M. Lower. He was born and raised in Barrie, Ontario, and recalled that in 1907 when he was eighteen years old he 'had not been more than sixty or seventy miles away from home'. Lower wondered whether he was 'exceptional' in being thus rooted. 'It is remarkable,' he then added, 'how local everyone was in those days.'[51]

Another basically important fact to be borne in mind was that there was limited economic growth during this period and that in contrast to the United States, for example, there was no dramatic advance of industrial capitalism. Even the Laurier 'boom years' after 1900 rested on the development of agriculture in the West, and well into the first decade of the twentieth century contemporaries still regarded Canada's economy as essentially an agricultural one.[52] In 1896 Bryon Walker wrote in the *Monetary Times* that agriculture was 'the substratum of our well-being'.[53] Two years later D.R. Wilkie in a speech before the Canadian Bankers Association explained that Canada 'was essentially an agricultural country'[54] and in 1907 this characteristic was again referred to, that 'the real backbone of Canada is its agricultural and its dairy and pastoral interests.'[55] A 1906 piece in *Industrial Canada* pointed out that 'Canada is and always will be a great agricultural country ... [the farmer] is the very foundation stone of our social economy.'[56]

A natural consequence of this reality was the relative insignificance of the industrial, manufacturing sector of the Canadian economy in moulding the social structure and value system of Canada. Some caution is required in broaching this topic, for there is some disagreement among scholars about the nature and performance of the Canadian economy during this period. It used to be a conventional enough statement that there was little economic development between 1867 and 1900, at which point there was a take-off based on the wheat boom in the West. The picture of unrelieved gloom for the pre–1896 years can no longer be sustained, as Professor Waite has recently explained in his assessment of the new evidence.[57] There was steady growth in some manufactures; the GNP rose from $710,000,000 in 1873 to $1,800,000,000 in 1896. Clearly the economy did grow and the transportation and banking structures developed before 1900 proved a solid base from which the more rapid, diversified growth of the twentieth century could develop. Yet while acknowledging the reality of this economic growth its limitations must be kept in mind. The manufacturing firms in Canada were small, employed tiny work forces, and had a very restricted impact on the social structure.[58] In 1870 the average number of persons employed in each manufacturing establishment was 4.6; in 1890 it had risen to only 5.5.[59] Manufacturing was still small-scale, decentralized, and geographically dispersed.

These economic circumstances were important for sustaining such a flourishing patronage system. The key point is that there were limited job opportunities available in the private manufacturing sector and that as a consequence federal contracts and positions in the federal public service were important areas of career opportunities.[60] In a system in which there was dynamic capitalist growth as in the United States employment opportunities at the disposal of the federal government assumed a minor place, but in the case of Canada such opportunities were a foremost feature in the job market. The way in which the Donegan family immediately turned to political patronage for jobs is a good example of the role federal posts played in this respect. When it is further remembered that the major capitalist activity of the period—the Canadian Pacific Railway—was also controlled by the state, it is clear that federal patronage played a dominant role in job distribution in post-Confederation Canada. It is revealing to note that patronage started to decline once the economy began to develop and diversify. There were several reasons for the decline of patronage after the 1914–18 war but one of the basic ones was that the advance of manufacturing reduced the heavy dependence on the federal government (and therefore the federal political parties) for jobs and contracts.[61]

The slow development of industry in Canada had another social consequence that intensified the central significance of the patronage system. Again in contrast to contemporary United States, where capitalists and businessmen formed the dominant social class, these groups were numerically small and socially insignificant in Canada. In a society where industrial development was in its infancy and where manufacturing was small-scale, the professional middle classes flourished.[62] The prestige occupations in Canada lay in this area—barristers, solicitors, clergy, civil servants. In the case of Quebec the pre-eminence of these groups is accepted readily enough. Jean-Charles Falardeau has provided a good summary of the situation in Quebec, pointing out that by the mid-nineteenth century the professional middle classes had succeeded the traditional élites. 'La noblesse professionelle,' Falardeau notes,

'constituent effectivement, jusqu'à l'époque contemporaine, l'élite canadienne-française—c'est cette élite que l'on est tenté d'appeler et que l'on
appelle souvent notre bourgeoisie.'[63] But while this social phenomenon of a
'bourgeois' class composed mostly of professionals rather than businessmen
is normally associated with Quebec, it was equally a hallmark of English-
Canadian society before the industrialization of the twentieth century.
Because there was no rapid capitalist and industrial development in Canada,
there failed to develop a large and powerful middle class whose members
could earn a living in ways that were open to trained and educated men in
the United States and Britain. Opportunities for upward mobility through
business corporations or by selling technical skills were very limited in Canada. This weakened 'the development within Canadian society of capitalist,
urban middle-class social values and forms of social structure'.[64] In these
circumstances there was little choice for each generation between 1867 and
1911 but to earn a living and gain social status by entering the legal profession
or gaining a position in the public service.

A nice example of the social prestige a professional man could achieve in
this small-town society was given by the Civil Service Commission in their
1908 report. Looking back to the 1880s for an overview of the reasons why
public service was so attractive to Canadians, the commissioners pointed out
the advantages:

> Owing to the small mileage of railways and to the lack of communications most
> of the necessities of life raised in the different localities were consumed locally.
> Butter, eggs, meats, foodstuffs and articles entering into daily consumption were
> produced in the locality in which they were consumed. The same characteristic
> feature was applicable to domestic servants employed in the households of offi-
> cials in the public service. A generation ago there was no means by which the
> farmers' daughters could remove easily from the locality in which they were
> born, and as the supply of domestic servants was greater than the demand the
> wages were comparatively small . . . The civil servant in these days, although
> not in receipt of a large income, had his wants satisfied cheaply and without
> stint.[65]

Not all public employees could afford servants. Nevertheless it is a valid
proposition that for most of the 1867–1911 period, bearing in mind prevailing economic conditions, the public service was the biggest single area
of attractive, secure, and prestigious employment. Even as late as 1911
employees in the public service still talked in terms of the 'dignity' and
'respectability' of their position in society.[66] The only way to get one of these
jobs was to have some claim on one of the two political parties. It was these
basic social and economic realities that enabled the political parties to make
the patronage system such a powerful organizing force in Canadian society
and politics.

IV

These final two sections will put forward some general conclusions about the significance of the patronage system and its long-term consequences in Canadian political development. The first point to make is that the pervasive patronage system that lasted throughout these years confirmed the power and prestige of the professional middle classes who ran the two federal parties. In Canada these middle-class groups—barristers, solicitors, doctors, notaries—which controlled the political parties did not, as in Europe, face serious social or economic competition. There was no aristocratic or traditional landed class that still had an influence in public affairs; there was no lingering peasant presence upon which a political movement could be based; there was no rapidly expanding capitalist class deriving wealth and power from industrialization; there was no mass labour movement seeking to form its own party. In these conditions the federal political parties, representing the dominant middle class and particularly the professionals, were extraordinarily influential in Canadian society. To understand the ramifications of these circumstances it is useful to consider the observations made by Hans Daalder in his analysis of political development in Western Europe.[67] Daalder, in tackling the question of how political élites relate to other élite groups in society, has suggested that one method of assessing the relative power of élites is to gauge the extent to which important positions within society could be obtained without reference to the political élite, without going through party channels.[68] In Canada nearly every important position in society was available only through the two political parties. Judges were appointed on the basis of partisan loyalty; QCs were distributed to lawyers who had been active in party work; senators were purely political appointments; posts throughout the public service, from the most senior down to the temporary and from Halifax to Vancouver, were disposed of by the parties to those who had worked for them. Even men with technical qualifications, such as civil engineers seeking work on the railroads, thought it wise to let their party credentials be known.[69] And in filling these positions the party leaders were approached in a supplicating manner by archbishops, bishops, deacons, priests, ministers, university principals, manufacturers, and individuals from their prominent social groups. In Daalder's terms the political élite in Canada was the top power élite, no other group approaching it in terms of power and influence.[70]

The course of Canada's economy during these years helped sustain the dominant role of the parties and their patronage system. Again it is helpful to compare Canada with Europe and the United States. Jacques Ellul has written that 'the nation-state is the most important reality of our days. . . . Nowadays it is the state that directs the economy. . . . The state is not just a superstructure. Marxist analysis is only valid in the nineteenth century when the emergence of uncontrolled, explosive economic power relegated a weak, liberal and unclearly delineated state to the shadows and subjugated it.'[71] In Canada things did not happen this way. There was no explosive economic growth and the state was not relegated to a position of insignificance by the powerful forces of industrial capitalism. On the contrary, the state in Canada, the federal government, was the single most important energizing agency as it took the lead in stimulating economic growth, protecting infant industries, building a national transportation network as well as constructing its own physical presence in hundreds of public-work projects across the country in the form of harbours, bridges, railways, post offices, customs houses, and other buildings to house its bureaucracy. Upon entering office, each political party fell heir to this extensive sphere of government activity. In the United States the party in power had similar room for manoeuvre but in that country the party's scope for activity was circumscribed by other powerful interests in the expanding capitalist economy, whereas in Canada the parties faced no rivals. Quite simply in Canada the parties were dominant and pervasive. A contemporary observer in the 1880s caught this development in the new Confederation. There was in Canada, he wrote, 'an overgrowth of partyism.'[72] In these circumstances the patronage system was like water finding its own level as it permeated post-Confederation Canadian society.

Another important point to emerge from the ramifications of the patronage system is that in the 1867 to 1911 period English and French Canadians were more alike in their social and political behaviour than has commonly been accepted. Scholars have drawn attention to the fact that a major reason for the French-Canadian attachment to the Union (1840–67) was that the Québécois professional middle class received, through patronage, opportunities for social advancement. Jacques Monet has well described this phenomenon in the twenty years before Confederation. 'For two generations since 1800', explains Monet,

> the Canadian professional class had been struggling to secure an outlet for its ambitions: so now with a kind of bacterial thoroughness it began to invade every vital organ of government, and divide up among its members hundreds of posts of Judges, Queen's Counsels, Justices of the Peace, Medical Examiners, school inspectors, militia captains, postal clerks, mail conductors, census commissioners. And as the flatteries and salaries of office percolated down to other classes of society—from merchants who wanted seats on the Legislative Council down to impoverished habitants on the crowded seigneuries—the Canadians came to realize how parliamentary democracy could be more than a lovely ideal. It was also a profitable fact. And henceforth . . . there could be guaranteed for all French Canadians the possibility of room at the top.[73]

This process continued after 1867. Jean-Charles Bonenfant has described a typical pattern of upward mobility through politics—'l'homme politique était bourgeois d'une certaine aisance, ayant de préférence une formation juridique, se faisant élire à la chambre basse pour mourir plus tard conseiller législatif, sénateur ou juge.'[74] Jean-Charles Falardeau in his analysis of nineteenth-century Quebec society also draws attention to the relationships among politics, patronage, and social status. Falardeau makes distinctions between professionals and politicians, suggesting that the political bourgeoise represented by such leaders as La Fontaine and Laurier and the members elected to Ottawa were more susceptible to English values, while within the localities of Quebec the 'pure' professionals such as doctors, advocates, notaries, derived office and rewards from political patronage but remained rooted in Quebec language and culture. By the middle of the nineteenth century these professional and political elements, flourishing off the patronage system and all its ramifications, had replaced the ailing seigneurs as 'la class dirigeante' in Quebec. Falardeau describes them, in that perceptive phrase already noted, as 'la noblesse professionelle'.[75]

All this may be familiar enough, but such historical social analysis should not stop short at the Ottawa River. Most of the preceding observations about the mobility patterns, values, and social aspirations of the Quebec middle classes apply almost as well to English Canada between 1867 and 1911. Of course conditions were not identical in Canada and Quebec. In the English provinces there were more varied responses to business, finance, and commerce; there were more opportunities in these fields and more social credit attached to them. Also in English Canada there was no one dominant church to which all successful men had to defer or relate in some manner. Yet recent research has downplayed some of these conventional distinctions and shown that Quebec's response to economic change was not as reactionary as was once supposed.[76] Whatever the final verdict of scholars on these distinctions, it is essential to point out the similarities that did exist. Before industrialization developed in a dynamic manner in the decade after 1900, English Canada was a rural, small-town, and churched society with limited contacts with the secular and transforming world of industrial capitalism. The opportunities for posts and social advancement through businesses and companies were restricted. It was a society in which the most prestigious and important groups were the professional middle classes; a society in which patronage was normal, legitimate, and pervasive; a society in which patronage was the single most important route of upward mobility to sought-after positions that gave security and status. English-speaking Canadians like their counterparts in Quebec turned to the patronage of the parties to become judges, senators, QCs, post-office officials, customs-service officials, collectors of inland revenue, medical examiners, and a multitude of other positions in the public service. The operations of these social processes in English Canada may have been less intense than in Quebec, more directly linked to business and commercial goals, but the profound similarities between French and English

Canadians remain. There was then a fundamental convergence in how English and French Canadians regarded politics and political parties and the social ramifications of politics. In particular both major ethnic groups in Canada shared the same expectations and derived the same kind of rewards from the system of political patronage. On patronage English and French Canadians spoke the same language.

V

In turning to the long-term consequences of the patronage system, a paradox appears. On the one hand patronage helped to create and maintain political stability, an essential condition if Confederation were to succeed, but on the other hand it helped to entrench a political culture which because of its nature pushed problems concerning the nature of Confederation to the background. On the positive side the ability of the parties to utilize patronage on so grand a scale over so long a period helped them to attract and retain supporters and thereby establish a solid base in the population. The process of establishing political stability has been analysed by many scholars studying new nations in the modern world, and one conclusion they have come to is that political stability usually requires political parties to have an extensive and influential reach in society. The political parties must be able to show that they can effectively reward supporters and so encourage loyalty to the party. Often some form of patronage or corruption is the means by which a party establishes its position. As Joseph Palombara puts it, 'corruption or its functional equivalent may be critically important to a developing nation.'[77] For example, in such a new nation if merit alone were the criterion for appointment to the public service then there would be a growth of bureaucratic power which would push the parties to the sidelines and thus lead to political instability as the parties became unable to attract and reward supporters. In the Canadian case patronage functioned in this manner. Patronage cemented the support of both federal parties, enabled them to exert extensive influence throughout society, and thus helped create a stable party system.

Such an achievement should not be underestimated in a country as fragmented ethnically and regionally as Canada. But for the achievement of political stability there was a price to pay. One of the adverse consequences of the patronage system was that it encouraged the persistence of localism in Canadian politics. The way in which patronage was dispensed made every local party organization across Canada jealous of its own territory and suspicious of outsiders. Local exclusivity was sanctioned by the national party leaders. Indeed, this was a deliberate object of policy in order to create strong local organizations to fight election campaigns. This tendency must be kept in perspective. Localism, given the social, economic, and geographic setting of Canada at the time, was bound to be a natural characteristic of Canadian politics.[78] The parties were moulded by the type of society in which they functioned. It is therefore a question of degree. Localism was bound to exist and the parties could either simply live with this reality or try to lessen its impact or encourage its persistence. They did the latter. The patronage system of the two parties encouraged Canadian political culture to remain localized. From a party viewpoint this was a good thing since it created strong, loyal, hard-working local associations that could be managed by skilled leadership in Ottawa from the centre of the patronage web. But it also restricted the vision of those in politics: MPs and local party notables were not encouraged by the system to interest themselves in affairs outside their own areas. The system worked in the direction of local inwardness. Because of this the Canadian House of Commons was in a metaphorical sense 'la maison sans fenêtres'.[79] The MP's vision was narrowly focused back into his locality and the windows on national issues were closed or obscured. The long reign of the patronage system contributed to a persistent parochialism in Canadian politics.

The great paradox lying at the centre of Canadian political culture in this period was that this emphasis on localism and avoidance of debate on the relationships between the two racial groups were the very reasons for the success of the party system in maintaining stability prior to 1911. To explain this paradox it is useful to relate the case advanced in this article to recent work done by Arend Lijphart on élite accommodation and consociational democracy.[80] Lijphart's model seems a fruitful one to apply to Canada. He argues that European countries which have an ethnically segmented population have developed a peculiar form of democracy. In these systems each major ethnic group supports its own political party, and the leaders of these parties, the representative élites, negotiate and mediate to form governments and maintain stability without sacrificing the interests of one particular group. Thus while there may be little communication and even great tension between the various linguistic blocs the élites of each group compromise in an attempt to reach solutions to national problems. The system then is characterized by élite accommodation. In a stimulating and thoughtful study Kenneth McRae has applied the consociational democracy model to the Canadian case.[81] McRae points out that the model can be useful for Canada only if it is modified to account for the fact that the two major ethnic blocs have never been represented by separate political parties at the national level. If accommodation does take place between the élites of each society, it must take place within the parties rather than between ethnically based parties. Having made this adjustment to the model, McRae analysed how the system has worked in Canada and concluded that 'even by the most charitable interpretation, the political system's capacity to learn and adapt to linguistic-cultural diversity has not been high.'[82] The federal parties have not been able to work out solutions to national problems but have instead created a situation of 'immobilism and stalemate' in which the federal government seems weak and ineffective. Accommodation within the parties which should have been going on since 1867 has not taken place. On the contrary, the gulf between English and French Canadians has widened to the point where the continued survival of the nation is in doubt. McRae concludes that the Canadian political system has a low learning capacity.[83]

This is a complex topic which requires multi-factor analysis. Yet one of the principal reasons for the apparent ineffectiveness of the federal party system lies in the structure of parties as they developed between 1878 and 1911. The cardinal point here is that both parties relied on patronage so heavily that they reduced the need for any genuine accommodation on such issues, for example, as language in the public service. As Brown and Cook have recently pointed out, communication between the two races hardly existed except in the realm of politics. In 1902 Lord Minto remarked that he found 'the leaders of society of both races unacquainted with each other'.[84] In these conditions much depended on the intercourse among the politicians of each race within the two federal parties and they found it easier and more congenial to deal with patronage and localized politics rather than 'questions of race'.[85]

The impact of patronage limited accommodation in the whole system of appointments and promotions in the public service. As far back as 1877 William Le Sueur drew attention to the fact that in the Canadian public service no heed was paid to whether or not an employee or candidate was bilingual and no recognition or reward was given to those who happened to be bilingual. Le Sueur pointed out that

> in a service where two languages are used it is obviously unfair that a man who brings to the Service a knowledge of both, and whose knowledge of both is made use of by the Department in which he serves, should derive no advantage whatever from the fact. Such, however, is the fact. In the Department in which I serve a man who knows both French and English is made to do work requiring a knowledge of both those languages and to do it for his seniors. A senior clerk may send to a junior clerk that portion of his work which requires knowledge of a second language and the junior gets nothing at all in the way of promotion for this special qualification.[86]

It is important to emphasize that both English- and French-speaking politicians were responsible for this non-recognition of the value of two-language people in the public service—it was not a policy concocted by bigoted Anglo-Canadian politicians. The fact that a contemporary like Le Sueur could put his finger on a fundamental issue like this shows that it is not anachronistic to suggest that more could have been done by the parties to incorporate linguistic duality more securely and formally into the structure of the federal administration. The parties did not do so because it did not occur to them to do so. Whether they came from the Gaspé or western

Ontario or Halifax or Vancouver the politicians of the day were interested in the public service from the viewpoint, above all, of patronage. Their interest lay in placing party workers in the service, not in trying to make the civil service a setting for reasonable accommodation of French- and English-Canadian interests.[87] In such ways the patronage system, while satisfying the immediate needs of local party associations in Quebec and the rest of Canada, constricted any incipient structural accommodation between the two racial blocs.

Canadians of the twentieth century are reaping the harvest of patronage politics during the 1867 to 1911 period. Parties relied heavily on patronage to satisfy ethnic groups within each party and so avoided the need to think about genuine accommodation in terms of the relationship of English and French Canadians in Confederation. Patronage was a great strength yet also a great weakness in the Canadian party system. It enabled the parties to flourish and maintain political stability as long as social and economic conditions were fertile ground for patronage and as long as society placed no major demands upon the parties. But once conditions changed, as Canada became an industrialized, urbanized society, as the provinces became more powerful and, above all, as Quebec modernized and began demanding that attention be paid to the basic meaning and structure of Confederation, then the parties which had been successful before 1911 began to become less effective. Their historical development had not prepared them for finding solutions to national problems.[88]

Suggestions for Further Reading

J.E. Hodgetts *et al.*, *The Biography of an Institution: The Civil Service Commission of Canada 1908–1967* (Montreal, 1972).
W.T.R. Preston, *My Generation of Politics and Politicians* (Toronto, 1927).
P.B. Waite, *Canada 1874–1896* (Toronto, 1971).

Notes

[1] W.L. Morton, 'The Cabinet of 1867', in F.W. Gibson, ed., *Cabinet Formation and Bicultural Relations* (Ottawa, 1970), 3; an example of a source-book treatment of the topic is J.H. Steward Reid, Kenneth McNaught, Harry S. Crowe, *A Source Book of Canadian History* (Toronto, 1964), 331–46.

[2] Morton, 'The Cabinet of 1867', 2. Political reminiscences of the period are full of references, charges, and counter-charges to patronage and corruption. Richard Cartwright, *Reminiscences* (Toronto, 1912), is particularly rich in this regard. So too is W.T.R. Preston, *My Generation of Politics and Politicians* (Toronto, 1927).

[3] Peter B. Waite, *Canada 1874–1896* (Toronto, 1971), 96.

[4]Commission to Inquire into the Present State and Probable Requirements of the Civil Service (1868–70), 1st and 2nd Reports in Sessional Papers, #19 (1869), 3rd Report in Sessional Papers, #64 (1870); Royal Commission to Inquire into the Organization of the Civil Service Commission (1880–1), 1st Report in Sessional Papers, #113 (1880–1), 2nd Report in Sessional Papers #32 (1882); Royal Commission to Inquire into the Present State of the Civil Service at Ottawa (1891–2), Report in Sessional Papers #16C (1892); Report of the Civil Service Commission (1907–8), Sessional Papers, #29A (1907–8); Commission to Inquire into the Public Service (1911–12), Sessional Papers, #57 (1913).

[5]Report of Investigation into the Department of Marine and Fisheries, Sessional Papers, #38 (1909).

[6]Waite, *Canada 1874–1896*, 218–21, 230.

[7]J.E. Hodgetts, William McClockey, Reginald Whitaker, V. Seymour Wilson, *The Biography of an Institution. The Civil Service Commission of Canada 1908–1967* (Montreal, 1972), 8.

[8]The evidence is taken from John A. Macdonald Papers, Public Archives of Canada [hereafter PAC], vol. 14, Kingston Patronage. On the formalities of the process see John McIntyre to John A. Macdonald, 11 October 1891.

[9]Edward Smythe to John A. Macdonald, Kingston, 13 November 1889, Private, Macdonald Papers, vol. 14, PAC.

[10]Smythe to Macdonald, Kingston, 17 September 1889, Private, Macdonald Papers, vo. 14, PAC.

[11]J.A. Metcalfe to John A. Macdonald, Kingston, 18 January 1890, Macdonald Papers, vol. 14, PAC.

[12]Mackenzie Bowell to John A. Macdonald, Ottawa, 8 January 1891, Macdonald Papers, vol. 14, PAC.

[13]Thomas H. McGuire to John A. Macdonald, Kingston, 9 January 1891, Macdonald Papers, vol. 14, PAC.

[14]J.A. Metcalfe to John A. Macdonald, Kingston, 29 November 1890, Private, Macdonald Papers, vol. 14, PAC.

[15]S.M. Conger to John A. Macdonald, Picton, 26 December 1890, Macdonald Papers, vol. 14, PAC. The militia appointment involved the interests of several ridings in south-east Ontario.

[16]R.R. Pringle to John A. Macdonald, Cobourg, 28 December 1890, Macdonald Papers, vol. 14, PAC.

[17]H. Ward to John A. Macdonald, Port Hope, 23 December 1890, Private. On the relationship of this piece of patronage to local party 'strength' see also Sam Hughes to Charles Tupper, Jr, Lindsay, Ontario, 25 December 1890, Macdonald Papers, vol. 14, PAC.

[18]George Fitzpatrick to John A. Macdonald, Kingston, 8 January 1891, Private. Macdonald Papers, vol. 14 PAC.

[19]John McIntyre to John A. Macdonald, 10 January 1891, Private.

[20]John Haggart to John A. Macdonald, Ottawa, 19 September 1889. In another case Edward Smythe discussed with the prime minister the plight of 'our old friend B. McConville', a party activist who had been given a contract for carrying the mail and now wished the amount to be increased. See Smythe to Macdonald, Kingston, 17 September 1889. Private, Macdonald Papers, vol. 14, PAC.

[21]Report of Investigation into Department of Marine and Fisheries (1909), 10.

[22] *Ibid.*, 41.

[23] *Ibid.*, 44.

[24] *Ibid.*, 42–3.

[25] Report of the Civil Service Commission (1907–8), 37, 27.

[26] *Ibid.*, 28.

[27] *Ibid.*, 89–90.

[28] *Ibid.*, 7, 28, 440–3.

[29] *Ibid.*, 28.

[30] Hugh Falconer to Wilfrid Laurier, Shelburne, Ontario 13 January 1908; Laurier to Falconer, Ottawa, 15 January 1908, Private, Laurier Papers, PAC, vol. 950.

[31] John Small to John A. Macdonald, Toronto, 5 April 1887, Confidential, Macdonald Papers, PAC, vol. 24.

[32] Robert Birmingham to John A. Macdonald, Toronto, 10 October 1889, Macdonald Papers, PAC, vol. 24. Macdonald kept a list of all the barristers in Toronto and noted opposite each name the party affiliation. He also estimated the composition of the Ontario bar as a whole according to party membership. The Toronto bar had 150 barristers eligible for the QC—95 were Conservatives, 55 were 'Reformers'. See List of Barristers in Toronto, Macdonald Papers, PAC, vol. 24.

[33] B.L. Doyle to Frank Smith, Goderich, 28 November 1879, Private, Macdonald papers, PAC, vol. 25 II.

[34] Frank Smith to John A. Macdonald, [?], 1 December 1879, Macdonald Papers, PAC, vol. 25 II.

[35] N.O. Coté, *Political Appointments, Parliaments and the Judicial Bench in Canada 1890–1903 (Ottawa, 1903)*, 571–2.

[36] H.C. Gwyn to John A. Macdonald, Dundas, 22 April 1885, Macdonald Papers, PAC, vol. 26.

[37] S. Dawson to John A. Macdonald, Ottawa, 13 May 1884, Macdonald Papers, PAC, vol. 26.

[38] N.C. Wallace to John A. Macdonald, Ottawa, 15 July 1885, Private, Macdonald Papers, PAC, vol. 26.

[39] A.M. Boswell to John A. Macdonald, Toronto, 7 July 1887, Macdonald Papers, PAC, vol. 27 II.

[40] George Reid to James Sutherland, London, 4 May 1900, Laurier Papers, PAC, vol. 873.

[41] *Ibid.*

[42] Roy Choquette to Wilfrid Laurier, Ottawa, 12 September 1896, Personelle, Laurier Papers, PAC, vol. 833.

[43] *Ibid.*

[44] *Ibid.* Laurier himself would act on these patronage requests, even down to the most minor, by notifying (as Macdonald had done) the appropriate minister of the necessary appointments. For example, in response to one request for Liberal appointees to the Intercolonial Railway, Laurier made out a memorandum naming those employees to be dismissed and indicating their replacements. See H.G. Carroll to Wilfrid Laurier, Quebec, 29 December 1896; Memorandum by Laurier in Reply, n.d., Laurier Papers, PAC, vol. 833.

[45] Royal Commission on the Public Service (1911–12), 1292. Macpherson's evidence was given on 30 and 31 July 1912.

[46] *Ibid.*, 1416–17.

47With the changes wrought by industrialization and urbanization the Canadian government was forced to acknowledge that the patronage-ridden public-service system was inefficient and ineffective in the new conditions. This was a basic factor pushing for change. Public opinion, increasingly critical of patronage after 1900, and an increasing sense of professionalism within the service were additional factors. Public employees in the western provinces were particularly critical in their appearance and representation to the Royal Commission of 1911–12. See R.C. Brown and R. Cook, *Canada 1896–1921. A Nation Transformed* (Toronto, 1974), 192–4, 321; Norman Ward, *The Canadian House of Commons* (Toronto, 1950), 275–81; Royal Commission on the Public Service (1911–12), 16–20, 337–8; Civil Service Commission (1908–9), 13. The latter report noted that 'it was the universal feeling amongst the officials who gave evidence . . . that this patronage evil was the curse of the public service.'

48P.B. White, *Canada 1873–1896* (Toronto, 1971), 8–9.

49M.C. Urquhart and K.A.H. Buckley, eds, *Historical Statistics of Canada* (Toronto, 1965), 5, 14–15, Series A 15–19 and A 20–24. On 5–7 Urquhart and Buckley discuss the problems of 'urban' and 'rural' classification in this period.

50F. Gibson, ed., *Cabinet Formation and Bicultural Relations* (Ottawa, 1970), 171.

51A.R.M. Lower, *My First Seventy-five Years* (Toronto, 1967), 33. Some examples of suspicion of 'outsiders' appear in this article. The patronage papers of both Macdonald and Laurier are full of other instances. For example a lawyer looking for work in London, Ontario, was regarded with deep antipathy because he had no roots in the area. Another individual who was not known locally was described as an 'unscrupulous professional man'—i.e., with no base in the local church or community, simply interested in pursuing a career wherever he could get a job. See John Barwick to John A. Macdonald, Woodstock, 10 February 1879, Macdonald Papers, PAC, vol. 251; A. McKean to John A. Macdonald, Bothwell, Ontario, 19 September 1887, Macdonald Papers, PAC, vol. 271. Also see note 30 above for an example in the Laurier Papers.

52Michael Bliss, 'A Living Profit: Studies in the Social History of Canadian Business 1883–1911', PhD thesis, University of Toronto, 331.

53*Monetary Times*, 21 June 1896, quoted in Bliss, 'A Living Profit', 331.

54*Journal of Commerce*, 4 November 1898, 634–5; Byron Walker to G.F. Little, 10 October 1907, both quoted in Bliss, 'A Living Profit', 332.

55Byron Walker to G.F. Little, 10 October 1907, quoted in Bliss, 'A Living Profit', 331.

56*Industrial Canada*, March 1906, 484, quoted in Bliss, 'A Living Profit', 332.

57Waite, *Canada 1893–1896*, 74–8.

58S.D. Clark, 'The Canadian Manufacturers Association', *Canadian Journal of Economics and Political Science*, IV (1938), 506–8. R.T. Naylor, *The History of Canadian Business 1867–1914*, 2 vols. (Toronto, 1975), vol. 2, 276–84, argues that Canadian industrial development was stultified during these decades.

59Urquhart and Buckley, eds, *Canadian Historical Statistics*, 463, Series Q 1–11.

60Naylor, *History of Canadian Business 1867–1914*, vol. 2, 276–84. Contemporaries talked of the very recent growth of industrial capitalism in Canada and referred to the fact that there was not as yet a class of entrepreneurs who could sit back and enjoy their profits. W.T.R. Preston in *My Generation of Politics* (Toronto, 1927), 204, 487, described the 1880s and 1890s as 'the twenty years [which witnessed] the creation and establishment of a capitalist system'. Robert Laird Borden in his *Memoirs* (Toronto, 1938), 151, pointed out that 'we have no men of leisure or of means'. Goldwin Smith in his *Reminiscences* (New York, 1910) 456–7, 487, remarked that 'Toronto wealth is not munificent. It certainly is not compared with the United States'. All these points reflect the fact that Canadian industry was as yet only a struggling part of the social and economic structure.

[61]The Report of the Civil Service Commission (1907–8), 14, 17, pointed out that public-service positions, while still sought after, were becoming less attractive as opportunities expanded in the economy. They pointed to the significance of the fact that the lower levels of the public service were being increasingly filled by women. Norman Ward in his study of Canadian MPs emphasizes that many of them went on to important patronage positions. 'The evidence is fairly strong', he writes, 'that politics in Canada is by no means the precarious occupation it is often assumed to be. Until very recently, only a small number of private businesses were in a position to provide positions for 30 per cent of their employees.' See Ward, *House of Commons*, 98–101, 103, 146.

[62]Bliss, 'A Living Profit', 1, 321, 341; S.D. Clark, *The Developing Canadian Community* (Toronto, 1968), 227, 234. Clark argued that 'in a way scarcely true of any other Western nation, the middle class in Canada has been the Establishment.'

[63]J.C. Falardeau, *Évolution des structures sociales et des élites au Canada français* (Quebec, 1960), 10–11.

[64]Clark, *The Developing Canadian Community*, 243–52.

[65]Report of the Civil Service Commission (1907–8), 14–17.

[66]Royal Commission on the Public Service (1911–12), 1213.

[67]Hans Daalder, 'Parties, Elites and Political Development in Western Europe', in Joseph Palombara and Myron Weiner, eds, *Political Parties and Political Revolution* (Princeton, 1966).

[68]*Ibid.*, 75. Daalder talks of the 'reach' or 'permeation' in society of political parties.

[69]For example, George Grant to John A. Macdonald, Kingston, 26 November 1883, Macdonald Papers, PAC, vol. 26, Bishop of Hamilton to Macdonald, Hamilton, 15 October 1880, Macdonald Papers, PAC, vol. 25 II, Bishop of Peterborough to Macdonald, Peterborough, 23 November 1887, Macdonald Papers, PAC, vol. 27 I, Reverend A. McKean to Macdonald, Bothwell, 19 September 1887, Macdonald Papers, PAC, vol. 27 I, Byron Nicholson to William Gibson, Quebec, 28 November 1908 (Nicholson was a newspaper editor and 'littérateur'), Laurier Papers, PAC, vol. 950, Thomas Swan to John A. Macdonald, Mount Forest, Ontario, 17 March 1883, Macdonald Papers, PAC, vol. 5 (Swan owned a carriage works business), R. McKechnie to Macdonald, Dundas, 11 March 1891, Macdonald Papers, PAC, vol. 22 (McKechnie was head of a manufacturing company and former President of the Canadian Manufacturers Association). On railroad patronage see N.A. Belcourt to Laurier, Ottawa, 31 August 1904, Laurier Papers, PAC, vol. 950. Also, Waite, *Canada 1873–96*, 136–7, Brown and Cook, *Canada 1896–1921*, 147–53.

[70]Alexander Tilloch Galt caught the essence of this condition in the new confederation when he wrote that 'politics form the only short cut from the middle to the upper ranks'. See O.D. Skelton, *The Life and Times of Sir Alexander Tilloch Galt* (Toronto, 1920), 377–9. In 1880 an observer noted the dominance of fashionable society in Ottawa by politicians, civil servants, and associated professionals. See J.E. Collins, *Canada Under Lord Lorne*, 309. See also Lady Aberdeen's comments in

Saywell, ed., *The Canadian Journal of Lady Aberdeen* (Toronto, 1960), 42. J.W. Dafoe, 'Canadian Problems of Government', *CJEPS*, v (1939), 288, pointed out that a career in politics in pre-1914 Canada carried more 'personal distinction' than since that time and that to be an MP 'meant a good deal more than it does now; and to be a member was a very general, if not all but universal desire among ambitious men'.

[71]Jacques Ellul, *The Political Illusion* (New York, 1967), 9.

[72]Hans Muller, *Canada, Past, Present and Future* (Montreal, 1880), 7. J.D. McClokie back in 1948 described a new state form, 'the party state', in which the political party was the most dominant power. See McClokie, 'The Modern Party State'. *CJEPS* XIV (1948), 143.

[73]Jacques Monet, 'Les Idées politiques de Baldwin et Lafontaine', in Hamelin, ed., *The Political Ideas of the Prime Ministers of Canada* (Ottawa, 1969), 16–17. See also l'Hon. Charles Langelier, *Souvenirs Politiques* (Quebec, 1912), 25–6.

[74]Jean-Charles Bonenfant, 'L'Évolution du statut de l'homme politique canadien-français', in Fernand Dumont et Jean-Paul Montmigny, éd., *Le Pouvoir dans la société canadienne-française* (Quebec, 1966), 117–18.

[75]Falardeau, *Évolution des structures*, 11. The phrase 'La noblesse professionelle' comes from P.J.O. Chauveau, *Charles Guérin: roman de moeurs canadiennes* (Montreal, 1853), 55–6.

[76]For example, William F. Ryan, *The Clergy and Economic Growth in Quebec 1896–1914* (Quebec, 1966). Two other studies put Quebec economic development in a much clearer light than traditional works. See Albert Faucher, *Québec en Amérique au XIX siècle* (Montreal, 1971). Faucher, for example, deals with the economic divergence between Quebec and Ontario in terms of technical development, regional pulls, and so on, rather than in terms of differences in value systems. See too the assessment in Brown and Cook, *Canada 1896–1921*, 127–43.

[77]Joseph Palombara, ed., *Bureaucracy and Political Development* (Princeton, 1963) 11; Hodgetts *et al.*, *Biography of an Institution*, 14–16.

[78]Gibson, ed., *Cabinet Formation*, 171. See note 51.

[79]Daalder, 'Parties, Elites and Political Development', 64–5.

[80]Arend Lijphart, *The Politics of Accommodation: Pluralism and Democracy in the Netherlands* (Berkeley, 1968). 'Typologies of Democratic Systems', *Comparative Political Studies* I (1968), 17–35, 'Consociational Democracy', *World Politics* 21 (1969), 207–25.

[81]Kenneth D. McRae, *Consociational Democracy: Political Accommodation in Segmented Societies* (Toronto, 1974).

[82]*Ibid.*, 250, 259–60.

[83]*Ibid.*, 245, 261.

[84]Brown and Cook, *Canada 1896–1921*, 164–5.

[85]In a letter written shortly before his death Macdonald complained, almost in a tone of surprise, that such issues should arise in Canada, that it was 'a great pity that these questions of race should arise so frequently'. John A. Macdonald to Alphonse Desjardins, Ottawa, 6 January 1891, Alphonse Desjardins Papers, PAC, MG 271, E22.

[86]Notes on Civil Service Reform by William D. LeSueur Select Committee on Present Conditions of the Civil Service (1877), 106.

[87]McRae's comments are pertinent here. 'In retrospect,' he writes, 'the quest to accommodate linguistic diversity in Canada may be viewed as a series of lost oppor-

tunities . . . and it seems likely that this low capacity of the system to devise effective solutions has helped to increase the intensity of linguistic and cultural cleavage in recent decades.' McRae, *Consociational Democracy*, 259.

[88]It is necessary not to press this case too far lest the tone become anachronistic. Professor Creighton has warned against placing politicians of post-Confederation Canada in an alien context. They were not eighteenth-century politicians interested in ethnic and cultural issues. They were Victorian politicians who were successful in building a viable Canada in arduous circumstances. D.G. Creighton, *Canada's First Century 1867–1967* (Toronto, 1970), 8. These are weighty reminders of the dangers of anachronistic analysis. Yet, as the 1877 evidence of LeSueur shows, there were alternatives even in the context of the times. Macdonald and Laurier then can be characterized as limited in their response to the basic problem of Confederation—and these limitations took root and flourished because the patronage system enabled the political leader to close their minds to structural responses to the 'question of race'.

2

Politics in Quebec after Confederation

Brian Young

The acquisition of the West was an outstanding item on the agenda of the new federal government, but the acceptance of the union by its component parts, including the new province of Quebec and its French-Canadian inhabitants, was equally important. The problems caused by French Canada in the administration of the province of Canada had been a major factor in the drive to eliminate the need for concurrent majorities and resulted in the movement for Confederation. The drafters of the British North America Act hoped that the establishment of a separate French-Canadian province would guarantee that cultural and religious rights would work more effectively. From almost the first day of union, however, there were potential threats to harmony. Francophones and Roman Catholics outside the province of Quebec whose cultural and religious rights were not guaranteed came under attack. Ontario's reaction to the Riel resistance in 1869–70 and the

federal government's failure to grant an amnesty to Riel; the moves against Catholic schools in New Brunswick in 1871; and the second Riel uprising in the West in 1855 —all tested Quebec's acceptance of what the majority of Canadians saw as the tacit understanding of Confederation: that Quebec would have a fair measure of autonomy and protection for French-Canadian rights within the province, but would allow anglophones to get on with governing the remainder of the nation. For an entire generation, however, Quebec remained loyally attached to the Conservative Party that governed as the Confederation Party, and did not seriously question the nature of the union.

Brian Young discusses the nature of Quebec's implementation of Confederation. One of the keys was the continued close relationship between Ottawa and the *Bleu* leaders of Quebec, who were supported by economic interests and the hierarchy of the Roman Catholic

Church. The *Bleus*, Young observes, were experienced politicians who found Quebec's autonomous government satisfactory as long as they could continue to control it. A system of dual representation in Ottawa and Quebec City certainly helped, as did the attention the Macdonald government normally paid to Quebec interests and sensitivities. Centralization seemed to be working with Quebec, although there were some signs of restiveness. Nevertheless, Young concludes, Quebec did not mount a strong stand for provincial rights until 1887.

Was the working relationship between politicians in Quebec and Ottawa based on genuine acceptance of the Macdonald principles of Confederation, particularly centralization of authority? To what extent did *Bleu* success depend on *Rouge* weakness? What non-political factors helped lock Quebec into Confederation? How important is public opinion in Young's analysis? By implication, what would be required to turn Quebec against the *status quo*? And finally, in what ways are Quebec's initial twenty years of support for Confederation important?

This article first appeared in Bruce W. Hodgins, Don Wright, and W.H. Heick, eds, *Federalism in Canada and Australia: The Early Years* (Waterloo, 1978), 97–108.

Even without the added strain of Confederation, Quebec in the 1860s was labouring under serious economic and social ills.[1] In addition to traditional ethnic and religious difficulties, there was a growing metropolitan struggle between the province's two major cities, Montreal and Quebec City. Aggressive and expansionist, Montreal's entrepreneurs dominated the province. The concentration of industry in Montreal's harbour and canal area brought an increase of 56.6 per cent in the city's population in the decade 1851–61 and another 18.7 per cent from 1861–71. Powerful Montreal families such as the Molsons, Redpaths, Ogilvies, and Allans strengthened their hold on the province's brewing, banking, refining, milling, and transportation industries. Montreal's stranglehold had been increased by the completion in 1859 of the Victoria Bridge, the only rail link in the province between the north and south shores of the St Lawrence. In the face of this challenge, other cities in Quebec became what one journalist described as 'sloughs of despond'. In particular, Quebec City suffered from the growing north-south orientation of trade and the decline in its square-timber business. While the ancient capital retained her political and ecclesiastical power, she became a peripheral economic centre.

The province's political parties reflected these tensions. The leader of the Quebec wing of the Conservative Party, or *Bleus*, was George-Étienne Cartier. Preoccupied with heavy responsibilities in Ottawa, including a major cabinet portfolio, Cartier became isolated from the provincial reality. In his

Montreal base, he found it increasingly difficult to bridge the clashing ambitions of the old Grand Trunk Railway and the aggressive Pacific-railway interests. At the same time, his party's long-standing alliance with the Roman Catholic Church was weakening in the face of growing clerical support for aggressive right-wing theology. As early as 1861 a struggle for power in Montreal between the Sulpician and Jesuit orders had implicated the *Bleu* leadership. Cartier backed the Sulpicians while Ignace Bourget, the Bishop of Montreal, supported the stricter Jesuits. The publication of the *programme catholique* in 1871 emphasized the political importance of these religious differences. This ultramontane document called on Catholics to give their political support to uncompromising candidates far to the right of mainline *Bleus*. Although its base of support was much smaller, the province's Liberal party, known as the *Rouges*, experienced the same difficulty in maintaining a united front. While radical *Rouges* like Joseph Doutre insisted on the traditional platform of religious and economic liberalism, more moderate members of the party like A.A. Dorion, Henri Joly, and Wilfrid Laurier moved to encroach on the centrist position of the weakened Conservatives. These moderates called for an end to the perennial bloodletting between the *Rouge*-dominated *Institut canadien* and the Catholic hierarchy. In 1871 the moderates formed a short-lived but important movement, *le parti national*. To attract nationalist and ultramontanist support they opted for peace with the Church, political liberalism, economic expansion, efficient government, and improved communications. Capitalizing on Cartier's weakness and the commercial and religious divisions in his riding of Montreal-East, *le parti national* succeeded in defeating the *Bleu* leader in 1872.

The defeat of Quebec's leading politician emphasized the difficulties of holding responsibilities in Ottawa while trying to maintain control of provincial affairs. Within his own riding of Montreal-East, Cartier was unable to straddle the gap between the national interests of his party and the particular demands of his constituents. Powerful entrepreneurs were able to apply pressure on him within the riding and in Ottawa. His opponent ran as defender of local French-Canadian interests; Cartier had to defend himself against charges that he was a *vendu* to the Grand Trunk Railway. As a federal politician Cartier was also embarrassed by having to explain the reality of the country's religious diversity to his strict ultramontanist Bishop.[2]

Despite the outward signs of stability, Quebec was characterized in the Confederation period by deep political, social, and economic divisions. The federal structure grafted onto the province in 1867 had been a conservative and empirical solution to the larger problems facing the politicians of British North America. Given the ethnic rivalry, the regional differences, and the *ad hoc* division of administrative structures in the union period, it had been impossible to impose a legislative union. By default many Conservative politicians had turned to federalism as the best means of ensuring political stability and economic expansion. After Confederation many of the same politicians worked to ensure the centralization of the new state and the dominance of Ottawa over the provinces.

Unlike its sister province, Quebec made little attempt to emphasize its autonomy in political and economic matters in the early years after Confederation. Some Quebec politicians even regretted that Canada had opted for a federal system. M.W. Baby, a Conservative advocate of legislative union, believed federalism had been a mistake for French Canada because 'it is now admitted on all hands that the English members, thirteen in all, control the legislature, and we have a system more extensive than the old one and of no avail to protect the French element.'[3] Despite Baby's pessimism, there was always some opposition in the province to federal domination. In the first session of the provincial legislature in 1868, Provincial Treasurer Christopher Dunkin spoke out against efforts to subordinate the province and argued that the provincial and federal legislatures should have 'the character of co-ordination'. Narcisse Belleau, the first Lieutenant-Governor of the province, protested against the centralizing tendencies of Ottawa and the arrogance of Langevin and other federal officials. He was joined by Cauchon's *Le Journal de Québec*, which attacked Langevin for damaging 'the independence of our provincial institutions'. There was also resentment against the divided loyalty of politicians who sat in both the provincial and the federal legislature. The dual-representation issue allowed Wilfrid Laurier to revive the old *Rouge* legacy of local autonomy; in 1871 he urged that the provincial legislature be independent 'from any federal control'.[4] Within the province, F.G. Marchand led Liberal opposition to dual representation but he was embarrassed by the fact that both the provincial and the federal leader of the Liberal Party exercised it. Before 1874 bills to abolish dual representation were blocked by the Legislative Council. *Le Journal des Trois-Rivières*, a Conservative and ultramontanist newspaper, was worried about the arbitration of the pre-Confederation debts of Ontario and Quebec; perhaps the silence of Cartier and Langevin on this issue was because 'their role as federal ministers entirely absorbed their duties as provincial deputies'?[5]

Bleu leaders in Quebec reflected the conservatism and practicality of their allies in other provinces. They sought stability and a continuation of the *status quo*, control of patronage, a denial of political power to the *Rouges*, and commercial development for their constituencies. The *Bleus* achieved these goals by careful manipulation of the nationalist issue, the implementation of conservative, British institutions, the strict control of the party at both the provincial and the federal level, the subordination of the provincial government to its federal counterpart, and reassuring the province's English minority. In the decade after Confederation, *Bleu* leaders exemplified what Arthur Lower has called 'the cunning of experienced hands'.[6] While loudly defending French Canada from external threats, they quietly extended their control over the province.

Leaders like George-Étienne Cartier, Hector Langevin, and Joseph Cauchon had been nurtured on the politics of Lafontaine. A common feature
of this experience had been the realization that British institutions—responsible government, the cabinet system, and parliamentary committees—along
now with a new, formalized federal system could satisfy demands for commercial expansion and cultural autonomy while ensuring their own continued dominance over French Canada. Both before and after Confederation,
conservative French-Canadian leaders rejected the radical experiments of
France and the United States and accepted federalism as a compromise solution. Cartier was typical in applauding the British Conquest, which saved
French Canada from 'the shame' of the French Revolution. Thirteen years
after Confederation, Langevin praised life under the British flag as offering
'perfect freedom, but no license'.[7] Younger Conservatives followed the examples of their mentors. In the first election campaign after Confederation, J.A.
Mousseau wrote of 'a heart beating with indescribable joy' that only a hundred years after the Conquest, Britain had restored 'our complete autonomy'.
Joseph Chapleau was another who subscribed to the rhetoric of his *Bleu*
elders. Although he speculated privately that Quebec's role in Confederation
was 'to carry water to the mills of others', his public pose was as a defender
of the system. He interpreted the federal union as 'an idea of conciliation
between the different nationalities' and described Confederation and the
Conservative party as the defenders of 'the autonomy of our Province'.[8]

Although they often spoke in favour of provincial autonomy, *Bleu* leaders
like Cartier and Langevin were centralists in the Macdonald tradition. Most
Bleus supported double representation, whereby politicians could sit simultaneously in the provincial and federal legislatures. Sittings of the Quebec
Legislative Assembly were timed to coincide with recesses of the House of
Commons. In general, French-speaking Conservatives showed little respect
for the provincial, or 'local' house as they preferred to call it. 'You are at the
helm of the ship,' P.J.O. Chauveau, the first premier of Quebec (1867–73),
wrote to Macdonald, 'well, I have done the best way I can to paddle the
smaller skiff.'[9] The province's English-speaking Conservatives agreed. The
Montreal *Gazette* was probably representative of this feeling when it urged
biennial sessions of the provincial house as an economy measure; it also
attacked the development of parties at the provincial level since the assembly
should deal with 'local questions from local stand-points'. A year after taking
power in the province, Chapleau in 1880 assured the prime minister that his
government would attempt 'to harmonize the action of the Province with
the general progress of federal institutions'.[10] Minimizing the importance and
independence of the provincial government went along with attempts to
reassure the province's influential English minority. English-speaking members like Alexander Galt had long had a powerful voice in the Conservative
Party; Galt was instrumental in promoting the idea of federation in the late
1850s and in winning over Cartier. The special electoral districts established

in the Eastern Townships, the Protestant school system confirmed in the first session of the provincial legislature, and the nomination of English judges and cabinet ministers were part of the careful attention paid to the English minority by Cartier, Langevin, and other *Bleu* leaders. In 1867 Galt and Christopher Dunkin successfully blocked Joseph Cauchon from forming the province's first ministry. This was by way of retribution for Cauchon's opposition in 1865 to the principle of autonomous Protestant schools. A decade later, federal leaders used their influence with Premier de Boucherville to ensure that six out of the twenty-four seats in the Legislative Council were retained by English appointees even though the percentage of English in the province was declining.[11]

If the *Bleus* were avowed centralists on most economic and political issues, they found it practical to defend provincial autonomy in the New Brunswick school question. The suppression of Catholic schools in 1871 by the New Brunswick government embarrassed French-Canadian Conservatives; important ultramontane leaders like Bishop Bourget called on them to defend the faith by disallowing the provincial act. The *Bleus* skirted the issue and finally diverted it to the courts. In voting against a motion of disallowance Langevin described the British North America Act and its provisions for provincial autonomy as '*le palladium de nos libertés provinciales*'.[12]

Like their *Bleu* counterparts, the *Rouges* were adept politicians who proved quite flexible in adapting to the exigencies of a federal system. By 1874 the major *Rouge* critics of Confederation were out of public life. The *parti national* with its plank of provincial autonomy was dormant, Jean-Baptiste-Eric Dorion was dead, his brother Antoine was on the bench, and radicals like Médéric Lanctot had been destroyed. Most Liberals proved to be able compromisers. While Wilfrid Laurier was an opponent of dual representation, the provincial Liberal leader, H.G. Joly, sat in both the federal and provincial legislatures until 1874. Luther Holton, an outspoken Quebec Liberal, described the provincial legislature as 'moribund', and in 1878 refused to join the Joly cabinet. Joly's provincial administration, like its Conservative predecessors, was weak and subservient to Ottawa. 'Where none but Provl [*sic*] interests are concerned,' he complained to Francis Hincks, 'where the autonomy and self Govt of the Province are in Question, is the Province not to be heard?'[13]

Between 1867 and 1873 the fledgeling Quebec government was dominated by Sir John A. Macdonald and his French-Canadian lieutenants; Macdonald never permitted Quebec to be an exception to his restricted concept of provincial sovereignty. The Prime Minister rewrote provincial bills that did not suit him or that did not conform to the wishes of prominent Montreal Conservatives like Hugh Allan:

I have read Chauveau's bill with not a little astonishment. It gives the local legislature infinitely greater power than we have here or the Lords or Commons have in England. The Bill will not do at all but you need not say anything to him about it. I will draft a Bill which I think will hold water and do all that is necessary and will give it to you when you come up.[14]

The provincial premier was sometimes the last to learn of the prime minister's decision. 'By the way,' Macdonald wrote Premier Chauveau in 1869, 'the disallowance of your Privileges of Parliament Act will come out in the next Gazette with that of the Province of Ontario. Cartier and Langevin both thought this would be better than your repealing it.'[15]

With Cartier ill and preoccupied with Ottawa affairs, Macdonald's usual emissary to Quebec City was his Minister of Public Works, Hector Langevin. The Conservative party in Quebec functioned as a single unit, and Langevin does not seem to have drawn any particular distinction between provincial and federal matters; he believed that his influence on events in the provincial capital was necessary *'pour mettre la Confédération en mouvement'*.[16] One of Langevin's major duties was to reinforce the weak Chauveau adminstration. Worried that the government of the 'trembling and fearful' premier would collapse, Langevin treated Chauveau as a loyal subordinate.[17] He criticized provincial expenditures and spent long periods in Quebec City to reconcile differences. Langevin also met on occasion with the provincial cabinet to ask for specific provincial measures concerning patronage, railway subsidies, education, or the licensing of inns and grocery stores. Nor was Langevin the only liaison between Quebec City and Ottawa. For important matters the entire provincial cabinet travelled to Ottawa to meet with their federal counterparts.[18]

Langevin's influence in provincial affairs was not restricted to the Chauveau period. When the premier resigned early in 1873, Langevin went to Montreal for the weekend and helped construct the Ouimet cabinet subject, in the words of a prominent Liberal, 'to the approbation of Sir John and the Ottawa Cabinet'.[19] Even when the Conservatives were out of power in Ottawa their influence was still felt in Quebec City. In September 1874 the Tanneries scandal forced another restructuring of the Quebec cabinet and again Langevin was involved. The task was difficult, he wrote Macdonald, but he approved the choice of Charles Boucher de Boucerville as premier and the addition to the cabinet of A.R. Angers and J.G. Robertson. The growing provincial debt and de Boucherville's inept handling of railway and financial policy brought Conservative leaders back to the province in 1878. The provincial treasurer had sent Macdonald his tax legislation for approval: 'As our House reopens the day after tomorrow, and as I would like to present the financial statement as soon after the opening as may be possible, may I ask if you have had time to look over the draft act that I sent you?'[20] Entangled in a web of railway politics, Premier de Boucherville had weakened his party by choosing a route for the government railway which favoured the Terrebonne County interest of L.F.R. Masson and Joseph Chapleau. In doing so, de Boucherville had alienated powerful Conservatives in neighbouring counties and in Montreal. Macdonald was prepared to come to Quebec himself to avoid a 'disastrous' breakup, but Langevin was able to assure Prime Minister that he had 'come to an understanding' with de Boucherville's leading *Bleu* opponent.[21]

The system of dual representation was a useful tool in enforcing the will of the *Bleu* leadership. Among the Conservatives who sat in both the provincial and the federal legislature in 1867 were Langevin, Cartier, Joseph Cauchon, Christopher Dunkin, George Irvine, John Jones Ross, L.A. Sénécal, and Premier Chauveau. Committees of the provincial legislature were another source of influence. Of the above members, only Langevin did not sit on the important provincial committee on railways, canals, telegraph lines, and mining and manufacturing corporations. The use of federal patronage was a less subtle form of control. A militia post, a judgeship, an appointment to a government commission, a federal contract, a lieutenant-governorship, or a senate seat were treasured plums. For the less prominent the federal government had positions in the Post Office, Customs Department, or Intercolonial Railway; for errant sons of constituents the North West Mounted Police offered a respectable and yet distant career. Pressures from Ottawa could also be used to encourage entrepreneurs with federal contracts to donate to party coffers at the provincial level. Joseph Chapleau, like Langevin and Cartier, played the patronage game to good effect. Chapleau's brother served as secretary to Langevin, and some of his great respect for Macdonald may have been due to handouts he received from the Prime Minister. In 1879 Chapleau, leader of the opposition in Quebec after the formation of the brief Liberal régime of Henri Joly, asked Macdonald for the 'paltry sum' of £2000 and reminded the Prime Minister that 'times are hard', 'elections frequent', and that the government had been 'stingy' with him.[22]

The financial terms of Confederation reinforced Quebec's subservience to Ottawa. Over half of the province's income was in the form of a federal subsidy. Despite the warnings and admonitions of federal politicians, the province's financial situation steadily deteriorated. In 1876 the provincial Liberal leader predicted that Quebec would have to accept a legislative union if it did not curtail its spending. Alexander Galt, a leading architect of the financial arrangements of Confederation, wrote to the new premier in 1878 that 'you have a most difficult task before you, if the Province is to be saved from bankruptcy. If you fail, then Confederation must give place to a legislative union.'[23] Railway subsidies were the main cause of the province's financial embarrassment. Government expenditures to aid railway construction jumped from $48,171 in 1871 to $1,013,099 in 1875; by 1882 the province had spent $12,537,980 for a railway joining Quebec City, Montreal, and Ottawa. To pay for its railway expenditures, Quebec repeatedly had to make provincial loans, and by 1880 debt charges accounted for 23 per cent of the province's total expenditures.[24] Provincial politicians of both parties, while publicly avowing provincial autonomy, directed public revenues to railways that would lock the province into a transcontinental economic grid.

In the years immediately after Confederation, the strong presence in Ottawa of Cartier, Langevin, and other prominent *Bleus* had assured the attentiveness of the Macdonald government to the needs of Quebec. However, the provincial administrations of Gédéon Ouimet (1873–4) and Charles Boucher de Boucherville (1874–8) had little leverage with the federal Liberal government of Alexander Mackenzie. After Dorion was named to the bench, the Mackenzie administration had only weak representation from Quebec. Nor was the appointment to the federal Liberal cabinet of the renegade Conservative, Joseph Cauchon, a success. *Persona non grata* with both Liberals and Conservatives, Cauchon was finally put out to pasture as lieutenant-governor of Manitoba. The outspoken attack by Mackenzie's postmaster general, Lucius Huntington, on the alliance between the *Bleus* and the Roman Catholic hierarchy damaged efforts by provincial Liberals to moderate the hostility of the Church. Whereas Macdonald, Cartier, and Langevin had administered patronage in the province with ease and for useful political goals, Mackenzie's fussing over the temerity of French-Canadian office-seekers led to weak appointments. The Prime Minister was not opposed to railways, but he objected to the constant demands for railway subsidies from the *Bleu* backers of Quebec's north-shore railways. The Prime Minister did show concern for the state of Quebec finances, and in 1876 helped the province float a loan on the British market. On the issue of a Canadian supreme court, Mackenzie was bolder than John A. Macdonald. As Prime Minister, Macdonald had backed off from establishing a supreme court in the face of opposition from his Quebec advisers, Cartier, Langevin, and Thomas Chapais. Mackenzie went ahead and instituted the court despite the protests of French-Canadian Conservatives, who worried about the treatment of Quebec civil law in a federal court. His Minister of Justice, Télésphore Fournier, argued that a supreme court on which two of the six judges would be French Canadian would be an improvement on the Privy Council in England.[25] For a few months in 1878 there were Liberal governments in both Ottawa and Quebec City. Mackenzie and Premier Henri Joly were able to make minor agreements such as the cession of federal property in Quebec City for the construction of a station for the province's railway. However, the period of Liberal dominance was shortlived.

Joly and the Liberals had been brought to power in March 1878 by Lieutenant-Governor Letellier's dismissal of the de Boucherville government. Late in 1877 relations had deteriorated between Letellier, an outspoken Liberal, and the Conservative cabinet. In addition to growing personal hostility, Letellier contested the cabinet's financial and railway policies and its practice of excluding him from their councils. After dismissing the Conservatives he invited the Liberals to form a government. The Lieutenant-Governor's precipitate action augmented the debate on federalism in Quebec. Provincial and federal elections in 1878 did not ease the situation. In Quebec, Joly's government, with a majority of one, barely maintained its hold on office. The federal election brought John A. Macdonald back to power supported by an overwhelming Conservative vote in Quebec. The resulting months of debate in both Ottawa and Quebec City gave both Liberal and Conservative orators an opportunity to argue their diverse concepts of federalism. The Conservatives, sounding like good Whigs, emphasized the constitutional rights of the people and pressured Macdonald to dismiss the Lieutenant-Governor. Israel Tarte, Joseph Chapleau, and Conservative newspapers charged that the Liberals had gained power by authoritarian tactics. The Lieutenant-Governor, the Montreal *Gazette* charged, had been backed by George Brown and Alexander Mackenzie in 'filching power in the Province of Quebec'. In a speech to the House of Commons, Langevin concentrated on the unconstitutionality of the Lieutenant-Governor's action:

> If the Crown could set aside the laws passed by both Houses of Parliament, then our Responsible Government and constitution would come to nothing, because the Crown alone would rule the country . . . . The will of the people, as expressed by their representatives, had always been respected. Whenever votes of money had been given by the people through Parliament, the Queen had been most thankful to her faithful Commons, and it was left for Mr Letellier to do otherwise, and violate the Constitution of the country.[26]

Not surprisingly, the Liberals loudly defended provincial autonomy. 'Our federal system is a fraud,' an angry Mackenzie exclaimed, 'if this Parliament is to constantly exercise surveillance over the actions of the local legislatures and local Governors.' To Wilfrid Laurier, the Lieutenant-Governor should be left in office as a matter of liberty and self-government:

> . . . what I ask in the name of the Province to which I belong is that we be allowed the privilege of being governed according to our own standard—that we should be allowed the privilege of being badly governed, if being governed by ourselves meant bad government; but, at all events to be governed by ourselves. This I ask in the name of liberty and self-government.[27]

In October 1879 the Joly government fell. Recurring difficulties over its north-shore railway policy, the mounting provincial debt, lingering bitterness from the Letellier affair, and a hostile Conservative majority in the Legislative Council contributed to the Liberals' collapse. The new premier, Joseph Chapleau, brought a new strength to provincial leadership. Never a lackey to Macdonald, Chapleau was, however, an experienced professional politician who understood the reality of power in the Canadian federal structure. While solicitous of Macdonald, the premier was an old hand at hard bargaining with the federal government. Throughout much of his tenure, Chapleau pressed the Prime Minister to resolve Quebec's deepening financial crisis. In October 1880 he warned Macdonald that 'the financial existence of the province' depended on the sale of the provincial railway and that a decision could not 'be long delayed without exposing our Treasury to a disaster.'[28] Chapleau wanted the federal government to increase its subsidy to Quebec, to purchase the government railway or to force the Canadian Pacific Railway to buy it. In March 1882 he settled for half a loaf. The Canadian Pacific bought the line from Montreal to Ottawa; the remaining section, from Montreal to Quebec City, was sold to Chapleau's friend and crony, Louis Sénécal.

While Chapleau used all the traditional *Bleu* tricks to wangle aid from Ottawa, politicians in other provinces acted as watchdogs against any special concessions to Quebec. In 1884, for example, Edward Blake attacked the flexible system of provincial subsidies as 'destructive of the independence and autonomy of the Provinces' and urged that they be placed on a 'permanent and lasting basis'. He pointed out that the system of subsidies wrecked economical government by the provinces and had an adverse 'moral and financial influence' on the Confederation agreement.[29]

The most important theoretical attack on the increasing centralization of the Macdonald system came from Thomas J.J. Loranger. Member of a prominent Conservative family and a judge of the provincial Supreme Court, Loranger was worried by Quebec's loss of corporate identity. Confederation seemed to be working to the detriment of French Canada: 'Political Union, which for other nations means increased force, natural development, and concentration of authority, means, for us, feebleness, isolation and menace, and Legislative Union, political absorption!' To counteract the increasing focus on Ottawa, he emphasized the autonomy of the provinces and the independence of the lieutenant governors and argued in favour of what became known as the compact theory:

> In constituting themselves into a confederation, the provinces did not intend to renounce, and in fact never did renounce their autonomy. This autonomy with their rights, powers and prerogatives they expressly preserved for all that concerns their internal government; by forming themselves into a federal association, under political and legislative aspects, they formed a central government, only for interprovincial objects, and far from having created the provincial powers, it is from these provincial powers that has arisen the federal government, to which the provinces have ceded a portion of their rights, property and revenues.[30]

These protests had little effect before 1887. In accepting the subordination of Quebec to Ottawa, the politicians may only have been accepting the reality of the province's situation. Confederation had locked Quebec into a federal state in which, for the moment at least, the great powers lay with the central government. At the same time, expanding railways were tying Quebec into transcontinental systems. The province's major city, Montreal, was making its bid to be the metropolis of the new Canadian state. The city's bankers, shippers, and entrepreneurs, caught up in the rush for capital, western trade, and new industries, had little time for constitutional niceties or federal-provincial relations. The Liberal party, never a serious threat to the *Bleus* before 1878, was still exorcising itself of the devils of old radical *rouge-isme*. The *Rouge* leaders—A.A. Dorion, L.A. Jetté, Wilfrid Laurier, and Henri Joly—were moderates for whom provincial autonomy was only one of many planks which had to await the accession to power.

The province, torn after Confederation by divisions between Quebec City and Montreal, religious controversies, recurring scandals, and a mounting economic crisis, lacked both the strength and the desire to do battle with the centralizers. Only with Honoré Mercier's accession to the premiership in 1887 would Quebec politicians learn to exploit effectively the issue of provincial rights.

Suggestions for Further Reading

Paul-André Linteau, René Durocher, and Jean-Claude Robert, *Quebec: A History 1867–1929* (Toronto, 1983).

Susan Mann Trofimenkoff, *The Dream of Nation: A Social and Intellectual History of Quebec* (Toronto, 1983).

Brian J. Young, *George-Étienne Cartier: Montreal Bourgeois* (Montreal, 1981).

Notes

[1] A general treatment of economic tensions is contained in Jean Hamelin and Yves Roby, *Histoire économique de Québec, 1851–1896* (Montreal, 1971).

[2] Cartier's defeat is examined in detail in the author's article, 'The Defeat of George-Étienne Cartier in Montreal-East in 1872', *Canadian Historical Review*, 51 (December 1970): 386–406.

[3] Archives of the University of Montreal, Baby Collection, M.W. Baby to George Baby, 16 December 1869.

[4] *Le Journal de Québec*, 4 July 1873; Quebec, *Report of the Royal Commission of Inquiry on Constitutional Problems* (Quebec, 1956), 1: 61, 63.

[5] *Le Journal des Trois-Rivières*, 14 November 1870.

[6] A.R.M. Lower, 'Theories of Canadian Federalism', in A.R.M. Lower *et. al.*, *Evolving Canadian Federalism* (Durham, N.C., 1958), 8.

[7] J. Boyd, *Sir George Etienne Cartier* (Toronto, 1914), 319; Langevin is quoted in *The Pacific Railway Speeches Delivered . . . in the House of Commons, 1880* (Montreal, 1880), 49.

[8]Mousseau's election pamphlet was quoted by W. Laurier in Canada, House of Commons, *Debates*, 12 March 1879, 330; Archives of the Province of Quebec, Labelle Papers, J. Chapleau to Curé Labelle, 27 November 1883; Montreal *Gazette*, 25 September 1878.

[9]PAC, John A. Macdonald Papers, P.J.O. Chauveau to J.A. Macdonald, 19 July 1867.

[10]Montreal *Gazette*, 25 March 1882; Macdonald Papers, no. 86537, J. Chapleau to J.A. Macdonald, 31 October 1880.

[11]Macdonald Papers, H. Lagevin to J.A. Macdonald, 18 January 1877.

[12]H. Langevin to Jean Langevin, 22 June 1873, quoted in A. Désilets, *Hector-Louis Langevin: un père de la confédération canadienne* (Quebec, 1969), 238.

[13]*L'Evènement*, 10 November 1875; Archives of the Province of Quebec, Joly Papers, H.G. Joly to F. Hincks, 12 April 1879.

[14]Macdonald Papers, J.A. Macdonald to H. Langevin, 28 December 1869.

[15]*Ibid.*, J.A. Macdonald to P.J.O. Chauveau, 30 November 1869.

[16]Désilets, *Hector-Louis Langevin*, 195.

[17]Archives of the Province of Quebec, Chapais Collection, H. Langevin to Jean Langevin, 11 February 1868.

[18]The whole provincial cabinet went to Ottawa in March 1873, and in February 1884 all but Premier Ross waited upon the federal cabinet. *Ibid.*, H. Langevin to Macdonald, 28 January 1879.

[19]PAC, Mackenzie Papers, no. 257, A.A. Dorion to A. Mackenzie, 11 February 1873.

[20]Macdonald Papers, L.R. Church to J.A. Macdonald, 15 January 1878.

[21]*Ibid.*, H. Langevin to Macdonald, 28 January 1879.

[22]*Ibid.*, J.A. Chapleau to Macdonald, 13 May 1879.

[23]Joly Papers, no 425A, Alexander Galt to H.G. Joly, 20 April 1878.

[24]Quebec, *Sessional Papers, 1882–83*, no. 71; *Report of the Railway Commission* (Quebec, 1882–83); S. Bates, *A Financial History of Canadian Governments* (Ottawa, 1939), 148.

[25]P.B. Waite, *Canada, 1874–1896: Arduous Destiny* (Toronto, 1971), 39.

[26]Canada, House of Commons, *Debates*, 12 April 1878, 1944.

[27]Mackenzie is quoted in Dale C. Thomson, *Alexander Mackenzie: Clear Grit* (Toronto, 1960), 350; Laurier was speaking in *Debates*, 12 March 1879, 329.

[28]Macdonald Papers, no. 86519, Chapleau to Macdonald, 15 October 1880.

[29]Canada, House of Commons, *Debates*, 12 April 1884, 1529.

[30]T.J.J. Loranger, *Letters Upon the Interpretation of the Federal Constitution* (Quebec, 1884), 7. For more on the compact theory see R. Arès, *Dossier sur le pacte fédératif de 1867* (Montreal, 1967), and Ramsay Cook, *Provincial Autonomy, Minority Rights and the Compact Theory, 1867–1921* (Ottawa, 1969).

3

Provincial Rights and Dominion–Provincial Relations

Christopher Armstrong

While most of the Fathers of Confederation clearly intended the new nation they were forging to be a strongly centralized federal state, many countervailing pressures were built into the situation that led to the drafting of the British North America Act, and these prevailed after its implementation. The provinces and their governments had not been eliminated in the new constitutional arrangements—protection for French Canada made such a step impossible to contemplate, even apart from the Maritime provinces' lack of enthusiasm—and in the ensuing years they successfully asserted their power in practical and legal terms. Ironically, much of the impetus for 'provincial rights' came not from Quebec or the Maritimes but from the province that had initially provided most of the national vision in the making of Confederation: Ontario. Even more ironically, the man most responsible for Ontario's early stand—Premier Oliver Mowat—had been a staunch

advocate of a strong central government in the 1860s. But as the most populous and economically successful province, Ontario had no desire to see its policies constrained or its riches disbursed to its less prosperous neighbours; it consistently dug in its heels to resist federal encroachments on its freedom of action, particularly in economic matters.

Christopher Armstrong outlines the Ontario position in federal-provincial relations, concentrating on the period before the First World War but going beyond it to demonstrate the continuity of policy and problems. Ontario's first concern, he argues, was to preserve control over its own economic development, especially in the matter of resource development, where the province frequently found little advantage in a 'National Policy'. It was also consistently opposed to anything akin to today's 'equalization payments' to the less affluent provinces, seeing such redistribution of revenue as occurring at

Ontario's expense. To support its position, Armstrong continues, Ontario helped frame the 'Compact Theory of Confederation', a view that insisted that the unification of British North America was a result of treaties made among the provinces and implied the entitlement of provinces to a veto over constitutional changes. The Compact Theory acquired a new meaning when French Canada came to see Confederation as an agreement between races as well as provinces, but in its original formulation Ontario played the major role. Unlike Quebec, Armstrong concludes, Ontario had no need to call upon the federal government to protect minority rights outside the province (in the Manitoba Schools Question, for example); therefore its advocacy of provincial rights could be unqualified.

Did Ontario's place in Confederation entitle it to special consideration? Did Ontario consistently oppose a National Policy, or only when it ran counter to Ontario's interests? How did Ontario's advocacy of provincial rights limit the powers of the federal government, and how did it affect other provinces? Was provincial rights a constructive force in Canadian development? Finally, has Ontario's position and policy changed appreciably in recent years?

This article first appeared, titled 'The Mowat Heritage in Federal-Provincial Relations', in Donald Swainson, ed., *Oliver Mowat's Ontario* (Toronto, 1972), 93–118.

Sir Oliver Mowat deserves the title, 'father of the provincial-rights movement in Canada'. It was he who challenged Sir John Macdonald upon the use of the power of disallowance, over the granting of 'better terms' to some provinces without the others being consulted, and over the functions of the lieutenant-governor. He took a hand in the calling of the first Interprovincial Conference, which dutifully passed a number of resolutions he had drafted demanding for the provinces sovereign control of their affairs within their sphere of jurisdiction. He appeared personally before the Judicial Committee of the Privy Council with conspicuous success and persuaded them to accept his contentions in a number of important constitutional cases. All in all, he made it certain that the provinces would be far more than the glorified municipalities which some Fathers of Confederation, not least himself, had envisaged.[1]

Some might say that Canadians have little reason to be grateful to Mowat for his efforts. It must be admitted that the conduct of federal-provincial relations seems to bring out the worst in our political leaders. In the intervals between delivering long-winded speeches, most of which are no more than platitudinous humbug, premiers and prime ministers alike have engaged in backbiting and name-calling on a grand scale. Witness, for example, Mackenzie King's description of Howard Ferguson as a 'skunk', or Sir James Whitney declaring that the federal minister of justice, "Baby" Aylesworth, '. . . is without exception the most infantile specimen of politician or statesman that ever came to my notice', or that master of invective, Mitchell Hepburn, reviling King in 1941 as an 'assassin of Confederation', fiddling with the Canadian constitution while London burned.[2] None of this has raised the tone of our political life, and such bitterness might be said to have retarded the growth of Canadian national feeling.

Mowat, of course, can hardly be blamed for the whole unedifying spectacle. What should be remembered is that during almost twenty-five years as premier of Ontario he defined the objectives of the province's external policy, of its relations with the federal government and with the other provinces. These his successors continued to pursue long after his retirement. He recognized that Ontario occupied a unique place in the Canadian federation owing to its size, its wealth, and its population. The poorer provinces might look upon federalism as a means of overcoming regional disparities, but Ontarians, loyal to the Clear Grit tradition, valued separation more than equalization. The province wished to be left on its own to develop its bountiful resources without outside interference. Mowat sensed that 'Empire Ontario' must have its emperor, and during his premiership did his best to enhance the province's power and influence along with his own.[3]

Mowat's first objective then was to secure the fullest control over the province's economic development. Federal policies which threatened to restrict this must be strenuously resisted. Indeed, there developed a sort of dialectic in federal-provincial relations: any 'interference' by Ottawa was opposed by provincial politicians, almost as a conditioned reflex. Whenever federal policies failed to meet Ontario's needs, or threatened to work against her best interests, the province tried to substitute its authority for that of the federal government. More often than not, it should be noted, the dynamic force which provoked such clashes was a private interest group, attempting to use whichever level of government best met its needs and desires. The province would take up the cudgels on behalf of its clients, whose opponents were usually pressing just as hard for Ottawa's aid.

Because of its vast domain Ontario was rich enough to resist the efforts of the federal government to bully it or bribe it into line. While the other provinces clamoured for 'better terms', Ontario held aloof. Since almost half of federal tax revenues were supplied by Ontarians, any increase in federal transfer payments to the other provinces held a limited appeal for them. When the other premiers went cap in hand to Ottawa, Mowat could afford to stay at home and denounce any changes made in the financial relations between the Dominion and the provinces without consulting him. Occasionally, however, Ontario might wish the support of the other provinces for some demand it was making upon the federal authorities. Then the premier could unbend a little and ensure the necessary backing by approving the demands of the poor relations for increased subsidies.

Sir Oliver was quick to realize that both of these objectives could better be attained if Ontario were to secure a veto over constitutional change. He could not only torpedo those amendments of which he disapproved but demand favours in return for his assent. Since the British North America Act contained no formula for its own amendment, there was no statutory basis for such a demand, but the 'Compact Theory' of Confederation, which explained the constitution as a treaty between the provinces, offered a historical and conventional justification for this claim. Mowat early became an ardent exponent of the theory, and while his efforts bore little fruit during Macdonald's lifetime, his successors reaped the benefits.

Only a few illustrations can be offered here of the way in which Mowat and his successors pursued these aims, but they are sufficient to show that the premiers of Ontario, regardless of party, have been surprisingly faithful to them. As a result the Mowat heritage in federal-provincial relations long remained a vital part of our national life.

The most serious threat to the Ontario domain during Mowat's premiership arose from Macdonald's determination to cut the province down to size by handing over a huge area west of the Lakehead to the new province of Manitoba. To the *Globe* the issue was a simple one:

> Shall Ontario be deprived of the railway terminus on Lake Superior, with the city which is certain to spring up there?
>
> Shall Ontario be robbed of 60,000 acres of fertile land?
>
> Shall Ontario lose the revenue of $125,000,000, the sum which the pine timber alone, to say nothing of other valuable timber on the disputed territory, is computed to be worth?
>
> Shall Ontario be defrauded of a mineral region the wealth of which may exceed anything else in the known world?

Mowat threw himself vigorously into the fight; in 1882 he went so far as to threaten secession, boldly stating that

> if they could only maintain Confederation by giving up half their province, then Confederation must go . . . and if they could not demand the large amount of property to which they were entitled without foregoing the advantages of Confederation then it was not worth maintaining.[4]

Eventually the matter was fought out before the Judicial Committee. With Mowat personally arguing the province's case, Ontario won its point. He returned home to a hero's welcome, and while touring the province the premier told the crowd at a reception in Niagara Falls,

> I rejoice to know that the one great cause, the principal cause of your enthusiasm, is that you love Ontario as I love it. The display that you have made this

night shows that you are for Ontario, and that you are for those who maintain Ontario's cause.[5]

When Macdonald continued to claim the timber and minerals in the disputed area, Mowat entered another suit to establish full possession. In 1888 the Privy Council again upheld him, and a settlement with the Dominion was finally arrived at in 1889.

The way in which private interest groups could create tension between the Dominion and the province was also dramatically demonstrated in Mowat's time by the row over the Rivers and Streams Act. The significant fact was that one of the lumbermen involved in the dispute was a Grit, the other a Tory. The Grit naturally turned to the provincial government for help, while the Tory hitched his fortunes to the government in Ottawa. Four times the legislature passed the act and three times it was disallowed by Macdonald. The two levels of government were drawn into serious conflict through a private quarrel. Neither premier nor prime minister emerged from this fracas with an enhanced reputation, but a pattern had been fixed which would frequently be repeated in future.[6]

Macdonald was convinced that Canada's economic development could best be achieved through the National Policy. So long as it seemed to promote the fullest development of Ontario resources and the creation of an industrial base there, the province's politicians were content to accept its benefits. But as soon as Ontario's interests seemed threatened, the province stood ready to challenge federal policies, to substitute an 'Ontario policy' of its own. The need did not arise during Mowat's premiership, but in 1897 the Dingley Tariff imposed a duty of $2 per thousand board feet on Canadian pine lumber, while the unprocessed raw material, pine sawlogs, was admitted free to the United States. Ontario lumbermen were naturally upset at the closing of the huge and profitable American market. They pressed the federal government to impose an export duty on sawlogs to force the McKinley administration to negotiate. But Sir Wilfrid Laurier was reluctant to act, not only because the Dingley Tariff included certain retaliatory provisions, but because he had fixed his hopes for freer trade on the pending negotiations aimed at settling all Canadian-American differences.

Unable to get relief in Ottawa, some Ontario lumbermen turned to the provincial government and demanded that it require the sawing of all Ontario pine in Canada. They succeeded in convincing the public and both political parties that Ontarians would become mere 'hewers of wood and drawers of water' for their richer, industrialized American neighbours if they failed to act. Facing a provincial election in 1889, Mowat's successor and long-time subordinate, Arthur S. Hardy, bowed to this skilfully promoted public clamour and inserted a manufacturing condition in all timber licences so that the exportation of pine sawlogs cut on Crown land was forbidden.[7]

American lumbermen who owned limits in Ontario protested both to Washington and to Ottawa. Secretary of State Day suggested that the federal government might disallow the export embargo legislation. Premier Hardy began to fear that the federal government might do so in order to persuade the McKinley administration to accept a reciprocity agreement. Laurier refused, however, to interfere with the provincial policy, for Hardy had warned that this would seriously damage the Liberal party's prospects in Ontario. Efforts were then made by the American lumber interests to have prohibitive duties imposed on lumber and other Canadian imports. Meanwhile, the Colonial Office urged Laurier to persuade Hardy to suspend the embargo until the courts decided whether it was a regulation of trade and commerce and, hence, a federal responsibility. The premier stood firm in the face of pressure from Washington, London, and Ottawa. He refused to suspend the act or to join in a reference to the courts, and eventually the embargo was declared valid by the Judicial Committee in a private suit.

As Professor Nelles has shown, the government of Ontario wished to force companies exploiting the province's natural resources for sale in the United States to do their processing in Canada. This was intended to create jobs as well as capital investment in plant. The success of the sawlog export embargo in forcing the relocation of a number of American sawmills in the province led the government to extend the manufacturing condition to pulpwood, nickel ore, and hydroelectricity too, though with varying degrees of success. Ontario sought, then, to impose her own development policy, which sometimes clashed with the consistent federal policy of seeking to secure free access to the American market for Canadian raw materials.

The mediating influence of party loyalty, both Hardy and Laurier being Liberals, had helped to prevent any open federal-provincial conflict over the sawlog embargo. With the election of the Conservative Whitney administration in 1905 this influence disappeared. Over the next half-dozen years bitter rows between the two levels of government over development policy were frequent. Technological innovations in the fields of transportation, hydroelectricity, and pulp and paper held out the lure of such large profits that one observer was moved to declare, 'If Solomon were on hand today, he would say, "With all your getting, get a water power and a lighting and electric railway franchise." '[8] Astute entrepreneurs were quick to take note of these opportunities; owing to the vagueness of the BNA Act about the division of authority to incorporate companies,[9] men like James Conmee became convinced that they could play a kind of game and evade provincial control by obtaining federal charters. Attempts at regulation by the Ontario government could then be denounced as attacks upon vested interests and the sacred right of private property.

Conmee himself was specially favourably situated as a Liberal Member of Parliament, able to call upon the government to back his schemes. But others were quick to follow his lead in seeking to obtain at Ottawa what they were denied at Toronto. So complaisant did the Laurier administration prove in meeting the demands of company promoters, that Whitney was forced to retain the services of a watchdog in Ottawa to alert him to trouble ahead.[10] A good deal of time and energy was spent by both provincial and federal Conservatives in denouncing charter-mongering by the Liberals, though their protests usually fell upon deaf ears. A reservoir of ill-will built up which did much to embitter the relations of the province and the Dominion as long as Laurier remained in power.

Ontario's single most valuable resource was hydroelectricity, the province's only domestic power source. For over thirty years Mowat's successors resisted federal attempts to take control of the electrical industry. Here, too, the conflict was rooted in a constitutional ambiguity. While the province owned its lands and natural resources, the BNA Act gave the Dominion control of navigation. The greatest hydro potential lay on navigable rivers like the St Lawrence and the Ottawa. If the existing canals were improved, creating new waterpowers, the federal government might claim them as 'incidental' to navigation. Or else it might block the construction of provincially owned generating stations indefinitely as impediments to shipping. Once the province had taken the decision to develop all its power through an arm of the provincial government, the Hydro-Electric Power Commission, conflict between Ontario and the Dominion seemed unavoidable.

The First World War produced an enormous upsurge in the demand for electricity, and by the mid 1920s the HEPC was casting longing eyes at a share of the two-million-horsepower potential of the International Section of the St Lawrence. This development obviously required the co-operation of the United States government which was ready to support the construction of the St Lawrence Seaway as a joint power-navigation project. However, Prime Minister Mackenzie King was determined that if there was to be a Seaway it should be paid for through the sale of power and not from federal revenues. Should the federal government establish control over this development, it would have sufficient leverage to establish a national electricity policy.

Premier Howard Ferguson of Ontario was equally determined to prevent this. The very idea of a national electricity policy was repugnant to his government, and he rejected the notion that the HEPC's customers should finance the Seaway through higher electricity rates. To bolster its position the province fell back upon the Compact Theory of Confederation:

Canada was created by the act of the separate provinces. They established a federal union, yielding to the union the rights and functions appropriate to the national endeavour. Navigation went to the federal authority in the interests of national trade and commerce. . . . On the other hand, it was only natural that the more local aspects, the more particular property rights, the power, the domestic and sanitary uses [of waterways], which physically are applicable only to local industry and endeavour and should be retained within the sphere of the Provinces.

Ottawa's claim that power was 'incidental' to navigation was

a concealed assault upon the provincial position under our federal system. In effect, if admitted, it would mean that federal action could completely oust the province from all benefits whenever a stream could be made navigable.

Such tactics 'could slowly convert Canada from a federal union into a legislative union under supreme control of the Parliament at Ottawa'.[11]

Efforts to clarify the constitutional position through a reference to the Supreme Court in 1928 proved abortive, for the learned judges confined their replies almost entirely to vague hypotheticals. Efforts to negotiate a settlement during the next two years were equally fruitless. During the federal election campaign of 1930 Ferguson and King traded insults over who was to blame for the delay. The new prime minister, R.B. Bennett, was more enthusiastic about the Seaway than his predecessor; and a fellow-Conservative, George Henry of Ontario, proved more co-operative once it was clear that Bennett was prepared to concede the province's demands. By the Canada–Ontario agreement, which preceded the St Lawrence Deep Waterway Treaty of 1932 with the United States, the federal government agreed to pay the entire cost of works required for navigation alone plus 30 per cent of the cost of joint navigation and power works. The remaining 70 percent, about $37.7 million, along with the $66.5 million to equip the powerhouses, was to be met by the province. The HEPC would own all the power.

The treaty failed to get approval in the United States Senate, but Ferguson's struggle had not been in vain. When the Roosevelt administration persuaded Mackenzie King to take up the Seaway project again in the late 1930s, it was simply assumed that Ontario would control Canada's share of the power. Under the St Lawrence Basin Agreement of 1941 the province's share of the cost of joint works was also reduced from 70 per cent to 62.5 per cent. Just as Mowat had done in the case of the Manitoba boundary, his successors successfully defended the province's control of a vital resource on which its industrial base and future prosperity were heavily dependent.

The second part of Mowat's legacy was opposition to increases in federal transfer payments to the provinces. As early as 1869 Edward Blake led the Ontario Reform party in denouncing the grant of better terms to Nova Scotia as a violation of the Confederation compact. Ontario's first premier, Sandfield Macdonald, accumulated such a large surplus that the provincial government weathered the depression of the 1870s with relatively little difficulty. However, when the Mowat administration found itself faced with large deficits in the early eighties, his ministers turned their fire upon Macdonald's habit of soothing discontented provinces with financial titbits taken from the pockets of Ontarians. Christopher Fraser, the Commissioner of Public Works, told the legislature in 1885:

[W]e who have charge of Ontario affairs would be recreant to our trust, if in the face of what we see going on, and what is absolutely certain to occur again, we made no sign, and did not indicate that Ontario would not continue submitting to these raids by the other Provinces . . . .We do not care to get these indirect and unwarranted grants, and that Ontario shall be the milk cow for the whole concern.[12]

When Honoré Mercier suggested an Interprovincial Conference in 1887, Mowat at once agreed that federal encroachment on provincial autonomy must be resisted, but added pointedly that Ontario 'was satisfied with the provisions of the British North America Act, and would still prefer them to any changes if the principle on which they are based were faithfully carried out by the Dominion Parliament with the approval of all the provinces.'[13] Yet he realized that subsidy increases were the chief concern of Mercier and the other premiers. In what would become a classic ploy for Ontario leaders, he agreed to throw his weight behind their demands, despite his reservations, in return for the backing of the other provinces in his demand for greater provincial autonomy. The conference called for hefty increases in the scale of grants to civil government (in Ontario's case involving a rise from $80,000 to $240,000 per year), and proposed that the annual per capita subsidy of 80 cents be tied to the current census figures rather than the 1861 ones. Such a 'basis for a final and unalterable settlement' meant, of course, that the Mowat administration would get the tidy sum of $600,000 a year to dispose of.[14]

Macdonald simply ignored the resolutions passed at the conference. The subsidy question was not raised again until 1900 when the Liberal premiers of Quebec and the Maritime provinces secured better terms. Premier George W. Ross of Ontario immediately protested to Laurier 'about the reopening of questions of public policy which were considered settled years ago'.[15] The other provinces were insistent on an all-round subsidy increase, however, and an Interprovincial Conference met in December 1902. Ross, who was occupied with a crucial series of by-elections, did not even bother to attend or to send an Ontario representative. In a memorandum read to the delegates, he simply reaffirmed support for all the resolutions passed in 1887, although he did suggest more generous grants for the support of civil government. Premier S.N. Parent of Quebec, by contrast, wanted the per-capita subsidy fixed at $1. In the end the delegates merely repassed the earlier resolutions.

Laurier showed no more inclination to act upon these demands than had Macdonald, but as the federal surplus mounted the provinces became increasingly restive. By 1904 even Ontario faced a deficit of $800,000 on ordinary account, although the proceeds from the sale of timber limits covered this. Ross was still convinced that piecemeal grants of better terms were a poor way to cope with financial difficulties. Nevertheless, the financial pinch made him less high-minded; he pleaded with Laurier for a subsidy of $6,400 per mile for the provincially owned Temiskaming and Northern Ontario Railway. Laurier refused, however, to treat the province like 'an ordinary railway company', opening the way for a flood of similar demands from the other provinces.[16]

The election of Whitney's Conservative government in 1905, ending almost thirty-five years of Liberal rule, saw no reversal of the province's policy on transfer payments. When Premier Lomer Gouin of Quebec sought the new premier's support for another Interprovincial Conference, Whitney agreed coolly that 'fixity of arrangement between the Federal Government and the Provinces . . . would, for more than one reason, be very desirable. . . .'[17] It was left to the Liberal premiers to persuade Laurier to call a meeting in October of 1906. Whitney recognized that the original subsidies had become quite inadequate. The 1887 proposal to tie the per capita subsidy to the growth of population had several attractions. It had been twice approved by Interprovincial Conferences. The subsidy would automatically increase through time, so that periodic revisions would be unnecessary. Such an arrangement would be both elastic and yet permanent. Last but not least, the largest province would get the biggest increase. Whitney therefore decided to propose that the conference simply endorse the 1887 subsidy resolution once more.

The other premiers were prepared to agree to this, but insisted that each province should have the right to demand additional special allowances. Whitney fought a stubborn rearguard action against this, but was eventually overborne. He then proposed that British Columbia, the most importunate in its demands, should receive a special grant of $100,000 annually for ten years. An attempt by the other western provinces to obtain similar grants was turned down largely at Whitney's insistence. Laurier agreed to accept these terms as a 'final and unalterable' settlement of the subsidy question, and the BNA Act was amended the following year.

The steadily increasing demand for provincial services like highways and education soon absorbed these increases completely. The years immediately before the First World War found even a rich province like Ontario sufficiently hard pressed that its opposition to greater federal transfer payments was again relaxed somewhat. The election of Robert Borden in 1911 was the signal for the repayment of a number of political debts owed to Conservative premiers like Whitney, Rodmond Roblin, and Richard McBride. The boundaries of both Ontario and Manitoba were extended, and conditional grants to agricultural education and highway construction proposed. Still provincial spending mounted inexorably. In 1913 another Interprovincial Conference was held to consider the subsidies. Whitney and the other premiers approved a resolution demanding that 10 per cent of federal tariff revenue by channelled into subsidies. Grants to civil governments were to be increased 50 per cent to $2,610,000, while the remaining $10,710,000 (for 1913) would be distributed according to population. The beauty of this scheme, from Whitney's point of view, was that it would return to Ontarians a fairer share of the money which the federal government would collect from them in any case, so that any increase in transfer payments financed by the province would be comparatively small. Despite strongly worded pleas from Whitney, Borden refused to consider this ingenious suggestion, which would have made every tariff revision the occasion for a federal-provincial donnybrook.

In 1927 there came another occasion when the Mowat ploy proved effective. A Dominion-Provincial Conference was called by Mackenzie King in the midst of his dispute with Howard Ferguson over the control of water-power on navigable rivers. Since the prime minister was content to drag his feet, to refuse to negotiate seriously, Ontario faced a severe power shortage with no prospect of early development of either the St Lawrence or the Ottawa river. Ferguson and Premier L.A. Taschereau of Quebec were confident that the courts would uphold the claims of the provinces, but a reference case required the consent of the federal cabinet. The conference provided a heaven-sent opportunity for forcing King's hand.

Both the Maritimes and the western provinces wanted better terms. When the question of subsidies was raised, Ferguson seized his chance. He reminded the delegates that Ontario paid the largest amount into the federal treasury, yet he supported the demands of the poorer provinces. 'He did not', he said,

> intend . . . to cavil about small things. He regarded it as supremely important to bring about a situation which would be satisfactory to all the provinces.
>
> The basis of financing laid down by the British North America Act could not be regarded as permanent and must be subject to readjustment. . . . This big problem was to promote satisfaction and prosperity by giving fresh inspiration to those who needed help. . . . The expenditure of a few hundred thousand dollars was nothing if optimism, harmony, and industry could be inspired.[18]

Lest the other premiers forget their duty, he suggested that the power question should be eliminated from the agenda and referred to the courts. Despite an invitation from the prime minister to discuss this matter the other premiers remained quiet as mice. Doubtless they were too busy savouring the 'fresh inspiration' of 'a few hundred thousand dollars'. Outmanoeuvred, King gave way and allowed the matter to go to the Supreme Court, though not without taking care to frame the questions so as to render most of the answers irrelevant.

The Compact Theory of Confederation, the third element in the Mowat heritage, provided an underpinning for the other objectives. It could be called into play to defend Ontario's interest in controlling its development or in the financing of the federal system. To insist upon consultation concerning constitutional change proved the surest defence of provincial rights against federal encroachment. The grant of better terms of Nova Scotia had been attacked by Edward Blake in 1869, on the grounds that the assent of all the provinces was required to change the financial terms of the BNA Act. As Blake's successor, Mowat quickly adopted the Compact Theory as a weapon in his disputes with Macdonald.

The Interprovincial Conference of 1887 was represented as the reconvening of the Quebec Conference of 1864, at which the original compact had been agreed to. Under Mowat's influence, the 1887 meeting resolved that the provincial legislatures 'should at the earliest moment take steps with a view of securing the enactment by the Imperial Parliament of amendments to the British North America Act . . .'. In return for his agreement to support an an allround subsidy increase, the premiers gave their support to Mowat's proposals to widen the powers of the provinces and make them even more immune to federal interference.

Mowat's successors were equally loyal to the Compact Theory. George Ross declard that it was

> quite evident that in every stage of its progress it [the BNA Act] was regarded by its framers as a treaty under which the Provinces agreed to transfer a certain portion of their sovereignty to a central Government, which would undertake to discharge the duties common to all, while at the same time leaving the residuum of their sovereignty intact and unimpaired. . . .
>
> Now is it not clear that a trusteeship so formed cannot be dissolved, or its powers abridged or increased without the consent of the parties by whom it was made?[19]

By the turn of the century, indeed, politicians of both parties paid lip service to some version of the Compact Theory. The influence of Blake and Mowat remained strong within the Liberal Party, and Robert Borden admitted that

> In very many matters touching the everyday life of the people, the policy and aims of any provincial administration are of the greatest possible interest and importance. The Liberal-Conservative party for many years past has been inclined to regard Provincial issues as of somewhat minor consequence.

This he now promised to change.[20]

Nevertheless, the provinces did not succeed in establishing a firm conventional right to be consulted about constitutional change. The 1907 subsidy revision was agreed upon at the Interprovincial Conference, and its recommendations accepted by Laurier, but later amendments were not the product of consultation. However, at the 1927 Dominion-Provincial Conference

Ernest Lapointe laid before the delegates an amending formula for the BNA Act, declaring that

> The Government has taken the ground that the BNA Act is an agreement between different parties and that no substantial change should be made without consulting the contracting parties. The BNA Act is the charter of the provinces in which powers have been fixed and determined between the Dominion and the provinces. Consequently, the provinces have the right to be consulted about establishing a new procedure to amend it.[21]

Lapointe's plan would have allowed amendments concerning exclusively federal matters to be made without reference to the provinces. Changes concerning education, the use of French, the administration of justice, property rights, and the like, would have required unanimous provincial consent, and other changes could be made with the consent of any six of the nine provinces.

The dangers inherent in this proposition cannot have escaped Ferguson. Federal powers could now be altered without any reference to the provinces. More important, on all but a few matters, any six provinces could join with the federal government to approve an amendment even if both Ontario and Quebec opposed it. Better to allow the existing confusion to continue, meanwhile loudly claiming the right to be consulted about every alteration, than to tie oneself up in such an unsatisfactory arrangement. Ferguson felt the change might 'affect the fundamental structure of our constitution' and declared that he could 'see no substantial reason in favour of it'. Strong support for this stand came from Premier Taschereau, and Lapointe had to abandon his efforts.

In 1930 the problem recurred. Newly elected, R.B. Bennett prepared to depart for London and an Imperial Conference to approve a draft of the Statute of Westminster, which would have repealed the Colonial Laws Validity Act of 1865 insofar as the Dominions were concerned. Thereafter, British legislation would apply to Canada only if the Dominion expressly requested that it should do so. But the BNA Act was a British statute. Could the division of powers between Dominion and province be altered at the request of the federal Parliament alone once the Statute of Westminster took effect, leaving the provinces with no recourse?

Premier Ferguson was much upset, and suggested to Taschereau

> that the provinces should enter a vigorous protest against what is being done without the original parties to the Confederation agreement being consulted . . . . [W]e should at least be consulted about it before representations are made to the Imperial Parliament. I have made strong protest to Mr. Bennett in one or two discussions I have had with him, and at his suggestion I am putting my views in writing and have asked him to give voice to them at the Conference.[22]

The premier put his position in an open letter to Bennett.[23] Confederation had been 'brought about by the action of the Provinces', and the constitution was 'the crystallization into law . . . of an agreement made by the provinces . . . '. Accordingly, Ferguson claimed the right to veto any changes: 'The Province of Ontario holds strongly to the view that this agreement should not be altered without the consent of the parties to it.' He protested vigorously against the proposed statute and demanded that nothing be done until 'the parties to the original compact' had been consulted and were satisfied. Any other course, he warned, would 'not only greatly disturb the present harmonious operation of our Constitution, but I fear may seriously disrupt the whole structure of our Confederation.'

In an accompanying memorandum the Compact Theory of Confederation was further explained. First came a number of bald assertions: 'The Quebec resolutions . . . were in the nature of a treaty between the provinces . . . '; 'the Dominion was . . . created at the instance of the provinces . . . '. Then came the 'proof': Macdonald, Cartier, and Brown had all referred to the agreement as a 'treaty' at various times. Moreover, the federal Parliament had not been given the power to amend the constitution; if it had such power 'the long and hitherto successful controversy [*sic*] as to the constitutional rights of the provinces would have had a very different outcome, because at any stage of the struggle the Dominion Parliament would have had the power to enact legislation setting aside the pretensions of the provinces.' Skating lightly around the difficult question of who was now party to the compact, the memorandum merely insisted that all the provinces, even those created since 1867, had the same rights. The fact that the provinces had only been formally consulted about a constitutional change on one occasion was dismissed; it simply showed the perfidy of the federal authorities. After all, Ontario had been demanding to be consulted since 1869. A new era had begun in 1927, when Lapointe had at last admitted that the provinces had a right to be consulted. There could be no turning back now, and Ontario would bring all its influence to bear to prevent the power to amend the constitution unilaterally from being handed over to Ottawa by the British parliament.

Coming from the Conservative premier of the largest province, this protest proved effective. The Imperial Conference was adjourned 'until an opportunity has been given to the provinces to determine whether their rights would be adversely affected . . . '.[24] In April 1931 a Dominion-Provincial Conference met, and Bennett somewhat reluctantly agreed that the statute should be amended so that it conferred no new powers upon either the Dominion or the provinces to amend the BNA Act or to alter their legislative jurisdiction. The broader question of an amending formula was ignored. The outcome satisfied Premier Henry of Ontario, since provincial powers had not been reduced.

Pressure for constitutional amendment was naturally increased by the Depression. The fashion of the day in many quarters was to insist that the federal government should assume full responsibility for unemployment and for relief. Not surprisingly, however, neither the Henry government nor the Liberal administration of Mitchell Hepburn was enthusiastic about such a constitutional change. Both premiers suspected that proposed amendments would simply be designed to place all effective power in federal hands. Arthur Roebuck, Hepburn's attorney general, was alarmed by Bennett's aggressive attitude towards the provinces: 'Wherein lies the need for immediate revision?' he asked J.W. Dafoe. 'The tory-minded would like to centralize power. The Divine Righters always did, and every battle for freedom has been directed to decentralization.' In any event, Roebuck added, nothing should be done until the provinces all agreed upon an amending formula. He was confident that tactical skill in these negotiations could 'head off a Dominion grab'.[25]

In 1935 Mackenzie King accepted the recommendation of a Select Committee of the Commons that an amending formula should be discussed at a Dominion-provincial conference. Roebuck insisted that any method must be 'satisfactory to all provinces'.[26] Some progress was made; he and W.J. Major of Manitoba proposed that all the constitutional statutes should be consolidated and divided into four categories, each with a different amending procedure. Matters exclusively federal, like disallowance or the creation of new provinces, could be handled by Parliament alone. Changes concerning the Dominion and some, but not all, the provinces could be made if the provinces concerned concurred in amendments approved by Parliament. All ten legislative bodies would have to approve changes in minority rights. The remainder of the constitution, in particular the distribution of powers under Sections 91 and 92 of the BNA Act, could be altered with the consent of Parliament and two-thirds of the provinces if they represented 55 per cent of the population.

A number of meetings of a committee of attorneys general were held to discuss this plan during 1936. It was approved in principle, although fears expressed by Maritimers that the other six provinces might gang up on them were met by treating 'property and civil rights' and 'all matters of a merely local or private nature' in the same way as minority rights. Moreover, a province was to be permitted to opt out of any amendments and to retain its exclusive jurisdiction. Ontario certainly supported this formula; with one-third of Canada's population, its veto would operate unless all the other provinces united against it. The attraction of the formula, as the province's deputy attorney general pointed out, was that 'This method definitely recognized the compact or contract theory. Changes cannot be made without the consent of the provinces affected, and this settles for all time the question as to whether the provinces should be consulted or not.'[27] The long struggle begun under Mowat and carried on by his successors had apparently been won.

Unfortunately, it proved impossible to secure the unqualified assent of all the provincial governments to the formula. Mackenzie King's announcement in the spring of 1937 that a Royal Commission would be appointed to study Dominion-provincial relations led to the suspension of negotiations pending its report. Premier Hepburn considered the Rowell-Sirois Commission a waste of time and money. Loyal to the Compact Theory, he bluntly told the Commissioners: 'I have always regarded Confederation as the outcome of a conference. . . . If there is to be a change in Confederation, it can be brought about only by renewed conference of the representatives of the people and with unanimity of approval.'[28] The *Report*, therefore, realized his worst fears. Already at odds with Mackenzie King over his handling of the war effort, the Premier drafted a blistering speech for delivery to the Dominion-Pro-vincial Conference in January 1941. He described the Commission's rec-ommendations as 'a scrapping of Confederation, that robs the provinces of their fiscal independence and of their full autonomy'. When the conference opened he immediately declared that he would not be a party to 'national vandalism', to the handing over of the constitution to the tender mercies of any 'mushroom government that may in future take office at Ottawa . . .'. When Premier John Bracken of Manitoba suggested that the Ontario leader should show the same breadth of vision that George Brown had displayed in joining the Great Coalition of 1864, Hepburn was defended by his High-ways Minister, T.B. McQuesten: '[I]n taking the attitude he has, Hon. Mr Hepburn has been living up to the tradition of Brown and has defended and upheld all that Brown stood for, and is safeguarding the rights and respon-sibilities vested in the separate provinces by Confederation.'[29] In the face of such opposition the conference hastily adjourned. Hepburn's performance, if not his manners, had been firmly in the Mowat tradition, and the aim of securing provincial consultation concerning constitutional change had at last been achieved.

Although the illustrations given here cover only the period up to the Second World War, there is evidence that Mowat's legacy retains its vitality. Premier William Davis has declared that if federal action is not forthcoming to offset the effects of the 10 per cent surcharge on imports, imposed by President Richard Nixon in August 1971, upon Ontario businesses, then the provincial government will take independent action. Arthur Wishart, attorney general in the Robarts administration, expressed his belief in the Compact Theory of Confederation on a number of occasions. And in April 1971, former Premier Robarts attacked the increase in the federal equalization payments drawn from Ontario taxpayers, which he claimed had risen from $1.4 billion in 1970 to $2 billion in 1971, or over 40 per cent in one year.[30]

Since the Mowat heritage has been so consistent and long-lasting, it seems proper to ask whether it has been a constructive force in Canadian development. Mowat's own achievements have not been kindly dealt with. He has been criticized for misleading the Privy Council, and they for heeding his arguments in favour of provincial rights. It has been pointed out, quite rightly, that Mowat was inspired as much by partisanship as by principle. More important, his heedless use of the provincial-rights movement is said to have hindered the development of national feeling in Canada. As early as 1889 D'Alton McCarthy argued that

> The worship of local autonomy, which some gentlemen have become addicted to, is fraught . . . with great evils to this Dominion. Our allegiance is due to the Dominion of Canada. Our separation into provinces, the rights of local self-government which we possess, is [sic] not to make us less anxious for the promotion of the welfare of the Dominion.

Canada's uncertain response to the economic crisis of the 1930s seemed to many to confirm that Mowat's legal and political guile had subverted the intentions of the Fathers of Confederation. The nation had been reduced to a collection of enfeebled but semi-independent principalities, no longer capable of providing Canada with a minimum level of social and economic services, and resistant to the development of a strong and cohesive national identity.[31]

Mowat and his successors were certainly partisans. They identified their possession of power with the public good. But the very relentlessness with which they pursued their objectives in federal-provincial relations suggests that they sensed a strong, deep-laid Ontario particularism, on which they could draw. The Clear Grits had expressed this feeling before Confederation, and it did not disappear in 1867. Reinforced by Mowat's political skills and legal successes, it became a resource upon which the politically astute, the Whitneys, the Fergusons, and the Hepburns, could depend. Ontarians resent being the 'milk cow' of Confederation just as much in 1971 as in 1941 or 1885. The Compact Theory of Confederation, however shoddy historically or legally, is important as an expression of the province's self-consciousness.

Perhaps, however, sectional loyalties like this do pose a bar to the development of strong national feeling. Certainly, it has usually been assumed that they do so, but David Potter has recently pointed out 'the general similarity between nationalism and other forms of group loyalty'. The attachment of the citizen to his nation can be a by-product of loyalty to non-national groups and goals, for in Morton Grodzin's words, ' . . . one is loyal not to nation but to family, business, religion, friends. One fights for the joys of his [sic] pinochle club, when he is said to fight for his country.' Nationalism and sectionalism are not necessarily antithetical, though they may sometimes conflict. The editor of the *Globe* grasped as much when he wrote in 1883: 'Only upon condition that Provincial rights are respected is there any hope of building up a Canadian nationality.' National loyalty flourishes not by overpowering other loyalties but by subsuming them and keeping them in a mutually supportive relationship. Loyal Canadians can also be loyal Ontarians.[32]

Professor Maurice Careless has suggested that we should explore 'limited identities' in Canada.[33] Big, rich, and successful, Ontario has not hesitated to express its feelings, its distinctive identity. Indeed, its government has been the foremost crusader for provincial rights. The cultural and ethnic distinctiveness of Quebec has made it particularist, too, yet French-Canadian politicians have never been able to ignore the existence of the minority outside Quebec. The Manitoba Schools Question showed vividly how minority rights and provincial rights could collide. How, then, could French Canadians commit themselves fully to provincial rights for Quebec if this meant the sacrifice of the diaspora? Federal power, as they saw, could be called upon to serve ethnic ends, for the Official Languages Act has a lengthy pedigree. But Ontario's leaders have been hampered by no such ambivalence. They have committed themselves fully to the cause of provincial rights and so given expression to Ontario's particularism or, as some might say, its imperial ambitions. In this they have reflected the desire of Ontarians to fasten their version of Canadian nationalism upon the rest of the country, making little copies of what they see as the 'real' Canada.

Where Mowat led, his successors have followed. He taught them all the moves; how to rally the other provinces against Ottawa; when to form accords and when to go it alone; above all, he revealed the value of persistence and tenacity. He was not an enemy of the national spirit, but one who understood how it would develop in a new country, by grafting itself onto older, deeper loyalties. His vision of Canada's development was different from Macdonald's, but time has proved him more far-sighted. When the Ontario legislature met in 1897, that stubby, determined, myopic figure was absent from the premier's chair for the first time in a quarter of a century. Andrew Pattullo recalled his past triumphs for the cause of provincial rights. 'In this long series of constitutional victories', Pattullo told the Assembly,

> lies perhaps Oliver Mowat's highest claim to enduring fame and everlasting gratitude of his countrymen. For it was essential to the stability and very existence of Confederation that the rights and privileges of the Provincial and Federal Governments should be clearly and justly defined. Without such just consideration and protection of the rights of the Provinces by the Privy Council, it is quite certain that the Provinces would not have remained in the same union.[34]

Suggestions for Further Reading

Christopher Armstrong, *The Politics of Federalism: Ontario's Relations with the Federal Government, 1867–1942* (Toronto, 1981).

Ramsay Cook, *Provincial Autonomy, Minority Rights, and the Compact Theory 1867–1921* (Ottawa, 1969).

J.A. Maxwell, *Federal Subsidies to Provincial Governments in Canada* (Cambridge, Mass., 1937).

Notes

[1] All students must be indebted to J.C. Morrison's study, 'Oliver Mowat and the Development of Provincial Rights in Ontario: A Study in Dominion-Provincial Relations, 1867–1896', in *Three History Theses* (published under the auspices of the Ontario Department of Public Records and Archives, 1961).

[2] King Diary, 17 June 1930, quoted in H.B. Neatby, *William Lyon Mackenzie King.* vol. 2, *1924–1932, The Lonely Heights* (Toronto, 1963), 337; Public Archives of Ontario, Whitney Papers, Whitney to R.L. Borden, 11 September 1907; *ibid.*, Mitchell F. Hepburn Papers, draft of speech to Dominion-Provincial Conference, January 1941, 12.

[3] I am indebted to H.V. Nelles's essay in Donald Swainson, ed., *Oliver Mowat's Ontario* (Toronto, 1972), for this concept.

[4] *Globe*, 20 May 1882, quoted in Morrison, 'Mowat and Provincial Rights', 147–8, 296.

[5] *Globe*, 16 September 1884, quoted in K.A. Mackirdy, 'Regionalism: Canada and Australia' (unpublished PhD thesis, University of Toronto, 1959), 186.

[6] For an analysis of the conflict over the Rivers and Streams Act, see Morrison, 'Mowat and Provincial Rights', 206–15.

[7] See Professor Nelles's essay for a more detailed analysis of the manufacturing condition.

[8] PAC, Willison Papers, Alex. Smith to J.S. Willison, 2 October 1905, 27826–7; Smith was the secretary of the Ontario Reform (Liberal) Association.

[9] The provinces could charter companies 'with provincial objects', but it was not clear whether this phrase was to be construed territorially, so that only concerns operating within one province were covered, or jurisdictionally, so that any company with objects covered by Section 92 was included. The federal government could incorporate companies whose objects were covered by Section 91, such as banking and shipping concerns, and also claimed the right to charter any company whose works were declared to be 'for the general advantage of Canada'. The province contested the latter claim and pressed for the jurisdictional interpretation of provincial objects.

[10] The provincial agent was an Ottawa lawyer, R.G. Code; see the Code-Whitney correspondence, 1905–10, in the Whitney Papers.

[11] Unsigned memorandum entitled 'Federal and Provincial Rights in Waterways, Georgian Bay Canal Charter and Dominion Lease of Carillon Rapids to National Hydro Electric Company', 24 February 1927, 8, in PAO, Howard Ferguson Papers.

[12] *Globe*, 23 February 1885, quoted in Morrison, 'Mowat and Provincial Rights', 260–1.

[13] *Globe*, 31 March 1887, quoted in Morrison, 'Mowat and Provincial Rights', 263.

[14]The deliberations of this conference, and the subsequent ones, may be studied in *Dominion-Provincial and Interprovincial Conferences from 1887 to 1926*, and *Dominion-Provincial Conferences, 3–10 November 1927, 9–13 December 1935, 14–15 January 1941* (Ottawa, 1951). See also J.A. Maxwell, *Federal Subsidies to Provincial Governments in Canada* (Cambridge, Mass., 1937).

[15]PAC, Laurier Papers, Ross to Laurier, 14 May 1901, Private, 56180–1.

[16]*Ibid.*, Laurier to Ross, 29 February 1904, 82607–12.

[17]Whitney Papers, Whitney to Gouin, 18 September 1905.

[18]'Precis of Discussions, Dominion-Provincial Conference, 3 to 10 November 1927', 25, in *Dominion-Provincial Conferences, 1927, 1935, 1941.*

[19]Sir George Ross, *The Senate of Canada, Its Constitution, Powers and Duties Historically Considered* (Toronto, 1914), 31–2.

[20]PAC, Borden Papers, Borden to W.B.A. Ritchie, 15 June 1909, 6646–7.

[21]*PAC*, Bennett Papers, Precis of Discussion, Dominion-Provincial Conference, 1927, 16298–312.

[22]Ferguson Papers, Ferguson to Taschereau, 10 September 1930.

[23]This letter and the accompanying memorandum were published as a pamphlet entitled *Amendment of the Canadian Constitution, Statement and Protest by the Prime Minister of the Province of Ontario* (Toronto, 1930).

[24]Bennett Papers, Bennett to George S. Henry, 23 February 1931; Ferguson had been succeeded by Henry upon the former's appointment as Canadian High Commissioner in London by Bennett. J.W. Dafoe greeted the news this way: 'What a gift for Ontario but imagine him at Canada House! Part of the harvest of the regime of bunk, blather, bluster, blasting, braggadocio, Bennett—a swarm of B's.' PAC, Dafoe Papers, Dafoe to Harry Sifton, 29 November 1930.

[25]*Ibid.*, Roebuck to Dafoe, 7 January 1935.

[26]'Dominion-Provincial Conference, 1935, Record of Proceedings, Ottawa, 9–13 December 1935', 50, in *Dominion-Provincial Conferences, 1927, 1935, 1941.*

[27]I.A. Humphries. *Observations on a Proposed Method of Amending the British North America Act* (n.p., n.d.), 17–18.

[28]Royal Commission on Dominion-Provincial Relations, *Statement by the Government of Ontario* (n.p., 1938), Book I, Statement by Premier M.F. Hepburn, 3–4.

[29]Mitchell F. Hepburn Papers, draft of speech to Dominion-Provincial Conference, January 1941, 14; 'Dominion-Provincial Conference, Tuesday 14 January 1941, and Wednesday 15 January 1941', 15, 76, in *Dominion-Provincial Conferences, 1927, 1935, 1941.*

[30]For Robart's speech, see *Globe and Mail*, 20 April 1971.

[31]Sir Charles Tupper quoted McCarthy in Canada, House of Commons, *Debates*, 17 March 1896, 3700; D.G. Creighton has severely criticized the trend towards decentralization in his essay, 'Federal Relations in Canada Since 1914', in Chester Martin, ed., *Canada in Peace and War: Eight Studies in National Trends Since 1914* (Toronto, 1941), 48; similar criticisms may be found in F.R. Scott, 'The Development of Canadian Federalism', *Proceedings of the Canadian Political Science Association* (1931), 231–58.

[32]David M. Potter, 'The Historian's Use of Nationalism and Vice Versa', *American Historical Review*, 67 (1962), 931; Morton Grodzins, *The Loyal and the Disloyal: Social Boundaries of Patriotism and Treason* (Chicago, 1956), 29; *Globe*, 5 February 1883, quoted in Morrison, 'Mowat and Provincial Rights', 299; John Robarts remarked

in the spring of 1971 that Ontario now had the 'capability to devise and offer alternatives to major federal policies and programmes. While the alternatives are developed in Ontario, they cannot be based only on an Ontario standpoint. Rather, if they are to serve Ontario's interest, they must represent national alternatives, and by national I do not mean simply federal. They must be based on a recognition of the fact that what is good for Canada is good for Ontario, . . . ' *Globe and Mail*, 20 April 1971.

[33]J.M.S. Careless, ' "Limited Identities" in Canada', *Canadian Historical Review* L (1969), 1–10.

[34]*Globe*, 12 February 1897.

4

The West and Louis Riel

J.M. Bumsted

In 1869–70 the Métis in the Red River Settlement of Rupert's Land organized a resistance against the Dominion of Canada, which had recently purchased the territory from the Hudson's Bay Company and sought to prepare it for settlement. The Métis had not been consulted about the transfer of Rupert's Land to the Dominion, and they were fearful for their land rights and their status under Canadian sovereignty. A provisional government, led by Louis Riel, succeeded in forcing Canada to negotiate and to create through the Manitoba Act the new, albeit small, province of Manitoba.

Riel himself was not able to enjoy the fruits of this victory. Held responsible in eastern Canada for the 'murder' of the Orangeman Thomas Scott, who was executed by a firing squad after being convicted of insubordination by a court martial made up of his Métis captors, Riel was forced into exile. He spent the next fifteen years in a meta-phorical wilderness. Elected to the Canadian House of Commons, he was unable to take his seat; granted an amnesty in 1875, he was forbidden re-admittance into Canada for another five years; he suffered what amounted to a nervous breakdown and was institutionalized until early 1878. Eventually he made his way back west, settling in Montana in 1879, where he became a naturalized American citizen, married, became a father, and appeared to have achieved stability. Nevertheless, when representatives from the valley of the Saskatchewan visited him in Montana in 1884 and invited him to return, to assist their continuing struggles with the Canadian government, he accepted with a minimum of agonizing over the question. Within a year he would be dead, executed for treason after a judicial process that was highly political.

The following essay discusses the 1985 publication of Louis Riel's collected writings—he is the only Canadian whose papers have received such scholarly treatment—and attempts to explore Riel both as historical actor and as figure of Canadian mythology. Whether the two Riels can ever be successfully separated is, indeed, another matter. In any event, within his own lifetime Riel was something of an enigma, a man who struggled with considerable inner emotional turmoil and who has left us with few attempts at self-explanation or self-justification. Was Riel a 'great man'? What are the cases to be made on either side of this question? Could the Canadian government have treated Riel differently—in 1870, in 1875, or in 1885? Why did Canada not show Riel more compassion? Was he a classic 'victim' of circumstances beyond his control, or the unstable architect of his own destiny?

This article first appeared, titled 'The "Mahdi" of Western Canada? Louis Riel and His Papers', in *The Beaver* 67, 4 (August–September 1987), 47–54.

Canada has not often executed traitors, and probably the only instance most Canadians could conjure up if asked about the matter is that of Louis Riel, hanged for high treason in Regina on 16 November 1885. That Riel is the nation's most famous traitor is only the tip of the iceberg of ironies surrounding his life and death. For 'traitor' Riel was a duly naturalized American citizen, leader of a transnational group of people, the Métis, and perhaps insane at the time of the commitment of his acts of treachery. In keeping with the complexity that was Riel, he vehemently denied insanity, although acceptance of such a defence might well have saved his life.

The overriding irony, of course, is that in the years since his death Riel has become a major hero for large numbers of Canadians, a legendary larger-than-life figure who looms far more significantly over western Canadian history for the facts of his death. If the Canadian government hoped through exacting the ultimate penalty for his actions to put paid to his crusade, it failed miserably. For not only is Riel one of our few mythic heroes, he is the only major Canadian whose papers have been collected and published with the full panoply of scholarly apparatus developed for figures like Thomas Jefferson, George Washington, Benjamin Franklin, and John Adams. And given the shutdown of the granting program under which the Riel Papers were funded, they are likely to stand in unique splendour for many years to come.

Canada has generally always lagged badly behind other nations in terms of the publication of the documentary sources of its history. We have had nothing comparable with the collected editions of papers of individuals and institutions produced in Great Britain, France, and the United States in the nineteenth and twentieth centuries. Governments have produced regular collections of sessional papers, the Public Archives of Canada published some documents—mainly between 1880 and 1920—and various private ventures such as the Champlain Society, the Hudson's Bay Record Society (now defunct although revived in another guise), and the Manitoba Record Society have soldiered on despite largely indifferent public support. But the recent trend, particularly in the United States, to produce accurate scholarly editions of the papers of major American leaders, chiefly from the ranks of the so-called 'founding fathers', very nearly passed Canada by. The Social Sciences and Humanities Research Council of Canada did get involved in large-scale editorial projects in the early 1970s, funding such ventures as the Disraeli Papers, the John Stuart Mill Papers, and the Erasmus Papers. Louis Riel was its first—and last—experiment with a Canadian figure, at least on the scale of major funding.

At first glance Louis Riel does not appear to be a likely candidate for such loving, painstaking, and expensive academic treatment. He was, after all, a rebel executed for treason. But it must be remembered that many of the American figures given similar treatment were also rebels. The difference was that they were successful, although men like Franklin certainly appreciated that failure would probably be followed by the rope. It must also be kept in mind that Riel's execution was a highly political act by the Canadian government, one which not only ignored his mental state but the recommendation of the jury that had convicted him. That jury, while agreeing easily that he was guilty as charged, also recommended mercy, on the grounds that the inadequacies of government policy for the North West Territories constituted mitigating circumstances. Moreover, given the waves of controversy that have surrounded Riel since his first appearance in the public spotlight at the head of the Red River Resistance of 1869–70, given the academic disputes to which his career has given rise, and particularly given his appropriation for the mythology of all sorts of elements of Canadian society, ranging from French-Canadian Catholic Nationalism to Native Rights to Canadian New Left student movements, the full publication of his writings offers a natural opening to 'set the record straight'. Whether there should be consonance between the Riel of the papers and the Louis Riel whose name was invoked by radical students at Simon Fraser University to rename a residence financed by private capitalism (and initially called 'Shell House') is another matter entirely. Riel is clearly a complicated personality whose actions and thoughts have struck many different and even divergent resonances, and the publication of his papers probably creates as many problems as it resolves. Many factors contribute to the continuing confusion unresolved by the papers.

In the first place, Riel appears to have lacked whatever instinct leads human beings to generate and save their writings for posterity and the historical record. To some extent, the oral tradition of the people he was leading probably militated against the production of very much day-to-day written material. To some extent, the fact that he was only briefly a man of action, and in both cases leading movements lacking the institutional legitimacy that the American rebels were able to bring to their struggle with the British, contributed to a paucity of papers for the critical periods of activity. Riel was not an unlettered man, and he was to some extent a man of letters, a point brought home by an entire volume of the published papers devoted to his poetry. But he was also a man of a mystical bent, who doubtless felt that the hundreds of pages describing his various visions and visitations were as important as the keeping of a daily diary. Indeed, when he did keep such a diary, as at Batoche in 1885, it is filled with visions rather more than the ordinary activities of a rebel commander in the field. In short, we learn little of the prosaic details of his life from Riel's writings and correspondence. He lacked the eye for the ordinary of a Pepys or a Boswell, and even his letters to his family are singularly unrewarding in this respect.

What the Riel papers document best are Riel's peculiar abnormalities, especially what his contemporary William James labelled for other religious visionaries the 'sick soul', the inner emotional turmoil of the spiritual quest for truth and certainty, and the enormous difficulties of exile that Riel faced. The problems of Louis Riel as political refugee are a major point in these documents, one that has not received much attention from most scholars, who have concentrated on Riel's periods of political activity and have seen the intervening years often in terms of the manoeuvring in Ottawa and Manitoba among the various contending parties. While the manoeuvring went on, however, Louis Riel lived in exile.

One of our leading authorities on Riel has written, 'Louis Riel was not a great man; he was not even what Carlyle would call a near great' (G.F.G. Stanley, *Louis Riel: Patriot or Rebel?* Ottawa, CHA, 1954, 24). Whether George Stanley, who served as editor-in-chief of the Riel Papers project, would now change that verdict is not clear from his own editorial comments in the volumes; he does not directly confront his own earlier judgment. But Riel was certainly a complex man, whose life was shaped and even warped by circumstances beyond his control. In the last analysis, there is a tragic greatness to Louis Riel, and the careful reader of his collected surviving testament cannot help but be struck by the ways in which *Dame Fortuna* conspired continually against him. While he may be, as Stanley put it in 1954, 'a sad, pathetic, unstable man, who led his followers in a suicidal crusade and whose brief glory rests upon a distortion of history', he was also the classic rebel visionary who became the classic victim of a government and society he wanted less to overthrow than, along with his Métis people, to join. First they exiled him, then they executed him.

In any individual's life there are certain key turning points. For Louis Riel there can be no doubt that the event dominating the subsequent unfolding of his life occurred in early March 1870, when he ordered the execution of

Thomas Scott. The Riel papers contain virtually no material for the period of his leadership of the Red River Uprising, and so it is hardly surprising that there is no contemporary documentation for this controversial action. From Riel's subsequent justifications and explanations, as well as from the testimony of some of his collaborators, a story of sorts emerges. Scott was part of an armed band of opponents to Riel's provisional government captured at Portage la Prairie in February 1870. The party's leader, Major Charles Boulton, was condemned to death by a Métis court martial, but his life was spared through Donald Smith's intervention. In captivity Scott was surly and unruly, probably provocatively insulting to the Métis. He was charged with insubordination before another court martial, convicted, and executed the following day under Riel's orders by a firing squad. Riel never attempted to evade his personal responsibility for the execution by arguing that his followers had insisted upon it; his constantly reiterated argument was that the situation demanded such action, to make his government respected and to prevent others from challenging it. The summary nature of the deed suggests that Riel did not long agonize over the decision, and certainly did not appreciate its larger potential significance.

Up to the point of the Scott execution, Riel's leadership of the Métis Uprising had been masterful. Whether or not he was the principal strategist behind the series of moves that had resulted in the negotiations with Canada occurring at the very moment of Scott's death is impossible to determine, nor is it relevant. As the head of the armed Métis he could have thwarted the plans of others, and even if he did not initiate, he carried them out. He was probably not fully aware of the deep embarrassment that the uprising was causing the Canadian government simply by exposing the lack of fore-sight shown in its own behaviour in annexing the West without informing, much less consulting, its inhabitants. He certainly could not appreciate that the execution of the Orangeman Thomas Scott would serve as the catalyst for turning Ontario's attention to the West and reacting against the Métis. As Canada Firster George Denison would later recall, until news of the death of a 'loyal Ontario man, an Orangeman' reached the east, 'it had been found difficult to excite any interest in Ontario in the fact that a number of Canadians had been thrown into prison.' But 'by denouncing the murder of Scott,' it was 'possible to arouse the indignation of the people, and foment a public opinion that would force the Government to send up an armed expedition to restore order' (George T. Denison, *The Struggle for Imperial Unity, Recollections & Experience*, Toronto, 1909).

While Riel can be excused for his failure to appreciate the uses to which Scott's execution (his 'murder', as Riel's opponents always put it) could be put, a bit of reflection might have led him to appreciate that the action was out of keeping with the overall image of legitimacy that the provisional government was generally and successfully maintaining. Riel himself would be 'murdered' by the Canadian authorities in 1885. Interesting enough, if John A. Macdonald had his way, Riel's case would not have been carried through the full judicial appeal process possible under the British North America Act, but he was overruled by his governor-general. But Riel's own execution, however political in its way, was legitimized by the Canadian and imperial judicial system, while that of Scott was carried out by a firing squad based upon a decision by an *ad hoc* tribunal. Even in 1870 there was a difference between Riel's suppression of opposition through force, in which people might lose their lives in armed resistance, and summary executions of prisoners, however much such action was part of the Métis tradition. Indeed, such tradition was part of the Canadian case against the Métis, and having taken such great pains to establish legitimate authority in his provisional government, it behooved Riel not to undermine the position through an action which nobody could defend as legal, however justified it might be.

No political organization has ever appreciated being forced to do the right thing at the point of a gun, and the government of Canada in 1870 was no exception, especially when one of the principal demands of those negotiating on behalf of the 'rebels' was a general amnesty for all illegal acts committed by any parties involved in the disturbances in Red River. Two points are worth making here. One is that the uproar in Ontario over the death of Thomas Scott occurred in the midst of the negotiations, making a general amnesty doubly difficult for the Canadian government to swallow. The second is that the delegates of the provisional government headed by Riel were dealing not with representatives of the British Empire accustomed to making such arrangements in distant parts of the Empire and not directly responsible to the population of the territories involved, but with a Canadian government both delicately placed politically in attempting to balance a variety of political constituencies and agreeing to include Red River as a full-fledged province of the relatively new Dominion. These last considerations were particularly important for Riel, since it was likely—indeed almost certain—that he would become a major political figure in Manitoba, either as one of its representatives to the Canadian House of Commons or, after the achievement of full responsible government, as its premier. Riel's behaviour—and his correspondence in his papers—over the next few years suggest that such political leadership was exactly what he had in mind for himself, and with an amnesty would have achieved. When Riel wrote in 1884, probably to W.H. Jackson, that 'Mr Norquay is playing a glorious part, at the head of the Manitoba responsible government,' referring to the Manitoba premier's efforts to extract better terms for his province from Ottawa, one suspects not only that Riel identified with Norquay's cause but with his position.

Without the promised amnesty, never guaranteed in writing by the Canadians because of its political sensitivity, Riel was reduced to exercising political influence from afar, pressing continually but ineffectually for the execution of the guarantees given his delegates, and ultimately to direct confrontation with Ottawa by getting himself elected to the Canadian House of Commons. No one more than Riel appreciated the farcical aspects of his appearance in the House in 1874, and in one of his rare flashes of conscious humour Riel told a reporter in 1883 that he had not hidden out in the legislative building on the day of the opening of Parliament, but stood 'about in the lobbies like any other member and I did not make any effort to keep out of the way. I just acted in an ordinary manner.' But while standing aimlessly around in lobbies obviously called no attention to himself, signing the roll and attempting to take his seat did. Like those rebellious men before him who had attempted such a ploy—one thinks of John Wilkes a century earlier—he was rapidly expelled from the Commons for infringement of its privileges. The one ultimate advantage gained from his action was on the question of his status; a year later he was granted amnesty 'conditional on five years' banishment from Her Majesty's Dominions'.

Instead of resolving his situation, banishment appears to have been more than Riel could handle. It is in dealing with these matters that the full publication of Riel's correspondence is so useful. By 1875 Riel had been on the run for nearly five years, living mainly in the homes of friends and friendly priests in the United States and occasionally venturing back into Manitoba, obviously with some trepidation. By 1874 he had left Minnesota and moved further east to northern New York, where he was closer to Ottawa. The papers suggest no gainful employment. He was of course always hoping that the amnesty would be proclaimed and he could take his proper place among his people and his province. Some money came from sales of land, but mainly support came from Bishop Taché, perhaps laundering a government payout to keep him away, and from the charity of friends. Finances were plainly not a happy business for a proud Riel in the early 1870s, as his correspondence demonstrates. Five years as a wandering (and stateless) mendicant, unable to do much productive work and isolated from his family, friends, and people, would be difficult for anyone to survive without some considerable strain.

Riel might have reacted to his new five-year banishment in a variety of ways, although it must be added that an additional five years of exile was a cruel blow, too long a period to meet with equanimity, too short a time to decide to put paid to his hopes of a normal life in his own country. Banishment for life would probably have been easier to accept. In any event, Riel might have done what thousands of other exiles before and since have done, by finding somewhere to settle in for the duration and making the best of it, perhaps among congenial fellow refugees. The United States certainly had a number of communities of political refugees in its larger eastern cities to which he might have attached himself. Alternatively, Riel might have decided to break with his past, and again like thousands of exiles before and since, to start a new life in the United States. Riel, of course, chose neither of these options in 1875. Instead he fell apart emotionally and suffered what amounted to a nervous breakdown, a reaction further complicated by his spiritual state. We can understand and appreciate his emotional collapse, given the strain under which he had been operating for years, but we must also keep in mind that the collapse was accompanied by religious visions and revelations that move it out of the realm of simple insanity.

The spiritual nature of Riel's mental and emotional state after 1875 introduces a sort of wild card into the situation, making his behaviour particularly difficult to interpret and properly appreciate. The Judeo-Christian tradition has a long history of acceptance of supranatural human experience. Visions, visitations, and revelations, as well as other occurrences such as the appearance of stigmata, have been recognized for nearly 2,000 years by the Roman Catholic Church as potentially legitimate, although the Church has developed elaborate criteria for judging such matters. But Roman Catholicism has had no monopoly on extraordinary spiritual experience, and within North America, Protestantism has produced a long series of messianic and prophetic figures whose religious state is no more unrational than that of Louis Riel. Indeed, Riel's prophetic messianism probably makes more sense seen in the context of nineteenth-century American Protestant millenialism than Catholic supranaturalism, and comparisons with spiritual leaders like Joseph Smith and Brigham Young are hardly farfetched. Unlike the Mormons, who were able to establish themselves in a new promised land in advance of civil authority, Riel and the Métis of the Canadian northwest had to deal with the Canadian government backed by armies and the paramilitary forces of the Mounted Police. Finally, there is some tradition of the supranatural even in the secular system and even in Canada. A Canadian prime minister only half a century after Riel's death had dream visions and conversed with the spirit world, and, we are told, such experiences did not greatly affect his ability to govern Canada on a pragmatic political basis. Both because of the historical context and because of our own greater appreciation of the complexities of abnormal behaviour (and its constantly shifting definition by society), we are perhaps more likely to shy away from simple attributions of insanity to people like Louis Riel.

Nevertheless, Riel was institutionalized in several mental hospitals of his day between 1876 and 1878, less because of his spiritual experiences than because of his observed behaviour, which made it difficult for him to lead anything resembling an outwardly normal life. This edition of the papers is never strong on context, and the casual reader of Riel's writings during these years might not fully appreciate the extreme nature of his condition. 'Alienists' and medical people of the time might be unreliable witnesses as to the nature of his problem, but there is no reason to doubt their recorded observations of his mental and emotional complete withdrawal from the world around him. His mental state makes it difficult to interpret the documents written in periods surrounding his institutionalization. What are we to make, for example, of the memoir to American president Ulysses S. Grant, dated by the editors as written late in 1875 (and probably never communicated)? Here Riel outlines the grievances of the Métis against the Canadian government accumulated since 1870, arguing 'Undoubtedly it is m[os]t just that we should, in consequence, reassume our former attitude' (II, p. 8). While the presentation of grievances is quite lucid and credible, his calculations of his potential support and opposition ('In all, I have, in manitoba and north-west, about 68,000 souls to support my policy. The Canadian government have not more than 10,000 souls, to resist my forces.') are less than compelling. In 1875, Riel anticipated total armed backing from the English and French Métis, three to four thousand 'of adventurers who are against Canada to a man', and the 'favourable dispositions' of 38,000 Indians. He discounted 3,000 of the pro-Canadians as Mennonites who would not fight, and as for the Mounted Police, they 'can hardly take care of their horses'. Moreover, he expected hundreds of French-Canadians and Irishmen to flock to his standard as new emigrants to Manitoba. Were these the calculations of an impotent rebel exile indulging his fantasies, or the ravings of a man demented? In any event, if this sort of thinking coloured his decision to return to the Canadian North West in 1884, he joins other armed rebels in Canadian history (William Lyon Mackenzie and L.J. Papineau, for example) in totally over-optimistic expectations about the strength of his employable forces.

After his emergence from institutionalization early in 1878, Riel returned to upstate New York and made his way back west to Montana in 1879. Once again, the complete run of documentation for his years in Montana is extremely useful in illuminating one of the least well-known aspects of his life. It would appear that Riel had finally decided to come to terms with exile and to make a new life for himself in the United States. In Montana he made himself useful to the authorities as an intermediary with both the Indians and the Métis, supporting the Republicans rather than the Democrats, a reminder that in this period the modern stereotypes of the American parties are quite irrelevant. The Republicans tended to be the liberals and radicals, and the Democrats the backroom boys committed to the status quo. After several early abortive attempts at courtship, one in Montreal in the 1860s and one during his first period of exile, Riel married in 1881, initially à la façon du pays but later in a religious ceremony. His wife, Marguerite Monet, was a Red River Métis, ill-educated and (unlike the previous candidates) not of a prominent and upwardly-mobile French-Canadian family. He obtained steady employment as a schoolmaster at St. Peter's Mission, became a father, and applied successfully for American citizenship. What could be more conventional?

Even a careful reader sensitized with hindsight would have trouble in finding in Riel's Montana papers evidence of instability (mental or otherwise), religious mania, or even discontent. He continued to be interested in his 'people', the Métis or 'Halfbreeds', as he himself referred to the mixed bloods of Dakota and Montana. His writing about the American Halfbreed Question was judicious and balanced, mainly in English, a language Riel used for business but not for passionate matters. There is a sense of distance between Riel the observer/commentator and his subject, whether liquor for halfbreeds (a Montana newspaper described his views as 'An Intelligent Statement of the Case by Louis Riel') or the American refusal to permit the immigration of Asiatics. There is quiet humour; the newspaper interview noted earlier is from this period, as is Riel's English wordplay (he refers to 'the United Moral States' in connection with Asiatic immigration, observing ' . . . because the States are Moral, as I say; and because the Mongols have no moral state enough to present the States, they are unwilling, they hesitate' (II, p. 370). Nothing in the Montana documents of volume II prepares the reader for the opening documents of volume III, dealing with Riel's response to the invitation of a delegation of North West inhabitants to come and advise them in their disputes with the Canadian government. Three drafts precede the final letter of acceptance, the first neutral, the second dubious, the third positive but hedged with qualifications. This material represents our only hint as to the thought process by which Riel became involved in the events that would lead to his execution.

There exists a curious tendency when dealing with Riel to look for parallels and comparisons. His arch-opponent, Sir John A. Macdonald, compared him in 1885 with the Mahdi, the Muslim messianic prophet who was leading his people against the British government in the Sudan and who was held responsible for the death of General Gordon at Khartoum early in the same year as the North West Uprising led by Louis Riel. The Prime Minister of Canada obviously sought to associate Riel and his rebellion with the series of events in northern Africa that had the British Empire in an uproar, but the comparison was not entirely fanciful or ridiculous. The implicit parallel between Duck Lake and Khartoum may have been useful politically, but the event most closely resembling Duck Lake, where armed Métis confronted a party of North-West Mounted Police and settlers with disastrous results for the Mounties, is Seven Oaks, where in 1816 a party of settlers led by Red River governor Robert Semple was decimated by the Métis. In both cases the ensuing carnage of the encounters was accidental and responsibility for invoking violence impossible to assess. The difference between Seven Oaks and Duck Lake, of course, was that the Red River settlers of 1816 could not invoke external reinforcement, since Semple's authority came from the Hudson's Bay Company and for complex reasons was not supported by the imperial authorities, while the Canadian government found both the will and the means to bring military forces into play that were beyond the capabilities of the Métis to resist. Nevertheless, Duck Lake was a critical turning point for Riel, who had been advocating a peaceable demonstration of discontent rather than a war. Once the territory burst into armed conflict, the road to the gallows was almost inexorable.

Suggestions for Further Reading

Thomas Flanagan, *Louis 'David' Riel* (Toronto, 1979).

G.F.G. Stanley, *The Birth of Western Canada* (Toronto, 1960).

G.F.G. Stanley, ed., *Louis Riel: The Collected Writings/Les Ecrits complets*, 5 vols (Edmonton, 1985).

5

The Economy of Atlantic Canada

Eric W. Sager

One of the many reasons the provinces of the Atlantic region had so reluctantly participated in the creation of the Dominion of Canada was the strength of their shipping industry. In the region's 'Golden Age of Sail', the middle years of the nineteenth century, its merchant marine was one of the largest in the world, turning the attention of many Maritimers away from the interior of the continent. Some of the region's residents, including many of its politicians, seized on Confederation as a way to open new markets; unhappily, in the years after 1867 the Maritime provinces (Newfoundland remained outside Confederation until 1949) were unable to take advantage of protective tariffs and transcontinental railway subsidies to develop a successful industrial strategy.

Economic historians have long debated the relationship between an outmoded and increasingly obsolescent shipping industry and Maritime industrialization. One of the most pervasive views is that declining profits in shipping (especially in wooden sailing ships that were being replaced by iron and steel steam-driven vessels) forced regional investors to shift their capital into industrial enterprises having few advantages in the open marketplace.

Eric Sager's discussion of the shipping industry in Atlantic Canada postulates that the situation was considerably more complex than conventional wisdom holds. He is particularly interested in understanding the contemporary thinking that was 'part of economic reality'. In this context, he finds it striking that Maritime investors did not invest in supposedly more profitable iron sailing ships; a pervasive pessimism about the shipping industry became its own self-fulfilling prophecy. Sager suggests that instead of expanding and modernizing the region's merchant marine, thus taking advantage of Maritime strengths, the shipowners joined other interest groups in pressing for a landward industrial development that did not build on what the region could do best. At the same time, they permitted their own industry to remain unprotected and unsupported. Thus, Sager suggests, the Maritimes ended up with the worst of both possible economic options that faced the region after Confederation. Did the shipping industry decline? How would one define 'decline' in this context? What problems do the question of decline present to the historian? Why did pessimism about ship-owning become a self-fulfilling prophecy? What alternatives were not explored or exploited by the merchant capitalists of the Maritime region? How do these arguments fit into the overall discussion of the economic decline of the Atlantic region after Confederation?

This article first appeared, titled ' "Buying Cheap and Selling Dear": Merchant Shipowners and the Decline of the Shipping Industry in Atlantic Canada', in Peter Baskerville, ed., *Canadian Papers in Business History* I (Victoria; University of Victoria, 1989), 59–74.

One day early in April 1881, a shipowner in Charlottetown sat at his desk and wrote an irritable letter to a shipbroker in Galveston, Texas. 'My feelings at the moment are none of the pleasantest,' wrote Robert F. Quirk. 'Shipowning nowadays is such a poor business that every attention must be given to the minutest details.' Quirk proceeded to give attention to his ship docked in Galveston, and pestered the shipbroker with letters and telegrams about the vessel's cargo, the rate of freight, loading days, and the size of the broker's commission. Quirk represents the sailing ship managing-owner *in extremis*: faced with declining freight rates and falling profits, he struggled to reduce operating costs, to shed labour, and to speed up his vessels. 'Shipowning is not what it was in 1870,' said Quirk, 'and things must be worked on a different basis altogether.'[1] In a few years' time, frustrated beyond endurance by the struggle to earn profits in this business, Quirk followed the path of many other shipowners in the Maritimes: he quit the shipping industry altogether.

The shipowner's frustration supports an obvious hypothesis about the decline of the shipping industry in Atlantic Canada: with the increasing competition of iron and steam in major trades, profits collapsed, and shipowners withdrew from the industry. This paper suggests that the story is much more complex. If we study the shipping industry only to learn that collapsing profits were a cause of declining investment, we should have learned very little. We might still follow a traditional path and display the various 'causes' of the decline of shipping. Of greater interest, however, is the information which the industry and its decline may yield about the nature and structure of merchant capital in the Atlantic colonies. This paper suggests that the decline of the shipping industry was part of the evolution of merchant capital in the region, and part of mercantile responses to the combined impact of Confederation and industrial capitalism.

This approach does not dismiss Robert Quirk's frustration or his analysis, but accepts them and asks that they be set in a social and cultural context extending far beyond the walls of his office in Charlottetown. Quirk was quite right when he said that shipowning had changed between 1870 and 1881. We know that rates of return were high in the early 1860s and in the early 1870s: returns to capital of 20 per cent and more were likely to have been very common.[2] C.K. Harley's recent attempt to suggest that profits in sailing ships were negative, even in the early 1870s, is unconvincing, to say the least.[3] If indeed sailing ships were losing money, even when freight rates were relatively high, then several critical questions must be answered. First, why would Maritimers say that sailing ships were profitable, if their ledgers suggested otherwise? Second, why should Canadian sailing ships lose money when Norwegian sailing ships, working in the same trades, were making good profits?[4] Finally, why should Maritimers continue to build up their sailing ship fleets through the 1870s, while those ships were losing money? Harley does not answer such questions, and there is really no need to answer them, since all available evidence suggests that shipowning was a profitable business in the early 1870s.

By the early 1880s it was still possible to make money in sailing ships, but rates of return were falling. By the mid-1880s there can be no doubt that many sailing ships were losing money. The decline of the shipping industry, it would seem, is easily explained. Profit is the driving force of capitalist activity, and where returns declined steeply over a short period of time, it is little wonder that investors should seek other opportunities and move their capital out of shipping.

Declining profits may serve as a beginning of our analysis, but they are not a complete explanation for the decline of the shipping industry. There are, first of all, problems in connecting falling returns with the timing of declining investment in specific places. In some places, such as Halifax, the decline began in the mid-1870s, when freight rates were still high. In others, such as Windsor, investment did not peak until 1891, long after freight rates and profits had collapsed. Norwegian investment in sailing ship tonnage increased in the 1880s, and even closer to home, investment in sailing vessels in Newfoundland did not peak until 1919. The point is that it was possible for investment to continue in certain places even when most sailing-ship owners experienced falling rates of return. It is unlikely that non-pecuniary benefits, such as pride or love of sailing ships, motivated shipowners in some places to persist with an obsolescent technology.[5] It is much more likely that an industry survived, even where profits were falling, because it conferred a benefit in another industry which it served. With shipping this often occurs, since shipping is in the ambiguous situation that it is an industry in its own right, and at the same time an input in another trade or industry. There may be several advantages to the merchant-exporter in owning and controlling his own transportation services (this occurred, for instance, in the timber trade of the early nineteenth century). The fact that ocean freight rates were declining may be uninteresting and irrelevant. The real question may be: why did Maritime exporters no longer wish to possess their own shipping service, even when export volumes and the demand for tonnage in their ports were increasing?

There is another problem with explaining declining investment as a function of declining profits. Sometimes investors withdraw from an industry in which rates of return are high. This leaves us with a troubling thought: even if there had been substantial profits, the shipping industry might have declined anyway.[6] We might easily dismiss such speculation were it not for the fact that this very phenomenon did occur in a shipping industry located very near to the Maritimes. In the 1860s and 1870s the deep-sea merchant marine of the eastern United States declined, despite the fact that demand for tonnage in United States ports was growing rapidly, and despite the increase in freight rates in the early 1860s and early 1870s. There are differing interpretations of the decline of the United States merchant marine, but one view is that capital was shifted into landward industries regardless of the profits to be made in shipping.[7]

It is tempting to say that rates of return must have been higher in other industries, and that capital was thereby pulled out of shipping and into expanding landward economies, first in the United States and, slightly later, in Canada. But at this point the historian stumbles over a thorny problem in neo-classical economic logic. Neo-classical economics assumes a direct relationship between investment choices and returns: given pervasive scarcity and the desire to maximize returns, human beings will invest in whatever capital stock has the highest rate of return. To predict investment behaviour—or to explain such behaviour in the past—it is necessary to define the investor's utility function and to discover which activities exhibited high returns. As Douglass C. North reminds us,

A powerful insight of neoclassical theory, with fundamental implications for economic history, is that under conditions of uncertainty it is impossible for individual profit, or wealth maximization to exist (since no one knows with certainty the outcome of a decision), but that the wealth-maximizing result nevertheless occurs. It occurs simply because competition in the face of ubiquitous scarcity dictates that the more efficient institution, policy, or individual action will survive and the inefficient ones perish.[8]

The first problem for the historian results from the fact that conditions of uncertainty were pervasive in the past, and information was never perfect.

Even if the evidence for high returns in railway stock is sound, for instance, consequential investment in railways assumes that the investors knew about those high returns. It is entirely possible that imperfect information prevented investors from perceiving high rates of return where they existed, or persuaded them that returns were high where in fact they were low. Information and knowledge are differently distributed between individuals, between social classes, and between regions. To assume a dependent relationship between profit and subsequent investment merely begs all the interesting questions: what information was available, how was it transmitted, and what factors conditioned the environment in which investors made choices?

A second problem with the neo-classical formulation is the risk of circular argument. The sentence quoted above merely repeats the tautology inherent in Darwinian 'survival of the fittest' evolutionary theory: those institutions or firms best adapted for survival have a better chance of surviving than those not so well adapted.[9] The proposition cannot be tested against evidence, since it is a truism. The historian then sets out to 'prove' that industries of low productivity collapsed, while those experiencing productivity gains survived, but the conclusions follow from assumptions rather than from evidence. In the history of the Maritimes Peter McClelland offers the best example of a Darwinian tautology: 'Our expectations for regional economies are analogous to our expectations for firms. There are going to be winners and losers. It is reasonable to expect that in competitive regional development there should be some winners and some losers.'[10] The risk in such assumptions are that they direct the historian toward particular evidence—the evidence of poor productivity and low rates of return in regional industry. Having found such evidence (as McClelland did) it is declared to be sufficient. It is little wonder that David Frank and Gregory Kealey, upon hearing this, should ask if the inevitability of 'winners and losers' is not mere apologia, and urge regional historians to consider theoretical tools other than that hoary chestnut, comparative advantage.[11]

This does not mean that economic historians have ignored these problems. For Douglass C. North such problems are central to economic history. Precisely because knowledge is imperfect, and because information and expectations intrude upon market mechanisms, neo-classical economists have grappled with 'the economics of information and knowledge'.[12] It is not clear how any of this literature helps the economic historian, however, especially when (as in Israel Kirzner) it concludes with fatuous moralizing about 'the social importance of freedom' and 'the need for individuals to discover for themselves the available range of alternatives'.[13]

The choices made by businessmen cannot be understood simply as the outcome of a maximizing calculus and opportunity costs. The merchant capitalists of Atlantic Canada operated in conditions of pervasive uncertainty. Very often they were investing in industries with which they had no prior experience. Their prediction of future returns on capital was not based upon personal or local experience, but upon information transmitted from elsewhere. They knew that the same information might be available to others, and that others might respond to the same predictions of high returns in particular industries, thereby encouraging over-production and reducing or eliminating anticipated profits.

Control of information was critical, and there is no better testimony to this fact than the action of the directors of the Truro Condensed Milk and Canning Company in January 1887, after paying a fifteen per cent dividend:

> We have had such a good year that we are not having any statements printed and it was the wish of all the stockholders that were at the annual meeting yesterday that nothing be said about it in order to prevent, as far as possible, competition.[14]

The discussion of investment choices became a debate over the lessons of experience outside the Maritimes—a debate in which the equation of information with economic power was fully understood:

> We have been for the last year or two urging, by all the means in our power, the capitalists of Yarmouth to invest some of their surplus funds in the erection of a Cotton Mill. We have pointed out to them that if cotton cloth can be manufactured in Massachusetts at a fair profit, it can be made here at a heavy profit, the large import duties on the foreign article being taken into account. . . . 'something must be done' and that in short order. . . .[15]

It is precisely at this point that the subject of profits in shipowning acquires more than merely antiquarian or regional interest. What did the merchant capitalist know, and how did he know it? The question takes us beyond neoclassical economics, to the point where the history of culture and communications must intersect with economic history. The subject is an old one, of course—it is a long time since Max Weber grappled with the paradoxical effects of theology and morality on economic behaviour. And today, when recent theorists have so forcefully reminded us of the domains of 'power/ knowledge' (Foucault's term), discourse and language, and the ability of these to define and limit fields of perceived truth, the economic historian can no longer be content with truisms about opportunity costs and profit maximization as determinants of investment behaviour.[16] We must recognize that theorists of economic development in the so-called 'third world' have done irreparable damage to the old tools of comparative advantage. And while using quantitative methods and learning what we can from the social science disciplines, we must be aware that the positivist roots of neo-classical economic 'science' have been under attack for decades.[17] None of this recent theoretical work offers clear guidance to the business historian, and it is regrettable that Brian Young's appeal for a wider discussion of theory and method (at the Canadian Business History Conference to which this paper was presented) yielded no response other than total silence.[18] Outside Canadian business history, however, lies theoretical ferment, which may have no other implications for the subject of the shipping industry than the following: if information is treated, at least initially, as an independent variable in the arena of investment choices, then it follows that the decline of a regional industry may have less to do with differential rates of return between industries than with the transmission of information and its receipt by a specific social class at the point of transition from merchant to industrial capitalism.

What the merchant-shipowner appears to have known in the third quarter of the nineteenth century was that the shipping industry was doomed to decline or extinction. This knowledge did not come from his reading of his ledgers, since those ledgers showed positive and often healthy profits even into the 1880s. 'The shipping business is a comparatively profitable one generally,' Frank Killam of Yarmouth informed a Select Committee of the Canadian House of Common in 1876. Moments later, asked if there was a depression in his industry, Killam's answer was unequivocal: depression was 'universal'.[19] Depression, it seems, was 'universal'—despite the fact that average returns on capital were above 15 per cent, and despite the fact that 'Yarmouth ships . . . made a better return for the money and labour invested in them than almost any industry in the Province.'[20] In 1876 Killam's pessimism followed not from past experience but from a specific prediction about the future—a prediction which Edward Willis heard and repeated a few years later in his Report on industry in the wake of the National Policy tariffs:

> The competition of iron steamers and iron ships with wooden craft in the carrying trade of the world, revolutionized the shipbuilding interest and destroyed the magnificent business which had made for many citizens of this place comfortable competencies, if not colossal fortunes.[21]

Not only was the industry doomed, but nothing could be done to save it, said Willis: 'Government edicts could not be made to shackle the wheels of progress. . . .'

Willis's analysis tells us about the contemporary thinking which was fully part of economic reality. For one thing, he was treating shipbuilding and shipowning as a single industry, and begging an obvious question: if iron steamers were more productive, then why did local shipowners not purchase them? Even shipowners used the same flawed analysis, with all its revealing pessimism. 'I regret to say that this great shipping industry of the lower Provinces has almost virtually ceased,' said Thomas Kenny in 1888—despite the fact that Canada had the fifth largest merchant marine in the world. 'That has been caused by the improvement in steam—and also by the iron sailing ships. We, who wish to continue in the shipping business, have discovered that the iron sailing ship is a more profitable investment than our wooden ships. . . .'[22] But the point was that Kenny and his fellows were not investing in iron ships at all, whatever the proven advantage of those ships. His decision to pull his capital out of shipping flew in the face of his own economic analysis. In the 1890s we find Kenny's pessimism reaching even odder conclusions: 'the depression in shipping is owing to the fact that we cannot build iron ships in this Dominion, not at least on the Atlantic coast. . . .'[23] Kenny did not stop to ask how it was that iron ships were then being built elsewhere in Canada. Nor did he explain why he did not purchase iron ships, and it is little wonder that one of his listeners should say: 'I do not understand why a maritime people . . . cannot keep pace with the times, in shipping.'[24]

What was the source of this pervasive pessimism about the shipping industry? The speaker who followed Thomas Kenny in the legislature, A.H. Gillmor, had a perceptive answer:

> It has occurred to me during this debate that we are looking now with our mind's eye towards the great Atlantic; whereas all the time in the past we have been looking to the west, as though the whole Dominion and all its interests were settled in the great prairie.[25]

Of course there were Maritimers in the Confederation era who looked both west and east, and saw railroads to the west as part of a seaborne and landward transportation system linking Canada and Britain and thereby encouraging the local shipping and shipbuilding industries.[26] An interest in western development was certainly not incompatible with an interest in shipping. Nevertheless, Gillmor had a point: Confederation and railway development had put the west in 'our mind's eye'. Even for Joseph Howe the critical thing about railways was their capacity to expand commercial activity and population growth in landward directions. All railroads in America are made to pay, he said, 'by directing latent resources and by growth of internal commerce and manufacturing. . . .'[27] And as Rosemary Langhout has pointed out, the development strategy behind railroads was that of 'entrepôt growth', whereby trade was concentrated in specific locations.[28] The benefits would come from the expansion of commerce and port development—the expansion of shipowning was a corollary, or an ancillary benefit, not a primary stimulant of development in its own right.

In the decades following Confederation, in Halifax and Saint John, attention focused increasingly upon port development.[29] Politicians and civic boosters often lost sight of shipowning altogether. Shipping and entrepôt development were equated, and the word 'shipping' acquired a new and profoundly ambiguous meaning: it refers both to the export and import of goods—the work of the *shipper*—and to the business of carrying goods in ships, the work of the *shipowner*. These two activities were not the same, and after mid-century they were less often combined in the operations of merchant-shipowning firms. Very often the word 'shipping' refers not to ship-owning at all, still less to shipbuilding, but to entrepôt growth and commodity exchange.[30] Confederation turned the 'mind's eye' and altered economic discourse in the Maritimes.

It is impossible to define with statistical precision the flow of information available to merchant capital and politicians in the Maritimes. But newspapers were transmitters or receptacles of much of that information, and it is reasonable to ask what views they expressed about shipbuilding and shipowning, as these industries expanded and declined. The answer one finds is sometimes astonishing, and it bears directly upon the pervasive pessimism which preceded and accompanied the decline of these industries. The press of Yarmouth, Halifax and Saint John reflected almost nothing about the huge locally owned merchant marine. One knows that the industry existed from the 'Shipping Intelligence' columns which reported the movement of vessels. Otherwise one might wonder if the industry existed at all. A content analysis of the *Yarmouth Herald* in 1867 suggests that the fate of the United States merchant marine was of more interest than the fate of local shipowning and shipbuilding after Confederation. There was no discussion of the anticipated impact of Confederation upon shipowning. The local shipowning and shipbuilding industries were the principal topics of only two per cent of all articles in the paper in 1867.[31] Shipbuilding in the United States 'is all but completely destroyed', and a 'high tariff operates severely against the shipping interest', but even in this anti-Confederation newspaper the fate of local shipowning appears to be irrelevant to the discussion of Confederation.[32] A random sample of ten per cent of issues of the Saint John *Globe* (a daily) in 1867 produced a similar result: there were more articles on shipbuilding outside the Maritimes than on shipbuilding in New Brunswick, but in either case the message was almost uniformly pessimistic.[33] 'Many of the [ship] yards are now closed with ships half unfinished upon the docks' because of 'the ruinously low prices' for wooden ships in Britain.[34] Insofar as there was a lesson from this experience, it was not that local shipowners could now benefit from the lower initial capital cost of ships. The lesson was that iron ships and steamships were now in demand, and that there should be a 'handsome subsidy' from the new Dominion government to attract these new steamships into local ports.[35] The steamships would be owned by Cunard or Allan or British firms—the fact that they would then compete with local ships, drive down freight rates in Saint John, and contribute ultimately to the collapse of shipowners' profits, appears to have excited no concern. The decline of wooden shipbuilding in the 1860s must certainly have encouraged many to turn their eyes westward, and to assume that shipowning would soon meet the same fate as shipbuilding.

All of this is testimony to the commonplace equation of economic development with commodity exchange in continental markets. The equation follows not only from local experience, but from the massive borrowing of information about economic development from elsewhere. That information carried the message that commodities would henceforth be transported by rail, and some even concluded that all waterborne transportation was becoming obsolete:

> Trade will continue to grow, but it will not be carried on through the instrumentality of wooden ships, under sail. In fact, a large and continually increasing proportion will not use ships at all. Not many years ago, the trade between New Brunswick and Nova Scotia, as well as between this province and the upper provinces, was carried on by water. . . . The Intercolonial and other railways have changed all this, and the coasting trade has suffered accordingly; but the same thing, on a large scale, has happened the world over! . . . Commerce may easily increase without increase in water carriage. . . .[36]

This analysis was, of course, entirely incorrect, even with respect to Canadian coastal traffic, where the demand for carrying capacity and even for sailing ships was still increasing. It is not necessary to show that this analysis was typical or even widely shared—the fact that such an argument could be heard at all, in one of the major shipowning ports in the British Empire, is testimony to the massive impact of landward development upon economic discourse in the Maritimes. Given such pessimistic analysis, and given the accumulation of vested interests in the Intercolonial Railway, it is no surprise to find even shipowners arguing that coastal shipping between the Maritimes and Montreal was dead, since the railway was now 'the great national highway', and 'without a perfect railway system we would almost fall back on our old Provincial prejudices and isolated condition.'[37] Pessimism about shipowning became a self-fulfilling prophecy. Only a few years later Norwegian vessels were carrying coal from Cape Breton to Montreal.

Railways, cotton, iron, and sugar—these were the bedrock of economic development. Such were the lessons of external experience. But these lessons were also filtered through the experience of merchant capitalists long since engaged in exchange rather than production. Of course they were interested in industrial manufacturing, and many invested in it.[38] One cannot use the story of merchant-shipowners in the Maritimes to prove that a dominant commercial sector led, in R.T. Naylor's words, to a 'stultification of industrial entrepreneurship'.[39] But one can show that industrialization reinforced an existing mercantile interest in commercial exchange, transportation, and port development.[40] Often manufacturing was the servant of commerce: it was another means of 'buying cheap and selling dear'. The mercantile interest in trade goods guided much of the lobbying by merchants and politicians in the Maritimes after Confederation. They would not unite to demand protection for shipowning or shipbuilding; instead they demanded a readjustments of the sugar tariffs, extension of the Intercolonial Railway, the creation of a 'winter port', and the building of grain elevators. These were the causes for which even the erstwhile shipowner now fought, and these were the concessions which Dominion governments slowly gave. All of these causes were intended to benefit 'shipping' in its new sense—not the work of the shipowner, but of the shipper of goods.

The merchant-shipowners of Halifax and Saint John were merchants first and shipowners second. After Confederation the interests of the shipper collided with the interests of the shipowner as they never had before—and the interests of the shipper took precedence. The division came to a head over the issue of government subsidies to steamships. In the 1870s we find Maritimers blaming the decline of the West Indies trade on the absence of regular steam communications and linking this to the sugar tariffs.[41] Members of Parliament from the Maritimes were quite capable of pointing out that if subsidies could be given to a Canadian Pacific Railway, then they could be given to steamships to serve the vital West Indies trade: 'I would like to know what difference there is between granting a subsidy to a steamship line like this, and a line of railway?'[42] But there was a problem with steamship subsidies: the steamships would compete with vessels owned by Maritimers themselves. William Welsh of P.E.I. and A.G. Jones of Halifax led the charge:

> Do hon. gentlemen want to destroy the marine interests of this country? . . . I shall, in all cases, oppose any subsidy for any steamboat service for commercial purposes. I want to see steamers and sailing vessels try and compete with each other on a free trade basis. I do not want to subsidise one man and leave another out.[43]

The shipowners lost this debate. And they lost to other shipowners from the Maritimes, such as Thomas Kenny of Halifax:

> As a ship-owner I can say that the great depression which now exists in the Lower Provinces is mainly due to the fact that our shipping is so unremunerative; but I think our duty here is to facilitate in every way our export trade, and we cannot accomplish this unless by means of steam. I regret to have to say that sail as a competitor with steam has now no chance on the ocean; I regret it because I am a sailing-ship-owner myself. But we must do all we possibly can to cultivate our export trade. . . . We cannot develop a large export without regularity of shipment, and that can only be attained by the use of steam.[44]

Embedded in this bitter exchange over steamship subsidies lie the reasons for the decline of the local shipping industry. On one side a shipowner argued for subsidies to encourage his competitors, the British and central Canadian firms who owned steamships. On the other side shipowners argued against subsidies which were essential if Canadians were to make the transition to the new industrial technology. Maritimers would not unite, either to invest in new shipping technologies, or to demand policies which would encourage such investment.

Both sides argued from the same premise. The premise was that of merchant capital—'buying cheap and selling dear'—and vessels were always a means to this end. This was true even for the shipowners who argued against steamship subsidies. They were not trying to maintain artificially high freight rates by keeping steamships from their ports. They were trying to keep steamships out of the West Indies fish trade, because steamships threatened to glut the markets and so lower the prices received.

> In a market like Porto Rico, where we ship 150,000 to 160,000 quintals of fish a year, a steamer would require to take about 8,000 to 9,000 quintals of fish every trip, of two trips per month. . . . The arrival of such a quantity of fish . . . in the West Indies, would cause the price to go down at least $1 a quintal. . . .[45]

By threatening the winter employment of schooners and fishermen, the steamers might also discourage fishermen and reduce the size of the local labour force in fishing, to the further disadvantage of the merchant. The shipowner was a trader first and a shipowner second.

This, then, is why even shipowners were so receptive to a landward development strategy purveyed by the local press and by pro-Confederation politicians. Even as shipowners they were primarily interested in commodity exchange, and Confederation afforded new opportunities for commercial activity because of the promise of railroads and entrepôt growth. Shipowners have a vested interest in high freight rates; commodity traders have a vested interest in low freight rates. Even when ocean freight rates reached a peak in the early 1870s, the shipowners' interest in those freight returns was dissolving. It dissolved under the influence of external models of industrial development, and the merchant capitalists' reception of those models. A merchant marine would require protection: cargo reservation policies, preferential port charges for Canadian vessels, or the reservation of steamship and mail subsidies for Canadian-flag ships. Maritimers did not unite in support of these policies. They failed to unite because such policies would raise, not lower, the cost of freight. Such policies were therefore outside the merchant capitalist's perception of his self-interest. Instead of protection, most merchants and politicians in the Maritimes argued for precisely the opposite:

> My strong opinion is that it is the bounden duty of the Government of Canada in the interests of the trade of Canada to make the great ports of Canada absolutely free to the shipping of the Dominion, aye, open to the shipping of the world.[46]

Even the coastal shipping of Atlantic Canada would remain largely unprotected, despite the protests of schooner-owners in the early 1900s. Only a few men of business sought to preserve the merchant marine. The decision to shift capital from the sea began, not with falling rates of return, but with the experience of the merchant capitalist who worked to buy cheap and sell dear.

Suggestions for Further Reading

David Alexander, *Atlantic Canada and Confederation: Essays in Canadian Political Economy* (Toronto, 1983).

Lewis Fischer and Eric W. Sager, eds, *The Enterprising Canadians: Entrepreneurs and Economic Development in Eastern Canada, 1820–1914* (St John's, 1979).

Eric Sager with Gerald E. Panting, *Maritime Capital: The Shipping Industry in Atlantic Canada, 1820–1914* (Montreal, 1990).

Notes

The author is indebted to Chris Roberts and Christine Godfrey for research assistance, to the Social Sciences and Humanities Research Council, and to Gerry Panting of the Maritime History Research Unit at Memorial University. This paper grows out of research undertaken for the Atlantic Canada Shipping Project, and for a book on the history of the shipping industry, being written jointly with Gerry Panting.

[1] Public Archives of P.E.I. [PAPEI], Duncan Letterbooks, Robert Quirk to James Moller and Co., Galveston, 1 April 1881; Quirk to R.M.C. Stumbles, 5 May 1881.

[2] The evidence on profits is contained in a book recently submitted for publication, co-authored with Gerry Panting, and entitled *Maritime Capital: The Shipping Industry in Atlantic Canada, 1820–1914.* Our estimates are based on the following procedures. I took cargoes and quantities for Atlantic Canadian ships entering Liverpool and London from the U.K. *Bills of Entry* for the years stated. From the shipping newspapers (mainly the *New York Maritime Register* and *Mitchell's Maritime Register*) I took freight rates current for those cargoes at the time of departure, and used these to estimate gross revenues per voyage. From gross revenues I deducted estimated costs, including wages, port charges, brokerage charges, repairs, provisions, insurance, and depreciation. These cost estimates were checked against known costs on specific trade routes from shipowners' account books in the Moran Papers, New Brunswick Museum, Colin Campbell Papers, Dalhousie University Archives, and other such sources. Depreciation is estimated to be 7 per cent a year to 1880 and 9 per cent a year thereafter. The average number of voyages per year is known from our analysis of Crew Lists. The number of voyages analyzed was as follows: for 1863 n=83 (mainly timber, cotton, petroleum, grain, guano and molasses, with each cargo weighted according to proportion of U.K. entrances); for 1873 n=168 (mainly timber, cotton, petroleum, grain and rice); for 1883 n=51. The method is described more completely in Eric W. Sager and Lewis R. Fischer, 'The Pursuit of Profits: An Analysis of the Returns from the Shipping Industry of Atlantic Canada' (paper presented to the Atlantic Canada Studies Conference, Saint John, May 1983). Returns from several individual vessels have also been analysed, using records of actual dividends paid to shareholders. For six vessels operating mainly in the 1870s and 1880s, and for a total of 66 vessel-years, the

average annual return on depreciated capital was 15.6 per cent. In 1878 Peter Mitchell, the former Minister of Marine and Fisheries, said: 'They [shipowners in the Maritimes] had made ships the savings banks of some portions of the Dominion. . . . There was no doubt that the Yarmouth ships, for example, made a better return for the money and labour invested in them than almost any industry in the province.' Canada, House of Commons *Debates*, 18 February 1878, 363.

³C.K. Harley and Yrjö Kaukiainen, 'Panel Review: The Atlantic Canada Shipping Project', *Newfoundland Studies*, 4, 1 (Spring 1988), 87–97.

⁴Lewis R. Fischer and Helge W. Nordvik, 'From Broager to Borgen: The Risks and Rewards of Peter Jebsen, Shipowner, 1864–1892', *Sjofartshistorisk Arbok* (Bergen 1986).

⁵This is a possibility, as Ralph Davis reminds us in quoting an 18th century authority: 'There was a time, *in my memory*, when merchants prided themselves in charming gallies they sent to sea; they saw and admired them with a lover's eye, and did not reckon on *much gain* on them, merely as a *ship-account . . .* ' *Reasons for an Augmentation of at least Twelve Thousand Mariners, to be Employed in the Merchants' Service and Coasting Trade* (1759), cited in Ralph Davis, *The Rise of the English Shipping Industry* (London 1962), 387.

⁶Seven years ago James M. Gillmour pointed out this possibility to me, and I have not forgotten what he said.

⁷A very useful summary is by Jeffrey J. Safford, 'The Decline of the American Merchant Marine, 1850–1914: An Historiographic Appraisal', in Lewis R. Fischer and Gerald E. Panting, *Change and Adaptation in Maritime History: The North Atlantic Fleets in the Nineteenth Century* (St John's 1985), 53–85.

⁸Douglass C. North, *Structure and Change in Economic History* (New York 1981), 6–7.

⁹'For it may be little more than a truism to state that the individuals that are best adapted to survive have a better chance of surviving than those not so well adapted to survive.' T.H. Morgan, cited in Francis Hitching, *The Neck of the Giraffe, or Where Darwin Went Wrong* (London 1982), 104.

¹⁰Peter McClelland, 'Commentary: On Demand and Supply in Shipping and Regional Economic Development', in Lewis R. Fischer and Eric W. Sager, *Merchant Shipping and Economic Development in Atlantic Canada* (St John's 1982), 115. McClelland's doctoral thesis remains, however, one of the most important works on the history of the region: 'The New Brunswick Economy in the Nineteenth Century' (PhD thesis, Harvard University, 1966).

¹¹Comments by Frank and Kealey in Lewis R. Fischer and Eric W. Sager, *Merchant Shipping and Economic Development in Atlantic Canada* (St John's 1982), 120–1.

¹²Much of the discussion begins with F.A. Hayek, 'Economics and Knowledge', *Economica* (February 1937) and Hayek, *Individualism and Economic Order* (London 1949). Much of the literature is cited in Israel M. Kirzner, *Perception, Opportunity and Profit; Studies in the Theory of Entrepreneurship* (Chicago 1979).

¹³These are the conclusions of Kirzner's *Perception, Opportunity and Profit*, 237.

¹⁴Martin Dickie to James E. Dickie, 21 January 1887, Dalhousie University Archives, Dickie Correspondence.

¹⁵Undated article from the *Yarmouth Tribune*, cited in *Halifax Herald*, 3 January 1881.

[16]The implications of all of this Marxism are worth noting: see, for instance, Mark Poster, *Foucault, Marxism and History; Mode of Production versus Mode of Information* (Oxford 1984); Julius Sensat, *Habermas and Marxism; An Appraisal* (London 1979).

[17]See, for instance, Donald N. McCloskey, *The Rhetoric of Economics* (Madison 1985); and from another perspective, Martin Hollis and Edward J. Nell, *Rational Economic Man: A Philosophical Critique of Neo-Classical Economics* (Cambridge 1975).

[18]One honourable exception here was the commentary by Chad Gaffield on papers by Ian Radforth and Elizabeth Bloomfield.

[19]'Report of the Select Committee on the Causes of the Present Depression', Canada House of Commons *Journals*, 1876, vol. 10, Appendix 3, 164.

[20]Peter Mitchell, MP, in House of Commons *Debates*, 18 February 1878, 363. Mitchell's remarks went unquestioned, even by Frank Killam, who spoke earlier in the same debate.

[21]Canada *Sessional Papers*, 1885, no. 37, 42.

[22]Canada House of Commons *Debates*, 1888, 389.

[23]Canada House of Commons *Debates*, 2 March 1893, 1606.

[24]*Ibid.*, 1606 (Mr Gillmor).

[25]*Ibid.*, 1606 (Gillmor).

[26]See, for instance, Joseph Howe, *Speech of the Hon. Joseph Howe on Intercolonial Railroads, and Colonization, Delivered at Halifax, Nova Scotia, May, 1851* (Halifax 1851).

[27]Joseph Howe to Thomas Baring, 31 December 1861, cited in Rosemary Langhout, 'Developing Nova Scotia: Railways and Public Accounts, 1849–1867', *Acadiensis* XIV, 2 (Spring 1985), 8 n.17.

[28]*Ibid.*, 8.

[29]See Elizabeth W. McGahan, *The Port of Saint John* (Saint John 1982), 2 vols.

[30]See, for instance, Edmund Flynn of Richmond, N.S. in the debate on Halifax as a winter port: Canada House of Commons *Debates*, 20 December 1880, 160.

[31]Short two and three line fillers were omitted from the count. Articles were subdivided into leaders, editorial page articles, and miscellaneous, and into three categories by length of article. Of 1,364 short articles only 16 had local or Maritimes shipowning, and only 14 had local shipbuilding, as a principal topic; of 517 articles of medium length, only 10 had shipowning or shipbuilding as principal topics; of 256 long articles only two had shipowning or shipbuilding as principal topics.

[32]*Yarmouth Herald*, 14 February 1867.

[33]Of 649 articles in the 52 issues in the sample, only sixteen had local shipowning or shipbuilding as a principal topic.

[34]St John *Globe*, 18 January 1867.

[35]*Ibid.*, 10 December 1867.

[36]'The Outlook for the Future', St John *Daily Sun*, Supplement, 3 April 1889, 13.

[37]Thomas Kenny, then President of the Merchants' Bank of Halifax, cited in 'Report of the Select Committee on Inter-Provincial Trade', Canada *Sessional Papers*, 1883, Appendix no. 4, 22.

[38]See Gerry Panting's data in Eric W. Sager and Gerry Panting, 'Staple Economies and the Rise and Decline of the Shipping Industry in Atlantic Canada, 1820–1914', in Lewis R. Fischer and Gerald E. Panting, eds, *Change and Adaptation in Maritime History: The North Atlantic Fleets in the Nineteenth Century* (St John's 1985), 29–34.

Note that the opponents of Confederation in 1867 also assumed that manufacturing growth would occur, alongside the traditional marine-based industries. They argued, however, that Canadian control of Dominion tariffs, and 'throwing our markets open to Canadian manufactures' would 'destroy' manufacturing industry in the Maritimes: *Morning Chronicle*, 22 July 1867, cited in Delphin A. Muise, 'The Federal Election of 1867 in Nova Scotia: An Economic Interpretation', *Collection of the Nova Scotia Historical Society* 36 (1968), 340–1.

[39] R.T. Naylor, *The History of Canadian Business* (Toronto 1975), vol. 2, 283.

[40] On the mercantile heritage the essential works include T.W. Acheson, *Saint John: The Making of a Colonial Urban Community* (Toronto 1985); David A. Sutherland, 'The Merchants of Halifax, 1815–1850: A Commercial Class in Pursuit of Metropolitan Status' (PhD thesis, University of Toronto, 1975).

[41] See, for instance, Jones, Mitchell, Davies, Forbes and others in House of Commons *Debates*, 28 February 1876.

[42] John V. Ellis of Saint John in House of Commons *Debates*, 14 March 1890, 1963.

[43] William Welsh (Queen's, P.E.I.) in House of Commons *Debates*, 18 April 1888, 908.

[44] Canada House of Commons *Debates*, 14 June 1887, 989.

[45] A.G. Jones in House of Commons *Debates*, 14 June 1887, 992.

[46] George Robertson of Saint John in PAC RG 33–3, *Royal Commission on Transportation: Evidence*, 1 (1904–5), 74–5.

6

The Settlement of Western Canada

Wendy Owen

A major development of the period between Confederation and
World War I was the settlement
of the Canadian West, particularly
the prairie provinces. Between the
transfer of Rupert's Land to Canada
and the Great War, thousands of
migrants and immigrants poured
into Western Canada. Most were
drawn by dreams of independent
farm ownership, although many
ended up in the region's burgeoning
cities rather than on the land. Concomitant to the visions of freehold
farms wrought out of inexpensive
land grants or even free homesteads,
the West also generated strong mythologies, none more powerful than
the myth of the self-made man. Anyone could come to western Canada,
the land of opportunity, and by virtue
of hard work and constant application eventually succeed in achieving
that elusive goal: financial independence.

As Wendy Owen points out in
her study of farm-making in early
Manitoba, the realities of agricultural settlement in the prairie west
were quite different from the contemporary mythologies. The establishment of successful farms required
more than merely hard work. Even
free homestead land required substantial capital to develop properly.
In addition to capital, the successful
prairie farmer also required considerable agricultural experience, good
fortune, and some kind of devel-
opmental strategy. Employing the
account books and correspondence
of Almon James Cotton, Owen outlines the agricultural strategy of one
successful prairie farmer. That strategy was not based on the rapid
acquisition of freehold land, but
rather on the exploitation of tenancy on the land of others. It offered
a scheme for utilizing capital in
reducing debt, based upon the
assumption that investment in land
ownership should wait until the
farmer was out of debt and had cash
in hand. Cotton was both a good
farmer and a good businessman, and
even he required a number of years

of initial privation in order to 'turn the corner' and achieve prosperity.

Was Cotton a 'typical' farmer? Why is his record important, whether or not he was typical? What were the components of Cotton's agricultural success? Were they replicable by others? Did tenancy necessarily exploit the farmer? Would you have accepted Cotton's 1903 offer to farm in the Swan River Valley? Why or why not?

This article first appeared, titled 'The Cost of Farm-Making in Early Manitoba: The Strategy of Almon James Cotton as a Case Study', in *Manitoba History* 18 (Autumn, 1989), 4–11.

Between 1870 and 1914 hundreds of thousands of men and women poured into the prairie region of Western Canada, both into its cities and onto its land. Part of the attraction of the prairie West, of course, was its perpetuation of the long-standing New World dream of beginning—in economic terms —with virtually nothing, and achieving great prosperity. Newcomers came west to seek their fortunes, and in urban and rural surroundings some few succeeded. Perhaps the greatest single source of rapid economic gain was successful land speculation, but James Ashdown parlayed a small tinsmith's workshop behind a Red River hotel into a large wholesale trading empire, and on a homestead near Minnedosa Pat Burns began a career as one of Canada's most successful entrepreneurs. Few working farmers ever struck it rich, but the local histories of the region are full of stories of farmers who rose to prosperity from humble origins. The myth of the self-made man, so powerful everywhere in North America, had a special currency in the Canadian West.

At the same time, the records are equally full of the evidence of failure: abandoned farms, disastrous attempts at homesteading, and a high incidence of transiency.[1] As has always been the case, those who did not succeed have left far less impress upon the historical record than those who did well. Nevertheless, by the turn of the twentieth century, both immigration literature and the popular journals had come to recognize that the image of the totally self-made farmer was flawed. For the agrarian newcomer, the cost of establishment on the land—even if it were obtained at low expense under homestead conditions—was always a serious problem.[2]

Even were the land free, and frequently it was not, establishment upon it required some capital and involved many hidden costs. In recent years a considerable debate has emerged in the scholarly literature over the minimal amount of capital necessary to establish a Canadian prairie farm.[3] In addressing the problem of farm-making costs, however, the focus has been on initial establishment rather than the subsequent progress and viability of the farms involved. While it is possible to assume that those farmers who came with the barest minimum took longer to achieve financial independence (and ran more risk of going bust in the process) than more substantial newcomers, there has been little attempt in the literature to provide any framework for the process of farm establishment over time, or to evaluate alternative strategies. Examining establishment costs in a vacuum frozen in time does little to help clarify the mechanics of successful prairie farming. The following case study of Almon James Cotton, one of the prairie region's many 'Wheat Kings' in the boom years before World War I, attempts to contribute to the cost-of-farm-making debate by analysing how one farmer did succeed. Cotton is one of the few farmers in early Manitoba for whom extensive financial records and personal papers are available. Detailed analysis of Cotton's surviving account books makes it possible to follow the gradual process by which Cotton achieved his success.

Almon James (A.J.) Cotton was born near Port Granby, Ontario, in 1858. He began his farming career in 1881 by taking over on leasehold a small family holding in Durham County, which he expanded by purchase of adjacent property in 1884. Three years later Cotton decided to abandon Ontario, 'having farmed down there', he later recalled, 'until we could farm no longer at a profit'.[4] Cotton sold his farm for less than he had paid for it, but he was able to dispose at auction of much of his livestock and equipment to provide some working capital, and he brought a railcar of goods with him to his new home in Treherne, Manitoba. The land to which Cotton migrated in 1888 belonged to a Port Hope, Ontario, businessman, who was prepared to lease the land to Cotton for five years at an annual rental of one dollar per acre providing the landlord acquired all improvements at the conclusion of the lease. Cotton was thus able to acquire well-located fertile land without tying up his limited capital, with no mortgage costs, and with few financial responsibilities for it. Providing he did not over-improve the property, he was getting first cultivation of it for a relative pittance. Cotton eventually parleyed his success at Treherne into a major landholding in the newly opened Swan River Valley, removing there in 1901. He would farm in the Valley until his death in 1942.

In many ways, establishment costs to a farmer were inseparable from subsequent cash flow and continual availability of capital. One of the most difficult problems for many settlers was finding the cash necessary for farm expansion. The homesteader could not mortgage his land until he received the patent. Farm equipment could often be bought by giving a 'note', assuming one's credit was 'good', but credit often entrapped the farmer into an endless round of refinancing at increased cost. Paying off debt could be accomplished from the sale of a cash crop, whether grain or other farm produce such as eggs or butter. The beginning farmers frequently hired out their labour to others more prosperous in an attempt to bring in cash in the early years. While expansion of land under cultivation was one of any new farmer's major priorities, at some point the cost of expansion had to be exceeded by the rewards of expansion. In the first years, when margins tended to be tight and cash flow a perennial problem, any untoward occurrence such as the loss of livestock, the need to replace damaged equipment, or poor yields, could place the beginning farmer in a perilous position. A key part of the 'cost of farm-making' question, therefore, is how the farmer dealt with these first critical years. Obviously some long-term calculated strategy worked best, and A.J. Cotton had one.

In 1903 Cotton offered his sister-in-law and her husband, Mr and Mrs John Hislop, the opportunity to farm one of his recently acquired half-sections in the Swan River Valley on terms even more generous than those he had himself received in Treherne. Cotton provided the Hislops with a detailed breakdown of what he considered their progress should be over the four years of the proposed contract.[5] The Hislops were expected to erect a house and stable on the property, fence the entire 320 acres, and pay the taxes. In return, John Hislop would receive what Cotton had earlier gotten: the opportunity to take first crops over virgin land at minimal expense. Cotton's calculations were based on considerable experience, particularly his own. They offer an interesting opportunity to view the kind of strategy which Cotton felt he himself had followed at Treherne, upon which the Hislop offer was clearly based.

According to Cotton, the major expenses for the first year were in the provision of equipment and animals. Cotton suggested bringing the livestock and most of the implements from Ontario, as they were cheaper there, but he emphasized that the seeder and plows should be obtained in the West, where those available suited prairie conditions. The freight charges for the railcar ($117) were exactly the same in 1903 that Cotton had paid in 1888, and the cost of implements, stock, and freight charges amounted to $933. Additional expenses in the first year included $60 for shingles, windows, and nails for the house and stable; $21 for fence wire; $35 for taxes; and $105 provisioning for family and livestock. The total was $1,154. This estimate was considerably higher than the minimal figures discussed in the cost of farm establishment debate; Cotton obviously did not set his expenditures at the minimum. The only income he envisioned to set against the necessary costs would be $100 earned by Hislop helping his neighbours at harvest and threshing time. The first year (1903) would be taken up with building shelter for the family and animals, and in breaking land. Cotton estimated that sixty acres could be broken the first year, close to his own figure of 1888. But in retrospect, he did not recommend trying to crop the first year of settlement, thus reducing potential income.

Cotton envisaged the Hislops entering their second year with a debt of $1054 and interest at seven per cent, or $1,127.78 on the debit side. Expenses for 1904 would amount to an additional $378. Broken down, this figure included $47.50 for seed to plant fifty acres of wheat and fifteen acres of oats. Feed oats and provisions for the family would add $80 to the expense and the taxes would add another $35. Shingles and nails for a granary would come to $38. In addition to sundry expenses of $25, there would be the cost of harvesting the grain crop, which Cotton estimated at $155 ($30 for binder twine, $45 for threshing wheat, $30 for threshing oats, and $50 for hired help). The total expenses for the second year, added to the previous year's debt, would produce a liability of $1,505.78, offset by sale of 880 bushels of wheat at fifty cents a bushel. For purposes of his exercise, Cotton estimated average yields at twenty bushels per acre and average prices for wheat at fifty cents per bushel over the whole of the four-year period. These estimates were not, given the records of the time, unduly optimistic. At the end of their second year of farming, therefore, the Hislops would be $1,065.78 in debt, a small increase over the previous year. Again, this general calculation paralleled Cotton's own earlier experience.

A further sixty acres would have been broken in the second year, Cotton estimated, so that Hislop would begin 1905 (year three) with 125 acres of broken land and enough seed carried over from the previous year to raise the 1905 crop. With interest on the debt, the Hislops began 1905 in the hole to the tune of $1,140.38. But year three was critical. Cotton anticipated that 110 acres would be seeded in wheat and fifteen acres in oats, yielding 2,200 bushels of wheat and 750 of oats. Expenses for harvesting this crop would amount to $129 for threshing, $56.25 for binder cord, and $75 for hired help, or $260.25. In addition to these costs, expense for cultivation would require another horse at $200, an additional half-set of harness at $15, and another stubble plow at $18. Cotton increased the amount for family provisions to $75, probably to take into account the feeding of hired help. With taxes up to $40 and $25 for sundries, total expenses in year three came to $633.25. In all, expenses for this year plus previous liabilities amounted to $1,773.63. To set against such debits, Cotton envisioned selling 1,930 of the 2,200 bushels threshed, realizing $965 and reducing the Hislop indebtedness at the end of 1905 to $808.63.

For the fourth and final year of their contract, the Hislops would have 205 acres ready for crop, an increase of eighty acres over the previous year; 180 acres would be sown with wheat and twenty-five with oats. Seed for this planting would be carried over from the previous year. Such expanded acreage would require the help of a hired hand for seven months, as well as additional hands for harvesting and threshing. The projected wage bill would be $275, but part of this expense could be offset by hiring out to break fifty acres of land for others, bringing in $150. The major task for this year besides growing grain would be the completion of the fencing of the half section at an additional cost of $84. The expanded acreage would require another wagon to carry the wheat to the elevator, at a cost of $70. Threshing expenses for 3,600 bushels of wheat and 1,200 bushels of oats came to $273.50. With sundries of $50 and taxes of $40, total outgoings would be $771.90. To this figure was added the $808.63 indebtedness (plus interest of $56.60) from the previous year, totalling $1,637.13. But with receipts estimated at $2,325 from the sale of the grain, the Hislops would end year four with $688.81 cash on hand, plus all their chattels, 750 bushels of oats, and 270 bushels of wheat.

As we shall see, this calculation of progress was marginally faster than that managed by Cotton himself. It took him five years to have cash on hand. However, Cotton had expenses that the Hislops did not, including hired help and horses. As with most such projections, Cotton assumed fixed prices and yields, making no allowance for any of the disasters that might beset the western farmer. But even under the most favourable conditions, he did not anticipate a beginning farmer turning a profit in less than four years, and then only providing he had access to over a thousand dollars in unsecured credit at an uncompounded seven per cent—and had minimal land expenses. What Cotton expected the Hislops to do at the end of their four years of tenancy is not clear, since most of his land at Swan River was ultimately destined for his sons. Apparently he thought that the farming experience and their assets after four years would provide the Hislops with a good start on land of their own. Not surprisingly, the Hislops did not take Cotton up on his offer. When laid out in such graphic terms, starting up in Manitoba must not have sounded terribly attractive. Cotton had great difficulty in attracting tenants to his land in Swan River, partly because most newcomers had a fixation with land ownership. But Cotton here did something that little contemporary literature or modern scholarship has repeated. He thought in terms of a lengthy process of gradual expansion and reduction of debt based upon the market. He did not pretend that farming could begin without capital or debt, but he offered a scheme for reducing debt in an orderly and relatively swift fashion. He also assumed that the beginner should not own land until he had cash in hand.

Equally importantly, A.J. Cotton was not simply engaging in abstract theorizing in order to attract some tenants. The plan paralleled his own experience as it can be reconstructed from his financial records, although the Hislop situation was not identical to his own some fifteen years earlier. In the first place, Cotton did have some equipment and livestock, worth perhaps $800 to $1,000, as well as access to small amounts of family capital in Ontario. In the second place, Cotton brought not only his horses to Manitoba but a hired man as well. Finally, 1888 was not 1903, as Cotton himself appreciated, writing to the Hislops, 'Of course, the more capital you can put into it, the easier you can get through. Pioneering now is not what it used to be.'[6] Nevertheless, Cotton's own first years provide a context for his advice to the Hislops.

The Cotton family left Ontario for Manitoba in March of 1888, and on 4 May of that year, A.J. sowed his first crop in Manitoba: two and one-half acres of oats. On 23 May he began to sow twenty-three acres of barley, and he also planted an acre of potatoes. In all, during the first year Cotton planted twenty-six and one-half acres and broke a total of sixty acres. He was able to do so because of a spring arrival, the presence of a hired man, and the willingness of the family to camp out in the abandoned shell of a neighbouring farm while Cotton devoted his major effort to his new land. Recollection of these early days, particularly hard on his wife and family, helped contribute to Cotton's advice to the Hislops not to attempt to plant in their first year.

At the conclusion of his first year, Cotton's accounts showed a profit of $1.96. This figure, however, did not reflect the true picture. Cotton's 1888 costs included $165.10 for the move to Treherne, plus $216.86 in ongoing expenses. He did not have much outlay for buildings in this initial year. Combining money borrowed from kin, the money raised by working for others ($36.50) and from sale of crops and produce (194 bushels of barley at forty cents a bushel—or $78.90—plus twelve bushels of potatoes, twenty-five pounds of butter, and seven and one-half dozen eggs for $7.41), he had an income of $337.81. Although it is not clear from his accounting, Cotton must have used notes to finance part of his expenses, probably a stubble plow and a threshing bill. Nevertheless, at the end of his first year, Cotton had his livestock (including some animals obtained in Manitoba), as well as 160 bushels of barley, twenty-five of oats, fifty-eight of potatoes—plus sixty acres of broken land.[7] Since the province did not publish agricultural statistics in 1888, it is impossible to put Cotton's yields in a larger context. However, at Pipestone, James Lothian's oat yield was forty-eight bushels per acre as compared with Cotton's ten.[8] Cotton's yields appear relatively low, perhaps reflecting his lack of experience with the new environment. Although he had planted and harvested a crop, it had amounted to very little, doubtless another factor in his subsequent advice to wait until the second year to plant.

In 1889 Cotton sowed his first wheat, on 25 March of that year. By the time of sowing, two more acres of land had been cleared, and the entire sixty-two acres were planted with wheat.[9] According to the *Manitoba Crop Bulletin* for this year, seeding of spring wheat was earlier than any other year in the history of the province to date, and in thirty-two years of subsequent record-keeping Cotton only began seeding this early in one other year.[10] After his wheat sowing had been completed on 11 April 1889, Cotton began the next day to break land for a barley crop. By 24 May he had broken and seeded thirty acres of barley.[11] Having been sown relatively late, Cotton's barley crop escaped the late May frosts that decimated the crop already above the ground, but it fell victim to summer drought and was a complete failure.[12] Early seeding of wheat was followed by a fairly early harvest, with Cotton beginning cutting wheat on 8 August.[13] This harvest was generally disappointing across the province, with the yield the lowest on record. The problem was exacerbated by the fact that much of the rain-starved grain was too short to cut and bind in sheaves. Although the provincial yield was light, the grain threshed was considered of good quality, 'being pronounced bright and hard', and both high quality and scarceness drove up the price. The average wheat yield per acre across the province was 12.4 bushels, while the return for the district in which Cotton's land was located was better at 19.5 bushels per acre. Cotton topped both figures with an average of 23 bushels per acre.[14]

In all, Cotton harvested 1,256 bushels of wheat in 1889. Of this total, 840 bushels were taken directly from the threshing machine to the Farmer's Elevator at Treherne, and the remaining 416 bushels were stored in the back kitchen.[15] A month later Cotton sold the elevator wheat to R.S. Alexander for $536.80, which with wastage represented a price of $.65 per bushel, $.07 more than James Lothian received for his wheat at Virden.[16] Cotton's yields were also considerably better than Lothian's, the latter averaging 15.5 bushels per acre on land that had been cropped the previous year and (surprising in a drought year) only nine bushels per acre on fallow land.[17] Cotton's earning of $14.95 per acre was thus substantially greater than Lothian's, marking the beginning of a long run of such superior returns, which when combined with a constantly increasing acreage sown would form the basis of Cotton's prosperity.

The year 1889 had been a busy and costly one for Cotton. One of his first actions had been the purchase of another horse, completing two full teams. The horse was purchased from his landlord in Ontario and cost $180, Cotton giving a note for the amount due on 1 December 1889. Only if Cotton were unable to redeem the note at that time would interest be charged at the rate of seven per cent.[18] Such access to interest-free short-term capital was obviously enormously advantageous to Cotton. With two teams and two men (in addition to hired man Albert Taylor, Mrs Cotton's brother Will Ford was now at Treherne), Cotton was able to break another seventy-five acres in 1889, as well as planting nearly 100. Two teams and the move into wheat brought additional expenses. Cotton had to buy another breaking plow, this time a Moline at $27. He also had to obtain a second stubble plow at $20. The major expense in equipment, however, was a $200 Massey-Harris binder, although Cotton spent as well $49.20 on 615 pounds of wire to complete the fencing of the land and $13 for a permit to cut wood for posts, logs, and firewood.[19] Cotton was not merely concerned in 1889 with a crop and breaking land, for in addition to the fencing he had on 21 March laid the foundation for a house on his leasehold. Lumber and shingles for the house cost $118.41, although Cotton also paid $3.10 interest on the outstanding bill up to 16 October, when he used part of the proceeds from the sale of his wheat to retire the debt.[20] Unlike many a Manitoba farmer, A.J. Cotton appreciated the burden that interest charges placed on his operation, and he never allowed interest-bearing debt to remain a moment longer than necessary.

Cotton's rate of land breaking slowed in 1890, with only thirty-six fresh acres broken, bringing the total of broken land on the farm to 171 acres.[21] In this slowdown Cotton appears to have been in line with many others in the province, as a definite decline in the level of new breaking was noted in 1890.[22] Spring had been late in 1890, which may account for the reduction. Weather certainly retarded seeding. Beginning his seeding on 7 April, Cotton was a full week in advance of the general date for the province. This year he sowed 120 acres of wheat and ten acres of oats.[23] Rainfall was generally good in the spring and early summer, although there was still a shortage of moisture due to the drought of the previous year. Probably all would have been well but for a disastrous hailstorm over a large portion of the southern part of the province on 2 August. In some areas the crops were completely destroyed; in total, 31,851 acres of wheat, 8,403 of oats, and 1,108 of barley were wiped out.[24] Cotton does not seem to have been affected by this storm, although he was undoubtedly struck with the rain which fell generally from August through October. Although a week ahead in sowing, Cotton was almost a week behind the general date for cutting, beginning on 20 August.[25]

Cotton's average yield of 21.3 bushels per acre was marginally below the 21.5 bushels for his district and barely above the 20.1 bushels per acre which was the province-wide average. His oats yield was 32 bushels per acre, compared with 25.3 for the district and 41.3 for the province.[26] While these yields were doubtless disappointing to him, the doubling of his acreage took away some of the sting. Cotton managed a respectable crop in a year of personal consolidation. Making no major equipment or livestock purchases and no substantial improvements to his buildings, Cotton noted at the end of the year that his incomings were $832.95 and his outgoings only $444.84. Since part of the outgoings included retirement of $167.79 of debt, it was clear that 1890 was a critical year for A.J. Cotton.

Cotton accounts for 1891 show that this year was an easier one financially for the entire family. More money was spent on incidentals, and a large Christmas order was despatched from T. Eaton in Toronto.[27] Cotton increased his wheat acreage by another twenty acres, bringing the total to 130 acres, but in so doing he was below the twenty-two per cent increase general across the province.[28] The weather had been particularly favourable for putting in the wheat crop, and with the aid of his new press drill Cotton had finished planting by 12 May.[29] He also sowed twenty acres of oats and ten of barley. The July weather was good for the crop and a large one was anticipated, but in fact the crop year was rather mixed.[30] Although the crop was unusually heavy, a frost had affected at least forty per cent of the yield, and a late, slow harvest due to shortage of farm labour probably influenced the grading if not the quantity harvested.

Cotton appears to have escaped the worst of the problems, typical of his fortune in the early 1890s. His wheat averaged 28 bushels per acre, above the district level of 26.5 and the provincial figure of 25.3 bushels per acre.

His oats produced his best average yield ever at 55 bushels per acre, again ahead of both the district at 48.7 bushels and the province at 48.3 bushels.[31] Cotton's yields were persistently above both the district and provincial figures in the 1890s, and while account books cannot be made to yield the secret of his success, they do demonstrate that he was a highly skilled farmer. To what extent expansion onto virgin land assisted the total yields cannot be calculated.

At year's end, Cotton had only 360 bushels remaining of his 3,920 threshed bushels of wheat, indicating that his marketing was not delayed as was that of many other farmers in the province.[32] In addition to his cereal crops, Cotton continued to sell other produce from the farm. Although obviously a market-oriented wheat farmer, Cotton also ran a mixed farm operation. Sales of hay, potatoes, eggs, butter, as well as a steer for $19, all added to income in 1891. Cotton augmented his livestock this year, buying two more horses. The 'span of colts' cost $280. The animals represented the major purchase of the year, although in general Cotton's expanded acreage cost more to farm. He had to buy oats and barley for seed, and his harvesting costs were up, both for threshing and for binder twine.

At the end of the year Cotton calculated his assets and liabilities. The list of assets, which included grain on hand, livestock and farm implements, as well as his $25 share in the Treherne Farmer's Elevator, amounted to $2,280.25. The liabilities, including a note due on 11 October 1892 for the insurance of the farm house and its contents (together valued at $500) and $151 still outstanding to a relative in Ontario, amounted to $355. Cotton considered his net worth at the end of the year to be $1,825.25, perhaps double that with which he had arrived in Manitoba four years earlier. Nevertheless, his income was $2,696.08 and his outlay $2,716.84.[33] Despite the substantial increase in assets, Cotton had still not reached Mr. Micawber's golden mean. As we have already seen, Cotton would later project a substantial annual profit for year four of the Hislop operation, although he had not actually achieved such a state himself.

1892 was a good year for Manitoba wheat and for A.J. Cotton. Manitoba wheat won the gold medal at the International Millers Exhibition in London, England, a recognition that could not have come at a more opportune time.[34] The large harvest of the previous year had shown that the Manitoba wheat crop had outstripped the demand in North America, and the province would have to look more seriously for markets in Britain and Europe.[35] In 1892 Cotton planted 153 acres of wheat, as well as ten acres of barley and twenty-three of oats.[36] The total of 186 acres planted meant that he was continuing to bring new land under cultivation. During the early summer, farmers looked forward to a bumper harvest, but this expectation was not realized everywhere. Dry weather caused the wheat to ripen too quickly, there were the usual local storms and frosts, and in some sections wheat did not fill to the top.[37]

According to the analysts, another reason for the light yield of 1892 was overexpansion; some farmers were breaking more land than they could properly cultivate.[38] A.J. Cotton, however, had not allowed his land to get out of control, and he was lucky with the weather as well. His wheat yield in 1892 was 29 bushels to the acre, nearly double that of either his district (16.33 bushels) or the province (16.50 bushels). Oats and barley yields were equally good for Cotton, barley more than doubling the district average and nearly doubling that of the province. Oats averaged 61.5 bushels, compared with 35.7 for the district and 35 for the province. Altogether Cotton had 4,437 bushels of wheat, 1,414 of oats, and 570 of barley.[39] Christmas in the Cotton household of 1892 reflected the prosperity derived from these results. In addition to a fifteen-pound turkey, there were candies and raisins, nuts, oranges, lemons and pears.[40] While last year's holiday had been a good one, this one was even better.

When Cotton sat down to his annual year end's reckoning, for the first time he could record that he had $228.36 cash on hand. His assets this year came to $2,668 and the liabilities were $348.61, down slightly from the previous year. Some debt had been retired and some added. Cotton now owed his aunt in Ontario $166.06, the increase reflecting the six per cent interest being charged on the remaining principal. Cotton's net worth had increased by $772.50 over the previous year, now standing at $2,547.75. It had taken him five years in Manitoba to 'turn the corner', and he had begun with some advantages and progressed without any major setbacks. Despite Cotton's later calculations for the Hislops, it would appear that five years represented the minimum span of time during which a farmer beginning in Manitoba in the late 1880s could expect to become a profit-maker.

Over the remaining years of the 1890s, Cotton continued to expand his holdings in rented virgin land and his acreage under cultivation, reaching his maximum wheat acreage in Treherne and the Swan River Valley in 1900 at 730 acres. In 1895, with 314 acres under cultivation, Cotton produced 12,745 bushels of wheat (a spectacular 40 bushels per acre in a bumper year in which the provincial average was 27 bushels per acre). Harvesting early, by 27 September of that year he had 12,585 bushels of wheat filling nineteen rail cars heading for Fort William, thirteen of them filled with No. 1 hard and six with No. 1 northern. He received an advance of thirty cents on the bushel, and between his $2,600 advance and an additional sales worth $4053.77 of other produce he was able to clear his remaining debts and increase his net worth substantially to $6,237.15.[41] After this year it becomes impossible to relate his annual revenue to his annual production, since he was now sufficiently well off to be able to hold wheat back for the best price. By 1899 he had assets of $19,103.68, including $6,306.56 out on loan. According to his calculations that year, he had made a profit of $.22 on every bushel of wheat he had threshed.[42] Small wonder he was labelled 'The Wheat King' in several newspapers and journals.

Table 1. A.J. Cotton: Acres under Crop, 1888–1900

Year	Total	Wheat	Oats	Barley
1888	25.5	—	2.5	23
1889	62	62	—	—
1890	130	120	10	—
1891	170	140	20	10
1892	186	153	23	10
1893	235	200	25	10
1894	330	280	35	15
1895	380	314	52	14
1896	412	320	80	12
1897	544	475	59	10
1898	760	515	13	
			2	13
1899	690	650	40	—
1900	810	730	80	—

What can we learn from the foregoing detailed examination of A.J. Cotton's farming progress from 1888 to 1893? In the first place, it must be emphasized that he was a hardworking and skilled farmer. The land at Treherne was among the best in the province, but Cotton consistently outproduced his neighbours, year after year. Continual expansion onto new land undoubtedly aided his yields, and may also have kept down some of the collateral problems of weeds and pests. In the second place, while his annual planning seemed centred around constant expansion of acreage under cultivation, Cotton did have an overall strategy and a good business sense. He had become established without investing in land, and he operated on a pay-as-you-go basis as much as possible.[43] He kept his equipment purchases to the minimum, and seems to have engaged in little mechanization. In the third place, of course, Cotton built his success in a period in which constant expansion of acreage under cultivation worked, and in which the costs of mechanization had not yet emerged. He was thus able to expand without incurring the substantial costs of mechanized agriculture. Horses remained his major equipment investment. In the fourth place, Cotton was very fortunate, particularly in escaping the many disasters that ravaged parts of the provincial grain crop in the period. Finally, Cotton exploited all possible sources of income, including ploughing land for neighbours (195 acres for $400 in 1892, 280 acres for $500 in 1893) and the production of mixed farming (dressed hogs, eggs, butter, lard, and cattle brought in an additional $289.65 in 1893).[44] At the same time, Cotton was not able to resolve the problems of marketing. Despite his success he was no better off than his

Table 2. A.J. Cotton: Comparative Wheat Yields per Acre

Year	Acreage	Total bu.	Bu/acre	District–ave/acre	Prov. ave/acre
1888	—				
1889	62	1371	23	19.5	12.4
1890	120	2566	21.3	21.5	20.1
1891	140	3920	28	26.5	25.3
1892	153	4437	29	16.33	16.5
1893	200	4378	22	20	15.5
1894	280	8400	30	20.5	17.0
1895	314	12745	40	29	27.0
1896	320	4536	14.25	11.9	14.33
1897	475	12350	26	14.7	14.14
1898	515	16206	31	19	17.01
1899	650	18632	29	19	17.13
1900	730	6025	8.5	7.6	8.9

neighbours once his threshing was completed, and various strategies of marketing wheat all proved of limited satisfaction. Cotton never managed to beat the system to his own advantage in all his years of farming.

But A.J. Cotton had succeeded, and the advice he gave to his kinfolk was based on that experience. As he wrote to the Hislops in 1903 regarding successful establishment as a prairie farmer,

> . . . to accomplish this . . . means *industry* and *good management*, and doing the proper thing at the proper time. You cannot be promised ease or luxury. There will be a certain amount of hardship to endure, obstacles to overcome. Your first four years would be your greatest worry, after that you would be into shape to go ahead.[45]

These observations bring us back to the scholarly debate over the cost of farm-making in prairie Canada before World War I.

It is difficult to fault A.J. Cotton's strategy and tactics—or good fortune—apart from his concentration on rented virgin land adjacent to rail transportation as an alternative to purchase or homestead. Land ownership might in the long run have brought him greater returns by enabling him to sell out at inflated prices when he decided to move to Swan River. But much depended on where the land he might have purchased or homesteaded in 1888 was located, and if purchased how much additional debt he would have incurred in the process. As matters stood, he had begun with capital of nearly $1,000, relatively few debts, and access to short-term interest-free funds. He had enjoyed yields continually above average, experienced much good fortune with weather, and run a tight business-like operation that kept interest

charges low and maximized all sources of revenue. Even under these conditions, it took A.J. Cotton five years to turn the profit corner. During those
five years he and his family had been forced to work hard, defer expectations,
and watch expenses carefully. As Cotton had noted to the Hislops, capital,
careful management, and perseverance were the keys to successful farm establishment. Capital was certainly a prerequisite, but it was not by itself sufficient. Given Cotton's experiences, the minimum amount of capital desirable
was clearly in the range of $1,000, to which must be added the immeasurable
patience and fortitude to continue to lose money and forego luxury annually
for four or five more years before achieving success. Not all prairie farmers
possessed such resources, and many would fail regardless of the size of their
initial capital investment. Given A.J. Cotton's evidence, it is difficult to see
how it could have been otherwise.

Suggestions for Further Reading

Lyle Dick, *Farmers 'Making Good': The Development of Abernethy District, Saskatchewan,
1880–1920* (Ottawa, 1989).
David C. Jones, *Empire of Dust: Settling and Abandoning the Prairie Dry Belt* (Edmonton, 1987).
Paul Voisey, *Vulcan: The Making of a Prairie Community* (Toronto, 1988).

Notes

[1] For recent studies of these themes for the prairie West, see Paul Voisey, *Vulcan: The
Making of a Prairie Community* (Toronto, 1988) and David C. Jones, *Empire of Dust:
Settling and Abandoning the Prairie Dry Belt* (Edmonton, 1987).
[2] See, for example, Lyle Dick, 'Factors Affecting Prairie Settlement: A Case Study
of Abernethy, Saskatchewan in the 1880s', *Canadian Historical Association Historical
Papers*, 1985, 11–28.
[3] See, for example, Robert E. Anklin and Robert M. Litt, 'The Growth of Prairie
Agriculture: Economic Considerations', in Donald H. Akenson, ed., *Canadian
Papers in Rural History*, I (1978), 33–66; Lyle Dick, 'Estimates of Farm-Making
Costs in Saskatchewan, 1881–1914', *Prairie Forum*, VI (1981), 183–201; Irene M.
Spry, 'The Cost of Making a Farm on the Prairies', *Prairie Forum*, VII (1982),
95–100; Lyle Dick, 'A Reply to Professor Spry's Critique "The Cost of Making
a Farm on the Prairies" ', *Prairie Forum* VII (1982), 101. Anklin and Litt suggest
$1,000 as a minimum for 1900, and while Dick accepts $1,000 as average, he
suggests that $300 was an absolute minimum. Spry disagrees with some of Dick's
'expenses', arguing that they were not properly a part of 'farm-making', but accepts
his conclusion that it was possible to succeed with little initial capital.
[4] For the career of Almon James Cotton, consult Wendy J. Owen, 'Prairie Patriarch:
A History of Almon James Cotton, 1858–1942', unpublished MA thesis, University
of Manitoba, 1986; Wendy Owen, ed., *The Wheat King: The Selected Letters and
Papers of A.J. Cotton, 1888–1913* (Winnipeg, 1985). The bulk of the Cotton Papers

are located in the Provincial Archives of Manitoba, Winnipeg (hereafter cited as CPPAM), although some papers and photographs are still in the possession of the family in Swan River, Manitoba.

[5]A.J. Cotton to John and Sadie Hislop, 28 January 1903, CPPAM. This letter, although not its accompanying material, is reprinted in Owen, ed., *The Wheat King*, 68–70.

[6]*Ibid.*

[7]Cotton Account Books, 1888, 1889, CPPAM.

[8]James Lothian Papers, 1888, Provincial Archives of Manitoba.

[9]Cotton Account Books, 25 March 1889, CPPAM.

[10]Manitoba Department of Agriculture and Immigration, *Crop Bulletin*, n. 22 (1889), 3. Hereafter this source will be cited as *Crop Bulletin*, with relevant number.

[11]Cotton Account Books, 11 April, 12 April, 24 May 1889, CPPAM.

[12]*Crop Bulletin* 23, 7; Cotton Account Books, 1889.

[13]Cotton Account Books, 1889.

[14]*Crop Bulletin* 24, 8; Cotton Account Books, 1889.

[15]Cotton Account Books, 11 September 1889.

[16]Cotton Account Books, 16 October 1889; James Lothian Papers, PAM.

[17]James Lothian Papers, 16–21 September 1889, PAM.

[18]Cotton Account Books, January 1889.

[19]Cotton Account Books, 1889.

[20]*Ibid.*

[21]Cotton Account Books, 30 December 1890.

[22]*Crop Bulletin* 26, 11.

[23]Cotton Account Books, 7 April 1890; *Crop Bulletin* 25, 5.

[24]*Crop Bulletin* 26, 14.

[25]Cotton Account Books, 20 August 1890; *Crop Bulletin* 27, 5.

[26]Cotton Account Books, 1890; *Crop Bulletin* 27, 6.

[27]Cotton Account Books, 9 May, 15 May, 22 December 1891.

[28]Cotton Account Books, 1891; *Crop Bulletin* 28, 4.

[29]Cotton Account Books, 12 May 1891.

[30]*Crop Bulletin* 30, 6 and *Crop Bulletin* 31, 5.

[31]Cotton Account Books, 1891; *Crop Bulletin* 31, 5.

[32]Cotton Account Books, 1891; *Crop Bulletin* 31, 8.

[33]Cotton Account Books, 1891.

[34]*Crop Bulletin* 33, 15.

[35]*Crop Bulletin* 32, 3.

[36]Cotton Account Books, 1892.

[37]*Crop Bulletin* 37, 4.

[38]*Crop Bulletin* 31, 11, and *Crop Bulletin* 36, 12.

[39]Cotton Account Books, 1892.

[40]Cotton Account Books, 24 December 1892.

[41]Cotton Account Books, 1895.

[42]Cotton Account Books, 1899.

[43]The issue of ownership versus tenancy has not been much addressed in the Canadian literature, although Voisey suggests in *Vulcan*, 135ff, that Alberta farmers

expanded their holdings through the use of rental land. There is a substantial American literature on tenancy, however, much of which suggests that it was a functional economic strategy rather than a factor necessarily involving exploitation of poor tenant farmers, a point with which Voisey concurs.

[44]Cotton Account Books, 1892, 1893.
[45]Cotton to Hislops, 28 January 1903.

7

Race in Victorian Canada

Judith Fingard

Society in Victorian Canada was comprised of a number of separate and distinct strands, with distinctions invidious and otherwise made on grounds of religion, ethnicity, race, gender, and class. Few Victorians genuinely believed in social equality, before the law or otherwise, although a prevailing tenet of the age was the notion of progress. Things were supposed to be getting better, which in social terms meant that there was continual evidence of upward mobility. So long as the poor had a chance to advance, Victorians remained content. What was worrisome (then as now) was when certain minorities among the population became structurally trapped in situations of permanent inferiority cutting across a number of the categories but dominated by one, such as race.

Canadians have traditionally almost ignored the historical presence of racial minorities such as blacks, people from Asia, and native peoples within their ranks, often assuming that such groups have only recently appeared in numbers. Certainly one minority with high potential for structural entrapment was the black population of Victorian Nova Scotia, especially of Halifax. Descendants of black Loyalists and immigrants from the Caribbean and the United States, blacks (or 'coloureds', as they would have called themselves) represented a substantial minority with considerable roots in the Halifax region. Whether they could enjoy a constant upward mobility was another matter.

In her study of the black community of Victorian Halifax, Judith Fingard attempts to understand the nature of that community, as well as its aspirations and limitations. According to Fingard, the élite members of the black community in Halifax had crossed a mystical line into 'respectability'. There was a stable group of black leaders with middle-class aspirations for improvement, particularly in education.

Halifax blacks made some gains in desegregating the schools, gains ultimately limited by the attitude of the white community, which refused to treat the blacks with respect. In the end, Halifax blacks gave up efforts at integration in favour of black consciousness. Why was 'respectability' such an important attribute in Victorian Halifax? How was it measured? Had the black leadership of the city truly achieved it? Why did education become the battleground for the black community? How did the Bruce case precipitate trouble? In the end, what limited black advancement?

This article first appeared, titled 'Race and Respectability in Victorian Halifax', in *Journal of Imperial and Commonwealth History* 20, 2 (May 1992), 169–95.

The strains of 'God Save the Queen' reverberated melodiously through the black churches of Halifax on two symbolically crucial occasions in the late nineteenth century. The first was a November evening in 1883 when a meeting, assembled in the African Baptist Church, passed resolutions in favour of racially integrated schools.[1] The second was nine years later in June 1892 when another meeting of black citizens, convened in Zion African Methodist Episcopal Church, voted in favour of the dismissal of an 'entirely and absolutely unfit and improper' public school teacher.[2] Given the degree of anger and frustration which lay beneath the surface of the dignified and polite behaviour at these meetings, the concluding ceremonial of the national anthem represented less a demonstration of loyalty and obedience than an expression of proper and respectable conduct. Pride in Britishness was part of the imperial fervour of the age shared by all upwardly mobile elements of the community. It did not imply unquestioning acceptance of the *status quo*. As one leading Afro-Nova Scotian explained: 'We are Britishers and we have the law and constitution of our glorious Empire to support us, and our rights we claim and our rights we will demand.'[3] Another was reported to have suggested that 'They were a down trodden race under a British flag and they would have justice or know the reason why.'[4]

Since both initiatives were in fact ultimately successful, black power under the British flag appears to have made some headway in late Victorian Halifax. Support from liberal whites may have been valuable but it was not indispensable to the articulation of goals and strategies of 'the most influential and respectable of the colored citizens of the city'.[5] The assertion of black rights, which integrating the schools and forcing out an unpopular teacher represented, occurred before out-migration, economic competition, and racist attitudes of the Jim Crow variety effectively thwarted black aspirations.

Existing studies provide little insight into these modest victories because historians and sociologists of race relations in Nova Scotia have chosen to ignore the second half of the nineteenth century. They have concentrated instead on the pitiful settlement experience of the period between the 1780s and the 1830s and the institutional discrimination in the twentieth century represented by such factors as racist military policies and the plight and destruction of the black ghetto of Africville.[6] Yet, between the occurrence of these two lamentable types of experience, a black élite emerged in Halifax with all the trappings of Victorian respectability. The American literature on the socio-economic progress of blacks during the post-bellum era suggests that surely Halifax, a city with a larger proportion of blacks in its population in 1881 than Boston, twice the percentage of Cleveland, and almost three times that of Chicago, should yield some interesting parallels in social mobility.[7] That upward mobility was likely to have involved the quest for respectability is indicated by the British literature. Either as an ideology based on thrift, industry, and sobriety, or a role distinguishing correct from rough behaviour, respectability appealed to social climbers. So vital was the concept in some racially mixed communities of the late nineteenth-century Empire that 'the true gulf in society was between those who were respectable and those who were not, rather than between whites and non-whites.'[8]

In 1881 blacks in Halifax lived in the sixth largest city in Canada. They shared it with some 35,000 other civilians and between two and three thousand British soldiers. The official census count identified 1,039 blacks, which is a slight under-enumeration given the failure to identify several prominent black families as African in origin. Nearly one and a half times as many blacks lived in the county of Halifax, from whence they commuted to the city for trade, casual labour, and marriage partners. By the late nineteenth century intermarriage with whites had produced many mixed-blood offspring. Regardless of skin colour, however, members of the Afro-Nova Scotia community were universally identified as 'coloured'. Only rarely was the term 'negro' employed and the designation 'black', so universally acceptable now, never appeared in print. Unlike usage in other parts of the British Empire, 'coloured' meant any person of colour who was of African extraction. It was also the term used by blacks to describe themselves.

Families of African ancestry, who persisted in Halifax over several generations, were invariably caught up in economic change and urban growth. Although the city continued to be a fishing, shipping, and military centre, it had entered a significant period of industrialization in the 1870s, which intensified after the introduction of the 'National Policy' of protectionism in 1879. Black citizens were affected more by the gradual shift from ocean-related to railway-centred transportation than the transition from commercial to industrial city. The men's participation in seafaring, marine-related trades, construction and haulage, which were prominent occupations in the 1850s, 1860s, and 1870s, expanded during the 1880s and 1890s into a more diversified range of jobs, especially in service (on land and rail as well as sea), and also in offices, shops, and the professions. Few opportunities for industrial employment, however, appear to have come their way.[9]

The total civilian population increased by 22 per cent between 1871 and 1881, with a slightly lower rate of increase for the black population. This development influenced residential patterns. For blacks, the creation of more class-based neighbourhoods in a period of growing class consciousness, the separation of home and workplace, and nascent racial intolerance meant greater concentrations of black households in clearly definable areas. Between 1871 and 1881 there was a marked movement of blacks away from the south and central wards of the city which encompassed the original commercial core and residential district of the servant-employing élite, located between Citadel Hill and the south Common to the west and the waterfront to the east. Many of the blacks relocated in what was called the north end, where they joined the descendants of the original early nineteenth-century black community just to the north of Citadel Hill in Ward 5. Within this area, the cluster of streets most populated by blacks became Maynard, Creighton, and Maitland, adjacent streets running north–south, and the cross streets and lanes. Another, much smaller concentration of blacks resided in Africville, a poor and struggling enclave with a strong sense of identity, a mile and a half farther north on the edge of Ward 6 where Campbell Road skirted the Intercolonial Railway line parallel to the shore of Halifax Harbour as it opened out into the Bedford Basin. The long-term effect of residential segregation was ghettoization; in the short term, however, the closer contact gave the blacks a sense of unity needed to resist the attempts by whites to shape their destiny.

Neighbourhood was not the main organizing mechanism for political action by the blacks. Instead, they relied on city-wide institutions which they established for religious, fraternal, and economic purposes. While the black community had access to the services of most of the publicly supported institutions, they had direct influence only over their own segregated, voluntary institutions, which included, in the mid-Victorian period, three church congregations, a mutual benefit society, a militia company, two fraternal lodges, a temperance society, and at least one labour-based association. Passion for temperance and interest in party politics won the leading black citizens influential friends among whites.

Although the people of African descent in Halifax may have emulated white institutions and trends, they were also connected to the wider Afro-American world as a result of the continuous arrival of sailors from the Caribbean, preachers from American black churches and, until the Civil War, runaway slaves from the United States. Their wider horizons gave them a sense of solidarity which characterized their all-black organizations. But they also expected enough integration to enable them to share the benefits of society as a whole. The realization of these expectations took a number of different forms. They participated in civic celebrations as members of the Victoria Rifles, the Coloured Truckmen's Association and the African

Friendly Society or Anglo-African Society, as it had become by the 1870s; their separate lodges of freemasons, templars, and oddfellows were, respectively, full members of the multi-racial parent organizations, the Grand Lodge of Nova Scotia, the IOGT Grand Lodge of the World, and the Acadia District of the Independent Order of Oddfellows, Manchester Union. They had separate schools dating back to the African School established by the Bray Associates in 1785, but they expected to place their more talented and ambitious children in integrated schools for advanced instruction and to have the option of sending their young ones to the neighbourhood schools of their choice.[10]

While they could not take integration for granted, access to education, property ownership, voting privileges, and European fashions in culture increased their self-worth and ostensibly equipped them with the trappings for achieving success in the white man's world. United by colour, they were nonetheless clearly divided by attitude and behaviour. Upwardly mobile blacks had about as much sympathy for the social misfits and 'undeserving' poor among their own people as their white counterparts had for theirs. What set them apart from their lesser brethren was not greater wealth or more prestigious occupations but their devotion to respectability. The worthy black citizens of Halifax considered respectability to be the key, not only to their superiority over their rough brethren, but to equality with whites, dignity in status, and justice in the public sphere.

This article addresses Afro-Nova Scotian perceptions of respectability in late nineteenth-century Halifax by focussing on three issues: the nature of black community leadership which established the material basis for respectability; the controversy over school segregation and integration in the 1870s and 1880s in which public respectability was defined largely in terms of citizenship; and the campaign in the 1890s to get rid of a white teacher in an all-black school, which provides insights into the norms of respectable behaviour in the private sphere.

I

We can identify the black leadership, with its middle-class aspirations and its insistence on its own respectability, as the signatories to the major extant petition asking for school integration in the early 1880s.[11] The petition identifies over one hundred 'colored' men, all of whom appear to have signed their names, though at least twelve can be verified, on the basis of other sources, as being unable to write. This black community leadership comprised 40 per cent of the black adult male population of 1881 (258 over 20 years of age). Although women participated actively in the citizens' meetings, served as the main vigilantes of the treatment of their children within the schools, and petitioned at least once as a distinct group, they were not involved in the major petition as signatories. They appear here as supporters rather than as principal actors. Nonetheless their influence was undoubtedly significant since they comprised over 60 per cent of the adult black population and were accustomed, especially in seafaring families, to managing their own domestic affairs.

Using decennial federal censuses (1871–91), almanacs, city directories, provincial marriage registrations, undertakers' and burial records, society and church papers, newspaper obituaries, wills and probate court records, positive identifications have been made of 98 (90 per cent) of the 108 black men concerned.[12] At least 55 of the 98 were in their 30s or 40s, years when they would have been most concerned about their children's schooling. Another twenty were men over 50 whose interest was in their grandchildren rather than their children, though several had fathered children in old age. Some of the elderly men were patriarchs who had been prominent in the city for many years. One of these was Jesse Coleman, a former slave from Baltimore, who had settled in the city as a stonemason in 1839 after escaping from the south, first to Boston, where he had been encouraged to change his destination from Upper Canada to Halifax. Although he was 83 in 1883, his direct interest in the school question was still of recent memory since he had a 17-year-old daughter by his third wife.[13] Another was John McKechnie (McKeagney), a shipwright from the British West Indies, who had arrived in Halifax about 1835. In his mid-60s, he was the great uncle of a number of school-children and lived with a niece, Elizabeth Lewis, wife of a ship's cook and steward, who emerged as an active and vocal other in the school controversy.[14] A third representative of the older generation and the most venerable by far was thrice-married John Shaw, an ex-slave and former coachman, who had arrived in 1816 and was aged 89 in 1881.[15]

Three of the signatories derived their position in the black community from their relationship to one of the black matriarchs, Esther Allison, a shopkeeper and Creighton Street property-owner in her 70s. One was her tenant, Daniel E. Jacobs, a Jamaican tailor. The others were her son, Robert S. Allison, a crockery packer and father of two small children, and her son-in-law, William Walker, a ship's steward married to her daughter Esther, who had one small daughter, all of whom lived with her at the time of the 1881 census.

Esther Allison's grandchildren were scarcely school-aged by the time of the submission of the petition. Like her son and son-in-law, a number of other married men signed the petition as prospective fathers of schoolchildren, with at least 17 of the petitioners being in their 20s. Alexander P. Davidson, a sometime porter, packer, and clerk with a drug company, had an infant son, as did George Brown, an Africville nailmaker. Charles Pinheiro, a Barbadian waiter who later became a railway porter, storekeeper for the commissary department of the ICR, and finally porter-instructor for the CNR, got married in 1882 in the midst of the school question and had no school-aged offspring until the 1890s.[16] Other interested parties were mature couples whose children had left home. William Crawley, a broom-maker, and his wife, Louisa, had no children living with them in 1881; neither did James Saunders, an umbrella mender, and his wife, Maria; John Green, a cook-steward from Antigua, and his wife, Margaret, a shopkeeper; George Jackson, a labouring man, and his wife, Susan; or John Whitfield, a Jamaican truckman, and his wife, Elizabeth. On the other hand, stevedore Henry and Jane Whebb's children were young adults still in their parents' household.

The petitioners also included several single men, both old and young, bachelors and widowers, most of whom had no close family connection to the schoolchildren and their parents. Their interest clearly established the issue as a community concern. They comprised, in addition to Daniel E. Jacobs, Daniel Gross (Grose), an old seaman, George Liston, a middle-aged boatman, Thomas G.D. Scotland, a young British West Indian bookkeeper with the black fur and hat firm of Thomas & Co. as well as Martin Lucas, a servant in the household where the furrier partners lived, George Barrett, a young barber living with his widowed mother and his sisters, and William T. Davis, an elderly uncle to several of the other petitioners, who had a long career as a head waiter in a number of high-class hotels and boarding houses. George Roache was the youngest petitioner, at 17 in 1881. The stepson of mariner James H. Martin, another petitioner, who had several younger children, Roache was destined to become the most successful of the petitioners in material terms as a caterer and restaurant proprietor.[17]

The petitioners' shared characteristics derived from four areas of respectability. First, most of these men were prominent in the city's organizational life, particularly in the temperance movement and fraternal societies. George Davis, a barber by trade, and Peter E. McKerrow, a Thomas & Co. furrier, originally from Antigua, were leading members not only of the Morning Glory Lodge of Good Templars, an all-black chapter, but also of the provincial grand lodge. When this organization seceded from the original Templars in 1876 over the issue of the 'color line', Nova Scotia joined the pro-integrationist minority. In 1877 George Davis crossed the Atlantic to represent the IOGT of Nova Scotia in 1880, Nova Scotians of both races reaffirmed their loyalty to the secessionist Lodge of the World, and three Halifax West Indians—Peter E. McKerrow, Thomas G. Scotland, and John L. French, an undertaker—were appointed to provincial standing committees.[18] Given the amount of drunkenness among the rough segment of black society, the teetotal position of the leaders graphically distinguished between the respectable and non-respectable. The drink trade in all its forms was anathema to them and contributed to their moral indignation about the exclusion of their children from the public schools of their choice. As John L. French emphasized: 'The children of the [white] rumseller were admitted and no questions asked, but his were [*sic*] refused because she was a little darker, and her color might cast a dark cloud over the school.'[19] Another badge of respectability was membership in the Ancient Free and Accepted Masons. Peter E. McKerrow became a member of Union Lodge No. 18 in 1861, wrote its history, and served as secretary at the time of his death in 1906. Altogether 28 (28.6 per cent) of the petitioners were sometime members of Union Lodge.[20] The Wilberforce Lodge of Oddfellows arrived on the scene last and attracted the younger men and their sons, becoming by 1900 an organization with over 80 members.[21]

A second measure of respectability related to the leaders' roles within their churches. Although not all the black petitioners belonged to the African Baptist or African Methodist Episcopal churches, an overwhelming 89 per cent did, identified as 55 Baptists and 32 Methodists. Jesse Coleman, who had been a founder of Zion African Methodist Episcopal Church in Halifax, became its long-time stalwart and a part-time local preacher. His obituarist noted that 'He followed masonry for a living and preached between whiles, as did the Apostles of old in the midst of their manual occupations.'[22] William D. Howell, a Barbadian-born waiter who reared two daughters to become teachers, one of whom was the first black woman to attend the city's Dalhousie University, was 'a lifelong and valued member' of the same church.[23] Indeed the American and West Indian immigrants contributed the major Methodist membership. In some cases marriage to local Baptist women resulted in gradual assimilation for both Methodists and others to the church of the black majority.

The names of 13 of the Baptist petitioners appear in the 1895 list of church officers of Cornwallis Street African Baptist Church, printed in McKerrow's *Brief History of the Colored Baptists of Nova Scotia*. Among the deacons were Charles F. Biddle, a coal hawker, Elijah, Jacob, and Joseph Flint, truckmen, shoemaker William Johnston, James Saunders, William B. Thomas, furrier, and Robert J. White, ship's steward. Two of the ushers and collectors were William Carter and Demus Skinner, both truckmen. The trustees included McKerrow himself, who was also secretary of the African Baptist Association, Henry Russell, coal hawker, and John Turner, shoemaker.[24] The annual reports of the Nova Scotian African Baptist Association identify another six petitioners who were active members of Cornwallis Baptist Church, four of whom (truckman Alexander Bailey, coal hawker Albert Brown, Daniel Gross, and truckman Richard Symonds) had died by 1895. Four other members of the provincial association were petitioners from Africville, which had its own congregation.[25]

A number of the Baptist petitioners were, like Methodist Coleman, part-time preachers. Although Alexander Bailey made his living as a truckman, he preached in the Baptist church at one of the black settlements in the county, Beech Hill, for many years. After his death, his niche in the Baptist church was taken by his wife, Louisa, who was a Sunday School teacher, delegate to the African Baptist Association, and president of the Pastor's Aid Society.[26] Edward Dixon, another truckman and a resident of Africville, was, by the time of his death in 1908, a preacher of 32 years' standing.[27] William B. Thomas combined work in the family fur business with the charge of a succession of pastorates in the county and beyond.[28] Whether preachers or officers in their churches, these particular petitioners accepted responsibility for the religious and moral leadership of the black community of the city and much of the surrounding area.

Third, the black leadership looked for tangible evidence of respect from whites. Often they got it in a condescending manner. William T. Davis, possibly because of his occupation as a waiter, was described as being 'of an exemplary and courteous disposition'.[29] The esteem, even if tinged with paternalism, was often genuine and lifelong. Necrology provides some evidence of the nature of that respect. At a time when control of the press was entirely monopolized by whites, and obituaries were selective rather than universal, the petitioners received the same kind of eulogies accorded prominent white members of the community. Alexander Bailey was one of the 'landmarks removed'; Charles F. Biddle was 'highly respected by all who knew him, and his demise leaves a blank in a large circle, particularly of the colored population, to whom the deceased for generations had been guide, philosopher and friend'. Truckman James M. Davidson, George Davis, Joseph Flint, Peter E. McKerrow, George Roache, and Demus Skinner, all of whom died between 1892 and 1920, were described as 'highly respected' or 'good citizens'.[30] Their funerals were also a time for the white citizenry to demonstrate that respect. Among the procession of 300 people in Jesse Coleman's cortège in 1884 were 'a number of merchants, aldermen, civic officials and others, which showed the high place the deceased occupied in the respect of the citizens of Halifax'.[31] One of the four clergymen who officiated at William Johnston's funeral in 1910 was Dr John Forrest, leading Presbyterian divine and president of Dalhousie University. In his address he referred to 'the universal respect in which Mr Johnston was held'.[32]

Fourth, the black petitioners saw themselves as worthy citizens. Their own arguments about status and respectability were not based on their role within their own small circle but rather on their participation in the wider Halifax community. Their economic circumstances contributed to their sense of self-worth. Some of them were members of the aristocracy of labour noted for its middle-class, respectable goals. Artisan William Johnston was unsuccessfully urged by whites to seek nomination for city councillor for Ward 4 in the election of 1897. Both Peter Bushenpin, a cooper, and George Davis were active in provincial politics.[33]

One of the petitioners' main arguments for equal educational opportunity was their status as taxpayers. This did not mean that all of them owned property: some rented their dwellings and paid poll tax, such as porter William T. Bailey, seaman John Barrett, Peter Bushenpin, barber William J. Chearnley, William Crawley, tinsmith Benjamin N. Davis, porter Charles Dixon, Elijah Flint, Daniel E. Jacobs, and Charles Pinheiro. But in the incomplete assessment records for the early 1890s (available in fragments for Wards 3, 4, and 5), 19 of the men (or their widows) were assessed for real property.[34] Estate papers indicate that at least 18 men were the sole owners of real estate, often mortgaged of course, at the time of their deaths.[35] Property-ownership did not necessarily go with a high status occupation. A significant number of the property-owners were truckmen, most of whom owned their own means of production (horse, harness, cart, sleigh) but often spent their time carting 'night soil'.[36] Residential stability and local family roots were far more significant factors than occupation for predicting property-ownership.

The stake in the community of such individuals was reinforced by their continuity of residence. Despite the mobile features of urban life in general and Nova Scotia life in particular during the onset of the 'brain drain', domiciliary addresses within the city remained the same for about ten per cent of the petitioners over a long period of time. Found in the same houses for several decades were Creighton Street residents Robert S. Allison, James M. Davidson, Elijah, Jacob and Joseph Flint, and John McKechnie, as well as Benjamin N. Davis of Grafton Street, seaman Adolphus D. Francis of Gerrish Street, William Johnston of Gerrish Lane, Henry Russell of Maynard Street, and Robert J. White of Maitland Street. Some of the other long-time residents lived in Africville. Despite the increasing concentration in Wards 5 and 6, the black petitioners suggested that their pattern of residency made them citizens of Halifax, not of a particular neighbourhood, and they did not think in terms of residential segregation. In their 1883 petition, they referred to two families in Ward 1, six families in Ward 2, twenty families in Ward 3, sixteen families in Ward 4, one hundred families in Ward 5 and forty families in Ward 6.[37]

Prolonged residence did not necessarily mean that Nova Scotia was their birthplace. While Canadian historians have had a great deal to say about out-migration, to which the black community certainly contributed, many of these black leaders were part of the less well-known in-migration to the city. They came long after the major influxes of immigrant groups, including the refugee blacks of the War of 1812. Predictably some of the Halifax black leaders were runaway slaves of the pre-Civil War era. Another group, arguably the most significant in terms of lay leadership in this period, consisted of some seventeen natives of the British West Indies and Bermuda. Eight of the seventeen shared a more specific occupational identity as mariners on arrival in Halifax. They were part of a much larger marriage pool for local black women, who were as likely to wed West Indian mariners as their white counterparts were to marry British soldiers.[38]

As one would expect in a small community of about 1,000 members, kinship was another feature of the black leadership. The petitioners included brothers, cousins, and cross-generational relatives. One of the most respectable extended families was composed of the children of the Reverend James Thomas, a white, Welsh-born preacher and furrier, with a Jewish mother, and Hannah Saunders, his Afro-Nova Scotian wife. Three of the petitioners were their son, William B. Thomas, and sons-in-law, William Johnston and Peter E. McKerrow, two of whom were prominent in the family fur and hat business. Another, Thomas J. Ewing, a boilermaker, was married to Eliza Bailey, the widow of Thomas' eldest son, who was herself the daughter of petitioner Alexander Bailey. James and Hannah Thomas's grandchildren, who went for their elementary education to the black separate schools, supplied the first two black men to matriculate at Dalhousie, James R. Johnston and his cousin Horace G. McKerrow.[39] White or light parentage seems to have contributed to the integrationist preferences of Halifax's black community. Many of them had white cousins and, given their faith in all things British, they may have seen marriage to whites as desirable. Although interracial marriages appear to have declined towards the end of the century, aspirations for lighter skin shaped the attitudes of the Halifax black community as it did those in contemporary cities of the northern United States. Several of the petitioners had white, British-born wives. Others, such as John L. French, Peter E. McKerrow, and William B. Thomas, were so light-skinned that they were not listed in the 1881 census as African in origin.[40]

The occupations of the black leaders were ones which historians normally associate with either working-class or lower-middle-class status. All the known occupations can be grouped into four categories: transport, packing and carting; service, including white collar and professional; trades; and unspecified labour.[41] As the example of the worker-preachers indicates, occupational pluralism, both concurrent and serial, was as frequent among blacks as among the rest of the population. It was not a sign of a lack of skills. In the period between the 1870s and 1910s, only 7 of the 98 were consistently identified as labourers, a term associated with casuality and privation. While some of the job flexibility appears to have been horizontal, vertical movement also occurred, with some men rising in the world and others declining. Thomas Spriggs, a labourer in 1871, had become a coal dealer by 1881, and had a servant to help his wife with the care of their seven children, albeit the eldest was herself a servant. Henry T. Johnston, a carpenter from Bermuda, supervised white men as a foreman employed for 19 years by J.W. Rhuland, a white building contractor, and did well enough to enjoy a period of retirement before he died in 1911 worth $4,000 in bank savings.[42] Diminished status, though not necessarily less income and security, was involved in John T. Brown's transition from schoolteacher to truckman and Robert S. Allison's from carpenter to packer.

Self-employment may have been a common experience for a number of the black leaders but only a few appear to have been able to maintain an existence as independent masters, employers, or businessmen over the longer term. Old Jesse Coleman, the master mason, was one. Richard Whidden was another. He had a clothes dyeing and cleaning business and was known to be 'industrious, conscientious, and self-respecting'.[43] John L. French, one of the most outspoken blacks, expanded his carpentry to become a self-employed undertaker, successful enough to have a servant in 1871 and a bold-print listing in the city directory as late as the mid-1880s. But he had disappeared from the city by 1890 and the number of undertakers in the city as a whole declined from ten in 1880 to three in 1890.

Career prospects for the sons of the petitioners were certainly enhanced by the fathers' hard work and sacrifice, and possibly also by their relationships with whites. One of William Johnston's sons became the city's first black lawyer and Peter E. McKerrow's youngest son became a medical doctor, though, significantly, not in his native province but in Massachusetts, where he was joined by many Halifax blacks of his generation. George Davis, an independent barber, turned over his business to several of his five sons, beginning with the eldest, Charles S., the first black public high school graduate in the city. Having moved aside, Davis senior had enough political connections to secure a berth in the federal service as a postman and became an active member of the Letter Carriers' Association of Canada before retiring on a pension after 25 years' service. Peter Bushenpin, who gave up coopering to work in the commissary department of the ICR, had two sons who left the city to seek their livelihoods in Montreal as railway porters, where they died young of tuberculosis. William D. Howell's 'refined' school-teacher daughters both married railway porters, the occupation which, like going to sea as stewards, offered reliable and preferred employment for Halifax blacks.[44]

The prospects for Howell's daughters may have been improved by the extra income brought into the household by their mother, Mary Ann, who reported the occupation of dressmaker in both 1881 and 1891. Few wives of petitioners admitted to paid employment but we know from other sources that it occurred. Truckman Frederick Byers' wife Caroline was a school-teacher in Africville for a couple of years in the early 1880s and James M. Davidson's wife, Letitia, acquired an independent income by taking in sewing and washing. Widows of petitioners often made their livings by washing, cleaning, or shopkeeping. Such activities, as in the case of shopkeeper Mary Allison, widow of Robert S., were more likely to be a continuation or extension of earlier unreported activities than new departures.[45]

If occupations tell us the range of job choices, the nature of personal property provides some insight into levels of material comfort and family activities. Estate inventories highlight the centrality of music in the lives of the black élite. Among Charles and Lucy Biddle's humble possessions was a broken flute. Jesse Coleman's house on Creighton Street was equipped with a cabinet organ, as was James M. Davidson's on the same street, for which he paid $75 in 1883. Richard Symonds' estate included an organ; Alexander Bailey's two. George Davis left a piano to his daughter. The Bushenpins' genteelly furnished house in King's Place was well stocked with sheet music.[46] Other luxury items which were frequently enumerated included books, clocks and silver watches, cast-iron stoves, sewing machines, and cash in the Dominion Savings Bank.

Although estates of fourteen of the petitioners, who died during the more uncertain decades after 1900, can be found in the probate records, only five left property worth more than $3,000. Some of the other petitioners died in abject circumstances. George Liston, for example, ended his days in 1922 in the City Home, Halifax's poor house. Yet even he received confirmation of his good citizenship when, shortly before his death, the mayor presented him with a gold life-saving medal to acknowledge his courage in pulling many drowning people from the waters of the harbour in his capacity as a boatman.[47] Material success was not, therefore, a reliable basis for black respectability. Far more instrumental was the zest for improvement.

II

The late nineteenth-century black élite was committed to improvement and improvement meant education. Education galvanized the black leaders to define their sense of respectability as citizens. The school segregation controversy arose in the 1870s for three reasons. First, black residents whose children attended Zion school, an all-black institution within the public school system, located in the African Methodist Episcopal Church, demanded, as they had done before, better facilities and better teachers. The first petition in this particular round was in 1873 from mothers who shared the common desire of the day for sex-segregated instruction for their children.[48] Respectability depended on separate spheres. Three years later another petition from black citizens in the north end of the city, where the school was located, signified that it did not give 'general satisfaction to them as ratepayers'.[49] The clear implication was that other city schools could more successfully meet their needs.

Second, Zion school on Gottingen Street was all-black but the schools in the city centre were not all-white. Although the parents of black children who attended the other public schools considered them to be better than Zion, the experience was not always a positive one. In the early 1870s several black parents lodged individual complaints about the treatment their children received in these integrated schools. School board investigations of complaints by such black leaders as Peter E. McKerrow, George Davis, and John L. French concluded unconvincingly that there was no racial discrimination behind the incidents in question.[50] None the less the problems encountered by black children served to encourage rather than discourage the drastic official solution of removing them permanently from these schools. Third, children of some of the poorest blacks attended a racially integrated charity school operated since 1869 by the North End City Mission. Their presence there in disproportionate numbers, together with the spasmodic interest in education displayed by the residents of the struggling black suburb of Africville, created an impression in the minds of the white school authorities that low standards and primitive conditions were endemic features of black schooling.[51] Hence, few whites initially objected to the institutionalization of educational discrimination.

The school board's solution was to ask the Council of Public Instruction to approve a resolution in 1876 invoking a permissive clause in the provincial school legislation which allowed for the provision of separate schools for blacks.[52] The board tried to make the controversial policy palatable by expressing its intention to improve the quality of the schooling at the same time as it confined blacks totally to their own schools. Zion school provided a useful precedent for this policy of segregation; indeed, some whites deflected attention away from their own biases by arguing that blacks preferred their own schools.[53] The blacks themselves could not deny that they had originally wanted separate schools but claimed that they had every right to change their minds.[54] Even the minority black separatist lobby in Halifax became convinced that segregated schooling would never mean equal schooling; that they would always get the worst facilities, equipment, and teachers, as well as outmoded pedagogical practices, and that only integrated schools would reduce prejudice.[55] In these circumstances separatism would be a source of weakness rather than of strength.

When Zion school was closed in 1877, the school board opened the Maynard Street school for black boys in the North End City Mission and a school for black girls on Lockman Street. The black élite hated these schools and were very resentful of the expulsion of their children from the inner city schools. John L. French vowed in 1878 to fight the new policy but was thwarted at every turn.[56] Citizens' meetings and group petitions became the vehicle for protest against the exclusion, beginning in 1880. They did not command much notice until Henry Russell complained that his daughter Blanche (formerly a pupil at Lockman Street girls' school) had been denied admission to the two secondary schools in her neighbourhood and that he had footed the bill in 1882–83 for a year's attendance in the integrated school system of the Boston area.[57] His predicament finally focused attention on one of the major shortcomings of the black schools. They provided education only at the primary level. What was a bright and ambitious black child to do then? The children of the middle-aged members of the black élite were reaching their teens and faced a bleak prospect in Halifax if they could not even finish their schooling. This problem resulted in a new round of meetings and petitions, including the one signed by the leadership whose composition is analysed in the first part of this article. That petition provides us with a useful summary of the arguments against the black schools.

What the petitioners objected to most in the educational system that evolved after 1876 was the denial of their freedom of choice and their treatment as second-class citizens. Why should they be confined to two 'inferior', elementary schools, 'little better than those heretofore kept up by charity for vagrants and outcasts' when 'the children of the very dregs of the city, if white, so called, can go through a regular course of graded schools up to the high school'? Why should their schools be located in the 'most degraded quarter of the city' and taught by 'the rejected and tainted teachers of other schools'?[58] Why should taxpaying citizens be denied the right to neighbourhood schools for their children and be forced, in the absence of access to qualify public education, to maintain four private schools in the city for their children? Halifax blacks believed that their predicament was unique in Canada and that the consequent educational dead-end meant that the city held no future for their children. They also felt they were being treated as though 'the rates we as a people pay towards the support of schools do not possess the same intrinsic value as the coin similarly denominated which is paid by other citizens.'[59]

Most of their arguments could be effectively substantiated. As one parent claimed in a letter to the *Morning Chronicle*: 'the desks in them have been in use over forty years, and when some of the other schools are supplied with new and improved furniture the ancient debris is carted away to the colored schools for the use of the pupils attending them, as much as to say, "anything is good enough for the colored schools".'[60] Their criticisms of the white teachers were also apposite. Some of them were the flotsam and jetsam of other schools. James A. Artz, expelled from Albro Street school as an ineffective disciplinarian, fulfilled the expectations of black parents when he was dismissed from the Maynard Street boys' school in 1881 for incompetence. Although James A. Smith had been discharged from the service of the Halifax school board for drunkenness in 1874, he was reinstated as the first teacher of the Lockman Street school for girls. He remained sober enough to finish his long career in 1892 at the Africville school.[61]

The campaign against separate schooling proved to be effective in the short term, especially for the more ambitious and highly motivated members of the black community. When the new conciliatory regulations came into effect in 1884 in response to their agitation and widespread white support for their rights, black children were allowed to attend schools in the wards in which they lived, something which a few male pupils had in fact continued to do unofficially.[62] This meant that even in the two wards where the separate primary schools continued, and where most blacks resided, children were not precluded from access to secondary education with whites. In 1884, for example, Blanche Russell entered Brunswick Street school, one of the schools from which she had previously been banned, and Charles S. Davis, formerly an 'illegal' pupil at the National school, went to the protestant high school.[63] Thereafter black children transferred to the white schools fairly regularly and attended senior high school, though in very small numbers. In fact there is some evidence to suggest that members of the black élite had initially tried to strike a deal with the school authorities by which they would ensure that in return for the acknowledgment of their right to attend the public schools unimpeded, the right would never be exercised by more than 25 per cent of the black school children.[64] The campaign to desegregate the schools, even if it was not totally successful in Wards 5 and 6, achieved the basic aims of the black élite. Their limited boycott, evidenced in the maintenance of private schools, their petitions, drawn up at well-publicized meetings, their unsuccessful demand, endorsed by the political opposition, for representation on the offensive school board, and the support they finally received from white clergymen, lawyers, politicians, school commissioners, and school administrators brought matters to a head at a crucial time for their cause.[65]

In the meantime, in 1884, the Lockman Street girls' school and the Maynard Street boys' school were amalgamated to create a quasi-graded school at the expense of sex-segregated classes. The school took over the space rented from the North End City Mission formerly used by the boys' school and the mission's charity school. It remained in this location until it was permanently closed 18 years later.[66] The school functioned as a nursery for the new generation of the black élite. It did so despite the fact that the blacks continued to loathe it and took a strong dislike to its white principal and major teacher between 1884 and 1892, Jane Bruce.[67]

III

Bruce, a middle-aged woman with experience as a teacher in Boston and first-class credentials, had entered the employment of the Halifax Board of School Commissioners with the hope of securing a position in the Acadian girls' school in the inner city, a school which was notorious in the 1870s for its expulsion of black pupils. Instead, she was appointed to teach black children. Bruce's willingness to remain at Maynard Street much longer than any turn-of-the-century teacher—black or white—in black schools was probably attributable to a relatively good salary and status as principal. Neither was within the reach of most female teachers of her day. Bruce also saw the position as a challenge. 'I am determined,' she said after her appointment to the Lockman Street girls' school, 'to show that these girls can compete with other schools if they will only give me the opportunity.'[68] There is some evidence that Bruce was a strict taskmaster; on the other hand she seems to have been a very effective, though eccentric, teacher. During her decade as the major teacher of black children, her school registers include the names of the children of the well-established members of the black élite: the McKerrows, the Johnstons, the Howells, the Davises. One of the school petitioners, Adolphus D. Francis, brought a charge against her in court in 1886 for mistreating his daughter but, after that was dismissed, the school continued without incident until 1892.[69] It should be noted, however, that Bruce must have been the most carefully watched and scrutinized teacher in the employ of the board. Her school registers record the unusual attendance day after day of parents of her pupils, particularly mothers, and of black community leaders, particularly the African Baptist and African Methodist Episcopal pastors. Unfortunately the attendance of the pupils was not so good, the school inspector discovering that many of them did not arrive until 11 a.m. In addition to the erratic attendance, the effectiveness of the school also declined because of Bruce's workload. Left without an assistant teacher in 1890, she had little opportunity to prepare the more advanced pupils beyond the fifth grade. Luckily, a sympathetic inspector transferred a few children each year to higher grades in better staffed primary schools in the neighbourhood and thereby relieved Bruce, while at the same time improving the prospects of the brightest pupils for admission to the secondary schools.[70]

The peace between Bruce and her parents, uneasy though it may have been in very unsatisfactory conditions, was destroyed by another court case in 1892 in which the school board, acting on Bruce's behalf, charged Maud Batters, the mother of one of her pupils, with using abusive and 'filthy' language in the school.[71] This case, which resulted in the conviction of Batters, unsettled the black élite because it suggested that their hard-won respectability could not be taken for granted. The conflict between teacher and mother exposed such disrespectable features of black home life as child battering, cohabitation, foul language, and truancy. The black leaders tried to obscure the unflattering aspects of the evidence by launching a full-scale attack on the teacher which lasted for the rest of the school year and finally resulted in Bruce's resignation the following autumn just after they threatened to secure an injunction prohibiting the commissioners from employing her in their school.[72] Indeed, the self-respect of the black community leadership depended on the termination of her services. Although they considered themselves to be far removed from the world of Maud Batters, they knew full well that they would be tarred with the same brush if they did not challenge the evidence and promote solidarity. They therefore set out to make Bruce look like the epitome of the disrespectable white woman. Fortunately for them, the eccentric Bruce was an easy target. A petition of 30 June 1892 set out the reasons for demanding her dismissal:

> 1. She has written unwomanly and unbecoming letters to the [school] board reflecting upon the children.

2. Without authority or consent she has made a lodging room of the school house for sometime until quite recently to the disgust of pupils and all right thinking people.

3. She has maltreated children by kicking and whipping them so as to cause bruises and cause blood, such acts of violence being at least of three years' continuation.

4. She has abused them also by calling them low names and making vile comparisons.

5. She has made use of her position and authority to say and make undue and impudent enquiries into our family affairs, and to ask the children disgusting and vulgar questions, calculated to reflect on the probity, integrity and chastity of the parents.

6. She has used the water bucket to wash her underclothing in the presence of a [sexually] mixed school, spread the articles to dry on the backs of chairs and the stove, using for the remainder of the day the same bucket for drinking purposes.

7. She has sent our children during school hours to the Wellington barracks to beg for soldiers' cast off clothing to make mats for her own use.

8. She has endeavored to induce our children to commit perjury, and in one case going so far as to offer a large sum of money if a certain falsehood would be sworn to.

9. She has conspicuously figured in law suits and whether a good teacher or a bad one, she has had the misfortune to fight a quarrel with fully one half of the families sending their children to the school.

10. Her continuance in Maynard St. School can but engender dislike and hatred in the bosums of parents and will do more to corrupt the morals than any other teacher can repair in ten years.

11. A reputation in the city on account of the foregoing reasons of a kind fatal to her usefulness as a teacher, and altogether her whole school career a bad one so far as we can ascertain. We therefore discard her and request her immediate dismissal.[73]

Bruce raised questions that cast aspersions on black respectability. When little Beatrice Carrol, Batters' 'adopted' daughter turned up at school hungry and disfigured by scratches and bruises, a conscientious teacher grilled her about what had happened, asking such questions as 'Who goes to your house? Who stops there? What do you have for breakfast? What do you have for dinner? Is your mother married to your father?' The community closed ranks against 'insolent, vulgar, pimping, inquisitive busy-body teachers' who 'delve into the privacy of our actions, the sanctity of homes and gormandize their vulture like instincts with a knowledge of our most private and sacred affairs'.[74] Not only were the black leaders aware that the Batters' case would confirm racist stereotypes, but they also feared that investigation of their own private lives might reveal charges for drunkenness and wife abuse and reliance on charity and other non-respectable forms of behaviour in their own not-so-distant pasts.[75] Such exposure would damage their self-esteem and discredit Afro-Nova Scotian respectability. They had to counter such an outcome by exaggerating the unacceptable behaviour of Jane Bruce.

The leaders had previously claimed to speak only for the respectable part of the community. In the 1883 petition, for example, they had objected to the location of the Maynard Street school because it was 'in the most degraded quarter of the city, the haunt of the vicious and lawless and of the outcasts of *both races* and all nationalities'.[76] Like respectable workers in Britain and blacks in the United States and the West Indies, they had an ambivalent attitude towards their rough brethren.[77] Even their wills underscore the sanctity of respectability. On Jesse Coleman's death in 1884, he provided for the rental of his property

> on condition that all and every person and persons who shall or may live in the dwelling house and premises shall be found to keep a quiet, orderly and respectable house—that is, no fiddling or dancing be allowed therein, nor the same to be converted into a Public House or place of Entertainment or a place of rendezvous for idle and unprincipled people. Should my executor see any violation of my will in this respect, he is to remove the tenants and let the property to decent, quiet orderly people.[78]

Coleman was of course a preacher. But many years later in the 1917 will of George Roache, we find the stipulation that his flats should 'be let to respectable coloured people only'.[79]

In 1892, however, the respectable blacks closed ranks with their less acceptable brethren in the face of a common enemy, the prying Jane Bruce. In doing so they employed sexism to fight racism. In the 1883 campaign the opinion had been expressed that the prejudices of white female teachers lay behind the expulsion of their children from the common schools. McKerrow claimed that: 'It was the snobbish girl teachers who were complained of, and who made most of the trouble.'[80] This parental suspicion made matters difficult for Jane Bruce even at the best of times. What it tells us about the attitudes of black fathers towards their daughters who sought to replace the white teachers in the separate schools is unclear. The men appear to have done little to promote the employment of their daughters. Given the prevailing notions of racial superiority and the white monopoly of the school board, the prospects for black teachers were negligible without such support. Occasionally women did supply teaching or got jobs in a black school in the nearby town of Dartmouth or in the county. But in Halifax until the end of the century they always lost out in the competition for permanent jobs to men or white women. The black leadership did not mobilize to protest that injustice. Not until 1896 did a black female teacher secure a regular position in the city. Laura Howell was the daughter of a petitioner. Ironically she was also a protégée of none other than Jane Bruce.[81]

IV

Jane Bruce's unwitting attack on precarious black respectability was echoed throughout the Halifax white community in the 1880s and 1890s. The views of illiberal whites help to place the struggle of the black community within a wider context. As Elizabeth Pleck observed in the case of black Bostonians: 'Middle-class cultural values should have propelled them forward, but . . . persistent racial prejudice held them back.'[82] Popular prejudices emanating from the white working and lower middle classes of the wards most heavily populated by blacks did not distinguish between different classes of blacks, between the rough and the respectable. During the educational controversies of the last quarter of the century, blacks were dismissed by all but the most liberal whites as ungrateful, unclean, and uncouth, and their claims to equal rights as citizens were treated with contempt.

The main measure of their ingratitude was held to be their poor school attendance. Although the estimates of the number of school-aged black children varied from 250 to 500, with the 1881 census indicating 167, the average attendance of 70–110 clearly reflected a low rate of attendance. In their discussions of this issue, neither whites nor blacks referred to economic necessity as a contributory factor. The white inference that public schooling was too good for the blacks was countered by the black charge that the curriculum in the segregated black schools was based on the lowest common denominator, which meant that able children became discouraged after unnecessarily spending two or three years on the same school reader.[83]

The argument about uncleanliness was implicit rather than explicit and was inverted by upper middle class liberals who made repeated references to how clean the 'respectable' blacks were. The physical overtones in the protests of white north end parents against the admission of Blanche Russell to Brunswick Street school were also strongly sexual, with warnings about where racial intermixing would lead.[84] The black reaction to the issue of cleanliness was neatly expressed in the objections to Jane Bruce's domestic habits as squatter in the Maynard Street school: 'she slept in the building and did not air it in the morning before the children arrived.'[85] Her knickers, drying in the stuffy classroom, were the very antithesis of the respectable housewife's spotless linen billowing on the outdoor clothesline.

That blacks were vulgar and uncouth was a message which the white press strongly reinforced in the nineteenth century. The school controversy exposed Maud Batters' off-colour language. It was apparently far worse that she described Bruce as a 'fagot' than that Bruce described her pupils as 'apes', 'goats', 'monkeys', 'darkeys'.[86] In fact the black leadership was acutely aware of the importance of correct language as part of the paraphernalia of respectability. They sometimes engaged in public displays of self-congratulation when one of their number got through an address without making any grammatical errors.[87] Moreover, black dialect had to be suppressed in order to avoid the ridicule for which the white press was notorious. When McKerrow referred to the failure of the school commissioners to uphold the complaints against Jane Bruce, he protested that 'the charges which the colored people had presented against the teacher were not made in ordinary vernacular, they had been made in good old Anglo-Saxon.'[88]

Finally, the claim to equality on the ground of citizenship was given short shrift by the racists. It was not enough to be a taxpayer: what counted was the quantity of one's taxes, not the quality. Black taxes were inconsequential in amount; therefore black rights could be violated with impunity. Petitioners against Blanche Russell's admission to Brunswick Street school in 1884, who described themselves as 'mechanics', fatuously claimed that 'the school tax imposed individually upon many of the parents, who have been patronizing the school, would probably amount to more than the aggregate taxes paid into the revenue by the whole colored population.'[89] In the face of such arguments, the blacks' reliance on British traditions of justice and fair play and on moderate, reformist approaches represented by meetings, petitions, and dialogue did little to protect them against ridicule and contempt. Respectability failed to mediate racial prejudice. If the humbler whites in society received the 'Order of Respectability, Second Class', as Trygve R. Tholfsen suggests, the order accorded blacks was not much better than third class. Since respectability failed to give them effective integration, the new generation of black leaders turned increasingly to the promotion of separatism as a crucible for encouraging race pride and racial unity in turn-of-the-century Halifax.[90]

Suggestions for Further Reading

Donald H. Clairmont, *Africville: The Life and Death of a Canadian Black Community* (Toronto, 1974).
Judith Fingard, *The Dark Side of Life in Victorian Halifax* (Porter's Lake, N.S., 1989).
Robin W. Winks, *The Blacks in Canada: A History* (Montreal, 1971).

Notes

The research for this article was supported by a grant from the Social Sciences and Humanities Research Council of Canada, whose assistance is gratefully acknowledged. An earlier version was presented as a paper at the annual meeting of the Canadian Historical Association in Victoria, British Columbia in 1990. I would like to thank Peter Bailey and John O'Brien for their comments, Philip Girard, Bonnie Huskins, Ian McKay, Suzanne Morton, and Joan Payzant for sharing references with me, and Marc Epprecht for his research assistance.
[1]*Morning Chronicle* (hereafter *MC*), Halifax, 6 November 1883. The church was also called the Cornwallis Street Baptist Church.

²*MC*, 17 June 1892. The actual quotation comes from an earlier meeting about the same matter in March which also concluded with the National Anthem, *MC*, 16 March 1892. Zion church was affiliated with the British Methodist Episcopal Church for several decades in the second half of the nineteenth century.

³*Halifax Herald* (hereafter *HH*), 24 June 1892.

⁴*HH*, 17 June 1892.

⁵*Morning Herald* (hereafter *MH*), Halifax, 30 October 1883. Some of the strongest white supporters were the Rev. Allan Simpson: *MH*, 22 September 1884; Robert Sedgewick: Public Archives of Nova Scotia (hereafter PANS), minutes, Halifax Board of School Commissioners, Vol. 6, 17 February 1881; *MC*, 18 February 1881, 12 December 1883; J.T. Bulmer; PANS, minutes, Halifax Board of School Commissioners, Vol. 7, 4 October 1883; *Acadian Recorder* (hereafter *AR*), Halifax, 1 November 1883; Philip Girard, ' "His whole life was one of continual warfare": John Thomas Bulmer, Lawyer, Librarian and Social Reformer'. *Dalhousie Law Journal* 13, 1 (May 1990), 376–405. On white liberals in the United States in this period, see James M. McPherson, *The Abolitionist Legacy from Reconstruction to the NAACP* (Princeton, 1975).

⁶A recent illustration of this is James W. St G. Walker, 'Black History in the Maritimes: Major Themes and Teaching Strategies', in Philip Buckner (ed.), *Teaching Maritime Studies* (Fredericton, 1986), 96–102. See also Pearleen Oliver, *A Brief History of the Colored Baptists of Nova Scotia, 1782–1953* (Halifax, 1953); R.W. Winks, 'Negro School Segregation in Ontario and Nova Scotia', *Canadian Historical Review* I, 2 (June 1969), 164–91, and *The Blacks in Canada: A History* (Montreal, New Haven, and London, 1971); John N. Grant, 'Black Immigrants into Nova Scotia, 1776–1815', *Journal of Negro History*, LVIII, 3 (July 1973), 253–70; Donald H. Clairmont and Dennis William Magill, *Africville: The Life and Death of a Canadian Black Community* (Toronto, 1974); James W. St G. Walker, *The Black Loyalists: The Search for a Promised Land in Nova Scotia and Sierra Leone, 1783–1870* (London and New York, 1976), and 'The Establishment of a Free Black Community in Nova Scotia, 1783–1840', in M. Kilson and R. Rotherg (eds), *African Diaspora, Interpretive Essays* (Cambridge, Mass., 1976), 205–36; Calvin W. Ruck, *The Black Battalion 1916–1920: Canada's Best Kept Military Secret* (Halifax, 1987). Some of the analysis of occupations and spatial mobility draws on an unpublished essay written in the late 1970s by Linda Lever, 'The Black Community in Halifax, 1871–1881'. The only Victorian book is a Baptist genealogy, reissued by Frank Stanley Boyd (ed.), *A Brief History of the Coloured Baptists of Nova Scotia . . . by P.E. McKerrow (Halifax, 1895)* (Halifax, 1976).

⁷The American literature in the form of books, let alone articles, is voluminous. Relevant to this study are Elizabeth Hafkin Pleck, *Black Migration and Poverty, Boston 1865–1900* (New York, 1979), especially Ch. IV; Kenneth L. Kusmer, *A Ghetto Takes Shape; Black Cleveland, 1870–1930* (Urbana, Chicago, and London, 1976), especially Chs 5 & 6; Allen H. Spear, *Black Chicago: The Making of a Negro Ghetto, 1890–1920* (Chicago, and London, 1967); Howard N. Rabinowitz, *Race Relations in the Urban South, 1865–1950: The Shadow of the Dream* (Chicago and London, 1981); Gary B. Nash, *Forging Freedom: The Formation of Philadelphia's Black Community, 1720–1840* (Cambridge, Mass. and London, 1988). For a contemporary

analysis, see W.E.B. DuBois' classic *The Philadelphia Negro: A Social Study* (New York, 1899; reissued 1967). For Afro-American strategies of the period, see August Meier, *Negro Thought in America, 1880–1915: Racial Ideologies in the Age of Booker T. Washington* (Ann Arbor, 1963).

[8]For interesting perspectives and analyses of the historiography of respectability, see Peter Bailey, ' "Will the Real Bill Banks Please Stand Up?" Towards a Role Analysis of Mid-Victorian Working-Class Respectability', *Journal of Social History* 12, 3 (Spring 1979), 336–53, Brian Harrison, 'Traditions of Respectability in British Labour History', in his *Peaceable Kingdom: Stability and Change in Modern Britain* (Oxford, 1982), 157–216; and Neville Kirk, *The Growth of Working Class Reformism in Mid-Victorian England* (Urbana & Chicago, 1985), Ch. 5. For the West Indian perspective contained in the quotation, see Bridget Brereton, *Race Relations in Colonial Trinidad, 1870–1900* (Cambridge, 1979), 211.

[9]For insights on economic and social developments in Halifax during this period, see Phyllis R. Blakeley, *Glimpses of Halifax 1867–1900* (Halifax, 1949); T.W. Acheson, 'The National Policy and the Industrialization of the Maritimes, 1880–1910', *Acadiensis*, I, 2 (Spring 1972), 3–28; Ian McKay, 'The Working Class of Metropolitan Halifax 1850–1889', unpublished honours thesis, Dalhousie University, 1975; L.D. McCann, 'Staples and the New Industrialism in the Growth of Post-Confederation Halifax', *Acadiensis*, VIII, 2 (Spring 1979), 47–79; Janet Guildford, 'Public School Reform and the Halifax Middle Class 1850–1870', unpublished PhD thesis, Dalhousie University, 1990.

[10]For the participation of blacks in celebrations see Bonnie Huskins, 'Public Celebrations in Victorian Saint John and Halifax', unpublished PhD thesis, Dalhousie University, 1991. For the first schools for blacks see Judith Fingard, 'Attitudes toward the Education of the Poor in Colonial Halifax', *Acadiensis*, II, 2 (Spring 1973), 15–42.

[11]Petition dated 5 April 1883, PANS, RG 5, Series P, Vol. 78, Nos 88 and 154. The signatures (No. 88) were separated from the petition (No. 154) during sorting and therefore two references are necessary for the retrieval of the whole document. This petition may have been drawn up and/or signed as early as 1881 since two of the preachers whose names appear had left the province by 1883. Boyd notes this in his edition of McKerrow's *History*, 36–7. This is the only extant petition as far as I have been so far able to discover. Printed copies of some others appear in the press but without a complete list of names. For another group profile of urban black leaders, see Emma Jones Lapsansky, 'Friends, Wives and Strivings: Networks and Community Values Among Nineteenth-Century Philadelphia Afro-american Elites', *Pennyslvania Magazine of History and Biography* 108, 1 (January 1984), 3–24.

[12]In the analysis that follows I have added to the 105 petitioners three other male residents of Halifax who were very prominent in black protest meetings and citizen committees of the 1880s and 1890s. They may have been absent from the city when the petition was circulated. The actual petition contains 106 names but one is a duplicate. The total of the names canvassed is therefore 108. Two of the ten unknowns are in fact 'known' in the sense that they were American preachers but their residence was strictly temporary as indicated in note 11.

[13]*AR*, 4 October 1883, 22 and 24 November 1884; *MC*, 24 November 1884. The press erroneously identified him as a Virginian slave. Most of the information on individuals comes from the sources enumerated in the text. Only additional ones and specific newspaper references are cited. A petitioner's principal 1880s occupation is mentioned the first time his name appears and repeated only when it is relevant to the issue under discussion.

[14]PANS, minutes, Halifax Board of School Commissioners, Vol. 8, 30 August 1888; *MC*, 17 June 1892; *AR*, 13 May 1905.

[15]*MC*, 7 October 1889.

[16]*Halifax Chronicle*, 22 July 1944.

[17]*MC*, 7 November 1892; Halifax County Probate Court, George Roache, No. 8952.

[18]*MC*, 25 July 1877; *MH*, 8 July 1880. On the secession see *MC*, 26 and 29 July, 22 and 23 September 1876.

[19]*AR*, 30 October 1883.

[20]*MC*, 26 December 1906; annual returns, Union Lodge, No. 18, R.N.S., A.F. and A.M., PANS, MG 20, Vol. 2012, No. 2. On black masonry in the United States, see William A. Muraskin, *Middle-class Blacks in a White Society: Prince Hall Freemasonry in America* (Berkeley, 1975).

[21]Minutes of the Grand Lodge Sessions, 1900–1916, Oddfellows Collection, PANS, MG 20, Vol. 1164.

[22]*AR*, 22 November 1884. For his own reminiscences, see *AR*, 4 October 1883. On similar occupational profiles in the United States, see Curry, *The Free Black in Urban America*, 23. For the West Indians there is some overlap in identity between Methodists and Anglicans.

[23]*AR*, 28 December 1906; Dalhousie University Registrations, 1896–97, Dalhousie University Archives (DUA).

[24]*A Brief History of the Coloured Baptists of Nova Scotia*, 25.

[25]*Minutes of the Sessions of the African Baptist Association of Nova Scotia*, 24th–55th, 1877–1908 (incomplete), Acadia University Archives, Baptist Collection.

[26]*Belcher's Farmer's Almanack*, 1877–86; *AR*, 19 January 1886, 30 December 1911.

[27]*AR* 26 June 1908.

[28]*AR* 28 June 1937.

[29]*MC*, 7 November 1892.

[30]*AR* 19 January 1886, 15 February 1897, 28 January 1893; *MC*, 20 January 1908; *MC*, 7 November 1892, 9 December 1911; *AR*, 26 December 1900; *MC*, 26 December 1906, 19 April 1918; *AR*, 19 April 1918; *MC*, 3 August 1920.

[31]*AR*, 24 November 1884.

[32]*MC*, 28 October 1910.

[33]*AR*, 11 and 13 March 1897, 25 November 1909; *MC*, 20 January 1908.

[34]See incomplete assessment books, PANS RG 35A, 5, Nos. 2, 7, 9, 10, 13.

[35]The evidence indicates that several of the renters of the 1890s owned real estate before they died. Halifax County Probate Court, George Alexander, seaman/labourer (Africville), No. 4473, Alexander Bailey, No. 3422, William Brown, cooper (Africville), No. 5890, Esther Ann Bushenpin, widow of Peter, No. 7191, Thomas J. Clayton, storekeeper, No. 4967, Jesse Coleman, No. 3306, Alexander P. Davidson, No. 5696, James M. Davidson, No. 4365, Benjamin N. Davis, No. 7578, George Davis, No. 6567, Elijah Flint, No. 11396, Jacob Flint, No. 12408,

Joseph Flint, No. 7271, Adolphus D. Francis, No. 5425, William Johnston, No. 7032, George Roache, No. 8952, Josiah Smith, butcher, No. 8620, Richard Symonds, No. 3631.

36See list of annual night cart and truck licences for 1887–88 and 1899–1904, PANS, RG 35–102, Series 11, D, 6 and 8.

37PANS, RG 5, Series P, Vol. 78, No. 154. Although nominal identification was applied to the manuscript census schedules, there are no aggregate racial data in the 1891 census. The printed reports on the 1901 census indicate a decline in the black population of 31 per cent between 1881 and 1901 but the data on blacks are thought to be flawed. See John N. Grant, *Black Nova Scotians* (Halifax, 1980), 36.

38For the relationship between black seafaring and family life in another seaport setting, see W. Jeffrey Bolster, ' "To Feel Like a Man": Black Seamen in the Northern States, 1800–1860', *Journal of American History*, 76, 4 (March 1990), 1173–99. James W. St G. Walker fails to grasp the significance of West Indians in nineteenth-century Halifax with the sole exception of the well-known leadership of P.E. McKerrow: *The West Indians in Canada*, Canadian Historical Association, Canada's Ethnic Groups, Booklet No. 6 (Ottawa, 1984), 8. On out-migration, see Alan A. Brookes, 'Out-Migration from the Maritime Provinces, 1860–1900: Some Preliminary Considerations', *Acadiensis*, V, 2 (Spring 1976), 26–56, and Patricia A. Thornton, 'The Problem of Out-Migration from Atlantic Canada, 1871–1921: A New Look', *Acadiensis*, XV, 1 (Autumn 1985), 3–34.

39The Halifax school registers are bound alphabetically by name of school for each year in PANS, RG 14; Dalhousie University Registrations, 1892–93 to 1897–98, DUA.

40Those who *may* have been married to white wives include Robert Byers, retired, William J. Chearnley, George Davis, Joseph Flint, and John J. Parker, printer. On the significance of skin colour in Boston, see Pleck, *Black Migration and Poverty*, 93–94.

41Occupations included as transport, packing and carting consist of boatman, coachman, coal hawker/dealer, expressman, hackman, mariner (increasingly stewards and therefore closely related to service), packer, stevedore, storeman, teamster, truckman; those in service consisted of butcher, caterer, clerk, chimney sweep, clothes cleaner/dyer, conductor, letter carrier, porter, preacher, servant, steward, store/shopkeeper, teacher, tobacconist, umbrella mender, undertaker, waiter/butler, whitewasher; those in trades included barber, boilermaker, broom-maker, carpenter, cooper, furrier, machinist, mason, printer, shipwright/caulker, shoemaker, tinsmith, tailor, woodsawyer.

42HH, 19 June 1911; Halifax County Probate Court, Henry T. Johnston, No. 7171. Since he had Halifax-born relatives, Johnston's father had probably been born in the city.

43AR, 6 November 1899.

44McAlpine's City Directory, 1900–01, lists Branch No. 9, Federated Association of Letter Carriers; MC, 20 January 1908. For the deaths in Montreal of Bushenpin's sons, see PANS, Snow's Funeral Homes Register 2, 2 June 1904 and 6 February 1905. The starting point for identifying Howell's sons-in-law was his obituary, AR, 28 December 1906. For the movement of blacks to Montreal to seek work with the railroad and the high morality rates they suffered, see Winks, *The Blacks in Canada: A History*, 332–3. For a study of black railway porters which mentions the turn-of-the-century period, see Agnes Calliste, 'Sleeping Car Porters in Canada: An Ethnically Submerged Split Labour Market', *Canadian Ethnic Studies*, XIX, 1 (1987), 1–20.

[45]PANS, minutes, Halifax Board of School Commissioners, Vol. 6, 22 June 1880, 16 June 1881, 5 October 1882; Halifax County Probate Court, James M. Davidson, No. 4365, Robert S. Allison, No. 4590. Two women brought property into their marriages which they subsequently left to favourite daughters. See Halifax County Probate Court, Adelaide Martin (widow of James H.), No. 6107 and Laura A. Thomas (who died before her husband, William B., but bequeathed the residue of her estate, after his death, to her youngest daughter), No. 14371. On the nature of work undertaken by black women in the United States during this period, see Sharon Harley, 'For the Good of Family and Race: Gender, Work and Domestic Roles in the Black Community, 1880–1930', *Signs: Journal of Women in Culture and Society*, 15, 2 (Winter, 1990), 336–49.

[46]Halifax County Probate Court, Lucy Biddle, No. 4894, Jessie Coleman, No. 3306, James M. Davidson, No. 4365, Richard Symonds, No. 3631, Alexander Bailey, No. 3422, George Davis, No. 6567, Esther Ann Bushenpin, No. 7191.

[47]*AR*, 13 March 1922. The five with property valued at over $3000 were A.P. Davidson, B.N. Davis, George Davis, H.T. Johnston and George Roache.

[48]PANS, minutes, Halifax Board of School Commissioners, Vol. 4, 7 June 1873.

[49]*Ibid.*, Vol. 5, 28 June 1876; *MC*, 29 June 1876.

[50]PANS, Minutes, Halifax Board of School Commissioners, Vol. 3, 3 April and 19 June 1871; Vol. 4, 20 November 1872, 1 and 29 April 1874; Vol. 5, 2 December 1875, 16 and 23 February 1876.

[51]On the mission school see PANS, minutes, Halifax Board of School Commissioners, Vol. 5, 26 April 1876; Judith Fingard, *The Dark Side of Life in Victorian Halifax* (Halifax, 1989), 129–30, and 'The North End City Mission: Building Use in the Old North End', paper presented to the Royal Nova Scotia Historical Society, February 1991; on the Africville school before 1883, see PANS, minutes, Halifax Board of School Commissioners, Vol. 3, 20 June and 11 July 1870; Vol. 5, 2 June and 2 December 1875, 20 December 1876; Vol. 6, 9 September 1878, 22 June 1880, 17 March 1881; Vol. 7, 4 January 1883.

[52]PANS, minutes, Halifax Board of School Commissioners, Vol. 5, 16 August and 29 November 1876; *MC*, 17 and 25 August 1876.

[53]*Presbyterian Witness (PW)*, Halifax, 19 January 1884; *Dartmouth Times*, 23 February 1884.

[54]*MC*, 27 September 1883.

[55]*MC*, 6 November 1883; Kusmer, *A Ghetto Takes Shape*, 131.

[56]PANS, Minutes, Halifax Board of School Commissioners, Vol. 5, 28 February and 28 March 1877; Vol. 6, 2 November 1878.

[57]*MH*, 9 December 1880; PANS, Minutes, Halifax Board of School Commissioners, Vol. 6, 31 August 1882; Vol. 7, 2 August 1883; *MC*, 4 August 1883; *MH*, 12 February 1884. On the integration of Boston schools in the 1850s, see Stanley K. Schultz, *The Culture Factory: Boston Public Schools, 1789–1860* (New York, 1973), Chs. 7 and 8.

[58]PANS, RG 5, Series P, Vol. 78, No. 154.

[59]*MC*, 28 September 1883.

[60]*Ibid.*

[61]PANS, Minutes, Halifax Board of School Commissioners, Vol. 4, 29 April, 13 May, 3 June 1874; Vol. 5, 15 December 1875; Vol. 6, 3 and 16 June 1881; Vol. 7, 18 June 1885; *MH*, 9 December 1880; Rabinowitz, *Race Relations in the Urban South*, 173–4.

[62]Despite the 1876 resolution, a few black children continued to be admitted to the National, St. Mary's, Beech Street, St. Patrick's and Morris Street schools, according to various contemporary sources. PANS, minutes, Halifax Board of School Commissioners, Vol. 7, 18 September 1884; *PW*, 27 November 1880; *MC*, 2 February, 14 March, 12 April 1884.

[63]PANS, Minutes, Halifax Board of School Commissioners, Vol. 7, 4 September 1884; *MH*, 12 February and 31 October 1884.

[64]*MC*, 2 and 5 February 1884.

[65]*MC*, 31 October 1883; *AR*, 2 November 1883.

[66]PANS, minutes, Halifax Board of School Commissioners, Vol. 7, 3 July 1884; Vol. 10, 3 April 1902.

[67]Bruce had been appointed the teacher of the Lockman Street girls' school a year before the amalgamation. Judith Fingard, 'Jane Bruce', *Dictionary of Canadian Biography*, Vol. XIII, forthcoming.

[68]*Dartmouth Times*, 23 February 1884; PANS, RG 14.

[69]PANS, minutes, Halifax Board of School Commissioners, Vol. 7, 2 September 1886; Vol. 8, 2 December 1886; *AR*, 9 July 1886.

[70]Inspector's reports on teachers in schools in Halifax, 1890–91, PANS, RG 14, Vol. 156, No. 37.

[71]The best press account is provided by the *Evening Mail* (hereafter *EM*), which is not extant for this period, but clippings of relevant articles are preserved in the school board minutes, Vol. 8, between the meetings of 5 February and 3 March 1892. See also *AR* 1, 2, 4 March 1892.

[72]PANS, minutes, Halifax Board of School Commissioners, Vol. 9, 29 September 1892.

[73]*HH*, 2 July 1892; also *MC*, 15 March 1892.

[74]Articles from *EM*, 13 March 1892, in school board minutes, Vol. 8.

[75]The ways in which some blacks may have slipped in and out of respectability have yet to be explored, but indications are that some of the petitioners were well known in the police court as public drunkards (e.g., Thomas Kellum, umbrella mender, *MH*, 15 November 1881) and that the Society for the Prevention of Cruelty intervened on behalf of neglected mothers (Alexander Bailey, 20, 23, 26, 28 February 1885, Daily Journal, Society for the Prevention of Cruelty, PANS, MG 20, Vol. 516, No. 6) and abused wives (Alexander Carvery, labourer, *AR*, 18 and 19 June 1889). See Bailey, ' "Will the Real Bill Banks Please Stand Up?" Towards a Role Analysis of Mid-Victorian Working-Class Respectability', *loc. cit.*

[76]My italics, PANS, RG 5, Series P, Vol. 78, No. 154.

[77]Harrison, *Peaceable Kingdom*, 176; Brereton, *Race Relations in Colonial Trinidad*, 103–4.

[78]Halifax County Probate Court, Jesse Coleman, No. 3306.

[79]Halifax County Probate Court, George Roache, No. 8952.

[80]*MH*, 30 October 1883.

[81]In 1891 Howell taught in the Dartmouth segregated school. She was in charge of the Maynard Street school from 1896 to 1899. Caroline Byers (Africville) was not

a regular teacher. Martha E. Jones, who completed her studies at the age of 21 with Bruce in 1885, tried unsuccessfully through the 1880s and 1890s to obtain a position in Halifax. Howell was succeeded by Agnes A. Davis, youngest daughter of George Davis, who remained at the school until the attendance dwindled so low that in 1902 the school board closed it. Thereafter black children went to the integrated schools in the city centre, but those in Africville continued to have their own school. See the school board minutes.

82Pleck, *Black Migration and Poverty*, 119.

83Both whites and blacks seem to have exaggerated the number of school-aged children, the former mainly to indicate black laxness, the latter mainly to indicate black dissatisfaction. For black complaints about the children's lack of progress see *HH*, 24 June 1892.

84*MC*, 24 January 1884.

85*HH*, 17 June 1892.

86*EM*, 14 March 1892, in school board minutes, Vol. 8; *AR*, 10 March 1892, *MC*, 17 June 1892. Judge Benjamin Russell had a Sunday School class of black boys in Dartmouth in the mid-nineteenth century. He preferred the term 'darkie' to 'nigger': ' "Darkie" is not so objectionable. It is a kindly and friendly diminutive and I have no compunction in using it to describe the members of my Sunday-School class.' *Autobiography of Benjamin Russell* (Halifax, 1932), 26.

87*MC*, 5 August 1876.

88*HH*, 17 June 1892.

89*MC*, 19 September 1884.

90*MH*, 9 December 1880; *MC*, 1 July 1904; Trygve R. Tholfsen, *Working Class Radicalism in Mid-Victorian England* (New York, 1977), 218. Pleck points out that it 'seems paradoxical that the adoption of white values and beliefs could have stimulated black consciousness. But blacks had to first regard themselves as the social equals of whites before they could recognize the need for group solidarity.' *Black Migration and Poverty*, 117. See also Meier, *Negro Thought in America*, 24. For a similar appreciation of the need for class unity, see Kirk, *The Growth of Working Class Reformism in Mid-Victorian England*, 231.

II

Society and Culture

1867–1914

8

Industrialization and the Family

Bettina Bradbury

The process of industrialization was clearly one of the major developments in Canada in the years after Confederation. It had an impact not only on the Canadian economy but also on its social structure, particularly in the urban environments that were affected by rapid population growth and expansion, and by an alteration in the nature of working conditions and working experiences. Though no city in Canada escaped change, Montreal underwent one of the most significant transitions as industry expanded and employed a growing labour force in its shops and factories. From the standpoint of the social historian Montreal is particularly fascinating because of its position within French Canada. This society, which had established its values largely in terms of a rural and agrarian experience, was not substantially augmented or internally influenced by the process of new European immigration that affected other parts of eastern Canada. The many rural

French Canadians who could no longer expect opportunities in agriculture—for good land was increasingly in short supply in Quebec—and had for several generations been supplying New England factories with many of their workers now joined Irish immigrants to provide the labour force that fuelled Montreal's industrial growth.

Bettina Bradbury examines the effects of the process of industrialization in Montreal on that central core of French-Canadian society and existence: the family. As she observes, there has been much international debate over the interplay of class, cultural background, and the nature of production in the emergence of industrial capitalism. From the standpoint of families, the most important aspect of the Montreal experience was the heavy emphasis on female and child labour. There was nothing unusual about the utilization of women and children in industrialization, since they provided a cheap labour force in factories where traditional skills were not required. From the perspective of family survival, Bradbury argues, the income from women and children was essential. Focussing on two working-class wards within the city—one predominantly French-Canadian, the other Irish— Bradbury examines family structure in detail and offers some comparative dimensions for the testing of her generalizations. While she finds some differences, Bradbury argues that both wards demonstrate the close interconnections between family structure and industrial production.

Why were women and children such an important component of the early Montreal industrial labour force? What are the relationships between the industrial situation and the earlier rural and pre-industrial one? In what ways is Bradbury limited by her data? Why are the low percentages of 'nuclear families classified as occupying a whole household' in Montreal important? Are the differences or the similarities between French-Canadian and Irish responses to industrialization in Montreal more striking? In what ways and to what extent did the traditional French-Canadian cultural and social values influence the Montreal experience?

This article first appeared, titled 'The Family Economy and Work in an Industrializing City: Montreal in the 1870s', in *Canadian Historical Association Historical Papers* (1979), 71–96.

Introduction

The impact of industrial capitalism on the structure, size, and nature of the family has recently been attracting the interest of historians, demographers, sociologists, and anthropologists.[1] The topic has produced some lively debates between feminists and family historians, between historians and sociologists, and between Marxists and liberals.[2] Did industrialization lead to the emergence of the nuclear family as early sociologists believed?[3] Were the separation of home and workplace and the creation of a separate sphere in the home a result of industrialization?[4] Was the family a passive agent automatically adjusting its size and structure to economic change?[5] Was the advent of capitalism or industrialization the important factor?[6]

This paper aims to cast light on some of these broad questions. It examines how class position, cultural values, and changes in the nature of production influenced the family economy in the period of early industrial capitalism. It attempts to relate the work of family members to the particular nature of industrialization in one place at one time—Montreal in the 1870s. The aim is to see what data from the manuscript census reveal about the family economy in a period of transition, and to examine beyond the figures of census-based material the interaction between the family as an institution and the economy. The link between the two, here, is in the paid work of family members. Other important aspects of the family economy and family life—unpaid work at home, socialization, reproduction—are not dealt with in this paper.

To illustrate the interrelationships and relative importance of class, cultural tradition, and the nature of production, five topics are studied. The first section briefly examines major aspects of Montreal's industrialization. The following three sections examine aspects of the family economy; the relationship between the number of workers per family and the father's occupation, the prevalence and nature of work by young children, and the work of wives and mothers. Finally, household structure is examined to see whether sharing housing offered an alternative survival strategy for families.

The major sources for the study are random samples taken of households resident in two Montreal wards, Sainte-Anne and Saint-Jacques, in 1871.[7] These data are complemented by a complete survey of all working wives in these two areas and of the manuscript returns of the industrial census.[8] Thus, while much of what is argued is relevant to all of Montreal in this period, the data are specifically focused on the immigrant, industrial, working-class suburb of Sainte-Anne and the predominantly French-Canadian and more artisanal suburb of Saint-Jacques. Ideally, families and industrial change should be traced over several decades at least. However, even a static examination of one period begins to show important patterns.[9]

Industrialization

Families living in Montreal in 1871 were part of a city in transition. For two to three decades industrial capital had unevenly but persistently been reshaping the geography of the city, the organization of production, and the nature of work.[10] The rhythm of people's lives and the bases of family life were radically altered. In trades like shoemaking, carpentry, and tailoring, old forms of production and apprenticeship had largely disappeared. Most workers were collected together under the control of one master, often manufacturing only a single part of a whole commodity.[11] Artisans had not been eliminated in most trades, but were increasingly confined to certain lines of luxury production, to repair work, and to the less industrial parts of town. The transition from mercantile to industrial city involved both the growth of large-scale industries and the proliferation of small-scale ones. Highly mechanized factory production coexisted with small workshops and artisanal production. Machine work in many cases multiplied the amount of hard work that had to be done.[12]

The city became increasingly differentiated by function. The residential areas of the bourgeoisie were concentrated together, separate from the homes of workers and from commerce and industry. Commerce was still centred largely in the old city, but retail merchants were beginning to move their shops up the hill toward Sainte-Catharine Street. In the west of the city, Canada's first major concentration of industry was clustered around the basins and locks of the Lachine Canal, which the government had developed to produce water power of the emerging industrial bourgeoisie. Stretching along both sides of the canal among and beyond the factories was Sainte-Anne, the first industrial working-class suburb. Within its boundaries was Griffin-town, the Irish immigrant area. Here were housed what remained of those people H.C. Pentland has identified as forming Canada's early proletariat two decades earlier.[13] Now they were supplemented by their children and by an influx of French Canadians and newer immigrant families from Ireland, England, and Scotland.

On the eastern boundary of Montreal, Sainte-Marie was beginning to emerge as the major French-Canadian industrial suburb.[14] Between it and Saint-Laurent ward lay Saint-Jacques. It and Sainte-Anne were like two different worlds in 1871. The first was definitely an immigrant suburb, a mixture of Irish, English, Scots and French Canadians. Sainte-Anne was Montreal's industrial area, whereas in Saint-Jacques production was largely artisanal or at a handicraft stage. The most common enterprise there was a small workshop, with between one and four employees—often the crafts-man, an apprentice, and members of the family. The crafts that predominated were woodworking ones, especially carpentry and joiners' shops; food-processing, including small bakers and butchers with stalls at the local markets; and shoemaking and dressmaking.

The contrast between Sainte-Anne and Saint-Jacques clearly illustrated three major aspects of Montreal's industrialization. First, the scale of enterprises was growing steadily. More and more workers were involved in large factories. Work processes were constantly being modified, old skills were rendered obsolete, and new ones created. Machinery, especially powered by steam or water, was increasingly being used.[15] Mechanization and the application of power to one part of the labour process usually created the need for additional and often tedious hand work in unchanged parts. Some of this was done in departments of the factories. In shoemaking and clothing, much was 'put out', especially to women and children working at home. It was into this kind of work that the women and children of Saint-Jacques were drawn in large numbers.

Secondly, despite the overall increase in scale, industrial-capitalist and pre-industrial forms continued to coexist for a long period of time. In Sainte-Anne, the presence of a few large, mechanized primary-processing plants for flour and sugar seemed to have spurred the growth of small baking and confectionery establishments in the neighbourhood. Coopers and black-smiths continued to run their shops, despite the fact that most of the large foundries and factories had coopering and blacksmith departments. The whole ward of Saint-Jacques existed as an almost pre-industrial, artisanal enclave in the changing city. Two-thirds of its productive establishments employed under five workers. Yet even there one large tobacco factory and two tanneries employed nearly half the ward's enumerated 'industrial' workers.[16]

The third feature of Montreal's industrialization, and one most important for its families, was the heavy reliance on child and female labour. As work processes were cut down into their component parts, women and children were drawn into sections of the production process. In the city's type foundry, for example, a complex machine cast type 'so rapidly that 200 small type could be cast in a minute'. However, a small 'jet' remained on the type. This was broken off by young boys. Then

> The type is next given over to a number of girls, who sit around a circular stone table. These young women rapidly pick up a type each and rub it upon the table . . . to smooth the surface. The dexterity . . . is astonishing.[17]

Or, in Lyman's chemical plant, where most of the workers were men, and waterpowered machinery operated powerful presses and complicated cutting systems, women were 'kept constantly employed in the washing of bottles'.[18] Similarly, in DeWitt's Buckskin Glove Factory on the Lachine Canal:

> A machine at one stroke takes out pieces the shape of the thumb and fingers of the human hand. . . . In an adjacent room a number of young women, operating on sewing machines stitched them together with great rapidity.[19]

In shoemaking, cigarmaking, and confectionery, the story was the same. A cigar maker complained in 1889 that

> in 1863 there was a mould invented. . . . Before that time we did not know what it was to have a lot of apprentices in the shops. The system of making cigars by moulds caused a great many children to go to work at the trade. Manufacturers found they could get cigars more cheaply by children.[20]

Women and children thus came to constitute a vital element of Montreal's industrial labour force.[21] In 1871 three types of production dominated in Montreal: leather, boots, and shoe manufacture; clothing manufactures; and metal work and transportation-related industry. In the first two, the proportion of women and children was 50 per cent and 80 per cent, respectively. Overall, women and children made up nearly 42 per cent of the industrial workforce reported in the 1871 census. Montreal's industries appear to have employed significantly more women and children than did Toronto's, where the proportion was 33 per cent.[22] Thus, although the employment of large numbers of women and children appears to have been a general characteristic of early industrial capitalism everywhere, the proportions involved varied immensely. In a mill town like Lowell, Massachussetts, for instance, women constituted 56 per cent of the workforce, compared to Montreal's 33 per cent. In Preston, Lancashire, England, by the time boys were fourteen, 88 per cent of them were working. In Montreal around 25 per cent of boys eleven to fifteen years old worked.[23] Obviously, the different opportunities for work for family members in any one locale conditioned the particular nature of the impact of industrialization of the family.

The Family Economy: Average Numbers of Family Workers

Montreal's labour market was characterized by seasonal and cyclical unemployment and by low wages. In the winter many workers were without jobs. The Port, which in summer fed both commerce and industry, was open only seven to eight months a year. With its closure the rhythm of business and employment for the whole city slowed down. Labourers and carters found themselves seeking alternative winter employment, although there was very little work available. City lumberyards closed down between November and May. Even shoemakers and moulders expected to lose two or three months during the winter. Competition for jobs became tough. Winter wages in most jobs dropped. 'When they don't find work at anything else,' explained a moulder in the 1880s, 'they walk the streets and wait till work commences, and when the bosses see they are hard up for work, they try to reduce wages and put them as low as possible.'[24]

While winter wages dropped, living expenses usually soared. The winter of 1871–2 was exceptionally severe, and fuel costs rose to what were reported as 'famine prices' of between ten and fifteen dollars a cord.[25] Obviously a labourer earning between one and two dollars a week could not afford to pay such a price, when a cord of wood would heat the home for only a week.[26]

Given the need for extra money in the winter for fuel, clothing, and food, and the low wages that prevailed in most jobs, it is not surprising that it was fairly generally accepted that many working-class families needed more than one worker if they were to survive adequately. Employers and charity workers alike agreed on this a decade later before the Royal Commission on the Relations of Labour and Capital. Some, while arguing that young children should not work, admitted that 'many are necessitated to do so from the fact that their parents probably earn very little, not sufficient to keep a large family unless the little fellows are sent to work at tender years.'[27] Employers pleaded pressure from widows and poverty-striken parents as the reason for hiring very young children.[28]

In 1871 families in Sainte-Anne and Saint-Jacques averaged 1.6 workers each. Averages, however, are generally deceptive, masking more than they show. The father's occupation was crucial in influencing the work of other

Table 1. *Average Number of Workers in Families Classified by the Father's Occupational Group, 1871*[29]

	Sainte-Anne	Saint-Jacques
Professionals	1.0	1.3
Proprietors	1.2	1.6
'White-collar' workers	1.2	1.4
Skilled workers	1.5	1.5
Semi-skilled and unskilled workers	1.8	1.8

family members. In the few Sainte-Anne families that were headed by proprietors, the average number of workers was only 1.2. In both wards, semi-skilled and unskilled workers in contrast averaged 1.8 workers each. Skilled workers averaged only 1.5. The one divergence between the wards interestingly reflected the fundamental difference in the nature of production in the two wards. Saint-Jacques's proprietors averaged more workers per family than did local skilled workers or 'white-collar workers' (see Table 1). The reason lay in the nature of their enterprises. For these artisans and small shopkeepers, their business was often a family undertaking. Few employed large numbers of workers. Most were helped by apprentices, sons, daughters, or wives.[30]

If the apparent strong relationship between class and the number of family workers is examined further, to see actual rather than average numbers of workers, roughly 40 per cent of unskilled families in Saint-Jacques had more than one worker compared to 30 per cent of skilled and 20 to 25 per cent of white-collar and professional families.

The Family Economy: Working Children

Both Saint-Jacques and Sainte-Anne were working-class wards, with 60 to 80 per cent of their residents involved in manual wage labour, skilled or otherwise. French Canadians predominated in skilled trades in both wards, while the Irish of Sainte-Anne clustered significantly in unskilled positions, especially as labourers and carters. Small proprietors, artisans and shop-owners were much more prevalent among Saint-Jacques's workers, especially within the small non-French-Canadian population (see Table 2).

It was definitely the norm in families of all classes and backgrounds for the husband to be the primary breadwinner. Two-thirds of all workers in both wards were the male heads of their families. Virtually all husbands listed occupations in the 1871 census, although this did not imply that they had steady work or were currently employed. Nor did it mean that the occupation listed was their only one. 'Certain establishments', the writer of the 1871 census monograph explained,

Table 2. Occupational Groups by Origins: Sainte-Anne and Saint-Jacques Wards Compared 1871[31]

Sainte-Anne

	French Canadian		Irish		Other		Overall
	Number	%	Number	%	Number	%	%
Professional	1	1.1					.3
Proprietor	3	3.3	8	6.2	8	9.9	5.0
Commercial employee	1	1.1	10	7.7	8	9.9	6.3
Public service			2	1.5	1	1.2	1.0
Service	2	2.2	5	3.8	4	4.9	3.6
Skilled	58	63.7	43	33.1	41	50.7	48.3
Semi-skilled & unskilled	26	28.6	60	46.2	18	22.2	34.5
Other			2	1.5	1	1.2	1.0
	91	100.0	130	100.0	81	100.0	100.0
% of total population		26.5		50.0		23.5	

Saint-Jacques

	French Canadian		Other		Overall
	Number	%	Number	%	%
Professional	16	3.2	10	11.0	4.4
Proprietor	43	8.6	20	22.0	10.5
Commercial employee	45	9.0	11	12.1	9.5
Public service	9	1.8	1	1.1	1.7
Service	18	3.6	13	14.3	5.3
Skilled	241	48.3	15	16.5	43.5
Semi-skilled & skilled	97	19.4	17	18.7	19.3
Other	30	6.0	4	4.3	5.8
	499	100.0	91	100.0	100.0
% of total population		82.5		17.5	

do not employ workmen or labourers during the whole year, nor in a regular manner . . . men following certain occupations are successively engaged in the course of the year in various employments.[32]

The few husbands not listing jobs were either retired and living with one of their adult children, or newly married and living, together with their brides, with one of the families of origin.

Older sons still resident at home were the most usual second wage-earners. Almost all sons over twenty worked, while only half the daughters of that age did. About 75 per cent of sixteen- to twenty-year-old sons had jobs, while only around 40 per cent of daughters did. If there were boys in the family, the older girls were likely to remain at home to help with housework and care of younger children. At all ages sons were much more likely to work than daughters (see Table 3).

More interesting is the number of children between the ages of eleven and fifteen who worked. It was the work of children of these ages in factories and sweatshops that was to capture the imagination and elicit the horror of reformers a decade or so later. Newspapers, Royal Commissions, and labour unions would all proclaim the evils of child labour. Laws would be passed attempting to control it, not always with great success. In 1871, however, there was no legislation to prevent the work of young children and there was little public outcry compared to the reforming voices of subsequent decades.[33] Graphic descriptions of the hours and conditions of child labour exist, but little real idea of how widespread it was, of what families it occurred in, of the role that it played in the economy of businesses and families, and of what parents thought about their young children being involved in wage labour.

Around 25 per cent of boys aged between eleven and fifteen reported occupations to the 1871 Census taker, while about 10 per cent of girls did so (see Table 3). Focusing on those families which had these youngsters at work, the following section will attempt to describe the work they were doing and some of the factors that determined whether or not children of this age would work in any particular family.

First, it should be reiterated that a demand for child labour existed in Montreal. A large proportion of the city's major industries were dependent on children's cheap labour. With industrialization Montreal appears to have developed a variety of jobs that were age-specific, which children did for a while until they became too old or too experienced to be paid such cheap wages.

Most of Sainte-Anne's young worked in factory jobs—in the local cotton mill or tobacco factories, or as typecasters or nailers. A Sainte-Anne cotton mill reported twenty-four workers aged under sixteen to the 1871 Census taker, although there may well have been more. Two-thirds of the employees were female.[34] Young children in the mill were confined to specific tasks such as carrying thread and hose or working in the mule and spinning rooms as 'doffers'. Most of the women and children were French Canadians. Several of the working families had been brought from the rural Saguenay country as cheaper 'green' labour. Many children in the mill also had brothers and sisters there and sometimes fathers or widowed mothers as well.[35]

Fines in cotton mills were high and a daily experience, especially for the children. As a result the pay they took home was often drastically reduced.[36]

Table 3. Children, Work, and School Attendance, 1871[37]

Sainte-Anne

	Work Number(%)	School Number(%)	Neither Number(%)	Total Number
Sons				
0–5		6(8%)	67(92%)	73
6–10	1(2%)	38(67%)	18(31%)	57
11–15	9(24%)	22(58%)	7(18%)	38
16–20	40(75.5%)	1(2%)	12(22.5%)	53
Daughters				
0–5		4(5%)	74(95%)	78
6–10		48(76%)	15(24%)	63
11–15	5(7%)	32(48%)	33(47%)	70
16–20	21(40%)	47(7.5%)	28(52.5%)	53

Saint-Jacques

	Work Number(%)	School Number(%)	Neither Number(%)	Total Number
Sons				
0–5		8(6%)	124(94%)	132
6–10	2(2%)	48(54%)	39(44%)	89
11–15	25(26%)	43(45%)	28(29%)	96
16–20	61(75%)	5(6%)	15(19%)	81
Daughters				
0–5		8(6%)	132(94%)	140
6–10		54(60%)	46(40%)	90
11–15	12(13%)	39(42%)	47(45%)	92
16–20	41(40%)	1(1%)	60(59%)	102

Fines were also the standard method of disciplining youngsters in the tobacco factories of both wards. There, too, children tended to work on specific jobs, often separate from the skilled tradesmen who might have taught them the trade. While some were technically employed as apprentices, indentureship for most children did not guarantee induction into the mysteries of a trade. Most 'apprentices' in cigar-making spent their time watching a machine or only rolling cigars. In Saint-Jacques ward in 1871, there were still some children who appear to have been apprenticed to a small master running his own shop, some to their father. They worked in trades such as tinsmithing, not in cigar-making or shoemaking, both of which had radically altered over the decades.

It was from the semi- and unskilled Irish and French-Canadian families of Sainte-Anne, Saint-Jacques, and other areas of Montreal that the bulk of

Table 4. Percentage of Non-Manual, Skilled, and Unskilled Families with Working
Children under Sixteen[38]

	Sainte-Anne, 1871 11–15 %	Saint-Jacques, 1871 11–15 %
Non-manual	0	22.5
Skilled	11.8	13.6
Unskilled	33.3	29.0

the city's young workers were drawn. These families were more than twice
as likely to have children under sixteen at work as were skilled families. Such
children worked in around 30 per cent of unskilled families compared to 12
per cent of skilled. In Sainte-Anne, the children of non-manual workers
seldom had jobs, whereas Saint-Jacques's artisans and entrepreneurs did put
their children to work at an early age (see Table 4). Family work for the
latter was part of an old tradition, but was also necessary because of the
increasing competition they were experiencing from industrial production.

In large families, especially those with unskilled fathers, it was much more
common for young children to be sent out to work. In families of four (that
is, with two children) only 5.5 per cent had eleven- to fifteen-year-olds at
work, while 30 per cent of families of eight did so. The presence of older
siblings does not seem to have militated against a younger child also being
sent out to work. Indeed, the opposite seemed true. Where older brothers
or sisters worked, children between eleven and fifteen were more likely to
also work than those who had older siblings who did not. Certainly, the
wages of one working child were not high enough to give much of a boost
to family income in large families. The larger the family, the more likely a
young child would be sent out to work.

French Canadians appear to have been somewhat more likely to send
their younger children to work than other groups. In Saint-Jacques, nearly
25 per cent of French-Canadian families with children aged between eleven
and fifteen had at least one of them at work in 1871, compared only to 13
per cent of non-French Canadians. More French-Canadian families had
children of all ages at work than other groups. Studies of families from
Quebec in the United States have shown similar patterns. In Cohoes, New
York, during the 1880s, for instance, 27.3 per cent of female French-Canadian workers in textile plants were under fourteen compared to 13.5 per
cent of English and 15.6 per cent of Irish workers.[39] Similarly in Manchester, New Hampshire, in the early twentieth century, Tamara Hareven
found that French Canadians had more textile workers per family than
other groups. She argues that the

basic tradition of family work and of the economic role of each member . . . was carried over from the agricultural background. The important continuity was in the perception and experience of the family as a work unit, even when the location of the job and the work processes were different.[40]

Cultural attitudes to work and to the idea of the role of children certainly seem to have supported child labour in French-Canadian families. However, the relationship between ethnicity and the work of young children should not be overstressed. Class was still more important than ethnic background. In Sainte-Anne, where the Irish constituted most of the unskilled workers, more of their families had children at work than did French Canadians— even unskilled French Canadians. The family economy had been part of rural Irish life too, although most of Sainte-Anne's residents with young children were second-generation immigrants, brought up far from the land. For families of all backgrounds, basic need arising from the insecurities of a father's work was as important as cultural values and tradition, so that for all groups unskilled families were more likely to have their children at work than other families (see Table 5).

Finding work for these children appears to have been a family responsibility. In the textile industry especially, capitalists preferred to hire whole families. Indeed, they advertised for families in the newspapers, specifying that young children would be welcomed.[41] And they recruited whole families of 'green labour' from the rural areas. Manufacturers saw it as a distinct advantage to hire whole families and by the 1880s were providing 'cottages, so as to give the employees of the mill nice comfortable homes'. Girls working in such factories were assumed to be living with their parents. They 'would not undertake the work otherwise', an employer pointed out.[42] For parents, it was desirable to have their young children in the same workplace. It enabled mothers to work. Traditional ties between children and parents could be maintained, even though the family as a unit of production which had once worked their land together had been transformed. Employers often argued that the hiring of very young children resulted from parental pressure. A mill overseer explained:

> . . . a man will be working at the mill, and his daughter working there also, and he may have a small child, whom he desires to have there, for instance, in the spooling room. Often you don't want to take the child, but if you do not, he and his daughter will go out, and they will go to some mill where the whole three will be employed.[43]

It was apparently common for mothers to seek work for their daughters and sons and to act as go-betweens. For instance, when Madame Sara Fontaine's two daughters were dismissed, first from the Sainte-Anne Mill and then from the Hudon Mill at Hochelaga, it was she who went to the 'boss' asking 'Why did you dismiss my daughters? I have need of their assistance

Table 5. Ethnicity and Working Children

The percentage of families with children over age eleven who have at least one child at work.

	Sainte-Anne		Saint-Jacques	
	French-Canadian	Other	French-Canadian	Other
	%	%	%	%
Non-skilled	0	0	55	38
Skilled	80	82	58	25
Unskilled	86	94	77	50

to live.'[44] The manager explained that when girls came to the mill their 'mothers often come with them, and beg the chance of getting them on to work.'

> For instance, there was a mother brought a girl the other day. I said she was small. The mother replied: 'I went into the mill about that age.' I told her . . . at first she would get very little pay. She replied that she understood that.[45]

The relationship between young working children, their employer, and the parent or parents was complex. Work for whole families offered a chance for the family unit to stay intact, at least within the confines of one factory. It also meant that the employer could pay lower wages and that parents could be expected to exercise some discipline over their children. The whole family could thus be moulded to the demands of industrial work with minimum friction. However, family employment appeared to have been largely limited to the textile trade. Elsewhere, fathers and sons, or several siblings, frequently worked in the same plant. Mothers and daughters often worked at home as sewing girls. In the situations where children worked alone, parents appeared to have endowed the employer with the patriarchal and disciplinary powers usually attributed to the father. In the 1880s, Mr Fortier, Montreal's infamous exploiter and abuser of child labour, claimed that parents asked him to discipline their children. When 'apprentices' in his factory failed to turn up on time, they first notified the parents, then 'had the child arrested. We have had parents come to us over and over again,' he argued, 'and threaten to hold us responsible if we did not make the apprentices attend to their work.' Other tobacco manufacturers reported having been requested by parents 'to correct the children'. Still others sent the children home to their parents when they did wrong.[46]

Obviously children needed discipline to conform to the demands of factory routine. Adults too had to learn the punctuality and application that these new work processes demanded. However, in the relationship between children, employer, and parents, the last apparently assumed that employers performed the same role as masters of apprentices had done in former times. Yet most employers were concerned only with employing and disciplining a cheap labour force. The family and the child did not gain the benefits of a trade well learned in return. They merely earned some money. This, the employer appeared to have considered a family responsibility. Fines, one employer explained, were imposed

> in order that the parents may see it marked on the envelope, that it may thus attract the parent's attention—they see 10¢ marked as a fine and they will know about it. They will then find out from the children how it occurred, or they will go to the overseer and speak about it and that generally effects the result we desire.[47]

How parents felt about sending their young children to work in factories and workshops is hard to determine. Certainly French Canadians and Irish immigrants from rural backgrounds were used to labouring together as a family. Many children had meant many hands to work the land. The farm economy had been a family economy. Even where children had left the land to work elsewhere, it was apparently common for French-Canadian children to return much of their earnings to their father. Fathers, in return, had been responsible for finding land, employment, or dowries for those children who would not inherit.[48]

In the city this family economy was fundamentally undermined, but did not disappear totally. For most families production and ownership were no longer linked. Now they had only their labour to sell, at whatever price the capitalists were offering. Only those with sufficient capital or skills could set up small family businesses or artisanal shops, and the latter were increasingly suffering from the competition of industrial capital. However, the old values of family work may well have continued to function. They served well in a situation where many fathers could not earn enough to support a family. Need and tradition seemed to have combined to maintain the idea of family work and the fact of child labour within the growing and changing city.

Until reformers reacted against child labour and legislation was passed to control it in the 1880s and 1890s, the work of many family members continued to be a feature of the urban family economy. 'The working family' continued to 'suffer generally from lack of means, and there is no doubt that in the families of working people, where the average of children is 8, 9 or even 10, there is need of the handwork of children under 14'.[49] Until well-organized unions began to push for a working wage adequate to nurture a whole family, child labour would continue to be vital to family survival. What the parents thought about it in private could have no influence until they had the means to express their wishes.

Research on attitudes about the family and children in English Canada suggests that ideas about childhood may have undergone a fundamental transformation in the years following the 1870s. Whether similar changes occurred in Quebec remains to be studied. Before the 1890s English Canadians generally showed little awareness of children as individual persons with an emotional life of their own. Children were viewed by many as partially formed, potential adults.[50] Or, for men like Egerton Ryerson, as small men differing from adults in the need for greater restraint. Work was seen as crucial to the formation of character, as one of the best forms of education. Childhood and education were part of a brief, passing phase which, to the dismay of educators, many parents expected to be quickly finished so that children could 'enter the working world'.[51]

The widespread practice of child labour in Montreal suggests that attitudes there were similar. Whatever the ideal was, the labour of children was obviously vital to the economy of many of the city's families. Many children did not work, however. Despite the fact that there were no compulsory school laws in Montreal, around one-half of the boys and girls between the ages of eleven and fifteen reported attending school in 1871. Once boys reached sixteen, 'the working world' was the major educating agent, while for girls the home was more important. At all ages large numbers of children neither worked nor went to school (see Table 3). Some of them may have had jobs that were not reported to the census taker. Others may have swelled the ranks of the 'Arabs of the street' who worried contemporary middle-class observers. Some of these street children were reported to earn 'a few pence by retailing newspapers or, as is sometimes the case, supplement the labour of begging by the sale of daily journals', forming an 'irregular squad of urchins who may be seen around the printing offices at the hour of publication'. Others, observers believed, were 'thrust forth this morning from a comfortless home' to beg or to steal.[52]

The Family Economy: Working Wives

Not all families could rely on the work of their children to prop up the family income, as many had no children old enough to work. In both Sainte-Anne and Saint-Jacques over two-thirds of the families were dependent on the wages of only one worker at the time the 1871 census was taken. Of these, 75 per cent of Sainte-Anne's and 65 per cent of Saint-Jacques's families were at the stage of their life cycle when all children were under eleven years old. This was a period in the process of family formation when a steady income was more needed than ever, but when children were too young to help supplement it. Where the income of the father was insufficient, alternative survival strategies had to be followed. Either the wife and mother could go to work, or housing could be shared with friends, relatives, or boarders to cut down on rental and heating costs.

A few wives took on steady jobs and reported occupations to the census taker. Still more probably worked occasionally, taking in washing, ironing, sewing, mending, or babysitting for neighbours, relatives, or friends. Their work, and the day-to-day labour of women in the home, is absent from the statistics and from most of the observations of the period. Likely even steady work for wages by married women was under-enumerated by census takers.[53] Yet even if under-enumeration was common, the wife was clearly the one family member least likely to have a paid job at any period of her married life. Only 2.5 per cent of all wives resident with their husbands reported occupations.[54] Despite its relative infrequency, the work of these women is worth examining in some depth, as it clearly illustrated the way family economies were both influenced by, and interacted with, the particular nature of industrialization in any area.

Working wives were clustered in the poorer sections of both wards. Virtually all had husbands with unskilled or skilled jobs. Nearly 25 per cent were married to labourers. Shoemakers in Saint-Jacques (21 per cent) and factory workers in Sainte-Anne (25 per cent) were the next most common occupation of husbands. Sixty per cent of the wives worked as seamstresses (73 per cent in Saint-Jacques and 53 per cent in Sainte-Anne), another 11 per cent as chars and washerwomen, and 5 per cent as labourers of an unspecified nature. A few wives in both wards worked as grocers or traders and in other small corner businesses, often helping their husbands.

Fairly similar patterns of occupations in the two wards masked a basic difference in the relationship between the work of mothers and their families. While dressmaking and sewing occupations predominated in both wards, they were more prevalent and of a different nature in Saint-Jacques. There, sewing at home appears to have been part of the putting-out system, so basic to Montreal's clothing industry. While in Sainte-Anne only two of the wives worked as dressmakers along with their children or other relatives, in Saint-Jacques 31 per cent of the women had other members of the family who listed the same occupation. Work at home was a family enterprise enabling the mothers to keep an eye on their young children while working and to work with their daughters. The former was important, as 20 per cent of the women who worked had children under the age of two and 45 per cent had children under five.

In the clothing trade, mechanization revolutionized production both in and outside the growing number of factories. In a trade that was particularly unstable in the years before the initiation of the National Policy's tariffs, capitalists sought ways to keep costs as low as possible.[55] 'Putting out', 'sweating', or 'homework' saved on overhead rental, machinery costs, and labour costs. As the old craft of the tailor or seamstress was deskilled, as immigrants from the countryside and abroad were drawn into the city, homework especially for women and children multiplied. Thus, labour that resulted directly from the mechanization of some parts of the labour process brought to these women no separation of work and home, but rather the increased likelihood of work for wages at home.

Most employees in the clothing trade worked outside the factory. Work was shipped both to families in the city and as far as twenty or thirty miles away to Saint-Jérôme, Saint-Hyacinthe, and Sainte-Rose, where there were reported to be 'hundreds of hands'.[56] Employers often knew little of what went on outside their factory. 'We don't know how many hands work at it,' explained one Montreal clothier who employed seventy to one hundred people preparing the work to go out. 'We only know one woman, but don't know how many she employs.' He believed that in 1874 he probably employed a total of seven hundred to one thousand people including the hundred or so 'inside'.[57]

Mr Muir, a Montreal clothier, explained the relationship between factory work and home work. In his factory there was

> a 15 horsepower engine running three machines having 50 needles each, and a knife which cuts cloth by steam, so that four cutters will do the work of from twelve to fifteen.

In homes around Montreal the next stage was carried out:

> We employ a large number of women who live in their own homes. These women sit down when their breakfasts, dinner and supper is over, and make a garment, but are not exclusively employed at this work all day.[58]

It was convenient for employers to believe that for these mothers and daughters sewing was a secondary family occupation, something done in their spare time. They could thus justify the extraordinarily low wages paid. 'Those people who work in their own homes work very cheap,' Mr Muir explained, 'and they will earn comparatively little' compared even to unskilled factory hands who were earning only $1.50 to $2.00 a week in his factory. He told the 1874 Select Committee that 'most of them are wives and daughters of mechanics, who earn enough to keep the house.' The women were, he argued, earning enough money which enabled them 'to buy finery . . . which they would not be able to buy but for this industry'.[59]

The working wives of Saint-Jacques and most of those of Sainte-Anne were certainly not in this position. The majority of their husbands listed their occupations as labourers, workers in the building trade, factory workers, or shoemakers. The first two had always been highly seasonal and precarious jobs. The latter had been rendered precarious by technological and organizational change.[60] Work by wives thus appears to have been much more the result of necessity than of the desire or need for extra finery.

Homework brought minimal pay, with wages almost always paid by the piece. The more people who could work, therefore, the better for the family.

In one-third of the families in Saint-Jacques where the mother was a seamstress, daughters worked with her. It was not uncommon to find three to four sisters, ranging in age from eleven to twenty-eight, all working, presumably together, as sewing girls. In the Aliron family, for instance, Demithilde and her four daughters aged fourteen to nineteen worked as sewing girls, while the father worked as a saddlemaker.[61] In some families daughters but not the mothers worked. Thus, in the Moisan family four daughters all worked as sewing girls, the wife did not work, and the father worked when he could as a labourer.[62] For widows, work at home offered both a means of support and a way to remain with their children.

The clothing industry was thus a vital part of the life of many Saint-Jacques families. Not surprisingly, seamstress was the ward's leading occupation, ranking even above labourer. It was definitely women's work, and employers were able to take advantage of the large numbers of families desperately needing work for their members. Virtually all those involved were French Canadian, as was typical in the industry. 'Your labour supply is chiefly French?' clothier Muir was asked by the 1874 committee.

> It was almost exclusively French.
> —You have a surplus population in Montreal which enables you to get cheap labour?—Yes, in fact it makes my heart ache to have the women come crying for work.
> —Then your labour is very cheap?—Yes; too cheap.
> —I fancy that from the surplus in Montreal, you get labour cheaper than you could in any other part of the country?—We think so . . . Irish women, for instance, if they come to this country and do not get the wages they want, will emigrate.[63]

The demography of the Quebec family, the exhaustion of easily available good land in the province, and the tradition of family work thus combined to enable capitalists in clothing and other trades to count on a steady supply of cheap labour.

Families working at home were not involved only in handwork. By 1872 advertisements in the newspapers for sewing machines for family use were common.[64] A journalist for the *Montreal Daily Witness* explained how families were contacted by sewing-machine salesmen:

> A set of canvassers are first sent out in order to induce workingmen's wives to buy a machine. In reality they do not buy the machine, but are induced to sign a form of lease by the terms of which, without the intervention of a lawyer, this machine can be taken back again within any period of time, if the entire amount cannot be paid. If, therefore, by sickness or death . . . the poor woman is unable to pay the installment when due, she loses all that she has paid upon the machine.[65]

How many of the women listing themselves as dressmakers had sewing machines is hard to tell. Definitely in this category were two sisters in Sainte-Anne, Philomène and Aurélie Leduc. They each reported ownership of a sewing machine valued at sixty-five dollars to the industrial census taker. Working on 'cloth etc. furnished by merchants', they produced around four hundred and three hundred dollars' worth of coats, pants, and vests each. Unlike most Saint-Jacques women, these sisters appear to have employed one extra woman each, to whom they paid a total of $276 in wages annually.[66]

Probably some of Sainte-Anne's working wives worked as seamstresses in the local merchant tailor's shops which employed three to nine people, or in the larger workshops of clothiers, dressmakers, and milliners in the neighbourhood. Some too may have worked in one of the large clothing or hat-making factories. Only three of the married women dressmakers of Sainte-Anne ran establishments of their own that were reported to the industrial census taker. Of these one reported an annual production of fifty dollars' worth of dresses, the other two three hundred dollars.[67] Not one of Saint-Jacques's women was reported as proprietor of her own establishment. The six hundred to nine hundred dollars capital mustered by the three Sainte-Anne women was probably well beyond most of their saving abilities. Homework for them would continue to be the piecework of the putting-out system.

Why these married women worked and how they viewed their participation in wage labour can only be surmised. Some of those who had no children may have worked because they wanted to, because they enjoyed their work, or to help save up money for the future. Most probably worked, however, because they needed to. That married Saint-Jacques women took the opportunity offered by homework suggests the importance placed on being near growing children. Many of the other women's occupations—charwomen, housekeepers, and small traders—were the ones that did not require a full-time absence from the family and home. Some of the sewing women may have worked in factories, although not one listed an easily identifiable factory occupation. Such work would have meant a full day away from the home.

Most importantly, the work of wives provided a supplement or stabilizer to the father's income at those stages of the life cycle when children were too young to work (see Table 6). In Sainte-Anne, most wives appear to have stopped work once their children were old enough to find jobs. There, under 20 per cent of the wives had working children. In Saint-Jacques, in contrast, most working wives did have children old enough to work. They continued to work largely because they could do so at home sewing.

The Family Life Cycle and Household Structure

Both Michael Anderson and John Foster, in studies on mid-nineteenth century English working-class families, have stressed that few were permanently

Table 6. The Life Cycle Stage of Working Wives[68]

	Sainte–Anne		Saint-Jacques	
	Number	%	Number	%
No children	21	27	13	17
Children 1 and under only	15	19	14	18
Children all 10 and under	12	15	5	7
Some children 11-15, none older	19	25	11	15
Some children over 16	11	14	32	43
Total	78		75	

free of poverty. Work by several family members there, as in Montreal, could ensure a less precarious survival. However, for those families who only had children too young to work, over one-half fell below the poverty line.[69] No poverty line has as yet been established for Montreal in this period. Clearly, however, large numbers of Montreal families were vulnerable to poverty at this stage. Certainly, until children were old enough to work, most families relied on one worker (see Table 7).

Some may have turned to charity to survive. Figures from Protestant and Catholic organizations attest to vast numbers of families who were visited in their homes and given relief, especially during the winters. In February of 1872, 279 families received firewood, clothing, blankets, and provisions from the Board of Outdoor Relief of the Protestant House of Industry and Refuge alone.[70] The Grey Nuns and Sisters of Providence probably visited and provided help to three times that number of needy Catholic families.[71] Others, especially in Saint-Jacques, shared their living space with other families or relatives, or took in boarders.

Michael Katz has argued that in Hamilton in 1861, 'the presence of boarders and relatives in any given household appears to have been largely accidental.'[72] This was not so in Montreal in 1871. There, household structure was closely related to the family life cycle.

Over one-half the couples in Sainte-Anne and Saint-Jacques began their married lives sharing their households, especially with unrelated families and couples. As children were born and grew older and as the family's size grew they were more likely to live alone. Seventy-five to 80 per cent of families lived alone when half their children were fifteen and under. For most families this was a crucial and difficult stage. Most children were too young to work and families were at their largest. As families grew, the strain of sharing cramped quarters appears to have become intolerable for all but the most needy. While only 20 per cent of families shared with relatives or other

Table 7. Average Number of Workers at Different Stages of the Family Life Cycle[73]

	Sainte-Anne		Saint-Jacques	
	Average Number of Workers	Number of Families	Average Number of Workers	Number of Families
1. Wife under 45, no children	1	13	1.1	50
2. 1 child under 1	1	12	1	19
3. All children 10 and under	1.03	55	1.03	94
4. Half or more 15 and under	1.83	36	1.7	67
5. Half or more over 15	3.05	19	3.2	34
6. All over 15	2.5	13	2.3	28
7. Over 45, no children at home	1	5	.8	24
Single Parents				
1. Half children under 15	2.0	2	.75	4
2. Half children over 15	2.5	2	2.75	10

families at this stage, more took in boarders. Boarders provided some income without extreme overcrowding. As children left home families were once again likely to share living space, especially with relatives—often their married children (see Table 8).

At all stages of the life cycle it was the unskilled families who were least likely to live alone. Only 47 per cent of Saint-Jacques's unskilled families, compared to 66 per cent of professional families, lived in a simple nuclear household (see Table 9). People were sharing houses not because they wanted to, but because they needed to. A contemporary citizen observed that 'under the present state of things, overcrowding is inevitable and only the cheapest and most inferior class of rookeries can be paid for out of the current rate of wages.' He stressed the double and linked need for 'better dwellings for the working classes and increased income for all wage earners of the city'.[74]

The percentage of nuclear families classified as occupying whole households in both Saint-Jacques and, to a lesser extent, Sainte-Anne was much lower than that found in other studies in Canada or elsewhere in the western world. It is also much lower than the 76 per cent found by Louise Dechêne in Montreal two centuries earlier in 1681.[75] In Hamilton, Canada West, Katz found that nearly 80 per cent of households contained only a simple nuclear

Table 8. The Family Life Cycle and Household Structure[76]

	Simple Family	Extended Family	Multiple Some Related	Multiple Not Related	Total Families
Sainte-Anne					
1. No children	46.7%			53.3%	15
2. 1 under 1	75.0%	8.3%		16.7%	12
3. All under 11	71.4%	5.4%	3.6%	19.6%	56
4. Half under 15	81.1%	8.1%	2.7%	8.1%	37
5. Half over 15	85.0%	0	0	15.0%	20
6. All over 15	60.0%	6.7%	26.7%		15
7. No children	66.7%			33.3%	6
Overall household structure	71.9%	5.4%	2.4%	20.4%	167
With boarder(s)	16.6%	11.1%	25.0%	20.6%	18.4%
Saint-Jacques					
1. No children	40.8%	4.1%	14.3%	40.8%	49
2. 1 under 1	36.8%	5.3%	15.8%	42.1%	19
3. All under 11	63.4%	8.6%	5.4%	22.6%	93
4. Half under 15	74.6%	4.5%	0	19.4%	67
5. Half over 15	50.0%	8.8%	2.9%	38.2%	34
6. All over 15	57.1%	14.3%	17.9%	10.7%	28
7. No children	33.3%	0	8.3%	58.3%	24
Overall household structure	56.4%	6.7%	7.3%	29.3%	328
With boarder(s)	17.2%	16.0%	22.2%	11.7%	15.7%

family in 1851 and 1861.[77] This compares with 56.4 per cent in Saint-Jacques and 63 per cent in Sainte-Anne in 1871. Anderson's work on Lancashire led him to suggest that industrialization, rather than leading to the decline of the nuclear family as early sociologists had posited, led to an increase in the importance of kinship. Kin, he argued, chose to live both with and near each other, helped each other find jobs, and provided essential support in critical situations. Yet even there, 72 per cent of married couples occupied a whole house, 15 per cent shared with non-relatives, 5 per cent shared with kin, and 8 per cent lived as lodgers.[78] Thus, the high proportion of Montreal families sharing dwelling space with other couples, families, and boarders appears to have been peculiar to that city.[79]

There are several possible explanations. First, French-Canadian family-oriented values were probably very important in leading to the sharing of

Table 9. Saint-Jacques, 1871—Household Structure and the Occupation of the Father

	Professional & Proprietor		Service		Skilled		Unskilled		Other	
No family	1	2%	1	3%	1	1%	1	1%	1	14%
Simple family	40	6%	19	59%	78	53%	40	47%	3	44%
Extended family	4	6%	1	3%	10	7%	7	8%	1	14%
Multiple —Some related	4	6%	1	3%	14	10%	5	6%	1	14%
Multiple —None related	12	20%	10	32%	43	29%	32	38%	1	14%
Total number of families	61	100%	32	100%	146	100%	85	100%	7	100%

households by relatives. As an example, in Saint-Jacques, the French-Canadian suburb, the percentage of families sharing with relatives was double that of Sainte-Anne. Furthermore, the residents of Sainte-Anne, like those of Preston, Lancashire, and Hamilton, were largely immigrants who were less likely to have large numbers of kin near at hand. French Canadians in Montreal, in contrast, would have been constantly augmented by kin from the rural areas. Certainly, in both wards, French Canadians were less likely to live as a single nuclear family than the Irish or other groups (see Table 10). Yet there were differences too in the extent of sharing. All Saint-Jacques families were more likely to double up with others than were those of Sainte-Anne. This may have been a result of the nature of housing in the two areas. Or it may have reflected the fewer work opportunities near the Saint-Jacques area.

Secondly, it is possible that the high percentage of families sharing households was not a real phenomenon at all, but the result of fuzzy definitions of households on the part of the census takers, who may have called all people resident in one dwelling, with separate apartments, a 'household'. This does not, however, appear to have been the case.[80] Qualitative evidence of overcrowding lends support to the statistical data. Fifteen years later 'doubling up' was described as common and did not appear to be viewed as a recent phenomenon, although increased migration to the city as well as the effects of the Depression may well have exacerbated it. A doctor testifying before the Commission on the Relations between Labour and Capital suggested then that the average labourer's tenement would have three to four rooms and would be occupied by

> two to three families, or sometimes two families using one stove between them, and if there are several families, each family will have one room for a sleeping

Table 10. French–Canadian and Others' House Structure Compared

	Sainte-Anne				Saint-Jacques			
	French Canadian		Other		French Canadian		Other	
Solitaires					2	1%	3	5%
Simple family	37	69%	78	76%	145	53%	35	61%
Extended family	1	2%	6	6%	20	7%	2	4%
Multiple—Some related	4	7%			23	8%	3	5%
Multiple—Not related	12	22%	19	18%	84	31%	14	25%
Totals	54	100%	103	100%	274	100%	57	100%

room, and use the kitchen for a dining room—the kitchen and stove in common with others.

An even greater number of families would share the same water closet or privy outside.[81] The same doctor reported finding as many as 'seventeen or eighteen souls residing in a house of five or six rooms'.[82]

Conclusion

Class position, the stage of the family life-cycle, and cultural values thus combined to condition not only the number of workers in any family and the age at which the children would be sent to work, but also the very composition of the households within which they would grow up. Many of the children in the families of Montreal's unskilled workers, at least those of Sainte-Anne and Saint-Jacques wards, were likely to go to work before they were fifteen and to grow up in families that at some point of their life shared living space with large numbers of other people. Children in such families were also less likely than others to spend much of their life in school.

In what Pollard has referred to as the transformation of a 'society of peasants, craftsmen and versatile labourers' into 'modern industrial workers', the family played an important role.[83] The hiring of whole families in the textile trade, the continued use of outmoded apprenticeship contracts, systems of fining children, the putting-out arrangement, and, indeed, the very employment of children: all drew on old ideas and familial traditions within a new context. Families thus served as a medium of socialization to new and strange work habits.

Montreal in 1871 appears to have been in a phase common to most nineteenth-century communities undergoing an 'industrial revolution'. Labour was viewed as a commodity to be bought as cheaply as possible. Workers' families were not seen by producers as potential units of consumption. There was thus little impetus to raise individual workers' wages to the level necessary to properly support a family. Low wages, the changing organization of production, and the large numbers of jobs opened up to women and children combined to make the work of several family members both possible and necessary in all but the best-paid of skilled working-class families.

The desire of capitalists for cheap female and child labour coincided with the need of families with children old enough to send them out to work. The surplus of such unskilled labour helped in turn to keep wages down. Thus for a while the needs and values of working-class families and of capitalists coincided to shape both the family economy and some of the characteristics of industrial production.[84]

Suggestions for Further Reading

Herbert Brown Ames, *The City Below the Hill* (Montreal, 1897, reprinted Toronto, 1972).

Terry Copp, *The Anatomy of Poverty: The Condition of the Working Class in Montreal, 1897–1929* (Toronto, 1974).

Michael J. Piva, *The Condition of the Working Class in Toronto, 1900–21* (Ottawa, 1981).

Notes

[1]For reviews of recent historical literature on the family and industrialization, see especially Lutz K. Berkner, 'Recent Research on the History of the Family in Western Europe', *Journal of Marriage and the Family* XXXV (August 1973); Elizabeth Pleck, 'Two Worlds in One—Work and Family', *Journal of Social History* (Winter 1976); and Lise Vogel, 'The Contested Domain: A Note on the Family in the Transition to Capitalism', *Marxist Perspectives*, I (Spring 1978). For books dealing explicitly with the topic, see Michael Anderson, *Family Structure in Nineteenth Century Lancashire* (Cambridge, 1971); William Goode, *World Revolution and Family Patterns* (New York, 1963); Peter Laslett and Richard Wall, *Household and Family in Past Time* (Cambridge, 1972); David Levine, *Family Formation in An Age of Nascent Capitalism* (New York, 1977); Edward Shorter, *The Making of the Modern Family* (New York, 1975); and Neil J. Smelser, *Social Change in the Industrial Revolution* (London, 1959).

[2]For a feminist rejoinder to Shorter's work, see Louise Tilly and Joan Scott, 'Women's Work and the Family in Nineteenth Century Europe', *Comparative Studies in Society and History*, XVII (1975); and Louise Tilly, Joan Scott, and Miriam Cohen, 'Women's Work and European Fertility Patterns', *Journal of Interdisciplinary History* VI (Winter 1976). For Shorter's rejoinder to the earlier article, see 'Women's Work: What Difference Did Capitalism Make?', *Theory of Society*, III (Winter 1976). For Marxist critiques, see Veronica Beechy, 'Some Notes on Female Wage Labour in Capitalist Production', *Capital and Class*, III (Autumn 1977); Jane Humphries, 'The

Working Class Family, Women's Liberation and Class Struggle: The Case of Nineteenth Century British History', *The Review of Radical Political Economics*, IX (Fall 1977); Jane Humphries, 'Class Struggle and the Persistence of the Working Class Family', *Cambridge Journal of Economics*, I (1978); and Lise Vogel, 'The Contested Domain'.

[3]Talcott Parsons, 'The Social Structure of the Family', S.M. Farber *et al.*, *The Family's Search for Survival* (New York, 1965). For sociologists questioning this view, see especially Goode, *World Revolution and Family Patterns* (1963), and Laslett and Wall, *Household and Family in Past Time* (1972).

[4]Pleck, 'Two Worlds in One'.

[5]Humphries, 'The Working Class Family' and 'Class Struggle and the Persistence of the Working Class Family'; Tamara Hareven, 'Cycles, Courses and Cohorts: Reflections on Theoretical and Methodological Approaches to the Historical Study of Family Development', *Journal of Social History*, XII (Fall 1978); Virginia Yans McLaughlin, 'Patterns of Work and Family Organization: Buffalo's Italians', *Journal of Interdisciplinary History*, II (Autumn 1971); and 'A Flexible Tradition: South Italian Immigrants Confront a New Work Experience', *Journal of Social History*, VII (Summer 1976).

[6]Berkner, 'Recent Research'; and Vogel 'The Contested Domain'.

[7]A 5 per cent random sample was taken of households enumerated in Sainte-Anne ward in 1871, using a standard table of random numbers and taking one household in twenty at random from within each census subdivision, thus ensuring geographical coverage. In Saint-Jacques the same process was followed, except that a 10 per cent sample was taken. The latter proved more adequate, as at times the numbers involved in Sainte-Anne proved too small for some analyses. The samples taken approximated published material on the two wards as regards place of birth, origins, and age and sex structure.

[8]Because of the small number of working wives in the two samples, I skimmed the returns for the two wards, pulling out all working wives, resident with their husbands. All institutions enumerated by the 1871 Industrial Census takers in these two wards were studied. It should be noted that industrial returns for Subdistrict 8 of Sainte-Anne ward are missing, so that the amount of industry in that ward is consistently underestimated by about 10 per cent. Public Archives of Canada, Manuscript Census, 1871, Schedule 6, Microfilm Reels Numbers 10041, 10042, 10044, 10045.

[9]On the importance of longitudinal family studies, see Tamara Hareven, 'The Family as Process: The Historical Study of the Family Cycle', *Journal of Social History*, VII (Spring 1974). In my doctoral thesis I hope to be able to trace families from 1861 to 1881. This paper represents an initial attempt to sort out some elements of the relationship between families and industrialization from the information in the 1871 manuscript census.

[10]For an excellent description of the unevenness of industrial change and the coexistence of highly mechanized and very labour-intensive industries in the 1850s and 1860s in Great Britain, see Raphael Samuels, 'The Workshop of the World: Steam Power and Hand Technology in Mid-Victorian Britain', *History Workshop*, III (Spring 1977). On early industrial development in Montreal, see especially Gerald J.J. Tulchinsky, *The River Barons: Montreal Businessmen and the Growth of Industry and Transportation, 1837–1853* (Toronto, 1977), especially chapter 12.

[11]Joanne Burgess, 'L'Industrie de la chaussure à Montréal: 1840–1870—le passage de l'artisanat à la fabrique', *Revue d'histoire de l'Amérique française* XXXI (September 1977), 198.

[12]*Ibid.*, 204; and *Manuscript Census, Industrial Schedules* 1861 and 1871.

[13]H. Clare Pentland, 'The Development of a Capitalistic Labour Market in Canada', *Canadian Journal of Economics and Political Science*, XXV (1956), 456.

[14]C. Goucy-Roy, 'Le Quartier Sainte-Marie à Montréal, 1850–1900' (MA Thesis, Université du Québec à Montréal, 1977).

[15]Just over one-third of Sainte-Anne's manufacturing and industrial enterprises reported the use of steam or water power in 1871. In Saint-Jacques, in contrast, under 5 per cent used any kind of motor power.

[16]Manuscript Census, 1871, Schedule 6. Saint-Jacques ward.

[17]*The Montreal Gazette*, 19 July 1864, 4; and *Montreal Business Sketches . . . with a description of the city of Montreal, its Public Buildings and Places of Interest* (Montreal, 1865), 18–19.

[18]*Montreal Business Sketches*, 13.

[19]*Ibid.*

[20]Royal Commission on the Relations of Labor and Capital, *Quebec Evidence*, 1889, 369. (Hereafter RCRLC, 1889, *Quebec Evidence*).

[21]For women's role in the Montreal economy from 1871 to 1891, see Suzanne Cross, 'The Neglected Majority: The Changing Role of Women in 19th Century Montreal', Susan Mann Trofimenkoff and Alison Prentice, eds, *The Neglected Majority: Essays in Canadian Women's History* (Toronto, 1977).

[22]Greg Kealey, *Hogtown: Working Class Toronto at the Turn of the Century* (Toronto, 1974), 4.

[23]The Lowell figure is from a personal communication from Francis Early. Anderson, *Family Structure in Nineteenth Century Lancashire*, 75.

[24]RCRLC, 1889, *Quebec Evidence*, 313.

[25]'Report of the United Board of Outdoor Relief for Winter 1871–72', *Ninth Annual Report of the Montreal Protestant House of Industry and Refuge* (1872), 1.

[26]The Montreal Council of Social Agencies estimated that a family required one cord of hard, best wood per week, and one cord of soft wood and coal and coal oil. See Terry Copp, *The Anatomy of Poverty: The Condition of the Working Class in Montreal 1897–1929* (Toronto, 1974), Appendix A. On the variable availability and price of fuel, see Huguette Lapointe Roy, 'Paupérisme et assistance sociale à Montréal, 1832–1865' (MA thesis, McGill University, 1972).

[27]RCRLC, 1889, *Quebec Evidence*, 290.

[28]*Ibid.*, 4 and 18.

[29]Evidence from matching personal and industrial returns.

[30]The figures presented in Table 1 and in all following tables are derived from the random samples of personal returns for each ward. The classification of occupations is based on that in Michael Katz, 'Occupational Classification in History', *Journal of Interdisciplinary History* III (Summer 1972), Table 2, modified taking into account the work of the Philadelphia Social History Project, *Historical Methods Newsletter*, IX (March-June 1976). In this table public service, private service, and commercial employee have been arbitrarily collapsed to form the 'white collar' category.

[31]See footnote 30. The percentage of the total population is from Canada, *Census of 1870–1871*, Table III. Origins of the People, 288–9.

[32]Canada, *Census of 1870–1871*, vol. III, 5.

[33]On subsequent legislation and its supplementation, see Roger Chartier, 'L'Inspection des établissements industriels, 1885–1900', *Relations industrielles*, XVII (January 1962).

[34]Manuscript Census, 1871, Schedule 6, Sainte-Anne, Subdistrict 9, 2.

[35]RCRLC, 1889, *Quebec Evidence*, 281, 315, 318, 348, 393. Evidence of Sainte-Anne cotton-mill workers.

[36]*Ibid.*, 279, 280, 317, 392.

[37]This table refers to all children resident in the two wards, not just those resident with their parents.

[38]Here the categories Professional, Proprietor, Commercial Employee, and Service, Public and Private, are collapsed to create the non-manual category.

[39]Daniel J. Walkowitz, 'Working Class Women in the Gilded Age: Factory, Community and Family Life Among Cohoes, New York, Cotton Workers', *Journal of Social History*, V (Summer 1972), 474.

[40]Tamara Hareven, 'Family Time and Industrial Time: Family and Work in a Planned Corporation Town, 1900–1924', *Journal of Urban History*, I (May 1975), 371.

[41]*Le Canadien*, 27 July 1889, cited in Jean Hamelin and Yves Roby, *Histoire économique du Québec, 1851–1896* (Montreal, 1971), 307.

[42]RCRLC, 1889, *Quebec Evidence*, 380, 397.

[43]*Ibid.*, 394.

[44]*Ibid.*, 641.

[45]*Ibid.*, 397.

[46]*Ibid.*, 103, 140.

[47]*Ibid.*, 392.

[48]Attempts to describe traditional family economies may be found in Gauldrée-Boileau, *La Paysan de Sainte-Irénée* (1861), cited in Léon Gerin, 'The French-Canadian Family—Its Strengths and Weaknesses', M. Rioux and Y. Martin, eds, *French-Canadian Society* (Toronto, 1964), 34. On the family economy in twentieth-century rural Quebec, see Gérald Fortin, 'Socio-Cultural Changes in an Agricultural Parish', Rioux and Martin, eds, *French-Canadian Society*, 94; Everett Hughes, *French-Canada in Transition* (Chicago, 1943, 1964), 172; and Horace Miner, *St. Denis: A French-Canadian Parish* (Chicago, 1939), 64.

[49]RCRLC, 1889, *Quebec Evidence*, 4.

[50]Neil Sutherland, *Children in English-Canadian Society: Framing the Twentieth-Century Consensus* (Toronto, 1976), 6, 10–1.

[51]Alison Prentice, *The School Promoters, Education and Social Class in Mid-Nineteenth Century Upper Canada* (Toronto, 1977), 35–6.

[52]*The Saturday Reader*, Montreal, IV (1867), 22.

[53]On this problem see Sally Alexander, 'Women's Work in Nineteenth Century London: A Study of the Years 1820–1850', Juliett Mitchell and Ann Oakley, eds, *The Rights and Wrongs of Women* (1976), 63–6.

[54]The following section is based on analysis of all working wives in the two wards. They numbered seventy-five in Saint-Jacques and seventy-eight in Sainte-Anne.

[55]*Report: Select Committee on the Manufacturing Interests of the Dominion*, Journals, House of Commons, Appendix III, 1874, 8, 22. (Hereafter, *Report: Manufacturing Interests*, 1874).

[56]RCRLC, 1889, *Quebec Evidence*, 284, 295.

[57]*Report: Manufacturing Interests*, 1874, 23.

[58]*Ibid.*, 36.

[59]*Ibid.*

[60]See Burgess, 'L'Industrie de la chaussure'.

[61]Manuscript Census, 1871, Personal Returns, Saint-Jacques, Subdistrict 6, Household 137.

[62]*Ibid.*, Subdistrict 2, Family 53.

[63]*Report: Manufacturing Interests*, 1874, 38.

[64]*La Minerve*, any day in April, 1872, for example, 20 April, 1. 'George Harvey, marchand de toutes espèces de Machines à coudres de première classe à point nué pour familles et manufactures'. In the same paper he advertised for a bilingual agent collector with good references.

[65]RCRLC, 1889, *Quebec Evidence*, 603–4.

[66]Manuscript Census, 1871, Schedule 6, Sainte-Anne, Subdistrict 5, 1.

[67]Manuscript Census, 1871, Personal Returns and Schedule 6, matched, Subdistrict 3, Households 105, 128, and 156.

[68]This table based on *all* working wives, not a sample.

[69]Anderson, *Family Structure*, 31, John Foster, *Class Struggle and the Industrial Revolution, Early Industrial Capitalism in Three English Towns* (London, 1974), 96.

[70]*Ninth Annual Report of the Protestant House of Industry and Refuge*, 1872, 1.

[71]On their work in the previous decade, see Roy, 'Paupérisme et assistance sociale', 115–16. Between 1856 and 1863 she reports that the Grey Nuns helped an average of 225 families in their own homes annually. The Sisters of Providence helped as many as five hundred.

[72]Michael B. Katz, *The People of Hamilton, Canada West: Family and Class in a Mid-Nineteenth Century City* (Cambridge, Mass., 1975), 244.

[73]This table is based on the samples of families. This explains why the average number of workers at stage 2 can be one, while in the previous table some working wives had children under one. The stages of the life cycle are based on those developed in Anderson, *Family Structure*, 202, modified so that whether children work or not is not defined within the life cycle.

[74]RCRLC, 1889, *Quebec Evidence*, 732.

[75]Louise Dechêne, *Habitants et Marchands de Montréal au XVII Siècle* (Paris, 1974), 416.

[76]The categories of household structure are derived from those of Peter Laslett, 'Introduction: The History of the Family', Laslett and Wall, *Household and Family in Past Times*, 31.

[77]Katz, *The People of Hamilton*, 223.

[78]Anderson, *Family Structure*, 49.

[79]Taking in boarders was not unique to Montreal. Tamara Hareven has suggested that 'at any particular point in time' the proportion of households in American cities having lodgers was between 15 and 20 per cent. 'Urbanization and the Malleable Household: An Examination of Boarding and Lodging in American Families', *Journal of Marriage and the Family* (August 1973), 460. What was apparently unique to Montreal was the high percentage of families sharing houses.

[80]Generally the census takers appear to have been careful to make the distinction between a shared address (building) and a shared household.

[81]RCRLC, 1889, *Quebec Evidence*, 606.

[82]*Ibid.*, 609.

[83]Sydney Pollard, *Genesis of Modern Management* (London, 1965), 160, 208.

[84]For an examination of changes in the family economy between 1861 and 1881 see Bettina Bradbury, 'The Working Class Family Economy, Montreal, 1861–1881', PhD dissertation, History, Concordia, 1984.

9

Sport and Canadian Society after Confederation

Colin D. Howell

The period from Confederation to the Great War saw substantial developments in the nature of sport in Canada. The increasingly formal organization and rules made it possible for a number of Canadian sports to become not only genuinely popular but highly visible. British North Americans had engaged in sports and games before Confederation, but typically in an unorganized and often highly individualistic or improvised fashion. The regional and national organization of sport, which ran parallel to the organization of the nation, was probably less a result of Confederation than a product of the impulse of the time for greater structure.

Sports like lacrosse and snowshoeing developed almost entirely within Canada to great popularity in the post-Confederation period; hockey, football, and baseball adapted European games to North American conditions. While Canadians plainly took the lead in hockey, in football and, especially, in baseball, changes occurred virtually simultaneously in both the United States and British North America. There is some evidence that Upper Canadians were playing a game with baseball-like rules in the 1830s, and precursors of baseball—like rounders—were common everywhere before Confederation.

In his analysis of baseball in the Maritimes after Confederation, Colin Howell is concerned less with the sport's origins than with its rapid expansion. He examines the linkage of baseball to Victorian ideas of respectability (see Reading 7) and other middle-class values. But baseball was played by young men from the working classes, and industrialization created an audience, often unruly, that commercialized and professionalized the game. In the later years of the nineteenth century, women and minorities (especially blacks) became involved as well, while in the early twentieth century the national debate over amateurism in sports reached baseball and the

Maritimes. Howell concludes that out of a variety of conflicts and contradictions, baseball was ultimately transformed into an acceptable kind of mass leisure.

Why did baseball expand in popularity so rapidly? What sorts of internal conflicts did it produce?

Why did professional baseball collapse in the Atlantic region? What emerged to replace it? What were the underlying issues in the amateur-professional debate? Why does the author argue it does not matter in the end which philosophy won out? Do you agree?

This article first appeared, titled 'Baseball, Class, and Community in the Maritime Provinces, 1870–1910', in *Histoire sociale/Social History* 22, 44 (November 1989), 265–86.

In the past few years, historical writing on the history of sport has concentrated upon the relationship of sport to society, rather than merely chronicling the accomplishments of great athletes or celebrating sport as a form of character building. Serious academic work, such as Tony Mason's history of Association Football, Wray Vamplew's analysis of professional sport in Victorian Britain, or Alan Metcalfe's study of the emergence of a disciplined and organized sporting culture in Canada, has drawn widely upon the insights of the 'new' social history to understand how sport shaped community identities and, yet, was shaped itself by class, ethnic and gender rivalries.[1] This analysis of the early history of baseball in the Maritime Provinces and New England looks at how the development of the game was linked to Victorian notions of respectability and to the growing discourse that emerged with respect to the public organization of play and leisure.[2] In so doing, it investigates the subtle and often unpredictable ways in which reformers, entrepreneurs, gamblers, working people, athletes and spectators shaped the game to meet their own needs. Seen in this light, the history of baseball involves what Raymond Williams refers to as the 'social relations of cultural production', social processes actively shaped by human agents, neither fully determined by nor independent of the capitalist mode of production.[3]

The study of baseball provides a useful window into the continuing redefinition of class relations, gender roles and community identity that accompanied the industrial transformation of the Maritimes in the last third of the nineteenth century.[4] Baseball's early development was closely linked to the expansion of urban centers in the region in the industrial age. Some historians have suggested that the game's appeal lay in its ability to evoke images of rural simplicity in an age of industrial dislocation;[5] others argue that the game replicated the attitudes of the industrial workplace in its emphasis on organization, precision and discipline.[6] Whatever its appeal, baseball originated and flourished in urban centers and small towns. Promoted by a group of middle and upper-class reformers who regarded sport as a powerful antidote to crime, rowdiness and class hatred, the game was played primarily by adolescents and young men who had only recently entered the world of work. But the interests of reformers and players did not always coincide. If reformers prized baseball for its blending of teamwork and individual initiative, its cultivation of the 'manly virtues' and its uplifting character, they also remained suspicious of the way in which players, spectators and speculators approached the sport.

Baseball first came to the Maritimes during the 1860s and, over the next two decades, grew rapidly in popularity, spreading from the larger metropolitan centers such as Saint John, Halifax and Moncton to smaller communities like Woodstock, St Stephen, Fredericton, New Glasgow, Westville and Kentville. Although a number of Saint John residents had earlier played pick-up games of 'rounders'—a precursor of the modern game of baseball —it was not until 1869 that Mr P.A. Melville, a prominent newspaperman, introduced baseball to Saint John. Within five years, a number of local club teams, including the Invincibles, the Mutuals, the St Johns, the Shamrocks, the Athletes and the Royals, were playing each other and occasionally challenging teams from St. Croix, Fredericton and Bangor, Maine. Organized largely along occupational, ethnic and religious lines, the teams were still exclusively amateur. As of yet, the promoters of the game thought more of its civilizing influence than its profit potential. There was little gate money, and given the limited provision for field security, spectators often crawled over and under fences to escape admission.[7]

Baseball came to Halifax at about the same time it originated in Saint John. In May 1868, the Halifax *Reporter* announced a meeting of the Halifax Baseball Club at Doran's Hotel, followed a few days later by an announcement of an organizational meeting at the Masonic Hall of another independent club and the election of the team's officers.[8] The Halifax club's first president was Dr A.C. Cogswell, a long-time proponent of organized recreation in Halifax. Like many of his contemporaries, Cogswell saw sport as a remedy to youthful idleness and indolence, and a force contributing to mental well-being and physical health. A few years earlier, Cogswell had led a campaign for a public gymnasium, which, the *Acadian Recorder* predicted, would rescue Halifax youth from 'gawking lazily at street corners to stare at passers-by, lounging about drinking saloons, smoking and guzzling' and partaking of 'other irrational modes of getting over life'. Another of Cogswell's contemporaries, Superintendent John Grierson of the Halifax Protestant Boy's Industrial School, shared this faith in the uplifting character of organized recreation. 'The necessity of providing recreation for lads of this class', wrote Grierson about the boys in his charge, 'is now universally admitted.'[10] The Industrial School sported a gymnasium and playing ground for cricket and baseball, and the boys played challenge matches against the Young Atlantas and Young Oxfords of Halifax.[11]

Table 1. Occupation of Halifax Baseball Players, 1874–1888

	Number	%
Clerks (including bookkeepers and accountants)	29	21.8
Labourers (including teamsters, janitors, messengers, seamen, porters and stable boys)	32	24.0
Tradesmen	42	31.5
Students, merchants and professionals	30	22.7

Baseball was particularly attractive to reformers because it brought into play the so-called 'manly virtues': courage, strength, agility, teamwork, decision-making and foresight. It was inexpensive and took little time to play or witness, so that 'a busy man can gain in two hours on the ball field rest and relaxation that elsewhere he would seek in vain.'[12] Another virtue, from the reformer's perspective, was that it appealed in particular to working-class youth. A sample of players whose names appeared in newspaper box-scores in Halifax, between 1874 and 1888, makes this clear. Of the 133 players whose occupation can be traced through census records and city directories, the vast majority came from working-class backgrounds. Clerks, labourers and unskilled workers made up 45.8 per cent of the sample: tradesmen such as cabinet-makers, carpenters, tailors, blacksmiths, machinists, brass-finishers, gasfitters, printers, bakers, plumbers, coopers and bricklayers comprised another 31.5 per cent: and merchants, students and professionals made up the remaining 22.7 per cent. (See Table 1.)

If baseball was basically a working man's sport, it was also a young man's game. The ages of those who appeared in box-scores for the first time ranged from a 12-year-old student to a 46-year-old physician, Chandler Crane. Most players, however, began their careers in their late teens or early twenties and few continued to play into their thirties. The average age of those appearing in box-scores for the first time was 22.6 years. Given that some continued to play after that, it is reasonable to assume that the average age of those who played the sport was somewhat higher, but did not exceed twenty-five years.

Data available with respect to the ethnic origin and religious preference of 153 players also reveals a heavy concentration of Irish Catholics on Halifax's ball diamonds. Irish and black players made up 59.4 per cent of the sample; those of English origin 20.9 per cent; Scots and Germans 7.8 per cent each. With respect to religious denominations, Catholics comprised 60.7 per cent of players (compared to slightly more than 40 per cent of the total population), Anglicans 15.7 per cent, Baptists (including African Baptists) 11.1 per cent and Presbyterians 7.8 per cent.

Working men also made up a substantial portion of the audience for base-ball games. At the end of the 1877 season in Halifax, for example, Thomas Lambert, a well-known labour leader and employee at Taylor's Boot and Shoe Factory, presented a silver ball and bat to the city champion, Atlantas, on behalf of the mechanics of Halifax. (The *Acadian Recorder* reported that the prize was offered by the mechanics of the city alone, in recognition of their dedication to the game.)[13] Lambert's involvement in baseball is intriguing. A major figure in the working-class movement, he had come to Halifax in 1865 with the 2nd Battalion of the Leicestershire regiment.[14] Soon after, he took up employment at Taylor's factory and became one of the first trade unionists in Halifax to attain international prominence. In 1869, he was elected an international officer of the Knights of St Crispin and he became First Grand Trustee of the International Lodge in 1872.[15] Although there is no evidence that Lambert ever played baseball, he was instrumental in organizing a team at Taylor's after the company defeated the shoemakers in a bitter strike at the factory. Subsequently, in September 1877, Lambert appears as scorekeeper in a game between the Crispin Club of Taylor & Company and a team representing W.C. Brennan & Co. Later in the same month, two teams from Taylor's—'Lambert's Nine' and 'Baldwin's Nine'—squared off, with the Lambert's playing to a 28–18 victory.[16]

Workers, then, were involved in the game as organizers, players and spectators. As spectators, they seemed more than willing to pay the standard 25 cents admission fee for competitive club or inter-city matches. Although not much is yet known about the impact of industrialization on the real wages of working men and women in the urban centers of the Maritimes, or upon the family wage, it is likely that factory workers such as Lambert were enjoying an increasing real income, similar to workers elsewhere in Britain and North America at this time.[17] The gradual tightening of workplace discipline, the growing separation of work and leisure and the concomitant shortening of the workday, moreover, nurtured an increased demand for organized leisure by working people and bourgeois proponents of rational recreation alike.[18] The movement of women into industrial and clerical work also led them to seek out ways to fill their leisure time, one of which was attendance at sporting events.[19] In the last quarter of the 19th century, therefore, the changes wrought by industrialization had engineered the basic prerequisite for the commercialization of baseball—the creation of an audience.

For spectators and players alike, class, ethnic and community identities, and rivalries provided an important impetus to the game. In Halifax, for example, challenge matches between the 'Mechanics' and the 'Laborers', the 'Barkers' and the 'Growlers', the 'Southends' and the 'Northends', the 'Young Atlantas' and the 'Young Oxfords', the 'True Blues' and the 'Green-stockings' involved rivalries based upon occupation, location, ethnicity and age. In addition, teams representing various employers such as the 'Heralds', the 'Recorders', the 'Chronicles', the 'Dolphins' (for Dolphin's Factory) and Taylor's Factory, sometimes served to secure an identity to the firm and, in other cases, encouraged worker solidarity. While the Taylor Factory teams seem to have been made up exclusively of working men, the Dolphins had a lineup which in addition to factory hands included manager K.J. Dolphin.[20] Now and then, novelty games attracted sizeable crowds, as was true of the match in July 1878 between the Fat-Men—Dolphin was suited up here as well—and the Atlantas, a competitive team who agreed to pitch, bat and throw left-handed in order to give their obese opponents a chance at victory. 'The match . . . was a complete success', reported the *Acadian Recorder*, 'and the crowd assembled, numbering nearly 500 persons, was kept in continual roars of laughter by the blunders and exertions of the Fat Men.'[21]

The rivalries that attracted the greatest spectator interest were those between teams representing various towns and cities throughout the Maritimes and New England. Particularly significant here was the impetus to the game provided by the completion of the Intercolonial Railway to Halifax in 1876. The Intercolonial linked the major urban centers of the region and allowed for dependability in the scheduling of challenge matches. Railway service made it possible for barnstorming New England club and college teams to tour the region during the summer, while telegraph communication allowed promoters to schedule games with touring teams in return for expenses and a guaranteed portion of the gate. By the last half of the 1870s, regional championships were being held annually. In 1875, for example, the Halifax Atlantas travelled to Saint John and defeated the Mutuals and Shamrocks of that city and, in the following year, the Moncton Invincibles travelled to Halifax to play the Atlantas and Resolutes to determine the Maritime champion. The Atlantas prepared for the match by enclosing their grounds and charging an admission fee, and before a large crowd, defeated Moncton 15 to 12.

By the 1880s, inter-urban contests had become regular fare. Indeed, when pioneer baseball player James Pender announced his retirement in 1888, after fourteen years on the most competitive Halifax teams, he could count among his appearances victories over the Saint John Mutuals and Shamrocks, the Moncton Redstockings and various other teams from Londonderry, Fredericton, Houlton, St Stephen, Bangor, and Boston.[22] By this time, too, the baseball culture of the Maritimes was becoming more intimately linked with that of New England, a hardly surprising development considering the significant exodus of young Maritimers during the seventies and eighties to the 'Boston States'.[23]

The gradual integration of Maritime and New England baseball during the 1880s brought a number of changes in the nature of the sport in this region. During the 1885 season, baseball promoters in Saint John contracted with the Queen City team of Bangor, Maine, to play a challenge match in

Saint John. Although this was an error-filled match (17 errors on one side and 28 on the other), the lopsided 17-5 victory for Bangor provided an impetus for Maritime teams to import coaches and players from the United States. During the 1888 season, the Saint John Nationals imported two college ball players, Wagg and Larabee, from Colby College, and in so doing, ushered in an era of professional baseball. The following year, three more imports, Small, Rogers, and Parsons were added to the team and the Shamrocks secured the services of Edward Kelly of Portland, Maine, and William Donovan of Bangor. In 1980, Fredericton and Moncton established professional teams, and a four-team New Brunswick professional league was established relying heavily upon imported players. The Nationals (now called the Saint John Athletic Association) discarded Rogers and signed Jack Priest, Billy Pushor, Billy Merritt and pitcher 'Harvard' Howe. The Shamrocks cut Kelly and added Jim and Joe Sullivan, Abel Lezotte, Jack Griffin and John 'Chewing Gum' O'Brien.

The development of professional baseball during the late 1880s contributed to the sharpening of metropolitan rivalries that accompanied the coming of industrial capitalism to the region. This was particularly true of the region's two largest urban centers, Saint John and Halifax, neither of which could establish a commercial industrial hegemony over the entire region. Whenever it could, the Saint John press contrasted the bustling exuberance of the New Brunswick centre to that of somnolent Halifax. A dispatch from the Saint John *Telegraph*, carried in Halifax newspapers on 31 July 1888, described games between the Nationals of Saint John and the Atlantas of Halifax as a 'very easy contract' and suggested that if Halifax remained uncompetitive, the Nats would have to go south of the border to find better competition. 'The Atlantas play good ball in the quiet town of Halifax', the *Telegraph* concluded, 'but when they come to a great city like Saint John, the noise and bustle and excitement seem to unnerve them.'[25] In the following year, when the Socials travelled to Saint John to play a challenge match during the Saint John city carnival, they were treated to a city parade which routinely burlesqued Halifax. One float was a replica of the mail steamer *Atlas* detained in fog eighty hours outside Halifax Harbour. Another was adorned with a banner 'Little Sister Halifax, Haligonian Specialties, Fog in summer, harbour skating in Winter.' When the Socials were subsequently defeated by the Saint John Club, one newspaper wrote that 'bright, active, energetic Saint John scored one against her old and unprogressive rival yesterday, and she did not require the assistance of . . . (the umpire) to make that score either.'[26]

Halifax held its own summer carnival in early August 1889. The roster of activities included a match between a New York cricket team and the Garrison team, single scull races, a Labrador whaler boat challenge, fencing and gymnastic displays, wrestling and even a mock military battle at Point Pleasant Park. The highlight of the carnival, however, was a series of baseball games between the Halifax Socials and the John P. Lovell Arms Company and Woven Hose teams of Boston. These teams were made up of players signed and paid to advertise the companies' wares, and were probably the strongest teams in the United States outside of organized baseball. The Socials fared well against high calibre competition such as this. During the 1889 season, the Socials played twenty-one matches against teams from other cities, winning eleven. In addition to the two teams from Boston, their opponents, in 1889, included Portland, Bath, Gardner and Bangor, Maine: Bates College—as 'gentlemanly a set of fellows as ever graced a diamond'—and the Boston St Stephens. In the following season, the Holy Cross Collegians, the Worcester professionals and a regular assortment of teams from Maritime centres provided Halifax with stiff competition.[27]

Although the establishment of professional baseball enhanced the calibre of competition in the Maritimes, it also raised questions about the essential purpose of sport itself. Initially, sport advocates hoped that baseball would serve, as cricket and rugby had done, to enhance 'gentlemanly' values.[28] Bedecked in uniforms that occasionally included high sneakers and bow-ties, players were often admonished against uttering derogatory remarks about their opponents and the umpire. Newspaper accounts of games regularly criticized the practice of 'kicking', or disputing an umpire's decision, and derided those players who would not accede to the arbiter's authority. Protests of calls were seen to be the responsibility of the team captain, and individual players were urged to defer to the captain's authority. The extent to which 'kicking' was criticized, however, reveals that the players themselves did not conform easily to the 'gentlemanly code' that others wished to bring to the game.

Nor were umpires always the neutral officials that they were supposed to be. Poorly trained and often not completely cognizant of the rules, umpires were frequently biased in favour of their home teams during inter-urban matches. After a game between the Saint John Nationals and the Halifax Socials in 1888, for example, the Saint John press charged umpire William Pickering, who regularly played second base with the Socials, with 'bare-faced cheating', and also alleged that a Mr F. Robinson of Halifax had bribed the umpire. Robinson admitted boasting to friends in a local hotel that he had bought Pickering, but denied actually having done so.[29] In the following year, Pickering was again the subject of criticism for his partisanship during a double-header between the Socials and a team from South Portland, Maine. Both games, said the Halifax *Acadian Recorder*, featured obviously partisan umpiring and, in the second, Pickering was calling strikes against Portland batters that were nowhere near the plate.[30]

Despite these instances of favouritism, it was generally conceded that the authority of the umpire was an essential component of the game. This was a common theme in the columns of F.J. Power, sporting editor for both the *Acadian Recorder* and the Halifax *Daily Echo,* and a well-respected umpire whose career behind the plate spanned four decades. Power's career began during the 1870s as a player for the Atlantas, but he soon turned to umpiring on a regular basis. As an umpire, Power was an authoritarian figure, respected for his integrity and decisiveness in dealing both with players and unruly fans. Even spectators came to recognize his authority. At one point, for example, Power demanded the ejection of a spectator for joking that the umpire had a glass eye. 'He simply raised his arm', said the *Acadian Recorder,* 'and a big policeman escorted . . . [the fan] out.'[31]

Incidents such as these reveal the hope of many sports reformers that baseball would encourage cultivated behaviour and respect for authority. Players were expected to approach the game in a mannerly and respectable fashion, playing for the love of the sport and avoiding disparaging remarks about their opponents. But the importation of professional players from the United States during the late 1880s raised doubts that these goals could be achieved. In July 1888, a crowd of 1,200 Haligonians, including a 'large gathering of the fair sex,'[32] turned out to see the Saint John Nationals and their star import player named Wagg. A pitcher from Colby College, playing under an assumed name in order to maintain his eligibility for college base-ball, Wagg struck one newspaperman as resembling 'the lecturer outside a side-show at the circus'. In the sixth inning, a number of 'hoodlums' tried to stop Wagg's 'continual prattle by endeavouring to irritate him . . . , but it was useless.' The same reporter criticized William Pickering, the second baseman and notorious umpire, for loud and uncontrolled language and chided Fitzgerald of the Atlantas for talking too much while guarding his base.[33]

Now and then, games degenerated into actual violence. During one game involving two Saint John teams in September 1901, pitcher Webber of the Alerts was 'grossly insulted' by first baseman Friars of the Roses, caught hold of him by the neck and shook him. There was immediate confusion, the bleacherites swarmed on the field, and fisticuffs broke out between Protestant and Catholic spectators. The second baseman, Bill O'Neil called for the cops. 'It was not nice for the people present, especially the ladies, and players should restrain themselves no matter how great the insult,' said the Saint John *Globe.* ' . . . If a player makes a habit of using nasty, insulting epithets to opposing players, he should certainly be suppressed. There is some excuse for a man who in the heat of passion shows a disposition to administer bodily punishment, but nothing but contemptuous loathing for one who prefers to waggle an unguarded and insulting tongue.'[34]

The concern of most sport reformers was that undisciplined behaviour by the players would encourage similar rowdiness amongst the audience. Pro-moters of the game especially feared the effect of unruly behaviour and 'bad manners' upon women spectators. Women, of course, were important to the future of the game, not only as patrons, but also as symbols of respectability; their attendance provided the game with the hallmark of gentility that reformers wished to establish. Boorish behaviour by male spectators, of course, undermined the quest for respectability. Aware of this, the Saint John *Progress* of 11 August 1888 apologized for the behaviour of a few boors who crowded in the press box and smoked persistently, even though ladies were present. The columnist took further pains to assure female spectators that the perpetrators of this 'crudeness' were not pressmen.[35] The *Acadian Recorder* was equally concerned about 'hoodlums', 'toughs', and 'persons of a similar character', many of whom sneaked into the grandstands and took the seats of paying patrons.[36] Soldiers from the Garrison at Halifax were another source of displeasure. During a game between Saint Mary's and the Garrison, before a crowd of 1,200 spectators, about a hundred men of the ranks 'shouted, jeered, hooted and made all sorts of remarks about the opposing players'. Noting a similar occurrence in a recent match in the United States, the columnist judged the incident in Halifax to be particularly unsavoury. In the American game, 'the language was of a more humorous nature, and there were no remarks unfit for ladies to hear as in this instance. It is said that such actions take place in Montreal', the reporter concluded, but he found no reason for them to occur in Halifax.[37]

Unruly crowd behaviour obviously contradicted the conception of base-ball as a 'gentleman's game' played before a respectable audience. Bourgeois sport reformers, many of them medical doctors, educators, ministers, or jour-nalists, hoped that the extension of organized sport to working people would help create a common culture that transcended class interest, and dreamt of a world of play where class distinctions would be eradicated. The editor of the Sydney *Record*, for exmple, believed that sport and physical exercise would help empty prisons, asylums, workhouses and relieve unemployment. With more recreation, he concluded 'a good half of our social problems might disappear.'[38] When the reality fell short of the ideal, these bourgeois sportsmen blamed the subversion of the game upon professionalism. The commercialization and professionalization of team sport, they argued, attracted less dignified members of the working class who put financial reward above the values of self-discipline, self-sacrifice and teamwork, and who indulged in various forms of desultory and unsavoury behaviour. These attitudes were no doubt confirmed when the off-field activities of two of the early imports to Saint John, James Guthrie and Edward Kelly, blossomed into a public scandal in September 1889. These two Irish-American ball players had arrived in Saint John from Maine, in the summer of 1889, accompanied by a number of young girls destined for employment in a bordello run by Mattie Perry, sometimes known as 'French Mattie'. One of the girls was a young teenager from Bangor named Annie Tuttle who had been recruited by Guthrie's companion Lizzie Duffy. When Annie Tuttle's mother travelled to Saint John in search of her daughter and reported her disappearance to the authorities, the police raided Mattie's Brittain Street house and found the young girl there. Mattie was told to leave the city at once and accompanied by Kelly, 'one of her boon companions in Saint John for some weeks', left that night on the American Express for Presque Isle, Maine. Guthrie, also 'well known in baseball circles' in both Bangor and Saint John left on the same train with Lizzie Duffy.[39]

Of greater concern to reformers than this connection between the world's oldest and youngest profession was the increasing influence that betting men seemed to exercise upon the sport. Critics of professionalism noted the greater likelihood of corruption, gambling and match-fixing among professional players, no doubt sympathizing with the Toronto *Mail*'s description of a professional as a 'double cross athlete who would cut his throat to keep his reputation as crooked if he thought that anyone was betting that he would live.'[40] Indeed, gambling was widespread and substantial sums of money changed hands, particularly in matches involving urban rivals or barnstorming clubs from the United States. Players were by no means immune from the lure of quick money and when the odds warranted, occasionally had friends place bets against them. One such incident took place in Halifax in September 1890, when a number of Saint John players threw a game against the Halifax Socials. Beginning in the third inning, a number of curious incidents raised the suspicion of many in the crowd of over 1,000. It was in that inning that a Saint John man whose money was being wagered on the Socials walked across the field to the Saint John players' bench. Shortly thereafter, the umpire, himself from Saint John, began to make calls that favoured Halifax, giving bases on balls to the Socials on obvious strikes. For Saint John, Priest the pitcher struck out by swinging at balls nowhere near the plate, and third-baseman Parsons, after hitting safely, removed his hand from the base and allowed a Socials player to tag him out.[41] This transparently fixed match, said the *Daily Echo*, provided an indication of the depth that professional players could sink to when betting men were interested.[42]

A number of reasons were given to explain the fix. In the first place, the Socials were going to Saint John the following week and a victory for the Halifax team would ensure Saint John promoters a big crowd. It was also widely believed that revenge was the motive, because the better who had fixed the match had been taken advantage of by a Halifax gambler who bet $300 on the Saint John team at two-one odds during the first game of the series. Haligonians were further outraged when a correspondent of the Moncton *Times* reported that upon returning home, a banquet was held for the Saint John players, despite their acknowledged throwing of the game. Seven of the nine men, the *Times* correspondent reported, were involved in the fix and they 'openly avow and boast of it'. At the dinner, an MPP from

Saint John chaired the festivities which included a succession of speeches glorifying the players. 'This barefaced outrage on public morals', the correspondent concluded, 'will perhaps bring a gulled public to some sense of the honour involved in professional baseball.'[43]

The thrown match at the end of the 1890 season had a devastating impact upon professional baseball in the region. Prior to that time, the elevated standard of play that accompanied the importation and payment of athletes had attracted a growing clientele. Players were performing before crowds that averaged about 1,200 in Halifax and Moncton, and about three times that number in Saint John. In the latter city, fan interest was so great that the King Street merchants installed a telephone at the baseball grounds, in August 1888, so that after each inning, the score of the game in progress could be telephoned to the DeForest and March store, at the corner of King and Germane Streets, and placed on a large blackboard which could be seen from a considerable distance.[44] This enthusiasm for the game attracted sports entrepreneurs, who with admission prices of 25 cents and an extra 10 cents for admission to the grandstand and prize purses that sometimes were as high at $500, could bring in as much as $1,500 for a single match in Saint John, or $1,000 in Halifax or Moncton.

During the 1890s, fan interest waned. In the wake of the discrediting of the game's integrity, the Halifax Socials disbanded and, through the 1890s, baseball in Halifax was played on a decidely amateur level. Rivalries between employees at manufacturing or commercial establishments, or between ethnic groups, or recreational clubs provided the community with interesting but not outstanding baseball. Matches with other city clubs or touring teams were rare, and although there were sporadic attempts to revive competitive baseball in the City, there was little enthusiasm for the professional game. In Saint John, the nineties saw the emergence of a great rivalry between two city teams, the Alerts and the Roses, the former supported largely by the Irish Catholic community and the latter appealing to an Anglo-Protestant constituency.

The collapse of professional baseball in the 1890s accompanied the diffusion of the amateur game throughout the Maritimes. In Pictou County, Nova Scotia, baseball originated as a result of the efforts of newspaperman R.S. Theakston.[45] The nineties also saw the flourishing of the game in the coal-towns of Joggins, Westville and Springhill, where baseball was an important cultural component of worker solidarity, and in 'busy Amherst', one of the most rapidly growing industrial towns in the region. 'The baseball craze has struck Springhill', said the *Springhill News and Advertiser* of 13 August 1896, 'there are about three teams at Miller's Corner ranging from 6 years of age to 60, also two teams on Herritt Road and two or three in town.' Springhill was by no means unique. Rivalries based both upon propinquity and shared occupational and cultural identities, invigorated matches between

Joggins, Springhill and Westville. Before long, towns from Truro to Annapolis were playing each other and accepting American challenges. Similar rivalries emerged in the western counties of Nova Scotia between Windsor, Kentville and Middleton; further south in Digby and Yarmouth; across the Bay of Fundy in Macadam and Woodstock; and in a number of border towns in Maine.

If the 1890s witnessed the diffusion of the sport beyond the large metropolitan centers to the smaller towns of the region, the absence of high level inter-urban competition in Halifax, Moncton and Saint John provided a boon to the development of baseball for women and racial minorities during the 1890s. In 1891, a touring ladies team from the United States caused great excitement, playing in a number of towns in the region. In Nova Scotia, the women defeated all-male clubs in Amherst, Annapolis and Middleton and before a crowd of 3,000, beat a Halifax amateur club by an 18–15 score. Tours of this sort helped secure the legitimacy of female participation in organized team sport, much to the delight of feminists such as Grace Ritchie of Halifax who regularly advocated women's greater involvement in sporting activity. The reaction to the entrance of women into baseball's male domain, however, was mixed. Those who feared the emergence of the 'new woman' were concerned that participation in sports such as baseball contradicted the ideal feminine personality, while others regarded physical training for women an antidote to nervous exhaustion or 'neurasthenia'. Prevailing notions of biology emphasized woman's nurturing character, her physical frailty and her nervous irritability, and suggested that women were particularly susceptible to an imbalance of physical and mental faculties.[47] Involvement in competitive sport and physical exercise still had its critics, but by the 1890s, there was a growing acceptance of female athleticism because it compensated for nervous debilitation.[48]

The tour of the 'Chicago Ladies', in 1891, brought the debate over women and sport to center stage. The Truro *Daily News* reported that a clergyman in New Glasgow had spoken strongly against the tour at a local prayer meeting while in Truro, a delegation of citizens unsuccessfully lobbied the Mayor to prevent the team from playing.[49] On the day of the game, the Truro newspaper noted that 'many people, doubtless, will be there to witness the antics of the girls, but if all reports be true, the propriety of attending is very questionable.'[50] After the games in Truro and New Glasgow, the local press criticized the women as frauds who could not compete on equal terms with men although they presumed to do so. 'They are nothing better than a lot of hoodlums from a crowded city', said the New Glasgow *Eastern Chronicle*, '. . . they are frauds of the first order.'[51]

Despite these criticisms, a few days later, a crowd of 3,000 assembled at the Wanderer's Grounds, in Halifax, to watch the women. In addition to the paying patrons, boys climbed electric light poles and trees outside the grounds and a crowd 'containing people of all classes of life' assembled on Citadel Hill, overlooking the field.[52] In Halifax, there was little of the hostility that accompanied the team's visit to New Glasgow and Truro. The women were popular as well in Amherst, where the victory of the girls over the local boys' team was 'both interesting and exciting'. In the opinion of the Amherst *Evening News*, there was 'nothing, whatever, here which would warrant their being refused the privilege or opportunity of playing'.[53] The Moncton *Transcript* agreed and announced the intention of local officials to invite the women to play another match in the city of their return from Nova Scotia.[54]

The tour of the Chicago team provided an important impetus to the organization of women's baseball teams throughout the region. Women were playing baseball in most of the major urban centers before 1900 and even in smaller communities such as Bocabec, New Brunswick, and Oxford, Nova Scotia, teams of women baseballists risked the wrath of the churches as they pushed forward into a formerly male sporting domain. This activity seems to suggest that the idea of maternal feminism and the doctrine of 'separate spheres' were by no means universally accepted by turn of the century Maritime women.[55]

Black teams also flourished in a number of Maritime communities during the 1890s. The most powerful of these was the Halifax-based Eurekas who during the 1890s lost only one match, that to the Amherst Royals in 1897. Other black teams active in this period were the Fredericton Celestials, the Truro Victorians, the Dartmouth Stanleys and Seasides and the Independent Stars and North Ends of Halifax. For the black minority in the region, baseball and other sports provided an avenue to respectability and relative acceptance by the white majority. Involvement in athletics created local heroes and encouraged black pride, but also offered a chance for black athletes to visit other communities in the region and demonstrate their skills. While black teams rarely played against their white counterparts, they nonetheless contributed to the more organized character of 19th-century sporting life, establishing regional championships and attracting sizeable paid gates. Although the press was inclined to emphasize the 'ludicrous incidents' that took place in black baseball, it is fair to say that the coverage of black sporting activity was one of the more positive elements in the press's treatment of the black community in the 19th-century Maritimes.[56]

If the 1890s saw the diffusion of the sport throughout the region and the emergence of women and blacks on the baseball diamond, the opening of the new century witnessed the renewed ascendancy of professional baseball in the Maritimes. Professional teams once again graced the diamonds of Halifax, Fredericton, Saint John and Moncton, and smaller communities also began importing players. Many of these imports were college students from American universities such as 'Colby Jack' Coombs, a Moncton pitcher who would later star in the major leagues and ultimately be inducted into the Hall of Fame. Others, who would play or had at one time played in the big leagues, were Bill O'Neill, the Saint John native and starting leftfielder for the Chicago White Sox in the 1906 World Series, Larry McLean of the Halifax Resolutes and Bill Hallman, a former second-baseman for the Philadelphia Athletics turned thespian, who played on the touring Volunteer-Organist baseball and theatre company team.[57]

The opening decade of the 20th century also witnessed the first connections between organized baseball activity on the mainland and on Cape Breton Island. Baseball was slow to arrive in Cape Breton, but by 1905, teams in Sydney, Sydney Mines, Reserve Mines and Glace Bay were importing players. The Sydney *Record* of 21 August 1905 reported that better baseball than had ever been witnessed on the Island was now being played, 'though the results are getting to depend too much on which team can import the most and best men.'[58] The Dominion No. 1 team was the only team in this colliery district league that chose not to import men. Crowds of 800 per game were common in Cape Breton during the 1905 season, and seeing the potential for lucrative gates, sports promoters like M.J. Dryden of Sydney began to call for a strictly professional baseball operation for the 1906 season.

Although there were those who regarded the provision of recreation to the colliers of Cape Breton as a valuable antidote to class antagonism, not everyone supported the introduction of professional baseball. The editor of the Sydney *Record* regarded it warily, thinking it a scheme of unscrupulous promoters who, in preying upon the mining districts, would encourage idle habits amongst the working class. The summer months, the editor continued, were already busy with sports, picnics, excursions and holidays which took people away from the workplace. 'We should be the last to deny to anybody a reasonable amount of recreation and a reasonable amount of holidays', the editor wrote, 'but this taking a day or a half day off at frequent intervals disorganizes the working man. England today is suffering from an excess of the sporting and holidaying spirit and she is in consequence feeling the competition of the steadier and more industrious continental nations.'[59] In taking this stand, the newspaper was echoing the position of the operators of the Dominion Coal Company who complained that the scheduling of games before 5 o'clock resulted in 'a considerable number leaving work early in the day, three or four times a week.'[60]

Another concern was that the commercialization of baseball undermined respect for the sancity of contract. Contract jumping was widespread in the early years of baseball, and without a rigorous governing body for the sport, there were few prohibitions against athletes selling their services to teams on a game-by-game basis. In a game between the Saint John Roses and Fredericton Tartars, in August 1890, for example, the Roses were without four of their players. Friars and Shannon abandoned the club to play a game for Eastport against Calais, Maine. Cunningham was in Houlton playing for the Alerts, while Bill O'Neill was at Black River training for a race for a money purse.[61]

During the same season, the Halifax Resolutes offered a sizeable sum to Fredericton's pitcher 'Harvard' Howe to pitch a single challenge match against Moncton. Due to the expense, ladies, who had earlier been admitted free, now were required to pay a fee of 15 cents.[62] The Resolutes followed a similar course later in the 1900 season, securing a pitcher by the name of Holland from the Saint John Roses to pitch against the Alerts.[63] The inability or unwillingness of clubs to enforce player contracts encouraged widespread player raiding between teams. During the 1901 season, for example, trainer John J. Mack, a professional athletic coach of the Wanderer's Amateur Athletic Club in Halifax, was implicated in an attempt to induce the star battery of the Alerts (Webber and Dolan) to jump the club and sign with the Halifax Resolutes. The Saint John *Globe* noted that Mack and Mr Nevill, who was attached to the Resolutes club, offered the players salaries higher than those presently offered in the fast New England League. 'All this goes to show', said the *Globe*, 'how the baseball craze is taking hold of Halifax; how the ring of sporting men, whose sole idea of sport is to gamble on it, are getting in their fine work and are turning the game into a money making speculation, robbing it of all that is genuine and lowering its standard to those of cock-fighting or pugilism.'[64] Without an effective regulatory body that could tighten up these loopholes, there was little hope of overcoming the problems of contract jumping. If clubs tried to enforce their contracts, the players would simply play for a release. League officials also found that the lax administration of contracts left them unable to discipline players who broke league regulations. They could only shake their heads in annoyance when players like first baseman Joe Donnelly, suspended from the Maine-New Brunswick League one week, became a regular in the lineup of the Halifax Socials the next.[65]

By the middle of the first decade of this century, then, the contradictions professional baseball presented to the dream of recreational respectability were abundantly clear. Rather than encouraging a oneness of sentiment that transcended class lines, the development of baseball seemed to reveal the worst influences of commercialism, a flagrant disrespect for the sanctity of contract, an encouragement of reckless gambling and unruly crowd activity. Competitive baseball also undermined the participatory character of amateur athletics. Rather than playing themselves, spectators preferred 'to watch a few experts whose business it is to play for the public amusement', and, in turn, while neighbouring provinces were scoured for ball players in return for 'a good salary, a lazy time and the small boys' idol', local amateur sport withered.[66]

There were other problems. On the field of play, the working men who played alongside college students seemed not to be uplifted to respectability, but in the eyes of sports reformers, posed a threat to the respectable character of young college men. This concern was by no means confined to critics of professionalism in the Maritimes. Dr E.H. Nicholas of Harvard University opposed college students playing alongside professionals in summer leagues and voiced the increasingly widespread belief that the longer a person stays in pro-ball 'the worse he becomes'.[67] Between the turn of the century and World War One, therefore, reformers made a concerted effort to separate amateur and professional sport and to define new standards of play that would distinguish professional baseball from the 'gentlemanly amateurism' of the college game. In the United States, the NCAA took steps towards this end, striking a Committee, in 1913, to rid college baseball of objectionable practices. Reporting in the following year, the Committee made a number of suggestions for changes in the game. The Committee recommended:

1) strict adherence to base-coaching rules, especially those prohibiting coaches from inciting or gesticulating to the crowd or using defamatory language;

2) enforcement of rules against blocking the runner, prying runners off base or other forms of trickery, in order to bring a decorum to the game;

3) prohibition of verbal coaching from the bench;

4) prohibition of encouragement of the pitcher from outfielders. 'Remarks of endless iteration' were deemed disagreeable to spectators, thus, encouragement should only come from the infield;

5) prohibition of catchers talking to batters;

6) restriction of indecorous or unseemly behaviour.

The report concluded that 'a college baseball game is a splendid contest of skill between two opposing nines before an academic throng of spectators. It is not a contest between a visiting team and a local team assisted by a disorderly rabble.'[68]

The debate over amateurism was equally energetic in the Maritimes by 1910. In that year, the Halifax *Herald* ran a series of fifty columns on amateurism and professionalism in regional sporting life. Much of the debate centered upon the rapid growth of professionalism in hockey, but baseball was also a matter of lively concern. The *Herald*'s position was clear. The main evil was not payment, but the system of amateurs and professionals playing alongside each other. What justification was there for promoters paying one athlete while exploiting another? This inequality of treatment encouraged amateurs to turn professional, many of whom would still be playing for the love of the game, except that someone was 'getting the green on the side'.[69] At the same time, the *Herald* admitted that working-class athletes needed compensation for lost wages and the sacrifice of time, noting the argument of a well-known Maritime catcher who pointed out that he could not afford to play ball on a Saturday afternoon without compensation for docked wages. But the same player's suggestion that the Maritimes Provinces Amateur Athletic Association (MPAAA) give up its jurisdiction over baseball and let amateurs and pros play side by side was given a hasty rejection. 'Amateurs and Pros Mix', said a headline of 25 February, 'No! No! All in chorus!'[70]

The growing support for a clearer demarcation of amateur and professional sport led the Maritime Provinces Amateur Athletic Association to tighten its regulations with respect to amateur standing. Critical here was the resignation of James G. Lithgow as President of the MPAAA and his replacement, in 1909, by a new president, Dr H.D. Johnson of Charlottetown. Lithgow, actively involved in sporting organizations in the region and at one time president of the Nova Scotia Amateur Hockey league, had often turned a blind eye to violations of amateur standing. He must have been naive, the Halifax *Herald* concluded, not to know that professionalism was widespread, particularly after a lawsuit involving a Fredericton hockey club revealed that all its players, in the 1908 season, were under salary and that many of them were playing in Nova Scotia during the 1909–1910 season.[71] As incoming president of the MPAAA, Johnston took immediate steps to separate amateur and professional play and instituted a tighter transfer rule to discourage player raiding in both hockey and baseball. Johnson's position on amateurism was to let bygones be bygones; subsequent violations of amateur standing, however would be severely dealt with. In the future, Johnson declared, there would be no reprieve. 'Once a professional, always a professional' now served as the ruling maxim of the MPAAA.[72]

Ironically, these new regulations tended not to encourage the development of competitive amateur baseball in the region, but led to a more thoroughgoing system of importing professionals, some of whom were on option from major league teams, others who continued to play ball in the summer, while attending American universities in the off-season. In 1911, a professional New Brunswick-Maine baseball league was formed which, though not formally part of organized baseball, relied heavily on players from major league organizations. A four-team professional league followed in Nova Scotia, in 1912, with teams in Stellarton, Westville and Halifax. Other independent professional teams operated in Cape Breton, Yarmouth and in the coal mining town of Springhill. The success of these leagues—in August 1912, over 8,000 spectators attended a game between the Saint John Marathons and Houlton, Maine—quickly attracted American promoters such as Frank J. Leonard of the Lynn Baseball Club of the New England league who envisaged a prosperous new league in Maine and the Maritimes.[73]

Although Leonard's initial attempt to create a regional professional league ended in failure, it was taken up once again in the spring of 1914. The new organizer was Montrealer Joe Page, sports agent for the Canadian Pacific

Railway. Operating on behalf of officials of the Saint John baseball teams, Page hoped to spearhead a new professional league in the Maritimes. This league, slated to operate as a Class 'D' circuit within organized baseball, was to include teams in Halifax, Saint John, Moncton, Stellarton and New Glasgow. Page, who also envisaged his trains transporting players and fans to and from matches, helped secure a number of name players for the new circuit, including former Boston, Detroit and Cleveland player Cy Ferry. Unfortunately for Page, when Moncton and New Glasgow demanded guarantees of $2,745 for thirty-eight appearances in Halifax and an equal amount from Saint John, yet offered none in return to the other clubs, the scheme was scuttled.[74] With the coming of the war in Europe, the prospects of reviving the experiment were permanently dashed. In future years, the distinctions between amateur and professional were strictly maintained. The Depression of the twenties and thirties ensured that professional play would no longer be the widespread phenomenon that it had been before 1914.

Between the origins of Maritime baseball in the late 1860s and the outbreak of World War One, then, life on the region's sandlots changed drastically. Emerging out of the transformation of the region that accompanied the development of industrial capitalism in the 1870s and 1880s, baseball appealed initially to bourgeois reformers intent upon establishing appropriate standards of respectability and gentlemanly play. But the gamblers, promoters, players, spectators, ethnic groups and women athletes who also played a role in shaping the game brought their own needs to the sport. By the turn of the century, therefore, most reformers recognized their inability to use baseball as a means of social control, and were beginning to demand the separation of amateur and professional play.

The results of the drive to separate amateurism and professionalism were somewhat ironic. Although successful in encouraging a clearer demarcation between amateur and professional sport, reformers such as Dr Johnson and F.J. Power were faced with the growing public acceptance of professional athletics. Yet, in the longer run, the triumph of professionalism over amateurism served the interests of the bourgeoisie just as well.[75] The period between 1870 and 1914 was one in which baseball was transformed from a cultural struggle involving reformers and 'rowdies' to a more manageable form of organized mass leisure. And, if the transformation of baseball from an instrument of socialization to that of a marketable spectacle failed to eradicate class conflict as reformers had hoped, baseball gradually became one of the unifying enthusiasms that bridged class divisions and encouraged community solidarity.[76] The roots that baseball sank in the towns and cities of the region prior to World War One, in fact, were so deep that they would nurture the sport for another half century. Only in recent years, with the coming of television and the increasing sophistication of the consumer marketplace, has baseball become essentially commodified and detached from its community roots. The result has been the withering of community baseball in the Maritimes and the incorporation of the region into a modern baseball culture of mass-produced Toronto Blue Jay caps and Montreal Expos sweatshirts. That, however, is another story altogether.

Suggestions for Further Reading

Maxwell and Reet A. Howell, eds, *History of Sport in Canada* (Champaign, Ill., 1985).
Alan Metcalfe, *Canada Learns to Play: The Emergence of Organized Sport 1807–1914* (Toronto, 1987).
Don Morrow *et al.*, *A Concise History of Sport in Canada* (Don Mills, Ont., 1989).

Notes

The author wishes to thank Ian MacKay, Keith Walden, Gerald Redmond, John Thompson, David Bercuson and members of the Halifax History Seminar for their helpful suggestions in the development of this paper.

[1]Tony Mason, *Association Football and English Society, 1863–1915,* Brighton, 1980; Alan Metcalfe, *Canada Learns to Play. The Emergence of Organized Sport, 1807–1914,* Toronto, 1987; Wray Vamplew, *Pay Up and Play the Game. Professional Sport in Britain, 1875–1914,* Cambridge, England, 1988. See also James Walvin, *The People's Game: A Social History of British Football,* Bristol, 1975.

[2]On the centrality of the idea of respectability in Victorian thought, see F.M.L. Thompson, *The Rise of Respectable Society. A Social History of Victorian Britain, 1830–1900,* Cambridge, Mass., 1988. For an appreciation of the relationship of respectability to the reform of leisure and recreation, see Peter Bailey, *Leisure and Class in Victorian England. Rational Recreation and the Contest for Control,* London, 1978; Eileen Yeo and Stephen Yeo, *Popular Culture and Class Conflict: Explorations in the History of Labour and Leisure,* Sussex, 1981.

[3]Raymond Williams, *Culture,* Glasgow, 1981, 67.

[4]The literature on the industrialization of the Maritimes is extensive. See in particular T.W. Acheson, 'The National Policy and the Industrialization of the Maritimes, 1880–1910', *Acadiensis,* 1, 2(Spring 1972) 3–28; L.D. McCann, 'The Mercantile-Industrial Transition in the Metal Towns of Pictou County, 1857–1931', *Acadiensis,* 10, 2(Spring 1981), 29–64.

[5]Allan Guttmann, *From Ritual to Record: The Nature of Modern Sports,* New York, 1978, 100–8.

[6]Steven M. Gelber, 'Working at Playing: The Culture of the Workplace and the Rise of Baseball', *Journal of Social History,* 16, 4(Summer 1983) 3–22.

[7]Saint John, *The Globe,* 14 December 1901, section 4, p. 7.

[8]Halifax *Reporter,* 9, 12 May 1868.

[9]*Acadian Recorder,* 18 July 1857.

[10]First *Annual Report,* Halifax Industrial Boy's School, 1864. See in particular the section entitled 'Amusements'.

[11]See, for example, *Acadian Recorder,* 15 October 1877.

[12]*Acadian Recorder*, 11 August 1888.

[13]*Acadian Recorder*, 11 September 1877.

[14]*Ibid.*, 7 March 1891.

[15]Knights of St Crispin, 'Proceedings of the 5th Annual Meeting of Grand Lodge, April 1872', New York: Journeymen Printer's Cooperative Association, 1872.

[16]*Acadian Recorder*, 6, 18 September 1877.

[17]For Great Britain, see E. Hopkins, 'Working Hours and Conditions During the Industrial Revolution: A Reappraisal', *Economic History Review*, XXXV, 1982. For the United States, see John Modell, 'Patterns of Consumption, Acculturation and Family Income Strategy in Late Nineteenth Century America' in Tamara K. Hareven and Maris Vinovskis, eds., *Family and Population in Nineteenth Century America*, Princeton, 1978; Clarence Long, *Wages and Earnings in the United States, 1860–1890*, Princeton, 1960.

[18]Ray Rosenzweig, *Eight Hours for What We Will. Workers and Leisure in an Industrial City*, London, 1983. The development of organized sport, amateur athletic associations and the YMCA also provided alternatives to the tavern as the focus of leisure activity. See, for example, Peter Delottinville, 'Joe Beef of Montreal: Working Class Culture and the Tavern, 1869–1889', *Labour/Le Travailleur*, 8 (1981), 34–5.

[19]Kathy Peiss, *Cheap Amusements: Working Women and Leisure in Turn-of-the-Century New York*, Philadelphia, 1986.

[20]*Acadian Recorder*, 8 July 1881.

[21]*Ibid.*, 11 July 1878.

[22]*Ibid.*, 27 September 1888.

[23]Alan A. Brookes, 'Outmigration from the Maritime Provinces, 1860–1900: Some Preliminary Considerations', *Acadiensis* 5, 2 (Spring 1976) 26–55.

[24]Saint John *Globe*, 14 December 1901.

[25]Quoted in *Acadian Recorder*, 27 July 1889. See also *ibid.*, 3 October 1889.

[26]*Ibid.*, 27 July 1889.

[27]*Ibid.*, 5 August 1889. On the Bates College nine, see *ibid.*, 8 June 1889.

[28]On the relationship between team sport and Victorian notions of manliness and the inculcation of ideals of teamwork, patriotism, courage and respectability, see Morris Mott, 'The British Protestant Pioneers and the Establishment of Manly Sports in Manitoba', *Journal of Sport History* 7, 3 (Winter 1980), 25–6; 'One Solution to the Urban Crisis: Manly Sports and Winnipegers, 1890–1914', *Urban History Review* XXII, 2 (October 1983) 57–70; Norman Vance, *The Sinews of the Spirit: The Ideal of Manliness in Victorian Literature and Religious Thought*, Cambridge, 1985; Brian Dobbs, *Edwardians at Play*, London, 1973; S.F. Wise, 'Sport and Class Values in Old Ontario and Quebec', in W. Heick and R. Graham, eds., *His Own Man. Essays in Honour of A.R.M. Lower*, Montreal, 1974. For a contemporary view, see J. Castell Hopkins, 'Youthful Canada and the Boys' Brigade', *Canadian Magazine* IV, 6, 551–66. On working-class opposition to bourgeois reformism, see Joe Maguire, 'Images of Manliness and Competing Ways of Living in Late Edwardian Britain', *British Journal of Sports History*, 3 (December 1986) 256–87.

[29]*Acadian Recorder*, 20, 21 September 1888.

[30]*Ibid.*, 30 May 1889.

[31]*Acadian Recorder*, 24 July 1900. During the 1870s Power had played and umpired games for money, but this was 'when the distinction between amateur and professional athletics was unknown in this city'. Despite subsequent protests that his earlier

actions violated his amateur standing, Power was reinstated as an amateur by the Maritime Provinces Amateur Athletic Association's Executive Committee in 1888. *Ibid.*, 23 May 1888.

[34]Saint John *Globe*, 12 September 1901.

[35]Saint John *Progress*, 11 August 1888.

[36]*Acadian Recorder*, 25 May 1900.

[37]*Ibid.*

[38]Sydney *Record*, 19 July 1905.

[39]*Acadian Recorder*, 18 September 1889.

[40]Quoted in Frank Cosentino, 'Ned Hanlan—Canada's Premier Oarsman—A Case Study in 19th Century Professionalism', *Canadian Journal of the History of Sport and Physical Education*, v 2(December 1974) 7.

[41]*Acadian Recorder*, 8 September 1890.

[42]Halifax *Daily Echo*, 11 September 1890.

[43]*Acadian Recorder*, 8 September 1890.

[44]*Ibid.*, 4 August 1888.

[45]Halifax *Chronicle Herald*, 16 August 1951.

[46]Springhill *News and Advertiser*, 13 August 1896.

[47]Carole Smith Rosenberg and Charles Rosenberg, 'The Female Animal: Medical and Biological Views of Woman and Her Role in Nineteenth Century America', *Journal of American History*, 60 (September 1973) 332–56.

[48]Michael J.E. Smith, 'Graceful Athleticism or Robust Womanhood: The Sporting Culture of Women in Victorian Nova Scotia, 1870–1914', *Journal of Canadian Studies*, 23, 1–2 (Spring-Summer 1988) 120–37; Helen Lensky, *Out of Bounds, Women, Sport, and Sexuality*, Toronto, 1986; Kathleen E. McCrone, *Playing the Game, Sport and the Physical Emancipation of English Women, 1870–1914*, Lexington, Kentucky, 1988.

[49]Truro *Daily News*, 18 August 1891.

[50]*Ibid.*, 19 August 1891.

[51]New Glasgow *Eastern Chronicle*, 21 August 1891.

[52]*Acadian Recorder*, 24 August 1891.

[53]Amherst, *The Evening News*, 20 August 1891.

[54]Quoted in the *Acadian Recorder*, 20 August 1891.

[55]Cf. Michael J.E. Smith, 'Female Reformers in Victorian Nova Scotia: Architects of a New Womanhood', MA thesis, Saint Mary's University, 1984.

[56]On the propensity to comment upon ludicrous incidents, see the *Acadian Recorder*, 14 August 1900, for a game between the Eurekas and Seasides before an audience of 250. Black baseball originated in the 1880s and by the end of the century, there was an annual regional championship, *ibid.*, 28 August, 11 September, 18 September 1900.

[57]Joseph Reischler, *The Encyclopedia of Baseball*, 5th ed. New York, 1983; Sydney *Record*, 8 August 1906.

[58]Sydney *Record*, 30 July, 21 August 1906.

[59]*Ibid.*, 2 August 1906.

[60]*Acadian Recorder*, 4 August 1906. The coal operators argued that the scheduling of baseball before 5 o'clock seriously embarrassed the company and diminished output. 'Picnics have also contributed their share of adverse influence', said the *Recorder*, 'but baseball is the principal sinner.' The company prevailed upon the league to

move the starting time to 5 o'clock from 3:30 p.m., but this proved inconvenient. The company also proposed that all games be held on Sunday, but the miners refused this interference in their leisure and opposed Sunday baseball on religious grounds. See also Sydney *Recorder*, 23 July 1906.

[61] *Acadian Recorder*, 27 August 1900.

[62] *Ibid.*, 18 July 1900.

[63] *Ibid.*, 24 July 1900.

[64] Saint John *Globe*, 25 June 1901. Born in 1870 in Chelsea, England, Mack was an accomplished coach, athletic director at Columbia College, New York, in the 1899–1900 term and trainer for the Wanderers' Amateur Athletic Club in the summer season for a number of years. Mack denied allegations of unfair practice, but admitted writing to Webber who was 'under his care in the University of Maine all last winter and spring' and who contacted Mack expressing his desire to play in Halifax. Halifax *Herald*, 26 June 1901. In 1905, Mack was hired as Yale's athletic director. *Acadian Recorder*, 15 August 1905.

[65] Saint John *Globe*, 11 August 1911.

[66] Sydney *Recorder*, 23 July 1906.

[67] Dr E.H. Nichols, 'Discussion of Summer Baseball', *American Physical Education Review* XIX, 4 (April 1914), 292–300.

[68] 'Committee on Ridding College Baseball of Its Objectionable Features', *American Physical Education Review*, vol XIX, 4 (April 1904) 313–14.

[69] Halifax *Herald*, 11, 14 January 1910.

[70] *Ibid.*, 25 February 1910.

[71] *Ibid.*, 11, 22 January 1910.

[72] *Ibid.*, 6, 7 January 1910.

[73] *Acadian Recorder*, 14, 30 August 1912.

[74] *Ibid.*, 18 April, 6, 15 May.

[75] The separation of amateurism and professionalism in athletics may be seen as part of a broader sorting out of high-brow and low-brow culture at the end of the 19th century. In this regard, see Lawrence W. Levine, *Highbrow/Lowbrow: The Emergence of Cultural Hierarchy in America*, Cambridge, Mass., 1988.

[76] Ian Gordon McKay, 'Industry, Work, and Community in the Cumberland Coal-fields, 1848–1927', pt. 1, PhD thesis, Dalhousie University, 1983, 370–3. McKay makes a similar argument with respect to baseball in the town of Springhill.

10

Canada and its Native Peoples

The Canadian government after Confederation, like its British predecessors or provincial counterparts, had no genuinely constructive policy for dealing with the aboriginal peoples who inhabited large expanses of territory, especially in the west and north. The federal government continued the pre-Confederation policy of negotiating 'treaties' with the native peoples, and creating reserves—mainly on marginal lands not desired by Europeans. In 1876 it gathered a variety of precedents, policies, and attitudes into a federal Indian Act which would shape the regulation of Indian life for generations to come. Perhaps the 1876 Indian Act's most important immediate feature was to define Indian status, and to exclude the remainder of native peoples from its coverage. For those defined as Indians, the federal government's Department of Indian Affairs continued to hope for ultimate assimilation into European society through education and the gradual settlement of Indians as small freehold farmers.

Sarah Carter discusses some of the activities of the Department of Indian Affairs through an analysis of its 'showpiece' agricultural colony at File Hills, in southeastern Saskatchewan. The File Hills colony, she argues, was one of the few reserves where the government actively pursued its declared agricultural goals. A principal concern was the tendency of educated natives to return to a traditional life style, and careful segregation was pursued at File Hills. Carter compares the colony with other model villages in British Columbia, Alabama, and elsewhere, as well as other community experiments in western Canada. She also documents the internal resistance of an outwardly conformist population to the loss of their traditional culture. The colony succeeded in the first years of the twentieth century, she argues, for a variety of reasons, but mainly because of the energy of its founder, William Morris Graham. Why was the File Hills Farm Colony regarded as so unusual? What was the distinctive purpose of the colony? What does its establishment and operation tell us about Canadian policy towards the native peoples? Were there limitations upon the success of the colony from the government's perspective?

This article first appeared, titled 'Demonstrating Success: The File Hills Farm Colony', in *Prairie Forum* 16, 2 (Fall 1991), 157–83.

'Canada's Prosperous Red Men' was the title of a 1925 article in the New York *Literary Digest*.[1] It was noted that the aboriginal people of Canada, under 'wise leadership and intelligent encouragement', made important contributions to the nation's chief industry of agriculture. Most of the item was devoted to the southeastern Saskatchewan File Hills farm colony for ex-pupils of residential schools. The colony was singled out as a fine example of the policies of the Canadian government. The scheme, credited with wonderful results, was briefly described. A portion of a reserve was surveyed into eighty-acre lots for the colonists who were each loaned $125 to buy housing material, a yoke of oxen, harness and a plough. From humble beginnings in 1901 when three colonists enlisted, by 1915 the community had grown to thirty-six farmers and their families and they had over 3,000 acres under cultivation. Readers of the *Digest* were told that the contribution of the colonists to the World War I effort was particularly noteworthy. Per capita it was higher than that of any white community in the province; with but one exception, every able-bodied man enlisted for overseas service.

The File Hills colonists were accustomed to such attention. The colony was featured in numerous journal and newspaper articles as an example of the sound administration of Canada's Department of Indian Affairs which resulted in a happy, contented, even prosperous people. During the war years the colony was used to illustrate the intense patriotism that these 'wards' exhibited in return for the kind treatment they received. A 1924 history of Saskatchewan devoted several pages to the colony, 'the solution of the Indian problem', and its founder William Morris Graham, who 'thoroughly deserved' his recent promotion to Indian commissioner.[2] Here were Native farmers with 'big barns, bank accounts and automobiles'. The two churches, hospital and farms on the colony 'would do credit to white men'. Commissioner Graham was quoted as saying that the Natives 'instead of being a leech on the country, as might be expected . . . are an asset to it'.

The greatest pride however was taken in the 'international' attention the colony received. As part of his 1914 eight-week study of the methods and policies of Native administration in Canada, Frederick Abbott, secretary of the American Board of Indian Commissioners, toured the File Hills colony. His 1915 publication, which was highly complimentary of the 'simplicity, comprehensiveness, elasticity and efficiency' of Canadian Native policy, presented the File Hills colony as the best illustration of the Canadian system.[3] Abbott's findings were boasted of for many years in the Canadian press. In a 1921 item in the Winnipeg *Free Press* it was proclaimed that the File Hills colony had become 'famous over the whole continent of America and has drawn visitors from officialdom at Washington to find out "how it is done".'[4] Many other dignitaries, including royalty, toured through the colony. Earl Grey, governor general of Canada, took a special interest and visited on several occasions, as did his successor, the Duke of Connaught.

Readers of the articles and newspaper reports of distinguished visitors to the colony might well be excused for imagining that all reserve residents in western Canada were exceedingly comfortable, if not prosperous, with homes, outbuildings and equipment comparable to those of the surrounding settlers. This was certainly the impression that the Department of Indian Affairs, and especially Graham, the mastermind of the colony, wished to convey. The colony was created with a view to the needs of the non-Native visitor. It was never intended to be a model farm for other aboriginal people. Tours for them were not arranged, nor were they encouraged to visit individually. The colony did not mark the inauguration of a more widespread scheme aimed at the improvement of living conditions on all reserves. Most prairie reserves were pockets of rural poverty. The poorly fed and poorly clad residents lived in log shacks in winter, canvas tents in summer, and attempted to farm with increasingly out-of-date and out-of-commission equipment. The colony addressed the need, long felt by government officials, to have a 'showpiece' reserve which could advertise Canada's sound administration. Through vigorous promotion of the colony the impression was left that this was representative of the work of the department.

The Department of Indian Affairs had always shown concern for public image, particularly in the wake of criticism of its activities following the resistance of 1885. Annual reports from Indian agents and inspectors of agencies were frequently 'altered by the excise of paragraphs which it is considered inadvisable to print', before they were sent to the publisher.[5] (One example was the excise of a report of a northern Manitoba agent who found children in a so-called school on one reserve squatting on the ground, huddled in a small canvas tent blackened with smoke.)[6] The department took pride especially in its sterling record in comparison to American policy, and this theme was often emphasized in the partisan press. American crimes against Natives were catalogued, and contrasted with the more just and honourable methods of Canada. The department was congratulated for the 'fairness, good faith and liberal consideration which our country has always displayed towards the aboriginal population.'[7] A very special effort to exhibit the work of the department was made at the Chicago World's Fair in 1893. Young people from Manitoba and the North West were taken to Chicago to demonstrate their skills at a variety of trades and household duties, while alongside them were displayed remnants of the 'warpath' days, including, according to one reporter 'horrid, bloody scalps'.[8] A Montreal correspondent wrote that the exhibit 'portrayed to all visitors the splendid treatment and intelligent supervision and provision of the Canadian Government for these wards of the country . . . it is an "object" lesson indeed for other nations.'[9]

Those who had an opportunity to view actual conditions on western Canadian reserves seldom boasted about Canada's treatment of aboriginal people. A missionary in the Touchwood Hills reported in 1893 that the exhibit at the World's Fair and the annual reports of the department reminded him of 'the drawing classes at school just before show or inspection day, at the end of a term. They do not convey a fair idea of the general state of the Indian, and are only a fancy picture of the situation.'[10] While the department successfully created a favourable impression of its work through newspaper reports and distant exhibitions, the question of where to send dignitaries such as the governor general when they actually visited the west in order to emerge with the same impression, had long posed a problem. Certain reserves were considered much more 'advanced' than others, but prairie conditions were unpredictable from day to day, and visiting dignitaries could be left gazing at wastelands of shrivelled up stalks dried out by hot winds or at barren fields flattened by hail. For an 1895 visit of the governor general the agent at one of the 'advanced' reserves was instructed to send word immediately 'if by any means you do not desire him to visit you, owing to failure of crops or otherwise.'[11] Other considerations had to be taken into account. Where reserve residents keenly felt certain grievances they were likely to place these before distinguished guests, particularly if they were given advance warning of the visit. Some of these problems were sidestepped for the 1901 visit of the Duke and Duchess of Cornwall and York as the department carefully staged a 'demonstration' at Shaganappi Point near Calgary, not on any reserve. Such displays however, involving the movement and provisioning of people, were expensive and regarded as disruptive to farm work.

The establishment of the File Hills colony solved the problem of where to take dignitaries. With its churches and cottage hospital, neatly whitewashed homes surrounded by vegetable and flower gardens, and tree-lined roads, the community presented a most pleasing appearance of pastoral charm, even if crops should happen to fail. This was at a time when it was difficult to find any 'advanced' reserves. Government policies of the 1890s prevented reserve farmers from using the technology required to be successful on the prairies, and brought agriculture to a standstill on many reserves.[12] A change in government in 1896 did not brighten prospects for reserve residents. The new Liberal administration slashed the budget for Indian Affairs, dismissing many employees including farm instructors and lowering the salaries of those who remained.[13] This administration showed no commitment to the advancement of agriculture on reserves. This was made vividly clear in a preoccupation with reserve land surrender, which ran counter to efforts to create a stable agricultural economy on reserves. The rationale for the encouragement of land surrenders was that Natives held land out of all proportion to their needs, that they did not effectively use this land, and that it should be placed in the hands of more capable owners.

In western Canada land surrenders were enthusiastically pursued by Graham. He handled the negotiations for the surrender of large tracts of land from the Pasquah, Muscowpetung, Cowesses and Kakewistahaw bands between 1906 and 1909, reserves in the same district as File Hills. At the same time as he urged bands to sell their agricultural land, Graham was heralded as the person who had done more than any other to promote farming among aboriginal people. 'To him,' it was boasted in a 1921 *Free Press* article, 'belongs the very proud distinction of being the first man to solve the problem of making the Indian take kindly and successfully to farming.'[14] Graham was an extremely astute promoter, conveying the impression through the colony that a great deal was being done to assist reserve farmers. The colony was a carefully orchestrated showpiece for the public, and a means of enhancing Graham's own reputation and opportunity for advancement.

The File Hills colony also demonstrated the wisdom of the government's new goals for the education of aboriginal people. The Liberal administration was skeptical of the large sums spent on education unless 'the certainty of some practical results could justify the large expense.'[15] There was concern that children were being educated 'above the possibilities of their station' and that a 'distaste for what is certain to be their environment in life' was being created.[16] Deputy superintendent general of Indian Affairs James Smart wrote in 1901 that in the western provinces especially 'it may well be that the graduates are for the present doing the greatest amount of good in the direction of elevating their race, by returning to live on their reserves, and . . . it would appear that for the large majority there is no alternative.'[17] In Smart's opinion experience had shown that graduates returned 'to the communities of their own race' and 'to all intents and purposes remain Indians, with all their deepest interests, affections and ambitions centred in their reserves.' Indian Commissioner David Laird reported in 1903 that as agriculture and stock raising were likely to be the pursuits of ex-pupils, only those skills that would prove useful in connection with farm work were to be taught to the boys, and for the girls the emphasis was to be upon practical housewifery, so that as farmers' wives they could become 'useful helpmates'.[18]

This approach to the education of 'backward races' was evident elsewhere in the English-speaking world at this time. Curriculums of 'low expectations and practical lessons' predominated. The thinking was that Native people should be taught only those subjects that would directly apply to their daily experience. Instead of giving these people unrealistic ambitions, they should be educated to return to their own rural communities where they could be the 'leaven' of civilization. The File Hills colony demonstrated to the public that the place for ex-pupils was indeed back on the reserves which they could help mould into thriving communities. The department's duty was to guard against 'retrogression', the tendency of ex-pupils to return to a traditional lifestyle once they graduated, and for this reason it was announced in 1901 that experiments were being undertaken 'in the direction of the establishment of little colonies of these graduates on their reserves, in the hope that they will not only retain for themselves the benefits received at the schools but exert a beneficial influence upon their own people.'[19]

Graham's colony scheme began modestly and without fanfare in 1901, and for several years the 'school-boy colony' was referred to as an 'experiment'. In February 1901, Graham wrote to the superintendent general of Indian Affairs asking for a share of the funds provided for the assistance of ex-pupils and a month later, $1,500 of the $2,000 set aside in the estimates that year were made available to him.[20] Graham proposed that the southeastern portion of the Peepeekisis reserve in the File Hills be subdivided into eighty-acre lots, and the survey of ninety-six of these was completed in 1902. The File Hills appears to have been chosen, not because of its agricultural suitability and potential, but because this was Graham's scheme, and he had been the Indian agent for these reserves since 1896.

The four File Hills reserves were surveyed in a grid-like fashion in the fall of 1880 for the bands of Little Black Bear, Star Blanket, Okanese, and Peepeekisis, which were predominantly Cree. It was soon recognized from the point of view of agriculture that the File Hills was a poor choice. Surveyor J.C. Nelson visited these reserves in 1884 and found that well over half the land was dotted with swamps, ponds and lakes, poplar bluffs and clumps of willow.[21] This was the western slope. In the centre of the reserves, at the height of the hills, were heavy woods. Prairie land suitable for farming was found only along the eastern slope. (See Figure 1.) Agent Allan MacDonald lamented in 1883 that the reserves were so cut up by lakes and marshes that large fields could not be made.[22] The File Hills reserves also suffered in the late nineteenth century as they were well back of the settlements that hugged the Canadian Pacific Railway, and were thus remote from any markets for labour or produce. A further disadvantage suffered by these bands was that, after the resistance of 1885, the government regarded them as 'disloyal'. Their annuities were withheld, and they were ordered to surrender their arms, which limited their abilities to hunt what game there was. The Indian commissioner at Regina, Hayter Reed, formulated a plan to break up the agency altogether, and distribute the people on other reserves in order to put an end to what was regarded as their 'fractious' behaviour.[23] Other reasons he

Figure 1. File Hills reserves, 1881. Canada. House of Commons. Sessional Papers, vol. 15, no. 6 (1881).

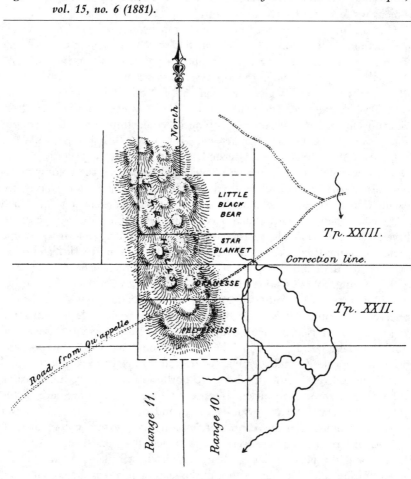

Sketch Showing Reserves in the File Hills, the dotted lines are yet to be run.

cited for this move were 'the disadvantages of the district for the cultivation of grain, the dearth of game, and the absence of a market for the industries of the Indians, and of opportunity for them to get freighting or other work.' The scheme was never implemented even though Ottawa officials concurred with Reed's view.

Matters were not quite as dismal for the File Hills people by 1900. They sold cattle, hay and seneca root, and were gradually increasing their acreage under cultivation. The establishment of a railway branch line in 1905, which ran along the southeast boundary of the Peepeekesis reserve, made this a more attractive situation as there was a ready market for grain and stock, which was formerly hauled to Indian Head, a round trip of eighty miles.

Graham and his superiors in Ottawa initially hoped that any possible obstructions to the colony plan could be removed by inducing the four bands to amalgamate, and to congregate on one, or perhaps two, of the reserves.[24] Altogether the population of the four reserves was then 234. Graham thought the bands would 'readily give their consent', but this never proved to be the case, even though the effort was made over a number of years. In 1906 Graham reported that he did everything he could think of to bring about an agreement but the Star Blanket and Little Black Bear bands would not consent.[25] Amalgamation and 'abandonment' of the Peepeekisis reserve would have allowed Graham a free hand in administering the colony; without this, he had to consult with the band. Admission to the colony, for example, had to be made through a vote of the Peepeekisis band which included all the male voting members, but in the beginning there appears to have been little difficulty getting applicants admitted. Colonists became members of the Peepeekisis band, were allowed a share in the land and other privileges of the band, and gave up membership in their band of origin.

The young colonists were all from other bands; some were from other File Hills reserves but others were from farther afield, such as St. Peter's reserve in Manitoba. It is likely that candidates were not selected from the Peepeekisis band itself as the philosophy was that colonists had to be separated from their family and associates. The colonists soon began to outnumber the original Peepeekisis band members who came to be referred to as the 'old guard'. They lived on the unsubdivided portion of the reserve, raised cattle and sold hay, wood, and pickets but grew little grain. The presence of the colony left them little opportunity to expand their industries, or to ever consider farming. After the second subdivision survey for the colony in 1906 the original band members were left with less than one-quarter of their reserve, and the portion left to them was the least suitable to agriculture. Their housing and clothing was not of the same standard as the colonists but in their appearance they served a useful function for department propaganda purposes by way of contrast as visitors could clearly appreciate what was being done for the rising generation.

In selecting the colonists, Graham worked closely with the principals of boarding and industrial schools, especially Father Joseph Hugonard of the Qu'Appelle Industrial school at Lebret, and Katherine Gillespie of the File Hills Presbyterian Boarding School which adjoined the Okanese reserve. Gillespie was appointed principal in 1902, the year after the colony was established, and she maintained an avid interest even after 1908 when she left missionary work to marry W.R. Motherwell, a local farmer and Liberal politician. Motherwell became minister of Agriculture in the first Saskatchewan government (1905–1919) and later federal minister of Agriculture (1921–1930). As his wife visited the colony regularly so did the minister of Agriculture, often giving lectures on farming, and this connection with government may account for some of the public attention the colony received over the years.

Educators and government officials were concerned with what was called 'retrogression', the tendency of ex-pupils to 'revert' to a traditional lifestyle once they returned to their reserves, or to go 'back to the blanket'. Some attributed the difficulties of ex-pupils to the chasm between student and parent created by the long period of separation. Most authorities however believed that the progress of ex-pupils was retarded not by the chasm between parents and children but by the 'proximity to, and influence of, family connections of the old type who oppose submission to the new order of things.'[26] It was part of the 'official mind' of the department of Indian Affairs to routinely blame aboriginal people for obstinately clinging to tradition, and for refusing to modify, modernize or improve their lifestyle.

There was recognition however that ex-pupils did not have the means to start farming for themselves, and the department began a program of assisting select graduates who showed an inclination to begin farming on their reserves. Aid in the way of oxen, wagons, harness, seed and materials for home building were loaned to the male ex-pupils, their value to be repaid within four years.[27] Females were given a small sum with which to purchase 'useful' articles such as sewing machines or furniture, particularly if they were married to another graduate. As a powerful incentive to return to their reserves immediately, assistance was only offered for two years from their date of discharge.[28] Indian agents were instructed in 1914 to 'carefully select the most favourable location for ex-pupils, and [they] should also consider the advisability of forming them into separate colonies or settlements removed to some extent from the older Indians.'[29] Lengthy lists were drawn up, recommending some ex-pupils as clean, industrious and worthy of assistance, and describing others as simply 'no good'.[30] There appear to have been no concerted efforts on other reserves however to establish colonies on the scale of that at File Hills. Elsewhere government officials were disappointed, even with some ex-pupils who were given assistance. The authorities generally agreed with Reverend W. McWhinney of the Crowstand Boarding School who believed that the problem lay with the proximity to the older 'lodge' Natives. 'It is not pleasant,' he wrote, 'to see our best and most hopeful boys shipwrecked by these derelicts.'[31]

The separation of the 'lodge' people from the school people was the method pursued at File Hills, extending the process begun in the educational institutions. In its discipline and daily supervision the colony was also very much like the schools. 'Hardly a day passes,' Graham wrote in 1911, 'that some officer of the department does not visit them, and if there had been success, it has been the result of this close and constant supervision.'[32] As Indian agent, Graham already enjoyed considerable authority. Agents were responsible for enforcing the Indian Act and were justices of the peace under that act. Graham was vigilant in enforcing the act, and the other rigid rules and regulations that governed the colony. Women, for example, were not allowed to visit frequently with each other as they were to be attending to their duties at home, and the use of Native languages was strictly forbidden.[33] Church personnel helped oversee the activities of the colonists. Sermons imparted correct values and attitudes such as industry, self-discipline, and punctuality. Leisure time was controlled as well. Traditional popular recreations or ceremonies, even fiddle dances, were prohibited and were replaced with a brass band, a sewing circle, and lecture groups. The colony had a fine brass band that entertained not only on the colony but in the schoolhouses and towns of the surrounding settlements. Two of the musicians were 'natural comedians' who never failed to 'bring down the house'.[34] In the winter months there were literary evenings and a Farmers' Institute which sponsored visiting lecturers. Baseball was the acceptable summer recreation, as was the annual File Hills agricultural exhibition.

A high premium was placed upon the creation of Christian family homes. One of the steadfast rules of the colony was that no couples were allowed to live together unless 'lawfully married by the laws of the country or their respective churches.'[35] When a new colonist had his house built he was encouraged to marry. It was explained that this was because 'the bachelors with no home ties soon became restless and discouraged.'[36] Only graduates of residential schools were regarded as suitable candidates for marriage. Graham explained that these women were the key to making respected and prosperous citizens out of their husbands, and it was also their responsibility to use the skills they learned at school to see their children were brought up in a 'civilized way'.[37]

The File Hills colony appears to have been unique during its time, but it bears striking resemblances to the model Christian Tsimshian village of Metlakatla established in 1862 by Methodist missionary William Duncan.[38] The residents of this village appeared to its many distinguished visitors to have completely adopted the religious and social values of Victorian England. They wore European-style clothing, attended church, worked at a variety of industries, and observed a set of strict and specific guidelines governing behaviour. They had neat white houses, gardens and picket fences. The Metlakatla system was similarly all-embracing, involving leisure hours that were devoted to brass bands, games such as football, and to the library and museum. This settlement also owed much to the authority and ambition of one man. This 'utopia' had broken down by 1887. One of the legacies of the system was a highly politicized people who pressured for recognition of their aboriginal rights and refused to recognize the authority of the Indian agent.[39]

A similar kind of model settlement called Greenwood Village was situated near the Tuskegee Institute in Alabama. This 'Model Negro Village', a residential counterpart of the institute, was intended to demonstrate 'that blacks could live in the clean, orderly, middle-class way.'[40] The colony at File Hills also bore some resemblances to the settlements advocated by individuals and charitable organizations as a means of improving and reforming the needy, the urban working class, and a wide variety of groups such as criminals.[41] The Salvation Army, for example, created farm colonies which aimed at uplifting and reclaiming the thieves, drunkards and other 'lost souls' of the city, and making honest, pious, thrifty citizens of them. In 'social settlements' such as two in Gary, Indiana in the early twentieth century, Europeans, Mexicans and Afro-Americans were weaned away from their cultures and indoctrinated with American customs and values.[42]

A wide variety of rural community experiments were undertaken in the Canadian west in the settlement era from 1885 to 1910.[43] Invariably called colonies, these ranged from the 'sacred to secular, from aristocratic and arcadian to democratic and futuristic, from ethnic to nationalist, and from conservative to communistic.'[44] Some, like the colony at Wapella sponsored by the Jewish Colonization Association, were, like File Hills, intended to demonstrate that a certain people had a capacity for farming. But the File Hills colony differed from most of these experiments as the primary motive for them was to preserve minorities persecuted elsewhere, to defend religious beliefs and customs. File Hills was established to indoctrinate a group of people to majoritarian values. In many ways they had less freedom to manoeuvre than other prairie colonists. If they withdrew or 'migrated', as a few did in the early days, they had few alternatives open to them since they had given up membership in their band of origin, and as status Indians they were not eligible to take up homesteads.

The 18-year-old pioneers of the File Hills colony in 1901 were Fred Dieter, Ben Stonechild, Marius Peekutch, Remi Crow and William Bird. Peekutch and Crow soon deserted, and Bird died of tuberculosis in 1903; Dieter and Stonechild became model colonists for others to follow. Dieter, a grandson of Chief Okanese, attended the Regina Industrial School. Graham liked to boast that this boy was taken from 'a home which is today one of the worst hovels on the reserve and where his people were purely Indian in all their habits and do no farming.'[45] Dieter had a five-room home with a basement cellar, and in 1911 he had built, on contract, one of the finest barns in the district. He kept cows, pigs and hens, had four 'magnificent Canadian horses' and a full complement of farm machinery. Dieter had a hired hand, a non-Native, whom he paid $30 per month. For many years in a row Dieter won a bronze 'challenge' shield, donated by Earl Frey in 1907 to 'the boys' of the colony. It was to go to the farmer with the best wheat crop and serve as an incentive to all members. Dieter's wife, Marybelle

Coté, a grandaughter of Chief Gabriel Coté, was the first bride in the colony. She had also attended the Regina Industrial School.

Among the other names cited in Graham's annual reports as the most successful farmers were John Thomas, Frank Dumont, John Bellegard, Mark Ward and Joseph Ironquill. Ironquill joined the colony in 1905, at the late age of 24. Graham boasted in 1914 that Ironquill's fields were a 'magnificent sight', and his buildings 'splendid'.[46] He had an enormous barn with the name of his farmstead 'Lakeview Farm' lettered on the front. Ironquill shipped grain by the carload, and in 1914 had ten head of heavy horses, twenty head of cattle, as well as pigs and poultry. He managed this farm by employing a non-Native and his wife year-round, paying them $500. Ironquill's cloths were 'made-to-order' and he used printed stationery for his business correspondence.[47] In 1917–1918 he attended the Manitoba Agricultural College to make a special study of traction engines and their management, and he became expert with motor engines, doing all his own repairs.

Not even Graham had anticipated that colony farmers would have such large operations. He initially thought that eighty acres would be adequate, and had not settled the original settlers on alternate lots. By 1907 nearly every member occupied from 160 to 240 acres. The result was that some of the farmers had a patchwork of eighty-acre lots. Ben Stonechild, for example, had one lot interrupted to the south by P. Jackson's, then the agent's, before his next lot could be reached.[48] This meant more road allowances than in ordinary townships, as well as the awkward moving about of men and machinery. By 1906 Graham alerted Ottawa that all the 'good farming plots' in the colony were taken up, and that an extension of the survey was required.[49] He felt this had to be done with some haste as he could not 'now keep the Indians from plowing fields just outside of the Colony', nor could he 'insist on men remaining in their Colony and farming inferior lands when there is better just outside the Colony that they have an equal right to.' Graham required the extended survey, which was granted, to maintain his control over the expansion of the colonists, and to permit new applicants. The fact that the 'old guard' was to have access to less and even more inferior land does not appear to have concerned officials. (See Figure 2.)

While the colony gave every outward appearance of conformity, the ideal of a model Christian settlement, there is evidence that the colonists were not prepared to give up their cultural heritage. Traditional ceremonies and rituals were carried on, despite injunctions against them. These included feasts and funerals, as well as illicit 'fiddle dances'.[50] There were persistent efforts to hold traditional dances at File Hills, although Graham and his staff attempted to break these up. An 1895 amendment to the Indian Act intended to undermine dancing and other types of ceremonial behaviour was vigorously applied in the prairie region by Graham. In February 1902 the North

Figure 2. By 1906 most of the Peepeekisis reserve was surveyed into 80-acre plots for the colonists. National Archives of Canada. National Map Collection No. 0023712.

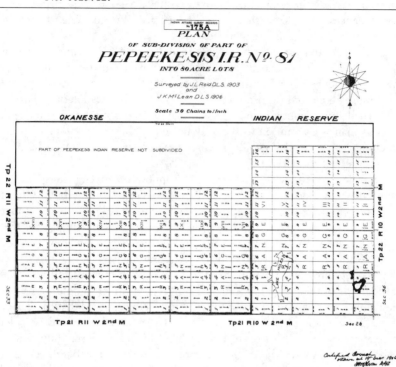

West Mounted Police were alerted to the situation at File Hills as the principal of the school there had learned that 'the Indians . . . were going to attack and destroy the school, in revenge for the Agent having pulled down a building used as a dance house.'[51] The assistant commissioner of the police explained that the Indian agent (Graham) had 'made many radical changes in the management of the Reserves, some of which, I believe the Indians resent.' The attack on the school did not take place but efforts to hold traditional dances continued, and these efforts were not confined to the 'old guard'. Joseph Ironquill headed a 1910 movement to 'start dancing on the colony'.[52] In 1914 Graham again complained that he was experiencing difficulty with 'an element who are determined to revive dancing which has been a thing of the past for the last 12 years.'[53] While he was away in Winnipeg the residents gathered for a dance which was successfully dispersed with the assistance of the clerk and farm instructor. Graham blamed the movement this time on Chief Star Blanket, who had always been 'more or less a serious drawback to progress', but was certain that dancing would not be confined to the old Natives if it was allowed to begin. A year later Graham complained that the File Hills Natives wished to go to other agencies to attend dances, and asked that these be stopped altogether, as they had a 'demoralizing' effect on the graduates.

Colonists could not simply be ousted if Graham found their behaviour unsuitable. They were expected to assist the agent to 'further the interests of the Department', but when they did not yield to this authority they could not simply be ejected from the colony.[54] Privately for example, Graham was concerned about Ironquill and believed that 'a serious mistake was made the day this man was admitted to the Colony, and if there is any way by which he could be removed it would mean a great deal for the future harmony and progress of the Colony.'[55]

It was Ironquill who also led the 1911 opposition to Graham's desire to admit fifty new colonists and change the method of admitting them. Graham encountered 'quite a lot of opposition', particularly from colony members, to the entry of new colonists.[56] He found a 'tendency on the part of these young Indians who have been doing well, not to listen so readily to advice as they did when they were in poorer circumstances.' The colonists were likely taking into consideration the expansion of their own operations as well as the needs of their children. Graham however wished to continue to be at the helm of an ongoing program for ex-pupils. He proposed that the balance of the Peepeekisis reserve be surveyed and that each of the 150 resident members be given a cash settlement of $20 'on the understanding that the Department will have the right, without reference to the Band, to admit, say sixty male graduates.'[57] (Graham was well-known for his use of ready cash as an incentive to Indian bands, and he always insisted that the department provide him with money at the time he presented documents for approval.) This money would gradually be repaid by the persons who joined the colony under this agreement. Graham wanted the new people to be settled as quickly as possible, perhaps anticipating the growth of opposition again, and proposed that funds be made available to 'grub stake' them while they were breaking land and building homes. In the past beginners had to provide themselves with provisions. In order to avoid future and further defiance of his wishes the new colonists were 'to clearly understand when they are admitted, that they must carry out the instructions of the Officers in charge.'

The law clerk in Ottawa drafted an agreement which was sent to the band for approval along with a cheque so that distribution could be made immediately. The agreement gave the superintendent general the right to locate future graduates on whatever quantity of land. To Graham's surprise the band voted against the agreement. Ironquill was blamed for this, because he resented authority according to the agent. It was reported to Graham that Ironquill 'went to the elders of the original band, who were in favour of the deal at one time and influenced them to oppose the agreement by making false statements.'[58] About a month later however, the agreement was submitted to the band again, and the necessary approval was given. It is unclear just what strategies Graham used to overcome opposition, but his persistence was rewarded and he was pleased to report that now 'one of the greatest obstacles in starting up graduates has been removed.'[59] By 1915 there were nine new admissions to the colony under the new agreement.

Among other evidence that colonists were not prepared to bow to authority was their campaign to have a day school in the settlement rather than send their children to residential schools, but once again they were unsuccessful. This had long been a grievance of reserve parents, but their opinions were seldom taken into consideration. Graham supported the colonists in this, perhaps to maintain good relations and silence opposition but also because a modern day school would make the settlement appear even more like the off-reserve communities he was always comparing it to. The children could carry their lunches to school 'as white farmers' children do'.[60] He wrote however that 'of course I am counting on the Department insisting that Industrial and Boarding schools shall not draft children from this Colony.' For a time Ottawa officials agreed that the school should be built, and that the other educational institutions would not be allowed to recruit pupils. The secretary of the department, J.D. McLean, explained that as these Natives were 'well advanced in civilization, the Department does not think it politic to separate children from their parents by lengthy periods of residence in boarding or industrial schools but on the contrary wishes to keep the home ties intact.'[61]

Father Hugonard, who was alarmed at not being able to recruit for the Qu'Appelle school, and at the prospect of Catholic children attending a secular school, was told that the department thought it well to meet the wishes of the colonists, and that the children could be trained at home in household work and agriculture, 'as is the case with the children of white people'. Hugonard quickly alerted Archbishop Adelard in St. Boniface who warned that public discussion, as well as the knowledge and consent of Parliament, was required for this departure in practice, as a secular school system could not simply be inaugurated by the department. Restrictions upon recruiting children at File Hills were hastily withdrawn. It appears that the colony did not get a day school until 1949, despite repeated requests from the residents.

The public heard nothing of what went on behind the scenes at the colony as Graham presented only those aspects that reflected well on himself and his work. In his annual reports several themes were continually emphasized. One was that the colony would compare favourably with any other community. 'I have lived in this country all my life,' Graham wrote in 1907, 'and can say without hesitation that, to my mind, no white community has made such a showing as these young people have. The style of farming here is not surpassed in any of the farming districts in the country.'[62] He stressed that Native languages were not used, that colonists attended church regularly, and that there were seldom infractions of the Indian Act. The housing on the colony was the most tangible evidence of the success of the program. All were one and a half stories so that sleeping quarters were separate from the living quarters. In the early years the homes were all made of logs which were plastered and whitewashed, but after 1910 more frame structures were built. That the 'old ways' had been left behind was also visible in the interiors of these homes which were comfortably furnished with carpets or linoleum, wallpaper, pictures on the walls, sideboards, chairs, sewing machines, clocks, and lace curtains. The annual report of the department of 1904 showed a photograph of three people at the table in Ben Stonechild's house, with the tablecloth, tea service, crystal, a pump organ, clock and calendar all in view. (Most homes on reserves at this time were one room, with rough planks for flooring, mud fireplaces rather than stoves and no furniture, not even bed-steads.) It was boasted that the women of the colony maintained their homes systematically, 'the result of the training they have received at school . . . If one would visit this colony on a Monday, one would see clothes hanging out to dry at almost every house. If one should go on Saturday, one would find them scrubbing.'[63]

Graham claimed that the colonists raised larger and healthier families, and that there was 'less sickness in this colony than there is among other Indians on the reserve, which fact is attributable, no doubt, to the manner in which their food is prepared and to the generally improved conditions under which they are living.'[64] Eight of the male colonists however died of tuberculosis before 1911, as did thirteen children. The chief medical officer, P.H. Bryce, concluded in 1911 that the men 'were almost certainly infected before enter-ing the colony.'[65] Several came from File Hills school which had a particularly high rate of death. At the end of its first sixteen years of operation 75 per cent of all pupils who had been at the school were dead.[66] The colony death rate however was not high when compared with the situation on other reserves. In his 1922 pamphlet, 'The Story of a National Crime', Bryce used the colony as his example of how under normal conditions of housing and sanitation, Native reserve populations could have a low mortality rate.[67] Bryce did not put File Hills statistics to their usual purpose—to show how healthy and prosperous reserve residents were—but used them as a means of highlighting the very different and dismal living conditions of most other aboriginal people of the west. The colonists enjoyed improved health care after 1911 when the department built an attractive 'cottage hospital', situated in the centre of the reserve. A trained nurse was placed in charge, and a doctor visited upon request. The hospital demonstrated that the young graduates put their faith in 'modern medicine' rather than in the powers of the medicine man. This too was an amenity enjoyed by few other reserve residents. There was a hospital on the Blackfoot reserve, for example, but it was run by the Roman Catholic church, not by the government.

The File Hills colonists distinguished themselves during World War I, and at this time they received their most extensive press coverage. A brief item in a 1915 issue of *Saturday Night*, 'The Fire [*sic*] Hills Indians Do Their Bit', was typical of the attention they received.[68] The work of these people, 'an example to many of paler complexion', illustrated the enthusiasm the Native people of Canada had for the cause of Great Britain. Even those who had within recent memory 'rebelled' against the Crown were now showing their loyalty and commitment, as 'among the younger men who contributed to the Patriotic Fund, were two sons and a nephew of Gabriel Dumont, a lieutenant of Louis Riel in the Rebellion of 1885.' The contributions of the farmers to the Patriotic Fund, and of the women to the Red Cross Society were detailed, and it was noted that in the surrounding towns the File Hills brass band gave concerts to raise money for the Belgian Relief Fund. It was pointed out that the older 'pagan' people were every bit as enthusiastic as the modern farming colonists. *Saturday Night* included the story of an 'aged medicine man, Kee wist [who] brought to Mr Graham a dollar one day, saying, "It's for those poor, poor people, far across the big water, who suffer so terribly from the war".'

The File Hills people were also featured in a 1916 issue of *The Courier* on 'How Dark Men Help the Empire', which was accompanied by a photograph with the caption: 'Sepoys, once enemies of England in the East, now in the trenches at Kut'.[69] Readers were told that Canadian Natives were also defending the empire. Twenty-four men from the colony enlisted, out of a total adult male population of thirty-eight, and several others wished to go but were found to be medically unfit. After rendering assistance at recruitment meetings in the province most of the brass band enlisted. Bandmaster Alex Brass was awarded the Military Cross for conspicuous gallantry in action. In 1917 Graham claimed that 'no white community in Saskatchewan . . . has given more on an average than these Indians,' and after the war it was widely circulated that 'the Indians of the File Hills Reserve . . . contributed more per capita than any other community in Canada when due allowance is made for their station in life.'[70]

With such a high rate of enlistment the war years were difficult for those who remained on the colony. Graham's correspondence for these years was full of complaints that he and his staff shouldered massive added responsibilities. They had to look after the accounts of a large number of women and children, and there were many farms which had to be kept under active operation.[71] It was impossible to place these farms in the hands of tenants because of the shortage of labour. When Graham's 1917 request to have an extra clerk at the agency was turned down he threatened to resign but his dispute with his superiors was resolved by the next year when he was appointed Indian commissioner, moved to Regina, given a greatly increased salary and placed in charge of a 'greater production' scheme, which aimed at increasing the amount of reserve land under cultivation.

World War I was the golden age of the colony, at least as far as the public attention it gained. The community was still mentioned in articles of the 1920s such as 'Canada's Prosperous Red Men', but even in this the statistics quoted were from ten years earlier. The colony's major promoter was in Regina, dealing with the affairs of many other agencies, and only visited File Hills once a year. From his distant desk Graham was frustrated by what he knew of the affairs of the colony. His targets were the agent and farm instructors whom he never found up to standard. By 1924 Graham had made up his mind to fire farm instructor Charles Wills because the agency 'had not made the progress I expected', and because Wills did not 'go round enough amongst the boys'.[72] (No matter how aged the colonists got they were often referred to by officials as 'the boys'.) Wills was given three more months and warned that he was to pursue an energetic policy.

Graham's wrath then descended upon Indian agent F.L. Deacon who was 'suspended' for two weeks in November of 1924 for deliberately ignoring instructions. According to the commissioner the cattle herd had decreased by 100 since 1920, and farming operations had increased by only 372 acres in four years.[73] This agency, Graham informed Deacon, had more employees than many others with a much larger population. (Although Graham himself had always claimed that agencies should not be graded according to the number of people supervised, and that where there were more farming Natives the office work load was much heavier.) By August 1926 Graham had turned once again on Wills who was fired for being 'much too easy going to properly handle Indians'.[74] 'The land on the colony', Graham wrote, 'is in a deplorable state, and drastic steps are going to be taken to clear the situation up.' Wills had apparently not carried out instructions with regard to wild oats and many of the fields were infested with the weed. Shortly after this, agent Deacon resigned because of ill health, and was replaced by George Dodds.

It is not certain which agent author and colonist Eleanor Brass referred to when she wrote that one of Graham's successors 'had very dictatorial methods and administered in a negative way. As a result many couples became discouraged and left the colony. Some rented their farms to white farmers and thus avoided having any business with the Indian agent.'[75] She and her husband got along well with Deacon so this was likely Dodds, who 'came in with the idea that he was either going to make a success of the reserve or break us all. He was a real dictator. It seems as though I was always fighting with him.' The Brasses, a young couple, eventually left the reserve altogether. Even some of the original colonists left their farms, especially during the 1930s. Alex Brass, for example, found work off the reserve as a carpenter. Like other reserves during the Depression, the File Hills reserves were short of equipment, horses, seed, feed, houses, and food, and hundreds of acres once under cultivation were idle.[76]

One legacy of the colony was that the Peepeekisis reserve had an unusually high population.[77] Because of this, there was little 'vacant' or 'unused' land that officials might regard as available for surrender. During the Depression however, when many fields were abandoned, there was pressure placed on the band to lease land to outsiders. It is ironic that in one case pressure to lease was put to bear by the colonists' old friend, W.R. Motherwell, who wanted some land for his farm manager.[78] Band members were very much opposed to the lease of any land as they had to first 'surrender' it, and there was concern that 'if they surrender they will not get the land back again.'[79] In order to make them change their minds, they were refused whatever assistance they were receiving from the department. As always, surrenders or leases of land were regarded by officials as of great benefit to reserve residents. Inspector of Agencies Thomas Robertson explained the reasons for with-holding assistance from the band. 'The Band can, by leasing some of this land, do a great deal to expedite improvements for themselves and children, and if they do so we will give them all further assistance possible, but I wish to make it clear that we are not wasting money by attempting to help those who will not do anything to help themselves.'[80] Not surprisingly, the band eventually consented to a five-year lease although the lease was never renewed.

By 1930, in the annual reports of the Department of Indian Affairs, any special reference to the colony as distinct from the File Hills agency had disappeared, but the settlement was still referred to as a colony as late as 1950 when the File Hills Indian Colony Day School was opened. During the 1950s however, another set of events led to the dispersal of many of the people. In the spring of 1952 some members of the Peepeekisis band pro-tested the status of the original colonists and their descendants, involving over 400 people.[81] An amendment to the Indian Act provided that if ten members of a band protested the rights of any person living on a reserve, a hearing could be held to determine if that person rightfully belonged to the band. Several Saskatchewan bands precipitated action against band members but the Peepeekisis case was unique as it involved not just one or two indi-viduals; much of the population of the reserve was threatened with eviction. If the protests had been allowed membership in the band would have been reduced from 500 to 75 or less. At stake was a loss of status and privileges, a loss of the right to farm or to live on the reserve. The action might be called the 'revenge of the old guard' as the protesters were descendants of the original band; they lived on the subdivided portion of the reserve and did not farm.[82] In 1954 a federal commission held a four-day hearing into the charges at Lorlie but reserved a decision. The controversy was not resolved until 1956 when Judge J.H. McFadden of the District Court of Melville, held an eight-day hearing and in December made his decision which preserved the status of the colonists.

During the years that the case remained in limbo the colonists became discouraged as they faced the possibility of leaving their reserve and home. Many had been resident at File Hills for over fifty years and others had been born there and knew no other home. Among the members protested were six widows, nearly all elderly, who would have found it difficult to adjust to new surroundings. Noel J. Pinay, a colony farmer and wounded veteran of World War II, told the press in September 1956 that 'this matter has been prolonged too long and has affected our people economically and morally.'[83] Ida Drake of the Women's Missionary Society wrote that 'after the first hearing many of our people lost heart and felt that there was no use in cultivating their land or improving their homes for someone else's benefit. Many left their homes altogether and took work off the reserve where possible. Band funds were also tied up due to the uncertainty of membership status, so that no help towards improvements, etc. could be obtained. During these years much of the land has become infested with weeds.'[84]

For a time however, especially during the first two decades of the twentieth century, the File Hills colony achieved a standard of living unparalleled on other prairie reserves. What factors account for this? Graham believed that this was due to the policy of the separation of the elders from the young graduates, and to the constant supervision of the colonists. He also once wrote that any success was due to the fact that the operations of the colonists had increased beyond the point where all proceeds were required to pay for such things as twine, threshing, and repairs.[85] When anthropologist David Mandelbaum visited the File Hills in 1934 the agent and clerk gave him the impression that the colony had received large infusions of money during Graham's time. Mandlebaum wrote in his notebook that

> this Agency is the old stamping ground of Graham who was Indian Commissioner for many years. As a result it has better grounds and more buildings than most Agencies . . . Graham got the idea that if only he could get the young fellows off by themselves, away from the influence of the older people, they would become 'good Indians'. And so he picked out the land in the Pipikisis [sic] Reserve and went through the schools, picking out the likely boys and getting them into the Pipikisis [sic] band. Few of the boys were full-bloods. The Colony looked good on paper because a great deal of money was pored [sic] into it. But actually there were only three or four good farmers among all the graduates of the schools on the land. When money was not put in at as great a rate, the whole business sagged badly.[86]

Voices of the Plains Cree author and Anglican priest Edward Ahenakew wrote that the key to the functioning of the colony was that the young people accepted the authority of one man, as they had learned to do in school. The colonists

> are under the guidance of an official who has more authority than most, and he is an able man whose authority these young people accept in the way to which they become accustomed in boarding school . . . I do not think that if he were asked to do the same thing again, that he would be willing. That colony is a tribute to his own ability and to his strong desire to improve the Indian, but I do not believe that it is a natural development.[87]

Eleanor Brass, who was born and raised on the colony, wrote that the achievements at File Hills 'may be attributed to the initiative of the colonists, who were allowed to conduct their own affairs,' combined with the constant encouragement of missionaries and officials. She referred to 'by-laws' that the colonists made themselves.[88]

It is unlikely that the agricultural accomplishments of the colony could be attributed to the separation of the elders from the younger school graduates. Officials customarily blamed the state of reserve agriculture on the supposed stubborn resistance of aboriginal people to change, and they overlooked economic and environmental factors, as well as the role of government policy. Although Graham regularly credited himself with introducing the aboriginal people of the West to agriculture, he arrived on the scene two decades after the beginning of reserve agriculture. Many Plains chiefs and prominent spokesmen of the 1870s, former buffalo hunters, led the way in this respect including Mistawasis, Ahtakakoop, Kakewistahaw, Day Star, Pasquah, Poundmaker, and Louis O'Soup. There was no widespread opposition to agriculture, indeed at the treaty negotiations and subsequent assemblies it was aboriginal people who insisted that they would be allowed the means to farm in return for their land. That there was very little to show for these efforts after twenty years was due to a wide variety of factors, including in some cases poor land, limited oxen and implements, seed shortages, restricted access to markets, and setbacks due to drought, frost, hail and prairie fire.[89] Government policies, particularly those of the 1890s, placed obstacles in the way of agricultural expansion. Many had very little choice but to pursue whatever other options were available including the sale of wood, hay, and seneca root, but this was not because of opposition to agriculture.

On the File Hills colony there was concern to create conditions that would allow for the establishment of agriculture, beginning with the initial loan. While loans were offered to select ex-pupils on other reserves, they were not available to any person wishing to begin farming; nor were they eligible to apply for bank loans. Spokesmen made it clear that this was a great grievance of reserve residents. Many were induced to surrender large tracts of their land in the early twentieth century largely because they were promised funds to outfit those wishing to begin farming. By 1913 however, the department declared it would no longer make loans to farmers from the land surrender money it held in trust, unless in the form of short-term loans to be repaid from the sale of the crops harvested.[90] If the crops did not cover expenses 'farming may be considered a failure and it would be unwise to continue it.' There was little concern about whether farming succeeded or not.

The issue of threshing machinery allows comparison between the situation at File Hills and on other reserves. By 1911 the colonists owned, in common, two steam threshing outfits; the department did not purchase these but the farmers were allowed to go into debt with implement dealers. On other reserves the farmers were not allowed to enter into such arrangements. Agents were told that this should not be encouraged, that they would be burdened with collecting debts, and that if one reserve was allowed to make such a purchase it would only lead to others making similar requests.[91] The equipment on reserves, particularly threshing machinery, became increasingly out-of-date and out-of-commission, and was rarely replaced. Agent H. Nichol of the Muscowpetung agency near the File Hills complained in 1913 that there was not an operable threshing outfit in his agency, and he outlined the many reasons why it was impossible for the Natives to pay for one themselves.[92] The department would not allow the farmers to purchase machinery out of capital funds derived from land already surrendered, and the only solution the agent could see was to surrender more land in order to raise the funds. The want of threshing machinery became a chronic problem throughout the prairie reserves. In 1922, for example, it was reported that the Battleford agency, which had a large acreage under cultivation, was greatly handicapped for the want of proper threshing outfits.[93] The son of a farm instructor on one western reserve recalled how difficult it was for Native farmers as they 'were fifty years behind the times in their machinery'.[94] His father 'had an awful time trying to get the Indian agent to buy even one mower for twenty-seven farmers. You can imagine how much hay was harvested with one mower.'

The File Hills colony farmers were allowed to purchase the machinery necessary to their enterprise while other reserve farmers were not. It was not so much that money was 'poured in' to the colony but that there was concern to create conditions that would allow farmers to enjoy some success. As Graham himself recognized, the colonists got beyond the point of seeing their entire proceeds going to pay their debts, and this allowed them to acquire amenities unheard of on other reserves. Because of their relative prosperity, the colonists were perhaps able to demand a greater say in the management of their own affairs, as Eleanor Brass wrote. Certainly Graham was concerned about the tendency of those who were doing well not to 'listen so readily to advice'. In his annual published reports Graham claimed to encourage this independence. He wrote in 1911 that

> particular attention is paid to the matter of giving those Indians who are able to conduct their own affairs, a chance to do so, as I consider this most essential. We have a few among those who first entered the colony who have a comparative free hand in conducting their own business. Several of these Indians have private bank accounts, which show a credit balance the year round, and against this they draw cheques from time to time.[95]

Graham may simply have been making the best of a situation that presented itself to him, as it seems unlikely that he would have encouraged such independence.

Without doubt some credit for the agricultural achievements of the colony must go to its energetic founder and promoter. Graham's constant supervision of the colonists and the dedication he demanded of his staff must have had its drawbacks, but may also have been of assistance. It is unfortunate that the same energy was not applied to other prairie reserves where farming floundered. Graham was interested in the success of farming only on the colony. Elsewhere Graham sought to alienate Native reserve lands, an initiative that most certainly worked against the best interests of reserve farming.

Suggestions for Further Reading

Sarah Carter, *Lost Harvests: Prairie Indian Reserve Farmers and Government Policy* (Montreal: 1990).

J.R. Miller, *Skyscrapers Hide the Heavens: A History of Indian-white Relations in Canada*, rev. ed. (Toronto: 1991).

E. Palmer Patterson, *The Canadian Indian: A History since 1500* (Toronto: 1972).

Notes

[1] *The Literary Digest* (New York), 7 March 1925.

[2] John Hawkes, *The Story of Saskatchewan and its People* (Regina: The S.J. Clarke Publishing Co., 1924), 104. William M. Graham was born in Ontario in 1867 and came west with his family in the 1870s. His father James Graham was Indian superintendent for the Manitoba district. He began work with Indian Affairs in 1884, first as a clerk in the Birtle and Moose Mountain agencies. File Hills was the first agency Graham was placed in charge of, in 1896, and he remained resident there for twenty-one years, although he was appointed inspector of agencies in 1904. Graham was promoted to Indian Commissioner in 1918 when he left File Hills for Regina, and retired in 1932. See E. Brian Titley, 'W.M. Graham: Indian Agent Extraordinaire', *Prairie Forum* 8, 1 (1983): 25–41; Titley, *A Narrow Vision: Duncan Campbell Scott and the Administration of Indian Affairs in Canada* (Vancouver:

University of British Columbia Press, 1986), chapter 10, 'The Ambitions of Commissioner Graham', 184–99.

[3]Frederick H. Abbott, *The Administration of Indian Affairs in Canada* (Washington: 1915), 51.

[4]*Free Press* (Winnipeg), 1 January 1921.

[5]National Archives of Canada (NAC), Records relating to Indian Affairs, RG 10, vol. 3784, file 41/61, Robert Sinclair to Edgar Dewdney, 27 July 1887.

[6]*Ibid.*, Angus Mckay's report, 4 October 1885.

[7]*The Empire* (Toronto), 19 January 1891. See also *The Tribune* (Winnipeg), 23 December 1890 and *The Week* (Toronto), 13 December 1890.

[8]*The Mail* (Toronto), 15 September 1893.

[9]*The Gazette* (Montreal), 19 September 1893.

[10]*Leader Post* (Regina), 6 July 1893 and *Mail*, 11 July 1893.

[11]NAC, RG 10, Deputy Superintendent General Letterbooks, vol. 1117, 319, Hayter Reed to Amédée Forget, 20 July 1895.

[12]Sarah Carter, 'Two Acres and a Cow: "Peasant" Farming for the Indians of the Northwest, 1889–1897', *Canadian Historical Review* 70, 1 (1989), 27–52.

[13]D.J. Hall, 'Clifford Sifton and Canadian Indian Administration, 1896–1905', *Prairie Forum* 2, 2 (1977), 129.

[14]*Free Press*, 1 January 1921.

[15]Canada. House of Commons (CHC), *Sessional Papers*, Annual Report of the Department of Indian Affairs for 1901, xxix.

[16]Jean Barman, 'Separate and Unequal: Indian and White Girls at All Hallows School, 1884–1920', in *Indian Education in Canada*, vol. 1, *The Legacy* (Vancouver: University of British Columbia Press, 1986), 120.

[17]CHC, *Sessional Papers*, 36, 27 (1901), xxix.

[18]*Ibid.* 38, 27, (1903), 238–9.

[19]Frederick E. Hoxie, *A Final Promise: The Campaign to Assimilate the Indians, 1880–1920* (Cambridge: Cambridge University Press, 1989), 196. See also Kenneth James King, *Pan-Africanism and Education: A Study of Race Philanthropy and Education in the Southern States of America and East Africa* (Oxford: Clarendon Press, 1971).

[20]NAC, RG 10, vol. 7768, file 27111-2, W.M. Graham to the superintendent general of Indian Affairs, 4 February 1901.

[21]*Ibid.*, vol. 3703, file 17,728, J.C. Nelson to Dewdney, 31 December 1884.

[22]CHC, *Sessional Papers*, 17, 4 (1883), 72.

[23]NAC, Hayter Reed Papers, vol. 21, large letterbook, no. 94, Hayter Reed to L. Vankoughnet, November 1889.

[24]NAC, RG 10, vol. 7768, file 27111-2, David Laird to the secretary, superintendent general of Indian Affairs, 30 September 1902.

[25]*Ibid.*, Graham to Laird, 31 March 1906.

[26]CHC, *Sessional Papers*, 45, 27, (1911), 347.

[27]NAC, RG 10, vol. 1392, circular letter D.C. Scott, 12 March 1914.

[28]*Ibid.*

[29]*Ibid.*

[30]Glenbow-Alberta Institute (GAI), Blood Indian Agency Correspondence, File 97, W.J. Dilworth to D.C. Scott, 1914.

[31]NAC, RG 10, vol. 4072, file 431,636, Rev. W. McWhinney to the assistant deputy and secretary, 26 February 1913.

[32]CHC, *Sessional Papers*, 46, 27 (1911), 520.

[33]Eleanor Brass, *I Walk in Two Worlds* (Calgary: Glenbow Museum, 1987), 11.

[34]W.W. Gibson, 'Indians at Work for the War', *East and West: A Paper for Young Canadians* (Toronto), 14 April 1917.

[35]Eleanor Brass, 'The File Hills Ex-Pupil Colony', *Saskatchewan History* 6, 2 (1953), 67.

[36]Alice W. Tye, 'Indian Farmers at File Hills Colony', *Nor'West Farmer*, 5 September 1912, 1169.

[37]CHC, *Sessional Papers*, 42, 27 (1907), 158–9.

[38]Jean Friesen (Usher), *William Duncan of Metlakatla: A Victorian Missionary in British Columbia* (Ottawa: National Museums of Canada, 1974).

[39]*Ibid.*, 127.

[40]Louis R. Harlan, *Booker T. Washington: The Wizard of Tuskegee, 1901–1915* (New York: Oxford University Press, 1983), 169–70.

[41]Clark C. Spence, *The Salvation Army Farm Colonies* (Tuscon: University of Arizona Press, 1985).

[42]Raymond A. Mohl and Neil Betten, 'Paternalism and Pluralism: Immigrants and Social Welfare in Gary, Indiana, 1906–1940', *American Studies* 15, 1 (1974).

[43]A.W. Rasporich, 'Utopia, Sect and Millenium in Western Canada, 1870–1940', *Prairie Forum* 12, 2 (1987), 217–43.

[44]*Ibid.*, 222.

[45]CHC, *Sessional Papers*, 42, 27 (1907), 157.

[46]*Ibid.*, 50, 27 (1914), 229.

[47]*Free Press*, March 1918, clipping in NAC RG 10, vol. 7768, file 27111-2.

[48]See the map in NAC, RG 10, vol. 6300, file 641-1, part 1.

[49]NAC, RG 10, vol. 7768, file 27111-2, Graham to J. McLean, 9 March 1906. The strip Graham recommended was three miles wide and extended to the west boundary of the reserve. It contained 120 lots of 80 acres and 12 of about 120 acres. This left 6,500 acres of the reserve unsubdivided.

[50]Brass, *I Walk in Two Worlds*, 13.

[51]NAC, RG 10, vol. 6307, file 653-1, pt. 1, J.H. McIllree to comptroller, 4 February 1902.

[52]*Ibid.*, vol. 7768, file 27111-2, Graham to J. McLean, 17 June 1911.

[53]*Ibid.*, vol. 1394, Graham to McLean, 31 July 1914.

[54]*Ibid.*, vol. 7768, file 27111-2, Graham to McLean, 17 June 1911.

[55]*Ibid.*

[56]*Ibid.*, Graham to the secretary, Department of Indian Affairs, 18 October 1910.

[57]*Ibid.*

[58]*Ibid.*, 24 July 1911.

[59]*Ibid.*, Graham to McLean, 23 August 1911.

[60]*Ibid.*, vol. 6300, file 641-1, pt. 1, Graham to Scott, 28 September 1909.

[61]*Ibid.*, McLean, 17 March 1909.

[62]CHC, *Sessional Papers*, 42, 27 (1907), 156.

[63]*Ibid.*, 46, 27 (1912), 520.

[64]*Ibid.*, 42, 27 (1907), 159.

[65]*Ibid.*, 45, 27 (1911), 285.

[66]P.H. Bryce, *The Story of a National Crime: Being an Appeal for Justice to the Indians of Canada* (Ottawa: James Hope and Sons Ltd., 1922), 4.

[67] *Ibid.*, 10–11.

[68] *Saturday Night* (Toronto), 17 April 1915.

[69] *The Courier*, 25 March 1916, in NAC, RG 10, vol. 11198, scrapbook no. 1, 1884–35.

[70] NAC, RG 10, vol. 1394, Graham to Scott, 15 January 1917, and Hawkes, *Story of Saskatchewan*, 103.

[71] *Ibid.*, vol. 4070, file 427,063-A, Graham to Scott, 12 August 1917.

[72] *Ibid.*, vol. 9131, file 306-4, Chas. Will to Graham, 14 May 1924 and Graham to F.L. Deacon, 24 April 1924.

[73] *Ibid.*, Graham to Deacon, 3 November 1924.

[74] *Ibid.*, 24 September 1926.

[75] Brass, *I Walk in Two Worlds*, 19.

[76] NAC, RG 10, vol. 9135, file 306-6, T. Robertson to C. Dodds, 7 March 1938.

[77] According to the 1929 census there were 239 colonists as well as 45 others on the Peepeekisis reserve. On the other File Hills reserves the population was much lower—Star Blanket - 58, Little Black Bear - 40, Okanese - 31. By 1947 the population on the Peepeekisis reserve had increased to 390.

[78] NAC, RG 10, vol. 9135, file 306-6, G. Dodds to Thos. Robertson, 28 February 1938.

[79] *Ibid.*, Robertson to the secretary, Department of Mines and Resources, Indian Affairs Branch, 18 January 1939.

[80] *Ibid.*, Robertson to Dodds, 7 March 1938.

[81] Saskatchewan Archives Board (SAB), annual reports of the Women's Missionary Society of the Presbyterian and United churches, 1887–1956, typescript, 84–85.

[82] *Leader Post* (Regina), 9 June 1954.

[83] *Ibid.*, 17 September 1956.

[84] SAB, Women's Missionary Society reports, 85.

[85] NAC, RG 10, vol. 1390, Graham's annual report, 4 February 1914.

[86] Canadian Plains Research Center, Dr. David Mandlebaum Fieldnotes, File Hills 1.

[87] Edward Ahenakew, *Voices of the Plains Cree* (Toronto: McClelland and Stewart, 1973), 133.

[88] Brass, 'File Hills Ex-Pupil Colony', 66.

[89] Sarah Carter, *Lost Harvests: Prairie Indian Reserve Farmers and Government Policy* (Montreal: McGill-Queen's University Press, 1990).

[90] NAC, RG 10, vol. 7596, file 10116-11, pt. 1, McLean to H.A. Gunn, 17 May 1915.

[91] GAI, Battleford agency correspondence, box 5, file 24, W.J. Chisholm to Indian agent, 22 May 1902.

[92] NAC, RG 10, vol. 1993, H. Nichol to McLean, 20 September 1913.

[93] GAI, Battleford agency correspondence, box 1, file 2, S.L. McDonald to Graham, 6 October 1922.

[94] *Ibid.*, Hart Cantelon interview.

[95] CHC, *Sessional Papers*, 46, 27 (1911), 521.

11

Canadian Nationalism

Carl Berger

The nineteenth century was the Age of Nationalism, an era that unleashed new energies in both the political and cultural spheres. Much of nineteenth-century nationalism revolved around world-wide efforts to translate identifications of commonality among people—based on language, culture, and history—into self-governing nation-states. The process involved both political unification (such as that in Germany and Italy) and political separation (such as that in the Austro-Hungarian, Ottoman, and British empires). In both cases it was assumed that people who shared common cultural characteristics should be politically embodied in a single nation. Although Canada in this period was typical in longing for political unification and self-determination, the nation-state that resulted was scarcely a product of a common cultural identity. Canadian Confederation was a political, constitutional, and economic matter, and most of the currents of cultural

'nationalism' worked against rather than towards unification. Many Canadians were conscious of the absence of a 'true national feeling' for the newly created Canadian nation, and some worked hard to find suitable myths and symbols around which a national spirit might rally.

Carl Berger points out that the climate provided one of the few experiences common to most Canadians, and not surprisingly the rhetoric of Canadian nationalism quickly focused on it. A whole series of positive national characteristics could be derived from Canada's northern location, which transcended racial differences within the country, distinguished Canadians from Americans and integrated two of the critical watchwords of the age: liberty and progress. The concept of a northern race found intellectual and scientific support in a variety of theories then in vogue, and found expression in literature and art as well as in political utterance. The theme was mythical, Berger maintains, for it rested neither on objective reality nor on universally sustainable intellectual foundations. Nevertheless it represented a powerful and compelling series of beliefs and icons that had both contemporary implications in many areas of the nation's life and a potential for survival.

Why was the northern metaphor so compelling for Canadian nationalists in the late nineteenth century? Despite its ostensible commonality among English and French Canadians, was the northern theme equally appealing to both groups? Which group appears to have identified itself more strongly with northernness? What were the racist elements in the northern theme? How did the concept of northernness affect Canadian immigration policy and social attitudes? Was northernness a myth? Does the concept still retain vitality for Canadians today?

This article first appeared, titled 'The True North Strong and Free', in Peter Russell, ed., *Nationalism in Canada* (Toronto, 1966), 3–26.

Hail! Rugged monarch, Northern Winter, hail!
Come! Great Physician, vitalize the gale;
Dispense the ozone thou has purified,
With Frost and Fire, where Health and age reside,—
Where Northern Lights electrify the soul
Of Mother Earth, whose throne is near the Pole.

Why should the children of the North deny
The sanitary virtues of the sky?
Why should they fear the cold, or dread the snow,
When ruddier blood thro' their hot pulses flow?

. . .

We have the Viking blood, and Celtic bone,
The Saxons' muscled flesh, and scorn to groan,
Because we do not bask in Ceylon's Isle,
Where Heber said, that 'only man is vile'.

. . .

But we, as laymen, must get down to earth,
And praise the clime which gave our nation birth.
Kind Winter is our theme.

William Henry Taylor,
*Canadian Seasons. Spring: Summer: Autumn:
Winter: with a Medley of Reveries in Verse
and Prose and Other Curios* (Toronto, 1913)

Everybody talks about the weather and the climate: seldom have these been exalted as major attributes of nationality. Yet from the days of the French explorers, who often remarked that the future inhabitants of northern America must necessarily be as hardy as their environment, to John Diefenbaker's invocation of the northern destiny of the nation, detached observers and patriotic spokesmen alike have fixed upon the northern character of Canada as one of the chief attributes of her nationality. Canadian national feeling, like the nationalist impulse in other countries, has expressed itself in myths and legends about the past and anticipations of noble mission in the future, as well as in distinctive economic and international policies. Such myths and symbols nourish and sustain the emotional taproot of nationalism, and impart to it an intellectual content which itself has an attractive power. The purpose of this paper is to describe the elements and savour the texture of one such recurrent theme in Canadian nationalist thought which flowered in the half century after Confederation and which is, in muted form, still with us— the idea that Canada's unique character derived from her northern location, her severe winters, and her heritage of 'northern races'.

The True North, Strong and Free

In the rhetoric of the day, Canada was the 'Britain of the North', 'this northern kingdom', the 'True North' in Tennyson's phrase, the 'Lady of the Snows' in Kipling's. 'Canada is a young, fair and stalwart maiden of the north.'[1] 'The very atmosphere of her northern latitude, the breath of life that rose from lake and forest, prairie and mountain, was fast developing a race of men with bodies enduring as iron and minds as highly tempered as steel.'[2] Canada was the 'Young giant nation of the North', the 'Young scion of the northern zone'; her people, 'Our hardy northern race'; her location, those 'Stern latitudes'.[3] These images denote not merely geographical location or climatic condition but the combination of both, moulding racial character. The result of life in the northern latitudes was the creation and sustenance of self-reliance, strength, hardness—in short, all the attributes of a dominant race. 'Northern nations always excel southern ones in energy and stamina, which accounts for their prevailing power.'[4] In the north 'the race is compelled by nature to maintain its robust attributes, mental and physical, whereas in more sunny countries like Africa and Australia the tendency of the climate is toward deterioration.'[5] 'A constitution nursed upon the oxygen of our bright winter atmosphere', exclaimed Governor-General Dufferin, 'makes its owner feel as though he could toss about the pine trees in his glee . . .'[6] Just as 'northern' was synonymous with strength and self-reliance, so 'southern' was equated with degeneration, decay, and effeminacy. Our 'bracing northern winters', declared the *Globe* in 1869, 'will preserve us from the effeminacy which naturally steals over the most vigorous races when long under the relaxing influence of tropical or even generally mild and genial skies.'[7] Moreover, it was believed that liberty originated among the tribes of northern Europe and was dependent upon those very characteristics which the northern environment called forth. Canada, then, was not only the true north, but also strong and free.

In origin, ideas about the relationship between climate and the character of 'races' and their institutions were rooted in myths and stereotypes in classical, medieval, and renaissance Europe, most of which viewed the southern Mediterranean peoples as gay, lively, and individualistic, and the northerners as stupid and dull barbarians.[8] The first coherent Canadian statement of the idea of the northern race came from an associate of the Canada First Movement who was also a Fellow of the Royal Society of Northern Antiquaries of Copenhagen, Robert Grant Haliburton. Lamenting the fact that Confederation had been created with a little excitement among the masses as if a joint-stock company had been formed, he asked, 'Can the generous flame of national spirit be kindled and blaze in the icy bosom of the frozen north?' Convinced that the indispensable attribute of a nation, a 'national spirit', was the product of slow growth unless stimulated by a violent struggle, the memory of a glorious past, or the anticipation of a bright future, Haliburton added to the Canada First spirit the contention that Canada's future as a dominant nation was secure because of its northern character. 'We Are the Northern of the New World', his lecture to the Montreal Literary Club in 1869 on the men of the north and their place in history, was the seedbed of the northern race idea. Ironically, Haliburton's poor health compelled him to spend his winters in tropical climates, where he devoted himself to ethnological and anthropological investigations. In 1887 he discovered the existence of a race of pygmies in North Africa.

Haliburton's declaration that Canadians were a northern race was expressed in the language of science and the rich imagery of romantic history. 'Our corn fields, rich though they are, cannot compare with the fertile prairies of the West, and our long winters are a drain on the profits of business, but may not our snow and frost give us what is of more value than gold or silver, a healthy, hardy, virtuous, dominant race?' The peculiar characteristic of the new dominion, he asserted, 'must ever be that it is a Northern country inhabited by the descendants of Northern races'. This claim to dominance rested on two assumptions: firstly, the hardy northern races of Europe are attracted to Canada. The British people themselves are 'but a fusion of many northern elements which are here again meeting and mingling, and blending together to form a new nationality'. This new nationality must comprise at once 'the Celtic, the Teutonic, and the Scandinavian elements, and embrace the Celt, the Norman French, the Saxon and the Swede'. Secondly, to Haliburton, the climate itself was a creative force. 'Is it climate that produces varieties in our race or must we adopt the views of some eminent authorities of science, who hold that the striking diversities now apparent in the languages, temperament, and capacities of nations, must have existed *ab initio*? The Mosaic chronology must be rejected and the period of man's life on earth must be extended to million of years.' 'If climate has not had the effect of moulding races, how is it that southern nations have almost invariably been inferior to and subjugated by the men of the north?'

The stern climate would preserve in their pristine vigour the characteristics of the northern races and ensure that Canada would share the destiny of the northmen of the old world, who destroyed Rome after it 'had become essentially Southern in its characteristics'. Those northmen were not barbarians but the carriers of the germ of liberty. 'On investigating the history of our laws and of the rise of civil and political liberty in Europe', Haliburton found them rooted in the elemental institutions of the northmen. 'Almost all the Northern nations had similar systems of regulating the rights of property and the remedies of wrongs. Their laws were traditions called by them their *customs*, an unwritten code which still exists in England where it is known as the Common law, . . . [and] it is a remarkable fact that wherever these unwritten laws have been preserved, civil and political liberty has also survived.' In Canada, 'the cold north wind that rocked the cradle of our race, still blows through our forests, and breathes the spirit of liberty into our hearts.'[9] Thus, because of the climate and because Canadians are sprung from these men of the north—the 'Aryan' family—Canada must be a pre-eminent power, the home of a superior race, the heir of both the historical destiny of the ancient Scandinavians and their spirit of liberty.

In the exuberant optimism of Canada First nationalism, Haliburton took the Canadian climate—since the days of Voltaire's famous disparagement, the symbol of sterility, inhospitality, and worthlessness—and turned it into the dynamic element of national greatness. Though he was to break with Haliburton over the issue of Canadian independence, to the end of his days the irrepressible Colonel Denison could boast that 'We are the Northmen of the new world.'[10] Charles Mair, too, thought that 'whilst the south is in a great measure a region of effeminacy and disease, the north-west is a decided recuperator of decayed function and wasted tissue.'[11] And William Foster, in his address on the new nationality in 1871, said that 'The old Norse mythology, with its Thor hammers and Thor hammerings, appeals to us,—for we are a Northern people,—as the true out-crop of human nature, more manly, more real, than the weak marrow-bones superstition of an effeminate South.'[12] It is no accident that members of this youthful and intellectual nationalist group should appeal to what Mair, in his poem on Foster's death, called 'the unconquered North', that they should extol Alexander Morris's vision of 'the Great Britannic Empire of the North', or that they should be remembered a generation later as exponents of the northern destiny of Canada. Their most practical achievement in politics was the agitation for Canadian acquisition of the northwest territory, the importance of which they contended had been obscured by tales of ice and snow falsely broadcast by Hudson's Bay Company officials to protect their fur domain from settlement.

Climatic or Racial Determinism?

While Haliburton's address included much that was to receive progressive elaboration by others, such as the notion that French and English were, in racial terms, one people, it contained an ambivalence that was to become more obvious as the idea of the northern race became enmeshed in a popularized Darwinism. This dichotomy was simply between an optimistic, idealistic meliorism which took climate as moulding desirable qualities irrespective of the racial origins of the people, and a scientific determinism which saw racial capacities as fixed, or changeable only to a limited degree. Haliburton avoided such subtleties by implying that all future immigration into Canada would consist of those races already inured and adapted to the northern environment. Later, more pessimistic writers were to see the climate as a 'barrier' to certain kinds of immigrant, rather than an agency for totally transforming them. This dualism can be best illustrated by considering two different versions of the idea.

A most forceful statement of the view that assumed the complete malleability of character was made in 1877 by another Nova Scotian, Charles R. Tuttle. A self-educated schoolteacher who later made a career of journalism in Winnipeg and the United States, Tuttle produced a large number of now forgotten books including an imposing two-volume history of Canada. In this history he expressed the optimistic opinion that the institutions, soil, and climate of Canada would determine the character of the people. The immigrants, he wrote, come from the monarchical countries of Europe, 'ignorant, rude, and unmannerly', but their character is transformed, they become self-reliant, and exhibit a 'manly independence', under the influence of British institutions and the 'broad rivers, boundless prairies, high mountains, and pathless woods'.[13]

In Tuttle, a romantic ruralism was mixed with the conviction that man's capacity for improvement was infinite and, in a favourable environment, inevitable. Where he saw the 'ignorant, rude, and unmannerly' being formed into independent and hardy yeomen by the natural features of the country and British institutions, more pessimistic observers, while not denying the potent influence of environment, nevertheless emphasized rather the inherent and unchangeable aptitudes of the 'northern races'. That the northern climate constituted a national blessing because it excluded 'weaker' races was the persistent theme of the writings and orations of the Canadian imperialist

George Parkin. A native of New Brunswick, Parkin was one of the most forceful and idealistic spokesmen of the Imperial Federation League, Principal of Upper Canada College during the late 1890s, and subsequently one of the organizers of the Cecil Rhodes scholarship trust. Heavily influenced by the social Darwinism of the time, and acknowledging his debt to the historian Buckle for the idea of climatic influence upon the life of nations, Parkin called the Canadian climate 'one of our greatest blessings'. The 'severe winter climate of Canada', he said, 'is perhaps the most valuable asset that the country has.' A temperature of twenty degrees below zero which he found at Winnipeg 'seemed to give an added activity to people's steps and a buoyancy to their spirits'. The climate necessitates vigorous effort; 'it teaches foresight; it cures or kills the shiftless and improvident; history shows that in the long run it has made strong races.'

Where Tuttle viewed the capacity for self-government as the product of the environment, Parkin contended that fitness for self-government was itself the inherent function of the northern races. Without race vanity, he asserted, we may attribute to the Anglo-Saxon race a unique aptitude for self-government. The special importance of the Canadian climate, therefore, was not merely that it sustained the hardy character of the stronger races, but that it also constituted, in Darwinian terms, 'a persistent process of natural selection'. The northern winters ensured that Canada would have no Negro problem, 'which weighs like a troublesome nightmare upon the civilization of the United States'; and it seemed that nature itself had decreed that Canada would have no cities 'like New York, St Louis, Cincinnati, or New Orleans which attract even the vagrant population of Italy and other countries of Southern Europe'. 'Canada', Parkin emphasized, 'will belong to the sturdy races of the North-Saxon, and Celt, Scandinavian, Dane and Northern German, fighting their way under conditions sometimes rather more severe than those to which they have been accustomed in their old homes.' The climate 'is certain, in short, to secure for the Dominion and perpetuate there the vigour of the best northern races'.[14]

The Advantages of Northernness

To recapitulate and detail the elements of this concept is to indicate the basis of its credibility and the nature of its appeal. First of all, the very fact of northernness connoted strength and hardihood, vigour and purity. 'Strength and power', ran the familiar refrain, 'have ever been with the Northern peoples.'[15] In the struggle for existence, the northern conditions called forth the virtues of self-reliance and strength: only the fittest survived. On the other hand, the 'south' conjured up the image of enervation, of abundance stifling the Victorian values of self-help, work, and thrift, of effeminacy, of voluptuous living, and consequently of the decay and degeneration of character.

A whole series of desirable national characteristics were derived from Canada's northern location. It was implied that northern peoples expressed their hard individualism in an individualistic religion, stripped of the gorgeous luxuries congenial to southern Catholicism. The climate, said Parkin, imparts 'a Puritan turn of mind which gives moral strenuousness'.[16] A Methodist clergyman and editor, who attended the American centennial exhibition in 1876 and saw a representative collection of European paintings, reported his disgust with the Catholic art of the south, a reaction he attributed to the lax morals of the 'Latin' races. 'I must', he wrote, 'record my protest against the sensuous character of many of the foreign paintings, especially of France, Austria, and Spain. In this respect they are in striking contrast with the almost universal chaste and modest character of the English and American pictures, and those of Rothern [*sic*, Northern] Europe. I attribute this difference partly to the only partial moral restraints of the Roman Catholic religion, and partly to a survival, in the old Latin races, of the ancient pagan characteristics which created the odious art and literature, and social corruptions of the effete and dying Roman Empire.'[17] These impurities, of course, were due to much else besides climate, but the clear, cold, and frosty air itself seemed an insulation against lax morality. Another clergyman found in the Canadian winter the impulse to cultural and mental improvement. The winter 'is prophetic . . . of a race, in mind and body and moral culture, of the highest type'. Applying to Canada the remarks that Sir Charles Dilke had made in reference to Scotland, the Reverend F.A. Wightman cited with approval the opinion that the ' "long winters cultivate thrift, energy and fore-thought, without which civilization would perish, and at the same time give leisure for reading and study. So the Scottish, the Icelanders, the Swedes, and the northern races generally, are much better educated than the Latin and southern races." '[18]

The Canadian winter was not only considered to be conducive to mental improvement: in maintaining physical health and stimulating robustness, according to one of the foremost Canadian physicians of the day, it was unsurpassed. A belief in the healthful qualities of the climate was expressed in much of the literature on the northern theme, but it was left to a surgeon at the Hôtel-Dieu in Montreal to impart to this idea the authority of medical knowledge and statistical proof. William Hales Hingston had studied medicine at McGill and Edinburgh, as well as Berlin, Heidelberg, and Vienna; in 1854 he began practice in Montreal and was for many years surgeon at the largest hospital in Canada and a professor of clinical surgery at the Montreal School of Medicine. In 1884 Hingston published a series of papers under the title, *The Climate of Canada and its Relation to Life and Health.* Employing statistics provided by the surgeons at British and American army stations, he ascertained that as one passed northward the salubrity of the climate increased, that the ratios of mortality from digestive, respiratory, and nervous disorders decreased in a northward progression. After considering practically every known malady from diarrhoea to dysentery, consumption to cataract, he emphasized that there are no diseases indigenous to the country. The dry air and cold winter, moreover, are decided recuperators of disease. 'Indeed,' he concluded, 'in considering the few diseases which here afflict humanity relatively to elsewhere, we have great reason to be thankful to the All-powerful Controller of the seasons as of our fate. . . . He keeps us in health, comfort and safety.' If only such pernicious social habits as intemperance could be avoided, the climate was most 'favourable to the highest development of a hardy, long-lived, intelligent people'; the tendency 'is unmistakably in favour of increased muscular development'; 'the future occupants of the soil will be taller, straighter, leaner people—hair darker and drier and coarser; muscles more tendinous and prominent and less cushioned . . .' These future occupants of the soil will be, emphatically, a '*Canadian* people', for the distinct nationalities of Europe will blend here into a homogeneous race, the predominating characteristics of which will be determined 'after the fashion described by Darwin as the struggle for existence'. To this people 'will belong the privilege, the great privilege, of aiding in erecting, in what was so lately a wilderness, a monument of liberty and civilization, broader, deeper, firmer, than has ever yet been raised by the hand of man'.[19] There was much in Hingston's book—description of the variety of the climate, reflections on social habits, and the straight-faced observation that those frozen to death display on their visages a look of contentment achieved only by successful religious mystics—but its central burden was that the northern location will breed a distinctive, superior, and healthy people.

It seemed that scarcely any advantages accruing to Canada from the winter season went unnoticed or unsung. The winter snow covers and protects fall crops; the frost acts as a solvent on the soil, ploughing the ground and leaving it in springtime 'completely pulverized'; the cold freezes newly killed livestock and preserves them for market. It makes possible the commercial activity of lumbering, for the 'frost makes bridges without a cent of cost; the snow provides the best roads', 'the whole face of the country being literally Macadamized by nature'. Winter makes possible sleighing, tobogganing, snowshoeing, and skating. 'Jack Frost effectually and gratuitously guards us on three thousand miles of our northern coast, and in this he does us a distinct service, greatly relieving national expenditure and contributing much to our sense of security.'[20]

A Basis For Racial Unity

While Canada's northernness implied these desirable national advantages, in its second aspect it underlined the fundamental unity of the French and

British Canadians. According to most definitions of nationality offered in the late nineteenth century, a nation was held together by the ties of race, religion, and language, as well as by a general similarity in political and social institutions. The very existence of the French Canadians, however, and the 'racial conflict' and disunity their distinctive social and religious institutions helped to engender, seemed to belie the contention that Canada was a nation.

But the French Canadians, by the very facts of their colonization, settlement, and multiplication, had demonstrated their fitness to cope with the inhospitable northern environment. The stern climate and the winds of winter were uniform on both sides of the Ottawa River. The 'geographical contour of our Country', said F.B. Cumberland, Vice-President of the National Club of Toronto, 'assists by creating a Unity of Race. Living throughout in a region wherein winter is everywhere a distinct season of the year, inuring the body and stimulating to exertion, we are by nature led to be a provident, a thrifty, and a hardy people; no weakling can thrive among us, we must be as vigorous as our climate.' Through the 'natural selection' of immigration, only the northern races, including the 'Norman French', have settled here, and what selective immigration has effected 'nature is welding together into Unity and by this very similarity of climate creating in Canada a homogeneous Race, sturdy in frame, stable in character, which will be to America what their forefathers, the Northmen of old, were to the continent of Europe.'[21]

It was argued, moreover, that 'there is no real or vital difference in the origin of these two races; back beyond the foreground of history they were one.'[22] This identification of the common racial origin of both the British and French Canadians rested on the results of the research of genealogists, like Benjamin Sulte and Cyprien Tanguay, who had inquired into the origins of the original immigrants to New France. Between 1871 and 1890 Tanguay compiled no less than seven volumes of his *Dictionnaire généalogique des familles canadiennes* and demonstrated that the majority of French Canadians were descended from immigrants who had come from Brittany and Normandy. The 'French Canadian type', declared Sulte, 'is Norman, whether its origin be pure Norman, mixed Norman, Gascon or French-English.'[23] Since the Normans themselves were descendants of the Scandinavian invaders of the ninth and tenth centuries who had gone to conquer Britain, it could be claimed that both British and French were a northern race, or at least that both contained elements of the northern strains. It is an interesting fact, asserted the historian William Wood, 'that many of the French-Canadians are descended from the Norman-Franks, who conquered England seven hundred years before the English conquered La Nouvelle France, and that, however diverse they are now, the French and British peoples both have some Norman stock in common'.[24]

That the 'Norman blood' was a positive unifying force in Canada was emphasized by George Bourinot in his constitutional histories, and in 1925 G.M. Wrong, Professor of History in the University of Toronto, told the Canadian Historical Association that 'There is in reality no barrier of race to keep the English and French apart in Canada: the two peoples are identical in racial origins.'[25] As late as 1944, Abbé Arthur Maheux, Professor of History at Laval University, after condemning those 'people who think along the lines of blood, so being Hitlerites without knowing it', pointed out that 'the Norman blood, at least, is a real link between our two groups.' The French people, the Abbé explained, 'is a mixture of different bloods; the Gaul, the Briton, the Roman, the Norman each gave their share. The same is true with the English people, the Celt, the Briton, the Roman, the Saxon, the Dane, the Norman each gave their share of blood. It is easy to see that the elements are about the same and in about the same proportions in each of these two nations. Both are close relatives by blood from the very beginning of their national existences. And both Canadian groups have the same close kinship.'[26]

A Rationale For Anti-Americanism

The Canadian people were thus not only collectively a superior race, but their 'northernness' was constantly compared to the 'southernness' of the United States. The third use of the idea was a vigorous statement of the separateness of the two countries. When the annexationists asked 'why should the schism which divided our race on this continent 100 years ago, be perpetuated? . . . What do we gain by remaining apart?' and answered their own question by saying that 'Union would be the means of ultimately cementing the Anglo-Saxon race throughout the world,'[27] the usual retort was to deny that the Republic was an Anglo-Saxon country and to elaborate Canadian virtues derived from its northernness against the degeneration of 'the south'. While the northern climate of Canada was both moulding the northern elements and rejecting weaker, southern immigration, thus creating a homogeneous race, the southern climate of the United States was sapping the energies of even those descendants of vigorous races at the same time that it was attracting multitudes of the weaker races from Southern Europe, in addition to providing a hospitable home to the large Negro element. This destruction of the homogeneity of the Republic was regarded as 'diluting' its strength, as a species of 'deterioration'. This was because the southern immigrants were neither formed by a hardy climate in the homeland nor forced to adapt to one in the States. In Canada, Principal Falconer of the University of Toronto reassured his readers, 'the rigour of the northern climate has been, and will continue to be, a deterrent for the peoples of Southern Europe.'[28] Our climate, contended Parkin, excludes the lower races, 'squeezed out by that 30 or 40 degrees below zero'. Canada attracts 'the stronger people of the northern lands. That is the tendency to squeeze out the undesirable and pump in, as Kipling says, . . . the strong and desirable.' 'We have an advantage, this northern race, of a stern nature which makes us struggle for existence.' The 'submerged tenth', the weaker members of even the stronger races, are also excluded, and hence Canada does not suffer from the American labour troubles. Labour problems are unknown in Canada partly because of the abundance of land and partly because the 'Canadian winter exercises upon the tramp a silent but well-nigh irresistible persuasion to shift to a warmer latitude.' The United States itself thus serves as a 'safety-valve' for labour questions in the Dominion. The climate 'is a fundamental political and social advantage which the Dominion enjoys over the United States'. It ensures stability and ordered development as well as superiority.[29]

Northernness and Liberty

The notion of strength and superiority inhering in the quality of northernness included a fourth, and perhaps the most important, element of the general idea. Expressed in the words of Emerson, it was that 'Wherever snow falls, there is usually civil freedom.'[30] Not only did the northern climate foster exactly those characteristics without which self-government could not work, but it was held that, historically, the 'germs' of the institutions of liberty originated among the northern peoples and that northern races, inured by centuries of struggles with the elements and acquaintance with these institutions of self-government, enjoyed a superior capacity for governing themselves. Liberty itself depended upon self-reliance, a rugged independence, instilled by the struggle for existence. Thus to the equation of 'northern' with strength and the strenuous virtues, against 'southern' with degeneration and effeminacy, was added the identification of the former with liberty and the latter with tyranny.

Because 'liberty' was itself somehow the major stimulant to 'progress', the comparison was often made in terms of progress and regression. In a book review, the editor of the *Canadian Methodist Magazine* contrasted the result of Anglo-Saxon development in North America with that of the Latin races in South America. 'On the one side,' he wrote, 'a forward motion of society and the greatest development of agriculture, commerce and industry; on the other, society thrown backward and plunged to grovel in a morass of idle, unproductive town life, and given up to officialism and political revolutions. In the North we have the rising of the future, in the South the crumbling and decaying past.'[31] Wherein, asked a pamphleteer, lies the secret of such marvellous progress? 'It springs largely from the fact that the country was peopled by the Anglo-Saxon race. . . . When Rome was overshadowing the nations of Southern and Central Europe with its greatness, in the cheerless, uninviting north, a people was undergoing hardy discipline, on land and sea, in constant strife and endless foray, which produced a nobler type of manhood than Rome. . . . It is from these fearless freemen of North Germany, England is indebted in a large measure for her political liberties.'[32]

The idea that it was in the north 'that the liberties of the world had their birth' was sustained by the political science of the day. Influenced by the 'comparative politics' of E.A. Freeman in England and H.B. Adams in the United States, the constitutional and political writings of George Bourinot detailed the operations of the Teutonic germ theory in Canada. In biological analogy, freedom was a 'seed', a 'germ', which originated in the tribal assemblies of the ancient Scandinavians, was transplanted to England and subsequently to New England, and then to Canada by the migration of descendants of these Teutonic races. Wherever the favoured race appeared, its early institutional life was repeated and amplified because 'freedom' was in 'the blood'. Conversely, southern non-Teutonic peoples were either 'untutored' in self-government but were educable, or were incapable of governing themselves altogether. In the bracing climate of the north, so resembling freedom's original home, liberty, it was thought, would flourish in a purer form.[33]

It was this identification of liberty with northernness that gave such force to the anti-American emotion that Canadian, or 'British', liberty was far superior to the uproarious democracy of the United States. It was a charge taken directly from pessimistic American racists. The 'new immigration' coming from southern and southeastern Europe became the object of concern and then dread in the late 1880s, partly because it coincided with political and social disturbances arising from the transition from an agrarian to an industrial civilization. It was thought that this immigration not only destroyed the homogeneity of the American people, but also threatened the very existence of Anglo-Saxon leadership and Anglo-Saxon values. Commenting editorially on an article by Henry Cabot Lodge, the chief immigration restrictionist in the Senate, the *Empire* agreed that the old-stock families in the United States were losing their hold, that immigration and the multiplication of 'the dregs of the old world population' were increasing too rapidly for assimilation. 'The Anglo-Saxon element, the real strength of the nation, is not proportionally as influential now as it once was.'[34] Even earlier, Goldwin Smith feared that 'the Anglo-American race is declining in numbers; . . . The question is whether its remaining stock of vitality is sufficient to enable it, before it loses its tutelary ascendancy, to complete the political education of the other races.'[35] What Smith viewed with apprehension, others relished in the conviction that Canada was preserved from such a fate. 'Take the fact that one million two hundred thousand people passed through Ellis Island into the port of New York last year. Who were they,' asked Parkin, 'Italians, Greeks, Armenians, Bulgarians, the Latin races of the South. People unaccustomed to political freedom, unaccustomed to self-government, pouring in. . . . They did not come to Canada.'[36] In Canada, because of the climate, there were no Haymarket riots, no lynchings, no assassinations of public men. 'The United States', declared the *Dominion Illustrated* in 1891, 'are welcome to the Hungarians, Poles, Italians and others of that class; they are, as a rule, wretchedly poor, make very poor settlers, and bring with them many of the vices and socialistic tendencies which have caused much trouble to their hosts already. Renewed efforts should . . . be made by our government to induce more of the hardy German and Norwegian races to remain here.'[37]

The Imperialism of the Northern Race

For the imperialist the idea of the northern race had an importance which transcended its purely Canadian application. It supported the notion of the tutelary role of the stronger races in extending order and liberty to southern peoples who, either because of their climate alone, or because of their inherent weakness, could neither generate progress unassisted nor erect the institutions of self-government. Imperialists like Parkin had an immense pride in their native Canada: it alone, of all the Dominions, lay above the forty-fifth parallel. Because of the vigour implied in its northernness, Canada could exercise within the imperial framework a dynamic influence on the future, perhaps even exceeding that of the homeland. Because of the inevitable deterioration that was creeping over the urbanized and industrialized Englishman, cut off from the land, Canada was to be a kind of rejuvenator of the imperial blood. For all their rhetoric about the citizens of Canada regarding South Africa or Australia as their own country, this notion of northernness bolstered their feeling of a unique connection between Canada and Britain.

The imperial role of Canada depended on the character of the race, and it was with 'character' that imperialists like Parkin and Kipling were most concerned. Their apprehensions that the character of the imperial race had deteriorated, that the instinct of adventure and self-sacrifice which had been the motive force of imperial expansion had decayed, were coupled with the pervasive fear that the race was becoming 'soft', that it no longer manifested 'hardness'—hardness meaning not callousness but the stoical acceptance of the strenuous life and the performance of duty irrespective of rewards. It was this concern that lay at the bottom of their advocacy of a manly athleticism, their praise for what seemed to some a martial arrogance, and their exhortations to uplift the weaker races, not so much because they believed that the weaker races could be transformed but because the imperial race's assumption of the burden was in itself a test and an exaltation of their race's 'character'. The motive was as much self-regeneration as altruism. The northern race idea is subtly related to this concern, at least psychologically. In Canada, said Kipling, 'there is a fine, hard, bracing climate, the climate that puts iron and grit into men's bones.'[38] In moulding character this climate was a permanent fixture, unlike an abundance of free land. It instilled exactly those characteristics upon which the imperialists themselves placed the most value—hardness, strenuousness, endurance—so vital to dominance.

The aspect of northernness was associated with the historic imperialism of the northern races. The British Isles were conquered by the northmen, who transmitted to the Anglo-Saxons their love of the sea as well as their genius for self-government. 'The English came to America', wrote the secretary of the Navy League in Quebec, 'in obedience to the same racial seafaring instincts that led their ancestors to England itself.'[39] One of the reasons for British primacy, explained another historian, was that 'our northern climate has produced a race of sailors and adventurers from the days of the Vikings to the present, inured to all the perils of the sea and the rigours of climate.' The Icelandic sagas, he continued, 'are an interesting part of the native literature of our race, which owes much of its hardihood and enterprise to the admixture of northern blood'.[40] The celebrations of 1892 and 1897 of the voyages of Columbus and Cabot deepened interest in the Norsemen who had preceded both of them, an interest sometimes associated with the arguments of the navalists in the Navy League. Like liberty, the 'seafaring instincts' were racial properties. Parkin said that imperial expansion was not haphazard but the inevitable result of 'racial instincts' as well as national necessities. The mind which viewed expansive and hardy racial character as northern products saw the Norse voyages as something more than interesting details at the beginning of Canadian history books. 'Though nothing came of these Norse discoveries,' wrote Charles G.D. Roberts, 'they are interesting as the first recorded contact of our race with these lands which we now occupy. They are significant, because they were a direct result of that spirit of determined independence which dwells in our blood.'[41]

Moreover, this northernness of the imperial race was connected with the notion of the tendency of world power to shift northward as the phases of evolution proceeded. Parkin, who confessed finding confirmation and amplification of his own beliefs in Benjamin Kidd's *Social Evolution*, must have read with approval Kidd's prediction that northward the march of Empire makes its way:

> The successful peoples have moved westwards for physical reasons; the seat of power has moved continuously northwards for reasons connected with the evolution in character which the race is undergoing. Man, originally a creature of a warm climate and still multiplying most easily and rapidly there, has not attained his highest development where the conditions of existence have been easiest. Throughout history the centre of power has moved gradually but surely to the north into those stern regions where men have been trained for the rivalry of life in the strenuous conflict with nature in which they have acquired

energy, courage, integrity, and those characteristic qualities which contribute to raise them to a high state of social efficiency . . .[42]

Especially after 1890, the northern-race concept was frequently explained in the language of a popularized social Darwinism which imparted to it a scientific credibility surpassing in authority either vague rhetoric or poetic allusions. Parkin often employed the terminology of evolutionary science when expressing the notion, but it was left to an obscure writer in a university magazine to place the idea in the general context of 'The Theory of Evolution'. Beginning with a curt dismissal of the Mosaic account of creation as 'a mixture of Hebrew folk-lore and Christian teaching', he stated that 'man himself does not stand apart from the rest of living things as a separate creation, but has had a common origin with them and is governed by the same laws.' One of these laws is the progressive evolution of man which accompanied his migration from the tropical to the northern zones. 'The most primitive type of man at present existing is the Negro, who, like the Apes most nearly allied to Man, is essentially a tropical animal, and does not flourish in cold countries.' 'As the negro race, however, spread, it gradually reached the temperate regions, and here the struggle with Nature became fiercer and the whole civilization underwent development and a higher type of man—the yellow or Mongolian race was evolved.' This race, which included the Red Indians, Peruvians, Chinese, and Japanese, also came into contact with a more vigorous climate, either by expanding northward, or meeting the Ice Age as it moved southward. The result was progressive evolution: 'the struggle for the necessities of life, the need for bravery, endurance, and all the manly virtues, reached its climax, and the highest type of man was evolved—the Nordic type of white man, whose original home was on the fringe of the ice-sheet.' Subsequently, from Scandinavia and Russia, the Nordic race conquered Britain and temperate Europe. From this capsule history, 'as determined by zoological methods', the writer drew several 'comforting conclusions as to the future of Canada'. For one thing, the Canadian must be 'the conquering type of man', and this included the 'French-speaking fellow countrymen who, so far as they are of Norman descent, belong to the same race'. Moreover, the 'Nordic man is essentially an arctic animal and only flourishes in a cold climate—whilst in a warmer region he gradually loses virility and vitality. So that from a zoological point of view the outlook is bright for Canada.'[43]

The Northern Myth in Canadian Art

The image of Canada as a northern country with a strenuous and masterful people was reinforced and sustained in the novels, travelogues, and works of scientific exploration that abounded in the period. The adventure stories centering on life in the isolated Hudson Bay posts and the exploits of the lonely trapper had long been the staple themes of the novels of Robert M. Ballantyne and the boys' books of J. Macdonald Oxley. But after 1896, when the northwest became the locus of immigration and investment, imaginative writers found in that region not only a picturesque setting the indigenous historical incidents and themes but also an area which a large number of their readers had never experienced. Certainly it is significant that a number of the best-selling writers in the decade before the First World War, Ralph Connor, Robert Service, and William Fraser, not only set their works in the northerly setting but also lived there.

The very titles of these books are indicative of their focus: Agnes Laut's story of the fur-trader, *Lord of the North* (1900), and her history—*Canada, the Empire of the North* (1909); Gilbert Parker's *An Adventure of the North* (1905); H.A. Cody's life of Bishop Bompas, *An Apostle of the North* (1905); Ralph Connor's many manly novels set in the northwest, like *Corporal Cameron* (1912) with its inevitable blizzard; travelogues like Agnes D. Cameron's description of her journey through the Athabasca and Mackenzie River region of the Arctic, *The New North* (1909); chronicles of exploration, J.W. Tyrrell's *Across the Sub-Arctics of Canada* (1897), and Vilhjalmur Stefansson's *My Life with the Eskimo* (1913). In 1926, a literary critic complained that the 'whole of Canada has come to be identified with her northernmost reaches', and in 'modern folk-geography Canada means the North'.[44]

This image was strengthened by the paintings of the 'national movement' in Canadian art, the Group of Seven. While some of the most characteristic work of men like A.Y. Jackson and J.E.H. Macdonald was done in the post-war decades, it was during the years before 1914 that their nationalism was inspired and their determination made to express the essence of Canada through her landscape. Some of them were directly influenced by a Scandinavian art exhibition in 1912 which 'impressed them as an example of what other northern countries could do in art'. A member of the group admitted that in their minds Canada was 'a long, thin strip of civilization on the southern fringe of a vast expanse of immensely varied, virgin land reaching into the remote north. Our whole country is cleansed by the pristine and replenishing air which sweeps out of that great hinterland. It was the discovery of this great northern area as a field of art which enticed and inspired these painters.' But the north—with its sparkling clear air and sharp outlines which could never be apprehended with the techniques of Old World art—was much more than a field of art: it was the mirror of national character. After a trip into the Arctic with A.Y. Jackson, Lawren Harris reported that 'We came to know that it is only through the deep and vital experience of its total environment that a people identifies itself with its land and gradually a deep and satisfying awareness develops. We were convinced that no virile people could remain subservient to and dependent upon the creations in art of other peoples . . . To us there was also the strange brooding sense of another nature fostering a new race and new age.' Though they displayed a variety of personal styles and attitudes, the group was united in the effort to portray the rugged terrain of the Canadian Shield and the changing seasons in the northern woods. While present in J.E.H. Macdonald's *The Solemn Land* (1921) and other early works, the theme of northernness culminated in A.Y. Jackson's *The North Shore of Baffin Island* (*c.* 1929) and Lawren Harris's *Bylot Island* (1930) both of which exude the crystalline cold and seem themselves to be a part of the stark northern wastes.[45]

The Northern Theme in Retrospect

In retrospect, the northern theme, as it was expressed in the first half-century after Confederation, must be regarded as a myth, for not only did the observations it exalted conflict with objective appraisal, but its primary, intellectual assumptions became suspect. While it rested on the truism, confirmed by modern human geography, that certain climates are stimulating to human exertion, it too frequently glossed over the variety of climatic regions within Canada, and it tended to identify the whole country with that region of it which contained the fewest of her people. It was related and sustained, moreover, by the ebullient faith in the progress of the north-west, in the lusty but mistaken hopes of the wheat-boom years that the northern zone would become the home of millions of happy yeomen. The northern theme also assumed a racist aspect, holding that the capacity for freedom and progress were inherent in the blood of northern races. Not only was this belief progressively undermined by modern anthropological scholarship, but the identification of the Teutonic race with the spirit of liberty appeared especially specious after the First World War. In addition, the appeal of the northern-race idea was limited in the post-war period because its main usefulness had been to underline the differences between Canada and the United States. In the 1920s the focus of nationalist thought shifted, and one of its dominant preoccupations came to be the definition of Canadian character in terms of North American experience, to emphasize the similarities between Canada and the United States.

Intellectual styles change but the permanent facts they seek to interpret and render meaningful do not. As long as there exists a nationalist impulse in Canada the imagination of men will be challenged by the very existence of the fascinating north. Though racism and crude environmentalism have now largely been discredited, the effort to explain Canadian uniqueness in terms of the north has not. As late as 1948, Vincent Massey found several differences between the United States and Canada, such as 'the air of moderation in Canadian habits' to be derived from climate and race:

Climate plays a great part in giving us our special character, different from that of our southern neighbours. Quite apart from the huge annual bill our winter imposes on us in terms of building construction and clothing and fuel, it influences our mentality, produces a sober temperament. Our racial composition — and this is partly because of our climate — is different, too. A small percentage of our people comes from central or southern Europe. The vast majority springs either from the British Isles or Northern France, a good many, too, from Scandinavia and Germany, and it is in northwestern Europe that one finds the elements of human stability highly developed. Nothing is more characteristic of Canadians than the inclination to be moderate.[46]

Apart from the muted tone, these observations do not really differ in substance from the remarks made in ringing rhetoric and with scientific certainty in the late nineteenth century by George Parkin, who was, incidentally, Massey's father-in-law.

Very different, however, and of high political potency, was the emotional appeal to the Canadian northern mission evoked by John Diefenbaker in the election of 1958. Seizing upon a theme which his native northwest had inspired in poets and nationalists since Confederation, he declared, suitably enough at Winnipeg, that 'I see a new Canada' — not orientated east and west, but looking northward, responding to the challenges of that hinterland, its energies focused on the exploration and exploitation of the Arctic — 'A CANADA OF THE NORTH!' To this compelling theme, which runs so persistently through Canadian nationalist thought since the days of D'Arcy McGee, Canadians responded eagerly and with conviction.[47]

On a more sober and scholarly plane, but not less pungent and appealing, is another recent exposition of the northern theme articulated by a president of the Canadian Historical Association, W.L. Morton, also a native of the northwest. In an address delivered in 1960, Professor Morton fixed upon Canada's 'northern character', her origins in the expansion of a northern, maritime frontier, and her possession of a distinctive, staple economy, as factors which explained a substantial aspect of her development, her historical dependence upon Britain and the United States, the character of her literature, even the seasonal rhythm of Canadian life.[48]

The concept of Canada as a northern nation, like the idea that the unique character of the United States was shaped by the westward movement, is as important for understanding the intellectual content and emotional appeal of nationalism as it is for explaining the objective determinants of historical development. From the time of Benjamin Franklin, Americans saw 'the west' not so much as a geographical fact but as a symbol, around which they grouped the leading tenets of their nationalist faith — that their movement westward was carrying the American further and further away from effete Europe, that 'the garden' would become the home of an independent yeomanry in which alone reposed true Republican virtue, that the frontier was a safety valve which kept social conditions in the new world from ever approximating those in decadent, classridden Europe. Like the American symbol of the west, the Canadian symbol of the north subsumed a whole series of beliefs about the exalted past, the national character and the certain future. Unlike the American frontier of free land, however, the north itself was inexhaustible: as A.R.M. Lower has recently reminded us, it is a perpetual breath of fresh air.

If Canadian nationalism is to be understood, its meaning must be sought and apprehended not simply in the sphere of political decisions, but also in myths, legends, and symbols like these. For while some might think that Canadians have happily been immune to the wilder manifestations of the nationalist impulse and rhetoric, it seems that they too have had their utopian dreamers, and that they are not totally innocent of a tradition of racism and a falsified but glorious past, tendencies which have always been the invariable by-products of nationalism. For by its very nature, nationalism must seize upon objective dissimilarities and tendencies and invest them in the language of religion, mission, and destiny.

Suggestions for Further Reading

Kenneth Minogue, *Nationalism* (London, 1967).
W.L. Morton, *The Canadian Identity* (Toronto, 1961).
Peter Russell, ed., *Nationalism in Canada* (Toronto, 1966).

Notes

[1] William Pitman Lett, *Annexation and British Connection, Address to Brother Jonathan* (Ottawa, 1889), 10.

[2] Walter R. Nursey, *The Story of Isaac Brock* (Toronto), 1909, 173.

[3] Joseph Pope, *The Tour of Their Royal Highnesses the Duke and Duchess of Cornwall and York through the Dominion of Canada in the Year 1901* (Ottawa, 1903), 259; Hon. George W. Ross, *The Historical Significance of the Plains of Abraham, Address Delivered Before the Canadian Club of Hamilton, 27 April 1908* (n.p., n.d.), 18; *The Canadian Military Gazette*, XV (2 January 1900), 15; Silas Alward, *An Anglo-American Alliance* (Saint John, N.B., 1911).

[4] G.D. Griffin, *Canada Past, Present, Future, and New System of Government* (n.p. 1884), ii.

[5] George Parkin, address to the Canadian Club and Board of Trade in Saint John, N.B., reported in *The Daily Telegraph*, Saint John, N.B., 6 March 1907. Clipping in *Parkin Papers*, vol. 82 (Public Archives of Canada, hereinafter PAC).

[6] William Leggo, *History of the Administration of the Earl of Dufferin in Canada* (Toronto, 1878), 599.

[7] *Weekly Globe*, 2 April 1869.

[8]For a fascinating sketch of these myths see J.W. Johnson, ' "Of Differing Ages and Climes" ', *Journal of the History of Ideas*, XXI (October–December 1960) 465–80.

[9]R.G. Haliburton, *The Men of the North and their place in history. A Lecture delivered before the Montreal Literary Club, 31 March 1869* (Montreal, 1869) 2, 8, 16.

[10]Clipping from *The Globe*, 8 December 1904, in *Denison Scrapbook 1897–1915*, 167. *Denison Papers* (PAC).

[11]Charles Mair, 'The New Canada: its natural features and climate', *Canadian Monthly Magazine*, VIII (July, 1875), 5.

[12]*Canada First: A Memorial of the late William A. Foster* (Toronto, 1890), 25.

[13]Charles R. Tuttle, *Popular History of the Dominion of Canada*, 2 vols, Boston 1877 and 1879, vol. 1, 28.

[14]G.R. Parkin, *The Great Dominion, Studies of Canada*, London, 1895, 25, 211–15; 'The Railway Development of Canada', *The Scottish Geographical Magazine* (May, 1909), 249, reprint in *Parkin Papers* vol. 66 (PAC), address to Canadian Club and Board of Trade in Saint John, New Brunswick, reported in *The Daily Telegraph*, 6 March 1907. Clipping in *Parkin Papers*, vol. 82 (PAC).

[15]Edward Harris, *Canada, The Making of a Nation* (n.p., *c.* 1907), 7.

[16]G.R. Parkin, *The Great Dominion*, 216.

[17]W.H. Withrow, 'Notes of a Visit to the Centennial Exhibition', *Canadian Methodist Magazine* (December, 1876) 530.

[18]Rev. F.A. Wightman, *Our Canadian Heritage, Its Resources and Possibilities* (Toronto, 1905), 46.

[19]W.H. Hingston, *The Climate of Canada and its Relation to Life and Health* (Montreal, 1884), xviii, 94, 126–7, 260, 263, 265–6.

[20]Wightman, *Our Canadian Heritage*, 280, 44–5; J. Sheridan Hogan, *Canada, An Essay: to which was awarded the first prize by the Paris Exhibition Committee of Canada* (Montreal, 1855), 53–4.

[21]F.B. Cumberland, 'Introduction', *Maple Leaves: being the papers read before the National Club of Toronto at the 'National Evenings', during the Winter 1890–1* (Toronto, 1891), vii–viii.

[22]Wightman, as cited, 221.

[23]Benjamin Sulte, *Origin of the French Canadian. Read before the British Association, Toronto, August 1897* (Ottawa, 1897), 14. See also his essay of 1897, 'Défense de nos Origines' in *Mélanges historiques*, compiled by Gérard Malchelosse, vol. 17 (Montreal, 1930).

[24]*The Storied Province of Quebec, Past and Present*, W. Wood (ed.) vol. 1 (Toronto, 1931), 3.

[25]G.M. Wrong, *The Two Races in Canada, a Lecture delivered before the Canadian Historical Association, Montreal, 21 May 1925* (Montreal, 1925), 4–5.

[26]Abbé Arthur Maheux, *Canadian Unity: What Keeps Us Apart* (Quebec, 1944), 22, 23, 25.

[27]*Canada's Future! Political Union With the U.S. Desirable* (1891), 2–3.

[28]Principal R.A. Falconer, 'The Unification of Canada', *University Magazine*, VII (February, 1908), 4–5.

[29]George Parkin, 'Canada and the United States on the American Continent', reported in *Yarmouth Herald*, 3 March 1908. Clipping in *Parkin Papers*, vol. 84, (PAC); *The Great Dominion*, 214.

[30] Cited in Charles and Mary Beard, *The American Spirit, A Study of the Civilization of the United States* (New York, 1962), 173.

[31] *Canadian Methodist Magazine* (December 1898), 566–7.

[32] Silas Alward, as cited, 8–10.

[33] See especially, J.G. Bourinot, *Canadian Studies in Comparative Politics* (Montreal, 1890).

[34] *The Empire*, 24 January 1891.

[35] *The Week*, 1 January 1885.

[36] G. Parkin, in *Yarmouth Herald*, 3 March 1908.

[37] *Dominion Illustrated*, VI (11 April 1891).

[38] Cited in *Canadian Methodist Magazine* (June 1899), 536.

[39] William Wood, *The Fight for Canada* (Boston, 1906), 33.

[40] Rev. W.P. Creswell, *History of the Dominion of Canada* (Oxford, 1890), 11, 15.

[41] Charles G.D. Roberts, *A History of Canada* (Boston, 1897), 3.

[42] Benjamin Kidd, *Social Evolution* (London, 1895), 61–2.

[43] E.W. MacBride, 'The Theory of Evolution', *The McGill University Magazine*, I (April 1902), 244–62.

[44] Lionel Stevenson, *Appraisals of Canadian Literature* (Toronto, 1926), 245–53.

[45] R.H. Hubbard, *The Development of Canadian Art* (Ottawa, 1964), 88; L. Harris, 'The Group of Seven in Canadian History', *Canadian Historical Association Report* (1948) 30, 36–7.

[46] Vincent Massey, *On Being Canadian* (Toronto, 1948), 29–30.

[47] Peter Newman, *Renegade in Power: The Diefenbaker Years* (Toronto, 1964), 218.

[48] W.L. Morton, 'The Relevance of Canadian History' in *The Canadian Identity* (Toronto, 1961), 88–114.

12

Women and Reform

Carol Bacchi

In the latter part of the nineteenth century, when the impulse to reform society's ills was evident in most parts of the industrializing world—and when many of the leading reformers were women—the status of women as an object of reform quite naturally became an issue. In Canada the principal reform advocated in the 'women's issue' was the extension of the political franchise to women. Against much opposition the suffrage movement emerged victorious during the First World War, initially in the western provinces and ultimately at the federal level. But despite this success, and despite the important role played by women in other reform efforts—such as prohibition and child welfare—neither the suffrage movement nor the general reform impulse did much to confront or alter the underlying factors that kept women in an inferior position in society.

Carol Bacchi analyses the reform ideology of the suffrage movement in English Canada in an attempt to explain its differences from later women's movements. Suffragists— who were narrowly based in the ranks of the Protestant middle classes—did not so much seek to alter women's existing roles as to elevate their importance. Like their male compatriots in the imperialism debates, Canadian women active in reform were influenced by racist ideas, which they combined with prevailing assumptions about the importance of women as society's nurturers, forming a conception of themselves as 'Mothers of the race'. This framework led suffragists inevitably to child welfare; but it also led to attacks on social vice and to the advocacy of state intervention to improve the nation's moral fabric. Bacchi notes that concern over prostitution and the unwed mother achieved some recognition of male sexual exploitation of women, and that the campaign against female promiscuity may have contained the germ of a notion of sexual liberation from the tyranny of males. But she concludes that on the whole suffragists concentrated on their image as the 'upholders of conventional female virtues', and that most of the reformers sought to gain recognition for women's particular virtues in society at large, rather than to seek a radical restructuring of society.

What contemporary racial theories were most acceptable to suffragists? Why? Did the suffrage movement attempt to turn 'racial improvement' to the advantage of women? Why was 'racial purity' such an important catalyst for reform movements in this period? Is Bacchi's distinction between the defensive and offensive character of 'social purity' significant? What were the weaknesses of the suffragist movement—and of the reform impulse in general—in this period?

This article first appeared, titled 'Race Regeneration and Social Purity: A Study of the Social Attitudes of Canada's English-Speaking Suffragists', in *Histoire sociale/Social History* XI, 22 (November 1978), 460–74.

I

Feminist historians have recently pointed out that the female suffragists in Canada, Britain, the United States, and Australia had aims very different from today's liberation movement.[1] Attention has been drawn in particular to two facets of the women's ideology. First, the vast majority accepted that woman's most important contribution to society consisted of her role as wife and mother. As a result they usually assumed that a woman would stop working at marriage, to devote her full energy to her family. Second, rather than demanding sexual freedom for women, most upheld the Victorian idea that women stood above sex.

Though this synopsis of their social attitudes is accurate, little attempt has been made to understand why they held these views. This paper argues from the position that the women have to be understood within the context of the social group to which they belonged. Canada's English-speaking suffragists were members of a late-nineteenth-century reform coalition drawn from the Anglo-Saxon Protestant middle classes.[2] Such middle-class reformers suggested only minor changes. The family, for instance, remained sacrosanct in their eyes. The suffragists did not want to challenge the accepted female role but only to raise its status.

This paper examines two parts of the reform ideology: the commitment to race regeneration and the crusade for society purity. It shows how both these goals depended on traditional views of women's virtues. The desire to create a strong and healthy race placed an emphasis on woman's role as procreator and nurturer. The crusade for purity, an attempt by the Protestant élite to reimpose its values on a deviant society, made a patriotic virtue of women's asexuality. Given the suffragists' Protestant Anglo-Saxon background it ought not to be surprising that they endorsed this program. Their allegiance to their sex was not their sole allegiance. In fact, at times, the commitment to race, creed, and class superseded the commitment to sex.

II

Several studies of late Victorian and Edwardian society point to the fact that the English-speaking Anglo-Saxon community in Britain, its colonies, and the United States, felt defensive in this period.[3] Britain faced the particular trauma of declining imperial supremacy. The number of recruits for the Boer War who were rejected on the grounds of physical incapacity seemed to indicate that the British were becoming a race of weaklings. Bernard Semmel has labelled the reforms advanced in this period to upgrade the health of the population 'social imperialism'.[4]

The 'race suicide' scare, the suggestion that Anglo-Saxon numbers were declining while 'inferior' races proliferated, aroused particular concern. The old Malthusian fear that too many people were being born gave way to the idea that the English population had stopped growing. The problem was not simply numbers, though it was frequently expressed in this way. The real problem was that the best stock were being outbred by the unfit. Studies, for example, revealed an increasing number of feeble-minded in the population.

Canada's middle-class reformers came from sound Anglo-Saxon stock and were well aware of the warnings about the degeneration of the race. Social-gospel leaders S.D. Chown and W.W. Andrews viewed with alarm 'the diminishing birth rate in some sections of our population'. They considered it a great national evil 'that some of the best strains in our country are becoming extinct'.[5] The large influx of eastern and southern European immigrants between 1896 and World War I increased their anxiety. Much of the reform program aimed at finding ways to improve the calibre of tomorrow's citizens. A commitment to race-regeneration and nation-building dominated the movement.

The idea of evolution aroused interest since it seemed to suggest that the race was moving forward. All they had to do was harness this process. Unfortunately, scientists could not agree upon the mechanism by which evolution took place. Two contrary theories developed. Environmentalism, traceable to Jean-Baptiste de Lamarck, maintained that a modification in the environment produced in a person visible physical and mental changes which were transmittable to the next generation. The opposing school of thought, labelled 'eugenics' by its founder, Francis Galton, placed emphasis on nature (i.e., heredity) rather than nurture.[6]

The two schools of heredity offered different solutions to the race-degeneration and race-suicide problems. Lamarckians and neo-Lamarckians believed in the inheritance of acquired characteristics and recommended ameliorative legislation to improve the living and working conditions of underprivileged groups. According to their hypothesis this would produce higher types in the future. The simple answer to the birth-rate dilemma lay in reducing the infant death rate by upgrading the standard of living generally. Discounting the impact of environment, eugenists insisted that the only way to improve the race was through selective breeding. They advocated legislation to prevent the unfit from multiplying and to encourage the fit to have more children.

The middle-class reformers tended to be humanists who defended the need for environmental change. Environmentalism (or 'euthenics' as it came to be called in contradistinction to eugenics[7]) provided them with a *raison d'être* since it suggested that people living today could build for the future. But eugenics seemed to make social reform unnecessary. Worse still, it implied that reformers were actually contributing to the deterioration of the race by preserving weak specimens.[8]

Some reformers rejected eugenics outright since it seemed to deny their effectiveness. The Rev. A.E. Smith, a Methodist minister from Brandon, Manitoba, and an exponent of the social gospel, felt uncomfortable with the new creed: 'We do not believe in the survival of the fittest. We do not believe in the brushing on one side of the weak and the helpless.'[9] Others took up those parts of eugenics which retained environmental overtones, for example restricting the propagation of those with hereditary defects. Beyond this, they retained their faith in the benefits of environmental change.

Dr Peter Bryce, the President of the Canadian Purity-Education Association, provides a good example of this ability to integrate some eugenic arguments without abandoning a basically environmental approach. To control the spread of hereditary weakness he recommended stricter government regulation of marriage and the removal of the feeble-minded to state-supported homes. In the field of euthenics he called for a 'sanitary environment', improved housing, lessening of overcrowding, a reduction in local taxation and child labour, and lower costs for food and land. Bryce coined his own terms for the complementary processes. The 'Law of Heredity' doomed men and women to carry their ancestral physical structure and character with them. But the 'Gospel of Heredity' mitigated the doom, providing in environment the 'potentialities of almost infinite improvement'.[10]

Because of their reform orientation the suffragists also placed more faith in environment than in genes. Emily Stowe, the founder of Canada's first woman suffrage society, for example, blamed the environment, not heredity, for the production of the criminal.[11] Most reforms in the suffrage platform (factory legislation, compulsory education, city planning, health and hygiene, temperance, prison reform, pure-food laws) were euthenist and aimed at improving the living and working conditions of the poor.[12]

As with the reformers, however, the suffragists could not ignore the discoveries of genetics. Ethel Hurlbatt, a vocal member of the Montreal Suffrage

Association and Warden of McGill's Royal Victoria College in 1907, explained clearly the dilemma posed by eugenics and the way in which it challenged the basic assumption of reform:

> Is degeneracy in every form to be attributed to poverty, bad housing, unhealthy trades, drinking, industrial occupations of women, and other direct and indirect environmental influences on offspring? Can we, by education, by legislation, by social effort change the environmental conditions and raise the race to a markedly higher standard of physique and mentality? Or is social reform really incapable of effecting any substantial change, nay by lessening the selection death rate, may it not contribute to emphasizing the very evils it was intended to lessen? . . .
>
> Through investigations they [eugenists] show that improvement in social conditions will not compensate for bad hereditary influences; that the problem of physical and mental degeneration cannot be solved by preventing mothers from working, by closing public houses, by erecting model dwellings; that the only way to keep a nation strong mentally and physically is to see that each new generation is derived from the fitter members of the generation before.[13]

Placed on the defensive, the suffragists also proposed a compromise. They accepted that environmental reform could not affect mental capacity and therefore agreed upon the need to control strictly the breeding of the retarded. One Western woman wanted special industrial farms, segregation of the sexes, and in some cases sterilization to keep the feeble-minded from multiplying.[14] In the East, Constance Hamilton, the President of the National Equal Franchise Union, included drunkards among the unsalvageable. She recommended keeping them under restraint rather than leaving alcoholic mothers 'free to fill cradles with degenerate babies'.[15]

Beyond the regulation of the feeble-minded, however, most suffragists were unwilling to go. Strict eugenists were few. Only Carrie Derick, a student in McGill's Botanical Department between 1887 and 1890, and later a Professor of Evolution and Genetics, championed the direct application of scientific principles to human conditions. That is, she believed that the struggle for existence ought to be allowed to proceed unrestrained, so that the truly fittest would survive. She preferred a 'spirit of indifference' to the 'happy feeling' that education, pure air, good housing, proper food, and short hours of work may bring about a permanent improvement in people.[16] To justify her activities as a reformer and a suffragist, she argued that 'If men and women were taught to be chaste, clean living and high thinking, there would be an uplifting of the race without any special legislation.'[17] The higher education of women and the freeing of women from conventional ideas, Derick maintained, would help achieve this aim.

Generally, the application of theories of evolution, be they eugenist or environmental, tended to reinforce traditional sex roles. The obsession with the numbers and quality of the next generation accentuated woman's maternal function. The particular reforms one espoused depended on the school of heredity to which one belonged. The environmentalists concentrated on two things: improving the health and fitness of women on the grounds that their children would benefit and bettering the home environment in which those children would spend the first crucial formative years. The eugenists tried to popularize the idea of controlled breeding. The suffragists almost invariably favoured the Lamarckian program, firstly because they were environmentalists, and secondly because it allowed greater scope for women to contribute actively to the creation of a new race.

Eugenics reduced the maternal function to a mere biological capacity. The main concern for the future of the race, according to eugenic theory, was that those with hereditary defects were multiplying faster than those with desirable traits. The source of this problem was traced partly to the reluctance of intelligent women to stay home and have babies. Statistics revealed a lower marriage and birth rate among college women, proving to eugenists that these women were neglecting their duty.[18] Francis Galton, the well-known founder of the movement, was willing to force this duty upon them: 'If child-bearing women must be intellectually handicapped,' he explained, 'then the penalty to be paid for race predominance is the subjection of women.'[19]

This conclusion raised a real dilemma for the suffragists. Since most were well educated and since they shared the concern for the future of the race, what could they say to those who accused them of not doing their share? Ethel Hurlbatt did some soul-searching over the issue:

> If the philanthropists are right, there is no doubt that college women are contributing their share to movements which will secure better physical and moral conditions for the race. If the eugenists are right, are college women? Do college women maintain the same standard of physical efficiency as their less educated sisters? Do they as readily marry? Do they bring into the world as many children?[20]

She could only hope that the 'philanthropists' (or environmentalists) were right since that made women's contribution to the reform effort as important as their breeding function. Hurlbatt is not suggesting that female reformers might want to abandon the domestic sphere but that the improved environment they were helping to create was of more value than the simple multiplication of offspring. Environmental theory thus allowed a greater scope for activity, albeit within a restricted domain.

In a similar fashion the environmental approach to bettering the race was partly responsible for altering the traditional image of the Victorian woman. A belief in the inheritance of acquired characteristics produced a new concern for both woman's physical and her mental fitness. The 'frail vessel' fell into disrepute. Dr Edward Playter, an Ottawa reformer, announced that 'the age for regarding as fashionable and popular delicate women and girls is past.'[21] It had become 'a woman's duty to be well'.[22]

The dress-reform movement received a real fillip from this idea. Many medical men approved looser-fitting garments on the grounds that the 'corset curse' might damage the womb and/or its occupant.[23] More and more educators began to press for physical-education facilities for girls in order to improve the health of future mothers. All the new women's colleges in the period, such as the Royal Victoria College in Montreal, had large recreation rooms where women learned calisthenics.

Environmentalism could also be used to justify women's higher education. Many people, including many clerics, had begun to criticize the traditional academy education, which concentrated on needlework, dancing, and languages, on the grounds that it produced a flighty and frivolous woman. According to one champion of women's higher education, McGill's Principal William Dawson, the mental discipline of future wives and mothers had to be improved since the children were in their care all day.[24] This logic made university-level courses in moral philosophy, history, and Christian doctrine quite acceptable. But the education was still essentially education for motherhood. There was no suggestion that better-educated women move into the job market.

While the environmental approach encouraged women to break free from certain parts of Victorian convention, on balance the Lamarckian school reinforced traditional sex roles. Women were simply allowed the liberty to become better mothers. This is aptly demonstrated by the reformers' enthusiastic support for domestic-science education for women. Since the home life was crucial to the physical and mental development of an individual, they wanted more attention paid to the training of the homemaker. J.W. Dafoe, writing in the *Grain Growers' Guide*, believed that the health of the nation depended upon 'the proper balancing of foods in the bill of fare' and that upon its health depended its achievements in commerce, arts, and science. In brief, 'the gastric organs are the hub of the wheel.'[25] Consequently, above all else, women needed instruction in physiology, hygiene, and nutrition.

The idea of domestic-science training fitted in nicely with developments in education theory. Towards the end of the nineteenth century many educators began promoting a practical over a general liberal-arts program.[26] It was argued that the strength of the nation required that boys receive technical education in industrial schools. On the same grounds and given the traditional assumptions about the sexual division of labour it was decided that girls needed training in the skills of household management. Between 1893 and 1908 home-economics classes were established in the public schools of thirty-two Canadian cities.[27] In 1894 the Hamilton School of Domestic Science opened and in 1900 a Hamilton Normal School for training teachers of domestic science was established, with government aid.[28]

The reaction of the suffragists to domestic science provides a good example of the way in which they accepted and worked within the reform ideology. Because of their enthusiasm for improving the race, the majority warmly

approved the new education. In 1889 Emily Stowe asked for the incorporation of one grand Normal School for domestic instruction in every city.[29]
The Manitoba suffragist and journalist, Lillian Beynon Thomas, wanted girls
in public schools to receive a thorough training in domestic science because,
in her words, 'the health of the nation is largely in their hands.'[30] Only a
small feminist minority realized that home economics restricted women to
a purely domestic function: Carrie Derick saw the danger in the new trend.
She pointed out that centring woman's education around cooking and sewing restricted her choice of career.[31] The majority accepted this restriction.

The general acceptance of domestic science ought not to be surprising.
The suffragists shared the concern for the race which made it necessary that
the home life of the masses be improved. Also, the idea of scientific training
for motherhood provided a new status for a role most of them accepted. In
the eyes of the Manitoba suffragist Mrs Frances Graham, home economics
had dignified the old-time 'kitchen drudgery' into a delightful and controlled
science.[32] Moreover, few suffragists did their own housework and domestic-
science education promised to replenish the ever-diminishing supply of
domestic servants.

Other parts of the suffrage program illustrate the priority placed on racial
improvement. Their arguments in favour of factory legislation were essentially racial, that is, that women had to be kept healthy to protect their
offspring. The Toronto Suffrage Association, for example, included among
its list of reasons why women needed the vote '. . . because millions of
women are wage workers and their health and that *of our future citizens* are
often endangered by evil working conditions that can only be remedied by
legislation'.[33] In the early days of sweatshop labour some safeguards were
necessary, but the suffragists failed to consider that protective legislation burdened a working woman with a handicap which made her less employable.
Only a very few suffragists, notably Carrie Derick, argued the modern feminist position that restrictive legislation tended to drive women out of work
they were well able to perform.[34] Ideally, the majority of the suffragists
wanted women out of the factories altogether because of the threat such
work posed to their health.

This is not to say that the suffragists allowed the male reformers to define
their program but that they accepted the need for racial improvement and
hence had no intention of challenging the importance of woman as mother.
The motto adopted by the Child Welfare Exhibition, sponsored by the Montreal Suffrage Association in 1912, could well stand as the motto for the
suffrage movement: 'If we are to become a great nation, the well-being of
our children must be our first care.'[35]

Within this framework the women demanded the esteem they deserved
as the 'mothers of the race'. To justify their enfranchisement, they put forward the simple plea that they needed a vote to protect their homes and

children properly. Industrialization, they argued, had intruded into woman's sphere and transferred many of her functions to distant, impersonal, collective enterprises.[36] Factories made the food and clothing; schools educated the children; governments controlled the environment which affected her family's health. To guarantee that these tasks, which were actually her responsibilities, were performed well, woman needed to intrude into the world. Government had become housekeeping on a grand scale and women were still the most natural housekeepers.

The suffragists were thus able to capitalize on the paranoia over the deterioration of the race to raise their status. They sensibly aligned themselves with the environmentalists who at least promoted women above the level of breeding stock. But the obsession with racial perfection made women's maternal and nurturant functions far more important than any contribution she could make outside the home. This helps explain why very few suffragists suggested a serious restructuring of sex roles.

III

Social purity formed one of the most persistent themes running through both the suffrage and the general reform movements. According to David Pivar, it provided 'the moral cement that gave cohesiveness to otherwise disassociated reforms'.[37] Its central role tells us a great deal about the reform ideology and helps us understand the suffragists' prudery.

As with race regeneration, social purity was essentially defensive. The style of city living, brought on by the rapid urbanization of the end of the century, challenged the standards of the Protestant middle class. The numbers of foreigners who congregated in urban slums increased the feeling that they had lost control of the nation's character. Richard Hofstadter's 'status anxiety' still best describes their attitude.[38]

The most visible signs of disregard for the Christian way of life were the bar-rooms and the brothels. Numerous studies of the temperance campaign describe the reaction to the first of these and show how it aided the suffrage movement.[39] Only a few historians have examined the second.

Social-purity crusaders concentrated predominantly upon the problem of prostitution, which seemed to embody the challenge to Christian morality. Social-gospel preachers and civic leaders complained ceaselessly about the degree of 'social vice' rampant in Canada. In 1894 the Rev. W.J. Hunter reported that Montreal with a population of 220,000 supported 228 'houses of shame'.[40] J.S. Woodsworth drew attention to the problem in the West where, in 1911, Winnipeg had one hundred and fifty houses of ill-fame.[41]

Prostitution raised an additional problem for reformers dedicated to improving the race: venereal disease. Syphilis and gonorrhea reportedly had reached staggering proportions. Dr Charles Hastings, Toronto's public-health inspector, quoted the ominous findings of the 1901 New York State Commission of Seven which concluded that one New Yorker in five had venereal disease.[42] (Canadian reformers often looked to the United States to forecast their future.) The Alberta reformer, Emily Murphy, indicated the deteriorating situation in Canada. She found that one in three prisoners in Alberta's Provincial jail had to be treated for syphilis and gonorrhea.[43]

The impact on future generations magnified the seriousness of these diseases. In 1905 Fritz Schaudinn and Erich Hoffman discovered the spirochete which caused syphilis and proved that it could be transmitted from an infected mother to an unborn baby.[44] Subsequent studies claimed that syphilis produced other afflictions including insanity, paralysis, blindness, deformity, and sterility in the victim and the victim's offspring. Lillian Beynon Thomas blamed syphilis for 50 per cent of all mental deficiency.[45] Dr Hastings attributed to gonorrheal infection 20 to 25 per cent of all blindness, 17 to 25 per cent of all sterility, and 60 to 80 per cent of all miscarriages.[46]

Science proved no more helpful than in the heredity debate, for while it could list all the deplorable side-effects of venereal disease it could offer no cure. One treatment for syphilis, doses of mercury, used as early as 1479, killed many patients and made the medicine as dangerous as the disease. Arsphenamine or salvarsen, a derivative of arsenic, developed in 1910, proved more successful but a clinical cure still required repeated injections over a period of one and a half years.[47] Some stages of later syphilis proved refractory to all forms of therapy. Although Albert Neisser discovered the organism which caused gonorrhea in 1879, no effective treatment was developed until the 1940s.[48] Municipal authorities in Europe, Britain, and some American cities tried to control the problem by segregating prostitutes and subjecting them to compulsory medical inspection. The British Contagious Diseases Acts, introduced between 1864 and 1869, constituted a test case of social supervision.[49] But the Puritan reformers would not support this technique, which they interpreted as state sanctioning of moral evil. In any case the idea of regulation was doomed to failure for a far more practical reason: it failed to work. Prostitution simply went underground and venereal disease statistics rose.[50]

The reformers decided to attack the problem at its source and launched a crusade for the general reformation of the nation's morals. Several Canadian reform organizations joined in the purity crusade. Between 1906 and 1915 a Purity-Education Association, staffed mainly by doctors, operated out of Toronto.[51] A second group, the National Committee for the Suppression of the White Slave Traffic, founded in 1912, fought against the international trade in prostitutes. Social purity also operated as a subsidiary theme in associations committed to other causes. The Women's Christian Temperance Union, for example, had committees for press and literature censorship, as well as those dedicated to eliminating white slavery and the 'social evil'.[52]

The reformers adopted several types of tactics. For the 'fallen' they could only suggest that they be prevented from transmitting the disease to others.

In 1912 the Methodist Church demanded that all cases of venereal disease be reported to Medical Health officers and that no one be granted a marriage licence until he or she could produce a medical certificate that established freedom from venereal disease.[53] Dr Hastings suggested the provision of public laboratories where Wasserman tests (discovered in 1906) could be carried out.[54] In 1918 Mary McCallum, then woman's editor for the *Grain Growers' Guide*, recommended the strictest and closest quarantine of venereal-disease patients.[55] For those yet to fall, the strategy included censorship and sex education. The logic behind the latter was that, if more people were aware of the frightening consequences of 'loose morals', they would reform. A *Self and Sex* series, consisting of eight volumes and published in the United States between 1900 and 1915, became very popular among Canadian reformers. One volume, entitled *What a Young Man Ought to Know*, contained a sixty-page lecture on the frightful effects of venereal disease. Purity lecturers, notably Beatrice Brigden, William Lund Clark, and Arthur W. Beall, hired by the WCTU and the evangelical Churches, toured the country, imparting the secrets of life to the young.[56] The instruction they offered was filled with threats and warnings, encouraged continence, and discouraged sexual activity.

Victorian vitalist physiology, which maintained that the body contained a limited amount of energy, strengthened the reformers' contention that sexual activity ought to be discouraged for the sake of the race. The Rev. W.J. Hunter explained that sex depleted the body's working power, shortened human life, and burdened it with infirmities and diseases. He defended sexual abstinence on the grounds that the vigour of the race demanded it. Masturbation or the 'solitary evil' also stood condemned, since 'loss of semen is loss of blood.'[57]

The reformers' underlying strategy was to raise the status and influence of good Christian women. The Victorian female was popularly believed to be asexual. Moreover, it was obvious that male promiscuity was primarily to blame for the degree of prostitution. The simplest answer, therefore, was to enlist the asexual females to help impose a higher standard of morality upon men. The double standard which allowed a man to 'sow his wild oats' had to be demolished. Dr Hastings felt it most important to blot out the 'physiological fallacy of sexual necessity for men'.[58]

The revelation of police compliance in prostitution convinced many reformers that women needed a ballot in order to be effective in altering men's moral standards. Almost every reformer who supported woman suffrage believed that women would help improve the nation's morals. This involved no real change in woman's role or function. It merely meant capitalizing on woman's traditional perceived virtues: her conservatism and her chastity.

Canada's suffragists confirmed the reformers' faith in woman's purity and removed any hesitation they may have had to give women a vote. Almost without exception the women upheld a strict Victorian code of morality.

Emily Stowe approved of the 'anti-sex' sex education which taught the young 'all the consequences of the transgression'.[59] In a similar vein, Dr Amelia Youmans, founder of the Manitoba Equal Suffrage Club in 1894, issued a foreboding pamphlet entitled 'Warning Words', which recounted all the dire effects of venereal disease. Lillian Beynon Thomas advised women to wear modest dress in order to curb 'animal desire'.[60] Alice Chown, a Toronto feminist, wished to limit sex relations to purposes of reproduction.[61]

The campaigns against prostitution and white slavery attracted enthusiastic suffrage support. Dr Margaret Gordon, President of the Toronto Suffrage Association, called white slavery the strongest reason which made her a suffragist.[62] In 1908, Flora MacDonald Denison, the President of the National Suffrage Association, was even willing to violate cherished civil liberties to end the trade. She wanted the city to be divided into districts each having an officer with the power to go into any home and find out about its inmates.[63] The suffragists tried to protect young girls from the white-slave traders by raising the age of consent to twenty-one. Every suffrage society also demanded that proprietors be held responsible for the order and the respectability of their houses, an attack aimed directly at the brothel keepers.[64]

The purity problem seems to have been the main issue over which the suffragists displayed sex antagonism, uniting in a sisterhood of sorts against the men. It angered them that the prostitute consistently played the villain while the man got off with a nominal fine.[65] In their opinion the prostitute was less guilty since she often fell through hunger or was driven into sin because 'some man' paid her starvation wages.[66] Conversely the client always went through choice. Flora MacDonald Dension bemoaned the fact that 'hundreds of our sisters are forced to live lives of shame to keep body and soul together.'[67] Lillian Beynon Thomas wished to subject the men to equal mortification by having the names of those found in houses in the red-light district published in newspapers.[68]

The unwed mother, considered another victim of male licentiousness, also aroused sympathy. Agnes Chesley, women's editor for the *Montreal Star*, recommended that she be treated with infinite compassion: 'If a girl goes astray, the fault must be looked for in her heritage from her parents, her environment and, above all, in her upbringing.'[69] Existing parental custody laws made the father the sole legal guardian of legitimate offspring but left the illegitimate child the sole responsibility of its mother. The well-known Manitoba suffragist, Nellie McClung, pointed to the injustice of this situation: 'If a child is a treasure in a married happy home and clouds arise and a separation follows, who gets the child? The father! But who gets the illegitimate child that bears the brand of shame? The poor unfortunate mother. . . .'[70] Equal parental rights over legitimate and illegitimate children became a popular cause among the suffragists.

The move to liberalize divorce laws also aimed at freeing women from sexual exploitation. The suffragists objected most strongly to the clause which allowed a man a divorce on the grounds of adultery but which denied such a right to a woman unless she was forced to cohabit with her husband's mistress.[71] The option of divorce meant a woman no longer had to tolerate her husband's sexual whims, his brutality, or his promiscuity.

According to John and Robin Haller, Victorian feminists used purity reform to try to achieve a kind of sexual freedom.[72] Since contemporary social values would not countenance female promiscuity, the women went the other way and denied their sexuality, in an effort to keep from being considered or treated as sex objects. Their prudery was a mask that conveniently hid the more 'radical' effort to achieve freedom of person. Michael Bliss also links the movement for sexual repression to the movement to liberate women—'often, indeed, to liberate them from male sexual tyranny'.[73]

Canada's suffragists definitely tried to play down the physical side of relationships. They constantly exhorted women to become friends and companions to men rather than sexual toys or dolls.[74] They seemed to feel that physical strength still played a prominent role in work and in defence and that in order to claim equality women must emphasize the spiritual and the intellectual side of human nature. It could be argued then that they feared sex because it accentuated physical needs and kept the weaker woman in a subservient relationship. As Alice Chown explained, 'So long as woman accepts indiscriminate sex relations, so long will she be subject to man.'[75] For the same reason the suffragists were unable to assess the value to women of artificial birth control devices which they interpreted simply as one more means of facilitating male licentiousness.[76]

Purity reform was offensive as well as defensive. In a period plagued by revelations of corruption and disease, the claim to represent a higher morality became a very powerful weapon in the suffragists' arsenal. With a ballot in their hands they could bring their moral pressure to bear upon deviant males and become the moral arbiters for the nation. Their strength rested in the respect they gained by presenting themselves as upholders of conventional female virtues.

IV

In order to understand the suffragists' social attitudes we have to understand the values of the group with which they identified. As Anglo-Saxon, Protestant middle class, such women shared the anxieties and expectations of this group. They saw women's problems through glasses tinted with values shaped by this allegiance.

As demonstrated in the first section, the Anglo-Saxon élite in this period were attempting to preserve or regain racial predominance. Two schools advocated different means towards this end. Eugenists concentrated upon applying lessons in animal breeding to humans while a group of environmental reformers argued for the need to improve the living and health standards of the population. Both approaches stressed the importance of woman's role as mother. The suffragists wished to participate in the re-creation of the race and therefore accepted the priority of woman's maternal function. Environmentalists themselves, they found within this theory a justification for their activities in the reform movement. Environmentalism also promised women greater freedom of movement and more diverse activities. Finally, the approval of domestic-science training raised the status of home-maker. These factors together satisfied the suffragists' longing for recognition.

The same Anglo-Saxon Protestant élite faced another challenge in the growth of large cities, city slums, and resultant intemperance and social vice. The campaign to reinstate Protestant standards of chastity and sobriety naturally attracted the women since it glorified their particular virtues.

With an understanding of the suffragists' background their social attitudes become predictable. It would have been inconceivable to most of these women to suggest serious restructuring of sex roles or to suggest that women imitate male immorality. Rather, they took advantage of the new dignity bestowed on women to achieve certain victories. The vote and the acquisition of higher-education facilities, less restricting garments, and a wider range of physical activities ought to be counted among these.

Suggestions for Further Reading

Catherine Lyle Cleverdon, *The Women Suffrage Movement in Canada* (Toronto, 1950).
Linda Kealey, ed., *A Not Unreasonable Claim: Women and Reform in Canada, 1880s–1920s* (Toronto, 1979).
Veronica Strong-Boag, ed., *'A Woman with a Purpose': The Diaries of Elizabeth Smith 1872–1884* (Toronto, 1980).

Notes

[1] Aileen Kraditor, *The Ideas of the Women Suffrage Movement, 1890–1920* (New York: Anchor Books, 1971); Anne Summers, *Damned Whores and God's Police* (Victoria, 1975); C. Rover, *Women's Suffrage and Party Politics in Britain, 1866–1914* (London, 1967); R. Dalziel, 'The Colonial Helpmeet: Women's Role and the Vote in Nineteenth-Century New Zealand', *New Zealand Journal of History* (October 1977).

[2] Carol Bacchi, 'Liberation Deferred: The Ideas of the English-Canadian Suffragists, 1877–1918' (PhD dissertation, McGill University, 1976). In the thesis the instigators of the suffrage societies and some of their followers are described as more feminists than social reformers. This paper is not concerned with these since they were a distinct minority.

[3] Ronald Hyam, *Britain's Imperial Century, 1815–1914* (London, 1976); G.R. Searle, *The Quest for National Efficiency* (London, 1971).

[4] Bernard Semmel, *Imperialism and Social Reform* (Cambridge, Mass., 1960).

[5] Graeme Decarie, 'The Prohibition Movement in Ontario 1894–1916' (PhD dissertation, Queen's University, 1972), 261.

[6]The theory of acquired characteristics had been unchallenged until the middle of the nineteenth century. In 1869 Galton published *Hereditary Genius* which stressed the hereditary aspects of human existence and society. In 1883 the German embryologist and geneticist, August Weissman, developed his 'germ-plasm' theory which completely denied the impact of environment. The rediscovery of Mendel in 1900 strengthened the allegiance to hereditary determinism. Donald K. Pickens, *Eugenics and the Progressives* (Nashville, 1968), 26; Hans Stubbe, *History of Genetics* (Cambridge, Mass., 1972), 176; A.H. Sturtevant, *A History of Genetics* (New York, 1965), chapter 3.

[7]Mark H. Haller, *Eugenics: Hereditarian Attitudes in American Thought* (New Brunswick, N.J., 1963), 82.

[8]Kenneth M. Ludmerer, *Genetics and American Society: A Historical Appraisal* (Baltimore, 1972), 10.

[9]Rev. A.E. Smith, 'Cutting Down an Evil Tree' in Social Service Congress of Canada, *Report of the Proceedings and Addresses* (Toronto, 1914), 204.

[10]Peter H. Bryce, M.D., 'The Ethical Problems Underlying the Social Evil', reprinted from the *Journal of Preventive Medicine and Sociology*, Toronto (March 1914), 13. Bryce was also the Chief Medical Officer for the Department of Immigration, Ottawa.

[11]Waterloo Lutheran University Archives, Emily Stowe Papers, Scrapbook III, undated (*c.* 1897) letter from Stowe to the editor of the *Toronto Mail*.

[12]Bacchi, *op. cit.*, 234–7.

[13]*Montreal Witness*, 12 October 1910.

[14]Archives of Saskatchewan, Mrs. S.V. Haight Papers, Drafts of Speeches, undated speech on feeble-minded.

[15]National Council of Women of Canada, *Annual Report* (1912), 29.

[16]*Montreal Witness*, 23 February 1912.

[17]*Montreal Star*, 24 October 1914.

[18]Mark Haller, *op. cit.*, 81.

[19]Semmell, *op. cit.*, 46.

[20]*Montreal Witness*, 12 October 1910.

[21]Edward Playter, M.D., 'The Physical Culture of Women', in *Woman; Her Character, Culture and Calling*, ed. Rev. B.F. Austin (Ontario, 1890), 225.

[22]Dominion Women's Christian Temperance Union (WCTU), Annual Report (1891), Department of Heredity and Hygiene, 88.

[23]John S. and Robin M. Haller, *The Physician and Sexuality in Victorian America* (Urbana, 1974), 146.

[24]Suse Woolf, 'Women at McGill: the Ladies' Education Association of Montreal', McGill University, 1971, 9 (mimeographed).

[25]*Grain Growers' Guide*, 14 October 1914.

[26]R.J.W. Selleck, *The New Education, 1870–1914* (London, 1978).

[27]Mary Q. Innis, *The Clear Spirit* (Toronto, 1966), 109.

[28]National Council of Women of Canada, *Women of Canada: Their Life and Their Work*, ed. Ishbel Aberdeen (Paris International Exhibition, 1900), 110.

[29]Emily Stowe Papers, *op. cit.* Scrapbook IV, article entitled 'Housewifery' (May, 1889).

[30]*Winnipeg Free Press*, 8 April 1916.

[31]National Council of Women, *Report* (1904), 121.

[32]*Grain Growers' Guide*, 27 September 1911.

[33]Victoria College Library, Emily Stowe Papers, Scrapbook VI, Printed flier, 'Votes for Women! The Woman's Reason'.

[34]*Montreal Gazette*, 27 March 1912.

[35]Child Welfare Exhibition, *Souvenir Handbook*, 8–22 October 1912.

[36]Bacchi, *op. cit.* 167.

[37]David J. Pivar, 'The New Abolitionism: The Quest for Social Purity' (PhD dissertation, University of Pennsylvania, 1965).

[38]Richard Hofstadter, *The Age of Reform* (New York, 1955).

[39]Decarie, *op. cit.*; John H. Thompson, 'The Prohibition Question in Manitoba' (MA dissertation, University of Manitoba, 1969); Robert Irwin Maclean, 'A "Most Effectual" Remedy: Temperance and Prohibition in Alberta, 1875–1915' (MA dissertation, University of Calgary, 1969); Albert J. Hiebert, 'Prohibition in British Columbia' (MA dissertation, Simon Fraser University, 1969).

[40]Rev. W.J. Hunter, *Manhood Wrecked and Rescued* (Toronto, 1894), 71.

[41]J.S. Woodsworth, *My Neighbour* (Toronto, Reprint, 1972), chapter 8.

[42]Social Service Congress, *op. cit.*, 208.

[43]Emily Murphy, *The Black Candle* (Toronto, 1922), 307.

[44]William J. Brown, M.D., *Syphilis: A Synopsis* (Washington, 1968), 9–11.

[45]*Winnipeg Free Press*, 3 July 1915.

[46]Social Service Congress, *op. cit.*

[47]Brown, *op. cit.*

[48]D. Llewellyn-Jones, *Sex and Venereal Disease* (London, 1974), 42.

[49]Glen Petrie, *A Singular Iniquity: The Campaigns of Josephine Butler* (New York, 1971).

[50]Haller and Haller, *op. cit.*, 243.

[51]Michael Bliss, 'Pure Books on Avoided Subjects: Pre-Freudian Sexual Ideas in Canada', Canadian Historical Association, *Historical Papers* (1970), 104.

[52]WCTU, *Annual Reports*.

[53]Methodist Church, Department of Evangelism and Social Service, *Annual Report* (1912–1913), 10.

[54]Social Service Congress, *op. cit.*, 208.

[55]*Grain Growers' Guide*, 16 January 1918.

[56]Beatrice Brigden and William Lund Clark were hired by the Canadian Methodist Church. Arthur W. Beall lectured to the schoolboys of Ontario on behalf of the WCTU. Methodist Church, Board of Evangelical and Social Service, Correspondence between Beatrice Brigden and Dr Albert Moore; United Church Archives, Beatrice Brigden and William Lund Clark Papers.

[57]Hunter, *op. cit.*

[58]Social Service Congress, *op. cit.*, 213.

[59]Waterloo Lutheran University Archives, Emily Stowe Papers, *op. cit.*, Scrapbook IV, undated (*c.* 1877) newspaper clipping.

[60]*Winnipeg Free Press*, 19 August 1916.

[61]Alice A. Chown, *The Stairway* (Boston, 1921), 114.

[62]University of Toronto Archives, Flora MacDonald Denison Papers, collection of newspaper clippings, *Star Weekly*, Toronto, 23 March 1913.

[63]*Ibid.*, unpub. typescript, 'The White Slave Traffic', n.d.

[64]Saskatchewan Provincial Equal Franchise Board, *Minutes of Meetings*, 18 February 1916.

[65]*Montreal Herald*, Woman's Edition, 26 November 1913, 24.

[66]*B.C. Federationist*, 17 October 1916. A quote from a BC suffragist.

[67]*Toronto World*, 15 January 1911.

[68]*Winnipeg Free Press*, 7 October 1916.

[69]*Montreal Herald*, 24 September 1913.

[70]*Grain Growers' Guide*, 26 February 1913.

[71]Helen Gregory MacGill, *Daughters, Wives, and Mothers in British Columbia: Some Laws Regarding Them* (Vancouver, 1913), 31.

[72]Haller and Haller, *op. cit.*, xii.

[73]Bliss, *op. cit.*, 103.

[74]*Grain Growers' Guide*, 14 August 1912; *Winnipeg Free Press*, 28 August 1915; *Toronto World*, 31 October 1909; *Montreal Herald*, Woman's Edition, 26 November 1913, 17.

[75]Chown, *op. cit.*, 114.

[76]C. Rover, *Love, Morals, and the Feminists* (London, 1970).

13

Canadian Education before the Great War

Marta Danylewycz and Alison Prentice

Post-Confederation Canada focused on the extension of public school systems into new communities, and the expansion of school attendance in established communities through compulsory attendance legislation. The public schools were increasingly expected to serve as a principal instrument of the state in dealing with its citizens, and perhaps *the* principal agency of change in a variety of enterprises both large and small, ranging from improved public health to greater facility in dealing with modern industrial working conditions. The schools were expected to prepare new generations of Canadians for the challenges of a world of technology, to assimilate new immigrants to Canadian society, to inculcate good citizenship among the children of both old and new Canadians, and to serve as the vanguard for a variety of social reforms in Canadian cities. Not surprisingly, these manifold goals turned the education system into a substantial bureaucracy, or series of

provincial bureaucracies, with enormous amounts of paperwork to be performed. Equally unsurprisingly, the schools were expected to introduce students to a variety of new subjects as well as maintaining discipline and encouraging appropriate behaviour. Not all scholars have agreed that placing such a heavy burden on the public school system was necessary or desirable, but most would agree that Canada's schools increasingly performed a variety of functions.

Marta Danylewycz and Alison Prentice look at the effect of changing patterns in education upon its teachers, particularly in terms of the work responsibilities that teachers were increasingly obliged to perform. Especially in the primary grades those teachers were usually women, whose work has been ignored by scholars because it does not fit the standard patterns. Danylewycz and Prentice conclude that the new demands upon the school system bore heavily on teachers, in terms of both additional paperwork and new expectations, educational and otherwise. They offer a useful discussion of the new requirements and a number of comments on the current state of scholarship on the history of education. Why do the authors warn against the possibility of over-generalization? Are the sim- ilarities or the differences between the teacher's situation in Ontario and Quebec most striking? Were teachers different from other workers? How? Would you have chosen the teaching profession under the terms and conditions outlined by the authors? Has it much changed?

This article first appeared, titled 'Teachers' Work: Changing Patterns and Perceptions in the Emerging School Systems of Nineteenth- and Early Twentieth-Century Central Canada', in *Labour/Le Travail* 17 (Spring 1986), 59–80.

The contract of Miss Ellen McGuire, dated 1 June 1880, spelled out government teachers' duties as they were understood at that time in the province of Quebec. As mistress of District School No. 3 in the township of Lowe, she agreed to

> exercise an efficient supervision over the pupils attending the school; to teach such subjects as are authorized and to make use only of duly approved school books; to fill up all blank forms which may be sent her by the Department of Public Instruction, the Inspectors or Commissioners; to keep all school registers required; to preserve amongst the archives of the school such copy books and other works of the pupils which she may be ordered to put aside; to keep the school-rooms in good order and not to allow them to be used for any other purpose without permission to that effect; to follow such rules as may be established for discipline and punishment; to preserve carefully the *Journal of Education*; in a word to fulfill all the duties of a good teacher; to hold school every day, except on Sundays, and festivals and on the holidays authorized by the Commissioners or granted by proper authority.[1]

Miss McGuire's contract stated that it was 'in conformity with' the Quebec School Act of 1878 and, like many teacher contracts of the period, was on a printed form provided by the Quebec Department of Public Instruction. Her duties, as spelled out in the printed engagement, were those put forward by the department as the standard for any government schoolteacher in the province.

In subsequent years, provincial regulations and contract forms included further detail. Indeed, the very next year, the contract of Philomène Lachance of the parish of St Croix, St Flavien, already stipulated that it was the teacher's duty to supervise pupils, whether they were in or out of class, as long as they were 'under her view'. It was further agreed that Mlle Lachance would keep the school register and children's books in a cupboard especially designed for that purpose. The teacher was expressly forbidden to use any of the schoolrooms to entertain unauthorized visitors. The contract also sounded a cautionary note regarding the use of corporal punishment, which was to be discouraged. Finally, the teacher was to be properly dressed and to set a good example of 'cleanliness' and 'savoir vivre'.[2]

Teacher contracts such as those of Ellen McGuire and Philomène Lachance outline the major areas of teachers' work in state-supported elementary schools in the latter part of the nineteenth century. They deal with the subjects to be taught, the paperwork, and the discipline of both pupils and the teacher herself. They speak, if only briefly, of the teacher's duty to take care of the schoolroom and its property. On the other hand, the contracts say nothing about the responsibility of the school commissioners towards the teacher and the school. Although they failed to mention class size, the state of school buildings, heating and cleaning arrangements, or even the locations of schools, these factors too affected teachers' work. Teachers' contracts, therefore, left much unsaid.

They nevertheless serve as a useful starting point for examining the history of teachers' work in a vital period of transition. The following discussion, which is part of a larger, ongoing study of Quebec and Ontario public school teachers, focuses on the crucial years in the nineteenth and early twentieth centuries when state school systems were in the process of being established and teacher work forces were becoming disproportionately female across both provinces. We have probed elsewhere some of the major problems addressed by our explorations in this history, such as teachers' class and ethnic origins, the question of their changing ages, marital, and household status, and the overwhelmingly important issue of gender as it affected all of these questions, or was addressed by school reformers and teachers of the time.[3] In this exploratory essay, our focus is on the actual work of teachers in the schoolroom, as this appears to have been understood and as this understanding changed during the crucial years of school system development in the nineteenth and early twentieth centuries. It is taken as a given that, increasingly, the teachers we are studying were women.

As we analysed the history of teachers in this period, we were struck by two interesting lacunae in most previous historical considerations of the subject. Educational historians have tended on the whole to treat turn-of-the-century school mistresses and masters as incipient professionals or, more disparagingly, as professionals *manqués*, shying away from any concrete consideration of the work that they actually did. The story has often been told as a tragedy: an account of the failure of teaching to become a 'genuine profession'. In one Canadian analysis, this failure was explicitly attributed, at least in part, to the influx of inexperienced and malleable young girls into the occupation and the resulting devaluing of the work of experienced and well trained males. Equally, labour historians have not seen teachers as part of the changing work force that needs to be examined in their analyses of the emergence of industrial capitalism. As Graham Lowe has shown to be the case with clerical workers, teachers also have not fitted very well into the classic model of workers perceived to be men doing manual, as opposed to intellectual or managerial, work.[4] Teachers, on the contrary, have been seen and portrayed as 'brainworkers'; and as either actually or ideally the managers, at the very least, of children if not of other adults. In addition, they were very clearly not working *men*, since so many, as time went on, were in fact women. Thus, teachers *as workers* have been left out of nineteenth- and early twentieth-century labour history, just as they have been ignored in the history of education. Recently, investigations by Michael Apple on the position of twentieth-century American teachers, and Barry Bergen, Jennifer Ozga, and Martin Lawn on their late nineteenth- and twentieth-century British counterparts, have called into question both the tendency to focus exclusively on teachers' status as either incipient or failed professionals and the tendency to ignore them as workers. By looking carefully at the meaning of changes in teachers' work and working conditions, and by introducing the concept of gender, these studies begin, rather, to develop a convincing argument for the 'proletarianization' of the teacher labour force.[5]

Our task, in the light of these considerations, was to try to come to grips more concretely than has been the case in the past with what teachers did in their daily work and how this work changed during the period of state school system construction in central Canada. As our concern was to try to get a general picture, we have ignored many details and interesting comparative questions, perhaps blurring very real differences between teachers' work in Quebec and Ontario, in Catholic and Protestant, or rural and urban schools. Nor have we focused very sharply on emerging differences between the roles of teaching assistants and principal teachers or even between those of men and women. Our concern, rather, has been to look at what was going on in nearly all nineteenth-century state-supported elementary schools, in both provinces, in all their regional, religious, and ethnic variety, to try to find the common denominators that seemed to have been affecting nearly all teachers, whatever their backgrounds or places in schools and school systems. In a reading of the annual reports of the Ontario and Quebec provincial departments of public instruction, the reports of the Montreal Catholic School Commission and the Toronto Public School Board, the *Journal of Education for Upper Canada*, and the *Educational Record of the Province of Quebec*, as well as a sampling of the correspondence of the two provincial education departments and other scattered sources, we in fact discovered a number of recurring themes. These included the introduction of new subjects and new teaching methods into nineteenth- and early twentieth-century schoolrooms; the introduction and phenomenal growth of paperwork; and a growing emphasis on discipline and hierarchy, as well as on uniformity of practice and routine. Pupil and teacher health and the question of the physical maintenance of schools and classrooms also emerged as important questions for analysis. Documents of the period make it clear, in other words, that an understanding of teachers' work must include a consideration not only of their tasks, but also of the changing conditions under which they performed them. Finally, teachers' work was affected by less tangible factors. Their own perceptions, and the perceptions of their employers, regarding the economic and social position of schoolmistresses and schoolmasters, as well as assumptions about what work was compatible with that position, also played a role. Here great tensions were generated, tensions that explain the contradictory policies pursued by the women teachers' associations which emerged at the turn of the century, as they sought to improve their members' conditions of work and to define the position of women teachers in the labour force.

New Subjects, More Teaching

Despite the profound differences in the organization and structure of the Ontario and Quebec public school systems, both were settling into an era of consolidation and growth by the 1880s. Having weathered the storms of local opposition to the intervention of central authorities in the establishment of schools, and having asserted their dominance over teacher certification and classroom instruction, provincial educational leaders were now in a position to expand the functions of the institutions they increasingly controlled. The lengthening of the period of formal schooling and the broadening of the public school curriculum were part of that expansion and both developments directly affected the work of teachers. As children remained in school longer, classs sizes and schools grew proportionally; and as students had to master a broader range of subjects, the workload of many teachers increased.

The 1871 Ontario School Law, which made schooling compulsory for children between the ages of seven and twelve, also called for the addition of agriculture and drawing to the long established elementary school program of reading, writing, arithmetic, geography, and grammar. The 1880s saw the introduction in Ontario of hygiene, temperance, and calisthenics into the curriculum, and the turn of the century brought in manual training and domestic science. The annual reports of the Department of Education recording the number of children learning the new subjects following their introduction attest to the widening of teachers' responsibilities during the last quarter of the nineteenth century. The number of children studying drawing, for example, increased eight fold between 1870 and 1900; the number taking hygiene increased six fold; and the number taking drill and calisthenics increased three fold between 1880 and 1900.[6]

Similar developments occurred in Quebec, producing comparable alterations in the work of teachers. Although compulsory education was not legislated until 1940, a rise in school attendance, owing to growing enrolment and the lengthening of the period of formal schooling, was evident by the last quarter of the nineteenth century. Moreover, as was the case in Ontario, so too in Quebec were agriculture, drawing, hygiene, calisthenics, and domestic science beginning to be integrated into the public elementary school curriculum during the closing decades of the nineteenth century.[7]

In both provinces curricular reform created much consternation among teachers. Not having been consulted about or forewarned of changes in elementary school programs, they were frequently overwhelmed by the new demands being made of them. 'Can anyone tell us where we are drifting to in this matter of additional text-books and increasing number of subjects?' asked one Montreal teacher of a teachers' journal. It was this teacher's hope that the editor would throw some light on the 'impossible goal' towards which teachers were 'expected to hasten'. Teachers such as this correspondent were often troubled by their lack of preparation to teach the new subjects. Many responded by simply ignoring the pressure to introduce them, arguing that this was justified as long as the central authorities did not provide proper instruction manuals or opportunities for teacher retraining. Because both provinces were slow in helping teachers out of the conundrum the new subjects created, such resistance endured.[9]

Central authorities, for their part, may have counted on the high turnover rate among teachers to flush out the older and ill-equipped masters and mistresses who would, they must have reasoned, eventually be replaced by normal school graduates trained in the teaching of the new subjects. But normal school training remained the exception rather than the rule in both Ontario and Quebec. The majority of teachers moved into the occupation through other channels, generally by attending model or convent schools and then presenting themselves to local boards of examiners. Moreover, within the teaching corps there were increasing numbers of persisters or career teachers whose training pre-dated curricular reform. If in the early days educational authorities satisfied themselves by assuming that such teachers would train themselves in the new subjects or by reminding the recalcitrant that 'the *clever* teachers' would be able to master them 'without the aid of a manual',[10] by the last decades of the nineteenth century they began to supply some assistance. During the holidays, after school, and on weekends, schoolmistresses and masters were urged to attend provincially or locally organized classes and institutes, to learn not only the new subjects but the more modern methods of instruction and classroom management popularized by the 'new education' movement of the period. These extracurricular courses, *ad hoc* at first, soon became a regular part of teachers' work.[11]

Paperwork

If new subjects added to the teacher's workload, so did the rapidly growing mounds of paperwork. As early as 1847, the chief superintendent of schools for Upper Canada had foreshadowed this work when he wrote to a local school officer to the effect that what was not put in writing did not, for the purposes of the school system, exist. What was communicated 'verbally', he commented then, could not be considered 'official'. In this brief remark, tossed off so casually to an obscure Upper Canadian educator who must have failed to put some information crucial to his purposes on paper, the chief superintendent enunciated a principle which was to haunt teachers as well as the officers of school systems from then on.[12]

It may have been the local school officers who were legally required to fill out the forms demanded by provincial authorities—and by the 1860s in Ontario, local trustees' reports covered over a hundred different items—but it was usually the teacher who had to supply the basic information. And of the 'blank forms' mentioned in the Quebec teachers' contracts of early 1880s, the most time-consuming, as well as the most vital, was probably the individual class or school register. In Canada West the daily attendance register seems to have made its appearance as early as the 1840s. In 1850 it took on a crucial role for local schools, and parents and taxpayers, for after that date the Upper Canadian school grant was distributed on the basis of average attendance rates, with the highest grants going to the schools with the best attendance. Woe betide the teacher who did not keep an accurate daily account of pupils' presence or absence in the school, for falsification of the attendance register, according to the chief superintendent's report for 1859, met with 'punishment'. Failure to keep it altogether jeopardized the entire school grant to the section.[13]

By the 1880s in Quebec, it was clear that individual teachers had paperwork that went beyond the compiling of the daily registers. A correspondent to the *Educational Record* explained the methods whereby teachers could compute the averages from their daily records for half-yearly reports.[14] Rural Quebec teachers reported to local commissioners rather than to boards of trustees for individual schools, and an 1883 report from the county of Soulanges is evidence of some of the information that they had to include. This document, dated 19 February 1883, came from the pen of Marie Argonie Viau, *institutrice* of a school in the sixth *arrondissement* of the *Municipalité Scolaire de St Joseph*. It was two pages in length. One page listed the scholars in the school, along with their ages and the numbers of boys and girls who were studying various subjects or reading particular books. The other page consisted of a letter introducing this material, explaining its deficiencies, and requesting that the commissioners supply the teacher with a notebook so that she could comply with the requirement that an ongoing record be kept of inspectors' and commissioners' visits to her school.[15]

In the city of Toronto, the annual reports of the Public School Board are evidence of the reporting tasks that could be added to the work of urban teachers as school systems grew larger and more complex. In 1872, in addition to the statistical summaries of their schools' registers that were periodically required, headmasters and mistresses were asked to provide monthly lists of absentees for that month, along with the reasons for their non-attendance. In 1881, it was announced that every teacher had to keep a written record of all homework assigned to pupils. Finally, in 1891, written assessments of individual students' progress were added to the teachers' work. At the end of the school year, every teacher had to produce a 'mind chart' for each pupil, along with his or her recommendations regarding the individual pupils' promotions.[16]

If reporting to their superiors produced one kind of paperwork for teachers, the advent of written tests and examinations produced another. Gone was the era when everything depended on the oral questioning of both pupils and teachers. Examinations for teacher certification on the one hand, and the correction and assessment of students' workbooks and examinations on the other, loomed ever larger in the work of schools. Another part of the teacher's work lay in dealing with the anxiety that examinations inevitably produced. On the occasion of the introduction of provincial examinations in Quebec in 1895, a sarcastic letter from '*Amicus*' appeared in the *Educational Record*, revealing the extent to which one correspondent, at least, felt that schoolmistresses and masters in Ontario had already become slaves to the unreasonable central authorities who controlled such exams. *Amicus* produced a list of injunctions which reflected what this author clearly believed were the sins the Ontario examiners had all too often committed. Failing to phrase questions simply or arrange them clearly, or to proofread the printed copies of the examinations were only a few among many. Moreover, it was really the teachers who were being examined, not their pupils. What provincial examiners wanted, *Amicus* seemed to imply, was confusion and anxiety—in short, more work for the people who were actually on the firing line in the schools, their already overburdened teachers.[17]

The Work of Supervision—and Being Supervised

Both *Amicus* and Marie Argonie Viau outlined the difficulties teachers had in complying with the control mechanisms set in place by provincial schoolmen, and their comments reveal how wide the gulf could be between the expectations of central authorities and the realities teachers faced on the local level. If the laws and departmental or local regulations were problematic, even the pressures generated by reformers' supposedly helpful suggestions could have a disquieting effect. A teacher writing to the *Educational Record* in the mid-1880s captured the anxiety of many. The *Record*'s advice was good, the letter implied, but hard to follow in this teacher's country school.

The *Record* had suggested a school museum, but that was impossible. The 'scholars would likely kill one another with the mineral specimens.' Even the more standard activities of needlework and scripture reading were counted 'a loss of time' in this teacher's school, where pupils no doubt continued the tradition of attending only when farm or domestic work permitted them to do so: 'You have never taught schools in this country. I feel as I felt one summer when I rode for a month a very vicious horse, coaxing him a little, yet not too much, lest he should think, or rather find out, that I feared him, for then he would be sure to run away with me.'[18]

Individual teachers were caught between the exigencies of local conditions and the demands of their superiors, and both fell heavily on them. In the 1840s it had been possible for an elderly rural teacher from the Upper Canadian District of Gore to lie on a bench and allow the pupils to read out loud to him as they gradually drifted into the school over the course of the morning. But the district superintendent, on observing this approach to school teaching, had been shocked. As he related to the chief superintendent of the province, when all the pupils were assembled he had lectured both teacher and taught on the importance of punctuality; later on he had seen to it that the old man's certificate to teach was not renewed.[19] The situation of the teacher from Gore anticipated that of his successors for, as the nineteenth century wore on, the teacher's role in matters like punctuality was increasingly emphasized. One graphic illustration of how important such issues became was the astonishing drop from 69,456 cases of 'lateness' reported for Toronto board schools in 1874 to only 5,976 cases in 1880. This constituted a great improvement in the eyes of the city's newly appointed school superintendent, James Hughes; how it had been achieved was not explained. Clearly, though, classroom teachers must have been involved in Hughes' campaign to reduce tardiness.[20]

Teachers were also increasingly expected to take responsibility for the behaviour of students outside the classroom. This included pupils 'on their way to and from school' as well as during lunch hours and school breaks. Recognizing the fact that some parents sent children to school when they were sick, the Toronto board required each school to appoint a teacher to stay inside with such pupils during recess. All other teachers, according to a new regulation of 1879, had to be in the schoolyard during that period.[21] The supervision of children outside of the classroom, most educators believed, involved not just one's presence but also setting a good example. Thus an 1885 *Educational Record* article entitled 'Noontime' exhorted teachers to eat 'decorously' and use a napkin when having lunch with their pupils. After a short lunchtime rest, they were also encouraged to organize games for the children to keep them happy and occupied.[22]

As school officials increasingly used teachers to tighten the reins of control over students, they also introduced measures to insure that the teachers themselves performed their work as specified in the regulations. Through local institutes teachers were instructed in matters as personal as their tone of voice and as trivial as how many times to pull the rope when ringing the school bell, as well as in matters more clearly related to academic instruction.[23] But the more obvious controls were exerted by the visits of school inspectors and, where schools were growing larger, by principals or head teachers. The frequency and character of rural school inspection depended on a variety of factors, ranging from the personality of the inspector to the location of the school. Schools that were hard to reach were sometimes missed altogether when the inspector made his rounds.[24] Conversely, urban teachers were inspected more regularly than rural teachers and were subjected to more systematic and closer controls. In Toronto, for example, Public School Board teachers were visited by an increasing number of 'specialists', who supervised the teaching of subjects like drawing, domestic science, and drill. School-mistresses and some masters who taught for large urban boards were also visibly compartmentalized in the lower rungs of growing educational bureaucracies which subjected them to several levels of inspection, beginning with the school principal and ending with the district and provincial superintendency.[25]

Working for Better Health

The superintendency concerned itself not just with teachers, of course. It was also part of the inspector's job to supervise the local school boards them-selves, with a view to enforcing the laws requiring decent school accom-modation. Ontario authorities, for example, specified in 1871 exactly how much land, floor space, and air each school should have, depending on the number of pupils. Requirements governing fences, ventilation and heating, drinking water, school privies and equipment were vaguer, stating only that these items should be 'sufficent' or 'suitable'.[26] But whether they were spe-cific or vague, the regulations were hard to enforce and teachers all too often found their employers delinquent in these matters. As a result their work frequently had to be performed under the most trying conditions.

In a typical letter, dated 23 March 1883, a local inspector described to his superiors in the Quebec Department of Public Instruction the failure of the commissioners for St Jean de Rouville to provide proper accommodation for their village school. The school, he reported, was exactly as he had found it the year before, despite promises to repair and renovate it. The building was so cold that parts of it were uninhabitable; the rooms were so small that some of the children were literally 'crushed one against the other'. The inspector clearly felt that only provincial pressure could bring about an improvement and he buttressed his case by referring to the feelings of the school's two teachers. These schoolmistresses not only suffered considerable 'malaise' because of the conditions in their school, but, according to the inspector, were reluctant to complain because when their predecessor had done so, he had been reprimanded and forced to retract his complaints by the St Jean de Rouville commissioners.[27]

In Montreal, teachers employed by the Catholic School Commission did not even need to submit a grievance to be reprimanded. City health inspectors might achieve the same result, as in the case of Mlle Thibodeau in 1877. Because they found the conditions in her two-room school 'injurious to the health of the pupils' and reported that finding to her employers, Thibodeau's subsidy from the commission was cut off. This teacher, her employers decided, would be reinstated only after the required renovations were made or after she found a new building to house her 150 pupils.[28]

Thibodeau's predicament was not an isolated one in the history of Quebec schooling. Many Montreal women teachers toiled in poorly ventilated, ill-equipped, insufficiently lit, and overcrowded classrooms. When health inspectors presented a damning report, they and not their employers, the commissioners, faced the consequences, because schoolrooms and buildings were their responsibility.[29] Thibodeau was laid off for a month and a half; she needed that much time to find more suitable accommodation for her school. In the meantime, she and others like her suffered the loss of their salaries while moving from one site to another. Thibodeau, like many other teachers, also suffered from poor health, fatigue, and physical breakdown as a result of her working conditions, and eventually had to resign.

Clearly, if the health of the students was endangered by the poor condition of many schools, so too was that of their teachers. Léocadie Généreux, a contemporary of Thibodeau and mistress of a neighbouring school, requested a leave of absence in 1879 due 'to the precarious state of her health'. It was granted along with a $50.00 bonus in recognition of fifteen years of service to the school commission.[30] Généreux returned to the classroom one year later, to take up the front line in the battle against smallpox, diphtheria, and tuberculosis being waged by school officials and public health reformers. In the wake of scientific findings that many of the contagious diseases could be contained by vaccination and proper diet, late nineteenth- and early twentieth-century teachers increasingly found themselves instructing their pupils in hygiene and correct eating habits, insuring that they were vaccinated, inspecting them for contagious diseases, and sending the ill to the school clinic or home.[31]

The combination of poor working conditions and exposure to a variety of contagious diseases debilitated teachers, forcing many to take periodic leaves of absence. In recognition of this fact, the Toronto Public School Board in the 1870s began to hire 'occasional teachers' to replace those on sick leave.[32] While from the students' and employers' point of view substitute teachers were a solution to the absent teacher problem, they were hardly the answer as far as the ailing schoolmistresses were concerned. Their only recourse at time of sickness was family, kin, or charitable institutions. In this regard their situation was no different from that of nineteenth-century labourers, who also relied on these traditional, albeit frequently inadequate, support systems.

At the same time, however, teachers were pressuring provincial governments to make amends to pension funds (established in 1853 in Ontario and in 1856 in Quebec) in view of the ill effects working conditions had on their health. Individual and isolated requests of schoolmistresses like that of Eliza Pelletier from L'Islet, Quebec for an early retirement with a pension due to her anemic condition, became by the turn of the century collective demands voiced at meetings of teachers' associations.[33] The associations of Protestant and Catholic teachers of Montreal stood united in the early 1900s in an effort to pressure the provincial government to lower the age of retirement for women teachers from 56 to 50. Reasoning that 'the great majority of women teachers break down before reaching the present retiring age, and are utterly unfit to follow other occupations,' they demanded revisions to the pension fund scheme as well as, at least implicitly, a recognition by school officials that the work of women teachers was far more exacting than that of the men.[34]

In the same vein, women teachers began to publicize their concerns about health and working conditions through the medium of the press. Whenever the occasion presented itself, and it did in turn-of-the-century Montreal with the founding of the *Ligue d'enseignement*, they pleaded their case with the public.[35] They also rejoiced when support for their cause or recognition of the difficulties under which they laboured appeared outside their own circles. In 1891 the *Educational Record* reprinted an article from one of the province's newspapers that had taken notice of the teacher's plight and outlined ways in which teachers could prevent fatigue, anemia, or mere discouragement.[36]

School Maintenance and Housekeeping

If poor working conditions and health care were dominant themes for teachers in the second half of the nineteenth century and carried on unabated into the early twentieth, a related and muted theme was the teacher's continuing role in the physical maintenance of the school. The school had once been located in the teacher's home, a rented house, or a room in someone else's house; then, as provincial school systems were put into place, in most locations the school house became public property and, in theory, the responsibility for its maintenance shifted to local boards of trustees or commissioners. But, for the women who taught under the Montreal Catholic School Commission, as we have seen, this theory did not even begin to be put into practice. And for a long time the boundaries of responsibility for the maintenance and upkeep of school property remained blurred in other regions as well. Often school boards insisted that at least the minor work of school maintenance still belonged to teachers.

In Ontario, debate on the subject can be traced back to the 1840s. Queries to the office of the chief superintendent of schools suggest that Upper Canadian trustee boards and their teachers had already entered into dispute in two areas: who should lay the fires in schools and who should clean the schoolhouses. In 1848, Egerton Ryerson wrote that these were matters for negotiations between teachers and trustees, the law not specifying who was responsible for the work of school maintenance. He suggested that the trustees could give the teacher a higher salary in return for the work, grant a special allowance for the purpose, or agree to it being done by the pupils under the teacher's direction.[37] But arguments on the subject continued to reach the chief superintendent's desk, as trustees pressed the housework of the school on reluctant teachers who clearly regarded such tasks as 'extra' work, or beneath their dignity. By 1861 the provincial Education Office took a stronger stand on behalf of such teachers. The housekeeping work of the school, Egerton Ryerson now argued, was no longer a matter for negotiation; such work, he implied, did not belong to the men and women whose employment educational reformers were trying so hard to define as 'professional'. Under the heading 'Official Replies of the Chief Superintendent of Schools to Local School Authorities in Upper Canada', the *Journal of Education for Upper Canada* published the following brief statement: '*Teachers are not required to make Fires.* The Teacher is employed to teach the school, but he is not employed to make the fires and clean the school house, much less repair the school house.'[38]

Provincial educational authorities' pronouncements did not necessarily sway local school boards, however, and in an 1863 trustees' minute book for School Section No. 1, North West Oxford, building fires as well as ringing the school bell were explicitly laid out as the teacher's contracted work. In 1865 however, the superintendent from Oxford County reported that the more common solution in the country schools under his jurisdiction was to hire a lad to do the 'extra work' or to press it onto the pupils.[39]

Anna Paulin, who taught in the Quebec parish of Ste Marie de Manoir Rouville in the 1880s, engaged to keep the school clean and the path to the school clear, according to her contract.[40] But in Quebec as well, such work was subject to debate. Under the heading 'Enquiries', the *Educational Record* dealt with the topic in 1885. Was it 'part of the teacher's duty' to light the school fires each morning? The answer was unequivocal: 'Certainly not. The trouble and expense of lighting the fires must be provided for by the school commissioners through the school manager of the district.'[41] In 1889 the *Educational Record* argued that it was the teacher's job, with the help of her pupils, to keep the schoolroom neat and clean, but only provided that a proper caretaker cleaned it thoroughly once a week. The issue was of sufficient importance to merit attention once again in an 1893 editorial on how teachers could improve their position in society. Schoolmistresses and masters were advised to see to it that their contracts were signed and sealed and that no one dictated to them on the subject of where they should board. Last but not least they were told to arrange 'if possible, with the trustees to make someone look after the cleaning of the schoolroom and making the fires.'[42]

If these issues continued to be problematic for rural teachers as late as the 1890s, in the cities they were less often debated. At least wherever urban schools were larger than one or two rooms, the need for a separate staff of caretakers was generally recognized. By 1876 the Toronto Public School Board employed nineteen caretakers; fifteen years later their number had almost tripled. City school caretakers in the nineteenth century frequently lived on the school property; indeed it seems often to have been a family occupation and even a job for women. Wages compared favourably with those of teachers: in 1889 the top annual salary for a male caretaker was $600, for a woman $375. In 1891, nine women were among the board's 53 caretakers. Two of these women were succeeded, when they died, by their sons.[43]

If the heavy work of school cleaning and laying fires was a thing of the past for city schoolteachers, this did not mean that their jobs were entirely free of housekeeping tasks. Urban and rural teachers alike were exhorted to keep their schoolrooms tidy and to 'beautify' them.[44] Even the Montreal daily, *Le Canada*, in its support for the 'new education' movement, decried the unattractive appearance of Quebec schools compared to American ones: 'Our [schools] are devoid of decoration, while in the public and catholic schools of our neighbours, professors and students pride themselves on giving their schools as beautiful an appearance as possible.'[45] Schoolroom tidying and decorating, indeed, gradually moved in to replace the more mundane tasks of sweeping and dusting for late nineteenth-century teachers.

Tidying became important for both rural and city teachers because of the growing stock of globes, maps, and other material goods that modern schools required. In the city of Toronto as well as in rural and urban Quebec, school documents express concern about this work. As one of them put it, now that the teacher was responsible for school property it was only fair that each school or classroom should contain a cupboard for its safekeeping. In Toronto, the school board recognized in 1873 that teachers occasionally needed extra time for the work of tidying and organizing the classroom and its contents. That year, at least, the day before the Christmas holidays was set aside for teachers to put their rooms 'in good order'.[46]

The advent of caretakers also meant another kind of work for urban teachers: the work of negotiating when their interests and those of the caretakers clashed. Such a conflict occurred when the women employed in Toronto schools noticed that the oil used by the caretakers on the floors soiled the hems of their skirts. If it was part of the teacher's work to set a good example by looking clean and presentable—and Ellen McGuire's 1880 Quebec contract was not the only one to state explicitly that this was the case—then a measure initiated to reduce costs or caretakers' labour in maintaining floors had resulted in increased costs and labour for the women who taught in Toronto public schools.[47]

Resistance and Perceptions of the Woman Teacher's Ambiguous Position

It was this issue, along with those of their wages, that the Women Teachers' Association of Toronto brought to the trustees of the city twenty years after their organization's founding in 1885. Indeed, these were the problems, along with other long-standing concerns about health, working conditions, and the reorganization of the pension fund in light of the particular needs and experiences of women teachers, that eventually drove schoolmistresses to band together and establish protective associations. In central Canada, Toronto led the way with Montreal and then, somewhat later, rural teachers in both Ontario and Quebec followed suit. By the turn of the century, urban women teachers were speaking with collective voices, not only echoing the grievances their predecessors had so frequently raised in individual exchanges with their local and provincial superiors but also winning some concessions from their employers. In Toronto, for example, organization helped to bring the women teachers a salary scale based on seniority rather than grade level and the election of a woman to the school board.[48] In Montreal the associations of Catholic and Protestant women teachers succeeded in persuading the provincial government to make the pension plan more favourable to women teachers and to raise the annual pension by 50 per cent. The Catholic association also guaranteed ill or unemployed teachers some assistance during times of need.[49]

When schoolmistresses should be allowed to retire and the presence of women on school boards were hardly the major concerns of those promoting school system development and professionalism among teachers in the nineteenth and early twentieth centuries. The former were of such profound interest to Ontario and Quebec women teachers, on the other hand, that eventually they began to view themselves as a class apart from their male colleagues and state school employers. A sense of separateness, nourished by years of working conditions harsher than those endured by men (who generally could look forward to administrative positions or at least teaching the more advanced grades) and of a shared experience of inequality in salary and opportunity for advancement in the occupation, led many of the career women teachers to express their particular demands and grievances increasingly openly. As part of her contribution to the pension debate, a Quebec schoolmistress, who had 'roamed professionally' from one rural county to another for nearly twenty years, remarked in no uncertain terms that she, as a teacher, did 'more work for [her] country than some of our politicians'. This conviction prompted her to ask why no provision could be made for 'the few women' who made elementary teaching 'their life-work' and to offer the provincial government a list of suggested improvements.

> I would suggest that our Government provide a work house for superannuated female teachers, taxing highly-salaried teachers and school inspectors for its support. Another suggestion I beg leave to make is that women be eligible for the office of school inspector. It would be a comfortable berth for some of us that have been too long on starvation salaries.[50]

Such sentiments were behind the founding of separate women teachers' associations in both Ontario and Quebec. The frustrations and aspirations expressed by teachers making suggestions of this kind were also a reflection of the transition teachers' work had undergone in the period since 1840. Prior to the establishment of government school systems as well as during the early years of their creation, schoolmistresses and masters worked within informal, more personal, and less hierarchical structures. Centralization and the development of provincial elementary school systems brought about a major change in the form and content of schooling. Athénais Bibaud, the principal of Marchand Academy in Montreal, noted in 1911 that in the past 'the programme of studies was not as heavy', leaving time for frequent breaks and 'cordial chats between teachers and pupils, chats which were very useful because they *shed light on everything*'. But, as she further remarked, as all things go, this type of interaction between student and teacher had come to an end, and not just in her own school. Discipline had become 'more severe', pupils and teachers alike 'worked a bit harder', and younger mistresses were now supervised by the older, more experienced ones. By this time, too, the Montreal Catholic School Commission exercised more control over the academy.[51]

The reorganization of time, work, and discipline in the school did not improve the lot of the teacher. 'One thing that did not keep pace with the changing times', added Bibaud in her reflections, 'were the salaries of teaching assistants.'[52] A similar observation of the disjuncture between the enduring regime of low salaries and the changing mode of schooling led Elizabeth Binmore, a founder of the Montreal Protestant Women Teachers' Association, to speculate on the nature of the woman teacher's work in the public schoolroom and its relationship to her status in society. Did her employment fit with the title 'lady teacher' which was still so much in use? Elizabeth Binmore seemed to think not.[53] Her work was not leisure; therefore it was not appropriate to refer to the schoolmistress by using a term implying that it was. 'Lady teacher' belonged to a genteel past which by the turn of the century was but a dim memory to the vast majority of overworked and underpaid women teachers in Montreal.

While Binmore was able to make such a statement in the mid-1890s, a moment when Montreal teachers' salaries, owing to depressed economic conditions, may have been at a particularly low ebb, she and her colleagues in the three women teachers' associations that late nineteenth-century conditions spawned in Quebec and Ontario nevertheless had great difficulty grasping permanently a vision of themselves as workers. Wayne Urban has argued that in the three American cities he studied, the women teachers who organized were aware of their interests and fought mainly as interest groups rather than as incipient professionals, although their approaches varied according to local conditions.[54] It is very clear that Canadian women teachers, like their American counterparts, also formed their associations with bread and butter issues such as wages, working conditions, and pensions chiefly in mind. Yet, unlike the most radical Americans, Canadian teachers were reluctant to ally themselves with working-class organizations or identify with working-class groups that had comparable problems. In Toronto, the Woman Teachers' Association toyed with a labour affiliation in 1905, but backed off.[55]

Perhaps the key word here is 'comparable'. For, with hindsight, we can now see that the position of turn-of-the-century women teachers was similar to that of beleaguered industrial workers but, as the women teachers of the time perceived, it was also different. Women teachers had not necessarily been 'deskilled'; on the contrary, new skills were constantly being demanded of them. Nor were they necessarily subjected to seasonal unemployment and layoffs to the same extent as labourers, especially those who worked in the light manufacturing industries. Moreover, their work was supposedly intellectual and not manual, a division which, at least according to Harry Braverman, was 'the most decisive single step in the division of labour' taken by industrial capitalist societies.[56] Yet as 'brainworkers' they also at times toiled manually, beautifying their schools, keeping the path to the schoolhouse clear in the winter, and inspecting pupils for contagious diseases. They spent hours on the busy work of maintaining school records and looking after the objects that increasingly filled their classrooms. In fact, in their work they straddled both sides of Braverman's great divide and laboured on the margins of both. As far as their working conditions and salaries were concerned, however, they did share the plight of nineteenth-century workers.[57]

It was the uncertainty of their position in the labour force that helps to explain how women teachers could flirt with the mystique of professionalism while at the same time their members referred to themselves as the exploited or as toilers and hirelings. In recalling their double bind one returns, finally, to feminists' recognition of the need for a more nuanced analysis of work and a less dichotomous vision of the social order if we are to understand the work of women.[58] Elizabeth Binmore began to glimpse these truths in the mid-1890s. Teachers, she saw, were not 'ladies'. Nor, however, could they fully see themselves as workers, in spite of the poor wages and difficult working conditions they endured.

Michael Apple has rightly argued that teachers' 'deskilling and reskilling, intensification and loss of control, or the countervailing pressures of professionalization and proletarianization' that have affected the occupation, and continue to affect it to this day, are complex processes. They cannot be explained solely in terms of the sexual division of labour. Nevertheless, as he also contends, that division has been an essential component in these processes.[59] This brief study of central Canadian teachers during this period of state school system formation confirms Apple's contention. Turn-of-the-century women teachers in Ontario and Quebec were increasingly aware of their special problems and some were already aware of the ambiguity of their position. Many also knew that a major source of their difficulties was the fact that they were women in school systems largely designed for and controlled by men.[60]

Suggestions for Further Reading

Susan E. Houston and Alison Prentice, *Schooling and Scholars in Nineteenth-Century Ontario* (Toronto, 1988).
Roger Magnuson, *A Brief History of Quebec Education* (Montreal, 1980).
Neil Sutherland, *Children in English-Canadian Society: Framing the Twentieth Century Consensus* (Toronto, 1978).

Notes

[1] Engagement of Ellen McGuire, 1 June 1880, Education Records, E 13, Archives Nationales du Québec (hereafter ANQ).

[2] Engagement of Philomène Lachance, 11 July 1881, E 13, ANQ.

[3] Alison Prentice, 'The Feminization of Teaching in British North America and Canada, 1845–1875', *Social History/Histoire sociale* 8 (1975), 5–20; Marta Danylewycz, Beth Light, and Alison Prentice, 'The Evolution of the Sexual Division of Labour in Teaching: A Nineteenth Century Ontario and Quebec Case Study', *Social History/Histoire sociale* 16 (1983), 81–109; Marta Danylewycz and Alison Prentice, 'Teachers, Gender and Bureaucratizing School Systems in Nineteenth Century Montreal and Toronto', *History of Education Quarterly* 24 (1984), 75–100.

[4] André Labarrère-Paulé, *Les Instituteurs laiques au Canada français, 1836–1900,* (Québec 1965). J.G. Althouse, *The Ontario Teacher: A Historical Account of Progress, 1800–1910* (1929; Toronto 1967) focuses on the 'rise' of the professional teacher, but avoids discussing the question of gender. Graham S. Lowe, 'Class, Job and Gender in the Canadian Office', *Labour/Le Travail* 10 (1982), 11–37.

[5]Michael W. Apple, 'Work, Class and Teaching', in Stephen Walker and Len Barton, eds, *Gender, Class and Education* (New York 1983), 53–67; Jennifer Ozga and Martin Lawn, *Teachers, Professionalism and Class: A Study of Organized Teachers* (London 1981); Barry H. Bergen, 'Only a Schoolmaster: Gender, Class and the Effort to Professionalize Elementary Teaching in England, 1870–1910', *History of Education Quarterly* 22 (1982), 1–21.

[6]*Annual Reports of the Chief Superintendent of Schools for Ontario*, 1870–1900.

[7]*Ibid.* and *Annual Reports of the Superintendent for the Province of Quebec*, 1870–1900.

[8]*Educational Record of the Province of Quebec* 13, 1 (1893), 28.

[9]*Educational Record* 9, 12 (1889), 324. Resistance to curricular reform in Quebec can be traced in a variety of sources. For references to complaints coming from rural schools, see the letters in Education Records, E 13, 615-44, 614-50, 615-200, and 615-82, ANQ.

[10]A reference to parent resistance to too many new subjects, and the fact that the Toronto Public School Board supported the complaint against their introduction by the provincial government, may be found in the *Annual Reports of the Toronto Public School Board*, 1872 and 1873. Reports for the remainder of the 1870s and 1880s record the work of special subject masters hired to deal with new areas like music, drill, and drawing, including the introduction of after-hours classes to train the teachers. The tone of the special subject masters' reports suggests that many urban teachers were as slow as rural teachers to accept the new subjects.

[11]Miss Reid, 'How to keep the Little Ones Employed', *Educational Record* 2, 10 (1882), 413.

[12]Egerton Ryerson to C. Gregor, 5 May 1847, Education Records, RG 2, C-1, Letterbook C, 355, Public Archives of Ontario (hereafter PAO). On the role of the Ryerson administration in the increase of paperwork in Ontario Schools, see Alison Prentice, 'The Public Instructor: Egerton Ryerson and the Role of the Public School Administrator', in Neil McDonald and Alf Chaiton, eds, *Egerton Ryerson and His Times* (Toronto 1978), 129–59.

[13]*Annual Report of the Chief Superintendent of Schools for Ontario*, 1859, 16–7.

[14]*Educational Record* 6, 3 (1886), 81–2.

[15]Report of Marie Argonie Viau to the commissioners, 19 February 1883, E 13, ANQ.

[16]*Annual Reports of the Toronto Public School Board*, 1872, 12–5; 1881, 16; 1891, 28 ff.

[17]*Educational Record* 15, 3 (1895), 91–3.

[18]*Ibid.* 5, 2 (1885), 57.

[19]Patrick Thornton to Egerton Ryerson, 22 January 1849, RG 2, C-6-C, PAO.

[20]*Annual Report of the Toronto Public School Board*, 1880, 11.

[21]*Ibid.* 1873, 66; 1879, 29.

[22]*Educational Record* 5, 1 (1885), 7–8.

[23]*Annual Report of the Toronto Public School Board*, 1886, 18–9.

[24]J-P. Nantel to Hon. Surintendant de l'Instruction Publique, le 29 March 1884, E 13, 637-50, ANQ.

[25]*Annual Report of the Toronto Public School Board*, 1891, 33 ff., describes the addition of an assistant superintendent and four 'supervisory principals' to the Toronto administration.

[26]*Annual Report of the Chief Superintendent of Schools for Ontario*, 1870, 59.

[27]J.B. Delage to Gédéon Quimet, 23 March 1883, E 13, ANQ.

[28]Registre des délibérations du Bureau des Commissaires, Vol. II, 27 April, 4 May, 19 June 1877. Archives de la Commission des Écoles Catholiques de Montréal (ACCM).

[29]The Montreal Catholic School Commission was unusual in requiring women teachers to find accommodation for their own schools. The commission did not, until the 1900s, build schools for female teachers and students. A discussion of its policies may be found in Marta Danylewycz, 'Sexes et classes sociales dans l'enseignement: le cas de Montréal à la fin du 19e siècle', in N. Fahmy-Eid and Micheline Dumont, *Maîtresses de maison, maîtresses d'école* (Montreal 1983), 93–118.

[30]Registre des délibération, Vol. II, 5 March 1879; Généreux worked for the commission until her death in 1890, ACCM.

[31]For a discussion of public health reform and the role of teachers in it see Neil Sutherland, *Children in English-Canadian Society: Framing the Twentieth Century Consensus* (Toronto 1978).

[32]Teachers were permitted to take sick leaves of up to one month. For longer absences they had to pay for the substitute teachers out of their own pockets. See *Annual Reports of the Toronto Public School Board*, 1872, 98, and 1874, 85–90.

[33]Eliza Pelletier to V.T. Simard, 19 January 1884, E 13, 637–12. ANQ.

[34]'Miss Ferguson's Address to Convention on Pension Act', *Educational Record* 28, 12 (1903), 392.

[35]See the following in *La Patrie*, 'Causerie—Une Grande Fondation', 6 December 1902; '*Autour de l'école*', 11 October 1902.

[36]*Educational Record* 11, 1 (1891), 4–12.

[37]Egerton Ryerson to John Monger, 26 December 1848, RG 2, C-1, Letterbook D, 360.

[38]Letters of inquiry on the subject include C.W.D. De l'Armitage to Egerton Ryerson, 27 June 1849; Meade N. Wright to Ryerson, 26 June 1859; and Teacher to Ryerson, 1 April 1859, RG 2, C-6-C, PAO. 'Official Replies, . . . ' *Journal of Education for Upper Canada*, 14, 3 (1861), 40.

[39]North West Oxford Trustees' Minute Book, School Section No. 1, 15 January 1863, RG 51, 10816, No. 1, PAO, and *Annual Report of the Chief Superintendent of Schools for Ontario*, 1865, Appendix A, 53.

[40]Engagement of Anna Poulin, 1 June 1882, E 13, 826–13, ANQ.

[41]'Enquiries', *Educational Record* 5, 7/8 (1885), 199.

[42]*Educational Record* 13, 10 (1893), 286.

[43]*Annual Reports of the Toronto Public School Board*; see especially 1876, Appendix 1, 10, and 1891, 14–5 and 37–9.

[44]See *Ibid.*, 1876, 18; and 'Something for Country Teachers', *Educational Record* 4, 2 (1884), 51–3.

[45]'Les écoles primaires à Montreal et aux Etats Unis', *Le Canada*, 26 August 1903.

[46]*Annual Report of the Toronto Public School Board*, 1873, 87.

[47]Wendy Bryans, 'The Women Teachers' Association of Toronto', paper presented to the Canadian Association for American Studies, Ottawa, 1974.

[48]*Ibid.*

[49]Marie Lavigne and Jennifer Stoddart, 'Women's Work in Montreal at the Beginning of the Century', in Marylee Stephenson, ed., *Women in Canada* (Toronto 1977), 139. Marie Thivierge, 'La Syndicalisation des institutrices catholiques, 1900–1959', in *Maîtresses de maison.*

[50]'Correspondence', *Educational Record* 11, 9 (1891), 241–2.

[51]Athénais Bibaud, 'Nos écoles de Filles', *Revue Canadienne* 2 (1911), 138–9. In 1905 the Marchand Academy had been listed as 'receiving subsidies', but not 'under the control' of the Montreal Catholic School Commission. By 1909, the Catholic School Commission had replaced the former school with a new one built by itself and now directly under its control. Many girls' schools in Montreal underwent a similar transformation at this time.

[52]*Ibid.*, 139.

[53]Miss E. Binmore, 'The Financial Outlook of the Women Teachers of Montreal', *Educational Record* 13, 3 (1893), 69–74.

[54]Wayne Urban, *Why Teachers Organized* (Detroit 1983). The three cities studied were Chicago, New York, and Atlanta.

[55]Bryans, 'The Women Teachers' Association of Toronto', 13–4. See also Alison Prentice, 'Themes in the History of the Toronto Women Teachers' Association', in Paula Bourne, ed., *Women's Paid and Unpaid Work* (Toronto forthcoming). The most radical Americans were the leaders of the women teachers' association in Chicago.

[56]Harry Braverman, *Labor and Monopoly Capital* (New York and London 1974).

[57]Michael W. Apple has argued that twentieth-century teachers are 'located simultaneously in two classes', being members both of the petite bourgeoisie and the working class. See his 'Work, Class and Teaching', 53.

[58]Joan Kelly, 'The Doubled Vision of Feminist Theory', in Judith L. Newton, Mary Ryan, and Judith Walkowitz, eds, *Sex and Class in Women's History* (London 1983), 259–70.

[59]Michael W. Apple, 'Work, Class and Teaching', 64.

[60]Prentice, 'Themes in the History of the Toronto Women Teachers' Association'; Bryans, 'The Women Teachers' Association'; John R. Abbott, ' "A Man's Task": Women Teachers and the Turn-of-the-Century Public School Inspectorate in Ontario', paper presented to the Canadian Historical Association annual meeting, Montreal 1985.

14

Urban Reform

Margaret W. Andrews

A principal characteristic of the period from 1880–1914 was the increasing incidence of middle-class reform movements in Canada, all seeking to change patterns of life regarded as in desperate need of improvement and—usually—more elevation. Much of the pressure for change was put on the cities of Canada, which grew substantially in size and complexity in the period between 1860 and 1914. At the time of Confederation, only Montreal and Toronto could be regarded as anything other than large towns. The sheer swiftness of urbanization after Confederation, as well as its scope and meaning, took Canadians, still thinking in rural and small-town terms, by surprise. By the Great War Canada had a number of rapidly growing urban centres, including a whole series of cities in western Canada, that had not existed a few decades earlier. The populations of these cities had been drawn from elsewhere, and often faced considerable problems of readjustment to their new circumstances.

As Margaret Andrews points out in her analysis of the early years of the Vancouver Health Department, Vancouver had a responsible attitude toward public health not necessarily shared by all Canadian cities, and it created a considerable bureaucracy to deal with health matters, a bureaucracy that appears less the product of partisan politics than an acceptance of the wider standards of the professionals the city had put in charge. The result was non-partisan reform by a managerial and professionalized middle class that employed very little rhetoric to achieve its goals. What explanation does Andrews advance for the lack of debate in Vancouver over health care matters in these years? Are other explanations possible? Does the rise of bureaucracy seem a totally satisfactory context for the expansion of health facilities in Vancouver? What, if anything, has been left out of the discussion?

This article first appeared, titled, 'The Emergence of Bureaucracy: The Vancouver Health Department, 1886–1914', in *Journal of Urban History* 12, 2 (February 1986), 131–55.

Bureaucratization in municipal government in the United States has received historical notice largely as part of the progressive reform movement, specifically as a structural change introduced by upper- or middle-class reformers to limit the power of political bosses, replacing graft and ward-heeling by efficient management supervised by apolitical experts who could be expected to share the reformers' progressive views.[1] Standing in evidence against the importance of bossism to the development of bureaucracy is the transformation of US business that was well underway in the progressive era. In *The Visible Hand*, Alfred D. Chandler, Jr, has shown the traditional owner-manager of US business retreating into bureaucracy because he could not cope with the multiplicity of units dictated by continentwide operations or with the complex technology increasingly central to the practice of business.[2]

There is also direct evidence that political reform has been overemphasized as means and motive for bureaucratization in municipal government. In *The Unheralded Triumph*, Jon C. Teaford shows late nineteenth-century US cities bureaucratizing not only because of antimachine politics but also because of the same inability to cope with increasing scale and complexity that was changing the structure of business.[3] It is the purpose of this article to describe and analyse the development of the city health department of Vancouver, British Columbia, from the city's incorporation in 1886 to the outbreak of World War I. The rise of a businesslike expert-run department there in the absence of machine politics provides a clear view of the systematic or structural, as opposed to political, causes of municipal bureaucratization.

Vancouver shared with US cities of the time the dominance of an ancestral British culture and, at least to some extent, the American frontier experience. A fair proportion of its residents were born in the United States, and the city enjoyed strong commercial and cultural connections with Seattle and San Francisco.[4] Like US cities, it experienced rapid growth and the impact of burgeoning technology. On the other hand, the relation of Vancouver's lower economic classes to the political process was fundamentally different from that obtaining in the United States; for almost the whole period studied here, only those who owned or rented property assessed at $300 or more could vote for mayor and aldermen, and only property owners could vote on money bylaws.[5] Machine politics did not develop in Vancouver in that period. Robert A.J. McDonald, the most knowledgeable authority on the subject, assigns the city's 'benign social political environment' a causal role in the failure of attempts by its business élite to capture municipal power.[6]

From municipal incorporation in April 1886, Vancouver's municipal authorities, unlike those of many North American towns and cities of the

1880s, gave every appearance of a responsible attitude toward public health.[7] The health committee, established as a standing committee by the first city council, was an active and attentive executive. The initial health bylaw was among the lengthiest enactments of the city's first year; in more than five thousand words, it made detailed provision for medical care for the indigent, protection against and control of contagious diseases, regulation of privies, handling and removal of garbage, and prevention and abatement of filth, noxious smells, food adulteration, and unsanitary housing. Construction of a sewerage system was undertaken in May 1887; a municipal general hospital was opened in September 1888; pure water piped underwater across Burrard Inlet was available in March 1889; and an incinerator for refuse went into operation in October 1891.[8]

Administrative changes are the focus here, not achievements of the city, and the impression of a steady and sometimes rapid increase of health services that I trust will appear should be regarded as incidental. Such an impression must in any case be tempered with the realization that an increase in need was also ongoing through most of the period of this study. Population increased from less than 1,000 at incorporation to more than 14,000 at the end of 1891, in what was at least partly a speculative boom based on the city's expectations as the Canadian Pacific Railway's western terminus. Thereafter, population increased at a moderate rate of around five or six per cent a year from 1892 through 1897—years of economic depression—and again at a rapid rate from the Klondike gold rush year 1898 through 1912, reaching a peak of more than eighteen per cent in each of the years 1909 through 1911. It decreased from 1913 through 1916 under the impact of economic depression and war; at the end of 1914, it was approximately 106,000.[9]

The summer of 1914 is a convenient place to end this study of the rise of the medical expert in Vancouver's health department. By that time, medical or comparable expertise was established as a qualification for several department positions, eight staff members were affiliated with the Royal Sanitary Institute ('Vancouver Health Department' being the official address of the British Columbia branch), and in November of that year the criteria for selecting a new lady health inspector included status as a trained nurse, with reputation of the training institution also to be considered. The outbreak of war interrupted the pattern of development toward a larger, more specialized, and more medically oriented department—four members of the predominently British-born staff immediately enlisted for foreign military service and only two replacements were made—but the vacancies created were clearly marked as temporary.[10]

Throughout the period covered here, final authority for all city actions was vested in the city council of annually elected mayor and aldermen, who divided their time between municipal government and earning a livelihood.

Close supervision was delegated to the standing committees of council, each of which comprised an alderman from each ward of the city, with the mayor a member *ex officio*. The various standing committees' areas of responsibility were often (by 1914, nearly always) referred to as 'departments', although never formally established under that name. The subject of this article (which I shall hereafter continue to call 'health department') is thus, in fact, the set of employees, officers, and functions of city government overseen by the health committee (also known officially and otherwise as 'Board of Health'). The works department, overseen by the council committee known as 'Board of Works' is also involved here, partly because of its frequent cooperation with the health department and the occasional transfer of functions and officials between the two, but more importantly because it provided Vancouver a satisfactory experience of a bureau controlled by a scientifically trained expert—the sort of bureau the health department became.

While Vancouver was in its small-city phase, city employees were few and many were part time; most supervisory employees reported directly to committees of the city council, and positions were frequently rearranged. Inspection for violations of the health bylaw's sanitary provisions was the one health committee concern consistently met by a staff appointment. In May 1886, the council determined that the chief of police was to serve also as health inspector. In January 1887, it created a position of license, fire, and health inspector, offered a salary of $75 per month, and selected the chief of the volunteer fire brigade from the twenty applicants. Six months later it abolished the position (leaving health inspection once again in charge of the police), only to recreate it in February 1888, offering $65 per month.[11]

The February 1888 appointee was Joseph Huntly, an aggressive former rent and debt collector who went on to fill a variety of posts in the infant bureaucracy. A few months after his initial appointment, he added $10 per month to his salary by becoming street inspector and police court clerk as well. In January 1889, he was relieved of the added duties, presumably because of increasing demand for his work as license, health, and fire inspector; his total salary remained $75 per month. His work as health inspector continued to expand, as the council acknowledged by raising his salary to $100 per month in May 1890, relieving him of fire inspection duties in April 1891, and of license inspection in March 1892. On the last occasion, he was also appointed special constable so that he might be 'clothed with greater powers when performing his duties.[12]

By the time Huntly left his municipal job at the beginning of 1893, five money bylaws providing for sewerage and drainage and four for water works had been approved by qualified voters,[13] and proper installation of and connection with the resulting underground networks had replaced purity of wells and proper removal of night soil as a major concern of the city council. As a result of the new concern, health inspection was once again combined with other duties (this time with plumbing inspection), and once again a period of experimentation with various combinations of duties ensued. A health and sewer inspector was appointed in February 1893, an assistant health inspector in March, and a plumbing inspector (also reporting to the health committee) in May. In December 1894, the health inspector was relieved of responsibility for plumbing and sewer inspection, those duties being assigned to the works department. In September 1895, the council returned plumbing inspection to the health department, settled on the title 'health and plumbing inspector', and made a more lasting appointment; the men who had previously served as inspectors under the health committee were passed over in favor of Robert Marrion, at that time the master plumbers' representative on the municipal board of plumbing examiners. Marrion's initial salary as inspector seems to have been $65 per month.[14]

Marrion's plumbing expertise was obviously a primary consideration in his appointment, but his work as chief inspector was wide-ranging. He inspected lodging houses, cellar dwellings, schools, bakeries, saloons, hotels, vacant lots, back lanes, and whole suburban areas for unsanitary conditions, and he enforced (and sometimes supervised) clean-up operations. He was instructed to attend to a 'nuisance' of Gypsies, to visit the leprosarium on Darcy Island, to make some disused city premises habitable for two chronically ill women, to institute proceedings against doctors who failed to report cases of typhoid fever, and to oversee some minor construction projects (an improvement in city jail ventilation and an addition to the city hospital). He notified aldermen of opium smoking in Chinatown, served as bill collector for the isolation hospital, reported cases of destitution, and distributed relief.[15]

Although technical expertise was for the most part introduced gradually into the city's health inspectorate, some medical expertise was assumed from the beginning: The 1887 health bylaw provided that a physician might be appointed Medical Health Officer (MHO), to be responsible for recognizing and controlling smallpox and other infectious diseases and to be in charge of an isolation hospital. Until 1904, the position of MHO was a part-time one, in some years not filled at all. The first MHO was Dr A.M. Robertson, who filled the position in combination with that of medical attendant at the city hospital for a salary of $25 per month in the summer of 1887. Early in 1889, his salary was doubled in return for his providing medical care to those in quarantine and to indigents authorized to receive care at city expense. In August 1889, however, the city council gave both Robertson and the City hospital staff (matron, porter, and two nurses) a month's notice and authorized advertisement for a new matron, specifying that a 'middle-aged person' was required. One alderman considered it questionable whether the hospital was being run 'for pleasure or for use'. Whether the perceived fault was extravagance or some other impropriety is now purely conjectural.[16]

The office was next filled in July 1892, when a temporary MHO was appointed at a salary of $20 per day to deal with an outbreak of smallpox and to satisfy regulations issued that month by the provincial government;

the salary was reduced to $10 per day in August, when the smallpox had been 'got under control'. Presumably also to satisfy provincial regulations, the health committee chairman (a physician) accepted appointment to the post for a few weeks at the end of 1892, serving without pay. From January 1893 to June 1904, the position was continuously filled on a salaried basis, with four different physicians serving during that period. Salary ranged from $40 to $75 per month, and the incumbent also received fees from the city for work not required by the health bylaw. The latter seem to have been fair and amounted on several occasions to bills of about $200 for work done over a period of a few months.[17]

The work was not confined to that anticipated in the health bylaw. In addition to imposing quarantine and compiling physicians' reports of infectious disease, the MHO was specifically authorized at times to collect a fee from the city for attending births to indigent women, attending patients ill with infectious diseases (presumably also indigent), and, when 'necessary', examining corpses of Chinese people who died unattended; his duties also included attending sick prisoners in the city jail and examining people temporarily interned as probable lunatics. The MHO also often participated in health inspection; he reported unsanitary premises, improper street cleaning, pollution of English Bay beaches by offal from a fish cannery, and a danger to the city's water supply from cesspools near its source, the Capilano River. The MHO and health inspector together prepared a report on the sanitary condition of slaughterhouses, condemned and seized tinned food that they judged unfit for human consumption, and were jointly asked by the council to make a recommendation for improving scavenger service in the city.[18]

By 1904, the city health department staff included (in addition to the two principal officials) an assistant health inspector, a milk inspector, an assistant plumbing inspector, a bacteriologist, a crematory caretaker, an isolation hospital caretaker, and a caretaker and assistant caretaker for the cemetery. Until 1902, when the functions and facilities of the city hospital were taken over by the newly incorporated Vancouver General Hospital, the health committee was also responsible for hospital staff; at the time of the changeover, that comprised a house surgeon, a matron, three nurses, a housekeeper, a night porter, two day porters, a cook, two assistant cooks, and a charwoman. It is important to notice that additions to the health department staff up to 1904 for the most part broadened its structure without increasing its hierarchical depth. In 1902, for example, the health committee received separate regular reports from the MHO, the health inspector, the milk inspector, the crematory caretaker, the ambulance driver, the hospital house surgeon, and the city auditor (on hospital patients' accounts).[19]

Lack of any staff with primarily administrative responsibility left the health committee with the tasks of assigning duties, evaluating performance, responding to suggestions and complaints from the public, and attending directly to many details that fell between or above the responsibilities of existing staff. At various times the chairman or other delegates from the committee personally inspected piggeries and slaughterhouses, the city pound (then still used to contain wandering horses and cows, one should recall), and the city incinerator. The committee regularly concerned itself with details of individual relief cases, particularly when institutional care might be called for or when a case could be closed by providing a ticket on an outbound train. Operation of the city hospital was particularly demanding; the committee arranged for repairs and additions, selected staff, found accommodation for nurses, and considered ambulance maintenance in detail. One debate centered on the importance of rubber tires, which were not deemed necessary as of April 1902.[20]

The chairman was so frequently empowered to take 'such action as he may deem necessary' that he was, especially in the city's early years, functionally a member of the health department staff. He hired a temporary cook for the hospital, visited the Darcy Island leprosarium to determine whether a Chinese man sent there was in fact afflicted with leprosy, was required to sign all orders for supplies for the isolation hospital, and purchased underwear and clothing for a long-time hospital inmate. He accompanied the health inspector in a search for quarters for an isolation hospital and in inspection of slaughterhouses; along with the hospital house surgeon, he arranged for purchase and storage of a barrel of whiskey and for a photograph of the hospital to grace the diplomas of graduating nurses.[21] In the city's early years, lack of any kind of staff made it natural for the health committee to participate directly in the work for which it was responsible; subsequently, lack of administrative staff encouraged persistence of that practice.

The health committee's work at what a present-day administrator would consider an inappropriate level of detail was of course done in addition to its work at the level of planning and policy. The health department budget originated with it, as did the health bylaw, its amendments, and other health-related bylaws, such as those providing for licensing of milk vendors and inspection of milk, for the regulation (subsequently the prohibition) of slaughterhouses, for controlling the contents and weight of bread loaves sold in the city, and for regulating the arrangement, construction, maintenance, and inspection of lodging houses.[22] The committee was also the city's advisor in dealing with other levels of government on health matters; for example, when Health Inspector Marrion became concerned about lax enforcement of smallpox quarantine regulations at the B.C.-Washington border in 1902, he and the committee chairman traveled to Seattle to ascertain the level of danger, and communication between the city and the dominion government ensued.[23] The committee received complaints from the public it served and in serious cases investigated and resolved them; two notable examples are condemnation of a row of unsanitary (but apparently profitable) shacks in

Chinatown and a case of illness allegedly due to a faulty sewer connection.[24] In specifying the duties of the various inspectors, the MHO, and the hospital house surgeon, the committee established the health department's rudimentary structure.

From about the turn of the century until the reorganization of the health department under a full-time MHO in 1904, Health Inspector Marrion's initiative was increasingly important in providing the committee with staff assistance in its functioning at the planning and policy level, and his personal energy and alertness no doubt contributed to the *de facto* executive role his office came to exercise with respect to the other inspectorate offices. Marrion's initiative with respect to quarantine at the international border has already been mentioned. He also requested and was granted permission to travel to Victoria to gather information on isolation hospitals and thereafter suggested and implemented improvements in Vancouver facilities. He likewise visited Seattle to garner suggestions for improvement of the bylaw concerning milk inspection, he provided the committee with a draft lodging-house bylaw, and he called upon his own expertise as a master plumber to suggest amendment of the plumbing bylaw. Because of the growth of the inspectorate (which followed that of the city) and the limitation of the MHO's office to one part-time physician, the health inspector also took over a limited amount of the MHO's administrative work; Marrion's attention to quarantine matters illustrates this, as does the frequent inclusion of infectious disease statistics in his reports.[25]

In contrast to the health committee, the board of works had long been committed to dependence on expert assistance, and the works department evolved an admnistrative hierarchy well before 1904. Public works such as roads, sidewalks, water tanks, and sewers aroused heated public debate because of their great cost,[26] and aldermen did not hesitate to protect their reputations and their interests in the city's success and growth by hiring engineering experts. In 1887, the city hired Edward Mohun, a local civil engineer, to plan and supervise construction of the city's first sewers and Hermann Schussler, a civil engineer from San Francisco, to assess waterworks proposed by a private company. In 1890, the city paid Schussler $2,500 to come to Vancouver to test the waterworks system that had been constructed, and on the basis of his report proceeded to purchase the system.[27] It was the prospect of that purchase that led the council to make engineering expertise a permanent feature of the city's administration; two weeks after a second reading was given to a bylaw authorizing the purchase, advertisements were placed in both local and eastern papers for an 'Engineer in Chief' competent in both general and sanitary engineering work. H.B. Warren, the man selected from the fifty-seven applicants for the position in September 1890, rapidly alienated his assistant and most of the council and was dismissed within a few months, but the council remained committed to engineering expertise and advertised for an engineer experienced in sanitary and hydraulic work as his replacement. The successful candidate, T.H. Tracy, presided over both the waterworks and street and sewer engineering work (reporting to the water committee as well as the board of works). He held office for the next fourteen years and firmly established the role of the technical expert in Vancouver's municipal government.[28]

The city engineer, whose work was essential to the planning and policy-making of the board of works, was the city's highest-paid employee. In 1892, his salary was $2,700 per year; second place went to five positions, including that of assistant engineer, at $1,500 per year. By 1904, other expert professionals had been added to the city payroll, but the engineer's $2,700 annual salary was still first, with the city solicitor's $2,500 second. The board of works required the engineer's approval of building plans before giving their own, and obtained his advice, often in the form of a formal report, on such matters as the modification and extension of the sewerage system and revision of the building bylaw. This is not to say that the board of works functioned in an altogether different way from the health committee of the same period; as late as 1904, the whole board went on a tour of theaters in the city to inspect for fire equipment and exit doors.[29]

The city council elected in January 1904, larger than that of the previous year because of a realignment of the city's wards, comprised five returning and seven new members, at least one of the latter from each ward; of the former chairmen of standing committees, two had run for mayor (health committee chairman W.J. McGuigan being elected) and the rest were defeated in the election.[30] In February, the council requested all city department heads to submit names, salaries, duties, and hours of all employees along with a statement of rules and regulations governing their work; the large council turnover might sufficiently explain this, but it is also possible that there were thoughts of reorganization; the new mayor had expressed concern during the election for efficiency in government.[31] Whatever its intentions, this council did not undertake any general reorganization during its year in office, but it did make a fundamental and lasting change in the health department, making the MHO full-time department head and specifying new qualifications for that position.

The immediate impetus for restructuring the health department came from the Vancouver Medical Association, which (through its secretary) advised the city council in February that it considered essential the appointment of an MHO trained in bacteriology (the analysis of milk, in particular) and required to devote all his time to city work. Mayor McGuigan and Health Committee Chairman W.D. Brydone-Jack were both physicians and likely supported the association's advice. In June, on a motion of Brydone-Jack, the council called for applications for a full-time MHO, who, in addition to ordinary medical qualifications, was to have a diploma in 'Sanitary

Science, Public Health, or State Medicine'. A week after the call, the council, with applications in hand from two physicians from Montreal and one from Toronto, unanimously chose Frederick T. Underhill, who had served as city bacteriologist (unsalaried) since 1901.[32] Given the annual scale of city council work, the restructuring of the health department was reasonably deliberate; in contrast, Underhill's appointment, if considered as independent of the restructuring, was as precipitate as possible. The appointment was in effect an internal one, and (as often in such a case) the intention was to base the restructuring largely upon the available person.

Underhill, forty-six years old when appointed, continued as MHO and head of the health department for twenty-six years. Medicine was his family's profession; his father, his grandfathers, his two step-brothers, and three of his five brothers were physicians or surgeons; he began to wash bottles in a surgery and learn dispensing as soon as he left school in Tipton, Staffordshire, at the age of 15. He went on to the University of Edinburgh to study medicine, becoming an LRCP and L&LM in 1881, and an FRCS in 1884. He likely would not have left the general practice that he subsequently estab-lished in Tipton had he not suffered a systemic infection that left him in poor health. Through an advertisement in the *British Medical Journal*, he purchased a practice on the Fraser River at Mission and came to British Columbia in 1894 to recover his health; his first reward was the challenge of this Canadian frontier. He was flooded out of his Mission home within days of arrival; he reached patients by dugout canoe, on horseback, and on foot, facing forest fire and drifted snow as he traveled. He was sufficiently captured by the frontier to leave his family at Mission in 1896 and take up a provincial government post attending miners in the Cariboo. This was a last fling of youth, however, for in the following year he settled his family (he ultimately had thirteen children) in relatively sedate New Westminster and returned to Edinburgh to study public health (receiving the DPH in 1897). When Brydone-Jack asked him in 1904 if he was willing to give up his lucrative practice in Vancouver's West End to work full time as the city MHO, he 'could not resist the invitation'. A public health official in the state of Washington described him in 1912 as 'one of the most thoroughly alive health officials in the Northwest'. In a sense, he never stopped working, for his public and domestic lives intertwined: A family dinner out could end with an impromptu inspection of the restaurant kitchen, and an inspection of the water intakes in the Capilano and Seymour Rivers become a family outing. His energy could 'flame into righteous indignation' at those who tried to keep him from his duty, but more characteristically he 'patiently, courageously, but courteously withal, . . . did what he knew should be done, and insisted on those in authority doing the right thing.'[33]

The motives of leaders in the medical profession in this matter are rea-sonably clear. The establishment of a new government post to be filled by a physician was quite straightforwardly advantageous to the professional association as a guild, particularly when the post could be imagined—as Dr Brydone-Jack imagined it in his annual report as health committee chairman for 1904—as but the first in a series, with the health department growing to include divisions of school medical work, jail medical work, and an inspectorate of meat and food, each with its own supervising 'medical man'.[34] The requirement of special scientific training for the new position was also directly in the interest in the profession; scientific expertise is a cornerstone of professional authority and autonomy in our century.[35] I do not mean to imply that these motives are narrowly selfish; the elevation of people of Underhill's training and character, formed in the culture of professionalism, has been the primary means of applying scientific research to health needs.

The motives of the city council as a whole in accepting the new health department arrangements are also reasonably clear. The man to be in charge was thoroughly reliable, and the principle of professional management under responsible directorship, widely accepted in the world of business, was becoming acceptable in city government as well.[36] For the aldermen who had served for several years, the contrast between the authority and dependable assistance of the city engineer and the welter of detail that regularly faced the health committee should have been enough to win support.

In a list of duties drawn up in connection with Underhill's appointment and signed by Brydone-Jack as health committee chairman, the MHO was given 'entire charge of the Health Department and . . . full responsibility for the proper performance of the duties of those under him'. He was to be responsible for all health-related record keeping, accounting, and inspection and to perform all functions specified by health statutes and bylaws, including those of city bacteriologist, police surgeon, and public vaccinator. His responsibility for the traditional sanitary aspect of the department's work was stated briefly—'to supervise and direct all Sanitary arrangements'—while more detailed description was given to health work in vogue at the time: supervision of ventilation, sanitation, and disease control in the public schools, inspection of food and milk, and inspection of lighting, ventilation, and sanitation of buildings. He was to attend prisoners, patients in isolation hospitals ('when necessary'), and paupers (when authorized by the mayor or the health committee). At its last meeting, the 1904 health committee heartily approved Underhill's report on department progress to date, instructing that a copy be sent to the secretary of the provincial Board of Health, and affirmed its abdication of administrative responsibility, resolving 'that, as the Medical Health Officer is the head of the Health department, under the Health Committee, all those directly under his surveillance, as outlined in his list of duties, take their orders from him and be directly under his jurisdiction; and that all reports etc. must come through him to the Committee or Council.' The MHO's salary for 1905 was $2,500.[37]

The 1905 health committee similarly limited the extent of its involvement in departmental detail, specifically to the consideration of that which Underhill might report as necessary to put his department in 'good practical shape', and subsequent relations between committees and department continued the same pattern. The MHO's reports became in effect the agendas for health committee meetings, and the committee soon requested that they be received in advance of meeting days. Health committee minutes for the first years of his tenure are rife with such phrases as 'referred to MHO', 'left in the hands of the MHO', and 'left in the hands of the MHO and the City Engineer'.[38] The effectiveness of the health department reorganization can be seen from the virtually complete and immediate disappearance from the committee's minutes of Underhill's predecessor in providing this sort of assistance; Robert Marrion continued as a loyal health department employee until his retirement as chief sanitary inspector in 1912 and returned as temporary health inspector in 1914 in response to the wartime manpower shortage, but his position had become subordinate.[39]

In addition to relieving the health committee of responsibility for detail, Underhill also continued the practice of his predecessor in providing staff assistance and initiative in matters of planning and policy and in communication with other governmental entities. The health committee occasionally held special meetings to consider business he brought up, and he drafted and revised bylaws with remarkable industry; in May 1913, for example, he prepared draft bylaws dealing with milk, ice cream vendors, lodging houses, camping, and brush and vacant lots. Such work was often done in conjunction with staff and aldermen from other municipal departments: with the city solicitor for revision and consolidation of health bylaws; with the building committee for revision of the building bylaws; and with the solicitor and city engineer on a basement drain bylaw. He worked with the school board to inaugurate medical inspection of school children; with the provincial board of health to prepare a model lodging house bylaw; and with the dominion Indian agent to find a suitable stopping place for Indians visiting the city. His importance in intergovernmental affairs is also evident in his selection to join the mayor and an alderman as delegates to the 1909 convention of the Union of B.C. Municipalities. An unconscious admission of the extent to which Underhill took charge appears in 1906 finance committee minutes: instead of 'Health Committee', we find 'Medical Health Committee'. It is a testimony to his fiscal good sense as well as a measure of his authority in city government that the elements of his reports considered at length by the health committee were most often not those involving the greatest expense but, rather, highly visible matters affecting public sensibilities, such as the location of an isolation hospital for smallpox patients or of public urinals and water closets.[40]

The sort of hierarchy Brydone-Jack imagined in 1904 came fairly quickly into being. From its ten staff positions at the time of Underhill's appointment, the department grew to thirty-five in 1913, grouped under the MHO in ten divisions: infectious diseases (a physician, the ambulance driver, and a fumigation officer and his assistant), bacteriological (a bacteriologist who held a medical degree, his assistant, and a laboratory assistant), analytical (an analyst and his assistant, who was Underhill's son), milk and food inspection (an inspector and one assistant), district inspection (a chief sanitary inspector, five health inspectors, and a quarantine officer), rooming house and restaurant inspection (a chief inspector, three assistants, and a clerk), smallpox hospital (a caretaker and his assistant), cemetery (a superintendent and two assistants), and office staff (a chief indoor inspector, a stenographer, and a secretary). Whereas in 1904 Underhill was the only medical expert in the department, in 1913 there were three physicians and three other people with training in medical laboratory work.[41]

Extensive as the medical orientation of the health department was, it would have been more so if Underhill had had his every wish. At his strong urging, poor relief was partially removed from the health department in 1911; the city continued to provide funds for relief, but they were administered by a semiautonomous body, the Associated Charities of Vancouver, whose general secretary also served as city relief officer. In 1913, when high depression-induced unemployment made relief a matter of general concern, the city council tightened its control over funds administered by the Associated Charities and established the first of a series of committees charged with overseeing relief payments; relief was thereby effectively removed from the MHO's purview. With the outbreak of war, depletion of manpower in all city departments obliged Underhill to take charge of relief again, but in so doing he reiterated his position that 'casual relief or relief of the destitute men' should not be handled by the health department.[42] There was a similar effort with respect to cemetery matters; in 1906, the position of cemetery superintendent was created, and from then until 1914, cemetery expenses were not normally included in the health department budget, even though the cemetery superintendent was still considered a health department staff member and the health committee continued to consider some cemetery matters.[43]

The administration of refuse collection in this period provides another illustration of Underhill's efforts to specialize his department along medical lines, but also shows his overriding concern for public health. This function having been performed with indifferent success by private companies since the city's beginnings, Underhill obtained council approval to take it over in 1907; $20,000 was allocated and a superintendent appointed. At the end of the year, with the system fully operative, he gladly relinquished responsibility to the works department (already responsible for street cleaning).[44]

Implementing the health department's medical orientation by the hiring of physicians was naturally a matter of continuing interest to the Vancouver Medical Association. The following sequence of events indicates the degree of VMA concern and involvement. In December 1908, two physicians newly practicing in the city petitioned to be allowed to set up a free dispensary for the 'deserving poor' in disused city premises. The VMA objected, citing potential 'evils and abuses', and recommended instead further health department appointments to meet the perceived need. City appointments to meet the responsibilities for personal medical attendance specified in the MHO's list of duties had already been made; prisoner attendance had been transferred to the jail surgeon (a police department appointment) in 1905, and that position had been brought partly within the health department in 1908, with duties enlarged to include examination of suspected lunatics and medical care of paupers and inmates of the old men's home; furthermore, a physician had been employed on a temporary basis in the summer of 1908, and again early in 1909, to help with the smallpox epidemics. Still, with the growth of population, the need was likely real enough, and the health committee agreed to a new appointment, stipulated a salary of $2,000 per year, and asked the VMA to name the person they considered most suitable for the post. The association responded that the salary offered was too small to attract an able man full time and suggested creating two part-time positions instead. Their suggestions, which specified $1,200 for an assistant to be at the MHO's disposal and $800 for a bacteriologist, and which named the physicians to be appointed, were accepted, 'such arrangement having met with the approval of Dr Underhill'.[45]

However much the medical association's role in obtaining health department appointments for physicians might seem to resemble that of a union hiring hall, it had a deeper social significant—to promote the perception of physicians' services as essential in yet another walk of life. Underhill did not merely concur in that effort, he led it by diligently keeping public health medicine in public view. He attended council meetings well before department heads were required to do so, responding in person to questions on such topics as infant mortality and the quality of milk. He arranged for dissemination of articles on health as department circulars and press releases, and he provided for uniforms to be worn by health department inspectors when on duty. He served on the governing boards of the Vancouver General Hospital and the Victorian Order of Nurses, thereby sharing in the favorable reputation of those organizations and maintaining contact with influential fellow board members, and he expressed the importance of his department's work in public addresses.[46]

In the 1880s, the health committee had been confident of its ability to meet its responsibilities through enactment of a straightforward (if large) slate of sanitary regulations and employment of a diligent general-purpose inspector. The aldermen admitted certain scientific and technical limitations with the appointment of physicians as part-time MHOs and of an expert in plumbing matters as health and plumbing inspector, but the three-year period at the end of the 1880s in which there was no MHO shows that they did not see their limitations as essential. Growth of the city made some bureaucratic development in the health inspectorate a necessity, but the energy and initiative of Inspector Marrion limited the need, and his managerial ability allowed the development to take the form of budgetary increase rather than fundamental change in department organization.

By 1904, it had been more than a decade since anyone had expected direct aldermanic management of the works department (domain of the city engineer), and ready acceptance of expert management for the health department awaited only specifications for the appropriate expert—a medical man competent in bacteriology and especially trained in public health. A reorganization of the city council, the presence of doctors in two key positions, and the medical association's appeal for a full-time MHO combined to provide and accept those specifications, and Underhill took office.[47] After his appointment, a branching hierarchy for communication and command appeared. Underhill decided what information was passed on to the health committee, but he depended upon and usually accepted the reports of his subordinates. Effective decision making was thus diffused through the department, team loyalty developed, and there emerged the self-sustaining form of organization John Kenneth Galbraith has called the technostructure.[48]

Conclusion

It is clear from the foregoing account that the bureaucratization of the Vancouver health department did not occur as an element of political reform but, rather, in response to a belief on the part of aldermen overwhelmed by technology and changes in scale that the application of expertise beyond their own was called for—the same belief that had pushed businesses toward bureaucratization. This interpretation is consonant with those of the organizational school (named by Louis Galambos), who generally agree that, in the process of progressive reform, a large measure of authority was transferred to a new managerial middle class, relatively highly educated and respectful of specialist expertise.[49] While supporting that thesis, the present study suggests sharply diminishing the importance assigned to politics in the transfer of authority to the managerial class; in particular, it shows that the transfer can occur locally by entirely apolitical means.

Assuming, then, that politics had only an incidental role in the great changes occurring in city government and city life in the period studied here, it is appropriate to seek further for causes. A certain identifiable class succeeded to authority as a result of those changes, and its success was far from limited to city government and city life.[50] We discover at least a species of cause by considering the objective that class realized in its success: namely, amenity of life rather than power *per se*. In hard times, amenity and power stand starkly in the relation of end and means, but the period in question was one of unprecedented excess of wealth over greed; there could be amenity enough for so large a fraction of society that the employment of power in its defense was little needed. Thus, where political means were employed in favor of the rising managerial class, the thrust was generally to replace political with managerial institutions.[51] In Vancouver no political establishment stood in opposition, and political means were eschewed. The nature of the wealth that enabled the managerial class to institutionalize its authority reveals a deeper relation still: it was a wealth based on transport, communication, and information (the placement of capital); it was a wealth, that is to say, based on management. The rise of managerial authority in city government here merges with the industrial revolution itself, in which were created the complex conditions of life demanding hierarchies of experts.

In its present incarnation, bureaucracy emerged as the dominant feature of civil government in the European world in the expansive (wealth-increasing) phase highlighted by the disappearance of the American frontiers, and the preceding argument suggests a way to see this as natural: The culturally coherent group that had managed that phase of economic expansion effectively displaced an outmoded institution of leadership. According to Wiebe, 'the heart of progressivism was the ambition of the new middle class to fulfill its destiny through bureaucratic means',[52] and it is historiographically interesting to consider why he and other students of the progressive era retained their political focus despite this observation. A straightforward and possibly sufficient explanation is that their attention was naturally first drawn to cities notorious for political corruption and thus susceptible to political reform. Contemporary accounts of character and institutions are much more accessible for such cities than for those like Vancouver, in which managerial principles were implemented with less fanfare. On this view, it is simply the passage of time and the consequent proliferation of scholarship that has permitted the penetration of the facade of politics by the organizational school.

The study of political reform inherited a certain optimism from its object, even when emphasis was given to the adverse side of reform, the undermining of bosses' service to the otherwise underprivileged. The optimistic inference motivating all that study is that politics matters, that the role of the governed in government is significant. For our present that conclusion seems naive, and on a darker view, it is this that leads us to penetrate the façade of politics, inquiring the Progressive Era not how the battle went between bosses and reformers, but how the innocent, careless tangle of bureaucracy, with its dreary air of ultimate irresponsibility, succeeded both.

Suggestions for Further Reading

Patricia Roy, *Vancouver: An Illustrated History* (Toronto; 1980).
Paul Rutherford, ed., *Saving the Canadian City: The First Phase 1880–1920* (Toronto; 1974).

Maria Valverde, *The Age of Light, Soap, and Water: Moral Reform in English Canada, 1885–1925* (Toronto; 1991)

Notes

This research was supported by grants from the American Philosophical Society and Washington State University.

[1]Samuel P. Hays, *The Response to Industrialism, 1885–1914* (Chicago, 1957), 104–9; 'The Politics of Reform in Municipal Government in the Progressive Era', in Hays, *American Political History as Social Analysis* (Knoxville, 1980), 226–31; Robert H. Wiebe, *The Search for Order, 1877–1920* (New York, 1967), 164–76; Bradley Robert Rice, *Progressive Cities: The Commission Government Movement in America, 1901–1920* (Austin, 1977), 58–63; Martin J. Schiesl, *The Politics of Efficiency: Municipal Administration and Reform in America, 1800–1920* (Los Angeles, 1977), 3–5, 149–70; Jon C. Teaford, 'Finis for Tweed and Steffens: Rewriting the History of Urban Rule', *Reviews in American History* 10 (December 1982), 133–43.

[2]Alfred D. Chandler, Jr, *The Visible Hand: The Managerial Revolution in American Business* (Cambridge, 1977).

[3]Jon C. Teaford, *The Unheralded Triumph: City Government in America, 1870–1900* (Baltimore, 1984), 132–3, 187–8, 193–4.

[4]Walter N. Sage, 'British Columbia Becomes Canadian, 1871–1901', in J. Friesen and H.K. Ralston, eds, *Historical Essays on British Columbia* (Toronto, 1976), 57–68; Keith Ralston, 'Patterns of Trade and Investment on the Pacific Coast, 1867–1892: The Case of the British Columbia Salmon Canning Industry', in W. Peter Ward and Robert A.J. McDonald, eds, *British Columbia: Historical Readings* (Vancouver, 1981), 296–305; Patricia E. Roy, *Vancouver: An Illustrated History, the History of Canadian Cities* (Toronto, 1980), 61, 169; Robert A.J. McDonald, 'Victoria, Vancouver, and the Economic Development of British Columbia, 1886–1914', in Alan F.J. Artibise, ed, *Town and City: Aspects of Western Canadian Urban Development* (Regina, 1981), 31–55; Chad Evans, *Frontier Theatre: A History of Nineteenth-Century Theatrical Entertainment in the Canadian Far West and Alaska* (Victoria, 1983), chaps, 7, 9.

[5]James Bryce, *The American Commonwealth*, 2 vols (New York, 1921), vol. 1, 678, vol. 2, 379–84, 476; Robert A.J. McDonald, 'The Business Elite and Municipal Politics in Vancouver, 1886–1914', *Urban History Review/Revue d'histoire urbaine* 11 (February 1983), 13, n. 28.

[6]McDonald, 'Business Elite', 11.

[7]Margaret W. Andrews, 'The Best Advertisement a City Can Have: Public Health Services in Vancouver's First Years, 1886–1888', *Urban History Review/Revue d'histoire urbaine* 12 (February 1984), 19–27.

[8]Vancouver City Archives (VCA), Vancouver City Council, *Minutes*, 9 May 1887, 4 March 1889, 12 October 1891; *Daily News-Advertiser*, 23 September 1888.

[9]VCA, Vancouver City Council, *Annual Report* (Vancouver, 1922), 68–9.

[10]City Council, *Minutes*, 19 May 1913, 2 November 1914: VCA, City Clerk's Correspondence (Inward), 13-B-3, file '1914 Medical Health Officer', Underhill to Health Committee, 2 February, 31 August 1914; Vancouver Health Department,

Annual Report (Vancouver, 1914), 5. Thirty of the staff of thirty-five were born in Great Britain.

[11]VCA, Vancouver City Council Health Committee, *Minutes*, 23 May 1886; City Council, *Minutes*, 10, 17, 24, 31 January, 11 July 1887; *Daily News Advertiser*, 4, 14, 28 February 1888.

[12]City Council, *Minutes*, 14 May 1888, 21 January 1889, 5 May 1890, 13 April 1891, 21 March 1892.

[13]Vancouver Bylaws, 29, 64, 80, 97, 126, 127, 148, 150, 151.

[14]City Council, *Minutes*, 20 February, 20 March, 29 May 1893, 16 July, 17, 31 December 1894, 11 March, 4, 30 September 1895, 20 April 1896.

[15]City Council, *Minutes*, 23 March, 10 August 1896, 15 November 1897, 7 February, 14 March, 7 June, 22 August, 3 October, 7 November 1898, 22 May 1899, 11 June, 10 September 1900, 11 March, 9 April, 13 May, 10 June, 22 July 1901, 19 May, 8 September, 6 October, 24 November 1902, 23 November, 7 December 1903, 18 January, 7, 21 March, 11 April 1904.

[16]City Council, *Minutes*, 16 August 1887, 28 January, 12 August 1889; *Daily News-Advertiser*, 16 August 1887, 4; *Vancouver Daily World*, 13 August 1889, 1.

[17]City Council, *Minutes*, 8 August, 21 November 1892, 30 January, 20 March, 27 April 1893, 28 May 1894, 2 May 1895, 20 April 1896, 2 April, 5 May, 7 June 1897, 1 April 1898, 27 February 1899, 15 March 1900, 28 March, 8 September, 11 November 1901, 15 April, 26 May 1902, 25 March 1903, 18 April, 13 June 1904.

[18]City Council, *Minutes*, 30 January, 27 February, 13 March, 17 April 1893, 15 October 1894, 22 March, 28 June 1897, 7 February, 9 August 1898, 6 March, 22 May 1899, 22 January, 20 August 1900, 20 May 1901, 1 June 1903, 8, 22 February 1904.

[19]City Council, *Minutes*, 21 November 1892, 19 March, 17, 31 December 1894, 9 August 1898, 6 March, 12 June 1899, 12, 26 February, 11 June, 10 September, 26 November, 10, 21 December 1900, 9 December 1901, 15 April, 26 May, 21 July, 8 September 1902, 18 April 1904.

[20]City Council, *Minutes*, 22 August 1892, 11 November 1895, 17 April, 11, 18, May, 10, 24 August 1896, 6 March, 24 April 1899, 22 January, 11 June, 25 October 1900, 24 June, 26 August 1901, 24 March, 21 April, 1902, 16 February, 2 March 1903.

[21]City Council, *Minutes*, 9 October 1899, 29 February 1892, 27 February 1893, 29 October 1894, 25 February, 22 July 1895, 7 December 1896, 23 January, 7 August, 23 October 1899, 11 June 1900.

[22]City Council, *Minutes*, 7 May 1888, 25 August 1890, 20 April, 29 June 1891, 30 July 1894, 21 August 1899, 11 September 1899.

[23]City Council, *Minutes*, 24 February, 10, 24 March 1902.

[24]City Council, *Minutes*, January 1896, 3, 24 February, 2 March, 13, 20 July, 10, 24 August, 8, 14, 21 September, 5, 26 October 1896, 24 November 1902.

[25]City Council, *Minutes*, 6 February, 21 August 1899, 24 September, 21 December 1900, 21 October 1901, 22 June, 21 September 1903, 11, 25 April, 30 May 1904.

[26]For example, the debate over waterworks: *Daily News-Advertiser*, 10 May 1887–5 June 1887.

[27]City Council, *Minutes*, 11, 15 April, 2, 9 May, 11 July 1887, 13 May, 2, 30 June 1890; VCA, City Clerk's Correspondence (Inward), 12-A-1, file 11, Edward Mohun to Mayor and Council, 22 January 1888.

[28]City Council, *Minutes*, 14 July, 30 September 1890, 23 February, 20 March 1891; VCA, Add Mss 54, v. 13, file 'W.A. Clement'.

[29]13 March, 4 September 1900, 16 March 1903, 8 February, 18 April 1904.

[30]VCA (compiler), 'The Roll of Mayors and Aldermen, City of Vancouver . . . 1886–1946' (typescript, 1946); *Daily News-Advertiser*, 15 January 1904, 1.

[31]*Daily News-Advertiser*, 9 January 1904; City Council, *Minutes*, 15 February 1904. Reform of city administration in general was an active concern in the succeeding two years: McDonald, 'Business Elite', 10–11.

[32]City Council, *Minutes*, 10, 21 December 1900, 8 February, 13, 20 June 1904. Underhill dated his association with the health department from 1897, stating that he became city bacteriologist in that year—VCA, City Clerk's Correspondence (Inward), 13-B-3, file '1914 Medical Health Officer, 'Health Department Establishment List'—city council minutes show that he applied for appointment as public analyst in April 1898, and that his application was referred to the finance committee (25 April 1898), but there is no direct evidence that the appointment was made.

[33]VCA, Add Mss 54, v. 13, file 'F.T. Underhill', Washington Board of Health, *Monthly Bulletin* 2 (March 1912), 16.

[34]VCA, Vancouver City Council Health Committee, *Minutes*, newspaper clipping at back of Minute Book for May 1899–June 1906.

[35]See Burton J. Bledstein, *The Culture of Professionalism: The Middle Class and the Development of Higher Education in America* (New York, 1976), 326–7; Carol L. Kronus, 'The Evolution of Occupational Power: An Historical Study of Task Boundaries Between Physicians and Pharmacists', *Sociology of Work and Occupations* 3 (February 1976), 25; Jerold S. Auerback, *Unequal Justice: Lawyers and Social Change in Modern America* (New York, 1976), chap. 3.

[36]Chandler, *The Visible Hand*; Paul Rutherford, 'Tomorrow's Metropolis: The Urban Reform Movement in Canada, 1880–1920', in Gilbert A. Stelter and Alan F.J. Artibise, eds, *The Canadian City* (Toronto, 1977), 368–92, esp. 378–9; John C. Weaver, '"Tomorrow's Metropolis" Revisited: A Critical Assessment of Urban Reform in Canada, 1890–1920', in Stelter and Artibise, *The Canadian City*, 393–418, esp. 409–12.

[37]City Council, *Minutes*, 9 January 1905, 29 March 1905; VCA, City Council Health Committee, *Minutes*, sheet at back of Minute Book for May 1899–June 1906.

[38]City Council, *Minutes*, 6 February 1905, 13 May 1907, and *passim*. Examples of the sorts of relationship enumerated include 19 February 1906, 9 July 1906, 8 September 1908, 16 November 1908.

[39]Vancouver Health Department, *Annual Report* (Vancouver, 1911), 2, 9; *Annual Report* (Vancouver, 1914), 5; City Council, *Minutes*, 15 January 1912; VCA, City Clerk's Correspondence (Inward), 13-B-3, file '1914 Medical Health Officer', Underhill to Health Committee, 31 August 1914.

[40]City Council, *Minutes*, 25 September 1905, 8 January, 4 September 1906, 18 February, 16 September, 25 November 1907, 28 December 1908, 13 April, 30 August,

13 September 1909, 11 April, 10 October 1910, 13 February, 13 March, 22 May 1911, 27 January, 19 February, 19 May 1913; VCA, City Clerk's Correspondence (Inward), 12-D-6, file 'Health Petitions and Communications Dealt with, 1909–1910', Underhill to Health Committee, 3 November 1908; VCA, Vancouver Health Department, Environment Decision, 145-C-1, file 1, H.E. Young to F.T. Underhill, 11 December 1913.

[41]Vancouver Health Department, *Annual Report* (Vancouver, 1913), 3.

[42]City Council, *Minutes*, 10, 24, April, 8 May 1911, 27 January 1913, 9 February, 20 April 1914; Health Department, *Annual Report* (Vancouver, 1911), 2; VCA, City Clerk's Correspondence (Inward), 13-B-3, file '1914 Medical Health Officer', Underhill to Health Committee, 31 August 1914.

[43]City Council, *Minutes*, 5 February 1906. An item for cemetery 'new work' in the 1909 health department estimates (13 April 1909) is the sole exception.

[44]VCA, City Clerk's Correspondence (Inward), 12-D-1, file 13 'Miscellaneous Correspondence, 1905', Underhill to Health Committee, 15 November 1905; City Council, *Minutes*, 18 March, 2 April, 25 November, 5 December 1907.

[45]City Council, *Minutes*, 20 February 1905, 10 February, 15 June, 7 December 1908, 15 March, 10, 24 May 1909; College of Physicians and Surgeons of British Columbia, Master Register; VCA City Clerk's Correspondence (Inward), 12-D-7, file 'Medical Health Officer 1909–1910', undated petition from the Vancouver Medical Association.

[46]City Council, *Minutes*, 26 September 1904, 7 August 1905, 25 November 1907, 30 January 1911, 17 November 1913, 26 April 1915; *Daily News-Advertiser*, 2 June 1912, 6; *Vancouver Daily Sun*, 21 February 1917, 3; *Vancouver Daily Province*, 8 October 1918, 2, 17 October 1918, 16.

[47]The leading role of engineers in municipal bureaucratization in the United States is described in Stanley K. Schultz and Clay McShane, 'To Engineer the Metropolis: Sewers, Sanitation, and City Planning in Late-Nineteenth-Century America', *Journal of American History* 65 (1978), 389–411, esp. 399–400. The significant role of professionals (doctors, in this case) is consistent with the findings of Wiebe, *Search for Order*, Hays, 'Politics of Reform', Wayne K. Hobson, 'Professionals, Progressives, and Bureaucratization: A Reassessment', *The Historian* 39 (August 1977), 639–58; and Teaford, *Unheralded Triumph*, 198–214.

  The bureaucratization of health departments in other cities was not specifically mentioned in discussions surrounding the 1904 reorganization, but civic and professional leaders were no doubt aware of such developments in a general way. The contemporary state of affairs in the United States is indicated in Teaford, *Unheralded Triumph*, 153–6; that in Montreal in Terry Copp, *The Anatomy of Poverty: The Condition of the Working-Class in Montreal, 1897–1929* (Toronto, 1974), 91; that in Toronto in Heather MacDougall, 'Public Health in Toronto's Municipal Politics: The Canniff Years, 1883–1890', *Bulletin of the History of Medicine* 55 (1981), 199–200.

[48]John Kenneth Galbraith, *The New Industrial State* (New York, 1978), chap. 6.

[49]Richard Hofstadter, *The Age of Reform: From Bryan to F.D.R.* (New York, 1955), 148, 215, 258–9; Wiebe, *Search for Order*, 111–13; Louis Galambos, 'The Emerging Organizational Synthesis in Modern American History', *Business History Review* 44 (1970), 279–90; Samuel P. Hays, 'The New Organizational Society', in Hays, *American Political History as Social Analysis*, 244–63; Schiesl, *The Politics of Efficiency*, 4, 151–2. In 'The New Organizational Society', Hays presents the new class almost

exclusively in ideological terms; his remark that 'throughout the nineteenth as well as the twentieth century, modernization . . . drew men into relationships on a wider scale' (261) perhaps justifies his impersonal vocabulary.

[50]According to Daniel Joseph Singal, 'Beyond Consensus: Richard Hofstadter and American Historiography', *American Historical Review* 89 (1984), 997–1001, many scholars characterize the resulting society as dominated by an ideology rather than a class. So to characterize a society seems to me both misleading and unnecessary; ideologies are historically important precisely insofar as they serve to define effective social groups. My reaction (if not my reasoning) is supported by occasional historiographic outbursts directed at the organizational school: 'For those who persisted in asking what human intentions drove the great social engines . . . Hays's answers, still more than Wiebe's, seemed vexingly obscure', Daniel T. Rodgers, 'In Search of Progressivism', *Reviews in American History* 10 (December 1981), 119.

[51]Hays, 'Politics of Reform', 229–31; Wiebe, *Search for Order*, 165–70.

[52]Wiebe, *Search for Order*, 166.

15

The Rise of Organized Labour

Gregory S. Kealey

The process of industrialization had a considerable impact on the Canadian worker, particularly on the way the worker viewed and dealt with the employer. While the most familiar form of industrial institution, the factory, was employing relatively unskilled labour to work on machines (often women and children, see Chapter 8), not all industrial enterprise, especially in the transitional period, was highly mechanized. There was still an important place in many industrial enterprises for skilled artisans. Such workers may have clung tenaciously to traditional ways and resisted mechanization whenever possible, but they were also capable of facing the new order openly and adapting to it. Their adaptation usually took the form of collective organization into unions, which fought with employers to control the terms and conditions of their work. Skilled workers were the vanguard of union activity in Canada; they not only acquired considerable power in some industries but created most of the successful unions, which could then serve as models for others not yet organized. But mobilizing the unskilled labour force proved a more difficult task.

Gregory S. Kealey analyses the emergent response to industrialism of Toronto's skilled workers in the last third of the nineteenth century, focusing on the coopers, the printers, and the iron-moulders. He suggests that the experiences of these three crafts were quite different. The coopers tried to adapt to the new industrialism but lost much of their power to new technological innovations before they could achieve success. The iron-moulders were more successful in winning union struggles with the employers; they were able to remain powerful and to perfect their organization before they were seriously threatened by machinery. The printers were the best-organized and most highly skilled of the workers Kealey considers, and they experienced considerable success both in negotiation with management and in providing leadership for the Toronto working-class movement. The printers also managed to confront new technology without being overwhelmed by it, building it instead into their working environment. Kealey concludes that the most important aspect of early worker control in the skilled sector was the commitment to the trade union, although traditions of control frequently remained after the industries themselves had been greatly altered.

What does Kealey mean by 'worker control'? What factors contributed to the success or failure of various trades to achieve it? What does Kealey mean by working-class culture? To what extent do the unions he describes belong to the tradition of the medieval class guild rather than to the modern union? Could 'worker control' be easily extended into industries without skilled workers? To what sorts of industries was it best adapted?

This article first appeared, titled 'The Honest Workingman and Workers' Control: The Experience of Toronto Skilled Workers, 1860–1892', in *Labour/Le Travailleur*, I (1976), 32–68. © Committee on Canadian Labour History.

> And now Canadian workingmen,
>   Arise and do your duty;
> Behold these massive towers of stone,
>   In all their wondrous beauty.
> Who builds those lovely marble towers,
>   Who works and makes the plans?
> 'Tis he who sleepless thinks for hours—
>   The honest workingman.
>
> From 'The Toilers', written for
> *The Ontario Workman*, 17 July 1873

Skilled workers in the nineteenth century exercised far more power than we have previously realized. Well on into the industrial period craftsmen through their trade unions played important roles in community affairs, in the world of politics, and especially on the job. In Toronto workplaces, craftsmen employed their monopoly on skill and experience to dictate terms to their employers in a wide array of areas which, in modern parlance, gave to these late nineteenth-century craftsmen a high degree of workers' control of production. In this paper I will describe the practice of three Toronto unions from the 1860s to the early 1890s to illustrate the extent of this power.

The three unions under discussion have been chosen to exemplify significant variants of trade-union power in Toronto. They include: the relatively little known Coopers' International Union, Ontario No. 3, which played an important role in the Nine Hour Movement and the establishment of the Toronto Trades Assembly; the extensively studied International Typographical Union No. 91; and the Iron Molders International Union No. 28, employed in Toronto's heavily capitalized stove, machinery, and agricultural implements industry. This great diversity of experience demonstrates that the crafts analysed here, although each unique, are nevertheless not atypical of other Toronto skilled unions of this period. Other crafts could have been chosen and although the details would differ the overall patterns would remain much the same.

To date most discussion of artisanal resistance to the arrival of industrial capitalism has focused on the maintenance of pre-industrial work habits, the tenacious hold of ethnic cultural ties, and the deep suspicion craft workers felt for 'the new rules of the game' demanded by the advent of the market economy.[1] This analysis applies to workers undergoing the process of industrialization and will account for the Coopers' early Toronto experience, but in studying the history of Toronto moulders and printers we will need other explanations.

David Montgomery has suggested that we must look beyond pre-industrial cultural forms if we are to understand the behaviour of skilled workers in late nineteenth-century America. These workers often were 'veterans of industrial life' who 'had internalized the industrial sense of time, were highly disciplined in both individual and collective behaviour, and regarded both an extensive division of labour and machine production as their natural environment'.[2] This was the world of Toronto moulders; Toronto printers, or rather Toronto compositors, occupied a position somewhere between the experience of the cooper and that of the moulder. The world of moulders and printers certainly drew on old craft traditions but it also transcended them. Although drawing on 'residual' cultural categories there was much about their world that was 'emergent', if we can borrow the important theoretical distinction drawn by Raymond Williams.[3] In the late nineteenth century Toronto skilled workers came to terms with the new industrial society, but the terms they arrived at were those of constant resistance and struggle. The successes that they and other workers achieved forced management and government to devise entirely new strategies which have become commonly known as 'scientific management' and 'progressivism'. Those innovations remain, however, subjects for other papers; here we will limit ourselves to an analysis of how the workres struggled, often successfully, for control of the work place.[4]

I

The experience of coopers in Toronto and throughout Ontario in the late 1860s and early 1870s provides a classic case of the artisan response to industrial capitalism. Elsewhere I have described the confrontation that occurred between Toronto shoe manufacturers and the Knights of St Crispin.[5] Although less dramatic in their response than the Crispins' Luddism, the coopers shared with the shoemakers the unfortunate fate of watching the destruction of their craft by a combination of mechanization, the rise of factory production, the depression of the 1870s, and an all-out employer offensive.

Originally organized on a shop basis, coopers enjoyed all the prerogatives of the skilled artisan. One vivid description of the old-time cooper's life style follows:

> Early on Saturday morning, the big brewery wagon would drive up to the shop. Several of the coopers would club together, each paying his proper share, and one of them would call out the window to the driver, 'Bring me a goose egg', meaning a half-barrel of beer. Then others would buy 'Goose Eggs' and there would be a merry time all around . . . .Saturday night was a big night for the old time cooper. It meant going out, strolling around town, meeting friends usually at a local saloon, and having a good time generally after a hard week's work. Usually the good time continued over Sunday, so that on the following day he usually was not in the best condition to settle down to the regular day's work. Many coopers used to spend this day sharpening up their tools, carrying in stock, discussing current events and in getting things in shape for the big day of work on the morrow. Thus Blue Monday was something of a tradition with the coopers, and the day was also more or less lost as far as production was concerned. 'Can't do much today, but I'll give her hell tomorrow', seemed to be the Monday slogan. But bright and early Tuesday morning 'Give her hell' they would, banging away lustily for the rest of the week until Saturday, which was pay day again, and new thoughts of the 'Goose Eggs'.[6]

However, these older artisanal traditions were coming under attack at mid-century from trade unionists as well as efficiency-minded manufacturers. A St Louis cooper's 1871 letter depicts both the tenacity of the old tradition and the new attitudes of skilled workers:

> The shops are paid off every two weeks, on which occasion one of these shops is sure to celebrate that time-honoured festival, Blue Monday. When Blue Monday falls it usually lasts for three days. And the man who succeeds in working during the continuance of this carnival is a man of strong nerve and indomitable will. Mr Editor, did you ever hear of Black Monday? Perhaps not. But I tell you wherever Blue Monday is kept, there also is kept Black Monday. The only difference is, Blue Monday is celebrated at the shop, while Black Monday is observed at the cooper's home. The man celebrates Blue Monday, but the wife and family observe Black Monday.[7]

In 1870 craftsmen created the Coopers' International Union in order, as the Chicago *Workingman's Advocate* so aptly put it, to avoid the fate of the ship caulkers and ship carpenters, artisanal victims of the new age of iron and steam.[8] The new union with head offices in Cleveland was 'in many ways the model of a successful organization of skilled mid-nineteenth century American craftsmen'.[9] Its leaders were deeply embedded in the labour reform tradition which found its organizational expression through the National Labour Union in the US. In Canada Coopers' International Vice-President, John Hewitt, played an active role in organizing the Toronto Trades Assembly and the Canadian Labor Union, and was one of the major theorists of the nine-hour movement of 1872. The CIU created a union structure which provided sick and death benefits, an international strike fund, and a card system for tramping members. Entering Canada in 1870, the union organized 24 branches in the first two years of its existence.[10] In early 1872 on a visit to Chicago John Hewitt announced that 'the coopers in Canada were alive and active and increasing their organization rapidly'.[11] Their decline was to be equally precipitous, but let us first examine the basis of their strength.

Coopers, like most skilled workers in the late nineteenth century, can best be described as 'autonomous workmen'. This term, usefully defined by Benson Soffer, describes workers who possess:

> Some significant degree of control over the quantity and quality of the product; the choice and maintenance of equipment; the methods of wage payment and the determination of individual wages and hours; the scheduling and assignment of work; recruitment, hiring, lay-off and transfer; training and promotion of personnel; and other related conditions of work.[12]

A reading of *The Coopers' Journal*, the excellent newspaper of the CIU, provides copious evidence that Canadian coopers enjoyed most of these prerogatives.

As was the case with most unions of skilled workers in the nineteenth century, wages were not the subject of collective bargaining. The union met together, arrived at the 'price' of its labour, informed management of its decision, and either accepted the new rate with gratitude or struck if the boss refused. Local unions had no trouble dictating terms in prosperous times, as can be seen in the report of the Brantford local of August 1871 which simply notes that they had imposed a new price list and expected no trouble.[13] In January of 1872 representatives from seven of the fifteen existing Ontario CIU locals met in Toronto to arrive at a province-wide price list.[14] This document not only imposed prices but also called for a maximum ten-hour day province-wide. It dictated prices for 37 different categories of piecework and added a day rate of $1.75 for work not included on the list.

In addition to assuming control of hours and wages, coopers also restricted production, especially when work was short. In this way they could spread the work around and also prevent speed-ups or other infringements of their shop-floor control. In the Ontario reports stints are mentioned by locals in St Catharines, Seaforth, Oshawa, and London.[15] This union-dictated restriction of output was of course the greatest evil in the eyes of the manufacturer.

Coopers also struggled to control the methods of production as in this Brant-ford case:

> H.W. Read, a boss cooper of this place, has shown his dirty, mean spirit by discharging three flour bbl. [barrel] makers from his shop; they were making bbls. at nine cts. jointed staves and circled heading. The boss took the jointer boy away, so that the hands had to join their own staves, which they did until noon, when they refused to make any more barrels, unless the staves were jointed for them or they were paid extra. For thus demanding their rights, Boss Read discharged them. . . . But we fear him not, for no respectable cooper will take a berth in his shop under the circumstances.[16]

The union also enforced personnel decisions in the shop. The monitor of each shop assured that new workers' union cards were clear if members, and that 'nons' would abide by the shop rules. 'Nons' who refused often found themselves moving on to the next town sooner than anticipated. In Brantford in 1871 for example:

> A scab in one of our shops, by the name of David Clawson, made himself very obnoxious to our men by his persistent abuse of the Union. At our last meeting it was ordered that the shop should strike against him, which was accordingly done, the consequence of which was that the mean tool of a man tramped and our men were out but half a day.[17]

One year later in Seaforth:

> J. Carter (who was suspended in Jan. 1872) got a berth at Ament's shop . . . The monitor of the shop immediately went to him and asked him to pay up his dues . . . And also that if he did not pay up, either he or they should not work there. [After he refused] the monitor of the shop went to the boss and told him that he must either sack Carter or they would take their tools out of the shop. . . . [When he refused] they did instantly.[18]

Equally the coopers controlled admission to the craft and their ritual pledged them to 'allow no one to teach a new hand' in order 'to control the supply of help'.[19] Use of helpers and apprenticeship rules were tightly supervised by the union.[20]

But perhaps more striking even than the presence of workers' control is the pervasiveness of appeals to manliness evidenced throughout the coopers' materials. David Montgomery has argued that this was a crucial component of 'the craftsmen's ethical code'.[21] Skilled workers carried themselves with pride and felt themselves to be the equal of their boss. CIU President Martin Foran's novel, *The Other Side*,[22] illustrates this theme well. The hero is a proud and respectable workman surrounded by unscrupulous capitalists and unmanly workers who have given up their self-respect in order to carry out the evil tasks of the monopolistic bosses. Foran in discussing his didactic novel claimed that:

The main incidents of this story are founded upon 'notorious fact', so notorious that anyone wishing it can be furnished with irrefragable, incontestable proofs in support of all the charges made against the typical employer, Revalson; that working men have been—because being trade unionists—discharged, photographed on street corners, driven from their homes, hounded like convicted felons, prevented from obtaining work elsewhere, arrested at the beck of employers, thrown into loathsome prisons on ex parte evidence, or held to bail in sums beyond their reach by subsidized, prejudiced, bigoted dispensers of injustice, & in every mean dishonourable manner imaginable, inhumanly victimized and made to feel that public opinion, law & justice were Utopian 'unreal mockeries' except to men of position and money . . . [23]

Canadian coopers saw 'manliness' as the keystone of their struggle and for them honour and pride were sacrosanct. 'Owls' or 'nons' who broke pledges or violated oaths were less than men:

At our last monthly meeting, the name of George Morrow was erased from our books, it having been proven beyond a shadow of doubt that he had violated his obligation by making known the business of our meetings to his boss. This thing Morrow, for I cannot call him a man, has never been of any use to us, he has not only betrayed us, but degraded himself in the estimation of every good man in our community.[24]

The Hamilton corresponding secretary went on to describe Morrow as a 'compromise between man and beast'.[25]

The traditions of autonomous work and the culture which grew from it made the coopers men to be reckoned with. Yet if the rise of the CIU was rapid, its decline was even more precipitous.

By late 1873 only seventeen locals remained and by 1875 this number had plummeted to approximately five.[26] The Canadian case was in no way unique, and from a peak membership of over 8,000 in 1872 the union's total membership had declined to 1,500 by 1876. In that year *The Coopers' Journal* suspended publication.

This disastrous decline was related both to the depression of the mid-1870s and to a concerted employers' assault on the trade. The best account of the coopers' demise describes the displacement of the hand cooper by machines in the Standard Oil works in New York and Cleveland. These cities, which contained the largest concentrations of coopers in North America, saw an epic struggle as Standard Oil moved to crush the CIU, the one remaining obstacle in its path to modernization and total monopoly.[27]

A similar process took place in Ontario. Coopering began to break out of its artisanal mould in the late 1860s in Ontario when the need for well-made, tight oil barrels in Western Ontario led the London firm of R.W. and A. Burrows to introduce stave-making and stave-dressing machinery.[28] Until then the entire process had been performed by hand. This innovation was adopted by large cooperages in the province such as those at distilleries in Windsor and Toronto. These three shops, Burrows', Walker's and Gooderham's, also differed from the old-time cooper's shop owing to their larger size; they resembled small manufactories far more than artisans' shops. Gooderham, for example, employed forty coopers in Toronto while the next biggest Toronto shop in 1871 held only seven.[29]

Although creating some problems for the CIU, these early machines did not abolish the need for skilled workers. Skill and knowledge were still important components of barrel-making. Thus, as late as 1871, Martin Foran was taking consolation in the cooper's skill:

> Many of our members place far too much significance on machinery as a substitute for their labour. I have given the subject much thought and consideration, and am unable to see any serious cause for apprehension in barrel machinery . . . Ours is a trade that cannot be reduced to the thumbrule of unfailing uniformity. To make a general marketable piece of work, of any kind peculiar to our trade, it required tact, judgement and discrimination on the part of the maker . . . when the friends of barrel machinery succeed in inventing a thinking machine they will succeed in making a success.[30]

Within two years of this statement Standard Oil's version of 'a thinking machine' was a complete success.

The process was less revolutionary in Ontario, but the effects of increased mechanization can be seen in the reports of the Toronto local. Gooderham's defeated the union between 1870,[31] when hours and wages were dictated by the workers and CIU President Martin Foran acclaimed 'Gooderman's [*sic*] shop as without exception the finest cooper shop [he had] ever seen',[32] and late 1872 when John Hewitt reported that the shop

> contained the most inveterate set of owls to be found on this continent and the few good men we have there, not being able to control the shop, have concluded to sacrifice their principles and work on for whatever price the great Gooderham chooses to pay.[33]

As its peak strength in March of 1872 the Toronto local had had complete control over the trade.[34] The ability of the coopers to dictate terms was seriously undermined elsewhere in Ontario by the advent of machinery. In 1874 the Seaforth local noted that the installation of two barrel machines would throw a great number of coopers out of work.[35] Six months later they reported their failure to control the machines due to non-union coopers taking their jobs at low rates.[36] By the 1880s the struggle was over; the cooper's craft was dead. In 1887 a Windsor cooper argued before the Labour Commission that machinery had 'killed the trade' and that there no longer was 'a man in the world who would send his son to be a cooper'.[37]

The power that coopers had possessed as artisans they tried to adapt to the industrial age. Old models of the trade practices of independent craftsmen were transformed into union rules and struggled over with new-style bosses. However, one base of their power was disappearing rapidly in the 1870s as technological innovation stripped them of 'their monopoly of particular technical and managerial skills'.[38]

Yet we should always be careful in positing technological change as the crucial factor, for other workers, as we shall see here, were more successful than the coopers. A Seaforth cooper, P. Klinkhammer, recognized this only too clearly:

> The men here have much to say about the barrel machine. The machine is not to blame. If the union men had been supported by the nons last fall and the latter had not taken the berths vacated by the union men and worked at 4 cents the machine would not be making barrels now.[39]

Their one real hope was to ally with other workers as Klinkhammer suggested. Their important role in the US National Labour Union and the Toronto Trades Assembly, the Canadian Labor Union, and the Nine Hour Movement were steps in the right direction, but craft particularism remained very strong in the 1870s. However, unionism did not disappear totally from the barrel factory with the demise of the CIU. Like the shoemakers, the coopers learned from their experience. Toronto coopers retained an independent union after the demise of the CIU and were successful in raising their rates in the spring of 1882.[40] The next year they participated in attempts to create a new International.[41] In 1886 the Toronto local joined the Knights of Labor as 'Energy Assembly', LA 5742.[42] This path was followed by many other coopers' locals throughout Canada and the US.

II

Workshop-control traditions were extremely strong in foundry work. Late nineteenth-century moulders displayed all the characteristics that Soffer and Montgomery identify as typical of 'autonomous workmen'. Two things distinguish them from the coopers. First is their impressive success in tenaciously maintaining these traditions on into the twentieth century. Second was their presence from the start of this period at the centre of the industrial capitalist world. Moulders were not artisans working in small shops reminiscent of preindustrial society. In Toronto and Hamilton, and throughout Ontario, moulders worked in the important stove, machinery, and agricultural-implement industries. These firms, among the largest in nineteenth-century Ontario, led Canadian industry in attempting to fix prices and later to create multi-plant firms. Not surprisingly, these companies were also continually in the forefront of managerial innovations regarding labour.

Moulders in Toronto were first organized into a local union in 1857.[43] This local joined the Iron Molders International Union, organized in 1859, some time in 1860.[44] The International made clear its position on questions of shopfloor control from its inception. The original constitution claimed for the union the power 'to determine the customs and usages in regard to all matters pertaining to the craft'.[45] This gave the union control over the price of the moulders' labour. In stove shops, the union shop committee would meet and discuss the price to charge for moulding new patterns as the boss brought them in. The committee would meet with the boss or foreman and arrive at a mutually acceptable overall price for the whole stove but as there were always a number of pieces involved in the assembly of any stove the committee would then decide amongst itself how to split this price among its members working on the different castings. This 'board price' once established was considered to be almost non-negotiable and these prices very quickly became recognized as part of the established customs and usages that were the union's sole prerogative. This price was not the only source of the moulders' wages, for there was a second element termed the 'percentage', which was a supplement paid in addition to the piece rate. This percentage was negotiable, and wage conflicts in the industry generally revolved round the 'percentage', for very few bosses made the mistake of trying to challenge the 'board price'.[46]

This was one considerable area of strength for the union, but there were others. The shop committee also dictated the 'set' or 'set day's work', which was the number of pieces that a member was allowed to produce in one day. Thus production control was also taken out of the boss's hands. It was of course in the union's self-interest to 'set' a reasonable amount of work which an average craftsman could perform. Craft pride would dictate against 'setting' too low, but equally craft strength could prevent any attempt at a speed-up.[47] Peterborough moulders enforced the 'set' and brought charges against members who 'rushed up work'.[48] Generally part of each local's rules, the 'set' was made a part of the International Constitution at the 1886 convention in London: 'Resolved that all molders working at piece work be not allowed to make over $3.50 a day.' In 1888 this was struck from the Constitution and was again left to the discretion of each local. Canadian locals continued to enforce this control over production. In Peterborough, in June 1891 'Brother Burns brought a charge against Brother Donavan for earning over $3 a day.'[49]

An additional area in which the union dictated terms was hiring. Members who made the mistake of applying to the foreman instead of to the shop committee were often fined.[50] In one such case in Toronto moulders directly recruited by stove manufacturer Edward Gurney were casually turned away by the shop committee whom they had been directed to by the workers after asking for the foreman.[51] The number of apprentices allowed in a shop was also set by the union. The Peterborough local in 1889 refused to allow 'Mr Brooks to bring in any more apprentices' and in 1891 reasserted that the union would 'allow no more than the regular number of apprentices, one for every shop and one to any eight moulders'.[52] The union also controlled the use of 'bucks' or 'berkshires' (unskilled labourers). When used they were traditionally paid directly by the moulder out of his wages and thus were employed by the craftsman, not the employer. Later, when bosses tried to use 'bucks' to perform some of the work customarily performed by moulders, the latter did all in their power to prevent it.[53] This was the greatest area of contention with Toronto employers. Finally the union struggled to impose a closed shop on its employers and refused to work with non-union moulders. Thus in the moulding industry large areas of control in the setting of price, productivity, and hiring resided with the union.

The extent of the control that the union established was neither won nor maintained without constant struggle. Manufacturers used every device in their power to break the moulders' shop-floor control. In 1866 the newly founded employers' association in the industry passed a resolution to

> proceed at once to introduce into our shops all the apprentices or helpers we deem advisable and that we will not allow any union committees in our shops, and that we will in every way possible free our shops of all dictation or interference on the part of our employees.[54]

The 'Great Lock-out of 1866' that followed the employers' posting of the above 'obnoxious notice', which extended into Canada, culminated in a costly victory for the union. Canadian stove manufacturers also organized and were active in the 1870s in fixing prices, in advocating increased protection, and most significantly in pressing a concerted effort to deal the union a smashing defeat.[55] In this they too failed.

In the Toronto moulding industry, the union's claim to control was the central issue. Strikes were fought at least fourteen times in the years between the founding of Local No. 28 and 1895.[56] The moulders engaged in the major strikes to resist demands by the manufacturers that the customs and usages of the craft be sacrificed. Thus in 1867 McGee demanded that he be allowed to hire as many apprentices as he wished;[57] in 1870 Gurney tried to force his moulders to work with 'bucks',[58] in 1890 both Gurney and Massey offered their moulders a choice of either a substantive cut in the previously unchallenged board price or accepting 'bucks';[59] in 1892 Gurney demanded that his moulders not only accept a reduction on the percentage rate but also commit themselves to this rate for a year, a new scheme to prevent their raising the 'percentage' as soon as the economic climate changed.[60] The same battles were to be fought yet again in 1903–1904.[61]

These strikes were not minor struggles in the history of the Toronto working class. In the general employers' offensive of the late sixties and early seventies to counter the emergence of a strong and newly self-confident working-class movement the boss moulders used various techniques in their attempt to defeat the union. In this period they resorted most often to coercion, falling back on outmoded statutes and the power of the law. The frequently cited case of George Brown and the Toronto printers of 1872 was preceded in Toronto by numerous uses of the courts by stove manufacturers. In 1867 McGee charged six Buffalo moulders with deserting his employment. Recruited by his foreman for a one-year term, they quit work when they discovered that they were being used as scabs. The magistrate claimed he was being lenient owing to the implicit deception used, and fined them only $6.00 each.[62] Two apprentices who left McGee's before their terms were up because of the union blacklist of the shop were not so lucky. They received fifteen days in jail for deserting his employment.[63] Three years later Gurney, a large Toronto and Hamilton stove manufacturer, made use of the courts to fight the union in a slightly different way. He had two union members charged with conspiracy and assault for trying to prevent scabs from filling his shop after he turned out the union men for refusing to work with 'bucks' and a large number of apprentices. After the men were found guilty the Toronto Grand Jury commented that:

> It is with sincere regret that the Grand Jury have had before them . . . two persons charged with assault and conspiracy acting under the regulations of an association known as the Molders Union and they feel it their duty to mark in the most emphatic terms their disapproval of such societies being introduced into our new country calculated as they are to interfere with capital and labour, cramp our infant manufacturers and deprive the subject of his civil liberty. . . .[64]

During another strike that same summer Beard charged ten of his apprentices with 'unlawfully confederating to desert his service with the intent to injure the firm in their business'. Their real offence had been seeking a wage increase and then using the traditional moulders' weapon of restricting their output to enforce their demand. On their last day on the job they all did the same limited amount of work. They were found guilty.[65] Nevertheless the founders' tactics failed. The victory that the moulders won here was especially sweet given the force brought to bear against them. This victory was quite clearly contingent on their monopoly of skill and their ability to control the labour market. Thus it was reported that Gurney was forced to resort to employing moulders such as 'John Cowie who quit one job to go scabbing in Gurney's shop where he had never worked in before, simply because he was of so little account they would never hire him—circumstances sometimes make strange companions'.[66] The union 'defied anyone to produce such a lot of molders as were in Gurney'.[67] But if the victory over Gurney was pleasing that over Beard was valued even more highly:

> It appears that for a year or two past, Beard and Co. of Toronto, have been running an independent scab shop refusing to be 'dictated to by the Union as they felt competent to conduct their business in their own way'. . . . They

found that reliable men were all union men, they found that the sober men were all union men, and what was of more importance, they found that all the good molders were union men and they were obliged to take the off-scourings of creation, all the drunken scallawags and botch workmen, that found their way to Toronto. . . . Their scab foreman was not equal to the situation and they found that their trade was fast leaving them and to save themselves from utter ruin the nauseous dose had to be swallowed. . . .[68]

The 1880s saw the maturing of the system of industrial relations that was only emerging in the 1860s and 1870s. The foundrymen mounted no challenges to the basic rights of the union in the 1880s and only the percentage came under consideration. In 1880 moulders sought and gained a 10 per cent increase but when the economy turned in late 1883 they were forced to accept a 20 per cent reduction. In 1886 they won a 12.5 per cent advance but in 1887 their request for a 10 per cent increase was resisted by Gurney and after a nine-week strike a compromise 5 per cent advance was accepted. In early 1887 the Ontario branches of the IMIU came together to form a District Union. The thirteen Ontario locals with over 1,000 members were brought together to organize more efficiently and to run joint strikes more effectively.[69] In 1887, for example, the Hamilton moulders' strike against Gurney spread to Toronto when Gurney locked out his moulders there. Later in 1890 moulders at the Massey Hamilton plant refused to mould while their Toronto brothers were locked out. But perhaps the major example of these cross-industry strikes was the Bridge and Beach Strike of 1887 in the US. In March of that year moulders struck the Bridge and Beach Manufacturing Co. in St Louis with the sanction of the International. Immediately the new Stove Founders National Defense Association attempted to manufacture the required patterns for the company. Their moulders in turn refused to work on the patterns from the struck foundry. This process spread until at its height almost 5,000 moulders were locked out in fifteen centres. Finally, in June, the Defense Association called the patterns in and supplied the St Louis company with a force of non-union moulders and work resumed as before at the other shops. Both sides claimed victory but most important was that each side had demonstrated to the other their respective strength and staying power. Almost immediately after the end of this strike negotiations were commenced which were to lead to the establishment of national conciliation in the industry through conferences of the contending parties.[70]

The Canadian industry did not take part in these conferences, nor did conciliation apply to the machinery-moulding branches of the trade. Until these industry-wide agreements in stove foundries the strength of the moulders depended entirely on their skill and control of the work process and their ability through their union to maintain this and to exercise some degree of control over the labour market. This labour-market control was of great importance and has been admirably discussed before with reference to the moulders.[71] The importance of the union card to the moulder has been summarized: ' . . . within the jurisdiction of his own local a union card was a man's citizenship paper; in the jurisdiction of other locals it was his passport.'[72]

The early 1890s saw a new employer offensive in Hamilton and Toronto as Gurney and Massey both attempted to smash the moulders' continuing power in their plants. The Gurney strike which commenced in February 1890 lasted an amazing sixteen months before Local 28 ended it. The Massey strike covered ten months from October 1890 to July 1891.[73] In both cases the companies pursued a similar strategy. They shut down their moulding shops, ostensibly for repairs, and after a considerable lapse of time called in the shop committees and asked them to accept either a sizable reduction or work with 'bucks'.[74] In both cases the moulders refused, for 'union rules did not permit "bucks" and the men thought they saw in it their eventual displacement by these labourers and a menace to their trade'.[75] Both Gurney and Massey claimed that they could no longer afford union rates and compete successfully, but the moulders suspected 'a long conceived plan in the attempt at a reduction'.[76] In each case management and labour settled down for a protracted struggle. David Black, the secretary of Local 28, wrote after five months on strike:

> Our fight with Gurney still continues and bids fair to last quite a while longer, we succeed very well in relieving him of his good men, but he has plenty of money and it will take hard fighting and time to beat him.[77]

The Toronto local spared no expense or risk in this struggle, and a number of their members were arrested and tried for intimidating scabs.[78] In September the local issued an appeal 'To the Canadian Public' which explained they had been locked out 'because they refused to make their work cheaper than for any other employer in the same line in the city; and thus assist them to destroy their competitors and monopolize the Canadian market at our expense'. The public was called on to buy only union-made goods, since

> By this means our victory over monopoly will be assured; our right to organize and obtain fair wages for our labour will be vindicated; while the superior quality of your purchase will amply repay your preference.[79]

The union lost both these struggles, but the cost to capital was also high. Gurney in early 1891, when his victory seemed sure, brayed triumphantly that 'the only change resulting from the strike is that he now controlled his shop.' However, when he continued to claim that things were excellent, the *Globe* reporter noted that, faced with the open incredulity of the union representatives present, Gurney modified his statement, mentioning 'that of course the whole year had not been as smooth'. The key in these struggles in the early 1890s was control. As capital entered a new stage where it recognized the necessity of supervising more closely the process of production it had to confront and defeat its 'autonomous workmen'. This gives Gurney's parting chortle added significance:

> The men must work for someone else until they come to one of my proposals. I do not think (with a smile) that there is any likelihood of my going to local union 28 and asking them to come and take control of my foundry.[80]

Gurney's last laugh was too precipitate, however, for the IMIU came back strong in Toronto in the late 1890s and a new wave of struggle broke over the foundry business in 1902–04.[81] It is not the purpose of this paper to detail that struggle, but it is important to emphasize that the power of the moulders was not broken in the struggles of 1890–2. Gurney and Massey delivered only a partial defeat and the moulders came back strong. J.H. Barnett, Toronto IMIU secretary, described one 1903 struggle:

> Just after adjourning the meeting this afternoon the foreman of the Inglis shop, R. Goods, came to the hall and informed us that he had discharged all the scabs in his shop and that he wanted the union men in on Monday, that the firm was tired of the scabs and was willing to give the nine hours. . . .[82]

One year later in yet another struggle with Toronto foundrymen, now supported by the National Foundry Association, Barnett wrote again of the continued monopoly on skill that the moulders enjoyed:

> They are having greater losses in the foundry now than when they first started. They have been trying to make a big condenser and can't make it. They have started the old St Lawrence shop with some of the old country moulders who refused to work with Ersig, the NFA foreman up in the new shop. Jas Gillmore and Fred McGill is instruction [*sic*] them but ain't doing any better.[83]

Iron moulders then, unlike coopers, maintained a high degree of work-place control on into the twentieth century. This was primarily due to their strong organization but was also partially contingent on the slowness with which technology replaced their skill. Machines for moulding were experimented with in the mid-1880s but were an extremely expensive failure.[84] Massey imported its first machines in 1889.[85] Thus, unlike the coopers and shoemakers, the moulders had time to perfect their organization before their major contest with machinery.

Moulders also developed an early understanding of the need for solidarity with their unskilled co-workers. Thus, when the Knights of Labor struck the huge Massey works in Toronto in 1886, moulders left the job in their support. Peterborough IMIU Local no. 191 also co-operated with the Lindsay Knights of Labor.[86]

III

The workers' control enjoyed by Toronto moulders, and their struggle to retain it, was more than equalled by the experiences of Toronto printers. The printers' control of the shop floor demonstrates extremely well early union power. In the 1890s the President of the Toronto local of the ITU insisted:

> The work of the composing room is our business. To no one else can we depute it. It is absolutely ours. The talk of running another man's business will not hold. It is ours; we learned it and must control it.[87]

Unionism among the Toronto printers owed much to the customs and traditions of the craft. Organized first in 1832, the society lapsed in 1836 but was refounded in 1844 to resist a new Toronto employer's departure from the 'settled usages of the trade'.[88] In 1845, when forced again to fight the initiatives taken by George Brown, the printers issued a circular to the Toronto public demanding only 'to maintain that which is considered by all the respectable proprietors as a fair and just reward, for our labour and toil —"the labourer is worthy of his hire" '.[89] Here the tenacity of pre-industrial notions of traditional wages can be seen. Customary usage dictated wages— not any abstract notion of what the market might bear. Employers as well as workers had to learn the new rules of a market economy, and the disruptions caused by the Browns' arrival in the Toronto printing trades in the 1840s suggest that until then wages had been 'largely a customary and not a market calculation'.[90]

The printers possessed a strong tradition of craft pride and identification. In their 1845 statement to the Toronto public they resolved 'to maintain by all legitimate means in their power their just rights and privileges as one of the most important and useful groups in the industrious community'.[91]

Members of the 'art preservative', they saw themselves as the main carriers of rationalism and the enlightenment. No trade dinner or ball, and these were frequent, was complete without a set of toasts to the printers' patron, Benjamin Franklin, and to Gutenberg and other famous printers. Franklin replaced the older European craft tradition of saints, and his rationalism fitted very well with the printers' disdain for other societies who had recourse to secret signs and fiery oaths. The printers prided themselves on the fact that

> initiation ceremonies, melo-dramatic oaths, passwords, signs, grips, etc., though advocated by many worthy representatives, and repeatedly considered by the national union, never found a place in the national or subordinate constitutions.[92]

The printers saw their craft as crucial in maintaining all that was best in the western literary tradition. As one printer toasted at an 1849 Anniversary Dinner: 'To the art of printing—under whose powerful influence the mind of fallen and degraded man is raised from nature up to nature's God'.[93] Thus printers' shop committees were 'chapels' and the shop steward was 'the father of the chapel'. This pride in craft was manifested time and time again throughout the nineteenth century.

In 1869 the executive recommended the initiation of a reading room and library:

> where the members of the craft can have access in leisure hours for the enjoyment of study and mental recreation and where may be ever within their reach increasing facilities for the acquisition of whatever in our art is may be of advantage to know. . . . It is a laudable endeavour to support one's calling which two centuries ago was deemed the most honourable of all professions. . . .[94]

The union seal depicted a printing press with light emanating from all around it.[95]

The Toronto printers had a strong sense of the history of their craft and their union. They were particularly proud of being the oldest Toronto union and parts of their frequent fêtes were often spent on these themes. The 1888 picnic program, for example, contained original histories of both the art of printing and the Toronto Typographical Union.[96] All these traditions were put to use by the printers, and they brought the craft lore together in stirring addresses invoking custom in the struggle against oppression:

> Fellow-workingmen, knights of the stick and rule, preservers of 'the art preservative',—ye whose honourable calling is to make forever imperishable the noblest, truest, and most sublime thoughts of the statesman, the philosopher, and the poet,—to you is committed the mightiest agent for good or ill which has yet been pressed into the service of humanity. The printing press, the power mightier than kings, more powerful than armies, armaments, or navies, which shall yet overthrow ignorance and oppression and emancipate labour, is your slave. Without your consent, without the untiring labour of your skillful fingers and busy brain, this mighty giant, with his million tongued voices speeding on wings of steam all over this broad earth of ours, would be dumb. Shorn of his strength which your skill imparts, his throbbing sides and iron sinews might pant and strain in vain; no voice or cry of his or your oppressors could ever reach or be heard among men. Realizing this my friends it is easy to determine our proper station in the grand struggle that is now in progress all over the civilized world, the effort of the masses to throw off oppression's yoke. . . . We belong in the front rank, at the head of this column. Since the discovery of printing humanity has made great progress and already we see the dawn of the coming day when light and knowledge shall illuminate all lands and man shall no longer oppress his fellow-man.[97]

Central to the power of the International Typographical Union was the extent to which each local maintained its control over production. The composing room was the preserve of the printer. Management's only representative there, the foreman, was a union member and subject to the discipline of his brothers. This was true in Toronto from the inception of the TTU and was very important because the union also demanded that all hiring be done through the foreman.[98] In 1858 the ITU convention had ruled that:

> The foreman of an office is the proper person to whom application should be made for employment; and it is enjoined upon subordinate unions that they disapprove of any other mode of application.[99]

The new ITU constitution of 1867 fined members who applied for jobs to anyone other than the foreman. Four years later this control was reasserted but foremen were also warned:

> It is the opinion of your humble servant that the foreman of an office belongs to the union under which he works and the union does not belong to the foreman . . . and that no foreman has the right to discharge a regular hand . . . on any other ground than that of shortness of work or wilfull neglect of duty. . . .[100]

In an extraordinary 1873 case the ITU ruled that the Ottawa local was correct to strike against J.C. Boyce, the proprietor of *The Citizen*, when he took over operation of his own composing room. Only if Boyce submitted a clear card from the London (Eng.) Trades Society would he 'be allowed to work under the jurisdiction of the Ottawa Union'.[101]

This effective union control of the hiring practice was augmented by the role the foreman played in enforcing the printer's right to divide work. In newspaper offices each regular employee had a 'sit' and with this place came the right to choose a replacement any time the regular wanted time off. Although he was not technically employed by the regular printer that was actually what the practice amounted to. In Toronto the *Mail* paid the money to the regular who then paid the subs from his salary.[102] When bosses tried to regulate this custom by utilizing 'sub-lists' which delineated the substitutes from whom regulars were forced to choose, the International roundly condemned the practice and refused to allow locals to co-operate with it.[103] The union claimed ever more interest in the hiring process. In 1888 a resolution was introduced at the ITU convention 'that would have placed the regulation of hiring and discharging of employees entirely in the hands of the local unions'.[104] In 1890 'the priority law' was passed by which the grounds upon which foremen could discharge were even more tightly circumscribed. Only incompetence, violation of rules, neglect of duty, or decrease of labour force were acceptable causes for firing, and on discharge a member was entitled to a written statement of cause. In addition the final part of the law ruled that 'subs' in an office had priority when positions became available.[105] The power of the union, then, in controlling the selection of printers, was almost total.

The union also retained a strong position in bargaining. The union would first arrive at an approved scale of prices unilaterally and would then take it to the employers.[106] Some negotiation was possible, but much of the scale was regarded as non-negotiable. For example after the strike of 1872 for the nine-hour day never again were hours subject to consideration; having been won once they were off limits for further discussion.[107] The scale was a complex document divided into three major sections: timework; piecework, news and magazines; and piecework, books. Time work was not the traditional method of payment in the printing industry but throughout the late nineteenth century more and more job shops adopted it. However, the time rate was closely tied to the piece rate. In Toronto, where the piece rate was 33 $\frac{1}{3}$ cents per 1,000 ems, the time rate was 33 $\frac{1}{3}$ cents an hour—the general assumption being that a hand compositor averaged 1,000 ems an hour. In newspaper offices the usual method of payment was by the piece, which in the compositor's case was measured by the area of type that he composed and expressed in 'ems'. Printers were thus paid per 1,000 ems of matter. There were a number of areas of conflict implicit in this type of payment. Rates were set for the newspaper as a whole, but special rates were set for material classified as difficult, such as foreign languages or tables, or even for illegible copy.[108] As the century progressed more and more newspaper work consisted of advertising, which contained far more blank space than regular material. This copy became known as 'fat' matter and was the most lucrative for the printer. The printers insisted that rates were set for the paper as a whole, thus retaining the higher rate for fat matter as well. The traditional way of distributing the material was that all copy was hung on the 'hook' as it arrived in the composing room and the compositors picked it up in order, thus insuring an even distribution of the 'fat'. Bosses began to object to this, and tried to create 'departments' by which specific printers did the special composing. This the union resisted strenuously and forbade locals to accept 'departments'. They offered, as a compromise, to allow members to bid for the 'fat' matter. The successful bidder who gained the ads then paid back to the union the amount of his bid, usually a percentage of his earnings, which was then used to buy things in common for all the printers or to hire a person to clean everybody's type, or was distributed equally among the members.[109] The Toronto local, however, resisted all employer incursions in this area. Toronto employers certainly tried. In 1882 the *Mail* offered its printers an advance but in return demanded the return of the ads. Instead the new scale of 1883 reiterated that 'where weekly and piece hands are employed the piece hands shall have their proportionate share of "fat" matter.'[110] Seven years later another new scale still insisted that 'compositors on newspapers were entitled to equal distribution of any "phat".'[111] The complexity of the Toronto printers' scale is suggested by the 39 sections of the 1883 and 35 sections of the 1890 contract.[112] All this led one managerial strategist named DeVinne, who was later to play a major role in the United Typothetae, to moan that 'It is the composition room that is the great sink-hole. It is in type and the wages of compositors that the profits of the house are lost.'[113]

So far we have spoken entirely of only one branch of printing—the compositors. Until the middle of the century in the cities and until much later in small shops, a printer ran the press as well as composing. With the rise of power presses, the pressman's role became more and more complex, and increasingly the old-time printer who did both jobs disappeared and new specialists took over. By 1869 the Toronto local had special piece rates for pressmen, and the job definition of the compositor prevented him from performing press work. The pressmen's new consciousness led the ITU to begin to charter Pressmen's locals separately in 1873, and ten years later the Toronto Pressmen set up their own local. Disputes with Local 91, however, led them to join the new International Printing Pressmen's Union in 1889. This splintering of the printing crafts caused many problems, but the pressmen as an equally skilled group carried with them the traditions of printers' unionism. Time was spent at meetings, for example, in designing outfits for the various marches and parades that were so much a part of working-class life in Toronto in the 1880s.[114]

Although the major focus of this paper is the skilled worker's power on the job, one cannot discuss the Toronto printers without alluding also to their political strength in the city, in provincial and even in national politics. They provided the Toronto working-class community and movement with important leadership. It was natural for these literate working-class intellectuals to play key political roles, but the extent of their dominance is striking nevertheless. Although not the initiators of the Toronto Trades Assembly (this honour belongs to John Hewitt of the Coopers International Union), they did play an important part in this organization and in the Canadian Labour Union. In the 1880s they helped found the Toronto Trades and Labor Council after the meeting of the ITU in Toronto in 1881 and later were quite active in the meetings of the Trades and Labor Congress. Moreover, of the six labour papers published in Toronto between 1872 and 1892, three were published and edited by printers—*The Ontario Workman* under J.S. Williams, J.C. McMillan, and David Sleeth, all prominent members of Local 91; *The Trade Union Advocate/Wage Worker* of Eugene Donavon; and D.J. O'Donaghue's *Labor Record*. Other members of Local 91 also enjoyed prominent careers in labour reform—John Armstrong, a former International President of the ITU (1878–9), was appointed to Macdonald's Royal Commission on the Relations of Labour and Capital in 1886; D.J. O'Donoghue, prominent as an MPP, leading Canadian Knight of Labor, and later collector of labour statistics for the Ontario Bureau of Industries; E.F. Clarke, arrested in 1872 and later Mayor of Toronto, MPP and MP; and W.B. Prescott,

International President of the ITU from 1891–8. This was just one generation of Local 91's membership; the next was to include two mayors of Toronto and a senator.[115]

Local 91's political role stemmed from its union activities. Toronto printers, for example, had little use for George Brown's brand of Liberalism. As early as 1845 they had noted the irony implicit in his labour-relations policies:

> A person from the neighbouring Republic commenced business here and has ever since been unremitting in his Liberal endeavour to reduce as low as possible that justly considered fair and equitable rate of remuneration due to the humble operatives.[116]

His 'Liberal' endeavours were to lead him into conflict with the printers time and time again, culminating in the printer's strike for the nine-hour day in 1872.[117] Brown's use of antiquated British laws against combination to arrest the leaders of the ITU was turned against him by Macdonald's passage of the Trade Union Act. The Tories controlled Toronto working-class politics for a number of years following, until D.J. O'Donoghue, the Knights of Labor, and the legislative responsiveness of the Mowat Ontario government started a swing towards the Liberals.

The political expertise of the printers had of course grown throughout their various struggles, and the tactics perfected in 1872 were used again in the 1880s. Thus when John Ross Robertson's *Telegram* came under union attack in 1882 the union first turned to the boycott to bring pressure on the owner. They decided that in this way they could expose

> the treatment which union printers have received at the hands of JRR for many years past, and the manner in which that gentleman (?) invariably casts aspersions upon the union mechanics of this city generally through the columns of his vasculating [*sic*] paper.[118]

John Armstrong and D.J. O'Donoghue were appointed to visit the merchants who advertised in the *Telegram* and convince them to place their ads elsewhere. The next year when ITU No. 91 passed a new scale of prices they struck the *Telegram*, pulling most of the compositors out on strike. They then received the endorsement of the whole Toronto Trades and Labor Council for the boycott and late in March held a mass meeting at which speeches were delivered by most of the prominent Toronto labour leaders pledging support for Local 91.[119]

The strikes the following year against the *Mail* and the *Globe* were even more eventful and suggestive of the printers' political acumen. The papers united with the other Toronto publishers and print shops to demand a 10 per cent reduction on the printers' wages and gave only a week for consideration. The printers refused and struck. The union was successful in forcing job offices and smaller papers to withdraw the reduction, but the *Globe* and the *Mail* held out. The *Globe* insisted that it had never become a union shop because 'the boss needed absolute control in a newspaper office.'[120] The morning papers after a hard fight won the reduction to 30 cents per 1,000 ems, down from 33 $\frac{1}{3}$ cents, but their victory was short-lived. In 1885 the *Globe* reversed its position of a year before and the political game of the 1870s by becoming a union shop for the first time. This left only the Tory *Mail* holding out against the typos. The *Mail* succumbed in February of 1886 and became a union shop, withdrawing the iron-clad contract that it had adopted after the troubles in 1884.

What tactics had the ITU used to win these long-range victories after their apparent defeat in 1884? The printers had employed their usual measures against the papers. They first withdrew all their members from the shops and when they failed to prevent the shops' filling up with the much despised 'country-mice', non-union printers from small towns, they turned to the boycott and mass demonstrations of workingmen.[121] But this time they also requested all workingmen to boycott any candidates supported by the *Mail* in the municipal election campaigns of the winter of 1885–6.[122] Local 91 passed a resolution: 'That this union will oppose to its utmost any candidate for municipal honours who may be supported by the *Mail* newspaper'.[123] The following weeks saw union after union endorse the ITU motion and also saw a number of Tory ward heelers running for cover and abandoning the *Mail*. The union issued a circular exposing its dealings with the *Mail* since 1872 and then placed advertisements in the Toronto papers in January of 1886 strongly attacking Manning, the *Mail*'s candidate for Mayor:

> Resolved that this union consider Mr Manning a nominee of the Mail, he having advertised in that paper . . . and having been editorially supported by it, particularly so on Saturday morning January 2; and therefore we call on all workingmen and those in sympathy with organized labour to VOTE AGAINST MANNING, THE NOMINEE OF THE MAIL.[124]

The same Local 91 meeting also decided to blacklist aldermanic candidates who had not broken with the *Mail* and decided to issue 10,000 circulars denouncing Manning and these candidates. After Howland's stunning election as mayor, widely regarded as a working-class victory, the ITU issued this statement:

> To the Trades and Labour organizations of Toronto—Fellow unionists: Toronto Typographical Union No. 91 takes this opportunity of thanking the labour organizations of this city and their friends who so nobly supported us at the polls in our effort to defeat the Mail. To the workingmen of Toronto who have had the honour and manhood to rise above party ties in the cause of labour, the heartiest thanks of the 300 members of the TTU are due. . . . At a time when we needed your assistance you have shown that the motto of our union

'United to support not combined to injure' is the guiding stone of the honest toiler everywhere . . . [125]

This electoral defeat led to the *Mail*'s total reversal in February 1886, when it surrendered to the Union. Local 91 had to prove its strength at the polls, however, for as early as 1884 leading Tory printers had warned Macdonald of the possible repercussions of the *Mail*'s adventure. J.S. Williams had written in August, 1884:

> Not only will the matter complained of [*Mail* lock-out] alienate a very large proportion of the working men who have hitherto nobly supported the party, but it places a barrier in the way of any prominent or representative working-man actively working or speaking in the future.

Moreover he predicted that the *Mail*'s reactionary policies could cost the Tories two to three seats in Toronto and perhaps seats in other urban centres as well. E.F. Clarke, a prominent politician and member of Local 91, wrote to the same effect:

> A reduction of wages at a week's notice and a refusal of the Mail to leave the settlement of the question to arbitration will alienate the sympathies of a large number of workingmen who have hitherto supported the Conservative cause, and will weaken the influence of the journal with the masses. . . .

A non-working-class Tory politico wrote that the labour friends of the party were now in an impossible position since they 'cannot support the party that treats them so shabbily' and expressed the fear that the loss of the whole Toronto Trades and Labor Council might result in electoral defeat in the city.[126] Nevertheless these warnings were ignored until the humiliating defeats of January 1886. Then the party rushed in to settle the matter once and for all. Harry Piper, a Tory ward heeler, wrote to Macdonald in February to inform him that the ITU-*Mail* fight 'had of late assumed a very serious aspect' since a number of old-party workers had clearly transferred their allegiance in the election. As a result he arranged a meeting with John Armstrong, a Tory leader of Local 91 who had lost his own job at the *Mail* during the strike. Piper convinced Armstrong that 'the Union was *killing our Party* and the Grits were reaping the benefit of the trouble and using our own friends.' Armstrong promised to help if the iron-clad was removed. Piper then arranged with the manager and directors of the *Mail* that the document be ceremoniously burned before the printers, and Armstrong agreed to have the union lift the boycott.[127] Thus the seeming defeat of the summer of 1884 had been translated by political means into a striking victory for Local 91. Neither the *Globe* nor the *Mail* were to cause the union difficulty again in the late nineteenth century.

Similar tactics were employed successfully against J.H. Maclean of the *World* in 1888 when he tried to defeat the union's control of 'fat' matter.

The struggle was precipitated by a fight over the price to be paid for an advertisement that was inserted twice. The union rule was that if the advertisement was run in an identical manner then the compositor was only paid once but that if any changes were made the compositor was paid again for the whole advertisement. The foreman supported the printers' case but the Macleans, after paying the money owed, locked out the union. The ITU then reiterated its position on 'fat' matter:

> Only by the getting of the advertisements and other 'fat' matter are the men able to make anything like living wages, and this fact is recognized by all fair-minded employers as well as the men.[128]

In late July, after filing his shop with 'country-mice', Maclean sought an injunction against the ITU's boycott of the *World*. It was granted on an interim basis and then made permanent in mid-August.[129] The injunction did not solve Maclean's problems:

> The World is in sore straights as a result of the law compelling union men not to buy it or patronize merchants who advertise therein. Internal storms are of such common occurrence that a couple of weeks ago the vermin employed there went out on strike even but returned to the nest again.[130]

A few months later Maclean again sought to make his paper a union shop. Again the political dimensions of the settlement are clear. W.B. Prescott, the President of Local 91, wrote John A. Macdonald and sought his intervention with Maclean to insure that the *World* came around. Prescott pointed out that 'the cheap labour policies of the *World* antagonized organized labour.'[131] Perhaps one reason that Maclean and the *World* felt the pressure was that the Local had quickly found a way to circumvent the injunction by promoting union papers rather than naming those boycotted. They continued to use this technique, especially in a political context. In the municipal campaigns of 1891–2, for example, they issued the following circular:

> Having been informed that you are seeking municipal honours, we desire to call you attention to the fact that there are a few printing and publishing houses in this city who do not employ union labour, and we, believing it would be to your advantage to patronize only those who do employ such, request you to place your patronage and advertising in union offices only, as we can assure you that from past experience, your chances of election are greater by so doing.[132]

The circular then listed the dailies that were union shops, which by 1891 included all but the *Telegram*, which was shortly to enter the fold. In March 1892 the TTU also began the use of the union label.[133] Thus the power of the Toronto printers continued to grow throughout the late nineteenth century and a larger proportion of Toronto printers were unionized in the early 1890s than had been at any previous date.[134]

The initial encounter with mechanization served to strengthen their position. Until the invention of linotype and monotype machines in the late 1880s, typesetting had remained unchanged from the sixteenth century.[135] In Toronto the *News* introduced the Rogers typograph machine in 1892 and offered the printer-operators 14 cents/1,000 ems. The ITU had recommended in 1888 'that subordinate unions . . . take speedy action looking to their [linotype machines'] recognition and regulation, endeavouring everywhere to secure their operation by union men upon a scale of wages which shall secure compensation equal to that paid hand compositors'.[136] This was amended in 1889[137] to demand that in all union offices only practical printers could run the machines and that the rates on the machines would be governed by the local unions.[138] In Toronto the union's right to control the operation of the machine was not challenged initially and their *Typographical Journal* correspondent reported in March of 1892 'that so far we have not suffered from their use'. However, that summer the *News*, appealing to the craft custom of piece rates, refused to pay operators by the day. After a seven-week strike the union won its demand that the printers be paid by time. They were to receive $12.00 a week for six weeks while learning the machine operation and then $14.00 after they demonstrated their competence which was set at 2,000 ems per hour or 100,000 ems per week. This settlement brought the union not only control of the machine and the wage style it sought but also implicitly recognized the printers' right to limit production since the rate of competence set was far below the actual capabilities of the machine which were estimated to be anywhere from 3–8 times as fast as hand composition.[139] The International was also concerned to prevent any proliferation of speed-ups with the new machine and ruled that 'no member shall be allowed to accept work . . . where a task, stint, or deadline is imposed by the employer on operators of typesetting devices.'[140] The union later successfully resisted any attempts by employers to speed up work totals. The victory over the *News* and the union's previous success with Robertson's *Telegram* also brought Local 91 control of all Toronto newspapers for the first time in its history.[141] The printers had learned their lessons well. They left the century not only with their traditions intact but also with their power actually augmented. They had met the machine and triumphed.[142]

IV

What ramifications did shop-floor power have in terms of how workers thought about their society, how it was changing, and their own role in it? David Montgomery has argued that the major impact of this early workers' control was the skilled workers' growing awareness that the key institution for the transformation of society was the trade union.[143] From their understanding that they, through their unions, controlled production, it was a relatively easy step to the belief that all the capitalist brought to the process was capital. Thus an alternative source of capital would transform the society, ending the inequities of capitalist production and creating the producer's society that they all dreamed of. This ideology looked to co-operation administered through the trade union as the major agent of change. All the unions we have discussed favoured co-operation.

John Monteith, President of Toronto IMIU Local 28, wrote *Fincher's Trades Review* in 1863 to describe the work of Canada West members in discussing and investigating co-operation. A union moulders' committee had contacted Rochdale and now recommended both producers' and consumers' co-ops to their local unions. They sought co-operation because 'our present organization does not accomplish what we want. That is to take us from under the hand of our employers and place us on an equal footing.'[144] Co-operation of course would accomplish this very end. Five years later another Toronto moulder complained that 'We are but little better off than our forefathers who were serfs to the feudal barons. We are serfs to the capitalists of the present day. . . .' His solution:

> Let the next convention create a co-op fund to be devoted entirely to co-operation. . . . We have been co-operating all our lives, but it has been to make someone else rich. We have been the busy bees in the hives while the drones have run away with the honey and left us to slave in the day of adversity. . . . Day after day the wealth of the land is concentrating in the hands of a few persons. The little streams of wealth created and put in motion by the hard hands of labour gravitate into one vast reservoir, out of which but a few individuals drink from golden cups; while labour, poor, degraded and despised labour, must live in unhealthy hovels and feed upon scanty, unhealthy food from rusty dishes. . . .[145]

The IMIU founded as many as twenty co-operative foundries in the 1860s.[146]

Toronto printers started three co-operative newspapers. At the height of the nine-hour struggle in 1872 *The Ontario Workman* was started as a co-operative venture, as was D.J. O'Donoghue's *Labour Record* of 1886. In 1892 during the strike at the *News* a group of printers banded together and founded the *Star*.[147] The *Ontario Workman* operated as a co-op paper for only six months and the *Labor Record* and the *Star* each lasted about a year. Capital for the *Star* was raised from the TTU and TTLC. They initially used the presses of the *World*, since W.F. Maclean offered them his facilities in return for 51 per cent of the operation. This 'Paper for the People' enjoyed quick success in winning the readership of the *News*, which had from its inception in 1882 posed as the paper for Toronto workers.[148] Riordan, the owner of the *News*, attempted to buy the operation and Maclean tried to merge it with the *World* but the printers refused both offers and instead bought a press. However, they failed to make a go of it and the paper suspended publication in June of 1893. It was continued after its purchase as a pro-labour paper but control had passed out of the printers' hands.[149]

Machinists and blacksmiths in Toronto organized a co-operative foundry early in 1872 after losing a strike at the Soho works.[150] Six years later Toronto cigar makers established the Toronto Co-operative Cigar Manufactory Association. Here, as with the moulders in the 1860s, the push for co-operation came as logical extension of their knowledge of the trade and their refusal to accept management's reduction of wages. Alf Jury, a Toronto tailor and labour reformer, denounced 'the wage system as a modified form of slavery' and demonstrated that there could be 'no fraternal feeling between capital and labour' at a cigar-makers' strike meeting that year. Jury then cited production statistics to repudiate the employers' claims that the reduction was necessary. A number of bosses who had agreed to pay union rates supported this assertion. Jury's logical solution was the great aim of working-class struggle: 'to do away with the capitalists while using the capital ourselves'—the establishment of a co-operative factory.[151] An association was founded, shares were issued, a charter was obtained and the factory opened for business in March 1879. About a year later the Toronto local of the CMIU reported that the co-operative was 'progressing finely' and 'doing a good trade'.[152] Stratford cigar-makers also founded a co-operative factory in 1886 which was owned by the Knights of Labor and run under CMIU rules. It employed between 20 and 30 men and produced a brand known as 'The Little Knight'.[153] Toronto Bakers Assembly LA 3499 also set up a co-operative bakery which lasted about two years in the mid-1880s.[154]

The successes or failures of these co-operative ventures are of less importance than the ideological assumptions on which they were based. Often originated only in crisis situations, they nevertheless flowed directly from the shop-floor experience of skilled workers and the practices of their unions in struggling to control production. It was a relatively easy step from there to envisaging a system that was free of the boss who did so very little. A Chatham moulder wrote in 1864:

> This then shows both classes in their just relations towards each other—the capitalist and the mechanic; the one, the mechanic is the moving power—the capitalist bearing about the same relation to him that the cart does to the horse which draws it—differing in this respect, that the mechanic makes the capitalist and the horse does not make the cart; the capitalist without the mechanic being about as useful as the cart without the horse. The capitalist no doubt at times increases the sphere of usefulness of the mechanic; so does the cart that of the horse, and enables him to do more for his owner than otherwise he could do; but deprive him of it, and there is little that he can do with it that he could not accomplish without it. In short the workingman is the cause the capitalist the effect.[155]

The syntax may be confused but the moulder's meaning comes through clearly. In 1882 at the time of a Toronto carpenters' strike, during discussion of a co-operative planing mill, a reporter asked union leader Thomas Moor if the carpenters had the requisite skills. Moor's response was simple but profound: 'If the men can manage a mill and make it a success for their employers, surely they can do the same thing for an institution in which they have an interest.'[156]

Co-operation was one extension of workers' control, socialism was to be another.[157] Capital, however, also began to respond to the challenges raised by the growing tradition of workers' control. F.W. Taylor, capital's main workplace ideologue, understood very well the power of the 'autonomous workman':

> Now, in the best of the ordinary types of management, the managers recognize the fact that the 500 or 1000 workmen, included in the 20 or 30 trades, who are under them, possess this mass of traditional knowledge, a large part of which is not in the possession of management. . . . The foremen and superintendents know, better than anyone else, that their own knowledge and personal skill falls far short of the combined knowledge and dexterity of all the workingmen under them.[158]

Taylor also reminisced at length about his first job experience in a machine shop of the Midvale Steel Company in the late 1870s:

> As was usual then, and in fact as is still usual in most of the shops in this country [1912], the shop was really run by the workmen, and not by the bosses. The workmen together had carefully planned just how fast each job should be done, and they had set a pace for each machine throughout the shop, which was limited to about one-third of a good day's work. Every new workman who came into the shop was told at once by the other men exactly how much of each kind of work he was to do, and unless he obeyed these instructions he was sure before long to be driven out of the place by the men.[159]

After his appointment as foreman Taylor set out to increase production. He fired some of the men, lowered others' wages, hired 'green' hands, lowered the piece rate—in general engaged in what he described as a 'war'. His limited success in this 'bitter struggle' he attributed to not being of working-class origin. His middle-class status enabled him to convince management that worker sabotage, not the speed-up, was responsible for a sudden rash of machine breakdowns.[160]

The new popularity of Taylor and the other proponents of 'scientific management' in the early twentieth century, was indicative of capital's new attempt to rationalize production.[161] This, combined with the rise of the large corporation, the rapid growth of multi-plant firms, and the ever-increasing extension of labour-saving machinery, challenged directly not only workers' control traditions but also the very existence of the labour movement.

Toronto workers, who had struggled throughout the late nineteenth century for shop-floor control, were about to face new, more virulent battles. The custom of workers' control, widely regarded as a right, had become deeply embedded in working-class culture. The fight, initially to maintain and later to extend this control, became the major locus of class struggle in the opening decades of the twentieth century.

Thus even in the cases where craft unions abandoned the traditional practices of the 'autonomous workman' in return for concessions or out of weakness, the leadership could not always assure management that the membership would follow union dictates. As one investigator noted about the foundry business:

> The customs of the trade . . . do not always vanish with the omission of any recognition of 'the standard day's work' in wage agreements. Nor can it be expected that the entire membership of an organization will at once respond to the removal of limitations on output by a national convention of that organization. Trade customs, shop practices, grow; they become as much a part of the man as his skill as a molder. . . .[162]

Written in 1904, these cautions were as true of other skilled workers as they were of moulders. Customs of control, established by struggle, would not vanish; they had to be vanquished by persistent management assault.

Suggestions for Further Reading

Robert H. Babcock, *Gompers in Canada: A Study in American Continentalism before the First World War* (Toronto, 1974).

Gregory S. Kealey, *Toronto Workers Respond to Industrial Capitalism, 1867–1892* (Toronto, 1980).

Bryan D. Palmer, *A Culture in Conflict: Skilled Workers and Industrial Capitalism in Hamilton, Ontario 1880–1900* (Montreal, 1979).

Notes

[1] See Herbert Gutman, 'Class, Status and the Gilded Age Radical: A Reconsideration' in Gutman and Kealey (eds) *Many Pasts: Readings in American Social History*, vol. 2 (Englewood Cliffs, 1973), 125–51, and his 'Work, Culture, and Society in Industrializing America, 1815–1919', *American Historical Review*, 78 (1973), 531–88; see also E.J. Hobsbawm, 'Custom, Wages and Work-load', in *Labouring Men: Studies in the History of Labour* (London 1964), 344–70.

[2] David Montgomery, *Workers' Control in America: Studies in the History of Work, Technology, and Labour Struggles* (1980), 9–31. See also his 'Trade Union Practice and the Origins of Syndicalist Theory in the United States', unpublished paper,

and his 'The "New Unionism" and the Transformation of Workers' Consciousness in America, 1909–1922', *Journal of Social History*, 7 (1974), 509–29. All these are part of Montgomery's ongoing study, tentatively titled *The Rise and Fall of the House of Labor, 1880–1920*.

[3]Raymond Williams, 'Base and Super-structure in Marxist Cultural Theory', *New Left Review*, 82 (Nov.-Dec. 1973), 3–16. For an application of these categories to US working-class history see Leon Fink, 'Class Conflict and Class Consciousness in the Gilded Age: The Figure and the Phantom', *Radical History Review* (Winter 1975).

[4]On scientific management in the US see Milton Nadworny, *Scientific Management and the Unions* (Cambridge, Mass., 1955); Katherine Stone, 'The Origin of Job Structures in the Steel Industry', *Radical America*, 7 (1973), 19–66 and Bryan Palmer, 'Class, Conception and Class Conflict: The Thrust for Efficiency, Managerial Views of Labor and the Working Class Rebellion, 1903–1922', *The Review of Radical Political Economics*, 7 (1975), 31–49. For Canada see Bradley Rubin, 'Mackenzie King and the Writing of Canada's (Anti) Labour Laws', *Canadian Dimensions*, 8 (Jan. 1972); Michael Piva, 'The Decline of the Trade Union Movement in Toronto, 1900–1915', unpubl. paper, CHA, 1975; and Craig Heron and Bryan Palmer, 'Through the Prism of the Strike: The Contours and Context of Industrial Unrest in Southern Ontario, 1901–1914', *Canadian Historical Review* LVII, 4 (Dec. 1977), 423–58.

[5]Gregory S. Kealey, 'Artisans Respond to Industrialism: Shoemakers, Shoe Factories and the Knights of St. Crispin in Toronto', Canadian Historical Association, *Historical Papers* (1973), 137–57.

[6]Franklin E. Coyne, *The Development of the Cooperage Industry in the United States, 1620–1940* (Chicago, 1940), 24.

[7]*Coopers' Journal* [henceforth *CJ*], May 1871, 210–11.

[8]*Chicago Workingman's Advocate*, 19 March 1870.

[9]H.G. Gutman, 'The Labour Policies of the Large Corporation in the Gilded Age: the Case of the Standard Oil Company', unpublished paper, October 1966, 10.

[10]Organizational data are drawn from *CJ*, 1870–1875; Coopers' International Union of North America, *Proceedings*, 1871 and 1873; and Coopers' International Union of North America, Executive Department, *Names and Addresses of the Cor[responding] Secretaries of all the Unions* (Cleveland, 1873).

[11]*Workingman's Advocate*, 20 Jan. 1872.

[12]Benson Soffer, 'A Theory of Trade Union Department: The Role of the Autonomous Workman', *Labor History*, 1 (1960), 141.

[13]*CJ*, August 1871, 319.

[14]*Ibid.*, April 1872, 254, and Coopers' International Union of North America, Executive Board, *Price List* (Cleveland 1872), 32–3.

[15]*CF*, October 1872, 633; March 1873, 133–4; June 1873, 278.

[16]*Ibid.*, Sept. 1872, 566.

[17]*Ibid.*, June 1871, 248.

[18]*Ibid.*, June 1872, 373.

[19]*Coopers' Ritual* (Cleveland 1870), 8–9.

[20]*CJ*, May 1871, 211.

[21]Montgomery, 'Workers' Control of Machine Production', 7–9.

[22]Martin Foran, *The Other Side: A Social Study Based on Fact* (Washington, 1886). The novel originally appeared in serial form in *CJ* commencing in December 1871 and was reprinted in the *Ontario Workman* in 1872.

[23]*CJ*, July 1872, 426–9.

[24]*Ibid.*, March 1871, 153.

[25]*Ibid.*

[26]*Ibid.* and *Proceedings.*

[27]Gutman, 'Standard Oil'.

[28]H.B. Small, *The Products and Manufactures of the New Dominion* (Ottawa, 1868), 139–41. For a good description of hand production see T.A. Meister, *The Apple Barrel Industry in Nova Scotia* (Nova Scotia Museum, Halifax n.d.).

[29]For Gooderham's see *CJ*, Oct.-Nov. 1870, 25 July 1871, 268; April 1872, 235; August 1872, 500; September 1872, 566; December 1872, 741; March 1873, 133; Toronto *Mail*, 23 April 1872. For Walker's see *CJ*, January 1872, 47–8. For other Toronto shops see Canada, *Census*, 1871, Industrial Mss.

[30]CIU, *Proceedings*, 1871.

[31]*CJ*, Oct.-Nov. 1870, 25.

[32]*Ibid.*, July 1871, 268.

[33]*Ibid.*, December 1872, 741.

[34]*Ibid.*, March 1872, 182.

[35]*Ibid.*, December 1874.

[36]*Ibid.*, June 1875.

[37]Greg Kealey (ed.), *Canada Investigates Industrialism* (Toronto 1973), 113–16.

[38]B. Soffer, 'The "Autonomous Workman" ', 148.

[39]*CJ*, June 1875.

[40]*Globe*, 15, 24 April 1882.

[41]Iron Molders' Journal, August 1883.

[42]G.S. Kealey, 'The Knights of Labor in Toronto', unpublished paper, 1974.

[43]Paul C. Appleton, 'The Sunshine and the Shades: Labour Activism in Central Canada, 1850–1860', unpubl. MA thesis, University of Calgary, 1974.

[44]The best work on the Iron Molders International Union [henceforth IMIU] in Canada is C.B. Williams, 'Canadian-American Trade Union Relations: A Study of the Development of Binational Unionism', unpublished PhD thesis, Cornell, 1864, chs. 3–4. Although limited in scope the discussion of the Union is insightful.

[45]IMIU, *Constitution*, 1859 as cited in Williams, 'Canadian-American', 105.

[46]The discussion of wages in the industry is drawn from John P. Frey and John R. Commons, 'Conciliation in the Stove Industry', *Bulletin of the Bureau of Labor*, 62 (1906), 124–96, especially 125–30, and Frank T. Stockton, *The International Molders Union of North America* (Baltimore, 1921).

[47]Carroll D. Wright, 'Regulation and Restriction of Output', *Eleventh Special Report of the Commissioner of Labor* (Washington, 1904), 149–85.

[48]Peterborough Iron Moulders International Union, No. 191, *Minutes*, 4 September 1882, in Gainey Collection, Trent University Archives [henceforth *Minutes no. 191*].

[49]*Ibid.*, 19 June 1891.

[50]Jonathan Grossman, *William Sylvis, Pioneer of American Labor* (New York, 1945), 153.

[51]*Globe*, 21 January 1871.

[52]*Minutes no. 191*, 8 February 1889; 15 May 1891.

[53]Frey and Commons, 'Conciliation', 126–7, 176; Stockton, *International Molders Union*, 170–85.

[54]Williams, 'Canadian-American', 120.

[55]*Iron Molders Journal*, August–December 1874; February 1876; May 1876.

[56]Strike data drawn from Toronto press, 1867–92, and from *Iron Molders Journal*, 1864–95 and IMIU, *Proceedings*, 1864–95.

[57]*Globe*, 22 March, 3 April 1867.

[58]*Ibid.*, 21, 23, 27 December 1870; 20 January 1871. IMIU, *Proceedings*, 1872.

[59]*Globe*, 24 May, 2 June, 26 September 1890; 10 January 1891; Massey Clippings Files, vol. 1, 1886–1891, Massey Archives, Toronto. IMIU, *Proceedings*, 1890.

[60]IMIU, *Proceedings*, 1895.

[61]See especially J.H. Barnett to John Robertson, Toronto, 20 August 1903, and 30 May 1904, in IMIU no. 191, *Correspondence*, Gainey Collection [henceforth *Correspondence no. 191*].

[62]*Globe*, 22 March 1967.

[63]*Ibid.*, 3 April 1867.

[64]*Ibid.*, 20 January 1871. See also 21, 23, 27 December 1870; 21 April 1871.

[65]*Ibid.*, 15, 18 July, 18 November 1871. For the moulders' response to these legal initiatives see *Iron Molders Journal*, 31 January 1871.

[66]*Ibid.*, 28 February 1871. For other similar cases see *IMJ*, 30 September 1871; 31 December 1870.

[67]*Ibid.*, 30 September 1871.

[68]*Ibid.*, 31 December 1871.

[69]*Globe*, 8 January 1887; 6 January 1888; *Canadian Labor Reformer*, 8 January 1887.

[70]Frey and Commons, *Conciliation*, 104–47.

[71]Williams, 'Canadian-American', *passim*.

[72]Grossman, *Sylvis*, 110.

[73]Ontario Bureau of Industry, *Annual Report, 1892*; IMIU, *Proceedings*, 1892–5.

[74]*Globe*, 27 February, 22 August, 26 September, 3 October 1890; 10 January 1891; *News*, 25 August 1890; *Monetary Times*, 31 October 1890.

[75]*Globe*, 10 January 1891.

[76]*Ibid.*, 22 August 1890.

[77]David Black to F.W. Parkes, Peterborough, 29 June 1890, *Correspondence, no. 191*.

[78]*Globe*, 24 May, 2 June 1890.

[79]'To the Canadian Public', Toronto 1, September 1890, *Correspondence, no. 191*.

[80]*Globe*, 10 January 1891. Encouraged by his temporary victory in Toronto Gurney attacked his Hamilton moulders the next year. For this bitter struggle see IMIU, *Proceedings*, 1895; Fred Walters to F.W. Parkes, Peterborough, 20 March 1892; Executive Board IMIU, 'Circular letter', 3 March 1892; Hamilton IMIU Local No. 26, 'Labor Struggle against Capital', 28 March 1892. The last three items are in *Correspondence, no. 191*.

[81]For general material on the employee offensive see works cited in note 4 supra.

[82]J.H. Barnett to John Robertson, Jr. Peterborough, 20 August 1903, *Correspondence, no. 191.*

[83]Barnett to Robertson, 30 May 1904, *ibid.*

[84]Robert Ozanne, *A Century of Labour-Management Relations at McCormick and International Harvester* (Madison, 1967), ch. 1.

[85]Massey Account Books, Massey Archives, Toronto. For the best discussion of technological innovation in the moulding industry see James Cooke Mills, *Searchlights on Some American Industries* (Chicago 1911), ch. 7.

[86]For Massey Strike see Kealey 'Knights of Labor', 23–7; for Peterborough-Lindsay connection see *Minutes no. 191*, 1886–7. Ozanne, *A Century*, provides similar evidence of co-operation between Chicago moulders and the Knights.

[87]From William Powell's address to the fifty-first annual convention of the ITU. Cited in Wayne Roberts, 'The Last Artisans: Toronto Printers, 1896–1914', in Kealey and Warrian (eds), *Essays in Working Class History* (Toronto, 1976).

[88]Toronto Typographical Union *Minutes*, 5 March 1845 [henceforth TTU, *Minutes*].

[89]*Ibid.*, 2 July 1845.

[90]Hobshawm, 'Custom, Wages and Work-load', 347. See also Sally Zerker, 'The Development of Collective Bargaining in the Toronto Printing Industry in the Nineteenth Century', *Industrial Relations*, 30 (1975), 83–97.

[91]TTU, *Minutes*, 2 July 1845.

[92]George E. McNeill, *The Labour Movement* (Boston 1887), 185.

[93]TTU, *Minutes*, 7 March 1849.

[94]*Ibid.*, January 1869.

[95]*Ibid.*, 6 June 1891.

[96]*Globe*, 27 July 1888. The extensive historical interests of printers are also evidenced by two early offical ITU histories: John McVicar, *Origins and progress of the Typographical Union, 1850–1891* (Lansing, Mitch., 1891) and George A. Tracey, *History of the Typographical Union* (Indianapolis, 1913).

[97]International Typographical Union [henceforth ITU] *Proceedings*, 1881, 46.

[98]Carroll Wright, 'Restriction of Output', 88–91.

[99]National Typographical Union, *Proceedings*, 1858, 45–6.

[100]TTU, *Proceedings*, 1871, 47.

[101]*Ibid.*, 1873 and Elizabeth Baker, *Printers and Technology: A History of the Printing Pressmen and Assistants' Union* (New York 1957), 215.

[102]*Globe*, 21 July 1884.

[103]George A. Barnett, 'The Printers: A Study in American Trade Unionism', *American Economic Association Quarterly*, 3rd series, X (1909), esp. 218–21.

[104]*Ibid.*, 230.

[105]*Ibid.*, 228–42 and *Typographical Journal*, 15 July 1890.

[106]Zerker, 'Development of Collective Bargaining', 84–8.

[107]Sally Zerker, 'George Brown and the Printers' Union', *Journal of Canadian Studies*, 10, 1 (1975), 47.

[108]A humorous example of the last was the Vancouver 'cap "I" strike' of 1889. The printers struck the *World* for two days when management refused to pay for corrections in faulty copy. See George Bartley, *An Outline History of Typographical Union, no. 226 Vancouver, B.C., 1887–1938 (Vancouver 1938)*, 8.

[109]Barnett, 'The Printers', 108-42, and Sally Zerker,'A History of the Toronto Typographical Union', unpublished PhD thesis, Unviersity of Toronto, 1972, 1–14.

[110]TTU, 'Scale of Prices' in *Minutes*, 17 March 1883.

[111]*Ibid.*, 20 December 1890.

[112]*Ibid.*, 17 March 1883; 6, 20 December 1890; 28 March, 5 December 1891.

[113]Baker, *Printers and Technology*, 69. For a discussion of the historical roots of ITU strength and for contemporary twentieth-century examples see S.M. Lipset, M.A. Trow, J.S. Coleman, *Union Democracy: The Internal Politics of the ITU* (Glencoe, Ill. 1956), ch. 2.

[114]Toronto Printing Pressmen's Union, No. 10, [henceforth TPPU] *Minutes*, March 1883–December 1890, PAC, and Baker, *Printers and Technology*, *passim*.

[115]Roberts, 'Toronto Printers' and Ross Harkness, *J.E. Atkinson of the Star* (Toronto, 1963), 28.

[116]TTU, *Minutes*, 2 July 1845.

[117]Zerker, 'George Brown', *passim.* and for greater detail on TTU struggles in the 1850s see Appleton, 'The Sunshine and the Shade', 103–16.

[118]TTU, *Minutes*, 3 June 1882.

[119]*Globe*, 21, 23, 30 March 1882.

[120]*Ibid.*, 5 July 1884.

[121]*Ibid.*, 5, 6, 21, 22 July 1884 and ITU, *Proceedings*, 1885, 1886.

[122]TPPU, *Minutes*, 11 December 1885.

[123]*Globe*, 8, 11, 15, 16, 19, 22 December 1885.

[124]*Ibid.*, 4 January 1886. Emphasis in original.

[125]*Ibid.*, 5 January 1886.

[126]J.S. Williams to John A. Macdonald, Toronto, 4 August 1884, 196352–5; E.F. Clarke to Macdonald, Toronto, 5 August 1884, 196358–60; John Small to Macdonald, Toronto, 5 August 1884, 196369–70. *Macdonald Papers*, PAC.

[127]Harry Piper to Macdonald, 2, 3 February 1886, 205474–6, *Macdonald Papers*.

[128]*Globe*, 18 July 1888.

[129]*Ibid.*, 26, 27 July, 8, 15 August 1888.

[130]*Typographical Journal*, 15 September 1889.

[131]W.B. Prescott to Macdonald, Toronto, 5 May 1890, 241968, *Macdonald Papers*.

[132]TTU, *Minutes*, 5 December 1891.

[133]*Ibid.*, 5 March 1892.

[134]Zerker, 'A History', ch. 3.

[135]For the best discussion of the effects of mechanization on printers see George E. Barnett, 'The Introduction of the Linotype', *Yale Review* (Nov. 1904), 251–73. A good summary of all the literature on printers and mechanization is Harry Kalber and Carl Schlesinger, *Union Printers and Controlled Automation* (New York, 1967), especially ch. 1.

[136]ITU, *Proceedings*, 1888, and Barnett, 'The Printers', 197.

[137]ITU, *Proceedings*, 1889. For the struggle in New York which set the continental pattern see Kalber and Schlesinger, *Union Printers*, ch. 1.

[138]ITU, *Proceedings*, 1891.

[139]For a similar success in Vancouver see Bartley, *Outline History*, 12.

[140]ITU, *Proceedings*, 1893.

[141]Zerker, 'A History', 160–5, 202–7; Harkness, *Atkinson*, 25–6; Barnett, 'The Printers', ch. 11, and Wright, 'Restriction of Output', 35–55.

[142]For the English response to typesetting machines see Ellice Howe (ed.) *The London Compositor* (London 1947), ch. 19. For an excellent autobiographical account of

an Edwardian British compositor which illustrates many of the themes discussed here see John Barnett (ed.), *The Annals of Labour: Autobiographies of British Working Class People 1820–1920* (London 1974), 330–40.

[143] David Montgomery, 'Trade Union Practice', 16–25.

[144] *Fincher's Trades Review*, 15 August 1863.

[145] *Iron Molders Journal*, February 1868.

[146] James C. Sylvis, *The Life, Speeches, Labors and Essays of William H. Sylvis* (Philadelphia 1872), 390.

[147] For similar events in Vancouver see Bartley, *Outline History*, 11. There, during a strike in 1892, the printers founded *The New World*.

[148] Russel Hann, 'Brainworkers and the Kights of Labor: E.E. Sheppard, Phillips Thompson and the Toronto *News*', in Kealey and Warrian (eds), *Essays*.

[149] Harkness, *Atkinson*, 25–47.

[150] *Machinist and Blacksmiths' Journal*, December 1871, 451; January 1872, 486.

[151] *Globe*, 30 October, 5, 18, 27 November, 14 December 1878.

[152] *Cigar Makers Journal*, March 1879; April 1880.

[153] *Palladium of Labor*, 29 May, 3, 10 July 1886.

[154] *Globe*, 30, 31 January, 5, 8, 22, 25, 28 February,. 17 March, 28 April, 9, 15 May 1884; see also *Journal of United Labor*, 15 October 1885.

[155] *Fincher's Trades Review*, 23 April 1864.

[156] *Globe*, 5 April 1882.

[157] David Frank, 'Class Conflict in the Coal Industry: Cape Breton 1992', in Kealey and Warrian (eds), *Essays*.

[158] F.W. Taylor, *The Principles of Scientific Management* (New York 1967), 32. For a brilliant discussion of modern management strategies see Harry Braverman, *Labour and Monopoly Capital* (New York, 1974).

[159] Taylor, *Principles*, 49.

[160] *Ibid.*, 53.

[161] Palmer, 'Class, Conception and Conflict', 31–3.

[162] Wright, 'Restriction of Output', 174.

16

Immigration and Ethnicity

Ross McCormack

The years of the late nineteenth and early twentieth centuries saw a major influx of immigrants into Canada that matched the waves that had arrived in British North America in the middle years of the nineteenth century. Unlike the earlier migrations, however, which were composed largely of people from the British Isles, the migration of the period before the First World War was far more ethnically diverse, containing large numbers of newcomers from southern and eastern Europe who spoke different languages and imported distinctive cultural traditions. The question of how Canada could assimilate these new arrivals was an important one for contemporaries struck by the appearance of 'foreigners' in their midst. Discussion of the appearance of new ethnic groups has often overlooked the fact that the British Isles continued to be the main source of immigrants to Canada and, while such newcomers enjoyed substantial advantages over Italians or Ukrainians, they too were ethnics, experiencing the same problems of dislocation and adjustment.

Ross McCormack discusses the English as ethnics in the years before the First World War. Central to his analysis is a conceptual framework of ethnicity against which the English experience can be measured; therefore McCormack begins with a theoretical discussion that concludes with a working definition of ethnicity. Having defined an ethnic group as 'a collectivity which shares a culture, which recognizes a collective identity, and which is perceived as distinct by society', McCormack argues that the English were indeed ethnics, although with certain advantages. Nevertheless, they were discriminated against by Canadians and found difficulties in adjusting that led them to emphasize their collective identity and to establish institutions and patterns of behaviour that supported group cohesiveness. They were, however, able to use their identity to advantage in the labour market. McCormack concludes by speculating on the extent to which the Canadian experience created a British, rather than an English, Scots, or Welsh identity, and by suggesting that class may have been an important component in cultural persistence and group solidarity.

Is McCormack's definition of ethnicity an acceptable one? If not, what other dimensions or variables ought to be included? Given his definition, does McCormack make a convincing case for the English experience as one of ethnicity? Where are the weaknesses in the argument? In what ways are the English different from other ethnics? What are the implications of introducing class as an important component of ethnic experience in Canada?

This article first appeared, titled 'Cloth Caps and Jobs: The Ethnicity of English Immigrants in Canada 1900–1914', in Jorgen Dahlie and Tissa Fernando, eds, *Ethnicity, Power and Politics in Canada* (Toronto, 1981), 38–55.

Before Victor Marshall emigrated in 1910, he had been an agricultural labourer in Rolven, a small Kentish village. To alleviate the emotional and material hardships of migration, Victor lived with his elder brother on his arrival in Winnipeg. In keeping with the custom, work was found for him on a CPR section under the auspices of the gang foreman, who belonged to his brother's lodge. Later Victor married a fellow-countrywoman and opened a boarding house to which he admitted only British immigrants. At work, at home, and at leisure Victor honoured the customs and retained the values of the English working class.[1] Is Victor Marshall an 'ethnic'? The question is not gratuitous. Had he emigrated from Sicily or Galicia instead of Kent, scholars would routinely explain his behaviour as the properties of a shared cultural identity, ethnicity. Yet they indicate no similar disposition toward Victor and his compatriots in Canada, who appear, on the basis of even the most superficial observation, to have manifested precisely those characteristics that social scientists conventionally describe as 'ethnic'. Victor Marshall was typical of a group, the behaviour of which is best understood in terms of explanation forms and conceptual theories applied to ethnic collectives. This essay will argue, if only in a preliminary way, that English immigrants asserted a group identity based upon shared cultural forms because there were explicit social advantages to such ascription.

Social historians who wish to inform their inquiries into the immigrant experience with sociological models are confronted, and perhaps confounded, by a substantial degree of theoretical controversy in the field of ethnic studies. In large part a function of the field's 'revival', the debate basically pits scholars who subscribe to the traditional theory of assimilation against the new advocates of pluralism.[2] Sociologists frequently cite the observation that Vilfredo Pareto made over fifty years ago: 'The term "ethnic" is one of the vaguest known to sociology. We use it merely to designate a state of fact, going in no sense into the question of explaining the fact.' Apparently there has been little change in the intervening half-century. Certainly the present debate has not produced a theoretical consensus: in a recent article Manyoni warns that 'we do not yet have a reliable definition of ethnicity from which generalizations about ethnic groups can be made.'[3] The condition is reflected in the literature. Perhaps awaiting a new paradigm, ethnic studies are for the most part descriptive, enumerating and classifying observable cultural forms. Consequently, social historians find it difficult to derive their models from sociology.

Partly because they have not received theoretical direction from sociologists, historians of immigration in Canada have been highly conventional in their conceptualization of ethnicity and inter-group relations. They have catalogued characteristics founded on primordial sentiments and described Canadian perceptions of minority groups. Recently the inquiries of a few historians have been informed by some sophisticated theoretical models; the most notable and encouraging example is Harney's excellent work. Still, historical ethnic studies in Canada remain handicapped by two basic disabilities. On the one hand, the main qualification of many who work in the field is membership in the group under review; while their sensitivity to the culture is essential, their work lacks adequate theoretical underpinning. The result of such inquiries has too often been filio-pietism. On the other hand, too many professional historians of immigration lack the language skills which would allow them fully to appreciate and explain the dynamics of emergent ethnic cultures. By emphasizing instead state policy and popular prejudices, these scholars have reinforced the assimilationist assumptions of liberal sociologists.

Theoretical or methodological deficiencies in the general field are compounded in the case of immigrants from the United Kingdom by a professional tendency to ignore British ethnicity. Sociologists have been prepared to recognize such immigrants as an identifiably discrete group for some time, but the preoccupation in the discipline with collectivities which diverge most from the Canadian cultural norm has apparently produced a reluctance to study the British. Deutschmann has recently documented this inertia.[4] For their part historians appear to have assumed that ethnicity was a condition peculiar to low-status minorities, not to the 'easily assimilable' British. Perhaps only administrative fiat could have produced the 'Anglo-Celts', and even when the Secretary of State's Department published a history of Scots in Canada, it was preoccupied with a filio-pietistic recital of contributions and not group dynamics.[5] Such lack of perspective is consistent neither with recent studies of British immigration to other countries nor with the traditions of the field in Canada. Erickson's excellent examination of the

British in nineteenth-century America makes it plain that immigrant groups from the United Kingdom manifested a substantial degree of cultural integrity over time. That Britons identified themselves, and were perceived, as a distinct group in society is the clear implication of the precise and sensitive observations that Reynolds made of their community in Montreal over forty years ago.[6]

An examination of the historical experience of English immigrants in Canada should be informed by the work of sociologists who study ethnic groups. But first, given the state of the literature, it is necessary to hit upon an operative definition of the term ethnicity which, however tentative, may afford some consensual value. Descriptive studies of ethnic groups provide a starting point. From them the social historian can derive an appreciation of the sociologists' conception of the properties of ethnicity by which he can develop a kind of taxonomic model. All peoples possess observable customs, institutions, and values—in other words a distinctive culture—through which society is regulated, goals are defined, and experience is explained. In descriptive studies, the totality of these cultural forms appears to constitute ethnicity. Some recent theoretical work, however, encourages the conclusion that a viable definition cannot be merely categorical. To explain group behaviour, the concept of ethnicity must incorporate both cultural identity and social relationships. Barth has emphasized that ethnicity has mainly to do with 'boundaries' and that the essential characteristic of a discrete group is that it 'has a membership which identifies itself, and is identified by others, as constituting a category distinguishable from other categories of the same order'.[7] Ascription is, of course, the essential component of this definition of ethnicity. And it will be equally essential for the definition employed here. In this essay an ethnic group is defined as a collectivity which shares a culture, which recognizes a collective identity, and which is perceived as distinct by society. All academic neophytes, whether they be undergraduates or scholars venturing into new fields, derive comforting reassurance from textbooks. Thus it is a relief to note that this definition conforms, at least in essentials, to one set out in a standard introduction to Canadian sociology.[8] More to the point, Englishmen and women who immigrated to Canada before World War I conformed to this definition of ethnicity.

Canadians clearly ascribed a separate, and relatively superior, identity to English immigrants. The federal immigration service discriminated in their favour, at least to the extent that it emphasized recruitment in the British Isles. This policy was based on the assumption that immigrants from the 'Mother Country' assimilated more easily and on the recognition that workers with the technical skills needed to modernize the Canadian economy were available in the United Kingdom, especially in England's industrial heartland north of Birmingham. Popular opinion which usually shared the official preference for British immigrants was, nonetheless, more discriminating, largely because of the country's Celtic heritage. Canadians whose forebears had emigrated from Scotland and Ireland in the nineteenth century distinguished between emigrants from what they continued to consider the 'Old Country' and Englishmen. Nationalism in the United Kingdom ensured such discrimination. Still, given the pervasive Canadian imperialism and the burgeoning European population, the English were welcomed as immigrants who would help to keep the Dominion British. 'They are our own kith and kin', editorialized the Vancouver *Province* about one contingent, 'entertaining for British laws and customs and for the British flag the same respect which we ourselves hold, [that] makes them . . . doubly desirable as citizens.' Even John W. Dafoe of the Winnipeg *Free Press*, an ardent Canadian nationalist who traced his ancestry back through several generations of North Americans, resorted to imperialist imagery when he celebrated the English immigrants' contribution of 'Anglo-Saxon blood'.[9]

Canadian attitudes, both official and popular, were by no means wholly positive. From the beginning of large-scale immigration after 1900, there was a consensus that the country should not become the dumping ground for social casualties of English cities. This attitude was reflected in federal programs which purported to recruit only domestics and agricultural labourers in Britain and in popular suspicion of the large English emigration societies. Because of the association in the public mind between the Salvation Army or Barnardo Homes and the deportation of paupers, many immigrants from large cities were stigmatized. And greater public anxiety was expressed about the English than other immigrants from the United Kingdom. 'I have not told anybody here why I came out,' wrote a labourer working in Manitoba who had been assisted by a London charity; 'I have not mentioned anything about unemployment.' Popular fear of indigent immigrants caused even the *Canadian Churchman*, official voice of the country's Anglicans, to insist that every immigrant leaving Liverpool 'be able and willing to work for a living'.[10]

Popular resentment of the English—as indeed of immigrants in general —was most acute during periods of economic crisis. The reaction peaked during the depression of 1907–8 when 'No English Need Apply' notices proliferated and the victimized cockney passed into popular mythology.[11] The *Edmonton Journal* seemed to express the country's anxieties about jobless immigrants well when it complained that 'one cannot look at these hundreds of town-bred people without feeling that their presence is a mistake.' Certainly the depression demonstrated that the federal government was prepared to deal as harshly with the English as with any other immigrants. Of the nearly 1,800 persons deported in 1908, some 1,100, fully 70 per cent, were returned to the British Isles. This draconian measure was followed by new regulations designed to curtail assisted immigration and ensure economic self-sufficiency. The depression also generated one of the most extreme castigations of the English on record. After studying populations of Ontario mental institutions, a professor at the University of Toronto concluded that an alarming proportion of immigrants from England were 'sexual perverts of the most revolting kind, insane criminals, the criminal insane, slum degenerates, general paretics and weaklings of other varieties'.[12] Such prejudice naturally produced a reaction which reinforced the ascriptive identity of English immigrants.

Too much should not be made of this syndrome. Like British immigrants in other times and places, those who felt a sense of persecution most keenly were probably developing a rationale for unsuccessful economic adjustment.[13] The conviction that Canadians actively discriminated against Englishmen was without real foundation simply because the latter provided skills, in some cases virtually unique, essential to the developing Canadian economy. Within months of the end of the depression of 1907–8, the state and industry resumed active recruitment in England and the popular press returned to its emphasis on the desirability of immigrants from the 'Mother Country'. Even if the Victoria *Colonist* exaggerated when it assumed 'a disposition to give [Englishmen] the preference over all other immigrants', the Canadian perception of them was relatively advantageous.[14] The worst that can be said about Canadian ascriptions *vis-à-vis* the English is that the content of this identity apparently was less positive than that applied to Scots and Ulstermen.

For their part English immigrants adapted a shared identity which was part of their cultural baggage. Gorer argues that a collective identity had been a 'self-sufficient aspect' of English society since at least the seventeenth century.[15] The English tendency to maintain their identity overseas and resist acculturation to Canadian norms was probably fostered even before emigration by promotional literature which almost invariably emphasized that Canadian society really differed little from home. If this were the case, emigrants appear to have reasoned, there was no need for them to cast off traditional values and customs. Eisenstadt has described an analogous case of cultural persistnce among Jewish refugees in Israel.[16]

But Canada was, of course, a substantially different society. To minimize this difference is, at least implicitly, to dismiss more than a century of social development shaped by a number of environmental and cultural imperatives, not the least of which was the pervasive influence of the United States. The English quickly appreciated that their culture distinguished them from Canadians as well as the many other immigrant groups flooding into the country. Although their sense of distinctiveness had many sources, it was likely founded on obvious differences in aesthetic cultural forms. Language is a good case in point since it was considered as one of the essential bonds of unity in Greater Britain. Richardson has emphasized the dislocation produced by sensory change. 'Canadian English' had been developing through the nineteenth century, and by the Edwardian era immigrants' ears were assailed by what Englishmen considered a decided 'Yankee twang'. Some newcomers experienced serious frustrations in communication; a domestic who spoke Liverpool's rich brogue told a friend, 'Unless you speak very plain, it is hard to be understood by most people.'[17] Separated from Canadian society by real cultural distinctions, the English discovered that emigration is a disruptive, potentially traumatic experience.

To accommodate to an alien environment, English immigrants set about, as Breton explains, 'to reconstruct [their] interpersonal "fields".'[18] This was accomplished through the assertion of a collective identity based on a shared culture. In 1907, after interviewing immigrants in Ontario and the West, a London journalist reported, 'They talk of "the flag" and "the old country" and "the other side" with an effusive affection that startles the mere Englishmen.' And the identity persisted over time. In a recent survey of immigrants, some of whom arrived in this country as early as 1910, respondents invariably stated that their primary emotional allegiance was to England. A Peterborough woman who settled in Brandon said simply, 'We were always English, always English.'[19]

Imperialism was a basic dimension of this identity. Respondents in the survey tended to be staunch advocates of empire; because 'the British people owned half the world,' a Londoner recalled that he had found imperial grandeur 'magical'.[20] As in Britain, agrarian and lower-middle-class English immigrants appear to have subscribed to this ideology most fully. But members of the working class were also imperialists; a Lancashire man who arrived in Vancouver in 1907 believed that he was 'a partner in a glorious imperial system destined to civilize the world under the Union Jack'.[21] In the Edwardian era, English immigrants cheered jingoistic rhetoric, celebrated the Tommies' valour, promoted the unity of Great Britain, and basked in the glories of 'a greater Empire than has been'. They also accepted the grimmer responsibilities of an imperial destiny when they responded to Britain's call to arms in that most jingoistic of conflicts, the Boer War. An East Anglian farming in southern Ontario spoke for most of his compatriots when he told a friend, 'We are very much interested in the war here: . . . everybody is entirely loyal to old England.' They made bandages. They bought cavalry horses. And most significant, they enlisted; English immigrants were substantially overrepresented in the Canadian contingents that fought in South Africa.[22] Participation in such observance, in turn, tended to enhance group identity and thus cohesiveness.

Imperialism was Edwardian England's nationalism, and English identity in Canada was an overseas manifestation of that ideology. In the literature collective English pride is usually exaggerated and then trivialized as supercilious metropolitanism. But, in addition to indicating the natural insecurity of immigrants, the behaviour surely reflected a patriotic identification with the achievements of a great nation at the height of its economic and political power. Nationalism had a tremendous impact on England at the turn of the century. In the manner Gellner predicts, it naturally became basic to the identity of Englishmen who emigrated, not only in Canada but throughout the Empire. De Vos argues that 'nationality is indistinguishable from ethnicity; . . . national identity and subjective cultural identity cannot be distinguished, especially when ethnic identity and national identity have been one historically.'[23]

The networks which English immigrants developed to protect and promote their group identity grew out of the family. By filling its traditional role of furnishing both emotional and material support, the family constituted a model for other networks. Because it is a principal mediator of social identity in modern society, immigrants have traditionally used the family as a mechanism to reduce their sense of dislocation and to facilitate their adaptation.[24] Before World War I the structure of UK immigration facilitated this process for the English. British men and women entered Canada at a ratio of 3:2, while other Europeans arrived at a ratio of 5:1. Survey findings demonstrate that English immigrants established a traditional patriarchal system of family organization with the husband assigned a dominant and public role and the wife a subordinate and private one.[25] The home became the focus for the maintenance of 'Old Country' aesthetic cultural forms such as idiom, diet, and values. 'I love my home,' a London woman living in a B.C. coal camp wrote a friend, 'and make it as homely and English as I can. I generally get English jams, pickles, sauces, etc., and thus keep up our English taste of food.'[26]

In addition to providing immigrants with emotional support, the family filled a significant economic role. Among the English working class it was customary for the wife and older children living in the home to supplement the husband's income through wage-labour. The practice was transferred to Canada where immigrant women and adolescents worked, especially during the first two or three years while families got on their economic feet. As a matter of course, emigration societies assumed that this mechanism would be used to facilitate adjustment; the East End Emigration Fund defined the 'ideal family' as one composed of 'parents under forty, with four children, two of whom are working age'.[27] Many English families appear to have functioned as co-operative units with wives, sons, and daughters working in the home, going into domestic service or, especially in the case of adolescent boys, joining the labour force. A Cumberland woman who settled in Winnipeg when she was fifteen remembers, 'Father said, "Everybody out. You have all got to work." ' Reynolds found that among British working-class immigrants in Montreal this practice accounted for nearly 20 per cent of family income. Given the importance of a working spouse, it is not surprising that a London carpenter settled in Hochelaga described the benefits of marital bliss in purely economic terms: 'I have found the benefit of a good wife out here, as I have met single men . . . who have fared far worse than I during the past year.'[28]

To ensure the integrity of the family, English immigrants practised endogamy. Emigration propaganda emphasized that women should go out to Canada, marry a countryman, and start a family to maintain the 'British character' of the country. 'Canada is calling out for useful women,' the Girls Friendly Society informed its working-class constituency, 'men cannot make homes without them.'[29] Once in Canada English immigrants manifested a pronounced tendency to maintain group cohesiveness through intermarriage. The phenomenon is demonstrable through an examination of some 460 marriages in three Anglican parishes in and around Winnipeg in the years between 1903 and 1913.[30] Of the 231 English-born bridegrooms in the parishes, 65 per cent married countrywomen; 74 per cent of the 200 English brides entered endogamous unions. The pattern appears to have varied according to the status of the men. While only 48 per cent of the English bridegrooms in professional occupations intermarried, 73 per cent of unskilled manuual workers made endogamous matches. These rates of intermarriage are similar to those of Greeks and Italians in Australia described by Price and Zubrzycki, who found endogamy to be an important index of cultural persistence.[31]

The English also used chain migration, a social mechanism closely related to the family, to maintain group cohesiveness. The process, by which immigrants receive information, financial support, accommodation, and assistance in finding employment from compatriots settled in the receiving country, is usually associated in the literature with low-status southern and eastern Europeans.[32] In fact from the early nineteenth century such networks were part of the English experience in this country. British emigration societies promoted the process as one of the most effective means of facilitating economic adjustment. Because, as a popular cliché insisted, every Englishman had 'people' in Edwardian Canada, various forms of chain migration emerged. One of the most prevalent was the practice whereby men emigrated, established a home, and remitted family passages after a year or two. A Londoner who went out to Ontario in 1905 brought over one relative in each of the six succeeding years. But chain migration was not restricted to the family; when a Peterborough man arrived in Brandon, he sought out former townsmen who helped him secure employment.[33]

The centrality of these networks to the migration process is manifested in the experience of some 19,000 Londoners who immigrated between 1904 and 1913. Nearly 40 per cent went out to family and friends in Canada. As opportunities for sponsorship increased with the growing number of English settlers in this country, more individuals took advantage of them; while only 31 per cent migrated within a network at the beginning of the period, 56 per cent went out under personal auspices in 1913. Chain migration appears to have been most prevalent during times of economic crises; of the Londoners able to immigrate during the depression of 1907–8 fully 75 per cent were received by family or friends.[34] The social utility of chain migration was demonstrated when the process became institutionalized. Federal government regulations enacted after the depression of 1907–8 which required sponsors for economically marginal immigrants made chain migration, in effect, state policy. And specifically in the case of the British, Imperial Home Reunion Associations helped workers finance the passage of their families remaining in the United Kingdom.

English boarding houses and hostels were an extension of chain migration. In the same way that such institutions provided Harney's Italians with 'a means of living with one's own', they furnished English immigrants who did not enjoy access to a familiar home with emotional, and frequently material, support.[35] Boarding houses were, of course, primarily commercial enterprises, but they prospered by offering English immigrants familiar, often familial, environments. A Kentishman who kept a house in central Winnipeg boarded only his countrymen because clients shunned 'foreigners'.[36] But whatever the reason for exclusivity, such establishments with their familiar diets, accents, and conversation helped boarders overcome their sense of dislocation. Hostels, ordinarily supported by affluent Englishmen or emigration societies, consciously attempted to create surrogate families. Certainly emotional support was provided by a Calgary 'home' where 'everything seemed so much like England.' Each morning 'matron' sent 'the girls' out to work, a journalist reported, and each evening they shared each others' hopes and fears in an overfurnished parlour.[37] Like families, hostels and boarding houses facilitated the immigrants' economic adjustment. A Lancashire man who arrived in Winnipeg when 'times were bad' remembers securing work under the auspices of fellow-boarders at an English establishment in the city's west end.[38]

English homes and boarding houses appear to have been spatially segregated in Canadian cities. While final conclusions must wait on the availability of quantitative data, qualitative evidence strongly suggests that the English formed as many ghettoes as other immigrants. Reynolds found substantial levels of residential concentration among Montreal's British population, usually associated with high-technology industries such as the CPR shops.[39] An analogous pattern developed in boom-time Winnipeg. The city's west end, adjacent to the CPR shops, and Transcona, built around the CNR shops, were British neighbourhoods. Similarly, Elmwood, across the Red River from factories where many British artisans worked, had a distinctive English character. One street was populated by 'a bunch' of families from Leicester. Nearby an Ulsterwoman, whose husband had emigrated from Sheffield, was the 'only foreigner' on another English street.[40] Immigrants remember that neighbours in these communities practised various forms of mutuality, such as lending money, during economic crises. The custom of 'neighbouring', frequent and informal house visits, characteristic of the English working class, was practised in Canada, and this tended to insulate the immigrants from the larger community and increase group cohesiveness. In addition such districts concentrated populations adequate to the formation and maintenance of institutions which promoted a distinct cultural identity. English neighbourhoods supported football clubs, music halls, 'fish and chippers', and so on. In fact, the English manifested a distinct degree of what Breton has called 'institutional completeness', a condition which substantially reinforces group identity.[41] Significantly, the formation of these immigrant institutions involved a substantial measure of direct cultural transfer.

In the Anglican Church of Canada, the English found a well-established and vital organization through which they could protect and promote their identity. As a result of British immigration, the Church underwent extraordinary expansion in the first decade of this century. Between 1901 and 1911 its membership rose from 681,000 to 1,043,000; this growth rate of 53 per cent far surpassed all other denominations, with only the Presbyterians coming close with a rate of 32 per cent. Anglicans flourished most in provinces which had a high immigration rate. By 1911 they were the third largest denomination in Ontario, the second in Manitoba. In British Columbia, Englishmen's preferred destination, the Church enjoyed a growth rate of 129 per cent between 1901 and 1911 and emerged as the province's principal denomination.[42] English immigrants dominated the Church, at least in the West, by the early 1900s. This was, in fact, a condition that embarrassed a few Anglican divines who worried that their Church would be perceived 'as something for Englishmen alone'.[43]

Anglican parishes clearly provided immigrants with important emotional support. Reynolds found that churches were usually the first institutions which newcomers to Montreal joined. Synge's Hamilton interviews indicate that church attendance among British workers actually increased in Canada, a pattern which preliminary Winnipeg survey results suggest may have prevailed in that city as well.[44] This tendency was probably in part pragmatic; Anglican parishes functioned as networks for the distribution of charity and jobs, but more importantly it mitigated the immigrant's sense of dislocation. A devout Anglican remembers her profound sense of gratitude and relief because her welcome to a Winnipeg parish was 'so warm and friendly'. Among Protestant denominations, the Church of England was unique in that its liturgy and doctrine were identical to those observed in the United Kingdom; thus identification with England was regularly renewed. It also linked sending and receiving societies in a powerfully emotive way. 'When we are at church it seems so much like home,' a labourer from the southern counties wrote, 'and one feels the new life enter in him, after the toils of the week.'[45] The Church also promoted group cohesiveness by sponsoring collective activities, such as women's auxiliaries, musical societies, athletic clubs, and youth organizations, which brought the English together and promoted associations among the immigrants. The process insulated them from Canadian society, 'substituted', to use Breton's term, group institutions for native ones.

English immigrants also established a number of clubs and lodges, modelled on an important Victorian institution, which combined cultural and economic functions. Friendly societies were mutual-aid associations which provided British workers with insurance and a variety of other benefits and, as they became better established, a rich social life. Some Canadian lodges, such as the Independent Order of Oddfellows, were directly transferred from the United Kingdom. The Oddfellows, composed mainly of British immigrants, flourished across the country; in 1913 the lodge was estimated to have seven thousand members in British Columbia alone.[46] But English immigrants also formed mutual-aid societies which derived from their Canadian experience and which were remarkably ethnocentric. Western cities supported Cornish Associations, Devonian Societies, and Cumberland Clubs. British Columbia's Yorkshire community was so well organized that it was able to establish a provincial association by 1905.[47]

The largest and most important English cultural society was the Sons of England, which in 1913 had over forty thousand Canadian members. Lodges were formed across the country, usually led by affluent Englishmen, professionals, clergymen, and former military officers, who had joined local élites. With names ringing with imperial glory such as Balaclava, Trafalgar, and Blenheim, lodges averaged several hundred members in large cities, a few centres supporting two or three branches.[48] A Cumberland woman who was involved in the formation of a cultural society in Winnipeg recalls that she and her compatriots organized 'to keep the British tradition going, you know'.[49] In fact the Sons of England contributed substantially to the maintenance of aesthetic cultural forms. This was achieved in part through the sponsorship of traditional recreational activities; for instance, excursions to the seaside were popular in B.C. lodges. But the most important vehicle in this process was the social evenings modelled on English music halls which the Sons regularly held. 'At homes' allowed, indeed demanded, the most explicit exhibition of overt cultural signs; the evening succeeded only if all present indulged in wanton nostalgia. They thrilled to jingoistic songs; they wept at evocations of England's green and pleasant land; they savoured warm, dark ale; and they reverted to regional dialects. When groups are asserting an identity, De Vos explains, 'greater emphasis is put on aesthetic [cultural] features related to communication and social communion.'[50]

Consistent with friendly-society practices and, more important, immigrants' needs, the Sons of England furnished its members with economic support. The president of the Burlington lodge provided a description of the classic immigrants' mutual-benefit society when he reported that 'we get in touch with a lot of men from England and give them a helping hand, if they are deserving of it.' Emigration societies recommended membership in societies to facilitate economic adjustment. The Sons of England organized reception committees for newcomers, provided medical services and paid unemployment and disability benefits. Most important the lodge, with a country-wide organization and an élite leadership able to provide patronage, was an effective network for the distribution and control of jobs. A cockney working in Montreal considered the Sons of England 'a very handy society . . . [because] there are several foremen belonging to us and lots more all over the country.'[51]

The criticism could, of course, be offered that these cultural and social patterns merely identify a group of recent immigrants rather than signify the emergence of an ethnic tradition. But this is a distinction which sociologists, let alone historians, rarely draw. Indeed, some sociologists argue that the concept only applies to Europeans who have migrated to North America; the Bergers assert that ethnicity 'refers to those cultural traits retained by immigrant groups to [the United States] from their original home culture'.[52] In any case, for the purpose of this essay it will be assumed that English group identity is an observable phenomenon.

Though it is relatively easy to describe a culture through observation, it is a problem of a quite different order to explain the dynamics of identity. What binds individuals with a shared culture into solidary groups? The phenomenon appears to be best understood in terms of recent theoretical developments in sociology. An important dimension of the 'revival' of ethnic studies in the last decade or so has been the shift from a culture-population group frame of reference to a conceptualization which explains ethnicity as a reaction to social context, a dimension of social participation. In this structural view, ethnicity is instrumental; individuals consciously adopt a group identity to promote their collective self-interest. Immigrants use ethnicity, Howard and Wayne argue, 'in a search for greater power and control and in an attempt to create channels of access to scarce resources. . . . Ultimately, then, it is the number and kinds of resources to which access might be forged that accounts for the persistence, elaboration, or attenuation of ethnic networks.[53] The process is most prevalent in heterogeneous societies where roles are assigned on the basis of observable cultural characteristics; ethnic boundaries become crucial to the maintenance of status.[54]

Like other Europeans the English began their lives in Canada in a precarious economic position, a condition which resulted primarily from a surplus in the labour market caused by massive immigration. In this country's heterogeneous society where many immigrant groups competed for limited economic resources, the English were perceived as familiar by a xenophobic society and skilled by an industrializing one. Clearly it was relatively advantageous to be English. As a social strategy, then, English group identity became explicit and assertive because such ethnicity afforded enhanced status and competitive advantage by distinguishing the English from other immigrants. The focus here will be on the manner in which the English used their identity to secure the essential requirement for successful economic adjustment—jobs.

Canadian ethnocentricity and xenophobia have been well documented.[55] Popular perceptions of low-status immigrants need not be rehearsed, except to point out that these attitudes benefited the English in the labour market. They enjoyed the additional advantage of a reputation as skilled workers. The *Edmonton Journal* reflected a widely held opinion, when in an article urging British immigration it observed, 'Almost every industry in western Canada wants skilled workmen, and some of these industries are suffering . . . because they cannot get them.'[56] Canadian corporations, like their counterparts in other modernizing economies, considered the first industrial nation the best place to recruit highly trained workers, and their agents scoured Britain for specified skills, in some cases advancing passages to this country. The perceived importance of the United Kingdom as a source of skilled workers is illustrated by the role of the Canadian Manufacturers' Association in a typical English recruitment scheme. In 1903 the CMA requested the British Women's Emigration Association to supply several hundred experienced 'machinists' for central Canada's growing garment industry. Over the next two years the society, supplied with both detailed specifications and financial support from Canadian industrialists, recruited women from London's depressed needle trades. Once in Canada the garment workers were distributed from a CMA-financed hostel in Toronto.[57] That British immigrants, in fact, composed nearly 60 per cent of all artisans entering the country before 1914 only enhanced the English workers' reputation and improved their competitive advantage.[58]

The English clearly recognized the economic benefits of distinguishing themselves from other European and Asian immigrants. Synge found that immigrants emphasized their 'Englishness' as a means to ingratiate themselves with Hamilton's Anglophilic middle class. Maintenance of privileged status required English immigrants to practise ethnic exclusivity, to erect boundaries. Concerned with 'respectability', a Staffordshire woman who worked as a maid in Winnipeg remembers, 'To tell the truth, I didn't bother with any foreign people. I was too English for that.'[59] But the English strategy went beyond the passive maintenance of boundaries. They bludgeoned other immigrants with their identity whenever those groups were perceived as a threat. Berthoff suggests that British emigration deflected from the United Sates to Canada and other Dominions, in part, to escape growing competition from eastern and southern Europeans.[60] Clearly the English found competition from low-status immigrants both surprising and inappropriate in 'a British possession'. Because such competition was most intense in British Columbia, the province serves as the best case in point. A Lancashire labourer who had fled Vancouver complained that 'the Chinese swamp the labour market; it is impossible for an Englishman to work for the wages they are paid.' To overcome this threat, immigrants from the United Kingdom decried the animal incompetence of 'coolies', appealed to imperialist racism, and demanded 'the rights of Englishmen'. Conditions in the Vancouver Island coalfields where most Chinese worked, a sympathetic observer gravely warned, were 'pregnant with all that . . . an Englishman dislikes'.[61]

Sociologists have observed the use of ethnic networks to control and allocate jobs in industrial society, and the practice, to the extent that it was viable, was probably common among most immigrant groups. The networks that developed in the English community formed the basis of the group's competitive strategy. In fact such tactics were part of English cultural baggage; workers in Victorian Britain had successfully employed nativistic institutions to confine the Irish to low-status jobs.[62] Starting with the family, virtually every network in the community was used to circulate information and provide sponsorship to Englishmen seeking employment. In the Crowsnest Pass area the practice even extended to football clubs which north-country miners used to intimidate Ukrainian and Italian rivals.[63] The practical side of the process is well illustrated in the operation of hostels. These institutions were especially important in providing work for women, as domestics and factory hands but also in higher-status occupations such as stenographers and governesses. The Anglican director of Toronto's Welcome Hostel always advised her 'girls' that 'a retention of their respectable English manner is a valuable asset.' But to enhance the competitive advantage of identity, she systematically excluded other immigrant groups from her publicly funded institution; in 1911 literally 99 per cent of the hostel's clients were British. English women seeking jobs came to rely upon such networks, a condition explained by the effectiveness of Vancouver's exclusive Friendly Lodge run by a wealthy Anglican matron. In 1907 she found work for four hundred women; by 1911 she was able to place a thousand.[64]

English immigrants were clearly able to use their identity to secure preferential treatment from Canadian employers; the propositon will be illustrated here with two cases, one applying to women, one to men. The T. Eaton Company, the founder of which had emigrated from Ulster, became an important employer for British women. A Cumberland woman who worked in the Winnipeg store believes that 'Eaton's was very partial to old-country people . . . .I don't think they ever turned anybody down.'[65] Like other Canadian corporations, Eaton's recruited skilled workers in England. When the company began full-scale garment production in 1911, it despatched specifications to the British Women's Emigration Association which supplied several hundred seamstresses and shirt-makers. Brought out with company funds, the women, mainly Londoners, dominated Eaton's factories in Toronto before 1914.[66] If the company preferred English factory hands, it insisted that higher-status jobs be filled almost exclusively by British immigrants. Eaton's appears to have believed, as a matter of policy, that its reputation for honesty and reliability in trade would be best preserved by the 'respectability' of young women from the United Kingdom. Respondents, several of whom worked for the company, invariably describe sales clerks as British. A Suffolk woman and old Eatonian remembers, 'Most of them were girls, you know, like myself.'[67] Many Englishwomen won their private war for security and status on the playing fields of Eaton's.

Because the expanding Canadian Pacific Railway required large supplies of skilled workers, especially in the metal trades, the company became an important place of employment for English artisans. In addition to promoting the settlement of prairie land grants, CPR agents in the United Kingdom consistently recruited workers for the company's great repair shops. But the railway also introduced the innovative policy of using the union which organized metal-trades workers in Britain, the Amalgamated Society of Engineers, as a labour supplier. In 1904 the ASE, one of the few British unions established in Canada, estimated that 30 per cent of the artisans in some CPR divisions were union members.[68] The ASE was strongest in Montreal where British immigrants dominated the CPR shops. A Woolwich machinist who had found work with the company told a friend that 'they think a lot of the English here.' Reynolds explained the condition in terms of 'the strategic position of the foremen' in hiring. The ASE instructed members who had risen to supervisory positions that they fulfilled their 'duty . . . by employing our members', and foremen routinely gave preference in hiring to British immigrants. The railway's management accepted the custom as an efficacious means of securing skilled workers. The advantage of an English identity for CPR employees was nicely illustrated by the promotion of a London labourer working in the Montreal yards:

> . . . the boss asked me if I understood boiler making; so I told him no, but I understood hauling iron about and could use a 14 lb. hammer; so he says, come along with me and I will see what you are made of. He took me to another boss in the boiler shop, and he sent me to work next day. He asked me how I liked the job. So I told him I was satisfied with my job if I suited him. He says I will have 10 cents rise a day at once.[69]

These two cases, Eaton's and the CPR, demonstrate that their identity afforded English immigrants real advantages in the acquisition and retention of relatively high-status jobs in the short run. What about the long run? In this contest that time-frame may, in fact, not even be a historian's province; still, a few brief remarks seem in order.

Many studies demonstrate that the English group and their children have continued to enjoy advantages in the labour market over time. Indeed this social phenomenon has become one of the basic themes of Canadian ethnic studies. For instance, Donnelly, in a report submitted to the Royal Commission on Bilingualism and Biculturalism, found that in the mid-60s people of British origin dominated the best jobs in Winnipeg's civil service.[70] But perhaps it would be most appropriate here simply to invoke conventional wisdom. Commentators as disparate as John Porter and Pierre Berton have observed that long after the Englishmen's massive influx and the nation's imperial romance, a British identity affords real advantages in Canadian society.

Additional questions and further inquiries are still to be made. Two related issues seem to stand out. First, did a pan-British identity emerge in Canada? In other words, were Welshmen, Scotsmen, Ulstermen, and Englishmen subsumed in one ethnic group? International migration has produced several new collectivities formed by the integration of groups who were distinct, even antagonistic, in a former context but were identified or identified themselves as one in a new environment of greater heterogeneity. Indeed, precisely this process characterized the British experience in the United States when immigrants were confronted with aggressive Irish nationalism. Although the alien threats were of a different order in Canada, they nonetheless appear to have producd similar unifying tendencies. Conceivably Britishness, as it is understood in this country, is as much a product of the North American experience as the B'nai Brith. Second, did working-class Englishmen manifest a greater degree of cultural persistence and group solidarity than their middle-class compatriots? The condition is hypothetically predictable, and even empirically implicit. Liberal sociologists have explained the 'resurgence' of ethnicity, despite the assumed homogenizing imperatives of modern industrial society, in terms of the persistence of inequality. The findings of Breton and Porter, to name only two scholars, suggest that workers may be more assertive of a shared cultural identity. Because working-class English immigrants were confronted with substantially more competition in the labour market from eastern and southern Europeans than their more privileged compatriots, they probably found a distinct identity more advantageous. Perhaps the persistence of 'fish and chippers' in Vancouver has more to do with class polarization than tourism.

English ethnicity in Canada was real. Like other immigrant groups, the English ascribed a collective identity because it provided significant social advantages. Canadian society assigned status and roles on the basis of observable cultural characteristics. To accommodate this reality, English immigrants asserted a relatively advantageous identity, frequently quite explicitly because Canadians had learned to recognize aesthetic cultural signs. It was an Edwardian cliché that Englishmen could be 'spotted'. The phenomenon is manifest even today; looking at old photos, the observer who has walked the streets of Lancashire and Yorkshire industrial towns experiences a sense of *déjà vu*. In Canada the cloth cap became the Englishman's Afro.

Suggestions for Further Reading

Martin L. Kovacs, ed., *Ethnic Canadians: Culture and Education* (Regina, 1978).
Norman Macdonald, *Canada: Immigration and Colonization, 1841–1903* (Toronto, 1966).
Howard Palmer, ed., *Immigration and the Rise of Multiculturalism* (Toronto, 1975).

Notes

[1]Manitoba Museum of Man and Nature/University of Winnipeg Oral History Project, Interview No. 1-Wi-79-1.

[2]The various perspectives in the controversy are elaborated in Nathan Glazer and Daniel P. Moynihan, *Ethnicity: Theory and Experience* (Cambridge, Mass., 1975).

[3]Joseph R. Manyoni, 'Ethnics and Non-Ethnics: Facts and Fads in the Study of Inter-group Relations', *Ethnic Canadians: Culture and Education*, ed. Martin L. Kovacs (Regina, 1978), 31.

[4]Linda Bell Deutschmann, 'Decline of the Wasp? Dominant Group Identity in the Ethnic Plural Society', *Ethnic Canadians*, 411–18.

[5]W. Stanford Reid, *The Scottish Tradition in Canada* (Toronto, 1976).

[6]Charlotte Erickson, *Invisible Immigrants: The Adaptation of English and Scottish Immigrants in Nineteenth-Century America* (London, 1972); and Lloyd G. Reynolds, *The British Immigrant: His Social and Economic Adjustment in Canada* (Toronto, 1935).

[7]Frederik Barth, 'Introduction', *Ethnic Groups and Boundaries: The Social Organization of Culture Difference* (London, 1970), 11.

[8]Frank G. Vallee, 'Multi-Ethnic Societies: The Issues of Identity and Inequality', *Issues in Canadian Society: An Introduction to Sociology*, ed. Dennis Forcese and Stephen Richer (Scarborough, 1975), 167.

[9]Carl Berger, *The Sense of Power: Studies in the Ideas of Canadian Imperialism, 1867–1914* (Toronto, 1970), 145–51; *The Province*, 26 May 1902, and *Manitoba Free Press*, 22 March 1902.

[10]*Fourth Report: The Central (Unemployed) Body for London July 1909–June 1910*, 54, and *Canadian Churchman*, 23 February 1905.

[11]Basil Stewart, *No English Need Apply or Canada as a Field for Immigration* (London, 1909).

[12]*Edmonton Journal*, 29 November 1907; Mabel F. Timlin, 'Canada's Immigration Policy, 1896–1910', *Canadian Journal of Economics and Political Science*, 1960, 523; and C.I. Clarke, 'The Defective and Insane Immigrant', *The University Monthly*, 1907–8, 276.

[13]Alan Richardson, *British Immigrants and Australia: A Psychosocial Inquiry* (Canberra, 1974), 119–25; and Wilbur S. Shepperson, *Emigration and Disenchantment: Portraits of Englishmen Repatriated from the United States* (Norman, 1965), *passim*.

[14]*Victoria Daily Colonist*, 20 August 1910.

[15]Geoffrey Gorer, 'English Identity Over Time and Empire', *Ethnic Identity: Cultural Continuities and Change*, ed. George De Vos and Lole Romanucci-Ross (Palo Alto, 1975), 156.

[16]S.N. Eisenstadt, *The Absorption of Immigrants: A Comparative Study based mainly on the Jewish Community in Palestine and the State of Israel* (Glencoe, 1955), 91–2.

[17]Richardson, *British Immigrants*, 31, and *Friendly Leaves*, October 1911.

[18]Raymond Breton, 'Institutional Completeness of Ethnic Communities and the Personal Relations of Immigrants', *American Journal of Sociology*, 1964, 194.

[19]*The Clarion*, 13 December 1907 and Interview No. 1-Wi-79-8.

[20]Interview No. 1-Wi-79-15.

[21]Richard Price, *An Imperial War and the British Working Class* (Toronto, 1972), 201; Carman Miller, 'A Peliminary Analysis of the Socio-economic Composition of Canada South Africa War Contingents', *Histoire sociale/Social History*, 1975, 230; University of British Columbia Special Collection Division, Angus McInnis Collection, vol. 53–4, Faulkner to Steves, 5 March 1959.

[22]*East End Emigration Fund: Report 1900*, 9, and Miller, 'Canada's South African Contingents', 222.

[23]Ernest A. Gellner, *Thought and Change* (Chicago, 1965), 157, and George De Vos, 'Ethnic Pluralism: Conflict and Accommodation', *Ethnic Identity*, 11.

[24]Charles Tilly and C. Harold Brown, 'On Uprooting, Kinship and the Auspices of Migration', *International Journal of Comparative Sociology*, 1967, 67–75.

[25]Paul Thompson, *The Edwardians: The Remaking of British Society* (London, 1977), 287–95, and Michael Anderson, *Family Structure in Nineteenth Century Lancashire* (Cambridge, 1971).

[26]*Friendly Leaves*, August 1908.

[27]*East End Emigration Friend: Report 1905*, 4.

[28]Interview No. 1-Wi-79-7; Reynods, *British Immigrant*, 191, and *Church Emigration Society: Annual Report 1908*, 23.

[29]*Friendly Leaves*, June 1912.

[30]The Parishes are All Saints, St Andrew's, and St Paul's. The records of the first are housed in the vestry offices, while those of the latter two are on deposit in the Public Archives of Manitoba.

[31]C.A. Price and J. Zubrzycki, 'Immigrant Marriage Patterns in Australia', *Population Studies*, 1962, 124. Conceivably a more complete data base, similar to that employed by Price and Zubrzycki, would demonstrate even higher rates of endogamy among English immigrants in Canada. (C.A. Price and J. Zubrzycki, 'The Use of Inter-Marriage Statistics as an Index of Assimilation', *Population Studies*, 1962.)

[32]In a standard article John and Leatrice MacDonald appear to assume that chain migration was largely peculiar to the 'new immigrants'. 'Chain Migration, Ethnic Neighbourhood Formation and Social Networks', *Millbank Memorial Fund Quarterly*, 1964, 82–97.

[33]*East End Emigration Fund: Report 1911*, 2, and Interview No. 1-Wi-79-8.

[34]*British Dominions Emigration Society: Report 1913*, 18.

[35]Robert F. Harney, 'Boarding and Belonging', *Urban History Review*, 1978, 31.

[36]Interview No. 1-Wi-79-1. A Scotswoman employed a more arcane device to ensure the exclusivity of her house; she advertised in Gaelic. (Interview No. 2-Wi-79-4.)

[37]*British Women's Emigration Association: Report 1912*, 31, and Ella C. Sykes, 'At a Women's Hostel in Canada', *Cornhill Magazine*, 1912, 660–70.

[38]Interview No. 1-Wi-79-13.

[39]Reynolds, *British Immigrant*, 118–22.

[40]Interview No. 1-Wi-79-10 and Interview No. 4-Wi-79-1.

[41]Breton, 'Institutional Completeness', 193–205.

[42]*Census of Canada*, 1901 and 1911, vol. I, Table VII, and Vol. II, Table I.

[43]*Canadian Churchman*, 18 September 1902. The relationship between the Church of England and immigration is clearly complex. But answers to such questions as —what proportion of British immigrants joined Anglican churches? Methodist? or none?—must wait on the analysis of parish records. My work to date strongly suggests that the English-born constituted the bulk of western churchmen.

[44]Reynolds, *British Immigrant*, 137; Jane Synge, 'Immigrant Communities—British and Continental European—In Early Twentieth Century Hamilton, Canada', *Oral History*, 1976, 46.

[45]Interview No. 4-Wi-79-2 and *Church Emigration Society: Annual Report, 1910*, 21.

[46]*Victoria Daily Colonist*, 28 February 1913.

[47]*The Province*, 4 April 1905.

[48]*Ibid.*, 13 January 1900; *Victoria Daily Colonist*, 19 January 1911 and *Calgary Herald*, 2 July 1913.

[49]Interview No. 1-Wi-79-7.

[50]Peter Vailey, *Leisure and Class in Victorian England: Rational Recreation and the Contest for Control, 1830–1885* (London, 1978), 142–54, and De Vos, 'Ethnic Pluralism', 15.

[51]*East End Emigration Fund: Reports 1909 and 1901*, 24, 12.

[52]P.L. and B. Berger, *Sociology: A Biographical Approach* (New York, 1972), 119.

[53]Leslie Howard and Jack Wayne, 'Ethnicity in Canada A Social Structural View', *Journal of Comparative Sociology*, 1974, 41–2; Michael Hechter, 'The Political Economy of Ethnic Change', *American Journal of Sociology*, 1974, 1152–6; and Orlando Patterson, 'Context and Choice in Ethnic Allegiance: A Theoretical Framework and Caribbean Case Study', *Ethnicity: Theory and Experience*, 305–13.

[54]Barth, *Groups and Boundaries*, 9–17.

[55]Donald Avery. 'The Radical Alien and the Winnipeg General Strike of 1919', *The West and the Nation*, eds Carl Berger and Ramsay Cook (Toronto, 1976), 209–31, and J.E. Rea, "My main line is the kiddies . . . make them good Christians and good Canadians, which is the same thing."' *Identities: The Impact of Ethnicity on Canadian Society*, ed. Wsevolod Isajiw (Toronto, 1977), 3–10.

[56]*Edmonton Journal*, 17 March 1906.

[57]*British Women's Emigration Association: Report 1903*, 15; *Imperial Colonist*, April 1904; Fawcett Library, Central London Polytechnical Institute, British Women's Emigration Association Papers, vol. 3, 'Factory Scheme Sub-Committee', 3 November 1904.

[58]Reynolds, *British Immigrant*, 44.

[59]Synge, 'Immigrant Communities', 41, and Interview No. 1-Wi-79-3.

[60]Rowland T. Berthoff, *British Immigrants in Industrial America 1789–1950* (Cambridge, Mass., 1953), 21, 133.

[61] *The Clarion*, 17 July 1908 and Canada, *Sessional Papers*, 1904, Vol. XXXVIII, No. 13–36A. 'Evidence Taken Before the Royal Commission to Inquire into Industrial Disputes in the Province of British Columbia'. 454.

[62] Orvis Collins, 'Ethnic Behaviour in Industry: Sponsorship and Rejection in a New England Factory', *American Journal of Sociology*, 1945, 293–8; Oswald Hall, 'The Canadian Division of Labour Revisited', *Canadian Society: Pluralism, Change and Conflict* (Toronto, 1971), 219–25; L.P. Curtis, *Anglo-Saxons and Celts: A Study of Anti-Irish Prejudice in Victorian Britain* (Bridgeport, 1968), 24, 119.

[63] Allen Seager, 'Class Consciousness, Class Anarchy: Three Alberta Coal Towns During the Great Depression', paper presented to the 1979 Convention of the Canadian Historical Association, 12.

[64] *Imperial Colonist*, April 1906, and May 1912, and *Annual Report of the* [Toronto] *Women's Welcome Hostel for 1911*, 9–10.

[65] William Stephenson, *The Store That Timothy Built* (Toronto, 1969), 63, and Interview No. 1-Wi-79-7.

[66] *Friendly Leaves*, December 1911; *Imperial Colonist*, February 1912; *British Women's Emigration Association: Report 1913*, 48.

[67] Interview No. 1-Wi-79-12.

[68] *Amalgamated Engineers' Journal*, February 1904. For the development of British unions in the country, see Eugene Forsey, 'British Trade Unions in Canada, 1853–1924', unpublished paper, n.d.

[69] *East End Emigration Fund: Reports 1894 and 1903*, 19, 15; Reynolds, *British Immigrant*, 104, 167–8; *Amalgamated Engineers' Journal*, January 1900 and November 1903.

[70] M.S. Donnelly, 'Ethnic Participation in Municipal Government: Winnipeg, St Boniface and the Metropolitan Corporation of Greater Winnipeg,' report made to the Royal Commission on Bilingualism and Biculturalism, 1965, 63–7.

III

From World War I

to World War II

17

Canada and the Great War

Timothy H.E. Travers

In late 1914, hundreds of thousands of Canadians volunteered for military service overseas to fight against the German-led Central Powers. The Canadian government had willingly supported, as part of Canada's imperial commitments, the British declaration of war on Germany and its allies in the wake of the assassination of the Archduke Ferdinand of Austria at Sarajevo by a Serbian nationalist. Neither Canada nor its volunteer soldiers had any idea that the resulting war would be so long, so bloody, or so apparently futile. Only a handful of military specialists could appreciate the prospect of a war in which two entrenched armies battled over a few hundred yards of territory, or of the new technologies (gas, the submarine, the tank, the airplane, the machine gun, for example) that would render the fighting so destructive. For years before 1914, the Canadian government had been struggling to keep its military forces separate from the British. From the

beginning of the war Ottawa insisted on Canadian units being kept together (rather than scattered among British ones) and commanded by their own officers, however inexperienced those leaders might be. From the British perspective, raw Canadian volunteers led by neophyte commanders could never be successful soldiers; the British command (civil and military) failed persistently to understand Canadian or other colonial sensitivities regarding autonomy. The conflict continued in a variety of areas throughout the war.

As Timothy H.E. Travers points out, war-time British-Canadian disagreement over the deployment and leadership of Canadian troops carried on even into postwar official histories. The battle of Second Ypres was a critical one, both for the war itself and for the subsequent historians. Ypres, in Belgium, was the first major battle in which Canadian troops were involved. Employing chlorine gas for the first time, the Germans had opened a wide gap in Allied ranks, and 1 Canadian division was one of those joining with British troops to fill the gap and halt the advance. Canadian casualties were heavy and Canadians at home were proud of the way in which their troops had fought. The British were less certain about the extent to which the Canadian involvement—and especially its leadership—could be congratulated for Second Ypres. British reservations, expressed at the time, became part of the British official history of Second Ypres—a history that provoked strong objections from the Canadian perspective. The ensuing debate not only tells us a good deal about long-standing Anglo-Canadian military disagreements, but also reminds us that even histories based on as much contemporary and eye-witness documentation, as was the military account of Second Ypres, are subject to differing interpretations. What, essentially, were the underlying points at issue? Were the Canadian commanders as free from criticism as the Canadians wanted to make out, or as culpable as the British would have it? Why was there not more criticism of the British high command's ultimate responsibility for this and other battles of the war?

This article first appeared, titled 'Allies in Conflict: The British and Canadian Official Historians and the Real Story of Second Ypres (1915)' in *Journal of Contemporary History* 24 (1989), 301–25.

In 1927, the British Official Historian, Brigadier-General Sir James Edmonds, related to his friend Captain B.H. Liddell Hart the story of Brigadier-General A.W. Currie's difficulties when commanding the 2nd Canadian Infantry Brigade at Second Ypres on 24 and 25 April 1915. According to Edmond's version:

> Currie three times ordered the Canadians to retire, but his troops did not obey. Currie reported his orders to Alderson [Lieutenant-General E.A.H. Alderson, commanding 1 Canadian Division, containing the 2nd Canadian Infantry Brigade] and on telling Snow [Major-General T.D'O. Snow, commanding the neighbouring 27 Division] the latter said, 'If Currie was an English officer I would have had him put under arrest and he would probably have been shot'. This conversation was all taken down by Mildmay [a staff officer on 27 Division Staff]. When recorded in the [British] Official History, vol. 3, Currie begged for its deletion and this was granted. (It had hung over his head for 13 years.)[1]

Was there any truth to this statement, and to several other post-war charges and counter-accusations over the real story of Second Ypres?

Before dealing with post-war arguments, we shall briefly detail the events of 24–25 April 1915 which form the crux of this story. On 22 April 1915, 1 Canadian Division (GOC Lieutenant-General E.A.H. Alderson) was stationed in the Ypres salient when the first gas attack of the war took place. 1 Canadian Division comprised three Brigades, the 1st (GOC Brigadier-General Mercer) in reserve, with the 2nd (GOC Brigadier-General Currie) and the 3rd (GOC Brigadier-General Turner) both being in the line at the apex of the salient. The gas attack caused 45 Algerian Division (to the left of the Canadians) to retire in disorder, and it was left to 1 Canadian Division to restore the situation, including a counter-attack that night, and others the next day, 23 April. The German forces waited a day and then launched another gas attack at dawn on 24 April, and followed up with heavy attacks throughout that day. Both the 2nd and 3rd Canadian Brigades were involved in heavy fighting and at times the situation seemed critical. At about 11:45 a.m. on 24 April, Currie issued orders to his 5th and 8th Battalions (of 2nd Canadian Infantry Brigade) to retire, but this retirement did not take place. Again, at midday on 24 April the situation appeared so perilous that Currie left his headquarters to seek reinforcements for a counter-attack, and visited the headquarters of the neighbouring 27 Division (GOC Major-General T.D'O. Snow). Currie did not rejoin his 2nd Brigade staff until some time that evening partly because his staff had shifted from the forward command post to set up another headquarters at Wieltje, further to the rear.

Early the next morning, 25 April, a counter-attack by a largely British force was turned back, and in the ensuing withdrawal the front-line positions of Currie's 2nd Canadian Infantry Brigade again appeared to be in trouble. However, the line held until the afternoon when severe German attacks and false information caused Currie sufficient anxiety for him to again order portions of two of his Battalions (the 5th and 8th) to withdraw at approximately 5:00 p.m. Despite protests from the two Battalion commanders, the withdrawal took place to a depth of 1000 yards, but finding that other units were not making similar movements, the 5th and 8th Battalions (of 2nd Canadian Infantry Brigade) returned to their original positions. At 6:00 p.m., the 2nd Canadian Infantry Brigade came under the orders of General Bulfin (GOC 28 Division), and that night (25–26 April), was replaced in the line by 11th Infantry Brigade.[2]

Thus far it would seem that Brigadier-General Currie had made some mistakes (as had Brigadier-General Turner, to be discussed below) but the fundamental error had really been committed by Sir John French (Commander-in-Chief of the British Expeditionary Force), who persisted in defending a very awkward salient. When this was pointed out to him by his Second Army commander, General Sir Horace Smith-Dorrien, Sir John French took the chance to remove Smith-Dorrien, against whom he was harbouring a grudge. Not long after, General Plumer was told to carry out the suggested retirement. Behind Sir John French's original decision to hold on to the Ypres salient was the old Aldershot maxim that warfare meant gaining ground and not giving it up—ground was the emotional benchmark of success or failure.

Nevertheless, when the British and Canadian Official Histories of Second Ypres came to be written in the 1920s and 1930s, the wider responsibility for the battle was to a large extent subordinated to an investigation of the details of the campaign. In this investigation Edmonds came to feel that 1 Canadian Division, and especially Currie, had behaved poorly, and that the Canadian Official Historian, Colonel Duguid, was launched on a campaign to cover up the real story. For their part, Colonel Duguid and General Currie came to believe that Edmonds was deliberately minimizing the role of the Canadians, while maximizing that of the British, and that Edmonds had also set out to be deliberately critical of 1 Canadian Division and its leadership and staff work, as well as of the conduct of Currie and Turner. This post-war battle opened in 1924 when Edmonds conveyed a first draft of the British Official History version of Second Ypres to Duguid, who transmitted his comments on it to him early in 1925.[3]

Duguid's comments on the British Official History drafts were very detailed, and initiated a style of debate between Duguid and Edmonds in which Edmonds often made critical and sarcastic handwritten notes on Duguid's lengthy typewritten comments. Edmonds's handwritten notes, therefore, usefully reveal the points of difference between the two historians, especially since Edmonds's notes were not intended to be seen by Duguid. For example, when Duguid wrote that 'Currie went to Hqrs. 27th Div. at about 3:30 p.m. [on 24 April] to try to hurry reinforcements . . . ', Edmonds noted 'much earlier'. And when Duguid continued, 'He [Currie] does not appear to have required or received any counsel' (from Major-General Snow, GOC 27 Division), Edmonds underlined the last three words ('received any counsel') and remarked 'Didn't he!' Or when Duguid stated that the 5th Canadian Infantry Battalion (in Currie's 2nd Brigade) was in touch with its right-hand neighbours, the 3rd Royal Fusiliers, until the afternoon of 25 April, Edmonds simply writes: 'No they were *not*'.[4]

The next exchange between Duguid and Edmonds revealed two particular bones of contention: (1) the reliability of the narrative and maps of Lieuten-ant-General Alderson (GOC 1 Canadian Division); and (2) the argument that 1 Canadian Division was really out of touch with the battle on 24 and 25 April, and in ignorance of the situation, so that the real commander of the battle was General Snow, GOC 27 Division.[5] Edmonds simply stated: 'Neither Alderson's narrative nor his maps will stand examination. He and his staff were too far away, and don't seem to have known what was happening.' Elsewhere in the same document, Edmonds wrote in hand that the 1 Cana-dian Division map for 26 April was 'a Fake', and that the several officers whom Duguid claimed had compiled the 1 Canadian Division narrative had not in fact done so: 'There was only one Compiler a Canadian. See Genl Alderson's letter.' Moreover, according to Edmonds, at least two of those whom Duguid claimed had helped compile the 1 Canadian Division's narrative, Colonel Romer and Captain Butler (ADC to Lieutenant-General Alderson), each 'disclaims all knowledge of narrative'.[6]

In this particular instance, Duguid was apparently proved wrong, for Edmonds later quoted a letter from Lieutenant-General Alderson:

> I [Alderson] am not surprised that you [Edmonds] found the [1 Canadian Division] account and maps inaccurate. It was written soon after [in fact 13 May 1915] by one of my Canadian staff. I did not want to hurt his feelings. I sent it in much as he wrote it. They were very sensitive and I often had to do that.'[7]

According to Edmonds, the 1 Canadian Division Diary contained an entry for 22 April 1915 which read: 'For remainder of diary till 10 a.m. 4th May 1914, [this should read 1915] see copy of report (attached).' Moreover, Edmonds had learnt from Colonel Romer that there *had* been a 1 Canadian Division Diary for the missing period, 'but heaven alone knows what happened to it'.[8] The obvious implication was that 1 Canadian Division, meaning Lieutenant-General Alderson in particular, had not liked what was in the Division Diary for the period 23 April 1915 to 4 May 1915, and had substituted a presumably more appealing narrative or report. General Snow reinforced Edmonds's mistrust of 1 Canadian Division's report/narrative by writing to him that, 'I saw the Canadian report on the battle and I know it is quite erroneous and was written by someone far in rear and only said what ought to have been done not what was done'. For his part, Colonel Duguid was forced to issue a rather lame retraction to Edmonds: 'I did not suggest the report of the 1st Canadian Division should be taken as the final authority . . .', but perhaps could be accepted as a framework. This was certainly a retreat from his previous statement that Alderson's narrative and maps' 'completeness is remarkable and their accuracy astonishing. . . .'[9]

The second area of difficulty in Duguid's comments related to 1 Canadian Division's control of the battle. Edmonds's basic contention was that 1 Canadian Division was out of touch and in ignorance of the situation so that Major-General Snow, GOC of the neighbouring 27 Division, really ran their battle. This contention was reinforced in a letter that Edmonds sent to Colonel Romer, in which he stated that Currie had wanted to take his Brigade out of the battle, while Snow had persuaded him to keep it in! If true, this was a situation that should clearly have been dealt with by General Alderson and not by Snow.[10] Meanwhile, the next set of draft chapters, commented on by Duguid on 25 July 1925, also maintained the same line of argument, and Duguid forcibly objected to Edmonds's statements that 'events forced General Snow to a great extent to take general charge of the defence . . .', and that Major-General Snow's 27 Division Headquarters became the focus of communication and information due to a telephone breakdown at 1 Canadian Division, apparently on 24 April. Duguid declared that the Canadian Signal Company did repair lines as soon as they were broken, but

Edmonds wrote in pencil: 'Evidence that not a telephone was heard at Can. Div. Headquarters'. Some support for Edmonds's assertion comes from a message from Major-General Snow to Brigadier-General Turner (GOC 3rd Canadian Infantry Brigade) on 24 April, timed at 2:15 p.m., and included in Duguid's published Canadian Official History *Appendices*. The message reads in part: 'I [Snow] am issuing these orders as I am on the spot and communication appears to be dislocated and time is of the highest importance. Act with vigor.'[11] It would also appear that early on 25 April, 1 Canadian Division was sending and receiving messages by hand and not by wire, although it is not clear how long this situation lasted. At a lower level, a Canadian junior officer reported that by 25 April, 'In spite of the untiring efforts of the men in charge, the telephone communication had permanently broken down'.[12]

This line of reasoning continued with Duguid's comments, dated 19 November 1925, on another draft chapter from Edmonds. Edmonds had evidently written, regarding 25 April: 'Information from Can Div scrappy', and Duguid retorted: 'There seems to be little reason for reprinting such a gross calumny as this from an unknown pen'. Against this, Edmonds noted in pencil that his source of the information was the '[V] Corps diary', and added that his information was 'only too true'.[13] Next, Edmonds turned his attention to Brigadier-General Currie and his 2nd Canadian Infantry Brigade on the evening of 25 April. Edmonds had evidently written that Currie and his staff 'could give no information' to the 11th Infantry Brigade that had come up to relieve Currie's Brigade. This Duguid labelled 'a plain misstatement', partly because Currie 'knew the area' well. However, Edmonds underlined the words 'knew the area', and noted 'but he [Currie] was "crashed" ', meaning that Currie was exhausted and so not in control of the situation. Further down the page, Edmonds had also evidently stated: 'It was learnt through the 85th Bde. that the 2nd Canadian Brigade had disappeared'. Duguid simply retorted, 'It had not.' Against this, Edmonds wrote in pencil, 'Yes, but this was true unfortunately', and against another paragraph detailing 11th Infantry Brigade's search for the 2nd Canadian Infantry Brigade, Edmonds remarked '. . . the 2nd Can. Brigade had practically disappeared & BM [Brigade Major] 2nd CIB found it.'[14]

Edmonds had been making some serious allegations, and perhaps feeling the need for support, he turned to two official historians who had worked on Second Ypres, C.F. Atkinson (later a Fellow of Exeter College, Oxford) and Captain A.F. Becke (who worked on the maps for Second Ypres). Both Atkinson and Becke professed to find serious discrepancies between the British and Canadian war diaries, especially for 24 and 25 April and particularly between the report of Currie's 2nd Canadian Infantry Brigade (the 2nd Canadian Infantry Brigade war diary had been replaced between 23 and 27 April with a narrative written by General Currie), and those of neighbouring

British units, the 8th Durham Light Infantry and the 3rd Royal Fusiliers. Edmonds sent the Atkinson-Becke reports to Duguid, who simply asked whether the two authors had read 1 Canadian Division's report and his own comments, but he did not make any other specific remarks or defence.[15] However, Edmonds seems to have become fixated with the lack of war diaries from 1 Canadian Division and from 2nd and 3rd Canadian Infantry Brigades (only the 1st Canadian Infantry Brigade had kept a proper diary), and would continually return to this subject. In fact, as the correspondence between Edmonds and Duguid progressed, it would seem that Edmonds began to concentrate on three main areas of difficulty during 24 and 25 April: (1) the disappearance or non-existence of the war diaries of 1 Canadian Division, and of 2nd and 3rd Canadian Infantry Brigades; (2) the conduct of Brigadier-General Currie and his 2nd Canadian Infantry Brigade; and (3) the question of whether Major-General Snow (27 Division) or 1 Canadian Division (especially the GSO 1, Romer) really controlled 1 Canadian Division's battle during these two days.

Thus, the next set of comments by Colonel Duguid on 9 December 1925 were largely devoted to defending the unexpected and unannounced visit of Brigadier-General Currie to Snow's 27 Division Headquarters at Potijze on 24 April. Edmonds evidently felt that Duguid was 'covering up' General Currie's visit, but Duguid was able to point out that Currie's own 2nd Canadian Infantry Brigade report made no secret of his movements that day, while his effort to get reinforcements from 27 Division fitted in with his prior and subsequent actions. Ironically, if there was a cover-up here, it was actually in Major-General Snow's own confidential report, which made no mention of Currie's visit to him on the 24th![16] Duguid's next set of comments stated that it was Colonel Romer who fought 1 Canadian Division's battle under the direction of V Corps; that other documents and reports adequately replaced the missing Canadian war diaries, which in any case had not been kept due to pressures of time; and that Edmonds's view of Second Ypres was really coloured by 27 Division staff's 'sinister insinuations' concerning Currie's visit to General Snow's dug-out.[17] A further letter in March 1926 from Duguid to Edmonds argued that 'Currie went to 27th Division Headquarters expecting to find a better wire to the rear from the Divisional signal office than from any Brigade signal office nearer the front'. Duguid also refuted Edmonds's repeated assertion that Currie attempted to 'take his brigade out of the line' early on 25 April, and when Currie *did* order his Brigade to withdraw around 5:00 p.m. on 25 April, it was for 'tactical rather than humanitarian motives'. Duguid then promised to send in the comments of Canadian officers on the British Official History drafts,[18] which he had apparently not yet circulated, although he had received the first draft in late 1924, a year and a half earlier.

The circulation of the British Official History drafts to Canadian participants of Second Ypres caused a turning-point in this story, for these drafts aroused such feelings of amazement, indignation and dismay that the C. of S. [Canadian Chief of Staff, Major-General MacBrien] has felt impelled to write to General Sir George Milne [the British Chief of the Imperial General Staff] asking officially for the submission of a further draft for Canadian comment before publication.

Another letter, from the author of the Official History of the Medical Services of the Canadian Forces in World War One, Andrew McPhail, to L.S. Amery, the Secretary of State for Dominion Affairs, strongly attacked Edmonds's drafts, and claimed that 'the whole Imperial relation and future co-operation in war is involved. . . .'[19] In other words, the rivalry between Duguid and Edmonds over Second Ypres had now been elevated to a political dimension, and it seemed likely that some of the contested incidents[20] would come into sharper focus, as well as any biases held by the two Official Historians. Indeed, Edmonds was now called upon to defend his version of events by General Sir George Milne.

Edmonds's defence of his allegations fell into three categories. Firstly, that the GOC of 1 Canadian Division, Lieutenant-General Alderson, had passed Edmonds's draft as 'excellent and fair' (although Alderson's GSO 1, Colonel Romer, had warned that if '*any credit*' was given to General Snow, 'there would be trouble with the Canadians'). Secondly, Edmonds defended the British draft with blunt assertions of British superiority, and his right to censor colonial versions of the war. The Australians, he wrote, had published much that was 'offensive', and had not even consulted the 'Mother country in any way'. Meanwhile, the Canadian story was not to be believed—Field-Marshal Haig had once said to Edmonds: 'The Canadians seldom were where they said they were: at Festubert [May 1915] I had to send an aeroplane to look for them.' Perhaps partly for the consumption of Milne, Edmonds also made the remarkable statement: 'As the history proceeds, many and very serious difficulties with the Canadians will crop up—there was no limit to their lying as the war went on. It is important to make a stand now.' Thirdly, Edmonds once again expanded at length on the discrepancies between Canadian and British war diaries, reports and narratives. Edmonds also claimed that Duguid had tried to foist his own typewritten file of messages onto him, plus 'timed pieces of narrative' without authority to back them up. Edmonds concluded by saying that 'if the Canadian Historical Section wants a vainglorious account it better write its own as the Australians have done. I am afraid nothing I can write will satisfy them.'[21]

For their part, Currie, Duguid and other Canadian officers launched their own campaign against Edmonds. Currie wrote to Major-General MacBrien, to reinforce that officer's correspondence with Milne,[22] while Edmonds wrote to L.S. Amery further defending his interpretation, and mentioning that he had permission from the Committee of Imperial Defence to proceed with printing.[23] Colonel Romer (now Major-General Sir C.F. Romer) also wrote to Edmonds, and objected to various points, one of which concerned the now notorious visit of Currie to Snow on 24 April. Although the Canadian version had Currie visiting Snow's 27 Division Headquarters in order to obtain reinforcements and to use the better communications of 27 Division, the British version had Currie going to Snow for 'information and help'. Romer suggested to Edmonds that he reword the interview between Snow and Currie: 'I fancy this has upset Duguid and after all you can easily reword it so as to eliminate any idea that Curry [*sic*] wanted to come back.' Edmonds replied that in his first draft of Second Ypres, he had deliberately worded the 'Interview' of Currie and Snow 'obscurely', meaning that he had toned it down. Thus the first draft read according to Edmonds: ' "Br.-General Currie proceeded to General Snow's headquarters to obtain his advice" or words to that effect. Duguid wouldn't have that. Currie's anxiety to pull his Brigade out—he eventually did it—and Snow's endeavour to keep it in the line cannot be altogether omitted.'[24]

Thus far, Edmonds's views had been represented by his handwritten notes on Duguid's own comments on the first and second British Official History drafts, and his letters to individuals such as Romer and Milne. But at the end of 1926, by which time the British Official History Second Ypres volume had gone to press, Edmonds summarized the whole controversy in a hitherto unknown and extraordinary report to the Cabinet Office.[25]

Edmonds commenced this report by noting that Duguid had not circulated the first draft of the British Official History of Second Ypres to Canadian officers, but did circulate the second draft, at which point the trouble began:

> Private letters from a little group of Canadians who are supporters of General Sir A. Currie were received by various persons in England, complaining that the narrative was not impartial, etc. Among others who received a letter from General Currie's particular friend [presumably Andrew McPhail] was Mr. Amery, Secretary of State for Dominion Affairs.

Amery apparently supported Edmonds, as did another officer who received a letter, Major-General Sir Percy Radcliffe. Indeed, Edmonds claimed that far from being biased:

> I had . . . covered up a number of unpleasant incidents, and particularly the unsoldierly behaviour of General Currie and some of the higher officers, appointed apparently by the late Sir Sam Hughes for political services. Their conduct, *inter alia*, had the result that their commands left the front without waiting to be relieved by other troops.[26]

After these unkind remarks, Edmonds reported that the next stage in the controversy was the arrival of the Canadian officers' comments. These comments, claimed Edmonds, mostly concerned matters of detail, or complaints of unfairness, such as those of Brigadier-General Sir F. Loomis, who complained of 'unfair, unfriendly and ungenerous treatment', and that the narrative was 'contemptible . . . and unsportsman-like'. But two of the key Canadian figures, Brigadier-Generals Currie and Turner, had zeroed in on Major-General Snow. The comments of Currie, wrote Edmonds, 'principally [concerned] abuse of General Snow, who did his best to prevent him [Currie] withdrawing his brigade prematurely'. On the other hand, Turner 'denied sending a message from General Snow's headquarters, and said he only went there through "simple curiosity, to see their wonderful dugouts" '.[27]

Meanwhile, Duguid, who had by now amassed and sent forty pages of criticism and comment on Second Ypres to Edmonds, arrived in Britain in August 1926. Duguid was ostensibly on holiday, but apparently he wished to confront Edmonds over the latter's version of Second Ypres. After four days' discussion, with Edmonds claiming that Duguid had retreated over many of his comments, Edmonds asked Duguid why he had not simply sent him redrafts of the sections that he (Duguid) did not like. According to Edmonds, Duguid replied that:

> he had direct orders of the C.G.S. [MacBrien] NOT to do this, but to find every possible fault with the draft. He had checked the rank and initials of every officer mentioned, the spelling of every name and place name and the hour of every event; when accounts, time, or even spelling of Belgian place names varied, he had suggested the opposite to that one which I had accepted. (This is evident in the comments.) The object of all this smoke and dust was to obscure the real issue which Colonel Duguid said was to get expunged from the record that on the 24th April Sir A. Currie and his staff had made grave mistakes, and on the morning of the 25th April, regardless of the troops alongside, had ordered the retirement of his brigade, reported his action in writing (the message is preserved) to the Canadian Division and verbally to General Snow (who used rather strong language to him). The publication of the whole story of General Currie's conduct would ruin his position in Canada—where he is passing as a staunch supporter of the Imperial connection. To my natural comment, why didn't you write this to me and save all this bother, he said that he had not been allowed to do so in writing. Further, though admitting that at the time too much credit had been given to the Canadians and too little to the British (I have this in writing), he begged for more praise for the Canadians, and that the share in the battle of General Snow might not be made so prominent.[28]

Edmonds states that he did add more praise for the Canadians,

> and omitted the incident of General Currie's orders and his other dubious conduct at Ypres, though it had an effect on the position of troops which it is a little difficult to hide; and in general I accepted Colonel Duguid's proposed

corrections . . . in particular that the Canadian retirements had been made in good order. . . .[29]

Edmonds ended his account of Duguid's visit by reporting that the latter had said that the Canadian strategy was not to publish their Official History version first, but 'to force' the Canadian narrative onto the British Official History.[30]

Edmonds then repeated his earlier statements regarding the missing war diaries, and argued that the substituted narratives conflicted with other war diaries, quoting Lieutenant-General Alderson's corroboration of this allegation regarding 1 Canadian Division. Finally as a parting shot, Edmonds pointed out that Duguid had broken a promise not to publish without joint consultation, but had in fact published an anonymous account of Second Ypres in the *Encyclopedia Britannica Supplement*, vol. 3, just issued. Ironically, the shoe was now on the other foot, for Edmonds complained that the British role was barely mentioned and the Canadian Division was the central focus, so that Duguid entirely omitted 'the Canadian retirement on the 24th and 25th April 1915 by which a large piece of the salient was lost'.[31]

Edmonds's remarkable outburst to the Cabinet Office, and the sending of the British Official History third draft to the printers at the end of 1926, really concluded the strange private war between Edmonds and Duguid over Second Ypres. One or two more letters passed between the two historians, in one of which Edmonds continued his line of thought regarding the 'disappearance' of the 2nd Canadian Infantry Brigade on the evening of 25 April.[32] Then in 1927 the British Official History version of Second Ypres was published, although the Canadian Official History volumes, covering both 1914 and 1915, appeared very much later, in 1938.

The British Official History published version was circumspect, and did not mention Currie's visit to Snow on 24 April, nor was there any reference to orders to retire that Currie may have issued early on 25 April. However, Currie's retirement orders of 24 April, and those issued at 5:00 p.m. on 25 April, were recorded in the text. And there was only a veiled reference to 2nd Canadian Infantry Brigade's problems late on 25 April.[33] On the other hand, the Canadian Official History was surprisingly detailed, and included a separate *Appendices* volume of telegrams and messages that did reveal evidence of problems to the careful reader. Currie's visit to Snow was included and explained by Duguid as a search for reinforcements, but Duguid did include in the *Appendices* volume the full text of the telegram Currie sent from 27 Division Headquarters in the afternoon of 24 April. Moreover, the *Appendices* volume contained a checklist of the House of Commons debates on Currie's conduct at Second Ypres and later in the war, as well as postwar speeches concerning Currie's command generally. Duguid's text also referred to Currie's various orders to withdraw on 24 and 25 April, although omitting any reference to Currie's alleged orders early on 25 April. Duguid praised the Canadian defence of the Ypres salient, although hinting that control of the battle by 1 Canadian Division was not what it might have been. (1 Canadian Division Headquarters was 6½ miles to the rear, while Snow's 27 Division Headquarters was only 3 miles from the front. On the other hand, 28 Division Headquarters was even further away from the front line than 1 Canadian Division Headquarters.) Finally, Duguid was relatively cautious in his evaluation of the state of the 2nd Canadian Infantry Brigade on the evening of 25 April, and of the fact that Currie was then at 2nd Canadian Infantry Brigade Headquarters (at Wieltje), and evidently did not really know what was happening some 2½ miles further forward at the front line.[34]

Between the versions of Edmonds and Duguid, can the truth of 24 and 25 April 1915, at Second Ypres, be discerned? There appear to be five key areas of contention: (1) the question of the 'disappearing' war diaries, and the reliability of the replacement reports/narratives; (2) Currie's orders to retire on 24 and 25 April; (3) the reason for Currie's visit to Snow's 27 Division Headquarters on 24 April; (4) the question of whether Snow or 1 Canadian Division really ran the Canadian side of the battle; and (5) the 'disappearance' of 2nd Canadian Infantry Brigade on the evening of 25 April.

On the question of the 1 Canadian Division War Diary for the period 22 April to 4 May 1915, it does seem that a diary of some kind did once exist, that it was replaced by a report, and that this report was not entirely reliable. Indeed, Duguid did conceal evidence from Edmonds which pointed to the deliberate removal of the 1 Canadian Division diary. On the other hand, some Canadian staff officers denied the existence of a diary, while it may well be the case that the reports which replaced the war diaries of both the 2nd and 3rd Canadian Infantry Brigade were necessary because of the intense pressure of events from 22 April following, which prevented the keeping of a regular war diary. Nevertheless, the observations of two other official historians, C.F. Atkinson and Captain A.F. Becke, indicate that the two Brigade reports should also be approached with some caution.[35]

Secondly, Currie's orders to his Battalions to retire on 24 April, and again in the late afternoon of 25 April, are recorded in Duguid's text and appendices, together with the reluctance of his Battalions actually to retire, and the resentment of the neighbouring 85th Brigade (on the right of the 2nd Canadian Infantry Brigade). This story can be followed through a series of telegrams, commencing around 11:00 a.m. on 24 April, and ending in the late afternoon.[36] A message from 28 Division (to which 85 Brigade belonged) to 1 Canadian Division was especially impelling: 'Have replied imploring him [Currie's 2nd Canadian Infantry Brigade] not to retire . . . ', and, 'Will you please ask Canadian Divn. to stop any retirement contemplated . . . '[37]

If anything, the situation was worse during the late afternoon of the next day, 25 April, when around 5:00 p.m. Currie issued his retirement orders, and both his Battalion commanders, Lieutenant Colonels Lipsett and Tuxford, objected. At approximately 6:30 p.m., after retiring for around 1000 yards, three companies of the 8th Battalion (Lipsett) discovered that their neighbours, the 85th Brigade, had not withdrawn, and so the 8th Battalion returned to their former positions. (The situation in the late afternoon of 25 April was very complex. It is also possible that the retirement of the neighbouring Durham Light Infantry was the real cause of the initial retirement of the Canadian 8th Battalion.) The 5th Battalion Headquarters (Tuxford) and elements of the 5th Battalion also returned to their former positions.[38] It would seem that Currie was perhaps unduly pessimistic on both occasions, on 24 and 25 April. On the other hand, apart from a series of cryptic telegrams during the night of 24/25 April, there is very little evidence of Edmonds's repeated assertions that Currie wanted to take the 2nd Canadian Infantry Brigade out of the line early on 25 April.[39]

Ironically, however, the real culprit of the problems of these two days was actually Turner, and not Currie, since it was Turner's decision unexpectedly to take his own 3rd Canadian Brigade out of the line on 24 April without orders to do so, that opened up a large and dangerous gap to the left of Currie's Brigade. It was in fact this gap that Currie had been trying to fill when he visited Snow on 24 April to seek reinforcements. Why then did Edmonds continue to focus on Currie's difficulties, when the real object of his attentions should have been Turner? The answer seems to be twofold. Firstly, Edmonds evidently followed Snow's version of events, which blamed Currie for the difficulties of 1 Canadian Division (Edmonds had been Snow's GSO 1 in 1974, and therefore was likely to listen to Snow). Secondly, Edmonds focused on Currie rather than Turner because both Alderson and Duguid had deliberately either downplayed or concealed both Turner's role in ordering his troops (including two British battalions) back to the GHQ line without instructions, and the severe repercussions of this withdrawal.[40]

Turner's action, and his subsequent failure to close the 3000-yard gap in the line that he had created, led to Currie's visit to Snow's 27 Division Headquarters, and thus the *third* area of contention. It seems obvious, therefore, that Currie *did* go to Snow's Headquarters on 24 April to obtain reinforcements, and he also visited the 5th Durham Light Infantry and their Brigade Commander, Brigadier-General Bush, for the same reason. But it can also be inferred from accounts of the interview that Currie did seek advice and counsel from Snow, for Currie was new to trench warfare, whereas Snow had had six months' experience, and was not easily rattled.[41] According to Currie, there was a misunderstanding between him and Snow, since the latter believed Currie wanted to take his Brigade out of the line, because there were reports that Currie had ordered this action at around

1:00 p.m. that day (24 April). Certainly, 28 Division had to act around 5:00 p.m. on the same day to fill some gaps left by elements of the 2nd Canadian Infantry Brigade.[42] In any case, it was these reports of Currie's earlier orders to 2nd Canadian Infantry Brigade to withdraw (later cancelled by Currie), which no doubt created the misunderstanding between him and Snow. Subsequently, Major-General Romer revealed that Snow had told Edmonds that Currie had considered the advisability of withdrawing his Brigade to the GHQ line. Romer did not know if Currie remembered this part of the conversation as accurate, but 'I suppose in any case Currie had in his mind all throughout that day [24 April] the possibility of having to withdraw.'[43]

The difficult atmosphere at this meeting was later recalled by Currie, who remembered that he introduced himself to Snow, explained his requirements, and described his Brigade's critical situation:

> As soon as I mentioned that apparently there was a gap between the left of my 8th Bn. and the 3rd [Canadian] Brigade troops, he [Snow] shouted at me and asked how dare I allow such a gap to occur. To hear him you would think that I personally and solely was responsible for that gap. . . . He roundly abused me and told me to get out, shouting at me to 'give them hell, give them hell'. I asked if I might send a message to the 1st [Canadian] Division, but had no sooner sat down at a table to write the message when I was told that I was taking much too long over it. That was an insult and so at variance to the treatment which one officer should receive from another of superior rank that I was almost dumbfounded. . . . I left Snow's dugout and there followed me out a British officer . . . [who] told me not to mind what the General had said to me and that Snow had the reputation of being the rudest officer in the British army.

An independent witness to this interview, a Major Lynn of the Canadian Engineers, added a few of Snow's choice remarks that he remembered. For example, to Currie's request for reinforcements from Snow's division, Snow replied: 'Have you come here to teach me my profession and dictate to me how I shall handle my division?' Currie tried again, and Snow replied: 'Do you expect me to wet-nurse your Brigade? You have got yourself and your men into a mess and you will have to get them out as best you can.' Finally, Snow closed the interview: 'Enough of this, I have heard enough of your harangue. Get out of here. Take care of your own line, etc.' Needless to say, Currie left without the reinforcements he sought![44]

The truth of this interview seems to be that Currie's main aim was to obtain reinforcements, but that Snow expected the worst of Currie because of Currie's earlier withdrawal orders. Snow therefore overestimated Currie's anxiety, and passed this evaluation of Currie's attitude along to Edmonds. In turn, Edmonds over-emphasized Currie's intention to withdraw his troops, and wished to put this interpretation into the Official History.

However, Currie's visit to Snow did have one other result, namely, that Currie's absence from his Brigade apparently left his staff in confusion. At least three messages from his staff between noon and 2:00 p.m. on 24 April seem to indicate that any pre-arrangements with his staff were not capable of sustaining a long absence. At 5:00 p.m. Currie was still not back at his Headquarters, although he had rejoined his staff by 11:00 p.m. that evening.[45] It had been a bad day for Currie, yet by that night he seemed once more in control of the situation—despite writing later of his state of mind on 24 April: 'I had no sleep for days and nights and didn't care what happened'.[46]

The next, and *fourth*, area of contention was the question of whether 1 Canadian Division ran their own battle or not. It will be convenient just to focus on one day—24 April—to evaluate this problem. There is no doubt that on 24 April, a temporary command vacuum emerged. Into this vacuum stepped Snow, who actually ordered Turner's 3rd Canadian Infantry Brigade forward in the afternoon of 24 April although he had no authority to do so—obviously 1 Canadian Division should have done any ordering that was to be done. Snow's information that the Germans were in the area of Currie's 2nd Canadian Infantry Brigade Headquarters appears to have been wrong, but Snow's hurried action is an indication that 1 Canadian Division was thought to be out of touch with the situation. Currie's decision to go back to the General Headquarters line to seek reinforcements is also another strong indication that Currie at least felt that 1 Canadian Division was not doing enough to restore the situation. Judging by several wires to various units, it is also clear that 1 Canadian Division did not know where Turner's 3rd Canadian Infantry Brigade was, due to the latter's unexpected withdrawal. Moreover, this Brigade seemed to be reporting to Snow's 27 Division as well as to 1 Canadian Division. Meanwhile, Currie's 2nd Canadian Infantry Brigade Headquarters was out of touch with 1 Canadian Division on the evening of 24 April, and had to use 28 Division Headquarters as a communication conduit, while even Duguid admitted that Snow's 27 Division Headquarters was also conveniently situated for communications.[47]

1 Canadian Division continued to send messages throughout 24 April, but they did seem to be perplexed by changing conditions and to have lost control of their 2nd and 3rd Canadian Infantry Brigades from time to time while neighbouring British units were at times clearly concerned at 1 Canadian Division's actions, and frequently protested. Snow did at times intervene in the battle on behalf of 1 Canadian Division. Indeed, Brigadier-General Turner himself later wrote that around midnight on 24/25 April, he was forced to go by motorcycle to 1 Canadian Division Headquarters and request that Lieutenant-General Alderson give him 'definite instructions', since he was receiving 'conflicting orders from Major-General Snow'. In addition, 1 Canadian Division's GSO 1, Colonel Romer, made several post-war statements which clearly gave Snow a role in running the battle on 24 April. Finally, in a post-war letter to Edmonds, one of Snow's staff declared that

General Snow, alone of Divisional commanders, was able to keep in some sort of touch with what went on in the [Ypres] Salient during the Battle. Other Divisional commanders, with Headquarters west of Ypres [i.e. 1 Canadian Division and 28 Division] could not keep thus informed, for wires were so continually cut by shell fire that such means of communication became valueless.[48]

By the late afternoon of 25 April, however, the *fifth* and last area of disagreement between Duguid and Edmonds—the 'disappearance' of 2nd Canadian Infantry Brigade—had now come into play. On the night of 24 April, Currie was evidently worn out, and apparently Lieutenant-Colonel Lipsett temporarily took over command of the Brigade. However, at about 3:00 a.m. on 25 April, Currie was active in surveying the defensive lines of the 2nd Canadian Infantry Brigade, and at that point the Brigade was a cohesive unit.[49] Severe attacks throughout the afternoon of 25 April caused Currie grave anxiety, and two incorrect messages around 5:00 p.m. (plus the retreat of a neighbouring British unit) seemed to indicate that the only situation was a withdrawal, which he ordered for 'dusk'. It appears, however, that Currie was not fully in touch with the situation, because from about 3:00 p.m. onward, he was not with his Brigade in the front line command centre at Gravenstafel, but some three miles back, at 2nd Canadian Infantry Brigade Headquarters at Wieltje. This was proper enough, but telephone communication between the two places was cut off, and messages sent via runners had become very unreliable. Indeed Currie himself reported communications between the two places to be 'very slow and very uncertain', with more than one message never received.[50]

The situation for 2nd Canadian Infantry Brigade now deteriorated—Currie was apparently out of touch—and, as previously mentioned, elements of the 5th and 8th Battalions retired on Currie's orders and then returned to Gravenstafel ridge.[51] However, under relentless attack, the 2nd Canadian Infantry Brigade were then driven from Gravenstafel ridge, and began to withdraw. According to three different infantry units, the location of the 2nd Canadian Infantry Brigade was hard to find. The 85th Battalion, for example, claimed the 2nd Canadian Infantry Brigade 'had disappeared', while at 10:20 p.m. on 25 April the 1 Canadian Division had to ask Currie: 'Have you heard anything of a retirement of your Brigade?' (Edmonds commented opposite this message: 'Yes but the Brigadier was in Wieltje not with his Brigade.' Edmonds was implying that Currie was not close enough to his Brigade to know the situation, or command his Brigade.)[52] Currie replied to 1 Canadian Division with a message around 11:00 p.m. on 25 April, saying that he essentially did not know where his 5th Battalion was, but that the remnants of his Battalions were being collected at 2nd Canadian Brigade Headquarters at Wieltje.[53] In fact, most elements of 2nd Canadian Infantry Brigade remained in their front line positions until the early hours of 26 April.[54] It seems, therefore, that the allegation by Edmonds that the 2nd

Canadian Infantry Brigade had 'disappeared' on 25 April was not quite correct. What Edmonds apparently meant, and what actually happened, was that Currie was not sufficiently in touch with his Brigade to know exactly where it was, and that it was left to his Brigade Major to locate it for the relieving troops.[55]

Finally, what of the statement by Edmonds via Liddell Hart mentioned at the beginning of this article—that Currie had three times ordered his Brigade to retire, but that they had refused—and that this was deleted from the British Official History? In his very forceful report to Cabinet of 1 December 1926, Edmonds refers to two incidents involving Currie's orders to retire that were expunged from the record, one on 24 April and one on the morning of 25 April. The former incident did take place, but the latter cannot be substantiated, and is not mentioned in Duguid's *Official History* or *Appendices*. Since Edmonds had claimed to remove references to these orders, they are of course not to be found in the British *Official History*. No doubt Edmonds was principally referring to Currie's orders to retire on the morning of 24 April around 11:45 a.m., which were not acted upon (and which were later followed by Currie's visit to Snow), and also to Currie's orders to his Brigade to retire around 5:00 p.m. on 25 April, which were later reversed. It can be fairly said, therefore, that Currie did issue orders for retirement twice, but not three times, and that these retirements did not subsequently take place. However, as this article shows, there were also extenuating circumstances for Currie's orders in both cases.[56]

The post-war struggle between Duguid and Edmonds over the role of 1 Canadian Division, and especially over the actions of Currie and his 2nd Canadian Infantry Brigade, really reveals a conflict between the anti-colonial bias of the British Official Historian, Edmonds, and the difficulties of the Canadian Official Historian, Duguid, in protecting the reputation of Currie and 1 Canadian Division generally. Edmonds was over-critical of the fight of 1 Canadian Division in an impossible salient during two particularly difficult days, 24 and 25 April, and tended to underplay the fact that 1 Canadian Division had saved the situation on 22 April during the first gas attack of the war, and that the three Brigades of 1 Canadian Division had suffered 1839, 1829 and 1838 casualties respectively between 22 April and 3 May 1915—around 46 per cent of 1 Canadian Division's total infantry strength. On the other hand, it is clear that Turner, and to a lesser extent Currie, did make some mistakes which their Battalion commanders and front line soldiers had to retrieve, while Lieutenant-General Alderson and the staff of 1 Canadian Division were not always in command of the situation. This was really a matter of experience, since 1 Canadian Division was to become one of the four or five outstanding Divisions of the Western Front, while Currie in particular was to emerge as a successful Corps commander, especially in 1918.

However, what this episode also shows is the way in which official military history came to be written after the first world war. The British and Canadian Official Historians argued and haggled over the events of two key days during Second Ypres before deciding on what could be included and what omitted. Thus a sanitized version of the battle emerged, which can only now be properly evaluated. A second major result of the feuding over Second Ypres was the revelation of the mutually suspicious relationship between British and Canadian officers both during the war and after. Indeed, it is clear that the difficulty over Second Ypres was not an isolated incident. Quite apart from similar kinds of arguments between Edmonds and the Australian official historians, Second Ypres set the stage for further unpleasant recriminations regarding actions at Mont Sorrel and the St Eloi Craters; and after the war, Currie was still trying to obtain greater recognition for the contribution of the Canadian Corps in 1918 from a reluctant Lord Horne (GOC First Army), who made the remarkable statement that the Canadian 'Corps is perhaps rather apt to take all the credit it can for everything, and to consider that the BEF consists of the Canadian Corps and some other troops'.[57]

British and Dominion co-operation was not an easy matter during and after the first world war, but perhaps the level of conflict and resentment between the partners has yet to be fully appreciated.

Suggestions for Further Reading

D.J. Goodspeed, *The Road Past Vimy: The Canadian Corps 1914–1918* (Toronto, 1969).

Desmond Morton, *A Peculiar Kind of Politics: Canada's Overseas Ministry in the First World War* (Toronto, 1982).

G.W.L. Nicholson, *Canadian Expeditionary Force, 1914–1919* (Ottawa, 1962).

Notes

[1] Liddell Hart, Talk with Edmonds, 7 October 1927, 11/1927/17, Liddell Hart Papers, King's College Library, London University (hereinafter KCL).

[2] This brief outline has been based on Colonel F. Duguid, *Official History of the Canadian Forces in the Great War 1914–1919*, General Series, vol. 1, and *Chronology, Appendices and Maps*, General Series, vol. 1 (Ottawa 1938); Brigadier-General J.E. Edmonds and Captain G.C. Wynne, *Military Operations France and Belgium 1915 Winter 1914–15: Battle of Neuve Chapelle: Battle of Ypres* (London 1927); Hugh Urquhart, *Arthur Currie: The Biography of a Great Canadian* (Toronto and Vancouver 1950); D.J. Goodspeed, *The Road Past Vimy: The Canadian Corps 1914–1918* (Toronto 1969); Daniel Dancocks, *Sir Arthur Currie, A Biography* (Toronto 1985), A.M.J. Hyatt, *General Sir Arthur Currie: A Military Biography* (Toronto 1987).

[3] It seems likely that the first draft was conveyed to Duguid by Edmonds in 1924, Duguid to Edmonds, 14 September 1924, and the comments came in Duguid to

Edmonds, 8 January 1925; Cab 45/155, Public Record Office, London (hereinafter PRO). This file, and Cab 45/156, are solely concerned with Official History correspondence on the Canadian role at Second Ypres, and are central to an understanding of both this role and the post-war arguments.

[4] Duguid's comments on First Draft, and Edmonds's handwritten notes, with Duguid to Edmonds, 8 January 1925, 16, 15, 20, Cab 45/155, PRO.

[5] Duguid to Edmonds, 18 May 1925, 4, 5, 8, 10, Cab 45/155, PRO.

[6] *Ibid.*, 10, 4, 5, 8. The denial of Romer's and Butler's involvement is in C.F. Romer to Edmonds, 24 June 1926, Cab 45/156, PRO.

[7] Alderson to Edmonds, no date, quoted in Edmonds, *Canadian Comments on '1915 (France)'*, vol. 1, 1 December 1926, Appendix 1, 34, Cabinet Office History file, Cab 16/52, PRO.

[8] C.F. Romer to Edmonds, 23 December 1925, Cab 45/156; also reported in Edmonds to General Sir George Milne (CIGS), 30 April 1926, Cab 45/155, PRO.

[9] Major-General T.D'O. Snow to Edmonds, 8 June 1921, Cab 45/156; Duguid to Edmonds, 26 June 1925, 8; and Duguid to Edmonds, 18 May 1925, 5; Cab 45/155, PRO.

[10] Duguid to Edmonds, 18 May 1925, *ibid.*, 10; Edmonds to Romer, 25 June 1926, Cab 45/155, PRO.

[11] Duguid to Edmonds, 25 July 1925, 13, Cab 45/155, PRO. Duguid, *Chronology, Appendices and Maps*, message no. 600 (Snow to Turner) and no. 633 (85 Infantry Brigade to 28 Division, 24 April 1915, 11:20 p.m.), 281 and 287. See also no. 635 (28 Division to Canadian Division, 24 April 1915, 11:38 p.m.), 288.

[12] Colonel Duguid, *Chronology, Appendices and Maps*, nos. 643 (1:30 a.m. 25 April), 644 (2:10 a.m.), 647 (3:30 a.m.), 649 (9:15 a.m.), 650 (7:55 a.m. but received 4:00 p.m.!), 289–99. *Confidential Report by Captain G.W. Northwood, 8th Canadian Infantry Battalion*, 1, Cab 45/156, PRO.

[13] Duguid to Edmonds, 19 November 1925, 8, Cab 45/155, PRO.

[14] *Ibid.*, 10.

[15] C.T. Atkinson to Edmonds, 5 December 1925, and A.F. Becke (handwritten report), no date; and Duguid to Edmonds, 28 June 1926, Cab 45/155, PRO.

[16] Duguid to Edmonds, 9 December 1925, 2, Cab 45/155; and Major-General T.D.'O. Snow, Confidential Report on the operations of 27 Division, 28 May 1915, in Smith-Dorrien Papers, Cab 45/206, Part 2, PRO.

[17] Duguid to Edmonds, 28 January 1926, Cab 45/155, PRO.

[18] Duguid to Edmonds, 17 March 1926, 3, 4, 1, Cab 45/155, PRO.

[19] Duguid to Edmonds, 14 April 1926, Cab 45/155; Andrew McPhail to L.S. Amery, 25 April 1926, Cab 45/156, PRO. MacBrien's phrase was 'alarm and despondency', J.H. MacBrien to Sir George [Milne], 16 April 1926, Cab 45/156, PRO.

[20] An interesting side incident that now emerged was Edmond's information that at a 4 Division dinner on 25 October 1926, two of the 11th Infantry Brigade officers present said they had been just west of Ypres on 24 April, around noon, and had seen Currie thrown from his horse. They had gone to his assistance. After several often intemperate letters, Edmonds seems reluctantly to have accepted that the unseated officer was not Currie but someone else; Edmonds to Duguid, 26 October 1926; Duguid to Edmonds, 9 November 1926; Edmonds to Duguid, 22 November 1926; Duguid to Edmonds, 10 December 1927; and Edmonds to Duguid, 2 January 1928; Cab 45/155, PRO.

[21]Edmonds to General Sir George Milne (CIGS), 30 April 1926, Cab 45/155, PRO.

[22]Currie to MacBrien, 1 June 1926, Cab 45/155, PRO. In this lengthy, four-page letter, Currie makes some specific criticisms of Edmonds's drafts, but on the whole his argument is that Edmonds overpraises the British and underpraises the Canadians, which could 'lead to serious Imperial consequences' (4). See also McPhail to Amery, 25 April 1926; and MacBrien to Milne, 16 April 1926; Cab 45/156, PRO.

[23]Edmonds to L.S. Amery, 30 June 1926, Cab 45/155, PRO. In this letter Edmonds refers to Major-General Sir Percy Radcliffe (BGGS, Canadian Corps) and Colonel Romer, who both saw nothing wrong with his views.

[24]Romer to Edmonds, 24 June 1926, Cab 45/156; and Edmonds to Romer, 25 June 1926, Cab 45/155, PRO. Edmonds's reference to those who went to Snow for 'information and help', evidently meaning Currie, is repeated in Duguid to Edmonds, 18 June 1926, 1, Cab 45/155, PRO. It would appear that Edmonds had a firsthand account of the Currie-Snow discussion on 24 April, in the person of a 27 Division staff officer, Mildmay of Hele; Duguid to Edmonds, 28 January 1926, 2, Cab 45/155; and Snow to Edmonds, 8 June 1921, Cab 45/156, PRO.

[25]Edmonds, *Canadian Comments on '1915 (France)'*, vol. 1, 1 December 1926, 29–35, Cab 16/52, PRO. To my knowledge this document has not previously been cited by historians.

[26]*Ibid.*, 29–30.

[27]*Ibid.*, 31–2. The visit by Turner to Snow's Headquarters took place on the afternoon of 26 April. The comments by Loomis and Turner came in F.O.W. Loomis to Duguid, no date, Cab 45/156 ('the Anti-Canadian atmosphere or spirit which permeates the narrative'); and R.E.W. Turner to Duguid, 20 April 1926, Cab 45/156 ('fails to do justice to the Canadians . . . '), PRO.

[28]Edmonds, *Canadian Comments, op. cit.*, 32–3.

[29]*Ibid.*, 33. This was a point of view that Edmonds had expressed earlier to Major-General Romer: 'The Germans came on each time when they were ready. It is no good pretending otherwise as the Germans will point it out', Edmonds to Romer, 25 June 1926, Cab 45/155, PRO. Romer evidently disagreed.

[30]Edmonds, *Canadian Comments, op. cit.*, 32–3.

[31]*Ibid.*, 34–5.

[32]Edmonds to Duguid, 6 December 1926, Cab 45/155, PRO. In this letter Edmonds cites the report of Colonel Lipsett (Officer Commanding 8th Battalion, 2nd Canadian Infantry Brigade) which stated that the 8th and 5th Battalions only held Gravenstafel until 'dark' on 25 April and thus missed seeing their replacements, the Hampshires.

[33]Edmonds, *Military Operations France and Belgium, 1915 . . . Battle of Ypres*, 227–8, 246–7, 251.

[34]Duguid, *Chronology, Appendices and Maps*, 267–96, especially Currie's telegram of 24 April from 27 Division Headquarters, no. 607, 282 and the checklist of post-war debates on Currie, no. 589, 279–80. Duguid, *Official History . . . General Series*, 285–367, especially 318–19, 360–7, and for hints of communication disruption at 1 Canadian Division Headquarters, 414–16. For general praise, 421–2. For Currie's problems on the evening of 25 April, 366–7.

[35]Duguid to Edmonds, 18 May 1925, 26 June 1925, 9 December 1925, 28 January 1926; C.F. Atkinson and A.F. Becke to Edmonds, 5 December 1925 and no date;

Cab 45/155, PRO. Canadian staff officers in a series of letters either admit the existence of a scrappy war diary or deny that there ever was one. Even Romer, perhaps for political reasons when writing to Duguid, could not recall whether there was one! *Extracts from letters of Officers on Staff of Canadian Division April and May 1915. Relative to War Diary* (including Romer to Duguid, 5 December 1925, professing no recollection of a diary) Cab 45/156, PRO. However, in Romer to Edmonds, 23 December 1925, Romer states there *was* a diary, Cab 45/156, PRO. Duguid's concealment of evidence is in Sutherland-Brown to MacBrien, 25 November 1925; Romer to MacBrien, 4 December 1925; Panet to MacBrien, 4 December 1925; in RG 24, vol. 2680, part 1, Public Archives, Ottawa.

[36]Duguid, *Chronology, Appendices and Maps*, nos. 560a, 563, 565a, 565b, 570, 577, 579, 582, 587, 587a, 615, 626, 274–86.

[37]*Ibid.*, 28 Division to 1 Canadian Division, 1:30 p.m. 24 April, no. 579, 277–8. An independent voice comes from Lieutenant-Colonel G.A. Stevens (then Captain and Adjutant, 8th Durham Light Infantry), who claimed that late on 25 April the 8th Battalion, 2nd Canadian Infantry Brigade, did not know where they were, or where their trenches were, when they were relieved, Stevens to Edmonds, 24 February 1925, Cab 45/141, PRO.

[38]Duguid, *Official History*, General Series, 360–3. Urquhart, *Currie, 98–100, Confidential Reports by Captain G.W. Northwood, 8th Canadian Infantry Battalion*, Cab 45/156, PRO.

[39]Urquhart gives Currie a clean bill of health on this allegation; *Currie*, 95–98. Duguid, *Chronology, Appendices and Maps*, 287–92; nos. 633, 85 Brigade to 28 Division, timed 11:20 p.m. 24 April (Currie is out of touch with his Division); 635, 28 Division to 1 Canadian Division, timed 11:38 p.m. 24 April (Colonel Lipsett takes over command temporarily of 2nd Canadian Infantry Brigade, no reason given); 649, 28 Division to 1 Canadian Division, timed 8:40 a.m. 25 April (Brigadier [85 Bde.] states battalion on his left [this would be 5th Battalion of 2nd Canadian Infantry Brigade] retired at the double that he hung on as long as he could . . . '); 654, 10th Infantry Brigade to 1 Canadian Division, timed 9:15 a.m. 25 April (confusion, no news of 2nd Canadian Infantry Brigade); and 660, timed 12 noon 25 April; OC 7th Battalion (of 2nd Infantry Brigade) to OC 8th Battalion (of 2nd Canadian Infantry Brigade), 'Please get in touch with G.O.C. 2nd Can. Inf. Bde. [Currie] and advise him of situation. Also ask for instructions.'

[40]*Ibid.*, 288, no. 634, timed 11:35 p.m. 24 April, V Corps to 1 Canadian Division (all troops of 3rd CIB, and those of 27 & 28 Divs ordered back to GHQ line by Gen. Turner, 'thus giving up all the ground for which such a struggle has been made today & leaving the second bde. in the air . . . ', reverse the order!). J. Sutherland Brown (DAQMG of 1 Canadian Division) to MacBrien (CGS), 25 November 1925, RG 24, vol. 2680, part 1, and Duguid to CGS (MacBrien), 23 April 1936, RG 24, vol. 2680, part 2; Public Archives, Ottawa.

[41]Brigadier-General Jeudwine, then BGGS at V Corps, later told Edmonds that Snow was cheerful at his Division Headquarters at Potijze, when 'all the most important members [presumably senior staff and commanders] were hopelessly rattled and defeatist', Jeudwine to Edmonds, 2 October 1937, 1/259/168, Liddell Hart Papers, KCL.

[42]This is reflected both in Snow's 27 Division Report and Bulfin's 28 Division Report; and in the contents of two wires from 28 Division to 1 Canadian Division,

in the late afternoon of 24 April. Snow's report reads that the 2nd Canadian Infantry Brigade had fallen back and created a gap to the left of 28 Division, which Snow attempted to make Brigadier-General Turner's 3rd Canadian Infantry Brigade fill; Major-General Snow, 27 Division Report, 28 May 1915, 3; and also the Report of Major-General Bulfin, GOC 28 Division; 'About 1:00 p.m. [on 24 April] reports were received that the 2nd Inf Bde, Can Div, had been ordered to retire', 17 May 1915; Smith-Dorrien Papers, Cab 45/201, Part 2, PRO. The two wires from 28 Division were timed at 5:10 and 5:15 p.m. on 24 April, and both essentially sought to fill in gaps on 28 Division's left flank, which had been created by the falling back of elements of 2nd Canadian Infantry Brigade. The most interesting was 28 Division to 1 Canadian Division, 5:15 p.m., 24 April, regarding the return of two Battalions: 'These battalions were sent to FORTUIN [Currie's 2nd Canadian Infantry Brigade Headquarters] at three pm today [either when Snow and Currie were talking, or just after] by General Snow's orders as he was out of touch with me and heard the Germans were occupying FORTUIN.' Duguid, *Chronology, Appendices and Maps*, no. 616, 284. See also *ibid.*, 28 Division to 85, 84, 83 Brigades, 5:10 p.m. 24 April, no. 615, 284; and 27 Division to Turner, 3rd Canadian Infantry Brigade, 2:15 p.m., no. 600, 281. However, *all this has to be seen in light of Currie's efforts to repair the damage left by Turner's precipitate withdrawal of his Brigade.*

[43]Urquhart, *Currie*, 91. C.F. Romer to Duguid, April 1926, Cab 45/156, PRO.

[44]Currie to Duguid, 24 April 1926, RG 24, vol. 1755, part 1, no page numbers, and for Major Lynn, Duguid to Edmonds (draft letter), October 1936, RG 24, vol. 1756, part 2, 4–5; Public Archives, Ottawa.

[45]Duguid, *Chronology, Appendices and Maps*, Mersereau to 3rd Canadian Infantry Brigade, *c.* 12:30 p.m., 24 April, no. 563, 274; H.K. Betty to 3rd Canadian Infantry Brigade, 1:45 p.m., 24 April, no. 587, 279; Brigade Major to 1 Canadian Division, 1:50 p.m. 24 April, no. 587a, 279. At 5:15 p.m. Currie was still not back at his 2nd Canadian Infantry Brigade Headquarters; General Mercer, 1 Canadian Infantry Brigade to General Turner, 5:15 p.m., 24 April, no. 617, 284. By 11:00 p.m., Currie was back in command, Currie to 1 Canadian Division, 11:00 p.m., 24 April, no. 632, 287.

[46]Urquhart, *Currie*, 97, 101.

[47]Turner to GOC 2nd Canadian Infantry Brigade, 1:45 p.m. 24 April, no. 590, 280; Snow to Turner, 2:15 p.m., no. 600, 281; 1 Canadian Division to V Corps, 27 and 28 Divisions, 4:50 p.m., no. 604, 282; V Corps to 1 Canadian Division, 3:25 p.m., no. 606, 282; 28 Division to 1 Canadian Division, 4:35 p.m., no. 609, 283; 1 Canadian Division to 3rd Canadian Infantry Brigade, 4:35 p.m., no. 612, 283; 28 Division to 1 Canadian Division, 5:15 p.m., no. 616, 284; 3rd Canadian Infantry Brigade to 27 Division, no time, no. 618, 284; 3rd Canadian Infantry Brigade to Royal Irish Fusiliers, 7:20 p.m., no. 625, 285; 28 Division to 1 Canadian Division, 7:55 p.m., no. 626, 285–6; 3rd Canadian Infantry Brigade to 27 Division, 9:35 p.m., no. 631, 287; 85 Brigade to 28 Division, 11:20 p.m. no. 633, 287; V Corps to 1 Canadian Division, 11:35 p.m., no. 634, 288; 28 Division to 1 Canadian Division, 11:38 p.m., no. 635, 288; 27 Division to 3rd Canadian Infantry Brigade, 1:45 a.m., 25 April, no. 642, 289; 3rd Canadian Infantry Brigade to 27 Division, 2:45 a.m., no. 645, 289; Durhams, 3:20 a.m., no. 646, 289–90; Duguid, *Chronology, Appendices and Maps*. Some of the key messages are those from 27 Division to 3rd Canadian Infantry Brigade, and from the latter to units other than 1 Canadian

Division. Dancocks, *Currie*, 50. Duguid to Edmonds, 18 May 1925, 9–10, Cab 45/155, PRO.

[48]Lieutenant-General R.E.W. Turner to Duguid, 20 April 1926, Cab 45/156. C.F. Romer to Duguid, April 1926, Cab 45/156; C.F. Romer to Edmonds, 23 December 1925, Cab 45/156; and cf. C.F. Romer to Edmonds, 24 June 1926, Cab 45/156, PRO. Mildmay of Hele (27 Div. Staff) to Edmonds, 18 July 1924, Cab 45/140, PRO. It is fair to add that a competing Divisional commander thought that Snow's role was over-emphasized, Maj.-Gen. E. Bulfin (GOC 27 Div.) to Edmonds, 28 October 1925, *ibid.*

[49]28 Division to 1 Canadian Division, 24 April, 11:38 p.m., no. 635, 288. Duguid, *Chronology, Appendices and Maps.* Urquhart, *Currie*, 97, Dancocks, *Currie*, 52.

[50]Currie, 'Comments on 2nd Draft, British Official History', Public Archives, Ottawa, cited in Dancocks, *Currie*, 53. Dancocks is misled in saying that Currie spent all of 25 April at the 2nd Canadian Infantry Brigade forward command post at Gravenstafel, since there are messages from Currie at 2nd Canadian Infantry Brigade Headquarters at Wieltje to Gravenstafel, e.g., Duguid, *op. cit.*, 2nd Canadian Infantry forward command post to OC (Officer Commanding) 2nd Canadian Infantry Brigade (Wieltje), 3:22 p.m., 25 April, no. 671, 294. See also Edmonds's comments regarding Currie's presence at Wieltje in Duguid to Edmonds, 19 November 1925, 6, 10, Cab 45/155, PRO.

[51]Dancocks is misled here; the 2nd Canadian Infantry Brigade retirement evidently was not 'an orderly withdrawal'; Dancocks, *Currie*, 53. Urquhart is more accurate on this point; Urquhart, *Currie*, 99–100.

[52]Duguid to Edmonds, 19 November 1925, and Edmonds's comments, 10.6 (for 85 Battalion and 11 Infantry Brigade), Cab 45/155; for 8th Durham Light Infantry, see Stevens to Edmonds, 24 February 1925, Cab 45/141; also Major-General Bulfin, 28 Division Report, 17 May 1915, Cab 45/206, Part 2, PRO.

[53]For Currie's reply to 1 Canadian Division, about 11 p.m., 25 April, from Wieltje, no. 679, 296; Duguid, *Chronology, Appendices and Maps.* It is curious that Duguid reproduces very few of the messages sent during the evening of 25 April, although he clearly had access to several, including 1 Canadian Division to 2nd Canadian Infantry Brigade, 10:20 p.m., 25 April.

[54]Duguid to Edmonds, 19 November 1925, 10, Cab 45/155, PRO; Urquhart, *Currie*, 100. Edmonds says that the 2nd Canadian Infantry Brigade eventually moved back under the orders of Brig.-Gen. Hasler, GOC 11 Infantry Brigade; Edmonds, *Military Operations France and Belgium 1915*, 247. Duguid gives the hours of withdrawal in *Official History*, General Series, 363–4.

[55]This is again evident in Duguid's text, *ibid.*, 366–7.

[56]Edmonds, *Canadian Comments on '1915 (France)'*, vol. 1, 1 December 1926, 32–3, Cab 16/52, PRO; see, however, 2nd Canadian Infantry Brigade Report/War Diary, Public Archives, Ottawa, for the morning of 25 April, cited in Dancocks, *Currie*, 53, which has Currie reporting his 2nd Canadian Infantry Brigade to have been in a 'predicament', with men very tired and 'terrific' machine-gun and shell fire, and no artillery support. One wire on the morning of 25 April does seem to indicate that the 2nd Canadian Infantry Brigade was in some difficulty, and that 'General Currie said to be in FORTUIN. Have sent cyclist orderly also mounted officer to clear up situation about FORTUIN,' MacBrien, 10 Infantry Brigade to 1 Canadian Division, 9:15 a.m., 25 April, no. 654, 291; Duguid, *Chronology, Appen-*

dices and Maps. One other piece of evidence comes from Captain Northwood, 8th Battalion, 2nd Canadian Infantry Brigade, who reported that a message came from the 5th Battalion, 2nd Canadian Infantry Brigade, during the night of 24/25 April, asking when the 8th Battalion was going to retire. Northwood replied that his instructions were to hold on, *Confidential Report by Captain G.W. Northwood—8th Cdn. Inf. Batt.*, Cab 45/156, PRO.

[57]According to Andrew McPhail: 'The treatment of later battles is also causing alarm,' McPhail to Amery, 25 April 1926, Cab 45/156, PRO. See, in particular, the Canadian and British files in Cab 45/210, PRO, especially Edmonds to the Secretary, Historical Section, CID (E.Y. Daniel), 25 June 1928, and Edmonds to Daniel, 9 January 1929. Currie to Lord Horne, 20 March 1919, and Lord Horne to Currie, 27 March 1919, 73/60/2, General Lord Horne Papers, Imperial War Museum.

18

Quebec and the Great War

Susan Mann Trofimenkoff

The First World War, initially supported with enthusiasm by most
Canadians, dragged on for over four
years, producing ever-lengthening
casualty lists as well as profound and
rapid change in almost all aspects of
life. It forced Canada to mobilize its
agricultural sector and increase its
industrial output. Farmers were encouraged to overborrow and over-
produce, with devastating results
in the long run. The war led the
Canadian government into new
initiatives in domestic regulation of
economic and social life, from
income tax to prohibition. And the
sacrifice of fighting men, in battles
about which Canadian leaders were
not being consulted, led the Canadian government to a greater insistence on external autonomy within
the British Empire. At the same
time, the war demanded a commitment and a level of uncritical support for nation and empire that
many Canadians found beyond their
capacity. Any comments about the
senseless stupidity of the carnage or

Canada's role in it were regarded as
evidence of disloyalty, and the
Anglo-Canadian majority fiercely
resented French Canada's growing
hostility to the war, while openly
persecuting those from Germany
and eastern Europe who had settled
in the country. The First World War
was a crucible for the development
of modern propaganda techniques
and intolerance. While it may have
unified Anglo-Canadians, it also
helped alienate them from the remainder of the Canadian population.

Susan Mann Trofimenkoff explores the impact of the First
World War on Quebec. As she
observes, the war was not immediately perceived as a major threat to
French Canada; educational issues,
such as a dispute over bilingual
schools in Ontario, seemed far more
pressing in the early years of war.
But as the conflict ground on, as
casualties mounted and volunteers
declined in number, the government became convinced it needed a
new policy to meet its military

commitments. Under heavy pressure to 'equalize sacrifice' the government turned to conscription, which among other advantages would increase a very low Quebec military involvement in the war. By 1917 conscription had become the central issue for all Canadians, testing the anglophone majority's capacity to appreciate the views of the nation's minorities as well as Quebec's ability to transcend a tendency to interpret all unpopular majority actions as a threat to its way of life.

Why did Regulation XVII in Ontario become such a bone of contention in the early years of the war? What was the attitude of Québécois to the war? How did the government justify conscription? Was 'military necessity' a compelling argument? Does an individual —or a group of people—have the right, during periods of national emergency (such as war), to oppose the will of the majority, or the dictates of the government?

This article first appeared, titled 'The Prussians Are Next Door: Quebec and World War I', in *The Dream of Nation: A Social and Intellectual History of Quebec* (Toronto, 1983), 201–17.

Nationalists in Quebec have never forgotten the First World War and Liberal politicians have been a close second in reminding voters of its political ravages. For many nationalists the war years turned French Canada into Quebec. For many Liberals the blunders of federal Conservatives during the same years provided electoral ammunition for generations to come. To some French Canadians, the war revealed the basic incompatibility of Canada's two peoples: alien cultures finally exposed, in total disagreement over the demands of imperialism, the force of nationalism, and the logic of feminism. For other French Canadians, the crises of the war years—from Ontario schools to conscription to votes for women—were just that, temporary aberrations from the Canadian norm of compromise and forbearance. The difference of opinion within French Canada troubled the nationalists as much as English-Canadian hostility, although no one seemed unhappy to see the momentary reference to separatism disappear from the headlines as quickly as it appeared late in 1917.

Certainly separatist thoughts were far from anyone's mind in the summer of 1914. Even the vaguely voiced notion of Canadian autonomy from Britain was swept aside in a wave of enthusiasm for European military adventures. The British declaration of war on Germany in early August bound the entire empire, if not to actual participation, then to a legal state of war. In fact no one lingered over legal niceties: there was no questioning of Canadian support for and participation in the British war effort. Crowds in the cities of Quebec vied with those in other Canadian centres to express their emotion.

The Quebec government was as generous as that of the other provinces in offering an assortment of Canadian agricultural products freely to Britain. Four million tons of Quebec cheese thus made its way across the Atlantic accompanied by the salmon, hay, cattle, apples, and potatoes of the Canadian cornucopia. Only Henri Bourassa wryly commented upon the supplementary freight trains required to haul all the generosity to Canadian ports and the likelihood of much of it rotting on the quays of Liverpool before it could be distributed and consumed. But even he, although acknowledging no constitutional obligation to be involved in Britain's wars, admitted to a moral interest in the outcome for the two European countries with which Canadians had historical and emotional ties.

Canadian assistance and support was easy enough to offer when no one knew the extent or the demands of the war. Wilfrid Laurier, leader of the Liberal opposition in the House of Commons, offered his entire support to the Conservative government of Robert Borden. From the Liberals would come no questioning, not a word of reproach, as long as there was danger on the European front; the friends and foes of Great Britain should know that Canadian hearts and minds were united. Such magnanimity was as shortly lived as it was eloquently expressed. But in the spirited summer days of 1914, this political co-operation enabled the Canadian government to pass the War Measures Act, which sanctioned extensive controls over the lives and economic activities of Canadians. In Quebec the lieutenant governor offered all the resources of the province for the defence of Canada; Sir Lomer Gouin, the premier, indicated that Quebec government employees could enlist and continue to receive full salary. The Archbishops of Quebec and Montreal spoke of the sacred duty of Canadians to aid Great Britain. Only later in the war were appeals made in the name of Canada's two 'mother countries'; in the early months some French Canadians seriously wondered whether the war was not divine retribution for a France that had strayed from the path of true religion. The mayors of Quebec City and Montreal joined the chorus of assistance to Great Britain and the popular press followed suit. After all, the war was only supposed to last a few months; those few Canadian soldiers who were likely even to go overseas—as volunteers, the prime minister carefully assured the country—would be home for Christmas after a pleasant European tour.

The recruiting stations were barely open when some French Canadians began wondering just where the real battle was. Indeed, a number of nationalist leaders were being recruited, not to the Canadian Expeditionary Force—although there were some there such as Oliver Asselin, a military enthusiast ever since his participation in the Spanish-American War at the end of the nineteenth century—but rather to assist their French-speaking compatriots in Ontario. There, the Prussians were not across the Atlantic but across the street, the trenches held not by allied forces but by mothers armed with hatpins. The military analogies in the exaggerated language of Ottawa's *Le Droit*, a paper begun in 1913 to speak for the growing number of French Canadians in eastern Ontario, revealed both an ignorance of the horror of European trench warfare and the depth of the hurt occasioned by the Ontario school question. The intermingling of the war's demands with English Ontario's implacable hostility to all things French dampened French-Canadian enthusiasm for the war effort and created a new breed of nationalist.

The increasing number of French Canadians in Ontario seems to have been at the origin of the dispute over bilingual schools that began in 1912. By that date, one-tenth of Ontario's population was French-speaking as newcomers moved in from Quebec to join well-established communities in southwestern Ontario, to add to the newer settlers in the north along the lines of the National Transcontinental, or to swell the French presence in Ottawa and the counties of eastern Ontario. Their arrival complicated the lives of English-speaking Catholics, particularly in the schools, and raised fears among English-speaking Protestants, always suspicious of Catholicism and even more so when it was linked to the French language. Moreover the concentrated presence of French Canadians in three distinct areas of the province also had political implications for the Conservative provincial government. When many of them also showed signs of imitating their Quebec relatives by organizing formal interest groups, English-speaking Ontarians became distinctly hostile. In 1910, for example, the *Association canadienne-française d'éducation d'Ontario* held its first conference in Ottawa. Twelve hundred delegates from French-speaking areas of the province voiced their concern for the twenty-five thousand youngsters attending bilingual primary schools in the province: they wanted their children properly taught by competent teachers with legislative grants for their schools.

Other Ontarians had similar worries but for quite different reasons. Bilingual schools had no legal existence in the province; they had simply developed along with the French-speaking population, usually as part of the Catholic separate-school system constitutionally guaranteed since 1867, but sometimes, if a given district had no separate school, within the public-school system. Administrators in the ministry of education had nightmares about the complexities and the very thought of a third school system with multiple demands for classrooms, teachers, inspectors, and programs. Where would one find competent seventeen-year-olds able to teach the entire primary program in both languages and frequently in a single classroom for the scant hundred dollars annual salary offered by most school boards? Should French be encouraged at all when Ontario's industrial future, and the youngsters' place in it, was assuredly English? Like Manitobans of the late nineteenth century, English-speaking Ontarians could only measure progress in English terms.

Quebec nationalists always had difficulty with the fact that the school question surfaced because of the complaints of a Catholic bishop. The ideological connection that had been developing since the late nineteenth century, thanks largely to ultramontane logic, between language, religion, and nationality could not quite hold in the face of bitter Irish-French disputes in Ontario. The villain was supposed to be clad as an Orangeman; instead, in his first appearance, he wore the cassock of a priest. Monseigneur Fallon, the Bishop of London, complained to the Ontario government and the press that the bilingual schools in his diocese were producing poorly trained children, inferior to those in the English-language separate schools. The public controversy that swirled around Fallon's remarks induced the provincial government to investigate the bilingual schools of the province and, once the investigation confirmed the accusations, to pass regulatory measures. On the assumption that a single language would cure all the practical problems which the investigator, Dr Merchant, spotted in certain of the bilingual schools, the ministry of education added Regulation XVII to its decrees for elementary schools. Beginning as a mere directive in 1912, the regulation, slightly modified in the face of Franco-Ontarian opposition, became law in 1915. By then its purpose was hopelessly enmeshed with the Canadian war effort, as nationalists from Quebec fanned the flames of resentment between English- and French-speaking Ontarians.

To both Québécois and Franco-Ontarians, Regulation XVII implied the end of French-language teaching in Ontario. Its stipulation that French could be used as a language of instruction only in the first two years of the primary program, after which pupils were expected to know enough English to continue their schooling in that language, and that French as a subject of study should be limited to one hour a day, raised all the old fears of assimilation. In vain, and indeed not very loudly, did the Ontario government protest that the regulation only applied to an annually construed list of bilingual schools where English was inadequately taught or where the teachers lacked the proper qualifications. In vain did it tinker with the inspection system of the regulation: no one within the ministry of education or outside knew precisely how the regulation was to work or just what it intended. French Canadians, ever fearful, and increasingly sensitive to the question of language as the early twentieth century tumbled people together, believed the regulation meant their demise.

Little during the war years was to relieve their anxiety. While the Ontario government threatened to cut off provincial funds from schools that did not obey Regulation XVII, fanatical Protestants in the province urged even more severe restrictions. The Orange Order, claiming to defend British principles and therefore the English language, urged the abolition of all bilingual schools since they were agents of French-Canadian infiltration into the province. Worse still for the Orangemen was that those French Canadians were probably disloyal, given their poor showing in the enlistment figures for the war. Just as unsettling for French Canadians was the feud with their fellow Catholics. Prompted by Monseigneur Fallon, English-speaking Catholics, with a population three times that of the French in Ontario, argued that the senseless struggle over language risked endangering the much greater principle of Catholic education. If the French Canadians annoyed the Ontario government to such an extent that it decided to turn on separate schooling itself, where would Catholics be then? The two groups of Catholics came to legal blows in Ottawa when the English and French sections of the Ottawa separate-school board disputed the majority French section's defiance of Regulation XVII. While lawyers contested the validity of the regulation and of the government's means of enforcing it, French-speaking children and their mothers defended the schools and the teachers of their choice. A Laval University student newspaper cheekily remarked that the real threat to French civilization in the world was no longer in Flanders but in the schools of Ottawa.

Although the school question was to assist them in doing so, French Canadians had not yet drawn a frontier along the provincial boundary. Those in Quebec gladly lent their ideological and financial support to *Le Droit* and the *Association canadienne-française d'éducation d'Ontario*. The Franco-Ontarian leaders were all relative newcomers and they called upon intellectual and nationalist sustenance from their home province. Nationalist spokesmen from Quebec visited Ontario and reported on the struggle to their colleagues in Montreal and Quebec. Henri Bourassa was a favourite guest at Ontario gatherings; his powers of logic and persuasion were solace to the embattled minority. Bourassa in fact saw the French-speaking minorities in the rest of Canada as the outposts of Quebec: their defence against the attacks of a bigoted majority assured Quebec's own survival; if they succumbed, Quebec would be next. Bourassa's paper *Le Devoir* thus gave full coverage of the events in Ontario. Nationalist associations in Quebec held fund-raising campaigns to assist the Ontarians in their educational and legal defiance of Regulation XVII. Quebec bishops encouraged the campaigns and approved clerical ones launched from the pulpits of parish churches. The Catholic school commission of Montreal voted funds to assist the bilingual campaign in Ontario. Even the Quebec government, gingerly stepping on the minefield of interference in another province's affairs, passed a motion regretting the divisions over the bilingual school question in Ontario. It also permitted municipalities in the province to make financial contributions to patriotic, national, or educational causes, the latter intended to cover the Franco-Ontarian situation. Businesses even began to register the cost of French-Canadian unhappiness as Quebec clients refused to place orders with Toronto firms. Through it all, the force of numbers became increasingly obvious, although seldom openly admitted. French-Canadians were only safe in numbers and only in Quebec did they have the numbers.

Quebec's federal politicians would never make such an admission, but they too had to swallow much of the bitterness of the school question. Indeed, with some of the more dramatic episodes of the struggle taking place within shouting distance of Parliament Hill, they could hardly avoid the issue even if they had wanted to stay on the neutral terrain of education being a provincial matter. The tattered remains of the nationalist alliance with the Conservatives in 1911 rallied sufficiently to have cabinet ministers Pierre-Edouard Blondin, Thomas-Chase Casgrain, and Esioff-Léon Patenaude request that Prime Minister Borden refer the entire question of the status of the French language in Canada to the Privy Council for clarification. Borden refused on the grounds that the British North America Act was perfectly clear: French had a legal existence in the debates and recordings of the federal parliament, in those of the Quebec provincial legislature, and before the federal and Quebec courts. He refrained from adding 'and no further' as many Conservatives then and since have muttered. Nor would he, along with most English-Canadians, accept an argument for French based on natural right or even on the legally imaginative grounds that French Canadians, in Saskatchewan for example, required education in French in order to be able to take a case to a federal court in that province in their own language. In fact none of the defenders of bilingual schools in Ontario denied the necessity of learning English; they simply wanted their children taught in French as well.

But when such views were expressed in the federal parliament, they encountered a blank and sometimes hostile wall. Borden refused a petition from senator Philippe Landry and most of the Quebec bishops requesting federal disallowance of Regulation XVII; in the background some of his Conservative colleagues began to grumble about French-Canadian participation in the war effort. In May 1916, the MPs voted down an intricately worded resolution from Ernest Lapointe, Liberal member for Kamouraska, requesting that the Ontario government not infringe upon the linguistic privileges of French-speaking school children. The Liberal leader, Laurier, barely kept his Ontario members in line for the vote as westerners openly balked and voted with the Conservative majority. Behind the defeat, legitimate enough on the grounds of federal non-interference in provincial matters, was also the grim sentiment expressed by the former western Liberal MP, Clifford Sifton: the Franco-Ontarian agitation was criminal and unpatriotic at a time of national crisis. For Sifton and many English Canadians the real national crisis was on the European battlefield; for many French Canadians it was in the linguistic heart of Canada. When Abbé Lionel Groulx, six years later, placed the federal debate over the school question at the centre of his novel *L'Appel de la race*, he barely mentioned the war. But he did sanction the dissolution of a marriage—a personified Confederation—on the grounds of linguistic and racial incompatibility.

In 1916, however, the war could not be forgotten. Canadian involvement was about to produce a clash between French and English that would make the Ontario schools question pale in comparison. Rumours of compulsory military service were already touring the country when some of the signs of appeasement appeared in the bilingual-schools dispute. The courts left no doubt that Regulation XVII was quite within the power of the Ontario government although the learned law lords in London confessed to finding the language obscure, the effect difficult to ascertain, and some of the methods of enforcement dubious. But they also decreed that the Ottawa separate-school board was overstepping its jurisdiction by defying the regulation. The Pope also had a word to say on the matter. Responding to the appeal of different groups of Canadian Catholics, he advised moderation and tolerance. The unity of the Canadian Catholic church was essential and he was not at all sure that Quebec clerical involvement on behalf of the Franco-Ontarians was serving that cause. While a few French-Canadian priests wondered privately about the power of the Irish in Rome and Henri Bourassa pointedly refrained from any comment in *Le Devoir*, the papal directive did in fact carry some weight in calming emotions. Among English-speaking Ontarians, some soothing voices began to be heard as Liberals and businessmen invented *bonne entente* in an effort to repair the broken bridges of politics and commerce. Meanwhile the Ontario government found its regulation increasingly difficult to enforce and ultimately abandoned it in 1927. Only the Orange Order was left to fulminate against separate schools themselves, but even its fury abated when conscription offered a more exciting battleground for denouncing French Canadians. Although the schools question trailed off somewhat ignominiously, its stark lesson of numbers, reinforced by the implication of brute force in the conscription issue, was not forgotten.

By late 1916 the war that had been expected to be brief had become an endless bloodbath. It sucked up men, munitions, and supplies and buried them all in the trenches and then the mud of western Europe. Ever since the initial heroic send-off of one hundred thousand Canadians in the early autumn of 1914 from the final training camp at Valcartier near Quebec City, the numbers of enthusiastic recruits had steadily declined. There were only so many able-bodied recent British immigrants in the western provinces; they had been the first to respond to the imperial summons. In contrast, native-born Canadians held back, their tie to empire easily calculated by the number of generations their families had been in the country. The appeal of patriotism and religion, used effectively in both French and English Canada, began to wear thin as God appeared quite indifferent to the slaughter. Moreover the war was economically beneficial to Canada: western farms and eastern industries competed much more effectively for man and woman power than did the Canadian Expeditionary Force. But as the number of casualties rose and the number of recruits declined, the murmurings began.

Population figures alone meant that English-Canadian families were receiving more of the dreaded beige telegrams announcing death; the lists of wounded, missing, and demised were automatically longer in the English-language newspapers. But when the murmurings turned into a slogan—'equalization of sacrifice'—then people began watching the enlistment figures and pointing to that part of the country producing the fewest recruits.

Naturally, Quebec was at the bottom of the list. As the oldest Canadians, Québécois had the least interest in the war; no emotional tie pulled them to Britain or France. Besides, they had never found a comfortable place in the Canadian military service. Even the frequent presence of a French Canadian as minister or deputy minister of the Department of the Militia could not camouflage the essentially alien character of the institution for French Canadians. Few of the higher officers were French-speaking. Only a tiny fraction of the cadets at the Royal Military College in Kingston, the training school for military officers, was French Canadian and all the instruction was in English. Being an officer meant being or becoming English. The senior officers of the permanent, as distinct from voluntary, militia tended in fact to be British and they shared imperial enthusiasms. They had neither time nor patience for developing military attachments among French Canadians. The suggestion that a distinctive uniform, modelled on that of the *Zouaves*, might add to the attractiveness of the military for young French Canadians was vetoed at the very time when some English-Canadian regiments were permitted to don the equally foreign and much less practical kilt. Not surprisingly, by 1912, there were only twenty-seven French-Canadian compared to two hundred and twenty-seven English-Canadian permanent officers in the Canadian militia.

Furthermore, nothing during the war years made French Canadians any more welcome in Canadian military ranks. The language of instruction and command remained English. The difficulty of raising and maintaining French-speaking units without having them dispersed to reinforce others was obvious in the amount of political pressure required to form and sustain the French Canadian Royal 22nd Battalion. There at least French Canadians were able to develop an outstanding military force of their own, envied indeed by English Canadians. But elsewhere, appointments or promotions of French Canadians to the higher ranks of the military were few and far between. Even the minister of the militia during the early years of the war, Sam Hughes, could not hide his hostility: he particularly did not wish to have French-speaking military units accompany Catholic popular processions. And he was careful to keep the one French-Canadian general, François-Louis Lessard, busy in Canada instead of sending him overseas. Also, his own department established crude enlistment quotas based on a simple proportion of the total Canadian population. With twenty-eight per cent of the population, Quebec should be producing twenty-eight per cent of the recruits. Proportionately to the other regions of the country, however, Quebec had fewer men of military age, fewer bachelors, fewer casual labourers, and fewer British born, all of whom tended to be first in line at the recruiting stations. No statistics measured the impact of the Ontario school question or of Henri Bourassa's increasingly virulent anti-war tirades in *Le Devoir*. Although dead silence greeted Armand Lavergne's outburst in the Quebec legislature early in 1916 that every penny spent on recruitment in Quebec was money stolen from the Ontario minority, the mass-circulation *La Presse* placed the controversy over bilingual schools in Ontario at the head of its list of reasons why French Canadians did not rush to enlist. Given so little encouragement to do so, it is perhaps surprising that as many as thirty-five thousand French Canadians found their way into Canada's armed forces by 1918 at all (approximately half of them before conscription and half after).

By early 1917 conscription was more than just a rumour. Prime Minister Borden was determined to raise the number of Canada's soldiers to half a million, a figure he had set a year earlier. But the task became all the more difficult as the number of recruits no longer kept pace with the increasing casualties. The war itself was particularly bleak, the outcome no longer sure, and the end nowhere in sight. Russia withdrew from the allied cause into revolutions and civil war; the United States had not yet rallied its forces; the French army was fed up and mutinous; successful submarine warfare sapped the strength and morale of Britain. All of that Borden absorbed in a visit to England in the spring of 1917. At the same time he admitted that volunteers were no longer forthcoming in Canada. Neither national registration nor the idea of a home defence force early in 1917 succeeded in producing new recruits. National registration in fact raised more suspicion than enthusiasm. This country-wide registration of talent and availability for various wartime jobs also recorded the number of military prospects, and French Canadians were not alone in suspecting a trap. Both the Liberal press and labour organizations across the country joined them in wondering about the political motives of the enquiry. At the same time, employers and unions alike resisted the government's suggestion that more female labour be hired in order to release men for military service. In last-minute efforts to attract men, the military itself consented to lowering its medical standards while recruiting agents took to haranguing crowds lined up for Saturday-night entertainment. French Canada's one general attempted his own campaign for volunteers in Quebec. But the indifference was constant and it was all across the country. The people who were by then shouting so loudly for conscription clearly were not the same people as those who were supposed to sign up.

One of the first victims of conscription may have been in the House of Commons itself where the Military Service Bill proposing conscription was introduced in June 1917. Sir Wilfrid Laurier, far too old for military service, may yet have felt most severely the brunt of compulsion in the bill. During the debate over the government proposal to raise one hundred thousand recruits from various categories of male British subjects aged between twenty and forty-five, Laurier was forced to preside over the disintegration of the Liberal party. His westerners had already balked over the Lapointe resolution a year earlier; now they were adamant supporters of the government's conscription bill. Some of them were already dickering with the Conservatives about a possible 'Union' government that would unite all right-thinking Canadians in a thorough prosecution of the war effort. Laurier himself wavered just long enough to sense that any co-operation on his part in imposing conscription would send Quebec voters in droves into the nationalist embrace of Henri Bourassa. He therefore drew back from the temptation to join a Union government. But the various votes on the conscription bill carried off many of Laurier's followers from Ontario and the Maritimes, voting with their western colleagues in favour of conscription. To his remnant of French-Canadian Liberals from Quebec was added a handful of one-time nationalists from the Conservative benches. Laurier was thus forced to abandon his concept of national unity and to take on the leadership of one group only, a group primarily defined by language and race. In opposing conscription Laurier was also forced to discard his own promise of 1914 of a united war effort; Canadian hearts and minds were far from united on this question and he could not pretend otherwise. Given that stand, Laurier was then forced to pursue his opposition to conscription all the way to a federal election. No unanimous consent was forthcoming to prolong the life of parliament as had happened in 1916 to avoid the disruptions of a wartime election. Unanimity no longer existed and the disruptions would have to take their course. That they did, and very bitterly too, in the federal election of December 1917.

Laurier's reasoned parliamentary opposition to conscription was a careful translation of the emotional opposition seething in Quebec. Laurier argued from law and precedent and politics: none of them sanctioned conscription. The government had no mandate to impose compulsory military service on the country. Some Liberals even accused the Conservatives of digging up conscription as a popular cause to cover up a moribund government. Certainly the measure was part of an increasing number of controls exercised by the federal government over the lives of ordinary Canadians. Justified by the war and facilitated by the War Measures Act, various controls from rationing to price-fixing, from decrees against hoarding to those against loitering, probably overwhelmed the civil service more than anyone else, but they did indicate the state's willingness to go beyond persuasion to actual coercion in directing the activities of its citizens. Provincial governments—all except Quebec's—had also imposed restrictions, most notably in supervising the drinking habits of people by means of prohibition; the federal government would follow suit in 1918, although none of the laws lasted very long. Even the votes and incomes of Canadians came under close scrutiny by the federal government. By means of the Wartime Elections Act in 1917, the Conservatives carefully disfranchised certain Canadians of European background and just as carefully enfranchised the female relatives of soldiers. And in the same year the government introduced the income tax, thereby controlling the revenues of all Canadians, supposedly as a temporary measure to meet the mounting costs of the war effort. In such a context conscription was hardly an unusual idea. To Laurier, however, the setting could be no excuse: conscription was an illegitimate ploy on the part of a flagging government. The least it could do was hold a referendum on the question. Laurier may have expected the government to lose such a referendum, given the opposition of the working classes and of French Canadians to conscription. And if it won, well, there would at least be some democratic justification for the measure.

The difficulty was that the democratic numbers game on such an issue was racially fixed. On the whole, English Canadians supported conscription and were easily able to silence the protests of farmers and workers in western Canada; French Canadians virtually unanimously opposed it. It was all very well for French-Canadian Liberal politicians in Ottawa or Quebec to follow Laurier's lead and claim that Quebec would accept a Canadian verdict in a referendum; they really could not be sure. The issue cut too close to the bone: it was a majority of a different language and culture imposing military service for a foreign war upon a minority. In that light democracy could be an instrument of force. No one spoke of rape, Canadians of the time being much too prudish; but many people did recall the Conquest. No one in the eighteenth century had asked permission for that use of force; no one was likely to do so in the twentieth. Laurier's amendment to the Military Service Bill, that it be submitted to a popular referendum, was soundly defeated.

With the passage of the Military Service Bill, popular passions over conscription intensified throughout the summer and early autumn of 1917. While Henri Bourassa wrote in *Le Devoir* of national suicide for a foreign cause, the *Globe* in Toronto referred to conscription as fresh dedication to the cause of liberty. Mass meetings in Quebec filled the Sunday air with protest. Some federal Conservatives from Quebec hastily resigned from the government; others, remaining and even voting for conscription, knew that their political days were numbered. Young men took off for the woods, preferring to camp out in hiding rather than risk the legal intricacies of the exemption process. Senior students in classical colleges suddenly sported clerical garb and earnestly declared their intention to become priests, an occupation exempt from conscription. A last-minute attempt at a voluntary recruiting netted a grand total of ninety young men in the province. In some minds, the possibility of civil war loomed as a logical, perhaps even a deserved, consequence of the government's insensitivity. The Ontario schools question surfaced again, tangled with the conscription debate in the Commons, and left French Canadians profoundly uneasy about their place in Confederation. Attacks on their language and their faith were crystallizing in the imposition of military service. Henri Bourassa claimed that the conscription law, enacted early in August 1917, was an open invitation for a popular uprising.

The uprising, such as it was, occurred in the form of a federal election. The Conservatives took no chances on the outcome. They lured conscriptionist Liberals from the West into a Union government and ensured even more western backing by exempting twenty-year-old farm workers from their military obligations. They even wooed the women with the strange beginnings of federal woman suffrage in Canada. Assuming that the wives, daughters, and sisters of Canadian soldiers would vote Conservative in order to bring their men home sooner, the government accorded them the vote. It also organized the overseas military vote in such a way as to favour Conservative candidates. The government hardly needed the popular press to fan passions and prejudices, but that was precisely what the elections of 1917 did. Of the many issues confronting the country from profiteering and the cost of living to immigration and the nationalization of the railways, the press preferred the sensationalism of Quebec's opposition to conscription and English Canada's reaction to it. The English-language press quoted Henri Bourassa's arguments against the war and treated him, and by extension all French Canadians, as a traitor. A vote for Laurier would be a vote for Bourassa, for Quebec control of the entire country, for withdrawal from the war, and for the imposition of bilingual schools throughout the land. Quebec was the spoiled child of Confederation and should be compelled to do its share for the war effort. A map of Canada depicted Quebec in black, the 'foul blot' on the country. Surrounded by such images, Unionist candidates in Quebec could hardly open their mouths. They were heckled, shouted down, pelted with rotten eggs, and threatened with revolver shots. No paper would carry their message to French-speaking voters. The nationalists, less of an organized political force than in 1911 but holding a much more volatile issue, urged support for Laurier, a mere six years after they had turned on him as a traitor. They insisted upon the suspension of the Military Service Act while Laurier stated more vaguely the Liberal policy of maintaining Canada's war effort by voluntary means. The result was predictable: all the ridings but three in Quebec voted Liberal; all the ridings but twenty in the rest of the country returned Unionist candidates. No one took heart in the mere three hundred thousand popular-vote difference between Unionists and Liberals, since the parliamentary composition was much more striking: Quebec in opposition and English Canada in power.

The first response came from the Quebec legislature. A rather sorrowful motion, introduced by Joseph-Napoléon Francoeur, raised the question of separatism. If Quebec was so despised, perhaps it should opt out. Although a few students and an obscure clerical paper trumpeted the power of an independent Quebec with its control of rail and shipping routes, Francoeur was much more despondent and the assembly greeted his motion in the same way. A rather desultory debate never even came to a vote on the dreary proposition that:

> This House is of the opinion that the province of Quebec would be disposed to accept the breaking of the Confederation pact of 1867 if, in the other provinces, it is believed that she is an obstacle to the union, progress and development of Canada.

With the onus put upon the rest of Canada, few Québécois presumed to read the minds of their English-speaking compatriots, minds that had spoken all too clearly in the recent elections.

Neither the election nor the hint of separatism put a stop to French-Canadian opposition to conscription nor even to government blundering in its relations with Quebec. Only in January 1918 were the first men requested to report for military induction and most of them successfully claimed exemptions. Conscription ultimately produced some eighty thousand soldiers in Canada, about a quarter of whom were from Quebec but not all French Canadians. Few of them went overseas, let alone to the battlefront, before the end of the war in November 1918. The numbers were minimal for the hostility aroused and the symbolism created. Few French-Canadian families would forget English-speaking agents ferreting out their young men. Few young men would forget the months in hiding to escape the law or, for those enrolled, the low status of a conscript especially if he spoke French. More dramatic, because more public, were the anti-conscription riots in Quebec City in the early spring of 1918. Sparked by mounted police rounding up presumed defaulters and fed by popular discontent over wartime prices and rationing, the unrest boiled around the provincial capital for three days. True to form and no doubt fearing complicity between rioters and French-Canadian troops, Borden had English-speaking soldiers from Toronto sent to assist in quelling the disturbances. Well might some Québécois wonder just where the war was being fought.

For other French Canadians an even greater threat to the social order was issuing from Ottawa. Relegating *Le Devoir*'s commentary on the Quebec City riots to his second-in-command, Henri Bourassa took on what he obviously considered a much more serious problem, that of suffrage for women. By 1917 all of the provinces west of Quebec had introduced the suffrage, and the women involved had no intention of limiting their voting to the provincial sphere. They argued their special interest in matters of social reform, from prohibition to public health. They pointed to their wartime activities in fund-raising, support to the troops, and actual military service as nurses. Speaking through the National Council of Women, various women's associations convinced Prime Minister Borden to enlarge his peculiar precedent of 1917 and introduce total woman suffrage for federal elections. The bill was progressing through its various stages in the Commons at the very time of the anti-conscription riots in Quebec City. Meanwhile, Bourassa was exposing in *Le Devoir* all the ill effects of woman suffrage. Once women had the vote they would no longer marry since they would be engaged in fearsome competition with men. The family would thereby disintegrate, the education of children would be abandoned, and the privileged position that women now merited because of their maternal functions would disappear. Social degradation would follow woman's degradation.

For Bourassa, the suffrage, like feminism, was one more foreign import threatening the social structure of French Canada. It was a direct consequence of the individualism of Protestant religions; perhaps it suited Anglo-Saxon women who had long since lost their ability to influence society by feminine charm and natural means, but it was quite alien to French and Catholic women. The latter, Bourassa was convinced, did not want the vote; they were surely glad to be free of the civil and military duties that accompany a say in public affairs. Nor would they wish to take part in the cabals and base intrigue of political warfare. Their place was quite literally in the home; only by staying there could they aspire to any social role at all, let alone one claiming superiority. To step into the public sphere was to defy their sex, to deny the family as the basic social unit, to disrupt all notion of hierarchy and authority, to destroy the subordination of right to duties. In spite of the feminist argument that the vote was a mere means of bringing women's moral and social concerns to bear more directly on society, Bourassa spotted the radicalism of the measure. Once women had the vote they would be in a position of equality with men in terms of their relationship to the state. That relationship would no longer be mediated by men and who knew what the social consequences of that challenge to the natural order might be? Expressing what the Montreal *Gazette* termed 'mouldy ideas', Bourassa and some of the French-Canadian opponents of the woman suffrage bill in the House of Commons—none of whom was able to stop the bill's passage—thought they knew what suffrage would lead to and they did not like the prospect at all. French Canada would be irretrievably changed, and for the worse.

A number of clerics added their amen to the views of Bourassa and the politicians. The theologian Louis-Adolphe Paquet, surveying the world from within the walls of the Quebec seminary where he taught candidates for the priesthood, also foresaw the evil of women in competition with men as a result of the suffrage. With Saint Paul, Saint Thomas, and the current Pope, Benedict XV, on his side, Paquet could safely condemn the challenge to authority, the family, and society that lay behind feminist demands. But he was not as sure as Bourassa that the demands were foreign. Rather he feared that much in contemporary French-Canadian society actually spawned feminism: the education of young girls was much too similar to that of boys; too many young women defied parental authority in their clothing and their behaviour; the economic necessity of jobs in industry and commerce, which Paquet acknowledged, took women out of their homes, tossed them together, and facilitated their developing new aspirations. Paquet would have girls carefully educated for their maternal and religious role, differentiating their training not by talent but by class. No matter whom they married, all young women would have the same basic function—to develop the virtue of their sons and sustain the faith of their husbands, although depending on whether their husband was a farmer or a judge, their station in life would be different and would require special training. The Cardinal Archbishop of Quebec, Monseigneur Bégin, echoed Paquet's views by carefully culling papal antipathy to woman suffrage and passing it on to his priests. In their teaching and preaching, they were to keep in mind that neither the interests of society nor natural law justified votes for women. The Catholic press dutifully followed suit in opposing suffrage for women.

The major feminist organization in Quebec, the *Fédération nationale Saint-Jean-Baptiste*, also followed the clerical directive and subordinated its early interest in the suffrage. Instead it concentrated on preparing women for the proper exercising of the vote. Working as closely as it did with clerical groups, the *Fédération* perhaps could not avoid the intense hostility the male hierarchy of the church evinced towards the idea of legal equality for women. Sharing similar views about the roles of women in the family, in society, and in the preservation of French-Canadian culture, the women of the *Fédération* may have been just as sensitive to the enormous wounds the war years delivered to French Canada. Those wounds in turn may have reinforced the feminists' compulsion to soothe rather than disrupt. Certainly the journalist Fadette, writing in *Le Devoir*, thought Quebec women would exercise their new-found and unasked-for federal political right with more moderation than English-Canadian women: she was half-pleased and half-alarmed to see the Montreal Women's Club, a member of the local branch of the National Council of Women, split over the issue of conscription. Once women entered politics, she surmised, all their endeavours would be contaminated.

The fear of contamination coloured many French-Canadian reactions during the years of the First World War. The English-Canadian association of imperialism and nationalism was fraught with dangers (notably that of fighting in distant wars) for French Canadians who associated nationalism with anti-imperialism. The French-Canadian link between language, religion, and nationality had proven to be tenuous when confronted with co-religionists who spoke another language and compatriots who professed another religion, all of whom tied the future of a quite different Canadian nation to the

English language. And in the face of a determined majority on the conscription issue, an equally determined minority could only succumb: conscription does not permit compromise. When that same majority went beyond trampling on the national sensitivities of French Canadians to threaten a fundamental notion of social order in the family by granting women the vote in 1918, the minority could only withdraw into self-protection, nursing its differences in an alien world. With Prussians in various guises on all the frontiers, it was time to shore up the defences.

Suggestions for Further Reading

Elizabeth H. Armstrong, *The Crisis of Quebec, 1914–1918* (New York, 1937).

J.L. Granatstein and J.M. Hitsman, *Broken Promises: A History of Conscription in Canada* (Toronto, 1977).

John Herd Thompson, *The Harvests of War: The Prairie West, 1914–1918* (Toronto, 1978).

19

Women and Work

Graham S. Lowe

From the mid-nineteenth century on, increasing numbers of Canadian women left the home and farm (and various employments within them) to enter the outside workforce. Most were motivated by financial considerations interacting with a constantly increasing sense of the need for autonomy and independence. Women did not become evenly distributed across the previously male labour force, however, in either a horizontal—across occupations—or vertical—within an occupation—sense. Instead, they tended to cluster at the bottom of certain occupations, which became 'feminized'. Most of those were in the service sector, often associated with the traditional female values of nurture and caring. Thus nursing (which had always had a strong female component) was joined by teaching, particularly at the elementary school level, and afterindustrialization by such occupations as telephone operator, sewing-machine operator, and department store

salesperson, as almost exclusively female preserves. In many of these occupations, women supplanted men, both because they worked for lower wages and because, given gender stereotypes, they seemed particularly appropriate and well-suited for the task involved.

The process of 'feminization' is analysed by Graham Lowe in terms of another occupation that produced a 'female job ghetto': office clerical work. According to Lowe, feminization was a central component of the administrative revolution that struck Canadian offices in the first third of the twentieth century. Lowe offers some alternative explanations of this behaviour, finally opting for a structural interpretation that concentrates on the restructuring of office work into a large number of fragmented, specialized, and regimented jobs unattractive to middle-class males. These jobs were seen as part-time or temporary, and thus suitable for women whose proper place was at any rate in the home. Feminization, emphasizes Lowe, did not simply mean the replacement of men with women, but also the creation of a new female underclass of worker, paid less and prevented from advancing up the administrative hierarchy by segmentation and segregation. What alternative explanations for the feminization process does Lowe advance? Why does he reject them? How does technology play its part in feminization? Could women have altered the process by behaving differently? Why or why not?

This article first appeared, titled 'Women, Work and the Office: The Feminization of Clerical Occupations in Canada, 1901–1931', in *Canadian Journal of Sociology* 5, 4 (1980), 361–81.

The spectacular growth of white-collar occupations in Canada since the turn of the century has fundamentally altered the nature of the labour force. One of the most striking features of the burgeoning white-collar sector has been the shift in the sex ratio of many jobs accompanying the rise in female labour force participation rates. Nowhere has this feminization trend been more pronounced than in clerical occupations. At the turn of the century the office was largely a male preserve. Yet by 1971, 30.5 per cent of the entire female labour force was engaged in clerical work. And with about 70 per cent of all clerical jobs held by women, the contemporary office is the prototypical female job ghetto (Armstrong and Armstrong, 1978; Braverman, 1974; Kanter, 1977; Lowe, 1979).[1] Much can be learned about the emergence and maintenance of female job ghettos by examining how the feminization of clerical work occurred.

The purpose of this paper is to analyse how women came to predominate numerically in the office. A main theme of the paper is that the feminization process was central to the administrative revolution which occurred in major Canadian offices during the first three decades of the twentieth century. The administrative revolution accompanied, and indeed facilitated, the transition from small-scale entrepreneurial capitalism to modern corporate capitalism.[2] The hallmark of this revolution was the rise of large, centralized office bureaucracies and the growing importance of administration in regulating economic activity (see Braverman, 1974; Mills, 1956; Lockwood, 1966; Lowe, 1979). The nature of clerical work was dramatically altered: clerical ranks expanded tremendously between 1901 and 1931; the relative socio-economic position of the clerk was eroded;[3] and office organization and the clerical labour process were rationalized.

The feminization process is fundamental to all of these changes. For example, the influx of women into the office largely accounted for the growth of clerical occupations. This in turn undermined the socio-economic position of the clerical group, as women were paid less than men. And scientifically oriented managers, seeking greater administrative efficiency and more direct control over the office, created a new stratum of routine clerical jobs into which women were channelled. Thus, by the start of the depression, the old-style male bookkeeper had been replaced by an army of subordinate female clerks. As any observer of the contemporary office is quick to recognize, the legacy of this feminization process is still vital.

Four major questions will guide our analysis. First, how did clerical jobs come to be defined as 'women's work'? Second, what factors motivated employers to shift their source of labour supply in this manner? Third, to what extent do the characteristics of female clerks (relatively low wages, low skill levels, lack of opportunities, powerlessness, lower aspirations, and tenuous attachment to the labour force) reflect the nature of the jobs into which they have traditionally been channelled? And fourth, did women *displace* men in existing clerical jobs or *replace* them in qualitatively different kinds of work? Our investigation of these issues will proceed as follows: The first section of the paper will use census data to trace the major contours in the historical evolution of the female clerical labour force in Canada. The second section will evaluate various theoretical perspectives on female labour force participation in light of our research concerns. Emphasis will be placed on developing a historical analysis which relates changing labour force characteristics to transformations in the workplace. The third section will document how the female clerical labour market has its roots in the administrative revolution by examining three case studies of how changes occurred in the clerical labour process and office organization.

The Feminization of Clerical Work: Historical Trends

The entry of women into the office can be traced back to the closing decades of the nineteenth century. In the post-Confederation period women were usually relegated to servile domestic chores. In 1868, for example, the federal civil service employed only one woman, a housekeeper (Dawson, 1929: 190). This situation began to change, and by 1885 there were twenty female clerks working in the federal government (Payne, 1907: 511).[4] Yet many of today's major offices were slow to hire women. Sun Life Assurance Company in Montreal, for example, did not appoint its first female clerk until 1894 (*Sunshine*, November 1911: 142). Attitudes towards the employment of women in offices were becoming more tolerant. Jean Scott (1889: 24) was thus able to observe in 1889 that 'women seem as fitted for (office) work as men, and have proved as competent where the work was not too severe.'

The small number of women found in Canadian offices prior to 1900 reflected generally low female labour force participation rates. The 1891 Dominion Census, the earliest to break down occupational data by sex, shows that 11.4 per cent of the female population over the age of ten were

gainfully employed, comprising only 12.6 per cent of the entire labour force
(Canada, DBS, 1939: 4). After the turn of the century, however, powerful
new economic forces began restructuring the division of labour in industry.
By the end of the First World War, the foundation for a modern industrial
capitalist economy had been laid (Firestone, 1953: 152). A number of other
factors—the development of the modern joint stock corporation and the
public bureaucracy; changing attitudes towards the employment of women;
labour shortages during World War I; and the growing importance of more
efficient forms of administration—combined with industrialization to shape
the pattern of clerical feminization.

Tables 1 and 2 indicate that women made significant advances in clerical
employment after 1901. There were relatively few clerks in the labour force
in 1891, the vast majority being male (Table 1). The number of female clerks
increased from 4,710 to 12,660 between 1891 and 1901. While this represents a relative growth rate of 168.8 per cent (Table 2), almost ten times that
for the total female labour force, the female share of clerical jobs only
increased from 14.3 per cent to 22.1 per cent (Table 1). But this marked the
emergence of a trend which, by 1971, had resulted in the concentration of
30.5 per cent of all female workers in clerical occupations (Table 1).

The segregation of women into specific industries and occupations has
remained surprisingly stable since 1900 (Armstrong and Armstrong,
1978: 20). This is especially true in the case of clerical work. From 1901 to
1971, the share of clerical jobs held by females jumped from 22.1 per cent
to 68.9 per cent. Segregation was even more pronounced within particular
office jobs. In stenography and typing, for example, the 'female' label became
firmly affixed as the proportion of jobs held by women increased from 80
per cent to 95 per cent between 1901 and 1931.[5] Furthermore, changes in
the industrial concentration of clerical employment between 1911 and 1931
set the course of future developments (Lowe, 1979: 187). By 1931, manufacturing, finance and trade each accounted for over 20 per cent of all female
clerical employment (Lowe, 1979: 189).[6] These industries were at the forefront of corporate capitalism and their development required the rapid
expansion of administration.

The growth of administration is evident in Table 2. From 1891 to 1921,
the inter-censal decade growth rate for female clerks exceeded 166 per cent,
far outstripping increases in the total female labour force. In other words,
clerical feminization originated during the 1890s and accelerated dramatically
between 1901 and 1921. Indeed, the 1911–21 decade was pivotal to the
development of the modern office, containing the greatest surge in clerical
employment of the century. Clerical growth tapered off somewhat during
the 1920s, but changes in the nature of clerical work make this a decisive
period for the creation of a female job ghetto in the office. Women were
well on their way to predominating in the office by 1931, holding 45.1 per
cent of all clerical jobs (Table 1).

Table 1. Total labour force, clerical workers and female clerical workers, Canada, 1891–1971*

	Total labour force	Total clerical	Clerical workers as a percentage of total labour force	Female clerical	Females as a percentage of total clerical	Female clerks as a percentage of total female labour force
1891	1,659,335	33,017	2.0	4,710	14.3	2.3
1901	1,782,832	57,231	3.2	12,660	22.1	5.3
1911	2,723,634	103,543	3.8	33,723	32.6	9.1
1921	3,164,348	216,691	6.8	90,577	41.8	18.5
1931	3,917,612	260,674	6.7	117,637	45.1	17.7
1941	4,195,951	303,655	7.2	152,216	50.1	18.3
1951	5,214,913	563,083	10.8	319,183	56.7	27.4
1961	6,342,289	818,912	12.9	503,660	61.5	28.6
1971	8,626,930	1,310,910	15.2	903,395	68.9	30.5

SOURCES:

1. Canada D.B.S., Census Branch, *Occupational Trends in Canada, 1891–1931* (Ottawa, 1939), Table 5.

2. Meltz, *Manpower in Canada* (Ottawa: Queen's Printer, 1969), Section 1, Table A–1, A–2 and A–3.

3. 1971 Census of Canada, Volume 3, Part 2, Table 2.

*Data adjusted to 1951 Census occupation classification.

Table 2. Percentage increases, female labour force and female clerical workers,
Canada, 1891–1971*

	Female labour force	Female clerical workers
1891–1901	17.7	168.8
1901–1911	53.3	166.4
1911–1921	34.0	168.6
1921–1931	36.0	29.9
1931–1941	27.1	29.4
1941–1951	39.7	109.7
1951–1961	51.3	57.8
1961–1971	68.2	79.4

SOURCES:

1. Canada D.B.S., Census Branch, *Occupational Trends in Canada, 1891–1931* (Ottawa, 1939), Table 5.
2. Meltz, *Manpower in Canada* (Ottawa: Queen's Printer, 1969), Section 1, Tables A-1, A-2 and A-3.
3. 1971 Census of Canada, Volume 3, Part 2, Table 2.

*Based on data adjusted to 1951 Census occupation classification.

Chart 1 compares the actual number of male and female clerks in 1971 with what these numbers would have been had the occupational structure and sex composition of the labour force remained constant since 1901. The chart confirms that the clerical sector was a major source of new employment during this century. Furthermore, it illustrates the importance of female employment to the overall growth of clerical occupations.

We have traced the institutionalization of women as the major source of labour for modern clerical work. This underscores a central theme of the paper: that the entry of women into the office coincided with the proliferation of many new fragmented, routine jobs in the lower reaches of administrative hierarchies. Truncated employment opportunities for women and deeply engrained sex-based wage differentials resulted. We thus find that in 1901, female clerks earned 53 per cent of the average male clerical salary, inching up only slightly to 58 per cent by 1971 (Lowe, 1979: 223).[7]

The working conditions faced by female clerks have created a vicious circle. Low wages tend to produce the kind of work patterns—high turnover, short-term labour force attachment, and low aspirations—which reinforce employers' discriminatory attitudes and trap women in a relatively small number of female-dominated jobs. The underlying causes of these employment patterns deserve careful theoretical consideration.

Theoretical Perspectives

Why, then, did women become concentrated into a handful of lower level occupations as growing numbers of them entered the work force after 1900?

Chart 1. Changes in the clerical sector of the Canadian labour force, by sex, 1901–1971*

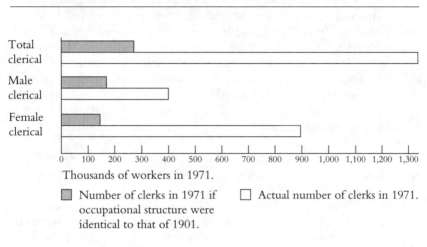

Thousands of workers in 1971.

■ Number of clerks in 1971 if occupational structure were identical to that of 1901.   □ Actual number of clerks in 1971.

* *Comparison between social distribution in 1971 and distribution calculated on basis of 1901 occupational structure, standardized to 1951 base.*

Explanations of this can be classified into four basic models: the consumer choice model, the reserve army of labour model, the demand model, and the segmentation model. In considering each of these theoretical perspectives below, we will assess its ability to account for the changing sex ratio of clerical jobs during the early twentieth century in Canada.

The consumer choice model
The consumer choice model, a common explanation of changing female work rates, is based on the concept of rational economic choice. The model is principally concerned with how married women decide to allocate their time between work within the home, work outside the home, and leisure. A central assumption is that employment decisions are rooted in the family context. For example, a wife may decide to work for pay outside the home because of a family consensus that the husband's income should be supplemented. Variables such as the wife's age, education, fertility, and potential earning power; stage in the family lifecycle; and husband's income, education, and occupation are also deemed important in the decisions regarding work (see Ostry, 1967).

The social, economic, and demographic variables included in the model may merely *reflect* rather than *affect* work rates (Madden, 1973: 9). The assumption that a woman's choice of whether or not to work is based on factors over which she has control tends to obscure the influence of social and economic structures (Connelly, 1978: 6; Armstrong and Armstrong, 1975). Furthermore, the model's emphasis on how family expectations shape a woman's work decision suggests that subjective processes ultimately determine behaviour. Consequently, insufficient attention is given to the limitations placed on female work rates by structural factors outside the home, such as the type of job opportunities and earnings available to women and the family's class position. Moreover, the model tends to discount the importance of interaction between the supply of women workers and the type of employer demand for their labour. Why, for example, did employers begin to hire increasing numbers of women for specific clerical jobs after 1900 and how was this shift in demand linked to changing office organization?

The reserve army of labour model

Some analysts (Armstrong and Armstrong, 1978; Braverman, 1974; Connelly, 1978) have used Marx's concept of a reserve army of labour to explain the position of women in the labour force. The model examines how capitalists create a fluid supply of cheap labour, capable of employment or deployment in response to changing industrial requirements (see Braverman, 1974: 386–8). Because of their availability and cheapness (see Connelly, 1978: 21), women increasingly have been drawn into the reserve army for the expanding clerical, sales, and service sectors. According to Braverman (1974: 385), 'women form the ideal reservoir of labour for the new mass occupations. The barrier which confined women to much lower pay scales is reinforced by the vast numbers in which they are available to capital.'

Yet to classify women who are trapped in unrewarding jobs as part of a reserve army tells us little about how this condition developed. Assuming that capitalism requires a permanent reserve army of labour, what would lead capitalists to distinguish between men and women workers when delimiting this reserve for certain occupations? Would it not be more accurate to refer to women in female job ghettos, such as the office, as part of the active labour force? Our concern is with how sex-based inequalities were built into the labour market as changes occurred in office organization and the clerical labour process. Yet the reserve army thesis is of little value in this respect because it falls short of providing a more precise analysis of (a) why women at a certain point in time became incorporated into the active labour supply for specific occupations; (b) the extent to which women are segregated from men in 'female' occupations; and (c) how their inferior position within job hierarchies has been maintained over time.

The demand model

Best exemplified in the work of Oppenheimer (1970) and Madden (1973), this model examines how employers segregate women into specific occupations by manipulating job requirements. Oppenheimer, rejecting the supply-based consumer choice model, argues that the growing demand for women in certain occupations and industries has brought increased supply and higher labour force participation (1970: 160). Madden (1973: 52, 58–60), on the other hand, demonstrates that the imperfect competition which pervades the labour market facilitates discrimination by employers who possess excessive market power. Both of these arguments use two concepts—labour market segregation and sex labelling—to explain sex-based employment differences. Because men and women tend to be segregated into separate, noncompetitive labour markets, one may therefore talk about a demand specifically for female workers (Oppenheimer, 1970). In other words, a demand for female labour results from the general demand for workers in nursing, elementary school teaching, clerical and sales work, and other jobs which are predominately female.

The restriction of female workers to a small number of female-dominated occupations is reinforced by the process of sex labelling. By manipulating demand characteristics of a job—such as skill and educational requirements, working conditions, and salary levels—employers can tailor the labour supply. Thus, job requirements such as physical exertion, geographic mobility, or an unbroken career path are barriers to women. On the other hand, stereotypes of women as more manually dexterous and patient but less effective at supervision than men and as secondary wage earners channel females into jobs at the lower end of the occupational spectrum (Oppenheimer, 1970: 115). These stereotypes furnish the rationale for discrimination against women in terms of remuneration and opportunities for upward mobility. Madden (1973: 78) explains that 'if job requirements are structured so as to preclude part-time work, to require peak effort between the ages of twenty and thirty-five, or to require career continuity with one employer, that job will never be a female occupation.' Strong norms develop to exclude women from those occupations defined as male. Moreover, once women are established in an occupation, their lower wage rates give employers little incentive to revert to higher-priced male labour. Discrimination tends to be cumulative, reproducing in the female labour market characteristics defined as unacceptable for more rewarding jobs.

Clerical work is an outstanding example of how sex-related job requirements limit female employment opportunities (see Oppenheimer, 1970: 115). Once a clerical job acquired a 'female only' label, future demand was not just for cheap labour but for cheap *female* labour. But the demand model does not address how changing job characteristics motivated employers to hire women in the first place. In some cases (Stevenson, 1975; Prather, 1971), it is merely suggested that a high degree of occupational segregation is itself responsible for the inferior economic position of women. Yet the sexual division of labour is undoubtedly one of the strongest bases for balkanizing the labour market into unequal segments (Kessler-Harris,

1975: 217). What we need, though, is an explanation of how sex-based discrimination became incorporated into both the institutionalized processes of the labour market and the organization of the workplace.

The segmentation model

A number of useful concepts, notably sex labelling and labour market segmentation, can be drawn from our discussion of the three models. More generally, the deficiencies of the models underline the need for a historical analysis of the origins of female job ghettos and, further, a thorough examination of the relationship between transformations in the work context and changing labour force characteristics. A more structural perspective would help us to trace the feminization of clerical occupations back to its origins. A strong connection undoubtedly exists between changes in the organization of office work and the characteristics of the office work force. As Kanter (1977: 18) suggests:

> . . . managerial and clerical jobs are the major sex-segregated, white-collar occupations, brought into being by the development of the large corporation and its administrative apparatus. A sex-linked ethos became identified with each of the occupational groupings. Ideologies surrounding the pursuit of these occupations and justifying their position in the organization came to define both the labour pool from which these occupations drew and ideal images of the attributes of the people in that pool.

It is therefore essential that we examine the sex-based dimensions of power and inequality inherent in the office, as well as the influence of broad economic and organizational forces on occupational characteristics. Recent work on labour market segmentation is instructive in this respect (see Gordon, 1972; Edwards *et al.*, 1975; Freedman, 1976; Edwards, 1979). Prominent in this literature is the hypothesis that the development of corporate capitalism has fragmented a once homogeneous working class by segmenting the labour process within firms and, as a consequence, within the labour market (Gordon, 1972: 43; Edwards *et al.*, 1975: xi).[8] Segmentation occurs when changes in the productive process create submarkets based on different occupational characteristics, behavioural rules, and working conditions. By linking changes in labour market sectors to the transformation of the workplace under corporate capitalism, segmentation theory indicates that sex is not the key to explaining male-female occupational differences. The segmentation of the labour market into non-competing male and female components results not from challenges in the market itself, but rather from the way labour power is utilized and organized hierarchically by employers. The fragmentation of the labour process over the course of this century, especially within large corporations, has led employers to clearly distinguish between types of jobs and therefore types of workers required. The main criterion shaping job requirements is the degree of stability the organization requires from the job holder (Gordon, 1972: 71). Methods of ensuring various degrees of stability are anchored in different systems of control in the workplace. Employers increasingly separated jobs requiring stability from those which did not, recognizing that devices for maintaining stability within, for example, professional, technical, and middle level administrative positions were too expensive and elaborate to apply to the lower strata of clerical and menial labour.

Edwards (1979) argues that variations in labour market behaviour can be explained in terms of the systems of control employers have instituted in the workplace.[9] For instance, given the interchangeability of workers in routine clerical jobs there is no reason for employers to offer high rewards in terms of pay, good working conditions, and career prospects. Hence, the creation of a 'secondary' labour market characterized by truncated career paths, part-time or short-term employment, relatively low salaries, subordination, and powerlessness. This connection between labour market subgroups and different job control systems lends support to our suggestion that the administrative revolution in Canadian offices brought about changes in clerical occupations. Segmentation theory shows that sex discrimination has become imbedded over time into the very structure of work. This structural perspective is lacking in one respect, however. It does not directly address how changing entrance requirements for certain jobs created a decisive, and permanent, shift from male to female workers. This deficiency can be remedied by combining the structural orientation of segmentation theory with the concept of sex labelling. This will equip us to analyse the origins of the persistent dichotomy of the female clerk and the male office manager to which Kanter (1977) refers above.

A Structural Explanation of Clerical Feminization: Selected Historical Evidence

In this section of the paper, we will document how major structural changes in office organization and the clerical labour process underlay the shift in demand from male to female clerical workers. Three case studies will be presented. The first will focus on the rise of a female labour market for bank clerks during the First World War. The second examines the clustering of female clerks in the lowest strata of the federal civil service. And the third outlines the mechanization of clerical work in major offices, arguing that this aspect of work rationalizations was fundamental to the feminization process. All three cases highlight the connection between the administrative revolution and changing occupational characteristics. The emphasis will be on how the dynamics of labour market segmentation and sex labelling were borne out in the office.

Before considering the historical evidence, a brief outline of the structural basis of clerical feminization is in order. The rise of corporate capitalism in Canada after 1900 precipitated a revolution in the means of administration. Two trends converged, transforming the nature of clerical work. First, the flood of paperwork generated by the expanding economy required growing numbers of clerks. Second, managers came to rely on the office as the nerve centre of administration. As organizations expanded, managers replaced traditional, unsystematic methods of administration with 'scientific' programs founded on the rational concepts of efficiency in organizational operations and control over the labour process. By the end of the First World War, these trends had greatly magnified the scope and complexity of office procedures. But the burgeoning layers of administration became a source of inefficiency, threatening to undermine the managerial powers vested in the office. This sparked a surge of rationalization in major Canadian offices, particularly during the twenties. By the end of the decade, the typical large central office exhibited certain factory-like features. Work had become fragmented and standardized; hierarchy and regimentation prevailed.

Task specialization was fundamental to this revolution in the means of administration. As the burden of office work increased, managers found that clerks performing simple tasks in rapid succession were cheaper to employ, produced more, and were more easily regulated. The new jobs created in this manner lacked the skill components found in the craft-like work of the bookkeeper. Consequently, they were unattractive to middle class male clerks expecting upward mobility and comfortable salaries. Employers were pragmatic enough to recognize the clear advantages of women's higher average education, traditionally lower pay, and greater availability for menial tasks. A permanent secondary labour market of female clerks thus developed. Its emergence was buttressed by a number of socio-economic factors, such as the rise of mass public education, male labour shortages during the First World War, the gradual loosening of social norms regarding women's employment, and the fact that female wages were generally better in offices than in domestic or sales work. In short, a hallmark of the modern office is the replacement of the general male bookkeeper by an army of female workers. As women flooded into these subordinate positions which employers had defined as 'female', they became entrenched as the modern clerical corps.

The impact of World War I on women in banking

Severe labour force disruptions during both world wars directly influenced the sex ratio of many occupations. It has been argued that far from transforming the economic role of Canadian women, World War I merely accelerated an earlier trend by creating a temporary influx of women into the world of men's work (Ramkhalawansingh, 1974: 261). This generalization underestimates how the war precipitated lasting shifts in the balance of the sexes in the office.[10] The more enduring effects of the war on clerical occupations resulted from the development of shortages of male clerks at a time when major structural readjustments were occurring in the office. The fact that the war coincided with the administrative revolution helped to break down traditional barriers to female employment in some industries.[11] In banking, for example, the war was instrumental in establishing women as the most economical source of labour for routine clerical jobs.

Banks traditionally considered the ideal clerk to be a young 'gentleman' from a solid middle class background. When there was an under-supply of Canadians of this description, the banks recruited in Britain. But acute shortages of male bank clerks during the war forced a reconsideration of staffing policies. We find, for instance, that the proportion of female clerks in the Bank of Nova Scotia's Ontario region rocketed from 8.5 per cent in 1911 to 40.7 per cent in 1916 (Lowe, 1979: 204). The war had shattered old restrictions, and even with postwar readjustments women still held over 30 per cent of these positions in 1931.

Women were a rarity in turn-of-the-century banks. One of the largest banks in the Dominion employed only five women in 1901 (*Journal of the Canadian Banker's Association*, July 1916: 316). A major stumbling block was that bankers considered women unable to create the public confidence necessary for a successful branch operation. One branch manager, when faced with his first female employee in 1901, 'discussed with the head office in all seriousness the advisability of having a screen—a good high one, too—placed around her to shut her off completely from the observation of the public' (*Journal of the Canadian Banker's Association*, July 1916: 316).

Prior to the war, women tended to fill jobs requiring no public contact, such as stenographic and secretarial positions and menial head office jobs. One bank, for example, employed 350 female stenographers and 273 female general clerks in 1916. These jobs were mainly at head office; only seven women held teller positions in branches. As the war escalated, bank officials had little choice but to deploy females to the branches as vacancies created by enlisting male clerks[12] combined with the general expansion of banking to precipitate a labour supply crisis. A female employee described the resulting diffusion of women throughout the bank's clerical hierarchies in these terms:

> The posts open to women in a bank are, of course, both stenographic and clerical, and on the former it is unnecessary to touch. In the head offices until quite recently the proportion of clerical openings was small, but it is rapidly increasing and affording, as the business of each bank expands, opportunities in the way of special openings calling for special ability. In addition to the ordinary run of clerical positions, women have been employed for the past few years in the branches of at least some of our leading banks in collection departments

and on the ledgers; yes, on the ledgers. . . . Since the outbreak of the war, women have been filling positions both as clerks and as heads of departments which were formerly held by men. . . . In fact, the only two posts which are not at present occupied by women in a greater or lesser proportion are those of accountant and manager. (*Journal of the Canadian Banker's Association*, July 1916: 314–15).

Bank management reluctantly adjusted to the realities of the wartime labour market. In 1916, the Bank of Nova Scotia officially directed its branch managers to replace enlisted male clerks with women. Recognizing that the scarcity of male clerks would likely continue, bankers considered the possibility of placing women into previously male dominated jobs: 'we might just as well realize at once that the services of young women will have to be utilized for ledger-keepers, and at the smaller branches for tellers, so that attention should be paid to their training with this kind of service in mind.'[13] While a good number of branch managers were unwavering in their conviction that the male clerk was indispensible for business,[14] some were acknowledging the merits of female clerks. But this was tempered by the assumption that after the war most would return to the higher callings of homemaking and motherhood.

The economic necessities of the war clashed with the traditional social norms governing female conduct. Women were thus confronted with a dilemma. Many of the newly recruited female clerks proclaimed their intention to remain employed 'not merely as the assistants of men but as their equals in service and remuneration' (*Journal of the Canadian Banker's Association*, July 1917: 316–17). Yet numerous other women demurred in the face of this challenge, thereby fulfilling the prophecy that 'with the return of peace scores of girls will joyfully lay down their pens and return to their homes' (*Monetary Times*, 8 August 1919: 10).

The immediate postwar boom carried wartime feminization into the twenties. The *Monetary Times* (8 August 1919: 10) reported that 'Canadian banks are busier than ever before, and by their policy of opening many new branches at the present time they are able to absorb their returning employees and still retain some of the temporary (female) help.' The expansion of bank hierarchies channelled numerous former male clerks into supervisory positions. The recession in the early twenties resulted in many branch closures, curbing the hiring of women for a time. But when the economy picked up later in the decade, banks actively recruited women into their lower clerical ranks.

Changes in the clerical labour process, especially in large branches and head offices, tended to make the banks' time-tested recruitment and training procedures obsolete. Curiously, some bankers considered male juniors cheaper to hire than women. The *Monetary Times* (20 May 1927: 11) offered this explanation:

Women do not cultivate 'mobility' which is such a characteristic part of Canadian banking. Again, they are not suitable for very small branches, where the employees act to a certain degree as protectors. Moreover, they do not respond to opportunities for promotion as readily as men, who are in the business as a life work. They have not so large a capacity for work as the average male, and consequently more clerks are necessary.

In other words, men were an investment, contributing considerably more to the bank in the long run by working their way up to responsible positions.

Even before the war, however, growing task specialization had increased the number of routine clerical jobs at the expense of the general clerkships which served as the training ground for aspiring males. As the banks modernized their administrative structures, there arose a 'good deal of discontent among the younger men who . . . enter the banking service at low salaries with the expectation of rising to more responsible and highly paid positions' (*Journal of the Canadian Banker's Association*, January 1911: 11). In sum, the wartime labour crisis exacerbated organizational changes in the banks to bring about a demand shift in the lower clerical echelons.

In order for women to become a permanent labour source by the end of the 1920s, the banks' occupational structure had to be segmented along sex lines. It was this segmentation which facilitated the creation of a secondary female labour market. At the root of occupational and wage discrimination in the office was the nineteenth century attitude that while women were handicapped in pursuing 'male' occupations because of inherent disadvantages, they nevertheless possessed certain qualities useful in a limited range of subordinate jobs. Scott (1889: 25) explains:

Woman has manifestly been designed by nature as a complement, not as a substitute for man. If society has put her under certain political disabilities, her creator has put her under certain physical disabilities. Even independently of the curse of Eve, the average woman cannot calculate on her ability to work continuously with as well-grounded confidence as the average man, while in bodily strength she cannot compare with him. On the other hand, she excels him in delicacy of touch, in lightness of step, in softness of voice.

Because their natural calling was thought to be in the home, women were relegated to part-time, temporary employment. Strong social sanctions prohibited the employment of married women.[15] Women tended to internalize these prevailing norms, making it that much easier for employers to build sex-based inequities into the division of labour. A vicious circle developed. Tasks defined as suitable for women were typically monotonous and unrewarding. This helped to turn the assumptions underlying occupational discrimination—the female's tentative labour force attachment, her primary vocation of homemaker and mother, her lower aspirations—into self-fulfilling prophecies, manifested in a lack of job interest and high quit rates. The way women reacted to their relatively disadvantaged working conditions provided employers with supporting evidence for the negative stereotypes which justified their recruitment into routine jobs.[16]

Labour market segmentation and job sex labelling in the federal civil service
The treatment of women in the federal civil service is a classic example of the use of legislation and formal hiring policies to severely restrict female employment opportunities. Beginning in the late nineteenth century, the flow of women into the lower ranks of the Ottawa 'inside service' steadily mounted. The relatively high government salaries and the introduction of merit-based entrance examinations in 1908 attracted many women into the swelling bureaucracy. This leads Archibald (1970: 16) to conclude that the 'generally low labour force participation rates of women in the early part of this century were more a result of restricted opportunities than of female lack of interest in working.' Women initially entered the civil service in response to a *general* demand for clerical labour. But the Civil Service Commission resorted to rules, regulations, and legislation to segment the supply of clerical workers into male and female groups, confining the demand for female labour to menial jobs in the lowest reaches of the clerical hierarchy.

The inequality of opportunity built into the civil services bureaucracy early in the century helped create a cheap female labour pool (Hodgetts *et al.*, 1972: 483). But other factors also contributed to the discrimination against women in the service. Closer examination of employment practices reveals direct links between the processes of segmentation and sex labelling, traditional attitudes regarding woman's role and the growth and rationalization of government offices.

By 1891, women had been accepted as a permanent part of the service and were considered as efficient as male clerks (Dawson, 1929: 191). Their numbers steadily increased, and in 1908, 700 of the 3,000 inside jobs were occupied by women (Hodgetts *et al.*, 1972: 483). The Civil Service Commission, however, reacted with alarm, predicting administrative chaos were the trend to continue. The Commission was even more concerned that the preponderance of women in the lower echelons of the service would eliminate these positions as a training ground for male officials. The Commission's solution was simple: restrict women to certain routine clerical jobs. In 1910 it limited appointments in the first and second division to men, leaving only the third division open to women. And blatant sex labelling was used to prevent women from monopolizing the third division:

> In the first place, there is certain work incidental to clerical duties, as in the handling of large registers, carrying of files and books up and down ladders, etc., which on physical grounds is not suitable for women. There are other positions in which, from time to time, the clerk may be called upon to travel considerable distances from Ottawa, alone or in the capacity as secretary of

assistant. For obvious reasons, male clerks are required in positions involving such duties. (Canada, *Civil Service Commission Annual Report*, 1910: 17).

The new rules forced women who passed the qualifying exam for the second division to take a position in the third. Temporary clerks had to pass typing or stenography tests, skills rare among males. Occupational segmentation was furthered by allowing department heads to label jobs 'male' or 'female'. Women therefore became stenographers and typists; men became general clerks (Archibald, 1970: 14). These measures had the desired effect. Yet the Commission did not consider the problem solved until the 1918 Civil Service Act limited job competitions on the basis of sex and a 1921 ruling barred most women from permanent posts (Archibald, 1970: 16).[17]

It is significant that during the same period the civil service job classification system was being overhauled by a team of Chicago efficiency experts (see Lowe, 1979: 312–18). The 'scientific' reforms increased the specialization and standardization of clerical procedures. The administrative division of labour advanced, adding to the pool of female jobs a growing array of routine tasks. Inequalities in the opportunity structure were becoming more rigid. Even though they constituted a stable supply of clerical workers, the status of the female civil servant can be best described as marginal. This sometimes had rather severe ramifications. For example, when the job market was tight, women were considered to have less right to employment than men (Hodgetts *et al.*, 1972: 487). In sum, the experience of the female civil service clerk supports Oppenheimer's (1970) contention that the effects of sex labelling are self-perpetuating. Early discriminatory policies have thus left an indelible mark on the present occupational structure of the federal civil service (Archibald, 1970: 19).

The female office machine operator
Mechanization had a disintegrating effect on traditional clerical occupations. It simplified tasks, reduced skill levels, standardized procedures, and intensified the pace of work and the level of supervision. The women who now operate modern office machines are considered the most 'proletarianized' sector of the white-collar work force (*Work in America*, 1973: 38; Rinehart, 1975: 92; Glenn and Feldberg, 1977). Mechanized clerical jobs were a byproduct of the progressive rationalization of the office. Women did not displace men, for a female label was always attached to this kind of work. Because office mechanization is so closely interconnected with feminization, it provides clear evidence of how structural changes in the office underlay the shifting ratio of clerical jobs.

Stenography became the first female office occupation for a unique combination of reasons. Because of the arduous nature of the work, the special training required, and the lack of obvious social or economic advantages, male clerks did not find stenography very attractive. Young women were being trained in typing in the early 1880s, at least a decade before the typewriter was modified into a practical office appliance. Typewriters thus helped create a new subgroup outside the male-dominated, mainstream clerical occupations. By 1900, any remaining doubts about women's ability to operate the new office machines had been supplanted. Prevailing social norms sanctioned these developments, provided women did not pose a competitive threat to the male clerk.

> A woman is to be preferred for the secretarial position for she is not averse to doing minor tasks, work involving the handling of petty details, which would irk and irritate ambitious young men, who usually feel that the work they are doing is of no importance if it can be performed by some person with a lower salary. Most such men are also anxious to get ahead and to be promoted from position to position, and consequently if there is much work of a detail (sic) character to be done, and they are expected to perform it, they will not remain satisfied and will probably seek a position elsewhere. (Leffingwell, 1925: 621)

Stenography presents somewhat of a paradox in terms of the position of women in the office. On one hand, we have shown that women were shunted into the bottom layers of administrative structures. Yet on the other hand, mechanization afforded considerable socio-economic status and craft-like work to a select group of female clerks. Early stenographers closely approximated the ideal of craft work, as evident in the range of their skills and their greater mastery and control over the work process. These conditions were significantly better than those in other clerical jobs, so much so that stenographers became career-oriented and tended to develop a strong occupational identification. This accounts for their longer years of service and greater earning potential. Consequently, we find that from 1911 to 1926 stenographers were the highest paid group *of either sex* in the Bank of Nova Scotia, with starting wages consistently higher than those for general clerks (Lowe, 1979: 231).

The privileged position of the stenographer was undermined, however, by the advance of rationalization. By the start of the First World War, the two central elements of the job, dictation and typing, were being separated. The introduction of dictation machines facilitated the organization of central typing pools. Furthermore, there was a great surge of women into the occupation in search of high wages and steady employment (*Labour Gazette*, 1913: *passim*). In 1915, Toronto had twenty-eight business schools turning out stenographers and typists (Ontario, *Report of the Commission on Unemployment*, 1916: 182).[18] The market became glutted. Unemployment among stenographers reached 25 per cent in Toronto that year (*Labour Gazette*, February 1915: 924) and only the most experienced operators could command top wages.

Management viewed the typing pool as more efficient, cheaper, and easier to control than individual stenographers scattered throughout the office. Typing pools combined technical and organizational changes, giving rise to the 'office-machine age' (Mills, 1956: 195) which has culminated in the 'word processing systems' and 'administrative support centres' of today. By the mid-twenties, many large Canadian offices had central typing pools (Lowe, 1979: 363–7). These paper-generating assembly lines obtained optimal efficiency from typewriters by keeping them in continuous use. Employees viewed the pool concept with suspicion. One insurance company reported that:

> Most stenographers who had seen or heard of transcribing machines were very much prejudiced against them, and the belief was almost generally entertained that the machine would ultimately force all stenographers to abandon their careers in favour of the much lower priced transcribing machine operators. . . . There was also a natural prejudice . . . against working in a Stenographic Department as compared with the more intimate contacts surrounding positions where they were required to take the work of only one or two dictators. (Life Office Management Association, *Proceedings*, 1926: 82)

Without downplaying the impact of the typewriter on the feminization process, it is accurate to say that the Hollerith machine fully launched the mechanical transformation of the clerical work process. The Hollerith punch card system was the most dramatic innovation in office technology prior to computers. International Business Machines was the main supplier, and by the early 1930s it had 105 major Canadian offices among its Hollerith customers (Lowe, 1979: 377–8). The job title of 'office machine operator' first appeared in the 1921 Census, signalling that a minor revolution in office technology was well underway.

The impact of the Hollerith machine was heightened by increasing bureaucratization and the introduction of scientific office management during the twenties. The women operators no doubt found that the machines tended to fragment and de-skill work. As Shepard (1971: 63) puts it, such devices 'greatly accelerated the trend toward functional specialization. Many more special purpose machine-operating jobs evolved, placing employees filling these jobs in a relationship to technology similar to the mass-production factory worker. Work in these jobs is repetitive, mechanically paced, and minutely sub-divided.' In short, the female office machine operator had become a standard feature of the large bureaucratic office by the late 1920s. These women constituted what in Marxist terms might be called the 'machine minders' of the modern office.

Conclusion

This article has attempted to develop a new perspective on the feminization process. By incorporating features of existing models into a structural explanation, we have been able to trace the origins of a secondary female clerical labour market back to transformations in the means of administration. The historical evidence presented supports Meissner's (1977: 162) contention that 'the structure of functional distinctions and social inequalities becomes visible in job assignments, wage differences, and job classifications.' The evolution of modern administration during the first three decades of this century in Canada created a new stratum of clerical jobs. As the number of these routine jobs grew, they became increasingly rationalized. Employers shifted their demand for clerks from men to women mainly because the requirements of the new administrative tasks were inconsistent with the established occupational characteristics of male clerks. Feminization was not simply a case of women displacing men. Rather, women became an administrative underclass because the division of labour had advanced to the point where male clerks were unsuited and unwilling, for a variety of social and economic reasons, to perform the new menial tasks. Segmentation resulted; men became office managers and technical or professional personnel and women occupied the subordinate clerical jobs.

The article raises a number of issues worthy of further investigation, but two in particular stand out. The first has to do with the relationship between sex segregation in clerical jobs and the hierarchical organization of the office (Stevenson, 1975: 251, 253). Specifically, how has the concentration of women workers in the lower reaches of administration helped maintain the hierarchical arrangement of control in the modern office? The second question links the workplace to the larger society. We have argued that in order to understand labour market processes, it is imperative to examine the social relations of production in the office. But to what extent are the social relations of office work reflected in the class structure? Davis (1975: 279) claims that lower level clerks form an integral part of the working class. Certainly our research suggests that office working conditions became 'proletarianized' during the administrative revolution, at least to the extent that they became more factory-like. But does this mean that the women recruited into clerical jobs comprise a segment of the working class? Both of these questions present intriguing theoretical possibilities and will hopefully spark future research.

Let us conclude with a comment on the present situation. Clerical occupations now contain the greatest concentration of women in the labour force. The thrust of sex labelling and segmentation, when combined with the progressive rationalization of the office, have increasingly locked women into subordinate clerical jobs. Presumably, attitudes towards women's position in society have liberalized considerably since the 1920s. But sex-based inequalities and discrimination are so deeply embedded in the structure of the contemporary office that only the utmost tenacity on the part of women's groups and unions holds prospects for greater equality.

Suggestions for Further Reading

Graham S. Lowe, *Women in the Administrative Revolution: The Feminization of Clerical Work* (Toronto, 1987).

Michele Martin, *'Hello Central?' Gender, Technology, and Culture in the Formation of Telephone Systems* (Montreal, 1991).

Joy Parr, *The Gender of Breadwinners: Women, Men, and Change in Two Industrial Towns, 1880–1950* (Toronto, 1990).

Notes

This is a revised version of a paper presented to the Political Economy Section of the Canadian Political Science Association Annual Meetings, June 1979, Saskatoon, Saskatchewan. I would like to thank Dennis Magill, Noah Meltz, Lorna Marsden, Rosalind Sydie, as well as three anonymous *CJS* reviewers, for helpful comments on an earlier draft. I would also like to acknowledge the Canada Council's financial support of the research.

[1] See Table 1 for exact figures. It should be noted that clerical employment data from the census used in this paper are reclassified to conform with the 1951 Census definition of clerk. This allows for accurate inter-censal comparison. However, these adjustments mean that employment data in Tables 1 and 2 for 1971 are slightly below those found in the actual census.

[2] The concepts of corporate capitalism and entrepreneurial capitalism have been drawn from Clement (1975: 71–80).

[3] Between 1901 and 1921, the average clerical salary rose from 116 to 125% of the average wage for the total Canadian labour force. Yet after 1921, clerical earnings entered a steady decline cutting below the labour force average in 1951. In 1971, the average clerical salary was only 77% of the labour force average (Lowe, 1979 224). Research by Lockwood (1966) in Britain and Burns (1954) and Braverman (1974) in the United States also documents how the explosion of white-collar occupations since the turn of the century has been accompanied by a relative decline in clerical wages.

[4] In 1881, the Civil Service Commissioners argued that if more female clerks were hired, 'it would be necessary that they should be placed in rooms by themselves, and that they should be under the immediate supervision of a person of their own sex, but we doubt very much if sufficient work of similar character can be found in any one Department to furnish occupation for any considerable number of female clerks, and it would certainly be inadvisable to place them in small numbers throughout the Departments' (Canada, *First Report of the Civil Service Commission*, 1881: 26).

[5] In 1971, 96.8% of all stenographers and typists were women (Canada, 1971 Census, Vol. III, Part 2, Table 2).

[6] Over the 1901–31 decades, women increased their share of clerical jobs in manufacturing from 16.5% to 40.7%; 22.7 to 52.9% in trade; 0.8% to 49.6% in finance; and 5.5% to 37.6% in government (Lowe, 1979: 184). For an interesting discussion

of the impact of changing industrial structure on female employment, see Singelmann and Tienda (1979).

[7]This is consistent with the broad labour force trend. In 1971 the average income for women doing paid work was about half that of men (Armstrong and Armstrong, 1975: 371). Yet within the female labour force, clerks were quite well off. For example, a 1921 survey (*Canada Year Book*, 1928: 779) indicated that female office clerks earned more than twenty-two other female occupations. Only telegraph operators in Montreal and tailoresses, teachers as well as telegraph operators in Toronto earned more. In 1901, female clerks earned 45% more than the average female wage. This fluctuated over the next several decades, rising to a high of 49% in 1941. This advantage gradually diminished, with female clerks only making 6% more than the female labour force average by 1971 (Lowe, 1979: 224).

[8]The term labour process refers to the way in which labour power is organized and regulated in the activity of production. The term labour market refers to those institutions which influence, directly or indirectly, the purchase and sale of labour power (Edwards *et al.*, 1975: xi).

[9]Edwards (1979) has advanced segmentation theory furthest by proposing three market segments, each defined in terms of a different form of job control found in the workplace. In other words, differences among jobs explain basic differences among workers (166). A thorough evaluation of Edwards' work is beyond the scope of the present paper. However, we should note that his model does not appear to have solved the problem of accounting for clerical occupations as more than just a 'deviant case' within the major labour submarkets (see Piore, 1975: 130).

[10]The tremendous expansion of the clerical sector during the war decade further segmented the labour market. For example, clerical jobs increased their share of the total female work force from 9.1% in 1911 to 18.5% in 1921. Fully 50.2% of the growth in office occupations over the decade was accounted for by women flooding into offices. In fact, 69,165 more clerical jobs were created during the 1911–21 decade than during the twenties. This works out to approximately four times more jobs, and therefore about four times more women entering the office.

[11]The impact of the war on clerical employment opportunities for women was not even across all industries. In Montreal, for example, munitions plants hired women clerks to help administer war production as well as regular business (Price, 1919: 26). On the other hand, Montreal's post offices employed mainly female clerks in 1914 and the war brought about little change (Price, 1919: 60). Similarly, in the Manufacturers Life Assurance Company the war merely tilted the balance in favour of women, something which would have happened anyway (Lowe, 1979).

[12]By early 1919, a total of 9,069 male bank clerks had enlisted in Canada (Lowe, 1979: 284).

[13]'Circular No. 1,699 from the General Manager, 6 April 1916', Bank of Nova Scotia Archives, Toronto.

[14]When conscription was imposed, the banks lobbied the government to exempt their male clerks, arguing that these employees possessed special qualifications and performed a vital role in the economy (*Monetary Times*, 29 March 1918: 22).

[15]In the early twentieth century, approximately 90% of women in the Canadian labour force were single (Vipond, 1977: 117).

[16]Ironically, women who entered the labour force typically were somewhat better educated than men. This was an added bonus for employers, but how was the discrepancy between occupational status and education rationalized? Part of the answer is found in the ideology surrounding woman's social role. The 'cult of domesticity' required that women, as the transmitters of culture to children, should have an adequate base of knowledge from which to work (Brownlee and Brownlee, 1976: 18). The growing number of women who entered the clerical labour market had to balance the contradictory demands of the world of work with those of home and family. Encouraged to gain specialized clerical skills by enrolling in one of the plethora of business colleges, yet all the while knowing her destiny was in the home, the young woman of the 1920s faced a basic quandry (see Vipond, 1977: 120).

[17]The 1921 regulation made exceptions for married women who were self-supporting or if other suitable candidates could not be found. Married women in the service were forced to resign and reapply as temporary workers at the minimum salary.

[18]Another contributing factor on the supply side was the attempt by typewriter companies to regulate the labour market for stenographers and typists through employment agencies (see Ontario, *Report of the Commission on Unemployment*, 1916: 182). The business schools and private employment agencies helped create a huge secondary labour pool of semi-skilled women, which employers drew on to fill routine typing jobs.

References

Armstrong, Hugh and Pat Armstrong
  1975   'The segregated participation of women in the Canadian labour force, 1941–71.' *Canadian Review of Sociology and Anthropology* 12: 370–84.

———
  1978   *The Double Ghetto: Canadian Women and their Segregated Work.* Toronto: McClelland and Stewart.
Archibald, Kathleen
  1970   *Sex and the Public Service.* Ottawa: Queen's Printer.
Braverman, Harry
  1974   *Labor and Monopoly Capital: The Degradation of Work in the Twentieth Century.* New York: Monthly Review Press.
Brownlee, W. Elliot and Mary M. Brownlee
  1976   *Women in the American Economy.* New Haven: Yale University Press.
Burns, Robert K.
  1954   'The comparative economic position of manual and white-collar employees.' *Journal of Business* 27: 257–67.
Canada
  n.d.   *Canada Year Book.*
  n.d.   Censuses, 1891–1971.
  n.d.   Civil-Service Commission, Annual Reports.
  1939   *Occupational Trends in Canada, 1891–1931,* Special bulletin, D.B.S., Ottawa.

Clement, Wallace
   1975   *The Canadian Corporate Elite*. Toronto: McClelland and Stewart.
Connelly, Patricia
   1978   *Last Hired, First Fired: Women and the Canadian Work Force*. Toronto: Women's Press.
Davies, Margery
   1975   'Women's place is at the typewriter: the feminization of the clerical labor force.' In *Labor Market Segmentation*, eds Richard Edwards *et al.* Lexington, Mass.: D.C. Heath.
Dawson, Robert M.
   1929   *The Civil Service of Canada*. London: Oxford University Press.
Edwards, Richard
   1979   *Contested Terrain: The Transformation of the Workplace in the Twentieth Century*. New York: Basic Books.
Edwards, Richard C., Michael Reich and David M. Gordon, eds
   1975   *Labor Market Segmentation*. Lexington, Mass.: D.C. Heath.
Firestone, O.J.
   1953   'Canada's economic development, 1867–1952.' Paper prepared for the Third Conference of the International Association for Research in Income and Wealth, Castelgandolfo, Italy.
Freedman, Marcia
   1976   *Labor Markets: Segments and Shelters*. Montclair, N.J.: Allanheld, Osmun.
Glenn, Evelyn N. and Roslyn L. Feldberg
   1977   'Degraded and deskilled: the proletarianization of clerical work.' *Social Problems* 25: 52–64.
Gordon, David M.
   1972   *Theories of Poverty and Underemployment: Orthodox, Radical, and Dual Labor Market Perspectives*. Lexington, Mass.: D.C. Heath.
Hodgetts, J.E., W. McCloskey, R. Whitaker and V.S. Wilson
   1972   *The Biography of an Institution: The Civil Service Commission of Canada, 1908–1967*. Montreal: McGill-Queen's University Press.
Journal of the Canadian Banker's Association
Kanter, Rosabeth Moss
   1977   *Men and Women of the Corporation*. New York: Basic Books.
Kessler-Harris, Alice
   1975   'Stratifying by sex: understanding the history of working women.' In *Labor Market Segmentation*, eds Richard Edwards *et al.* Lexington, Mass.: D.C. Heath.
Labour Gazette
Leffingwell, William H.
   1925   *Office Management, Principles and Practice*. Chicago: A.W. Shaw.
Life Office Management Association
   n.d.   *Proceedings of Annual Conferences*
Lockwood, David
   1966   *The Blackcoated Worker*. London: Allen and Unwin.

Lowe, Graham S.
  1979   'The administrative revolution: the growth of clerical occupations and the development of the modern office in Canada, 1911–1931.' Unpublished PhD thesis, University of Toronto.
Madden, Janice Fanning
  1973   *The Economics of Sex Discrimination*, Lexington, Mass.: Lexington Books.
Meissner, Martin
  1977   'Sexual division of labour and inequalities; labour and leisure.' In *Women in Canada*, second edition, ed. Marylee Stephenson. Don Mills: General Publishing.
Meltz, Noah M.
  1969   *Manpower in Canada, 1931 to 1961*. Ottawa: Queen's Printer.
Mills, C. Wright
  1956   *White Collar: The American Middle Classes*. New York: Oxford University Press.
Ontario
  1916   *Report of the Ontario Commission on Unemployment*. Toronto: A.T. Wilgress.
Oppenheimer, Valerie K.
  1970   *The Female Labor Force in the United States*. Berkeley: Institute of International Studies, University of California.
Ostry, S.
  1968   *The Female Worker in Canada*. Ottawa: Queen's Printer.
Payne, J.L.
  1907   'The civil servant.' *University Magazine* 6.
Piore, Michael J.
  1975   'Notes for a theory of labor market segmentation.' In *Labor Market Segmentation*, eds Richard Edwards *et al*. Lexington, Mass.: D.C. Heath.
Prather, Jane E.
  1971   'When the girls move in: a sociological analysis of the feminization of the bank teller's job.' *Journal of Marriage and the Family* 13: 777–82.
Price, Enid M.
  1919   'Changes in the industrial occupations of women in the environment of Montreal during the period of the war, 1914–1918.' Unpublished MA thesis, McGill University.
Ramkhalawansingh, Ceta
  1974   'Women during the Great War.' In *Women at Work: Ontario 1850–1930*, eds Janice Action, Penny Goldsmith and Bonnie Shepard. Toronto: Canadian Women's Educational Press.
Rinehart, James W.
  1975   *The Tyranny of Work*. Don Mills: Longman Canada.
Scott, Jean Thompson
  1889   'The conditions of female labor in Ontario.' *Studies in Political Science*, Series III, ed. W.J. Ashely. Toronto: University of Toronto.
Shepard, Jon M.
  1971   *Automation and Alienation: A Study of Office and Factory Workers*. Cambridge, Mass.: M.I.T. Press.

Singelmann, Joachim and Marta Tienda
  1979 'Changes in industry structure and female employment in Latin America: 1950–1970.' *Sociology and Social Research* 63: 745–69.
Stevenson, Mary
  1975 'Women's wages and job segregation.' In *Labor Market Segmentation*, eds Richard Edwards *et al.* Lexington, Mass.: D.C. Heath.
Sun Life Assurance Company
  n.d.   *Sunshine*, employee magazine
Vipond, Mary
  1977 'The images of women in mass circulation magazines in the 1920s.' In *The Neglected Majority*, eds Susan Mann Trofimenkoff and Alison Prentice. Toronto: McClelland and Stewart.
Work in America
  1973 Report of a Special Task Force to the U.S. Secretary of Health, Education and Welfare prepared by the W.E. Upjohn Institute for Employment Research. Cambridge, Mass.: M.I.T. Press.

20

Regional Political Protest in the 20s

Ernest R. Forbes

Postwar readjustment was difficult for many Canadians, and the 1920s represented less the era of untrammelled prosperity and hedonism usually associated with its characterization as 'The Roaring Twenties' than a decade of serious regional discontent and protest. Canadian agriculture was particularly vulnerable, but the entire resource sector of the economy sagged badly. Prairie farmers proved unable to comprehend the realities of the new postwar economic order, where virtually bankrupt European nations could no longer afford to buy the products of Canadian farms at the wartime price levels that everyone took for granted. Faced with heavy interest charges, high protective tariffs for manufactured goods, discriminatory freight rates, and marketing chaos, the Prairies turned against the traditional parties and organized their own political response, the Progressive Party, which flourished in the first half of the 1920s, electing sufficient members to Parliament in

1921 to hold the political balance of power. But Western Canada was not alone in feeling ill-used and victimized by regional disparities. The Maritime provinces also faced the postwar era with considerable disquiet. Like the Prairies, the Maritimes relied heavily on primary production—fishing, lumbering, mining, agriculture—which no longer enjoyed the markets or commanded the prices previously enjoyed. Moreover, Maritime manufacturing was suffering badly from an inability to remain competitive. The regional recession drove thousands of Maritimers to migrate to a seemingly more prosperous United States, and led their political and business leaders to seek desperately for solutions through political action.

Ernest R. Forbes discusses the emergence of the regional protest movement known as the Maritime Rights Movement, an attempt to organize a unified political response to regional disparities through the existing party machinery. As Forbes points out, complex economic issues were reduced on the popular level to a version of the 'Compact' theory of Confederation—and a demand for equality with the Western provinces. Federal insensitivity turned Maritimers against the Conservative Party in power and to the Liberals, who became the spokesmen for regional interests in the 1921 election. But even the election of a strong regional representation to the new Liberal government in Ottawa, headed by W.L. Mackenzie King, did the Maritimes little good, for the King government was far more dependent on the votes of western Progressives, who saw their interests as totally opposed to those of the Maritimes. While both the Maritimes and the Prairies were protesting against Central Canada and shared many common grievances, they ended up battling one another, and the Maritimes lost.

In what form did the Maritime region invoke the 'Compact' theory? Why are regional interests so often take up by Opposition parties in Canada? Why were the Maritimes and the Prairies natural enemies? Why were the protesting regions unable to combine in opposition to Central Canada?

This article first appeared, titled 'The Emergence of the Campaign for Maritime Rights, 1921–2', in Ernest R. Forbes, *Maritime Rights: The Maritime Rights Movement 1919–1927, A Study in Canadian Regionalism* (Montreal, 1979), 73–95.

The main rationale of the campaign for Maritime Rights was widely articulated throughout the three provinces before the end of 1921. The two grievances common to all were the still-unsettled demand for subsidies in lieu of Crown lands and the incorporation of the Intercolonial in the Canadian National Railways. With these were associated orders of more local application—the failure to nationalize a revenue-draining Saint John and Quebec railway, to provide adequate car-ferry facilities and replace narrow-gauge railways in Prince Edward Island, to expand facilities and encourage the use of Maritime ports, and to give the rural communities of the region a greater share in national programs to attract immigrants.

The railway grievance was at once the most important and the most difficult to articulate. Anger at the transfer of the Intercolonial's headquarters to Toronto derived from regional pride and such concrete issues as supply purchasing,[1] employment opportunities, and seniority. Of greatest concern to the whole region was the increase in freight rates. But the technicalities of rates and rate-making were of such complexity as to be imperfectly understood, even by the businessmen most directly affected.

Nonetheless the various strands of the railway grievance were brought together and reduced to a formula suitable for popular agitation by the development of a variation of the then-fashionable 'Compact' theory of

Confederation. Maritime spokesmen repeatedly argued that the Intercolonial, as the chief quid pro quo of the Maritimes' entry into Confederation, formed an integral part of the compact among the provinces upon
which the federal union was based. Section 145 of the British North America Act had proclaimed the construction of the road to be 'essential to the
consolidation of the Union and to the assent thereto of Nova Scotia and
New Brunswick'. In their public utterances the Fathers of Confederation
had further explained the purposes of the road as the development of interprovincial trade and the provision of national outlets on the Atlantic for
the Central provinces.[2]

These purposes, either stated or implied in the Confederation pact, were,
the Maritimers contended, largely political and could not be fulfilled by a
commercial railway. Until the war the political role had been paramount; the
compact had been honoured. The road was built at public expense, no
attempt was made to secure a return on capital invested, and operating revenues frequently fell short of expenditures. But in 1918 appointees from the
Canadian Northern had taken charge and applied to the Intercolonial the
principles of operation and rate-making which had evolved to meet the
needs of the private capital and commercial lines in Western and Central
Canada. These proved quite inappropriate for both the railway and the
region, and created serious barriers to interprovincial trade. The introduction
of such methods, the Maritimers argued, repudiated the intentions of the
Fathers in creating the railway and violated the 'rights' of the Maritime
provinces under the compact of Confederation, which required either the
separation of the Intercolonial from the CNR or its inclusion in a separate
unit with sufficient autonomy to fix rates and adopt practices which would
meet local needs and encourage interprovincial trade. Essentially it would
necessitate the restoration of the headquarters at Moncton under management knowledgeable of and sympathetic to local conditions and independent
of the jurisdiction of the Board of Railway Commissioners.

Similarly the defenders of Maritime ports claimed a commitment in the
'compact' to make Halifax and Saint John the chief outlets for Canada's
winter trade on the Atlantic. Here too they cited the 'promises' of the Fathers
in the negotiations preceding Confederation as constituting part of the
understanding upon which the Maritimers had been persuaded to enter.
Their demands included a more rapid development of their ports and an
adjustment of freight rates to channel trade through them rather than Portland or New York.[3]

Prince Edward Islanders also invoked the Compact thesis in their call for
a second railway-car ferry. That province had been successful on previous
occasions in securing recognition of the federal responsibility of maintaining
the 'continuous communication' promised the island on its entry.[4] In 1917
the steamers which fulfilled this function were replaced by an ice-breaking

railway-car ferry. Within three years the island's expanding trade with the mainland taxed that facility to the utmost. As they grew more dependent upon the ferry, islanders became alarmed at the effect on their trade of any interruption of service. Their vulnerability in depending on a single ship was underlined late in 1919 when government officials proposed diverting the ferry to aid a vessel trapped in the ice at the entrance to the St Lawrence. Prince Edward Island producers protested vigorously and redoubled their efforts to secure a second car ferry as a further guarantee of 'continuous communication'.[5] The extraordinary slowness in the widening of the Prince Edward Island railways was a related grievance, for it prevented island residents from taking advantage of the direct freight transport which the ferry allowed. Although the federal government had begun the standardization of the line in 1912, they had completed only fifty miles in nine years. Most of the farmers still faced the delay and inconvenience of having all their freight shifted from one car to another before it reached its destination.[6]

New Brunswick's claim for relief from responsibility for the Saint John and Quebec Railway rested partly on the argument that changes in federal policy accounted for the latter's financial difficulties and partly on a demand for equality in treatment with the Western provinces. In 1912 New Brunswick had entered a complex agreement with the federal government for the construction and operation of a railway running from Saint John to Grand Falls on the National Transcontinental. The province guaranteed bonds of more than $7 million for the road's construction. On its completion the government railways would operate the road in return for 60 per cent of the gross revenue. In 1916 the federal government, under the pressure of wartime expenditure, cancelled the first agreement, which would have necessitated an expenditure of $3 million on bridges, and persuaded the province to settle for a less efficient route. The provincial government accepted the compromise, the New Brunswickers claimed, out of a realization of the need for wartime economy and in the expectation that the road would be taken over by the federal government at the end of the war. As a local road the Saint John and Quebec Railway paid but a quarter of the bond interest for which the New Brunswick government was responsible. The province held the federal government liable for the failure of the road to develop as a part of the Transcontinental and for the additional investment required by the province in building the road to Transcontinental specifications. They also compared their position to that of the Western provinces, which had been relieved of liabilities of more than $100 million by the government takeover of the Canadian Northern and the Grand Trunk. Surely, New Brunswickers argued, it would be no more than justice if their province were bailed out in similar fashion.[7]

Early in 1920 the legislatures of the Maritime provinces resolved on joint action in presenting their claims, and their representatives met in Halifax to co-ordinate strategy.[8] Freight rates posed a dilemma. The three governments did not want to recognize the jurisdiction of the Board of Railway Commissioners over the Intercolonial. But although the road was still technically outside the board's control Railway Minister J.D. Reid had already been applying its judgements to Maritime lines.[9] The Maritime leaders realized that they could no longer afford to remain unrepresented before a board which was making basic decisions affecting their region.

In August 1920 the two larger provinces, in co-operation with the Maritime Board of Trade, sent a delegation to the Ottawa hearings on a proposed 40 per cent rate increase. The delegation, consisting of E.M. Macdonald, former MP for Pictou, R.E. Finn, Nova Scotia's minister of public works, and R.B. Armstrong of the Saint John Board of Trade, opposed the increase and attempted to prevent its application to the Intercolonial. Their case focused primarily on the magnitude of the increases already imposed on the Maritimes, the potential damage to local industry, and the 'peculiar' nature of the Intercolonial as a noncommercial road. The 40 per cent increase, E.M. Macdonald claimed, would represent a jump in first-class rates on traffic to Ontario of from 20 cents prior to 1916 to 48.5 cents when the new rate took effect. Increases on the Montreal arbitraries already meant that 'the Maritime Provinces can no longer successfully compete in the markets of Central and Western Canada which they are obliged to do to market their surplus production.' Further increases would 'put some Maritime industries out of existence or force them to locate elsewhere'.[10] The Intercolonial, Macdonald contended, was never intended to be operated solely on commercial principles; its purpose was the consolidation of Confederation and the development of interprovincial trade. It was, as John A. Macdonald had called it, 'a political consequence of a political union'. 'From 1874 to 1916,' Macdonald stated, 'every political party in power in this country, every Minister of Railways, everyone who had anything to do with the operation of the railway recognized that it was a railway that should be dealt with on that basis.'[11] The Maritime delegates appealed to the board to consider the rates on the Intercolonial from the perspective of its purpose and function in Confederation, rather than on strict commercial principles. Specifically, R.E. Finn urged the commissioners to 'divorce themselves absolutely from the position taken by Sir Henry Drayton' that freight rates 'could not be made for the purpose of removing geographical distances'.[12] The board was not impressed and imposed the full 40 per cent increase on the Maritimes.

In December 1920 the Maritime governments launched a formal complaint before the board, calling for a 'restoration of the arbitraries' and 'revision' of the other rate structures to, from, and within the Maritime provinces.[13] In the preliminary hearing the commissioners flatly rejected the main element of the Maritime case, the claim for special consideration because of the national or political purposes of the Intercolonial. 'We have nothing to do with any of the political conditions, or with very much of the past history,' stated Frank Carvell, the chief commissioner; 'we are trying to consider this matter purely from legal and business standpoints'.[14] For other aspects of the case they would have to 'go to the government'.

Go to the government they did in the summer of 1921. First, they arranged a display of regional support for their demands. In their spring sessions, the New Brunswick and Nova Scotia legislatures addressed identical resolutions to the federal cabinet, stating their case for lower freight rates and a separate management for the Intercolonial Railway. The New Brunswick legislature added a second resolution to the Saint John and Quebec Railway. Prince Edward Island contented itself with a memorial to the federal government requesting a second car ferry and the completion of the widening of their railway.[15]

At Moncton a conference of Maritime organizations, meeting to consider methods of encouraging regional promotion and industrial development, issued a strong statement of the Intercolonial's right to special status and proposed that a delegation formally present the Maritime case to the federal cabinet. Represented at the conference were Maritime boards of trade, shipper and manufacturing associations, co-operative and farmers' groups (including the United Farmers of New Brunswick), and various government departments of the two larger provinces. The resolution, which passed unanimously, affirmed that the 'Intercolonial Railway should be operated directly under the Department of Railways and that the freight and passenger rates . . . should be made in accordance with the terms and promises under which Nova Scotia, New Brunswick and Prince Edward Island entered Confederation'. The conference called upon 'civil, commercial, labour and agricultural organizations' to send delegates to Ottawa in support of the Maritime case.[16]

Approximately fifty delegates were on hand at the meeting with the federal cabinet on June 1, 1921. Hance J. Logan outlined in some detail the historical argument underlying their case. Quoting extensively from statements by John A. Macdonald, George-Étienne Cartier, George Brown, E.P. Taché, and other Fathers of Confederation, he tried to show that the Intercolonial was originally understood to be a military and political rather than commercial railway. Indeed, he observed, some had predicted that it 'would never pay for the grease on the axles of the carriages'. R.E. Finn recounted the Maritimes' unhappy experience before the Board of Railway Commissioners, which had refused to consider the original purpose of the road or regional needs in the setting of rates, and requested the exemption of the Intercolonial from the rulings of the board and the restoration of the railway's headquarters to the Maritimes under a management 'in sympathy to the aspirations of the people of the Maritime Provinces . . . who will so adjust the freight rates as to permit the industries of the Maritime Provinces to . . . get into the competitive markets of Canada'.[17]

In less measured tones, H.R. McLennan, representing the New Brunswick Commercial Club, complained of the steady encroachment of the Central provinces on Maritime rights under the compact of Confederation. The fault lay partly with Maritime representatives' slavish adherence to party politics and partly with the narrow preoccupation of representatives of other regions who failed to 'supervise the needs of those portions of Canada other than' their own. Nevertheless Maritimers were undergoing 'an intellectual awakening' and would no longer tolerate a continued denial of their 'rights'. They were, McLennan asserted, appealing to the country as a whole for relief from 'that autocracy which has been displayed by Ontario and Quebec'. If this appeal failed, 'those who are responsible . . . must take their political lives in their hands'.[18]

Ironically enough, unknown to McLennan and other Maritimers, some of the strongest support for the Maritime position came from A.E. Kemp, minister without portfolio from Toronto. Kemp committed his views to paper in a private letter to Arthur Meighen and included a memorandum for circulation among the other members of the government. Beginning with the assumption that 'the object of Confederation was principally to build up a strong nation and bind it together by inter-provincial trade,' Kemp was highly critical of the railway commissioners' failure 'to differentiate where territorial necessity demanded' in the application of the rate increases. This, he stated, was in sharp contrast to the 'recent advances' by the Interstate Commission in the United States which allowed the rates to 'vary according to national and territorial necessities'. The railways, too, were to blame. In their 'anxiety . . . to secure more revenue' they had 'entirely overlooked' the fact that 'only by the encouragement of the railways' were Maritime manufacturers 'able to obtain markets for their products which are now found in all the Western Provinces of the Dominion'. Kemp suggested that perhaps the commissioners had 'assumed that it was not within the scope of their duty to deal with a matter of general or broad national policy'. In any case it was '*now* the responsibility of the Government'. Kemp recommended that, if 'radical' changes were impractical, they should at least exempt the long-haul traffic of the Maritimes from the 40 per cent increase.[19]

Kemp's views did not prevail in the cabinet. The only answer to their delegation which expectant Maritimers received came in a press release from Conservative Party headquarters at Ottawa. Essentially it was a point-by-point rebuttal of a garbled version of the Maritime case. The Intercolonial claim to special rates, it argued, could not come from government ownership; most of the railways were now government-owned. It could not come from the Confederation pact since the BNA Act mentioned only the construction of the road and said nothing of its operation. There was no parallel with the toll-free Ontario canals because the charges on these had been removed by international treaty. Complaints against the freight increases, it conceded, were widespread so that 'A general reduction may be necessary in the public interest, but it would be rank sectionalism to lower rates in one part of the country and keep them up in another.' The dispatch concluded with the suggestion that such outrageous demands must have been politically motivated.[20]

Whatever debating points the Conservatives may have scored in the rest of the country, their response appeared needlessly provocative in the Maritimes. H.R. McLennan suggested that the government's reply left the Maritimes two choices: 'fighting the case by instructing our people as to their rights and having the Maritime Provinces co-operate in sending representatives to fight for them' or forming 'a colony of our own under British protection. We can not do worse and the chances of doing better are many.' The traditionally Conservative Saint John *Standard*, explaining the government's callous response as dictated by a fear of further inciting the more populous West, predicted that it would lead to the party's defeat in the Maritimes in the next election.[21]

The Maritimers were no more successful in pressing for subsidies in lieu of grants of Crown land. In 1920 the three legislatures had passed resolutions repeating their demands. These were discussed in the Maritime premiers' conference in Halifax and were mentioned again in various Speeches from the Throne in 1921.[22] Prime Minister Meighen assigned the task of investigating their claims to J.D. Reid, minister of railways from Ontario.

The report which Reid submitted to the cabinet in April 1921 was a remarkable document. It rejected the Maritime claims to compensation, not because the provincial governments lacked a proprietary interest in the Dominion lands, but because the Canadian government never had any. Canada had not purchased Rupert's Land from the Hudson's Bay Company; it merely paid to facilitate the extinction of the company's claims. All proprietary interest had reverted to the British Crown. The Rupert's Land Act and the order in council of 23 June 1870, which admitted the North-West Territory to the Dominion, conveyed no proprietary right but only the authority to administer these areas for 'the future welfare and good government of the territory', and for the 'Peace, Order and Good Government of Her Majesty's subjects and others therein . . . '. In enlarging the boundaries of Quebec and Ontario the Canadian government was not, Reid concluded, conveying proprietary interest, but merely arranging for the 'good government of Patricia and Ungava'. Since the action primarily involved 'good government', it affected only the people of the area and provinces immediately concerned. The rights of the Maritimes had been in no way infringed. A similar line of argument was employed in the case of the school and Crown lands of the Prairie provinces. Until Maritimers could prove that the federal government actually had a proprietary interest in the lands and that the land sales and transference were not concerned with the good government of the people in them, they could have no claim to compensation.[23]

The purpose of such legalistic rationalization is not difficult to surmise. The attempt by the Maritimes to secure a closer equity in subsidies with the Western provinces by attaching their claims to those of the Prairies was resented by Prairie leaders and posed an embarrassment in devising a formula for the transfer of the Crown lands to the Prairie governments. The subsidy claims of the two regions were mutually exclusive. Reid's obvious intent was not merely to destroy the Maritime case but to do so in a fashion which would facilitate a future settlement with the Prairies.

Reid's total lack of sympathy for the Maritime position was even more apparent in the memorandum which he appended to his report for the consideration of the prime minister. Here he suggested, rightly enough, that fiscal need underlay the Maritime demands. His solution, however, was not an increase in subsidies but rather to allow financial difficulties to lead the three provinces to political union. In business affairs a concentration of effort on the part of the management can sometimes lead to 'such a reduction of overhead charges that prosperity follows instead of threatened bankruptcy'. In totalling all subsidies and revenues from Crown domains in the three Maritime provinces, Reid found that they were roughly equivalent to those of Saskatchewan, the most populous Western province, which had about three-quarters of the population of the Maritimes. If the extra costs of three separate administrations were removed, such a sum, he believed, should be quite adequate for Maritime needs.[24]

The cabinet's insensitivity to Maritime problems resulted in the demoralization of the Conservative Party in the region and largely explains its inability to marshal an effective organization for the election of 1921. Regional anger had created a force stronger than party loyalty. Until it could offer Maritimers a reasonable expectation that their grievances would be adjusted by a Conservative government, the party held little attraction for any but the most dedicated supporters. In the Nova Scotia provincial election of July 1920, a Conservative stalwart, W.H. Dennis, publisher and managing director of the Halifax *Herald, Mail,* and *Sunday Leader,* reported the 'absolute lethargy of influential Conservative leaders'. Four months later J.A. Macdonald of Amherst, a wealthy industrialist, outlined in a tactful letter to Meighen the prospects for party organization in the province. But first, he stated, they would need 'three months of adjusting old grievances'. The attention to 'old grievances' was not forthcoming. In mid-September 1921, with the election less than three months away, Dennis reported that they were 'without organization and in many constituencies suitable men were not in sight as candidates'. 'A newspaper campaign', he continued, 'would be useless unless backed up with thorough organization and immediate attention given to great injustices to our people.'[25]

For Maritime Liberals the motives of regional concern and political ambition neatly coalesced. In associating themselves with the movement for

Maritime Rights they could not lose. If the government yielded to Maritime demands their regions would benefit; if it did not their party would be in a position to ride the resulting wave of popular anger to power. It is thus not surprising that Liberal leadership predominated in the campaign. Hance J. Logan of Amherst, whose pre-eminence in the Maritime Rights movement was recognized by two consecutive elections as president of the Maritime Board of Trade, was a former Liberal MP (1896–1908). In 1920 local Liberals made him president of their organization in Nova Scotia.[26] E.M. Macdonald of Pictou, also a veteran parliamentarian (1904–17) and leading party strategist in that province, had established himself publicly as the regional spokesman on railways. Other Liberals prominent in the campaign included J.C. Tory, MLA for Guysborough, noted for his contribution to the Maritime case for subsidies in lieu of Crown lands, New Brunswick Premier W.E. Foster of Saint John, who publicized the Maritime case both in the legislature and in national magazines, and Acadian leader P.J. Veinot of Bathurst, the New Brunswick minister of public works, who chaired the committee on Maritime claims at their national *fête* of 1921.

Liberals sought to capitalize on their association with the movement by proclaiming their party the Maritime Rights party in the election of 6 December 1921. E.M. Macdonald struck the keynote early in the campaign when, having denounced at length the Conservative government's sins against the region, he called upon Maritimers to 'rally round the Liberal banner . . . so that we may . . . regain our proper prestige and participation in the business of this dominion'.[27] Liberals were also encouraged in their regional stance by the activity and statements of their federal leader, W.L. Mackenzie King. King at this time was technically a Maritimer, having re-entered Parliament in 1919 as a member for Prince Edward Island. The offer of the nomination to the new Liberal leader was itself a bid by the Liberals of the island for local and regional recognition. With only four representatives in the House of Commons, the islanders were quick to seize upon any political leverage available. By securing the leader of the opposition as their representative, they could hope to make him better acquainted with their problems and place him under an obligation which might pay dividends when he came to power. Before long they had reason to feel pleased with their choice. King took up such local causes as cold-storage plants for fox-meat, lower freight rates on mussel-mud, and the demand for a second car ferry.[28] More gratifying to other Maritimers was his apparent interest in the whole region. He launched a speaking and organizational tour of the three provinces early in 1920 and based his first motion of nonconfidence on the lack of Maritime representation in the cabinet.[29] The tour was repeated in October of the following year in preparation for the election.

King's speeches on these occasions, although usually negative and ambiguous in their criticism of the government, gave ample scope for his listeners to believe that they heard in them the promises they wished to hear, particularly after they had been interpreted by the candidates and the Liberal press. His criticism of the government's centralization of the railways at Toronto was regarded in the Maritimes as a commitment to regional control.[30] In reporting the Liberal convention of 5 October at Amherst, the Halifax *Morning Chronicle* was highly laudatory of King's address as 'the greatest he has yet delivered in this part of the country'. But the reporter had little else to say about it. Most of the article dealt with H.J. Logan's speech advocating regional management of the Intercolonial, a 'national coal policy', and a vigorous defence of Maritime interests. 'Maritime rights must be our motto,' Logan had stated. 'In Parliament I pledge myself to advocate and stand by Maritime rights first, last and all the time.' The reporter's skill in interweaving Logan's statements in a report of King's speech conveyed the impression that the regional protest had the leader's full support. The article even confused the *Canadian Annual Review* of that year, which quoted Logan's pronouncements on the tariff as coming from Mackenzie King.[31] Locally the Liberals worked to confirm the impression of regional concern provided by the leader's visit. At Truro, Logan told his audience that he had given up plans to run as an independent Maritime Rights candidate only after King's promises respecting the Intercolonial had convinced him that Maritime needs could best be achieved within the Liberal Party.[32]

The Liberals' attempt to monopolize regional sentiment did not go unchallenged. In Nova Scotia the W.H. Dennis papers sought to maintain the credibility of their regional concern by commending the efforts of Logan, Tory, and the boards of trade. J.B.M. Baxter, leader of the Conservative opposition in New Brunswick, was also careful to make public his role in helping to draft the joint New Brunswick-Nova Scotia resolutions on the Intercolonial.[33] But local Conservatives could do little in competing with the Liberals for support from the movement without co-operation from the federal government, and this was not forthcoming until the election campaign had actually begun. Arthur Meighen took a step in that direction in the cabinet shuffle of late September when he replaced R.W. Wigmore, tainted by a year's association with a cabinet unresponsive to Maritime demands, with J.B.M. Baxter, a former Saint John alderman known for his commitment to port and region.[34] At the same time Meighen permitted the announcement of a new policy of regional management for the Canadian National Railways. On September 24 F.B. McCurdy criticized the local Liberal proposals to take the Intercolonial out of the Canadian National Railways and suggested that Maritimers should instead seek to retain the advantages of participation in a 'great transportation system' while maintaining regional control through the creation of an eastern unit with its headquarters in the Maritimes. Baxter followed with a similar suggestion, adding that the headquarters of the unit should be located at Moncton.[35]

In the course of his tour of the Maritimes in October, Meighen encountered intense pressure for a firmer commitment on railway policy. In an editorial in the *Herald* on the eve of his arrival, W.H. Dennis tried to impress Meighen with the importance of the railway issue in the campaign, while publicly defending his failure to act sooner on the matter. One could not expect a busy prime minister to 'follow, day and day, the details of management of such a colossal transportation system'. But once he became acquainted with the 'true conditions' one would expect that 'the just grievances of the maritimes' would 'meet with his sympathetic consideration'. Control of the Intercolonial 'must be taken from under the unsympathetic pushbuttons of Toronto and localized at Moncton'. The railway issue was the 'daily talk and conversation of Nova Scotia, New Brunswick and Prince Edward Island' and the prime minister, Dennis promised, would 'be acquainted with these facts during his visit'.[36]

From Nova Scotia Meighen cabled railway leaders for their comment on a proposed statement that 'upon formal taking of Grand Trunk into National system a policy of decentralization will be followed under which eastern end of amalgamated system will be operated from Moncton with necessary organization there for that purpose'. Their response was far from encouraging. J.A. Stewart and J.D. Reid, respectively new and retired railway ministers, stressed the 'necessity for strong central control' and warned of possible adverse political effects of such an announcement in other parts of the country. Sir Joseph Flavelle, the Toronto financier in charge of the Grand Trunk who had recently advanced his own scheme for railway organization, was flatly opposed. It would, he telegraphed, 'lead to misunderstanding and create difficult situation for railway executive when appointed'.[37] Nevertheless Meighen proceeded as planned and at Moncton gave a firm pledge that the CNR would establish a regional division with its headquarters at Moncton.[38]

The Dennis papers in Halifax took advantage of the new policy to charge to the forefront of the Maritime Rights movement, trying to convey the impression that they and their party had been there all the time. In November W.H. Dennis polled local candidates for their views on the railway issue. His statement referred to 'the campaign which our newspapers have consistently supported for the restoration of Maritime Rights in connection with the CNR', and explained regional demands on the issue in terms very close to the new policy announced by the government.[39] But the government's sudden concern for Maritime interests came too late. With no concrete evidence before the election that a new railway policy was in fact being implemented, Meighen's promise was simply not believed. In the last days of the campaign the prime minister was besieged with telegrams from party workers seeking a denial of rumours circulating among local railwaymen that the division of the lines had been 'indefinitely postponed'.[40]

The striking change in voting patterns in the election of 1921 was an indication of the Maritimers' attempt to secure their 'rights' through a change in government. In Nova Scotia the Liberals won every seat and the Conservative popular vote dropped to 32 per cent or about 10 per cent below their previous low of 1874. Liberals were also victorious in the four seats in Prince Edward Island and led their Conservative opponents by 8.5 per cent of the popular vote—the first time that more than 2 per cent had separated the two parties in a federal election in nearly thirty-five years. In New Brunswick, still strongly polarized between French and English, Liberal majorities increased in largely Acadian constituencies and Conservative majorities dwindled or were eliminated in the remainder.[41]

The role of regional issues was particularly apparent in the constituencies along the Intercolonial. In Westmorland county, which had formerly contained the railway headquarters, A.B. Copp's majority rose by 6,099 votes or by considerably more than one-quarter of the total votes cast. Hance J. Logan swept the former Conservative constituency of Cumberland by 5,355 votes and both his opponents forfeited their deposits. In Colchester F.B. McCurdy's 1,444-vote majority of only a year before disappeared as he was defeated by a freshman candidate, Harold Putnam.[42] In Halifax, where both the railway and ports were important issues, Liberal candidates won majorities of about 5,000 or half again more than their Conservative rivals.

The regional issues were, of course, not the only ones, nor were they necessarily the most in all constituencies. In Acadian counties the Conservative organization had been destroyed by conscription and the threat of *impérialisme* was kept alive by Acadian newspapers, particularly after Arthur Meighen became prime minister.[43] In the predominantly English-speaking counties of New Brunswick the old cries of race and religion were played up to divert attention from economic or regional questions embarrassing to the party in power. In the May 1921 by-election in York-Sunbury, for example, R.B. Hanson appealed directly to the Protestants of the constituency and applied to H.C. Hockin, grand master of the Orange Order in Canada, to send down the grand organizer to help in establishing the religious issue in the campaign.[44] Sectarian strife was also apparent in the two-member constituency of Saint John-Albert where Mackenzie King, in his October visit, reported the religious division to be working against the Liberals. The situation, he recorded, was 'as bad as can be, like Killkenny cats fighting each other, Irish Catholics & English Protestant, and the feuds of 1917 and earlier years perpetuated'.[45] Yet here, too, the impact of regional economic issues was apparent. The Conservative majority, which had exceeded 4,000 for R.W. Wigmore in 1920, all but disappeared in 1921. One Conservative candidate, Murray MacLaren, won by a narrow margin of 370 votes and even the highly respected Baxter secured a majority of only 1,115. Despite the presence of other issues in the campaign, regional grievances, rendered acute by economic recession, largely accounted for the sweeping Liberal gains throughout the Maritime provinces.

After the election, Maritimers quickly discovered that the realization of regional goals was not simply a matter of electing a new government, even when supported by a regional bloc from the Maritimes. They found, in fact, that their representatives were in a relatively weak position. The election produced a new Liberal government but a government dependent for its survival upon a much larger regional bloc of Progressives from the Prairies and rural Ontario.[46] The Progressives, like other Prairie representatives before them, were hostile to the Maritime position on subsidies, railways, the use of Maritime ports, and the preservation of the tariff on steel and coal. In his discussions with the prime minister on Christmas Eve 1921, Progressive leader T.A. Crerar called for the reduction of Nova Scotia's representation in the cabinet.[47]

In any contest of influence with the Progressives the Maritimers were at a serious disadvantage. Deficient in numbers—the Liberals held 25 of 31 Maritime seats but the Progressives had elected 64 members—and bound by party discipline, the Maritimers lacked the Progressives' ultimate weapon in bargaining, the threat to defeat the government should their demands not be met. Furthermore, despite all their talk of regional unity the Maritime Liberals formed an even less cohesive group than did the Progressives. The wedge upon which they tended to divide was the tariff. Unlike Prairie regionalism, firmly rooted in a common agricultural base, the Maritime variety had to span the conflicting interests of a more diversified economy. The Liberals were able to sweep the Maritimes on regional issues only by obscuring fundamental differences in economic interest and ideology. Their strategy had been to announce as their economic policy a return to the 'Fielding tariff'.[48] This was interpreted as the protective tariff in the central towns and as reciprocity with the United States in outlying farm and fishing communities. At Sydney, for example, the Liberal press headlined Mackenzie King's promises that the Liberal tariff would not harm the coal and steel industries. 'It is our policy to conserve and develop, not to shake, these great basic industries,' he had stated. Attributing the original industrial development to 'a Liberal tariff—Fielding tariff', King promised that 'the new "Liberal tariff" ' would bring 'a return to the general prosperity enjoyed by Canada after 1896'. A Conservative party worker returning from a trip along the east shore of Nova Scotia reported that there the Liberal candidates had 'actually got many people to believe that real free trade with the U.S. is in sight'.[49] Such contradictory aspirations predominating within different Maritime constituencies almost inevitably found expression in divisions among their representatives at the federal level as some joined the high- and others the low-tariff faction within the Liberal caucus.

Even the apparent advantage of an unusually large Maritime representation in government was deceptive. W.S. Fielding, the senior member of the Maritime quartet in the cabinet,[50] was far more a representative of Central Canada than of the Maritimes, which he had left a quarter of a century before. After his defeat in 1911, he had become part-owner and editor of a Quebec business journal, the *Daily Journal of Commerce*. Like other Central Canadian businessmen, he was alarmed by the political revolt of the Prairies but had little understanding of or sympathy for the Maritime protest.[51] Even in his private correspondence with Nova Scotia Premier E.H. Armstrong, he was not prepared to concede any basis for Maritime complaint. 'It would not be easy', Fielding wrote, 'to put one's finger upon any matter within the control of this Government in which injustice has been done to the Maritime Provinces'. Fielding's view was shared neither by his colleagues resident in the Maritimes nor by the large majority of their constituents.[52]

In the conflict between the Maritimers and the Progressives there was no question which side Mackenzie King would take. The cultivation of the Progressives became a central feature of his government's strategy for survival. In pursuing this policy, he found the Maritime demands an embarrassing nuisance. His sympathies were quite apparent in the rationalizations of which his diaries are so largely composed. King liked to justify his decisions on moral grounds with himself appearing on the side of the angels. After the election of 1921 he implicitly defended his lack of response to Maritime discontent in a continual disparagement of the motives, character, and ability of the chief exponents of Maritime Rights. When the Maritime Liberal members called for immediate action on their railway demands in a special meeting with the prime minister before the opening of Parliament, they were quickly put on the defensive. Led by Hance J. Logan and E.M. Macdonald, they reminded Mackenzie King of his promises in the Maritimes and requested the immediate restoration of the Intercolonial to independent management. They 'came in an ugly and Belligerent spirit,' King's diary recorded.

> I opened fire on Logan & told before the entire delegation of his intention to run as an Independent not as a Liberal until he had seen how things were going & that I had made no promise to any one to induce him to run. My own belief is that Logan had the article he referred to inserted in the Amherst [Halifax?] paper at the time & used it to serve his own ends at my expense. I am instinctively revolted vs such behaviour. It is apparent to me that both McDonald & Logan are resentful at not having been taken into the cabinet & intend to cause trouble. McDonald spoke of not wanting to stay in public life etc. etc. I shall recall this later when question of Cabinet appointments come up. A man like McDonald is not to be trusted in any way. I reminded the deputation the Liberal party had not a majority in the house & that on the Ry. Comm. there was room for the farmers & the tories to combine.[53]

King's scolding was followed by a lecture from the Liberal Toronto *Star*. The *Star* accused the Maritime Liberals of 'sectionalism' and 'political black-mail', reminded them of their relative weakness in numbers which would become even greater after the next redistribution, and warned that their region could easily become the victim of similar tactics from others. 'If they set this fashion,' the *Star* warned, 'the West or Ontario may imitate with demands which the Maritime Provinces acutely dislike', and might insist, for example, that 'in order to save paying heavy freight rates, Portland should be made more use of as a winter port'.[54]

The prime minister's initial response on the railway issue served notice how little help Maritimers might expect from the government in securing any of their 'rights'. Maritime subsidy claims received even less consideration from the new administration than from the old. Like their predecessors, the Liberals sought to isolate the Western claims and dispose of them in a fashion which would enable them to avoid a general readjustment of subsidies. In a letter to T.A. Crerar early in 1922, W.S. Fielding urged the Prairie provinces to state their claims for subsidies and the transfer of Crown lands in a manner which would not encourage claims by the other provinces. Mackenzie King made the same point in his letter to the three Prairie premiers later in the same month. Emphasizing that the subsidies in lieu of lands would cease with the transfer, King offered 'an accounting between the Dominion and the Provinces from the beginning, by an independent tribunal' to see if any money was due the provinces from the management of the resources. Any award by the tribunal could be 'capitalized and the interest adjusted in con-nection with the annual provincial subsidy'. King was, in fact, accepting the fine distinction between subsidies in lieu of lands and subsidies as compen-sation for previous 'unjust' treatment which the Prairie governments had by then begun to draw.[55] In their replies the premiers made quite clear that, prior to any judgement, the federal government would have to accept responsibility in the broadest sense for the monetary value of all land alienated while administered by the Dominion. However rationalized, it was obvious from their letters that no Prairie government was prepared to accept any decrease in subsidies in return for control of their natural resources. Indeed, from the breadth of their claims it is probable that they were hoping to increase them. This was not surprising. The real purpose of the subsidies had been to meet genuine fiscal needs. The need had not decreased. But if the financial problems for the Prairies were serious, those of the Maritimes, virtually excluded from the subsidy increases of 1906–11, were critical. The federal policy of dealing with the claims of the more powerful region as a separate case meant that, whatever happened there, Maritime needs and claims would remain unattended.

Government silence in the face of Progressive hostility also characterized the debate on the Maritime case for federal assistance in directing trade through Canadian ports. The subject was introduced in a resolution, presented by H.J. Logan in co-operation with J.B.M. Baxter, which proposed that 'the British tariff preference should be confined to goods brought into Canada through Canadian seaports'. The measure, Logan argued, would help both national ports and national railways and would honour a promise made by Sir Wilfrid Laurier in 1903 and reaffirmed in 1907.[56] He did not, he explained, want to force the issue to a vote but rather to test sentiment in the House in the hope of persuading the government to include some such measure in the budget.[57] Progressives and low-tariff Liberals, however, seemed to see the proposal as a dark plot by 'protected interests' to subvert the British preference. Progressive John Evans (Saskatoon) called it 'a camouflage of intent to curtail British competition'. Crerar condemned the resolution in principle because it would 'throw trade out of its normal, natural channel into an artificial channel created by this government'. Liberal James Malcolm (North Bruce) shifted the grounds for attack slightly in claiming that the measure meant 'discrimination' against Portland, which as a result of the government takeover of the Grand Trunk had become a 'national asset' and should be developed accordingly.[58]

Only two voices in favour of the resolution came from non-Maritime members, L.J. Ladner (Vancouver South) and W.F. Maclean (South York), both Conservatives. Indeed, amid the chorus of outraged free-trade principles provoked by the proposal came a quavering cry from within the Maritimes. A freshman Liberal MP, L.H. Martell (Hants), in a brief impromptu statement near the close of the debate, declared that he personally could not support anything which might increase the cost of food to the people of his constituency. In his budget a few weeks later, Fielding made no mention of any attempt to direct imperial trade through Canadian ports.

The closest the Maritimers came to a victory of any kind in the first year of the new government was on the issue of freight rates. The matter received a full airing in the house in the dispute occasioned by the imminent lapse of legislation suspending the Crowsnest Pass rates. In return for a federal subsidy on building a line through the Crowsnest Pass, the CPR in 1897 had reduced freight rates on grain and flour moving eastward, and on a variety of westbound commodities required by the settlers. The rates remained operative until 1918 when they were suspended by order in council to permit the railway to cope with wartime inflation. In 1919 the suspension was extended for an additional three-year period. A return to the old rates in 1922 would have been expensive for the railways, which claimed it would prevent the implementation of a 'voluntary' 20 per cent reduction on basic commodities across the country.[59] The Progressives, undoubtedly aware that their case for the renewal of the special rates stood little or no chance before the Board of Railway Commissioners, expressed their lack of confidence in that body and sought a political settlement in the house. They won an initial victory when the government referred the matter to a Special Committee on Transportation Costs.[60]

In the lengthy hearings before the committee, Maritime representatives called for a repeal of the earlier increases in the Maritimes as disruptive of interprovincial trade guaranteed by the Confederation agreement. British Columbians cited their own terms of union in demanding an equalization of their rates with those of the Prairies. Prairie representatives demanded the return of the Crowsnest Pass rates as necessary to provide their region the same protection against excessive rate increases which the Eastern provinces derived from competitive water rates and American railways.[61]

The ultimate report of the committee was determined less by the content of arguments than the exigencies of political power. Within the committee E.M. Macdonald led the attack on the Progressive position, arguing that the reduction should be applied to the basic commodities of the whole country rather than those of a single region. Realizing that he could not carry the committee in a complete restoration of the Crowsnest Pass rates, T.A. Crerar proposed their limitation to grain and flour only. Such a compromise, he suggested, would still leave room for reductions on other commodities on a national basis. Although narrowly voted down, Crerar's suggestion effectively divided the Liberal members in the committee, as such low-tariff sympathizers as W.D. Euler, James Malcolm, and even A.E. MacLean of Prince Edward Island voted with the Progressives. The split became even wider in the Liberal caucus as some of the low-tariff wing were reported to have used the rhetoric of a revolt against 'Montreal domination' in supporting the Progressive compromise. Aided by Progressive lobbying and threats of 'a determined opposition', the pro-Progressive faction won the vote in the Liberal caucus. The committee was hastily reassembled (though the Conservatives refused to associate further with a body whose decisions were determined elsewhere) and changed its recommendations to include the restoration of the Crowsnest Pass rates on grain and flour. The committee also declared 'a general reduction in railway rates' to be 'essential to the economic life of the country', but left this matter, as well as the claims of the Maritimes and British Columbia, for consideration by the Board of Railway Commissioners.[62]

The committee's decision, endorsed by the government, acutely embarrassed the Liberal exponents of Maritime Rights. E.M. Macdonald could not reveal the bitter fight which he had waged in the committee or the Liberal caucus without attacking the position ultimately taken by his party. In Parliament he gave a lengthy exposition of the Maritime case for lower freight rates but lamely concluded with the pious hope that the minister of railways would deal 'speedily' with the Maritime case. It remained for J.B.M. Baxter to point out the added sense of regional injustice which the government's policy would create in the Maritimes and the interpretation which would be placed upon the Maritime Liberals' apparent support of it. There seemed to be, he stated, 'two absolutely separate freight rate tribunals in Canada, one for the gentlemen with whom it is desirous to continue a political alliance, the other for the people who are absolutely in opposition or whose loyalty is so unquestioned or unquestionable that it is known in advance that they will swallow this or any other dose in the name of docile support to their leaders'.[63]

The cost of the Prairie victory became apparent in the meagreness of the reductions awarded on other commodities. The railway commissioners, taking the cost-revenue figures of the CPR as their criterion, calculated that there was an $8,338,469 surplus available for rate reductions. But $7,159,537 of this would be absorbed by the restoration of the old rates on grain and flour. The remainder, they ruled, would permit a reduction of only 7.5 more percentage points in the original 40 per cent increase.[64] Meanwhile the lengthy and detailed submission which the Maritime representatives had completed before the board early in 1922 finally bore fruit in a favourable decision on one aspect of their case. The commissioners still did not accept the Maritime claim for fixed arbitraries to protect the competitive position of Maritime industry, nor did they find any obligation to maintain low rates in the Confederation pact. But they did rule that the Montreal-Saint John portion of the rates of traffic to and from points west of Winnipeg was too high and 'did not indicate an equitable continuation of a long haul rate'. Their recommendation that such rates should be reduced from 42.5 cents to 24 cents first class was a virtual restoration of one group of arbitraries as they had existed prior to 1918.[65]

The final disillusionment of those who had looked to a Liberal government for recognition of Maritime railway claims came with the regional division of the CNR. The Liberal railway statement contained in the Speech from the Throne in 1922 called for a 'fair trial' for public ownership. More specific declarations of policy had to await the appointment of a new board of directors, which was not completed until October. By the end of the year the board had adopted the policy of maintaining strong central control of the railways but permitting the organization of five regional divisions. They shifted the general headquarters from Toronto to Montreal and established a local headquarters for the Atlantic region at Moncton.[66]

Whatever credit the Liberals might have derived from this partial concession to Maritime sentiment was largely destroyed by the board's decision to terminate the Maritime division not at Montreal, the western terminus of the Intercolonial since its extension in 1897, but 200 miles eastward at Rivière-du-Loup. The loss of control of a few hundred miles of railway was not the primary cause of renewed Maritime anger. The truncation of the Intercolonial assumed such great importance because it finally brought home to the Maritime public that the creation of a regional division did not imply anything like a return to the condition of regional independence which had prevailed prior to integration. Not only could they not regain control of rates to Montreal, but Maritimers would soon discover that they had little influence over rates within their own region. Furthermore, the drain in railway personnel from Moncton to the metropolitan headquarters continued.[67] Reminded of the brave promises by Liberal candidates before the election, Harold Putnam (Colchester) tacitly admitted the failure to implement them and remarked that, like Joseph Howe with Confederation, they chose to 'make the very best of a bad bargain'.[68] Like Howe's anti-Confederation supporters, however, the protesters of the 1920s proved less philosophical than their leaders in the acceptance of 'bad bargains'. Convinced of the betrayal of their interests by the Liberals, they would take their revenge at the polls at the earliest opportunity.

By the end of 1922 one phase of the campaign for Maritime Rights had come to a close. Maritimers had begun the decade on an optimistic note, proclaiming that they could restore their region to its 'rightful' position in the Dominion through unity and organization. The three Maritime governments had adopted a common case and co-ordinated their strategy in presenting it. They received the public support of the representatives and newspapers of all political parties and the vociferous endorsation of the leading commercial associations in their region. Snubbed by the Meighen government, the movement had demonstrated its strength by helping to produce a greater shift in the Maritime popular vote than in any previous election. But still it failed.

The reason for the failure had less to do with Maritime methods than with the clash of interests and imbalance of regional forces at the federal level. In the early 1920s the Maritimes and the Prairies were both in revolt against the central metropolises. Both shared common interests in their need for higher provincial subsidies and lower freight rates. The two Central provinces, with the large tax base from a growing consolidation of industry within their borders and less dependent upon long-haul transportation, were concerned with guarding the federal treasury against the costs of either subsidies or freight-rate reductions. The conventional approach taken by the Maritimes and the Prairies of preparing individual 'special cases' for subsidy and freight-rate changes brought them into conflict and facilitated the strategy of the railways and the Central Canadian politicians in playing one off against the other.

The urgency of the Maritime plight, especially on the railway issue, was apparent to some Central Canadian ministers and under normal circumstances might have yielded concessions. But the Central Canadian business community was badly frightened by the spectre of the Prairie revolt on the tariff. Unwilling to pay the price necessary to conciliate the Prairies, the

Meighen government avoided even the appearance of concessions to the Maritimes. This policy changed little with the new government. Indeed, the irony persisted of the two regional protests against the metropolitan region dissipating their firepower against each other instead of co-operating against a common enemy. Mackenzie King's government presided over the struggle like a referee at a wrestling match, but interfering occasionally to adjust the rules in favour of the stronger contender. The contest frustrated Maritime observers, whose champions under the rules of the game appeared doomed to perpetual defeat. By the following year they were desperately searching for means of changing the rules and threatening to withdraw from the game altogether.

Suggestions for Further Reading

Ernest R. Forbes, *Maritime Rights: The Maritime Rights Movement, 1919–1927, A Study in Canadian Regionalism* (Montreal, 1979).
W.L. Morton, *The Progressive Party in Canada* (Toronto, 1950).
John Herd Thompson with Allan Seager, *Canada 1922–1939: Decades of Discord* (Toronto, 1985).

Notes

[1] E.M. Macdonald to W.L.M. King, 8 December 1922, King Papers, PAC.
[2] It is not clear who first developed the compact thesis with respect to the railway. It was used in 1919 by Maritime MPs, newspapers, and boards of trade in opposing integration.
[3] 'Minutes', Halifax Board of Trade, 24 January 1922, PANS.
[4] M.K. Cullen, 'The Transportation Issue 1873–1973', in F.W.P. Bolger, ed., *Canada's Smallest Province* (Charlottetown, Prince Edward Island: Centennial Commission, 1973), 251.
[5] Premier Bell to J.D. Reid *et al.*, 31 December 1919, in 'Reports of Board of Trade Council Meetings, Charlottetown, P.E.I.', in the possession of A.W. Gaudet, Charlottetown; P.E.I., *Journals*, 1919, 127–8.
[6] 'Reports of Board of Trade Council Meetings', 17 February 1921, and P.E.I., *Journals*, 1921, 26.
[7] W.E. Foster, 'Justice for the Maritimes', *Maclean's Magazine*, July 1921, 30–1.
[8] N.S., *Journals*, 1921, 7.
[9] See Ernest R. Forbes, *Maritime Rights* (Montreal, 1979), chap. 4, n. 76.
[10] Evidence, Board of Railway Commissioners, 1920, 5323–4.
[11] *Ibid.*, 5336.
[12] *Ibid.*, 5478.
[13] *Ibid.*, 11701.
[14] *Ibid.*, 11704–5.

[15]N.B., *Journals*, 1921, 146–9; N.S., *Journals*, 1921, 357–61; P.E.I., *Journals*, 26–7.

[16]Sackville, *Busy East of Canada*, May 1921.

[17]'Report of Meeting with the Prime Minister and the members of the Government, Delegation from the Maritime Provinces, June 1st, 1921', R.B. Bennett Papers, 10139–43, PAC.

[18]*Ibid.*, 10147–8.

[19]A.E. Kemp to Arthur Meighen, 27 September 1920. Meighen Papers, PAC.

[20]Saint John *Standard*, 7 June 1921.

[21]*Ibid.*

[22]See N.S., *Journals*, 1920, 11–12, 1921, 7; N.B., *Journals*, 1920, 3, 1921, 5; P.E.I., *Journals*, 1920, 41–2, 1921, 5.

[23]'In re claims of Maritime Provinces for compensation in connection with grants made from public domain to other provinces', 18 April 1921, Meighen Papers, 023384, PAC. Reid was obviously employing against the Maritimes' case the ingenious rationalizations developed by Chester Martin in a historical justification of Manitoba's claims commissioned by the Manitoba government two years before. Chester Martin, *'The Natural Resources Question': The Historical Basis of Provincial Claims* (Winnipeg, 1920).

[24]J.D. Reid also announced at this time the postponement of work on the island railway until 'next year', *Debates*, 1921, 4568.

[25]Dennis to Arthur Meighen, 29 July 1920, Meighen Papers, PAC; Macdonald to Meighen, 23 November 1920, *ibid.*, Dennis to Meighen, 16 September 1921, *ibid.*

[26]Logan to Mackenzie King, 24 March 1920, King Papers, PAC.

[27]New Glasgow *Eastern Chronicle*, 7 October 1921.

[28]Charlottetown *Patriot*, 26 May 1920.

[29]W.L.M. King Diaries, 11 January 1920 (typescript), PAC (hereafter cited as King Diaries, PAC); *Debates*, 1920, 33.

[30]Amherst *Daily News*, 5 October 1921.

[31]Halifax *Morning Chronicle*, 6 October 1921, and *CAR*, 1921, 459.

[32]*Morning Chronicle*, 16 November 1921.

[33]Halifax *Atlantic Leader*, 16 and 23 May 1920; *Sunday Leader* (renamed), 15 May 1921; New Brunswick, *Synoptic Report of the Proceedings of the Legislative Assembly of the Province of New Brunswick*, 1921, 155.

[34]See Michael Hatfield, 'J.B.M. Baxter and Maritime Rights', 20, 24–5.

[35]Halifax, *Herald*, 25 September 1921; *CAR*, 1921, 394.

[36]*Herald*, 5 October 1921.

[37]Meighen to G.F. Buskard, 8 October 1921, Meighen Papers, PAC; Buskard to Meighen, 9 October 1921, *ibid.*

[38]Moncton *L'Évangéline*, 13 October 1921.

[39]Dennis to Hector McInnes, Hector McInnes Papers, 26 November 1921, in the possession of Donald McInnes, Halifax, N.S. (hereafter cited as McInnes Papers); Halifax *Evening Mail*, 28 November 1921.

[40]W.H. Dennis to Arthur Meighen, 22 November 1921, Meighen Papers, PAC; F.B. McCurdy to Meighen, 2 December 1921, *ibid.*; J.F. Boyce to Meighen, 2 December 1921, *ibid.*

[41]Popular-vote percentages are calculated from J.M. Beck, *Pendulum of Power*, vote totals are taken from the reports of the chief electoral officers, *Sessional Papers*, 1920, no. 13; 1921, no. 13; 1922, no. 13.

[42]In Colchester the Liberals added a new twist to the old grievances by claiming that the diversion of wheat to Portland and Boston was responsible for the lay-offs on the Intercolonial resulting from lack of freight. Truro *News*, 5 December 1921.

[43]*L'Évangéline*, 19 July 1920, 26 September 1921.

[44]According to his Progressive opponents, Hanson had said that he wanted 'no Catholic votes and is appealing for Orange support on the ground that they should not vote for the man the Catholics vote for'. T.A. Crerar to R.W.E. Burnaby, 15 May 1921, Crerar Papers, QUA; Hanson to H.C. Hockin, 22 April 1921, R.B. Hanson Papers, PANB.

[45]King Diaries, 16 October 1921, PAC.

[46]The Progressives had 64 seats, the Conservatives 50, compared with 116 for the Liberals. Four of the other five seats, 2 Labour and 3 Independent, were held by MPs from the Prairies who might be expected to side with the Progressives on regional issues.

[47]King Diaries, 24 December 1921, PAC.

[48]*Debates*, 1923, 102–3. To quote L.H. Martell (Hants), 'again we were told yesterday that the Liberal party came into power on a platform of lower tariffs. That is not the case. On every political platform that I had an opportunity of speaking in the Province of Nova Scotia, whenever I heard a colleague from Nova Scotia speak, and whenever I heard any of our leaders in Nova Scotia speak, no pronouncement whatever was made on the tariff. What we said was this, that we had it on good authority that . . . Mr. Fielding would be Minister of Finance . . . That was our tariff policy—Mr. Fielding as Minister of Finance.'

[49]Sydney *Record*, 27 December 1921; G.B. Kenny to Hector McInnes, 21 November 1921. McInnes Papers. See also *Morning Chronicle*, 18 November 1921.

[50]They were: W.S. Fielding (Shelburne and Queens), minister of finance and receiver general; D.D. MacKenzie (Cape Breton North and Victoria), solicitor general; A.B. Copp (Westmorland), secretary of state; and J.E. Sinclair (Queens, P.E.I.), minister without portfolio.

[51]A.K. Cameron, 'Memorandum of significant events and actions in the life of Rt. Hon. William Stevens Fielding; Prepared for Mr. Norman McL. Rogers,' W.S. Fielding Papers, vol. I, PANS.

[52]Fielding to Armstrong, 26 February 1923, *ibid.*, vol. 6.

[53]King Diaries, 1 February 1922, PAC.

[54]Quoted in *Debates*, 1922, 355.

[55]Fielding to Crerar, 1 February 1922, W.S. Fielding Papers, vol. 1. PANS; see King to the three Prairie premiers, 20 February 1922, and their replies in *Sessional Papers*, 1922, no. 142a.

[56]*Debates*, 1922, 708–10.

[57]*Ibid.*, 712.

[58]*Ibid.*, 718–21.

[59]9–10 Geo. v, c. 68, sec. 325 (5); *Debates*, 1922, 3552.

[60]A.W. Currie ascribed the West's 'lost faith' in the Railway Commission 'largely' to some 'injudicious' remarks by Chief Commissioner Frank Carvell. A.W. Currie, *Economics of Canadian Transportation*, 76. In this he seemed to be taking the excuse for the cause. The maintenance of such a special group of rates for one region would have been a complete reversal of the rate-making principles which the commissioners had proclaimed in their decisions over the previous decade.

[61]'Report of the Special Committee to Consider Railway Transportation Costs', Canada, House of Commons, *Journals*, 1922, 496.

[62]*Ibid.*, 498. A narrative of negotiations in the committee and reports from the Liberal caucus are contained in a lengthy letter, Crerar to J.W. Dafoe, 26 June 1922, Crerar Papers, QUA.

[63]*Debates*, 1922, 3570–6, 3582.

[64]Report of the Railway Commissioners for Canada, 1922, *Sessional Papers*, 1923, no. 33, 16, 90.

[65]*Ibid.*, 92–3.

[66]*Debates*, 1923, 62–3.

[67]*Ibid.*, 575.

[68]*Ibid.*, 13.

21

~•~

Nationalism in the 20s

Mary Vipond

The First World War brought change in many areas, from domestic labour relations to international economic trends. It certainly helped transform the prewar view of the role of Canada within the British Empire and in world affairs, though few Canadians—except in Quebec—explicitly criticized the relatively automatic loyalty to Britain that had been characteristic of Canadian policy at the onset of war. During the conflict the nation's political leaders had become increasingly aware of the disadvantages that followed from being entirely under Britain's imperial umbrella, and had begun to insist on Canadian input, if not independence of action. Many Canadians, moreover, had taken pride in their nation's participation in the war, and had developed a sense of distinctiveness from Europe. The failure of Europe's statesmen to find ways to halt the war helped produce a sense of disillusionment with the existing Eurocentric world order; the result was a considerable

positive response to President Wilson's 'Fourteen Points' and his proposals for a League of Nations. Canada insisted on joining the League, and began to build up its own international presence abroad. Meanwhile the postwar decade saw a renewed interest in the problems of Canadian identity and Canadian nationhood.

Mary Vipond analyses the nationalist response of the 1920s in Canada, focusing on the creation of an institutional network of organizations and individuals among English Canada's intellectual and artistic élite. As she points out, these men and women were little different in the background or outlook from the nation's political leadership, and were not so much interested in overturning the existing order as desirous of finding for it a new focus and a new sense of purpose, particularly in the area of cultural life, including broadcasting, literature, and the fine arts. Recognizing that political nationhood was not sufficient, they sought to mobilize a new national consciousness. But since these people were an élite, Vipond contends, their discussions hardly included the average Canadian except as a recipient of their ideas. While the intellectuals may have found a common purpose, they did not succeed in involving the general populace in their concerns.

How had the war served as a catalyst for a new spirit of nationalism? What parallels can be seen between the activities of the intellectual élite of English Canada in the 1920s and the social reformers of the prewar period? How did the nationalists conceptualize the problem of Canada and their role in it? Why were they unable to communicate with the general population? Did they adequately understand the realities of Canada? What factors and forces did they overlook? Have the problems of Canadian intellectuals changed over the years?

This article first appeared, titled 'The Nationalist Network: English Canada's Intellectuals and Artists in the 1920s', in *Canadian Review of Studies in Nationalism* v (Spring, 1980), 32–52.

Historians have consistently portrayed the 1920s as a nationalistic decade in Canada. The writers of textbooks still treat the years after World War I primarily as a key period in the 'colony to nation' saga; other students of the postwar decade point out that it also spawned an artistic and literary nationalism more vital than anything Canada had previously seen. In either case, however, whether the political/diplomatic or the cultural manifestations of English-Canadian nationalism in the 1920s are being examined, attention tends to centre on the small, close-knit, articulate, and concerned English-Canadian intellectual and artistic élite. The lengthy debates conducted in newspapers and journals, at public meetings and in faculty lounges, clubs, salons, and saloons about the twin issues of cultural survival and international status by professors, artists, authors, journalists, and their friends and acquaintances, have received a good deal of analysis at the hands of the historians of the 1920s. In most instances it is the content of the debates which has been studied: what did those thoughtful English Canadians mean by the term 'Canadian nationalism'; what did they think should be Canada's relationship with Britain, with the United States, with the League of Nations; what did they mean when they talked of national unity, of national literature, of national art?

But there was more to those discussions than their content. A few commentators on the period have noticed that fact, and have turned their attention beyond *what* was said to *who* said it and *how*. Graham Spry, for example, in reminiscing about the English Canada of the 1920s, commented on the 'intimate, trusting, confident, strong but really unorganized' web of personal relationships and friendships which linked together a 'network' of professionals, academics, businessmen, and other members of the English-Canadian élite in 'informal patterns of communication'.[1] Significantly, however, Spry made these observations in a short piece in the *Canadian Historical Review* on the founding of the Canadian Radio League. The phenomenon to which Spry was really addressing himself, and which others such as Brooke Claxton and Margaret Prang have also remarked upon, was not really the *in*formal communication patterns which existed within the English Canadian élite in the 1920s, but rather their *formulization*. Prang has pointed out, for example, that 'throughout the first post-war decade national organizations were born with a frequency unprecedented in Canadian history, while old ones took on fresh vitality.'[2] She lays particular emphasis on the spirit of 'Canada First' found in the 1920s among 'the small groups of young university teachers and professional men in the major cities across the country who established the *Canadian Forum* and debated public issues through its pages and who founded the Canadian League and later the Canadian Institute of International Affairs . . .'.[3] Claxton, too, referred specifically to four organizations with which he was asociated during the decade and after, the Association of Canadian Clubs, the Canadian League, the CIIA, and the League of Nations Society in Canada, and emphasized that

> To a considerable degree the objectives of these four organizations coincided and their membership overlapped. For quite a long time the key people in each organization came from much the same groups of people in Ottawa, Winnipeg, Montréal, Toronto and other Canadian cities. They had 'interlocking directorates'.[4]

This essay aims to investigate the hints dropped by Spry, Prang, and Claxton, by examining as *structure* a group of nationalist voluntary and cultural organizations which were formed or revitalized in the 1920s and which were led by or substantially composed of members of the English-Canadian artistic and intellectual élite. What is most important about the decade in this respect is not the informal communication patterns binding Canadian artists and intellectuals, but the extent to which these links became formalized, institutionalized, and made nation-wide during the postwar decade. Interpersonal relationships which previously had been relatively casual and localized were transformed at a rapid rate during the 1920s into a multiplicity of active national organizations with specific goals, constitutions, regular meetings, and frequent newsletters. The English-Canadian nationalist élite organized itself during this decade, and the questions are why and how? Why was the need for structures of communication so strongly felt in the 1920s, and how were personal and informal links used to build these structures?[5]

The focus here is on the English-Canadian intelligentsia of the 1920s, on the creative artists, the writers, the university professors—the intellectual élite. But the ties, whether personal or organizational, among these artists and intellectuals cannot be isolated from those which they shared with others. By and large the individuals who may be identified as English Canada's intellectuals in the 1920s were of the same class and background as the business, political, and professional leaders across the country. Family, marriage, war service, university, clubs, outlook—all tied them together. The intelligentsia was an integral part of a broader English-Canadian élite, formed by both birth and merit, but still an élite of education and position, almost entirely British Canadian and resident in the major urban centres. The intelligentsia was not radical, then; its members were not so much social critics as aspiring social leaders and moulders of public opinion. Few of them advocated fundamental social change; they all, however, felt that more rapid change than they had ever known before was enveloping them and other Canadians, and believed it to be their duty both to form responses to the new situation and to develop institutions which could cope with it. They saw themselves, as intellectuals and artists, performing the critical function of crystallizing community identity by dispensing meaningful symbols and articulating common goals.[6]

National feeling manifested itself in many forms among English-Canadian intellectuals in the 1920s: traditional, modern, Britannic, North American, and anti-American.[7] Even the imperialists of the 1920s were in many respects nationalists, for the differences between nationalism and imperialism were often more of emphasis than of substance, and imperialists such as A.J. Glazebrook, J.M. Macdonnell, and Hume Wrong were frequently active members of nationalist associations.[8] But however one 'classifies' them, all of these men and women shared a preoccupation with the current debate about Canada, its past, present, and future, its relationship with other nations and empires, its culture, its unity, and its identity. Within the wide boundaries of that common interest, they had much to say to one another. They were not all nationalists in the strict definition of the term, but they were all deeply concerned about the Canadian nation.

English Canada's nationalist intellectuals were not narrowly parochial either; they kept abreast of the major British and American literature, attended international conferences, and corresponded with friends in other countries, although their connections with French Canada were relatively few and weak.[9] Their external links, however, were usually carry-overs from earlier days, from birth or education elsewhere. Only rarely were significant new relationships being established across the seas or across the border during the 1920s. Most of the energy was being spent on expanding links with other English Canadians; the dynamism, the urgency, and the excitement were to be found moving along the lines of communication being built by nationalist intellectuals and artists *within* their English–Canadian world in the 1920s.

Canada's most prestigious intellectual organization in the 1920s was the Royal Society of Canada. Founded in 1882 with a political and nationalistic intent, the Society consisted of five sections embracing English and French humanistic and scientific disciplines.[10] Its founders hoped that the Royal Society would aid in 'the establishment of a bond of union between the scattered workers now widely separated in different parts of the Dominion', and this remained an important function in the 1920s.[11] Membership was by election for distinguished contributions to Canadian intellectual life. In 1930 there were two hundred Fellows, including such prominent scholars and writers as Chester Martin, O.D. Skelton, W.S. Wallace, L.J. Burpee, Lorne Pierce, Duncan McArthur, J.W. Dafoe, B.K. Sandwell, and Henry Marshall Tory. Royal Society Fellows met annually for business meetings and the reading of learned papers. Attendance was remarkably good, so that the annual meetings genuinely served the function of enabling intercommunication among the member scholars. The papers presented were published in the *Proceedings and Transactions of the Royal Society of Canada*, which went to individuals and libraries across the country. Despite, or because of, its exclusivity, the Royal Society was the genuine focal point of Canadian intellectual life in the 1920s. Few of the nationalist voluntary associations which sprang up during the decade would have survived without the initiative and aid of individual FRSCs. English Canada's nationalist intellectuals in the 1920s were not necessarily young 'moderns', then; on the contrary, many of them were middle-aged, well respected, and well established.

By the 1920s, several other academic organizations had grown out of the Royal Society. Since 1907, the Historic Landmarks Association (HLA) had worked to preserve Canadian historic sites. At its 1921 annual meeting, the HLA transformed itself, under the leadership of L.J. Burpee, a distinguished civil servant, prolific author, and historian, into the Canadian Historical Association.[12] The CHA was intended to be as inclusive in membership as possible, embracing all those interested in Canadian history.[13] Its first members were the former members of the HLA, about three hundred amateur historians, representatives of local historical societies, and wealthy social leaders. Over the decade the membership grew and changed; by 1930 academics predominated, especially at the annual meetings where papers were read and business discussed.[14] Links with the Royal Society remained strong, and many of the CHA's executive and council members were FRSCs. By the early 1930s the CHA's most important function, aside from encouraging scholarly research, was probably its nurturing of a sense of community, a sense of 'wider brotherhood' among Canadian historians.[15] Inevitably its meetings and activities came to provide a point of contact, a meeting place for amateur and professional historians interested not only in Canada's past but in its future. Two CHA publications helped to spread information about Canadian history among professionals and to a certain extent to a wider audience. The papers presented at the annual meetings as well as accounts of business and other activities were published in the CHA's *Annual Reports*, commencing in the year the association was founded. As well, after 1925 the University-of-

Toronto-centred *Canadian Historical Review*, featuring scholarly articles, book reviews, and occasional comment on contemporary affairs, was sent automatically to all members.[16]

The Royal Society and the CHA were almost the only Canadian academic organizations providing links for anglophone scholars in the 1920s. Few professors of English concerned themselves with Canadian literature in the 1920s, and they had no academic association to bind them together. The Canadian Political Science Association had been founded in 1913 at the instigation of Adam Shortt and O.D. Skelton, but after the first general meeting in Ottawa the war intervened, and the CPSA lapsed until 1929. Social scientists read and wrote for such Canadian publications as the *Bulletins* of the Queen's History and Political Science Departments (begun in 1910), various monograph series such as the McGill University Economic Studies, and, after 1928, *Contributions to Canadian Economics*, published under the direction of Harold Innis at the University of Toronto. By the 1920s it was common practice for Canadian economists, political scientists, and anthropologists to work for the government at some point in their careers, so Ottawa contacts and government publications provided an important communication link.[17] Since most Canadian social scientists at the time were historically oriented, many of them belonged to the CHA and published in the *CHR*. To a lesser extent, students of Canadian literature found their way to the *CHR* as well, because the compilation of its history still accounted for the bulk of research on Canadian literature.

Two university-associated journals also enabled Canadian academics to keep in touch both with one another and with a somewhat broader public. *The University Magazine* failed shortly after the war, but its place was partially filled by the *Dalhousie Review*, which commenced publication in April 1921. Edited throughout the 1920s by Herbert L. Stewart, an Irish-born philosophy professor, the *Review*'s declared purpose was to provide a vehicle by which scholars, teachers, and men of affairs could reach a wider audience.[18] Although domiciled in the Maritimes, the *Dalhousie Review* discussed both national and international affairs and attracted readers and writers from everywhere in Canada as well as from abroad. It maintained a strong concern for Canadian literature, and over the course of the decade revealed a growing sense of a non-British Canadian identity.[19] The other major surviving university journal, the *Queen's Quarterly*, had been founded in 1893. Like the *Dalhousie Review*, it was intended not so much as a scholarly journal as a means whereby scholars might reach a readership of intelligent ordinary citizens. The 'Current Events' section, written by a variety of men of different opinions, but dominated by economist O.D. Skelton and historian Duncan McArthur, kept up to date on British and Canadian events and provided wide coverage of Europe as well. As in the Dalhousie journal, references to the United States or French Canada were meagre. Despite their professed intent, the *Dalhousie Review* and the *Queen's Quarterly* seem to have appealed only to a small and specialized readership; by the end of the 1920s they had only 500 and 1500 subscribers respectively.

These university-linked organizations and journals provided Canadian academics with opportunities to meet, establish friendships, and explore common interests, but they were neither activist nor explicitly nationalist in their function. A host of other voluntary associations, to which many of these same intellectuals also belonged, did however provide opportunities for mutual exploration of views on the contemporary Canadian nation and for co-operation to reach nationalist goals.

The origin of the Canadian Institute of International Affairs (CIIA) in the Canadian League, the Canadian section of the British (after 1926 Royal) Institute of International Affairs, and the Institute of Pacific Relations has been described in detail by Edward Greathed.[20] All four organizations provided important links among Canadian academics and between them and other thoughtful Canadian men and women. The Canadian League, the least formal of these associations, consisted of about thirty small groups in fifteen cities. Members met approximately fortnightly 'to inform themselves about the country and its problems, to discuss these with other Canadians, to learn what other Canadians feel about them', and so to 'promote a general interest in the Country and its affairs'.[21] Based originally on wartime and university friendships, the Canadian League was organized in 1925 and held together primarily by J.M. Macdonnell, W.D. Herridge, Sandy Urquhart, Brooke Claxton, and Graham Spry.[22] The Institute of Pacific Relations was a mainly American organization founded in 1925 to promote understanding in the Pacific area. Among the Canadians active in it were a number of YMCA people from the West Coast, John Nelson, writer and editor from Vancouver, and Ontario Liberal Newton Rowell. The Royal Institute of International Affairs had a few Canadian members, such as Professor G.M. Wrong, Vincent Masey, A.J. Glazebrook, Loring Christie, Professor N.A.M. Mackenzie, and Newton Rowell, from the time of its establishment in 1920. The formation of a separate CIIA was sparked, according to Greathed, by a co-operative link between Nelson of the IPR and Rowell of the RIIA.[23] The CIIA began at the local level in Montréal, Toronto, Winnipeg, and Vancouver (in Winnipeg, especially, on a Canadian League base), and became a national organization in 1928.[24] It was neither a large nor a broad organization. Its founders intended to establish

> a small group of well-informed men and women in Canada who, because of their training, knowledge and position, may be of some assistance in dealing with the external affairs of our country, and who may help to form an intelligent public opinion on such questions.[25]

CIIA members were also sensitive, however, to the need for a somewhat broader base if they wished to exert real influence upon Canadian public opinion. For a 'popular arm' they often turned to the League of Nations Society in Canada.[26]

The League of Nations Society was formed in 1921 at the instigation of a group which included Newton Rowell, Sir Robert Borden, Vincent Massey, and A.J. Glazebrook. Contacts made through the Canadian Round Table group were instrumental in setting up the organization; as well, much proselytizing was undertaken on the Canadian Club luncheon circuit.[27] Academics were involved principally in the Society's educational wing, where they worked among other things to inform teachers and school children of the values and virtues of the League.[28] By the end of 1924 the membership of the Society was only 5,250, a figure which caused some consternation to an executive devoted to making the body a force in Canadian affairs. After special campaigns under the leadership first of Sir George Foster and later of Graham Spry and Ottawa businessman C.G. Cowan there were over 13,000 members at the end of 1928—still far below the original goals, and still including much dead wood—but at least forming a broader spectrum of interested, concerned Canadians than most such organizations. The League of Nations Society also published a *Bulletin*, after 1928 called *Interdependence* and edited by Graham Spry, in which issues of Canada's status in world affairs were debated at length.

Considerably larger and probably more significant in its function as an educational and opinion-moulding organization in the 1920s was the Association of Canadian Clubs. The Canadian Club movement, which had originated in 1892, had lapsed into a state of suspended animation during World War I. In 1919, instead of reviving, membership began to fall off sharply; the competition of newly formed service clubs such as Rotary, Kiwanis, and Lions was no small factor in this decline. The seemingly imminent collapse of the movement did not go unnoticed, however, by those who still believed in the purposes for which it had been created, namely, to 'foster Canadian patriotism and to stimulate intelligent citizenship'.[29] Under the leadership of E.J. Tarr, a prominent Winnipeg lawyer and president of Monarch Life, the Association of Canadian Clubs was reorganized in 1925 and 1926 and gained a new lease on life.

At the time of reorganization the Association of Canadian Clubs established permanent national headquarters in Ottawa and appointed a full-time secretary, twenty-six-year-old Graham Spry, just back from Oxford and a job with the ILO in Geneva. Spry's most important duties as secretary were coordination and distribution. He arranged programs, made them easily available to local clubs, and toured the country each year to deal with local problems and to rally support for the national Association. A measure of Spry's success was the climb in the number of clubs affiliated with the Association from 53 to 115 within two years, so that over 40,000 Canadians were Club members by the end of the decade.[30]

Spry had one additional important function: he edited the Canadian Club journal, the *Canadian Nation*. This little review, which was for a short period very successful (reaching a circulation of 37,000 in early 1929),³¹ contained thoughtful editorials on Canadian and Canadian Club goals written by Spry, reprints of significant Club speeches, articles on cultural affairs, stories by Canadian writers, and sketches by Canadian artists. In the optimistic days of late 1928 when Spry hoped to enlarge the magazine, Marius Barbeau and Frederick Philip Grove were named associate editors, but within a few months, owing to financial stringencies, the magazine instead folded.³²

The Canadian Club organization was much larger and more broadly based than any of the other associations mentioned so far. Its membership clearly extended far beyond the intelligentsia—so too did its speakers' lists. But its ties with the intellectual élite were relatively close and very important; intellectuals both used it and were influenced by it.³³ As is typical of any voluntary association, a small minority—in this case most particularly one individual, Graham Spry, the sole paid officer—exerted a large measure of control over the activities of the Canadian Club organization.³⁴ Spry, through his intimate knowledge of the week-to-week activities of all the clubs, through his power to initiate speakers' tours, and through his editorship of the Association's journal, was able to mould the A of CC to the purpose to which he felt it should be put, namely, to acquaint a large group of influential Canadians with one another and with their evolving world, and so to cultivate in Canada 'an informed, tolerant, national public opinion'.³⁵ Many Canadian intellectuals, through the liaison of Spry, were able to communicate directly with large numbers of men and women of local influence and power through the Association of Canadian Clubs.

A superb example of the extent and efficiency of the nationalist network of contacts which was developed among men of affairs and academics in the 1920s may be found in the Canadian Radio League.³⁶ Formed in 1930 by Graham Spry and Alan Plaunt as a pressure group to urge on the government the adoption of a national radio policy, the League was built on the personal and organizational bonds which had grown up in the previous decade. Spry's contacts were extensive, from his university years at Manitoba and Oxford, from the League of Nations Society, from the Canadian League, and especially from the Association of Canadian Clubs. Plaunt, who had graduated from the University of Toronto in 1927 and then spent two years at Oxford, was a member of the CIIA and active in the IPR. When the two young men decided to set up the Canadian Radio League, they turned to their friends and acquaintances—young, aspiring members of the leadership élite in the CIIA, Canadian League, Canadian Clubs, and the universities, including Brooke Claxton, E.A. Corbett, K.A. Green, R.K. Finlayson, and Norman Smith. The Canadian Radio League was a small association, but its members had contacts in influential circles in all the major urban centres and knew how to exploit them to full advantage. It was able to spring up so quickly and effectively owing to the careful orchestration of its two young founders and their brilliant use of a series of personal, professional, and organizational links among 'informed', 'concerned', and 'thoughtful' Canadians which were well in place by the end of the 1920s.[37]

The development of Canadian culture was a matter of intense interest to English-Canadian nationalists of the 1920s. Some of the academic and public-affairs-oriented organizations concerned themselves from time to time with cultural questions. As well, certain groups of artists, both literary and graphic, devoted themselves primarily to the nationalist cultural cause, and in turn had ties with academics and publicists.

Despite its relatively small size (approximately eight hundred regular and associate members), the Canadian Authors' Association (CAA) was one of the best-known nationalistic voluntary associations of the 1920s. Founded in March 1921, the CAA was primarily intended to be a trades guild for Canadian writers—to lobby for their interests (especially with regard to copyright legislation), and to provide a forum for the exchange of information and opinion on such matters as fees and contracts.[38] By the end of the 1920s, however, the Association had allowed so many 'associate' members into its local branches that it had become less a professional pressure group than a society of a wide variety of men and women interested in vaguely cultural activities.[39] Within the CAA writers, both professional and amateur, academics, and ordinary men and women were able to meet and discuss around the common focal point of an interest in Canadian literature; those who were so inclined (and these were the ones who dominated the Association by 1930) were also able to use the organization to attempt to imbue other Canadians with their enthusiasm for and dedication to the proposition that a national literature was essential to a true sense of Canadian nationhood.[40]

Aside from meeting at the annual national conventions (deliberately held in May or June to enable university people to attend more easily), CAA members kept in touch through two magazines. At first the *Canadian Bookman* was the society's official organ. Founded in 1919, the *Bookman* was edited by B.K. Sandwell with a deliberately nationalist intent. It was devoted almost entirely to comment on Canadian literature, and it tended to treat that literature very kindly indeed.[41] After the *Bookman* changed management at the end of 1922, the CAA commenced publication of its own *Authors' Bulletin* to convey news and to reprint speeches. Undoubtedly many members continued to read the *Bookman* as well, for it still provided the best coverage of Canadian literary news; by the end of the decade it had a circulation of 1,800.

Some Canadian artists also grouped together to proclaim themselves nationalists, and had contacts with nationalists in the universities and other circles. Best-known, of course, were the members of the Group of Seven, deliberate interpreters of the Canadian experience and propagandists for a 'national' art. The Group members not only painted and showed together, but spent a considerable amount of their time proselytizing. They wrote for and spoke to the public fairly frequently, and took full advantage of the publicity value of such imbroglios as the Wembley affair of 1923.[42] Contrary to myth, the members of the Group of Seven were not isolated from or ridiculed by Canadians in the 1920s—at least not more than occasionally. They received both moral and financial support from private individuals such as Dr J.M. MacCallum, from National Gallery officials such as Eric Brown and Sir Edmund Walker, from parts of the press, and from local and municipal art galleries, school boards, and individuals who purchased their works.

One of the important institutions which helped weld together the Group members and other men of culture in Toronto was the Arts and Letters Club. Established in 1908, the Arts and Letters Club was a gathering place for men interested in all the arts. Not only could members lunch at the Club on Elm Street, but they could stage plays, hang paintings, and contribute to the Club's own little magazine *Lamps*.[43] At the Club artists, musicians, actors, and their patrons could meet and become acquainted. There, through Lawren Harris, the other Group of Seven members met patrons, friends, and critics. Some of the most vigorous and perceptive of the Group's early supporters were members of the Club—most notably Fred Housser, the sympathetic author of the earliest full-length study of the Group, *A Canadian Art Movement*, published in 1926, whose wife Bess, also a painter, was the editor of the art page of the *Canadian Bookman*. The Arts and Letters Club has been called 'the centre of living culture in Toronto' after 1910.[44] Toronto itself was undeniably the cultural centre of English Canada, as the experience of artists in other parts of the country attests. The self-conscious nationalism of the Group and the stimulation they received from like-minded friends gave these painters a boost which those living elsewhere, such as David Milne or Emily Carr, were denied.[45]

Works by members of the Group of Seven were frequently published in Graham Spry's little *Canadian Nation*. They appeared occasionally in more popular periodicals such as the *Canadian Magazine* too. The greatest support for the Group, however, came from *The Rebel*, the little University of Toronto journal published between 1917 and 1920, and from its more broadly based successor, the *Canadian Forum*. Margaret Davidson has convincingly demonstrated the 'symbiotic' relationship which existed between the Group of Seven and the *Forum*; the periodical found the painters the perfect example of the new postwar Canadian cultural spirit for which it was searching; in turn the artists were encourged by the attention and publicity the *Forum* gave them.[46] Two members from the Group, J.E.H. MacDonald and Lawren Harris, served on the magazine's editorial board in the 1920s, as did Group friends and supporters Barker Fairley and Merrill Denison; prints and articles by and about the Group members appeared frequently. The *Forum* could not pay its contributors and its circulation was small, but its 2,500 subscribers, the cultural and intellectual élite of Canada, became very familiar with the work and the ideas of the Group of Seven by the end of the 1920s.

The *Canadian Forum* of course concerned itself with more than Canadian art. It was founded in 1920 to provide a forum for the 'freer and more informed discussion of public questions' and 'to trace and value those developments of arts and letters which are distinctly Canadian'.[47] Almost every well-known (or aspiring) English-Canadian intellectual or artist appeared in its pages at some point in the 1920s. It is no exaggeration to see the *Forum* as the single most important journal of the Canadian intelligentsia in the 1920s—or indeed for many years after.[48]

The *Canadian Forum* was not naively nationalistic. It strongly championed the application of the best critical standards to Canadian culture. It was sharply scornful of the 'boosting' in which organizations such as the Canadian Authors' Association engaged, and along with the tiny and evanescent *Canadian Mercury* and *McGill Fortnightly Review* published caustic criticism by young 'moderns' such as F.R. Scott, A.J.M. Smith, Morley Callaghan, and Douglas Bush of the orgy of sentimental nationalism in which so many Canadians of the 1920s were indulging. But these young writers were nationalists too, of a different type from the older generation, but still deeply concerned, in the manner of so many intellectuals and artists, with the growth of national culture, policy, and identity. Their goal was expressed by an editorial in the first issue of the *Forum*: 'Real independence is not the product of tariffs and treaties. It is a spiritual thing. No country has reached its full statute, which makes its goods at home, but not its faith and its philosophy.'[49] To the English Canadian intellectuals of the 1920s, it often seemed that the Canadian Manufacturers' Association had been far more effective in protecting and developing the nation's potential than they had; they firmly believed, however, that not only lamps and lingerie but 'OPINION should be MADE IN CANADA'[50]—and that it was up to them to make it.

This catalogue, while by no means exhaustive, gives an indication of the striking number and range of organizations and journals through which English-Canadian intellectuals institutionalized a set of friendships and essentially common interests during the 1920s. The interconnections are obvious; the same names—especially those of pivotal individuals such as L.J. Burpee and Graham Spry—appear again and again. A 'growing transcontinental network of concerns and personal relationships'[51] was utilized in the postwar decade to set up voluntary associations which would work to create national sentiment and to focus it on specific issues; the organizations themselves in turn extended and enriched the personal ties.

But why did so many of English Canada's intellectuals and artists during the 1920s feel such a need for the elaboration and institutionalization of previously informal or nonexistent links? The answer to that question relates both to general factors in post-World-War-I Canadian society and to the role of intellectuals in any society.

Canada had emerged from World War I insisting on its status as a self-governing nation in the world arena. Intellectuals were among the many Canadians who had developed a new sense of pride and identity as a result of their country's wartime achievements. Frank Underhill, who served overseas in both the Canadian and the British armies, wrote home to his mother in 1917: 'I'm much more a Canadian now than ever I was.'[52] A.R.M. Lower, who served in the British navy, similarly recalled in his autobiography: 'I came back from the war much more of a Canadian than I went to it.'[53] But the new consciousness of Canada and of its world role led as well to a new awareness of the country's weaknesses. The war had brought social disruptions and economic changes which exposed to view the many difficulties of the emerging nation. English-Canadian nationalists were only too familiar with the litany of Canada's problems: the ebbing of population growth, the increasing cultural and economic penetration of the United States, the rupturing of the East-West unity of the old National Policy, still-simmering ethnic antagonisms, the acceleration of urbanization and industrialization, the breakdown of traditional morality—and with it all, the lingering colonial mentality, now referred to in psychological terms as Canada's 'inferiority complex'. Canada was almost a nation in a political sense, but it still lacked the spiritual cement of a national will or purpose—or at least that was the intellectuals' diagnosis.

And the cure? That, they assumed, lay in their hands. They believed it to be their responsibility to 'mould public opinion' in the direction of a national consciousness. They were the 'innovative minority'; it was their job to formulate social goals, to give direction to the national will, and thus to give cohesion to Canadian society.[54] They were Canada's leaders, and as such their obligation was clear. J.W. Dafoe, for example, threw out the challenge to the Canadian Authors' Association: 'National consciousness doesn't happen,' he told the members at their annual banquet in 1925. 'It can be encouraged. It is a product of vision, imagination, and courage, and can be created and established by men and women who devote themselves to it.'[55] Similarly, literary critic W.A. Deacon wrote:

> Our struggle for nationhood needs writers and national magazines with native force behind them, filled with Canadian thought from the gifted Canadian pens which we drive out each year. 'Moulders of public opinion' is a phrase I hate. It indicates bulldozing on the part of the press. Yet, in a less offensive way, they are what we need—men who will take the nebulous ideas and vague stirrings of emotion and 'mould' them into concise and beautiful forms; we need to be expressed by our press, not harangued.[56]

Here then lay the role of the intelligentsia, the artists and the writers—to create a national feeling and to focus and direct it. It was a role with equal appeal to those who already saw themselves as Canada's leaders and to those aspiring to take their place among that select group.

Like many early twentieth-century 'progressives', these Canadian intellectuals were convinced that the acquisition of information was the first step toward the solution of national problems. If Canadians only knew one another and understood one another's point of view, they argued, regional and ethnic and class rivalries would vanish. And who was better suited to the research, study, thought, and writing needed than the nation's intellectuals? They were the experts; they would gather information and convey it to the public. Upon the artists a slightly different task devolved—the creation of myths and symbols which expressed the Canadian identity and clarified its meaning. Between them, the artists and intellectuals would work to provide all Canadians with a secure sense of their own identity as they ventured forth upon the world stage for the first time.

This, then, was the concrete task of education and proselytization which Canadian nationalist intellectuals in the postwar decade set themselves, and they were very conscious that they had in the past been 'shirking their duty to the state' in this respect.[57] But to achieve this goal they must organize. Such a difficult and challenging job could not be accomplished by the struggles of isolated individuals. All who shared the vision must come together in a united and directed effort. The establishment of voluntary associations and journals was a step toward accomplishing the grand duty to which Canada's idealistic intellectuals had been called.

But did the organizations and publications which the intellectuals created in the 1920s really aid them in moulding public opinion? Kenneth McRoberts, in an analysis of Karl Deutsch's *Nationalism and Social Communication*, commented that there are two distinct variables in the process of disseminating nationalist ideas from the élite to the mass: first the élite must desire to spread nationalism 'actively', and secondly the mass must be willing to pay attention. He elaborates:

> Turning . . . to the question of whether or not an élite disseminates nationalist ideology to the mass, we can assume that this will most likely occur if certain elements among the élite discover that their own personal needs might be advanced if a national political community were to come into existence. . . . But, more importantly, even if élites develop nationalist ideas, they might still fail to disseminate them to the mass with the energy and thoroughness necessary for adequate absorption. Communication between élites and mass might, in fact, be quite limited or profitless. Nationalist ideas might circulate intensively among the élites, yet not reach the mass.[58]

We have seen here that nationalist ideas did 'circulate intensively' within certain élite groups in Canada in the 1920s, and that the members of these groups believed that they had a duty to spread them further. But did they succeed in doing so; indeed, did they really try?

Intellectuals and artists certainly did communicate intensively with a group of business and political leaders who were their equals. But their links beyond this circle were sporadic at best.[59] Most of the associations and journals they used were small, specialized, and exclusive. Some of them made no attempt at all to cater to a wide audience; others, while more general in interest, only attracted small numbers. Even the largest and broadest of the organizations discussed here—the League of Nations Society and the Association of Canadian Clubs—were exclusive rather than inclusive. The former had at its decade peak 13,000 not very faithful members; the latter, while considerably larger, was invariably composed, in any given community, of the wealthier, the more powerful, the more 'important' men and women—those who could afford to attend lengthy luncheon meetings in the interests of self-improvement or for the opportunity to rub shoulders with touring 'greats'.[60]

But the fact that the organizations through which they claimed to wish to mould public opinion in truth directly touched only a small minority of Canadians seemed to worry the nationalist intellectuals very little. To a large extent this was because of their conception of public opinion. When they talked about moulding the minds of Canadians, what they really meant was that they wished to mould the minds of the literate, the influential, the informed—those who carried weight in the eyes of the community and of the government. The intellectuals saw themselves as the 'tutors' of the leaders of Canadian society—of the businessmen and the politicians. In the universities they prepared 'a class of leaders imbued with the right ideals and the necessary training'; in the community they continued the same job.[61] The mingling of intellectuals, businessmen, and politicians in the voluntary associations thus facilitated the communication of nationalist ideas within the élite; it was both built on and helped to create a sense of community among them.[62] That these organizations devoted more time to the Masseys than to the masses was not accidental; it derived from class and leadership assumptions which gave ordinary Canadians little role to play except as the consumers of nationalist propaganda. A good example of this attitude is to be found in the memorandum issued in July 1925 to explain the need for and purposes of the network of study groups which would be linked together as the Canadian League. Although the members of the League claimed that they wished to 'affect public opinion in every way that lay in their power',[63] they in fact had a very narrow definition of that task:

> So far as influence on what is called the positive side is concerned, it is a commonplace that the actions of governments are always influenced, not by the many, but by the few, and in this case the few will have the double advantage of having carefully studied the subjects on which they put forward their views and of being able to state that their view is held from coast to coast by thoughtful men. Moreover, the groups, although small in number, would really represent a substantial element in the community and could, if necessary, obtain a

measure of support from others like them. Various means of exercising their influence suggest themselves, such as pressure through the newspapers, petitions, influence on private members, direct representation to the Government which after all, if the conclusions were sound, would in many cases be only too glad to adopt them.[64]

Most striking about this statement, aside from the naiveté of its concluding phrase, is the emphasis it placed on the influence of the 'few' on the sources of power, and its complete lack of interest in the 'many'. Insofar as the intellectuals led anyone, they led other leaders. Only very indirectly was their influence to filter down to the rank and file.

The process of forming nationalist organizations also filled a deep need felt by the intellectuals themselves. First, these associations served a purely social function. Many of them were good excuses for people who enjoyed each other's company to get together regularly.[65] But there was more to them too. Despite the fact that the number of Canadian academics, artists, and authors was growing in the 1920s, and the fact that they were, relatively speaking, affluent, they still felt ill at ease, unloved and unwanted in what they perceived to be a superficial, pleasure-loving, growth-oriented society. Indeed, even the burgeoning of their own numbers had negative effects, for it led to impersonality, separation, and the loss of some of the old tight feeling of comradeship. The postwar recession, social confusion, and political uncertainty exacerbated these feelings of insecurity; any claims Canadian intellectuals had ever had to spiritual or social status seemed to be eroding in the wave of materialism inundating the country in the decade following World War I. Carleton Stanley, who had a foot in both the business and the university worlds, expressed it well in the *Hibbert Journal* in 1923:

> Forty or fifty years ago a Canadian university professor was one of the well-to-do men of the community. He could enter any social circle he chose. Not only in the lecture-room but also in the community at large he moulded public opinion. To-day he has the social position of a Roman client, and is the butt of the newspapers. A generation ago in the smaller Canadian towns the parson and the schoolmaster, along with the lawyer and the judge, were the intellectual aristocracy. To-day, except in a Catholic or Lutheran village, there is not a schoolboy who would raise his cap to the cloth; and the schoolmistress (for the schoolmaster is extinct) ranks with a telephone operator, and is not so well paid. The magnate of the place, whose views are canvassed on politics or the town library, is usually the owner of a shirt factory, or an automobile agent.[66]

To attribute the involvement of the intelligentsia in nationalist movements directly to its perceived loss of status would be impossible, but the idea merits consideration. By joining nationalist voluntary associations, professors, writers, and artists found forums in which their abilities were respected. Occasionally they found pecuniary advantage. Even more importantly, they found a cause for which to fight, and colleagues with whom to fight it. They were searching for a meaningful role to play in Canadian life in a period of rapid change, and nationalist organizations gave them one. Carlton J.H. Hayes has aptly summed up the appeal of nationalism to such groups:

> In the propagation of nationalism as in the propagation of any doctrine, there is always an opportunity for the person who likes to stand in the limelight and to feel that he is a man (or she is a woman) of no small importance. Especially has this been true in the propagation of a continuously and rapidly effective doctrine like nationalism in the nineteenth and twentieth centuries. To preside over a patriotic society, to deliver an address at the unveiling of a monument to a national hero, to march be-ribboned and be-medalled at the head of a patriotic procession, is calculated to feed one's self-esteem and at the same time to increase one's respect for that which has enabled one to be so conspicuous and so important. Vanity may be a fault, but if so it is a broadly human fault. It crops out in clergyman, in nobleman, in businessman, in professor. It has given us of late from every class many spectacular propagandists of nationalism.[67]

The organization and institutionalization of previously informal links in the 1920s thus fulfilled a personal and psychological purpose for the members of Canada's intelligentsia. At national conferences, in journals, at meetings, through friendships made there and correspondence begun, they gathered information, shared ideas, discussed hopes and plans; they stimulated one another, reinforced one another, and created a feeling of cohesiveness, community, and common purpose. Whether their cause bore fruit or not, they belonged.

Brooke Claxton, in a much-quoted excerpt, reminisced about the 1920s:

> Every kind of organization, national and local, cultural and religious, political and commercial was at a peak of activity hardly equalled since. . . . All these were manifestations of the growth of national feeling—it was nationwide, spon-taneous, inevitable. It cut across political, racial and social lines, indeed, it was curiously apolitical.[68]

The number of nationalist organizations and magazines which sprang up in the postwar decade was indeed remarkable. Only three or four of the many central associations or journals discussed here existed in an influential form prior to World War I; some of those founded in the 1920s were evanescent, but an impressive number of them has endured into the 1970s.

But the birth of these various organizations and periodicals was not quite as spontaneous as Claxton claimed. They blossomed as a result of the active work of a small group of English Canadians who felt certain personal needs, perceived certain national problems, and postulated a certain leadership role for themselves. To a significant extent the war was the catalyst in this process. It not only fostered national pride and revealed national problems, but it helped to create the personal and informal network which was used to build the associations of the 1920s. These nationalist organizations did not appear out of thin air; they were deliberately created for very particular purposes. The formation of the Group of Seven, for example, was a 'political' act. Abandoning individual isolation and becoming a 'group' may not have helped the artists to paint Canada better, but it did enable them to speak out more powerfully in the battles of the Canadian art world, and to transmit their nationalist vision to a wider audience. The self-conscious 'boosting' of the Canadian Authors' Association fulfilled a similar purpose. So, more or less, did the creation of all the groups discussed. One does not necessarily have to agree completely with Merrill Denison's analysis that the national sentiment of the 1920s was 'superimposed and artificial'[69] to recognize that in many cases its manifestations were deliberate, political, and élitist.

The nationalist intellectuals of the 1920s had certain ends which they wished to accomplish, and they perceived that organization was essential to success. From the war experience and from the business world they had learned much about how to bring ideas to fruition.[70] Their tactic of forming a number of separate associations, each with a fairly specific and focused purpose but with 'interlocking directorates'; their emphasis upon strong executive leadership within the associations; their use of publicity and of government lobbies—these were not accidents of circumstance but an indication of the growing sophistication of Canadian management techniques in the 1920s. The intellectuals, like their business and professional friends, had learned the need for formal structures to ensure effective and efficient communication. Nationalism is never spontaneous; it is an ideology which must be fostered. Because of their own needs, intellectual élites are usually among the first in a society to nurture nationalism.[71] That was the case in English Canada in the 1920s.

Suggestions for Further Reading

James Eayrs, *In Defence of Canada, I: From the Great War to the Great Depression* (Toronto, 1964).
S.M. Trofimenkoff, ed., *The Twenties in Western Canada* (Ottawa, 1973).
P.G. Wigley, *Canada and the Transition to Commonwealth: British-American Relations 1917–1926* (Cambridge, 1977).

Notes

[1]G. Spry, 'Broadcasting in Canada: A Comment', *Canadian Historical Review* (*CHR*) 46 (1965), 136–7.
[2]M. Prang, 'The Origins of Public Broadcasting in Canada', *CHR* 46 (1965), 2.
[3]M. Prang, 'Nationalism in Canada's First Century', Canadian Historical Association *Papers* (1968), 115.

[4]Brooke Claxton Papers, Manuscript Memoirs, II, 287, quoted in R.L. Faris, 'Adult Education for Social Action or Enlightenment? An Assessment of the Development of the Canadian Association for Adult Education and its Radio Forums from 1935 to 1952', Unpublished doctoral dissertation, University of Toronto, 1971, 47.

[5]This is not to say, of course, that national organizations did not exist before the 1920s, but only that the rate of formation of organizations devoted primarily to national questions was strikingly high during that decade.

[6]S.N. Eisenstadt, 'Intellectuals and Tradition', *Daedalus* 101 (Spring, 1972), 17.

[7]See M. Vipond, 'National Consciousness in English-speaking Canada in the 1920s: Seven Studies'. Unpublished doctoral dissertation, University of Toronto, 1974, *passim.*

[8]For more on the interrelationship of imperialism, nationalism, and internationalism within individuals and groups, see R.L. Faris, 'Adult Education', 48–9. For more on imperialists, see C. Berger, *The Sense of Power* (Toronto, 1970); D. Cole, 'The Problem of "Nationalism" and "Imperialism" in British Settlement Colonies', *Journal of British Studies* 10 (1971), 160–82; J. Weaver, 'Imperilled Dreams: Canadian Opposition to American Empire, 1918–1920'. Unpublished doctoral dissertation, Duke University, 1973, 86–104; Carrol Quigley, 'The Round Table Groups in Canada, 1908–1938', *CHR* 43 (1962), 204–24.

[9]The correspondence of G.M. Wrong and of F.H. Underhill, to cite two examples, is filled with letters to friends overseas and across the border. On Wrong's contacts, see Alan F. Bowker, 'Truly Useful Men: Maurice Hutton, George Wrong, James Mavor and the University of Toronto, 1880–1927'. Unpublished doctoral dissertation, University of Toronto, 1975, 77–8, 88–9.

[10]See P. Bowler, 'The Early Development of Scientific Societies in Canada'. Unpublished paper delivered to Canadian Historical Association Convention, 1972, 24.

[11]Dr J.W. Dawson, first President of the Royal Society, quoted by L.J. Burpee, 'Introduction to The Royal Society of Canada', in *Fifty Years Retrospect 1882–1932* (n.p., n.d.), 3.

[12]See J.F. Kenney, 'The Canadian Historical Association', *CHR* 3 (1992), 218–20; L.J. Burpee, 'Presidential Address', CHA *Annual Report* (1922), 7–8.

[13]J.F. Kenney, 'The CHA', 219; L.J. Burpee, 'Presidential Address', CHA *Annual Report* (1923), 10.

[14]Although there were about 850 CHA members at the end of the decade, attendance at the annual meetings was relatively small (for example, 69 in 1928), and predominantly professional. See PAC, Canadian Historical Association Papers, I, Registers.

[15]Long summers of research together in Ottawa also contributed to this sense of community. See A.R.M. Lower, *My First Seventy-five Years* (Toronto, 1969), 75, 181.

[16]For analysis of the contents of the *Canadian Historical Review* in its first ten years (as well as the next forty) see J.M.S. Careless, 'The *Review* Reviewed or Fifty Years with the Beaver Patrol', *CHR* 51 (1970), 48–71.

[17]C.D.W. Goodwin, *Canadian Economic Thought: The Political Economy of a Developing Nation 1818–1914* (Durham, N.C., 1961), 174; J.H. Dales, 'Canadian Scholarship in Economics', in R.H. Hubbard, ed., *Scholarship in Canada 1967* (Toronto, 1968), 93.

18See Editorial, 'Salutation', *Dalhousie Review* 1 (1921), 3.

19See PAC, Mackenzie King Papers, Correspondence, CLXXIV, A. Hawkes to King, 18 March 1930.

20E.D. Greathed, 'Antecedents and Origins of the Canadian Institute of International Affairs', in H.L. Dyck and H.P. Krosby, eds, *Empires and Nations* (Toronto, 1969), 91–115.

21*Canadian Nation* 1 (February, 1928), 22.

22Active local members included J.W. Dafoe, Chester Martin, T.A. Crerar, and E.J. Tarr (Winnipeg) and F.R. Scott, Eugene Forsey, Carleton Stanley, and Percy Corbett (Montreal). The occupations of the 480 members and supporters of the League in 1927 broke down as follows: businessmen 23%, barristers 21%, educators 10%, civil servants, doctors, journalists, and engineers, each 6%. R.L. Faris, 'Adult Education', 29.

23E.D. Greathed, 'Antecedents', 101; M. Prang, *N.W. Rowell: Ontario Nationalist* (Toronto, 1975), 442–3.

24Active academic members of the CIIA, in addition to those already mentioned, included R.A. Mackay, F.H. Underhill, Watson Kirkconnell, Percy Corbett, Chester Martin, A.L. Burt, Henry Marshall Tory, Mack Eastman, and F.H. Soward; other non-academics included J.W. Dafoe, Hume Wrong, and L.J. Burpee. See 'The Canadian Institute of International Affairs: Its Organization, Objects and Constitution' (n.p., 1929); Escott Reid, 'The C.I.I.A. After Ten Years 1927–1937', CIIA Mimeograph No. 52–200 (Toronto, 1937); E.D. Greathed, 'Antecedents', *passim*.

25N.A.M. Mackenzie Papers, Mackenzie to W.A. Mackintosh, 22 April 1929, quoted in E.D. Greathed, 'Antecedents', 111.

26D.M. Page, 'Canadians and the League of Nations Before the Manchurian Crisis'. Unpublished doctoral dissertation, University of Toronto, 1972, 303.

27It is worth noting that the founders chose to launch their organization in Ottawa in late May of 1921—while Parliament and the Royal Society were both meeting. D.M. Page, 'Canadians', 175; M. Prang, *N.W. Rowell*, 377–9.

28Participating academics included Chester Martin, A.L. Burt, D.C. Harvey, F.H. Soward, Percy Corbett, R.A. Mackay, N.A.M. Mackenzie, Mack Eastman, Henry Marshall Tory, and F.H. Underhill. Active non-academics included J.M. Macdonnell, Warwick Chipman, Sir George Foster, Mrs. J.A. Wilson, K.A. Greene, Brooke Claxton, E.J. Tarr, and Alan Plaunt. D.M. Page, 'Canadians', 337, n. 134; PAC, F.H. Underhill Papers, I, Underhill to C.P. Meredith, 4 November 1926.

29J.C. Hopkins, ed., *Canadian Annual Review, 1927–28*, 672. For a more detailed treatment of the Association of Canadian Clubs in the 1920s see M. Vipond, 'National Consciousness', chapter IV.

30On the list of members of the National Council of the A of CC in the late 1920s were such familiar names as J.M. Macdonell, L.J. Burpee, C.G. Cowan, Marius Barbeau, and Henry Marshall Tory. Interview with Spry, 28 November 1969; *Canadian Nation* I (April, 1928), 19.

31'The Work of the Association', *Canadian Nation* 2 (March-April 1929), 1.

32Public Archives of Manitoba, Canadian Clubs in Winnipeg, '26th Annual Report of the Executive Committee', 1930.

[33]PAC, Brooke Claxton Papers, V, Canadian League file, National Executive Committee Minutes, 1928 and 1929; A.R.M. Lower, *My First Seventy-five Years*, 140.

[34]R. Michaels, *Political Parties* (Glencoe, Illinois, 1948), *passim*; B. Barber, 'Participation and Mass Apathy in Associations', in A.W. Gouldner, ed., *Studies in Leadership* (New York, 1965), 498; D.L. Sills, 'Voluntary Associations: Sociological Aspects', *International Encyclopedia of the Social Sciences* (1968), XVI, 369.

[35]Editorial, 'The Canadian Club Job', *Canadian Nation* 1 (December, 1928), 18. See also Editorial, 'The Work of the Association', *Canadian Nation* 2 (March-April, 1929), 1; and Editorial, *Canadian Nation* 1 (February, 1928), 21.

[36]R.L. Faris, 'Adult Education', 100.

[37]For more on the Canadian Radio League see J.E. O'Brien, S.J., 'A History of the Canadian Radio League 1930–1936'. Unpublished doctoral dissertation, University of Southern California, 1964; M. Prang, 'The Origins of Public Broadcasting in Canada: A Comment'.

[38]See 'The Convention of Canadian Authors', *Canadian Bookman* 3 (June, 1921), 9.

[39]For a more detailed treatment of the Canadian Authors' Association in the 1920s see M. Vipond, 'National Consciousness', Chapter VI.

[40]Among the most active members of the national CAA were J.M. Gibbon, L.J. Burpee, Arthur Stringer, Madge Macbeth, Watson Kirkconnell, W.A. Deacon, and R.J.C. Stead. G.M. Wrong, C. Marius Barbeau, Graham Spry, J.W. Dafoe, H.M. Tory, Merrill Denison, and Barker Fairley were all involved in the CAA at the local level.

[41]Editorial, 'Standards of Criticism', *Canadian Bookman* 1 (April, 1919), 7–8.

[42]See Ann Davis, 'The Wembley Controversy in Canadian Art', *CHR* 54 (1973), 48–74.

[43]See A. Bridle, *The Story of the Club* (Toronto, 1945), *passim*.

[44]D. Reid, *The Group of Seven* (Ottawa, 1970), 128.

[45]For details of how Carr was 'discovered' by Barbeau, Brown, and the Group of Seven see P. Mellen, *The Group of Seven* (Toronto, 1970), 167.

[46]M. Davidson, 'A New Approach to the Group of Seven', *Journal of Canadian Studies* 4 (November, 1969), 9–16.

[47]Editorial, *Canadian Forum* 1 (October, 1920), 3.

[48]For more on the *Canadian Forum* in the 1920s see M. Prang, 'Some Opinions of Political Radicalism in Canada between the Two World Wars'. Unpublished MA dissertation, University of Toronto, 1953.

[49]Editorial, *Canadian Forum* 1 (October, 1920), 3.

[50]Advertisement, *Canadian Forum* 2 (May, 1922), back cover.

[51]M. Prang, 'Nationalism in Canada's First Century', 116. Margaret R. Stobie recounts a splendid example of how the network was instrumental in the 'discovery' of one unknown in her *Frederick Philip Grove* (New York, 1973), 89, 92.

[52]PAC, F.H. Underhill Papers, XVI, Underhill to Mother, 23 September 1917.

[53]A.R.M. Lower, *My First Seventy-five Years*, 139.

[54]Editorial, *Interdependence* 6 (December, 1928), 2.

[55]CAA *Authors' Bulletin* 3 (1925), 29.

[56]W.A. Deacon, *Pens and Pirates* (Toronto, 1923). 95.

[57]L.A. Mackay, 'The Intellectual Hunger-Strike', *Saturday Night* 44 (16 March 1929), 24; see also PAC, Brooke Claxton Papers, V, Canadian League File, Memorandum re 'Group Association', 30 July 1925, 4.

[58]K.W. Deutsch, *Nationalism and Social Commuication: An Inquiry into the Foundations of Nationality* (Cambridge, Mass., 1966), 2nd ed.; K. McRoberts, 'Social Communication and Mass Nationalism', *Canadian Review of Studies in Nationalism* 2 (Autumn, 1974), 149.

[59]Indeed, Faris emphasizes how little contact there was even with other élites, such as agrarian and labour leaders. R.L. Faris, 'Adult Education', *passim*.

[60]See PAC, F.H. Underhill Papers, III, Underhill to Lionel Curtis, 21 August 1925.

[61]A. Bowker, 'Truly Useful Men', 276.

[62]For a discussion of 'cluster patterns' in élites, see K.W. Deutsch, *Nationalism*, 32–6.

[63]E.K. Williams at the 1928 national conference of the Canadian League, quoted in R.L. Faris, 'Adult Education', 31.

[64]PAC, Brooke Claxton Papers, V, Canadian League File, Memorandum re 'Group Association', 30 July 1925, 4.

[65]See for example, *ibid.*, 'Minutes of National Conference', *Bulletin* of Canadian League, No. 6 (December, 1927), 11–12.

[66]Carleton W. Stanley, 'Spiritual Conditions in Canada', *Hibbert Journal* 21 (1923), 281.

[67]C.J.H. Hayes, 'The Propagation of Nationalism', in *Essays on Nationalism* (New York, 1926), 77.

[68]Quoted in E.A. Corbett, *We Have with Us Tonight* (Toronto, 1957), 104.

[69]M. Denison, 'The Omniscienta', *Canadian Bookman* 5 (January, 1923), 10.

[70]See, for example, Spry's editorial in *Interdependence* 6 (December, 1928), 1, in which he emphasizes the concrete, businesslike approach of the League of Nations Society.

[71]B. Akzin, *States and Nations* (New York, 1966), 72.

22

The Canadian Economy in the Great Depression

R.B. Bryce

The economic disaster which struck Canada in 1929 and lasted virtually until the start of the Second World War ten years later in 1939 was a cataclysmic event for millions of Canadians. It probably affected more families than the seemingly ubiquitous casualty lists of the Great War. That the problem was worldwide was little solace to those made unemployed or left without income by the severe drop in international demand—and prices—for Canadian goods. Official unemployment statistics only touched the tip of the suffering, for the government statisticians did not count most women looking for jobs as unemployed, and farming and fishing families—technically viewed as small business-people—were omitted from unemployment rolls despite their destitution because they were self-employed. Because unemployment understated destitution, it could hardly serve as a basis for relief. But to make matters worse, the question of the responsibility for whatever relief was extended became a constitutional football between the federal government and the provinces. Not until after the Depression was the question of jurisdiction over such matters resolved. For most Canadians, remembering the Thirties meant recalling days when the British North America Act did not seem an adequate document to deal with their problems.

R.B. Bryce, who was a civil servant in the Ministry of Finance during the period, examines the problem of unemployment relief during the thirties. He begins by pointing out the vulnerability of Canadian society in an era before most social welfare measures—including unemployment insurance—that we today take for granted. He then outlines in tabular form and in prose the various forms of relief undertaken by the various governments of Canada during the period, concluding that despite government reluctance, the Canadian relief system had become more systematic.

Why did the various Canadian governments not undertake a more massive campaign of emergency assistance during the 1930s? Why did the work-relief camps become such a problem? Was their problem connected with their effectiveness as relief measures? What questions and issues does Bryce omit from this 'brief account' of relief measures undertaken during the 1930s? What else would you need to know to make an appropriate assessment of unemployment relief under Bennett and Mackenzie King?

This article first appeared, titled 'The Canadian Economy in the 1930s: Unemployment Relief under Bennett and Mackenzie King', in Duncan Cameron, ed., *Explorations in Canadian Economic History: Essays in Honour of Irene M. Spry* (Ottawa, 1985), 7–26.

The Great Depression of 1929–1939 was deep, worldwide, and persistent. It was particularly severe in North America, where the United States and Canada had enjoyed a high level of prosperity in the late 1920s. For Canada it involved a rapid decline in exports of farm products, notably wheat; of raw materials, such as lumber; and of major manufactured products such as newsprint and automobiles. Prices of farm products and raw materials declined drastically along with the decline in the volume of trade; the prices of manufactured products declined less severely, depending on the circumstances in each industry. Widespread unemployment began to appear in 1930; it became severe during 1931, and was at its worst in 1932 and 1933. The low prices of farm products, and recurrent years of drought in the Prairie Provinces, caused severe hardship for many farmers and their families.

This severe unemployment had serious social effects upon a nation that had no unemployment insurance, and very few and inadequate arrangements to provide assistance to the poor in general, or to particular groups made destitute by unemployment, drought, or the catastrophically low prices for their farm, fishery, or forest products.

This essay gives a brief account of the main relief measures undertaken during the 1930s to deal with these severe social effects of the Depression.

Poverty and Relief in Canada[1]

Even during the prosperous period of the late 1920s, there were many poor people in Canada—the subsistence farmers of Quebec and the Maritimes eking out a bare living with small farms and perhaps some fishing or work in the woods, the unorganized workers in low-wage and seasonal industries, the unskilled drifters who took what work they could get, and a variety of unemployables who were physically or mentally unable to work, including the old, and single mothers with children. Little was done by governments to help any of these groups until the Old Age Pension Act of 1927, under which the Dominion government would share the cost with any province of a $20-a-month pension to those over seventy years of age and in need. This old age pension plan had been taken up by only the four western provinces before 1930, when it commenced in Ontario. In Nova Scotia, Ontario, and the western provinces there had also been provincial programs of mothers' allowances to help support dependent children when the male parent was unable to do so for various reasons. But for others, the poor in general, who were in need by reason of unemployment or inability to work, it was left to the local municipality or the churches or other charities to provide whatever aid they felt they should or could provide. When times were hard, as was the case in the period of substantial unemployment that followed the post-war economic crisis of 1920, the Dominion and several provincial governments provided funds to municipalities when they were needed. There were few professionally trained social workers and nearly all of them worked for the voluntary charitable organizations in the major cities.

Thus, when the Depression began in 1929 and became serious in 1930 it imposed unemployment, and reduced farm and fishery prices and incomes, on a society that already included many who were poor and vulnerable and for whom there was little organized means of help. The Constitution had assigned the jurisdiction and responsibility for helping the poor to the provincial legislatures, who in turn delegated it to the municipalities, many of whom could not, or would not, provide relief on any significant scale. Once the severity of the problem became apparent in the mid-1930s, the Dominion government, while disclaiming constitutional responsibility, recognized the emergency and brought in the Dominion Unemployment Relief Act of 1930 which appropriated $20 million to aid the provinces and municipalities to cope with the situation. The main action under this initial legislation was the provision of work projects for the unemployed, although these were very slow in starting. There were also the beginnings of direct relief, for example, material aid provided for food, fuel, clothing, and shelter for those in need, usually in kind or by vouchers, not cash. In late 1930 and early 1931 only about $20 million was disbursed for all relief purposes by all governments. At this stage most of the unemployed were having to get along as best they could. Dorothy King, director of the Montreal School of Social Work, wrote in 1938:

> In the early days of the depression, the difficulties of securing aid and its frequent inadequacy were responsible for cases of acute suffering and the breakdown of morale. Many of the unemployed sold their homes and other possessions, ran into debt till their credit was exhausted, and endured serious privations before reaching the unemployed aid lists. In many areas no rent was paid and evictions were common; in a still greater number, householders could secure no allotment in lieu of rent, with the result that payments on taxes and insurance were impossible and foreclosures on mortgages occurred frequently.[2]

In 1931 the main emphasis in relief programs continued to be on municipal work projects, but the need for direct unemployment relief increased, and in the West the drought in Saskatchewan and some areas of Alberta led to special Dominion assistance there. The problem of transient unemployed men, women, and even families was being recognized and resented seriously by municipalities who had enough trouble dealing with their own residents. As a result, the provincial and Dominion governments agreed to share equally the whole of the costs of relief for transients. The total expenditures for relief reached $95 million dollars by the 1931–32 fiscal year, and the Dominion had to finance just over one-half of this amount.

By 1932, unemployment had reached massive proportions—26 per cent of the wage earners were unemployed, and this did not include the young, or the wives who had never had a job, or the destitute farmers and fishermen. Moreover, the widespread nature of the collapse in the international financial system and the banking systems in the United States and central Europe caused many to recognize that there was no early end in sight for the serious situation. While work projects were preferred as the way to provide support for the unemployed, they could not be financed (or properly organized) on the scale necessary to meet the urgent needs of the hundreds of thousands requiring aid. Consequently, at the request of the provincial governments[3] public works were greatly curtailed under the 1932 legislation and there was a decided shift towards direct relief. In this year the Dominion Department of Labour began collecting statistics on the numbers of people receiving aid; these are summarized by years and various categories in Tables 1 and 2 (pp. 472, 474). It was also necessary to develop special plans for looking after unemployed homeless men, usually by establishing provincial camps for them in western Canada, and by placing them on farms, with only a few dollars a month in cash for each, or for the farmer for whom he worked.

The Dominion-Provincial Conference of January 1933 was organized primarily to discuss relief, and some progress was made. It was decided that there should be more emphasis on work projects. The Dominion agreed to co-operate with any province that set up its own provincial arrangements to dispense direct aid, as Saskatchewan did, rather than leaving it to the municipalities. The provinces agreed that those provinces in greatest need should get a larger proportion of support from the Dominion. Later in the year drought was more widespread in the West and all three Prairie Provinces got special assistance for the dried-out areas. After July 1933, the Dominion, through the Department of National Defence, took over direct responsibility for looking after the unemployed homeless men in camps. This action had the initial advantage of keeping them off the trains and out of the cities, but eventually the camps became centres of criticism and, ultimately, of political agitation. The meagre twenty cents a day allowed for pocket money (in addition to their accommodation, food, and clothes) was a matter of derision.

By this time two programs were well under way to place the unemployed on farms: one to subsidize single persons as hired help for farmers; and the other for the permanent settlement of poor families on new farms, some of these families being from the drought areas in the West. There were rather less successful ventures in Ontario to support those already sunk in rural poverty and in Quebec to colonize underdeveloped areas with poor urban families.

In 1934 and the first half of 1935 the policies and programs of the preceding years were continued, but with greater numbers needing aid in the drought areas and very little reduction in those requiring direct relief elsewhere, despite the beginning of some economic recovery and a modest increase in the number of employed wage-earners. It was probable, however, that during those years the number of employable persons on relief was increasing relative to the estimated number of 'unemployed wage earners' (as shown in line 10 of Table 1) for reasons which Grauer, in his research report for the Royal Commission on Dominion-Provincial Relations, described as follows:

> The deficiencies and lack of standards in the administration of unemployment aid become more serious for the individual family on relief as the duration of the depression lengthens. The needs of the individual family increase for a variety of reasons,—the wearing out of clothing and household equipment of all sorts, the exhausting of available financial help from friends and relatives, the piling up of dental and medical requirements, etc.[4]

The Trek to Ottawa

The only major political demonstration against the relief system of the Depression occurred in June 1935.[5] It began in some strikes organized by the unrecognized Relief Camp Workers' Union in the British Columbia relief camps in April and May. These resulted in a number of parades, 'tag days', and scuffles with the police in Vancouver, where the strikers were endeavouring to raise some money for their cause and to relieve their boredom and frustration. Then they organized an 'on-to-Ottawa trek', beginning about one thousand strong, seeking to make their way east on railway freight cars. They were welcomed and fed in some towns, and picked up supporters along their way. In Calgary, local sympathizers had arranged an orderly march across the city and they provided food for the trekkers, who rested a few days on the Exhibition grounds. But the trekkers heard ominous news about police reinforcements being assembled to meet them in Regina, and the militia being alerted. They were halted in Regina by the RCMP under instructions from Ottawa, but they had accommodation there, and enough to eat, and a chance to hold marches and meetings. The government in

Table 1. Number of Persons and Expenditures on Relief

	1932	1933	1934	1935	1936	1937	1938	1939
1. Total on direct relief	833,989	1,227,588	1,135,901	1,162,729	1,148,083	965,907	870,103	808,040
2. Total on drought-area relief	74,667	80,396	156,412	134,179	127,933	—	—	—
3. Total on agricultural relief	—	—	—	—	283,252	305,951	312,261	219,882
4. Total on unemployment relief	759,322	1,147,162	979,489	1,027,551	913,351	659,956	557,842	588,158
5. Total on unemployment relief—highest month	1,170,290	1,427,746	1,205,863	1,161,579	1,240,074	879,283	652,690	704,694
6. Total on unemployment relief—lowest month	456,713	920,310	824,533	886,463	707,293	455,839	444,732	488,984
7. Heads of families on unemployment relief—highest month	223,037	267,803	257,503	244,862	257,284	186,292	144,696	155,291
8. Employable persons on unemployment relief	212,610	321,205	274,256	287,947	282,757	187,204	148,289	156,780
9. Wage earners unemployed	639,000	646,000	521,000	483,000	430,000	337,000	407,000	386,000
10. Employable persons on relief as percentage of wage earners unemployed	33.3	49.7	52.6	59.6	65.8	55.6	36.4	40.6

11. Ex post estimates of 'persons without jobs and seeking work',— June	741,000	826,000	631,000	625,000	571,000	411,000	522,000	529,000
12. Number with jobs in agriculture	1,237,000	1,257,000	1,277,000	1,298,000	1,319,000	1,339,000	1,359,000	1,379,000
13. Heads of families/individual cases on agricultural relief	—	—	—	—	—	66,162	69,584	48,339
14. Heads of families/individual cases on agricultural relief as percentage of those with jobs in agriculture	—	—	—	—	—	4.9	5.1	3.5
15. Total relief expenditures ($ millions)	95	98	158	173	160	165	—	—

Rows 1-6 Figures given are monthly averages. Totals include heads of families, dependants and 'individual cases' receiving relief. *The Unemployment and Agricultural Assistance Act, 1940: Report of Dominion Commissioner of Unemployment Relief for the Fiscal Year Ending March 31, 1941* (Ottawa, 1941).

Rows 2-3 After August 1936, the category 'drought area' was no longer used in the annual reports of the Dominion Commissioner of Unemployment Relief. Instead, the number of persons receiving relief was divided into 'agricultural' and 'urban' categories.

Row 4 Total on unemployment relief = (total number on direct relief) − (total number on drought and agricultural relief).

Row 7 Annual reports of the Dominion Commissioner of Unemployment Relief, 1932–39.

Row 8 Figures given are monthly averages. For 1932–36 the number of persons on relief = (total number on relief) − (dependants, farmers, and unemployable persons on relief) as calculated in J.K. Houston, *Dominion Unemployment Relief: An Appreciation of Relief as Related to Economic and Employment Tendencies in Canada* (Ottawa, 1936). For 1937 figure, see S.A. Saunders, 'Nature and Extent of Unemployment', *Canada's Unemployment Problem* (Toronto, 1939), 36. For 1938–39 figures, the number of persons on relief = number of fully employable persons on urban aid. *The Canada Year Book*, 1940, 762.

Row 9 *The Canada Year Book*, 1940, 751.

Rows 11-12 Urquhart and Buckley, *Historical Statistics of Canada*, series C47–55, 61.

Row 13 *Report of the Dominion Commissioner of Unemployment Relief for the Fiscal Year Ending March 31, 1941.*

Row 15 Expenditure figures are not for calendar years; rather, they refer to the fiscal year ending closest to the December of the year given in the table. For example, the 1932 expenditure figure refers to the 1932–33 fiscal year.

Table 2. Number of Persons Receiving Indirect Relief and Total Number Receiving Relief, Direct and Indirect, 1932–1939

	1932	1933	1934	1935	1936	1937	1938	1939
1. Total assisted other than by direct relief—highest month	73,020	140,452	146,061	118,859	85,607	83,052	100,087	104,985
2. Total assisted other than by direct relief—lowest month	19,032	64,711	90,290	60,269	17,912	31,368	30,377	42,605
3. Persons employed on municipal relief works (monthly average)	15,506	7,422	20,833	1,909	1,170	694	1,365	4,301
4. Persons employed on provincial relief works (monthly average)	1,948	14,565	36,873	22,181	18,518	11,741	7,146	11,859
5. Persons employed on federal relief works or special projects	182	188	426	958	525	2,736	1,093	1,055
6. Persons on National Forestry Programme	—	—	—	—	—	—	—	1,320
7. Single homeless men on camps and farms	20,237	48,038	38,318	35,724	15,175	1,330	—	—
8. Persons on 'Farm Placement' program	817	4,999	4,636	4,011	7,612	18,389	14,416	8,598
9. Persons on relief settlements (cumulative total)	2,469	9,668	15,834	18,383	18,350	19,963	27,549	37,382
10. Persons on youth training program	—	—	—	—	—	3,558	13,785	7,512
11. Older persons on rehabilitation program	—	—	—	—	—	—	40	1,658

12. Total (including dependants) receiving relief, direct and indirect (monthly averages)	875,149	1,312,437	1,252,850	1,245,916	1,209,894	1,024,535	935,495	881,724
13. Total receiving relief, direct and indirect, as percentage of Canadian population	8.3	12.3	11.7	11.5	11.0	9.3	8.4	7.8

Rows 1-13 Compiled from information in *Report of the Dominion Commissioner of Unemployment for the Fiscal Year Ending March 31, 1941.*
Row 4   Number employed on provincial relief works includes those employed on Trans-Canada Highway.

Ottawa agreed to meet with a delegation of eight trekkers, who proceeded by train to see Bennett and some other ministers. The meeting went very badly: Bennett rejected all their demands (even though R.J. Manion, Minister of Railways, confided to the Prime Minister that several of these demands could be accepted in a general way). Both in the meeting and in his report on it to Parliament, Bennett began by concentrating his response on the Communist affiliations and criminal record of the spokesman for the group, Arthur Evans. The delegation had probably been ill-chosen, aggressive, and not really representative of most of the trekkers. But after their representatives were dismissed in Ottawa as 'an organized effort on the part of the various communist organizations throughout Canada to effect the overthrow of constituted authority in defiance of the laws of the land'[6]—a ludicrous caricature—there was a riot back in Regina on Dominion Day in which the RCMP clashed with some three thousand 'relief-camp deserters' and sympathizers. There were quite a number of injuries, dozens of 'strikers' were arrested, and one city policeman was killed. A special train was provided to take the relief camp workers back to British Columbia, and the crowd dispersed. Bennett had won the battle—though he was soon to lose the election.

Bennett's intemperate reaction to the trekkers in mid-1935 was not typical of his general recognition, during 1934 and 1935, of the need both for recovery from the Depression and for reform of the system.

The Bennett 'New Deal'

During 1934, Bennett introduced a number of reforms by legislation. One was a special statutory plan for bankruptcy and relief of debt for farmers—the Farmer's Creditors Arrangement Act, which fell under the jurisdiction of the Department of Finance. A second was the Public Works Construction Act, which Bennett characterized as a recovery rather than a reform measure. It was a special program of public works to create employment, financed by an expansion of the Dominion note issue—the main source of bank reserves—during the last eight months before the Bank of Canada commenced operations. There were important amendments made to the Canadian Farm Loan Act to enable it to be used more extensively at a time when credit was sorely needed, and also to enable it to be used in the process of renegotiating outstanding mortgages and other loans. Finally, and most ambitiously, there was the Natural Products Marketing Act, introduced in the spring of 1934, which gave a Dominion marketing board powers to regulate the marketing of natural products, and articles of food and drink derived from such products. It authorized the government to approve marketing schemes organized by a representative number of persons engaged in the production or marketing of specified natural products. The law would also permit the government to control the import or export of designated natural products in order to regulate or enforce marketing strategies for those products.

Bennett was subject to a number of influences during 1934 and the two preceding years which had some effect in causing him to embark on these reforms. The first and most important was the action of President Roosevelt, his various advisers, and the United States Congress in originating and implementing their 'New Deal' program, which involved not only new economic doctrines but broad new social and political ideas as well. These American thoughts and actions appealed to many in Canada, politicians and intellectuals alike, and some members of the business community. Bennett learned of the US ideas and legislation chiefly through his brother-in-law, W.D. Herridge, who was the Minister in charge of the Canadian legation in Washington, and who cultivated a range of close contacts with leading personalities in the New Deal circles there. Herridge made repeated suggestions to Bennett in 1933–34 about a variety of subjects, including a trade treaty and the building of a St Lawrence Seaway, as well as Canadian legislation and programs similar to those undertaken in the United States. He tried to persuade Bennett to adopt a more active interventionist philosophy with which to confront the Liberals in 1935.

A second, and secondary, influence came from the legal side, with two decisions by the Judicial Committee of the Privy Council on appeal from the Supreme Court of Canada. In these two cases—one concerning jurisdiction over aeronautics and the other, jurisdiction over radio broadcasting —the Judicial Committee ruled in favour of the Dominion Parliament having jurisdiction, mainly by reason of the general power granted Parliament under the 'peace, order and good government' clause of Section 91 of the BNA Act. These rulings encouraged Bennett and other Canadian lawyers and politicians (but not all) to believe that the Judicial Committee might well approve other legislation that was not clearly within the specified powers of Parliament or the provinces. The Natural Products Marketing Act was one example. Unemployment insurance might be another. Bennett had favoured legislation of this kind before 1934 and set his private secretary, Rod Finlayson, and others to work on it.[7]

A third and more disturbing influence during 1934 came from the actions of H.H. Stevens, the volatile Minister of Trade and Commerce. Early in the year, Stevens delivered a strong speech in Toronto criticizing the department stores and other mass retailers and wholesalers for using their bargaining strength to force down prices and wages in many of the weaker industries from which they bought, while themselves selling at quite profitable prices. Bennett soon after appointed Stevens chairman of a House of Commons Select Committee on Price Spreads which found much evidence that supported Stevens' case. The enquiry was not finished when Parliament prorogued early in July 1934, and Bennett agreed that it should continue as a Royal Commission, with Stevens as chairman. Meanwhile, Stevens made another inflammatory speech, attacking specific businesses, to a group of MPs. Copies of it reached the press and caused intense controversy and threats of lawsuits. When he was severely criticized in Cabinet by Cahan, a senior minister from Montreal who had close ties with conservative business interests, and it was suggested that he should apologize, Stevens resigned from the Cabinet and as chairman, but not as a member, of the Commission.

The Commission reported at length to Parliament in April 1935, making a whole list of recommendations relating to commercial and competitive practices, the Combines Investigation Act, the Companies Act, changes in labour laws and their administration, encouragement of trade unions, the establishment of minimum prices for primary products, and many other more specific items. Indeed, it was not clear whether the Commission really favoured competition or not. The principal organization proposed was a 'Dominion Trade and Industry Commission' to regulate many of these matters.[8]

Before the Price Spreads Commission had reported, Bennett had captured the initiative from Stevens and emerged as an ardent reformer, with the assistance of Herridge and Finlayson. The Prime Minister made five speeches over the radio early in January 1935. He described how bad things had been during the Depression, the measures that had been taken by the government, and the distinction he saw between recovery measures to increase employment and prices, and reform measures to improve the capitalist system. He proclaimed himself in favour of reform and against *laissez faire*. He proposed bringing in unemployment insurance and a new contributory old age pension system, and doing 'likewise' for health insurance.[9] He would take action on the recommendations of the Price Spreads Commission when they submitted their report, if they made a good case. He proposed to establish an Economic Council of Canada. He ended his final address by speaking about the difference between the *laissez-faire* Liberal party and his own party, which stood for the reform of capitalism.

These flamboyant speeches were the object of much puzzlement and concern both in Ottawa and across the country. Were they a program for Parliament in its final year or a platform for an early election? This was quickly resolved. Parliament was opened soon after the addresses, and the Throne Speech, which exaggerated the degree of recovery that had been achieved, stated that reform measures would be submitted to that session 'as part of a comprehensive plan designed to remedy the social and economic injustices now prevailing'.[10]

Substantial reform measures were, in fact, enacted at that session despite Bennett's absence, first due to illness and later because he was in London. Six International Labour Organization Conventions were ratified in order to lay a legal basis for acts to establish minimum wages, a weekly day of rest, and an eight-hour working day. The most important measure was the 'Employment and Social Insurance Act', which was to establish a system of unemployment insurance and an Employment and Social Insurance Commission. The Commission was to have only investigatory and advisory powers regarding national health insurance and payment of 'assistance' to unemployed persons not qualified for insurance benefits. A second rather sweeping measure was the Dominion Trade and Industry Commission Act, intended to carry out many of the detailed recommendations of the Price Spreads Commission. Initially, at least, the members of the Tariff Board were to serve as commissioners. They were to administer the Combines Investigation Act, and to investigate industries to determine whether or not 'wasteful or demoralizing competition'[11] existed. If the Commission found that such competition did exist, it could recommend that the Governor-in-Council approve agreements regulating that industry's prices and production. The Commission was given other, less sweeping powers of investigation and reporting. The Companies Act was amended to carry out recommendations of the Price Spreads Commission relating to 'watered stock'. Several other statutes were amended. Finally, Bennett's government introduced a compromise Wheat Board Act, which was passed with the agreement of the Liberals.

Some reform was accomplished in that session, or appeared to have been accomplished, but Stevens expressed his deep disappointment with the legislation. Mackenzie King, as Leader of the Opposition, did not oppose the reform legislation or even let his followers debate it at length, although he did occasionally question the constitutional status of what was proposed. He encouraged the split between Bennett and Stevens, which he thought would reduce the public impression of Bennett as a reformer. And so it did. Before the session was over Stevens was strongly critical and quit the Conservative party. He sought to form his own Reconstruction Party to fight the election that summer but he was its only member to be elected.

In the election of 14 October 1935, the Liberals gained an overwhelming victory and King was quickly back in office. One of the first actions of the new government was to refer Bennett's 'New Deal' measures to the Supreme Court to ascertain whether or not they were *ultra vires*. The Supreme Court's decisions had to be appealed to the Judicial Committee of the Privy Council to get final rulings. These were handed down on 28 January 1937. As many had expected, the Judicial Committee struck down a majority of these reform statutes as *ultra vires*. These included the whole of the Natural Products Marketing Act, and the Employment and Social Insurance Act. These two most important reform measures had also been found *ultra vires* by the Supreme Court of Canada. The three labour acts, intended to implement Conventions of the International Labour Organizations, were also declared *ultra vires*; on them the Supreme Court had been evenly divided. The

Dominion Trade and Industry Act, which was largely a response to the Price Spreads Report, was declared *ultra vires* because of its main provision, which authorized the Governor-in-Council to legitimize agreements regulating prices and production where 'wasteful or demoralizing competition exists'. The rest of that Act was considered within the powers of Parliament but it related chiefly to organization and procedure rather than to substantive powers. On the whole, there was little left of the reform legislation except the Farmer's Creditors Arrangement Act—which was not originally thought of as part of the 'New Deal'—and a new section of the Criminal Code penalizing discriminatory or predatory pricing, which probably was of importance in meeting some of the problems identified by Stevens and his Commission. The generally negative decisions of the Judicial Committee were an object of much criticism and expert argument in Canada. Even if the decisions had gone the other way, it would have done little to expedite recovery from the Depression in Canada, although unemployment insurance would have begun several years earlier than it did, and marketing schemes for natural products might have blossomed in the late years of the Depression to the benefit of a minority of farmers, fishermen, and others, at the expense of consumers.

The Slow and Incomplete Recovery, 1936–1939

In his biography of King during the 1930s, Blair Neatby opens his chapter on the Liberal response to the Depression by saying: 'In 1936 Mackenzie King would learn that even with a Liberal government in office at Ottawa the depression was still there, shading every aspect of Canadian life in sombre gray'.[12] Gray it would remain for the life of that Parliament, until the fall of France in 1940 coloured all with the flaming light of unexpected danger.

In October 1935, Mackenzie King selected a Cabinet which was both smaller and more capable than the former Bennett Cabinet. It included many strong ministers—among them Ernest Lapointe, Charles Dunning, C.D. Howe, T.A. Crerar, Norman Rogers, and J.L. Ilsley—but they were handicapped at the beginning by a very conservative economic and financial policy in which King, influenced by his easy economic experience of the 1920s, devoutly believed. He selected Dunning, another believer strong enough to carry out a program of financial restraint, to be Minister of Finance. Both King and Dunning favoured lower tariffs obtained by trade organizations as the chief instrument of recovery.

In his budget of May 1936 (so different from his complacent optimism of May 1930), Dunning had to begin with these serious qualifications:

> The most welcome feature in the fiscal year which has just closed has been what it indicates of a movement toward recovery. I do not wish to exaggerate the extent of that recovery, for to those who are charged with the responsibil-

ities of government in these hard times the distance yet to go and the problems still to be solved are the features of our economic record which are most impressive—and at the same time most distressing.[13]

The Minister found that the government's deficit for the previous year had been $162 million. He announced a new policy of making 'an immediate approach to a balanced budget'[14] which would 'show that complete equilibrium can be reached within a reasonable time', a policy which he identified as 'a doctrine of deflation'.[15] He announced new restrictions on expenditures, and increased rates both of income and sales tax. This mis-timed austerity had been worked out only a few months after the appearance of John Maynard Keynes's *General Theory of Employment, Interest and Money*, which was to be the intellectual foundation for a framework of analysis which would show that such a doctrine of deflation, and the measures giving it effect, were quite wrong in the circumstances of 1936.

Relief Reconsidered[16]

In the 1935 election campaign, King did not try to match Bennett's 'New Deal' promise of an unemployment insurance program. He preached financial restraint, arguing that the country could ill afford the expense of a large extension of social services. But despite his reluctance to increase federal expenditures on relief, King was aware that there were many inadequacies in the existing relief system. His selection of Norman Rogers, an intelligent and able political science professor from Queen's, as his Minister of Labour was evidence of the seriousness with which King approached the problem. Rogers very quickly attempted to make some major reforms of the Canadian relief system.

He began his assualt on the problem by investigating what was undoubtedly the most criticized of all federal relief programs, the relief camps organized and run by the Department of National Defence. In November 1935, a committee was appointed to review the relief camp situation and to make recommendations to the Minister of Labour as to how it could be improved.

The Dominion-Provincial Conference of December 1935 provided the first opportunity for the provincial premiers to discuss the problem of the costs of relief with members of the newly elected federal government. In order to help the provinces through the winter months, the Dominion government agreed to a substantial increase in its grants to the provinces. This increase in funding was, however, only a temporary measure designed to tide the provinces over until the existing relief system was revamped. Under Rogers as Chairman, a Conference Committee on Unemployment and Relief proposed a series of measures to improve the efficiency of the relief system. Among the Committee's recommendations was a nationwide registration and classification of all relief recipients. The Committee also suggested a possible division of the responsibility for providing relief among the various levels of government. The federal government would provide relief to all employable men and women and their dependants; all others in need of relief would be the responsibility of the provincial and/or municipal governments. The most significant recommendation of the Committee was that a national Commission on Employment and Relief should be established. This commission was intended to assist the provinces and municipalities in organizing the nationwide registration of all relief recipients, to establish standards and regulations which the provinces should meet in order to qualify for federal assistance, to supervise the distribution of Dominion grants, and to plan and co-ordinate a consistent program of public works and employment projects. Altogether, the Committee's recommendations called for a closer supervision of a more uniform relief system. The provincial premiers were anxious to receive the additional funding promised by the Dominion government, and they readily agreed to the establishment of the federal commission. Thus, from December 1935 to March 1936 the provinces received larger grants from the federal government for relief purposes. However, in April 1936, when King and Dunning were shocked at the increase in the federal deficit, they convinced the Cabinet to agree to a cut in federal grants to the provinces.

Early in 1936, the committee reviewing the relief camps made its recommendation to Rogers. On 26 February, he announced in the House of Commons that the Dominion government planned to close the camps by the summer. In order to provide alternate employment for those in the camps, the government had made arrangements with the Canadian National and Canadian Pacific Railways to hire an extra ten thousand men to perform maintenance work on the railway tracks. In addition, Rogers hoped that with the co-operation of the provinces it would be possible to extend the farm placement program to absorb some of the men who were working in the camps, and that others would find employment in forestry conservation and other development projects. The co-ordination of the placement of these men would, he commented, be handled by the National Employment Commission, which had yet to be set up.

In April 1936, an act was passed by Parliament authorizing the establishment of a National Employment Commission. This Commission, chaired by Arthur Purvis, one of the most able Canadian businessmen, was to investigate and make recommendations concerning the country's relief system.[17] In order to do so, the Commission began the first nationwide registration and classification of all relief recipients. The Commission was also granted the authority to control the disbursement of Dominion government expenditures on relief.

While the Commission conducted its study, the Dominion government continued to provide financial and material aid to the provinces for relief purposes. Various agreements were entered into by the Dominion and provincial governments for the construction of numerous public works projects, including the Trans-Canada Highway and provincial highways. The Dominion government also continued to contribute to the relief-settlement program.

By July 1936, the National Defence relief camps were closed. Many of the men in the camps were offered employment with the Canadian National and Canadian Pacific Railways. Others were placed on farms, in accordance with special agreements made between the Dominion government and the provinces (with the exception of Ontario and Nova Scotia). In order to ensure further employment for the relief camp workers, the Dominion government agreed to pay 50 per cent of the costs of operating forestry and other works undertaken by the provincial governments of British Columbia, Alberta, Manitoba, and New Brunswick, for the specific purpose of employing single persons unsuitable for farm labour.

Because of the acute drought in the Prairie Provinces, special assistance was given to the provincial governments of Alberta, Saskatchewan, and Manitoba in 1936 and 1937. The Dominion government assumed all costs for direct relief in the drought areas of these provinces from 1 September 1936 to 31 August 1937. The Dominion government also allocated funds to pay for the cost of feed and fodder for livestock in these areas.

Saskatchewan was by far the province most seriously affected by drought, which came on top of the disastrously low grain prices of 1931 to 1935. There were five successive years of drought, reaching a climax in 1937 when the average yield of wheat per seeded acre in Saskatchewan was about one-sixth of the average yield per acre during the decade 1920–29. In that disastrous year, two-thirds of the farm population of the province were destitute and on relief, and 96 per cent of the rural municipalities sought financial assistance from the provincial government; it, in turn, required special assistance on a large scale from the Dominion government. For the whole period from 1930 to 1937, total relief costs in Saskatchewan were 13.3 per cent of total provincial incomes; the average for all provinces was 3.6 per cent. It is remarkable that the province and its people survived without permanent damage.

By July 1937, the National Employment Commission had published an interim report, which included the results of its nationwide registration of relief recipients. This compilation of all persons receiving relief was used, whenever possible, as the list from which candidates were selected to work on public works projects. The Commission was also instrumental in establishing a training program for unemployed young persons. Following its recommendation, Parliament approved the expenditure of one million dollars for this purpose.

Before the Commission completed its final report, King was informed of its major recommendation. Mary Sutherland, a member of the Commission, forewarned King of the intention of the majority of the commissioners to recommend that the Dominion assume full responsibility for the provision of relief to all unemployed employable persons (in addition to unemployment insurance, to which the government was committed in principle and about which it had proposed to the provinces, in November 1937, a constitutional amendment giving the Dominion exclusive jurisdiction over the subject). King was both alarmed and dismayed by the financial implications of this recommendation. He argued that it was beyond the terms of reference of the Commission (which appears to have been the case) and showed the political naiveté and irresponsibility of the commissioners (which was not the case!). King blamed this on Purvis, who he thought was too much of an insensitive businessman, and on W.A. Mackintosh, another member of the Commission, whom King considered academic and theoretical. The Prime Minister had further harsh words for trade union leader Tom Moore, also of the Commission, who he claimed had 'been helped more than anyone else by this government'.[18]

The Commission's decision had apparently been the subject of some discussion with Rogers, who defended it when King reported Sutherland's conversation in a meeting of the Cabinet. King's faith in his Minister of Labour was undoubtedly shaken. He insisted that Rogers see Purvis and get the Commission to change its decision. Rogers resisted, although he did talk with Purvis. In due course, Purvis and Mackintosh suggested some changes to their colleagues on the Commission, which persuaded them to hold to their view against that of Sutherland, as expressed in her dissenting memorandum.

In essence, the majority report of the National Employment Commission stated that when the proposed change in the Constitution led to the establishment of a nationally administered system of unemployment insurance and an employment service, it would require 'a supplementary system of Unemployment Aid to meet those phases of unemployment need which experience abroad has shown cannot be covered by Unemployment Insurance'.[19] The Commission then stated that such a supplementary system would in its opinion be best administered by the Dominion. This further step would require determination by the Royal Commission on Dominion-Provincial Relations of the financial basis upon which such a system should be established, and, in light of all relevant considerations, of the wisdom of further constitutional and financial changes.

Sutherland alone dissented from these carefully worded conclusions, and her views were strongly commended by the Prime Minister to his colleagues.

But King was not displeased with the final result of the Commission's recommendations. Although the commissioners had refused to abandon their view of the desirability of Dominion government responsibility over the provision of relief, they had backed down to the degree of admitting that because of the financial implications of their recommendation the matter required further study by the Rowell-Sirois Commission. Thus, the determination of whether or not the relief system proposed by the Employment Commission was financially feasible was shunted off to another royal commission. The desperate need for a comprehensive reform of the relief system fell victim to Ottawa's desire for a more general review of Dominion-provincial financial relations.

Dominion contributions for relief purposes in 1938 and 1939 continued much as they had in 1937, although the work of the National Employment Commission had some impact on the allocation of government expenditures and the creation of relief programs. Grants to the provinces continued, and special assistance continued to be provided to the drought areas of Saskatchewan and Alberta. Relief applicants and recipients were registered and classified according to the specifications first established by the Employment Commission. Dominion contributions to the relief-settlement program and public-works projects were maintained. A Youth Training act was passed by Parliament to provide for the continuation of the youth training program, which was expanded in 1938–39. Parliament also appropriated funds in 1938–39 for the rehabilitation of older unemployed persons, as had been recommended in the report of the National Employment Commission. Although far from perfect and despite government reluctance, by the end of the 1930s the Canadian relief system had become more organized and uniform.

The unemployment situation remained serious, as the economic recovery remained quite incomplete, up to the outbreak of war in September 1939, particularly in the field of construction and other capital investment by business. In terms of our current concepts it has been estimated that 11.4 per cent of the total labour force (including the 30 per cent still in agriculture) were out of work and seeking jobs. The situation required the continuation of relief measures for the first eighteen months of war. During this period the Constitution was amended to give the Parliament of Canada specific jurisdiction over 'Unemployment Insurance' (but not over 'aid' for other employable unemployed persons), and the Unemployment Insurance Act was passed in August 1940. By the time the first benefits under it were payable in 1942 they were hardly needed, as the war had by then brought about practically full employment.

Suggestions for Further Reading

Barry Broadfoot, *Ten Lost Years, 1929–1939: Memories of Canadians Who Survived the Depression* (Toronto, 1973).

Robert B. Bryce, *Maturing in Hard Times: Canada's Department of Finance through the Great Depression* (Kingston, 1986).

H. Blair Neatby, *The Politics of Chaos: Canada in the Thirties* (Toronto, 1986).

Notes

This essay draws upon writing and research by the author in connection with a study of the history of the Department of Finance.

[1] The following sources were helpful in writing about relief in the 1930s: A.E. Grauer, *Public Assistance and Social Insurance: A Study Prepared for the Royal Commission and Dominion-Provincial Relations*, Appendix 6 (Ottawa, 1939); M. Horn, *The Dirty Thirties: Canadians in the Great Depression* (Canada, 1972); L.C. Marsh, *Health and Unemployment* (England, 1938); L.C. Marsh, *Canadians In and Out of Work* (England, 1940); L. Richter, ed., *Canada's Unemployment Problem* (Toronto, 1939); National Employment Commission, *Final Report* (Ottawa, 1938); Annual Reports of the Dominion Director of Unemployment Relief, 1931–32; Annual Reports of the Dominion Commissioner of Unemployment Relief, 1933–41.

[2] D. King, 'Unemployment Aid (Direct Relief)', in L. Richter, *op. cit.*, 106.

[3] Grauer, *op. cit.*, 18.

[4] *Ibid.*, 24.

[5] An interesting account of the 'On-to-Ottawa' trek can be found in Horn, *op. cit.*, 344–89.

[6] House of Commons (HC) *Debates*, 24 June 1935.

[7] Horn, *op. cit.*, 586.

[8] *Ibid.*, 511. See also Royal Commission on Price Spreads, *Report*, 1935.

[9] 'The Premier Speaks to the People', pamphlet of Bennett's second radio broadcast, 4 January 1935, R.B. Bennett Papers, PAC, microfilm reel M1401, 437387. All further references to the Bennett Papers are those located in the PAC.

[10] Speech from the Throne, HC *Debates*, 17 January 1935, 17.

[11] R.B. Hanson, *ibid.*, 11 June 1935, 17.

[12] B. Neatby, *William Lyon Mackenzie King: A Political Biography*, vol. 3, *The Prism of Unity* (Toronto, 1976), 153.

[13] Dunning, HC *Debates*, 1 May 1936, 2362.

[14] *Ibid.*, 2384.

[15] *Ibid.*

[16] Much of the 'Relief Reconsidered' section was drawn from the following sources: Annual reports of the Dominion Director of Unemployment Relief, 1931–32; Annual reports of the Dominion Commissioner of Unemployment Relief, 1933–41; National Employment Commission, *op. cit.*; Grauer, *op. cit.*

[17] The National Employment Commission consisted of Arthur Purvis (Chairman), Tom Moore (Vice-chairman), W.A. Mackintosh, Alfred Marois, A.N. McLean, Mary Sutherland, and E.J. Young.

[18] National Archives, King's Diary, 12 January 1938, Ottawa, Ontario.

[19] National Employment Commission, *op. cit.*, 28.

23

The Rise of Tourism

Ian McKay

Mass tourism has become a major industry in postwar Canada, representing in some provinces the largest generator of commercial revenue. Yet its earlier history has only begun to be investigated. The rise of tourism is inextricably connected with the development of the middle classes, urbanization, affluence, the concept of leisure, transportation— and various aesthetic considerations. Before 1850 only the very wealthy could afford to take the protracted 'Grand Tour' of Europe or America, much less venture into the exotic corners of the world. By 1900 large numbers of well-to-do urban Canadians were heading off regularly in the summer to beaches and unspoiled wilderness, and by 1950 almost every Canadian family expected annually to be able to 'take a holiday' somewhere.

As Ian McKay demonstrates in his discussion of Peggy's Cove, popular aesthetic considerations have been extremely important in constructing the framework for tour-

ism; at the same time, many of the objects of those aesthetics are too fragile to bear the weight put upon them. Through an analysis of the development of the public image of the 'archetypical' Nova Scotia fishing village, McKay explores some of the implications of the aesthetics of place that became crucial to mass tourism. For Canadian journalist J.F.B. Livesay, Peggy's Cove represented an idyllic coastal landscape (the more so for its occasional flaw) in which real fisherfolk worked. Peggy's Cove was wonderful both because it was so beautiful, and because its community was so natural and unspoiled. Earlier generations of observers had held a far less benign view of the Peggy's Cove landscape and of its inhabitants, and the difference between Livesay's report and those of his predecessors is exactly what McKay wishes to explore. Part of the explanation lies in Livesay's artistry, of course, but much also resides in the changing iconography of the Maritime region

and in Canadian society's newly valued nostalgia. Only when Peggy's
Cove becomes a semi-sacred regional image of a simpler and better ordered pastoral innocence does
it take on its new persona. And such
a persona is at odds with the influx
of tourists it attracts. In what sense

did J.F.B. Livesay 'invent' Peggy's
Cove? What other inputs besides his
artistry are important in the process?
What exactly has been preserved at
Peggy's Cove for the 200,000
annual tourists who stop there for
an average of less than two hours
each?

This article first appeared, titled 'Among the Fisherfolk: J.F.B. Livesay and the Invention of Peggy's Cove', in *Journal of Canadian Studies*, 23, 1 & 2 (Spring, 1988),
23–45.

A timely book by a famous author begins life with favourable odds. There
was something inevitable about the acclaim that greeted J.F.B. Livesay's *Peggy's Cove*, published by Ryerson Press in 1944. Livesay's national reputation
as the chief architect of the Canadian Press, and his death on 15 June 1944,
half a year before his book appeared, guaranteed that it would be treasured
as a valedictory message from a well-regarded and influential Canadian journalist. In other ways as well, the publisher's timing was perfect. *Peggy's Cove*
spoke soothingly of a tiny coastal community at peace with itself, of gulls
wheeling in the blue sky overhead, of an atmosphere fragrant with hay and
seaweed and fish, of friendly chats with fisherfolk in a snug little building at
the tide's edge. Canadians at war responded with an understandable enthusiasm to the prospect of what one of the many enthusiastic reviews called
'Escape Through Seascapes'. Depicted here, this reviewer noted, was a land
far removed from the grim realities of the 1940s, an 'ideal land where green
grass grows by sometimes verdant water; where golden fields of grain dis-
tantly nod to the silver harvest of the sea'.[1] Yet Livesay offered more than
mere escapism, added the reviewer for the Halifax *Chronicle*: *Peggy's Cove*,
in addition to appealing to 'lovers of the quaint and picturesque' also presented the 'typical Nova Scotian in his true character'.[2]

Forty years later, *Peggy's Cove*, now out of print and rarely consulted, is still
well worth reading. It has three enduring virtues. First, it represents the con-
summation of literary travel writing in the Maritimes, a genre which was
largely superseded after the Second World War by dreary motorists' guides
and cliché-ridden tourist promotions. Livesay's short volume, by contrast, is a
subtle, deft, and coherent work which, as a displaced pastoral romance, engineers an escape for its readers as deeply satisfying now as it was four decades
ago.[3] Second, *Peggy's Cove* can give us a new insight into modern ways of
seeing the fisherfolk and the rockbound coastline of Nova Scotia's South
Shore. Peggy's Cove, quaint fisherfolk, lighthouses, the *Bluenose*: none of these
signs of regionality were in common usage before the 1920s. Livesay, along

with other cultural producers, 'invented' Peggy's Cove, projecting onto the past and present of this one St Margaret's Bay fishing community his own concerns and values. Understanding how he did so gives us some valuable clues about regional culture in general. The third reason to re-read *Peggy's Cove* today is to stimulate thought about the ironies of post-1945 mass tourism. The heartfelt anti-modernist enthusiasms of Livesay and other writers of his era became the standard fare of tourism promotion after the Second World War. Those fleeing the twentieth century thus served as the forerunners of the very modernity from which they were trying so hard to escape.

I

Peggy's Cove, a book of only one hundred pages, contains twelve written sketches and thirty-five photographs describing J.F.B. Livesay's visit to Peggy's Cove from 16 July to 23 August 1943. Livesay was born in Ventnor, Isle of Wight, on 23 January 1875. He emigrated to Canada in the 1890s, having had a promising academic career cut short by his preference for reading the novels of Zola over studying for university examinations. After a series of odd jobs in lumber camps and gold mines, he landed a position on the Winnipeg *Tribune*. By 1920, as General Manager of the Canadian Press, he had scaled the heights of Canadian journalism, and as a reporter covering the Canadian Corps in Europe he had won a large audience with his journalism and his book, *Canada's Hundred Days*.[4]

Outwardly, Livesay was a tough man who treated both words and professional colleagues with a brisk, occasionally ruthless, decisiveness. The Canadian Press survived the Depression intact at least partly on the strength of his will. Few in the trade disputed *Newsweek*'s view that Livesay may well have been 'the most important Canadian newspaperman of his day'.[5] Inwardly, however, he felt that his life and talents had largely been wasted. 'People won't believe it, but I always felt I was a square peg, etc.', he confided to a friend. 'I wanted more than anything else to writ[e]—not that I have that illusion now. . . . Some of the extravagant things that have been written about me make me tired, because they don't touch the real man, who's had to fight all his life things like alcohol, but make a sort of plaster image. The Chinese buried these with their dead—I have to live with mine perhaps quite a bit yet!'[6] In a revealing short story entitled 'The High White Bed', Livesay has his bed-ridden protagonist, a retired newspaperman, reflect bitterly on his wasted literary talents and on the insatiable demands of the daily newspaper: 'With some bitterness he saw the daily newspaper a monster, pitiless, all-devouring, that sucked the life-blood from those that ministered to its unquenched appetite—and these, he saw again, as pebbles thrown into a bottomless well, their brief ripple closing over them, leaving unchanged its glassy surface.'[7] Livesay was not unusual among journalists in harbouring literary aspirations, but he did suffer to an unusual degree from the feeling that he had been trapped by his career. The creative work he did produce was rejected.[8] His daughter Dorothy, who was beginning to achieve the literary success he dreamt of, depicted the connection between her father's inner frustration and outward manner in her poem 'Inheritance':

> They called you shy; a blusterer—
> Two poles, stretched agony between
> And some might wonder why the grass grew green
> Where acid words had lately been.[9]

When Charles Bruce, his friend and colleague, remarked, 'To say that Fred Livesay's works are in the steel filing cabinets of The Canadian Press, the news agency with which his life was identified, is literal truth', he summed up not only Livesay's life work but, as well, his personal dilemma.[10]

Livesay's was a painful, common problem. Much as he loved nature and those writers—Whitman, Tolstoy and Thoreau—who had lived unconventional, 'natural' lives, he was far too burdened by material cares to quit his job. In 'The High White Bed', Livesay has his fictional hero work on an essay focusing on the theme of how 'the everlasting drive of modern life' claimed its victims among professionals and factory workers who were condemned to take their 'crushed and broken spirits' to hospital wards and asylums.[11] The newspaperman who publicly embodied hard-nosed objectivity, the proponent of the wire service's cold mechanization of the word, was, in an ironic way, the victim of his own philosophy.

Retirement was not easy for him. Diabetes, a bad heart, shingles, deafness: against all of these he fought, working, walking, gardening, ingesting large doses of nitroglycerine. He felt bitterly that it was now too late to write, and with equal force that he had no choice but to try. 'As a young man', Livesay wrote in 1942, 'I passionately wanted to write fiction but the office drive was too hard. And then I said: "When I get old and retire I'll do it." And when that time approached I found the will to write, even the technique, was gone. Inspiration slumbered by the fireside, feet on the fender . . . . There is so much beauty in the world, among growing things, and men and women. I would like to make a good "shot" of a tiny piece of it and pass it on when I go. I am hag-ridden until this book is done.'[12] The 'book' in question was his autobiography, and it never was done. Published in its stead was the The Making of a Canadian (1947), edited by his wife, a miscellany of reminiscences, testimonials from friends and associates, and fiction.

In the summer of 1943 Livesay set his autobiography aside and turned to the writing of a travel account. Here, as it happened, was a genre in which he could combine the discipline of journalism with the essayist's creative freedom. It was an ideal outlet for him.

Livesay had started 'going down to the sea' in 1922, and discovered Peggy's Cove about 1925. It was, for him, a return to the landscape of his Isle of

Wight childhood. Part of the Cove's deep appeal lay in its island-like quality, which Livesay thought had stamped its folk with the sympathy and understanding notable among island people.[13] His wife would later recall that Livesay, no fisherman himself, 'had the greatest sympathy with and for the folk whom he got to know so well. He found with them his spiritual home.'[14] He generally stayed at Peggy's Cove for only a week at a time, and could not afford to go every year.[15] As his 1943 diary suggests, Livesay was an energetic traveller. He went with the fishermen as they set nets, attended dances, bought presents (including the obligatory model lobster trap), taught a boy of the Cove how to swim, and collected conversations for his sketches. Even though he had suffered a heart attack on 22 July, to which he responded with his customary 'two nitro', on 4 August he 'Bathed in Cove in driving rainstorm' though he required help to get back to his lodgings.[16]

Peggy's Cove began as a series of sketches for the Vancouver *Province*. Livesay started serious work on his book on the train back to Ontario. Once home, he drove himself to finish it, looking over and selecting from the hundreds of photographs he had taken ('Some quite marvellous', he told his diary proudly). There was nothing relaxed about this work. By 17 October, ten of the sketches were in 'fair copy', and he noted in his diary that he reworked 'No. 11 in bed till 3 [o'clock]', and stayed awake until 4:30–5:00 a.m. 'Bad night but good job', he noted stoically.[17]

It is a credit to Livesay's discipline as a journalist that his book betrays nothing of the nervous energy he invested in writing it. *Peggy's Cove* begins with his first visit to the Cove in the mid-1920s, in the company of Andrew Merkel, Atlantic Superintendent of Canadian Press. They went to hear a guest sermon preached at St John's Church by Rev. Robert Norwood, a well-known poet and minister. Livesay's sketch of this first visit to the Cove moves strongly from his affectionate reminiscence of Norwood to his own first dazzling sight of the Cove itself.

> Stepping out of the porch, it lay before me as in a panorama, a unique spectacle. . . . Surely in all the world there is nothing, in its small way, so complete, so compact, all aglitter with rock and sea and sky . . . the Cove on that first glance was still quite perfect, nothing to be added and nothing to be taken away, a little pulsing human cosmos set in the uneasy sea.[18]

This passage is the closest Livesay comes to an extended description of the Cove. The next six sketches portray scenes from daily life, each concluded by an evening conversation with the fishermen in the small waterfront store which Livesay nicknamed 'Parliament House' in honour of the arguments that resounded there. In the course of these conversations we meet Lawson Innes, the 'Poet of the Cove', explore outport politics and the building of a lavish but useless government wharf, and overhear a number of fish stories. The remaining sketches take us to a Cove dance, out to nearby McGrath's

Cove, and along the shore, with one return to Parliament House for a rum-running story.

Nothing really happens in *Peggy's Cove*. Livesay adopted a plain style and used imagery sparingly. It is dialogue, not description, that carries the book. Portraying himself as a whimsical and charming English gentleman, Livesay becomes his own central character. He often plays the role of mischievous pixie in conversations with the taciturn fisherfolk. Here he is, for example, in conversation with Lawson Innes on Politics:

> . . . I turned to Lawson Innes, the Cove's philosopher and poet, now entering his eighties.
>
> 'Laws, do you remember the time you were building the new road on the Liberal side of the Cove and blew in all the windows of the Conservative committee room?'
>
> 'Why bring that up?' says he, nudging me sharply with his elbow. 'Some things are best forgot . . . .'
>
> 'Wasn't it in 1938, Laws?' I asked. 'I remember well how you and your gang of half a dozen Liberals blasted great boulders out in the Barrens to make the fill, with a yoke of oxen drawing the stuff to where you were working. Yes,' says I, warming up, 'and I remember the score or so of Conservatives, headed by Albert here, standing by, criticizing and jeering.'
>
> 'Hold on,' says Lawson, 'That's not so. I put all those fellows across the Cove to work on the job.'
>
> Alas, the years have their penalties! No one contradicted him, but we all remember how that little squad of Grits toiled away those weeks, when the price of fish was that low, a bit of roadwork was not to be despised.[19]

This passage is typical of the book's narrative strategy. We view such conversations from the whimsical perspective of Livesay, who regards his own mischievous gambits with distanced amusement. The narrative voice is culturally complex. In this instance, Livesay portrays himself as an intimate of the fishermen (calling them by their nicknames, for example), uses a conversational vernacular in dialogue, but reverts to a more educated English when, as author, he comes to impose his own interpretation on the conversation. We are on the fishermen's level (although one notes that we never discover how *they* addressed *him*), but we are also apart, able to remove ourselves and view the action from a wry, sceptical perspective.

Livesay's narrative voice delights because he is so unpretentious and candid about his folkloric romanticism. In one bit of slapstick, which gently spoofs the contemporary vogue for Norse myths, the narrator, commanding a view of the ocean from the door of one fisherman's house with nothing between himself and Portugal but the traffic of sea, ponders how 'this far-flung outlook must have moulded the stout generations, nurtured beneath that ancient rooftree, shouldering strong against the gales.' Distracted suddenly by a low-flying airplane, he proceeds to bump his 'philosophizing skull' on the doorway lintel.[20] Equally effective, and more subtle, is his strategy of introducing disparate subjects into the narrative. A book which finds no room for a down-to-earth realistic description of the natural or social history of Peggy's Cove devotes six pages to a description of Robert Norwood and over three pages to the Ontario CCF and its leader. This casual approach establishes the narrator's friendly and whimsical character and links Livesay to the English literary travellers of the interwar period.

As one conversation follows another in the little store Livesay nicknamed 'Parliament House', the breezy tone of the narrator establishes a trust between the author and the reader analogous to the bonds we are told link Livesay to the fisherfolk. When Livesay makes a direct statement of his pastoral interpretation—'The charter of Peggy's Cove dates from 1808, and through that long span the character of its folk has changed no more than the rocks that encompass it'—he reinforces it effectively by means of this brief interchange with Mrs Ethel Manuel, with whom he boarded: ' "Wouldn't you like an electric washing-machine?" I had once asked her. "No," she said, "I like the old ways best. Those contraptions don't really get the dirt out." ' An overt statement of Livesay's vision of Peggy's Cove as a 'true commonwealth' where all 'were of an equality'[21] convinces, because we have already heard the gentle, warm conversations of these citizens in 'Parliament House'. His moral theme—the plainspoken goodness of those who lead the natural life—becomes appealing and plausible precisely because of such 'spontaneous' dialogue.

Livesay does not overplay his hand. His portrait of this folk society is made all the more persuasive by tactical concessions to realism. We learn of fish prices so low that families abandoned the fishery altogether in 1938 and took in boarders instead. The Cove, moreover, is often dirty and stinks at low tide. Such details, however, when blended into the whole portrait, make the idyllic image stronger. For instance, after a wet spell, 'at last the sun comes out and the little rockgrit hay patches are ripe for the scythe, nets are abandoned and the Cove is merry to the sound of stone on steel. To the women and children, with rake and fork, falls the job of cocking up, a gay scene in that scented air.'[22] Interpretation triumphs over mere description in this passage; Livesay effects 'a triumphant mediation between two different dimensions: the dimension of individual physical things, on the one hand, and the dimension of universal significance, on the other'.[23] The labour of women and children in the folk community is scented, merry, harmonious, and pure; we are left with a delightful sense of wholeness.

Readers and reviewers were right to be impressed by this portrait of the fisherfolk. 'From these pages come a smell of salt, the straight talk of fisherfolk, hand-fashioned lobster traps smashed by the storm, a cup of hot tea in the kitchen, women pitching rain-soaked hay on the bare rocks to dry, an expert painting wet fog on his easel to stay long after the sun's shining,' wrote one reviewer, emphasizing Livesay's grasp of the physical world. Another praised his insights into the character of the fishermen: 'Here are his memories of fisher folk, hard as Northern Spies and sweet to the very core. . . .'[24]

II

Peggy's Cove belongs unmistakably to a distinct period: 1920–1950. In its content and form, it documents a gentle art of vacationing far removed from today's professionalized tourism. It also suggests a way of seeing this coastline and these communities that differs significantly from nineteenth-century responses. To earlier articulate observers the coastline was ugly and uninteresting and the fisherfolk primitive, pitiable outcasts from the 'march of improvement'. Rockbound coastlines and grizzled fisherfolk were not seen as uplifting symbols of Nova Scotia. Rather than admiring the province's 'older and better ways', most local and foreign commentators prior to 1920 hailed the transformations wrought by industrial capitalism, the natural sciences, and social reform.[25]

This warmly appreciative view of economic advance accorded with the Victorian taste for serene, ordered landscapes. Beauty and civilization were implicitly linked, and those parts of the province were esteemed that most resembled the gently rolling, fertile fields of the southern English countryside. The Annapolis Valley, Truro, at a pinch Halifax—though it was a bit on the dirty side—and the gentler parts of Cape Breton: these were the provincial settings Victorians held in high regard. The rockbound coasts of the South Shore, by contrast, were regularly condemned for their bleak sterility, monstrous barrenness, and 'wildness'. They merely made up one of those many provincial scenes 'from which the eye turns with painful dissatisfaction'.[26] 'When we landed at Yarmouth, far down near the southern tip of Nova Scotia, and saw the monotonous country which is characteristic of that part of the province, something very much like gloom settled upon our spirits,' wrote Frank Bolles in *From Blomidon to Smoky and Other Papers* (1894), while both T.C. Haliburton in 1823 and Thomas F. Anderson in 1893 felt compelled to remind their readers that Nova Scotia should on no account be judged on the basis of the stony, sterile, and thinly inhabited shores that the visitor saw from the Atlantic.[27] Hugh Murray, in his *Historical and Descriptive Account of British America*, thought the barren sod and stunted trees of the countryside near Halifax 'give a monstrous character to the scene'. Even a locally prepared guide for emigrants noted that 'The sea-coast is very rough, rugged, and rockbound, and travellers who have seen the coast only, or have stopped an hour at Halifax, can form no idea of the beauty and fertility of the interior of the country.' One pious writer, struggling to explain why God would have fashioned such a bleak coast, concluded that the 'Great Architect' had intended the huge rocks as a protective wall against the waves of the Atlantic.[28]

There is some evidence of a slight change in this point of view—possibly associated with a rise in the number of American and Canadian travellers—during the 1880s and 1890s, but it was not substantial enough to promote the rockbound coast and its fishing population to the position of regional icons.[29] Even those guidebooks devoted to the South Shore and the environs of Halifax tended to ignore nearby coastal scenery. They concentrated instead on the urban and civilized attractions of South Shore towns (Liverpool's electricity, Yarmouth's hedgerows), or on scenic drives with historical associations, such as the one from Halifax to Waverley along the Bedford Basin.[30] The same Peggy's Cove that wins two stars and is praised as 'the most attractive of all the settlements on the coast' from the demanding *Michelin Guide* (1985) does not appear in Baedeker (1907) at all. Though some weight should be attached to the sheer difficulty of getting to Peggy's Cove by road before the First World War,[31] an explanation based strictly on the difficulties of transportation can only go so far, for the Cove was easily accessible by water.

Although Victorian travellers tended to ignore or reject this coastline, there is one valuable collection of writings on Peggy's Cove and St Margaret's Bay: the letters and publications of the Jerseyman and Anglican missionary, John Stannage, who was appointed in 1834 by the Society for the Propagation of the Gospel in Foreign Parts. His job was to head (in most years, single-handedly to be) the Mission of St Margaret's Bay, covering 220 Anglican families scattered along the Atlantic coast. Before taking up his appointment, Stannage's friends warned him about St Margaret's Bay, a place with 'such a bad name for the roughness and the wildness of the inhabitants, that I never heard it mentioned in any other part of the province except with feelings of the deepest aversion. The people were represented to me as half men and half fish.'[32] Stannage was driven to nervous collapse in his efforts to civilize these curious people. As early as 1839, the year in which Stannage had a school house built in Peggy's Cove, he talked about leaving for another post.[33] He nonetheless stayed on a further seventeen years and enjoyed some success.

Impoverished, isolated, insecure, backward: Stannage captured all these qualities in the one word, 'wild'. The fisherfolk lived in small, half-finished wooden houses and subsisted on fish, potatoes, tobacco, and rum. The average wife could be found 'working as hard as a slave both about the fish and the land', with her ten (or more) children running about her, 'half clad, and more used to swear & curse, to dance and play cards, to wrangle and fight, than to read their Bibles, to pray, or to keep holy the Lord's day'.[34] 'The destitution . . . is such that no clergyman of any feeling can labour long in such places without going beyond his power or his means, both as regards his phisical [*sic*] strength, and his pecuniary resources,' Stannage wrote in 1847. Consumption—'a disease most particularly addicted to this bay'— and subsistence crises stalked the fisherfolk with dismaying frequency.[35] Both Stannage and local newspapers identified the credit system as an important element of the area's backwardness. He noted in 1855, 'it is hoped that many of the people will be enabled to pay their long arrears of debt to their merchants in Halifax which has for so many years weighed heavily upon our shoulders,' adding that such hopes were bound to be disappointed in fishery and that cod was not 'within our reach'.[36] More forceful was the analysis signed by 'A Mechanic' in the Halifax *Acadian Recorder* at the height of the 'starvation' of 1867. 'There are few of our fishermen, even in the most prosperous times, that are able to keep clear of the merchant's books,' he argued, and proceeded to condemn the 25 per cent mark-up for supplies provided on credit and to contrast the wealthy merchants with the over-worked, starving fishermen.[37]

Stannage's coast is a bleak place, where 'adultery, pollygamy [*sic*], incest, drunkeness &c. &c.' have become 'almost fashionable', where child labour sabotaged educational advancement, and where the fishermen's migratory habits undermined civilization. Stannage exempted Peggy's Cove from certain of these strictures, but not others: he described it as a community of migratory fishermen who did not observe the Sabbath and were too poor to found their own church.[38] He conveyed the common nineteenth-century image of the area, but with an uncommon verve and lyrical intensity. His description of the shack of a dying fisherman was especially vivid. After a harrowing trip across bog and barren, Stannage arrived at 'a house so open on all sides that an old sail that was under our feet was actually blown up by the air through the seams in the floor; while over head it was not much better there being no floor there either, & the outside itself not being shingled, so that in the morning I could see day-light through every part of the building.' In this 'dismal and solitary place', by the light of a candle in the mouth of a bottle, 'the most comfortable Sacrament of the body & blood of Christ our Saviour was administered. . . .' Afterwards, the poor family compelled Stannage to sleep in their one bed, and there he spent a restless night, listening to the crowing of a cock in the kitchen, to the crying of a sick child, to the raging storm outside, and to the groans of the dying fisherman.[39]

III

The contrast between Stannage's and Livesay's visions of Peggy's Cove epitomizes the gap between Victorian and post-1920 ways of seeing the fishing communities. We can use this difference in perceptions: first, to locate elements of invention in Livesay's account; second, to suggest the deeper implications of these two ways of seeing; and third, to trace the impact of the transition from one to the other on Maritime regional culture in the 1920s and 1930s.

Stannage wrote from a British imperial perspective, and much of his dark vision of the poverty and instability of lives dependent upon fishing can be traced back to Victorian conceptions of respectability and an English preference for garden scenery.[40] Like many missionaries, he saw only moral chaos where there was, perhaps, merely a way of life different from his own. However, his accounts do contain facts, not simply reducible to his cultural bias, that flatly contradict Livesay's pastoral version of the Cove's history. Within the pastoral tradition, the city and the country are treated as separate categories—indeed, as Raymond Williams observes, the very idea of 'landscape' implies separation and observation. The simplicity, order, and stability of the rural village—we think, here, of Livesay's claim that 'the character of its folk has changed no more than the rocks that encompass it'[41]—is counterposed to the complexity, chaos, and instability of the city. This pastoral anti-modernist description flies in the face of much evidence. So migratory and shifting was the population Stannage described in 1848 that most of those attending church at Peggy's Cove migrated to this spot in summer; furthermore, of the families living at Peggy's Cove in 1956, none bore a surname listed on George III's 800-acre grant of land, fish rooms, and pasture grounds, made in 1811.[42] The claim for cultural homogeneity finds warrant only after the 1880s when, following the outmigration of fishermen from other religious and ethnic backgrounds, a solidly Church of England and Orange population (anchored, probably, by the church planted by Stannage) remained at Peggy's Cove.[43] The Atlantic Coast of Nova Scotia is generally an inappropriate setting for a pastoral celebration of the stability and tranquillity of rural life. Through much of its history it has been dominated by transients and unsettled by war. Townsfolk attacked by privateers, or refugees—American, Loyalist, and 'Foreign Protestant'—flung onto this strategic coast by a century of war, scarcely embodied rural tranquillity.[44]

The independence, happiness, and freedom of rural folk are important themes within the pastoral tradition, but this pastoral vision is a poor guide to social history. There are no reasonable grounds for rejecting the first-hand testimony of Stannage and the reports of others documenting extreme hardship in these communities. Frequently reduced to charity in their recurrent crises, the debt-ridden fishermen of nineteenth-century St Margaret's Bay were not sturdy, 'independent yeomen'. In their defence of collective fishing rights against the claims of other area fishermen, and against at least one thrusting entrepreneur in the Cove itself, they acted collectively, not individually, in defending the 'common use of the Fishery'.[45]

Livesay did not, of course, claim to be an historian. His account of the past presents us with a pastoral vision of what the Cove's history *should have been* more than an account of what actually happened. However, the same reservations apply to his portrait of the Cove in the 1940s. In the role of the summer visitor both 'in' and 'outside' the community, Livesay proclaimed Peggy's Cove his 'spiritual home', but before his retirement he had stayed there only briefly, and as late as 1943 had not met many of its residents. His relations with people in the Cove were, naturally, cordial rather than intimate. (Otherwise, he might have avoided the reference to premarital sex—circumspectly pruned from the 1945 edition—that guaranteed his book a pained and chilly reception in many homes in the Cove.[46]) In much British travel literature, Paul Fussell notes, the traveller is richer and freer than those with whom he associates; the description of his ease with simple peasants links such literature with the pastoral tradition, which has been defined as a mode of presentation implying a beautiful relation between rich and poor.[47] Livesay conforms to this model exactly. The tone of his conversations with the fisherfolk is one of an ambiguous jocularity; in the end we know little more about them as individuals than we did when we started. Even Ethel Manuel, with whom Livesay stayed, is a *papier-maché* figure, the romantic essence of the contented fisherman's wife, the 'veritable mistress of the sea, both daughter and spouse of its mystery', and a stalwart foe of such modern appliances as washing machines. (Although Livesay implies she rejected modern technology for cultural reasons, there were practical difficulties in installing new plumbing in a community built on solid rock. Significantly, he does not tell us that her household possessed the Cove's one telephone, although we can glimpse the pole in his photograph of her home.[48])

Livesay did not wilfully misrepresent the facts. Like any writer, he highlighted those he found most interesting, important, and congenial. The facts never speak for themselves; they speak only with the aid of an enabling interpretive framework. Livesay *does* mention key facts—the terrible hardship and poverty of the fishermen in 1938, the bitter cold and damp of the fishermen's work, the drastic drop in the Cove's population—any one of which, in a different framework, could have aroused indignation. An instructive parallel here is provided by his disarming passage on editing the visual image of Peggy's Cove by erasing from sight a modern two-storey house and the Government Wharf, which he considered inappropriate 'eyesores' in this setting.[49] As with photography, so with prose: he freely edited. We need only remember how Livesay has 'edited' himself: the 'I' of *Peggy's Cove*, this whimsical, gregarious narrator, is an imaginary Livesay, free at last from his depressions, drinking problem, and premonitions of death.

Livesay 'edits' the fisherfolk to emphasize their serene and untroubled essence. He works with the same formula Raymond Williams ascribes to George Eliot, that of 'the "fine old", "dear old", quaint-talking, honest-living country characters,' which was as complacently successful in Nova Scotia as in England.[50] His fisherfolk always speak 'judicially' or 'cautiously' in their diminutive 'Parliament House', and this carefulness is somehow in comic contrast with the ordinariness of what they have to say. The very name Livesay invented—'Parliament House'—mocks by its grandiloquence the idea of a serious politics in this community. Here, it seems, things taken seriously in the outside world can be put in a fresh, sunny perspective. For example, were they set in Quebec under Duplessis, the passages dealing with patronage in local road- and wharf-building might have been accompanied by a critique of the powerlessness such political corruption instills in both its clients and its victims. Set in Livesay's Nova Scotia, they provide further evidence of quaintness.

That Livesay transformed himself and his material in the act of writing is not grounds for an indictment. *Peggy's Cove* is in fact an interpretive achievement, a Nova Scotian instance of a respected tradition of travel writing with a close affinity to fiction. 'My father died a sick, unhappy man,' remembers his daughter in a moving poem;[51] but in *Peggy's Cove* he 'edited' and transformed both himself and the seaside community he loved. He became the jovial guide to his own carefree, windswept heaven. Who could begrudge him that?

IV

We could leave the matter there if the way of seeing we find in Livesay were confined to travel writing. However, exactly the same problem of invention we find in Livesay can be documented in scores of other cultural realms. Indeed, *Peggy's Cove* touches upon a central contradiction—perhaps the central contradiction?—of post-1920 representations of Nova Scotia and the Maritimes. This is the problem of pastoral romance, the perspective through which most middle-class, urban writers described the inner life of Maritime folk communities. In the Maritimes, pastoral longings held very generally throughout the postwar Western world fused with traditions and grievances peculiar to the region to produce the myth of the Golden Age.

The central pastoral propositions—that there is something intrinsically quieter and simpler about the Maritime region, that what is most worthy of commemoration in regional history are the folk ways and dying crafts of the nineteenth century—have become a kind of popular 'commonsense'. Steeped in history, surrounded by the beauties of a rugged land and a turbulent sea, safely removed from the perils and temptations of the twentieth century—living, one apologist enthused (in 1976) 'as simply and as happily as their ancestors did before them'[52]—Maritimers find their sense of collective identity in their folk traditions, in their fiercely independent hamlets, in their amiable rejection of the twentieth century. Storm-tossed Peggy's Cove, securely nestled around its harbour, provides this social myth with the full guarantee of nature. The transition from the 'march of improvement' to the 'Golden Age' as the dominant *motif* of bourgeois thought was evidently a response to the collapse of the region's industries. The transition could as aptly be traced in regional literature, in the mass enthusiasm for the schooner *Bluenose*, and in the conscious reinvention and manipulation of Scottish traditions, as in the symbolic history of Peggy's Cove.[53]

One of the difficulties in coming to grips with this transition is that it involved not merely the selection of various landscapes and and the high-lighting of various aspects of history, but also a fundamental shift in outlook. It is necessary here to return to Stannage and Livesay. Their differences on a number of empirical points have been explored, but the fundamental dif-ference between them is epistemological. Stannage's position was that of the activist. His way of knowing the fisherfolk involved a dialectical relationship between his Christian principles and an empirical world he analysed in order to transform. After wrestling with rural poverty and disease, after scrambling over rocks and trudging through bogs, he did come to identify with his community but was unlikely ever to idealize it. The working pastor's vision and the pastoral vision had nothing in common. Livesay's position, by con-trast, is that of the traveller who brings to his reportage a journalist's sense of ironic detachment, and who composes the scenery and sights around him into a coherent landscape. Those who find Livesay compassionate and Stan-nage intolerant miss an essential point. Within Livesay's writing, nothing—neither the evidence of political corruption nor the performances of the 'Poet of the Cove'—is, or can be, taken seriously; everything is absorbed by a gentle, accepting patronage. In Stannage's world-view, the fisherfolk are not images to savour but souls to save, and this means that everything which stands in the way—poverty, disease, migratory habits—must be transformed. Narrow-minded as it frequently appears to be, Stannage's very Victorian outlook contains a politically creative potential, for saving souls means taking the rural population seriously. Conversely, Livesay's perspective on rural folk—dominant among the urban, middle-class cultural producers of the region since the 1920s—confines his subjects in a prison-house of patronage from which there can ultimately be no escape. Humble folk living in har-mony with their essential natures need not have a complex history, merely an unchanging and constant 'heritage'. Within this essentialist epistemology, they cannot be construed as men and women shaping their own future; they become, instead, objects of curiosity, prisoners of a perpetual present.

This newly dominant 'structure of feeling' can be found in one field of regional culture after another in the second quarter of the twentieth century: in the transitions from commissioned marine paintings of vessels to senti-mental seascapes and coastal views, from photographs documenting individ-uals and industries to Turneresque photographic studies of the sea, from rural manufactories to recently revived (or contrived) 'traditional' handicraft 'industries'. What can, in Livesay, be regarded as the harmless transubstan-tiation of reality into whimsy must be taken more seriously when it becomes the way in which a region generally gains access to its past and imagines its future.

Exploring the ways in which writers after years of neglect elevated Peggy's Cove to the status of the region's primary symbolic landscape opens one small window upon this considerable problem in regional culture.[54] Why Peggy's Cove is beautiful could be analysed in terms of psychoanalytical theory (Freud would have enjoyed deciphering the symbolism of a womb-like Cove flanked by a tower), behavioural theories of landscape (which ambitiously postulate a universal tendency, traceable back to our animal inheritance, to prefer spots that provide us with both refuge and prospect), or aesthetic categories (Peggy's Cove offering us an experience of both the 'sublime' as we watch unbridled nature hurl waves into the bare rocks, and the 'picturesque' as we savour the tranquillity of wharves and fishing boats). Such universal theories do not, however, help explain why twentieth-century observers of Peggy's Cove reversed the stock Victorian ways of seeing the same landscape.[55] It is more helpful to note the vogue of automobile tourism in the 1930s, which allowed middle-class motorists from Halifax to drive out to Peggy's Cove on Sunday to paint and to picnic, but this alone does not explain their choice of this site over others.

Peggy's Cove 'became beautiful' when it came to stand for the essence of the region's way of life. Its use as an icon of regionality is an invented tradition which could hardly have come into existence if it did not fill sig-nificant social and political functions.[56] While twentieth-century reverence for Peggy's Cove can be seen simply as the result of changing fashions in international tourism, its invention cannot be reduced to them. These chang-ing fashions interacted with a local culture of consolation elaborated by intel-lectuals and artists in response to the collapse of the regional economy in the 1920s. The local inventors of Peggy's Cove and other elements of regional rhetoric embraced but simultaneously transformed the negative stereotype of the Maritimes: they admitted regional backwardness, but then placed it under a positive sign. Communities lacking modern amenities and precariously dependent upon natural resources could now be re-imagined as unspoiled hamlets, havens of authenticity in an artificial world. A completed rhetoric of regionalism—a set of fixed, regulated, insistent figures conveying 'the essence of the Maritimes'—emerged in the 1920s and 1930s. Peggy's Cove was the nearest landscape to Halifax, where most of the local cultural pro-ducers lived, that was distinctive enough to serve as a regional icon.

Yet as soon as we have registered the claim for local authorship, we are instantly compelled to qualify it. An enthusiasm for primitive folk and regional distinctiveness was a common aspect of middle-class thought in the interwar period, and in part represented a rejection of the 'civilization' that had made the Great War. Consequently, by the 1920s, it was very difficult to draw a line between locally produced and externally imposed interpre-tations of the fisherfolk and of the 'Maritime identity'; indeed it is often pointless to attempt to assign key figures of the transition (such as Frank Parker Day, Hugh MacLennan, or F.W. Wallace) to one category or another.

That the assertion of the uniqueness and value of the region should have so closely followed standards and tastes universally affecting the bourgeois world, that middle-class observers in Halifax and Toronto should have seen the fisherfolk in roughly the same simplistic ways,[57] that Golden Age mythology was as easily used to rationalize Maritime underdevelopment as to protest against it: these were, and are, the contradictions of a regionalist culture of consolation lacking an alternative social or political perspective.[58] It cannot be plausibly argued that the new way of seeing was merely a patronizing interpretation of regional life foisted on the Maritimes from without, or that it emerged completely from within. In the case of regional art, for example, it was no coincidence that the South Shore was embraced at the same time that Lake Superior and Georgian Bay came to dominate the Canadian visual imagination. The Group of Seven had a direct influence on a number of Nova Scotia painters who selected similar kinds of landscapes.[59] They did so, ironically, with the intention of founding an authentically regional art.

Tourism and travel writing changed very rapidly after the 1920s. Until then, tourism in Nova Scotia, apart from specialized sportsmen's activities, had remained firmly wedded to such civilized attractions as Evangeline and garden scenery. Only after the First World War did provincial tourism fully conform to a new 'primitivist' style in which tourism became 'a flight from civilisation and progress in search of a "world of pleasure" '.[60] In Europe, the transition to primitivism meant a massive colonization of the Mediterranean and the celebration of its fisherfolk, an escape to settings untainted by the pressures and complexities of twentieth-century life. In Nova Scotia, it meant not only changing the message, but also revolutionizing the machinery of tourism in the 1920s, a decade of extensive road improvements and the first major state involvement in the tourist trade.

The new tourism meant the gradual winding-down of delightfully *ersatz* 'Land of Evangeline' historicism, and an emphasis on an appropriately hedonist motto: 'Canada's Ocean Playground'.[61] The severely clipped hedgerows, tidy streets, and gardens with which guide books had once enticed tourists to Nova Scotia were now superseded by rugged seascapes, merry peasants, and winding coastal roads. Pastoralism had cash value. Tourists were promised an experience of older, better, and simpler life-styles. As one travel writer wrote in 1925, Nova Scotia became an 'old-world land that civilization has not yet robbed of its charm', a land where tourists could savour the sight of the ox carts creeping along the roads, with 'weather-beaten old men' by their sides 'who look with annoyance and disdain on the conveyances of modern life'.[62]

In 1903, when 'W.D.T.'—likely the Halifax journalist W.D. Taunton— wrote the earliest extant account of a tourist's impressions of Peggy's Cove, he lamented that, although nearby Chester had long since been colonized as a resort by Americans, visitors to Peggy's Cove were 'few and far between'.[63]

In the 1920s, and especially in the 1930s, relative neglect was transformed into international fame. Peggy's Cove's triumph over countless other coastal villages depended on its being just the right distance from Halifax: remote enough to be an adventure, but close enough to permit a busy motorist to get there and back to Halifax in a day, albeit rather jarringly. 'Through a six-mile stretch of boulders, across a waste of undulating country, mottled with lichens, rain pools and gorse, on a road of trenches worn by iron tires for more than a century, and today harsh to rubber treads, our car pitched and careened in the general direction of the ocean.' So one adventurous traveller described the trip in 1934.[64] Poor road conditions helped the Cove's new boarding trade, for travellers recovering from their trip out welcomed the idea of staying awhile before retracing their steps.

The first widely distributed image of the Cove appears to have been W.R. MacAskill's 1921 photograph, 'Quiet Cove'. He captured several more famous images of the Cove in the two decades which followed.[65] His artistic work was quickly taken up by state tourism promotion, and the Peggy's Cove vista was given prominent play in the province's 1927 propaganda with the caption, 'A wind ridden sea hurls thundering floods of green upon the headlands at Peggy's Cove'. By 1929 a MacAskill photograph of Peggy's Cove was promoted in the province's major tourist pamphlet with the caption, 'Visitors to Nova Scotia find new life in the sharp breath of the sea'. Three years later, Peggy's Cove was singled out for the first time by name in official tourist literature.[66]

The wild and the primitive, once ignored, denied or derided, became positive attractions. What might now be considered a somewhat demeaning simplification of provincial imagery was undertaken by the provincial government itself. Its own official publication in 1928 printed the caption, 'A Nova Scotia type', beneath a photograph of a grizzled old fisherman mending his nets.[67] No less simplistic was the state-sponsored pastoral prose. 'The people of this Province are weathered human souls,' wrote George Matthew Adams, the syndicated newspaper columnist and positive thinker hired by the provincial government as a promotional writer. 'You love their simple and honest ways, their straightforward manner and genial consideration for you.'[68]

There was surprisingly little difference between local newspapers and national magazines in the development of the pastoral outlook. In 'Touring the Maritimes', a column in the Halifax *Mail*, Bob Davis described a visit in 1934 to Peggy's Cove. After his companion had spoken of the quaintness and grandeur of the Cove, Davis exclaimed: 'Step on it for Peggy's Cove. The primitive always appeals to me.' Once at the 'Capital of Content', he turned to a stock rhetorical device: the listing of all the 'defining absences' that made Peggy's Cove unique: no problems, no unemployment, no discontent with life, no fear of death—'The nameless iniquities that disturb civilizations, breed war, destroy generations and shake the very foundations of faith in mankind, are not of the Cove. . . . Factions which foment disorder and pestilential individuals who sow seeds of discord are unknown.' Exploring this 'Seaside Shangri-La' in 1947, Ian Sclanders found no need for psychiatrists, no crimes, and no divorces, in a hamlet where 'life flows on smoothly and peacefully, as it has for 140 years'.[69]

Simplicity, harmony, order: what better tonic could be prescribed for the beleaguered citizens of a world plagued by Depression and War? 'As everywhere that people lead a simple wholesome outdoors life,' we read in T. Morris Longstreth's 1935 account, 'the very statement of their days is caviar to our ears,' and we swiftly plunge into yet another list of things not to be found at Peggy's Cove:

> These people have never been kept awake by trolley-cars, newsboys, street radios, or klaxons. They do not make out laundry-lists. They never have to telephone and ask 'Are you dressing?' They do not lose latchkeys. They never have to tip bell-hops, coatroom attendants, and taxi-drivers. They never have occasion to say 'What an awful picture!' They neither make speeches at banquets nor have to listen to them. . . .[70]

Peggy's Cove thus served as a sign, not just of the regional identity, but of a lost, innocent world. It was, in fact, an *island* of calm, a friendly haven from the confusions of the world. Islands have long been potent images of man's formerly idyllic natural state, the true homelands of the noble savage.[71] Some travel writers combined the metaphor of insularity with excited coverage of actual islands. Sight unseen, Nova Scotia's islands enthralled Dorothy Duncan, who in *Bluenose: A Portrait of Nova Scotia* was delighted by the idea of the survival of 'small, isolated communities of descendants of shipwrecks' on the 'dots of rocky islands sprinkled along the South Shore', island dwellers who had never seen a motor car, an electric light (except on a passing steamer), or a dollar bill. Their lives were, necessarily, rather spartan, 'but the color they lend to the Nova Scotian scene is unquestionable in the eyes of the outsider, once he hears about them.' The fishermen of Peggy's Cove, who survived 'because they were sufficient unto themselves', and were said to 'know nothing and want nothing of cities', were the next best thing to these imaginary Crusoes in Duncan's account.[72]

Here we find a connection between the depiction of the region in travel and in mainstream literature. Thomas Raddall's *The Nymph and the Lamp* (1950) is set in the aftermath of the Great War on the thinly disguised Sable Island, which emerges as a natural alternative to the artificiality of urban Halifax. Evelyn Richardson's immensely popular memoir, *We Keep A Light* (1945), appealed to readers as a vivid and realistic portrait of wholesome family life in conditions of splendid isolation (although she wrote it while working year-round as a small cog in Canada's integrated national coastal defence system), while Frank Parker Day began his novel, *Rockbound*, on the isolated island of the same name only to move the action to the even *more* isolated, stark, and tempest-tossed Barren Island, 'a gaunt plateau' where 'life was stripped of all its shams'.[73]

Travel writing and regional fiction moved in tandem to elevate insularity to the status of a defining cultural trait of Nova Scotians. Hugh MacLennan, who was active in both fields, went so far as to argue that insularity made the difference between the maritime provinces and Ontario more basic than the difference between Quebec and English Canada had ever been.[74] The triumph of insularity in Maritime literature reflected a search for primitive purity which, in the second quarter of the twentieth century, united travellers and poets, painters and novelists, and pushed Peggy's Cove from nineteenth-century obscurity to twentieth-century renown.

V

Things have changed a great deal since the heyday of pastoral travel writing in the 1930s and 1940s. Road improvements have brought Peggy's Cove within easy reach of a vast motoring public. Travel has been rationalized and transformed into tourism. Although one columnist has derided Peggy's Cove as the 'Las Vegas of Quaint', thereby indicating that the Cove is wearing thin as a sign of the Maritime essence, some fishing families still live there.[75] When, in the summertime, they gaze out to sea to watch homecoming vessels laden with fish, they must first look past another sea of vehicles and anonymous strangers. Some feel that their privacy has been violated. In 1984 the annual number of tourists to a community with 47 permanent residents was estimated at 200,000. According to a recent study the average tourist stays one hour and forty-five minutes in the Cove.[76] Tourists rarely leave the bubble of the gift shop, lighthouse, and tour bus to meet the fisherfolk whose authenticity they purport to savour. It is in many ways a pathetic parody of travel forty years earlier.

Despite these changes, Peggy's Cove has not outwardly altered a great deal. Since 1962, development has been restricted by provincial statute; a non-elected Peggy's Cove Commission exercises a mandate to preserve the atmosphere of the village.[77] This entails restricting advertising, regulating the design of buildings, and curtailing out-of-doors entrepreneurship. Without these state controls, Peggy's Cove would be visibly, rather than discreetly, commercialized. Even with them, its one restaurant has mushroomed in size, two large parking lots serve thousands of tourists, and those employed in tourism far outnumber the dwindling ranks of the fishermen. The effect of state intervention has been to guarantee that, even if all the fishermen leave Peggy's Cove, it will maintain the appearance of a pre-industrial fishing village.

What is it, exactly, that is being preserved? Nature, perhaps? The rocks are sprayed with rock-coloured paint or with acid to remove the appreciative graffiti of past visitors, and over $25,000 per year is spent to 'maintain' the natural beauty of the site.[78] In pursuit of preserving the unspoiled 'sublime' it seems that the danger of having the odd tourist swept off the cliffs is preferable to erecting a safety barrier. However, it cannot simply be nature that is being preserved. The experience of watching waves crash against rock would *in itself* be little affected if, for example, a large observation tower or a modern boardwalk and marina were build on this site.[79]

Perhaps, then, it is 'heritage'? Is it a reverence for the past which explains an instinctive revulsion to the thought of bringing modern buildings to the Cove? Peggy's Cove is indeed filled with many nostalgic traces of the nineteenth century, from the English-made figurines of fisherfolk in the giftshop to paintings echoing and re-echoing a faded century-old landscape tradition. But is this, in any genuine sense, 'the past'? Most mementoes from Peggy's Cove impress one by their generic quality: the English busts of Jack Tars, the paintings of fisherfolk lounging about the wharves, the bric-a-brac incorporating brass and rope: all these call to mind some general 'romance of the sea' more than 'the past' of this particular village or of Nova Scotia. In fact, the fascinating and intricate history of the inshore fishing industry, the story of its achievements and tragedies, of hunger and prosperity, of enduring and the more common experience of leaving—none of this history is evident at Peggy's Cove at all.

It seems that what is really being preserved at Peggy's Cove is not nature, or the past, but Livesay's pastoral dream of a natural, redeemed past. This is why to demand that there be more than a faint shadow of real historical events and experiences at Peggy's Cove is to demand that it become something other than what it is, a sign which functions within a consoling myth of the Maritime essence. A museum that offered a realistic presentation of the history of the inshore fishery would only complicate and spoil an image marketed on the basis of its tranquil simplicity. 'Myth,' writes Roland Barthes, 'deprives the object of which it speaks of all history. All that is left for one to do is enjoy this beautiful object without wondering where it came from.'[80] Even to allow the normal holiday hustle-and-bustle of hot-dog stands and other vendors would break the spell of enchantment and disturb us as we consume this image. What need is there for a tedious rehearsal of historical details when we 'know', when we can 'see with our own eyes', the reassuring folk essence at history's core? The pastoral vision, once the foible of a few cultural producers, has not become an officially sanctioned and accepted way of seeing. It organizes festivals. It dominates popular magazines, books, and television shows. It issues or withholds building permits in Peggy's Cove.

Once upon a time, before progress robbed us of our innocence, life was full of content. People were truly individuals. They were happy then. They lived in balance with nature on an island outside history. Everyone was, as Livesay says, of an equality. In splendid isolation on a rockbound coast, they lived beautiful and simple lives, as their ancestors had done before them, never questioning their place in the world, never troubled by the politics of an uncertain age. They live this way still, pure and unspotted in a troubled and difficult world. Don't take my word for it. Go to Peggy's Cove, park your car in the provincial parking lot, and see for yourself.

Suggestions for Further Reading

E.J. Hart, *Selling of Canada: The CPR and the Beginnings of Candian Tourism* (Banff, 1983).

John A. Jakle, *The Tourist: Travel in Twentieth-century North America* (Lincoln, Neb., 1985).

Notes

The author would like to thank Gary Burrill and Dr Dorothy Livesay for helpful comments, Yorke Manuel of Peggy's Cove for his memories of Livesay and early travellers to the Cove, and John Hemple of Winnipeg for research assistance.

[1] J.F.B. Livesay Papers, Public Archives of Manitoba, MG 9, A 100, clipping (undated) of a review by W.J. Hurlow in the Ottawa *Evening Citizen*.

[2] *Chronicle* (Halifax), 16 December 1944. See also the favourable review in *Hospitality* (Halifax), 4, 2 (March 1945), 1. The most telling indication of the book's success was a second printing by Ryerson in 1945.

[3] See Paul Fussell, *Abroad: British Literary Traveling Between the Wars* (New York: Oxford UP, 1980), 210–14.

[4] J.F.B. Livesay, *Canada's Hundred Days: With the Canadian Corps from Amiens to Mons, Aug. 8–Nov. 11, 1918* (Toronto: Allen, 1919).

[5] See J.F.B. Livesay, *The Making of a Canadian* (Toronto: Ryerson, 1947); *Newsweek*, 26 June 1944.

[6] Livesay Papers, File 7, Livesay to Ken Clark, 10 February 1939.

[7] Livesay, *Canadian*, 145–6.

[8] Livesay Papers, File 7, Carl G. Milligan to J.F.B. Livesay, 27 March 1922; E. Norman Smith to Livesay, 1 December 1921. Florence Randal Livesay, his wife, was a poet and novelist in her own right, and *Savour of Salt* (Toronto: Dent, 1927) resembles *Peggy's Cove* in humorously describing the customs, traditions, and superstitions of a quaint Ontario community.

[9] Dorothy Livesay, 'Heritage', in *Collected Poems: The Two Seasons* (Toronto: McGraw-Hill Ryerson, 1972), 348.

[10] Livesay, *Canadian*, v.

[11] Livesay, *Canadian*, 148–9.

[12] Livesay, *Canadian*, 173.

[13] See Livesay Papers, File 9, Memos and Notes, note dated 7/1/1928: 'There is something about Island people that is different: there is sympathy and understanding the one of the other, especially if the island is small. Thus an Isle-o-Wighter feels

more at home on P.E.I. than in New Brunswick, in Cape Breton than on the
mainland. Peggy's Cove itself is to all intents and purposes is [sic] an island and a
tiny teeny weeny one at that: it has the essential quality of concrete compact unity.'

[14]Livesay, *Canadian*, 92.

[15]Livesay Papers, File 5, Daily Journal, 30 April 1941: 'Budget . . . and increase in
taxation makes problem for this menage—abandoned trip to Peggy's Cove'.

[16]Livesay Papers, File 6, Diary, 22 July, 4 August 1943.

[17]Livesay Diary, 27 September, 17 October 1943.

[18]J.F.B. Livesay, *Peggy's Cove* (Toronto: Ryerson, 1944), 8–9.

[19]Livesay, *Peggy's Cove*, 40–41.

[20]Livesay, *Peggy's Cove*, 24.

[21]Livesay, *Peggy's Cove*, 33, 52, 92–93.

[22]Livesay, *Peggy's Cove*, 76, 32.

[23]Fussell, *Abroad*, 214.

[24]Review by I.N.S. in the Ottawa *Journal*, undated clipping, Livesay papers, File 10;
Saturday Night, as cited in Livesay, *Canadian*, 16.

[25]For representative books, see R.R. McLeod, *Markland or Nova Scotia: Its History,
Natural Resources and Native Beauties* (Halifax: Markland Publishing Company,
1903); Herbert Crosskill, *Nova Scotia: Its Climate, Resources and Advantages. Being a
General Description of the Province for the Information of Intending Emigrants* (Halifax,
1872); and even Beckles Willson, *Nova Scotia: The Province that has been Passed By*
(Toronto: McClelland & Goodchild, [1912]), which is, despite its title, most enthusiastic about the triumph of progress in the province.

[26]Andrew Learmont Spedon, *Rambles among the Blue-Noses: Or, Reminiscences of a Tour
Through New Brunswick and Nova Scotia, During the Summer of 1862* (Montreal,
1863), 124.

[27]T.C. Haliburton, *A General Description of Nova Scotia: Illustrated by a New and Correct
Map* (Halifax, 1823), 5; Thomas F. Anderson, 'Nova Scotia', *New England Magazine*,
8 (August 1893), 731.

[28]Hugh Murray, *An Historical and Descriptive Account of British America*, 2nd ed., 2 vols
(Edinburgh, 1839), 2: 154; *A Description of the Province of Nova Scotia, Contrasted:
with a Glance at the Probable Future* (Halifax, 1860), 40.

[29]There is Charles Hallock's 1873 opinion that the coast from Lahave to Indian River
is 'of the most picturesque description, and full of novelty to the tourist' (Charles
Hallock, *The Fishing Tourist* [New York, 1873], 125); while Reverend R. Murray
and Mrs A. Simpson, 'Nova Scotia', in George M. Grand, ed., *Picturesque Canada:
The Country as it was and is*, 2 vols (Toronto, 1882), 2; 789–852, were enthusiastically
detailed about fishing communities and recommended Nova Scotia's Atlantic coast
as a splendid refuge from North America's summer heat waves. They did not,
however, celebrate natural fisherfolk as a tourist attraction or highlight any particular
Nova Scotia fishing village. Basil King, *In the Garden of Charity* (New York: Harper
& Brothers, 1903), an early novel of the Banks fishermen, also acknowledges a
certain wild splendour in the rockbound coast.

[30]McLeod, *Markland*, 247; *Vacation Days in Nova Scotia: 'The Land of Evangeline'* (N.p.:
Dominion Atlantic Railway, n.d. [1910]), 52–4; G.F. Parker, *A Tripod Trip along the
South Shore of Nova Scotia* (Yarmouth, 1899).

[31]Karl Baedeker [J.F. Muirhead], *The Dominion of Canada with Newfoundland and an
Excursion to Alaska: Handbook for Travellers* (Leipzig: Karl Baedeker, 1907); Michelin

Tires, *Canada* (Clemont-Ferrand, France: Michelin, 1985), 193. Robinson's Tours, *'Peeps at Nova Scotia'* (Halifax: Imperial Publishing Company, [c. 1913]) advertised a tour to French Village, Dover, Shad Bay and back via the Prospect Road, which lasted no fewer than three days over a road even the tour company conceded was 'not one of the best'.

[32]Reverend John Stannage, *Some Account of the Mission of St. Margaret's Bay, Nova Scotia: In a Letter, Drawn up at the Request of Some Friends in Jersey* (Jersey, England, 1844), 5.

[33]Stannage, *Account*, 3; Public Archives of Nova Scotia, Society for the Propagation of the Gospel in Foreign Parts, Originals, Microfilm, Reel 29, Stannage to Lord Bishop of Nova Scotia, 31 December 1843. In 1850, Stannage reported that his labours had been stopped 'by a total prostration of my strength' (Stannage to Archdeacon Willis, 31 December 1850). Stannage to the Secretary of the S.P.G., 1 January 1836.

[34]Stannage, *Account*, 8.

[35]Stannage to the S.P.G., 11 March 1847, 31 December 1839, 31 December 1845; *Novascotian* (Halifax), 30 December 1867; *Acadian Recorder* (Halifax), 4 November 1889; *Morning Chronicle* (Halifax), 29 January 1890; *Herald* (Halifax), 23 September 1920.

[36]Stannage to Rev. E. Hawkins, Secretary of the S.P.G., 18 August 1885.

[37]*Acadian Recorder*, 2 December 1867. Such images of the coast's poverty and wilderness recurred frequently in later nineteenth-century accounts. *Amherst Evening Press*, 3 September 1891 (on illiteracy); *Trades Journal* (Stellarton), 7 November 1883.

[38]Stannage to the S.P.G., 31 December 1845, 31 December 1848, 31 December 1841.

[39]Fowl were often kept in the kitchens of the dwellings of the poor of St Margaret's Bay during the winter. Stannage to S.P.G., 31 December 1845.

[40]See Mary Sparling, *Great Expectations: The European Vision in Nova Scotia 1749–1848* (Halifax: Mount Saint Vincent University, 1980); for parallel assessments of primary industry in New Brunswick, see Graeme Wynn, ' "Deplorably Dark and Demoralized Lumberers"? Rhetoric and Reality in Early Nineteenth-Century New Brunswick', *Journal of Forest History* 24, 4 (1980): 168–87.

[41]Raymond Williams, *The Country and the City* (Frogmore, U.K.: Paladin, 1975), 149. See, as well, Denis Cosgrove, *Social Formation and Symbolic Landscape* (London: Croom Helm, 1984); Livesay, *Peggy's Cove*, 33.

[42]William deGarthe, *This is Peggy's Cove* ([Halifax]: [1956]), n. pag.

[43]The 1871 manuscript suggests the dominance of the Church of England, but notes Baptists (the Manuel family) and Methodists (the Crooks) at Peggy's Cove. By 1903, 'There is not a man, woman or child who is not an Episcopalian and nearly every man is an Orangeman' (Halifax *Morning Chronicle*, 30 September 1903).

[44]See, especially, Winthrop Pickard Bell, *'The Foreign Protestants' and the Settlement of Nova Scotia: The History of a Piece of Arrested British Colonial Policy in the Eighteenth Century* (Toronto: U of Toronto P, 1961); and John Faibisy, 'Privateering and Piracy: The Effects of New England Raiding Upon Nova Scotia During the American Revolution', PhD Thesis, University of Massachusetts, 1972.

[45]Quotation from PANS, RG 20, Series 'C', Vol. 31, 1847, Petition of the Inhabitants of Peggy's Cove. See also PANS, RG 5, Series 'G', Petition of the inhabitants of Peggy's Cove, Indian Harbour, and elsewhere, 1849; and PANS, RG 20, Series 'C',

Vol. 31, 1847, Petition of the inhabitants of Peggy's Cove. Echoes of this collective tradition can be heard once again in the great anti-trawler campaign of the 1930s, in which the inshore fishermen of Halifax County urged Ottawa to stop licensing the beam trawlers they accused of hurting 'their' fish stocks (*Herald*, 27 May 1938). For a discussion of such collective traditions further down the South Shore, see Anthony Davis, 'Property Rights and Access, Management in the Small Boat Fishery: A Case Study from Southwest Nova Scotia', in Cynthia Lamson and Arthur J. Hanson, eds, *Atlantic Fisheries and Coastal Communities: Fisheries Decision-Making Case Studies* (Halifax: Dalhousie University, 1984), 133–64.

[46]His diaries, which are admittedly somewhat cryptic, seem to qualify the impression that Livesay was a regular visitor to 'Parliament House' where so many of the book's conversations are set. Livesay, *Peggy's Cove*, 96, contains the reference to pre-marital sex and unwanted pregancies removed in the second edition.

[47]Fussell, *Abroad*, 210.

[48]Livesay, *Peggy's Cove*, 81, 59. Moreover, she later bought a washing machine.

[49]Livesay, *Peggy's Cove*, 36.

[50]Williams, *Country*, 208.

[51]Dorothy Livesay, 'Heritage', 348.

[52]Jim Jamieson, 'Why Tourists Return to Atlantic Canada', *Axiom*, 1, 1:23.

[53]See E.J. Hobsbawm and Terence Ranger, eds, *The Invention of Tradition* (Cambridge: Cambridge UP, 1985), for models of interest to Maritime intellectual history.

[54]It is also a topic which might tempt one to assign too much emphasis to the part of tourism in creating a 'pastoral commonsense' in the region, for in the case of other traditions invented in the 1920s, such as the *Herald*'s sponsorship of the International Fishermen's Races and the entire *Bluenose* phenomenon, it would appear that local cultural producers and an overtly regionalist discourse played a more important and distinctive role than they did in this case. In fields less sensitively attuned to external tastes, pastoralism and its antithesis, 'improvement', may well have coexisted for a longer period.

[55]For a discussion of the interpretation of landscape which raises many suggestive parallels with the Nova Scotia experience, see Maria Tippett and Douglas Cole, *From Desolation to Splendour; Changing Perceptions of the British Columbia Landscape* (Toronto: Clarke, Irwin, 1977). For behavioural theory, see Jay Appleton, *The Experience of Landscape* (New York: Wiley, 1975).

[56]E.J. Hobsbawm, 'Mass Producing Traditions: Europe 1870–1914', in Hobsbawm and Ranger, *Invention of Tradition*, 307.

[57]Many would exempt Frank Parker Day's *Rockbound* (1928, Toronto: U of Toronto P, 1973) because of the grim realism with which it depicts life and labour in one island community. This seems at best debatable, however, given Day's extreme interest in viewing the fishermen as natural, child-like, primitive men, overgrown boys: in effect, he reduces their history to nature. More compelling is the vision of whole people and a natural community developed by the Maine painter Marsden Hartley, who, in *Cleophas and His Own: A North Atlantic Tragedy* (Halifax: A Press, 1982), eulogized two South Shore fishermen he loved who drowned while he was boarding with their family in 1936. Like Day, he too sees a 'primitive' quality in his fisherfolk, and he shares Day's sense of their being unrepressed in their sexuality.

Unlike Day, however, Hartley was not trying to establish a general thesis but to commemorate and mourn two particular individuals, and one never feels that the people in his poem are there to illustrate some didactic point, nor that he is feigning admiration for a style of life for which he had no genuine understanding. For all its unpolished quality, it convinces us where so many other evocations of 'simplicity' do not, perhaps because it emerged from the author's overpowering sense of loss.

[58] An important illustration of this contradiction is Hugh MacLennan, who passed rapidly from Nova Scotian to pan-Canadian nationalism, and whose explanation of Maritime underdevelopment (in 'The Miracle That's Changing Nova Scotia', *Mayfair* 27:7 [July 1953], 60) stressed one aspect of local culture in particular: the excessive conservative thriftiness of an older generation.

[59] For the role of J.E.H. MacDonald, see [Alex S. Mowat, comp.], *200 Years of Art in Halifax: An Exhibition prepared in honour of the Bicentenary of the Founding of the City of Halifax, N.S. 1749–1949* (n.p. [Halifax], n.d. [1949]).

[60] Louis Turner and John Ash, *The Golden Hordes: International Tourism and the Pleasure Periphery* (New York: St Martin's Press, 1976), 49.

[61] There were rather unhappy attempts to marry the old and new approaches—'The Playground With a History' was the curious slogan of 1927—before the slogan assumed its present form ('Canada's Ocean Playground') in 1929. See *Vacation Days in Nova Scotia, The Land of Evangeline Route* (n.p.: [1972]); *Nova Scotia, Canada's Ocean Playground* (Halifax: [1929]).

[62] Emma-Lindsay Squier, *An Autumn Trails and Adventures in Captivity* (London: T. Fisher Unwin, 1925), 9.

[63] *Chronicle*, 30 September 1903. W.D. Taunton is well remembered in Peggy's Cove as one of its main boosters.

[64] *Halifax Mail*, 28 August 1934.

[65] See Harris Grant, 'A Distinguished Photographer', *Mayfair* (June 1947), 78.

[66] *Vacation Days in Nova Scotia, The Land of Evangeline Route*; *Nova Scotia, Canada's Ocean Playground*, 38; J.H. Mitchell, comp., *Rambles Through Scenic Nova Scotia* (Halifax, 1932), 65.

[67] *Nova Scotia By The Sea* (n.p. [Halifax], n.d. [1928]).

[68] George Matthew Adams, *Glimpses of Nova Scotia* (n.p. [Halifax]: Nova Scotia Bureau of Information, [1932]), 1, 32.

[69] *Evening Mail* (Halifax), 28, 30 August 1934; Ian Sclanders, 'Seaside Shangri-La', *Maclean's Magazine*, 1 August 1947, 12, 31.

[70] T. Morris Longstreth, *To Nova Scotia, The Sunrise Province* (1935; Toronto: Ryerson, 1947), 15–16.

[71] Turner and Ash, *The Golden Hordes*, 151.

[72] Dorothy Duncan, *Bluenose: A Portrait of Nova Scotia* (New York: Harper & Bros. 1942), 150, 131.

[73] Evelyn Richardson, *B . . . was for Butter and Enemy Craft* (Halifax: Petheric, 1976), 5; Day, *Rockbound*, 106.

[74] Hugh MacLennan, 'The Miracle', 31; see also William B. Hamilton, *The Nova Scotia Traveller: A Maritimer's Guide to his Home Province* (Toronto: Macmillan of Canada, 1981), 245; and Howard T. Walden *Anchorage Northeast* (New York: William Morrow & Co., 1971), 146, who rather sensibly points out that if people

were really as enthusiastic about island life as romantic lip service suggests, far fewer Nova Scotia islands would be uninhabited.

75 *Globe and Mail* (Toronto), 27 April 1984.

76 Heather Conn, "It's Unreal": The Tourist Invasion of Peggy's Cove', *New Maritimes* 5, 11/12 (July-August 1987), 11; *Chronicle-Herald* (Halifax), 14 April 1984; Lynn Davis *et al.*, *Planning Choices for Peggy's Cove: A Report prepared by the Nova Scotia College of Art and Design* (Halifax: Nova Scotia College of Art and Design, 1983), 12.

77 *Statutes of Nova Scotia*, 11 Elizabeth II, Chapter 10, 1962, 'An Act to Create a Peggy's Cove Preservation Area and to Establish a Peggy's Cove Commission'.

78 For discussions of cleaning the rocks with acid, see Municipality of the County of Halifax, Peggy's Cove Commission, Minutes, 20 April 1978; for lifesaving, see the Minutes of 30 January 1980.

79 In fact, plans for a boardwalk, to incorporate a seafood restaurant, restroom facilities, and studios, were drawn up in the 1970s by one architect and town planner, although significantly she stressed how important it was to conform to the prevailing architecture. See Peggy's Cove Commission Papers, Correspondence File.

80 Roland Barthes, *Mythologies* (Frogmore, U.K.: Paladin, 1973), 151.

24

Political Protest in the Canadian Depression

Peter R. Sinclair

The great international economic collapse of the 1930s hit Canada hard, for the nation's dependence on foreign sales of its farming, mining, and forest products was substantial. While all sections of the country and all segments of the population were affected, none was harder hit than western farmers and all those dependent on their prosperity. The price of prime wheat plummeted from $1.03 per bushel in 1928 to 29¢ per bushel in 1932, and foreign protectionism in agricultural products further limited the market for almost everything farmers could produce. Still suffering from the financial problems of earlier expansion, the farmers of southern Alberta and Saskatchewan, who were working land located on the margins of adequate rainfall, experienced drought years in the early 1930s that turned much of their region into a veritable dust bowl. For many farmers the 1930s inflicted a series of annual net losses of income; only the fact that they

were considered to be self-employed prevented their swelling the official unemployment statistics to startling levels. The agrarian community of the West, which had never been sympathetic to the abstract realities of international finance, had already mounted several movements of protest against external 'interests'— including the Progressive Party, and the United Farmers of Alberta (UFA), which governed Alberta in the early years of the Depression. Not surprisingly, the western provinces were a hotbed of political unrest during the Depression. Out of the turmoil came two major political movements: Social Credit in Alberta and the Co-operative Commonwealth Federation (CCF) in Saskatchewan.

Sociologist Peter Sinclair argues that in western Canada Social Credit and the CCF were alternative populist responses to the Depression. He identifies four characteristics of populism, and evaluates CCF and Social Credit policy in this context. Sinclair then explains the appearance of western Canadian populist movements in terms of social class, focusing particularly on farmers as members of the *petit-bourgeois* class. The difference between the populist responses in Alberta and Saskatchewan, he argues, was rooted in the different development of farmer activism in the two provinces.

What, according to Sinclair, is populism? Apart from those social/political developments he considers, what others were possible? How does Sinclair define class? Are there alternative definitions? Is this a 'Marxist' interpretation? Are his explanations for the different responses of Saskatchewan and Alberta credible? What other factors might be taken into account?

This article first appeared, titled 'Class Structure and Popular Protest: The Case of Western Canada', in the *Canadian Journal of Sociology* 1 (1975), 1–15, and was reprinted with minor editorial changes in C. Caldarola, ed., *Society and Politics in Alberta: Research Papers* (Agincourt, 1979), 73–86.

The emergence of Social Credit and the Co-operative Commonwealth Federation (CCF) from similar social conditions in Alberta and Saskatchewan is best explained by stressing how the populist elements in each were consistent with the *petit-bourgeois* character of the most numerous class in each province. Differences in the historical development of each province prior to the Depression explain the acceptance of separate expressions of populism in Alberta and Saskatchewan. This is the thesis to be elaborated and defined in this paper.

In 1968 S.M. Lipset concluded that there had been no 'adequate explanation, or even a detailed descriptive account of the factors involved that resulted in such different reactions from two quite similar social units'.[1] Shortly afterwards David Smith[2] proposed that the federal system of government was a key explanatory factor. This did indeed make separate political development possible, but in itself is no explanation of the nature of that development. Walter Young[3] reconstructed the history of the Progressives, the CCF (which he treated as a national movement), and Social Credit. However, each political movement was treated in isolation, with no attempt to present an explicit comparison. More recently Naylor has stressed the similarity of Social Credit and the CCF as answers to the problems faced by the agrarian *petite bourgeoisie*:

> As to the contradiction between Social Credit and the CCF emerging from identical conditions, it ceases to exist once these movements are viewed in terms of objective class standards rather than the subjective standards of the leaders. The two movements are indistinguishable. For the farm constituency, the policy proposals of both groups were identical.[4]

In this paper the similar class base of Social Credit and the CCF is also emphasized, but these movements are certainly not 'indistinguishable'. There is still a need to account for their separate development in neighbouring provinces.

What is Populism?

My contention is that *both* Social Credit and Saskatchewan CCF developed as populist protest parties. But what are the salient characteristics of populism? The concept has certainly been among the most difficult to pin down in the sociology of politics because it has been applied indiscriminately to such disparate groups as North American cash-crop farmers and the *narodniki* of nineteenth-century Russia, as well as twentieth-century rural and urban movements in Africa, Asia, and South America. Proposed definitions vary from those which are so general in their emphasis on popular participation as to be equivalent to many definitions of democracy to those which tend to emphasize the characteristics of the particular movement which the author has studied in depth.[5] In part, the failure to agree on a definition reflects the difficulty of trying to include in one concept a large number of political movements which developed separately on different continents and with no influence on each other.

If we are to develop an adequate concept of populism, it is necessary to investigate what the 'examples' have in common. Yet, when this is attempted, similarities are found only at a highly abstract or general level. Attempts to be very specific seem doomed, as in the work of Peter Wiles, to whom populism is:

> any creed or movement based on the following major premise: *virtue resides in the simple people, who are the overwhelming majority, and in their collective traditions.*
> I hold that this premise causes a political syndrome of surprising constancy, albeit with now more, now fewer, socialist overtones.[6]

Wiles's syndrome lists 24 characteristics of populism, and he recognizes that no single case will have all of them. While this is to be expected in all ideal-type constructions, it is less acceptable that for most hypotheses in the list we can find examples of political movements which have been classified as populist and which contradict Wiles's assertions. The point is that statements which attempt to be specific about populism's ideology and organization must be qualified by exceptions. This does not mean that the category should be abandoned, but we must recognize that populism is a highly general category which must be qualified when looking at specific cases, just as categories such as socialism, communism, and capitalism must be qualified when applied to particular examples. It is still valuable to know what disparate events and situations have in common.

I shall now attempt to establish several general populist characteristics and indicate the correspondence of Social Credit and the CCF to them.

First, populist ideology stresses the worth of the common people and advocates their political supremacy. Reports of how William Aberhart, the Social Credit leader, stirred the people of Alberta in the thirties suggest his emotional commitment to their plight. For example, a small-town business-man claimed that 'above all, he had an absolutely great love for the suffering of the common people,' and a farmer reported that 'He took up our prob-lems and made them his own. That's why I worked for him.'[7] By explaining to the unemployed how the Depression was not a consequence of their personal failings, Aberhart restored a lost dignity. In more abstract terms, Social Credit theory proclaimed that the general will of the people must be realized, and this could be done through the inspired leadership of William Aberhart. The Social Credit League was to represent the will of all the people in one organization, which would be morally superior to the corrupt and socially divisive parties of the old political system.

Within the CCF, a close identification with the common people also existed. For example, Tommy Douglas[8] stated that 'This is more than a political movement, it is a people's movement, a movement of men and women who have dedicated their lives to making the brotherhood of man a living reality.' However, whereas in Social Credit populist emphasis on the worth of the people was shown mostly in the paternalistic concern of the leadership for the suffering of the people, in the Saskatchewan CCF it was most evident in the ideological commitment to popular control of the polit-ical organization.

This leads to the second characteristic of populism, that is, the rejection of intermediate associations between the mass and leaders. Of course, polit-ical organizations do develop, but their structure is influenced by the populist desire for direct democracy. In this respect, the Saskatchewan CCF followed the common practice of North American populism by requiring that orga-nization leaders be controlled from the mass base. Therefore, the CCF devel-oped a form of delegate democracy, which provided institutional means for the mass membership to retain control over its representatives. For example, the party leader was subject to election by convention each year, and policy resolutions, which might originate at any level of the organization, were not considered binding until passed by the annual convention. Whether such attempts to avoid the problems of oligarchical control in the CCF were suc-cessful is a disputed matter, but I am only concerned here to show the influence of democratic populist ideas on the formal organization.

In the case of Social Credit, the commitment to direct democracy took an authoritarian form. William Aberhart, claiming to represent the general will, was charismatically legitimated and had personal control of decision-making. In matters of policy, candidate selection, and administration, general conventions had given Aberhart the final say. Party conventions became more than convenient locations for the leaders to distribute information and give inspirational addresses. Aberhart retained his 'direct' relationship with the people through his frequent public meetings and his regular radio broadcasts. This kind of authoritarian populism is rare in North America and develops, as we shall see, when the more democratic form is discredited. Although more extreme and less popular than Social Credit, the American movements led by Coughlin, Long, Winrod, and Pelly were similar cases of authoritarian populism.[9]

A third characteristic of populism, closely linked with its emphasis on the common people, is the tendency for populist protest to be directed against some group which lies outside the local society. When deprivations are experienced, the stress on the homogeneity and virtue of the people means that external causes must be sought. This is the basis of the nationalist and isolationist sentiment of much populism. Among the most common scapegoats have been colonial capitalist states, monopoly industry and finance, industrial labour unions, Jews, and other ethnic minorities. In their frustration, supporters of both Social Credit and the CCF turned against the 'Big Interests' from the metropolitan East and against their representatives in the West. In attacking the eastern-controlled corporations, they were continuing a long tradition of protest by Western Canadian farmers. The thrust of Social Credit was against financial institutions, leading in its most extreme development to a theory that there was a world Jewish conspiracy to dominate the common people. (This minority group was disowned by the Social Credit leadership.) There was no evidence of such scapegoat theorizing in the CCF, but there was certainly a recognition that monopoly capitalism lay at the root of the farmers' problem and that the Saskatchewan party stood for the West against the East.

A fourth and critical quality of populism is that it demands the reform of capitalist structure rather than social revolution. Several writers refer to the Janus quality of populism, looking forward and backward at the same time.[10] Innovation is accepted provided the aim is to modify the existing order by making it more bearable for the common people Occasionally such innovation has taken on a socialist façade (for example, the setting up of state-owned grain elevators in some parts of North America), but in populist programs there is never any commitment to a fundamental change in property relations as they pertain to the small producer. Populist ideology reflects a desire to shore up what exists, or even to revert to some imagined golden age.

The debate about the ideological nature of American populism in the late nineteenth century has considerable theoretical relevance for an understanding of the Canadian cases. I shall not enter here the dispute about the rationality, nativist, or anti-Semitic character of American populism; rather I shall

limit my comment to the economic ideology. Norman Pollack's[11] provocative work argued that populists had strong support from and close ties with
eastern labour, but Goldschmidt[12] has presented evidence that New York
workers looked on populism as a movement of agrarian class interests that
had little to offer as a solution to the labourers' problems. Whether popular
with labour or not, populism was not socialist. For example, Durden[13]
records that H.D. Lloyd joined the populists in order to advance socialism,
but his collectivist proposals were rejected.[14] Most convincing is Nugent's[15]
study of Kansas, in which populism is shown as a practical reform movement
aiming to solve problems of land control, monopoly in transportation, and,
especially, money supply. Similarly, the Nonpartisan League of North Dakota
advocated policies of state intervention to prop up the position of the
farmer.[16] It had a direct influence on Canadian populism, particularly on the
United Farmers of Alberta.

Populism in Western Canada

In western Canada, similar reformist solutions were presented, as both Social
Credit and the CCF claimed to solve the class problems of the *petite bourgeoisie*
within the framework of capitalism. Social Crediters emphasized that they
did not threaten private property, savings, or the principle of free enterprise
but they did claim that the freedom and prosperity of the people could be
restored by reforming the monetary system of capitalism. The cause of poverty, they said, was a lack of purchasing power, which could be resolved by
controlling financial institutions and issuing dividends of social credit to each
member of society.[17] Having accepted the panacea of monetary reform, there
was less emphasis on other favoured techniques of populist defence. Therefore, in the Social Credit program we find little attention to promotion of
co-operatives, state control of monopolies, and state-welfare provisions, all
of which were part of CCF policy. These solutions would be unnecessary
after the financial system had been reformed.

By 1934 the Saskatchewan CCF was in the process of dropping its socialist
program for the state ownership of land and was becoming a party of populist
reform.[18] The elements of socialism in the CCF's program did not challenge
the dominant form of the organization of production in Saskatchewan (small-
scale private enterprise in the form of the family farm), but rather provided
for its continuation. That such a policy might involve government control,
or even ownership, of the forces which were affecting the farmer was consistent with populist ideology. The CCF leaders rejected Social Credit monetary reform, although there was considerable pressure in the thirties for
some co-operation with Aberhart,[19] and so they fell back on the staples of
North American agrarian populism—support for the co-operatives, control
of the banks and industrial monopolies, state medicine, etc. The Saskatch-

ewan CCF was also influenced by the urban labour background of some of its leaders and by its association with the national party, which was not farmer-dominated. Therefore, the party proposed and later enacted legislation which was more favourable to the rights of labour than that found anywhere else in the country. Yet, as Lipset[20] recognized, this was a trade-union program, not a socialist one. Even in the CCF's state enterprises, there was no commitment to workers' participation in management.

In assessing the CCF's ideology as populism, it is necessary to come to terms with the evidence that many leaders of the CCF saw it as a socialist party in opposition to capitalism. But when we understand the meaning of capitalism and socialism in Saskatchewan, there is no longer any reason to withdraw the populist label. When CCF leaders attacked capitalism, they were not attacking the idea of private ownership of productive property or the private accumulation of profit, which is essential for a long-term commitment to socialism. (Using this criterion, many of Europe's social-democratic parties could not be considered socialist either.) As evidence of the CCF position on profits, we may take a speech by party leader George Williams, who argued that small businessmen had nothing to fear from a supposed attack on profits because:

> From an economic point of view, a profit is something over and above a fair and just reward for a service rendered. . . . But the small margin our retail merchants receive is not in that class at all.[21]

To be against capitalism in Saskatchewan meant to be against monopoly exploitation; it did not mean to be against small-scale private enterprise, because this would have meant challenging the whole way of life of prairie farmers. The meaning of capitalism is made clear in a statement by T.C. Douglas, replying to a charge that his new government's proposals to help private enterprise were in contradiction to the official CCF policy of eradicating capitalism:

> Premier Douglas said 'private enterprise' and 'capitalism' were not synonymous terms. The reference to capitalism meant monopoly capitalism where a small group of men were able to control the whole economy of a community. . . . The government recognized three types of enterprise, public, co-operative and private, and all had a place in the province's economy. It was the government's intention to encourage private enterprise wherever it did not interfere with the welfare of the people.[22]

In the late thirties, public reference to socialism was usually avoided in CCF speeches and literature. When Douglas replaced Williams as party leader, the concept of socialism reappeared, but it now meant either opposition to monopolies or extension of the co-operative movement. In this, the CCF continued the tradition of pragmatic agrarian populism under another label.

The co-operative commonwealth is still based on capitalist property relations. Thus, it is true that:

> the co-operative movement does not advocate a basic change in capitalist institutional structure. It accepts profits and private entrepreneurship; indeed, it seeks to extend the benefits of these institutions to a large number.[23]

Therefore, we should question the CCF's own statement about the relationship between co-operatives and socialism—that 'their fundamental principles and objectives are the same.'[24] This could only be true if socialism can be defined to exclude a social revolution. In 1945, enabling legislation was passed to allow the establishment of collective farms in Saskatchewan, but only 29 were actually set up. This was the limit of the socialization of agriculture.

The preceding paragraphs have tried to establish the populist character of Social Credit and the Saskatchewan CCF, but why did populism develop in Western Canada? The explanation to be presented here stresses the influence of a person's class position on his political action. While this is hardly a novel idea, the concept of class has been used in such varied ways in the sociological literature that it is not clear what is intended by this statement. For example, with reference to the emergence of agrarian class-consciousness, Lipset employs a concept of economic class in which a class is defined in terms of relationship to the market. Such an approach to class is realist in the sense that 'it considers social class as a real ensemble defined at one and the same time by material facts and by the collective consciousness which individuals form of it.'[25] It is possible to conceive of such a group as an acting unit. However, in his analysis of the social base of CCF support, Lipset changes his use of class. Now the status-group categories favoured by many American sociologists appear. These categories describe aggregates of individuals and do not carry the implication that the groups are acting units. This would only be possible if they formed communities. Here class will be used consistently in the former sense.

The best attempt to analyse the class basis of prairie politics is C.B. Macpherson's *Democracy in Alberta*, in which he argues that the most useful way of categorizing people in order to understand political action is based on their relationship to the productive process—in particular, 'how much freedom they retain over the disposal of their own labour, and how much control they exercise over the disposal of others' labour'.[26] Those who occupy similar positions in these respects are liable to develop similar assumptions and outlooks as a result of their common life experience.[27] From this perspective, the farmers of Western Canada form part of the *petite bourgeoisie*, a concept which denotes a class of small-scale entrepreneurs who are self-employed and employ little or no labour from outside the family. In twentieth-century Canada, as the scale of organized production constantly increases, they form

Table 1. Occupational Distribution of the Labour Force, 1911–15
  (in Percentages)

	1911	1921	1931	1941	1951
Alberta					
Professional managerial	7.9	10.5	9.9	10.6	14.0
Other white-collar	6.4	9.6	9.3	9.4	14.7
Agricultural	49.9	52.8	50.9	49.0	32.5
Blue-collar	29.6	20.0	22.4	22.1	28.3
Service	6.3	6.6	7.7	9.0	10.0
Not stated		0.1		0.1	0.6
Saskatchewan					
Professional managerial	6.0	9.7	9.2	9.8	12.9
Other white-collar	5.2	8.0	7.6	7.7	11.7
Agricultural	63.9	65.2	60.3	59.3	48.8
Blue-collar	19.7	11.3	15.9	14.4	18.6
Service	5.3	5.6	7.1	8.8	7.7
Not stated				0.2	0.5

SOURCE: Calculated from data in Dominion Bureau of Statistics. Census of Canada, 1961. Bulletin 3.1–2.

Note: The Canadian census uses occupational categories which are not suitable for conventional sociological analysis. This table has been constructed by collapsing census categories. While the result is far from ideal, it is the best that can be achieved with the available data. Percentages may not add to 100 owing to rounding error.

the transitional marginal remnants of a past era.[28] The various sections of the class are united by their insecurity and their belief that they are *independent*. As Macpherson noted, the belief in independence, although it is an important determinant of their action, is an illusion, because the *petit-bourgeois* class is subordinate to large-scale, labour-utilizing capitalists, who control the price system. The small producer is independent, perhaps, in that he may still be able to decide for himself when and how to use his own labour.

Before commenting on the divisions within the *petite bourgeoisie*, the *petit-bourgeois* character of agricultural production in both Alberta and Saskatchewan until mid-century will be documented. Using census data, Macpherson[29] was able to show that small independent commodity producers formed the largest class in Alberta during the period of concern here. From Table 1, it is clear that the dominance of agricultural occupations has been even greater in Saskatchewan than in Alberta. Neither white-collar nor blue-collar occupations approached the agricultural in size. There is some indication in the table that agriculture is declining in importance, and later census reports show an acceleration of this trend.

Table 2 has been constructed to show that agriculture has been conducted largely by the *petite bourgeoisie*. Farming in the West has been overwhelmingly

Table 2. Employment in Agriculture, 1921–51 (in Percentages)

	1921	1931	1936	1941	1946	1951
Farmers as Percentage of Labour Force						
Alberta	37.9	32.2	31.3	29.5	28.2	23.2
Saskatchewan	43.5	36.2	36.6	36.4	37.9	36.0
Farmers plus Unpaid Family Labour as Percentage of Labour Force						
Alberta		41.6	42.1	37.9		27.0
Saskatchewan	NA[b]	49.1	50.7	46.9	NA	42.7
Wage Earners as Percentage of Agricultural Labour Force						
Alberta	14.7	18.0	20.1	16.3	12.3	16.6
Saskatchewan	18.0	18.5	18.9	14.7	10.7	12.6
Farms Having Hired Labour as Percentage of all Farms[a]						
Alberta		40.5	43.2	36.4	31.4	39.2
Saskatchewan	NA	41.8	43.2	34.0	29.6	38.7
Average Weeks of Hired Labour per Farm Having Any Hired Labour						
Alberta		26.3	28.4	27.9	23.8	
Saskatchewan	NA	27.1	24.5	23.9	20.4	NA

SOURCE: Calculated from data available in Dominion Bureau of Statistics, Census of Canada, 1921 to 1951; Census of the Prairie Provinces, 1936 and 1946.

[a]The figures here refer to the year preceding that of the census.
[b]NA = relevant statistic not available.

conducted by family units of commodity producers employing little or no hired labour. Normally, wage-earners account for less than 20 per cent of the agricultural labour force and are employed largely on a seasonal basis. Since 1936, less than 40 per cent of farms have used any hired labour at all, and there has been a continual decline in the number of weeks for which this labour has been employed. Thus, the trend towards larger farms has not resulted in greater dependence on wage labour; rather, increased mechanization has created the conditions which are summarized in Table 2.

Finally, from Table 3 we see that the class position of some farmers is complicated by the fact that there is a trend for them to become both owners and tenants, because this is the easiest way to expand as the price of land rises. Only about one per cent of farms were being operated by managers. Considering all the census data available, there can be little doubt that farming in both provinces was mainly a *petit-bourgeois* occupation.

It is now appropriate to turn to the problem of the unity of the *petite bourgeoisie* as a class. When a large number of people occupy a similar class

Table 3. Farm Tenure, 1921–51 (in Percentages)

	1921	1931	1941	1951
Alberta				
Owner-operated	79.5	72.6	62.5	62.7
Tenant-operated	9.7	12.2	17.1	11.6
Part owner-operated[a]	9.9	14.9	19.8	25.0
Manager-operated	0.9	0.3	0.6	0.7
Total	100	100	100	100
Saskatchewan				
Owner-operated	76.7	66.1	52.6	54.6
Tenant-operated	10.8	15.4	24.6	14.7
Part owner-operated	11.6	18.2	22.4	30.2
Manager-operated	0.9	0.3	0.4	0.5
Total	100	100	100	100

SOURCE: Dominion Bureau of Statistics, Census of Canada, 1961, Bulletin 5.3.

[a]'Part owner-operated farms' refers to those farms which are composed of land which is owned by the operator and additional land which he has rented.

position it does not follow that all of them will be conscious of their class identity and act in terms of it. The *petite bourgeoisie* has seldom done so. Indeed, different strata of the class have frequently been in conflict with each other. For a class to exist as an active force, there must be a communal sentiment and an organization to bring people in similar circumstances together. This has rarely been the case in western Canada. For example, there have been important differences in political alignment between small businessmen and farmers, because their common problem of insecurity in a state of economic oligarchy has seldom been sufficient to compensate for the antagonistic relations between them in other respects. The *petit-bourgeois* businessman in the towns and villages of Alberta and Saskatchewan is an artisan or merchant capitalist, who derives profit from providing a service. Perhaps the retail merchant is most interesting. In order to survive, he must dispose of the products of capitalist enterprise at a price which leaves him a surplus. The alternative of being a wage-earning distributor of goods conflicts with his image of self-independence. For these reasons the retailer becomes a supporter of liberal capitalist ideology, particularly when he is threatened by agrarian co-operatives. During depressions, the merchant is often defined by the farmer as a nonproductive parasite on his labour, and consumer co-operatives have been established to bypass the merchant.[30] In this situation, we would expect the village *petite bourgeoisie* to be susceptible to appeals from Liberals and Conservatives to support the old parties, thus saving the West from socialism. However, when the small businessmen recognize their dependence on trade with farmers, they may be attracted to reformist groups at times when the price system is operating to reduce farm income. Then, platforms which propose monetary reform in order to restore purchasing power to the consumer can make a significant impact on this stratum. This is probably why Social Credit was able to get its initial support and much of its leadership from the urban *petite bourgeoisie*, to whom the CCF appeared too radical. Also, the Reconstruction Party, which flourished briefly in 1935, proposed an investigation of monetary problems as well as a series of mild economic reforms and drew most of its support from small businessmen who had previously been Conservatives.

United *petit-bourgeois* action is rare, even when attention is restricted to the agrarian sector of the *petite bourgeoisie*. In Alberta and Saskatchewan, the 'vigorous consciousness of common interests' to which Macpherson[31] refers was not experienced by all farmers, and it is doubtful whether 'agrarian class unity was emerging out of economic conflict'[32] to the extent that we can talk about united class action. Of course, this is not to deny that large numbers of farmers did periodically act together for common political and economic ends. We must now consider the conditions on the Canadian prairies which contributed to or hindered the development of class-conscious political protest.

It may safely be assumed that for organized class protest to develop there must be some widespread experience of deprivation. For prairie farmers this has always been related to the problems of income insecurity. Given this, there must also be adequate means of communication among those who are subject to deprivation or exploitation in order that they develop some feeling of common identity. Although interaction in Alberta and Saskatchewan was limited by geographical factors until telephones, radios, and cars became numerous, agrarian problems were constantly aired in widely circulated farm journals, such as the *Grain Growers' Guide*. Political ideas were also promoted through the co-operative associations and grain growers' associations which emerged after the turn of the century.[33] These organizations were the training ground for protest leaders among the farmers; the roots of CCF and Social Credit populism lie there; it was the Depression of the thirties which stimulated a more radical expression of populism than was found in the Progressive movement[34] or in the provincial Liberal parties.

Class-conscious organization develops only when people feel more united by their common interests than they are divided on other grounds. In Western Canada, those in a common class position have often been divided by differences of social status. Thus, the *petit-bourgeois* farmers have been internally stratified by wealth, by type of agriculture, by ethnic origin, and religion. This disunity was shown in Saskatchewan elections between 1934 and 1944 when the CCF received less than average support in French, German, and Mennonite districts. The highest level of CCF support was in municipalities dominated by Anglo-Saxons, which casts doubts on Milnor's[35] thesis that the CCF was more a party of ethnic protest than a class movement. Differences based on type of agriculture were pointed out by John Bennett,[36] who found that ranchers in southwest Saskatchewan enjoyed greater economic security than grain growers and were also more inclined to oppose government intervention in economic affairs. Such differences within the agrarian stratum of the *petite bourgeoisie* have often gone unnoticed, because enough farmers have combined with urban labour (in Saskatchewan) or with other *petit-bourgeois* strata (in Alberta) to elect populist governments to the provincial legislatures.

I have argued that class-conscious *petit-bourgeois* action is likely to take a populist form. Put another way, the mass support of populism is typically *petit-bourgeois*. Although the CCF began as a socialist party and the Social Credit League was eventually transformed into a conventional conservative party, the conclusion is warranted that from 1934 to 1944 both were populist parties, advocating reform wherever necessary to protect or restore the way of life of the *petite bourgeoisie*. Yet the two parties did differ considerably in organizational structure and the nature of the reforms for which they pressed. Therefore, it becomes necessary to account for the development of different forms of populism in Alberta and Saskatchewan. Here the sociologist must pay close attention to the historical background of each province.[37]

Different Historical Backgrounds

What is crucial to our understanding of why an authoritarian populism emerged in Alberta is that Social Credit sprouted from the failure of an earlier democratic populism, the United Farmers of Alberta (UFA), to control the effects of the depression. The UFA was dominated by Henry Wise Wood, whose political beliefs on group government owed much to his knowledge of the populist tradition of the American mid-west. According to Wood, social life in industrial society is a history of conflict between a plutocracy and the masses. In this competitive society, only the plutocracy was organized. This enabled industrial producers to exploit others, who participated in the market as disorganized individuals. Farmers were especially exploited. Wood's solution lay in co-operative production and class organization; the organized strength of each class would then prevent the exploitation of any one class. Morton quotes Wood as follows:

> When you get class and class equally efficient in competition, as the less developed classes develop higher, I don't think the conflict in the last analysis will be very destructive, I think before it reaches the acute stage the better judgment of all will prevail.[38]

This approach assumes either common interests or the inability of one organized group to dominate others, both of which are unlikely. However, in a province where farmers were so numerous, it proved popular, especially when coupled with a denunciation of the party system. Instead of parties, Wood supported a system of political representation by democratically organized occupational groups, each nominating its delegates to the legislature and instructing them about what to support. Failure to comply would lead to the recall of the member. The organization of a new party was rejected because it was felt that parties led inevitably to corruption. Rather, a new co-operative government would be formed by elected representatives of class organizations. This was a Canadian corporatist theory.

Nevertheless the UFA proceeded to act much like a conventional party, winning the election of 1921 and governing the province for the next years by traditional means. It was thus the misfortune of the UFA to be in power during the early thirties. Crop failures, coupled with declining prices, generated a severe depression in rural areas. Like other governments in similar circumstances, the UFA proved incapable of producing legislation to protect the interests of the *petit-bourgeois* population. Urban dwellers were already alienated from the government because they were barred from membership in the UFA. Now the farmers also found themselves rejecting their own populist organization, whose leaders had grown distant from the rank and file. Yet they could not turn to the Liberal and Conservative parties, since these were both associated with the forces of exploitation. The UFA had been directly involved with the founding of the CCF and was stigmatized by its association with the early CCF socialism. Therefore, with all existing political associations discredited for some reasons, there was a political vacuum in Alberta. It could not be filled by a revolutionary movement because of the *petit-bourgeois* commitment to existing property institutions; any new mass movement would have to be consistent with this commitment. The situation of Alberta in the thirties made possible the development of a kind of populism in which allegiance is given to an authoritarian leader, who claims divine inspiration for his simple plan to solve the unsolvable—in this case, William Aberhart and Social Credit. From the conjunction of economic crisis and the failure of democratic populism, Social Credit was able to develop as a powerful authoritarian populism.

Saskatchewan history was such that the development of authoritarian populism was unlikely. In 1921, a year of much discontent, the Liberal government called an election before the Grain Growers' Association met, thereby eliminating the possibility of a farmers' government like that of the UFA in Alberta. When the first Depression election was held in 1934, however, the Liberals were out of office and were not tarnished by the economic disaster. Although the Liberals were linked by many people to the monopolies of eastern Canada, the provincial party had absorbed many of the most able farm leaders and had been receptive to the demands of agrarian spokesmen to some extent. Therefore, the Liberals were returned to power in 1934 with a large majority over the new CCF, which suffered mainly from a lack of funds and from popular opposition to its socialist land policy.

Although populism had not been discredited in Saskatchewan by failure to control the effects of Depression, the CCF had to wait ten more years before winning power. Meanwhile, Aberhart tried to expand Social Credit into Saskatchewan in the 1938 election, but by this time he was suffering a crisis of legitimation in Alberta, having failed to introduce Social Credit monetary reforms. The CCF emerged from this test as the only plausible alternative to the Liberals, despite falling far behind the Liberal total of elected representatives. At this time, portions of the Palliser Triangle in Saskatchewan were so chronically depressed that neither populist party made much headway. An apathetic, suffering people had neither the economic nor psychological resources to build an effective protest party. As economic conditions improved, the CCF was more successful in organizing support in these areas, until in 1944 a block of constituencies in the centre of the Triangle was in the top quartile of CCF support. Similarly, the poorest areas of Regina and Saskatoon were now among the strongest areas of CCF support.[39]

If this analysis of the emergence of Social Credit and the CCF is to be adequate, the failure of the New Democracy and National Reform movements must be accounted for, since they had similar populist ideologies. The answer lies in the interrelationship among these movements. Basically, National Reform and New Democracy developed when Social Credit and the CCF were already well established, with the result that the leaders of each had a vested interest in retaining their independence.

In the 1938 Saskatchewan election, two Social Credit and two United Reform candidates were victorious. Three of them had won with informal support from the CCF, and the CCF had hopes of forming a united opposition in Regina. However, when J.F. Herman accepted a position as Social Credit house leader, his invitation to join the CCF caucus was withdrawn.[40] Having failed to link up with the CCF, the four other opposition members formed a new national Reform group with a populist program including low tariffs, development of co-operatives, and the enforcement of anti-monopoly legislation.[41] The new group tried to encourage co-operation with the CCF by suggesting that they avoid fighting each other at any future election, but this was rejected by the CCF's annual convention, which marked the end of National Reform as a provincial force.

A greater threat to both the CCF and Social Credit was New Democracy, a national movement organized by William Herridge. Until 1938, he worked inside the Conservative Party but could not persuade that organization to adopt his policies. Herridge's frequent references to the need for monetary reform and more purchasing power attracted several Social Crediters, whose support was instrumental in leading him to announce, at the beginning of March 1938, that he would lead a drive to unite all progressive people under the banner of New Democracy.[42]

The national CCF reacted ambiguously to New Democracy. A circular instructed every section of the CCF not to attack it, yet there was to be no collaboration either. Wherever possible, all public discussion was to be avoided and the door left ajar for interested people to come to the CCF.[43] However, some weeks later, George Williams publicly rejected co-operation with New Democracy on the grounds that it was a capitalist reform organization, backed by the Communist Party[44] and out to destroy the CCF.[45] Despite the efforts of M.J. Coldwell, it was no longer possible for New Democracy to succeed in Saskatchewan. A few months later, New Democrats approached the CCF to join them in order to implement a reform program which was very similar to the CCF's. Unspecified economic and monetary reforms were proposed to promote maximum production and consumer purchasing. Government intervention was called for to promote co-operatives, improve collective-bargaining laws, establish minimum prices for farmers, set minimum wages, control monopolies, and increase social services.[46] However, the united-front approach was rejected by the CCF's convention. Now the national office felt safe in putting out a statement rejecting Herridge as just another reformer.[47]

For a time Herridge was more successful with Social Credit. Aberhart was quick to express 'encouragement and inspiration' from the announcement of New Democracy.[48] He was keen for Herridge to adopt Social Credit as his official policy, but Herridge preferred an umbrella movement. The alliance was successful to the point where federal Social Credit MPs called themselves New Democrats, and it held up until the 1940 federal election. However, the relationship deteriorated in the fall over the issue of conscription. Subsequently, Social Credit members simply produced their own program and called it New Democracy over the strong objections of Herridge.[49]

From this brief history, we can see that New Democracy and National Reform had a populist orientation but could not be successful in the West because the CCF and Social Credit, already well established, refused to integrate with them.

Conclusion

The thrust of this paper has been to demonstrate that the development of Social Credit and the CCF in Alberta and Saskatchewan can be explained by the appeal of their populist ideologies to the *petit-bourgeois* population. The class has been divided and its members have seldom agreed on their main interests, being, as Macpherson demonstrated, both committed to and exploited by capitalist relations. However, a sufficient number became convinced of the need to *reform* society that they could bring to power two parties, which we may describe as populist, while recognizing the different means by which each tried to protect the *petite bourgeoisie*. Today this is no longer the largest class in western Canada; the era of agrarian populism is disappearing with the decline of the class which promoted it.

Suggestions for Further Reading

John A. Irving, *The Social Credit Movement in Alberta* (Toronto, 1959).
Seymour M. Lipset, *Agrarian Socialism* (New York, 1968).
Walter D. Young, *Democracy and Discontent: Progressivism, Socialism and Social Credit in the Canadian West* (Toronto, 1978).

Notes

[1]S.M. Lipset, *Agrarian Socialism* (New York, 1968), xxii.
[2]David E. Smith, 'A Comparison of Prairie Political Developments in Saskatchewan and Alberta', *Journal of Canadian Studies* 4 (1969), 17–26.
[3]Walter D. Young, *Democracy and Discontent* (Toronto, 1969).
[4]R.T. Naylor, 'The Ideological Foundations of Social Democracy and Social Credit', Gary Teeple, ed., *Capitalism and the National Question in Canada* (Toronto, 1972), 251–6.
[5]For reviews of the concept see J.B. Allcock, ' "Populism": A Brief Biography', *Sociology* 5 (1971), 371–87. See also G. Ionescu and E. Gellner, eds, *Populism: Its Meaning and National Characteristics* (London, 1969).
[6]Peter Wiles, 'A Syndrome, Not a Doctrine: Some Elementary Theses on Populism', in G. Ionescu and E. Gellner, eds, *Populism*, 166.
[7]John A. Irving, *The Social Credit Movement in Alberta* (Toronto, 1959), 266.
[8]T.C. Douglas, speech reported in CCF Minutes, Eighth Annual Convention, Archives of Saskatchewan (1943).
[9]See Victor C. Ferkiss, 'Populist Influences on American Fascism', *Western Political Quarterly* 10 (1956), 350–73. See also S.M. Lipset and Earl Raab, *The Politics of Unreason: Right Wing Extremism in America* (New York, 1970).
[10]See, for example, Angus Stewart, 'The Social Roots', in G. Ionescu and E. Gellner, eds, *Populism*, 186–91. See also A. Walicki, *The Controversy over Capitalism: Studies in the Social Philosophy of the Russian Populists* (London, 1969), 22.
[11]Norman Pollack, *The Populist Response to Industrial America* (Cambridge, Mass., 1962).
[12]Eli Goldschmidt, 'Labor and Populism: New York City, 1891–1896', *Labour History* 13 (1972), 520–32.
[13]Robert F. Durden, *The Climax of Populism* (Lexington, 1965), 3–5.
[14]One might object here that socialists often try to advance their ideas by playing on the same deprivations as populists. It might be argued that the Russian 'populists', although they looked backward to a revival of the peasant *mir* community, also looked forward to a decentralized socialist society. (See Franco Venturi, *The Roots of Revolution: A History of the Populist and Socialist Movements in Nineteenth Century Russia*, London, 1960.) However, Russian populism, while anti-intellectual in its pronouncements, was largely a movement of intellectuals who did not have a mass appeal for the peasantry. They were usually treated with great suspicion. My argument is, essentially, that the socialist revolution is too radical for the *petite bourgeoisie* to accept. It is true, nevertheless, that Russian populism creates the biggest obstacle for the concept of populism presented here. Perhaps it would be best to agree with

Walicki (*The Controversy over Capitalism*, 93) that the distinctive features of the Russian intellectuals are best captured if the Russian term *narodnichestvo* is retained.

[15] Walter T.K. Nugent, *The Tolerant Populists: Kansas Populism and Nativism* (Chicago, 1963).

[16] See Robert L. Morian, *Political Prairie Fire: The Nonpartisan League 1915–1922* (Minneapolis, 1955). See also Theodore Saloutos, 'The Rise of the Nonpartisan League in North Dakota, 1915–1917', *Agricultural History* 20 (1946), 43–61; and Paul F. Sharp, *The Agrarian revolt in Western Canada* (Minneapolis, 1948).

[17] See Caldarola's paper, 'The Social Credit in Alberta, 1935–1971', in C. Caldarola, ed., *Society and Politics in Alberta: Research Papers* (Agincourt, 1979).

[18] Peter R. Sinclair, 'The Saskatchewan CCF: Ascent to Power and the Decline of Socialism', *Canadian Historical Review* 54 (1973), 419–33.

[19] *Ibid.*, 426–30.

[20] S.M. Lipset, *Agrarian Socialism*, 180.

[21] George Williams, 'Problems Confronting the Retail Merchants of Western Canada', transcript of Radio Broadcast, CCF Papers, pamphlet collection, Archives of Saskatchewan, 1939.

[22] *Regina Leader-Post*, 1 April 1947.

[23] John W. Bennett and Cynthia Krueger, 'Agrarian Pragmatism and Radical Politics', in S.M. Lipset, *Agrarian Socialism*, 351.

[24] CCF Papers, 'Socialism and Cooperatives', Archives of Saskatchewan, 1944. Even E.C. Manning, who hardly qualifies as a socialist, felt able on several occasions to give strong support to co-operatives and credit unions. See, for example, E.C. Manning, Budget Speech, Edmonton, Government of Alberta, 1945.

[25] Raymond Aron, 'Two Definitions of Class', in A. Beteille, ed., *Social Inequality* (London, 1969), 76.

[26] C.B. Macpherson, *Democracy in Alberta* (Toronto, 2nd edn, 1962), 225.

[27] For a similar interpretation of the class position of the farmer, see James McCroirie, 'Changes and Paradox in Agrarian Social Movements', in R.J. Ossenberg, ed., *Canadian Society: Pluralism, Change and Conflict* (Scarborough, 1971), 36–51.

[28] On the decline of the *petite bourgeoisie* in Canada as a whole, see Leo Johnson, 'The Development of Class in Canada in the Twentieth Century', in Gary Teeple, ed., *Capitalism and the National Question in Canada*, 141–83.

[29] C.B. Macpherson, *Democracy in Alberta*, 10–20.

[30] Jim F.C. Wright, *Prairie Progress: Consumer Cooperation in Saskatchewan* (Saskatoon, 1956).

[31] C.B. Macpherson, *Democracy in Alberta*, 226.

[32] S.M. Lipset, *Agrarian Socialism*, 69.

[33] See the following studies: Hugh Boyd, *New Breaking: An Outline of Cooperation among the Farmers of Western Canada* (Toronto, 1938); S.M. Lipset, *Agrarian Socialism*, 1968; W.A. Mackintosh, *Agricultural Cooperation in Western Canada* (Toronto, 1924); Harold S. Patton, *Grain Growers' Cooperation in Western Canada* (Cambridge, Massachusetts, 1928); and Paul F. Sharp, *The Agrarian Revolt in Western Canada*, 1948.

[34] See W.L. Morton, *The Progressive Party in Canada* (Toronto, 1950).

[35] Andrew J. Milnor, 'Agrarian Protest in Saskatchewan, 1929–1948: A Study in Ethnic Politics' (unpublished PhD thesis, Duke University, Durham, 1962).

[36]John Bennett, *Northrn Plainsmen* (Chicago, 1969).

[37]For a more detailed analysis of the historical background of Alberta and Saskatchewan, see Johnson's paper, 'The Failure of the CCF in Alberta: An Accident of History', in C. Caldarola, ed., *Society and Politics in Alberta.*

[38]W.L. Morton, 'The Social Philosophy of Henry Wise Wood, Canadian Agrarian Leader', *Agricultural History* 22 (1948), 118. See also: William K. Rolph, *Henry Wise Wood of Alberta* (Toronto, 1950); W.L. Morton, *The Progressive Party in Canada*; and C.B. Macpherson, *Democracy in Alberta.*

[39]For a more complete account of the rise of the CCF, see Peter R. Sinclair, 'The Saskatchewan CCF'.

[40]George Williams, Williams to J.F. Herman, 25 October 1938, CCF Papers, file no. 163, Archives of Saskatchewan.

[41]J.F. Herman *et al.*, press statement, CCF Papers, file no. 239, Archives of Saskatchewan (no date, but probably 1939).

[42]Mary Hallett, 'The Social Credit Party and the New Democracy Movement: 1939–1940', *Canadian Historical Review* 47 (1966), 302–4.

[43]CCF National Office, National Office to National Council Members, 12 March 1938, CCF Papers, file no. 240, Archives of Saskatchewan.

[44]The Communists appeared much more delighted with the new political development. In Regina, Tim Buck announced Communist backing for the New Democracy group, although it was not as socialist as he would have liked (*Regina Leader-Post* 27 April 1939). Howver, this was an endorsement which New Democrats did not want. When a Communist official was nominated as the New Democracy candidate in Maple Creek, he was not recognized by party officials (*Regina Leader-Post*, 6 September 1939); the New Democracy was Christian, Canadian, and British, opposed to fascism and communism, and committed to reforming and modernizing the present system. (See G.H. Barr, Barr to G. Williams, 4 November 1939, CCF Papers, file no. 240, Archives of Saskatchewan.)

[45]*Regina Leader-Post*, 27 April 1939.

[46]*Ibid.*, 4 July 1939.

[47]*Ibid.*, 25 July 1939.

[48]*Ibid.*, 6 March 1939.

[49]*Ibid.*, 21 October 1939.

25

Origins of the Welfare State in Canada

Alvin Finkel

The economic and social problems that faced Canada in the Great Depression of the 1930s were not so much new ones as familiar difficulties exacerbated and highlighted by the extent of the international economic collapse and by the trouble government experienced in responding. Governments in Canada at every level had never regarded active intervention in either the economy or the social well-being of the citizenry as an essential part of their functions; and while Canada was little different in this respect from other countries in North America and western Europe, it did have unique constitutional problems because of the distribution of powers under the British North America Act. The social and political unrest of the 1930s—particularly after the 'New Deal' policies of the American government headed by Franklin Delano Roosevelt were publicized—led to a major debate in Canada over social and economic planning and the role of govern-

ment. This debate occurred at both a practical and a theoretical level. On the practical level, for example, the failure of government to offer any relief for the millions of unemployed—beyond handouts and charity—led to demands for an improved system of dealing with unemployment, particularly by providing federal assistance to cut through the financial problems of the provincial and municipal governments responsible for such matters. On the theoretical level many Canadian groups, led by the labour unions and the League for Social Reconstruction, called for an entirely new conception of the responsibility of government.

Alvin Finkel discusses the debate over social welfare in the 1930s and the eventual implementation in Canada of the programs we have come to associate with the modern welfare state at the close of the Second World War. Finkel's perspective is that of the Left, and he tends to see the welfare state less as a positive triumph of social planning than as an attempt by a beleaguered capitalistic system to prevent its collapse by a patchwork of policies that left it intrinsically unreformed. Finkel points out that much of the impetus for the social policies of the welfare state, particularly those programs advocated by R.B. Bennett in 1935 as part of the so-called 'Bennett New Deal', came from the leaders of the Canadian business community. Businessmen, moreover, supported increased federal power at the expense of the provinces. Although initially unenthusiastic, by the end of the Second World War W.L. Mackenzie King was ready to act, responding to pressures from the other political parties and public opinion, as well as to concerns about dealing with the problems of postwar readjustment without economic planning and social safety nets.

How would Finkel characterize the Bennett New Deal? Are other interpretations possible? Why did many Canadian businessmen favour social-welfare policies in the 1930s? Why was Mackenzie King reluctant to implement social insurance? What evidence does Finkel offer for his view that, by the time of the war, 'capitalism was threatened by a working-class uprising if reforms were not forthcoming'? Why did the Liberals accept the welfare state in 1945? Was Liberal policy as 'conservative' as Finkel suggests?

This article first appeared in Leo Panitch, ed., *The Canadian State: Political Economy and Political Power* (Toronto, 1977), 344–70.

I

Social democrats have argued that the movement since the 1930s towards greater state provision of social security for citizens is evidence that capitalism can be controlled and that the political power of the bourgeoisie can be reduced without fundamental changes occurring in the structure of ownership and control of industry. The CCF-NDP threat; the influence of middle-class professionals; the bleeding hearts of depression and wartime politicians; and the collective national spirit that characterized the war and postwar reconstruction period: all are invoked to explain the expansion of the state's role in providing social security. The major survivors of the League for Social Reconstruction (LSR), founded during the depression as the intellectual brain trust of the nascent CCF, recalled forty years later:

> What is difficult for us to grasp today is that the social planning which was prescribed by the LSR in the thirties was a major heresy for those in government and in the business community. Government had its role and business had its role and the two roles had to be kept separate. Government's 'interference' in business was restricted to the enactment and enforcement of safety and health standards in factories and mines, subsistence minimum wages, and regulations for the adjudication of industrial disputes—at best a guardian and umpire role.

But for the government to intervene in the self-regulating economic system for the purpose of setting social goals that might inhibit the full play of the profit motive was regarded as a cardinal sin. To suggest further that government should plan the nation's economic life in the interests of the good of the majority of its people was to challenge the foundations of the faith.[1]

The problem with the LSR analysis is that it totally ignores the class nature of the state. It is assumed that where government planning exists and where a number of welfare programs exist—although Canada's welfare state is generally conceded to be incomplete—that the direction of economic planning is 'in the interests of the majority of the people'. What is to be argued here, however, is that the 'welfare state', while it places a floor on the standard of living of working people, was not constituted, even in its incomplete Canadian form, to reduce the economic and political power of the business leaders.[2] Indeed, the opposite is the case. It was devised by governments that wished to preserve the power of the ruling class but saw that power threatened by working-class militancy directed against an economic system that seemed unable to provide jobs or security. The upsurge of radicalism in the working class first in the Great Depression and then during the war forced an important section of the bourgeoisie to rethink its strategies with regard to the role of the state. The Canadian state had financed much of the infrastructure for Canadian industry and had intervened, when necessary, to defeat working-class attempts to improve wages and living standards through the formation of unions and the waging of strikes. Now, however, the provision of police and railroads alone could not create sufficient economic stability to fend off the working-class attack. The result was a rethinking among many businessmen of the proper relations between the state, industry, and the people.

In the first place, however, it is important to question whether the term 'welfare state' does not conceal more about Canada than it reveals. It is true of course that welfare programs place a floor on income and to that extent the winning of such programs has been a victory for the Canadian working class. Nevertheless, the Economic Council of Canada reported in 1972 that at least 27 per cent of Canadians must be said to be living in poverty if poverty were defined as 'an insufficient access to certain goods, services, and conditions of life which are available to everyone else and have come to be accepted as basic to a decent, minimum standard of living'.[3] A study prepared for the council indicated that governments, while establishing programs that transferred wealth to the lowest income group, used methods of taxation that involved 'extreme regressivity . . . at the lower end of the income scale and the lack of any significant progressivity over the remainder of the income range'.[4] Statistics Canada data indicate that negligible redistribution of wealth has occurred in Canada since 1950.[5] Moreover human 'welfare' is not an easily quantifiable economic proposition. Ecological destruction, the destruction of health in many factory and mine jobs, and the psychological problems created for people who do seemingly mindless work over which they have no control are less quantifiable but no less important measures of human welfare.

What is to be examined here are the origins of the 'welfare state' in Canada. The period studied covers the years 1930 through to 1945, that is, from the onset of the Great Depression to the end of the war that terminated the depression. It was during this period that the dictates of political economy created the debate on the 'welfare state' and finally the establishment of certain policies that provided the framework of the Canadian 'welfare state'. Of course, there were further programs added after 1945 that are not dealt with here. Nor are all the programs introduced by 1945 examined in detail. But the motivations behind welfarist policies as a whole are suggested by the debate on the particular policies discussed here. In short, by focusing on a few policies at a particular period, an attempt is made to reconstruct the motivations of the Canadian state in introducing welfarist policies. In particular, the question of the class nature of Canadian government is examined against the background of policies that certain critics, as above noted, thought to be of necessity directed against the bourgeoisie and in favour of the working class.

II

Social legislation in Canada before the Great Depression was minimal. The working class had not long been the majority group in the country and the agricultural class, over-represented in voting by rurally weighted electoral boundaries at both federal and provincial levels, had little understanding of urban society and largely supported the capitalist class in its resistance to social legislation. The trade-union movement, while it pressed for legislative changes, was weak and politically unimportant. Before the First World War the only victories it could claim were the winning of free public education and a number of public health services—though, in the case of Montreal and probably other cities, even these victories had not really been won by 1914. The public-education debate, it might be noted, centred in part on the need for a partially literate work force for industry.[6]

Additional social legislation came slowly. Workmen's compensation had been introduced by all provinces except Prince Edward Island by 1920. An American study of the introduction of compensation indicates that this measure was desired by large corporate interests as a means of fending off the more radical employer-liability type of legislation which made employers legally responsible for employees injured at work. A state-wide program would remove the onus on individual businessmen and thus remove the need for shorter working hours and costly safety measures. A recent study of the origins of workmen's compensation in Ontario suggests that Canadian employers thought along the same lines. While the Canadian Manufacturers' Association and its provincial branches often opposed specific features of proposed compensation legislation, they did not sway from their support of the principle itself. Before the introduction of workmen's compensation in Ontario in 1915, many employers taken to court by employees under the province's employer-liability legislation had been found negligent and therefore liable by juries sympathetic to the injured employees. Jury awards to injured employees for compensation by the employers were common enough and generous enough that many companies found themselves unable to find insurance companies that would provide them with insurance against liability.[7]

The high rate of unemployment before the First World War and the expected return to high unemployment at the war's end prompted the Ontario government to name a Royal Commission on Unemployment in 1916. The commission discussed and rejected the idea of a government-run employment-insurance scheme, though it urged the province to aid financially company and trade-union private programs for unemployment benefits.[8] The end of the war did bring some social legislation in the form of federal pensions for war widows and legislation in most provinces for mother's allowances. Throughout the 1920s, however, the Trades and Labor Congress pressed unsuccessfully for universal old-age pensions, unemployment insurance, sickness insurance, and disability insurance. And the only program passed by the federal government was a pension scheme for the needy poor. The scheme, which provided only twenty dollars a month and was available only from age seventy, was a concession won by the small Labour group in the House of Commons, under the leadership of J.S. Woodsworth, for support of King's precarious minority Liberal government of 1925.[9]

Few would have thought that the Conservative government of R.B. Bennett, elected in 1930 on a campaign of high tariffs for Canadian manufacturers and primary producers, would have been interested in introducing new programs for social security. Bennett was one of Canada's leading capitalists and had important holdings in almost all sectors of the economy. He had been a partner with Lord Beaverbrook in the financial manoeuvrings that had created such concerns as the monopolistic Canada Cement Company; he was the majority shareholder in the Eddy Match monopoly and in the E.B. Eddy Newsprint Company and had some say in Eddy policies even as prime minister; he had been western solicitor for the Canadian Pacific Railway; he was the second-largest individual shareholder in the Royal Bank; he had been president of the Turner Valley operations of Imperial Oil as well as Imperial's chief lawyer, and held thousands of shares in metal-mining companies; he was a past vice-president of Alberta Pacific Grain Elevators and a past director of such oligopolies as Imperial Tobacco and Canada Packers; at his death in 1947 he was worth forty million dollars.[10] Truly, here was a man who might claim to represent the big bourgeoisie as a whole and use the power of the state to achieve compromises among its different— though partly interlocked—sectors. Bennett's cabinet included many other men who had ties with big corporations, and the government's appointment of top civil servants and members of royal commissions reflected a belief that success in private business was a chief qualification for government service.[11] The tenor of Bennett's government might be thought to be best encapsulated by his oft-quoted statement that the 'iron heel of repression' was to be applied to those who rebelled against the existing order. Trade-union organizing attempts were suppressed with state aid, Communists were imprisoned, militants of foreign birth were deported, and unemployed young men were put in remote camps where they received no wages and were fired upon when they tried to come to Ottawa to seek redress.[12] Yet it was this clearly anti-labour government that introduced unemployment insurance, a federal manpower agency, government mortgage-lending, and a variety of marketing boards. It also promised in 1935, if re-elected, to introduce a universal pension program and health insurance. Why? A.E. Grauer, writing for the Royal Commission on Dominion-Provincial Relations in 1939, summed up the type of philosophy that began to make certain social reforms acceptable to conservatives not only in Canada but in many industrialized nations:

> Since the Great War, the Great Depression has been the chief stimulus to labour legislation and social insurance. The note sounded has not been so much the ideal of social justice as political and economic financial expediency. For instance, the shorter working week was favoured in unexpected quarters not because it would give the workers more leisure and possibilities for a fuller life but because it would spread work; and the current singling out of unemployment insurance for governmental attention in many countries is dictated by the appalling costs of direct relief and the hope that unemployment insurance benefits will give some protection to public treasuries in future depressions and will, by sustaining purchasing power, tend to mitigate these depressions.[13]

Social insurance, then, from this particular depression point of view, was intended to stabilize destabilized economies and not necessarily to redistribute wealth. That later studies should indicate that wealth had not been redistributed would only validate the view of conservatives who believed certain social reforms, if carried out in a certain way, would reinforce rather than disturb the status quo.

Sir Charles Gordon, president of Canada's then-leading bank, the Bank of Montreal, and president of Dominion Textiles, the country's leading textiles firm, was one conservative who argued that unemployment and old-age insurance programs were necessary to stabilize the economy. Accepting that structural unemployment was inevitable, Gordon told the Bank of Montreal annual meeting that an organized national system of social security was cheaper and more efficient than the haphazard municipal systems of relief that were in effect during the depression. The British experience was cited as proof that a country could weather better an economic recession if it collected funds in boom times to be released to the unemployed when the economy faltered.[14]

Gordon, who was second only to Sir Herbert Holt in assets over which he had trusteeship, was especially concerned that unemployment insurance be introduced. Reflecting the views of the bankers, Gordon wrote Bennett in January 1934 to urge unemployment insurance as an alternative to direct relief. The result of direct relief was that many municipalities and even provinces were in so much debt that they were 'threatening to strangle their general credit to the point where it would be difficult if not impossible to carry through refunding operations for any maturing issues, letting alone the finding of money for any new capital undertaking'.

The need to prevent future recourse to extensive direct relief convinced Gordon of 'the urgent desirability of invoking some system of unemployment insurance'. The British Parliament's recently reorganized unemployment insurance scheme was presented as a model, especially since it covered four-fifths of all working people. Concluded Gordon: 'May I suggest to you that *for our general self-preservation* some such arrangement will have to be worked out in Canada and that if it can be done soon so much the better.'[15]

The Bank of Nova Scotia's executives cautioned against expectations that unemployment insurance would completely obviate the necessity for direct relief. But they endorsed the principle as going at least part-way in decreasing the burden of relief on national and local budgets. Like many advocates of insurance, the bank advised that a workable insurance scheme must be tied to a better-developed and nationally co-ordinated system of unemployment bureaus such as existed in Great Britain. Only in this way could unemployment insurance become a scheme for re-employing the unemployed rather than a fund for 'malingerers'.[16]

The municipalities' supposed profligacy with relief was not the result of control of the lower levels of government by benevolent individuals glad to open up the public purse to those experiencing hard times. Rather it was the result of well-organized and generally Communist-led campaigns of the unemployed workers in the major municipalities. Supported by trade unionists, the massed unemployed presented the spectre of a revolt of the workers to the frightened pillars of communities in charge of municipal councils. The councils were forced to grant more relief, often at the price of defaulting on the cities' debts. As a result, both the municipal leaders and their banker-creditors looked to the federal government to provide programs that would calm the militancy of the unemployed and preserve the credit of the municipalities.[17]

Unemployment insurance was seen as the first plank of a program of social security that would take care of those out of work and reduce the number of people seeking jobs. A.O. Dawson, 1934–5 president of the Canadian Chamber of Commerce, president of Canadian Cottons, and director of many firms, was, like his fellow textile executive, Sir Charles Gordon, interested in copying the British example for social-security programs. Speaking on employer–employee relations to the Canadian Chamber of Commerce in September 1934, Dawson urged the government to establish a fund for sickness, unemployment, and old age. It would be financed through a compulsory contribution of 5 per cent of every employee's wages with contributions of an equivalent amount also to be made by the employers and the government. A reasonable pension for workers retiring at the age of sixty-five would be one of the benefits from this program, argued Dawson, who was concerned that technological changes would prevent the employment of all available hands even after the depression was over. (Canadian Cottons had endured a bitter strike in 1929 in its Hamilton plant where lay-offs accompanied the introduction of assembly-line techniques.[18]) Insurance programs would reduce the total labour force by retiring its oldest members and giving sustenance to younger workers laid off while they sought new jobs. The result would be that individual employers would not need to fear the consequences of labour-saving machinery and of speed-up techniques meant to reduce total labour requirements; responsibility for the unemployed and the aged would be socialized. Like Dawson, *Pulp and Paper of Canada*, the organ of the newsprint industry in Canada, saw a comprehensive insurance scheme as necessary to control working-class discontent. Pensions would be useful because they would vacate jobs for younger workers. The journal observed that keeping young people idle between the leaving of school and the time of finding a job 'breeds shiftlessness, discontent and ultimately disorder'.[19] Just as the militancy of the unemployed had forced increases in relief payments, it also forced a debate among businessmen on the question of social insurance as a means of preventing recurrences of such militancy during times of unemployment, whether caused by cyclical or structural factors.

Bennett largely shared the sentiments of people like Gordon and Dawson and the pulp and paper executives. Promising a universal old-age-pension scheme in the 1935 election as an extension of the social-security program that had been begun earlier that year with the introduction of unemployment insurance, Bennett vowed to reduce the age of retirement to sixty. 'Labour-saving machinery, elimination of duplication and growing concentration of business make it impossible to ever supply again work for all the people,' commented Bennett. On the other hand, these advances meant increased production and, if the state had some role in the distribution of the benefits of this increase in national income, more and more people could legitimately be removed from the labour force and provided for by the state.[20] Bennett, like Dawson, believed that unemployment insurance would head off the militancy that resulted from cyclical unemployment and that might also result from structural unemployment as it had in the case of Canadian Cottons.

'Iron-Heel' Bennett also recognized that repression alone might not be sufficient to preserve the existing system against the threat of socialism. As he wrote a New Brunswick publisher: 'Tim Buck has today a very strong position in the province of Ontario and he openly demands the abolition of the capitalist system. A good deal of pruning is sometimes necessary to save a tree and it would be well for us in Canada to remember that there is considerable pruning to be done if we are to preserve the fabric of the capitalist system.'[21]

Unemployment insurance was introduced as part of a 'reform' package in the parliamentary session of 1935, a package generally referred to as the 'Bennett New Deal'. The New Deal legislation, presented on the eve of a general election, was designed to reinvigorate a discredited Conservative government through a program of construction, social insurance, government mortgage-lending, and producers' marketing boards, which it was hoped would pacify demands of workers and farmers and restore investors' confidence. Unemployment insurance was introduced with a promise that health and old-age insurance would follow; a national minimum-wage and maximum-hours law was passed; the public-works program was expanded and the government entered the second-mortgage lending field in order to spur home construction; a producers' marketing-boards program introduced the previous year was also expanded.[22]

Workers and farmers were not impressed by the apparent death-bed conversion of the Bennett government. But it has been wrongly argued that the general reaction of the business community was negative. It is true that CPR president Edward Beatty and the Montreal *Gazette*, among others, were, as the *Gazette* put it, 'shocked and startled'.[23] But the response of the manufacturing and financial sectors which traditionally supported the Conservative party was generally one of positive support. The Conservatives, unable in the two years before the New Deal to collect corporate contributions, appeared to have been revived.[24] While the New Deal may not have been the major reason for this resurgence in party finances, it did not seem to hinder Tory fund-raising.

A veritable 'who's who' of Canadian manufacturing and finance wrote Bennett to pledge their support for the New Deal effort. Included were such luminaries of Canadian business as: A.O. Dawson, president of the Canadian Chamber of Commerce and president of Canadian Cottons; H.B. Henwood, president of the Bank of Toronto; C.H. Carlisle, president of Goodyear Tire and later also of the Dominion Bank of Canada; Colonel the Hon. H. Cockshutt, president of Cockshutt Plough; Thomas Bradshaw, president of North American Life; J.D. Johnson, president of Canada Cement; Ward Pitfield, president of Ward Pitfield Investments; W.W. Butler, president of Canadian Car and Foundry; J.W. McConnell, president of St Lawrence Sugar Refining and the *Montreal Star*; C.J. Ballantyne, president of Sherwin-Williams Paints; James McGroary, chairman of George Weston Bread; Arthur Purvis, president of CIL and Dupont; and F.N. Southam, president of Southam Publications.[25] Conspicuous by its absence was support from industrialists in the primary sectors.

There were business opponents of the New Deal. It is difficult to divorce business views on social welfare from their views on other subjects. For example, the leading department-store officials, having been roasted before the Stevens Royal Commission on Price Spreads, had no good words for any Tory policies even though Stevens had been forced to resign both from the chairmanship of the commission and from the cabinet. The department stores, as importers, were also opposed to the super-protective tariffs that were fundamental to the manufacturers' support of the Conservative party. Nevertheless, Sir Joseph Flavelle, chairman of the Canadian Bank of Commerce and former president of Simpson's as well as Canada Packers, had been a life-long Conservative. It is difficult to determine whether his denunciation by Stevens or his generally reactionary views or both caused him to turn against that party and support the King Liberals in 1935. Similarly, CPR president Edward Beatty, another Liberal convert, was also a thorough-going reactionary who might have switched allegiances even had the New Deal not been introduced. Beatty had attempted for five years to convince his friend Bennett, former chief western solicitor for the railroad, to hand over the publicly owned Canadian National Railways to the CPR. While Bennett introduced the policy of non-competition between the two railway systems, it was politically impossible for him to bequeath the CN to the CP. Beatty, obsessed with the idea of gobbling the CN, felt betrayed.[26]

The existence of these opponents of reform is hardly surprising. Bennett, after all, was himself a newcomer to the idea that these reforms were necessary to stabilize and legitimize the existing political and economic arrangements. The onset of an election no doubt played an important role in persuading Bennett to act. But one must remember that Bennett, as the head of the capitalist state, could not afford to wait until every capitalist was convinced that change was necessary. 'To save the fabric of the capitalist system' was his aim and, while certain individual capitalists and even capitalist sectors as a whole might disagree with his solutions, sufficient overall support and encouragement existed in the ruling class to allow him to act. Nor had Bennett completely rejected the 'iron-heel' approach to class conflict. The repression of the on-to-Ottawa trek of relief-camp inmates, after all, occurred after the New Deal session of Parliament. But Bennett had realized that the stick alone, while it could play some role in intimidating the working class, had proved an insufficient instrument for mediating class conflict in favour of the bourgeoisie. The carrot was also necessary.

Bennett lacked neither traditional Conservative business support nor newspaper support for his New Deal: the defeat of his government was less the rejection of the New Deal than of a government that had waited five years to act upon problems already obvious when it took power. Bennett had not launched the 'legislative assault on the corporate élite' which Richard Wilbur attributed to him and he was defeated not by the corporate élite but by the working people and farmers.[27]

Insurance and other programs, while meant to counter the communist threat, were not meant to redistribute wealth. Bennett made this clear in the debates on unemployment insurance in the House of Commons. In one debate, A.A. Heaps and the small Labour caucus argued for a non-contributory plan financed by a steeply graded income tax. A communist campaign among organizations of the unemployed, trade-union locals, and labour councils called for a similar plan. Bennett attacked such a plan and said that 'insurance involves premiums and premiums should be paid by the joint action alike of the insurer and the insured themselves and with the assistance of the state.'[28] Insurance programs then were seen as a kind of forced savings by workers for times of unemployment, old age, or infirmity rather than as a means of increasing the relative overall income for workers. As the *Financial Times*, speaking for St James Street, commented on 5 August 1932, workers did not have the foresight that corporations had, to build reserves 'against distress in the event of future unemployment'. Indeed, whatever redistribution might take place as a result of the contributions of the employers and the state was to be taken away by increasing the income tax collected from working people.

In 1930 only 3 or 4 per cent of working-age Canadians earned the $3,000 per annum above which income tax was paid. Bennett believed these men were treated unfairly since they also paid taxes on dividends, and the money from which dividends was received was, in turn, subject to corporation tax.[29] Bennett reduced the personal tax exemption to $2,000 and though inflation in the war and post-war period devalued the dollar time and again, governments did not raise the exemption. Workers who before the 1930s paid no direct taxes were faced then with both income taxes and insurance premiums to be deducted from their wages. Income that the worker once received to dispose of as he saw fit has been deducted from workers' wages for specific state 'welfare' programs. Such deductions from wages—as opposed to the stiff taxes on profits and salaries called for by the left—provide the state with an income for social programs without necessitating a redistribution of wealth. While the left wanted to rob Peter to pay Paul, the state saw fit to rob Paul to pay Paul. The worker would simply have his wages rationalized so that a large portion went, through taxes and premiums, to pay for services that he previously had to set aside money for on his own.[30]

The Mackenzie King Liberals, resurrected in 1935, were rooted in this period mainly in the primary industries—metal-mining companies, the Winnipeg Grain Exchange, the lumber industry—and supported by importers and exporters, in general. The export sector, while interested in achieving class harmony, thought the Bennett programs exacted too high a price. While the banks and the largely domestic-oriented manufacturing industries saw these programs as leading to a greater stability in the domestic market, the export-oriented sectors feared their result would be higher costs of operation.[31] The compromise that was worked out over time by the Liberals involved the granting of exemptions from various taxes to the exporters, particularly the mines, as compensation for the burden of insurance programs. Low taxes for these exporters have meant higher taxes on income for working Canadians.

The control of the export sector and particularly the mines over the provincial governments in whose spheres they largely operated was a constant complaint of Mackenzie King.[32] Ontario and Quebec, in particular, resisted King's attempts to reintroduce a federal unemployment-insurance scheme after the Bennett scheme was judged unconstitutional by the Judicial Committee of the Privy Council in 1937.[33] King, leading a federal party that traditionally emphasized provincial rights and which depended for much of its finances upon the same 'provincial' interest groups that dominated the junior governments,[34] was wary about reintroducing the Bennett schemes and rejected the requests of what he told his diary were 'Tory' big business interests who sought to impose expensive self-interested legislation without regard to the provisions of the constitution. For the most part, King, at this point quite opposite to Bennett, still rejected the idea that manufacturing was decisive in the Canadian economy or that the purchasing power of the urban workers was the crucial factor in the home market. In a revealing diary entry on 8 November 1937, King tells of his tariff discussions with American secretary of state Cordell Hull and indicates a hewers-of-wood, drawers-of-water conception of the Canadian economy: 'I spoke of the home market argument, pointing out that the home market in Canada was the purchasing power in the hands of our agriculturists for manufacturers while the home market in the United States was the purchasing power in the hands of the manufacturers and those employed in industries for the purpose of agricultural products. This, the result of Canada being an exporter chiefly in natural products; the United States an exporter wholly of manufactured products.'

The overall conversion of the 'national' business community to social insurance measures was indicated by the hostile reaction to the ruling of the Judicial Committee in 1937 that federal unemployment insurance was unconstitutional. The Ontario Associated Boards of Trade and Chambers of Commerce, representing all the boards in the province, congratulated King on his efforts to join with the provinces in securing an amendment to the British North America Act to permit unemployment insurance and labour agencies under federal authority.[35] In December 1937 *Canadian Business*, house organ of the Canadian Chamber of Commerce, attacked the 'constitutional fetish' of the three provinces—Quebec, Ontario, and New Brunswick—that were opposing federal insurance, largely, in the case of the first two provinces, at the behest of the mining companies.

The Royal Commission on Dominion-Provincial Relations, which was not empowered to deal with the merits of social insurance, nevertheless heard calls for such legislation from such groups as the Retail Merchants' Association, the Ontario Association of Real Estate Boards, and the Canadian Manufacturers' Association. The merchants argued for contributory unemployment insurance as a means of increasing purchasing power when recessions struck. The real-estate men added that unemployment insurance was a proper substitute for relief, which was paid by municipal property taxation; reduction in such taxation was necessary if the housing industry was to be revived, and unemployment insurance was the means to this end. The CMA, using the familiar forced-savings argument, called, as it had in the past, for a universal contributory pensions plan to replace the selective deserving-poor program.[36]

The major attempt to place a program of social insurance in the context of an overall program for economic stability was that of the National Employment Commission, which reported in 1938. Its chairman, Arthur Purvis, was one of Canada's most influential businessmen. He was president of the Canadian branches of CIL and Dupont Rubber and a director of a large number of firms. Purvis, like Bennett, advocated a conservative form of state planning to ensure the existing property and power relations among the various social classes in Canada. His vice-chairman on the commission was the veteran Trades and Labor Congress president Tom Moore, and the general concurrence of the two men on the best means to attack unemployment reflected the conservative ideology of the American-dominated crafts unions which predominated in the TLC.[37] Purvis believed that insurance and other spending programs could serve the purpose of lifting the economy when it began to sag and could also provide other benefits for industry. His report called for a 'co-ordinated attack' on unemployment. This would include unemployment insurance and perhaps other insurance programs, a national network of labour exchanges, expanded federal vocational education programs, and a comprehensive housing policy including subsidized rental housing for the poor and state loans to persons seeking home improvements. The emphasis was on a strengthening of the role of the central government in dealing with unemployment. For reasons of efficiency, the wasteful and unco-ordinated municipal relief programs had to be eliminated and replaced by a program of federal planning that would make the central government a major source of investment in the marketplace when the private investors, for whatever reasons, were not sufficiently carrying on the process of capital accumulation to maintain employment and hence demand at reasonable levels.

The Purvis report was rejected as 'Tory' by Mackenzie King. He was horrified by the commission's disregard for provincial rights and described Purvis's report contradictorily as an 'academic treatise' and a Tory big-business report.[38] Purvis had been suggested as chairman to King by Charles Dunning, minister of finance. King had appointed Dunning minister of finance because of his direct connections with Montreal capital and yet distrusted him and his appointees for these connections. Ironically, King, who always felt business exercised too great an influence over governments, both Liberal and Conservative, was to the right of many of the businessmen and rejected as 'Tory' certain social measures they proposed despite the fact that they went no further than his prescriptions twenty years earlier in *Industry and Humanity*.

The Purvis report reflected the attitudes of those businessmen who were most keen to use the state to prevent the repeated crises from which capitalism, through the marketplace alone, could find no protection. The 'national' business community, led by the Canadian Chamber of Commerce, gave support to the Purvis proposals and urged the federal government to alter the constitution so as to make possible its implementation. The Montreal Board of Trade told the Royal Commission on Dominion-Provincial Relations:

> taxation for the purpose of social services transfers purchasing power from the richer to the poorer classes, raises the standard of living of the poor, increases their demand for commodities and thereby tends towards industrial stability and prosperity. Furthermore, in a period of economic depression, heavier government expenditures, whether paid for by taxes or by loans, are justified and necessary in order to fill the gap resulting from the fear and inactivity which paralyze private enterprise.[39]

Indeed, the perspective of virtually all the business presentations before the Rowell-Sirois Commission was for increased federal-government control over areas traditionally within the provincial sphere and for the weakening of the provincial governments. But the resource industries, who had fattened the most from provincial troughs, were as absent from the long roll call of companies and business organizations making their views known to the commission as they were from the similar list of industrialists praising R.B. Bennett's New Deal.[40]

The combined urgings of 'Tory' businessmen and the depression militancy of farmers, workers, and the unemployed were insufficient to push cautious Mackenzie King to the point his Conservative predecessor had reached by 1935. But the onset of war strengthened the position of the working class and made it apparent that Bennett had been correct in his prognostication that capitalism was threatened by a working-class uprising if reforms were not forthcoming. During the 1930s, despite the general militancy of both workers and the unemployed, the state machinery had been used effectively to hold back attempts at unionization. The repression of Communists and the CIO, while it defeated neither group, held trade unionists in 1939 to a number not substantially greater than the 1930 figure. By the end of six years of war, however, the trade-union movement had more than doubled in membership, the result largely of the successful organization of mass-production industries.[41] Government labour policies during the war were extremely repressive. But it proved impossible to prevent unionization under wartime conditions of full employment and even labour shortages. As a result, by war's end King had turned his attention not to the question of whether there would be unions but what kind of unions there would be.[42]

The militancy of the trade-union movement had its counterpart in the rising popularity of left-wing political parties and especially the CCF.[43] The Conservative party, in the face of working-class agitation and the CCF threat, began to reassert its New Deal programs. Arthur Meighen, briefly resuscitated as party leader in late 1941, lost to a CCF candidate in a by-election in February 1942 in York South, a supposedly safe working-class Tory seat in Toronto. Meighen had made conscription and the war effort the issue; the CCF had successfully argued that the real issue was reconstruction after the war and what working people should expect from governments after having sacrificed so much to defeat facism.[44] Meighen, an admirer of the Roosevelt New Deal in the 1930s and a supporter of the Bennett reforms, had moved far to the right by the 1940s.[45]

Indeed, the oscillations of Meighen, like those of Bennett and King, between the use of repression and the use of social programs to diminish class conflict, indicates the extent to which the latter was regarded as tactical. Meighen, after all, had sent in troops to break the Winnipeg General Strike and had, as minister of justice, composed the infamous Section 98 which outlawed all activities that might be construed as falling within the rubric of a vaguely defined 'sedition'. Yet, faced in the 1930s with a widening gulf between the workers and capitalists, he had decided it was tactically correct to introduce social programs to pacify the workers and became the Tory spokesman in the Senate for the Bennett New Deal programs. Later he turned against such programs, believing that the war effort might be used to unite the 'nation' and obscure class conflicts.

But other Conservative party leaders, and especially J.M. Macdonnell, recognized that more than ever it was tactically necessary to use the state machinery to initiate reforms that would blunt the working-class offensive of the war years. Macdonnell, president of National Trust, had thought even before the war years that it was dangerous to wait for private economic forces to correct the depression. He told a Conservative party conference in 1933 that government had a role to play in stimulating demand during recessions. In an earlier address in the same year, Macdonnell had made his position clear: what was necessary was 'to remove the grit from the individualist machine and make it run smoothly—meanwhile allowing the process of the last century to continue, viz. the gradual socialization of those things which the sense of the community agrees should be socialized'. In September 1942 Macdonnell organized an unofficial conference of Conservatives in Port Hope, Ontario, to draw up a possible program for the party to deal with 'modern needs' and to prevent Canada from being engulfed by 'totalitarianism' of either left or right. The full range of reforms in the New Deal was reasserted and, reflecting the new political realities, other reforms were added. Not only would the workers have a variety of social-insurance programs for home-buying to protect them from the hazards of the marketplace, but they would have guaranteed rights to trade unions and collective bargaining.[46] Bennett, in 1935, had angrily rejected a CCF suggestion that blacklisting of trade unionists by employers be made illegal.[47] But, in 1942, with the trade-union movement having established itself in many mass-production industries despite repressive state policies, the Conservatives accepted the inevitable.

Though the Montreal *Gazette* and other elements in the Conservative party were still unconvinced that their party should commit itself to the welfare state, the party convention in December 1942 chose Macdonnell's candidate, John Bracken, the premier of Manitoba, as its new leader, and adopted substantially the Port Hope policies as the party platform.[48] The 'duty of the state', said the platform, was to maintain both a 'high level' of income for the individual and 'the principle of private initiative and enterprise'.[49]

Mackenzie King was finally being forced to act in this period. His earlier objections to the Purvis report's disregard for provincial rights were lessened by the report of the Rowell-Sirois Commission in 1940 that a strengthened federal government and correspondingly weaker provincial governments were necessary to equalize living standards across the country and to revive investor confidence shaken by the bankruptcies of many junior levels of government. Social-insurance programs, for example, it recommended, should be under federal jurisdiction. Shortly after the report was tabled, King, taking advantage of Maurice Duplessis's defeat by Adelard Godbout's Liberals in Quebec (largely thanks to the aid of federal ministers) and Ontario premier Mitch Hepburn's temporary willingness to make concessions for the war effort, was able to secure a constitutional amendment allowing the federal government to reintroduce the unemployment-insurance bill.[50]

The unemployment-insurance bill, however, was not followed by further reform legislation until 1944. In the interim, the King government had actually considered discontinuing the programs of government mortgage-lending begun by Bennett in 1935 with the Dominion Housing Act and extended slightly by the Liberals in 1937 in the National Housing Act. The life-insurance companies, mortgage companies, construction industry, and timber industry had all been active in convincing Bennett to include this legislation in the New Deal.[51] Now these business sectors all joined labour in opposing its removal; the legislation was left in place.[52]

But King, who had bowed to the most conservative elements of the business community before the war, was now faced with the certainty of political defeat if he did not act to create some or all of the programs that the other two major parties were advocating and which King had also supposedly supported since the First World War. The Liberal administration in Ontario had been badly defeated in the provincial election of 1943 and several federal Liberal seats had been lost in by-elections. A poll in September 1943 gave the CCF the support of 29 per cent of the electorate; the Liberals and Tories each had 28 per cent.[53] King had made, in a sense, his life's work the harmonizing of class relations in Canada and, during his years of employment with the Rockefellers, the United States. As deputy minister of labour, minister of labour, and finally prime minister, he had sought to devise means of ensuring labour peace and the unity of labour and capital 'under the ideal of social service'. In his 1918 book, *Industry and Humanity*, to which he would make endless references in the future, King, with the aid of confusing and semi-mystical charts, argued that public opinion was the major means of forcing the parties within industry to co-operate.[54] In practice, King's labour policies had been designed to maintain the status quo of social relations.[55] *Industry and Humanity* also spoke favourably of the British Labour party's idea of a National Minimum standard of living, which would be collectively guaranteed by society as a whole through state action. Minimum wages, maximum hours, and programs of social insurance were to be part of the State program to achieve the National Minimum. But again, in practice, King had been in office for many years without introducing such programs. Now, however, he was finally acting in order to introduce 'a wholly new conception of industry as being in the nature of social service for the benefit of all, not as something existing only for the benefit of a favoured few'.[56] A shift in class forces had occurred and made impossible the continuation of a do-nothing approach. King could at last dare to defy the more reactionary wing of the bourgeoisie and his party.

King, it might be emphasized, was not a businessman and did not pretend to act as a spokesman for business. His general views were compatible with business views but he always felt that businessmen were, at heart, Tories. He feared both the political and the economic consequences of offending the business community. Thus it is not surprising that programs to which King was committed twenty-five years earlier were not introduced until the mid-1940s. Given the Liberal party's need of business support and King's commitment to keeping the business community happy enough that new private investment in the Canadian economy would not be reduced, it is hardly surprising that little social legislation was introduced in the 1920s, a period when the trade-union movement was in retreat after its victories of the war period. Industry was hostile to social legislation at that time and there seemed to be no pressing need to act. While a shift in business thinking occurred in the 1930s as a result of the militancy of workers and the unemployed, such a shift was, as observed, less pronounced among Liberal businessmen than among traditionally Tory sectors of business. King could still not afford to go too far without committing political suicide. By 1944, however, he could argue that class conflict had reached such a point that social legislation was the only alternative to socialism. While some members of the ruling class remained unconvinced, and even actively opposed such legislation, the class as a whole was won over.

Jack Granatstein, in an excellent account of the wartime debate within government on the question of social-security legislation, argues correctly that at the root of the social reform programs of 1944 and 1945— family allowances, mortgage-lending programs, spending programs for reconversion of the wartime economy to a peacetime economy—'was the fear of postwar unemployment, depression and possible disorder'. He notes that these pro-grams were balanced by various programs of assistance to industry as part of 'an attractive—and expensive—package' to pacify the business community.[57] The 'package' approach to various state programs meant to produce stability of class relations was not new. The Bennett New Deal, the Purvis report, the Montreal Board of Trade report to the Rowell-Sirois Commission, the Conservative Port Hope platform, all similarly integrated programs such as housing construction, social insurance, marketing boards, bonuses to busi-ness, etc., in an attempt to devise a system that would use the state to smooth out certain contradictions within capitalism and thereby calm the restiveness of the working people. Interestingly, while the *Report on Social Security for Canada*, prepared by Professor Leonard Marsh for the Committee on Recon-struction set up by the Cabinet, received a great deal of government atten-tion, the actual legislation fell far short of its recommendations, particularly in the ignoring of the recommendation for health insurance.[58] Clearly, 'wel-fare state' measures in Canada were not to be introduced all at once.

III

The government *White Paper on Employment and Income* of 12 April 1945 was a further attempt to make clear that the state was to play a large role in stabilizing the economy in order to legitimize the private-enterprise system. So as to maintain a 'high and stable level of employment and income', the government would seek to keep its revenues and expenditures in balance not one year at a time but over longer—though unspecified— periods. This would allow the government to budget for surpluses when the economy was in a buoyant stage of the business cycle. When the cycle turned downward and unemployment threatened, the government would 'incur deficits and increases in the national debt resulting from its employment and income policy, whether that policy in the circumstances is best applied through increased expenditures or reduced taxation'.

While such crypto-Keynesianism was not a common demand of the business community, Granatstein exaggerates in commenting that 'before the war, budget deficits had been akin to sin; in 1945 they were simply an economic tool'.[59] It would be fairer to say that before the war proponents of greater government expenditure largely evaded the question of where the money for increased spending would be found. The Montreal Board of Trade, quoted above, seemed to regard financing by debt or taxation as equally acceptable measures, providing in both cases that the levels discussed were within reason.

The 'welfare state' from the beginning was regarded as a contradictory blessing by the governments and businessmen who felt obliged to support it. Michal Kalecki, arguing in 1943 that businessmen still largely opposed government measures for stimulating employment and particularly measures which would subsidize consumption, believed that even if mass pressure converted them to the opposite view they would soon be in the opposition camp once again. The 'maintenance of full employment', he argued, would remove from the bosses the threat of unemployment as a disciplinary measure. Working-class militancy would be increased and demands for wage increases and better working conditions would result in large numbers of strikes. This proved to be the case in the war years. And, as Kalecki noted, even the fact of increasing profits does not compensate capitalists for what appears to be a threat to their control over their factories. In this context, the attack against social insurance and government spending by the business community in recent years is a call for a return to the 'individualism' of a former day when a job or relief from the state was a privilege and not perceived as a right.[60]

How far, then, will the capitalist class go to undo the measures that they were willing to concede in an earlier day in order to pacify working-class militancy and stabilize the economic system? No easy answer can be given to this question. What has been suggested is that the radicalism of the depression years and the fears that such radicalism engendered brought the first abortive attempt in 1935 to introduce state policies for stabilization. The even greater working-class militancy of the war years forced even the cautious members of the ruling class to give way at the war's end. It can be assumed that the curbing of working-class militancy remains an aim of Canadian businessmen and, to some degree, the welfare state that was meant to pacify workers now appears, as Kalecki argued, to encourage their militancy. On the other hand, from the beginning, capitalists who supported 'welfare state' measures recognized the compensatory stimulus to consumption that these spending programs provided and their role in smoothing out the business cycle. It may be true, nevertheless, that the capitalist class as a whole would be willing to endure a steeper business cycle *if* this is the price of forcing the working class to be more insecure and less demanding. In this context, the extent to which workers resist cuts in state spending will play a crucial role, just as, at the present time, the future of wage controls appears dim because of the non-support of the working class.

The capitalist state's continued willingness and ability to maintain a high level of social expenditures is affected by still another factor—although more than a cursory discussion of this is beyond the scope of this essay—and that is the growth of the economy. From the beginning, ruling-class supporters of the welfare state believed that continuous economic growth was inevitable and that with the growth of the economic pie an analogous growth in social benefits could be allowed. Questions of what was produced and the question of relative distribution of wealth could be ignored as long as overall wealth increased and the share of income of various classes increased proportionately owing to state measures that put a floor on the income of the working class. But economic growth has slowed down, and state spending, involving spheres of activity that have little tendency to show increasing rates of productivity, has tended to increase at rates faster than the rates of economic growth.[61] It is clear that capitalists cannot continue to expect to get away with an availability of cheap resources, a continued neglect of environmental factors and the safety of workers, and the continued availability of an exploitable Third World from which super-profits can be extracted.

In these conditions, bourgeois politicians find themselves in the unpalatable role of having not only to justify temporary cutbacks in minimal social service programs, but more generally to 'resocialize' a populace weaned on the ideology of permanent capitalist affluence. As Pierre Trudeau himself recently put it, 'a large part of my message as a politician is to say: we have to put an end to rising expectations. We have to explain to people that we may even have to put an end to our love for our parents or old people in society, even our desire to give more for education and medical research.'[62]

Of course the capitalist state, acting on behalf of the interests of the capitalist class as a whole, can afford to ignore reactionary demands from particular individuals or even particular sectors of the ruling class. Trudeau's recently acquired illiberalism with respect to social legislation reflects the growing sense of crisis amongst the capitalist class as a whole. It is not that Trudeau opposes in principle social legislation or even that he is a direct representative of the big bourgeoisie. Rather it is simply that, like Mackenzie King, Trudeau takes existing class relations as a given and determines policies within limits set by these class relations. In part, these limits can be understood in terms of the class origins of these politicians and the class composition of the bourgeois parties. But there are other, more directly economic, limits that the politicians dedicated to the existing class relations must labour under. These are perhaps best outlined in a speech by Liberal finance minister Charles Dunning in 1938:

> We must follow policies which will enable it [private enterprise] to work in accordance with its essential principles. The most important of these principles is that decisions as to whether the individual shall spend and consume or shall save and invest or shall save and hoard are left to the individual's own initiative. If therefore the answers to the questions as to whether plants are to be built or extended, new houses are to be created and industry is going to expand or to stagnate, depend upon the decisions of tens of thousands of individuals who are free agents and not regimented sheep, it follows that governments must pursue policies which create confidence rather than fear and uncertainty, which give leadership and guidance and encouragement rather than stifle initiative and paralyze new enterprise.[63]

In short, then, the 'welfare state' changes nothing that is fundamental about capitalism. While it places a floor on workers' incomes, it leaves unaltered the control of means of production. Production for profit and not for use and the reduction of labour to an extension of the machines it operates for the benefit of capital remain the goals of the economic system. Indeed, the oscillations in support for state social spending among the ruling class result from disagreements in particular circumstances as to how useful that expenditure is towards these goals. It is clear that the working class must defend every 'welfare state' gain that it has won. On the other hand, there can be little doubt that government social programs do serve the function of legitimizing the system by making it appear that the worst aspects of *laissez-faire* have been compensated. At the present time, though, the ruling-class pendulum seems to have swung away from these programs and back towards the idea of a large dose of unemployment as a means of teaching the working class respect for its betters. It is dangerous to hazard a guess as to how serious the current *economic* crisis of capitalism really is—it has recovered from crises before—but there can be little doubt that the *legitimization* crisis of capitalism will increase as it attempts to force workers to accept both lower wages and fewer state benefits. But one should be careful not to assume the stupidity of one's enemy: the class struggle has forced the ruling class to concede various reforms in the past and, in the Canadian case, part of the ruling class was willing to make these concessions before it was absolutely necessary. It would be wrong to asume blithely that, given a strong working-class reaction against government cutbacks, the capitalist class will not relent again. While cutbacks must be opposed, such opposition must be placed within the context of an attack on the capitalist system as a whole or, like wage struggles, it may prove episodic and leave unchanged the relative force of bourgeois ideology in the working class.

Suggestions for Further Reading

Alvin Finkel, *Business and Social Reform in the Thirties* (Toronto, 1979).
Michiel Horn, ed., *The Dirty Thirties: Canadians in the Great Depression* (Toronto, 1972).
J.R.H. Wilbur, ed., *The Bennett New Deal: Fraud or Portent?* (Toronto, 1968).

Notes

[1]Research Committee of the League for Social Reconstruction, *Social Planning for Canada* (1935, Toronto, 1975), xix.

[2]Hugh G.J. Aitken, for example, says that the theory that the state acted merely as an agent for private economic interests in the nation-building period 'could probably be supported' and that the distinction between 'the state' and 'private enterprise' in Canada 'often seems artificial'. 'Defensive Expansionism: The State and Economic Growth in Canada', in Aitken, ed., *The State and Economic Growth* (New York 1959), 79–114. From a more radical perspective, H. Viv Nelles details the virtually complete power that resource companies had in dictating provincial 'regulatory' policies dealing with the resource industries. *The Politics of Development: Forests, Mines & Hydro-Electric Power in Ontario, 1849–1941* (Toronto, 1974).

[3]*Canada Year Book* (1972), 1218–19

[4]Allan M. Maslove, *The Pattern of Taxation in Canada* (Ottawa, 1972), 64.

[5]*Income Distribution by Size in Canada, Selected Years: Distribution of Family Incomes in Canada* (Ottawa, 1972) reported the following after-tax comparisons for quintiles of the population for 1951 and 1972:

	1951	1972
Top 20%	41.1%	39.1%
2nd 20	22.4	23.7
3rd 20	17.4	18.3
4th 20	12.9	12.9
5th 20	6.1	5.9

[6]See R.B. Splane, *Social Welfare in Ontario, 1791–1893: A Study of Public Welfare Administration* (Toronto, 1965); Dennis Trevor Guest, 'The Development of Income Maintenance Programmes in Canada, 1945–1967', unpublished PhD dissertation, University of London, 1968; Elisabeth Wallace, 'The Origin of the Social Welfare State in Canada, 1867–1900', *Canadian Journal of Economics and Political Science*, XVI, 4 (Aug. 1950), 383–93. On Montreal, see Terry Copp, *The Anatomy of Poverty: The Condition of the Working Class in Montreal, 1897–1929* (Toronto, 1974). On the education question, see Greg Kealey, ed., *Canada Investigates Industrialism: The Royal Commission on the Relations of Labor and Capital, 1889* (Toronto, 1973), xix, 15–16, 39–40.

[7]James Weinstein, *The Corporate Ideal in the Liberal State, 1900–1918* (Boston, 1969); Michael Bliss, *A Living Profit* (Toronto, 1974), 142; Michael Piva, 'Workmen's Compensation Movement in Ontario', *Ontario History* (March 1975), 39–56.

[8]Public Archives of Ontario, *Report of the Ontario Commission on Unemployment* (1916), 82–3.

[9]Kenneth McNaught, *A Prophet in Politics: A Biography of J.S. Woodsworth* (Toronto, 1959), 218–20.

[10]A complete list of Bennett holdings is found in Public Archives of Canada (PAC), R.B. Bennett Papers, v. 901, 563867–3900; Bennett's partnership with Beaverbrook is discussed in A.J.P. Taylor, *Beaverbrook* (London, 1972), 15, 34, 36–7, 86; Bennett's involvement with Eddy is detailed in Bennet Papers, v. 915, 916, and 917; the labelling of Canada Packers and Imperial Tobacco as oligopolies appears in *Report of the Royal Commission on Price Spreads and Mass Buying* (Ottawa, 1935), 53, 59.

[11]For example, C.H. Cahan, Bennett's only secretary of state, was a leading Montreal corporation attorney and industrialist and, like Bennett, a past Beaverbrook protégé. Cahan had been, on behalf of the Bank of Montreal, legal adviser and executive head of a vast array of tramway, electric light, and hydro-electric enterprises in South America, Trinidad, and Mexico. National revenue minister E.B. Ryckman was past president of Dunlop Tire and director of Gurney Foundry, IBM, Addressograph Company, Russell Motor Company, and others. When illness forced his retirement, he was replaced by a millionaire investment banker, R.C. Matthews, later a president of the Canadian Chamber of Commerce. Finance minister E.N. Rhodes was past president of the British America Nickel Corporation, later purchased by International Nickel. See *Canadian Parliamentary Guide* (1930–5). Links between politicians as well as leading civil servants and the corporations are traced in Libby C. and Frank W. Park, *Anatomy of Big Business* (Toronto, 1962); John Porter, *The Vertical Mosaic* (Toronto, 1965); Wallace Clement, *The Canadian Corporate Elite* (Toronto, 1975).

[12]See Ronald Liversedge, *Recollections of the On-to-Ottawa Trek*, ed. Victor Hoar (Toronto, 1973).

[13]*Labour Legislation: A Study Prepared for the Royal Commission on Dominion-Provincial Relations* (Ottawa, 1939), 5–6.

[14]*Report of the Annual Meeting of the Bank of Montreal* (3 December 1934).

[15]Gordon to Bennett, 6 January 1934, Bennett Papers, v. 811, 503059 (emphasis added).

[16]*Monthly Review of the Bank of Nova Scotia* (Aug. 1934), 4.

[17]See Oscar Ryan, *Tim Buck: A Conscience for Canada* (Toronto, 1975), 128–9; A.B. McKillop, 'The Communist as Conscience: Jacob Penner and Winnipeg Civic Politics, 1934–1935', A.R. McCormack and Ian Macpherson, eds, *Cities in the West* (Ottawa, 1974), 181–209; Liversedge, *Recollections*, 15–34; 'Some General Observations on the Administration of Unemployment Relief in Western Canada: Report for the Prime Minister's Office, 1932', Michiel Horn, ed., *The Dirty Thirties* (Toronto, 1972), 272–6.

[18]*Financial Times*, 21 September 1934; Dorothy Kidd, 'Women's Organization: Learning from Yesterday', in *Women at Work: Ontario, 1850–1930* (Toronto, 1974), 351–7.

[19](June 1935), 302.

[20]*Winnipeg Free Press*, 10 and 19 September 1935. There were, of course, businessmen who opposed unemployment insurance and indeed businessmen who opposed all of the Bennett reforms. Business opponents of unemployment insurance argued that it would add to the cost of doing business and hurt Canada's export position. It would encourage sloth and remove the insecurity of employees which allowed employers to impose labour discipline. Further, it would hit all industries equally

regardless of the incidence of unemployment in a given industry. Prominent opponents of unemployment insurance included CPR president Edward Beatty, Canadian Bank of Commerce vice-president Sir Thomas White, and the Montreal *Gazette*, among others.

[21]Bennett to Howard Robinson, 11 June 1935, Bennett Papers, v. 715.

[22]The philosophy and programs of the 'New Deal' were introduced in a series of radio speeches, which are reprinted in large part in Ernest Watkins, *R.B. Bennett: A Biography* (Toronto 1963), 253–63.

[23]J.R.H. Wilbur, *The Bennett Administration, 1930–1935,* CHA Booklet no. 24 (Ottawa, 1969), 14.

[24]The party's poor financial position in the period before the New Deal is discussed in J.R.H. Wilbur, 'H.H. Stevens and the Reconstruction Party', *Canadian Historical Review* XLV, 1 (March 1964), 6.

[25]Bennett Papers, v. 713, 714, 715, 718, 949.

[26]On Flavelle, see Michael Bliss, 'A Canadian Businessman and War: The Case of Joseph Flavelle', in J.L. Granatstein and Robert Cuff, eds, *War and Society in North America* (Toronto, 1971), 20–36; on Beaty, see D.H. Miller-Barstow, *Beatty of the CPR* (Toronto, 1950).

[27]The *Gazette's* defection must be balanced against the continued support in Montreal of the *Montreal Star*, presided over by financier Lord Atholstan and St Lawrence Sugar president J.W. McConnell. The Toronto *Evening Telegram* and the *Mail and Empire* gave enthusiastic support. Most importantly, F.N. Southam told Senator C.J. Ballantyne that he had directed his usually Liberal chain of newspapers to give positive support to Bennett and the New Deal. See Bennett Papers, v. 715 and 949. A detailed discussion of reaction to the New Deal is found in Alvin Finkel, 'Canadian Business and the "Reform" Process in Canada in the 1930's,' unpublished PhD thesis, University of Toronto, 1976, 125–8; and in Wilbur, *The Bennett Administration*, 20.

[28]*Can. H. of C. Debates*, 28 April 1931, 1077; 29 April 1931, 1104.

[29]*Ibid.*, 6 May 1930, 1831.

[30]See Leo Johnson, *Poverty in Wealth* (Toronto, 1974), 24–6.

[31]*Financial Post*, 1 June 1935.

[32]Mitch Hepburn, the premier of Ontario, for example, was seen by King as 'in the hands of McCullagh of the *Globe* and the *Globe* and McCullagh in the hands of financial mining interests'. PAC, King Diary, 13 April 1937. In general, King, in his diaries, regarded many Canadian politicians, both Liberal and Conservative, as 'in the hands' of various business interest groups.

[33]See Richard M.H. Alway, 'Hepburn, King, and the Rowell-Sirois Commission', *Canadian Historical Review* XLVIII, 2 (June 1967), 113–41.

[34]King's desire to maintain the support of the mining companies is indicated, for example, by his opposition in 1934 to the Conservative government's 10 per cent tax on the windfall profits gained by gold-mining companies when the price of gold increased from $21 to $35. He wrote an opponent of the tax: 'The present Government has made many blunders, but I think this one with respect to the ten per cent tax on the production of gold is perhaps the worst of the lot, considering, as you say, that it formed the major feature of this year's budget . . . I hope that some of those who have suffered as a result of the Government's policies will lend us a hand when the time comes to put the present Administration out of office.'

King to James E. Day, barrister, 5 May 1934, PAC, King papers, v. 199, 170306–7.

[35]12 November 1937, *ibid.*, v. 238, 204650.

[36]Royal Commission on Dominion-Provincial Relations, *Report of Hearings*, 31 May, 9691 (merchants); 19 January, 2739 (real estate); 17 January 1938, 2375 (CMA).

[37]The Canadian sections of CIO unions were, until 1939, still in the TLC. But they were clearly a minority within the organization and indeed only began to rival the crafts unions in their membership during the war period after their ouster from the TLC and the formation of their own federation, the Canadian Congress of Labour. See Irving M. Abella, *Nationalism, Communism, and Canadian Labour* (Toronto, 1973).

[38]King Diary, 4 April 1938. After calling the report an 'academic treatise', King said: 'It was a mistake having Purvis as chairman, he being a big businessman and a Tory at heart, not understanding methods of politics.'

[39]Royal Commission on Dominion-Provincial Relations, *Report of Hearings*, 524–5 (Chamber of Commerce); 8153 (Board of Trade).

[40]See Finkel, 'Canadian Business', 352–89.

[41]Estimated trade-union membership in Canada, according to the Dominion Department of Labour annual reports, was 310,534 in 1931 and 315,073 in 1939. Grauer, *Labour Legislation*, 68. There were 711,117 trade unionists in 1945. Canada, Department of Labour, Labour Organizations in Canada (1963).

[42]'Orders-in-council were passed freezing wage levels, facilitating the use of troops in labour disputes, and limiting the right to strike. The government also refused to force employers to negotiate with their workers and continued to appoint men whom the Congress [of Labour] considered "anti-labour" to government boards.' See Abella, *Nationalism, Communism*, 72; see also Stuart Jamieson, *Times of Trouble: Labour Unrest and Industrial Conflict in Canada, 1900–66* (Ottawa, 1968).

[43]See Jack Granatstein, *Canada's War: The Politics of the Mackenzie King Government, 1939–1945* (Toronto, 1975), 264–5.

[44]Jack Granatstein, *The Politics of Survival: The Conservative Party of Canada, 1939–1945* (Toronto, 1967), 110.

[45]Roger Graham, *Arthur Meighen: No Surrender* (Toronto, 1965), iii, 67, 117.

[46]Queen's University Archives, Macdonnell Papers, v. 52, 'Remarks on the History of Inflation: An Address Given to the Liberal-Conservative Summer School at Newmarket, September, 1933', and 'The Canadian Institute on Economics and Politics: Reports of Two of the Addresses'. The Port Hope conference is discussed in Granatstein, *Politics of Survival*, 125–50 and 207–10, and John R. Williams, *The Conservative Party of Canada, 1920–1949* (Durham, NC, 1956), 72.

[47]*Can. H. of C. Debates*, 18 February 1935, 949–52.

[48]Williams, *Conservative Party*, 70. Bracken, like Macdonnell, was no recent convert to the Port Hope philosophies. In a statement to Canadian Press in 1933 he had praised the Roosevelt New Deal and concluded that 'controlled inflation combined with new public works by the federal government would seem to be inevitable if the problems of the unemployed and the debtors in all classes are to be met in a constructive way.' *Winnipeg Free Press*, 10 August 1933.

[49]Granatstein, *Politics of Survival*, 213.

[50]Canada, *Report of the Royal Commission on Dominion-Provincial Relations*, Book Two: *Recommendations* (Ottawa, 1940), 151, 157, 270–4; J.W. Pickersgill, ed., *The Mackenzie King Record* (Toronto, 1960), I, 60–1.

[51]The Canadian Construction Association, in particular, took credit for the legislation. *Monetary Times*, 11 January 1936. The position of the mortgage companies was outlined by T. Darcy Leonard, solicitor of the Dominion Mortgages and Investments Association, in *Journal of the Canadian Bankers' Association* (April 1936), 297–303. See also *Canadian Lumberman*, 1 July 1934; and *Can. H. of C. Debates*, 25 June 1935, 3948.

[52]See PAC, Department of Finance Papers, 1942, v. 704–6.

[53]Granatstein, *Canada's War*, 264–5.

[54](1918, Toronto, 1973), 336.

[55]An especially trenchant evaluation of King's labour policies is provided by Jamieson in *Times of Trouble*, 128–32, 276–94. Jamieson's conclusions are substantially the same as those of the stridently anti-King study, H.S. Ferns and B. Ostry, *The Age of Mackenzie King: The Rise of the Leader* (1955, Toronto, 1976).

[56]*Can. H. of C. Debates*, 28 July 1944, 5535.

[57]*Canada's War*, 276, 278.

[58](Ottawa 1943, Toronto 1975).

[59]*Canada's War*, 277, 278.

[60]'Political Aspects of Full Employment', reprinted in E.K. Hunt and Jesse Schwartz, *A Critique of Economic Theory* (Middlesex, 1972), 426–9. I would disagree with Kalecki that, by 1943, the pressure of the masses had yet to make itself felt in the viewpoints adopted by big business, at least in Canada.

[61]The contradictions that confront the 'welfare state' are discussed in James O'Connor, *The Fiscal Crisis of the State* (New York, 1973); and Rick Deaton, 'The Fiscal Crisis of the State in Canada', in Dimitrios Roussopoulos, ed., *The Political Economy of the State* (Montreal, 1973), 18–56.

[62]*Maclean's*, 10 January 1977, 8.

[63]Quoted in *Canadian Business* (July 1938), 12.

26

Women in the Labour Force in World War II

Ruth Pierson

In 1939 Canada once again became involved in an international war. As in the First World War, conscription would become the major political issue; but more important developments were occurring that did not capture the public attention. The mobilization of resources during emergency conditions has often produced unexpected results. On the one hand war is always a devastating and destructive force—particularly for those who must fight it—but on the other, war for North American nations has usually meant economic prosperity and full employment, combined with major economic and social changes. From the standpoint of economic productivity, war is the ultimate consumer, requiring goods and services tailored for particular circumstances, often destroyed and quickly rendered obsolete. From the standpoint of employment, war took most of the able-bodied younger males out of the civilian labour market, making it necessary to tap new categories of

society to find replacements. In Canada, one of the groups whose labour became more valuable under wartime conditions was women.

Ruth Pierson analyses the impact of the Second World War on women and on the status of women in Canadian society, pointing out that in recruiting women into the labour force during the war the Canadian government was engaged in no long-term reconceptualization of the role of women. The government did not turn actively to women until the unemployment remaining from the Depression had been eliminated, and then it did so very selectively. Only gradually did the labour net expand into the recruitment of married and part-time female workers. Women responded to the calls for patriotic duty with enthusiasm, but the government found that working women, especially those who were married and/or had small children, provided special problems. Tax concessions were necessary, as was the provision of child-care facilities. Both were regarded as temporary wartime measures and were quickly dismantled as soon as the emergency had ended. After the war the government bureaucracy returned to its traditional attitudes towards women.

Why was the government reluctant to draw on the labour reserve represented by its female population? Was any thought given to the long-term implications of such recruitment? Why did women respond so eagerly to government mobilization? What concessions were necessary to accommodate the new work force? Did these concessions mark any genuine change in policy or attitudes towards women workers? Was there any long-range significance in the recruitment of women during the war?

This article first appeared in *Canadian Historical Association Historical Papers*, 1976, 142–71. Revised and expanded, it appears as Chapter One in Ruth Roach Pierson's *'They're Still Women After All': The Second World War and Canadian Womanhood* (Toronto: McClelland and Stewart, 1986).

It is often assumed that the employment of women in the labour force during World War II greatly advanced the emancipation of women, at least in the sense of women's struggle to achieve equal status with men in Canadian society.[1] Building on that assumption, feminists have lamented the ease with which many of the gains were lost at the war's end. One famous account, concerned with United States society but considered to have relevance for Canadian society as well, postulated the propagation of a 'feminine mystique' to account for the postwar reverses suffered by women's struggle for equality.[2] I should like to argue that both the assumption of great gains made by women during World War II and the bewilderment over the postwar reversals rest on an inadequate examination of the context of women's wartime employment and an inaccurate assessment of the degree to which attitudes towards women's proper role in society changed during the war. My basic proposition is that Canada's war effort, rather than any consideration of women's right to work, determined the recruitment of women into the labour force. The recruitment of women was part of a large-scale intervention by government in the labour market to control allocation of labour for effective prosecution of the war.

My first point is that National Selective Service and the federal Department of Labour, in their wartime mobilization of the work force, regarded women as constituting a large labour reserve, arranged in layers of employability, to be dipped into more and more deeply as the labour pool dried up: recruiting first young 'girls' and single women and then married women without children for full-time employment, next women encumbered with home responsibilities for part-time employment, and finally women with children for full-time employment. Starting with the most mobile, National

Selective Service pulled in these layers successively as the war effort intensified. In their public pronouncements, government officials stated a reluctance to draw upon those layers of the female labour reserve the mobilization of which would be most disruptive of the traditional family system.

Secondly, the government recruiting agencies viewed their task as service to Canada's war effort. Accordingly, the paramount appeal of recruitment campaigns was to patriotic duty and the necessity to make sacrifices for the nation at war. Not women's right to work, but women's obligation to work in wartime was the major theme.

Thirdly, accommodations to the particular needs of working women were made within the context of the war effort. These were generally introduced as temporary measures, to remain in effect only so long as the nation was at war.

I

Canada entered the Second World War with the effects of the Great Depression still in force. There were approximately 900,000 registered unemployed (Canada's work force at this time was approximately 3.8 million strong). In the following two years this reserve of unemployed persons largely met the increased demands for manpower created by military recruitment and the step-up of production stimulated by the war. By 1942 the slack in the labour market had been taken up. With war industry geared for full production and the Armed Forces continuing to withdraw large numbers of male workers from the labour force, the situation had changed from one of labour surplus and unemployment to one of labour shortage. 'To meet the pressure of war needs attention, therefore, became focussed on the reserve of potential women workers who had not yet been drawn into employment.'[3]

By thirteen orders-in-council, the National Selective Service program was established in March 1942 under the jurisdiction of the Minister of Labour.[4] Prime Minister Mackenzie King, in his 24 March 1942 address to Parliament on National Selective Service, declared that 'recruitment of women for employment was "the most important single feature of the program".'[5] He went on to outline a ten-point plan for drawing women into industry.[6]

In May 1942 a division of National Selective Service was created to deal with employment of women and with services related to women's employment. Mrs Rex (Fraudena) Eaton of Vancouver was appointed Assistant Director of National Selective Service in charge of the Women's Division. In December 1942 her title changed to Associate Director. Mrs Eaton sat on the Administrative and Advisory Boards of NSS and was immediately responsible to the Director of National Selective Service, a position held by Elliott M. Little until 19 November 1942, and thereafter by Deputy Minister of Labour Arthur MacNamara.

My first contention is that women were regarded as constituting a large labour reserve on which Canadian industry could draw to meet the special labour demands created by the war emergency. One of the first steps of National Selective Service regarding the recruitment of women into the work force was to assess the size of the top layer of this labour reserve: that consisting of young single women. 'It was decided to conduct a compulsory registration of *younger* women in order to ascertain more definitely what resources of woman power were available.'[7]

Under authority of order-in-council PC 1445, which directed the Minister of Labour 'to establish and maintain an inventory of employable persons' in Canada,[8] Humphrey Mitchell on 8 September 1942 ordered the registration of all female persons aged twenty to twenty-four (i.e., born in the years 1918 to 1922 inclusive), with the exception of members of religious orders, hospital patients, prison inmates, and women currently in insurable employment.[9] The registration was held during the week of 14 September through 19 September 1942.[10] In urban areas women reported to the local Employment and Selective Service office; in rural areas, to the nearest post office.[11]

Although women were required to register whether married or unmarried, it is clear that the main objective of this initial inventory of Canada's woman-power was to determine the size of the labour reserve made up of young single women so as to enable their effective mobilization. One major reason why the age group twenty to twenty-four was chosen was that: 'Single women would compose a higher percentage of the total than would be found in older age groups.'[12]

On 20 August 1942, Mrs Eaton convoked a conference in Ottawa of executive representatives of twenty-one national women's organizations so that she could enlist their co-operation and support for National Selective Service and the September Registration of Canadian Women. She explained that the registration of Canadian women aged twenty to twenty-four

> will show us exactly how many single women we have available to meet the increasing shortage of workers in our war industries. Then we will have a pool of single workers from which to draw when an employer asks for additional staff, and single women can be supplied immediately.[13]

At this time, the policy was not merely to mobilize single women, but to render unnecessary the employment of married women with children. Mrs Eaton stated emphatically: 'We shall not urge married women with children to go into industry.' Married women up until then had been allowed to drift into employment in war industries because, she was reported to have explained, 'no known reservoir of single workers existed.' It was hoped that the September 1942 registration of Canadian women would enable National Selective Service (NSS) 'to direct single women into essential war industries rather than to have employers building up huge staffs of married women with children'.[14]

On 15 December 1942, A. Chapman of the Research and Statistics Branch of the Department of Labour submitted a report on the 'Female Labour

Supply Situation'. Working with the results of the September 1942 Women's Registration, follow-up interviews carried out by local Employment and Selective Services offices, and detailed analyses by local offices of the relation of unfilled vacancies to unplaced applicants, he concluded:

> Study of the available information regarding the supply of and demand for female labour clearly indicates the existence of a large reserve of female labour throughout the country.[15]

Beyond 'the overall surplus of female labour', the figures more particularly indicated 'that the bulk of the readily available surplus of female labour is concentrated in those areas where war industry is least developed'. Even allowing for variation of response to the Registration in different parts of the country, Chapman insisted that the figures 'do emphasize the tremendous reservoir of female labour in areas such as the Maritimes and the Prairies where development of war industry has been slight'.[16]

National Selective Service (Women's Division) attached considerable significance to the fact that:

> There were 22,655 young single women without home responsibilities in Prince Edward Island, Nova Scotia, New Brunswick, Manitoba, Saskatchewan, Alberta and British Columbia, who were willing to work full-time either at home or in another area.[17]

The information disclosed by the Registration and follow-up interviews led to the adoption of a program for transferring young unmarried women workers, the most mobile segment of the female labour force, from areas of surplus to areas of short labour supply.

In May 1942 a survey of the expected demand for female labour 'showed that at least 75,000 additional women would be required in war industries before the end of the year'.[18] The Registration itself acted as a stimulus to young women to fill out applications for employment.[19] In addition, NSS launched a nation-wide publicity campaign, using radio and the press, to urge upon women 'the need to engage in some phase of the war effort'.[20] Newspaper publishers and magazine editors agreed to give space in their publications to pictures of women working on machines, of women war workers in their special work uniforms, and to stories of accomplishments by individual women. Papers published news releases on NSS and the problems it was facing. CBC presented over the national network 'a series of dramatic plays, written expressly for NSS around the theme of women war workers'.[21] The publicity campaign paid off. 'By January 1943, the additional 75,000 women required for war industries had been recruited.' It was calculated that by June 1943, 158,000 women had joined the industrial war effort since the beginning of 1942, bringing the total number of women engaged directly and indirectly in war industries to 255,000. During the same period, several thousand women had volunteered for service in the Women's Divisions of the various branches of the Armed Forces.[22] The 'readily available surplus of female labour'[23] had evaporated.

The September 1942 National Selective Service (Civilian) Regulations[24] provided the basis for controlling Canada's labour power during the war. They established schedules of labour priorities, to be revised periodically, which classified industries and firms under one of four categories: A) very high labour priority; B) high labour priority; C) low labour priority; D) no labour priority. Employment advertising was brought under the control of NSS: no employer could advertise for employees except by arrangement with a National Selective Service Officer. No employer could interview or hire a person for a job who did not possess an NSS permit to seek and accept employment. A seven days' notice of separation was required of an employer to fire and of an employee to quit. After January 1943 all persons between 16 and 65 years of age (excluding full-time students, housewives, and clergy) were required to register for work at local Employment and Selective Service offices if not gainfully employed for seven consecutive days.[25] NSS controlled the issuance of permits to seek or enter employment 'in a given community, industry, occupation or establishment' within Canada[26] and, after 29 October 1942, the issuance of 'Labour Exit Permits' to seek or accept employment in the United States.[27] Through these measures, NSS was able to supervise the movement of labour between establishment and to direct persons 'to employment in the order of importance to the war effort'[28] and to the maintenance of essential civilian services within Canada.

Women registering at local Employment and Selective Service offices for full-time employment were directed in the first instance to fill vacancies in establishments that had been given an 'A' or 'B' labour priority rating. But by the summer of 1943 serious labour shortages had developed in areas of the service sector long dependent on female labour. Women were leaving low-paid service jobs for more lucrative employment in war industries. Hospitals, restaurants, hotels, laundries, and dry-cleaning establishments were clamouring for help. Women were needed as ward aides in hospitals, as waitresses and kitchen help in restaurants, as chamber maids and waitresses in hotels, and for various subordinate positions in laundries and dry-cleaning establishments.[29] The labour pool of single women available for full-time employment was exhausted. 'It became necessary to appeal to housewives and those groups who would not ordinarily appear in the labour market.'[30] NSS (Women's Division) decided to launch a campaign to recruit women with home responsibilities for part-time work.

The NSS (Civilian) Regulations of September 1942 exempted from government control 'part-time subsidiary employment which is not [a person's] principal means of livelihood'.[31] Employers did not have to seek prior NSS approval to advertise for part-time help or keep a record of their part-time employees. Nor did persons seeking part-time subsidiary work have to register with an NSS local office. Therefore, the Women's Division of NSS in their campaigns to recruit housewives for part-time work needed the voluntary co-operation of employers as well as of women seeking part-time employment not exceeding twenty-four hours.

That use of part-time workers would become necessary was foreseen as early as November 1942.[32] Supervisors of the Women's Division of local Employment and Selective Service offices were instructed to begin persuading employers to make plans for employing women on a part-time basis. At first employers generally resisted the idea. In a memorandum dated 7 May 1943, Mary Eadie, Women's Division Supervisor, Toronto, reported that, although some had 'undertaken to use it with success . . . the employer as a whole "will not be bothered" . . . with part-time help'.[33] Employers cited higher costs stemming from additional clerical work, rearrangement of schedules, increased payroll work, need for increased supervision, and a feared rise in absenteeism and turnover as reasons for their opposition. But when firms in production of nonessentials, such as candy, tobacco, soft drinks, and luxury items, were informed that NSS would make no effort to send them 'full-time workers while essential services and war industries were short of labour'[34] and when by the spring of 1943 even establishments providing essential civilian services were suffering an acute labour shortage, many employers began to show a greater willingness to employ women part-time.

The first campaign for part-time women workers was mounted in Toronto from 12 July to 26 July 1943. To prepare for it, Toronto Selective Service first sought the co-operation of employers. 'Several conferences were called' with employers in hospitals, restaurants, hotels, laundries, and dry-cleaning establishments 'to discuss the possibility of [their] using part-time' women workers.[35] On 22 May 1943, Mary Eadie reported to Mrs Eaton that 'the Ontario Restaurant Association, the Laundry and Dry-Cleaning Association of Toronto and the Hospital Association of Toronto will co-operate with us because they are in such dire straits for help these days.'[36] When employers had placed with the Toronto Selective Service office a sufficient number of orders for part-time workers (approximately 1,500), the publicity campaign could be launched.

Meanwhile Toronto Selective Service also sought and won for the campaign the sponsorship and collaboration of the Local Council of Women.[37] According to Mrs Eaton, it was 'with great courage' that Mrs Norman C. Stephens, President of the Toronto Council of Women, 'offered to promote a publicity campaign inviting Toronto women to accept part-time work in these occupations which no one will claim to be glamorous or highly paid'.[38]

Not only employers in essential civilian services, for which the campaign was principally designed, but employers in some war industries decided to experiment with part-time workers. The appeal was 'particularly directed to housewives'.[39] At the same time 'no women with important home responsibilities were unduly urged to register.' Furthermore 'no appeal was made for women to work part-time in addition to a full-time job.' However, 'many women without children and with few home responsibilities consented, under pressure of the campaign, to accept full-time work.'[40]

In her report of 28 July 1943 to the National Selective Service Advisory Board, Mrs Eaton was enthusiastic over the results of the campaign. Two thousand, two hundred and sixty-seven women had responded to the call. Of these 1,518 had been placed in essential services, 643 in part-time and 875 in full-time positions. Another 599 had accepted part-time employment in war industries. The remainder (150) were yet to be placed. For Mrs Eaton, 'the success of the campaign offered some assurance that there is still a pool of women ready and willing to fill a breach when emergencies arise.'[41]

The Toronto campaign for part-time women workers served as a model for similar campaigns in other cities throughout Canada. NSS Circular no. 270–1, dated 18 August 1943, and sent to all local Employment and Selective Service offices, outlined the main purpose and features of the campaign. It was to relieve labour shortages in 'essential services such as hospitals, restaurants, hotel, laundries and dry-cleaning establishments'. It was directed at 'a new type of recruit', namely 'the housewife or others *who will do a Part-time Paid Job* for six days per week, perhaps only four hours per day, or perhaps three full days each week'. Not only was the campaign to be directed at housewives, the work they were being asked to do was seen as an extension of housework outside the home, as is clear from the circular's statement: 'It is possible for many women to streamline their housekeeping at home to do the housekeeping in the community for standard wages.' Local offices were first to secure the willingness of employers to provide definite orders for part-time workers, then to secure the sponsorship 'of an organization of women who have the high confidence of the comunity'. The Local Council of Women was specifically recommended. The publicity campaign would engage the combined efforts of the employers, the sponsors, and the staff of the local E. and S.S. office. The expenses of the campaign were to be borne by the benefiting employers and the Dominion Government on a fifty-fifty cost-sharing basis. Women of the sponsoring organization could help in the local office with registration of applicants, but all referrals to jobs would remain the responsibility of the local E. and S.S. office staff.[42]

The President of the National Council of Women, Mrs Edgar Hardy, agreed to endorse these campaigns. A letter signed on 31 August 1943 by A. MacNamara and Mrs Rex Eaton was sent to all Local Councils of Women enlisting their support of the campaigns for part-time women workers. Explaining the necessity for the campaigns, the letter stated: 'There is no reserve of men in Canada today. In fact there is little reserve of either men or women.'[43]

Working in close co-operation with the Local Council of Women, National Selective Service launched special recruiting campaigns for part-time women workers in fall of 1943 in Edmonton, Saskatoon, Regina, Brandon, Ottawa, Moncton, and Halifax. The drives sought part-time workers for jobs in the essential services already mentioned, but also in some centres, such as Edmonton, for jobs in the garment industry. In some places, such as Brandon and Edmonton, the part-time campaign was combined with a campaign aimed exclusively at encouraging women who were formerly employees of the civil service, but who were now married, to return to part-time or full-time work to alleviate the serious shortage of workers in war dapartments of government.[44]

Although for as long as possible only full-time workers were sought for war industries, by the end of 1943 and throughout 1944 women were hired for certain war jobs on a part-time basis. In some areas 'housewives' shifts' came into existence, so named because they were made up primarily or entirely of 'housewives who could work only in the evenings' from 6:00 or 7:00 to 10:00 or 11:00 p.m.[45]

Even before the conclusion of the part-time campaign in Toronto on 26 July 1943, National Selective Service was alerted to the existence of an acute labour shortage in war industries in the Toronto area. An estimated 3,500 women were urgently needed to fill full-time high-priority jobs in war industry.[46] The urgency of the need precluded its being filled by transferring women workers from other parts of Canada.[47] Toronto Selective Service met with representatives of the media to discuss how 'publicity could be used to impress women with the importance of employment in war industries.' Members of the War Council of the Artists' Guild proposed that NSS seek 'to recruit women for employment in war industries for full time work for a period of not less than three months'. At meetings of 23 and 26 July with representatives of management from Massey-Harris, Victory Aircraft, Goodyear, Small Arms, General Engineering, and York Arsenal, Toronto Selective Service sold these employers on the idea of launching a campaign to recruit full-time women war workers for a three-month period of service. As Mrs Eaton reported to the National Selective Service Advisory Board on 28 July 1943, although they felt their need to be for long-term full-time workers, the employers recognized certain advantages to the special appeal for three-month service: 1) it would give the media 'a new publicity angle to emphasize the needs of war industries for more workers'; 2) it might very well recruit many women who, once employed, would remain in employment; and 3) it would counteract 'the fear of being frozen to the job' which was seen as deterring many women from accepting 'employment full time in essential industry'.[48]

The keynote of the campaign was 'three months' service',[49] but attention was also given to the need in general for women workers in war plants to do full-time service on any one of three shifts. Although the call went out to all women, special appeal was made to housewives, with reference to the counselling service for mothers and the attempt to place women in war plants near their homes.[50] Radio publicity on the need of women in war industry began early in August. Originally set to open on 18 August, the full-fledged three-months' service campaign in the end got under way on 30 August and ran to 11 September. During the first week a 'war industrial show' was put on at the T. Eaton Company Auditorium. In booths set up by twelve industries, 'girls' from war plants demonstrated the operations which they carried out 'in their ordinary work at the plant' and a 'fashion show was given in which the girls wore their plant uniforms.'[51] In her final account of the results of the Toronto Campaign for Women in War Industries of 30 August to 11 September 1943, Mrs Eaton reported that 4,330 women had been referred to war industries, 300 women had applied for part-time war work but had not yet been placed, and 168 applicants were awaiting referral until day-nursery care for their children had been arranged.[52]

NSS continued to launch recruitment campaigns for full-time women workers as labour demands dictated. In early October 1943 an intensive campaign was mounted in Peterborough for 550 new women workers for full-time jobs in textile factories and other high-priority manufacturing firms.[53] Similarly in November 1943 special drives to recruit female textile workers for full-time jobs were carried out in the textile centres of Hamilton, Welland, St Catharines, and Dunnville.[54]

In late September 1943, NSS Regional and Local Officers in Montreal began planning a massive recruitment campaign to alleviate the area's recorded labour shortage of 19,000 women. But on 2 November 1943, a meeting of Montreal employers with Léonard Préfontaine, NSS Regional Superintendent for Quebec, decided to postpone indefinitely the large-scale general campaign. As opposition to women's employment still persisted in Quebec, feeling was that the public would be more receptive to a series of short, small, separate drives specifically for 'hotels, laundries, hospitals, textiles, etc.'[55]

In general the urgency for special recruitment campaigns let up in December 1943.[56] During the first months of 1944 'there was a slow but noticeable reduction in war industry.'[57] The number of women in the labour force actually declined by 10,000 to 15,000 in the first three months of the year. Although the end of the war was in sight, NSS was concerned that there be no slackening of the war effort until victory was secured. There was concern above all that women would begin to leave war industry in greater numbers than the slight slowdown in production warranted.[58] Married women might be wanting to return to their homes 'and a less strenuous life'; single women might be wanting to secure postwar jobs. 'Publicity was released through all channels asking . . . women [to] remain steadily on their jobs throughout the year.' NSS instructed the Supervisors of the Women's Divisions of local Employment and Selective Service offices to try to persuade all women asking for separation notices to stay on their jobs. To the reluctant they should suggest a few weeks' holiday; or offer transfer to a more convenient shift or, finally to 'a part-time job in essential work near their homes'. The efforts of NSS met with the desired results: 'there was no general exodus [of women] from war industries and essential services.'[59]

Then in June 1944 came a new emergency. The invasion of France made necessary a last large-scale special campaign to recruit women for war industry. The Department of Munitions and Supply informed NSS that shell and ammunition plants in Ontario and Quebec were going to have to operate at peak production in order to meet the needs of the Armed Forces on the newly opened European front. An estimated 10,000 additional women workers were required.

The campaign, which used the services of a commercial advertising agency, E.W. Reynolds Company Ltd, of Toronto, was organized by the Public Relations Office of the Department of Labour[60] and 'promoted co-operatively by the plants concerned'[61] with every assistance from National Selective Service. Local E. and S.S. offices near the shell and ammunition plants in Ontario and Quebec, such as Ajax, Pickering, Small Arms (Toronto), Massey-Harris (Weston and Woodstock), Moffats, and Bouchard (Montreal), 'redoubled their efforts to persuade women to accept jobs' in these war industries.[62]

In co-operation with recruiting agents of the shell and ammunition plants of Ontario and Quebec, National Selective Service resumed the transfer of women from Sydney, Edmonton, Saskatoon, Calgary, Regina, and Winnipeg to central Canada. Some 350 Alberta women, many of whom were schoolteachers, were persuaded to give up their summer vacations and take jobs at Ajax and Pickering, on the agreement they would be back in Alberta for school opening, 2 October.[63]

In addition to the wartime recruitment of women into industries and services, there was also recruitment of women into agriculture 'to fill some of the gaps in farm man power with female labour'.[64] In all provinces farmers' wives and daughters took over farm work in the absence of male relatives and farm workers who had left the land to join the Armed Forces or work in industry. In two provinces, however, special programs were organized to recruit farm labour on the basis of the Dominion-Provincial Farm Labour Agreement, entered into by Ontario in 1941 and by British Columbia in 1943. The Ontario Farm Service Force divided female farm-labour volunteers into three brigades: 1) the Farmerette Brigade for sixteen-year-old and older female students and teachers during their summer holidays; 2) the Women's Land Brigade for housewives and business and professional women on a day-to-day basis; and 3) the Farm Girls' Brigade, especially for farm women up to twenty-six years of age to lend a hand where and when necessary. The work was hard, usually nine to ten hours per day, and the wage rate low, 25 cents per hour. In 1943, '12,793 girls in addition to a considerable number of teachers' were enrolled in the Farmerette Brigade; approximately 4,200 women in the Women's Land Brigade; and about 1,000 in the Farm Girls' Brigade. After its creation, National Selective Service helped to publicize the appeals for Farm Labour Service.[65]

II

As is perhaps already apparent, Labour Department officials, National Selective Service officers, and Farm Service officials, charged with the recruitment of women into the labour force during World War II, viewed their task as service to the war effort. Accordingly, in their recruitment campaigns, they appealed first and foremost to patriotic duty and the necessity to make sacrifices for the nation in wartime.

This keynote was struck in the National Selective Service General Report on the Employment of Women of 1 November 1943. Next to determining the size of the existing labour reserve of women, the NSS's main task was 'to outline to all Canadian women the part they would be expected to play in the anticipated expansion of all war demands'.[66] It was the job of NSS to convince women 'that it was their duty to go to work' and to persuade women 'that work in war industries offered the most direct contribution which could be made to the prosecution of the war, apart from enlistment in the Armed Forces'.[67] The overalls and bandana of the woman war worker 'became a symbol of services'.[68] The 'vigorous publicity campaigns' of the Ontario Farm Labour Services laid 'considerable stress on patriotic service'.[69]

'There must be no let up in the supply of vital arms and equipment— no let up in food production—no let up in essential services' stated the letter sent by the Director of National Selective Service and Mrs Eaton to the Local Councils of Women enlisting their help for the fall 1943 campaigns to recruit women workers. The letter went on to make the following two suggestions:

> Arrange for an inspirational address in which the prestige and importance of any work essential to the war or to the home front is stressed, as well as a tribute to women now so employed.
> Stress the need of women for the armed services but point out essential employment as an opportunity for women not of military age to serve with equal effect.[70]

The NSS Circular of 18 August 1943 sent to all E. and S.S. offices, outlining the Campaign for Part-time Women Workers in hospitals, laundries, drycleaning establishments, restaurants, and hotels, opened with this ringing declaration: 'During the last three years in the spirit of service and adventure women have entered the war plants and the war factories.' The same circular ended on this hortatory note: 'The health and wellbeing of the Canadian people must be maintained while they participate in the March to Victory. The civilian essential services in the community are of vital importance.'[71] A 29 September 1943 meeting of NSS officials with personnel officers of various Peterborough firms agreed that the city's October 1943 drive for women workers had to 'supply the patriotic appeal to young people to come forward for part time storework'.[72]

'Roll Up Your Sleeves for VICTORY!' was the headline of the December 1943 design, prepared by the Information Division of the Dominion Department of Labour, for a full-page newspaper advertisement to recruit women for war industry. In the centre of the ad was a drawing of a woman, shoulders squared, rolling up her sleeves. Behind her, a montage of photographs of women working, one a taxi-driver, another a nurse, and the rest on production lines in war industry. The caption read:

> The women of Canada are doing a magnificent job . . . in the Munitions factories, making the tools of war, in the nursing services . . . in the women's active service units, on the land, and in many other essential industries. But the tempo of war is increasing, and will continue to increase until Victory is won. We need more and more women to take full or part time war work . . . Even if you can only spare an hour or two a day, you will be making an important contribution to the war effort.[73]

In May 1944, when it was feared that women were wearying of war work and might be leaving the labour force altogether or changing to jobs promising more of a future, Mrs Eaton drafted a letter to be circulated among the local E. and S.S. offices. It contained this directive:

> Try to change the attitude of mind represented in the words: 'I want to get a post-war job' or 'I am tired of making munitions.' We need to remind ourselves and others that the war has yet to be won and completed. It is too early to express other ideas. Service and sacrifice are yet the key words.[74]

Finally, in the massive campaign of July 1944 to recruit women to meet the sudden critical demands for labour in the Ontario shell and ammunition plants, the slogan was: 'Women! Back Them Up—To Bring Them Back.' This slogan appeared on advertisments placed in the major newspapers, reprints of which were delivered to thousands of homes in the neighbourhoods of the war plants, and on posters attached to the front and back of streetcars, displayed in store windows, outside movie theatres, and in theatre lobbies. The press release prepared by E.W. Reynolds & Company Ltd, Toronto, for Moffats Ltd, manufacturer of ammunition boxes for the 25-pounder gun, quoted this appeal from one of the company's officers:

> Only by the single and married women coming forward and offering their help will it be possible to get these ammunition boxes out in the required time and thus keep faith with the boys at the front.[75]

The call to patriotism, to sacrifice for the nation at war, to loyalty and service to the troops fighting overseas—that appeal dominated the recruitment of women workers from beginning to end.

At the same time Labour Department and NSS officials were not unaware that many women were in the labour force, or applying to enter it, out of economic rather than patriotic motives. In a 5 March 1943, memorandum to Mrs Eaton, Renée Morin of the Montreal NSS reported on her recent conversation with a personnel officer for the Dominion Rubber Company. Mlle Isabelle Groleau, who interviewed prospective workers for the plant, had stated that:

> Most of the married women with children who seek work in our factory are in need of money to help their family. Those who are working merely to buy luxuries have not the courage to stick to their work. Very few have in mind a contribution to the war effort.[76]

On 30 March 1943 the Women's Division of the Toronto E. and S.S. office ran a questionnaire on married female applicants over thirty-five years of age. In communicating the results to Mrs Eaton, Mr B.G. Sullivan, Ontario Regional Superintendent for NSS singled out the responses to Question No. 5 as 'the most interesting highlight'. The fifth question had asked: 'What is the prime object in your securing employment?' Of the women questioned, 9 per cent had indicated patriotic motives, 59 per cent 'desire to supplement family income', and 32 per cent 'personal needs'.[77] An 11 May 1943 memorandum brought to Mrs Eaton's attention that that month's issue of *Relations* carried an article by Germaine Bernier entitled 'Encore ce travail féminin'. It gave results from a 1942 investigation carried out by the Quebec Jocistes into the working experience of 700 of its gainfully employed female members. Amog the results was the statistic that 31.4 per cent of the women had given 'as their reason for working economic necessity—no other source of revenue'.[78] Although the representativeness of these studies is not established, it would appear that some discrepancy existed between the official emphasis on patriotism and the actual motivation of women workers.

Not all reports, however, to NSS on the motivation of female workers cast doubt on their patriotism. On 30 April 1943, the Director of Technical Education of Nova Scotia sent this account of the motivation of women workers in a munitions plant in his province: 'Their general attitude showed that they felt their effort was directly connected with war activity and based on a keen feeling of patriotism'.[79]

Actually advertisements for women workers recognized economic incentives, as at least of secondary importance. The caption on the December 1943 'Roll Up Your Sleeves for Victory' ad ended: 'By taking up some form of war work you will not only be showing your patriotism in a practical way, but you will also be adding to the family income.'[80] Above or below the slogan 'Back Them Up—To Bring Them Back' the advertisements in the July 1944 drive for women workers spoke of: 'Opportunity for Women in Modern War Plant . . . [for] doing an important job and at the same time making that extra money which you can use to plan your future.'[81] Nonetheless, patriotic service to the war effort was the main motif of campaigns to recruit women workers.

III

From the start of attempts to bring increasing numbers of women into the labour force, it was realized that accommodation would have to be made to the particular needs of working women, especially married women and women with young children. By and large, however, such accommodation was made in the context of the war emergency and regarded as having rationale only for the war's duration.

One accommodation, in the way of an economic incentive to married women, was the July 1942 amendment to the Income War Tax Act with respect to the income of married couples. Under the tax law in force up to July 1942, a married woman, whose husband also received an income, could earn up to but not more than $750 without her husband's losing the right to claim the full married-status exemption. The 1942 revision of the tax law as it affected married couples granted the husband whose wife was working the full married-status exemption 'regardless of how large his wife's earned income might be'.[82] The 'special concession' was regarded as a 'wartime provision'.[83] This amendment to the Income Tax Act was designed 'to keep married women from quitting employment'[84] and to 'encourage the entry of married women into gainful employment'.[85] Up through 1946, the husband paid no tax on any income up to $1,200 regardless of his wife's earnings. The wife paid tax on income exceeding $660.[86]

Then in September 1946, by Act of Parliament, the Income Tax Regulations were again amended with respect to married couples where the wife was working. The amendment to the Income Tax Act, effective 1 January 1947, repealed the wartime provision which granted the husband whose wife was working the full married-status exemption regardless of the size of her income. As of 1 January 1947, once a wife's income exceeded $250, the married-status exemption of her husband would be reduced by the amount of her income in excess of $250. Many married working women figured that the tax change would have a serious effect of their actual contribution to the family income after taxes. Many employers of married women feared the change would have a drastic effect of their skilled female labour force. Representations poured in to the federal Departments of Labour, Finance, and National Revenue. Officials in these Departments tended to think that the negative reaction was based on ignorance and misunderstanding. However, the Minister of Finance felt that an official statement by himself or 'a widespread programme of publicity might attract unnecessary attention to the subject.'[87] Instead he prepared an explanatory memorandum which pointed out that the changes in the Income Tax Act also included an increase in the full married-status exemption from $1,200 to $1,500 and a general reduction in tax rates. Further, it sought to clarify the actual effect of the tax changes on the combined income of husband and wife; a table demonstrating the effect on combined incomes at various levels was appended.[88] This memorandum was then sent to all Regional and Local Offices of the National Employment Service, with extra copies for distribution.[89]

Nonetheless, representations kept pouring in. The married female employee continued to calculate the effect her earnings in excess of $250 would have on reducing her husband's exemption and thus her actual contribution to the household income. Fruitpacking and canning firms complained that many of their most skilled female packers and sorters were quitting work once their earnings reached $250.[90] Textile firms complained that they were losing many of their most experienced power sewing machine operators, silk-cutters, winders, and carders.[91] Similarly business offices reported losing experienced stenographer-typists;[92] hospitals, married nurses;[93] school boards, married women teachers;[94] department stores, married female employees.[95] The Deputy Minister of Labour, Arthur Mac-Namara, denied that, 'in so far as the Labour Department [was] concerned', the intention of the tax change had been 'to drive married women out of employment', and certainly not 'out of nursing, teaching and any other line of employment where their services are so seriously needed'.[96] But as the spokesman for the Primary Textiles Institute of Toronto reasoned: since the 1942 revision, which conceded full married-status exemption to the husband irrespective of the wife's earnings, had been designed to draw married women into industry, its cancellation would have the opposite effect.[97] Nonetheless the official position of the federal government, as expressed in the memorandum prepared by the Minister of Finance in November 1946, was that the tax concession granted married working women in 1942 had been a war measure, 'justified only by the extreme state of emergency which then existed'.[98]

Perhaps the major accommodation to the particular needs of working women arranged during the war was the establishment of child-care facilities in Ontario and Quebec on the basis of the Dominion-Provincial Wartime Day Nurseries Agreement. But this accommodation too was made in the context of the war emergency and viewed to have a *raison d'être* only so long as the war emergency lasted.

In 1942, when it was realized that the Canadian economy would have to draw more extensively on women's labour than heretofore, it was also recognized that there might well be need to provide child-care facilities for working mothers. The Prime Minister's address to Parliament on 24 March 1942, explaining the necessity and plan for National Selective Service and outlining a ten-point program for bringing women into industry, had contained as its sixth point: 'The provision of nurseries and other means of caring for children'.[99]

Although the Women's Division of National Selective Service did not begin in 1942 to campaign for the employment of mothers, women with pre-school and school-age children had been in the labour force before the outbreak of war and had continued to enter it as production quickened.[100] As Mrs Eaton wrote in June 1942, 'without any urging on the part of Government, married women, usually on the basis of need of further income, have already gone into industry and are doing a good job.'[101] The mothers among these married women had had, of necessity, to make their own arrangements for the care of their children, with the help of relatives and neighbours.[102] 'But these unorganized arrangements'—here was government's and industry's material interest in day care in a time of labour shortage—'do not always work out so well and break down for days and weeks at a time.'[103] The number of existing private nurseries, run by churches and other charitable organizations, was inadequate. In 1942, in Ontario, especially in the greater Toronto area, public pressure for government provision of nurseries and after-school supervision of children increased. There was mounting concern over 'latch-key' children and the possible connection between working mothers and the rising rate of juvenile delinquency.[104] Asked to supply the Minister of Labour with ideas on child care for his upcoming meeting with Ontario and Quebec Ministers, Mrs Eaton referred to the rising concern for the welfare of children of working mothers as the main argument why government now had to step in:

> Consistent and well-founded reports lead one to believe that children are neglected—thus becoming unhappy, undernourished and delinquent. Such a situation must be accepted as a responsibility of government in these days, when it has become a burden too heavy for private agencies.[105]

Before the end of April 1942, the Director of NSS was in contact with the Government of Ontario concerning 'the setting-up of nurseries in co-operation with the provinces as needed'.[106] In May Mrs Eaton conferred with the Minister and Deputy Minister of Public Welfare in Ontario and with the Minister of Health and Social Welfare in Quebec.[107] Experts in the field of child care, such as George F. Davidson, Executive Director of the Canadian Welfare Council,[108] and Dr. W.E. Blatz, Director of the Institute of Child Study of the University of Toronto,[109] were consulted.

On the basis of these preliminary talks and consultations, a draft for a Dominion-Provincial agreement on child care was drawn up. On 16 June 1942, the federal Minister of Labour called a conference in Ottawa to discuss the proposed agreements with the Minister and Deputy Minister of Public Welfare of Ontario and the Minister of Health and Social Welfare of Quebec.

After clause-by-clause consideration of the draft agreement, it was approved.[110]

Then on 20 July 1942, through Order-in-Council PC 6242, the Minister of Labour, on behalf of the Dominion Government, was authorized to enter into agreements with any of the provinces to establish facilities for the care of children of mothers employed in war industries, in accordance with the draft agreement. A copy of the agreement and a letter inviting participation in the plan were sent to every province. The two most industrialized provinces signed that summer: Ontario on 29 July 1942; Quebec on 3 August.[111] The only other province to sign was Alberta, in September 1943.[112] But the Alberta Provincial Advisory Committee on Day Nurseries, set up to assess the need in that province, voted on 26 April 1944 that there was none,[113] despite considerable pressure from groups in Edmonton and Calgary for the establishment of day nurseries in those two cities.[114]

In the meantime, the administrative machinery was set up to implement the Dominion-Provincial Wartime Day Nurseries Agreement in the only two provinces which would make use of it, Ontario and Quebec. The Agreement itself provided that capital and operating costs were to be shared on a 50–50 basis between the Dominion and the province.[115] The initiative for establishing particular day nurseries rested with the provinces.[116] Ontario and Quebec each created a Provincial Advisory Committee on Day Nurseries, and local committees in urban centres, to determine where need existed. Provincial directors were appointed, and in Toronto, a director for the city.[117] At the federal level, Miss Margaret Grier was appointed in October 1942 Assistant Associate Director of NSS under Mrs Eaton, to have charge of the administration of the Dominion-Provincial Wartime Day Nurseries Agreement.[118] Local Employment and Selective Service Offices assumed the responsibility of interviewing applicants on need for child care, determining the eligibility of their children for day care, making referrals to operating child-care facilities, and keeping records of the numbers of applicants and referrals.[119]

The Dominion-Provincial child-care program was slow in getting off the ground. In fact, the first day nursery to open, at 95 Bellevue Avenue in Toronto on 6 October 1942, was initially a provincial project and was only later brought under the terms of the Dominion-Provincial Agreement.[120] A second day nursery in Ontario, actually the first under the Agreement, was opened in Brantford on 4 January 1943. February brought the opening of Ontario's third, fourth, and fifth day-nursery units in St Catharines, Oshawa, and Toronto; March, the sixth and seventh, also in Toronto.[121] To accommodate the increasing numbers of married women entering the labour force in the spring and summer of 1943, six more day nurseries were opened in Ontario between April and September.[122]

In addition to day-nursery care for children two to six years old, the Dominion-Provincial Wartime Day Nurseries Agreement also provided for:

foster-home care for children under two; and school supervision, outside school hours, for children between the ages of six and sixteen. The latter included supervision of school-age children during vacation periods as well as provision of hot noon meal and supervision before and after school during the regular school term. A special sub-category of the school-care program was developed, called Junior Day Care, which provided for the kindergarten child after the conclusion of the regular school session.[123]

By September 1945, there were twenty-eight day nurseries in operation in Ontario, 19 in Toronto, 3 in Hamilton, 2 in Brantford, and one each in St Catharines, Oshawa, Galt, and Sarnia, accommodating altogether approximately 900 children. In addition there were 44 school units, 39 of which were located in the Greater Toronto area; of the remaining five, Hamilton had two, and Windsor, Oshawa, and Sarnia each had one. The Wartime Day Care Program for School Children accommodated approximately 2,500 children.[124]

The child-care program was even slower getting off the ground in Quebec, and never developed there to the extent it did in Ontario. The first wartime day nursery in Quebec was opened on 1 March 1943 in Montreal. In 1943, five others were opened in Montreal, four on 1 May, and one on 1 October. As the latter closed on 31 December 1944, there were in September 1945 only five wartime day nurseries operating in Quebec, all in Montreal, and accommodating on the average only between 115 and 120 children.[125] There was no development in Quebec of the day-care program for school-age children.[126]

From the outset, the federal agencies involved viewed the establishment of child-care facilities for working mothers as a war emergency measure designed 'to secure the labour of women with young children' for 'war industry'.[127] In M
942, the Minister of Labour gave his approval to six principles which Labour Department and NSS officials, among them Mrs Eaton, had drawn up with reference to government aid for day nurseries. The sixth stated: 'That any such service should be strictly limited to provision for the children of women employees in war industries.'[128]

The actual Dominion-Provincial Day Nurseries agreement departed somewhat from the original intention to confine eligibility to pre-school children of mothers working in war industries.[129] The preamble clearly specified that the child-care facilities which the Dominion and provincial Governments would undertake to establish were intended for the young children of mothers working in war industries. But Clause 10 provided for the care of school-age children outside of school hours. And Clause 11 provided that up to 25 per cent of the capacity of any project could be opened to the children of working mothers employed in other than war-industrial occupations. Furthermore Clause 1 (d) gave a broad definition to 'war industries'.[130] In practice, however, only firms with an A or B labour priority rating were considered to be 'war industries'.[131] The federal government's position was that child care was 'normally the *responsibility* of the Province, in cooperation with its local groups'. Only the additional burden on the provinces 'caused by war conditions' justified the federal government's assuming a share of that responsibility. Therefore the program should 'relate *chiefly* to war industries'.[132]

In the course of 1943 strong objection was voiced to Clause 11 of the Day Nurseries Agreement, which set a quota of 25 per cent of a project's capacity for children of mothers not employed in essential industry. Most vociferous in their criticism were the Toronto Welfare Council and the Toronto Board of Education. C.H.R. Fuller, Business Administrator and Secretary-Treasurer of the Toronto Board of Education, made representation in a letter to Humphrey Mitchell, Minister of Labour, on 5 February 1943; R. Alan Sampson, Chairman of the Toronto Board of Education, wrote directly to Prime Minister Mackenzie King on 6 May 1943.[133] They asked that a most liberal interpretation be put on the definition of 'war work' as 'anything essential to the community at war' so that the children of all working mothers would be eligible. Application of the quota, they pointed out, put the school principals administering the school day-care program in the difficult position of having to refuse some children while accepting others. Limiting eligibility primarily to the children of mothers employed in firms with an A or B labour priority rating discriminated against mothers working in other firms. This was unfair, they argued, as all working mothers were contributing indirectly, if not directly, to the war effort. In many cases, the woman doing the 'non-essential' job was freeing a man or another woman for work in war industry. The children of all working mothers should be made eligible for the government-funded day-care services.

On 10 June 1943 Mrs Eaton chaired a meeting in Ottawa of NSS, Labour Department, and Quebec and Ontario officials to assess the Wartime Day Nurseries program a year after the draft agreement was first approved. First on the agenda was criticism of Clause 11. The meeting agreed that 'the ratio of 75 and 25 for mothers employed in war industry' should continue and that the interpretation of 'war industry' as firms with A or B labour priority rating should still hold. Labour Minister Humphrey Mitchell gave his approval to this decision.[134] 'If the Agreement is extended to include the children of all mothers who work, there is a further case that could be made out quite logically for the children of the woman who is ill or who is doing essential voluntary work,' Mrs Eaton had written to NSS Director Arthur MacNamara on 19 May 1943.[135]

But objections to Clause 11 persisted. Newspaper editorials took up the criticism:

> We are now into the fifth year of war. For at least three years the pressure has been heavy to get more women into industry. In the last year Government

agencies have urged women with children to fill the gaps so that the nation's economy could continue to function.

If mothers are to follow the advice of those agencies, then surely this division of children of working mothers into two classes is beyond common reason.[136]

So editorialized *The Globe and Mail* on 28 October 1943. 'It is a sort of crusade taken up by the papers, churches and women's organizations to get the children admitted regardless of any other consideration,' Mrs Eaton observed in a memorandum to NSS Director MacNamara on 1 December 1943.[137]

Under this mounting pressure the Ontario Minister of Public Welfare 'gave way publicly' in November 1943 and NSS officials began to reassess their stand.[138] Mary Eadie, Women's Division Supervisor of the Toronto local office, was asked to estimate the consequences in increased enrolments if the Day Nurseries Agreement were extended 'to cover the children of all employed mothers'.[139] By 1 December 1943, Mrs Eaton had concluded that: 'It is now apparent the 25 percent [Clause] does not altogether suffice'.[140] Negotiations with Ontario and Quebec to revise Clause 11 were begun. Finally by order-in-council on 6 April 1944, for Ontario, and on 18 May 1944 for Quebec, authority was granted to amend Clause 11 to extend the Wartime Day Nurseries Agreement to include children of all working mothers. Nonetheless the amendment stipulated that 'children of mothers working in war industry shall have priority at all times in admission' to any child-care facility established under the Agreement.[141]

That the Dominion-Provincial Day Nurseries Agreement was construed as a war-time emergency measure, however, is underscored by the relative swiftness of the program's discontinuance. On 23 August 1945 J.A. Paquette, Quebec's Minister of Health and Social Welfare, wrote to Labour Minister Humphrey Mitchell in Ottawa that he, Paquette, planned to close the day nurseries in Quebec on the first of October of that year. His argument read:

Article 23 of the Agreement, signed by the Federal Government and the Province of Quebec on the 3rd of August 1942, provides that the Agreement shall continue in force for the duration of the war.

Now that the war is over, I would be inclined to close these Day Nurseries immediately, but I feel that a month's notice to the parents would only be fair.[142]

Paquette's letter was referred to W.S. Boyd of National Registration. In Boyd's opinion, it could be contended on two grounds that Canada was still legally in a state of war: 1) a final peace treaty had not been signed and delivered; 2) neither His Majesty nor the Governor in Council had issued a proclamation that the war had ended (as Section 2 of the War Measures Act required).[143] Nonetheless on 1 September 1945 Humphrey Mitchell wrote to Paquette that he accepted Paquette's judgement and that Paquette, 'as chief administrator of the scheme', had the right to close the nurseries when he chose and 'upon such notice as is deemed advisable'.[144]

The closing of the Dominion-Provincial Wartime Day Nurseries in Quebec was set for 15 October 1945. In mid-September day-nursery staffs were sent a letter from the Deputy Minister of Health and Social Welfare that their services would no longer be required after 15 October.[145]

Margaret Grier, NSS Assistant Associate Director in charge of Day Nurseries, received appeals to keep open the five Montreal day nurseries from the Montreal Council of Social Agencies,[146] from officials of the Welfare Federation and the Federation of Catholic Charities, and from the Montreal Association of Protestant Women Teachers.[147] As early as 20 April 1945 mothers of children attending the first wartime day nursery established in Montreal had drawn up a letter urging the government to continue Day Nurseries after the close of the war.[148] In October, these same mothers gathered signatures for the Province of Quebec, protesting against their closing.[149] In both letter and petition, a major reason that mothers gave for requesting the continuance of the program was that the mothers who placed their children in the nurseries were compelled to work, because of death of husband, separation from husband, war injuries or sickness of the husband, or inadequate wages earned by the husband. Further the mothers argued that, compelled as they were to work outside the home, they could do so, thanks to the day nurseries, relieved of anxiety over the well-being of their children. In fact, their children were receiving better care in the day nurseries than they would have under any other circumstances: better health care, training, and diet. The day nurseries were actually helping the mothers keep their families together.

These appeals were of no avail. The Quebec Government's position remained firm: The Dominion-Provincial Day Nurseries program had been a war measure; the war was now over, and therefore the Agreement was no longer in force.

The situation was quite different in Ontario where many more wartime child-care facilities had been established and there was correspondingly greater pressure to keep them open after the close of the war. It was the federal government which took the initiative in opening discussions to end the Dominion-Provincial Wartime Day Nurseries Agreement in Ontario.

On 11 September 1945 Fraudena Eaton reported to Arthur MacNamara that applications for day care in Toronto had 'increased rather than diminished during the past two months'. She was having Miss Grier investigate 'this seemingly unreasonable situation'.[150] On 31 October 1945 the Wartime Day Nursery and School Day Care Centre in Oshawa were closed owing to decreasing enrolment.[151] But elsewhere in Ontario, especially in the Greater Toronto area, where 19 day nurseries and 39 day-care centres for school children were in operation, reports from local employment offices showed in November 'a continuing high demand for day care of children of working mothers'.[152]

Mrs Eaton's response to this information was to give a gentle nudge to Mr MacNamara with the suggestion that:

> The time will come fairly shortly when the employment of mothers will not necessarily be related to production for war purposes or for highly essential civilian goods. It brings the matter of providing day care for children back to the point where it may be reasonably looked upon as a responsibility of the Provincial Government.[153]

Mr MacNamara took the hint and instructed Mrs Eaton to draft a letter to the appropriate Minister in Ontario inviting discussion of a date to be fixed for terminating the Agreement on Day Care of Children.[154] In his letter of 22 November 1945 to the Deputy Minister of Public Welfare in Ontario, Mr MacNamara wrote:

> You understand that the financing of these and similar plans by the Dominion Government has been done as a war measure and our Treasury Board naturally takes the position 'now that the war is over why do you need money?'[155]

He suggested as a date of termination of the Agreement 'the end of Dominion Government fiscal year or soon thereafter'.[156]

Investigations indicated that of the mothers using the child-care facilities in Toronto, 50 per cent were working full-time out of economic need: some were widows without, or with very small, pensions; others were deserted and unmarried mothers; still others had husbands who were unemployed or ill or earning inadequate wages. In 5 per cent of the cases husbands had been 'apprehended because of conduct'. Thirty per cent of the mothers were working full-time to help husbands pay off debts, purchase homes, or get re-established in business. Fifteen per cent were working part-time to supplement family incomes.[157]

Hope was growing in Ontario that, after the Dominion Government pulled out of the Wartime Day Nurseries Agreement, the Provincial Government might pick up the whole tab. Margaret Grier informed Arthur MacNamara on 15 February 1946 that Deputy Minister of Public Welfare B.W. Heise himself had told her 'he now had every hope that the Province would continue to maintain the day nurseries.'[158] In early February deputations went to Toronto City Hall, the Board of Education, and the provincial Departments of Education and Public Welfare to press for the continuation of day care in Ontario. At an early February meeting 300 interested persons in Toronto founded a National Nursery School Association 'with the object of pressing for nursery school care in all Provinces and the maintenance of the standards set up in the Wartime Day Nurseries'.[159]

Meanwhile four months had elapsed since the Dominion Government first approached the Ontario Government proposing a date for the termination of federal participation in the Day Nursery project. On 18 February 1946 Mrs Eaton wrote to Mr MacNamara suggesting that, as Ontario might continue the operation of day nurseries, provincial authorities were in no hurry to see federal funds cut off. Now, however, the time for the cutoff had come, she argued, as:

> No suggestion could be made now or even four months ago, that the employ-ment of those women whose children are in day care centres is essential for work of national importance.[160]

This argument was taken up by federal Labour Minister Humphrey Mitchell in his letter of 26 February 1946 to W.A. Goodfellow, Ontario Minister of Public Welfare. 'As you know,' Mr Mitchell wrote, 'the Dominion share in financing this project was undertaken as *a war measure* for the reason that women whose children were in day care centres were engaged in *work of national importance.*' Implying that the gainfully employed mothers of Ontario were no longer engaged in work of national importance, the federal Minister of Labour communicated his Department's decision that it was necessary to set 1 April as the termination date for Dominion participation.[161]

Now a three-way passing of the buck began. W.A. Goodfellow's response to Humphrey Mitchell came in a letter of 7 March 1946. He informed the federal minister that enabling legislation was before the Ontario legislature to make day nurseries a municipal concern, with the provincial government sharing costs. The termination of federal contributions coming on 1 April, together with the planned transfer of day nurseries from the Department of Public Welfare to municipalities, threatened to disrupt the running of existing child-care facilities to the end of the school year. In view of that, the Ontario minister requested the federal minister to consider extension of the Domin-ion-Provincial Wartime Day Nurseries Agreement to 30 June 1946.[162]

Humphrey Mitchell approved the extension to 30 June of the Dominion-Provincial Wartime Day Nurseries Agreement, although this information got lost in the shuffle of intradepartmental memoranda and was not communi-cated to the Ontario Minister of Public Welfare until 2 April 1946.[163] In the interim, first and second reading had been given in the Ontario Legislature to Bill 124 authorizing municipalities to 'provide for the establishment of day nurseries for the care and feeding of young children' and the provincial government to contribute one-half of the costs of their operation and main-tenance. The bill passed third reading on 4 April and was enacted into law as the Day Nurseries Act, 1946.[164] Each municipality in which one or more daytime nurseries had been operating was notified of the new legislation. The day-care program for school-aged children was to be dropped altogether.

On 17 May 1946 the Ontario Minister of Public Welfare wrote the federal Minister of Labour with a new request. Some of the municipalities had indicated that, as their budgets for 1946 had already been passed, they had no budgetary provision enabling them to assume 50 per cent of the costs of keeping day nurseries in operation for the remaining six months of 1946. Therefore, W.A. Goodfellow was submitting for Humphrey Mitchell's consideration the following proposition:

> For those municipalities which indicate a desire to have the [day nursery] programme continued and which are prepared to assume the administrative responsibilities from July 1, would you consider continuing the 50 per cent net cost of the operation until December 31, 1946?[165]

On the same day Mrs G.D. Kirkpatrick, Chairman of the Board of Directors of the Welfare Council of Greater Toronto, forwarded to Humphrey Mitchell the Board's resolution not only that the Dominion Government continue to contribute 50 per cent of the funding for Ontario's day nurseries through 31 December 1946, but also that the provincial and Dominion Governments continue their support of the day care for school-age children.[166] A second letter from Mrs Kirkpatrick to Humphrey Mitchell on 29 May 1946 reiterated the concern of the Toronto Welfare Council's Board of Directors that the day-care program for school-age children not be eliminated.[167] Toronto, the city in which most of Ontario's wartime nurseries and day-care centres for school children were located, was one of the municipalities whose 1946 budget made no provision for assuming even the day-nursery costs.

On 21 May 1946 Humphrey Mitchell wrote to Brooke Claxton, Minister of National Health and Welfare. According to Mitchell's assessment of the situation, the current pressure on the federal government was the result of 'the Ontario Government's endeavouring to arrange for municipalities to pay the fifty per cent heretofore paid by the Dominion Government and the municipalities are objecting'.[168]

Claxton responded on 7 June. He and his Deputy Minister could 'see no reason why the Dominion Government should continue in peace-time to share in the costs of a program, the interest in which is apparently centred almost entirely within one province, and indeed largely within one large city in that province.' Claxton had learned from his deputy that Hamilton had agreed to absorb the municipal share of the day-nursery costs in its 1946 budget. In Claxton's opinion, if Hamilton could do that, 'even after the municipal tax rate has been struck and the budget set for the year', certainly other cities, such as Toronto and London, should have been able to do likewise.[169]

On 12 June 1946 Humphrey Mitchell communicated to W.A. Goodfellow the Dominion Government's decision not to grant Ontario a further extension.[170] On 30 June 1946 the Dominion-Provincial Wartime Day Nurseries Agreement with Ontario came to an end. The day-care program for school children ended in Ontario on that date. By the end of November 1946, nine out of the 28 day nurseries were closed.[171] To what extent the remaining 21 survived will require further research.

IV

The postwar abrogation of government-supported day nurseries in Quebec and day care for school children in Ontario, the postwar reduction of government support to day nurseries in Ontario, as well as the postwar cancellation of the tax concessions to employed married women, were all in keeping with the official attitudes towards working women which prevailed during the war itself. As labour shortages developed in 1942, women were regarded as a large labour reserve that Canadian industry could draw on in the war emergency. But women's place was in the home, and so initial recruitment was directed at young unmarried women and then married women without children. To meet increased labour shortages in 1943, recruitment had to dip more deeply into the female labour reserve, down to women with home responsibilities, even to mothers of young children. In deference to 'majority opinion' which tended 'to favour mothers remaining in the home, rather than working, where at all possible', NSS and Labour Department officials appealed to the fact of abnormal times, of war conditions, to justify their having to encourage mothers with young children 'to accept industrial employment, as an aid to our national effort'.[172] Even after the establishment of child-care facilities in Ontario and Quebec, the federal Department of Labour insisted that its policy was 'to put emphasis on the single or married women without children accepting employment in the first instance'.[173] As only war service justified a mother's leaving home for the public work place, the Dominion-Provincial Wartime Day Nurseries Agreement was intended to provide day care primarily for the children of mothers working in war industries. According to Mrs Eaton in April 1946, the Women's Division of NSS had 'found that women with children were unwisely deciding to look for employment', and had therefore in October 1943 advised the Counselling Service of local Employment and Selective Service offices 'to hold back from employment those who would seem to be neglecting their home and family'.[174]

In so far as there was opposition to the employment of women in industry, as there strongly was from certain quarters in Quebec,[175] the Women's Division of National Selective Service did not respond with arguments of women's equal right to work, but instead invoked the necessity of sacrifice for the nation at war and stressed the temporary nature of that sacrifice. In so far as women accepted jobs previously held only by men, they were generally regarded as replacing men temporarily. The large-scale part-time employment of women was obviously a temporary arrangement. The very increase in numbers of women in the labour force, from approximately 638,000 in 1939 to an estimated 1,077,000 by 1 October 1944,[176] was regarded as a temporary phenomenon. Therefore, it is not surprising that, faced with problems of women's unemployment and economic dislocation in the postwar period, the Women's Division of National Selective Service sought solutions in the return of married women to the home and the channelling of young unmarried women into those occupations in which women's services had been long accepted and were greatly needed: domestic service, nursing, and teaching.

Suggestions for Further Reading

Barry Broadfoot, *Six War Years 1939–1945: Memories of Canadians at Home and Abroad* (Toronto, 1974).

J.L. Granatstein, *Canada's War: The Politics of the Mackenzie King Government, 1939–1945* (Toronto, 1975).

C.P. Stacey, *Arms, Men and Governments: The War Policies of Canada, 1939–1945* (Ottawa, 1970).

Notes

[1]Barry Broadfoot, *Six War Years 1939–1945: Memories of Canadians at Home and Abroad* (Toronto, 1974), 353. Work is beginning to be done on the relation of women's wartime employment to the long-term trends in women's participation in the labour force. See Hugh and Pat Armstrong, 'The Segregated Participation of Women in the Canadian Labour Force, 1941–1971', *The Canadian Review of Sociology and Anthropology*, 12, 4 (Part 1), November 1975, 370–84; Paul Phillips, 'Women in the Manitoba Labour Market: A Study of the Changing Economic Role (or "plus ca change, plus la même")', Paper given at the Western Canadian Studies Conference, University of Calgary, 27–8 February 1976; and, for the First World War, Ceta Ramkhalawansingh, 'Women during the Great War', in *Women at Work: Ontario 1850–1930* (Toronto, 1974) 261–307.

[2]Betty Friedan, *The Feminine Mystique* (New York, 1963). For the impact of *The Feminine Mystique* on Canadian society, see the *Report of the Royal Commission on The Status of Women in Canada* (Ottaawa, 1970), 2.

[3]Chapter on 'Employment of Women and Day-Care of Children' (completed sometime before 24 August 1950), in the 'History of the Wartime Activities of the Department of Labour', Part 1, 5–6, Public Archives of Canada (PAC), Records of Unemployment Insurance Commission, RG 35, Series 7, vol. 20, file 10. Hereafter cited as 'Wartime History of Employment of Women . . .' or 'Wartime History of . . . Day-Care of Children.'

[4]'The Development of the National Selective Service (Civilian) Organization in World War II to December 31, 1945', n.d., 7, PAC, RG 35, Series 7, vol. 19, file 2; 'History of the National Employment Service 1939–1945', n.d., 5, PAC, RG 35, Series 7, vol. 19, file 3.

[5]'Wartime History of Employment of Women . . .', 6.

[6]PAC, RG 27, vol. 605, file no. 6–24–1, vol. 1.

[7]Emphasis mine. 'Wartime History of Employment of Women . . .', 15.

[8]'History of the National Employment Service 1939–1945', 6.

[9]Government Notice, 8 September 1942, Registration of Women, Order, Department of Labour/National Selective Service, PAC, Records of the Department of Labour, RG 27, vol. 605, file no. 6–24–1, vol. 1. By Order-in-Council PC 1955 (13 March 1942), every employer subject to the Unemployment Insurance Act (7

August 1940) was required to register all persons in his employ on forms provided by the Unemployment Insurance Commission. 'History of the National Employment Service 1939–1945', 6.

[10]Registration was extended for those who had not been able to register during the prescribed period.

[11]From the creation of National Selective Service in March 1942, the Minister of Labour and the Director of National Selective Service had found it necessary to draw upon the personnel and premises of the local offices of the National Employment Service of the Unemployment Insurance Commission for implementation of National Selective Service policies. By the terms of Order-in-Council PC 7994, dated 4 September 1942, the intimate association between the Unemployment Insurance Commission and National Selective Service was regularized for the duration of the war. The personnel and premises of the local Employment and Claims Offices of UIC were placed at the disposal of the Minister of Labour for administration and enforcement of National Selective Service Regulations; an Employment Service and Unemployment Insurance Branch of the Department of Labour was created with an Unemployment Insurance Commissioner at its Head (and in December 1942 this Director of Employment Service and Unemployment Insurance, Allan M. Mitchell, was put in charge of the Labour Supply Division of National Selective Service); local Employment and Claims Offices became Employment and Selective Service Offices and their managers became National Selective Service Officers. To handle the increased workload, the original 97 local offices of the National Employment Service had increased to 226 local Employment and Selective Service Offices by 1 November 1943. With respect to women's employment, separate Women's Divisions were set up within local Employment and Selective Service Offices in all larger urban centres. The supervisors of those Women's Divisions of local E. & S.S. offices were, in all but two or three instances, women, and their staff female. A Women's Division supervisor was responsible in the first instance to her local Employment and Selective Service office manager, but frequently in direct communication with Mrs Eaton, Associate Director of NSS (Women's Division), and the staff of her Ottawa office. See 'History of the National Employment Service 1939–1945', 5–15; 'The Development of the NSS (Civilian) Organization in WWII', 11. Also the General Report on National Selective Service—Employment of Women, 1 November 1943, PAC, RG 27, vol. 605, file no. 6–24–1, vol. 2; and 'Wartime History of Employment of Women . . . ', 13.

[12]'Wartime History of Women . . .', 16.

[13]'Listing of Women Starts September 14, Says Mrs Eaton', *The Globe and Mail*, 21 August 1942, 12; 'Mrs Rex Eaton Announces Registration of Canadian Women', PAC, RG 27, vol. 705, file no. 6–24–1, vol. 1.

[14]*Ibid.*

[15]A. Chapman, 'Female Labour Supply Situation', 15 December 1942, PAC, RG 27, vol. 605, file no. 6–24–1, vol. 1.

[16]*Ibid.*

[17]'Wartime History of Employment of Women . . .', 19.

[18]General Report on National Selective Service—Employment of Women, 1 November 1943.

[19]A. Chapman, 'Female Labour Supply Situation', 15 December 1942.

[20]General Report on National Selective Service—Employment of Women, 1 November 1943.

[21]'Wartime History of Employment of Women . . .', 8.

[22]General Report on NSS—Employment of Women, 1 November 1943.

[23]A. Chapman's phraseology.

[24]Embodied in Order-in-Council PC 7595, 26 August 1942, effective 1 September 1942 (*The Canada Gazette*, Vol. LXXVI, No. 94, 28 August 1942, 1–4); and consolidated and extended by Order-in-Council PC 246, 19 January 1943. 'The Development of the NSS (Civilian) Organization in WW II', 8–9, 12; 'History of the National Employment Service 1939–1945', 9–12, 18–19.

[25]'The Development of the NSS (Civilian) Organization in WW II', 12.

[26]'History of the National Employment Service 1939–1945', 10.

[27]Order-in-Council PC 9011, passed on 1 October 1942, put into effect 20 October 1942, and known as the 'Labour Exit Permit Order'. 'History of the National Employment Service 1939–1945', 16.

[28]*Ibid.*, 12.

[29]Letter of 18 May 1943, from Mary Eadie, Supervisor, Women's Division, E. & S.S. Office, Toronto, to Mrs Norman C. Stephens, President, Local Council of Women, Toronto. PAC, RG 27, vol. 605, file No. 6–24–1, vol. 1.

[30]General Report on NSS—Employment of Women, 1 November 1943.

[31]'Wartime History of Employment of Women, . . .', Appendix, Part 1. On 12 May 1943, in NSS Circular no. 234, Allan M. Mitchell, Director of Employment Service and Unemployment Insurance, clarified the definition of part-time subsidiary work. Henceforward, employment was not to be 'regarded as part-time subsidiary employment unless [it was] in addition to a regular full-time occupation or, unless, in the case of a person who [was not in] full-time regular employment, it [was] outside normal working hours', defined as between 8:00 a.m. and 6:00 p.m. 'In the case of housewives, employment [would be] regarded as part-time subsidiary employment if it [did] not exceed twenty-four hours in any week' inside or outside normal working hours.

[32]'Wartime History of Employment of Women . . .', 20.

[33]Memorandum of 7 May 1943, from Mary Eadie, Supervisor, Women's Division, Toronto, to Mr B.G. Sullivan, Ontario NSS Regional Superintendent, PAC, RG 27, vol. 605, file no. 6–24–1, vol. 1.

[34]'Wartime History of Employment of Women . . . ', 20.

[35]Report on Recruitment of Part-Time Workers—Toronto, by Mrs Rex Eaton to the National Selective Service Advisory Board, 28 July 1943. PAC, RG 27, vol. 605, file no. 6–24–1, vol. 1.

[36]Letter of 22 May 1943, from Mary Eadie to Mrs Rex Eaton. PAC, RG 27, vol. 605, file no. 6–24–1, vol. 1.

[37]The National Council of Women of Canada is a federation of women's organizations, organized nationally, provincially, and locally. For its early history, see Veronica Strong-Boag, *The Parliament of Women: The National Council of Women of Canada, 1893–1929* (Ottawa, 1976).

[38]Letter of 8 September 1943, from Mrs Rex Eaton to Mrs H.L. Stewart of the Local Council of Women, Halifax. PAC, RG 27, vol. 605, file no. 6–24–1, vol. 2.

[39]Report on Recruitment of Part-Time Workers—Toronto, by Mrs Rex Eaton to the National Selective Service Advisory Board, 28 July 1943.

[40]'Wartime History of Employment of Women . . .', 22.

[41]Report on Recruitment of Part-Time Workers—Toronto, by Mrs Rex Eaton to the NSS Advisory Board, 28 July 1943.

[42]NSS Circular No. 270–1, 18 August 1943, Employment of Women—Campaign for Part-time Women Workers. PAC RG 27, vol. 605, file no. 6–24–1, vol. 2.

[43]Draft letter of 31 August 1943, signed by Mr A. MacNamara and Mrs Rex Eaton, to be sent to Local Councils of Women. PAC, RG 27, vol. 605, file no. 6–24–1, vol. 2.

[44]'Wartime History of Employment of Women . . .', 23.

[45]*Ibid.*, 20–1.

[46]Draft Letter of 31 August 1943, signed by Mr A. MacNamara and Mrs Rex Eaton, to be sent to Local Councils of Women.

[47]'Wartime History of Employment of Women . . .', 24.

[48]Mrs Rex Eaton's Report to the National Selective Service Advisory Board on Recruitment of Women for Work in War Industries, 28 July 1943. PAC, RG 27, vol. 605, file no. 6–24–1, vol. 1.

[49]Letter of 16 August 1943 from B.G. Sullivan, Ontario Regional Superintendent, to Mrs Rex Eaton. PAC, RG 27, vol. 605, file no. 6–24–1, vol. 2.

[50]Minutes of 26 July 1943, Toronto, meeting of NSS with local Employers about the Campaign for War Plants. PAC, RG 27, vol. 605, file no. 6–24–1, vol. 1.

[51]Letter of 1 September 1943, from Mrs Rex Eaton to Mr A. MacNamara, with copy to Humphrey Mitchell. PAC, RG 27, vol. 605, file no. 6–24–1, vol. 2.

[52]Memo of 22 September 1943, from Mrs Rex Eaton to Mr. A. MacNamara. PAC, RG 27, vol. 605, file no. 6–24–1, vol. 2.

[53]Letter of 13 October 1943, from Mrs Rex Eaton to Mme Florence F. Martel, NSS Montreal. PAC, RG 27, vol. 605, file no. 6–24–1, vol. 2.

[54]'Wartime History of Employment of Women . . .', 23.

[55]Minutes of Employers' Committee Meeting held on 2 November 1943, in Mr Léonard Préfontaine's office, re Recruiting Campaign for Women War Workers. PAC, RG 27, vol. 1508, file no. 40–5–1.

[56]Letter of 2 December 1943, from V.C. Phelan, Director of Information, Information Division, Department of Labour to Mr MacNamara. PAC, RG 27, vol. 615, file no. 17–5–11, vol. 1.

[57]'Wartime History of Employment of Women . . .', 25.

[58]Memo of 8 May 1944, from Mrs Rex Eaton to Mr A. MacNamara. PAC, RG 27, vol. 605, file no. 6–24–1, vol. 3.

[59]'Wartime History of Employment of Women . . .', 25.

[60]Letter of 8 August 1944, from Gordon Anderson, Public Relations Officer, Department of Labour, to Mr Arthur MacNamara, Deputy Minister, Department of Labour. PAC, RG 27, vol. 615, file no. 17–5–11, vol. 1.

[61]'Wartime History of Employment of Women . . .', 26.

[62]*Ibid.*

[63]Memo of 25 July 1944, from Mrs Kate Lyons, Supervisor of Women's Work, Edmonton, to Mrs Rex Eaton. PAC, RG 27, vol. 605, file no. 6–24–1, vol. 3.

[64]NSS Report on 'Wartime Employment of Women in Canadian Agriculture', 17 April 1944. PAC, RG 27, vol. 985, file no. 7.

[65]*Ibid.*

[66]General Report on NSS—Employment of Women, 1 November 1943.

[67]'Wartime History of Employment of Women . . .', 8.

[68]'Comments re Wartime Programme', 5, Preface to 'Wartime History of Employment of Women . . .'

[69]NSS Report on 'Wartime Employment of Women in Canadian Agriculture', 17 April 1944.

[70]Draft letter of 31 August 1943, signed by Mr. A. MacNamara and Mrs Rex Eaton, to be sent to Local Councils of Women.

[71]NSS Circular no. 270–1, 18 August 1943, Employment of Women—Campaign for Part-Time Women Workers.

[72]Minutes of Meeting at NSS Offices, Peterborough, 29 September 1943. PAC, RG 27, vol. 605, file no. 6–24–1, vol. 2.

[73]December 1943 Design or Full-Page Newspaper Ad. to Recruit Women for War Industry. PAC, RG 27, vol. 615, file no. 17–5–11, vol. 1.

[74]Memo of 9 May 1944, from Mrs Rex Eaton to Mr A. MacNamara, with Suggested Draft Circular re Tightening of NSS Regulations for Women. PAC, RG 27, vol. 605, file no. 6–24–1, vol. 3.

[75]Moffats 'Help Wanted' Campaign Breaking 20 July 1944. PAC, RG 27, vol. 615, file no. 17–5–11, vol. 1.

[76]Memo of 5 March 1943, from Renée Morin, NSS Montreal, to Mrs Rex Eaton. PAC, RG 27, vol. 605, file no. 6–24–1, vol. 1.

[77]Letter of 8 April 1943, from B.G. Sullivan, Ontario Regional Superintendent, NSS, to Mrs Rex Eaton. PAC, RG 27, vol. 605, file no. 6–24–1, vol. 1. Unfortunately Sullivan's report of the questionnaire results does not give the number of women questioned.

[78]Memo of 11 May 1943, from Percy A. Robert, Montreal, to Mrs Eaton and Mr Goulet, PAC, RG 27, vol. 605, file no. 6–24–1, vol. 1.

[79]Memo of 30 April 1943, from Dr F.H. Sexton, Director of Technical Education, Department of Education, Technical Education Branch, Province of Nova Scotia. PAC, RG 27, vol. 605, file no. 6–24–1, vol. 1.

[80]December 1943 Design for Full-Page Newspaper Ad. to Recruit Women for War Industry.

[81]PAC, RG 27, vol. 615, file no. 17–5–11, vol. 1.

[82]'The Income Tax Change Applying to Married Employees in 1947', n.d. PAC, RG 27, vol. 606, file no. 6–24–11.

[83]Letter of 7 November 1946, from A. MacNamara, Deputy Minister of Labour, to Mr Fraser Elliott, Deputy Minister of National Revenue. PAC, RG 27, vol. 606, file no. 6–24–11.

[84]'Income Tax Change Benefits Employed Married Women/Aims to Keep Wives from Quitting Posts', *The Globe and Mail*, 16 July 1942, 1.

[85]Explanation received from the Minister of Finance, J.L. Ilsley, by Douglas Hallam, Secretary of the Primary Textiles Institute, Toronto, and conveyed in his letter of 4 November 1946 to Humphrey Mitchell, Minister of Labour, and in his letter of 13 November 1946 to A. MacNamara, Deputy Minister of Labour. PAC, RG 27, vol. 606, file no. 6–24–11.

[86]Full-page advertisement 'To the Man and Wife Who are *Both* Working', *London Free Press*, 26 December 1946, promoted through the Employer Relations Division

of the Unemployment Insurance Commission Office, London, Ontario, and sponsored by the London Chamber of Commerce. PAC, RG 27, vol. 606, file no. 6–24–11.

[87]Letter of 27 November 1946, from J.L. Ilsley, Minister of Finance, to Humphrey Mitchell, Minister of Labour. PAC, RG 27, vol. 606, file no. 6–24–11.

[88]'The Income Tax Change Applying to Married Employees in 1947', n.d.

[89]Memo of 30 November 1946, from A. MacNamara, Deputy Minister of Labour, to S.H. McLaren, Acting Chief Executive Officer, Unemployment Insurance Commission. PAC, RG 27, vol. 606, file no. 6–24–11.

[90]Minutes of the 24 January 1947 Meeting of the Vernon Local Employment Committee, a copy of which was sent to officials in the Department of Labour and National Revenue. PAC, RG 27, vol. 606, file no. 6–24–11.

[91]J.R. Moodie Company, Hamilton. Information conveyed in memo of 17 April 1947, from Margaret McIrvine, Acting Regional Employment Adviser, UIC, Toronto, to B.G. Sullivan, Ontario Regional Superintendent. PAC, RG 27, vol. 606, file no. 6–24–11.

[92]Memo of 31 December 1946, from George G. Greene, Private Secretary, Department of Labour, to A. MacNamara, Deputy Minister of Labour. PAC, RG 27, vol. 606, file no. 6–24–11.

[93]Memo of 30 January 1947, from W.L. Forrester, Manager, Local Employment Office, Prince George, B.C., to William Horrobin, Pacific Regional Employment Officer. PAC, RG 27, vol. 606, file no. 6–24–11.

[94]School Board of Charlotte County, New Brunswick. Information communicated in a telegram of 7 November 1946, from A.N. McLean, Saint John, New Brunswick, to A. MacNamara, Deputy Minister of Labour. PAC, RG 27, vol. 606, file no. 6–24–11.

[95]T. Eaton Company Ltd, Toronto, reported that 453 married women had left their employ since 1 January 1947. Information in a letter of 26 April 1947, from G.W. Ritchie, Chairman, Ontario Regional Advisory Board (Department of Labour), to A. MacNamara, Deputy Minister of Labour. PAC, RG 27, vol. 606, file no. 6–24–11.

[96]Letter of 12 February 1947, from A. MacNamara to F. Smelts, Chairman, Pacific Regional Advisory Board, Department of Labour. PAC, RG 27, vol. 606, file no. 6–24–11.

[97]Letter of 13 November 1946, to A. MacNamara from Douglas Hallam, Secretary, Primary Textiles Institute, Toronto. PAC, RG 27, vol. 606, file no. 6–24–11.

[98]'The Income Tax Change Applying to Married Employees in 1947', n.d. PAC, RG 27, vol. 606, file no. 6–24–11.

[99]Ten Points Enumerated in the Prime Minister's Speech of 24 March 1942, with a View to Bringing Women into Industry. PAC, RG 27, vol. 605, file no. 6–24–1, vol. 1.

[100]'According to the 1931 Census, there were 128,132 married women, including those divorced or widowed, who were gainfully occupied. Less than half that number were married women living with their husbands. In 1941, the single women who were working outside their own homes numbered about 688,000, and the others, 166,000.' See letter of 23 September 1943, from the Chief, Leg-

islation Branch, Department of Labour, Ottawa, to Miss Marion Royce, Secretary for Young Adult Membership, World's Young Christian Association, Washington, D.C. PAC, RG 27, vol. 610, file no. 6–52–2, vol. 2.

101Memo of 13 June 1942, from Mrs Rex Eaton to Mr George Greene, Private Secretary to the Minister of Labour, Ottawa. PAC, RG 27, vol. 609, file no. 6–52–1, vol. 1.

102Report on Day Care of Children, 1 July 1943. PAC, RG 27, vol. 609, file no. 6–52–1, vol. 1.

103Mrs Eaton's memo of 13 June 1942 to Mr George Greene.

104'Need for Day Nurseries', Editorial, *The Globe and Mail*, 16 July 1942, p. 6.

105Mrs Eaton's memo of 13 June 1942 to Mr George Green.

106Letter of 30 April 1942, from E.M. Little, Director of NSS, to G.S. Tattle, Deputy Minister, Department of Public Welfare, Ontario. PAC, RG 27, vol. 611, file no. 6–52–6–1, vol. 1.

107Letter of 14 May 1942, from Fraudena Eaton to E.M. Little, Director of NSS. PAC, RG 27, vol. 609, file no. 6–52–1, vol. 1.

108Letter of 28 April 1942, from George F. Davidson, Executive Director, The Canadian Welfare Council, to Mr E.M. Little, Director, NSS. PAC, RG 27, vol. 609, file no. 6–52–1, vol. 1.

109Memo of 30 April 1942, to E.M. Little, Director of NSS, and R.F. Thompson, Supervisor of Training, Training Branch, Department of Labour, subject: Conference with Dr W.E. Blatz, Director of the Institute of Child Study of the University of Toronto. PAC, RG 27, vol. 609, file no. 6–52–1, vol. 1.

110Report on 'Day Care of Children', 1 July 1943, no authorship specified. PAC, RG 27, vol. 609, file no. 6–52–1, vol. 1.

111Letter of 17 March 1943, from Miss Margaret Grier, Assistant Associate Director NSS to H.F. Caloren, Assistant Director of Administrative Services, Department of Labour. PAC, RG 27, vol. 609, file no. 6–52–1, vol. 1.

112Memo of 10 November 1943, fom Mrs Rex Eaton to Mr V.C. Phelan, Director of Information, Information Division, Department of Labour. PAC, RG 27, vol. 609, file no. 6–52–1, vol. 1.

113Letter of 27 April 1944, from E.C. (Marjorie) Pardee, NSS Representative on the Alberta Provincial Advisory Committee on Day Nurseries, to Mrs Rex Eaton. PAC, RG 27, vol. 611, file no. 6–52–9.

114PAC, RG 27, vol. 611, file no. 6–52–9.

115Memo of 27 May 1943, from Mrs Rex Eaton, to Mr George Greene, Private Secretary to the Minister of Labour. PAC, RG 27, vol. 609, file no. 6–52–1, vol. 1. Mothers were charged fees under the Agreement. For day-nursery care, mothers in Ontario paid 35¢ per day for the first child, 15¢ for additional children; in Quebec, the fee scale was 35¢ per day for the first child, 20¢ for additional children. Where both parents were working, the fee was 50¢ per child in both provinces. For day care of school children, mothers in Ontario were charged 25¢ per day for the first child, 10¢ for additional children. No school projects were established in Quebec.

116Memo of 8 February 1943, from Mrs Rex Eaton, to Mr. A. MacNamara. PAC, RG 27, vol. 609, file no. 6–52–1, vol. 1.

[117]Letter of 17 March 1943, from Miss Margaret Grier, to H.F. Caloren, Assistant Director of Administrative Services, Department of Labour. PAC, RG 27, vol. 609, file no. 6–52–1, vol. 1.

[118]'Wartime History of . . . Day-Care of Children', 3, PAC, RG 35, Series 7, vol. 20, file 10; Memo of 8 February 1943, from Mrs Rex Eaton, to Mr A. MacNamara. PAC, RG 27, vol. 609, file no. 6–52–1, vol. 1.

[119]Memo of 16 June 1943, from Mrs Eaton to Mr Eric Strangroom in response to request for information on Day Nurseries for the Minister of Labour. PAC, RG 27, vol. 609, file no. 6–52–1, vol. 1; NSS Circular No. 291, 15 October 1943, on Women Workers—Day Care of Children. PAC, RG 27, vol. 610, file no. 6–52–2, vol. 2.

[120]Memo of 4 March 1943, from Mrs Rex Eaton, to Mr A. MacNamara. PAC, RG 27, vol. 610, file no. 6–52–2, vol. 1. The Bellevue Avenue Nursery served not only as a child-care facility but also as a demonstration and training centre.

[121]July 1943 Monthly Summary of Dominion-Provincial Wartime Day Nurseries, Ontario. PAC, RG 27, vol. 611, file no. 6–52–6–1, vol. 1.

[122]September 1943 Monthly Summary of Dominion-Provincial Wartime Day Nurseries, Ontario. PAC, RG 27, vol. 611, file no. 6–52–6–1, vol. 1.

[123]Memo of 10 November 1944, from Mrs Rex Eaton, to Mr V.C. Phelan. PAC, RG 27, vol. 609, file no. 6–52–1, vol. 1.

[124]Survey of the Dominion-Provincial Wartime Day Nursery Program in Ontario submitted on 29 October 1945 to Mr B. Beaumont, Director of Child Welfare, Department of Public Welfare, Ontario, by Miss Dorothy A. Millichamp, Organizing Secretary, Wartime Day Nurseries, Dept of Public Welfare, Ontario. PAC, RG 27, vol. 611, file no. 6–52–6–1, vol. 3.

[125]Report of the Quebec Ministry of Health on the Dominion-Provincial Wartime Day Nurseries, 15 November 1946. PAC, RG 27, vol. 611, file no. 6–52–5–2, vol. 2.

[126]Memo of 7 July 1945, from Margaret Grier, to Miss Norris. PAC, RG 27, vol. 609, file no. 6–52–1, vol. 2.

[127]Letter of 30 April 1942, from E.M. Little, Director of NSS, to G.S. Tattle, Deputy Minister, Department of Public Welfare, Ontario. PAC, RG 27, vol. 611, file no. 6–52–6–1, vol. 1.

[128]Memo of 22 May 1942, on Proposals for Day Nurseries for Mothers Working in War Industry, for file in Deputy Minister's Office, Department of Labour. PAC, RG 27, vol. 609, file no. 6–52–1, vol. 1.

[129]Memo of 13 June 1942, from Mrs Rex Eaton, to Mr E.M. Little, Director, NSS. PAC, RG 27, vol. 609, file no. 6–52–1, vol. 1.

[130]'Wartime History of . . . Day-Care of Children', Appendix, Part 2. ' "War industry" means any industry or concern engaged in the manufacture, assembly, processing, transportation or handling of arms, ammunition, implements of war, naval, military or air stores, or any articles deemed capable of being converted thereto, or made useful in the production thereof intended for the use of His Majesty's naval, military or air forces or for the use of the forces of any of His Majesty's allies in the present war, including supplies, materials, equipment, ships, aircraft, automotive vehicles, goods, stores and articles or commodities of every kind which, in the

opinion of the Minister (of Labour), would be essential for the needs of the Government of Canada, of the aforesaid forces or of the community in war and anything which in the opinion of the Minister, is or is likely to be necessary for or in connection with the production, storage or supply of any such articles aforesaid.'

[131]NSS Circular No. 291, 15 October 1943, on Women Workers—Day-Care of Children.

[132]Report on 'Day-Care of Children', 1 July 1943.

[133]PAC, RG 27, vol. 610, file no. 6–52–2, vol. 1.

[134]Minutes of the 10 June 1943 Conference on the Day-Care of Children, Confederation Building, Ottawa, PAC, RG 27, vol. 609, file no. 6–52–1, vol. 1.

[135]Memo of 19 May 1943, from Mrs Eaton to Mr A. MacNamara. PAC, RG 27, vol. 610, file no. 6–52–2, vol. 1; vol. 1508, file no. 40–5–6.

[136]'An Inequitable Division', Editorial, *The Globe and Mail*, 28 October 1943, 6.

[137]Memo of 1 December 1943, from Mrs Rex Eaton, to Mr A. MacNamara. PAC, RG 27, vol. 610, file no. 6–52–2, vol. 3.

[138]*Ibid.*

[139]Memo of 22 November 1943, from Mrs Rex Eaton, to Mr A. MacNamara. PAC, RG 27, vol. 1508, file no. 40–5–6.

[140]Memo of 1 December 1943, from Mrs Rex Eaton, to Mr A. MacNamara.

[141]Order-in-Council PC 2503, 6 April 1944; and Order-in-Council PC 3733, 18 May 1944, PAC, RG 27, vol. 610, file no. 6–52–2, vols. 4–5.

[142]PAC, RG 27, vol. 609, file no. 6–52–1, vol. 2.

[143]Memo of 30 August 1945, from W.S. Boyd, National Registration, Department of Labour, Ottawa, to Mrs Rex Eaton. PAC, RG 27, vol. 609, file no. 6–52–1, vol. 2.

[144]PAC, RG 27, vol. 609, file no. 6–52–1, vol. 2.

[145]*Ibid.*

[146]Letter of 20 September 1945, from Miss Gwyneth Howell, Assistant Executive Director, Montreal Council of Social Agencies, to Miss Margaret Grier. PAC, RG 27, vol. 611, file no. 6–52–5–2, vol. 2.

[147]*Ibid.*, letter of 3 October 1945, from Renée Morin, NSS Welfare Officer, to Miss M. Grier.

[148]PAC, RG 27, vol. 609, file no. 6–52–1, vol. 2.

[149]See above note 147.

[150]Memo of 11 September 1945, from Mrs Rex Eaton to Mr Arthur MacNamara. PAC RG 27, vol. 609, file no. 6–52–1, vol. 2.

[151]*Ibid.*, letter of 22 October 1945, from B.W. Heise, Deputy Minister, Department of Public Welfare, Ontario, to Mrs Rex Eaton; letter of 29 October 1945, from A. MacNamara to Mr B.W. Heise.

[152]*Ibid.*, memo of 8 November 1945, from Mrs Rex Eaton to Mr Arthur MacNamara.

[153]*Ibid.*.

[154]*Ibid.*, memo of 9 November 1945, from A. MacNamara to Mrs Rex Eaton.

[155]*Ibid.*, letter of 22 November 1945, from A. MacNamara to Mr B.W. Heise, Deputy Minister, Department of Public Welfare, Ontario.

[156]*Ibid.*

[157]Letter of 17 December 1945, from Mary Eadie, Supervisor, Women's Division, Unemployment Insurance Commission, Toronto, to Miss Margaret Grier, Assistant

Associate Director, NSS, Ottawa. PAC, RG 27, vol. 611, file no. 6–52–6–1, vol. 3.

[158]Memo of 15 February 1946, from Margaret Grier to Mr Arthur MacNamara. PAC, RG 27, vol. 609, file no. 6–52–1, vol. 2.

[159]*Ibid.*

[160]*Ibid.*, letter of 18 February 1946, from Fraudena Eaton, Vancouver, to Mr A. MacNamara, Deputy Minister of Labour, Ottawa.

[161]*Ibid.*, letter of 26 February 1946, from Humphrey Mitchell, Minister of Labour, Ottawa, to W.A. Goodfellow, Minister of Public Welfare, Province of Ontario, Emphasis mine.

[162]*Ibid.*, letter of 7 March 1946, from W.A. Goodfellow, Minister of Public Welfare, Ontario, to Humphrey Mitchell, Minister of Labour, Ottawa.

[163]*Ibid.*, letter of 2 April 1946, from Humphrey Mitchell to W.A. Goodfellow.

[164]*Ibid.*, Bill No. 124, An Act respecting Day Nurseries, 1946.

[165]Letter of 17 May 1946, from W.A. Goodfellow, Minister of Public Welfare, Ontario, to Humphrey Mitchell, Minister of Labour, Ottawa. PAC, RG 27, vol. 611, file no. 6–52–6–1, vol. 3.

[166]*Ibid.*, letter of 17 May 1946, from Mrs G.D. (Beatrice H.) Kirkpatrick, Chairman, Board of Directors, United Welfare Chest, A Federation of Greater Toronto Social Services, Welfare Council Department, to Humphrey Mitchell.

[167]*Ibid.*, letter of 29 May 1946, from Mrs G.D. (Beatrice H.) Kirkpatrick to Humphrey Mitchell.

[168]*Ibid.*, letter of 21 May 1946, from Humphrey Mitchell, Minister of Labour, Ottawa, to Brooke Claxton, Minister of National Health and Welfare, Ottawa.

[169]*Ibid.*, letter of 7 June 1946, from Brooke Claxton to Humphrey Mitchell.

[170]*Ibid.*, letter of 12 June 1946, from Humphrey Mitchell to W.A. Goodfellow, Minister of Public Welfare, Ontario.

[171]Memo of 28 November 1946, from J.C. McK. to Mr MacNamara. PAC, RG 27, vol. 611, file no. 6–52–6–1, vol. 4.

[172]Report on 'Day Care of Children', 1 July 1943, PAC, RG 27, vol. 609, file no. 6–52–1, vol. 1.

[173]*Ibid.*

[174]Letter of 4 April 1946, from Mrs Rex Eaton, Associate Director, to Miss R.M. Grier, Assistant Associate Director, National Employment Service, Ottawa. PAC, RG 27, vol. 609, file no. 6–52–1, vol. 2.

[175]Marie T. Wadden, 'Newspaper Response to Female War Employment: *The Globe and Mail* and *Le Devoir* May-October 1942', History Honours Dissertation, Memorial University of Newfoundland, May 1976.

[176]'Wartime History of Employment of Women . . .', 80–1. In February 1944, Mrs Eaton estimated the number of women in the labour force at approximately 600,000 in 1939, rising to 1,200,000 by early 1944. Letter of 2 February 1944, from Mrs Rex Eaton, Associate Director NSS, to Mrs J.E.M. Bruce, Convenor, Trades and Professions Committee, Local Council of Women, Victoria, B.C. PAC, RG 27, vol. 605, file no. 6–24–1, vol. 3.

27

Dieppe, 1942

Brian Loring Villa

The names of a number of Great War battles—Ypres, the Somme—became part of the Canadian vocabulary. One World War II battle has stood out for fifty years—Dieppe. Most older Canadians, at least, have some sort of impression of Dieppe, one of the most controversial battles in which Canadian soldiers have ever fought. On 19 August 1942, a large amphibious raiding force crossed the English Channel and landed at the German-occupied port of Dieppe. Most of those 6,000 actually landed were Canadians in Canadian units. Despite support by a flotilla of small naval craft, 800 fighter planes, and 100 bombers, the landing was a complete disaster. In one morning's operation over 3,300 Canadian soldiers and officers were killed, wounded, or captured. The Dieppe raid produced controversy almost from the outset, with critics claiming that it had virtually no chance of success and ought never to have been mounted. For many Canadians, it constituted yet an-

other example of the way in which the British used (or misused) their Canadian allies; charges and countercharges have been hurled back and forth over the decades.

As Brian Villa emphasizes in his study of Canadian involvement in Dieppe, the question of responsibility for Dieppe is considerably more complex than one might at first imagine. Dieppe would never have happened had not the Canadian command in Britain, backed by the Canadian cabinet in Ottawa, been willing to allow Canadian troops to become involved. The really interesting question about Dieppe is why Canada should agree to a venture that had always been dubious and had on at least one occasion been cancelled. Villa finds the answer to this question in the murky area of wartime politics and public opinion. The government of Mackenzie King was far less eager to commit troops to battle than the Canadian public was to hear about its boys 'in action', and Canadian commanders were having difficulty in keeping up morale among their forces without evidence of battle activity. The Dieppe raid suited everyone's agenda, and so it went ahead. How did the Canadian government's commitment to limited war affect its ultimate attitude toward Dieppe?

How was Dieppe the 'perfect campaign' for Canadian forces in 1942? Why was North Africa an unacceptable theatre of war from the Canadian perspective? To what extent was Dieppe the logical consequence of the 1942 conscription referendum?

This article first appeared, titled 'How Canada Became Involved', in Brian Loring Villa: *Unauthorized Action: Mountbatten and the Dieppe Raid* (Toronto, 1989), 212–31.

The willingness of the Canadian commanders to undertake Dieppe made all the difference to Mountbatten and Hughes-Hallett in launching the raid. If the Canadian commander, General Andrew McNaughton, had not cooperated, it would probably not have taken place because no British commander would have been likely to hazard such a raid after the July cancellation and in the face of Montgomery's firm opposition to remounting. Mountbatten seemed to concede as much, saying '. . . they [the Canadians] paved an example of courage, and everything they possibly could be called upon to do, they did.' In such a generous moment he even said of General Roberts, whom he often criticized very bitterly: 'He did it [the raid] very gallantly.' Hughes-Hallett was even more effusive, saying after the war that '. . . the thing to remember was that they [the Canadians] did the operation and that's more than can be said for some of the crack formations which had been selected for earlier operations. The great thing was that the Canadians were not only brave but they were bold as well. They were prepared to chance their arm and it was that that made the Dieppe operation possible.' The justness of these remarks is scarely diminished by the fact that, in the brief period after *Rutter* had been cancelled, and Roberts thought it was honourable to question his original assignment, Hughes-Hallett bulldozed the doubtful Canadian commander, tacitly aided by McNaughton and Mountbatten. But it may also be noted that Canadian participation also served as a protective screen for Combined Operations Headquarters because whatever happened no British official was likely to raise much objection for fear of disturbing sensitive relations within the Empire.[1]

How did Canadians come to be involved and serve the purposes of the very determined Chief of Combined Operations and his no-less-determined Naval Adviser? The Canadian presence at Dieppe, far from being accidental, was the predictable outgrowth of Canadian ambivalence towards the military, as exemplified in the war policies of the Prime Minister, William Lyon Mackenzie King. So much has been written about his fear of stirring animosities between English- and French-speaking communities over the issue of foreign military service that little needs to be added here. Similarly, much has been written about the expedients he devised to give Canada the appearance of a vigorous war effort while avoiding combat casualties. What does need recalling is that King had placed at the head of the Canadian forces in Britain General McNaughton, who was committed to avoiding engagements until Canada could take a significant role in the final defeat against Germany. For the single Canadian division that had begun their training at Aldershot in January 1940 a largely garrison role was acceptable to McNaughton, even though the Canadian public, or at least its anglophone component, was growing increasingly restless. But King, with McNaughton's help, had the situation well in hand until the Fall of France, when their policy of a carefully measured war effort began to disintegrate. The growing feeling that Germany might really win the war made it all the harder to convince Canadians that garrison duty was enough. The Canadian high command was losing credibility. Even the still-neutral Americans seemed to be making as good an effort in terms of material support. The cumulative effect of these factors had great impact in shaping Canadian resolve to attempt the Dieppe raid.

The German blitzkrieg attack on the Low Countries and France in May 1940 shocked public opinion in Canada as much, perhaps more, than in any other allied nation. The leaders of the Opposition marched into Mackenzie King's office to inform him that the country was demanding a vigorous prosecution of the war. King, whose ear for public opinion was as sharp as ever, already knew this, and in Cabinet later that afternoon he raised no objection to going on more of a war footing with the enactment of a National Resources Mobilization Act, so long as everyone understood that there would be no conscription for overseas service. But in the coming weeks King found it increasingly difficult to contain the pressure for a more vigorous Canadian war effort. It certainly was not possible to maintain the charade of a decision he made in January, when to steal a march on the Opposition he had announced the eventual formation of a second division for overseas service, a measure that King probably never intended to carry out. With France collapsing he recognized that the division would really have to be raised. The energetic new Chief of the General Staff, General H.D.G. Crerar, had no intention of letting the Cabinet rest at that point, and by July he had pushed it into agreeing to a long-term expansion of the overseas force to five or even six divisions. He even got them to agree to raising a second and third division in the near term.[2]

Though King felt that this would strip Canadian home defences thin, he had boxed himself in, having committed Canada to Britain's defence without regret. He had noted earlier in his diary, on 24 May 1940, that 'we owe [Britain] such freedom as we have. It is right we should strike with her the last blow for the preservation of freedom.' But this noble sentiment did not mean that King would lose sight of his fundamental policy, which was to keep as many troops as he could out of combat for as long as this was possible. Even at the height of the crisis caused by the Fall of France, he never proposed to reverse the prohibition against conscription for overseas service. Moreover, he knew that after the British evacuation of Dunkirk in June 1940, sending troops to England would result in immediate fighting only if Hitler attempted to invade Britain. As the chances of this did not seem to be that great, and an attack on the Continent was out of the question for the foreseeable future, King was really opting for sending more men to garrison duty. Indeed, in late 1941 a combat role was still thought to be relatively remote when a Canadian Defence Staff study noted: 'In any event it would appear that if and when the Canadian Corps is disembarked on the Continent of Europe, the conditions which will then be found to exist will not be such as to demand prolonged major operations.' This hope was given life when Britain adopted a strategy of attrition, combined with strategic bombing, that lessened the importance of ground forces. It was under these circumstances that King, allowing his emotions to carry him away, agreed to the raising of the two additional divisions.[3]

But once so large a Canadian contingent had been created, it tended to assume a life of its own. General McNaughton, the commander of this force, excelled in managing public relations and getting maximum publicity for his troops. He and his friends had already demonstrated a marked ability for feeding stories to the press. As King's defence minister, J.L. Ralston, somewhat caustically noted, McNaughton was one who 'understands fully the value of publicity and has been widely publicized to the Canadian people'. Indeed, McNaughton made the cover not only of Canadian weeklies but also of *Life, Time,* and *Newsweek,* all of which lavished praise on 'McNaughton of the Canadians'.[4]

The *New York Times* was particularly generous in its coverage. On 9 February 1940, in an article datelined Ottawa, it spoke of the departure of the first Canadian division for Britain as 'only the beginning of a steady stream of manpower with which, as fast as Great Britain is able to accept and utilize it, Canada will reinforce her initial effort on the fighting front.' Two months later, in April, photographers were present when General Ironside, British Chief of the Imperial Staff, and the French commander, General Gamelin, visited McNaughton's headquarters. The caption in the *New York Times* suggested that three equals were planning offensive strategy. In July the press prominently carried news of McNaughton's promotion to Lieutenant-General and the suggestion that he would command a mixed British-Canadian corps. By June 1941 reports were circulating that McNaughton was going to replace Churchill as Minister of Defence in the British War Cabinet, a bit of impudence quickly denied by 10 Downing Street. Then in September came McNaughton's famous press conference when he boldly proclaimed that there would have to be an invasion of the Continent and suggested that

Canadian forces would be at the centre of this effort. As he put it, the Canadian Corps was 'a dagger pointed at the heart of Berlin, don't make any mistake about that.'[5]

Then in March 1942, in the midst of the strategic debate over the Second Front, McNaughton returned to Canada under klieg lights to consult with Mackenzie King. The press was even more intrigued by his wide detour to Washington, where he was reported to have had an hour-long strategy conference with President Roosevelt. Two weeks later the General was back in England deprecating Britain's war effort and seemingly joining the American campaign for an immediate Second Front. 'You don't win wars by sitting in defensive positions, no matter how important they are,' he declared, ignoring the fact that this was what Canadian troops had been doing since the start of the war. Canadians wanted to get into the business of a cross-Channel attack as soon as possible. 'We don't want a blow struck casually. We want a continuing effect on the enemy.' By June 1942 McNaughton began to realize that he was putting great pressure on the Canadian Government, creating expectations that would be hard to satisfy. He closed a speech of 24 June on a more restrained note, saying: 'And so the Army of Canada in Britain bides its time and waits with confidence and steady purpose knowing that for a while yet, patience is required.' From time to time McNaughton told the press to tone down its overly enthusiastic coverage, warning that it could lead only to disillusionment in Canada and to widespread disappointment. But of course the press, faced with the option of printing McNaughton's 'Go get 'em' releases and his and King's 'But not now', chose the former. The public wanted to hear what could be done, not what couldn't, and as always the press tended to give satisfaction.[6]

Nor could McNaughton afford to sound too cautious. After all, the conduct of war is thought to depend much on a peculiar psychological state: the willingness to risk lives for goals that in peacetime seem rather vague and intangible. War has ever been associated with its commanders' maintaining a confident, aggressive state of mind, for without such an attitude troops lose their fighting edge and commanders lose their credibility. McNaughton and his colleagues were indulging in 'pep talks', and it seems hard to question their basic validity without also questioning the whole art of command.

Not surprisingly, McNaughton's subordinate commanders entered the fray with enthusiasm. When General Victor Odlum arrived with the 2nd Canadian Division in 1940, the London *Evening News* headed a story with the line, 'Canadian want a smack at the Jerries', and quoted Odlum as saying, 'Germany has asked for it and she is going to get it.' *The Times* gave similar attention to his announcement that 'We are ready.' In May 1942 General Crerar, now in England as Commander of the First Corps, spoke with even more zeal. In an interview with 'Wes' Gallagher of the Associated Press he evoked memories of the Great War and the glorious Canadian victory at Vimy, and said that 'the Canadian Corps would raid enemy positions on the other side [of the Channel] as actively and effectively as it raided the German trenches in the last war.' This was brave talk indeed. In fact Odlum did not do a very good job of training the 2nd Division and it would not have been picked to do Dieppe had it not been for the fact that his successor, Roberts, brought it up to the highest standards.[7]

But Odlum's rhetoric was popular and was echoed at home. On 3 May 1942 Ralston took to the air waves to remind Canadians that the third job of the defence establishment was to 'train for new operations of every conceivable type; to be ready to strike anywhere and anyhow and any time. That army is under the command of Lieutenant-General McNaughton and to use his own words, it is a dagger pointed at the heart of Berlin.'[8]

Of course King tried to counteract the press campaign of his zealous commanders. As early as September 1940 a tour of Canadian defence installations had been arranged for the allied press, to whom the weakness of the Canadian forces and their lack of training and equipment was stressed. Hanson Baldwin, the respected military correspondent of the *New York Times*, wrote a four-column report titled 'War Effort's Peak in Canada Year Off', with such subtitles as 'Tour shows difficulties', 'Bottlenecks in skilled labour' and 'Dominion expected to become major factor in conflict only late in 1941'. Reflecting the briefing he had received, Baldwin reported that 'air-training [the Commonwealth Air Training Plan] is probably the only Canadian effort that may have a major influence upon the outcome of the war.' Undoubtedly many in Canada saw Baldwin's article as an arrant piece of American arrogance.[9]

King eventually succumbed to the relentless pressure to build an image of an aggressive, militant Canada. Though he knew that if he visited the troops in England he would be confronted by the much-resented fact of their inactivity and would be forced to make militant speeches, he alone of all the war leaders could not avoid such a trip. And of course what he feared would happen did. In September, King told his London audience that 'You all know how eager our Canadian soldiers are for action against the enemy. I cannot make too clear that the policy of the Canadian government is to have our troops serve in those theatres where, viewing the war as a whole it is believed their services will count the most.' This statement was designed to convey subtly to the British that Canada did not want any invitations to go to North Africa and that her troops should be kept in Britain facing the Channel. But as phrased, and more importantly as reported, it suggested that King wanted to be in on the big fighting regardless of the possible casualties. King's slow process of succumbing to the very rhetoric he found so objectionable in his military chiefs was reflected in the speech he made on his return from England: 'Every Canadian heart must have been thrilled by Mr. Churchill's words when he said that our Canadian soldiers stood at the very post where they would be the first to be hurled into a counterstroke against the invader.' No one should have been surprised by such rhetoric. A nation at war cannot easily avoid creating the impression that the first objective is to fight and win, and a government that cannot face that reality perhaps ought not to be at war. King realized this, and came to accept the need for presenting the public with images of Canadians fighting. But doing so meant that, sooner or later, he would exhaust the possibilities of rhetoric and be obliged to deliver the real thing.[10]

By early 1942 many in the Canadian Government were hoping that something more substantial than mere words could be found—though nothing too hazardous. To earn King's approval, any prospective military engagement would have to be so brief an action that it would be unlikely to cause many casualties or compel a recourse to conscription. To satisfy McNaughton it also should be against the principal enemy, Germany. Finally, to satisfy not only McNaughton as commander but also nationalist sentiment, the engagement must be one in which Canadian troops would lead. At all costs the splitting up of the small Canadian force or its dissolution into larger Commonwealth forces must be avoided. In sum, what was required was a combat mission against Germany big enough to convince the public that action was being undertaken, but small enough to be undertaken entirely by Canadians, and safe enough so that King would not have to be confronted with major casualties. Not only was this setting too many conditions on the employment of Canadian troops, but regrettably the idea of contributing to the speediest possible defeat of the enemy seemed to be playing a distinctly secondary role to considerations of image.

The search for the perfect campaign was not easy. In April 1940 McNaughton accepted, without reference to Ottawa, the idea of participating in the British attempt to parry German thrusts towards Norway. This met all of McNaughton's requirements, since it was likely to be a short expedition against German forces. But it soon became too hazardous and was cancelled, with McNaughton receiving a rebuke from Ottawa for having agreed to do it on his own initiative. In June 1940, in the midst of the shock of Dunkirk, approval was given to use Canadian forces in Brittany, though largely in a reserve capacity. They were soon withdrawn. (General Roberts, who was with the Canadian troops, returned, to the amazement of all, with more military equipment than he had arrived with, having collected abandoned British hardware. Obviously this was a very resourceful man.) When the possibility of engagement in France collapsed, the search for a Canadian field of battle began anew.[11]

In August 1941 a Canadian force took part in a bloodless raid on the Norwegian-owned islands in the Spitsbergen archipelago on the convoy route to Murmansk in northern Russia. Then in October 1941 the strangest of all attempts to find employment for Canadian troops was approved: the sending of two battalions to Hong Kong, a decision that probably fitted in with King's strategy of drawing Canadian attention to the Pacific theatre in the hope of keeping forces away from Europe. This gave the Canadian units their first taste of combat, after two years of being at war. Unfortunately the Japanese attack was overwhelming and the episode ended in a humiliating disaster. The quest for employment of the Canadian forces resumed. Thus the Canadian Government was in an embarrassing position by the spring and summer of 1942, for Hanson Baldwin's much-publicized date for a real peak of Canadian military effort in 1941 had come and gone and still Canadians had not seen action in Europe. McNaughton's bold talk made the embarrassment still more acute. If the dagger was pointed at Berlin, it seemed not to have moved an inch in a year.

As early as the summer of 1941 Canadian forces could have found employment in the Mediterranean theatre for the defence of Egypt. The Australians and South Africans were already in North Africa. If the Canadians had joined them, their contribution to the war might have been considerable, for Britain was incapable of any offensive operations until she had secured her lines of communication through the Mediterranean. A Mediterranean victory in 1941, followed by a consolidation in 1942, would have meant that a cross-Channel attack was possible in 1943—with the result that the war might have been shortened by a year at least. But McNaughton feared that his troops would be swallowed up into larger British formations in areas that would never be decisive. Vimy II could not possibly exist in North Africa; it must lie in Europe.

The possibilities for Canadian action in the Mediterranean/Middle East have been much obscured by military historians who suggest that Canadians never refused to undertake operations in the area. This has even been embellished to suggest that British and American planners deliberately hid the North African plan from Canadians to prevent them from joining. McNaughton's biographer has said that 'Though McNaughton would have welcomed fighting his army as such in North Africa, he did not even hear about the operation until September.' Nothing could be more misleading. After his arrival in England, McNaughton made it abundantly clear that he wanted his Canadian troops employed against the principal enemy; North Africa was, and would long continue to be, primarily an Italian theatre. McNaughton had a virtual veto on the employment of Canadian troops and the British, knowing his views, never pressed too hard. But they did ask. In October 1940, when Sir Anthony Eden approached a visiting Canadian minister to inquire whether there might be some possibility of sending Canadian troops to the Middle East, the minister consulted McNaughton and found his opposition had not changed. No Canadian authority ever picked up Eden's suggestion.[12]

Moreover, after the rebuke administered to McNaughton by the Canadian Government in April 1940 for committing troops for use in Norway without approval from Ottawa, the British Government also knew that any approval from McNaughton would have to be cleared in Ottawa. Indeed, a telegram King sent to Ralston on 6 December 1940 (drafted by O.D. Skelton) noted acidly: 'It is pretty certain to be felt that if troops are being sent to the Near East they should be sent from the parts of the Commonwealth which control policy in the Near East or which are more geographically concerned with the Near East. It is one thing for Canada to raise additional forces to assist Britain in the British Isles or in Western Europe, it might become a very different thing to get the support necessary for Canadian forces to be sent to other parts of the world.' A few days later the British Government gingerly explored the ground with Ralston, who visited London in the second half of December 1940. Eden first pointed out that major operations against North Africa might soon be possible and discreetly hinted that Canadian participation would be welcome. Ralston showed no interest. But Churchill, never one to accept a veiled no, raised the question at a subsequent meeting. Ralston's report spoke volumes about Canadian war policy:

> I mentioned that in Canada already there had been newspaper reports already intimating that it was proposed to send Canadians to the Middle East. I had advised the Government that such a proposal had never even been put forward and I intimated that we would assume that employment of our troops, outside of the United Kingdom, be left for our suggestion. His [Churchill's] reply was 'of course'.

Just to make sure that no unwanted invitations were extended, Ralston drafted a summary of their conversation and asked Churchill to confirm its accuracy. He did so, and a formal invitation to send Canadian troops to North Africa was effectively abandoned. Only indirect approaches were then possible.[13]

Nearly a year later, on the occasion of Ralston's trip to London in October 1941, another rather cautious British approach was made. It was preceded by vague hints from the British military planner, General Sir John Kennedy, to McNaughton's principal deputy, General Crerar, about possible help for operations in Spain or North Africa. When Ralston spoke to the British Secretary of State for War, he said the Canadian Government was prepared to consider employment of the Canadian Corps in any military operations the War Office might recommend, which perhaps might have been interpreted as an alteration of the stand he took with Churchill; but Ralston then proceeded to crawfish his way back, stressing that the Canadian Government was not pressing for the active employment of Canadian forces. Though the possibility of using some of them in Spain or Spanish Morocco was mentioned, Ralston did not respond. A few days later he explored the question of using troops in the Middle East with McNaughton, who made clear that he was still opposed to the idea: 'While such a step would be welcomed by the formation in question and undoubtedly would initially be well received by the Canadian public it would not serve to solve the larger issue of [the] general employment of all Canadian forces overseas.'[14]

Given Canadian attitudes, the British Government resigned itself to having the Canadian force as garrison troops. That was surely what King wanted, and until the opportunity for a potentially sensational engagement like Vimy Ridge came by, that was also what McNaughton wanted. It is not even clear that King desired another Vimy, judging from his outburst in May 1941, when the Minister of National Defence for Air suggested in the War Committee that Canada offer a brigade of troops for Egypt. King virtually exploded: 'I said at once that I would not countenance anything of the kind: that it might be my Scotch conscience, or it might be common sense, but I do not feel that any Government has the right to take the lives of any men for spectacular purposes.' Thus a careful examination of the record shows that, though it is technically correct to say that British authorities never made a formal approach to Canadian authorities for deployments in North Africa or the Middle East, it is misleading to suggest that tacit requests were not made, and even more misleading to suggest that Canadian authorities did not refuse them.[15]

This understanding—that unwelcome invitations should not be made— naturally left Canadian generals champing at the bit. As early as May 1941 the Department of Defence had reported to the Government that the 'absence of active participation of Canadians in recent operations is having a frustrating effect on public outlook in Canada'. General Maurice Pope, assigned to the Combined Chiefs of Staff mission in Washington, said it all when he wrote General Kenneth Stuart, Chief of the General Staff, in November 1942: 'I cannot help feeling that the continued inactivity of our forces in the United Kingdom is anything but in the national interest. And unless the intransigent policy in respect to their employment which has hitherto prevailed is modified in some degree, I greatly fear that our position will progressively become less enviable.'[16]

The whole problem was first thrashed out when Ralston visited McNaughton in October 1941. The minutes of their strategy review of 15 October record McNaughton as saying that the best employment of the Canadian Corps for the coming winter was to remain in Great Britain, but that in the spring it might be practicable to take part in operations elsewhere. The Minister asked whether he meant the Corps as a whole or in part. General McNaughton replied 'as a Corps', and to develop a specific theatre of operations. After a March 1942 conference with Mackenzie King, he noted that they were both agreed on keeping Canadian forces pointed against the principal enemy—that is, facing Germany across the Channel—and would brook no diversions to the Middle East. By this time, however, General Stuart was desperate to find some active employment for Canadian troops. In a letter to General Pope, he wrote that the continued prospect of nothing but garrison duty was bound to have a bad effect on the morale of the troops, and asked Pope to keep him posted on any opportunities for their deployment. The soldiers had no difficulty in recognizing who was responsible for their inactivity. When King visited the troops in August 1941 he was loudly booed from the ranks of the assembled formations. Rarely, if ever, had a Prime Minister been so publicly humiliated.[17]

In November 1941 a Gallup poll had showed that 60 per cent of the Canadian public wanted conscription, or in other words a more vigorous prosecution of the war. On 12 November 1941 Senator Arthur Meighen, a former Prime Minister, accepted the leadership of the Conservatives. In doing so he demanded a general policy of compulsory service. 'Our present methods', he asserted, 'are illogical, cruelly unjust, and tragically inefficient. I shall therefore urge with all the power I can bring to bear compulsory service over the whole field of war.' The Canadian Legion, tired of merely organizing welfare and education programs for soldiers overseas, had thrown its heart and soul into a 'Call for Total War', rallying 500 national organizations in its support. In January 1942 the Liberal premier of New Brunswick, J.B. McNair, publicly called for conscription, as did a Toronto committee of 200 that took out ads for conscription. And the Premier of Ontario, Mitchell Hepburn, gave tacit support to Meighen's political intentions. King characteristically tried to steal the march on his potential rivals by going to the electorate to ask for release from his no-conscription pledge in a plebiscite or, as some preferred to call it, a great national referendum. The decision to consult the electorate was announced in the Speech from the Throne on 22 January 1942, which revealed much about the dilemmas of Canadian defence policy. It recognized that without the formality of conscription, Canada's war effort was being denigrated outside the country and undervalued at home. King brought himself to express this attitude in a nation-wide radio address on 7 April:

> This restriction [the bar to conscription] is being represented as a bar to an all out effort on Canada's part. It makes no difference whether conscription for service overseas would add to Canada's total war effort or not, the fact that the government is not free to consider its adoption is made to appear as limiting Canada's war effort. The lack of power to impose such conscription has . . . placed our war effort in a wholly false light before our own citizens and what is worse before our allies.[18]

The polling took place on 27 April 1942. By almost two to one the electorate released the Government from its no-conscription pledge. But the vote also confirmed King's worst fears. In Quebec the *non*'s outweighed the *oui*'s by almost three to one. King, who had never really shown any desire to use conscription or to raise a large standing army, and had only wanted to steal the thunder from his possible rivals, was now more determined than ever to avoid conscription for overseas service—that is, refusing operations in Europe that might use manpower at rates that would necessitate its implementation. As he made clear in his diary, had the vote been on conscription, he would have voted against it himself. When Ralston pressed him to use the results to bring in conscription, King refused categorically, and when Ralston proposed that conscription be at least allowed in the northern hemisphere, King, though tempted, said that he would not consider it under the circumstances because 'I felt that it would concentrate the public mind on our not having an all-out war effort, and it was important that Canada's position should not be put in a false light. The whole purpose of the plebiscite had been to remove that.' But clearly there was a problem. King had posited that if Canada threw itself into war production, trained the pilots of the Commonwealth, sent a garrison force to Britain, and formally accepted the principle of conscription, Canadians would be satisfied and Canada would earn the homage of all Britain's allies. But now he was admitting this had not happened and implicitly recognized that something more must be done for Canadian pride at home and abroad—though, revealingly, he stressed the importance of the latter. The one thing he still would not countenance was placing a sizeable number of Canadian troops under fire.[19]

By June 1942 it was clear that Ralston was wavering in his support of King's policy of restraint. Ralston's Rotary Club speech of 16 June 1942 gives some indication of the tide King was swimming against:

> These troops shout for action. We all shout for action. The time will come for action; and when that time comes you can depend on it that Canadian troops will prove to be a powerful, hard hitting fighting force worthy in every way of the spirit that stormed Vimy Ridge twenty-five years ago.

King was in a dilemma. Any politician who was revealed as holding back the war effort would, in time, be gravely imperilled. King was certainly not going to let the situation deteriorate to a point where the public would echo the booing Canadian troops had given him. Always a realist in politics, King had begun to look for some way to demonstrate more vigorous action—while excluding anything that might require conscription, which he continued to regard as the greatest political danger of all. Thus the question was: how to project the image of more vigorous combat without risking conscription?[20]

As early as the summer of 1941 the Canadian military had been proposing to King that an active effort might focus on raids. They would do much for the image of Canadian military effectiveness, particularly if they could be represented as being daring. In April 1942 the argument made still better sense. Raids would give the lie to those who were saying that the plebiscite had been a phony issue because Canadians were serving nothing more than garrison duty. At the same time, raids offered the prospect of having the maximum possible effect at the lowest possible cost in casualties, since any raid would be relatively brief. For McNaughton, raiding operations would provide action without running the risk of dividing his army or sending it to dead-end theatres just to get battle experience. Indeed, the experience gained from raids on the Continent might earn Canadians a special right when the time finally came to point the dagger at Berlin. It is hard not to see in raiding operations the ideal solution to the problem of trying to get maximum prominence in the war at minimum cost. But approval for raids was not easily obtained. Ottawa was initially cool.

Securing approval had been made more difficult by the Trondheim project of May 1940, when McNaughton had committed 1,300 of his troops for use in Norway before he had asked Ottawa's permission. While the Minister of Defence, Ralston, was prepared to cover McNaughton a bit, saying that the 'Canadian government was consulted about the Norway expedition, and it gave its express approval', he also made clear that no one should assume that approval would be automatic in the future: 'I wish to say, just to clinch that, that the decision as to the employment of troops outside the United Kingdom is a matter for the Canadian government . . . the appropriate Canadian service authority cannot authorize the embarkation of Canadian forces from the United Kingdom without the authority of the Minister of National Defence.'[21]

A few months later, in July, the Cabinet in Ottawa made an attempt to develop a clear policy on military engagements. A key memorandum called the War Committee's attention to the fact that the 'absence of active participation of Canadians in recent operations is having a frustrating effect on public outlook' and asked whether the time had not come to give the Canadian commander blanket authority to conduct raids. The question was buried in a larger debate over the deployment of Canadian forces, so that in July, McNaughton had to ask the visiting Canadian Air Minister, C.G. Power, to raise the question with the Cabinet when he returned to Ottawa. This request in turn got side-tracked when the Spitsbergen project was being developed in July. At that time McNaughton in effect told the Government that he was preparing to go ahead until he received a very explicit veto. King was in fact inclined to give that veto. The minutes of the War Committee note that 'Mr. King said that he, himself, questioned the wisdom of such offensive operations, this year. As it was, the situation was developing favourably, with Russia, in large measure, engaging German energies. Further, the results of failure in operations of the kind would be to encourage our enemies and discourage our friends. The dangers appeared greater than the advantages which might accrue from success.' Only reluctantly did King go along with the majority, after insisting that McNaughton be warned that 'In arriving at decision you will no doubt have regard to question as to whether prospects of success are sufficient to warrant risks involved which include not only personnel but possible encouragement to enemy if results negative or worse.' In other words, McNaughton could commit his troops in this particular circumstance if there was absolutely no risk. When the Canadian raiders landed at Spitsbergen, the Germans were nowhere to be found; the seemingly daring gesture did not cost a single life. King could not have been more pleased. Undoubtedly the experience helped to undermine his initial dislike of raiding opportunities and to pave the way for his reluctant approval of the Dieppe raid.[22]

Ralston's trip to England in October 1941 gave McNaughton a chance to plead for general authorization to conduct raids, somewhat against his better judgement. Just days before his long conference with Ralston, McNaughton had observed that 'excluding the Spitsbergen Expedition all previous expeditions had been cancelled, subsequent to plans being laid, due to changes in the situation, which decision had proved right in each case.' Implicitly, then, he recognized they were not well-conceived operations. Nevertheless, at the end of October 1941 both McNaughton and Crerar lobbied hard with Ralston to get approval. Their representations indicate as clearly as anything could how keenly aware they were of King's desire to avoid anything risky that might produce significant casualties. McNaughton tried to pass the raids off as inconsequential, saying that raiding operations were regarded by the 'U.K. Government as [a] normal extension of [Home Forces] duties' and Crerar spoke of them as an extension of 'ordinary patrol activities' and as 'trivial'. General Kennedy, a key British planner, explained that there were few options, for besides raids there were available only the sort of operations that Canadian authorities had declined in the past. That convinced Ralston, who telegraphed a request for authority from the Cabinet in Ottawa. On his recommendation the War Committee gave McNaughton limited authority to conduct 'minor' raids.[23]

Thereafter senior Canadian military personnel in England threw heart and soul into securing the lead in raiding activities. This was not immediately forthcoming, because there were British units who wanted the opportunity, and perhaps also because London understood that McNaughton's authorization was somewhat circumscribed. This British resistance to giving Canadians the lead in raiding operations prompted a blistering reaction from Crerar. Writing on 5 February 1942 to General Montgomery, then commanding the South East Command (which had primary responsibility for raids in the Channel area), Crerar opened with the accusation that his Canadian troops had been unjustly denied any opportunity for combat. It was, he complained, a static situation not of their choosing. Somewhat ignoring the high-level exchanges that had transpired, Crerar insisted that Canadians had not refused to serve anywhere. In no uncertain terms he told Montgomery:

> This continued lack of active participation in operations provides neither pride nor pleasure to the officers and other ranks of the Canadian Army. . . . As the months go by and opportunities fail to materialize in which the officers and men of my present command can match their skill and courage against the enemy, the more difficult it will be to maintain in them the desired keenness and morale.

Crerar then proceeded to renew the Canadian request to participate in raiding operations:

> I believe that occasions will increasingly present themselves for small raids across the Channel opposite the Army front. I consider that it will be in the general interest if a very high proportion of these prospective raids, if not the total, should be undertaken by detachments from the Canadian Corps.

Thus he put the whole issue on the plane of professional pride, which he thought an officer like Montgomery would respect. Crerar closed his letter by recalling the very good reputation Canadian soldiers had made for themselves in the First World War and expressed confidence that the present generation, every bit as good, were particularly suited for the challenges implicit in aggressive raiding operations.[24]

Montgomery, who was not prepared to go so far as to give the Canadians the lion's share of the raids, replied vaguely that he would try to make available 'some' craft so that the Canadians could gain experience in raiding operations. He closed his letter pleasantly enough, noting Crerar's appeal to professional pride by saying that 'Your men should be quite first class at raiding,' which at least seemed to indicate that Canadians might be given some share of the raids. Crerar—either suspecting that he was getting the polite run-around, or determined to clinch matters—then took his appeal to higher levels. On 6 March he was making his case strongly (which long experience had given him practice in doing, often stridently) in the office of the Chief of the British Imperial staff, General Sir Alan Brooke. Crerar opened the meeting by indicating the 'importance he attached to Canadian participation [in raids] now that the prospects of an invasion during the early summer seemed to recede.' Canadian troops, he complained, had been in the UK—some for over two years—without 'having a chance to meet the enemy', a circumstance he found 'galling'. If this enforced inactivity continued it would have a serious effect on morale within the Canadian Corps.[25]

By blaming Britain for the failure to use Canadian troops, Crerar presented his case in terms of a personal grievance about which, officer to officer, something would have to be done. British authorities were thus faced with the choice of either contesting the accuracy of Crerar's presentation—which, because it would entail discussion of the tacit vetoes given by Canadian authorities, was pregnant with possibilities for recrimination—or accepting his demand. Brooke knew a losing argument when he saw one and offered to arrange a general meeting between the top Canadian officers and Mountbatten's Combined Operations staff to discuss a leading role for Canada in raiding operations. Crerar was pleased with this promise. But as he explained to one of his key staff officers, there must be no slackening; if Canadian troops were to get their chance, it would be necessary to keep up the 'pressure' on British authorities. Crerar was pushing hard down the road that would lead to Dieppe and the ruination of General Roberts' career.

The meeting with Brooke—the culmination of Crerar's campaign, though largely ignored by historians of Dieppe—had much to do with shaping that tragedy, for once Brooke had yielded, Mountbatten could do nothing but yield in turn. He did so most reluctantly, however, placing on record his opposition to giving the Canadians the principal role, which would be contrary to agreements made with the Commander of Home Forces that British Commandos should form the main element. Nevertheless, bowing to superior authority, he said he would find ways to include the Canadians in his next big raid, which turned out to be Dieppe.[26]

Leaving nothing to chance, McNaughton visited Mountbatten several times in April to clinch the accord and to offer British authorities an inducement to carry through: a promise that he would personally urge the Canadian Government to increase landing-craft production in a major way. He was as good as his word. Shortly thereafter he returned to Ottawa to review the position of Canadian troops with Mackenzie King and urge more landing-craft production. McNaughton's diary entry for his meeting with King is brief, indicating that they agreed that Canadian troops would remain concentrated in the 'decisive theatre of the war', which meant that British invitations for Canadian participation in the Middle East should be discouraged, as before, and that the only form of active combat for Canadian troops—in a year when no major cross-Channel attack was expected—would be raids. The General returned to England and again visited Mountbatten's headquarters on 21 April. Mountbatten must have been pleased with the report, for on 30 April the Canadians were officially invited, through Montgomery, to take the leading role in the Dieppe project.[27]

Months of pressuring had at last paid off. But though McNaughton had fought hard for this concession, it was not at all certain that the King government would approve. Ottawa had previously given McNaughton only authorization to conduct raids that he and Ralston had represented as being 'trivial'. McNaughton, aware that Dieppe represented an extraordinary expansion in size and scope, cabled Ottawa explaining that an operation was being planned that 'cannot properly be classed as minor', and requested specific authorization. Though McNaughton had avoided outright prevarication, he made no effort to tell Ralston that what was contemplated was the largest raid in modern history. Knowing how skittish the King government was about employing its troops in combat, he was judiciously reticent.[28]

The whole question was discussed in the Cabinet War Committee on 1 May 1942. King was inclined to refuse McNaughton's request to participate in Dieppe, pointing out that: 'It was essential that no such operations be undertaken without adequate preparations and a full appreciation of all factors involved, including the extent of the Forces available and the opposition that might be anticipated.' He also thought the same warning ought to be given to McNaughton as had been issued at the time of Spitsbergen: that he not commit himself unless he could give assurances of success. In short, the entire responsibility would be his. Only after Ralston erroneously assured the Committee that what was involved was merely on the scale of Spitsbergen, approval for 'a brigade or possibly larger' was given. King's own approval was so reluctant that, as his diary indicates, he continued to ponder the dangers after the Committee meeting: 'We asked McNaughton for more in the way of details as to the character of what was expected. . . . To these matters I must get into retreat and have time for thought . . . [and reflection on the] direction to be taken.'[29]

In reporting to McNaughton, Ralston rather downplayed the request for additional information. McNaughton continued to be guarded, suggesting only that 'the largest project in contemplation at present [Dieppe] might involve up to three brigades which might be all Canadian.' This was more accurate than Ralston's representations but still rather disingenuous, for three brigades were, in effect, a division. McNaughton may also have been counting on civilians' underestimating the size of a brigade. But King did not ask any more questions, and so McNaughton had his authorization. Had Canadian chiefs of staff wanted to ask difficult questions about the projected raid (*Rutter*), which McNaughton reported to them, they had such an opportunity when Mountbatten, after concluding his trip to Washington, flew to Ottawa to meet with them on 11 June. The record of the meeting, from which one infers that Mountbatten did most of the talking, does not even mention a division-size raid, much less *Jubilee*. On Dominion Day 1942 King said publicly that Canadian forces were poised to strike the next blow against Germany. British officials reacted with horror, fearing that he had compromised the Dieppe project. But McNaughton told them to relax, as King probably knew little or nothing about it, which certainly indicates how vaguely the General had briefed his Prime Minister and how few questions Ottawa had asked.[30]

On 7 July 1942 the first Dieppe project, Operation *Rutter*, was aborted —and General Montgomery recommended that the operation be cancelled 'for all time'. In July, under strange circumstances, the project was revived. Mountbatten told McNaughton that the project had approval from the British War Cabinet. McNaughton might have been expected to ask for a copy of the minute for Canadian records; but he never did, nor did he ever receive the least scrap of paper from any British authority indicating that *Jubilee* had been approved, or that he was being made in any way responsible for finding the forces or the commander for it. This was extraordinary from several viewpoints. The first law of military life is that everything concerning command and the execution of a military operation is supposed to be done by orders, from higher to lower command in an unbroken chain, preferably in quintuplicate. The absence of orders to McNaughton is startling, and he could not have failed to notice it. This should have led, and I suspect did lead, McNaughton to wonder whether the operation had in fact been approved. His suspicions would particularly have been aroused because he had been relentless, since the Dieppe project was first initiated, in demanding that everything be done regularly, and that he be kept scrupulously informed in writing of all projects in which the use of Canadian troops was contemplated. For instance, when *Rutter* was first approved by the Chiefs of Staff, McNaughton wrote to Lt-Gen. J.G. des R. Swayne, Chief General Staff Officer of Home Forces, to say:

> I suggest that in the future, [as regards] Combined Operations involving Canadian troops, the outline plan should be placed before me before submission to the Chiefs of Staff Committee and that the Chiefs of Staff Paper should show that in giving their approval they take note of my acceptance: also that I should be included in the distribution list.[31]

That was in May. Now, two months later, he was accepting the questionable revival of the project as *Jubilee*, after General Roberts had made known his complaints, and after Montgomery had recommended against it, without a word on paper about approval or authorization. Whatever one may think of his qualities as a commander, McNaughton had a razor-sharp mind. He could not have failed to realize what the complete and utter absence of any written authorization to Canadian headquarters meant: the operation had not been approved and the normal chain of command was not operating. A document in the files of RCAF Air Vice-Marshal Harold Edwards is virtually conclusive. On 9 August, McNaughton approached Edwards saying that as the responsible head of the Royal Canadian Air Force in Britain there was something that he should know, but that McNaughton feared he would not learn from the normal chain of command (i.e., from Portal). McNaughton was therefore taking it upon himself to inform Edwards privately that several RCAF squadrons would be taking part in *Jubilee*. There was no reason why Portal could not have given Edwards this information (unless he was trying to keep his distance from the operation). Edwards confirmed to McNaughton that his hunch was correct: he had not been informed. This exchange could not have left McNaughton in any doubt about the fact that *Jubilee* did not have official sanction—or status—in the highest command levels. By going to Edwards, McNaughton was in effect abetting Mountbatten, making up for the deficiences in the flow of commands, which resulted inescapably from Mountbatten's decision not to involve the Chiefs of Staff in the operation.

Apparently McNaughton, or at least his staff, was also aware that Mountbatten was being driven by ambition and the prospects of a major combat command in connection with the eventual cross-Channel invasion. For just a few days after the raid, Mountbatten showed up at US Army headquarters with a bushel-basket of medals to hand out to the minuscule American ranger force that had participated in the raid. As he had not done the same for the much larger Canadian force, C.P. Stacey could not help asking one of McNaughton's principal staff officers why Mountbatten wanted to pander so shamelessly to the Americans. The answer was that it was understood that Mountbatten wanted to become a 'Supreme Commander'.[32]

The reason for McNaughton's acquiescence is not hard to divine. Having obtained with such difficulty approval for Canadian involvement in a larger raid, needing to give force to his much-quoted metaphor about a dagger pointed at Germany's heart, and also needing to give his troops battle experience under conditions that would square all his and the government's requirements for such action, McNaughton was unwilling to throw away this unique opportunity by asking awkward questions.

King continued to agonize over the decision, even paraphrasing in a diary entry in May 1942 Stalin's words addressed to the British: 'What is the good of having an army if it does not fight?—for if an army once loses the habit of war it loses its spirit. Therefore, in our own interests we ought to conduct active military operations on the Continent or in the Near East.' King became convinced that the war represented a 'crucification' of mankind, referring to the impending decision as a 'Gethsemani', and noted that, in principal, the cup could not be refused. It was at this time that King continually made references in his diary to how meaningful he found the Book of Jeremiah, particularly Chapters 12–14, the theme of which is Jahweh's unhappiness with a rebellious people that 'must needs take their own false path, courting alien gods and submitting to their worship'. He came to regret his own part in the Dieppe decision. An extravagant spiritualist, King liked to record in his diary the promptings of the Almighty, but for Dieppe there was no sign that Providence had spoken. He was painfully conscious at the time of being swayed by other than purely military considerations. Knowing that his generals were demanding action, that the public was also demanding it, that he stood in danger of being accused of dishonesty with the plebiscite if he did not give some evidence of prosecuting the war more vigorously, and thinking that any other sort of operation might pose even greater dangers, he had acquiesced in Dieppe. But when, in 1943, the pressure for ground combat for Canadian forces grew again, he wrote in his diary: 'I have been afraid of a second Dieppe. By that I mean anxiety to do something to keep up morale.'[33]

Had Dieppe been successful, the Canadian public would have been filled with immense pride in its fighting forces as blazing the trail for the Americans. McNaughton might have been able to take heart in the knowledge that his troops had indeed been trained to the point where their striking at the heart of Germany in Berlin was not unrealistic. And King's hope of following the plebiscite with action that did not cause significant casualties or risk of conscription would have been solved for at least another year. These wished-for possibilities, born of an exceedingly difficult situation, are easily forgotten in hindsight.

In 1942 the concern to legitimize Canadian policies, ever-present in any decision-making process, was particularly acute after two-and-a-half years of Mackenzie King's unique style of waging war—of trying to project images of a total war effort while being unwilling to pay the real price for such an effort. King's endeavour had called into question Canada's wartime credibility and garnered tremendous public opposition. As engaging Canadian troops was becoming something of a political necessity in the summer of 1942, it is somewhat unfair to say Mountbatten was solely responsible for Dieppe because he was acting under 'institutional momentum', or because he needed to justify the worth of his organization. By July 1942 he had given a convincing display, in Saint Nazaire, of Combined Operations' ability to direct skilled forces in a daring raid. McNaughton was still waiting to prove that he and his men could do the same. Mountbatten already had his foot on the next rung of his climb to glory, for he had been given a major role in planning for *Torch*, the invasion of North Africa. McNaughton had also inspired some confidence in higher circles, having been offered in July 1942 responsibility for a full-scale invasion of Norway, but which he knew he would have to turn down because it was inherently too risky—quite apart from the difficulties involved in securing Mackenzie King's permission. (No such invasion took place.) In short, the next rung in McNaughton's career was not even in sight. He needed success at Dieppe much more than did Mountbatten. When one takes into account his bold, not to say foolhardy, statements to the press, and all the strenuous efforts he had made in Whitehall to get the chance to take part in the raid, it is clear McNaughton's prestige was, if anything, more deeply committed than Mountbatten's to pulling it off. If institutional momentum pushed forward this once-cancelled and inherently risky operation, there was as much of it at Canadian military headquarters in London as there was at Mountbatten's headquarters in Richmond Terrace.

In later years McNaughton tried to distance himself from the disaster— explaining that while he 'took full responsibility for the operation', this was on 'the general basis of his confidence in the officers concerned'. He told Stacey that 'In practice the actual control [he and Crerar exercised] over the planning . . . had been very slight.'[34]

The stubborn fact remains that at every important stage of the planning process McNaughton personally reviewed the work product and registered his approval under the authority delegated to him by the Canadian Government. On 30 April he approved the rough outline, on 15 May he approved the outline that had been submitted to the Chiefs of Staff, on 3 July he reviewed and then approved the final *Rutter* plan, and on 27 July he reviewed and approved the final *Jubilee* plan. This was surely more scrutiny and review than Mountbatten ever gave the plans.[35]

In McNaughton's defence it might be noted that he was somewhat boxed in by the activities of Crerar. Montgomery, to whom Crerar had appealed, got the distinct impression that 'if they [Canadian troops] were not allowed [to do Dieppe] . . . there would be trouble with the Canadian headquarters in England under General Andy McNaughton.' Once this impression had been given, McNaughton could hardly shatter it by then refusing the very thing that had been requested. Crerar, having pushed so hard to get the assignment, to the point of making a nuisance of himself, had compromised McNaughton's freedom to manoeuvre. As a rule it is not wise to go shopping in wartime for military operations. There is much to be said for staying in the barracks until you are needed and called. That, in fact, had been McNaughton's belief, and only the pressure of public opinion, following the furor over the plebiscite and King's method of waging war, had forced the General to depart from it.[36]

Suggestions for Further Reading

J.L. Granatstein, *Canada's War: The Politics of the Mackenzie King Government, 1939–1945* (Toronto, 1990).

C.P. Stacey, *Official History of the Canadian Army in the Second World War*, 3 vols (Ottawa, 1955–1960).

Brian Villa, *Unauthorized Action: Mountbatten and the Dieppe Raid* (Toronto, 1989).

Notes

[1]Mountbatten interview in 1978 with Terence Macartney-Filgate for CBC Program 'Echoes of Disaster', transcript in *DND* 79/567; Hughes-Hallett interview in 1967 with John Secondari for the ABC production, 'Rehearsal for D-Day', MB1/67/2— the only TV production on Dieppe (other than Mountbatten's own) of which Mountbatten is known to have approved; see Mountbatten to Lt-Gen. Guy Simonds, 4 February 1969, in Hughes-Hallett Papers, MG 30 E463, NAC.

[2]The evolution of Canada's war policy is ably laid out in C.P. Stacey's magisterial *Arms, Men and Governments: The War Policies of Canada, 1939–1945* (Ottawa, 1970), Part IV, 137–202. A more summary but still very insightful treatment is in Desmond Morton's *Canada and War: A Military and Political History* (Toronto, 1981), Chapter 5, 104–25. Noteworthy also is J.L. Granatstein, *Canada's War: The Politics of the Mackenzie King Government, 1939–1945* (Toronto, 1975) and John Swettenham, *McNaughton, 1939–1943*, II (Toronto, 1969). Valuable insights may also be garnered from J.W. Pickersgill and D.F. Foster, *The Mackenzie King Record (1939–1944)*, vol. 1 (Toronto, 1960), which, despite the title, draws on much more than King's diary. A recent and somewhat popularized, but still useful, treatment is Brian Nolan, *King's War: Mackenzie and the Politics of War, 1939–45* (Toronto, 1988). Dealing essentially with an earlier period, but pregnant with important insights into Canadian civil-military relations, is Stephen J. Harris, *Canadian Grass: The Making of a Professional Army 1860–1939* (Toronto, 1988), a study of fundamental importance.

[3]King Diary, 24 May 1940, MG 26 J13 1940; Canadian Defence Staff Study, 'Employment . . .' in the McNaughton Papers, MG 30, E133, Series III, Volume 182, folder 'PA 5-3-1, vol 1', NAC.

[4]Ralston's acerbic comment, and the record of his sometimes stormy relationship with McNaughton, can be traced in part in Ralston's 'McNaughton file', box 54, Ralston Papers, MG 27 III 311, NAC; see also, Stacey, *Arms, Men and Governments*, 208–9, and Swettenham, *McNaughton*, II, 192–3. *Life* devoted a cover story to the 'Commander of the Canadians' as early as 18 December 1939, which must have been the product of some effort, for as Canadians of the time ruefully observed, they did not often make the cover of a large-circulation American magazine.

[5]*New York Times*, 9 February 1940, 5 April 1941, 22 June 1941, 27 September 1941; Swettenham, *McNaughton*, II, 185.

[6]McNaughton diary for March 1942 (volume 248), MG 30 E 133; *New York Times* 9, 10, 11, 20, 22, 30 March 1942; 24 June 1942 speech, Ralston Papers (Box 171, McNaughton speech file), MG 27 III 311, NAC; Swettenham, *McNaughton*, II, 154. In fairness to McNaughton it should be pointed out that his papers contain a surprising number of refusals to meet the press; see McNaughton Papers (box 183, file P.A. 5-3-2-3), MG 30 E133, NAC.

[7]London *Evening News, The Times*, both of 3 August 1940; Crerar interview with Gallagher, Record Group 24, box 10768 (file 222C1-D205), NAC.

[8]Ralston speech, 3 May 1942, in Ralston Papers (box 171, 'Your Army' Radio Address file), MG 27 III 311, NAC.

[9]Hanson Baldwin in the *New York Times*, 10 October 1940; related notes in Baldwin Papers, Canada file, Yale University Archives, New Haven, Connecticut.

[10]Mackenzie King, 4 September 1941 speech, reprinted in King, *Canada and the Fight for Freedom* (Toronto, 1944), 15.

[11]Ralston's public rebuke (nearly a year after the event) is in *Hansard* (Ottawa, 1 April 1941); see also Swettenham, *McNaughton*, II, 50–4. The dispute itself is judiciously set out in C.P. Stacey, *Six Years*, 274–85. On the evacuation from Brittany and Roberts' role, see Swettenham, *McNaughton*, II, 107–9.

[12]Swettenham, *McNaughton*, II, 244–5; cf. Stacey, *Six Years of War*, 322–3. The Eden proposal, as conveyed to J.G. Gardiner, was even discussed at length in the Canadian War Committee; see King Diary, 4 December 1940, MG 26 J13 1940, NAC; Nathaniel A. Benson, *None of It Came Easy* (Toronto, 1955), 180.

[13]King to Ralston, 6 December 1940, King Papers, quoted in Stacey, *Arms*, 40; 'Notes on Mr Churchill's Conversation of Tuesday 17th December 1940', Ralston Papers ('Churchill, Brooke, etc.' file), MG 27 III 311, NAC.

[14]The Ralston-McNaughton exchange is reported in the Crerar War Diary for 14 October 1941, in the Ralston Papers (box 58), MG 27 III 311, NAC; entry for 25 October 1941, *ibid*.

[15]King Diary, 20 May 1941, MG 26 J13 1941, NAC.

[16]Pope to Stuart, 28 November 1942, in RG 24, box 11,004 (file D15), NAC.

[17]Minutes of Conference with the Minister of National Defence at CMHQ on Wednesday, 15 October 1941, McNaughton Papers, MG 30 E133 series III, vol. 183 (file P.A.5-3-1); Ralston-McNaughton meeting 15 October 1941; for the March King-McNaughton conference, see King Diary 16, 17 March 1942, in MG 26 J13 1942, and McNaughton War Diary in MG 30 E133, both NAC; Stuart quoted in Maurice Pope, *Soldiers and Politicians: The Memoirs of Lt. Gen. Maurice A. Pope* (Toronto, 1962), 202; King Diary, 23 August 1941, MG 26 J13 1941. On the booing, see also Pickersgill, *King Record*, I, 261. King learned his lesson, and shortly afterwards told Canadian troops 'not to let anyone say that it was the [Canadian] government's restraining hand' that was keeping them out of action. *Ibid.*, 261.

[18]Meighen speech is quoted in the *Montreal Gazette*, 10 December 1941; Throne Speech 22 January 1942, *Hansard* (Ottawa); King CBC Radio address, 7 April 1942, reprinted in King, *Canada and the Fight for Freedom* (Toronto, 1944), 135.

[19]For an interesting study of the referendum as Malcolm MacDonald reported it to the British Government, see WP (42) 103 of 28 February 1942 for an analysis before the vote, while a post-referendum analysis is to be found in WP (42) 202 of 13 May 1942. It was not often that Canadian affairs were brought formally to the attention of the London Cabinet. King Diary, 13 May 1942, MG 26 J13 1942; 7 May 1942, *ibid*.

[20]Ralston's Rotary Club speech of 16 June 1942, Ralston Papers (box 171, Rotary Club speech file), MG 27 III 311, NAC.

[21]See above, note 11.

[22]Stacey, *Six Years*, 307; McNaughton diary, 22 July 1941 (appendix XXXIV), McNaughton to Stuart and vice versa, 26 July and 31 July 1941, cited by Stacey, *Six Years of War*, 307–8, in RG 24, box 11004 (file D15), all in NAC.

[23]The McNaughton quote is in 'Minutes of a meeting at CMHQ, 15 October 1941', McNaughton Papers, MG 30 E133 (box 182, file P.A. 5-3-1, vol. 1) NAC; telegram from Ralston to Power, 26 October 1941, Ralston Papers (box 39, Canada-London file), MG 27 III 311, NAC; pencil notes of conversation with Crerar in Ralston Papers (box 58, English trips file), MG 27 III 311; *ibid*.; Crerar War Diary, 14 October–25 October 1941, *passim*, *ibid*. (box 58 war Office-minutes of meetings file), *ibid*.; Ralston to Power, 26 October 1941, in *ibid*., box 39 (Canada-London file), all NAC. It should be noted that McNaughton at times was beguiled by the prospects of super-raids. On 6 July 1941 Leo Amery noted in his diary that McNaughton was in favour of large raids. 'He . . . thinks that our superiority at sea coupled with air superiority once we get it, ought to enable us to do something in the nature of really big tip and run operations along the whole 1000 miles and more of German front facing us with regard to which we are on inner lines and can move

a force back from Norway to Brittany much quicker than the Germans can. . . .' Leo Amery Diary, 6 July 1941 in John Barnes and David Nicholson, eds, *The Empire at Bay: The Leo Amery Diaries, 1929–1945* (London, 1988), 696.

²⁴Crerar to Montgomery, 5 February 1942, in RG 24, vol. 10768 (File 222 C1 D189).

²⁵Montgomery to Crerar, 8 February 1942, RG 24, volume 10768; as reported by Crerar to BGS, 1 March 1942, RG 24, volume 10768, file 222 C1 (D17); on 6 March meeting, see 'Notes on Conference, 6 March 1942', RG 24, volume 10765. It is undoubtedly the memory of this meeting that caused General Simonds to write Mountbatten on 10 February 1969: 'I know for facts [*sic*], that as soon as Crerar heard of the Dieppe project, he brought every pressure he could bring to bear on the British Chiefs of Staff, and even Churchill himself: a) to nominate Canadian troops for the Operation [and] b) to have the operation carried out.' Copy in Hughes-Hallett Papers, MG 30 E463, NAC.

²⁶Ziegler, *Mountbatten*, 189. The clearest and most unequivocal statement of Mountbatten's opposition to using Canadian troops is in Mountbatten to Lt-Gen. Guy Simonds, 4 February 1969, in Hughes-Hallett Papers, *ibid*; on this point, Canadian records bear him out fairly well. The Canadian memorandum of record notes that 'Commodore Mountbatten said that the proposal to use a wholly Canadian detachment for raiding operations ran counter to the policy which had been settled upon . . . and that [Canadian] Army representation would take the form of "dilution" of raiding Commandos.' Notes on Conferences held on 6 March 1942 in RG 10765 NAC. (One could hardly expect Mountbatten to say that he did not think the Canadians were experienced enough, but his statement about 'dilution' came as close as one could expect him to come.)

²⁷On McNaughton's visits in April 1942 to COHQ, see his War Diary for April in (vol. 248) MG 30 E133; for the invitation to Canadians to participate, tendered through Montgomery to McNaughton, see *ibid*., entry for 30 April, NAC.

²⁸McNaughton to Stuart, 30 April 1942, in McNaughton file, Ralston Papers, MG 27 III 311, NAC.

²⁹Cabinet War Committee minutes of 1 May, Privy Council records, copy in Department of External Affairs files, II/4/6; King Diary, 1 May 1942, MG 26 J13 1942.

³⁰Minutes, Canadian Chiefs of Staff with Mountbatten, 11 June 1942, courtesy DND; King Dominion Day speech, 1 July 1942, *Hansard* (Ottawa). See also McNaughton Diary, Appendix L, 21 July 1942, for Mountbatten's complaints about the speech. It was a convenient pretext for Mountbatten, who was trying to convince McNaughton that Ottawa could not be trusted to keep a secret and should be told nothing about *Jubilee*. The reason probably was that Mountbatten was hoping to avoid presenting fictitious claims that *Jubilee* was authorized, and—knowing that if McNaughton communicated with Ottawa, authorization would have to be claimed—hoped to sever these communications before they got him in trouble. McNaughton, according to his own record, said that he was 'not disposed to withhold from the proper authorities in Canada, information which they should rightly have and which he was under obligation to furnish' (Appendix L, 21 July 1942). It was probably this exchange that forced Mountbatten to attempt to fill the void nine days later by conveying to McNaughton the erroneous impression that the War Cabinet had specifically authorized the revival of *Rutter* as *Jubilee*. By couching

all this in terms of War Cabinet discussions, it was easier to gloss over the problem of written authorization. See Appendix 'O', 25 July 1942, in McNaughton Diary, MG 30 E133 (vol. 248), NAC.

[31]McNaughton to Lt-Gen. J.G. des R. Swayne (Chief of Staff, Home Forces, GHQ), 15 May 1942, in Stacey, *Six Years*, 333.

[32]For the preceding paragraph the note is: Memo for file by M.H.S. Penhale, Brig. GS 1st Cdn Army (copy to file 8-3-5/ops HQ First CDN Army) 9 August 1942. The copy I have seen is drawn from the Air Marshal H. Edwards biographical file, DND; C.P. Stacey, *A Date with History* (Ottawa, n.d. but *c.* 1982), 94.

[33]King Diary, 24 May, 29 July 1942 (cf. diary for 11 March 1943); *ibid.*, 9, 13, 16, 17 May 1942, King Papers, MG 26 J13 1942, NAC.

[34]Handwritten note by C.P. Stacey in his copy of special report 100 in 594.013 (D17), DND.

[35]These approvals, which look so strange in hindsight, were all described carefully by C.P. Stacey in *Six Years of War* (329–43), essentially without commentary. Perhaps it was Stacey's affection for McNaughton that prevented him from any suggestion of criticism. The extent of their mutual trust and respect may be judged by the fact that McNaughton bequeathed control of his papers to Stacey. Their relationship is a poignant reminder of the difficulties inherent in the historian's calling.

[36]Montgomery 1962 interview, CBC 'Close-Up', 594.009 (D13), DND.

IV

After 1945

28

~∿~

The Beginnings of Post-War Nationalism in

Quebec

Michael D. Behiels

One of the constants of history is change, and societies are perennially in a state of transition. But it is the particular nature and incidence of change that mark one historical period from another. The period after 1945 saw extremely rapid change in all parts of Canada, not least in the province of Quebec. Typically perceived as a traditional agrarian society dominated by its clergy, Quebec had been altering for decades and now found itself in a dilemma. Modernization and the complete acceptance of industrialization threatened the uniqueness of French-Canadian society as it was traditionally understood. Most Canadians within Quebec or outside it had failed to realize the extent of the province's gradual transformation, or the extent to which Quebec had responded to postwar conditions before the emergence of the 'Quiet Revolution' of the 1960s or the separatism of the 1970s.

By 1960 it was clear that Quebec was no longer a rural, traditional, and agrarian society. It was an urban, industrial, and increasingly secular one. Its intellectual élite had long been debating the issues that would emerge as critical in the ensuing decades. During the 1950s especially, the whole nature of nationalism in French Canada was thoroughly aired. One group of revisionist critics, the 'neo-nationalists', understood that rural society was declining, that an industrial proletariat had developed, and that French-Canadian culture was slowly being transformed by external influences. The family and the church, the traditional bulwarks of French-Canadian society, were no longer adequate props. The neo-nationalists attempted to root nationalism in the new industrial order by linking it with the working class. But these critics were not alone in attacking the political and religious national élites of Quebec.

In the following selection Michael Behiels analyses another major thread in the critique of traditional nationalism in Quebec: the 'antinationalist' movement associated with Pierre Trudeau and *Cité libre* (1950–66). The young intellectuals associated with this journal were influenced by the Depression of the thirties, French social Catholicism, and modern social science. They desired a new Christian humanism freed from the outmoded principles of the Catholic Church as it then functioned in French Canada, one that would respond to the needs of the new urban-industrial society. Rejecting the clericalism and nationalism that had spawned the regime of Maurice Duplessis, they represented a non-Marxist democratic left. They were devastating critics of the old order, particularly of traditional Quebec nationalism, but they had little specific program to put in its place.

How revolutionary were the *Citélibristes*? In what way was their identification of nationalism with the particular problems of modern Quebec unfair? What was their alternative to nationalism? How was it thought that an open, democratic, pluralistic, secular, urban-industrial society could be harmonized with a distinctive French Canada? To what extent was Trudeau a representative spokesman for the *Citélibristes*?

This article first appeared, titled '*Cité libre* and Nationalism', in Michael D. Behiels, *Prelude to Quebec's Quiet Revolution: Liberalism versus Neo-Nationalism 1945–1960* (Kingston and Montreal, 1985, 84–96, 290–2).

Delivering oneself from traditionalism entails the suppression of clerical oppression and of nationalism which have until now prevented or impaired the emergence of a fruitful liberty.[1]

The liberal and social democrats in *Cité libre* were convinced from the outset that the greatest obstacle to the modernization of French-Canadian society was the omnipresence of a paranoid and distorted traditionalism. Originally this traditionalism had the laudable mission of preserving intact the values of French culture and civilization. But with the growing threat of contamination by Anglo-Saxon values this traditionalism adopted a state of siege mentality which had the nefarious effect of immobilizing 'in history the dynamism of the culture and of exhausting the creative energy of civilization'.[2] This siege mentality, reinforced by clericalism, served primarily the interests of the church. More important, however, was the fact that a corrupted traditionalism inspired the emergence of the ideology of nationalism. *Citélibristes* readily accepted Maurice Blain's assertion that since the turn of the century 'the demagoguery of various schools of nationalists, and particularly of nationalist history, perhaps has done more to provoke the stiffening of intellectual traditionalism and to precipitate the decline of the culture than the church had accomplished in an entire century'.[3] This perception of nationalism was going to draw the *Citélibristes* into undertaking a severe critique of French-Canadian nationalism, its major assumptions, aspirations, and specific proposals. As a result of this critique, they were charged with being not only antinationalist but anti-French-Canadian, in short, traitors to their own cultural community. *Citélibristes*, except for pessimists like Pierre Vadeboncoeur, were not anti-French-Canadian. In reality they were driven by a deeply rooted belief in the survival and *épanouissement* of the francophone culture in Canada and North America. They disagreed fundamentally with traditional French-Canadian nationalists about the nature and aspirations of what they considered to be a viable, modern French-Canadian society. *Citélibristes* were antinationalists because they believed sincerely that nationalism, like clericalism, had prevented the emergence of a dynamic, creative, indigenous, French-Canadian culture and society rooted in North America. French-Canadian society would survive and flourish, not because of any nationalist doctrine, but by maturing into an open, democratic, pluralistic, secular, urban-industrial society in harmony with, yet distinct from, that of the rest of North America.

The Critique of Nationalism

For some *Citélibristes* their distrust and scepticism of nationalism predated the founding of the movement. For Pierre Vadeboncoeur a national revolution was 'generally a failed opportunity to tackle an international problem which is that of mankind'.[4] Marcel Rioux, while stating his confidence in the continued survival of nations as viable and necessary cultural entities, concluded that 'the rights to survival, to individual and religious freedom, to property, to work and social security, are all rights of everyone living in society,' and thereby had priority over national rights.'[5] Guy Cormier complained bitterly that nationalism had never served the interests of the working class in Quebec and consequently the proletariat had no use for an ideology which stressed autonomy for the nation at the expense of autonomy for the individual.[6] Trudeau also revealed his distaste for the ideology when he rejected Filion's call for the creation of a republican and social movement to replace the moribund Conservative party. Trudeau preferred a new political movement based strictly on a platform of social democracy. The achievement of an independent Canadian Republic, while important, could wait until later.[7] The *Cité libre* group was thus well disposed to undertake a critical analysis of traditional French-Canadian nationalist thought. Events of the 1950s only reinforced their initial scepticism and impelled some members to question the viability of a society that had fostered and nurtured what they perceived as a highly conservative and at times reactionary ideology and culture.

The demise of the Bloc had prompted the young postwar nationalists to question the attachment of the French-Canadian working class to its cultural milieu. Neo-nationalists were provoked into a reassessment of traditional nationalism. The famous five-month strike in the asbestos mines in the Eastern Townships in 1949 served as a major catalyst in the formation of the *Cité libre* movement. The strike led the *Citélibristes* to question the nationalist ideology that, in their view, had given birth to the antisocial and antilabour Duplessis government during the depression and had returned it to power in 1944. The Duplessis regime was the incarnation of the petty bourgeois and clerical nationalism formulated in the pages of *L'Action française* during the 1920s and *L'Action nationale* in the 1930s and 1940s. The nationalists had clamoured for a French-Canadian republic on the banks of the St Lawrence. 'But', wrote Guy Cormier with a cutting sense of sarcasm, 'in this little republic which Mr Duplessis has given you (with a nice flag to boot), there are no republicans . . . The People, Mr Duplessis has sent to college. "The People are in college and strikes are its holidays." Mr Duplessis is the usher, the professor, and the spiritual guidance counsellor (Gospel in hand!).' As a result, the French-Canadian people were living a disguised separatist existence distinct from that of the rest of Canada and the international community. This led Cormier to ponder aloud whether the French Canadians would soon wake up one morning as citizens of a newly proclaimed fascist state! While his fears certainly were exaggerated, it was clear that *Cité libre* had opted for a society which placed a priority on the defence and development of civil rights and individual liberties rather than 'a political and religious state which oppresses consciences' in the name of an ideology called nationalism.[8]

According to the *Cité libre* interpretation, expressed by Trudeau, the asbestos strike occurred, in part, because the industrial workers of Quebec were suffocating in a society 'overburdened by inadequate ideologies and oppressive institutions'.[9] How had these two distinct yet related developments taken place? What did *Citélibristes* mean by the term 'inadequate ideologies'? Several members of the group, including Trudeau, Jean-Guy Blain, Vadeboncoeur, Dumont, and Rioux, contributed lengthy and revealing essays on this question. The central thesis and conclusion of all these essays was that an expanding gap had been allowed to develop between the socio-economic and cultural realities of modern Quebec and the unchallenged clerical and petty bourgeois ideology of nationalism that had been widely promulgated since the late nineteenth century.[10] French-Canadian social and economic thought had, as a result of historical events particular to French Canada, become synonymous with the prevailing nationalist thought. It thereby carried the burden of ensuring the survival of the French Canadians as a distinct collectivity. A heavy responsibility indeed.

It was this rigid identification of all French-Canadian social thought with nationalist thought that, in the view of the *Cité libre* group, created the dual socio-cultural and intellectual crisis confronting French Canadians in the 1950s. Nevertheless, the *Citélibristes* wanted it made clear that their critique of traditional nationalist thought should not be interpreted as an attack upon the integrity of the nationalists themselves. The latter, argued Trudeau, merited full respect, for they lacked 'neither creativity in their intentions, nor courage in their undertakings, nor firmness in their proposals, nor inventiveness in their resolutions'. Trudeau merely wanted to 'rid nationalist thought of the aspects which above all obstructed the present and prevented free and direct action'.[11] These nationalists, responding intuitively, had elaborated a security system to ensure the survival of a people that had been conquered, occupied, decapitated of its élites, forced out of the commercial sector and the urban centres, and reduced to the status of a minority with little influence in a country French Canadians had discovered, explored, and colonized. Nationalists and their doctrines, it was acknowledged, had played a role in saving French-Canadian culture and civil and religious liberties.[12] The point that *Citélibristes* hoped to make was that traditional nationalist doctrines simply had outlived their historical usefulness and had become burdensome intellectual anachronisms.

The major shortcoming of traditional nationalist thought was its excessive idealism. French-Canadian culture lacked an aspect fundamental to all dynamic cultures—an intimate contact with reality. Vadeboncoeur expressed the crisis confronting French Canadians in these harsh terms.

> We are nourished by myths, by ideals, whose relationship to reality is at the very best highly vague; this is a most irritating characteristic of our culture. This situation is quite evident in politics, for example. We envisage a highly patriotic national project without ensuring that an exciting and imperious reality provide the essential elements of a dynamic policy that is capable of being fulfilled. Our national mystique therefore remains necessarily sentimental and idealistic. It is not founded on a power base, it is not at the cutting edge of reality, because that reality is solvent. Our national mystique is based on an antiquated reality, fixed in tradition, which reached its zenith perhaps in the middle of the last century. This reality was for us the plausibility of becoming a small nation in the nineteenth-century conception of that term.[13]

What were these myths, these ideals, that inspired and motivated several generations of well-intentioned but naïve nationalists? In the *Cité libre* view of things, French-Canadian nationalists had constructed an ideal society that was totally unprogressive, antimodern, and destructive of the individual. French-Canadian nationalism, suggested Rioux, 'has always had the tendency to define a French Canadian not in his own terms but rather by what he was in relation to other groups. While the efforts of educators in other western societies concentrated on democracy, freedom, intellectual and scientific knowledge, the imperatives of our ideology were drawn from three characteristics which differentiated the French Canadian from his neighbours: minority, Catholic, and French.'[14] Clerical and petty bourgeois nationalists persisted in selling the virtues of a society which emphasized the superiority of spiritual and moral integrity to the fulfilment of mankind's material and social needs, a society which had as its mission the preservation and diffusion of Catholicism and the French culture on a continent dominated by secularism, materialism, and Anglo-Saxon values and institutions.[15] Traditional nationalism was characterized by a 'mythical' and 'historicist' mentality which made a cult of differences and the past and took account of a forbidding and treacherous present only in terms of its relationship to an idealized past and never to the future. This 'mythical' and 'historicist' mentality had rendered French Canadians prisoners of their past. It had made them incapable of assimilating the two major developments of the twentiety century—industrialization and urbanization.[16]

The psychological, intellectual, and institutional consequences of this monolithic, unrealistic, and doctrinaire nationalist system of thought were devastating and pervasive. Trudeau effectively demonstrated in his lengthy introduction to *La Grève de l'amiante* how doctrinaire nationalist ideology had prevented French-Canadian intellectuals from drawing upon creative and novel developments in the modern social sciences. It had also brought about, in Trudeau's estimation, a reactionary interpretation of the social thought of the Catholic church. On the political level, the nationalist influence made it virtually impossible for francophone politicians to implement socio-economic programs that had proved successful for the Protestant and materialistic English-speaking Canadians. Furthermore, the clerical nationalists' equation of state intervention with communism and socialism had made the implementation of meaningful provincial autonomy impossible, thereby impeding the growth of a democratic concept of authority and the role of the state. The five concrete solutions proposed by the nationalists—return to the land, support for small business, cooperatives, Catholic unionism, and Christian corporatism—were all, in *Cité libre*'s view, conservative, reactionary programs intended to impede the secularization and democratization of the society's values and institutions.[17]

Unfortunately, many of French Canada's important institutions—the Société Saint-Jean-Baptiste, the Ecole sociale populaire, *L'Action nationale*, the classical colleges and the universities, the church and the Catholic unions—had been thoroughly imbued with this clerical-nationalist ideology, making their transition to a modern secular world difficult, if not virtually impossible. 'Our ideologies', concluded Trudeau in somewhat overstated terms,

> full of mistrust of industrialization, clinging to a desire for isolation and rural nostalgia, no longer corresponded to our ethos, thrown into disarray by anonymous capitalism, swayed by foreign influences, and transported without baggage into a modern *capharnaüm* where the family, the community, the parish —traditional bulwarks against chaos—no longer offered the same security. In an industrial society, such as developed by capitalism, other remedies were required to deal with illness, accidents, and old age, than the parish school,

good neighbours, individual charity, and private initiative. But our social thought had imagined such inadequate solutions to these problems that it had managed to take root only in the written programs of artificial, useless, and debilitating associations. Meanwhile our living institutions, those whose very existence required them to remain in touch with reality, had to renounce all ideology or see their dynamism sacrificed.[18]

In his introduction to *La Grève de l'amiante* Trudeau demonstrated effectively, to the satisfaction of his *Cité libre* colleagues, what Maurice Blain had claimed in 1952. That is, that various schools of nationalists had since 1900 contributed as much if not more to the dissemination and entrenchment of a rigid, authoritarian intellectual traditionalism than the oppressive clericalism of the Catholic church had achieved in well over a century.

These harsh and extreme allegations by *Citélibristes* constituted, in effect, a form of secular moralizing. There were, undoubtedly, factors other than nationalist ideology which accounted for the lack of political and social modernization of French-Canadian society but the *Citélibristes* paid no attention to these. This narrowmindedness led a couple of *Citélibristes* to question seriously the future of French-Canadian society, its culture, and language. Pierre Vadeboncoeur, the most pessimistic *Cité libre* member, questioned the prospects of renewal for the French-Canadian society. Could a culture which he characterized as sterile, negative, passive, and authoritarian save itself from total decay and collapse? He concluded that French Canada's future was bleak indeed.[19] It was psychologically impossible, he argued, for a culture based on the idea of 'survival' to grasp the internal dynamic of its decadence because serious intellectual self-criticism of the essentials was considered taboo. Literary criticism, for example, was limited to secondary external problems—economic inferiority, failure of nationalist politics—'but the soul of the people, and in particular the soul of the individual, his level of energy, of courage, of independence, of intolerance, of injustice, of confidence, of liberty, and of the exercise of liberty, of intellectual toughness, of personalism, of internal autonomy, of determination, of spirit, of conquest, of passion, did not constitute subjects of analysis and certainly did not furnish the themes of major ideological movements.'[20] The signs of moral and cultural decay and popular inertia had never provoked nationalist intellectuals to revolt against the reigning culture or to examine it critically, but rather had led them blindly to reaffirm their faith in that culture and the institutions associated with it. Vadeboncoeur's pessimism and Rioux's scepticism stemmed from their conviction that traditional nationalist thought barred all original and creative revolutionary action without which, in their estimation, any modern society was doomed to disappear.[21] While Vadeboncoeur felt nothing could be done to revive the dying corpse of French-Canadian culture, all other *Citélibristes*, including Rioux, believed in the possibility of a modern, secular, democratic, and pluralistic French-Canadian society emerging if the appropriate strategy of thought and action was undertaken.

Cité libre's *Antidote to Nationalism*

How was the crisis to be resolved? *Cité libre's* first suggestion was to invite French Canadians to examine objectively their culture, to assess its relative strengths and weaknesses, to attempt to close the gap between the definition of the collective self-image and the realities of the socio-economic world in which their society functioned. Using arguments first developed by Maurice Tremblay, a Laval sociologist, Marcel Rioux contended that a national élite should not base its ideology on particularist and provincial elements or narrow class interests. An authentic national élite had the responsibility to use its prestige and influence to break 'the narrow circle of national egoism and to apply itself continuously to the purging and the surpassing of ethnic particularism, especially by working for its development and maturation through an enriching contact with foreign cultural values susceptible of being assimilated'.[22]

Again, following Tremblay's suggestion, *Cité libre* members questioned the traditional nationalists' definition of their culture as 'minority, Catholic, and French'. The majority of the French-Canadian people did not perceive themselves as members of an inferior minority, neither were they excessively nationalistic. Freed from the strait-jacket of nationalist doctrines, the majority of French Canadians, Rioux felt assured, would express their dynamism, confidence, and creativity. They would, in short, take their rightful place alongside other citizens of the world. Moreover, Catholicism in Quebec was not its highest and purest form, but rather a very specific French-Canadian Catholicism and in no way inherently superior to English-Canadian Protestantism. The Catholic French-Canadian culture could not claim to draw its distinctiveness from a theoretical moral and spiritual superiority. What counted was how French Canadians lived their Catholic beliefs.[23] Neither could the nationalists lay claim to defending the French culture and language in North America. Those elements, argued Rioux, had undergone a tremendous metamorphosis since the early days of New France. A specific French-Canadian culture and related language had taken root in Quebec and these should not be confused with the culture and language of modern France. French-Canadian literature was essentially North American literature of French inspiration. For nationalists to equate their culture with that of modern France was dishonest and misleading. The confusion prevented French Canadians from defining and coming to grips with the shortcomings of their own specific culture and language. The essence of the French mentality—a critical mind, a love of liberty, and a desire for creativity—had found refuge in a small group of French Canadians forced to live intellectually and psychologically, and in some cases physically, outside the mainstream of their own society.[24]

Vadeboncoeur, none the less, resigned himself to the eventual demise of the French-Canadian culture, a culture which lacked ambition, a sense of power, and the will to follow a cause to victory. French-Canadian politics and politicians were far too élitist, authoritarian, and nationalistic to fulfil in a revolutionary way the real needs of the people. Nationalism in a world dominated increasingly by the unifying and levelling forces of technology and economic development was a reactionary and anachronistic ideology. To believe in the importance of preserving national entities was futile, a pure waste of energy, and a sure sign of misinterpreting the forces of the modern world.[25] Working from a Marxist theory of superstructures, Vadeboncoeur suggested that French Canadians, if they wished to partake of the fruits of the modern world, follow existing socio-economic and geographic imperatives to their logical extreme.

> . . . a people of sparse population inhabits an immense territory, full of natural resources, neighbour of a nation which is in the process of engulfing the entire continent with its machines. Everything will be industrialized; wealth will create industry; industry will fully populate what is still a savage land. It is not we who will create the country but the machine and the foreigner. We have a political national vision, in tune with the rhythm of nature, with the natural increase of population, supported by the classical defences of distance and isolation in virgin territory, enjoying, in short, guarantees which are no longer in vogue. It is naïve to focus our attention on this national vision or to use it as an inspiration for our lives because it is no more than the ideological photograph of a situation whose conditions are in the process of disappearing. It is antidialectical to view our political situation first and to reason on the basis of the forces and an outdated situation that were able to provide us with some consistency. It is not this result which determines history, nor is it the ideal that these conditions created. What determines history are the actual forces at work—such as industrialization, our natural resources, the population those resources will attract, American expansion, progressive universal uniformization, the influx of high levels of foreign cultures, the forced contamination of our language, the general substitution of American values for ours—which are invading us on all sides and undermining us. To be dialectical is to perceive that these hidden forces constitute the essentials.[26]

The majority of *Citélibristes* were not amused. While accepting Vadeboncoeur's diagnosis they rejected his antinationalist Marxist cure. They spurned his overly pessimistic economic determinism and refused to despair of the survival of the French-Canadian society. Pelletier, expressing the group's strong dissent, quoted the French author André Malraux to the effect that 'For better or for worse, we are tied to the homeland. . . . The revolutionary who does not possess a sense of faithfulness will become despite himself a Fascist.'[27] The *Cité libre* group wanted the French-Canadian collectivity to strive to become an open, democratic, pluralistic, and humanistic society adjusted to the realities of the present and capable of confronting all reasonable challenges. *Citélibristes* firmly rejected a societal model based on mere survival or the nationalist imperative—*L'État français*—which according to Canon Groulx had to be imposed upon the history of North America. On the other hand, neither could they condone the argument that a collectivity, merely because it was weak and poor, should have to cut itself off from its past voluntarily by encouraging and collaborating with the unifying and levelling forces of technology, economic development, and American imperialistic nationalism. 'On the verge of the abyss,' countered Pelletier, 'I do not accept suicide. That the abyss kills us, this we cannot control. That is its business, not ours. It does not need our collaboration to carry out its task.'[28]

Fernand Dumont, agreeing wholeheartedly with *Cité libre*'s dissenting opinion, provided a solid sociological argument for the perpetuation of distinct cultural entities. From a socio-psychological perspective, he argued, the achievement of self-awareness constituted the deepest form of intellectual revolution. This self-knowledge was not attained through contact with a theoretical universal humanism, but rather by living and understanding one's own culture. Any attempt at short-circuiting the process would lead to an ideological outlook divorced from the realities of one's own society. Such had been the fate of traditional nationalism, which emphasized the attainment of self-awareness through the discovery of a mythical and systematized past interpreted so rigidly that it offered no options for future behaviour. In this framework the only alternatives were acceptance or rejection, neither of which led to a creative pursuit of humanist values. The homogeneous, petty bourgeois interpretation of French Canada's past had to be supplemented by a pluralistic account which considered the perspective and role of all classes, especially the working class. Only a new, more realistic, collective self-image, which took into consideration all social classes and contemporary socio-economic conditions, could ensure that French-Canadian culture possessed 'a destiny and a choice'.[29] In sum, French Canada needed a new history, or better still, a series of histories affirming the pluralist nature of its past.

Yet French Canada required more than a pluralistic interpretation of its past. What was also urgently required, according to the *Citélibristes*, was a strong and viable French-Canadian left-wing intelligentsia to serve as an ideological counter-force to the all-pervasive nationalist right. Nationalism and nationalists were, in the *Cité libre* perspective, inherently conservative, concerned with preserving and transmitting, with seeing the world strictly from a particularist, provincial perspective.[30] A strong and influential left-wing intelligentsia, however, could challenge the established order and work to establish a new social order based on Catholic personalist philosophy, secular humanism, and North American liberal and social democracy. Speaking for all *Citélibristes*, Marcel Rioux rejected the intense, sincere pessimism of Vadeboncoeur and opted for the creation of a 'gauche canadienne-française', which would, in due course, bring about the integration of a revitalized and dynamic French-Canadian society into the mainstream of North America.

> Far from despairing about the future of the French Canadians, the Left will know how to place them in the mainstream of history. At a time when the ideology of the Right is demonstrating its pessimism and wonders how many years the 'race' will endure, it is time to show confidence in one's people and to contest the ideology that has oppressed them for two centuries. The term leftist must not scare enlightened Catholics; to fight ignorance, narrow-mindedness, and caste interests is not doing the work of perdition. To rise against the stagnation and the unrealism of a fossilized ideology is to have faith in man, it is to rely upon the desire for improvement which appeared on earth with man and which is one of his highest and noblest characteristics.[31]

The Nationalists React

Naturally *Cité libre*'s strong critique and condemnation of traditional nationalist thought provoked a hostile reaction from its lay and clerical exponents. Father Marie-Joseph d'Anjou, the editor of the traditional nationalist Jesuit periodical *Relations*, denounced the group as irrepressible anticlericals and suggested a ban on *Cité libre*.[32] In fact, *Cité libre* was banned in some classical colleges and when Pelletier and Trudeau approached Bishop Léger they received a cool reception and no assurance that college rectors would be requested to lift the ban.[33] The event that sparked a concerted traditional nationalist counter-attack was the appearance in 1956 of Trudeau's comprehensive and devastating critique of French-Canadian nationalism in his introduction to *La Grève de l'amiante*. Robert Rumilly was infuriated, and he immediately set out to unmask and denounce what he considered to be a left-wing or socialist conspiracy to destroy the French-Canadian Catholic nation of Quebec. Rumilly considered French left-wing Catholics to be allied with what he regarded as anti-Catholic forces, namely, France's Socialist and Communist parties. The periodical *Ésprit*, founded by Emmanuel Mounier in 1932 and taken over in 1952 by Jean-Marie Domenach after the former's death, was considered by Rumilly to be in the vanguard of an influential movement of left-wing Catholics trying to 'humanize' socialist and communist doctrines to make them acceptable to a majority of Catholics.[34] *Cité libre* and its members, in Rumilly's view, were attempting to achieve the same objective in Quebec with the full support of Radio-Canada and the 'leftists' at *Le Devoir* and *L'Action nationale*, in the labour movement, and in the CCF.[35]

One forceful critic of Trudeau's and *Cité libre*'s condemnation of French-Canadian nationalism was the Jesuit Father Jacques Cousineau. As a member of the *Commission sacerdotale d'études sociales* and moral counsellor of the *Conseil central des syndicats de Montréal*, Father Cousineau participated in the Catholic church's eventually successful endeavours to resolve the asbestos strike in 1949. Cousineau charged that Trudeau's introduction to *La Grève de l'amiante*, by denigrating French-Canadian nationalist thought and ignoring the important role of the church in the resolution of the strike, 'empties of its essential meaning an important and painful event of our social life'.[36] Cousineau rejected Trudeau's interpretation that the asbestos strike was a break with the past because the asbestos workers, rejecting Catholic social doctrine and nationalist myths, had undertaken French Canada's first real movement of socio-economic emancipation. The strike, asserted Cousineau, marked the maturation and dynamism of the Catholic and national labour movement and was an expression of 'our' Catholic social doctrine.[37] Trudeau had idealized and mythologized the asbestos strike because such an interpretation reinforced his hypothesis that a monolithic, idealistic, and backward-looking nationalist creed had retarded the political and social modernization of French Canada. Trudeau's description and analysis of twentieth-century French-Canadian social thought was, in Cousineau's view, false because it was incomplete, methodologically flawed, and distorted by his personal doctrinal prejudices. 'His value judgements', concluded Cousineau, are based upon well-known norms, those of the CCF and PSD programs, both characterized by a rigid and passionate idealism bordering on utopianism.'[38] François-Albert Angers, promoted to the post of editor of *L'Action nationale* after the neo-nationalists had abandoned its editorial board in 1956, published a six-part diatribe against *Cité libre* focused on Trudeau's critique of French-Canadian nationalism.

Angers attempted to discredit the *Citélibristes* by denouncing what he called the 'libellous', 'socialist', 'revolutionary' overtones of their exaggerated declarations concerning French-Canadian nationalism and its adherents. 'In wanting to build from scratch a new society without using the materials or the methods of the old society,' *Cité libre*, contended Angers, 'was assuming responsibility for a society which will not be ours. It will be so similar to the Anglo-Canadian society which dominates Canada that, failing to distinguish themselves, both societies will almost inevitably assimilate one another.'[39] Taking his analysis one step further, Angers argued vigorously that the *Cité libre* interpretation of French-Canadian nationalism, like a house of cards, was built on a shaky foundation. *Cité libre*'s fatal hubris resided in the fact that its members were all unconscious prisoners of the corrupted sense of objectivity inherent in Marxist methodological concepts.[40] In short, educated French Canadians need not waste their time reading *Cité libre*. The assumptions and methodology of its authors were seriously in doubt and, consequently, little of intellectual value could flow from their pens! More importantly, *Cité libre*'s misguided antinationalism would only serve to bring about the assimilation of French Canadians by the English-Canadian majority.

Trudeau ignored F.-A. Angers' diatribe because he had always considered him to be extremely right-wing. He was, however, disturbed by Father Cousineau's critique, especially when it appeared in pamphlet form under the auspices of the *Institut social populaire* and was circulated widely throughout the province under the imprimatur of the church. What made Trudeau even more upset was Father Richard Arès' refusal to publish either Trudeau's 'critique d'une critique' or his short letter drawing the attention of *Relations*' readers to his assessment of Cousineau's critique. In his 'Critique d'une critique' Trudeau reasserted his interpretation of the asbestos strike by poking holes in Cousineau's counter-interpretation and by pointing out the contradictions, errors, slanders, distortions, sophisms, and sloppy methodology in Cousineau's attempt to undermine his critique of French-Canadian nationalism. Trudeau remained convinced that *La Grève de l'amiante*, despite its faults, had begun the process of demystifying the past and had laid the foundation for elaborating a clearly defined social philosophy, one capable to meeting the challenges of the industrial revolution.[41]

The neo-nationalist response to *Cité libre*'s critique of nationalism was, as we have seen, somewhat ambivalent. After all, neo-nationalists themselves had roundly condemned what they termed the excessive idealism of traditional French-Canadian nationalism. What made them feel uncomfortable with the *Cité libre* critique of French-Canadian nationalism was its authors' belief that all forms of nationalism were inherently unprogressive, undemocratic, and antimodern. Jean-Guy Blain questioned Trudeau's use of a single historical event to explain French Canada's isolationism and the inertia of its social values and institutional structure. 'This situation was due less to nationalist doctrine which, as compensation, served us as ideological fodder, than to an ethnic handicap which only history could explain fully.'[42] Others wondered how traditional nationalism, an ideology that was consciously opposed to secularism and industrialization, could reflect the socio-economic realities of such a society. Trudeau's essay, responded Laurendeau, was excellent polemic but unjust and inaccurate history. Nevertheless, his denunciation of nationalist thought for failing to recognize the inevitability of the industrial revolution was, in Laurendeau's view, quite valid. Trudeau had outlined the problem—the excessive idealism of nationalist thought—and described its practical consequences with great precision and scathing wit. What he had failed to do satisfactorily was to elucidate the 'why?', that is, the complex of historical reasons—social, cultural, economic, and political—that had fostered and nurtured the ideology. Despite Trudeau's polemical approach and oversimplified generalizations, Laurendeau willingly acknowledged that the essay revealed new insights, new truths. 'What is best in Trudeau, other than this technical competence, is his love of liberty; he welcomes its risks as well as its advantages. A remarkable personality is being revealed.'[43] The road for compromise and further discussion had been consciously left open by the neo-nationalists.

Conclusion

Cité libre's opposition to nationalism was both ideological and political. As Christian humanists and liberal and social democrats, the *Citélibristes* considered nationalism to be irrevocably and inherently conservative, anti-democratic, and reactionary. Nationalism placed a priority on collective values and interests at the cost of neglecting and, on occasion, opposing universal human values, such as freedom of expression, freedom of creed. Furthermore, nationalists seldom gave the appropriate priority to the socio-economic advancement of the individual or the weaker groups and classes in society. On the political level the ruling *Union nationale* party and its astute and wily *chef*, Maurice Duplessis, used nationalist rhetoric to retain office and prevent the modernization of Quebec society. In short, nationalism and nationalist programs, when they were implemented, served the vested interests of the established secular and clerical élites, anglophone and francophone, at the expense of the needs of the Quebec people. Nationalism, by camouflaging the real interests and ambitions of its advocates, distorted the true meaning and operation of parliamentary democracy. All in all, there was little in the *Cité libre* analysis to endear the group to either traditional or neo-nationalists. A close scrutiny of how both groups approached certain fundamental issues, such as the role of the modern state, will illustrate the basic divergences between their respective ideologies.

Suggestions for Further Reading

Donald Cameron, *Nationalism, Self Determination and the Quebec Question* (Toronto, 1974).

J.-C. Falardeau, ed., *Essays on Contemporary Quebec* (Quebec, 1953).

Kenneth McRoberts and Dale Postgate, *Quebec: Social Change and Political Crisis* (Toronto, 2nd edn rev., 1980).

Notes

[1] Maurice Blain, 'Sur la liberté de l'esprit', *Esprit* 20 (août–septembre 1952), 210.

[2] *Ibid.*, 209.

[3] *Ibid.*, 210.

[4] Pierre Vadeboncoeur, 'Notre Mission inattendue', *AN* 22 (octobre 1943), 107.

[5] 'Etat nation,' *AN* 27 (janvier 1946), 10–18 (10 quoted).

[6] Cormier, 'Pour un humanisme ouvrier: Notes sur l'autonomie quotidienne', *AN* 30 (novembre 1947), 172–83.

[7] Trudeau, 'D'abord social, puis républicain', *Devoir*, 6 juillet 1949. Vadeboncoeur supported Trudeau's arguments in his 'Portrait—ou caricature?—du "nationaliste" ', *ibid.*, 14 juillet 1949.

[8] Cormier, 'Petite Méditation sur l'existence canadienne-française', *Cité libre* 1 (juin 1950), 26–7, 28, 36.

[9]Trudeau, 'La Province de Québec au moment de la grève', 90.

[10]*Ibid.*, 11; Jean-Guy Blain, 'Pour une dynamique de notre culture', *Cité libre* 5 (juin–juillet 1952), 21; Vadeboncoeur, 'L'Irréalisme de notre culture', *ibid.*, 4 (décembre 1951), 20; Rioux, 'Idéologie et crise de conscience du Canada français', *ibid.*, 14 (décembre 1955), 3; and Dumont, 'De quelques obstacles à la prise de conscience chez les Canadiens français', *ibid.*, 19 (janvier 1958), 24.

[11]'La Province de Québec au moment de la grève', 13.

[12]*Ibid.*, 11–12; Blain, 'Pour une dynamique', 21.

[13]Vadeboncoeur, 'L'Irréalisme', 21.

[14]Rioux, 'Idéologie et crise de conscience', 14. For a similar statement see Trudeau, 'La Province de Québec au moment de la grève', 12.

[15]Cf. Maurice Tremblay, 'Orientations de la pensée sociale', in *Essais sur le Québec contemporain*, 194–208. Many of Tremblay's ideas had initially been expressed in a manuscript, 'La Pensée sociale au Canada français', Québec, June 1950; Blain, 'Pour une dynamique', 21.

[16]Rioux, 'Idéologie et crise de conscience', 14; Ernest Gagnon, 'Visage de l'intelligence', *Esprit* 20 (août–septembre 1952), 232.

[17]'La Province de Québec au moment de la grève', 14–37.

[18]*Ibid.*, 88. Jean-Charles Falardeau had raised most of these critical points in his conclusion to the 1952 Laval symposium on French Canada and industrialization. 'Perspectives' in *Essais sur le Québec contemporain*, 246–9.

[19]Vadeboncoeur, 'A Break with Tradition', *Queen's Quarterly* 65 (Spring 1958), 92.

[20]Vadeboncoeur, 'Pour une dynamique', 13.

[21]*Ibid.*, 16–17; Rioux, 'Idéologie et crise de conscience', 19.

[22]Tremblay, 'La Pensée sociale', 47, cited in Rioux, 'Idéologie et crise de conscience', 20.

[23]Tremblay, 'La Pensée sociale', 24. He wrote: 'partant du postulat de la transcendance du catholicisme sur le protestantisme, de la vérité sur l'erreur, l'auteur transpose inconsciemment cette transcendance sur le plan culturel, pour accorder à la culture canadienne-français catholique une supériorité absolue par rapport à la culture anglo-protestante.' For a published expression of his critique of the nationalist ideology see his 'Conflit d'allégeances chez les Canadiens français', *Ad Usum Sacerdotum* 13 (janvier 1958), 19–25; and his 'Réflexions sur le nationalisme', in *Ecrits du Canada français* 5 (1959), 11–43.

[24]Rioux, 'Idéologie et crise de conscience', 21–8; Maurice Blain, 'Sur la liberté', 201–4, 209.

[25]Vadeboncoeur, 'A Break with Tradition', 92–6; 'Critique de notre psychologie de l'action', *Cité libre* 8 (novembre 1953), 11–22.

[26]Vadeboncoeur, 'Critique de notre psychologie', 26–7. For another expression of these views see his 'A Break with Tradition', 97–102.

[27]Pelletier, 'Dissidence', *Cité libre* 8 (novembre 1953), 32.

[28]*Ibid.*, p. 33.

[29]Fernand Dumont, 'De quelques obstacles', *Cité libre* 19 (janvier 1958), 22–8.

[30]Trudeau, 'Conclusion', in *La Grève de l'amiante*, 396; Rioux, 'Idéologie et crise de conscience', 28–9.

[31]Rioux, 'Idéologie et crise de conscience', 29. For a similar response see Jean-Guy Blain, 'Pour une dynamique', 26.

[32]M.-J. d'Anjou, 'Le cas de "*Cité libre*"', *Relations* 11 (mars 1951), 69–70.

[33]Interview with Charles Lussier, 8 September 1976.

[34]Robert Rumilly, *L'Infiltration gauchiste au Canada*, 1–29.

[35]*Ibid.*, 77–95.

[36]Jacques Cousineau, *Réflexions en marge de 'la Grève de l'amiante'* (Montréal: Les cahiers de l'Institut social populaire, no. 4, septembre 1958), 6. Cf. Cousineau, *L'Eglise d'ici et le social 1940–1960* (Montréal, 1982), chap. 12, 'La Grève et l'Eglise d'ici (1949)', 168–84.

[37]*Réflexions et marge*, 16–22.

[38]*Ibid.*, 39.

[39]F.-A. Angers, 'Pierre Elliott Trudeau et *La Grève de l'amiante* I', 47 (septembre 1957), 10–22 (18 quoted).

[40]Angers, 'Trudeau et *La Grève de l'amiante*—VI', 48 (septembre–octobre 1958), 45–56.

[41]Trudeau, 'Le pere Consineau, s.j., et *La Grève de l'amiante*', *Cité libre* 23 (mai 1959), 34–48.

[42]Jean-Guy Blain, 'La grève de l'amiante', 46 (octobre 1956), 135; Cf. his 'La Province de Québec au tournant du demi-siècle: Evolutions de la pensée sociale', *Devoir*, 9 juin 1956.

[43]Laurendeau, 'Sur cent pages de P.E. Trudeau, I-II-III', *Devoir*, 6, 10, 11 octobre 1956 (article III quoted).

29

⤳

The 'Modernization' of Newfoundland

Ralph D. Matthews

When Newfoundland entered Confederation in 1949 Canada finally completed the unification process begun in 1867. Like most primary producing regions of North America, Newfoundland had suffered greatly between the wars, but the Depression obliged it to surrender its autonomy within the British Empire. Newfoundland had voluntarily returned to a colonial status—with no institutions of representative government—in which Britain administered its affairs. After the Second World War confederation with Canada was the only viable solution to Newfoundland's political difficulties, but it was not easy to persuade Newfoundlanders that there was no alternative, or to convince the government of Canada that it should assume the responsibility. The local movement for Confederation was led by a journalist and radio broadcaster, Joseph Smallwood, who became the province's first premier under Confederation. The alliance opened new sources of

revenue and income to Newfoundland and its people, and made possible the creation of new policies to deal with the province's recurring social and economic problems. The Smallwood government was prepared to confront Newfoundland's difficulties head-on, and its policies in the 1950s and 1960s were among the most innovative and interventionist of any Canadian province. Adapting Newfoundland to modern Canada was difficult, and Smallwood's policies provoked much debate.

Ralph Matthews assesses the Smallwood administration's response to Newfoundland's problems, particularly in the areas of social and economic development. Newfoundland attempted to deal with its high birth rate by centralizing its scattered population in hopes of providing a labour pool for economic growth. Its educational policies were extremely enlightened, despite high rates of illiteracy. The difficulty was that the destruction of a traditional way of life had to be justified by the development of satisfying alternatives—which did not emerge. Instead of a largely rural population, Newfoundland developed an urbanized society based not on industrial growth but on service and government support. Government attempts to diversify the economy through encouragement to private industry proved largely unsuccessful. Matthews argues that the Smallwood administration did have a comprehensive program for social and economic development, but relied too heavily on urban concentration and concessions to outside developers. In the end, he suggests, the failure to produce successful economic growth made the costs of the Smallwood policy extremely high.

What were the problems faced by Newfoundland after 1949? In what ways was the Smallwood government imaginative and innovative? Did it try to move too fast? Why did it concentrate so heavily on urbanization and economic diversification? What alternative strategies might have been adopted? Why did economic development fail? Was failure inevitable? On balance, how would you assess the Smallwood administration in Newfoundland?

This article first appeared in Neil B. Ridler, ed., *Issues in Regional/Urban Development of Atlantic Canada*, Social Sciences Monograph Series, II (Spring, 1978), 27–50. Copyright Division of Social Sciences, University of New Brunswick, Saint John.

Newfoundland, at the time of confederation with Canada in 1949, was lacking many of those things that have come to be regarded as basic and indispensable services and facilities in a modern society. The Fathers of Newfoundland's Confederation were faced with a formidable task, for they had to plan Newfoundland's modern development from the most basic level upward. Perhaps the depth of Newfoundland's needs are best revealed in this quote from her Premier for the first twenty-three years of Confederation, Joseph R. Smallwood.

84.
Eighty-four.
In all Newfoundland and Labrador.
84.
84 what?
84 schools with indoor toilets.
That was Newfoundland on the day that I became Premier.
Today: 838 schools have indoor toilets.
We have not in those years, produced any new or original education theory, philosophy or practice.
But we have put indoor toilets in 744 [sic] schools that didn't have them.
That's progress.[1]

In those early days of Confederation, the 'pursuit of progress' frequently was measured in terms of those things which other Canadians took for granted. Under such conditions dreams of 'human excellence' frequently had to be put aside.[2]

It is a measure of Smallwood's success that by 1972 living conditions had vastly improved for virtually every Newfoundlander. Though some of this improvement was simply the product of many Canadian social-service benefits which Newfoundlanders began to enjoy as soon as they became Canadians, much of the credit for these improved living conditions must go to Smallwood and his various governments. Smallwood spent a considerable portion of his provincial budget on improving provincial services. He was particularly imaginative in the areas of education and transportation and communication.

Regional schools were built, an impressive network of vocational schools were constructed, and Newfoundland's junior college grew into a university of considerable size and importance. Yet the Smallwood government's insight into the educational needs of Newfoundlanders went beyond the provision of facilities. As long as the average annual income from fishing remained less than $700, few ordinary Newfoundlanders would ever be able to afford higher education. Consequently, early in his term of office Smallwood established the most comprehensive system of scholarships and bursaries in Canada for all levels and types of education. For a while Newfoundland even had North America's only system of free university education. Newfoundland's traditional occupations were also assisted through a new fisheries college.

In the sphere of transportation, Newfoundland's traditional reliance on the sea for transport was replaced by land transportation. At the time of Confederation there was no trans-island highway, few local roads, and only 121 miles of pavement. Canada's west had been brought into Confederation with a promise of a railway link to central Canada. In 1949, Newfoundland was in no position to bargain for a similar highway link. Nevertheless, Smallwood continually demanded more than the 50 per cent of construction costs that the federal government had given other provinces to build the Trans-Canada Highway. In 1960 his efforts were rewarded when he wrested from Lester Pearson a pledge of 90 per cent of costs should Pearson and the Liberals regain power in Ottawa. When Pearson was successful, Newfoundland got its highway. But even though it stretched 600 miles across the island, Newfoundland's segment of the Trans-Canada Highway did not serve the large number of Newfoundlanders who lived on remote peninsulas and offshore islands. To assist them the provincial government built a network of secondary roads over 5,000 miles long.

Smallwood's administration also went beyond normal expectations in this sphere by founding an airline. Gander-based Eastern Provincial Airlines was originally a bush-pilot operation begun with a grant from the Newfoundland government and designed to link Newfoundland's isolated regions. It has been transformed into one of the largest regional airlines in the country. It is a valuable asset in everything from mining exploration to mail delivery. More important still, it remains the main transportation link between the island of Newfoundland and her rich Labrador hinterland. In recent years, EPA has also grown to be the regional carrier for the whole Atlantic region, providing daily jet service to all Maritime centres, and linking them with Montreal.

Newfoundland's post-Confederation government was both innovative and imaginative in recognizing and dealing with the problems of education and transportation which are so basic to any future course of development. However, these very services, which were demanded by the people and presumed to be necessary prerequisites to industrial development, may have actually hampered the long-term development of the province. By using his limited cash resources to provide infrastructural services, Smallwood drastically reduced the money available for resource and industrial development which could provide long-term jobs.[3] Much of Newfoundland's continuing economic difficulty and high rate of unemployment may be the result of these development policies. There were also other social and economic problems that the Smallwood administration did not face at all.

This paper will examine some of these social and economic problems and will assess the effectiveness of the Smallwood government's policies in dealing with them during the twenty-three years that he was in office. There are obvious demarcation difficulties. However, we will roughly divide the problem areas which the Smallwood government faced into social and economic problems. The two sections which immediately follow will examine the social problems and Smallwood's tactics for dealing with them. They will be followed by similar assessments of Newfoundland's economic problems and the Smallwood government's economic-development strategy.

Newfoundland's Social Problems

Newfoundland's main 'social' problems stem primarily from the growth and dispersion of her population.[4] The importance of population factors in economic development was succinctly expressed by a Newfoundland Royal Commission set up to investigate her economic development. In their words, 'Economic development embraces the whole socio-economic process whereby an economy's real income increased at a rate faster than its population growth.'[5] The Newfoundland population has tended to grow so rapidly that her economic gains have been largely dissipated.

While in many countries poverty and high birth rates tend to go together, Newfoundlanders seem to be more willing to bring children into the world in times of plenty than in times of economic depression. Thus her birth rate and population growth mirror her recent economic development (see Tables 1 and 2, p. 642). The high birth rate and low death rate which saw her population increase rapidly during the nineteenth century continued unabated into the twentieth century. Only the acute depression of the 1930s was able to force her phenomenal birth rate to fall slightly. But this trend was short-lived; the postwar 'baby boom' occurred in Newfoundland as it did in other western countries, and Newfoundland's birth rate shot to unprecedented levels. But just as the baby boom was ending elsewhere, Newfoundland joined Canada and began a new era of hope and prosperity. Moreover, the Canadian family-allowance system, by paying Newfoundlanders a 'baby bonus' for every new infant, brought scarce dollars into the traditional rural economy. As a result, the baby boom of the 1940s continued in Newfoundland until well into the 1960s, giving Newfoundland the highest birth rate of any Canadian province. This large juvenile population also tended to lower the death rate so as to give Newfoundland the lowest death rate in Canada as well.

The development implications of this rate of population growth are far-reaching. First, the large juvenile population means that a relatively small portion of the population must support the rest. By 1966, over 51 per cent of the population were in the age group 0–19, while those over age 65 made up another 5.9 per cent. This situation is made even more serious by the fact that, traditionally, few Newfoundland women have worked outside the home except in the pre-industrial fishing economy. As a result of these factors, those employed in 1968 averaged less than 24 per cent of the population.[6]

The high birth rate and large juvenile population also served to 'eat up' the very real economic gains achieved since Confederation. Between 1949 and 1967, Newfoundland's total personal income increased at an annual average of 8.5 per cent, the highest in Canada. But because of the population increase, some of these gains were dissipated across the larger population. Thus, in the same period, the per-capita income increased by only 6.5 per cent annually.[7] In 1970, the Newfoundland per-capita income was $1,784, a remarkable achievement over its 1949 level of $472. Nevertheless, it was still far lower than the Canadian average of $3,092 or the Ontario average of $3,584.[8] One way for Newfoundland to narrow this gap was to curb drastically its population growth.

The effects of Newfoundland's high birth rate on her social and economic development are by no means temporary. Even if the birth rate were immediately lowered, it would take twenty years for the large juvenile population already born to reach the labour force. This means that, in each of the next twenty years, Newfoundland will have many more people entering the labour force than leaving it through retirement and death. The Newfoundland government itself has estimated that it will have to produce 3,000 to 4,000 new jobs a year to absorb these additional workers, and their estimates are probably conservative.[9] While this may, at first glance, not appear to be an excessive demand, it means that upwards of 80,000 new jobs have to be developed in Newfoundland over the next twenty years if many Newfoundlanders are not to be unemployed or forced to migrate. Jobs have also, of course, to be found for the thousands who now find it impossible to get work, or who are only employed on a seasonal basis. This is an enormous demand for a province where the labour force is now only about 160,000.

Yet Newfoundland's rate of population growth is only part of her population problem. The dispersion of population creates still further difficulties. Only 40 per cent urban in 1949, by 1971 over 57 per cent of the population lived in centres of 1,000 or more people (see Table 3). Despite this apparent population shift, Newfoundland's rural population has not diminished but has also continued to grow, albeit at a slower rate. Moreover, the rural population is widely dispersed. Early proscriptions against settlement together with the desire to be as close as possible to the fishing grounds led many early settlers to pick the most barren headlands and offshore islands for their homesteads. In addition, the ecology of the traditional inshore fishery does not in general support large communities. As a consequence, as late as 1961, Newfoundland had 1,104 communities of which 815 had less than 300 inhabitants (see Table 4). Because of government programs which will be discussed in the following section, these numbers have been reduced. In 1971, there were only 878 separate communities. Nevertheless, there were still 545 with fewer than 300 residents and 226 with fewer than 100 occupants.

This dispersion of her rural population has been a major impediment to the provision of modern services in Newfoundland. As long as the people remained dispersed and isolated, it was simply too costly to provide many of them with facilities such as electricity, roads, telephones, hospitals, and modern schools. It was often impossible to find qualified doctors, nurses, and teachers who were willing to live in isolation. Despite this, Confederation led to rising expectations and few Newfoundlanders were willing to accept conditions as they had been. Their expectations were further enhanced by radio and television which brought them vivid impressions of the world outside their coastal villages.

Newfoundland's Social Development Policy

Even though one of Newfoundland's most basic social problems was her population growth, she has done virtually nothing to curb it. Indeed, throughout the whole of Smallwood's reign, Newfoundland's leaders actually boasted of her population growth and tended to equate larger population size with ultimate greatness and economic viability. The tenor of their beliefs

Table 1. Population of Newfoundland and Labrador 1836–1971.

Year	Population
1836	75,094
1857	124,288
1869	146,536
1874	161,374
1884	197,335
1891	202,040
1901	220,984
1911	242,619
1921	263,033
1935	289,588
1945	321,819
1951	361,416
1956	415,074
1961	457,853
1966	493,396
1971	522,104

SOURCES: *Census of Newfoundland and Labrador*, 1935, I: 9. Thahane: *Population Growth and Shifts in Newfoundland. Canada Year Book.* 1968, 1972.

Table 2. Newfoundland Live Birth, Death, and Natural Increase Rates per 1,000 Population by Periods 1921 to 1971.

Period	Average Live Birth Rate	Average Death Rate	Average Natural Increase Rate
1921 to 1925	26.7	14.0	12.7
1926 to 1930	25.1	13.7	11.4
1931 to 1935	23.4	12.8	10.6
1936 to 1940	25.8	12.4	13.4
1941 to 1945	29.8	11.8	18.0
1946 to 1950	36.2	9.3	26.9
1951 to 1955	34.1	7.6	26.5
1956 to 1960	34.6	7.2	27.4
1961 to 1965	31.5	6.6	24.9
1966 to 1970	25.8	6.2	19.6
1971	24.5	6.1	18.4

SOURCES: *Canada Year Book*, 1956, 1961, 1968, 1972. *Vital Statistics*, Preliminary Annual Report, 1971, Statistics Canada Cat. No. 84-201.

Table 3. Rural and Urban Population of Newfoundland and Percentage Rural and Urban for Census Years 1901 to 1971.

Census Year	Total Census Population	Rural Population (under 1,000)	Per cent Rural	Urban Population (over 1,000)	Per cent Urban
1901	220,984	171,368	77.5	49,616	22.5
1911	242,619	186,458	76.9	56,161	23.1
1921	263,033	198,555	75.5	64,478	24.5
1935	289,588	203,986	70.4	85,602	29.6
1945	321,819	218,886	68.0	102,933	32.0
1951	361,416	206,621	57.2	154,795	42.8
1961	457,853	225,833	49.3	232,020	50.7
1966	493,396	226,707	45.9	266,689	54.1
1971	522,104	223,304	42.8	298,800	57.2

SOURCES: For 1901 to 1945: compiled from statistics on communities of over 1,000 population given in *Census of Newfoundland*: 1945: 2. For 1951 to 1966: compiled from *Canada Year Book*, 1956, 1968. 1971 statistics provided by Statistics Canada. Urban and rural percentages calculated by this writer.

Table 4. Number of Communities in Newfoundland by Population of Community, Census Years, 1961, 1966, 1971.

Population of Community	Number of Communities		
	1961	1966	1971
0 to 49	238	153	113
50 to 99	174	148	113
100 to 199	263	222	196
200 to 299	140	125	123
300 to 399	83	91	82
400 to 499	69	48	44
500 to 999	83	116	126
1,000 to 4,999	47	60	71
5,000 to 9,999	5	7	8
10,000 and over	2	2	2

SOURCES: 1961: *Census of Canada*, 1961, 92–538, Bulletin SP-4, 'Population of Unincorporated Places of 50 Persons and Over'. *Canada Year Book*, 1968, 197. 'Incorporated Towns and Villages, 1961', and a supplement provided by Dominion Bureau of Statistics, St John's, Newfoundland, listing 'Unincorporated places with less than 50 persons'.

1966 & 1971: lists provided by Statistics Canada in St John's, Newfoundland, showing 'Province of Newfoundland: Unincorporated Communities with a Population of Less than 50 for 1966 and 1971'. 'Population of Unincorporated Places of 50 Persons and Over, Newfoundland 1966 and 1971'. 'Province of Newfoundland: Population of Incorporated Cities, Towns and Villages, Census Years 1951–1971'.

and the tenets of their argument are dramatically conveyed in the following quote from Smallwood's autobiography, *I Chose Canada*.

> I remember a brief conversation I once had in the air terminal at Gander with Prince Philip. There was an immense jam of cheering youngsters there from around central Newfoundland to greet the Queen and the Prince. 'We have the highest birth rate in North America,' I told him. 'Our population is growing at a faster rate than anywhere else in Canada.' He seemed to take a dim view of that fact, but his response changed quickly when I pointed out that we were only half a million souls in Newfoundland, which didn't make too good a market for industries catering to the Newfoundland market. 'When we have a million people in this province, they'll be able to support dozens of factories and other kinds of enterprise that couldn't survive today,' and he nodded in agreement.[10]

There is, of course, some truth in Smallwood's argument. A population double its present size would indeed require approximately twice as many goods and services. On the other hand, there would also be twice as many people to be employed to maintain even the current chronically poor employment level. Moreover, it is unlikely that twice as many people would be required to double the current production capacity, for large industries tend to employ proportionally fewer workers than small ones. Given an expanded population, many new industries would have to be attracted to maintain even current employment-unemployment rates. If this were not done, vast numbers of Newfoundlanders would either be unemployed or forced to migrate.

Smallwood appears to have realized this, for in 1969, he made the following statement.

> This is what I believe:
> —That Newfoundland is in danger of losing a large proportion of our young population:
> —That tens of thousand (yes, scores of thousands) of young Newfoundlanders will leave this Province to build up Ontario (and have a good living doing it) if we fail to give them a chance to build up our own Province and have a good living doing it:
> —That the loss of this young blood, the loss of this drive and energy and ambition would spell death for our Province.[11]

Unfortunately, Smallwood seems to have had the mistaken impression that he was succeeding in finding jobs for these young Newfoundlanders, and was thus keeping them at home. In the same work he claims:

> On the day I became Premier, our population was 347,000. Today it is 510,000. I am Premier today for 163,000 more Newfoundlanders than I was the first day. Because: Newfoundland, since Confederation, has had the highest birth-rate in Canada. And the lowest death-rate. And I have been successful in keeping most of our people home . . . keeping them in Newfoundland. It took a

lot of improvements, a lot of progress in many directions . . . but these did create an air of hope and confidence. But the mad rush away from Newfoundland was stopped.[12]

This statement ignores the fact that, despite the increased population, the emigration of Newfoundlanders was only halted during the first few years of his reign. In the later years of Smallwood's premiership, the rate of emigration from Newfoundland was higher than it had been in forty years.

It is possible to use census figures together with birth and death rates to calculate the exact net migration. This is the migration balance between those entering and leaving the province. The results of this calculation show that from 1957 to 1971 an annual average of 3,000 to 4,000 more Newfoundlanders left the province than there were outsiders entering it. Even when population size is taken into account, this is still a higher *rate* of emigration than occurred during the depression of the 1930s and 1940s. It is also particularly noteworthy that the net emigration approximates the number of additional jobs per year which the government has estimated it would have to produce in order to cope with Newfoundland's expanding population. Taken together these figures reflect an almost total inability to absorb Newfoundland's growing population into the labour force.

Even while the Newfoundland government tended to encourage the rapid growth of its population, it actively pursued policies to decrease population dispersion and move its population into selected 'growth centres'. The two programs of population resettlement that were launched can be seen as a deliberate attempt to amass large labour pools in order to entice new industry.[13] If such is the case, it was a particularly odious policy, for it placed the average worker directly at the mercy of the large corporations which could pick and choose, hire and fire, almost as they saw fit.

The first government 'centralization' program was a solely provincial-government operation begun in 1953, supposedly in response to repeated requests from Bonavista Bay residents for government assistance in moving from off-shore islands to the nearby mainland.[14] The declared goals of this program were essentially humanitarian ones. Its primary purpose was to assist those who already wanted to move away from the declining inshore fishery and devastated Labrador fishery, and closer to modern services and jobs in forestry and industry. Assistance of up to $600 per family was provided, but it was only granted after 100 per cent of the households in a community signed an official document indicating their willingness to move. Despite this restriction and the small sums involved, the program evacuated 115 communities, comprising 1,504 families and 7,500 persons, in the twelve years of its operation.[15]

By 1965, the federal government had begun to play a major role in policy planning in Newfoundland.[16] In that year a new Federal-Provincial 'Resettlement' Program replaced the previous program of community centralization. Though the goal was still community evacuation, economic development considerations were much more dominant under this program. For the first time, the place to which households moved became an issue, and assistance was granted only when this location was approved by a resettlement committee composed of federal and provincial civil servants. Also, for the first time, community relocation came to be regarded as part of a 'growth-centre strategy of development'. Seventy-seven growth centres were selected and those moving were encouraged to move to them. Though the aged and infirm might still move where they wished, able-bodied men and those with young families were directed into these selected communities. With the federal government paying the costs, each household which moved now received $1,000, plus $200 for each member, plus the costs of moving their personal effects. Finally, the stipulation in the Centralization Program that all households in a community had to agree to move was lowered under the Resettlement Program to first 90, then 80 per cent. Under this program, 137 communities containing 3,876 households and 19,197 residents were moved between 1 April 1965 and 30 April 1972.

Representatives of the Newfoundland government have frequently argued that the Resettlement Program was nothing new. They claim that Newfoundlanders have been moving for generations and that they were simply assisting (and perhaps speeding up) a process that would have occurred naturally, even if they were not involved. For this reason, almost every government tabulation of communities resettled makes reference to the forty-nine communities which disappeared without any assistance between 1946 and 1954.[17] This argument contains some truth, for Newfoundlanders do indeed have a long history of moving, and some of these forty-nine communities most certainly did disappear.[18] Indeed, it is probably valid to claim that the provincial centralization program in its early days *was* assisting a natural process. To claim that the resettlement process is a natural one, however, is to disregard totally *all* the sociological and anthropological literature on the subject. These studies repeatedly show that many of those who resettled had no intention of moving only a few months prior to doing so. They conclude that rumour and intimidation were very much a part of the resettlement process, as those who wanted to move attempted to sway others, so as to get the necessary 80 per cent required.[19]

The major complaint which has been levelled at resettlement is that it destroys a way of life without providing a viable alternative. The disenchantment of the critics with the selected growth centres is certainly understandable. Few of them had the economic base to sustain their own population, much less the influx of outsiders. Many who resettled were still forced to travel away from home in order to get work. Often the only advantage of such communities was their larger size, which justified their being provided with a few of the services and facilities lacking elsewhere. Such centres were a far cry from the 'growth pole' or 'growth centre' concept upon which the resettlement program was rooted.

The growth-centre theory posits that regional development is most likely to occur in those 'centres' which contain 'growth poles'. These are 'master industries' which, because of their large size, have what is described in the theory as 'propulsive potential'.[20] Though this is essentially an economics-based theory, it has obvious social implications. For any area to be able to support such large enterprises it must first have those infrastructural facilities which such industries require. These are usually available only in larger centres. There can be little doubt that such considerations were the underlying basis of Newfoundland's resettlement program, and indeed of a large part of its strategy of social development. The government persisted in this policy even when economic studies indicated that most of those who moved would take many years to obtain the level of housing and other facilities which they had prior to moving.[21]

Newfoundland's Economic Problems

Newfoundland's social problems and policies have been analysed by anthropologists, sociologists, and even economists interested in studying their economic implications. But there has been very little systematic analysis of the economic problems and economic-development potential of Newfoundland. An exception is the *Report* of the Royal Commission on the Economic State and Prospects of Newfoundland and Labrador, which is a most valuable compilation of data on Newfoundland's economic position.[22] Its recommendations, however, are overly general and piecemeal, and it lacks the thrust of an integrated development program. As a consequence of this dearth of previous work, the discussion which follows is somewhat sketchy. Partly to offset this lack of previous analysis, focus will again be placed on the more general 'background' factors affecting Newfoundland development.

The most critical background factor influencing Newfoundland's economic development is the fact that it is an island. Because of this, goods produced in Newfoundland cannot be transported overland to markets. The additional labour costs involved in loading goods from boats to trains or trucks for North American markets place Newfoundland products at a disadvantage as compared to those of, say, Nova Scotia and New Brunswick. Isolation hampers Newfoundland's economic prospects in other ways as well. It is worth noting that St John's is approximately the same distance by sea from Halifax as Halifax is distant from Boston. Thus goods produced in Newfoundland not only have to be loaded and unloaded several times, but they must also travel great distances to reach their markets.

Newfoundland's labour force presents further obstacles to economic development. Despite the major gains which have been made in education and training, a large segment of Newfoundland's labour force remains illiterate. In 1961, 18.0 per cent of all Newfoundlanders and 26.7 per cent of Newfoundland's rural population were illiterate, giving Newfoundland twice the national illiteracy rate. More important still, over 25 per cent of those between the ages of 35 and 44, and over 12 per cent of those between the ages of 25 and 34 were illiterate.[23] Much of the labour force (whether literate or illiterate) is unfitted for anything but manual labour and inshore fishing. It is occasionally suggested that Newfoundland's unskilled population and consequent low wage scale provide a cheap labour force which is attractive to industry. Indeed, this is one of the claims made by the advocates of growth centres. But the cost of training workers to perform the highly technical work demanded by many modern industries often makes unskilled labour prohibitively expensive.

An examination of the structure of Newfoundland's labour force gives further insight into her economic problems. At the turn of the century, almost the entire labour force of Newfoundland was made up of inshore fishermen.[24] Though there was some diversification in the 1940s, Newfoundland's 28,000 fishermen at the time of Confederation were still the backbone of the economy.[25] The years since Confederation have seen the number of fishermen stabilize at around 18,000, or about 20 per cent of the 1970 labour force (see Table 5). Despite the popular image of Newfoundlanders as primarily fishermen, loggers, and miners, these primary producers together now compose less than a quarter of the labour force.

By 1970, most Newfoundland workers were engaged in the secondary and tertiary sectors of the economy. This relatively rapid shift from a traditional rural fishing economy to a modern urban commercial one gave Newfoundland some of the characteristics of a 'dual society' in which there is a dichotomy between rural and urban areas in outlook and values.[26] Though many rural Newfoundlanders do move back and forth between the two sectors, there is ample evidence that most are simply using their occasional wage labour to make the traditional way of life more viable, and there is little change in their basic attitudes and values.[27] Indeed, there is strong evidence that basic value differences do exist in Newfoundland between the two ways of life.[28] Though there is a danger of over-emphasizing this dualism, it nevertheless has important development implications. Policies which focus on urban development and assume that the traditional rural sector of the society will automatically adjust may only increase the schism. Development planning must include rural-development planning. To be successful, rural-development planning should not simply be an extension of urban planning into rural areas but should be based on the natural skills, crafts, and resources of the traditional economy. It should not be aimed at annihilating the traditional sector, but at incorporating it into the overall economy.

The statistics on Newfoundland's labour force also reflect the Newfoundland government's general failure to attract manufacturing industry. Only

Table 5. Employment in Newfoundland by Selected Industry, 1970 (Yearly Averages).

Industry	Number of Employed
Primary:	
Forestry	2,200
Mining	5,900
* Fishing	17,765
(Fishing full-time)	(1,855)
(Fishing part-time)	(7,282)
(Fishing occasional)	(8,628)
Secondary:	
Manufacturing	12,600
(Non-durables)	(10,700)
(Durables)	(1,900)
Construction	7,600
Tertiary:	
Trade	18,200
(Wholesale)	(6,100)
(Retail)	(12,100)
Finance	2,300
Community, Business and Personal Services	30,300
(Non-commercial sector)	(21,600)
(Commercial sector)	(8,700)
Public Administration and Defence	8,600
Transportation, Communication, and Other Utilities	14,600

* As the Newfoundland fishery is seasonal, many Newfoundland inshore fishermen are listed as part-time and occasional, even though they would regard themselves as full-time fishermen. A small number of them may also be employed in other industries (notably forestry) during the off season.

SOURCES: Most of the data above are taken from 'Estimates of Employees by Province and Industry', February 1971, Statistics Canada, Cat. No. 72-008. This tabulation does not include fishermen, and the data on fishing were taken from 'Fisheries Statistics, Newfoundland 1971', Statistics Canada. Cat. No. 24-202.

12,600 of the approximately 160,000 persons employed in 1970 were engaged in manufacturing, and most of those were engaged in producing food products for the local market. Less than 2,000 were engaged in the production of durable goods. The employment structure also reflects the extensive amount of construction which has taken place in Newfoundland since Confederation. During the early 1960s, nearly 7 per cent of the labour force was engaged in construction,[29] slightly surpassing the national average.[30]

As Newfoundland's urgent construction needs were met, the government was faced with the spectre of having Newfoundland's few skilled workers added to the already large unemployment rolls.

Perhaps the most striking feature of the Newfoundland labour force is the large segment engaged in service (tertiary) activities. By the early 1970s this amounted to approximately 50 per cent of the labour force. While this is common in most advanced societies, it is somewhat unusual for a society with such a small manufacturing base. Of course, it is only possible because Newfoundland receives considerable sums of money in Canadian transfer payments.

Insularity, isolation, illiteracy, and a low level of skills were problems which faced the Newfoundland government at Confederation. In this sense, they can be regarded as background conditions which any future economic-development policy had to try to overcome or alter. But the problems of economic dualism, a small manufacturing base, an unbalanced labour force, and dependence on federal transfer payments seem to be of a different order. Though they are partly the result of insularity, isolation, and illiteracy, they are also the product of the government's handling of these problems. At this juncture, it seems impossible to separate Newfoundland's economic problems from the policies and programs which attempted to overcome them.

Newfoundland's Economic Development Policy

Any serious economic-development program attempts to overcome the fundamental obstacles to economic growth while capitalizing on whatever natural advantages may exist. Earlier we examined some of the steps taken by the Smallwood administration to overcome the obstacles of isolation, illiteracy, and lack of skills. These efforts were accompanied by attempts to capitalize on Newfoundland's major advantage, its natural resources: fish stocks, forest reserves, mineral wealth, and hydro potential.

There is a widely held belief among Newfoundlanders that, under Smallwood, the Newfoundland government and the Canadian government rejected the Newfoundland fishery. To prove their case, they point to the attempts to resettle fishermen and lure industry to the province, thus diversifying the economy, and the supposed directive of Smallwood in an early election campaign to 'pull up your boats, burn your flakes, and forget the fishery; there will be two jobs for every man in Newfoundland.'[31] However, as Peter Neary has noted, Smallwood's twenty-year electoral success can be seen as a loyal reaction to the largesse which he provided the fishermen, and their over-representation in Newfoundland's legislature.[32] Parzival Copes's documentation supports this thesis. He shows that assistance to the inshore fishery for the construction of boats, fishing gear, bait facilities, wharves, dredging, other capital works, and unemployment insurance surpassed the income generated by the inshore fishery.[33]

But even though the government provided considerable financial assistance to the fishery this, in itself, was not enough. To be successful the Newfoundland fishery needed planning as well as money. Though it received liberal supplies of money, the extent of comprehensive planning which took place appears to have been minimal. Wharves and bait facilities often seem to have been supplied with an eye on the location of voters rather than on the existence of plentiful fish stocks. Even when the facilities were actually needed, there seems to have been little attempt to see that they were used efficiently. As a result a frozen bait facility might quickly be transformed into a cooling chamber for the wares of the local beer merchant. There was a similar lack of management of fish stocks. If government pronouncements concerning the future of the fishery were relatively restrained, it was probably due to the bitter fact that the fish stocks which form the basis of that resource were being rapidly depleted. This was especially true of the inshore fishery, where the catch per man-year declined by 50 per cent in the decade from 1956 to 1966.[34]

Newfoundland's post-Confederation government faced further problems with regard to its forest resources. Over 60 per cent of the productive forest land in the island had already been leased to the two paper companies at Corner Brook and Grand Falls under 99-year agreements begun in 1902 and 1923 respectively. Only 14 per cent of the productive forest land in the island was still held by the Crown.[35] Despite this, the Liberal administration made desperate efforts to attract a third paper mill to Newfoundland and a fourth to Labrador. Their efforts went unrewarded[36] until, as a last resort, they turned to mining promoter John C. Doyle who was already engaged in the financial arrangements for iron-ore development in Labrador. Doyle's liner-board (cardboard) mill was built at Stephenville, on Newfoundland's west coast, for no other discernible reason than that there was great unemployment in that area due to the close-down of the local American airforce base. The wood for the mill had to be cut in Labrador and shipped several hundred miles at considerable cost. This alone placed a severe financial burden which militated against the success of the development. However, the greatest controversy surrounded the financial arrangements for its construction. The original announcements implied that the bulk of the financing would come from Doyle and his backers. But by the time Smallwood was voted out of office, the Newfoundland government had provided close to a hundred million dollars for the facility, even though ownership remained in Doyle's hands. One of the first acts of the Progressive Conservative administration which came to power in January 1972 was to buy out Doyle's interest in this mill. It was then operated as a Crown corporation until 1977, when the new administration announced that they were closing it. They contended that it cost more in subsidies than it benefited the Newfoundland economy.

The fishery and the forests had been the mainstay of Newfoundland's economy prior to 1949. However, such total dependence on two basic staples made the island's economy particularly vulnerable to world fluctuations in these commodities. Indeed, the collapse of the island's economy which began in the 1920s was brought on largely by the collapse of fish prices.[37] Moreover, as we have seen, both spheres offered little hope for economic expansion.

Yet Newfoundland's population was growing unchecked and Newfoundlanders needed jobs. To provide them, Smallwood's administration attempted to diversify the economy through the development of Newfoundland's mineral resources, the harnessing of its hydro-electric potential, and through industrial diversification. The path which Smallwood followed in developing all three areas was the same as that taken by Newfoundland's earlier régimes to obtain the province's trans-island railway and major paper mills. Large concessions were offered to mining and industrial concerns if they would come and establish in the province. At various times these concessions included tax relief, free land, government loans, and outright grants.

Unlike forestry, Newfoundland's mining potential was still largely untapped at the time of Confederation. In order to encourage mineral exploration in the province, the government offered interested mining companies exclusive exploration and mining rights to large concessions, often amounting to thousands of square miles. Though this strategy had some success,[38] the concession system displayed many of the same problems that proved detrimental to the further development of Newfoundland's forest resources. As the Commission on Newfoundland's Economic Prospects notes, few of the companies involved possessed the capital or the technical knowledge to explore their large holdings.[39] The commission recommended that regulations should be introduced governing the size of concessions and the extent of explorations required.[40]

The development of Newfoundland's hydro-electric potential represented her first major break with her traditional dependence on fishing, forestry, and mining. If the economy was to diversify, it would need new industry and these industries would need power. At Confederation, the province's power development was minimal. Existing industries were forced to curtail production because of lack of power.[41] Newfoundland was blessed, however, with an abundant hydro-electric potential which included the vast Churchill Falls waterway in Labrador and the large Bay d'Espoir waterway in southern Newfoundland. Smallwood has declared his greatest accomplishment (besides Confederation itself) to be development of the power potential at Churchill Falls.[42]

With seven million horsepower, the Churchill Falls project was (at that time) the largest power development in the western hemisphere and the second largest in the world. It cost over one billion dollars and took five thousand men four years to build. As almost 90 per cent of the work force was from Newfoundland this gave a massive boost to the economy. A project of this magnitude is certain to arouse comment. The two main sources of contention were the financial arrangements involved in the construction of the project, and the terms of agreement for the sale of power to Quebec.

As the right to develop Churchill Falls was given to private industrialists, there has been much argument about whether Newfoundland received a fair share of the profit. Philip Mathias argued that Newfoundland was awarded her fair share and he even praised the Smallwood government for its shrewdness. Indeed, he cites it as the one example of 'forced growth' in Canada which resulted in real economic benefit to the province making the deal. He argued that Newfoundland got a major development that it could not otherwise afford while 'it also created a source of revenue of $15 million a year, a sizeable source of funds for a province whose expenditures in 1966 were $131 million.'[43] Nevertheless, he admitted that Brinco, the backers of the development, 'can expect profits of $22–$23 million a year, even more than the revenue which will be received by the province which owns the waterfall'.[44]

Mathias's estimates were contradicted by statements from the new Progressive Conservative government which succeeded Smallwood. Finance Minister John Crosbie startled many Newfoundlanders when he claimed that the development of the Upper Churchill 'is far from a great benefit to this province from the point of view of revenue and employment'.[45] In a heavily documented presentation he indicated that revenue to Newfoundland from Churchill Falls would not reach $10 million annually until 1985, and would not reach annually the $15 million figure quoted by Mathias until after 2002.[46] But, according to Crosbie, even this profit is illusory. Under the federal-provincial Tax-Equalization Agreement, Newfoundland's payment from Ottawa will be reduced by at least an equal amount of her revenue from Churchill Falls.[47]

If matters were to stop at this point, Newfoundland would neither gain nor lose from Churchill Falls, while the Ottawa treasury would benefit. However, according to Mr Crosbie, under a 1965 act, the federal government agreed to return to the province ninety-five per cent of taxes collected annually from public utilities but that this amount would be subtracted from their tax-equalization payment. However, under its agreement with Brinco, the Newfoundland government agreed to return to that company one-half of its share of Brinco's contributions. As its tax-equalization payment would be reduced by this amount, Newfoundland would actually lose money through the operation of Churchill Falls. Indeed, the more successful Brinco became, the more Newfoundland would lose.

In the spring of 1974, the Progressive Conservative administration threatened Brinco with nationalization if they did not sell their shares in Churchill Falls to the Newfoundland government. After considerable bargaining the company reluctantly agreed. The new government was criticized for this action on the grounds that it tied up considerable development capital in something it already possessed. Yet, given the financial arrangements with Brinco, it was undoubtedly a wise move.

The wisdom of this move can be demonstrated on other grounds as well. When the Churchill Falls project was developed, technical difficulties made it impossible to transmit high-voltage power long distances under water, and so all of Labrador's power had to go to the continental power grid and not to the island of Newfoundland. According to Newfoundland government sources, technological advances since then make it possible for Newfoundland to receive Labrador power. However, Brinco's agreement with Hydro-Quebec for the purchase of Labrador power appears to have covered, not only the power from Churchill Falls, but also power from any other development on the lower Churchill River. If these reports are true, Quebec and not Newfoundland would reap most of the advantages from Labrador's power unless the Newfoundland government was in a position to renegotiate the terms of these agreements.

Recent revelations such as these certainly open to question Smallwood's much-touted accomplishments with regard to Churchill Falls power. However, his development of hydro resources did not stop there. As Labrador power could not be transported undersea to Newfoundland, in the early 1960s Smallwood's government began to develop the 600,000-horsepower potential at Bay d'Espoir on Newfoundland's south coast. If Newfoundland was to industrialize, this power was desperately needed. Significantly, no major concessions were made to private industry to develop this power; rather the power itself was made a concession in an effort to attract industries. Industries which used large amounts of electricity were offered subsidized power if they would relocate in Newfoundland. As a result one large chemical corporation did move to the island. However, since coming to Newfoundland it has been accused of polluting one of Newfoundland's most productive fishing grounds. It is also rumoured that the rate at which it was offered power was lower than can be considered beneficial to the economy. In any case, the needs of an expanding population quickly used up the available power and today the province faces power shortages unless new power plants run by expensive fossil fuels are quickly constructed.

Smallwood's industrial-development strategy was begun shortly after he took office. The immediate post-Confederation period saw a spate of twenty small industries started in the province as a result of government involvement and inducements. Most were poorly conceived, unrelated to Newfoundland's resources, and unrelated to one another. Only nine are still in operation but, given Newfoundland's isolation and lack of a propulsive industrial base, this can probably be considered a good record of achievement. Certainly Smallwood is willing to consider it so.

> We put a total of about $50 million altogether into these plants; and although, if you look at them from a narrow orthodox, private enterprise, balance-sheet

point of view, over half of them have been losers, the fact is that from the Province's point of view they have, taken as a whole, been a profit-maker. Substantially more than $50 million has gone back into the Province's economy in the form of wages and other disbursements by the industries concerned, and a lot more will get back in.[48]

In only four of these industries was there direct government ownership. In two of these cases this occurred when the government took over existing asphalt and creosoting plants which had been built during the war and which closed shortly after Confederation.[49] They were quickly sold to private interests. The other two were a cement mill and gypsum-board plant which the government built after several private operators had refused to participate in the venture. Again the government sold these shortly after they were completed. As Smallwood explained,

> I told Valdmanis [Director General of Economic Development] to go ahead with my preparations but wondered in my own mind who would build the two plants [a cement mill and gypsum-board factory] and own them when they were ready for operation. I had no thought whatever that the government should operate them; indeed I would have greatly preferred it if private enterprise had been willing to build and own the plants in the first place. . . .
>
> The two plants were built by us and went into production, and for a short period, they were operated by the Government. I looked about to find private operators who would be willing to buy both plants, but without luck. . . . I invited the Lundrigan firm in Corner Brook to put together a Newfoundland Company to take over the ownership and operation [of the gymsum-board plant]. This they did, and they continue to this day to operate the plant successfully. We made a similar arrangement for the cement mill.[50]

Why Smallwood 'had no thought whatever' of building and operating the two plants as state industries is not clear. Nor is it clear why these two operations were sold to private investors once they were in operation and, presumably, bringing in revenue. Perhaps state-owned industry was a 'socialist' tactic that simply did not come naturally to Smallwood, or the government may simply have been forced to sell these industries to obtain the capital needed to finance other ventures. Nevertheless, these two mills proved that at least some industry could be established in Newfoundland without lavish concessions, and they are among the few early enterprises which are still operating profitably today. The government did not use them as an example for other similar enterprises, and virtually all other industry in the province has been attracted there by the concession system.

The main example of this approach, and the pinnacle of Smallwood's industrial-development strategy, occurred in the concluding years of his reign. No longer content with enticing small industry to come to the province, Smallwood began negotiations for the construction of a major oil refinery. This $200-million project was the largest industrial undertaking ever attempted in the province. Again Newfoundland's pattern of enticements and concessions was involved. Though the refinery was built by a New York financier, John Shaheen, on funds secured primarily from British investors, a significant portion of the financing was backed by the Newfoundland government. In addition, the refinery was given special status as a provincial Crown corporation free from either federal or provincial taxes. Shaheen was to operate the refinery for a share of the income while retaining an option to purchase it for only a portion of its construction cost.[51]

Given her unemployment, low level of industrial skills, population dispersion, and generous supply of natural resources, Smallwood's government might well have been expected to encourage only small, labour-intensive, community-based industries engaged in refining local resources. Smallwood's plunge into oil refining was the direct opposite of this approach. Not only were there no operational oil reserves within 2,000 miles of Newfoundland, but its new oil refinery was a giant whose 'continuous-process' operation required very few employees, most of whom must possess a high level of training and skill. Few, if any, Newfoundlanders had such training.

Nevertheless, the Newfoundland government had several significant reasons for investing so heavily in oil refining. Although all phases of the refinery's operation would produce only 450 jobs, it was a significant source of employment while it was under construction. This construction boom came at a time when the Churchill Falls development was nearing completion and there was the threat of a major work shortage. But it this were her only gain, Newfoundland might have just as well built pyramids. Smallwood saw the oil refinery as a means of overcoming Newfoundland's major obstacle, her isolation. Oil is one of the few commodities which can be shipped great distances at minimal cost because of the low cost of ocean transport, and the vast size of modern oil tankers. Moreover, where such ships were involved, Newfoundland had a unique asset, for the southern Newfoundland coastline possesses two of the few ports in eastern North America which are deep enough to handle these giant vessels. In addition to these factors, the Newfoundland government's adventure into oil refining can be seen as an attempt to expand her economy and release her from total dependence on her traditional resource base. Smallwood justified this high investment in such a small source of employment with the argument that many smaller industries would be attracted to Newfoundland to use the oil by-products which such a large refinery would be capable of producing. In short, Smallwood's economic-development policy, like his social-development policy, was ultimately based on the growth-centre strategy of development which argued that the keys to development were 'propulsive industries' capable of bringing about a total transformation of the economy.

Newfoundland's huge investment in oil refining was a desperate effort to totally alter its economy. It was a gigantic gamble which involved a stake equal to two-thirds of the province's annual budget. Regrettably, the gamble failed. Not one additional industry was attracted to the province to use the refinery's by-products. Morever, the refinery was unable to obtain supplies of crude oil at sufficiently low prices to give it a competitive position on the North American market. By the mid-1970s it too had closed its doors and gone into receivership. Perhaps, in the long run, pyramids would have been a better alternative.

A Final Assessment

The Smallwood administration has often been severely criticized for failing to produce comprehensive social and economic development programs. A report prepared for the Canadian Council on Rural Development made the following ringing condemnation of Newfoundland's development planning.

> There is reason to believe that concepts such as community involvement or participation, planning and regional development, do not convey the same meaning and import in Newfoundland that they do in provinces such as New Brunswick and Manitoba. . . . One should not be surprised if 'planning' in Newfoundland amounts to nothing more than a disjointed series of ad-hoc handout programs, designed either to integrate the rural population in this manner with the commercial, semi-industrial urban based community, or keep the rural community content and indebted.[52]

One cannot but feel that this assessment is rather unfair. Putting aside the issue of whether a single development plan is desirable, we would argue that the Smallwood administration actually did have an underlying theme to much of their development planning, both economic and social. As we have demonstrated, Smallwood's administration appeared to define 'progress' in terms of urban growth and industrial size. If anything, they showed a single-minded commitment to urbanization and an unwavering tendency to encourage economic development through the offering of concessions.

Indeed, if Newfoundland's developers during the Smallwood administration are to be faulted, it is because they too often supported programs of urbanization and industrialization without sufficient regard to rural community development and the encouragement of small-scale, locally based industries. The report cited above makes a similar claim.

> . . . There needed to be reason to believe that the province had no real intention of becoming involved in comprehensive rural planning in the proper sense of that term. We were able to gather an impressive body of evidence—much of it confidential—which points in one direction; namely welfare programs.[53]

This neglect of rural areas virtually forced the resettlement of many rural communities where there was still a considerable social vitality.[54] The offering of large concessions to outside economic interests probably deprived New-foundland of some of the benefit which it could have obtained from its own resources.

In the twenty-three years of Smallwood's administration, Newfoundland certainly gained many services and facilities which had previously been only dreams. But the costs were enormous. Hundreds of communities were abandoned. More Newfoundlanders than ever were being forced to leave the province in order to obtain work. The unemployment rate was almost as high at the end as it had been at the start of his administration, and the total provincial debt was staggering. Under such circumstances, it is questionable whether it was a period of development, or of underdevelopment.

Suggestions for Further Reading

Richard Gwyn, *Smallwood: The Unlikely Revolutionary* (Toronto, 1968).
Ralph Matthews, *There's No Better Place than Here: Social Change in Three Newfoundland Communities* (Toronto, 1976).
Peter Neary, ed., *The Political Economy of Newfoundland, 1929–1972* (Toronto, 1973).

Notes

[1] Hon. Joseph R. Smallwood, *To You with Affection from Joey*, Action for Joey Committee (St John's, 1969), 37.
[2] Richard Gwyn, *Smallwood: The Unlikely Revolutionary* (Toronto, 1968), 31.
[3] For a more detailed discussion of Smallwood's spending priorities, see Ralph Matthews, 'The Smallwood Legacy: The Development of Underdevelopment in Newfoundland, 1949–1972', unpublished manuscript, 16–20.
[4] I should point out that Newfoundland has many difficulties which could be called social problems in that they are impediments to economic development. These include religious cleavages, attitudes toward work, and relatively rigid class divisions. However, in contrast with them, the population problems seem to be more general and more basic to development. Indeed, these other social problems are directly affected by Newfoundland's population patterns. For these reasons I have chosen to confine my examination to population-related issues and the effect that these have on Newfoundland's economic development.
[5] Government of Newfoundland, *Report of the Royal Commission on the Economic State and Prospects of Newfoundland and Labrador* (St John's, 1967), 2–3.
[6] Calculated from data supplied by Statistics Canada, St John's.
[7] Government of Newfoundland, *Newfoundland Bulletin*, December 1968.
[8] Government of Newfoundland, *Report of the Royal Commission on Labour Legislation in Newfoundland and Labrador* (St John's, 1972), 8.
[9] Government of Newfoundland, *A Social and Economic Development Program for Newfoundland and Labrador in the 1970s*. Prepared by the Hon. William N. Rowe, Minister of Community and Social Development (St John's, May 1970), ii.
[10] Hon. Joseph R. Smallwood, *I Chose Canada* (Toronto, 1973), 325.

[11]Smallwood (1969), 147.

[12]*Ibid.*

[13]This seems to be implied in Farley Mowat and John de Visser, *This Rock within the Sea: A Heritage Lost* (Toronto, 1968).

[14]C.M. Lane, 'Centralizing our Population', in J.R. Smallwood, ed., *The Book of Newfoundland*, vol. III (St John's, 1967), 564–7.

[15]Parzival Copes, *The Resettlement of Fishing Communities in Newfoundland*, Canadian Council on Rural Development (Ottawa, April 1972), 102.

[16]For a discussion of this changing federal role, see Ralph Matthews, *There's No Better Place than Here: Social Change in Three Newfoundland Communities* (Toronto, 1976), ch. 6.

[17]Lane (1967); Government of Newfoundland, *Statistics: Federal-Provincial Resettlement Program* (St John's, no date).

[18]The disappearance of others was simply the result of changing census practices and classifications.

[19]These include Noel Iverson and Ralph Matthews, *Communities in Decline: An Examination of Household Resettlement in Newfoundland*, Newfoundland Social and Economic Studies Number 6, Institute of Social and Economic Research, Memorial University of Newfoundland (St John's, 1966); Michael L. Skolnik, *Viewpoints on Communities in Crisis*, Newfoundland Social and Economic Papers, Number 1, Institute of Social and Economic Research, Memorial University of Newfoundland (St John's, 1968); Cato Wadel, *Marginal Adaptations and Modernization in Newfoundland*, Newfoundland Social and Economic Studies Number 7, Institute of Social and Economic Research, Memorial University of Newfoundland (St John's, 1969); Ralph Matthews, *Communities in Transition: An Examination of Government Initiated Community Migration in Rural Newfoundland*, unpublished PhD Thesis in Sociology, University of Minnesota (Minneapolis, 1970).

[20]These propulsive industries benefit from the advantages of 'agglomeration economics'. Furthermore, they are industries which have extensive 'frontward and backward linkages' with regional suppliers and extraregional distributors. These linkages lead them to spawn a network of related industries in the region while their propulsive nature accelerates the process of development at a faster than normal pace.

The concept of 'growth centre' as it is used in economics is discussed in Niles M. Hansen, ed., *Growth Centres in Regional Economic Development* (New York, 1973). The applicability of the growth-centre idea to the Atlantic region is discussed in the Atlantic Provinces Economic Council's *Sixth Annual Review: The Atlantic Economy* (Halifax, 1972). Its applicability to Newfoundland is examined in Stratford Canning, *Outport Newfoundland: The Potential for Development Planning*, unpublished thesis for the Diploma of Town and Regional Planning, University of Glasgow (Glasgow, 1971). An attempt to develop a growth centre in Atlantic Canada using this model of regional development is examined by Douglas Glover, 'The Astounding Ambitions of New Brunswick Multiplex', *Saturday Night* (September, 1973).

[21]Leslie Robb and Roberta Edgecombe Robb, *The Newfoundland Resettlement Program: A Cost Benefit Analysis*, Institute of Social and Economic Research, Memorial University of Newfoundland (St John's, 1968).

[22]Government of Newfoundland (St John's, 1967).

[23]Atlantic Development Board, *Profiles of Education in the Atlantic Provinces* (Ottawa, 1969), 1–6.

[24]In 1911, there were 43,795 persons employed in catching and curing fish. Government of Great Britain, *Newfoundland Royal Commission 1933: Report*, also known as the *Amulree Commission Report* (London, 1933), 236.

[25]David K. Roberts, *The Inshore Fishing Industry of Newfoundland: A Study of Its Operations from 1957 to 1966*, unpublished Bachelor of Commerce Thesis, Memorial University of Newfoundland (St John's, 1968).

[26]This statement appears to contradict the arguments of some Latin American theorists (notably Frank and Sunkel) who argue that there is no such thing as a dual society, for both developed and underdeveloped segments of a modern economy are the product of its contact with modern world capitalism. While agreeing that this is so, the two 'economies' are indeed both aspects of the same process, I see an important distinction between the economic and social aspects of the society at this point. My research on Newfoundland has convinced me that there are important cultural differences and differences in value-orientation between rural and urban areas. It is these which I am identifying when I use the term dual 'society'. Indeed, I would contend that much of Frank's writing concerns this very division, for he emphasizes the distinction between metropolis and hinterland. In sum, I would argue that a 'dual society' does indeed exist in Newfoundland, though I would not make a case for a 'dual economy'.

[27]Wadel (1969) documents this point.

[28]Chiaramonte has documented the unique character of business and exchange relations in rural Newfoundland. Louis J. Chiaramonte, *Craftsman-Client Contract: Interpersonal Relations in a Newfoundland Fishing Community*, Newfoundland Social and Economic Studies Number 10, Institute of Social and Economic Research, Memorial University of Newfoundland (St John's, 1973).

[29]Government of Newfoundland (1967), 123.

[30]*Canada Year Book 1968* (Ottawa), 759.

[31]Quoted in Cato Wadel, *Now, Whose Fault is That*, Memorial University of Newfoundland, Newfoundland Social and Economic Studies Number 11 (St John's, 1973), 10. Smallwood denies ever making such a statement, though it is now a firmly accepted part of Newfoundland folk culture.

[32]Peter Neary, 'Party Politics in Newfoundland 1949–71', *Journal of Canadian Studies* (November, 1971), 11.

[33]Copes (1972), 65–75, 230–43.

[34]Government of Newfoundland (1967), 184.

[35]Calculated from data contained in Government of Newfoundland (1967), 156.

[36]Smallwood (1973), 437–9.

[37]Government of Great Britain (1933).

[38]The value of mineral production has increased from $27.5 million in 1949 to $336 million in 1971. However, much of this increase is the result of the major iron-ore development in Labrador. Government of Newfoundland, *Historical Statistics of Newfoundland and Labrador* (St John's, 1970) and *Supplement to the Historical Statistics of Newfoundland and Labrador* (St John's, 1972).

[39]Government of Newfoundland (1967), 147.

[40]*Ibid.*, 147–50.

[41]*Ibid.*, 275.

[42]Quoted in Philip Mathias, *Forced Growth: Five Studies of Government Involvement in the Development of Canada* (Toronto, 1971). This book contains the only major analysis to date of the development and financing of the Churchill Falls hydro development.

[43]*Ibid.*

[44]*Ibid.*, 78.

[45]Thirty-sixth General Assembly of Newfoundland, *Verbatim Report*, vol. 1, no. 40 (Tuesday, 27 June 1972). Quoted in Peter Neary, ed., *The Political Economy of Newfoundland 1929–1972* (Toronto, 1973), 212.

[46]*Ibid.*, 214.

[47]*Ibid.*

[48]Smallwood (1973), 352.

[49]*Ibid.*, 351.

[50]*Ibid.*, 348.

[51]For details of this arrangement, see Gwyn (1972), 314–17; and Smallwood (1973), 472–83.

[52]James N. McCrorie, *A.R.D.A.: An Experiment in Development Planning*, Canadian Council on Rural Development (Ottawa, 1969), 86.

[53]*Ibid.*

[54]For a discussion on the social vitality and economic viability of rural life, see Ralph Matthews, *There's No Better Place than Here: Social Change in Three Newfoundland Communities* (Toronto, 1976).

30

The Conduct of External Relations under

Diefenbaker

John F. Hilliker

A central feature of the federal Liberal period of hegemony, 1935 to 1957, had been its direction of the nation's foreign policy and external affairs to a position of world leadership. Canada's place in the world was that of a 'middle power', acting as honest broker between the superpowers of the Cold War (especially the USSR and the United States) and much of the remainder of the world. This role had achieved international recognition in 1957 when Lester B. Pearson (minister of external affairs and soon to become leader of the federal Liberal party) was awarded the Nobel Peace Prize for his 'shuttle diplomacy' in the Suez Crisis of 1956. Many Canadians accepted not only the concept of middle-power status, but also the related notion that the nation had mainly managed to walk a fine line between Great Britain and the United States, not sacrificing its independence to either.

The federal Liberal party might well have been forgiven for accept-

ing the assessment of many political pundits that it had become Canada's 'governing party'. But not long after the announcement was made of Pearson's Nobel Prize, a dramatic election resulted in the overturn of the Liberals (who had become far too smug and complacent) by the Progressive Conserative party led by John Diefenbaker, returned to head a minority government. A year later the Diefenbaker PCs went again to the polls and swept the nation, even winning a huge majority in Quebec. John Diefenbaker remains one of the most fascinating and enigmatic Canadian politicians of our century, and his conduct of Canadian external affairs well demonstrates both his strengths and his weaknesses.

John Hilliker attempts to assess the Diefenbaker record in foreign policy. He argues that the mandarins in External Affairs were legitimately non-partisan, but admits that they had a more élitist style than the populist Diefenbaker, who preferred a moralistic approach. The government's general reputation for indecisiveness and policy confusion was reinforced by its record in the international arena, and contributed to its defeat in the election of 1963.

Why did Diefenbaker have so much early difficulty with foreign policy? What were the principal areas of concern for Howard Green?

What did the government's attitudes to nuclear disarmament, the Baltic states, and South Africa have in common? What was significant about the government's response to the European Economic Community? Could the government's anti-nuclear policy ever have proved acceptable?

This article first appeared, titled 'The Politicians and the "Pearsonalities": The Diefenbaker Government and the Conduct of Canadian External Relations', in *Canadian Historical Association Historical Papers*, 1984, 152–67.

When the Progressive Conservatives came to power in Ottawa under John Diefenbaker on 10 June 1957, they inherited, in the Department of External Affairs, a foreign policy establishment with an impressive reputation.[1] It was an asset, however, to be viewed with some caution by a new government, for it had grown to maturity during twenty-two years of Liberal rule. During about half that period, moreover, it had been under the direction, first at the under-secretarial and then at the cabinet level, of the outgoing minister, Lester Pearson, who, soon after the election, succeeded to the leadership of his party and hence of the parliamentary opposition. At worst, members of such a department might be suspected of giving clandestine help to Pearson and his political colleagues. Even if that possibility were dismissed as fanciful, there remained the more subtle danger that reliance on the department's capability and expertise might make the new government captive to priorities and policies established under Pearson rather than setting new ones of its own. These suspicions and anxieties are part of the background to the term 'Pearsonalities' which Diefenbaker coined to describe members of the Department of External Affairs.[2]

There is a good deal of testimony that members of the Department of External Affairs upheld the principle of nonpartisanship and indeed took considerable care to avoid even innocent social relationships with Pearson, which, if misunderstood, might give rise to suspicion.[3] While not all ministers were satisfied with the adjustment made by the department, the cause seems to have been nothing worse than insensitivity on the part of some officials.[4] Nor did members of the department expect that prevailing assumptions would survive unchallenged. Rather, according to an assistant under-secretary of the time, it had to be assumed that all decisions of the outgoing government were subject to revision. And even if they had wanted to mount a campaign of indoctrination, the resources were lacking. The department was short-staffed in the senior ranks in Ottawa,[5] there were no arrangements for comprehensive background briefing of the new ministers; and the style in department memoranda, developed to meet the requirements of an experienced minister and adhered to after his departure,[6] was to present not single-minded policy recommendations but a variety of options in the expectation that the minister himself would take the decision.

Diefenbaker did not rely on these constraints to operate unaided. Much concerned to preserve the autonomy of the elected executive, he made sure that Cabinet, rather than ministerial or interdepartmental committees, remained very much the locus of discussion and decision-making. In Cabinet, associates were aware, he kept a particularly close watch on those who seemed insufficiently independent of their civil-service advisers. At the same time, he maintained resources of his own to guide his judgement, for he kept in touch with and added to a broad acquaintance of informal advisers across the country which he had built up over his years in politics. External Affairs was affected by these practices in some ways more than most departments. Diefenbaker had preeminence in matters involving other heads of government and, for the first three months of his administration, had direct responsibility for the department as well, since he retained the portfolio himself. His conduct at that time was an indication of the division of labour he thought appropriate between the elected executive and officials in External Affairs. According to an assistant under-secretary who dealt with him then, Diefenbaker recognised that he could not expect to master the minutiae of the External Affairs portfolio and, especially on the technical side, would have to rely on the guidance of officials. His interest in substantive involvement was in major issues affecting the direction of the new government's policy.

There were good reasons for Diefenbaker to take this approach. While there was a considerable measure of agreement on foreign policy between the new government and its predecessor, for example on the usefulness of Canada's middle-power role in times of international tension, the recent election campaign had also revealed significant differences. In particular, such controversies as the previous government's conduct in the Suez crisis of 1956 and its handling of economic relations with the United States had enabled the Conservatives to exploit their traditional position as the party defending Canada's autonomy in North America while upholding the British and Commonwealth connection. As well, Diefenbaker, whose personality was the centrepiece of Conservative publicity, was identified with certain principles, such as concern for human rights, applicable to international as well as to domestic affairs. The campaign, however, did not produce a comprehensive program for the conduct of external relations. Rather, it left latent contradictions in the party's declared objectives and failed to anticipate some of the significant changes in the international situation which took place while the Conservatives were in office. External relations, therefore, were likely to provide a challenging test of the decision-making process under Diefenbaker.

The new prime minister got off to a rather uncertain start as a result of two episodes which caused the government some embarrassment: his suggestion that steps would be taken to shift 15 per cent of Canada's imports from United States to British sources, and his approval of joining the United States in an integrated North American air defence command (NORAD) without insisting on an intergovernmental agreement. In taking these actions without consulting cabinet or departmental officials beforehand,[7] Diefenbaker no doubt was the victim of inexperience, and the risks involved in ill-considered action were soon appreciated.[8] A potentially more serious problem was communication with External Affairs. Diefenbaker, those around him realised, had little patience with the shaded language of diplomacy, and he did not have either the time or the experience to deal with lengthy expositions of issues. What he needed was guidance, expressed succinctly, which alerted him to the implications of decisions he was being asked to take. But, despite advice on his requirements,[9] much of the paper reaching him remained more suited to a politician experienced in foreign affairs. The same was true of speech material. Diefenbaker, noted a contributor, wanted his speeches on foreign policy as on other matters to have relevance to the ordinary Canadian voter, but what he got from External Affairs often seemed to be pitched to the more specialised and élitist audience favoured by Pearson and his prime minister, Louis St Laurent.

These differences of style were another reason for Diefenbaker to regard members of the Department of External Affairs as 'Pearsonalities'. They affected not only the rank and file but also, an observer of their relationship has recalled, the under-secretary, Jules Léger, despite the high regard the prime minister had for him personally.[10] As a result of this problem in communications and his suspicion of the department as a creation of his political opponents, Diefenbaker at first tended to keep his distance from it in handling foreign affairs, excluding its representatives from his meetings with foreign leaders, omitting debriefing afterwards,[11] and neglecting to refer to it important communications which he received on international subjects. To overcome this problem, R.B. Bryce, Clerk of the Privy Council and Diefenbaker's most trusted civil-service adviser, arranged for the appointment of an experienced foreign service officer as special departmental assistant in the Prime Minister's Office. The first incumbent, Basil Robinson, who remained in place until 1962, became, on the basis of the confidence he earned from Diefenbaker and his associates, a highly effective means of communication between the prime minister and the department.[12] He also tried to educate the department about Diefenbaker's requirements, but some subjects had to be dealt with in complex and subtle terms. As a result,

Diefenbaker years later still remembered the departmental style for 'decorative uncertainty'.[13]

Another means of getting around the problem of communication between Diefenbaker and the Department of External Affairs of course was the appointment of a full-time minister. In September of 1957 Diefenbaker filled the position by going outside the Conservative caucus to choose Sidney Smith, president of the University of Toronto. Diefenbaker, however, kept in touch with the portfolio through copies of important telegrams and other communications from posts abroad, a daily summary of significant international developments,[14] and private communication which he encouraged with officials whose ideas he thought might be useful. Smith's performance probably caused the scrutiny to become more intense than it would otherwise have been. Although his reputation as a university administrator earned him a warm welcome from the press and the Conservative caucus,[15] it proved to be insufficient compensation for his inexperience in both electoral politics and foreign affairs. As a result, he was not a very effective spokesman for his area of responsibility, and Diefenbaker was concerned as well that he was overly reliant on his officials.[16] This concern no doubt increased after Norman Robertson, whom Smith favoured, succeeded Léger in the autumn of 1958, for the relationship between the prime minister and the new undersecretary was never better than strained.[17] It was not unusual, one writer has observed, for a secretary of state for external affairs to enjoy less latitude than Pearson had had under St Laurent but, while Smith held the office, prime ministerial involvement was sufficiently evident to leave the impression that there were two centres of decision-making.[18] Equally important, Smith's weakness in cabinet meant that his department's expertise was not always brought forcefully to bear on decisions to which it was relevant.

It was while Sidney Smith was secretary of state for external affairs that Diefenbaker's government took most of its decisions on acquiring weapons systems with nuclear capability for the Canadian armed forces. With encouragement from Léger,[19] Diefenbaker at the same time gave high priority to 'the search for disarmament with the Soviet Union',[20] but without anticipating the potential for conflict between the two courses of policy which was to be a source of difficulty for his government later on. One reason may have been the inexperience and comparative weakness of the secretary of state for external affairs. According to the Cabinet conclusions, diplomatic objectives did not feature in discussions of equipment for the armed forces, which concentrated on strategic, economic and domestic political consideration.

The sudden death of Sidney Smith on 17 March 1959 brought more forceful ministerial leadership to External Affairs in the person of Howard Green, whom Diefenbaker, after resuming the portfolio himself in the interim, named to take over in June. Formerly minister of public works,

Green brought to his new office long experience in the House of Commons, a solid position in Cabinet, and the confidence of the prime minister.[21] While some members of his new department were disconcerted by gaps in his knowledge of international affairs and by his lack of subtlety in negotiation,[22] his shrewdness and firmness were much admired by one of the most experienced diplomats in the service, Charles Ritchie at the United Nations.[23] At headquarters, he worked closely and confidently with the under-secretary[24] and other senior officers, but his habits were such that he did not give up his independence to them. He placed a good deal of confidence in his senior departmental assistant, Ross Campbell, who was by no means reluctant to raise considerations additional or contrary to those produced by the flow of advice from the department. Green also established direct contact with individual officers, down to the desk level, who were dealing with subjects that particularly interested him. He was careful to keep control himself of areas of policy he considered to be of special importance and, although he moderated his opinions and developed new interests to take account of his experience in office, he did not change his mind readily once he had made a commitment. Additionally, he tended to specialise, concentrating his energy on a limited range of issues which seemed to him of paramount importance.

The most important of these issues was nuclear disarmament. Closely related was Green's opposition to the acquisition of nuclear arms by Canadian forces and even more to their location within the country's borders, a condition which he feared would affect the credibility of his campaign for disarmament. These concerns were shared by Robertson, who had informed Diefenbaker of his views before Green took over External Affairs.[25] But Green, influenced by his memories of the First World War and reinforced by encouragement from his wife, a biochemist, and his friend C.J. Mackenzie, chairman of the Atomic Energy Control Board,[26] came to his own conclusions without prompting by Robertson. About a week after taking office at External Affairs, Green signalled his doubts about nuclear weapons[27] and it was only some time later, at the end of July of 1959, that Robertson set out his own position for the minister.[28] Green, moreover, remembered as the decisive influence on his thinking, not Robertson's submission, but the discussion, at the United Nations General Assembly in the autumn of 1959, of fallout from nuclear tests.[29] Robertson in fact did not at first always recommend as uncompromising a line on nuclear questions as Green favoured[30] or respond as promptly as the minister would have liked to requests for resources for work on disarmament. The minister, however, made sure that he got what he wanted, for these were subjects over which he maintained close personal scrutiny. An officer who felt the effects has recalled that pressure from the minister's office produced not only the creation of a Disarmament Division[31] but a noticeable diversion of energies to that subject from other parts of the department as well. In due course, Robertson, particularly as a result of shared concern over tendencies in United States' policy, moved towards the minister's position, so that together they constituted, a worried observer noted, 'a negative force of great importance' on the nuclear question.[32] But it was not an equal partnership, for throughout the pace was set by the minister rather than the under-secretary or other officials.

While Green had objectives of his own, he was also willing to serve as a vehicle for initiatives originating in his department. It was as a result of such an initiative and the minister's support that the Diefenbaker government decided to provide economic assistance to countries in francophone Africa. The suggestion originated with the deputy under-secretary, Marcel Cadieux, who was concerned about criticism in Quebec of the Commonwealth bias of Canadian aid programs.[33] He therefore suggested a new scheme of educational development directed to the francophone states of Africa which became independent in 1960. Other interested agencies, including the one directly responsible for overseas assistance, the External Aid Office, had doubts about this proposal. The principal concern, according to a leading critic, was whether the federal government could mount a program in French without further preparation. Cadieux's arguments, however, carried the day with Green, whose ministerial jurisdiction included the aid office as well as External Affairs. But Green did not accept them completely, for he feared that the proposed outlay, $600,000, would be considered too high by cabinet, and at his suggestion it was reduced by one-half.[34] This was a judgement founded on experience, for there were a number of objections recorded in the Cabinet Conclusions to this kind of expenditure, especially on nonfood aid to countries outside the Commonwealth. In this instance, cabinet, no doubt influenced by 'informal representations' which some ministers had received in favour of such a scheme, gave its approval, but only with the observation that even the amount of $300,000 might be 'disproportionately high when compared with the amounts allocated for other programs'.[35]

Notwithstanding the strength and the independence of bureaucratic control that Green displayed in handling such issues as disarmament and aid, the prime minister remained a potent force in the determination of foreign policy. By the time Green became minister, Diefenbaker was well equipped to assert his authority, for his normal experience of office had been reinforced by his world tour at the end of 1958. He also kept up his independent sources of information. The Prime Minister's Office received copies of all departmental memoranda to the minister, and later it requested copies of telegrams signed by Green and the under-secretary on certain sensitive subjects, including disarmament and nuclear tests.[36] Diefenbaker did not use these resources to become involved across the board in Green's area of activity, but he was active on a limited range of issues which interested him personally or were relevant to his role as prime minister.

Diefenbaker's personal interest and style, the product of his concern for democratic rights, his sensitivity to the views of Canadians of Eastern European origin and his fondness for direct and forceful language, had a marked effect on his government's approach to East-West relations. The Department of External Affairs favoured the soft line taken by the previous government and at first continued under Diefenbaker. This position, it was noted, was agreeable to Green because of his desire to promote an accommodating attitude towards disarmament in the Soviet Union. Diefenbaker, however, came to prefer a more vigorous approach, to which he gave expression in his address to the United Nations General Assembly in 1960. The effect of his involvement is clear from the evolution of the text, which started life in Eternal Affairs in the expectation that it would be given by Green. While expressing concern about recent deterioration in the international situation, his version did not assign blame to either side, and about half the text dealt with disarmament and related matters.[37] Diefenbaker then supplanted Green because of the decision of Khrushchev and a number of other heads of government to attend. Even before he was aware of Khrushchev's text, Diefenbaker was contemplating an attack on the Soviet Union's policies towards the Ukraine, the Baltic states and the European satellites.[38] Notwithstanding Khrushchev's denunciation of Western colonial policies, the officers in External Affairs responsible for drafting the speech were unenthusiastic about this approach. While they responded to Khrushchev by putting the onus for international tension on the Soviet Union,[39] they thought the speech would have the most useful effect if Diefenbaker took on the role of peacemaker. When he was unwilling to give up the offensive, the speechwriters then saw their task as marrying the prime minister's desire for pungent language with a text that would not itself become a cause of further deterioration in relations with the Soviet Union. This they did with reasonable success. A contributor remembered that Diefenbaker was pleased with the result, the speech was well received at home, and reports to the Department of External Affairs suggested a friendly response from Canada's allies.[40] Even so, by incorporating a stern critique of 'Soviet colonialism' as a major theme, the speech marked a significant departure from past practice, and introduced an important new component into the Diefenbaker government's position on East-West relations.

Two actions followed from Diefenbaker's speech of 1960. One was his decision to acknowledge the consular status claimed by representatives of the Baltic states, strongly indicated during the election campaign of 1962. This went against the advice of External Affairs, which feared complications in dealing with the power in control of the territories, the Soviet Union, on matters of interest to Canadians.[41] Diefenbaker, who remembered the department for insensitivity to 'the terrible persecutions behind the Iron Curtain', may well have regarded this advice as bureaucratic obstruction, part of a pattern going back to his expression of interest in the Baltic states early in his administration.[42] Certainly he suspected that such obstruction was a factor in the difficulties encountered in achieving his second objective, a resolution by the United Nations General Assembly in 1962 based on his earlier attack on Soviet policies.[43] In response to his criticism, the department made an intense effort to promote the resolution in friendly nations, but the response was negative and in due course cabinet decided that the initiative ought to be dropped.[44] Diefenbaker settled instead for a campaign of speech-making, but he made certain that it was based upon the tone he had favoured in 1960. While the opening salvo by Green was fairly mild, the climatic speech, delivered by his parliamentary secretary, Heath Macquarrie, was not. The first version of Macquarrie's speech, when submitted to the prime minister for approval, was rejected as 'pusillanimous':[45] as redrafted, it was described by the mission in New York as 'the harshest and most direct attack ever levelled against Soviet colonialism in the UN'.[46]

Diefenbaker's personal interests came together with his responsibility for dealing with other heads of government in the matter of South Africa's continued membership of the Commonwealth after it became a republic. As a civil libertarian with a rather stark view of right and wrong, Diefenbaker was not entirely comfortable with advice from the Department of External Affairs that Canada seek to avoid confrontation with South Africa over apartheid in the hope that, if lines of communication were kept open, the moderate forces in the country might operate to some effect.[47] Diefenbaker's party, however, was also identified with support for the old Commonwealth, and he did not feel strong pressure to depart from the course favoured by External Affairs until the Sharpeville massacre of 21 March 1960.[48] Even then there was no clear alternative. Bryce hoped that, to ensure the survival of the Commonwealth as a multiracial organisation, Canada might take the lead in pressing for the exclusion of South Africa, but there was not sufficient support from the Canadian cabinet or other Commonwealth leaders for Diefenbaker to take this line at the meeting of heads of government in 1960.[49] Instead, circumstances encouraged him to follow the recommendations of External Affairs that he try to exploit Canada's potential as a conciliator between South Africa and her critics[50] and to exercise his favourite strategy of playing for time in the hope that the problem would be overtaken by events. With material assistance from Diefenbaker, the heads of government agreed to postpone their decision on South Africa's continued membership until a referendum on republican status had been taken there.[51]

Diefenbaker's position was no easier when the Commonwealth heads of government met again in March of 1961, after the referendum held in South Africa had approved a republic. Most ministers in Ottawa wanted South Africa readmitted, while the position of a number of other heads of government was difficult to predict.[52] Diefenbaker was attracted by the possibility of postponing a decision yet again, on the ground—supplied by his high commissioner in London, George Drew—that no action was necessary until the constitutional change in South Africa, not due until after the Commonwealth meeting, had actually taken place.[53] By this time, however, Diefenbaker may well have developed a fall-back position: the creation of a situation which would force South Africa to solve the problem itself by withdrawing from the Commonwealth rather than accept onerous terms for continued membership. He had suspected, since his first heads of government meeting in 1957, that 'South Africa did not want to remain long in the Commonwealth',[54] and he had reason to believe that a declaration in support of racial equality, favoured by External Affairs as a means of placating South Africa's critics,[55] might be a means of getting her out. External Affairs had alerted him to this possibility, and a recent speech by Prime Minister Verwoerd suggested that he might be preparing his people for withdrawal if he could not remain in the Commonwealth on the terms he wanted.[56]

Diefenbaker was not able to take the initiative in promoting this solution because cabinet was against Canadian sponsorship of a Commonwealth declaration of rights. Such action, ministers believed, 'would probably provoke ridicule' at home since the Canadian Bill of Rights had not yet been tested.[57] But the idea remained useful when, the day before the discussion of South Africa was to begin, Diefenbaker learned that India, not hitherto expected to take the initiative, had decided on a hard line. A strong statement against apartheid, Diefenbaker suggested to the Indians, would likely cause South Africa to withdraw from the Commonwealth and so avert the necessity for direct action by the other members.[58] Diefenbaker did not mention this reasoning when he reported to cabinet on the early discussion of the issue in London, and his ministers did not give him further guidance.[59] So, although unable to take the lead in formulating a declaration of principles, he remained free to support the efforts of the nonwhite leaders. This produced the result he had anticipated when he learned of the Indian position. Unable to persuade Verwoerd to compromise and concluding that the South African application for continued membership would be rejected by all but Britain, Australia and New Zealand, the British prime minister, Harold Macmillan, secured its withdrawal.[60]

Among Diefenbaker's strengths in dealing with South Africa were his access to well-balanced information and his ultimate control of the decision-making process. These were not always easy to achieve, even on matters involving his relationship with other heads of government. The question of British membership in the European Economic Community was of material interest not only to Diefenbaker but also to the economic ministers and the Secretary of State for External Affairs. Equally important, it was one in which George Drew took a major and sustained interest. During Drew's time at Canada House, subjects in this category were very much the province of the high commissioner, who generated a large volume of private telephone calls, telegrams and letters to Diefenbaker and the ministers concerned. In preparing these communications and in carrying out his own activities in Britain, Drew acted on his own, without seeking the advice of his staff or the views of his departmental headquarters. As a former premier of Canada's wealthiest province and a former leader of his party still respected by its establishment, Drew could speak with authority on an economic subject such as the Common Market. He therefore could expect both considerable latitude in the way he handled his office and a receptive audience where it counted most, in cabinet. In short, he was a source of highly potent opinion and advice on the Common Market, which reached ministers uninfluenced by and uncoordinated with that going forward through the bureaucracy.

Drew and the government began to give serious attention to the Common Market in 1960, in response to indications that Britain was planning to apply for membership. What they feared were the possible economic and political consequences if Britain sacrificed Commonwealth preferences in order to meet the requirements of the community: erosion of Canada's competitive position in the British market, a weakening of Commonwealth ties based on shared economic interest, and the loss of a significant counterweight to United States economic and political influence on Canada. The Department of External Affairs, doubtful that the Canadian bargaining position was strong enough to do much about these problems, recommended that the government go to work on contingency plans.[61] Drew's position, founded on the belief that the community's conditions for membership were likely to be unpopular with a substantial element of British opinion, was very different. He favoured a vigorous campaign in Britain, reinforced as appropriate from home, to convince the public that the Canadian and Commonwealth markets were of continued and growing value, combined with a strong effort to get a commitment that British negotiators would protect the Commonwealth interest. The latter produced a public British assurance in May of 1961 of 'full consultation' with other Commonwealth governments,[62] a narrow interpretation of which formed the basis of Drew's subsequent action. This approach was more in line with ministerial attitudes in Ottawa than the cautious line favoured by External Affairs. 'Too weak!' was Green's comment on guidance prepared in his department for the prime minister.[63]

Drew's view of the British undertaking about consultation was that it might offer a means of thwarting negotiations with the community if they seemed likely to produce a result unfavourable to the Commonwealth. He therefore set a very high standard of what constituted acceptable consultation and counselled his government against accepting anything less. He did not regard a trip to Ottawa in July of 1961 by the Commonwealth Secretary, Duncan Sandys, as meeting his requirements, and his negative comments helped to produce a cool reception for the visitor.[64] When Macmillan, on

31 July, announced his government's intention to open negotiations with the community, Diefenbaker reiterated his preference, already expressed in connection with Sandys's visit, for a Commonwealth heads of government meeting as a forum of consultation. This idea, which would have complicated matters for the British a good deal more than a series of bilateral talks, was not very welcome to them.[65] It was made even less so by a Commonwealth ministerial meeting in Accra in September. There, it was reported, the Canadian ministers of Finance and of Trade and Commerce, Donald Fleming and George Hees, took the lead in mobilising opposition to the British plans.[66]

The bad press which Fleming and Hees received led the cabinet in Ottawa to moderate its position. On the initiative of the minister of Justice, Davie Fulton, it agreed 'that Canada should now accept as a fait accompli the United Kingdom decision to try to enter the European Economic Community'.[67] This position was smartly communicated to the two ministers and was reflected in the reports which they made to Parliament on their return.[68] Diefenbaker was concerned as well about the reaction in Britain, a fact which led him to believe that Canadian hostility to the negotiations, if continued, might even have the undesired effect of helping Labour to bring down Macmillan's government at the next election.[69] This was not a worry to Drew, who suspected that the criticism of the Canadian ministers in the British press was at least partly inspired by promarket ministers and officials.[70] He therefore did not follow the line adopted in Ottawa but kept on the offensive, getting into a prolonged argument with the British over their refusal to provide Commonwealth representatives with the full text of their opening statement in negotiations with the community, on the ground that they had agreed with the other parties not to release it.[71] Diefenbaker himself had to instruct Drew to moderate his opposition when the high commissioner's conduct in the dispute received unfavourable public attention in Canada[72] and in the end the struggle proved to have been ill-advised. The text, when it became available as a result of a press leak, turned out to contain nothing of substance which the British had not already revealed in oral briefings and written summaries.[73]

Despite this chastening experience, Drew's name continued to appear in the papers, although with less frequency, as a source of criticism of the Common Market in Britain.[74] He also maintained the flow of negative comment to Ottawa, notwithstanding British efforts to promote a better relationship with Canada, a policy which included two visits to Ottawa by the minister responsible for negotiations with the community, Edward Heath, and agreement to convene a Commonwealth heads of government meeting.

On the eve of a visit to Ottawa by Macmillan at the end of April 1962, Drew commented alarmingly on the political implications of the British approach to the community. Its success, he warned, would weaken the Commonwealth link and make Canada more vulnerable to control by the United States, an objective he suggested the Americans had in mind in encouraging the British effort.[75] This was not an aspect of the problem that occurred spontaneously to External Affairs, nor was it informed of Drew's concern or asked to comment. But Drew's argument was one to which Diefenbaker was susceptible[76] and it affected his approach to the British, including his preparations for the heads of government meeting. Unlike other Commonwealth leaders, he was not interested in contingency plans against Britain's possible entry. Instead, encouraged by public opinion polls showing low support for the Common Market in Britain, he preferred to hope that the conference would help to change the mind of the government there. Having been warned by officials against placing himself in a position to be blamed if the British bid should fail, he told Green, who accompanied him to London and who also continued to hope Britain would stay out, that they must achieve their objective without 'taking the part of the "dog in the manager".'[77] This proved to be an impossible task, for Diefenbaker had no success with Drew's ideas about expanding Commonwealth trade and the political dangers if Britain joined the community. All he did was to alarm the British and arouse a hostile press in London, and he did not recoup his position by proposing that the Commonwealth take the lead in organising a broader international conference on the lowering of trade barriers. Hence the conference ended without forcing a change upon the British. While the subsequent failure of their application to the community could not be blamed on Canada or the Commonwealth, as officials in Ottawa and Diefenbaker himself had feared might happen, the conference nonetheless did the prime minister more harm than good, by exposing his conduct to savage criticism in the press. It also helped disappoint the Conservatives' hopes for a warm relationship with London, contributing instead to the feeling, noted by a British high commissioner in Ottawa during the period, that there was 'something . . . awry' at the ministerial level.[78]

Diefenbaker might well have had better success in responding to the British negotiations with the European Economic Community had the advice from Drew been better integrated with that from public servants. Disparate advice, this time from different departments, was also a problem in dealing with the issue in external policy which was most troublesome for Diefenbaker's government, the crisis over nuclear weapons. Green's concern for Canada's credibility as an advocate of disarmament brought him into conflict with George Pearkes and his successor as minister of National Defence, Douglas Harkness, over their desire to reach agreement with the United States on the supply of nuclear equipment to the Canadian armed forces for their new weapons systems, and to American bases in Canada. This was an issue on which there had been differences between the departments of External Affairs and National Defence since Pearson's years as minister,[79] but they widened as a result of Green's personal interest in the subject and his approach to his work. Officials in External Affairs who dealt with the problem found that they could not count on Green to accept positions agreed to with their counterparts in National Defence. As a result, the matter became one for resolution between ministers or, if they could find common ground themselves, by the prime minister. His convictions, as expressed privately at the time, seem to have inclined towards the nuclear side. Although he acknowledged the desirability of disarmament, he was not convinced that it was realisable, and both his view of the Soviet Union and his appreciation of the economic benefits of defence production sharing encouraged a favourable approach to agreement with the United States.[80] But of more pressing concern to him than the substance of the issue were its political implications. The emergence of an organised antinuclear movement in Canada, which could take encouragement from the positions of the three opposition parties, was a factor here, but the greatest cause of difficulty was the division in cabinet. If one or other of the lead ministers were so offended by Diefenbaker's position that he withdrew, possibly taking supporters with him, the government's position obviously could become precarious, especially after it was reduced to a minority in the election of 1962.

For a long time, Diefenbaker was able to control the issue by blurring it, keeping both protagonists somewhat off-base, but that strategy was put to an end by the Cuban missile crisis in October of 1962. By revealing the weakness of Canada's defences resulting from the failure to acquire the weapons required by the new delivery systems, the crisis placed the government under greater pressure to take a decision. It appears, especially from Harkness's account, that Diefenbaker responded first and foremost as a politician under seige, anticipating an early election and anxious to find an issue which might provide a basis for recovering his majority in Parliament. Keeping his cabinet together was an important concern in this endeavour, but it was not the only one.

Harkness took advantage of the situation created by the missile crisis to secure cabinet agreement to proceed with negotiations with the United States about acquiring nuclear equipment for use both in Canada and by Canadian forces in Europe. Green did not cause serious difficulties about the latter. Because of his attitude, however, the government took the position that weapons for use in Canada, or vital parts of them, should be stored in the United States and moved across the border in an emergency. When meetings with the Americans failed to produce a workable arrangement for doing so, Diefenbaker held off making changes for the forces in Europe alone, arguing that he wanted to announce a solution to the whole problem at once. The objective as he saw it was to find a formula that could be used to the government's advantage in an election. An idea that appealed to him was to reach a comprehensive agreement with the United States and make that the issue in going to the country to restore the government's majority. This course, however, was opposed not only by Green but even by pronuclear ministers, who did not want to fight on the single issue of acquiring the weapons although they were willing to make it one of the planks in a campaign platform.[81]

Having failed to carry the idea of a pronuclear campaign, Diefenbaker, encouraged by the antinuclear bias of his mail,[82] found renewed attraction in seeking votes from the other side. Pearson's announcement on 12 January 1963, that he had decided that Canada was obligated to accept nuclear weapons, provided Diefenbaker with an obvious opportunity to appeal to antinuclear sentiment, but to do so he had to resist strong pressure to accept the logic of Pearson's reasoning. One source was the statement of the retiring supreme commander of NATO forces in Europe, General Lauris Norstad, that Canada ought to provide the nuclear equipment required by its forces there; another and more urgent one was Harkness's threat on 20 January to resign from the cabinet if the issue were allowed to remain unresolved until after another election. Diefenbaker's response was to promise a discussion of defence policy in Parliament and to appoint a committee of cabinet to examine the nuclear question. After a close study of the relevant documentation, the other members of the committee persuaded Green to acknowledge, 'reluctantly', that Canada had definite obligations to acquire nuclear weapons.[83] The committee then worked out an agreed position for presentation to the prime minister and cabinet. This provided for a request to NATO for clarification of Canada's nuclear role and, if that were reconfirmed, for acquisition of the appropriate weapons. With respect to NORAD, it was agreed that negotiations with the United States would 'be continued with a view to reaching agreement to secure the highest degree of availability to Canada.'[84]

If Green and Harkness were agreed on the report of the committee, it would seem that Diefenbaker need not have been concerned about an open split in cabinet if he accepted it. It is likely, therefore, that he was more influenced by doubts that a pronuclear position would be effective in an election and by the desire to be able to appear as a proponent of the other side if he considered it advantageous to do so. The outcome of the confused sequence of statement and counterstatement by himself and Harkness at the end of January reinforced these considerations. After the State Department in Washington released a note on 30 January taking issue with Diefenbaker's interpretation of Canada's obligations, he became if anything more resistant to Harkness's position, and informed his colleagues that he wanted to go to the country with an anti-American campaign.[85] Harkness, concluding that there was no hope of progress, carried out his threat to resign on 3 February and the government fell on an opposition vote of confidence two days later. Although he had not kept his cabinet together, Diefenbaker was able to go to the people in what he considered the most viable position on the nuclear issue: uncommitted to the nuclear option and able to exploit Canadian resentment of criticism of his action in the United States.

As events turned out, the election of 1963 was not a single-issue campaign, nor was foreign and defence policy its focal point. According to a Liberal strategist, domestic concerns were of more consistent interest to the voter, and the key to his party's success was concentrating in the final days of the campaign on the Diefenbaker government's reputation for indecisiveness, for which the Liberals offered an antidote in the form of 'sixty days of decision'.[86] But the outgoing government had to a considerable extent earned the reputation which helped defeat it in foreign policy, and hence the verdict of the electorate was in a sense a judgement on the way that activity had been conducted. The decision-making process under Diefenbaker enabled ministers to make good use of the bureaucratic resources available to them without giving up their autonomy. It did not guarantee, however, that they would always do so, or that they would keep out of trouble for other reasons. It may well be that the circumstances of Diefenbaker's fall deprived him and his government of credit for their achievements in foreign policy in a time of difficult transition in international affairs. Yet, as the handling of the Common Market and of defence policy shows, the problems were real, and they related as much to the way policy was made and implemented as to the principles on which it was based. It was reasonable, therefore, for the voters to be concerned about the process of making foreign policy when they went to the polls in 1963.

Suggestions for Further Reading

J.L. Granatstein, *The Ottawa Men: The Civil Service Mandarins, 1935–1957* (Toronto, 1982).

John W. Holmes, *Canada, A Middle-Aged Power* (Toronto, 1976).

Peter C. Newman, *Renegade in Power: The Diefenbaker Years* (Toronto, 1973).

Notes

[1] My understanding of this subject has been much assisted by interviews with a number of participants in the policy-making process, to all of whom I am very grateful. I have also benefited from the comments of Basil Robinson. The views expressed are mine and not necessarily those of the Department of External Affairs.

[2] Peter C. Newman, *Renegade in Power* (Carleton Library ed., Toronto, 1973), 252.

[3] See, for example, Charles Ritchie, *Storm Signals* (Toronto, 1983), 158, and J.L. Granatstein, *A Man of Influence* (Ottawa, 1981), 324.

[4] Peter Stursberg, *Diefenbaker: Leadership Gained* (Toronto, 1975), 147.

[5] Public Archives of Canada (hereafter PAC), Norman Robertson Papers, MG30 E163, Vol. 3A, J.W. Holmes to Robertson, 1 August 1957.

[6]See, for example, Department of External Affairs (hereinafter DEA), File 11246-40, Holmes to W.D. Matthews, 27 June 1957.

[7]Discussion of trade policy is recorded in DEA, File 50085-G-40, minutes of a meeting of the ministers of Finance and Trade and Commerce with officials . . . , 22 June 1957, and Privy Council Office (hereinafter PCO) Records, Cabinet Conclusions, 22 July 1957. I have not found confirmation in departmental sources that Diefenbaker consulted a senior member of External Affairs before agreeing to NORAD; cf. R.H. Roy, *For Most Distinguished Bravery* (Vancouver, 1977), 290.

[8]See, for example, PCO Records, Cabinet Conclusions, 11 April 1958.

[9]DEA, File 11246-40, Holmes to Matthews, 27 June 1957.

[10]Diefenbaker Centre, Saskatoon, Diefenbaker interview with John Munro, 4 December 1974.

[11]See, for example, PAC, Robertson Papers, MG30 E163, Vol. 3A, Holmes to Robertson, 1 August 1957.

[12]Granatstein, *Man of Influence*, 325–6.

[13]Diefenbaker Centre, Diefenbaker interview with John Munro, 14 December 1974.

[14]DEA, File 12685-40, R.B. Bryce to Jules Léger, 16 September 1957; *ibid.*, Léger to Bryce, 15 October 1957.

[15]Blair Fraser, 'Backstage at Ottawa', *Maclean's*, 12 October 1957, 2; *Telegram* (Toronto), 16 September 1957.

[16]Diefenbaker Centre, Diefenbaker interview with John Munro, 6 December 1974. See also Trevor Lloyd, *Canada in World Affairs, 1957–1959* (Toronto, 1968), 70, and Granatstein, *Man of Influence*, 326–7.

[17]See Granatstein, *Man of Influence*, 316, 320–1 and 323–6.

[18]Lloyd, *Canada in World Affairs*, 18, 20.

[19]DEA, File 50245-40, Léger to Prime Minister, 13 August 1958.

[20]House of Commons *Debates*, 20 February 1959, 1223.

[21]Stursberg, *Diefenbaker: Leadership Gained*, 185; Blair Fraser, 'The Lone Pine of Parliament Hill', *Maclean's*, 1 August 1959, 17 and 49–50.

[22]CJOH television, Ottawa, 'Insight', Peter Dobell interview with Douglas Fisher, 13 January 1980; Arnold Heeney, *The Things That Are Caesar's* (Toronto, 1972), 179.

[23]Charles Ritchie, *Diplomatic Passport* (Toronto, 1981), 171.

[24]See Granatstein, *Man of Influence*, 327–8.

[25]*Ibid.*, 338–9.

[26]Michael J. Tucker, 'Canada's Roles in the Disarmament Negotiations 1957–1971', PhD diss., University of Toronto, 1977, 81, 86 and n. 72.

[27]Granatstein, *Man of Influence*, 339.

[28]DEA, File 50210-F-40, Robertson to Léger, 10 August 1959.

[29]DEA, Historical Division, Howard Green interview, Vancouver, 2 March 1980.

[30]Granatstein, *Man of Influence*, 341.

[31]DEA, File 11336-10-A-40, Ross Campbell to Under-Secretary, 3 May 1961.

[32]Granatstein, *Man of Influence*, 343–9.

[33]PAC, Marcel Cadieux Papers, MG31 E31, Vol. 2, Cadieux to Under-Secretary, 21 April 1959.

[34]DEA, File 8260-15-40, Under-Secretary to Secretary of State for External Affairs (hereinafter SSEA), 7 November 1960.

[35]PCO Records, Cabinet Conclusions, 10 April 1961.

[36]DEA, File 11246-40, Far Eastern Division memorandum, 5 June 1959; File 10513-40, United Nations Division to Office of Under-Secretary, 9 March 1960.

[37]DEA, File 5475-DW-74-40, United Nations Division to Under-Secretary, 15 September 1960, and enclosure. I have benefitted in preparing this account from a review of the files by Anne Hillmer.

[38]Diefenbaker Centre, Diefenbaker Papers, Bryce to Prime Minister, 23 September 1960.

[39]DEA, File 5475-DW-70-40, New York (UN) to External, 23 September 1960, telegram 1541.

[40]Richard A. Preston, *Canada in World Affairs, 1959 to 1961* (Toronto, 1965), 270–1; DEA, Files 5475-DW-70-40 and 5475-DW-74-40.

[41]DEA, File 26-BEU-40, Under-Secretary to SSEA, 8 May 1962; File 633-40, Under-Secretary to Prime Minister, 8 May 1962. I have been assisted in dealing with this question by an account by D.M. Page.

[42]Diefenbaker Centre, Diefenbaker interview with John Munro, 4 December 1974; DEA, File 663-40, Under-Secretary to SSEA, 4 December 1957.

[43]PAC, Robertson Papers, MG30 E163, Vol. 18, Office of SSEA to Under-Secretary, 3 July 1962.

[44]PCO Records, Cabinet Conclusions, 6 September 1962.

[45]DEA, File 11389-A-40, Prime Minister's Office to Under-Secretary, 16 November 1962.

[46]*Ibid.*, New York (UN) to External, 24 November 1962, telegram 2370.

[47]See, for example, DEA, File 6230-40, Basil Robinson to Commonwealth division, 20 February 1959. I am grateful to F.J. McEvoy for a study which he has prepared on this subject.

[48]DEA, File 11827-40, Robinson to Commonwealth Division, 8 April 1960.

[49]DEA, File 50085-H-40, Bryce to Prime Minister, 18 April 1960.

[50]See, for example, *ibid.*, External to London, 7 May 1960, telegram K-164.

[51]John G. Diefenbaker, *One Canada: The Years of Achievement* (Toronto, 1976), 210–2.

[52]PCO records, Cabinet Conclusions, 11 and 25 February and 9 March 1961.

[53]DEA, File 50085-J-40, Drew to Prime Minister, 27 February 1961.

[54]PCO Records, Cabinet Conclusions, 6 July 1957.

[55]DEA, File 50085-J-40, SSEA to Prime Minister, 16 January 1961.

[56]*Ibid.*; PCO Records, Cabinet Conclusions, 11 February 1961.

[57]PCO Records, Cabinet Conclusions, 9 March 1961.

[58]DEA, File 50085-J-40, Bryce, memorandum, 12 March 1961.

[59]PCO Records, Cabinet Conclusions, 14 March 1961.

[60]Harold Macmillan, *Pointing the Way* (London, 1972), 299.

[61]DEA, File 12447-40, Under-Secretary to SSEA, 7 September 1960.

[62]*Ibid.*, London to Prime Minister, 18 May 1961, telegram 1833. Like many of Drew's recommendations on this subject, this document was not added to the External Affairs file until some years later.

[63]*Ibid.*, SSEA to Prime Minister, 2 March 1961 and minute, n.d.

[64]*Ibid.*, London to Prime Minister, 2 June 1961, telegram 2005, and *passim*; also Peyton Lyon, *Canada in World Affairs, 1961-1963* (Toronto, 1968), 447.

[65]DEA, File 12447-40, External to London, 1 August 1961, telegram E-1514; Lyon, *Canada in World Affairs*, 447–8.

[66]*Ibid.*, 448–50.

[67]PCO Records, Cabinet Conclusions, 14 September 1961.

[68]DEA, File 12447-40, External to Accra, 14 September 1961, telegram M67; Lyon, *Canada in World Affairs*, 450–2.

[69]PCO Records, Cabinet Conclusions, 26 September 1961.

[70]DEA, File 12447-40, London to Minister of Trade and Commerce, 24 September 1961, telegram 3454.

[71]*Ibid.*, London to Minister of Finance, 13 October 1961, telegram 3707.

[72]See, for example, PCO Records, Cabinet Conclusions, 15 November 1961.

[73]DEA, File 12447-40, SSEA to Prime Minister, 28 November 1961 and enclosure.

[74]'Mr Drew Writes a Letter', *Free Press* (Winnipeg), 7 May 1962.

[75]DEA, File 12447-40, London to Prime Minister, 29 April 1962, telegram 1588.

[76]See, for example, PCO Records, Cabinet Conclusions, 30 August 1962.

[77]PAC, Howard Green Papers, MG32 B13, Vol. 9, Diefenbaker to Green, 31 August 1962 and *passim*; PCO Reords, Cabinet Conclusions, 30 August 1962.

[78]Lord Garner, 'Britain and Canada in the 1940s and 1950s,' in *Britain and Canada*, Peter Lyon, ed. (London, 1976), 99–101; also Peyton Lyon, *Canada in World Affairs*, 463–76.

[79]George Ignatieff, 'Secrecy and Democratic Participation in the Formulation and Conduct of Canadian Foreign Policy', in *Secrecy and Foreign Policy*, Thomas M. Franck and Edward Weisband, eds (New York, 1974), 56.

[80]See, for example, PCO Records, Cabinet Conclusions, 14 January 1960; Jocelyn Maynard Ghent, 'Canadian-American Relations and the Nuclear Weapons Controversy, 1958–1963', PhD diss., University of Illinois at Urbana-Champaign, 1976, 81–3, 116–22.

[81]PAC, Douglas Harkness Papers, MG36 B19, Vol. 84, 'The Nuclear Arms Question and the Political Crisis Which Arose From It in January and February 1963'.

[82]Ghent, 'Did He Fall or Was He Pushed?' *International History Review*, Vol. I (1979), 258.

[83]Harkness, 'Nuclear Policy Muddled by Dief'. *Citizen* (Ottawa), 24 October 1977.

[84]PAC, Harkness Papers, MG36 B19, Vol. 84, 'Nuclear Arms question'.

[85]Harkness, 'A foolish move', *Citizen* (Ottawa), 25 October 1977.

[86]Walter L. Gordon, *A Political Memoir* (Toronto, 1977), 115–6, 120–1, 125–7.

31

The Canadian Constitution

David Milne

The post-1976 debates over constitutional change would probably
have astounded most Canadians of
the earlier part of the century, for
the thrust of change has largely been
to dismantle those centralizing
aspects of federalism so desperately
desired by previous generations. On
one level, the reaction against centralization merely represents the
latest turn in the wheel, for the
rise and decline of federal power
over time has been a constant of
Canadian politics since the 1860s.
On another level, the recent move
toward decentralization represents
the emergence of three separate
forces in Canadian politics (and
Canadian society): a reassertive,
nationalist, possibly separatistic,
Quebec; newly powerful and self-
confident provinces, resource-rich
and no longer willing to allow their
destinies to be subordinated to some
larger national needs; the collective
minorities, particularly the native
peoples, who would claim that their
'rights' require separate recognition
in any constitutional arrangement.
Attempting to satisfy all three forces
has tested the ingenuity of the constitutional negotiators: witness the
defeat of the Meech Lake and Charlottetown accords.

David Milne discusses the first
serious round of constitutional revision in his analysis of the Trudeau
initiatives of the early 1980s. As
Milne observes, Trudeau attempted
to preserve a fair measure of federalism in various features of his constitutional program, including the
employment of national referendums. Perhaps the most revolutionary part of the program was
expressed in the Canadian Charter
of Rights, which entrusted the protection of individual and collective
rights to the judicial rather than the
parliamentary system. How did the
Trudeau government attempt to
embody federalism in its constitutional package? In what sense were
referendums devices of federalism?
What was the effect of the Charter
of Rights on the system?

This article first appeared, titled 'Constitutional Politics', in David Milne: *Tug of War: Ottawa and the Provinces under Trudeau and Mulroney* (Toronto, 1986), 36–57.

By 1980 the constitution was the most important arena for the playing out of all of the developing federal-provincial tensions and conflicts. After more than a decade of intergovernmental discussions, the arrival of the Quebec referendum and its aftermath brought many of these issues to a head. At the centre lay the fight over Quebec independence, a political struggle that necessarily called into question the power and adequacy of Canadian state arrangements set against the dream of a new Quebec homeland. Here normal legal skirmishes were being entirely bypassed by reopening the debate about fundamentals—whether the people of Quebec would continue to live within the Canadian state at all and, if so, under what new promises and conditions. The PQ's idea of an independent French-speaking Quebec state, of a distinct people finally assuming control over its own destiny after years of colonial entanglements, was a powerful modern variant of nationalist ideology that challenged the logic and appeal of federalism for Quebeckers. In that subsequent battle of images, of politicians' portraits of people living in different patterns of association, the constitution was a symbol of possible new beginnings, and constitutional politics a way of taking stock of one's collective experience and attempting to redefine it either through renewal or revolution.

The federal-separatist war, which began in earnest after the PQ's electoral victory in 1976, could not be prosecuted without drawing on different meanings of community and of the good life. For the Parti Québécois, sovereignty-association, as the final extension of a long drive for increased Quebec legal powers since 1960, was advanced as a communal value of great importance. National self-realization through the achievement of an independent Quebec state was to be the fulfilment of every Quebecker's need, an essential precondition for a people's dignity, maturity and sense of itself. For the federal Liberals, the drive for a new Charter of Rights and Freedoms, containing language guarantees for francophones, was to compensate for the indignities the French had suffered during the first hundred years of association in Canada and was to provide the basis for a renewed sense of partnership with the English-speaking peoples in the country. It offered Quebeckers the modern liberal promise of guaranteed individual rights and freedoms throughout Canada in place of what federalists alleged to be the narrow separatist 'delusions of communal nationalism' behind Quebec's territorial picket fence.

But the constitution was a necessarily prominent element in a wider federal-provincial contest of wills. As a symbol of values and a statement on the future relations of peoples in different parts of the Canadian federation, the constitution gradually came to preoccupy even the anglophone leaders of the federation, especially in the West. They saw in the constitution an opportunity to right the wrongs of the past and to restructure a newer, more just and more equal federation. On the one hand, this objective was seen to be furthered by reforming federal institutions, principally the Senate and the Supreme Court, so that they could better reflect the interests of the less populated areas of the federation in federal policy. On the other, many premiers came to see the constitution as a potential playing field for the direct expansion of provincial power and for the consequent reduction of federal powers now considered inappropriate or outdated.[1]

Observers of the Canadian constitutional process were constantly exposed to the themes of disgruntled regionalism or alternatively to dualism and the new conflicting aspirations of Quebec leaders during the constitutional talks over the 1970s and 1980s. These ideas about the nature of the Canadian federation and the need to change it through constitutional bargaining had become ever more pressing issues on the public agenda, especially prior to the Quebec referendum. For each government there was a conscious link between its philosophy of federalism and its constitutional agenda, just as there was an understandable preoccupation with the power and interests of a particular government and its constitutional program. In most cases, that linkage was quite obvious, especially where the governments were discussing the transfer of more power in a particular area—for example, family law, natural resources, trade and commerce or the fisheries—from one level of government to another. But in some cases, the governmental stake in constitutional reform proposals was more obscure. The federally inspired Canadian Charter of Rights and Freedoms might be seen as a case in point. Presented disinterestedly by Ottawa as a 'people's' item that would not advance the powers of the federal government, its role in the government's overall philosophy of federalism and political program was much less evident.[2]

The federal constitutional program in 1980, it will be argued, in its determination to rebalance the federation contained in substance and in procedure quite a number of centralizing or unifying features, only some of which were finally acted upon in the constitutional settlement two years later. Moreover, the procedures that were rebuffed and the program elements that were dropped were generally those reflecting federal paternalism and central Canadian dominance, assumptions that, while relevant to the John A. Macdonald era, were no longer appropriate to the Canadian federation of the late twentieth century. In that respect, the Trudeau government's attempted resurrection of certain features of the older Macdonald tradition, most notably the primacy and adequacy of the national Parliament in the expression of the Canadian national interest in constitutional and other matters, was not in the end a successful counterweight in the government's program of restoring the balance of power in the federation. Its exclusion suggests the increasingly untenable nature of this model of federalism for the country.

On the other hand, the centralizing features of the federal proposals that were adopted in the form of the Charter of Rights and Freedoms were partially successful as counterweights only because of the popular and somewhat deceptive liberal ideology that sustained them. Unlike the explicit arguments for federal majoritarianism and parliamentary supremacy, this charter ideology as propounded by the federal government obscured rather than exposed the link to the question of the federal order of state and its institutions, while it made at least for a time a successful case for a 'peoples-based' nation-building instrument. Moreover, by entrenching minority language rights in the charter, this strategy had the potential of defusing or at least deflecting the country's oldest permanent conflict, namely, the French and English feud, away from the old government-to-government political arena of federalism (and away from separate state solutions like those of the PQ) toward a new nationally unified 'neutral' judicial forum where citizens could directly challenge and seek redress from governments for infringements of these rights. This shift toward defending matters of overriding national significance through a federal judiciary armed with a national charter, rather than a federal Parliament armed with rusty imperial legal tools and old-fashioned moral superiority, was nothing short of a master-stroke, since by this means a new and politically acceptable way was found to preserve the centre against centrifugal pulls on the balance.

The Defeat of Centralist Federalism

The part of the federal Liberals' constitutional program in 1980 that attempted to resurrect an older and more direct, if paternalistic, defence for the federal state emerged logically and yet paradoxically from the government's program to save federalism as a real balance-of-power system. If the latter were to be preserved, if Confederation were not to swing under current pressures entirely in the direction of 'ten autonomous states', then the case for the unique and superior position of the federal order of government had to be made, if not indeed overstated. That nationalist undertaking was exactly what the Trudeau government did in the context of threats to Canada's existence, which they believed were at least as grave as those that originally beset Confederation itself. The theory they mounted, tagged by some scholars as 'federal majoritarianism', was about as bold a restatement of the centralist assumptions of the bygone Macdonald era as has ever been propounded by a federal government in the twentieth century.[3] Trudeau gave succinct expression to that theory in a blunt and ringing declaration in the House of Commons on 15 April 1980:

We are the only group of men and women in this country who can speak for every Canadian. We are the only group, the only assembly in this country, which can speak for the whole nation, which can express the national will and the national interest.[4]

While in a subsequent aside Trudeau acknowledged that in our federal system 'the national government is [not] the sole voice' nor 'the national Parliament the sole instrument of the national interest in every area', he maintained that the national government does, however, enjoy the final 'right', indeed 'obligation', to 'uphold the national interest' against provinces 'even in areas of provincial jurisdiction' whenever these powers are being 'exercised in a way which [is] contrary to the national interest.' That, he declared, is the reason

> we find in the Constitution of Canada such things as the declaratory power, the reservation and disallowance powers, the spending power and the right to make orders in matters of education as provided by section 93, subsections (3) and (4).
>
> I am not saying that these rights cannot be limited or bargained away. As a matter of fact, our government beginning in 1968 and 1969, proposed ways of limiting the spending power. Our government, as recently as at the federal-provincial conference in February of 1979, proposed ways of limiting the declaratory power. But what I am saying is that when there is a conflict of interest, not of laws which will be judged by the courts, the citizens must be convinced that there is a national government which will speak for the national interest and will ensure that it does prevail.[5]

It was because of that insistence on the primacy of the national community and of the supremacy of the federal Parliament as the ultimate expression of that national will that Richard Simeon called Trudeau a latter-day Sir John A. Macdonald.[6] Trudeau's defence of parliamentary supremacy as the fount of this authority contrasted sharply with the premiers' demand that the national will lay ultimately in the collective wills of the provinces and the federal government as expressed perhaps through First Ministers' Conferences and subsequent legislative actions by both orders of government.[7] While Trudeau acknowledged that the latter view 'could be the essence of a federal state', he insisted that 'it *has not* been the essence of the Canadian federal state' and questioned whether it 'could be the essence of a parliamentary federal state'.[8]

Trudeau's defence of federal parliamentary pre-eminence based on past practice and the legal underpinnings of a colonial era was hardly a persuasive answer to the contemporary state of affairs of the Canadian federation, nor was it in keeping with Trudeau's rational acceptance of the Canadian state's evolution away from Macdonald's centralized federalism in his writings from the 1950s and 1960s. It appeared here in this bald form only because it formed a crucial part of the defence Ottawa would require if it were to move a single step in its unilateral program of rebalancing the federation. In that respect, the upshot of this argument was hardly academic, since upon it would rest the legitimacy of the Trudeau government's plans for unilateral action over the constitution, energy policy and many other matters.

Hence, once again, after decades of grudging acknowledgment of the powerful place of the provinces in the federation short of wartime conditions, the idea was advanced that in fundamental conflicts with the provinces only the federal Parliament could truly speak for Canada, that only the Canadian Parliament could exercise moral leadership in the defence of the Canadian economic union or tame the selfish regional and provincial interests then appearing to threaten the integrity of the country. This notion carried credence only in the context of the federal fight against Quebec separatism and its milder manifestations in the truculent provincialism of several other provinces. But these were precisely the conditions for the rebirth of many of the centralist assumptions which up to that time had been gradually discarded or suppressed as outmoded and incompatible with the evolving federation of the twentieth century. For although there had been periods of strong federal power during this century, such as the post-1945 period of federal pre-eminence activated by a functional social consensus around applied Keynesianism and the welfare state, they had not been simple reversions to the older nineteenth-century theory of centralized federalism.

This return in the 1980s to a quasi-imperial tradition rooted in the Macdonald legacy of Canadian federalism was clearest in the Liberal government's extraordinary decision to seek a fundamental change in the nature of the Canadian constitution without the consent of the provinces. While the government argued defensively that this move toward patriation was a decision taken reluctantly only after more than half a century of futile efforts to obtain the agreement of the provinces on an amending formula in the face of the 'trap of unanimity', it also staked out exceedingly bold legal and political claims against the very idea of a constitutional convention respecting provincial consent for changes to the constitution and in favour of the unilateral right of the federal Parliament to break any constitutional logjam with the provinces by going with a request to Westminster on its own.[9]

As Richard Simeon has noted, the defensive argument was somewhat 'specious', since Canada was not suffering from constitutional paralysis, the modern round of constitutional talks went back only to the mid-Sixties, and the opposition to federal unilateralism consisted of a good deal more than one or two 'recalcitrant premiers'. The federal government had decided to include not only patriation and its own amending formula in its request to Westminster, but also an important and massive new addition to the Canadian constitution in the form of a Canadian Charter of Rights and Freedoms. The latter could scarcely be justified by pointing to a long history of failed negotiations with the provinces, nor to an election result, nor even to a mandate for entrenching bilingual and other charter rights from its win in the 1980 Quebec referendum; the case rested instead on the final right of Parliament alone to discern and express the national interest on this matter and to ensure that its constitutional will prevailed.

The procedure used entailed repeating 'for one last time' the same humble request for the Parliament at Westminster to enact these constitutional measures for Canada and to have the Queen sign them into law. According to Edward McWhinney, that was in itself a very conservative and somewhat comical colonial exercise, hardly a new and stirring start to independent nationhood.[10] Instead of seeking a mandate from the Canadian people over the heads of 'right-wing, obstructionist premiers' and then using it (popular sovereignty) as the source for a forthright declaration of political independence, Trudeau's government had taken an 'ultra-positivistic' approach.[11] Under these circumstances, the government decided to use its exclusive power of drafting and forwarding constitutional resolutions to the Westminster Parliament as a unilateral instrument for a veritable 'constitutional *coup d'état*'.[12] That raised a whole thicket of ironies.

> We see [argued Simeon] the federal government seeking to achieve in Britain what it cannot achieve at home. There is a fine irony here: it is the very characteristic of our present constitution which Ottawa feels is so unconscionable which permits it to do what it is doing. For the government cannot win sufficient consent in Canada according to *any* of the formulae for amendment which have previously been proposed; nor can it even win consent by the very amendment procedure contained in the Resolution. Instead, it must by-pass the domestic process and ask Britain if we can be a colony one more time, asking Britain to change it before sending it back. I find it very strange that an action specifically prohibited by Section 91 (1) of the B.N.A. Act should be made by going to the U.K.[13]

However, having decided to go to Britain with no popular mandate from the regions of Canada and with only Ontario and New Brunswick in tow, the Trudeau government simply wrapped its actions in the language of parliamentary sovereignty and dared the Westminster Parliament to defy it. This attempted use of outdated colonial machinery to impose constitutional terms upon an unwilling Canadian community had disturbing parallels with the old paternalistic and heavy-handed practices of the nineteenth century. Citizens of the country could still remember, for example, how a combination of federal and imperial power had originally worked to keep Nova Scotia and New Brunswick in Confederation and to carve out a federal hegemonic position over the territories of the new West. While the popular Charter of Rights and Freedoms enjoyed considerable national support and provided some cover for the federal government's planned use of the imperial machinery, polls indicated that a majority of Canadians objected to this procedure. They recognized, as indeed the Supreme Court later did in its September

1981 landmark decision on the patriation case, that such an action violated a constitutional convention regarding provincial consent and that Canada had long since moved on from the days of the nineteenth century when mere requests from Ottawa for substantive changes were sufficient to amend the Canadian constitution.

This policy venture was only the most dramatic illustration of federal unilateralism.[14] The federal inclination to bypass the provinces and to govern the country increasingly from the centre was evident in a wide variety of other initiatives. At bottom these changes in direction pointed to a strategy of radical conservatism—an attempt to rearrange the balance of power toward the centre by reaching back to an earlier pattern of Canadian federalism for guidance and direction. While that strategy had the advantage of building from within the country's political culture and its own strong historical roots, it depended on a conception of the federal state that had become unrealistic. Provinces were now powerful, intergovernmental interdependence was unavoidable, foreign ownership had done much to erode the national dream of Canadian economic independence, and federal institutions and policies were regarded as so flawed that they no longer commanded national respect for their regional sensitivity and fairness. While the Trudeau government doubtless recognized the force of these countertrends and was aware that it could not simply resurrect the past—indeed, it did not wish merely to supplant provincialism with centralism—it was determined to borrow selectively from earlier periods of federal pre-eminence in its balance-of-power campaign. Often, as with its battle over fiscal federalism and social policy, the government's implicit reversionist strategy related more to the period of Canadian federalism following the Second World War than to the Macdonald regime. But it was all compositional variations on old thematic material, all decidedly *déjà vu*.

In the light of its apparent obsolescence, what is perhaps remarkable is the extent to which this federal approach was endorsed by a wide segment of the Canadian political community, including the national leadership of the NDP and the Conservative government of Ontario. Many of the centralizing unilateral federal initiatives—including the NEP and the constitutional program—were supported in procedure as well as in substance, particularly by anglophone party leaders and intellectuals from central Canada on both the left and the right. Most noteworthy is the strong and consistent support of the Ontario Conservative government; it joined forces with Ottawa in its plan to contain both Quebec separatism and western regionalism. Not surprisingly, many federal constitutional items and other policies appeared to reflect the *status quo* interests of Ontario at the expense of those forces seeking to reshape the country in their own interests. Central Canadian dominance was as prominent a feature of this brand of federalism as was its old-fashioned paternalism.

The same blend of elements could be seen in the federal case for defending the Canadian economic union against the alleged evils of economic provincialism. Whereas John A. Macdonald was able to employ the imperial tools of reservation and disallowance against provincial measures that threatened the integrity of the national economy, these were no longer available as practical instruments of policy in the 1980s. Although the removal of these legal powers, now regarded by convention as inappropriate and inoperative, was vigorously advanced by provincial leaders during the constitutional talks, the federal government did not cede them. By 1980, the government had decided that unless the provinces gave ground over the Charter of Rights, these overriding federal legal powers would be retained and, moreover, that the exercise of the federal discretionary powers permitting intrusions into provincial jurisdiction—the spending power, the declaratory power, the emergency power—would not be checked by any prior need for securing some measure of provincial consent. On the contrary, in the absence of a true give-and-take settlement with the provinces, these centre-defending instruments were justified as part of a legal balance devised by the founding fathers to ensure, in the face of conflict, the upholding of the national interest.[15]

Indeed, the government sought more effective means for controlling economic provincialism in proposed constitutional measures, the net effect of which would expand direct federal jurisdiction and subject provincial actions that interfered with the economic union to judicial review. These proposals were contained in the government's demands for 'powers over the economy' during the 1980 constitutional talks. In an exaggerated and one-sided attack on provincial restrictions and interference in the Canadian economic union, the government argued that only the federal order of government should be entrusted to defend the general national interest against these selfish, parochial and self-defeating measures. This could best be done by expanding federal powers over trade and commerce, by strengthening section 121 of the constitution to prohibit provincial nontariff barriers and, with respect to restrictive labour practices, by entrenching mobility rights for all Canadians in the new Charter of Rights and Freedoms. While this case was supported by a fairly simplistic free market rationale in a federal background paper written by A.E. Safarian, these extreme claims of damage to the union were not supported by later careful economic analysis.[16]

More disturbing was the political assumption that only provincial economic measures were seriously undermining the market efficiency of the Canadian economy and that similar federal restrictions would not be subject to judicial review. When the federal government tabled its draft proposals for the Canadian economic union, it became quickly evident that Parliament was to be largely exempt from the restrictions on the economic powers of governments whenever it acts in accordance 'with the principle of equalization and economic development' or whenever the matter is declared to be 'of overriding national interest'. As Thomas Courchene has noted:

> Ottawa's view is that it should be allowed to do the very things that it desires to prevent the provinces from doing. One is left with the very distinct impression that provincial actions in the economic sphere almost by definition leads to the fragmentation of the economic union, whereas similar federal initiatives, again almost by definition, are in the national interest.[17]

Such a self-serving view was hardly likely to convince the provinces during the constitutional talks or to justify the inclusion of this item in the government's unilateral initiative of 1980.[18] This strand of moral superiority and self-sufficiency in federal thinking carried over into much of the Trudeau government's economic policies. In view of the severe economic disparities in Canada and of widespread suspicion that federal policies under the guise of free market economics had long protected the interests of central Canada at the expense of the peripheries, it did not escape the attention of the western and eastern provinces that this federal constitutional initiative would most benefit Ontario. Once again, federal paternalism with a distinct central Canadian orientation was a noticeable part of Trudeau's constitutional program.

These patterns were also evident in the amending formula the Trudeau Liberals attempted to push through Westminster without the consent of the provinces. One feature of that formula suggested the superior federal role in initiating constitutional change by popular referenda rather than by some measure of intergovernmental consent. Although this part of the federal proposal appeared to enshrine democratic principles by allowing the people themselves to be the authors of constitutional amendments, there really was no way in which the mechanism could be used except by and with the consent of the federal Parliament. No provision was made for direct popular initiation of constitutional referenda (perhaps the ultimate logical instrument for a people actually exercising democratic control over a state's constitution, but probably for that very reason not yet accepted by any federal state, including Switzerland); nor was there provision for broader public participation in debating and approving amendments through constitutional conventions activated by subnational governments, an option already available to Americans under article V of their constitution. The provinces were given no means by which a given number of them could refer to the people constitutional proposals the federal Parliament was not prepared to consider. The assumption was that provincial government opposition might not truly reflect the opinions of the people on constitutional matters and, therefore, could hold back desirable change in the federation, whereas presumably the reverse could not reasonably be expected to happen. The federal Parliament would by definition reflect the public interest.

The centralist implications of this element of the federal amending proposal have been nicely highlighted by Alan Cairns:

> [The referendum mechanism] was potentially an immensely significant symbolic and practical redefinition of the constituent parts of the Canadian federal polity. It located ultimate sovereignty in an alliance between the federal government and national referendum electorates conceivably responding to amending proposals mainly of interest to the federal government and answering questions worded by federal officials. It was an incredibly ambitious attempt to strengthen the central government, elevate the status of the people as constitutional actors, and reduce provincial governments to the status of initial, but no longer final spokesmen for provincial interests. The fundamental thrust of the proposal was nation-building, if need be at the expense of provincial governments whose powers would henceforth be held on sufferance. The federal government, of course, preserved its own veto and had the exclusive power to activate the process, so there was no way in which it could be a loser.[19]

The proposal, drafted under the assumption that provincial electorates would be 'more pliable . . . in passing judgments on proposals from Ottawa for constitutional amendments' or certainly 'less tenacious' than provincial legislators and officials, was calculated to favour federal interests.[20] That fact was clear in the exclusive federal control over the initiation process. While such a provision already applied in the Australian constitution, experts there have recognized it as an inequality 'which is a little hard on the States if they want to get through an amendment which benefits them at the central legislature's expense'.[21] The Australian experience has also shown that the referendum device is an exceedingly tempting means for the central government to aggrandize its power by putting up self-serving amendment proposals; Australians have traditionally rejected most of these overtures, usually aimed at expanding central powers over economic matters, but they did accept a massive transfer of jurisdiction over much of social policy in a 1946 amendment.[22] These results may suggest linkages between the expansion of federal power and anticipated relatively clear-cut benefits to citizens for a successful referendum outcome, just as the same mix was needed for the successful political launching of the nation-building Canadian Charter of Rights and Freedoms. Whatever the future results of referenda might have been in Canada—Trudeau perhaps tongue-in-cheek had bet the provinces would win more often, though the matter is one of conjecture—there was little doubt that an avenue was being opened up for circumventing provincial governments and for establishing new direct relationships between Ottawa and the Canadian people on fundamental matters of state.

A considerable central Canadian bias was also reflected in the general Victoria formula the Trudeau government had been advancing for over a decade.[23] This formula granted Quebec and Ontario in perpetuity power to veto all future constitutional changes. Other provinces that acquired at least 25 per cent of the Canadian population might later be added to this preferred club. These provinces would in this respect enjoy equivalent status to that of the national Parliament—that is, exercise the power to strike down single-handedly any amendment proposal. While such a formula ensured that Quebec as the principal focus of francophone power would enjoy a veto, it also enshrined provincial inequality and central Canadian legal domination of the federation, since only the populated heartland of the country could expect to achieve these levels of concentration in the near future. Moreover, this formula carried no special protections of unanimity on any sensitive areas of constitutional concern to the other provinces.

This amendment formula essentially carried forward the older regional logic of Canadian Confederation, enshrined, for example, in Senate representation. There the whole of the East and West of the country—each region consisting of four separate provinces—was put on a par with the single dominant provinces of Ontario and Quebec. This arrangement had not helped the second chamber reflect and defend regional concerns against 'Empire Canada', but it did demonstrate rather graphically the lopsided nature of the Canadian federal union.

By the time of the 1981 constitutional negotiations, the opportunity to impose these constitutional principles onto the country had passed. In the final compromises of November, the federal amending proposal was sacrificed in favour of the provinces' preferred formula, while the battle against economic provincialism had shifted to other policy forums. The new general amending formula—Parliament plus seven provinces representing 50 per cent or more of the Canadian population—entrenched formal provincial equality as well as the 'noxious' feature of opting out, while the referendum idea was simply dropped.[24] Even the inclusion of mobility rights in the charter was compromised so that preferential labour restrictions could apply in essentially have-not provinces where the level of employment was below that of the Canadian average.

All of these setbacks suggested that it was unlikely the Trudeau government could quite so frontally turn back the clock, roll back provincial power and check the evolution of the Canadian federal system away from its centralized beginnings under John A. Macdonald. However, the Trudeau government's program for national unity and the defence of federalism was better advanced by the entrenchment of the Charter of Rights and Freedoms. This was the more important, subtle and popular element of its constitutional planning. Unlike the ill-fated reassertion of centralized federalism, this injection of liberal nationalism into a country hardly beginning to wake up from the conservatism of its colonial past was likely to be a lasting contribution to Canadian political culture, to federalism and to national unity.

The Entrenchment of Nationalist Liberalism

It is remarkable though scarcely surprising that the actual French Canadian nationalist underpinnings of Canada's new charter have not received much commentary or notice, at least in English-speaking Canada. The charter itself has drawn enormous interest but more for its broad humanitarian appeal to 'guaranteeing' rights in general than for the actual complex reasons for its placement in the constitution. It is especially sad to read those who explain the arrival of a new entrenched charter by pointing to the rise of modern liberalism and human rights advocates in English-speaking Canada. Though there were voices for the enactment of such a measure by progressives after the Second World War and though these demands found weak expression in the 1960 Diefenbaker government's Bill of Rights, there never was a sufficient consensus in English-speaking Canada for entrenchment of a rights charter. That is the reason why the Diefenbaker government had to content itself with a simple federal enactment applicable to itself rather than a constitutional measure binding on all the governments in the country. That is why, despite federal advocacy for such a measure over fifteen years, even fundamental human rights in the 1982 charter (as well as legal and equality rights) are still subject to legislative overrides.

Therefore, the meaning of the rights charter and certainly the reasons for its constitutional triumph in the 1982 settlement cannot be found in a sudden and inexplicable burst of liberal individualism in Canada. In that respect, the careful and useful retrospective study of the growth in a 'rights consciousness' in Canada done by Cynthia Williams and Alan Cairns for the Macdonald Commission is instructive.[25] The study shows the gradual and painstaking emergence over several decades of a notion of individual rights inherent in Canadian citizenship as a result of many factors, including international law and the increasingly popular recognition of group rights after the 1960s; yet the study also makes patently clear that, despite these promising tendencies in Canadian political culture, the whole entrenchment enterprise would never have been successful without the decisive push for a charter by the federal government in the late 1960s. It was the central government in response to the threats of Quebec nationalism and separatism that pushed nation-building through a rights charter, and while the earlier work of broader acculturation and lobbying by civil rights groups helped prepare a more fertile ideological ground in Canada than would otherwise have been the case, the way was always fraught with division and controversy. American liberalism in the form of a constitutionally entrenched charter of rights faced many ideological enemies both on the left and the right in English-speaking Canada, while in Quebec during the 1960s and the 1970s, it was anything but a mainstream ideological preoccupation. Hence, since the charter though popular was not the product of some coherent national ground swell of the citizenry, federal advocates of the idea had to struggle vigorously to find a place for it within the still-dominant traditions of federalism and parliamentary government.

Furthermore, it is by no means clear how an admittedly growing sensitivity and interest in the question of rights must necessarily culminate in an entrenched charter, nor that this particular means of securing and advancing rights would flow from a modern sophisticated rights advocate. What tilted a more rights-conscious Canada in that direction? Why the extraordinary stress in group or minority rights that necessarily find their footing in constitutional entrenchment? It may well be that answers to these and other related questions can be best achieved, not through a broader study of the diffuse sources of thinking and influence around rights, especially in English-speaking Canada, but by direct examination of the actual politics and longer indigenous traditions upon which a determined and powerful federal francophone élite built its case for entrenchment. Looking from within that longer Quebec tradition seems a preferable route to understanding the new national foundation for 'rights' and ultimately for accounting for the final emergence of the charter.

That perspective should be even more evident when the nature of the new constitutional rights in question are closely examined and when due regard is paid to the strategic role of the charter in the fight of the francophone federalists and their separatist enemies in Quebec. A substantial block of the most important rights in the charter—those put outside the scope of legislative infringement by the use of a notwithstanding clause—concern minority rights for francophones in anglophone Canada and for anglophones in an officially unilingual Quebec.[26] The defence of these collective rights of peoples is in some respects at odds with a purely individual defence of liberal freedoms, but the charter clearly gives these collective rights pride of place. In addition, declarations concerning the two official languages of the country and the exclusive rights belonging to the founding peoples find themselves curiously ensconced in an otherwise universalistic charter of individual liberal rights.

No doubt these inclusions would puzzle classical theorists, indeed anyone unfamiliar with Canada's history, for these sections hint at a nationalist liberalism concerned primarily with the politics of linguistic accommodation in the country but which has somehow managed to make a plausible case of grafting itself onto a classical liberal rights charter. It was essentially in this fashion that the Trudeau government managed to entrench the political vision of Quebec's Henri Bourassa in the Canadian constitution and thus to close off for a time the alternative separatist outlet for Quebec nationalism. If this is the real meaning and genesis of Canada's charter, it must be seen as one of the world's strangest routes to liberal constitutionalism.

It is true, as Cairns has noted, that the Canadian political identity had been undergoing rapid change in the postwar period with the decline in the

British connection and the power of the new American empire, the rise of French Canadian nationalism in the country, the rapid ethnic diversity of the population through immigration and the consequently painful struggle to reshape the meaning of Canadian political nationality.[27] The politics of dualism, multiculturalism, national self-determination for aboriginal peoples, and new rights for women all suggest that the old constitutional definitions of community in Canada were inadequate. It is also true, as noted earlier, that the rise of provincialism was forcing the Canadian government to seek better ways to defend the common purpose and integrity of the Canadian state. But it was the struggle against separatism that most threatened the federal government and preoccupied its attention. Indeed, the charter was actually drafted in the late 1960s when Quebec separatism was the only serious provincialist threat confronting Ottawa. And it was to the charter that federal leaders returned in the aftermath of the 1980 referendum, offering it to the people of Quebec as a plausible foundation for renewal of the federation, indeed as an alternative outlet for the expression of francophone nationalism.

Without this enormous political force behind it, the charter would never have seen the light of day during this century. It was by virtue of its role as a federal state measure to contain separatism that it was moved to the top of the government's constitutional priorities. Only later did public rights groups come to participate in the business of strengthening the rights provisions in the charter and of campaigning for it essentially on terms set by the federal goverment.[28] It was entirely instructive that with respect to the vigorous defence of the general human rights contained within the charter, it was always the public that prodded the federal government to close loopholes and strengthen wording so that general charter rights would receive more than cosmetic protection; but on language provisions the government had already staked out its program in forthright legal terms.[29] Similarly, when tradeoffs had to be made by the governments, it was always the language provisions on which the federal government would not budge. That was because these provisions enshrined the French Canadian nationalist vision and tradition that for almost a century had competed with separatism for the loyalty of the Quebec people.

This French Canadian nationalist foundation for the charter finds its roots far back in the history and political culture of Quebec. As A.I. Silver's splendid book *The French-Canadian Idea of Confederation* indicates, the Quebec-based vision of a country with a bilingual dual nationality only gradually emerged during the first thirty years of the Dominion, particularly in response to threats to francophones in western Canada. But by the 1890s the theory 'of the perfect equality of the two races before the law' and the idea of constitutional guarantees for minority language and school rights and of the constitution as the source of a new harmony between the English and French within their common homeland had taken root.[30] Already it was challenging the older idea of Quebec as the sole homeland for the French

Canadian nation, the logical intellectual antecedent for modern Quebec separatism. The new theory found its most consistent and dedicated champion in Henri Bourassa, and although Prime Minister Wilfrid Laurier failed miserably to give expression to it, the vision returned again in the 1960s in the recommendations of the Commission on Bilingualism and Biculturalism and later in Trudeau's constitutional charter between the two founding peoples.

It has been difficult for anglophones not steeped in that tradition to see the Canadian charter principally as the outcome of a long nationalist debate in Quebec and not so much as a simple export from the United States. Undoubtedly the latter American tradition has now been grafted onto the essentials of a bilingual vision of the country and was a necessary part of selling this whole strategy of nationhood to the Canadian people, especially in English-speaking Canada, but the centre and origins of this new constitutional edifice are uniquely Canadian. The powerful idea of the equal 'rights' of the French and English languages in the life of the nation, of the 'rights' belonging to the francophone and anglophone minorities in the country as a result of the Confederation bargain, was an antecedent of the nationalist liberalism that persisted in Quebec and coexisted uncomfortably and ambiguously with the idea of homeland Quebec. From the very beginning the bilingual vision never entirely dislodged the idea of the special role of Quebec as the francophone centre in the country, but it sought to reach out from that centre first in an early and vain attempt to defend francophones from attacks elsewhere in the country and later, in the face of an imminent threat of withdrawal from Canada by Quebec francophones, to reshape once again the linguistic partnership in the rest of the country. Here the liberal virtues of racial and linguistic equality, tolerance for differences, and the rolling back of past injustices to minorities were part of the Bourassa tradition Trudeau adopted. The emphasis on collective minority rights arises again here in the form of language and schooling rights, together with a national vision of a just and equal French-English partnership throughout Canada.

Another puzzle is resolved if this view of the charter's meaning is recognized. Why should an essentially conservative people, with little inclination to distrust governments on principle, have decided to bypass governments and entrust so many of its rights, especially language rights, to judges and not to politicians? This was the very debate around which the issue of the charter was fought, and the continued presence of the notwithstanding clause indicates that the federal government was only partially successful in making that transfer. Yet the decision to cede that power to the courts unequivocally in the case of language rights reflects once again this nationalist school in Quebec, which had learned through bitter historical experience that entrusting minority rights either to the goodwill of provincial governments or to federal remedial action was unacceptable. The politics of the late nineteenth century had taught Bourassa's successors the liberal lesson that reliance on any other mechanism short of constitutional guarantees was inadequate for a defence of fundamental rights.

Bourassa had purported to see a justification and guarantee of these rights, partly in a philosophical defence of language as a 'divine right' within the Catholic faith, but more fundamentally on broad historical and constitutional grounds.[31] His philosophical defence was important because it ended up embedding language rights in a social context—in the individual's relation to church and community—and not as absolute individual natural rights. That meant that such rights were scarcely marked off as natural rights that individuals held as against society, but were 'comprehensible only in relation to a group of . . . human beings with whom the language is shared and from which personal and cultural identity is achieved'.[32] It was therefore possible to claim language rights for a distinctive indigenous people with their own thriving identity while denying, for example, individual rights to education in the traditional language for immigrants and scattered communities.

When Bourassa was driven to defend his theory that French language rights were somehow legally 'guaranteed' throughout the Dominion of Canada, he could not point to any explicit liberal rights charter for support nor did he appear to have any such conception in mind as a possible remedy for protection of francophone minorities at that time. Instead, he pointed to the British North America (BNA) Act (now known as the Constitution Act 1867) itself—particularly to section 93, which empowered the federal government to protect denominational schools from provincial infringement, and to section 133, proclaiming the equality of the French and English languages in the national Parliament and the Quebec legislature—and to provisions of the Manitoba Act of 1870, which proclaimed English and French as the official languages of that province, as evidence that both languages were to 'have the right to coexist everywhere that the Canadian people leads a public life: at church, at school, in Parliament, in court, and in all public services'.[33] Such a claim was, strictly speaking, hardly sustained by these examples, but Bourassa was more interested in building his defence upon what he called the 'spirit' of Confederation as a gentlemen's 'double contract' between the two races of Canada, English and French, as well as between the union of British colonies. It was that moral bargain and not the legal niceties of the BNA Act that deserved to be respected if the Canadian experiment at union was to survive.

This constitutional defence was supported by appeals to history and to a sense of fair play from the majority anglophone populations in the other provinces. Had not French Canadians stood with their English-speaking neighbours in opposition to the Americans in the eighteenth and nineteenth centuries? Had they not steadfastly worked alongside the English in the building of the country they both now shared? From these common undertakings it appeared to Bourassa a matter of simple political justice to recognize 'the duality of races, the duality of languages, guaranteed by the equality of rights'.

It was only after the uselessness of these moral appeals had been amply demonstrated by political events, and after the manifest bankruptcy of the legal protections thought to be contained within the BNA Act, that ideological successors to Bourassa in Quebec, especially in the person of Pierre Elliott Trudeau, turned to an entrenched rights charter as a new vehicle for protection of these rights. But the earlier pan-Canadian liberal argument built around language rights was an indispensable antecedent to this development. Not only was Bourassa's view a logical foundation for the idea of a legally enforceable contract or 'charter' providing equal rights for the two founding peoples, his was also an accurate and prophetic warning of the dangers that would be done to national unity by his contemporaries' expunging the rights of francophone minorities in the Canadian Northwest, Ontario and elsewhere. It required only the later rise of separatism in Quebec to revive his vision of Canada as a homeland for both French and English and to prepare the way for its enshrinement in an otherwise broad and universal charter.

The merger is not accomplished without producing a bundle of curious ironies. The notion of a country putting in place a liberal charter with compromises permitting legislative overrides for what are described as fundamental freedoms (speech, conscience, assembly and other 'natural rights'), while denying such overrides for the 'hybrid' rights of language, speaks powerfully to the central purpose of the charter as it was defined and defended by its chief constitutional 'author' and 'advocate', the federal government of Canada under Justice Minister and, later, Prime Minister Trudeau. Moreover, the frequently advanced Liberal argument that the charter was essentially the nation's answer to francophones who had voted against sovereignty-association in the 1980 referendum was plausible only on a reading of the charter as an expression of the new partnership between the French and English. The fact that the federal government recognized that language rights were hybrids—that is, as belonging not to individuals as permanent natural rights but to individuals strictly by virtue of their membership in realistic minority communities—was clear in a number of revealing sections of the Charter of Rights and Freedoms.

First, rights to educational instruction in either of the country's official languages under section 23 do not extend equally and by natural right to all citizens of Canada. There is no freedom of choice for the language of instruction, least of all for members of the majority linguistic communities. Instead, only individuals who are members of minorities are granted these rights. Moreover, these rights continue only so long as the social conditions permit the continued vitality of these minority communities. Subsection 3a permits the enjoyment of these rights only 'where numbers warrant' and withdraws them whenever the social framework that had given them meaning disappears. In an even more telling homage to Bourassa, section 59 does not extend to immigrants' rights to minority language education in the mother tongue of English in Quebec unless that province later decides to extend such rights; on the contrary, language rights at least in Quebec are to be granted only to members of the indigenous minority communities, in striking contrast to the universal guarantees of fundamental, legal and equality rights given to 'everyone' under the charter.

These exceptions were made in deference to the government of Quebec, which had refused its assent to the constitutional settlement and refused to expose the majority community to what it regarded as a potential threat of assimilation from immigration. This gesture demonstrates how committed the charter founders were to protecting the collective right of communities against undue claims for purely individual rights. The same commitment can be read into the founders' acceptance of a notwithstanding clause in the charter, a provision that would permit legislatures to override certain basic charter rights, presumably in the name of the 'collective good'. That would turn out to be a highly debatable compromise, particularly in the light of the Saskatchewan government's relatively breezy use of section 33 to exempt its public sector back-to-work legislation in 1986. All of these curious compromising features in Canada's Charter of Rights and Freedoms suggest, at least at the level of élites, the uneasy and half-hearted marriage of constitutional liberalism to the country's traditional political institutions and practices.

However, on the question of language rights for established minorities in Canada, uneasy or not, the charter meant a fundamental change in the nature of their institutional protection, and with it a change in the nature of Canadian federalism. If it is remembered that it was the old British imperial idea of the crown as the final guarantor and protector of minorities that had actually been built into the Confederation agreement and provided the rationale for the federal power of remedial action under section 93 and partially for disallowance and reservation of provincial legislation, it is apparent that the adoption of constitutional liberalism and judicial guardianship arose from the direct failure of this imperial theory. Even by the 1890s—at the level of politics—language, schools and religious questions were clearly recognized as too explosive for any notion of political guardianship to work; at the level of federalism, the imperialist theory was seen even then as increasingly out of whack with the evolution of the Canadian federation away from its initially centralized roots. For all of these reasons, the rise of a Quebec-based theory of the country, with a new dual nationality entrenched in the constitution, was the most important and powerful domestic antecedent for Canada's new liberal charter.

It was the Trudeau government, first through the Official Languages Act and later through constitutional entrenchment, that carried forward this new

conception of Confederation into law. In one stroke it challenged the suf-
ficiency of parliamentary government for the defence of rights and relegated
to the dustbin the clumsy federal government paternalism that was expected
to compensate for provincial attacks on minority rights.[34] These actions did
not conform very comfortably with much of the centralist federal theory on
which the federal government was otherwise acting in the 1980s. The doctrine of federal majoritarianism, with its vigorous and relatively unqualified
defence of the adequacy of the federal Parliament in matters of the national
interest, hardly suited the rhetorical requirements of a charter advocate. Again
and again Prime Minister Trudeau was forced to draw out the limitations of
parliamentary institutions in the defence of the people's rights, while simultaneously advancing a forceful case for Parliament to speak and if necessary
act alone on some of the most vital concerns of the nation, including unilateral patriation of the constitution.

Yet, these contradictory tensions aside, rights and national unity are still
defended through central institutions. Francophone rights would not be
shielded by an independent Quebec homeland, but by constitutional
strengthening and extension. For the interpretation of these and other rights,
as well as the application of social policy that would flow from this exerise,
it was the centrally appointed members of the Supreme Court who would
declare and enforce common values in the federation. It was assumed that
the court, shielded by public acceptance of judicial neutrality and objectivity,
could act as a real guardian of minorities against indifferent or unruly provincial or national publics and governments. This would be a new and more
visible national institution with a mandate to protect the spirit of the linguistic accommodation in the constitution and, through that exercise, to
convince minorities, especially francophones, that Canada could be a tolerant
homeland for both founding peoples.

Although the Trudeau government had also sought to enshrine these values in a stirring new preamble to the constitution, this intention was left
behind as part of the unfinished negotiating agenda from 1980. But the
essentials of this part of the Quebec nationalist program were entrenched in
the new constitutional rights charter. Meanwhile, in the wake of this settlement, of social and economic change in the province and of a severe world-
wide recession, the forces of separatism began to weaken dramatically. In this
way, it appeared that at least for a time the tradition of Henri Bourassa was
overcoming that of Lionel Groulx and his separatist ideological descendants.

Suggestions for Further Reading

David Milne, *Tug of War: Ottawa and the Provinces under Trudeau and Mulroney*
(Toronto, 1986).

Edward McWhinney, *Canada and the Constitution 1979–1982: Patriation and the Charter of Rights* (Toronto, 1982).
Michel Vastel, *The Outsider: The Life of Pierre Elliott Trudeau* (Toronto, 1990).

Notes

[1] See Alan C. Cairns, 'Recent Federalist Constitutional Proposals: A Review Essay' in *Canadian Public Policy*, no. 3 (Summer 1979), 348–65. For an excellent review of the issues and problems in 'federalizing' central institutions, see Donald V. Smiley and Ronald L. Watts, *Intrastate Federalism in Canada*, vol. 39, Macdonald Commission Studies (Toronto: UTP, 1985).

[2] For a treatment of the constitutional agenda items and the distinction between the 'people's package' and the 'institutions package' and 'powers package', see David Milne, *The New Canadian Constitution* (Toronto: James Lorimer, 1982), 50. For a superb treatment of the fallacies in the federal sales pitch for the charter, see Peter Russell, 'Democratic Approach to Civil Liberties', *University of Toronto Law Journal*, (1969), 109, and 'The Political Purposes of the Canadian Charter of Rights and Freedoms', *Canadian Bar Review* 61 (March 1983), 30–54.

[3] Donald V. Smiley, 'The Challenge of Canadian Ambivalence', *Queen's Quarterly* 88, 1 (Spring 1981), 1–12.

[4] Pierre Elliott Trudeau, *Commons Debates*, 15 April 1980, 32.

[5] *Ibid.*, 33.

[6] Richard Simeon, 'An Overview of the Trudeau Constitutional Proposals', *Alberta Law Review* 19, 3 (1981), 395.

[7] See, for example, Allan Blakeney's declaration at the September 1980 Constitutional Conference, cited in Milne, *The New Canadian Constitution*, 75.

[8] My italics. An address by the Rt. Hon. Pierre Elliott Trudeau, Confederation Dinner, Toronto, 5 November 1980, 8.

[9] This action was in marked contrast to the careful restrictive approach to the matter of constitutional amendment by the federal government in 1949 when Parliament carefully limited its own direct unilateral power to amend the constitution to subjects of internal concern only. Although the constitutional issues here are not identical, they do raise the same broad question of the adequacy of the federal order of government making constitutional changes affecting the provinces on its own and provide two starkly opposing answers. Certainly the contention of the Trudeau government in 1980 was considerably closer to the older nineteenth-century model of a self-sufficient and paternal central government than it was to its Liberal predecessor only thirty-five years earlier.

[10] Edward McWhinney, *Canada and the Constitution, 1979–1982* (Toronto: UTP, 1982), 65–71.

[11] *Ibid.*, 46. It may be that this author's complaint arises from an unduly romantic attachment to the American and French routes to constitutionalism and that the government's course was one to which the government was driven by sheer political realism. Popular ratification of the contents of the federal constitutional resolution in every region of Canada was by no means certain.

[12]The expression belongs to Professor Ed Black of Queen's University, cited in Simeon, 'An Overview of the Trudeau Constitutional Proposals', 394.

[13]*Ibid.*, 393.

[14]See Kenneth McRoberts, 'Unilateralism, Bilateralism, and Multilateralism: Approaches to Canadian Federalism', in Richard Simeon, *Intergovernmental Relations*, vol. 63, Macdonald Commission Studies (Toronto: UTP, 1985), 71–129.

[15]See the prime minister's address to Parliament, 15 April 1980.

[16]See A.E. Safarian, *Canadian Federalism and Economic Integration*, Constitutional study prepared for the Government of Canada (Ottawa: Information Canada 1974); J. Chrétien, 'Securing the Canadian Economic Union in the Constitution', Discussion paper (Ottawa: Ministry of Supply and Services, 1980). For a careful review of this argument, see M.J. Trebilcock *et al.*, *Federalism and the Canadian Economic Union* (Toronto: Ontario Economic Council, 1983). Not even the Macdonald Commission was prepared to go along with these strong economic claims.

[17]Thomas J. Courchene, 'The Political Economy of Canadian Constitution-Making: The Canadian Economic-Union Issue', *Public Choice* 44 (1984), 227.

[18]Only mobility rights were included in the unilateral constitutional package as part of the charter, while the other demands were wisely dropped.

[19]Alan C. Cairns, 'The Canadian Constitutional Experiment: Constitution, Community, and Identity', Killam Lecture, Dalhousie University, 24 November 1983, 25.

[20]See Stephen A. Scott, 'The Canadian Constitutional Amendment Process', in Paul Davenport and Richard Leach, eds, *Reshaping Confederation: The 1982 Reform of the Canadian Constitution* (Durham, N.C.: Duke University Press, 1984), 268.

[21]P.H. Lane, *An Introduction to the Australian Constitution*, 3rd ed. (Sydney: The Law Book Company Ltd, 1983), 4.

[22]See *Melbourne University Law Review* 14 (June 1984), esp. 366; G. Walker, *The Australian Law Journal* 59 (July 1985), esp. 364; and Leslie Zines, ed., *Commentaries on the Australian Constitution* (Sydney: Butterworths, 1977), 235. Thus, while Australians may seem 'referendum shy' in turning down all but eight of the thirty-eight national referendum proposals put to them by the Commonwealth government since Federation, there is little warrant for arguing that they always vote 'no' to centralizing initiatives.

[23]For an examination of this and other formulae, see Milne, *The New Canadian Constitution*, 24–32, 189–95.

[24]This is not the place to go into the strengths and weaknesses of the amending formula actually adopted. For critical commentary, see Garth Stevenson, 'Constitutional Amendment: A Democratic Perspective', in *Socialist Studies* 2 (1984); 269–84; Stephen A. Scott, 'Canadian Constitutional Amendment'; D. Marc Kilgour and T.J. Lévesque, 'The Choice of a Permanent Amending Formula for Canada's Constitution', *Canadian Public Policy* 10 (September 1984).

[25]Alan Cairns and Cynthia Williams, 'Constitutionalism, Citizenship, and Society in Canada: An Overview', and Cynthia Williams, 'The Changing Nature of Citizen Rights', in Alan Cairns and Cynthia Williams, *Constitutionalism, Citizenship, and Society in Canada*, vol. 33, Macdonald Commission Studies (Toronto: UTP, 1986), 1–50, 99–132.

[26]Somewhat as an afterthought, rights for aboriginal peoples became added to the package of minority rights upon which the case for national unity was being based.

[27]See Cairns and Williams, 'Constitutionalism, Citizenship, and Society in Canada'.

[28]See Milne, *The New Canadian Constitution*, 86–8, 155–60.

[29]While public interventions also strengthened the language provisions, there was never any doubt that these were additions to an already toughly worded and specially entrenched section.

[30]A.I. Silver, *The French-Canadian Idea of Confederation, 1864–1900* (Toronto: UTP, 1982), 191–2.

[31]See C. Michael MacMillan, 'Henri Bourassa on the Defence of Language Rights', *Dalhousie Review* 62, 3 (Autumn 1982), 413–30.

[32]*Ibid.*, 420.

[33]H. Bourassa, 'The French Language and the Future of Our Race', cited in Mac-Millan, 'Henri Bourassa', 422. For extensive extracts on Bourassa's views on biculturalism, see Joseph Levitt, ed., *Henri Bourassa on Imperialism and Biculturalism, 1900–1918* (Toronto: Copp Clark, 1970).

[34]The legal pinnings to federal paternalism remained in section 93 and elsewhere in the Constitution Act, but the charter can only be seen as a clear repudiation of that legal and political machinery for a defence of minority rights.

32

Aboriginal Land Claims

William R. Morrison

After generations of relatively passive acceptance of exploitation, Canada's native peoples have gradually become active parts of the political process. Native activism quickened on a variety of fronts in the 1960s. Nowhere was it more evident than in the question of native land claims, which became the centre of native demands for justice from European society. Land claims were a graphic way of demonstrating the systematic abuse (ofttimes by a process of ignoring their existence) of the natives by European society, and of asserting a concept of aboriginal rights based upon principles of international law and justice which had been reasonably well defined. Land claims could often be considered in a court, subject to rules of evidence and precedent, rather than in the more highly charged legislative atmosphere. And they afforded some basis for one of the most difficult problems facing any government—deciding on compensation for past abuse. The

natives did not win every case they argued, but gradually the tide of justice began to turn in their direction.

In his analysis of the claims process in Canada's North, William R. Morrison distinguishes two sorts of claims: those arising from past treaties and agreements not honoured by government, and those arising from an absence of treaty (which means that native or aboriginal rights had never been dealt with, much less extinguished). The Northern natives had never given up their rights, and thus were in a strong position to assert them when in the 1960s the international climate of opinion began to change. For its part, the federal government became willing to discuss compensation for native peoples of the north, if only to extinguish the possibility of subsequent insistence on aboriginal rights. Not all native groups, Morrison points out, have agreed to the extinction of their rights in return for compensation, and the matter remains a hotly debated issue in native circles.

Why does Morrison insist that the government is pursuing essentially the same policy it has followed for 350 years? Why have some native groups accepted compensation in return for the extinction of rights? How have native rights become involved with native self-government?

This article first appeared, titled 'The Comprehensive Claims Process in Canada's North: New Rhetoric, Old Policies', in Kenneth S. Coates and William R. Morrison, eds, *For Purposes of Dominion: Essays in Honour of Morris Zaslow* (North York, Ont.: Captus Press, 1989), 261–74.

Over the past twenty years, Canada has experienced a remarkable upsurge in assertiveness on the part of her Native population, of which the most important manifestation has been the so-called 'comprehensive' claims. There are two categories of claims made by Canadian Native people (and accepted for negotiation by the federal government). The first, specific claims, are those which arise out of treaty obligations or the administration of lands and other assets under the Indian Act. Scores of such claims have been made over the years, and many settled, concerning improper use of Indian assets held in trust, use of Indian lands, and the like.[1]

The second category, the comprehensive claims, comes from those parts of Canada where no treaty has ever been signed,[2] and where as a result the aboriginal rights of the Native people have never been extinguished.[3] Comprehensive claims deal not with specific grievances but with a wide range of issues such as hunting rights, land use, political rights, and many other things.

In the late 1960s, partly as a result of the wave of liberalism and radicalism which at that time was forcing a re-evaluation of social and economic institutions all over North America, a conviction began to arise among some of the Native people of northern Canada that the old treaty-making process, in which Indians had agreed to the extinguishment of their aboriginal rights in return for annual cash payments and other compensation, had been a cruel fraud upon them. For a trivial sum they had sold their rights, and as a result had been shunted on to reserves, totally losing the power to influence the future development of what had been their land.

The Native people in the Canadian north were in a strong position to take advantage of the zeitgeist of the late sixties and early seventies, particularly after the advent of the energy crisis. Since they had never signed treaties, and since the British-Canadian legal tradition holds that aboriginal land can not be alienated from its inhabitants without the formality of a treaty,[4] they insisted, although with little success, that no economic development of their lands take place—no drilling, no pipelines laid—until their rights had been considered and dealt with.

A generation or two earlier the Canadian government would probably have brushed aside such objections. But by the late 1960s the emergence of dozens of countries from colonial status to independence had signalled the weakening of the ethnocentric impulse among the western nations, and 'participatory democracy' was a slogan of the Trudeau administration. A new generation of university-trained Native leaders had emerged in the 1960s. These people were much less likely than their fathers and grandfathers to accept government assurances and promises on trust, nor were they as susceptible to the threats, over or implied, which had generally accompanied the treaty process. There was also the example of Alaska, where the 1971 negotiations that led to the Alaska Native Claims Settlement Act seemed to herald a new era of rights for the Native people of the Canadian north as well.

Thus by 1970 the combination of a politically aware and educated Native leadership and a government willing to listen with fresh ears to Native people led to a dramatic change in the method by which the question of Native rights was dealt with. An indication of change was the reversal of the government's assimilationist policy, expressed on the notorious 'white paper' of 1969.[5] The outraged response from the Native communities and their supporters in the south as well as the north was such that within a year the government had completely reversed itself. In the same year the government appointed an Indian Claims Commissioner, and the next year began granting substantial sums to Native groups to carry out research into the legal and other basis for their claims. In 1974 the claims process was formalized with the establishment of the Office of Native Claims under the Department of Indian Affairs to deal with both specific and comprehensive claims.

On the government side, there was an openness and a willingness to compromise on negotiations (to a point) that would have been unthinkable in an earlier era. The basis government position on claims, outlined in the December 1981 policy statement 'In All Fairness—a Native Claims Policy', is rich with generous sentiments:

> . . . settlement benefits are [to be] provided in such form and manner as to facilitate the economic, social and cultural development of the native communities concerned, helping on the one hand to protect and promote their sense of identity while enabling their meaningful participation in contemporary society.[6]

And there are indications that this government rhetoric had some substance, for the 1980s have seen considerable movement on outstanding comprehensive claims.

Since 1973, six areas of Canada have been the subject of comprehensive claims.[7] The location and status of these claims is as follows:

1. The Yukon Territory, subject to a claim by the Council for Yukon Indians (CYI). This claim was nearly settled in 1976 and again in 1984, but

in both instances negotiations broke down at a late stage. A new agreement in principle was reached in 1988, and was quickly ratified by a special meeting of the CYI and band chiefs; the Yukon government has also ratified the accord. Final settlement of this agreement requires ratification at the band level.

2. The Mackenzie Delta-Beaufort Sea-Western Arctic Islands region, subject to a claim by the Committee for Original People's Entitlement (COPE), the organization of the Inuvialuit—the Inuit of the Western Arctic. This claim was settled in 1984 by the Western Arctic (Inuvialuit) Claim Settlement Act.

3. The Mackenzie Valley region, from the 60th parallel north to the Mackenzie Delta, subject to a claim by the Dene Nation (formerly the Indian Brotherhood of the NWT) and by the Métis Association of the NWT. This has been the best known of the claims, and was for many years the most intractable. No settlement has been reached in this claim, but shortly before the 1988 federal election, Prime Minister Brian Mulroney travelled to Rae, NWT to sign an agreement in principle with the Dene and the Métis. As in the Yukon, this deal must now be presented to the communities for ratification.

4. The eastern part of the NWT and the eastern Arctic islands, subject to a claim by the Inuit Tapirisat of Canada (the Nunavut claim). [An agreement in principle was reached in late 1992.]

5. The James Bay region, and the rest of northern Quebec, subject to claims by the Grand Council of the Cree of Quebec, the Northern Quebec Inuit Association, and the Naskapis of Schefferville. These claims were not subject to the same initial processes of negotiation as the others (they were presented to the courts rather than to the government), and were settled by the James Bay and Northern Quebec Agreement of 1975 and the supplementary Northeastern Quebec Agreement of 1978. The Conseil Attikamek-Montagnais of Quebec is currently negotiating a claim with the government.

6. Labrador, subject to the claims of the Labrador Inuit Association and the Naskapi Montagnais Innu Association. These claims have not yet been accepted by the government for negotiation, and thus remain in the early stages of the process.[8]

An important factor in the present comprehensive claims process is that fact that there was only one Indian Treaty signed in Canada which lay entirely north of the 60th parallel. This was Treaty 11, signed in 1921.[9] It is not true, as popular belief might have it, that the government avidly sought to negotiate the extinction of aboriginal rights through treaty with every Native group in Canada. In fact, the federal government refused treaties to the Native people of the territories (and the northern, non-agricultural regions of the provinces as well), until national priorities, generally economic ones, compelled them to do so.[10]

Nor were these treaties initiated solely by government. On the southern prairies, the Native people, realizing the inevitability of social and economic change, made treaty demands on the government which forced it to offer far more that it had originally intended, because Ottawa was anxious to alienate Indian title to the prairies in order to pave the way for agricultural settlement of the western wheat lands. The fact that the government subsequently reneged on some of its promises[11] does not alter the fact that the Native people were in large part initiators of the treaty process.

The basis of government policy for other Native people living north of lands suitable for agriculture was that they were 'best left as Indians'.[12] Administering a reserve system was expensive and unnecessary, and since there seemed no alternative to a hunter-gatherer economy, the Native people were best left alone. If non-Native development seemed likely, then treaties could be negotiated. An added disincentive to treaty-making in the Yukon was the possibility of new finds of gold. What would happen if the Yukon Indians were given a reserve and then gold was found on it?

This thinking is clearly evident in the events leading to the signing of Treaty 11. Before the first World War, the government refused to offer treaty to the Native people of the Mackenzie Valley area, despite the evident wish of many of them for one, and the pleas of local missionaries that they be protected from non-Native exploitation by treaty. This position, however, changed rapidly when in the summer of 1920 the Imperial Oil Company drilled a producing oil well at Norman Wells. Then the government found a reason for a treaty, and one was rapidly negotiated with the various Indian groups in the Mackenzie Valley.

Years after the signing of Treaty 11, as with the other treaties to the south, some of the Native groups found cause to regret having agreed to the government's wishes. But unlike the case with the other treaties, which had been signed much earlier,[13] some of the Native signatories and witnesses to Treaty 11 lived into the 1970s to testify to sympathetic listeners that they had been lied to by the government negotiators in 1921. A strong case has been made that the negotiations were hasty, and that the Native people were given oral assurances about their rights to hunt, fish and trap in the area covered by the treaty which were contrary to what the treaty in fact said.[14] Moreover, the reserves promised by the Treaty were never granted. So strong was the case that the federal government accepted for negotiation a comprehensive claim from the Native people in the Mackenzie as if the treaty did not exist.

The progress of individual claims negotiations has been based on one simple question: Were (are) the Native people involved prepared to surrender, forever, their aboriginal rights to the land? In those cases where the Natives were prepared to sign such an accord, negotiations proceeded relatively quickly towards a final settlement. When Natives have resisted this inflexible government demand, as have the Dene and the Council of Yukon Indians, negotiations have dragged on interminably, often dissolving in acrimony and frustration.

The classical examples of the first category, which is the most familiar, are the eleven treaties signed between 1871 and 1921. The basic premise of all these treaties was that the aboriginal rights of the Native people involved would be extinguished once and for all in return for various promises and payments. The purpose was to clear the title to public land in preparation for settlement or development. The James Bay agreement was a more generous and more sophisticated agreement of this type, as was the COPE settlement in the western Arctic and the earlier Alaska settlement.

It will noted immediately that another difference between these two types of comprehensive claims is that only those of the first category have been settled. The reason for this is quite simple: on the one hand, the government has insisted that as part of each claims agreement the aboriginal claims of the Native people be settled once and for all, so that the claim cannot be raised again in the future. On the other hand, the Native groups making these claims are fearful that if they surrender their aboriginal rights, at whatever price, they or their children will live to regret their action, as their land is developed without their consent, and they become, like the Indians of the southern prairies, powerless outsiders trapped in enclaves surrounded by land that was once theirs. There is also a strong sentiment in the northern communities that aboriginal rights cannot be surrendered, that they are a gift from God, not a power conferred by humankind.[15]

The first of the comprehensive claims to be settled was that of the Native people living in the province of Quebec, east of James Bay. This claim arose in response to the James Bay project, which, when launched in 1971, was one of the largest civil engineering works ever undertaken in North America. It was a giant hydro-electric project, creating a number of reservoirs in which would be penned the waters of several of Quebec's rivers, from the Great Whale in the north to the Eastmain in the south.[16] The fishing, hunting and trapping lands of the Cree of that region, and the Inuit to the north of them, would be seriously affected by the project, which would drown large areas of their lands.

This claim was handled differently from the ones that followed it, for the initial response of the Native people was to appeal to the courts. The government of Quebec took the position that the Cree and Inuit had no aboriginal rights, and that it had only the responsibility to pay them something for the damage done to their lands. However, when faced with the likelihood of lengthy delays in a multi-billion dollar project arising from a court challenge from Native groups funded by the federal government, the government of Quebec agreed to negotiate, and after two years' negotiation, a final agreement was signed in 1975.

The agreement involved about 6,600 Cree and 4,300 Inuit, living in eight Cree and fifteen Inuit communities. Initially the Native people had hesitated to sign an agreement which obliged them to 'cede, release, surrender and convey all their Native claims, right, titles and interests' to 400,000 square miles of territory.[17] But they had few allies in high places, and the pressure to sign were tremendous. Given the vast amounts of money involved—over a billion dollars had already been spent on the project by the time the agreement was signed, and the Quebec government was totally committed to it —it seemed unstoppable. So the Cree and the Inuit signed, and in 1978 the Naskapi Indians to the northeast were included, under the Northeastern Quebec Agreement.

In return for their rights, the Native people received $230 million, to be paid out over a maximum of 21 years (which works out very roughly to $1000 per capita per annum for 21 years). They also received outright ownership of 1,900 square miles of land for the Cree and 3,200 for the Inuit, and a further 25,000 square miles of land and 35,000 for the Inuit where they were to have exclusive hunting rights. There were numerous other provisions for local and regional governmental authority, economic development measures, and guarantees of a voice in (though not control over) future economic development of the region.

After the agreement was signed, the Cree and Inuit of Quebec were surprised to find themselves subject to criticism from some groups which had supported them in their struggle with the Quebec government. Canadian environmentalists who had backed them, considering the project an abomination, now called the Native people 'sell-outs'. Other Native groups, who had wished the Cree and Inuit to stand up for the principle of Native self-determination, accused them of betraying the Native cause.[18] But the Cree and Inuit of the James Bay region had acted pragmatically, securing what they considered to be the best terms under the circumstances, 'experiencing some success at maintaining their autonomy within the framework of the state apparatus'.[19]

In retrospect, some of the Native people covered by the James Bay agreement seem to have had second thoughts. Implementing the tremendously complex agreement proved to be a tortuous process, involving Native leaders in endless dealings with government bureaucracy. Chief Billy Diamond, one of the principal negotiators for the Cree, when asked in 1979 if he would sign the agreement again, said 'the same agreement today, four years later? No, I wouldn't sign it, not with the P.Q. [Parti Québécois] government.'[20]

The second comprehensive claim to be settled was the COPE claim, put forward by the Committee for Original People's Entitlement, the organization representing 2,500 Inuvialuit of the western Canadian Arctic—roughly, the Mackenzie Delta and Beaufort Sea areas. This claim was first submitted to the government in May 1977, signed in December 1983,[21] and ratified by the Western Arctic (Inuvialuit) Settlement Act of June 1984.[22]

The Inuvialuit, like the Cree and Inuit of James Bay, had in the 1970s found themselves in the path of southern economic imperatives. In this case it was the 'energy crisis', and the fact that the traditional lands and waters of the Inuvialuit were centred on the Beaufort Sea, whose rich oil reserves promised to free Canadians (and Americans) from the extortions of the Arab world. Economic urgency was a two-edged sword: on one hand it put pressure on the Inuit to negotiate, but by the same token, since the federal government was committed to the extinguishment of aboriginal rights it compelled them to negotiate a settlement before the massive projects slated for the region could go ahead. Oil wells could be and were drilled out in the Beaufort Sea before a settlement took place, but harbours, base camps and pipelines would use Inuvialuit land, lending urgency to negotiations (at least before the collapse of OPEC).

The Western Arctic (Inuvialuit) agreement was in essence the same as the James Bay agreement: it provided them with 'a range of rights, benefits and compensation in return for the surrender of their interest in and to certain lands in the Northwest Territories and Yukon and adjacent offshore islands and waters'.[23] The financial benefits were not given to the people directly; rather, $10 million went immediately to an 'economic development fund' and $7.5 million to a 'social development fund'. Future payments were to be made until 1997 to a total of $45 million in 1977 dollars, a sum equal to $18,000 for each person covered by the agreement. The Inuvialuit also retained title to 700 square miles surrounding each of six communities plus 770 square miles at Cape Bathurst as a protected, non-development area. They also retained title, but not subsurface rights to gas and oil, to a further 30,000 square miles in the region. Title to this land was vested in the Inuvialuit Land Corporation, owned by the Inuvialuit, and could be sold only to the individual Inuit or to the government.

These lands were selected by the Inuvialuit according to their use as traditional hunting and trapping grounds, because they were burial grounds, because they had other biological importance, or other economic potential, such as for tourism. The agreement contained a long list of ancillary socio-economic benefits. Nonetheless, the agreement, viewed with the eye of history, can be seen as essentially a very much more generous version of the 19th century treaties signed with the Indians of the southern prairies—rights to the land were surrendered in return for cash, land for reserves, and other benefits. There is a good deal of language suggesting future benefits—'they will also benefit from any special rights accorded to native peoples in the future through the process of ongoing constitutional development'[24]—but the government had what it has always wanted—the extinguishment of aboriginal claims to vast areas of potential economic value.

For the 1970s and much of the 1980s, other northern Native groups rejected the extinguishment request, and hoped for government flexibility on this score. They waited in vain, for as successive federal ministers and land claims negotiators made clear, the primary reason Ottawa participated in the claims was to eliminate the prospect of future Native demands based on aboriginal rights. The federal government did agree to a change in terminology. The initial term, 'extinguishment', which carried strong negative connotations among the Natives, was replaced by the gentler word 'certainty'. But the meaning was the same: the federal government would settle a comprehensive claim only if the Native negotiators agreed to a final and complete surrender of aboriginal rights on all non-settlement lands.[25] The best known of the negotiations of this type involves the Dene nation.

The Dene are an Athabaskan people numbering about 8,500, closely related in language and custom to Native people in Yukon and Alaska. Economic and political imperatives imposed upon them from the south have made them politically distinct, and their historical lands, Denendeh (roughly the Mackenzie basin north of the 60th parallel), a potentially distinct political unit. Though there are also about 4,500 people of mixed blood in the same region, sharing essentially the same way of life, southern imperatives have also caused these Métis and non-status Indians to feel distinct from the Dene.[26] Thus there are two comprehensive claims in the region—the Dene claim and that of the Métis Association of the Northwest Territories.

Perhaps more than other Native people in northern Canada, the Dene were aware of the implications of signing a treaty with the government which extinguished their aboriginal rights. By the 1970s the Dene were coming to believe that the treaty of 1921 had been a fraud. In the mid-1970s they found themselves astride the proposed Mackenzie Valley pipeline. This was the energy lifetime of the future, designed to bring oil and gas from the Beaufort Sea (and possibly gas from the north shore of Alaska) to the energy-hungry south. But by this time the government had admitted that much of Treaty 11 had become in fact void, and that the aboriginal rights of the Dene had not been properly dealt with. Thus this 'mega-project' could not go ahead until the claims of the Native people of the region (including the Inuvialuit of the north coast of Yukon) were settled.

In 1974 the federal government established the Mackenzie Valley Pipeline Inquiry to investigate all aspects of the proposed pipeline, particularly its effect on Native people in the region. The commission, headed by Mr Justice Thomas R. Berger, held hearings in 1975 and 1976, and issued its findings as the widely publicized Berger Report.[27] The report was arguably the most sensitive analysis of the effect of white development on Native society ever published in Canada; certainly it was the most widely read. Berger's most important recommendation was that no pipeline be built for ten years, a period that has now passed.[28]

This recommendation, and the great amount of sympathetic publicity that the Dene received as a result of the hearings, put them in a very strong position. The stakes were tremendous. The price of petroleum was rising almost daily, and warnings were coming from the oil companies that Canada's reserves, recently touted as almost limitless, were in danger of running dry. By 1976 Imperial Oil and Sun Oil had built fifteen drilling platforms in the Beaufort Sea, at enormous cost.

In October 1976 the Dene submitted a comprehensive claim to the federal government based on the 'Dene Declaration', a manifesto of Dene rights which had been approved in July 1975 by an assembly of three hundred Dene leaders representing twenty-five communities. The first sentence in this document is 'we the Dene of the NWT insist on the right to be regarded by ourselves and the world as a nation.' It goes on to say

> [T]he government of Canada is not the government of the Dene. The Government of the NWT is not the government of the Dene. . . . there are realities we are forced to submit to, such as the existence of a country called Canada, we insist on the right to self-determination as a distinct people. . . . We the Dene are part of the Fourth World. . . . What we seek then is independence and self-determination within the country of Canada.[29]

Although the Dene leadership quickly denied that the declaration was separatist in intention or content,[30] the document which followed it, 'Recognition of the Dene Nation through Dene Government',[31] was, if anything, even more radical, claiming virtually sovereign powers in the Mackenzie basin for the Dene.[32] The two documents became the basis for the Dene claim.[33]

The federal government was alarmed by this claim for two reasons. First, it came at a time when the avowedly separatist Parti Québécois had just come to power in Quebec; the federal government was unlikely to grant to the Dene rights which it would not dream of granting to Quebec. Second, the Dene claim ran directly counter to the long-standing government policy of extinguishing aboriginal claims. Since the government wished to define and limit Native rights, and the Dene declaration sought to expand them tremendously, there was bound to be friction.

Talks began between the Dene, the Métis and the government,[34] but as one government document delicately put it, 'prolonged difficulty [was experienced] in establishing positions and initiating meaningful negotiations.'[35] By March 1978 the Dene had received $2.4 million and the Métis $1.1 million to help with their side of the negotiations (in the form of an advance against the eventual settlement). In September of that year the government, dissatisfied with the tone and the pace of the negotiations, suspended them.[36] They were begun again in 1980, suspended again for a few months in 1983, and resulted in the signing of an agreement in principle five years later.

Since the original Dene declaration, the Dene position on extinguishment of aboriginal rights has been refined. The Dene negotiators now say that land ownership 'does not play as important a role in the present framework as in the original . . . position', because the Dene now realize that 'even if you own the land the government can still make laws about how the land is used . . .'. The focus has now shifted to 'aboriginal *political* rights':

> we are approaching the claim from the position of being able to hunt and trap on all the land in the settlement area, being able to have some say on how the land is used in the settlement area . . . getting a share of all the developments that occur in the settlement area. At the same time we are trying to get political influence and control . . . [37]

This position is essentially a more sophisticated version of the original Dene position recognizing that control of the land is equivalent to ownership of it. Years of costly negotiations took their toll. Unlike the federal government, which paid for its negotiators out of a seemingly inexhaustible national treasury, the Dene effort was mortgaged against the final accord; when negotiations reached an impasse, the government tried to bring the Dene to the table by cutting off their funding. As it became clear that the federal government would not budge on the main point, the Dene reluctantly accepted the reality that there would be no land claims deal without extinguishment.

Like the Dene, the Inuit Tapirisat, the organization representing the 14,000 Inuit of the central and eastern Arctic, put forward a comprehensive claim based on a sort of quasi-sovereignty. The original Nunavut ('our land') proposal of February 1976 had as its major provision the creation of a new Territory with the same powers as the existing Yukon and Northwest Territories, comprising the greater part of them—about a million square miles—and an equal area of water. The Inuit would own the surface rights to a large area of Nunavut, but not the oil and mineral rights. Within a year it was withdrawan, on the grounds that it represented the philosophy of the non-Native consultants who had helped draw it up rather than that of the Inuit.[38] It was replaced by a new claim, much closer to that of the Dene in tone, insisting on full mineral rights and an amendment to the Canadian Constitution to provide for the 'right of the Inuit to exist as an independent culture within Canada'. In 1982 the Tungavik Federation of Nunavut was set up to negotiate for the Inuit Tapirisat.[39]

Some progress has been made on this claim. As with the Dene claim, the government has been prepared to make concessions on a number of matters peripheral to its central goal, such as the location of Inuit traditional hunting areas. In October 1982 it agreed in principle to the division of the Northwest Territories.[40] But on more essential matters there has been little real movement. In 1983 the negotiators reached an impasse on the powers of the proposed Nunavut Impact Review Board, a body that was to review oil, gas and mining proposals and matters relating to the management of Nunavut land and resources. The government wanted it to be an advisory board, while the Inuit wanted it to have the power to veto development proposals. The Inuit believed that 'If northerners cannot participate effectively in developing their regional economy, and strengthening their economic participation in Canadian life, new structures of government are a delusion. . . . northerners will be living in a colony just as in the past.'[41] But as with the Dene, the government would not grant the Inuit of Nunavut the degree of autonomy or control they demanded.

The final major comprehensive claim discussed here is that of the Council of Yukon Indians, representing the 5,500 Native people of Yukon. This claim, the first accepted for negotiation by the federal government, has had perhaps the most tangled history of all. It was launched early in 1973 in a document entitled 'Together Today for our Children Tomorrow'. By 1976 negotiators (including representatives from the Yukon Territorial Government) had agreed on a draft agreement which was similar to the James Bay agreement, which in turn had resembled the Alaska agreement. The Yukon Indians' aboriginal rights were to be extinguished in return for lands owned outright, exclusive hunting rights on other land, social benefits and cash grants. But to the surprise of the negotiators, when the agreement was submitted to the local communities for discussion it was rejected, on the grounds that it was just a purchase of aboriginal title which denied the Indians any real participation in determining the future of the Territory.[42]

Negotiations began again, and by the spring of 1984 an agreement in principle satisfactory to negotiators on both sides was arrived at. This second version of the agreement was more generous than the first: nearly $190 million was to be paid to the beneficiaries over a twenty year period.[43] But to the surprise of the negotiators and the chagrin of the government, eight of the twelve bands in Yukon did not ratify the agreement within the deadline set by Ottawa, and the agreement collapsed amidst acrimony and charges of bad faith. The sticking point was again the issue of extinguishment, which several of the Indian communities still refused to endorse.

In 1988, a flurry of negotiations resulted in the negotiation of an agreement in principle (AIP) between the CYI and the federal and territorial governments. The deal has since been ratified by a special meeting of the CYI executive and the Yukon's 13 band chiefs, and by the Government of Yukon. Final ratification requires acceptance of the AIP by the individual bands, although the unanimity provisions of the 1984 AIP have been eliminated. The accord has been greeted more with relief than excitement, a potential end to 15 years of tiring, frustrating and often acrimonious negotiations.

Clearly, the northern land claims process is at a major turning point. The federal government has made only minor moves on the long-contentious issue of extinguishment. The federal government announced that 'in response to expressed concerns of . . . native groups, the Minister is reviewing the existing federal policy that requires the use of the wording "extinguishment of aboriginal rights" in all comprehensive land claims settlement.'[44] But whatever the wording may be, the government's intent did not change.

Given the federal negotiators' hard line, Native leaders faced a painful choice. They could continue negotiations, subject to federal control of Native funding, hoping to secure a shift in government policy. That policy had been pursued for a decade and a half, with virtually no movement on this critical point. There was, at the same time, the example of the COPE and James Bay settlements, with Native groups responding to the social, economic and cultural problems facing their people. The option, long resisted, was to accept the rigidity of the federal government's position of certainty/extinguishment and negotiate the best deal possible under the circumstances. In the last year, the CYI and Dene/Métis have taken the latter course, and have signed agreements in principle calling for the extinguishment of aboriginal rights on all non-settlement lands.

The question then arises as to why some Native groups quickly agreed to the extinguishment of their aboriginal rights while others resisted this demand for so long. Evidently the reasons are not racial, since one of the two settlements was with an Inuit group, and the other with a Cree and Inuit group. The Inuit of the Beaufort Sea signed; the Inuit of the eastern Arctic did not. Nor are they regional or geographical. They may perhaps be economic. The two agreements concluded were both in regions that were under heavy pressure from economic developers—the James Bay Hydro project and the Beaufort Sea oil drillers. But this rationale fails when the Dene are considered. They were under the same pressures as the Inuvialuit, yet they have been the most intractably opposed to extinguishment of aboriginal rights.

The most likely explanation is political, and this leads to questions such as why some Native groups consider that a bird in the hand is worth two in the bush, and others emphatically do not. At the beginning of the claims process the answers might have had something to do with the kind of advice the Native groups received from outside consultants and helpers: some were initially influenced by activists from southern-based organizations like the Company of Young Canadians, and others less so. But that period ended at least fifteen years ago; the Native groups have for some years now known their own minds on the issue, and do not need southerners to tell them what to think.

There is another possibility. Native organizations have struggled continuously to maintain a balance between the central office and Native people in the communities. The differences exist on several levels: an educated and politically motivated leadership negotiating on behalf of a less well educated population; the incomes of representatives and negotiators contrasting with the evident poverty in the communities; the urban, non-traditional lifestyles versus the land-based activities in the isolated settlements. The Dene and the

Council of Yukon Indians have had considerable difficulties maintaining a strong liaison between organizational headquarters and the communities; in the Yukon, the 1984 AIP was accepted by negotiators but rejected by the communities. The Inuvialuit and James Bay Natives have seemingly avoided these difficulties, a factor which doubtlessly aided the acceptance of agreements negotiated with the federal government.

It may be indeed that the question is unanswerable. It may also be that the question is not really the important one from the Native point of view. What really matters is whether the Native groups, in accepting the settlement of their comprehensive claims have acted in their own long-term best interests. It may be answered that time will tell, and it will take a generation or two to see if they have been wise. But this is to ignore history. In fact, as has already been suggested, the two comprehensive claims which have been settled are essentially modern versions of the eleven treaties signed between 1871 and 1921 (and in the tradition of the treaties signed by the British with the Indians since the beginning of their authority on this continent). They are vastly more generous than the old treaties, with one important difference: there is a limit to the annuity payments. Still, $1800 a year is better than the old sum of $5, which is still paid to tens of thousands of treaty Indians as an annuity, even if one is for twenty years and the other forever.

But these new claims agreements have exactly the same basic purpose from the point of view of the government. Leaving aside their fulsome and doubtless genuine protestations of concern for Native welfare, culture and the like, they have the same central aim as the old ones. Baldly put, it is to clear title to the land of northern Canada of the encumbrance of Native claims, so that southerners can get on with its development as they see fit. Its original inhabitants are to be consulted about this development, but they will have no power to prevent it or determine its course. It is surprising (or, given the imperatives of government, perhaps not so surprising) that the basic motives of the non-Native authorities have not changed in essence since Treaty 1 was signed outside the walls of Lower Fort Garry in 1871, or indeed, since the Puritans made agreements with the Indians of Massachusetts in the seventeenth century.

Native groups in Canada's north have recognized this fact. Observing that the Indians who signed the treaties in southern Canada have been relegated to the periphery of national development, and not wishing to see their own future develop along similar lines, they refused to sign away the rights to their lands.[45] They feared being confined to reserves, no matter how large, and no matter what they are called. But despite these concerns, and the fear that the day will come when their children will curse them for having sold their patrimony, northern Natives appear to have now accepted the inevitability of extinguishment. Like those who settled earlier, the Dene/Métis, CYI and Inuit Tapirisat have decided to make the best deal they can, either under pressure of economic development, because they see no chance of changing the government's mind, or because they believe that the immediate economic benefits and the increased power to determine their own local affairs outweigh the future dangers of the loss of their wider rights.

The Native leaders may be right, though history would indicate that the fears and suspicions of those who refuse to sign are amply justified. What is most remarkable is the difference between the rhetoric of government and the stark reality of the policy it has been steadfastly pursuing to date. From the publications and press releases emanating from the federal government, one might think that the authorities, freed of the ethnocentrism and indifference to the wishes of Native people that has characterised its past Indian policies, has entered upon a new dawn of generosity, understanding, and sensitivity to Native rights and desires. Instead, while cloaking its purposes in the language of sociology and cultural relativism, it is pursuing essentially the same policy as its predecessors have done for the past 350 years.

Suggestions for Further Reading

Michael Asch, *Home and Native Land: Aboriginal Rights and the Canadian Constitution* (Scarborough, Ont., 1988).

W.R. Morrison, *A Survey of the History and Claims of the Native Peoples of Northern Canada*, 2nd ed. rev. (Ottawa, 1985).

Donald J. Purich, *Our Land: Native Rights in Canada* (Toronto, 1986).

Notes

[1] The author wishes to thank the Treaties and Historical Research Centre of the Canadian Department of Indian and Northern Affairs, and particularly Robert Allen, Deputy Director, for assistance in obtaining research materials for this paper. The conclusions reached here do not, however, in any way reflect the opinions or policy of the department.

[2] With the exception of the Mackenzie valley, which is a special case.

[3] There is an extensive literature on the aboriginal rights of Canadian Native people. For an introduction to the subject, see W.R. Morrison, *A Survey of the History and Claims of the Native Peoples of Northern Canada*, 2nd ed., revised (Ottawa, 1985).

[4] British and Canadian law hold that aboriginal peoples have rights to their land, but these are 'usufructuary' rights—the right to use the land and what it produces. But they do not 'own' it, and thus cannot sell it, except to the government.

[5] Formally known as the *Statement of the Government of Canada on Indian Policy* (Ottawa, 1969).

[6] 'Background to the 1985 First Ministers Conference on the Constitution', prepared by Constitutional Affairs Directorate, Department of Indian Affairs and Northern Development, December 1984, 91.

[7] There are more than six claims, because some areas are subject to more than one claim, but it is easiest to treat the subject by geographical region rather than by

specific claim. The government will negoiate only six claims at any one time, so there is a backlog of claims waiting for negotiation.

[8]The government has also accepted for negotiation the comprehensive claim of the Nishga Tribal Council in British Columbia, but this is outside the geographical scope of this paper.

[9]Treaty 8, signed in 1899, encompassed part of the upper Mackenzie Valley.

[10]This is the central thesis of K.S. Coates and W.R. Morrison, *Treaty Research Report: Treaty 11 (1921)* (Ottawa, 1986).

[11]See John Tobias, 'Canada's Subjugation of the Plains Cree, 1879–1855,' *Canadian Historical Review*, LXIV, 4 (1983); Wayne Daugherty, *Treaty Research Report: Treaty One and Two* (Ottawa, 1983).

[12]K.S. Coates, 'Best Left as Indians: the Federal Government and the Indians of the Yukon, 1894–1950', *Canadian Journal of Native Studies*, 4, 2 (Fall 1984).

[13]The previous treaty was Treaty 10, signed in 1906. The northern adhesions to Treaty 5 were made in 1908. See K.S. Coates and W.R. Morrison, *Treaty Research Report: Treaty 5* and *Treaty Research Report: Treaty 10* (Ottawa, 1986).

[14]The case was made by Rene Fumoleau in his book *As Long as this Land Shall Last: A History of Treaty 8 and Treaty 11, 1870–1939* (Toronto, 1975).

[15]See *Day of Reckoning*, a program on the Mayo community, produced by Northern Native Broadcasting, Whitehorse, Yukon.

[16]There is a considerable literature on this project. For a chronological account, see Harvey A. Feit, 'Negotiating Recognition of Aboriginal Rights: History, Strategies and Reactions to the James Bay and Northern Quebec Agreements', *Canadian Journal of Anthropology*, 1/2 (Winter 1980). For the human aspect of the question, particularly a study of how the project affected the Cree, see Boyce Richardson, *Strangers Devour the Land* (Toronto, 1975).

[17]The text of the treaty, which runs to 450 printed pages, is in *The James Bay and Northern Quebec Agreement* (Quebec, 1976).

[18]B. Richardson, 320.

[19]H.A. Feit, 164.

[20]R. Wittenborn and C. Briegert, *James Bay Project—A River Drowned by Water* (Montreal, 1981), 147.

[21]Negotiations were not continuous; they broke down in May 1979 and were not formally resumed until January 1983.

[22]A short guide to the agreement is a booklet published by the federal department of Indian Affairs: *The Western Arctic Claim: a Guide to the Final Agreement* (Ottawa, 1984).

[23]*The Western Arctic Claim*, 1.

[24]*Ibid.*

[25]The Yukon agreement in principle provides for the continuation for aboriginal rights on lands retained by Native people.

[26]For an explanation of why this is so, see K.S. Coates and W.R. Morrison, 'More Than a Matter of Blood: The Government, the Churches and the Mixed Blood People of the Yukon and Mackenzie River Valley, 1870–1950', in L. Barron, ed., *1885 and After Native Society in Transition* (Regina, 1986).

[27]Berger, Mr Justice T.R. *Northern Frontier Northern Homeland: the Report of the Mackenzie Valley Pipeline Inquiry*, 2 vols (Ottawa, 1977). Volume one contains the social material from the Mackenzie Valley.

[28]For a number of reasons, not all having to do with concern for Native rights, the pipeline was not built. The oil fields at Norman Wells were later linked by pipeline to the southern pipeline system.

[29]'Draft [of the] Dene Declaration: For Discussion Purposes Only', n.a., n.d., Copy in Ottawa, Treaties and Historical Research Centre of the Department of Indian and Northern Affairs.

[30]'Notes for speech by James Wah-Shee [President of the Indian Brotherhood of the Northwest Territories, later renamed the Dene Nation] . . . to the National Conference, Oil, Chemical and Atomic Worker International Union, Toronto, 15 September 1975', Copy in Treaties and Historical Research Centre. That such a group would invite a Native leader as a guest speaker shows how times had changed since the early treaty period.

[31]Copy in the Treaties and Historical Research Centre.

[32]For a précis of this document, see W.R. Morrison, *A Survey of the History and Claims . . .*, 68–71.

[33]The Métis claim was presented at the same time under the title 'Proposed Agreement on Objectives between the Aboriginal Peoples of the Mackenzie Corridor and the Government of Canada for the Entrenchment of Rights to "Our Land, Our Culture, Our Future" '. It was a good deal less radical, since it fell short of asking for political autonomy. Since the government insisted that all aboriginal claims to the region be extinguished, the Métis claim could not be settled until the Dene claim was. This led to confusion and some acrimony between the two Native organizations.

[34]Including the government of the Northwest Territories.

[35]'Background to the 1985 First Ministers Conference', 100.

[36]'Funding Suspended for Mackenzie Valley Claims Negotiations', Department of Indian and Northern Affairs communique, 27 September 1978, Treaties and Historical Research Centre.

[37]Dene/Métis Negotiations Secretariat, *Dene/Métis Land Claim Information Package*, n.d., 8–9.

[38]See Keith J. Crowe, 'A Summary of Northern Native Claims in Canada: the Process and Progress of Negotiations', *Etudes/Inuit/Studies* 3/1 (1979), 35.

[39]See Quinn Duffy, *The Road to Nunavut* (Kingston, 1987).

[40]By the end of 1988 the residents of the NWT had not been able to agree on a boundary.

[41]Nunavut Constitutional Forum, 'Building Nunavut Today and Tomorrow', March 1985, 16.

[42]On this point, see National Indian Brotherhood, 'The Treaties, Yukon Proposal and the James Bay Agreement in Principle—A Comparison: Land Surrender, Resource Sharing, or Land Grabbing!!' October 1975. Copy in the Treaties and Historical Research Centre.

[43]This sounds like a huge sum for 5,500 people, but it works out to about $1800 per capita per annum for twenty years. Unlike the older treaties, the cash payments were not in perpetuity, and the money did not all go directly to the people; much of it went into various institutions designed to benefit them. Furthermore, the population could easily double in twenty years, which would halve the per capita benefits.

[44]'Background to the 1985 First Ministers' Conference', 100.

[45]No doubt their apprehensions were increased by news that many Alaskan Native people were not happy with their settlement. In 1983 Thomas Berger (of the Mackenzie Valley Pipeline Commission) conducted an inquiry into the Alaskan Native Claims Settlement Act of 1971 which publicized a great deal of bitterness on the part of the Alaskan Natives about the deal they had made. See T.R. Berger, *Village Journey* (New York, 1985.).